A SELECT LIBRARY OF THE CHRISTIAN CHURCH

NICENE AND POST-NICENE FATHERS

VOLUME 8

BASIL: LETTERS AND SELECT WORKS

SECOND SERIES

Edited by

PHILIP SCHAFF, D.D., LL.D. AND HENRY WACE, D.D.

Hendrickson Publishers, Inc.
P. O. Box 3473
Peabody, Massachusetts 01961-3473

ISBN 1-56563-124-2

Printed in the United States of America

First printing 1994

This is a reprint edition of the American Edition of the *Nicene and Post-Nicene Fathers, Second Series, Volume 8, St. Basil: Letters and Select Works*, originally published in the United States by the Christian Literature Publishing Company, 1895.

THE TREATISE DE SPIRITU SANCTO

THE NINE HOMILIES OF THE HEXAEMERON AND THE LETTERS

OF

SAINT BASIL THE GREAT

Archbishop of Cæsarea

Translated with Notes

BY

THE REV. BLOMFIELD JACKSON, M.A.

Vicar of Saint Bartholomew's, Moor Lane, and Fellow of King's College, London

PREFACE.

THIS translation of a portion of the works of St. Basil was originally begun under the editorial supervision of Dr. Wace. It was first announced that the translation would comprise the *De Spiritu Sancto* and *Select Letters*, but it was ultimately arranged with Dr. Wace that a volume of the series should be devoted to St. Basil, containing, as well as the *De Spiritu Sancto*, the whole of the *Letters*, and the *Hexaemeron*. The *De Spiritu Sancto* has already appeared in an English form, as have portions of the *Letters*, but I am not aware of an English translation of the *Hexaemeron*, or of all the *Letters*. The *De Spiritu Sancto* was presumably selected for publication as being at once the most famous, as it is among the most valuable, of the extant works of this Father. The *Letters* comprise short theological treatises and contain passages of historical and varied biographical interest, as well as valuable specimens of spiritual and consolatory exhortation. The *Hexaemeron* was added as being the most noted and popular of St. Basil's compositions in older days, and as illustrating his exegetic method and skill, and his power as an extempore preacher.

The edition used has been that of the Benedictine editors as issued by Migne, with the aid, in the case of the *De Spiritu Sancto*, of that published by Rev. C. F. H. Johnston.

The editorship of Dr. Wace terminated during the progress of the work, but I am indebted to him, and very gratefully acknowledge the obligation, for valuable counsel and suggestions. I also desire to record my thanks to the Rev. C. Hole, Lecturer in Ecclesiastical History at King's College, London, and to Mr. Reginald Geare, Head Master of the Grammar School, Bishop's Stortford, to the former for help in the revision of proof-sheets and important suggestions, and to the latter for aid in the translation of several of the *Letters*.

The works consulted in the process of translation and attempted illustration are sufficiently indicated in the notes.

LONDON, December, 1894.

CONTENTS.

GENEALOGICAL TABLES.

I.

THE FAMILY OF St. BASIL.

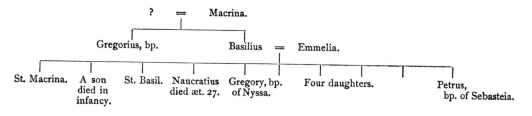

?   ═   Macrina.

Gregorius, bp.   Basilius ═ Emmelia.

St. Macrina.   A son died in infancy.   St. Basil.   Naucratius died æt. 27.   Gregory, bp. of Nyssa.   Four daughters.   Petrus, bp. of Sebasteia.

II.

THE FAMILY OF St. GREGORY OF NAZIANZUS, AND OF St. AMPHILOCHIUS.

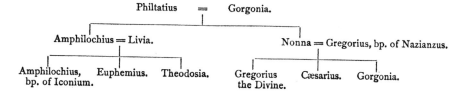

Philtatius ═ Gorgonia.

Amphilochius ═ Livia.   Nonna ═ Gregorius, bp. of Nazianzus.

Amphilochius, bp. of Iconium.   Euphemius.   Theodosia.   Gregorius the Divine.   Cæsarius.   Gorgonia.

CHRONOLOGICAL TABLE TO ACCOMPANY THE LIFE OF ST. BASIL.

A.D.
329 or 330. St. Basil born.
335. Council of Tyre.
336. Death of Arius.
337. *Death of Constantine.*
340. *Death of Constantine II.*
341. Dedication creed at Antioch.
343. *Julian and Gallus relegated to Macellum.*
     Basil probably sent from Annen to school at Cæsarea.
344. Macrostich, and Council of Sardica.
346. Basil goes to Constantinople.
350. *Death of Constans.*
351. Basil goes to Athens.
     1st Creed of Sirmium.
353. *Death of Magnentius.*
355. *Julian goes to Athens (latter part of year).*
356. Basil returns to Cæsarea.
357. The 2d Creed of Sirmium, or Blasphemy, subscribed by Hosius and Liberius.
     Basil baptized, and shortly afterwards ordained Reader.
358. Basil visits monastic establishments in Egypt, Syria, Palestine, and
     Mesopotamia, and retires to the monastery on the Iris.
359. The 3d Creed of Sirmium. *Dated* May 22. Councils of Seleucia and Ariminum.
360. Acacian synod of Constantinople.
     Basil, now ordained Deacon, disputes with Aetius.
     Dianius subscribes the Creed of Ariminum, and
     Basil in consequence leaves Cæsarea.
     He visits Gregory at Nazianzus.
361. *Death of Constantius and accession of Julian.*
     Basil writes the "Moralia."
362. Basil returns to Cæsarea.
     Dianius dies. Eusebius baptized, elected, and consecrated bishop.
     Lucifer consecrates Paulinus at Antioch.
     Julian at Cæsarea. Martyrdom of Eupsychius.
363. *Julian dies (June 27). Accession of Jovian.*
364. *Jovian dies. Accession of Valentinian and Valens.*
     Basil ordained Priest by Eusebius.
     Basil writes against Eunomius.
     Semiarian Council of Lampsacus.
365. *Revolt of Procopius.*
     Valens at Cæsarea.
366. Semiarian deputation to Rome satisfy Liberius of their orthodoxy.
     Death of Liberius. Damasus bp. of Rome.
     Procopius defeated.
367. *Gratian Augustus.*
     Valens favours the Arians.
     Council of Tyana.
368. Semiarian Council in Caria. Famine in Cappadocia.
369. Death of Emmelia. Basil visits Samosata.
370. Death of Eusebius of Cæsarea.
     Election and consecration of Basil to the see of Cæsarea.

PROLEGOMENA.

SKETCH OF THE LIFE AND WORKS OF SAINT BASIL.

I. LIFE.

I.—PARENTAGE AND BIRTH.

UNDER the persecution of the second Maximinus,[1] a Christian gentleman of good position and fair estate in Pontus,[2] and Macrina his wife, suffered severe hardships.[3] They escaped with their lives, and appear to have retained, or recovered, some of their property.[4] Of their children the names of two only have survived: Gregory[5] and Basil.[6] The former became bishop of one of the sees of Cappadocia. The latter acquired a high reputation in Pontus and the neighbouring districts as an advocate of eminence,[7] and as a teacher of rhetoric. His character in the Church for probity and piety stood very high.[8] He married an orphaned gentlewoman named Emmelia, whose father had suffered impoverishment and death for Christ's sake, and who was herself a conspicuous example of high-minded and gentle Christian womanhood. Of this happy union were born ten children,[9] five boys and five girls. One of the boys appears to have died in infancy, for on the death of the elder Basil four sons and five daughters were left to share the considerable wealth which he left behind him.[10] Of the nine survivors the eldest was a daughter, named, after her grandmother, Macrina. The eldest of the sons was Basil, the second Naucratius, and the third Gregory. Peter, the youngest of the whole family, was born shortly before his father's death., Of this remarkable group the eldest is commemorated as Saint Macrina in the biography written by her brother Gregory. Naucratius died in early manhood,[11] about the time of the ordination of Basil as reader. The three remaining brothers occupied respectively the sees of Cæsarea, Nyssa, and Sebasteia.

As to the date of St. Basil's birth opinions have varied between 316 and 330. The later, which is supported by Garnier, Tillemont, Maran,[12] Fessler,[13] and Böhringer, may probably be accepted as approximately correct.[14] It is true that Basil calls himself an old man in 374,[15] but he was prematurely worn out with work and bad health, and to his friends wrote freely and without concealment of his infirmities. There appears no reason to question the date 329 or 330.

Two cities, Cæsarea in Cappadocia and Neocæsarea in Pontus, have both been named as his birthplace. There must be some amount of uncertainty on this point, from the fact that no direct statement exists to clear it up, and that the word πατρίς was loosely employed

---

[1] Of sufferers in this supreme struggle of heathenism to delay the official recognition of the victory of the Gospel over the empire, the Reformed Kalendar of the English Church preserves the memory of St. Blaise (Blasius), bishop of Sebasteia in Armenia, St. George, St. Agnes, St. Lucy, St. Margaret of Antioch, St. Katharine of Alexandria.

[2] Greg. Naz., *Or.* xliii. (xx.). N.B. The reff. to the orations and letters of Greg. Naz. are to the *Ordo novus* in Migne.

[3] *Id.* [4] Greg. Nyss., *Vit. Mac.* 178, 191.

[5] Bishop of an unknown see. Of the foolish duplicity of Gregory of Nyssa in fabricating a letter from him, see the mention in *Epp.* lviii., lix., lx.

[6] Βασίλειος, *Basilius* = royal or *kingly*. The name was a common one. Fabricius catalogues "*alii Basilii ultra xxx.*," all of some fame. The derivation of Βασιλεύς is uncertain, and the connexion of the last syllable with λευς = λέως = λαός, people, almost certainly wrong. The root may be √BA, with the idea that the leader makes the followers march. With the type of name, *cf.* Melchi and the compounds of Melech (*e.g.* Abimelech) in Scripture, and King, LeRoy, Koenig, among modern names.

[7] Greg. Nyss., *Vit. Mac.* 392. [9] Greg. Nyss., *Vit. Mac.* 186. [11] Greg. Nyss., *Vit. Mac.* 182.

[8] Greg. Naz., *Or.* xliii. (xx.). [10] *Ib.* 181, 191.

[12] 329. Prudent Maran, the Ben. Ed. of Basil, was a Benedictine exiled for opposing the Bull Unigenitus. † 1762.

[13] "Natus. c. 330."

[14] Gregory of Nazianzus, so called, was born during the episcopate of his father, Gregory, bishop of Nazianzus. Gregory the elder died in 373, after holding the see forty-five years. The birth of Gregory the younger cannot therefore be put before 328, and Basil was a little younger than his friend. (Greg. Naz., *Ep.* xxxiii.) But the birth of Gregory in his father's episcopate has naturally been contested. *Vide D.C.B.* ii. p. 748, and L. Montaut, *Revue Critique* on Greg. of N. 1878.

[15] *Ep.* clxii.

to mean not only place of birth, but place of residence and occupation.[1] Basil's parents had property and interests both in Pontus and Cappadocia, and were as likely to be in the one as in the other. The early statement of Gregory of Nazianzus has been held to have weight, inasmuch as he speaks of Basil as a Cappadocian like himself before there was any other reason but that of birth for associating him with this province.[2] Assenting, then, to the considerations which have been held to afford reasonable ground for assigning Cæsarea as the birthplace, we may adopt the popular estimation of Basil as one of "The Three Cappadocians,"[3] and congratulate Cappadocia on the Christian associations which have rescued her fair fame from the slur of the epigram which described her as constituting with Crete and Cilicia a trinity of unsatisfactoriness.[4] Basil's birth nearly synchronizes with the transference of the chief seat of empire from Rome to Byzantium. He is born into a world where the victory already achieved by the Church has been now for sixteen years officially recognized.[5] He is born into a Church in which the first great Council has already given official expression to those cardinal doctrines of the faith, of which the final and formal vindication is not to be assured till after the struggles of the next six score of years. Rome, reduced, civilly, to the subordinate rank of a provincial city, is pausing before she realises all her loss, and waits for the crowning outrage of the barbarian invasions, ere she begins to make serious efforts to grasp, ecclesiastically, something of her lost imperial prestige. For a time the centre of ecclesiastical and theological interest is to be rather in the East than in the West.

II. — EDUCATION.

The place most closely connected with St. Basil's early years is neither Cæsarea nor Neocæsarea, but an insignificant village not far from the latter place, where he was brought up by his admirable grandmother, Macrina.[6] In this neighbourhood his family had considerable property, and here he afterwards resided. The estate was at Annesi, on the river Iris (Jekil-Irmak),[7] and lay in the neighbourhood of scenery of romantic beauty. Basil's own description[8] of his retreat on the opposite side of the Iris matches the reference of Gregory of Nazianzus[9] to the narrow glen among lofty mountains, which keep it always in shadow and darkness, while far below the river foams and roars in its narrow precipitous bed.

There is some little difficulty in understanding the statement of Basil in Letter CCXVI., that the house of his brother Peter, which he visited in 375, and which we may assume to have been on the family property (cf. Letter CX. § 1) was "not far from Neocæsarea." As a matter of fact, the Iris nowhere winds nearer to Neocæsarea than at a distance of about twenty miles, and Turkhal is not at the nearest point. But it is all a question of degree. Relatively to Cæsarea, Basil's usual place of residence, Annesi is near Neocæsarea. An analogy would be found in the statement of a writer usually residing in London, that if he came to Sheffield he would be not far from Doncaster.[10]

At Annesi his mother Emmelia erected a chapel in honour of the Forty Martyrs of Sebaste, to which their relics were translated. It is possible that Basil was present at the

---

[1] Gregory of Nazianzus calls Basil a Cappadocian in *Ep.* vi., and speaks of their both belonging to the same πατρίς. In his Homily *In Gordium martyrem*, Basil mentions the adornment of Cæsarea as being his own adornment. In *Epp.* lxxvi. and xcvi. he calls Cappadocia his πατρίς. In *Ep.* lxxiv., Cæsarea. In *Ep.* li. it is doubtful whether it is Pontus, whence he writes, which is his πατρίς, or Cæsarea, of which he is writing. In *Ep.* lxxxvii. it is apparently Pontus. Gregory of Nyssa (*Orat. I. in xl. Mart.*) calls Sebaste the πατρίς of his forefathers, possibly because Sebaste had at one time been under the jurisdiction of Cappadocia. So in the N.T. πατρίς is the place of the early life and education of our Lord.

[2] Maran, *Vit. Bas.* i.   [3] Böhringer.

[4] Καππάδοκες, Κρῆτες, Κίλικες, τρία κάππα κάκιστα. On Basil's own estimate of the Cappadocian character, *cf.* p. 153, n. *cf.* also Isidore of Pelusium, i. *Epp.* 351, 352, 281.

[5] The edict of Milan was issued in 313.   [6] *Epp.* cciv., ccx., ccxiii.

[7] *Epp.* iii., ccxxiii. The researches of Prof. W. M. Ramsay enable the exact spot to be identified with approximate certainty, and, with his guidance, a pilgrim to the scenes of Basil's boyhood and earlier monastic labours might feel himself on fairly sure ground. He refers to the description of St. Basil's hermitage given by Gregory of Nazianzus in his *Ep.* iv., a description which may be compared with that of Basil himself in *Ep.* xiv., as one which "can hardly refer to any other spot than the rocky glen below Turkhal. Ibora," in which diocese Annesi was situated, "cannot be placed further down, because it is the frontier bishopric of Pontus towards Sebasteia, and further up there is no rocky glen until the territory of Comana is reached. Gregory Nyssenus, in his treatise on baptism" (Migne, iii. 423 c.) "speaks of Comana as a neighbouring city. Tillemont, thinking that the treatise was written at Nyssa, infers that Nyssa and Comana were near each other. The truth is that Gregory must have written his treatise at Annesi. We may therefore infer that the territory of Ibora adjoined that of Comana on the east and that of Sebasteia on the south, and touched the Iris from the boundary of Comana down to the point below Turkhal. The boundary was probably near Tokat, and Ibora itself may have been actually situated near Turkhal." Prof. W. M. Ramsay, *Hist. Geog. of Asia Minor*, p. 326.   [8] *Ep.* xiv.   [9] Greg. Naz., *Ep.* iv.

[10] On the visits to Peter, Prof. W. M. Ramsay writes: "The first and more natural interpretation is that Peter lived at a place further up the Iris than Dazimon, in the direction of Neocæsarea. But on more careful consideration it is obvious that, after the troubles in Dazimon, Basil went to take a holiday with his brother Peter, and therefore he did not necessarily continue his journey onward from Dazimon. The expression of neighbourhood to the district of Neocæsarea is doubtless only comparative. Basil's usual residence was at Cæsarea. Moreover, as Ibora has now been placed, its territory probably touched that of Neocæsarea." *Hist. Geog. of A.M.* p. 328.

dedication services, lasting all night long, which are related to have sent his brother Gregory to sleep.[1] Here, then, Basil was taught the rudiments of religion by his grandmother,[2] and by his father,[3] in accordance with the teaching of the great Gregory the Wonder-worker.[4] Here he learned the Catholic faith.

At an early age he seems to have been sent to school at Cæsarea,[5] and there to have formed the acquaintance of an Eusebius, otherwise unknown,[6] Hesychius,[7] and Gregory of Nazianzus,[8] and to have conceived a boyish admiration for Dianius the archbishop.[9]

From Cæsarea Basil went to Constantinople, and there studied rhetoric and philosophy with success. Socrates[10] and Sozomen[11] say that he worked at Antioch under Libanius. It may be that both these writers have confounded Basil of Cæsarea with the Basil to whom Chrysostom dedicated his *De Sacerdotio*, and who was perhaps the bishop of Raphanea, who signed the creed of Constantinople.[12]

There is no corroboration of a sojourn of Basil of Cæsarea at Antioch. Libanius was at Constantinople in 347,[13] and there Basil may have attended his lectures.[14]

From Constantinople the young Cappadocian student proceeded in 351 to Athens. Of an university town of the 4th century we have a lively picture in the writings of his friend,[15] and are reminded that the rough horse-play of the modern undergraduate is a survival of a very ancient barbarism. The lads were affiliated to certain fraternities,[16] and looked out for the arrival of every new student at the city, with the object of attaching him to the classes of this or that teacher. Kinsmen were on the watch for kinsmen and acquaintances for acquaintances; sometimes it ·was mere good-humoured violence which secured the person of the freshman. The first step in this grotesque matriculation was an entertainment; then the guest of the day was conducted with ceremonial procession through the agora to the entrance of the baths. There they leaped round him with wild cries, and refused him admission. At last an entry was forced with mock fury, and the neophyte was made free of the mysteries of the baths and of the lecture halls. Gregory of Nazianzus, a student a little senior to Basil, succeeded in sparing him the ordeal of this initiation, and his dignity and sweetness of character seem to have secured him immunity from rough usage without loss of popularity.[17] At Athens the two young Cappadocians were noted among their contemporaries for three things: their diligence and success in work; their stainless and devout life; and their close mutual affection. Everything was common to them. They were as one soul. What formed the closest bond of union was their faith. God and their love of what is best made them one.[18] Himerius, a pagan, and Prohæresius, an Armenian Christian, are mentioned among the well-known professors whose classes Basil attended.[19] Among early friendships, formed possibly during his university career, Basil's own letters name those with Terentius[20] and Sophronius.[21]

If the Libanian correspondence be accepted as genuine, we may add Celsus, a pupil of Libanius, to the group.[22] But if we except Basil's affection for Gregory of Nazianzus, of none of these intimacies is the interest so great as of that which is recorded to have been formed between Basil and the young prince Julian.[23] One incident of the Athenian sojourn, which led to bitter consequences in after days, was the brief communication with Apollinarius, and the letter written "from layman to layman,"[24] which his opponents made a handle for much malevolence, and perhaps for forgery. Julian arrived at Athens after the middle of the year 355.[25] Basil's departure thence and return to Cæsarea may therefore

---

[1] Greg. Nyss., *Orat. in xl. Mart.*
[2] *Ep.* ccxxiii.
[3] Greg. Naz., *Or.* xliii.
[4] See *Ep.* cciv. and note on p. 250.
[5] *i.e.* the Cappadocian Cæsarea. The theory of Tillemont that Cæsarea of Palestine was the scene of Basil's early school life seems hardly to deserve the careful refutation of Maran (*Vit. Bas.* i. 5). *cf. Ep.* xlv. p. 148, and p. 145, n. *cf.* also note on p. 141 on a possible intercourse between the boy Basil and the young princes Gallus and Julian in their seclusion at Macellum. The park and palace of Macellum (Amm. Marc. "*fundus*") was near Mt. Argæus (Soz. v. 2) and close to Cæsarea. If Basil and Julian did ever study the Bible together, it seems more probable that they should do so at Macellum, while the prince was still being educated as a Christian, than afterwards at Athens, when the residence at Nicomedia had resulted in the apostasy. *cf.* Maran, *Vit. Bas.* ii. 4.
[6] *Ep.* cclxxi.
[7] *Ep.* lxiv.
[8] Greg. Naz. *Or.* xliii.
[9] *Ep.* li.
[10] *Ecc. Hist.* iv. 26.
[11] *Ecc. Hist.* vi. 17.
[12] Maran, *Vit. Bas.* ii., Fabricius, Ed. Harles. vol. ix.
[13] He does not seem to have been at Antioch until 353. *D.C.B.* iii. 710, when Basil was at Athens.
[14] *cf.* the correspondence with Libanius, of which the genuineness has been questioned, in *Letters* cccxxxv.–ccclix. *Letter* cccxxxix. suggests a possibility of some study of Hebrew. But Basil always uses the LXX.
[15] Greg. Naz., *Or.* xliii., and poem *De Vita Sua.*
[16] Φράτριαι. Greg., *De Vita Sua*, 215.
[17] A somewhat similar exemption is recorded of Dean Stanley at Rugby.
[18] Greg. Naz., *Or.* xliii. 20, 21; *Carm.* xi. 221-235:
"Ὁ δ᾿ εἰς ἓν ἡμᾶς διαφερόντως ἤγαγε
Τοῦτ᾿ ἦν θεός τε καὶ πόθος τῶν κρειοσόνων."
Ullman (*Life of Greg.*) quotes Cic., *De Amicitia*, xxv.: "*Amicitiæ vis est in eo ut unus quasi animus fiat ex pluribus.*"
[19] Soc. iv. 26 and Soz. vi. 17.
[20] *Ep.* lxiv.
[21] *Ep.* cclxxii.
[22] *Ep.* cccvi.
[23] Greg. Naz., *Or.* iv., *Epp.* xxxix., xl., xli., on the first of which see note.
[24] *Ep.* ccxxiv. 2.
[25] Amm. Mar. xv. 2, 8. "*Permissus*" is no doubt an euphemism for "*coactus.*"

be approximately fixed early in 356.[1] Basil starts for his life's work with the equipment of the most liberal education which the age could supply. He has studied Greek literature, rhetoric, and philosophy, under the most famous teachers. He has been brought into contact with every class of mind. His training has been no narrow hothouse forcing of theological opinion and ecclesiastical sentiment. The world which he is to renounce, to confront, to influence, is not a world unknown to him.[2] He has seen heathenism in all the autumn grace of its decline, and comes away victorious from seductions which were fatal to some young men of early Christian associations. Athens no doubt contributed its share of influence to the apostasy of Julian. Basil, happily, was found to be rooted more firmly in the faith.[3]

III. — LIFE AT CÆSAREA; BAPTISM; AND ADOPTION OF MONASTIC LIFE.

When Basil overcame the efforts of his companions to detain him at Athens, Gregory was prevailed on to remain for a while longer. Basil therefore made his rapid journey homeward alone. His Letter to Eustathius[4] alleges as the chief reason for his hurried departure the desire to profit by the instruction of that teacher. This may be the language of compliment. In the same letter he speaks of his fortitude in resisting all temptation to stop at the city on the Hellespont. This city I hesitate to recognise, with Maran, as Constantinople. There may have been inducements to Basil to stop at Lampsacus, and it is more probably Lampsacus that he avoided.[5] At Cæsarea he was welcomed as one of the most distinguished of her sons,[6] and there for a time taught rhetoric with conspicuous success.[7] A deputation came from Neocæsarea to request him to undertake educational work at that city,[8] and in vain endeavoured to detain[9] him by lavish promises. According to his friend Gregory, Basil had already determined to renounce the world, in the sense of devoting himself to an ascetic and philosophic life.[10] His brother Gregory, however,[11] represents him as at this period still under more mundane influences, and as shewing something of the self-confidence and conceit which are occasionally to be observed in young men who have just successfully completed an university career, and as being largely indebted to the persuasion and example of his sister Macrina for the resolution, with which he now carried out the determination to devote himself to a life of self-denial. To the same period may probably be referred Basil's baptism. The sacrament was administered by Dianius.[12] It would be quite consonant with the feelings of the times that pious parents like the elder Basil and Emmelia should shrink from admitting their boy to holy baptism before his encountering the temptations of school and university life.[13] The assigned date,

---

[1] "*Non enim citius contigit anno 355 exeunte aut incunte 356, si quidem ibi vidit Basilius Julianum, qui in hanc urbem venit jam me tia parte anni 355 elapsa: neque etiam serius, quia spatia inter studia litterarum et sacerdotium nimis contrahi non patitur rerum Basilii gestarum multitudo.*" Maran.

[2] On the education of Basil, Eug. Fialon remarks (*Étude Historique et Litteraire*, p. 15): " *Saint Grégoire, sur le trône patriarcal de Constantinople, déclarait ne pas savoir la langue de Rome. Il en fut de même de Saint Basile. Du moins, c'est vainement qu'on chercherait dans ses ouvrages quelque trace des poètes ou des prosateurs Latins. Si des passages de l'Hexaméron semblent tirés de Cicéron ou de Pline, il ne faut pas s'y méprendre. C'étaient de sortes de lieux communs qui se retrouvent dans Plutarque et dans Élien-ceux-ci les avaient empruntés à quelque vieil auteur, Aristotle, par exemple, et c'est à cette source première qu'avaient puisé Grecs et Latins. Les Grecs poussaient même si loin l'ignorance du Latin qu'un de leurs grammairiens ne semble pas se douter qu'il y ait des langues sans article, et que Grégoire de Nysse, ayant à dire comment le mot ciel s'exprime en Latin, l'écrit à peu près comme il devait l'entendre prononcer aux Romains,* Κέλουμ, *sans se préoccuper de la quantité ni de l'etymologie . . . La littérature Grecque était donc le fonds unique des études en Orient, et certes elle pouvait, à elle seule, satisfaire de nobles intelligences . . . C'est dans Homère que les jeunes Grecs apprenaient à lire. Pendant tout le cours de leurs études, ils expliquaient ses poèmes . . . Ses vers remplissent la correspondances des pères de l'église, et plus d'une comparaison profane passe de ses poèmes dans leurs homélies. Après Homère, venaient Hésiode et les tragiques Hérodote et Thucydide, Démosthène, Isocrate, et Lysias. Ainsi poètes, historiens, orateurs, formaient l'esprit, dirigeaient le cœur, élevaient l'âme des enfants. Mais ces auteurs étaient les coryphées du paganisme, et plus d'une passage de leur livres blessait la morale sévère du christianisme. Nul doute qu'un maître religieux, un saint, comme le père de Basile, à propos des dieux d'Homère, . . . dût plus d'une fois déplorer l'aveuglement d'un si beau génie. . . . Jusqu'ici, les études de Basile répondent à peu près à notre instruction secondaire. Alors, comme aujourd'hui ces premières études n'etaient qu'un acheminement à des travaux plus serieux. Muni de ce premier bagage littéraire, un jeune homme riche, et que voulait briller dans le monde, allait dans les grands centres, à Antioche, à Alexandrie, à Constantinople, et surtout à Athènes, étudier l'éloquence et la philosophie.*"

[3] cf. C. Ullman, *Life of Gregory of Naz.* chap. ii., and Greg. Naz., *Or.* xliii. 21. βλαβεραὶ μὲν τοῖς ἄλλοις Ἀθῆναι ἀτ εἰς ψυχήν. [4] *Ep.* i. [5] What these inducements can have been it seems vain to conjecture. cf. *Ep.* i. and note. [6] Greg. Naz., *Or.* xliii. [7] Rufinus xi. 9.

[8] *Ep.* ccx. § 2. The time assigned by Maran for the incident here narrated is no doubt the right one. But the deputation need have travelled no farther than to Annesi, if, as is tolerably certain, Basil on his return from Athens visited his relatives and the family estate.

[9] The word κατασχεῖν would be natural if they sought to keep him in Pontus; hardly, if their object was to bring him from Cæsarea. [10] *Or.* xliii. [11] *Vit. Mac.*

[12] cf. *De. Sp. Scto.* xxix., where the description of the bishop who both baptized and ordained Basil, and spent a long life in the ministry, can apply only to Dianius. cf. Maran, *Vit. Bas.* iii.

[13] According to the legendary life of St. Basil, attributed to St. Amphilochius, he was baptized at Jerusalem. Nor is it right to omit to notice the argument of Wall (*Infant Baptism*, ch. x.) founded on a coincidence between two passages in the writings of Greg. Naz. In *Or.* xl. *ad init.* he speaks of baptism as a γένεσις ἡμερινὴ καὶ ἐλευθέρα καὶ λυτικὴ παθῶν, πᾶν τὸ ἀπὸ γενέσεως κάλυμμα περιτέμνουσα, καὶ πρὸς τὴν ἄνω ζωὴν ἐπανάγουσα. In *Or.* xliii., he says of Basil that τὰ πρῶτα τῆς ἡλικίας ὑπὸ τῷ πατοὶ . . . σπαργανοῦται καὶ διαπλάττεται πλάσιν τὴν ἀρίστην τε καὶ καθαρωτάτην, ἣν ἡμερινὴν ὁ θεῖος Δαβὶδ καλῶς ὀνομάζει καὶ τῆς νυκτερινῆς ἀντίθετον. As they stand alone, there is something to be said for the conclusion Wall deduces from these

357, may be reasonably accepted, and shortly after his baptism he was ordained Reader.[1] It was about this time that he visited monastic settlements in Palestine, Mesopotamia, Cœle Syria, and Egypt,[2] though he was not so fortunate as to encounter the great pope Athanasius.[3] Probably during this tour he began the friendship with Eusebius of Samosata which lasted so long.

To the same period we may also refer his renunciation of his share of the family property.[4] Maran would appear to date this before the Syrian and Egyptian tour, a journey which can hardly have been accomplished without considerable expense. But, in truth, with every desire to do justice to the self-denial and unworldliness of St. Basil and of other like-minded and like-lived champions of the Faith, it cannot but be observed that, at all events in Basil's case, the renunciation must be understood with some reasonable reservation. The great archbishop has been claimed as a " socialist," whatever may be meant in these days by the term.[5] But St. Basil did not renounce all property himself, and had a keen sense of its rights in the case of his friends.[6] From his letter on behalf of his foster-brother, placed by Maran during his presbyterate,[7] it would appear that this foster-brother, Dorotheus, was allowed a life tenancy of a house and farm on the family estate, with a certain number of slaves, on condition that Basil should be supported out of the profits. Here we have landlord, tenant, rent, and unearned increment. St. Basil can scarcely be fairly cited as a practical apostle of some of the chapters of the socialist evangel of the end of the nineteenth century. But ancient eulogists of the great archbishop, anxious to represent him as a good monk, have not failed to foresee that this might be urged in objection to the completeness of his renunciation of the world, in their sense, and, to counterbalance it, have cited an anecdote related by Cassian.[8] One day a senator named Syncletius came to Basil to be admitted to his monastery, with the statement that he had renounced his property, excepting only a pittance to save him from manual labour. " You have spoilt a senator," said Basil, " without making a monk." Basil's own letter represents him as practically following the example of, or setting an example to, Syncletius.

Stimulated to carry out his purpose of embracing the ascetic life by what he saw of the monks and solitaries during his travels, Basil first of all thought of establishing a monastery in the district of Tiberina.[9] Here he would have been in the near neighbourhood of Arianzus, the home of his friend Gregory. But the attractions of Tiberina were ultimately postponed to those of Ibora, and Basil's place of retreat was fixed in the glen not far from the old home, and only separated from Annesi by the Iris, of which we have Basil's own picturesque description.[10] Gregory declined to do more than pay a visit to Pontus, and so is said to have caused Basil much disappointment.[11] It is a little characteristic of the imperious nature of the man of stronger will, that while he would not give up the society of his own mother and sister in order to be near his friend, he complained of his friend's not making a similar sacrifice in order to be near him.[12] Gregory[13] good-humouredly replies to Basil's depreciation of Tiberina by a counter attack on Cæsarea and Annesi.

At the Pontic retreat Basil now began that system of hard ascetic discipline which eventually contributed to the enfeeblement of his health and the shortening of his life. He complains again and again in his letters of the deplorable physical condition to which he is reduced, and he died at the age of fifty. It is a question whether a constitution better capable of sustaining the fatigue of long journeys, and a life prolonged beyond the Council of Constantinople, would or would not have left a larger mark upon the history of the Church. There can be no doubt, that in Basil's personal conflict with the decadent empire represented by Valens, his own cause was strengthened by his obvious superiority to the hopes and fears of vulgar ambitions. He ate no more than was actually necessary for daily sustenance, and his fare was of the poorest. Even when he was archbishop, no flesh meat was dressed in his kitchens.[14] His wardrobe consisted of one under and one

passages. Against it there is the tradition of the later baptism, with the indication of Dianius as having performed the rite in the *De Sp. Scto.* 29. On the other hand τα πρωτα της ηλικιας might possibly refer not to infancy, but to boyhood.
[1] *De S. Scto.* xxiv. On his growing seriousness of character, *cf. Ep.* ccxxiii.
[2] *Epp.* i. and ccxxiii. § 2.   [3] *Ep.* lxxx.   [4] *cf. Ep.* ccxxiii. § 2. Greg. Naz., *Or.* xliii.
[5] *e.g. The New Party*, 1894, pp. 82 and 83, quoting Bas., *In Isa.* i., *Hom. in illud Lucæ Destruam horrea*, § 7, and *Hom. in Divites.*   [6] *Epp.* iii., xxxvi. *cf.* Dr. Travers Smith, *Basil*, p. 33.   [7] *Ep.* xxxvii.
[8] *Inst.* vii. 19. *cf.* note on Cassian, vol. xi. p. 254 of this series.
[9] *Ep.* xiv. *ad fin.*   [10] *Ep.* xiv.   [11] Greg. Naz., *Ep.* i. or xliii. § 25.
[12] On the later difference between the friends at the time of Basil's consecration, De Broglie remarks : " *Ainsi se trahissait à chaque pas cette profonde diversité de caractère qui devait parfois troubler, mais plus sonnent ranimer et resserrer l'union de ces deux belles âmes : Basile, né pour le gouvernement des hommes et pour la lutte, prompt et précis dans ses resolutions, embrassant à coup d'œil le but à poursuivre et y marchant droit sans s'inquiéter des difficultés et du jugement des spectateurs ; Grégoire, atteint de cette délicatesse un peu maladive, qui est, chez les esprits d'élite, la source de l'inspiration poétique, sensible à la moindre renonce d'approbation ou de blâme, surtout à la moindre blessure de l'amitié, plus finement averti des obstacles, mais aussi plus aisément découragé, mélant a la poursuite des plus grands intérêts un soin peut être excessif de sa dignité et toutes les inquiétudes d'un cœur souffrant.*" *L'Église et l'Empire Romain au IVme Siècle*, v. p. 89.
[13] Greg. Naz., *Ep.* ii.   [14] *Ep.* xli.

over garment. By night he wore haircloth; not by day, lest he should seem ostentatious. He treated his body, says his brother, with a possible reference to St. Paul,[1] as an angry owner treats a runaway slave.[2] A consistent celibate, he was yet almost morbidly conscious of his unchastity, mindful of the Lord's words as to the adultery of the impure thought.[3] St. Basil relates in strong terms his admiration for the ascetic character cf Eustathius of Sebaste,[4] and at this time was closely associated with him. Indeed, Eustathius was probably the first to introduce the monastic system into Pontus, his part in the work being comparatively ignored in later days when his tergiversation had brought him into disrepute. Thus the credit of introducing monasticism into Asia Minor was given to Basil alone.[5] A novel feature of this monasticism was the Cœnobium,[6] for hitherto ascetics had lived in absolute solitude, or in groups of only two or three.[7] Thus it was partly relieved from the discredit of selfish isolation and unprofitable idleness.[8]

The example set by Basil and his companions spread. Companies of hard-working ascetics of both sexes were established in every part of Pontus, every one of them an active centre for the preaching of the Nicene doctrines, and their defence against Arian opposition and misconstruction.[9] Probably about this time, in conjunction with his friend Gregory, Basil compiled the collection of the beauties of Origen which was entitled *Philocalia*. Origen's authority stood high, and both of the main divisions of Christian thought, the Nicene and the Arian, endeavoured to support their respective views from his writings. Basil and Gregory were successful in vindicating his orthodoxy and using his aid in strengthening the Catholic position.[10]

IV. — BASIL AND THE COUNCILS, TO THE ACCESSION OF VALENS.

Up to this time St. Basil is not seen to have publicly taken an active part in the personal theological discussions of the age; but the ecclesiastical world was eagerly disputing while he was working in Pontus. Aetius, the uncompromising Arian, was openly favoured by Eudoxius of Germanicia, who had appropriated the see of Antioch in 357. This provoked the Semiarians to hold their council at Ancyra in 358, when the Sirmian "Blasphemy" of 357 was condemned. The Acacians were alarmed, and manœuvred for the division of the general council which Constantius was desirous of summoning. Then came Ariminum, Nike, and Seleucia, in 359, and " the world groaned to find itself Arian." Deputations from each of the great parties were sent to a council held under the personal presidency of Constantius at Constantinople, and to one of these the young deacon was attached. The date of the ordination to this grade is unknown. On the authority of Gregory of Nyssa[11] and Philostorgius,[12] it appears that Basil accompanied his namesake of Ancyra and Eustathius of Sebaste to the court, and supported Basil the bishop. Philostorgius would indeed represent the younger Basil as championing the Semiarian cause, though with some cowardice.[13] It may be concluded, with Maran, that he probably stood forward stoutly for the truth, not only at the capital itself, but also in the neighbouring cities of Chalcedon and Heraclea.[14] But his official position was a humble one, and his part in the discussions and amid the intrigues of the council was only too likely to be misrepresented by those with whom he did not agree, and even misunderstood by his own friends. In 360 Dianius signed the creed of Ariminum, brought to Cæsarea by George of Laodicea; and thereby Basil was so much distressed as henceforward to shun communion with his bishop.[15] He left Cæsarea and betook himself to Nazianzus to seek consolation in the society of his friend. But his feelings towards Dianius were always affectionate, and he indignantly repudiated a calumnious assertion that he had gone so far as to anathematize him. Two years later Dianius fell sick unto death and sent for Basil, protesting that at heart he had always been true to the Catholic creed. Basil acceded to the appeal, and in 362 once again communicated with his bishop and old friend.[16] In the interval between the

[1] 1 Cor. ix. 27.   [2] Greg. Nyss., *In Bas.* 314 c.   Cassian, *Inst.* vi. 19.   [4] *Ep.* ccxxiii. § 3.
[5] *cf.* Tillemont ix. *passim*, Walch iii. 552, Schröckh xiii. 25. quoted by Robertson, i. 366.
[6] κοινόβιον.   [7] Maran, *Vit. Bas.* vi.
[8] *cf.* Bas., *Reg. Fus. Resp.* vii., quoted by Robertson, i. 366. His rule has been compared to that of St. Benedict. *D.C.B.* i. 284. On the life in the Retreat, *cf. Epp.* ii. and ccvii.   [9] Soz. vi. 17.
[10] *cf.* Soc., *Ecc. Hist.* iv. 26. Of this work Gregory says, in sending it to a friend : ἵνα δέ τι καὶ ὑπόμνημα παρ' ἡμῶν ἔχῃς, τὸ δ' αὐτὸ καὶ τοῦ ἁγίου Βασιλείου πυκτίον ἀπεστάλκαμέν σοι τῆς Ὡριγενους Φιλοκαλίας, ἐκλογὰς ἔχων τῶν χρησίμων τοῖς φιλολόγοις. *Ep.* lxxxvii.   [11] i. Eunom.   [12] iv. 12.
[13] οἷς Βασίλειος ἕτερος παρῆν συναστίζων διακόνων ἔτι τάξιν ἔχων, δυνάμει μὲν τοῦ λέγειν πολλῶν προφέρων, τῷ δὲ τῆς γνώμης ἀθάρσει πρὸς τοὺς κοινοὺς ὑποστελλομένους ἀγῶνας. This is unlike Basil. "This may be the Arian way of saying that St. Basil withdrew from the Seleucian deputies when they yielded to the Acacians." Rev. C. F. H. Johnston, *De S. Scto. Int.* xxxvi.
[14] *Ep.* ccxxiii. § 5.   [15] *Ep.* li.   [16] *Epp.* viii. and li.

visit to Constantinople and this death-bed reconciliation, that form of error arose which was long known by the name of Macedonianism, and which St. Basil was in later years to combat with such signal success in the treatise *Of the Spirit.* It combined disloyalty to the Spirit and to the Son. But countervailing events were the acceptance of the Homoousion by the Council of Paris,[1] and the publication of Athanasius' letters to Serapion on the divinity of the two Persons assailed. To this period is referred the compilation by Basil of the *Moralia.*[2]

The brief reign of Julian would affect Basil, in common with the whole Church, in two ways: in the relief he would feel at the comparative toleration shewn to Catholics, and the consequent return of orthodox bishops to their sees;[3] in the distress with which he would witness his old friend's attempts to ridicule and undermine the Faith. Sorrow more personal and immediate must have been caused by the harsh treatment of Cæsarea[4] and the cruel imposts laid on Cappadocia. What conduct on the part of the Cæsareans may have led Gregory of Nazianzus[5] to speak of Julian as *justly* offended, we can only conjecture. It may have been the somewhat disorderly proceedings in connexion with the appointment of Eusebius to succeed Dianius. But there can be no doubt about the sufferings of Cæsarea, nor of the martyrdom of Eupsychius and Damas for their part in the destruction of the Temple of Fortune.[6]

The precise part taken by Basil in the election of Eusebius can only be conjectured. Eusebius, like Ambrose of Milan, a layman of rank and influence, was elevated *per saltum* to the episcopate. Efforts were made by Julian and by some Christian objectors to get the appointment annulled by means of Gregory, Bishop of Nazianzus, on the ground of its having been brought about by violence. Bishop Gregory refused to take any retrogressive steps, and thought the scandal of accepting the tumultuary appointment would be less than that of cancelling the consecration. Gregory the younger presumably supported his father, and he associates Basil with him as probable sufferers from the imperial vengeance.[7] But he was at Nazianzus at the time of the election, and Basil is more likely to have been an active agent.[8]

To this period may be referred Basil's receipt of the letter from Athanasius, mentioned in Letter CCIV., § 6.[9] On the accession of Jovian, in June, 363, Athanasius wrote to him asserting the Nicene Faith, but he was greeted also by a Semiarian manifesto from Antioch,[10] of which the first signatory was Meletius.

Valentinian and Valens, on their accession in the following year, thus found the Church still divided on its cardinal doctrines, and the lists were marked in which Basil was henceforward to be a more conspicuous combatant.

V. — THE PRESBYTERATE.

Not long after the accession of Valens, Basil was ordained presbyter by Eusebius.[11] An earlier date has been suggested, but the year 364 is accepted as fitting in better with the words of Gregory[12] on the free speech conceded to heretics. And from the same Letter it may be concluded that the ordination of Basil, like that of Gregory himself, was not wholly voluntary, and that he was forced against his inclinations to accept duties when he hesitated as to his liking and fitness for them. It was about this time that he wrote his Books against Eunomius;[13] and it may possibly have been this work which specially com-

---

[1] 360. Mansi, iii. 357-9.
[2] ἠθικά. "*Capita moralia christiana, ex meris Novi Testamenti dictis contexta et regulis* lxxx. *comprehensa.*" Fab. Closely connected with these are the *Regulæ fusius tractatæ* (ὅροι κατὰ πλάτος) lv., and the *Regulæ brevius tractatæ* (ὅροι κατ' ἐπιτόμην) cccxiii. (Migne, xxxi. pp. 890–1306) on which see later.
[3] The most important instance being that of Athanasius, who, on his return to Alexandria after his third exile, held a synod which condemned Macedonians as well as Arians. *cf.* Newman's *Arians,* v. I.
[4] Soz. v. 4. [5] *Or.* iv. § 92.
[6] *Epp.* c., cclii. Soz. v. 11. *cf.* also *Epp.* xxxix., xl., and xli., with the notes on pp. 141, 142, for the argument for and against the genuineness of the correspondence. Two Eupsychii of Cæsarea are named in the *Acta Sanctorum* and by the *Petits Bollandistes,* — one celebrated on April 9, said to have been martyred in the reign of Hadrian, the other the victim of Julian in 362, commemorated on Sept. 7. Tillemont identifies them. Baronius thinks them distinct. J. S. Stilting (*Act. Sanct.* ed. 1858) is inclined to distinguish them mainly on the ground that between 362 and the time of Basil's describing the festival as an established yearly commemoration there is not sufficient interval for the cultus to have arisen. This alone seems hardly convincing. The local interest in the victim of Julian's severity would naturally be great. Becket was murdered in 1170 and canonized in 1173, Dec. 29 being fixed for his feast; Lewis VII. of France was among the pilgrims in 1179. Bernadette Soubirous announced her vision at Lourdes in 1858; the church was begun there in 1862.
[7] *Or.* v. 39. [8] *cf.* Greg. Naz. *Ep.* viii. [9] Maran, *Vit. Bas.* viii. 8. [10] Soc. iii. 25.
[11] It will have been noted that I have accepted the authority of Philostorgius that he was already deacon. The argument employed by Tillemont against this statement is the fact of no distinct diaconate being mentioned by Gregory of Nazianzus. But the silence of Gregory does not conclusively outweigh the distinct ἔτι τάξιν διακόνου ἔχων of Philostorgius; and a diaconate is supported by the mistaken statement of Socrates (*H.E.* iv. 26) that the deacon's orders were conferred by Meletius.
[12] Greg. Naz., *Ep.* viii. [13] *cf. Ep.* xx.

mended him to Eusebius. However this may be, there is no doubt that he was soon actively engaged in the practical work of the diocese, and made himself very useful to Eusebius. But Basil's very vigour and value seem to have been the cause of some alienation between him and his bishop. His friend Gregory gives us no details, but it may be inferred from what he says that he thought Basil ill-used.[1] And allusions of Basil have been supposed to imply his own sense of discourtesy and neglect.[2] The position became serious. Bishops who had objected to the tumultuary nomination of Eusebius, and had with difficulty been induced to maintain the lawfulness of his consecration, were ready to consecrate Basil in his place. But Basil shewed at once his wisdom and his magnanimity. A division of the orthodox clergy of Cappadocia would be full of danger to the cause. He would accept no personal advancement to the damage of the Church. He retired with his friend Gregory to his Pontic monasteries,[3] and won the battle by flying from the field. Eusebius was left unmolested, and the character of Basil was higher than ever.[4]

The seclusion of Basil in Pontus seemed to afford an opportunity to his opponents in Cappadocia, and according to Sozomen,[5] Valens himself, in 365, was moved to threaten Cæsarea with a visit by the thought that the Catholics of Cappadocia were now deprived of the aid of their strongest champion. Eusebius would have invoked Gregory, and left Basil alone. Gregory, however, refused to act without his friend, and, with much tact and good feeling, succeeded in atoning the two offended parties.[6] Eusebius at first resented Gregory's earnest advocacy of his absent friend, and was inclined to resent what seemed the somewhat impertinent interference of a junior. But Gregory happily appealed to the archbishop's sense of justice and superiority to the common unwillingness of high dignitaries to accept counsel, and assured him that in all that he had written on the subject he had meant to avoid all possible offence, and to keep within the bounds of spiritual and philosophic discipline.[7] Basil returned to the metropolitan city, ready to coöperate loyally with Eusebius, and to employ all his eloquence and learning against the proposed Arian aggression. To the grateful Catholics it seemed as though the mere knowledge that Basil was in Cæsarea was enough to turn Valens with his bishops to flight,[8] and the tidings, brought by a furious rider, of the revolt of Procopius,[9] seemed a comparatively insignificant motive for the emperor's departure.

There was now a lull in the storm. Basil, completely reconciled to Eusebius, began to consolidate the archiepiscopal power which he afterward wielded as his own,[10] over the various provinces in which the metropolitan of Cæsarea exercised exarchic authority.[11] In the meantime the Semiarians were beginning to share with the Catholics the hardships inflicted by the imperial power. At Lampsacus in 364 they had condemned the results of Ariminum and Constantinople, and had reasserted the Antiochene Dedication Creed of 341. In 366 they sent deputies to Liberius at Rome, who proved their orthodoxy by subscribing the Nicene Creed. Basil had not been present at Lampsacus,[12] but he had met Eustathius and other bishops on their way thither, and had no doubt influenced the decisions of the synod. Now the deputation to the West consisted of three of those bishops with whom he was in communication, Eustathius of Sebasteia, Silvanus of Tarsus, and Theophilus of Castabala. To the first it was an opportunity for regaining a position among the orthodox prelates. It can hardly have been without the persuasion of Basil that the deputation went so far as they did in accepting the homoousion, but it is a little singular, and indicative of the comparatively slow awakening of the Church in general to the perils of the degradation of the Holy Ghost, that no profession of faith was demanded from the Lampsacene delegates on this subject.[13] In 367 the council of Tyana accepted the restitution of the Semiarian bishops, and so far peace had been promoted.[14] To this period may very probably be referred the compilation of the Liturgy which formed the basis of that which bears Basil's name.[15] The claims of theology and of ecclesiastical administration in Basil's

---

[1] Greg. Naz., *Orat.* xliii. 28, *Epp.* xvi.-xvii.   [2] *e.g. Hom. in Is.* i. 57, ἀλαζονεία γὰρ δεινὴ τὸ μηδενὸς οἴεσθαι χρῄζειν.
[3] Gregory has no doubt that Eusebius was in the wrong, even ridiculously in the wrong, if such be the true interpretation of his curious phrase (*Or.* xliii. 28), ἅπτεται γὰρ οὐ τῶν πολλῶν μόνον, ἀλλὰ καὶ τῶν ἀρίστων, ὁ Μῶμος. The monasteries to which Basil fled Gregory here (*id.* 29) calls φροντιστήρια, the word used by Aristophanes (*Clouds*, 94) of the house or school of Socrates, and apparently a comic parody on δικαστήριον. It might be rendered "reflectory." "Contemplatory" has been suggested. It is to be noted that Basil in the *De Sp. Scto.* (see p. 49, n.) appears to allude to the Acharnians. The friends probably read Aristophanes together at Athens.
[4] Greg. Naz., *Or.* xliii. Soz. vi. 15.   [5] vi. 15.   [6] Greg. Naz., *Epp.* xvi., xvii., xix., and *Or.* xx.
[7] οὐκ ὑβριστικῶς, ἀλλὰ πνευματικῶς τε καὶ φιλοσόφως.   [8] Soz. vi. 15.   [9] Amm. Marc. xxvi. 7, 2.
[10] ἐντεῦθεν αὐτῷ περιῆν καὶ τὸ κράτος τῆς ἐκκλησίας, εἰ καὶ τῆς καθέδρας εἶχε τὰ δεύτερα. Greg. Naz., *Or.* xliii.
[11] *cf.* Maran, *Vit. Bas.* xiv. and *D.C.A. s.v.* exarch. The archbishop of Cæsarea was exarch of the provinces (ἐπαρχίαι) comprised in the Pontic Diocese. Maran refers to *Letters* xxviii., xxx., and xxxiv., as all shewing the important functions discharged by Basil while yet a presbyter.
[12] *Ep.* ccxxiii.   [13] Hefele, § 88. Schröckh. *Kirch.* xii. 31. Swete, *Doctrine of the Holy Spirit*, 54.
[14] *Epp.* ccxliv. and cclxiii.   [15] Greg. Naz., *Or.* xliii.

time did not, however, prevent him from devoting much of his vast energy to works of charity. Probably the great hospital for the housing and relief of travellers and the poor, which he established in the suburbs of Cæsarea, was planned, if not begun, in the latter years of his presbyterate, for its size and importance were made pretexts for denouncing him to Elias, the governor of Cappadocia, in 372,[1] and at the same period Valens contributed to its endowment. It was so extensive as to go by the name of Newtown,[2] and was in later years known as the " Basileiad."[3] It was the mother of other similar institutions in the country-districts of the province, each under a Chorepiscopus.[4] But whether the Ptochotrophium[5] was or was not actually begun before Basil's episcopate, great demands were made on his sympathy and energy by the great drought and consequent famine which befell Cæsarea in 368.[6] He describes it with eloquence in his Homily *On the Famine and Drought.*[7] The distress was cruel and widespread. The distance of Cæsarea from the coast increased the difficulty of supplying provisions. Speculators, scratching, as it were, in their country's wounds, hoarded grain in the hope of selling at famine prices. These Basil moved to open their stores. He distributed lavishly at his own expense,[8] and ministered in person to the wants of the sufferers. Gregory of Nazianzus[9] gives us a picture of his illustrious friend standing in the midst of a great crowd of men and women and children, some scarcely able to breathe; of servants bringing in piles of such food as is best suited to the weak state of the famishing sufferers; of Basil with his own hands distributing nourishment, and with his own voice cheering and encouraging the sufferers.

About this time Basil suffered a great loss in the death of his mother,[10] and sought solace in a visit to his friend Eusebius at Samosata.[11] But the cheering effect of his journey was lessened by the news, which greeted him on his return, that the Arians had succeeded in placing one of their number in the see of Tarsus.[12] The loss of Silvanus was ere long followed by a death of yet graver moment to the Church. In the middle of 370 died Eusebius, breathing his last in the arms of Basil.[13]

VI. — BASIL AS ARCHBISHOP.

The archiepiscopal throne was now technically vacant. But the man who had practically filled it, " the keeper and tamer of the lion,"[14] was still alive in the plenitude of his power. What course was he to follow? Was he meekly to withdraw, and perhaps be compelled to support the candidature of another and an inferior? The indirect evidence[15] has seemed to some strong enough to compel the conclusion that he determined, if possible, to secure his election to the see.[16] Others, on the contrary, have thought him incapable of scheming for the nomination.[17] The truth probably lies between the two extreme views. No intelligent onlooker of the position at Cæsarea on the death of Eusebius, least of all the highly capable administrator of the province, could be blind to the fact that of all possible competitors for the vacant throne Basil himself was the ablest and most distinguished, and the likeliest to be capable of directing the course of events in the interests of orthodoxy. But it does not follow that Basil's appeal to Gregory to come to him was a deliberate step to secure this end. He craved for the support and counsel of his friend; but no one could

---

[1] *Ep.* xciv.　[2] ἡ καινὴ πόλις. Greg. Naz., *Or.* xliii. *cf.* Sir Thomas More's *Utopia*, Bk. II. Chap. V.
[3] Soz. vi. 34.　[4] *Epp.* cxlii., cxliii.
[5] πτωχοτροφεῖον. *Ep.* clxxvi. Professor Ramsay, in *The Church and the Roman Empire*, p. 464, remarks that " the ' New City ' of Basil seems to have caused the gradual concentration of the entire population of Cæsarea round the ecclesiastical centre, and the abandonment of the old city. Modern Kaisari is situated between one and two miles from the site of the Græco-Roman city."　[6] For the date, *cf.* Maran, *Vit. Bas.* ix. § 5.
[7] § 2, p. 63. *cf.* Greg. Naz., *Or.* xliii. 340-342, and Greg. Nyss., *In Eun.* i. 306.
[8] Greg. Nyss., *In Eunom.* i. § 10 (in this series, p. 45), remarks of Basil: τὴν πατρῴαν οὐσίαν καὶ πρὸ τῆς ἱερωσύνης ἀφειδῶς ἀναλώσας τοῖς πένησι καὶ μάλιστα ἐν τῷ τῆς σιτοδείας καιρῷ, καθ᾽ ὃν ἐπεστάτει τῆς ἐκκλησίας, ἔτι ἐν τῷ κλήρῳ τῶν πρεσβυτέρων ἱερατεύων καὶ μετὰ ταῦτα, μηδὲ τῶν ὑπολειφθέντων φεισάμενος. Maran (*Vit. Bas.* xi. § 4), with the object of proving that Basil had completely abandoned all property whatsoever, says that this must refer to a legacy from his mother. The terms used are far more consistent with the view already expressed (§ III.). So in his *Orat. in Bas.* Gregory speaks of Basil at the time as " selling his own possessions, and buying provisions with the proceeds."
[9] *Or.* xliii.　[10] Greg. Nyss., *Vit. Mac.* 187, *Ep.* xxx.　[11] *Ep.* xxxiv.　[12] *Id.*
[13] Greg. Naz., *Or.* xliii.　[14] Greg. Naz., *Or.* xliii. 33.
[15] *i.e.* the extant reply to his urgent request that Gregory would come to him. Greg. Naz., *Ep.* xl.
[16] " *Persuadé que, s'il échouait c'en était fait de la foi de Nicée en Cappadoce, il déploie toutes les ressources de son génie, aussi souple que puissant.*" Fialon, *Et. Hist.* p. 85.
" *Personne dans la ville, pas même Basile, malgré son humilité, ne douta que la succession ne lui fût acquise . . . il fit assez ouvertement ses préparatifs pour sa promotion.*" De Broglie, *L'Église et l'Empire R.* v. 88.
" Basil persuaded himself, and not altogether unwarrantably, that the cause of orthodoxy in Asia Minor was involved in his becoming his successor." Canon Venables in *D.C.B.*
" *Erselbst, so schwer er sich anfangs zur Uebernahme des Presbyterates hatte entschliessen können, jetzt, wo er sich in seine Stellung hinein gearbeitet hatte wünschte er nichts sehnlicher al seine Wahl zum Bischof.*" Böhringer the IVth c. p. 24. " Was it really from ambitious views? Certainly the suspicion, which even his friend entertained, attaches to him." Ullmann, *Life of Gregory of Naz.*, Cox's Trans. p. 117.
[17] " *Ne suspicatus quidem in se oculos conjectum iri.*" Maran, *Vit. Bas.*
" *Former une brigue pour parvenir à l'épiscopat était bien loin de sa pensée.*" Ceillier, iv. 354.

have known better that Gregory the younger was not the man to take prompt action or rule events. His invention of a fatal sickness, or exaggeration of a slight one, failed to secure even Gregory's presence at Cæsarea. Gregory burst into tears on receipt of the news of his friend's grave illness, and hastened to obey the summons to his side. But on the road he fell in with bishops hurrying to Cæsarea for the election of a successor to Eusebius, and detected the unreality of Basil's plea. He at once returned to Nazianzus and wrote the oft-quoted letter,[1] on the interpretation given to which depends the estimate formed of Basil's action at the important crisis.

Basil may or may not have taken Gregory's advice not to put himself forward. But Gregory and his father, the bishop, from this time strained every nerve to secure the election of Basil. It was felt that the cause of true religion was at stake. " The Holy Ghost must win."[2] Opposition had to be encountered from bishops who were in open or secret sympathy with Basil's theological opponents, from men of wealth and position with whom Basil was unpopular on account of his practice and preaching of stern self-denial, and from all the lewd fellows of the baser sort in Cæsarea.[3] Letters were written in the name of Gregory the bishop with an eloquence and literary skill which have led them to be generally regarded as the composition of Gregory the younger. To the people of Cæsarea Basil was represented as a man of saintly life and of unique capacity to stem the surging tide of heresy.[4] To the bishops of the province who had asked him to come to Cæsarea without saying why, in the hope perhaps that so strong a friend of Basil's might be kept away from the election without being afterwards able to contest it on the ground that he had had no summons to attend, he expresses an earnest hope that their choice is not a factious and foregone conclusion, and, anticipating possible objections on the score of Basil's weak health, reminds them that they have to elect not a gladiator, but a primate.[5] To Eusebius of Samosata he sends the letter included among those of Basil[6] in which he urges him to coöperate in securing the appointment of a worthy man. Despite his age and physical infirmity, he was laid in his litter, as his son says[7] like a corpse in a grave, and borne to Cæsarea to rise there with fresh vigour and carry the election by his vote.[8] All resistance was overborne, and Basil was seated on the throne of the great exarchate.

The success of the Catholics roused, as was inevitable, various feelings. Athanasius wrote from Alexandria[9] to congratulate Cappadocia on her privilege in being ruled by so illustrious a primate. Valens prepared to carry out the measures against the Catholic province, which had been interrupted by the revolt of Procopius. The bishops of the province who had been narrowly out-voted, and who had refused to take part in the consecration, abandoned communion with the new primate.[10] But even more distressing to the new archbishop than the disaffection of his suffragans was the refusal of his friend Gregory to come in person to support him on his throne. Gregory pleaded that it was better for Basil's own sake that there should be no suspicion of favour to personal friends, and begged to be excused for staying at Nazianzus.[11] Basil complained that his wishes and interests were disregarded,[12] and was hurt at Gregory's refusing to accept high responsibilities, possibly the coadjutor-bishopric, at Cæsarea.[13] A yet further cause of sorrow and annoyance was the blundering attempt of Gregory of Nyssa to effect a reconciliation between his uncle Gregory, who was in sympathy with the disaffected bishops, and his brother. He even went so far as to send more than one forged letter in their uncle's name. The clumsy counterfeit was naturally found out, and the widened breach not bridged without difficulty.[14] The episcopate thus began with troubles, both public and personal. Basil confidently confronted them. His magnanimity and capacity secured the adhesion of his immediate neighbours and subordinates,[15] and soon his energies took a wider range. He directed the theological campaign all over the East, and was ready alike to meet opponents in hand to hand encounter, and to aim the arrows of his epistolary eloquence far and wide.[16] He invokes the illustrious pope of Alexandria to join him in winning the support of the West for the orthodox cause.[17] He is keenly interested in the unfortunate controversy which distracted the Church of Antioch.[18] He makes an earnest appeal to Damasus for the wonted sympathy of the Church at Rome.[19] At the same time his industry in his see was indefatigable. He is keen to secure the

---

[1] Greg. N., *Ep.* xl. (xxi.).
[2] *Or.* xliii.
[3] *Or.* xliii. § 37.
[4] *Ep.* xli.
[5] *Ep.* xliii.
[6] *Ep.* xlvii.
[7] *Or.* xliii.
[8] *Or.* xviii., xliii.
[9] Athan., *Ad Pall.* 953; *Ad Johan, et Ant.* 951.
[10] This is inferred from the latter part of *Ep.* xlviii. *cf.* Maran, *Vit. Bas.* xiii. 3.
[11] Greg. Naz., *Ep.* xlv.
[12] *Id. Ep.* xlvi.
[13] τήνδε τῆς καθέδρας τίμην. Greg. Naz., *Or.* xliii.
[14] *Epp.* lviii., lix., lx.
[15] Greg. Naz., *Or.* xliii. § 40.
[16] *Id.* § 43.
[17] Basil, *Epp.* lxvi., lxvii.
[18] *Ep.* lxix.
[19] *Ep.* lxx.

purity of ordination and the fitness of candidates.[1] Crowds of working people come to hear him preach before they go to their work for the day.[2] He travels distances which would be thought noticeable even in our modern days of idolatry of the great goddess Locomotion. He manages vast institutions eleemosynary and collegiate. His correspondence is constant and complicated. He seems the personification of the active, rather than of the literary and scholarly, bishop. Yet all the while he is writing tracts and treatises which are monuments of industrious composition, and indicative of a memory stored with various learning, and of the daily and effective study of Holy Scripture.

Nevertheless, while thus actively engaged in fighting the battle of the faith, and in the conscientious discharge of his high duties, he was not to escape an unjust charge of pusillanimity, if not of questionable orthodoxy, from men who might have known him better. On September 7th, probably in 371,[3] was held the festival of St. Eupsychius. Basil preached the sermon. Among the hearers were many detractors.[4] A few days after the festival there was a dinner-party at Nazianzus, at which Gregory was present, with several persons of distinction, friends of Basil. Of the party was a certain unnamed guest, of religious dress and reputation, who claimed a character for philosophy, and said some very hard things against Basil. He had heard the archbishop at the festival preach admirably on the Father and the Son, but the Spirit, he alleged, Basil defamed.[5] While Gregory boldly called the Spirit God, Basil, from poor motives, refrained from any clear and distinct enunciation of the divinity of the Third Person. The unfavourable view of Basil was the popular one at the dinner-table, and Gregory was annoyed at not being able to convince the party that, while his own utterances were of comparatively little importance, Basil had to weigh every word, and to avoid, if possible, the banishment which was hanging over his head. It was better to use a wise " economy "[6] in preaching the truth than so to proclaim it as to ensure the extinction of the light of true religion. Basil[7] shewed some natural distress and astonishment on hearing that attacks against him were readily received.[8]

It was at the close of this same year 371[9] that Basil and his diocese suffered most severely from the hostility of the imperial government. Valens had never lost his antipathy to Cappadocia. In 370 he determined on dividing it into two provinces. Podandus, a poor little town at the foot of Mt. Taurus, was to be the chief seat of the new province, and thither half the executive was to be transferred. Basil depicts in lively terms the dismay and dejection of Cæsarea.[10] He even thought of proceeding in person to the court to plead the cause of his people, and his conduct is in itself a censure of those who would confine the sympathies of ecclesiastics within rigidly clerical limits. The division was insisted on. But, eventually, Tyana was substituted for Podandus as the new capital; and it has been conjectured[11] that possibly the act of kindness of the prefect mentioned in Ep. LXXVIII. may have been this transfer, due to the intervention of Basil and his influential friends.

But the imperial Arian was not content with this administrative mutilation. At the close of the year 371, flushed with successes against the barbarians,[12] fresh from the baptism of Endoxius, and eager to impose his creed on his subjects, Valens was travelling leisurely towards Syria. He is said to have shrunk from an encounter with the famous primate of Cæsarea, for he feared lest one strong man's firmness might lead others to resist.[13] Before him went Modestus, Prefect of the Prætorium, the minister of his severities,[14] and before Modestus, like the skirmishers in front of an advancing army, had come a troop of Arian

[1] Ep. liii.
[2] Hex. Hom. iii. p. 65.
[3] Maran, Vit. Bas. xviii. 4.
[4] Greg. Naz., Ep. lviii.
[5] παρασύρειν. Ib.
[6] οἰκονομηθῆναι.
[7] Ep. lxxi.
[8] Mr. C. F. H. Johnston (The Book of St. Basil the Great on the Holy Spirit), in noting that St. Basil in the De Sp. Scto. refrained from directly using the term Θεός of the Holy Ghost, remarks that he also avoided the use of the term ὁμοούσιος of the Son, " in accordance with his own opinion expressed in Ep. ix." In Ep. ix., however, he rather gives his reasons for preferring the homoousion. The epitome of the essay of C. G. Wuilcknis (Leipsig, 1724) on the economy or reserve of St. Basil, appended by Mr. Johnston, is a valuable and interesting summary of the best defence which can be made for such reticence. It is truly pointed out that the only possible motive in Basil's case was the desire of serving God, for no one could suspect or accuse him of ambition, fear, or covetousness. And if there was an avoidance of a particular phrase, there was no paltering with doctrine. As Dr. Swete (Doctrine of the H. S., p. 64) puts it: " He knew that the opponents of the Spirit's Deity were watching their opportunity. Had the actual name of God been used in reference to the Third Person of the Trinity, they would have risen, and, on the plea of resisting blasphemy, expelled St. Basil from his see, which would then have been immediately filled by a Macedonian prelate. In private conversations with Gregory, Basil not only asserted again and again the Godhead of the Spirit, but even confirmed his statement with a solemn imprecation, ἐπαρασάμενος ἑαυτῷ τὸ φρικωδέστατον, αὐτοῦ τοῦ πνεύματος ἐκπεσεῖν εἰ μὴ σέβοι τὸ πνεῦμα μετὰ πατρὸς καὶ Ὑιοῦ ὡς ὁμοούσιον καὶ ὁμότιμον." (Greg. Naz., Or. xliii.) In Letter viii. § 11 he distinctly calls the Spirit God, as in Adv. Eunomius, v., if the latter be genuine. In the De S. Scto. (p. 12) Basil uses the word οἰκονομία in the patristic sense nearly equivalent to incarnation. In the passage of Bp. Lightfoot, referred to in the note on p. 7, he points out how in Ign. ad Eph. xviii. the word has " already reached its first stage on the way to the sense of ' dissimulation,' which was afterwards connected with it, and which led to disastrous consequences in the theology and practice of a later age." On " Reserve " as taught by later casuists, see Scavini, Theolog. Mor. ii. 23, the letters of Pascal, and Jer. Taylor, Ductor Dubit. iii. 2.
[9] Maran, Vit. Bas. xx. 1.
[10] Epp. lxxiv., lxxv., lxxvi.
[11] Maran, Vit. Bas. xix. 3.
[12] Greg. Nyss., C. Eunom. i.
[13] Theod. iv. 16.
[14] Soc. iv. 16.

bishops, with Euippius, in all probability, at their head.[1] Modestus found on his arrival that Basil was making a firm stand, and summoned the archbishop to his presence with the hope of overawing him. He met with a dignity, if not with a pride, which was more than a match for his own. Modestus claimed submission in the name of the emperor, Basil refused it in the name of God. Modestus threatened impoverishment, exile, torture, death. Basil retorted that none of these threats frightened him : he had nothing to be confiscated except a few rags and a few books ; banishment could not send him beyond the lands of God ; torture had no terrors for a body already dead ; death could only come as a friend to hasten his last journey home. Modestus exclaimed in amazement that he had never been so spoken to before. " Perhaps," replied Basil, " you never met a bishop before." The prefect hastened to his master, and reported that ordinary means of intimidation appeared unlikely to move this undaunted prelate. The archbishop must be owned victorious, or crushed by more brutal violence. But Valens, like all weak natures, oscillated between compulsion and compliance. He so far abated his pretensions to force heresy on Cappadocia, as to consent to attend the services at the Church on the Festival of the Epiphany.[2] The Church was crowded. A mighty chant thundered over the sea of heads. At the end of the basilica, facing the multitude, stood Basil, statue-like, erect as Samuel among the prophets at Naioth,[3] and quite indifferent to the interruption of the imperial approach. The whole scene seemed rather of heaven than of earth, and the orderly enthusiasm of the worship to be rather of angels than of men. Valens half fainted, and staggered as he advanced to make his offering at God's Table. On the following day Basil admitted him within the curtain of the sanctuary, and conversed with him at length on sacred subjects.[4]

The surroundings and the personal appearance of the interlocutors were significant. The apse of the basilica was as a holy of holies secluded from the hum and turmoil of the vast city.[5] It was typical of what the Church was to the world. The health and strength of the Church were personified in Basil. He was now in the ripe prime of life, but bore marks of premature age. Upright in carriage, of commanding stature, thin, with brown hair and eyes, and long beard, slightly bald, with bent brow, high cheek bones, and smooth skin, he would shew in every tone and gesture at once his high birth and breeding, the supreme culture that comes of intercourse with the noblest of books and of men, and the dignity of a mind made up and of a heart of single purpose. The sovereign presented a marked contrast to the prelate.[6] Valens was of swarthy complexion, and by those who approached him nearly it was seen that one eye was defective. He was strongly built, and of middle height, but his person was obese, and his legs were crooked. He was hesitating and unready in speech and action.[7] It is on the occasion of this interview that Theodoret places the incident of Basil's humorous retort to Demosthenes,[8] the chief of the imperial kitchen, the Nebuzaradan, as the Gregories style him, of the petty fourth century Nebuchadnezzar. This Demosthenes had already threatened the archbishop with the knife, and been bidden to go back to his fire. Now he ventured to join in the imperial conversation, and made some blunder in Greek. "An illiterate Demosthenes!" exclaimed Basil; "better leave theology alone, and go back to your soups." The emperor was amused at the discomfiture of his satellite, and for a while seemed inclined to be friendly. He gave Basil lands, possibly part of the neighbouring estate of Macellum, to endow his hospital.[9]

But the reconciliation between the sovereign and the primate was only on the surface. Basil would not admit the Arians to communion, and Valens could not brook the refusal. The decree of exile was to be enforced, though the very pens had refused to form the letters of the imperial signature.[10] Valens, however, was in distress at the dangerous illness of

---

[1] cf. Epp. lxviii., cxxviii., ccxliv. and ccli., and Maran, Vit. Bas. xx. 1 ; possibly the bishops were in Cappadocia as early as the Eupsychian celebration.
[2] Jan. 6, 372. At this time in the Eastern Church the celebrations of the Nativity and of the Epiphany were combined. cf. D.C.A. i. 617.　　　[3] 1 Sam. xix. 20.
[4] Greg. Naz., Or. xliii., Greg. Nyss., Adv. Eunom. i., Soz. vi. 16, Theod. iv. 16. De Broglie well combines the variations which are not quite easy to harmonize in detail. On the admission within the sanctuary, cf. the concession of Ambrose to Theodosius in Theod. v. 18.
[5] Cæsarea, when sacked by Sapor in 260, is said to have contained 400,000 inhabitants (Zonaras, xii. 630). It may be presumed to have recovered and retained much, if not all, of its importance.
[6] The authority for the personal appearance of Basil is an anonymous Vatican document quoted by Baronius, Ann. 378: "Procero fuit habitu corporis et recto, siccus, gracilis ; color ejus fuscus, vultus temperatus pallore, justus nasus, supercilia in orbem inflexa et adducta ; cogitabundo similis fuit, paucæ in vultu rugæ, eæque renidentes, genæ oblongæ, tempora aliquantum cava, promissa barba, et mediocris canities."
[7] Amm. Marc. xxx. 14, 7: "Cessator et piger: nigri coloris, pupula oculi unius obstructa, sed ita ut non eminus appareret : figura bene compacta membrorum, staturæ nec proceræ nec humilis, incurvis cruribus, exstanteque mediocriter ventre." "Bon père, bon époux, arien fervent et zélé, mais faible, timide, Valens était né pour la vie privée, où il eût été un honnête citoyen et un des saints de l'Arianisme." Fialon, Et. Hist. 159.
[8] cf. Theod. v. 16 and note on p. 120 of Theod. in this series.
[9] Theod. iv. 16. Bas., Ep. xciv.　　　[10] Theod. iv. 16.

Galates, his infant son, and, on the very night of the threatened expatriation, summoned Basil to pray over him.   A brief rally was followed by relapse and death, which were afterwards thought to have been caused by the young prince's Arian baptism.[1]   Rudeness was from time to time shewn to the archbishop by discourteous and unsympathetic magistrates, as in the case of the Pontic Vicar, who tried to force an unwelcome marriage on a noble widow. The lady took refuge at the altar, and appealed to Basil for protection.   The magistrate descended to contemptible insinuation, and subjected the archbishop to gross rudeness.   His ragged upper garment was dragged from his shoulder, and his emaciated frame was threatened with torture.   He remarked that to remove his liver would relieve him of a great inconvenience.[2]

Nevertheless, so far as the civil power was concerned, Basil, after the famous visit of Valens, was left at peace.[3]   He had triumphed.   Was it a triumph for the nobler principles of the Gospel?   Had he exhibited a pride and an irritation unworthy of the Christian name?   Jerome, in a passage of doubtful genuineness and application, is reported to have regarded his good qualities as marred by the one bane of pride,[4] a "leaven" of which sin is admitted by Milman[5] to have been exhibited by Basil, as well as uncompromising firmness.   The temper of Basil in the encounter with Valens would probably have been somewhat differently regarded had it not been for the reputation of a hard and overbearing spirit which he has won from his part in transactions to be shortly touched on.   His attitude before Valens seems to have been dignified without personal haughtiness, and to have shewn sparks of that quiet humour which is rarely exhibited in great emergencies except by men who are conscious of right and careless of consequences to self.

VII. — THE BREACH WITH GREGORY OF NAZIANZUS.

Cappadocia, it has been seen, had been divided into two provinces, and of one of these Tyana had been constituted the chief town.   Anthimus, bishop of Tyana, now contended that an ecclesiastical partition should follow the civil, and that Tyana should enjoy parallel metropolitan privileges to those of Cæsarea.   To this claim Basil determined to offer an uncompromising resistance, and summoned Gregory of Nazianzus to his side.   Gregory replied in friendly and complimentary terms,[6] and pointed out that Basil's friendship for Eustathius of Sebaste was a cause of suspicion in the Church.   At the same time he placed himself at the archbishop's disposal.   The friends started together with a train of slaves and mules to collect the produce of the monastery of St. Orestes, in Cappadocia Secunda, which was the property of the see of Cæsarea.   Anthimus blocked the defiles with his retainers, and in the vicinity of Sasima[7] there was an unseemly struggle between the domestics of the two prelates.[8]   The friends proceeded to Nazianzus, and there, with imperious inconsiderateness, Basil insisted upon nominating Gregory to one of the bishoprics which he was founding in order to strengthen his position against Anthimus.[9]   For Gregory, the brother, Nyssa was selected, a town on the Halys, about a hundred miles distant from Cæsarea, so obscure that Eusebius of Samosata remonstrated with Basil on the unreasonableness of forcing such a man to undertake the episcopate of such a place.[10] For Gregory, the friend, a similar fate was ordered.   The spot chosen was Sasima, a townlet commanding the scene of the recent fray.[11]   It was an insignificant place at the bifurcation of the road leading northwards from Tyana to Doara and diverging westward to Nazianzus.[12]

---

[1] Theod. iv, 16. Soz. vi. 17. Soc. iv. 26. Greg. Naz., *Or.* xliii. Ruf. xi. 9.   [2] Greg. Naz., *Or.* xliii.
[3] "The archbishop, who asserted, with inflexible pride, the truth of his opinions and the dignity of his rank, was left in the free possession of his conscience and his throne." Gibbon, Chap. xxv.
"*Une sorte d'inviolabilité de fait demeurait acquise a Basile a Césarée comme a Athanase à Alexandrie.*" De Broglie.
[4] Quoted by Gibbon *l.c.* from Jerome's *Chron.* A.D. 380, and acknowledged by him to be not in Scaliger's edition.   The Benedictine editors of Jerome admit it, but refer it to Photinus.   *cf. D.C.B.* i. 288.
[5] *Hist. Christ.* iii. 45.   [6] Greg. Naz., *Ep.* xlvii.   [7] *cf.* Maran, *Vit. Bas.* xxiii. 4.
[8] Greg. Naz., *Or.* xliii. 58, and *Ep.* xlviii.   Bas., *Epp.* lxxiv., lxxv., lxxvi.
[9] It has been debated whether the *odium theologicum* was here mixed up with the *odium ecclesiasticum*.   Gregory (*Orat.* xliii. 58) represents Anthimus as defending his seizure of the metropolitan revenues on the ground that it was wrong δασμοφορειν κακοδόξοις, to pay tribute to men of evil opinions, and LeClerc (*Bibl. Univer.* xviii. p. 60) has condemned Anthimus as an Arian.   He was undoubtedly Αρήιος (Greg. Naz., *Ep.* xlviii.), a devotee of Ares, as he shewed in the skirmish by Sasima; but there is no reason to suppose him to have been Αρειανός, or Arian.   He probably looked askance at the orthodoxy of Basil. Basil would never have called him ὁμόψυχος (*Ep.* ccx. 5) if he had been unsound on the incarnation.   *cf.* Baronius, *Act. Sanc. Maj.* ii. p. 394.
[10] *Ep.* xcviii., but see note, p. 182, on the doubt as to this allusion.
[11] Greg. Naz., with grim humour, objects to be sent to Sasima to fight for Basil's supply of sucking pigs and poultry from St. Orestes.   *Ep.* xlviii.
[12] "Nyssa was more clearly than either Sasima or Doara a part of Cappadocia Secunda; it always retained its ecclesiastical dependence on Cæsarea, but politically it must have been subject to Tyana from 372 to 536, and afterwards to Mokissos. All three were apparently places to which Basil consecrated bishops during his contest with Anthimus and the civil power. His bishop of Nyssa, his own brother Gregory, was ejected by the dominant Arians, but the eminence and vigour of Gregory

Gregory speaks of it with contempt, and almost with disgust,[1] and never seems to have forgiven his old friend for forcing him to accept the responsibility of the episcopate, and in such a place.[2] Gregory resigned the distasteful post,[3] and with very bitter feelings. The utmost that can be said for Basil is that just possibly he was consulting for the interest of the Church, and meaning to honour his friend, by placing Gregory in an outpost of peril and difficulty. In the kingdom of heaven the place of trial is the place of trust.[4] But, unfortunately for the reputation of the archbishop, the war in this case was hardly the Holy War of truth against error, and of right against wrong. It was a rivalry between official and official, and it seemed hard to sacrifice Gregory to a dispute between the claims of the metropolitans of Tyana and Cæsarea.[5]

Gregory the elder joined in persuading his son. Basil had his way. He won a convenient suffragan for the moment. But he lost his friend. The sore was never healed, and even in the great funeral oration in which Basil's virtues and abilities are extolled, Gregory traces the main trouble of his chequered career to Basil's unkindness, and owns to feeling the smart still, though the hand that inflicted the wound was cold.[6]

secured his reinstatement and triumphant return. Basil's appointment was thus successful, and the connexion always continued. His appointment at Sasima was unsuccessful. Gregory of Nazianzus would not maintain the contest, and Sasima passed under the metropolitan of Tyana. At Doara, in like fashion, Basil's nominee was expelled, and apparently never reinstated. *Ep.* cccxxxix. Greg. Naz. *Or.*, xiii." Ramsay, *Hist. Geog. of A.M.* 305.

[1] As in Carm. *De Vita Sua* :

Σταθμός τις ἐστὶν ἐν μέσῃ λεωφόρῳ	" A post town on the king's high road,
Τῆς Καππαδοκῶν ὃς σχίζετ᾽ εἰς τρισσὴν ὁδόν.	Where three ways meet, is my abode;
Ἄνυδρος, ἄχλους, οὐδ᾽ ὅλως ἐλεύθερος,	No brooklet, not a blade of grass,
Δεινῶς ἐπευκτὸν καὶ στενὸν κωμύδριον,	Enlivens the dull hole, alas!
Κόνις τα πάντα, καὶ ψόφοι, σὺν ἅρμασι,	Dust, din, all day; the creak of wheels;
Θρῆνοι, στεναγμοὶ, πράκτορες, στρέβλαι, πέδαι·	Groans, yells, the exciseman at one's heels
Λαὸς δ᾽ ὅσοι ξένοι τε καὶ πλανώμενοι,	With screw and chain; the population
Αὕτη Σασίμων τῶν ἐμῶν ἐκκλησία.	A shifting horde from every nation.
[N.B. — The last line marks the quantity.]	A viler spot you long may search, '
	Than this Sasima, now my church!"

[2] It is curious that a place which had so important a connexion with Gregory the divine should have passed so completely into oblivion. From it he derived his episcopal rank. His consecration to Sasima was the main ground of the objection of his opponents at Constantinople in 381 to his occupying the see of the imperial city. He was bishop of Sasima, and, by the fifteenth Canon of Nicæa, could not be transferred to Constantinople. He never was bishop of Nazianzus, though he did administer that diocese before the appointment of Eulalius in 383. But while the name " Gregory of Nazianzus " has obscured the very existence of his father, who was really Gregory of Nazianzus, and is known even to the typical schoolboy, Gregory has never been described as " Gregory of Sasima." " The great plain which extends from Sasima nearly to Soandos is full of underground houses and churches, which are said to be of immense extent. The inhabitants are described by Leo Diaconus (p. 35) as having been originally named Troglodytes. . . . Every house in Hassa Keni has an underground story cut out of the rock; long narrow passages connect the underground rooms belonging to each house, and also run from house to house. A big solid disc of stone stands in a niche outside each underground house door, ready to be pulled in front of the door on any alarm. . . . Sasima was on the road between Nazianzus and Tyana. The distances point certainly to Hassa Keni. . . . An absolutely unhistorical legend about St. Makrina is related at Hassa Keni. Recently a good-sized church has been built in the village, dedicated to St. Makrina, who, as the village priest relates, fled hither from Kaisari to escape marriage, and to dedicate herself to a saintly life. The underground cell in which she lived is below the church." Ramsay, *Hist. Geog. of Asia Minor*, pp. 293, 294. Paul Lucas identified Sasima with Inschesu. [3] *cf.* Greg. Naz. *Ep.* l.

[4] *cf.* De Joinville's happy illustration of this in *Histoire du roi Saint Louis*, p. 18. Ed. 1617. The King of France would shew more confidence in the captain whom he might choose to defend La Rochelle, close to the English pale, than in the keeper of Monthléry, in the heart of the realm.

[5] At the same time it is disappointing to find Gregory mixing up with expressions of reluctance to assume awful responsibilities, objections on the score of the disagreeable position of Sasima. Perhaps something of the sentiments of Basil on this occasion may be inferred from what he says in *Letter* cii. on the postponement of private to public considerations in the case of the appointment of Pœmenius to Satala.

[6] *Or.* xliii. *cf.* Newman, *The Church of the Fathers*, p. 142, where the breach is impartially commented on : " An ascetic, like Gregory, ought not to have complained of the country as deficient in beauty and interest, even though he might be allowed to feel the responsibility of a situation which made him a neighbour of Anthimus. Yet such was his infirmity; and he repelled the accusations of his mind against himself by charging Basil with unkindness in placing him at Sasima. On the other hand, it is possible that Basil, in his eagerness for the settlement of his exarchate, too little consulted the character and taste of Gregory; and, above all, the feelings of duty which bound him to Nazianzus. . . . Henceforth no letters, which are preserved, passed between the two friends; nor are any acts of intercourse discoverable in their history. Anthimus appointed a rival bishop to Sasima; and Gregory, refusing to contest the see with him, returned to Nazianzus. Basil laboured by himself. Gregory retained his feelings of Basil's unkindness even after his death. . . . This lamentable occurrence took place eight or nine years before Basil's death; he had, before and after it, many trials, many sorrows; but this probably was the greatest of all." The statement that no letters which are preserved passed between the two friends henceforth will have to be modified, if we suppose *Letter* clxix. to be addressed to Gregory the Divine. But Professor Ramsay's arguments (*Hist. Geog. of Asia Minor*, p. 293) in favour of Gregory of Nazianzus the elder seem irresistible.

On *Letter* clxix. he writes: " For topographical purposes it is necessary to discover who was the Gregory into whose diocese Glycerius fled. Tillemont considers that either Gregory of Nyssa or Gregory of Nazianzus is meant. But the tone of the letter is not what we might expect if Basil were writing to either of them. It is not conceived in the spirit of authority in which Basil wrote to his brother or to his friend. It appears to me to show a certain deference which, considering the resolute, imperious, and uncompromising character of Basil (seen especially in his behaviour to Gregory Nazianzen in the matter of the bishopric of Sasima), I can explain only on the supposition that he is writing to the aged and venerable Gregory, bishop of Nazianzos. Then the whole situation is clear. Venasa was in the district of Malakopaia, or Suvermez, towards the limits of the diocese of Cæsarea. The adjoining bishopric was that of Nazianzos. Venasa being so far from Cæsarea was administered by one of the fifty *chorepiscopi* whom Basil had under him (Tillemont, *Mem. p. servir*, etc., ix. p. 120), and the authority of Basil was appealed to only in the final resort. Glycerius, when Basil decided against him, naturally fled over the border into the diocese of Nazianzos." (There is, however, not much reverence in *Letter* clxxi.)

" Comment l'homme qui avait tant souffert de l'injustice des autres, put-il être injuste envers son meilleur ami ? L'amitié est de tous les pays. Partout, on voit des hommes qui semblent faits l'un pour l'autre, se rapprocher par une estime mutuelle, par la conformité de leurs gouts et de leurs caractères partager les peines et les joies de la vie, et donner le spectacle du plus beau sentiment que nous ayons reçu de la divinité. Mais la Grèce avait singulièrement ennobli ce sentiment déjà si pur et si saint, en lui donnant pour but l'amour de la patrie. Les amis, destines a se servir l'un à l'autre de modèle et de soutien, s'aiment moins pour eux-mêmes, que pour rivaliser de vertu, se dévouer ensemble, s'immoler s'il le faut, au bien public. . . . C'est cette amitié de dévouement et de sacrifice, qu'au milieu de la mollesse du IVme siècle, Basile conçoit pour

With Anthimus peace was ultimately established. Basil vehemently desired it.[1] Eusebius of Samosata again intervened.[2] Nazianzus remained for a time subject to Cæsarea, but was eventually recognised as subject to the Metropolitan of Tyana.[3] The relations, however, between the two metropolitans remained for some time strained. When in Armenia in 372, Basil arranged some differences between the bishops of that district, and dissipated a cloud of calumny hanging over Cyril, an Armenian bishop.[4] He also acceded to a request on the part of the Church of Satala that he would nominate a bishop for that see, and accordingly appointed Pœmenius, a relation of his own.[5] Later on a certain Faustus, on the strength of a recommendation from a pope with whom he was residing, applied to Basil for consecration to the see, hitherto occupied by Cyril. With this request Basil declined to comply, and required as a necessary preliminary the authorisation of the Armenian bishops, specially of Theodotus of Nicopolis. Faustus then betook himself to Anthimus, and succeeded in obtaining uncanonical consecration from him. This was naturally a serious cause of disagreement.[6] However, by 375, a better feeling seems to have existed between the rivals. Basil is able at that date to speak of Anthimus as in complete agreement with him.[7]

VIII. — St. Basil and Eustathius.

It was Basil's doom to suffer through his friendships. If the fault lay with himself in the case of Gregory, the same cannot be said of his rupture with Eustathius of Sebaste. If in this connexion fault can be laid to his charge at all, it was the fault of entering into intimacy with an unworthy man. In the earlier days of the retirement in Pontus the austerities of Eustathius outweighed in Basil's mind any suspicions of his unorthodoxy.[8] Basil delighted in his society, spent days and nights in sweet converse with him, and introduced him to his mother and the happy family circle at Annesi.[9] And no doubt under the ascendency of Basil, Eustathius, always ready to be all things to all men who might be for the time in power and authority, would appear as a very orthodox ascetic. Basil likens him to the Ethiopian of immutable blackness, and the leopard who cannot change his spots.[10] But in truth his skin at various periods shewed every shade which could serve his purpose, and his spots shifted and changed colour with every change in his surroundings.[11] He is the patristic Proteus. There must have been something singularly winning in his more than human attractiveness.[12] But he signed almost every creed that went about for signature in his lifetime.[13] He was consistent only in inconsistency. It was long ere Basil was driven to withdraw his confidence and regard, although his constancy to Eustathius raised in not a few, and notably in Theodotus of Nicopolis, the metropolitan of Armenia, doubts as to Basil's soundness in the faith. When Basil was in Armenia in 373, a creed was drawn up, in consultation with Theodotus, to be offered to Eustathius for signature. It consisted of the Nicene confession, with certain additions relating to the Macedonian controversy.[14] Eustathius signed, together with Fronto and Severus. But, when another meeting with other bishops was arranged, he violated his pledge to attend. He wrote on the subject as though it were one of only small importance.[15] Eusebius endeavoured, but endeavoured in vain, to make peace.[16] Eustathius renounced communion with Basil, and at last, when an open attack on the archbishop seemed the paying game, he published an old letter of Basil's to Apollinarius, written by "layman to layman," many years before, and either introduced, or appended, heretical expressions of Apollinarius, which were made to pass as Basil's. In his virulent hostility he was aided, if not instigated, by Demosthenes the prefect's vicar, probably Basil's old opponent at Cæsarea in 372.[17] His duplicity and slanders roused Basil's indignant denunciation.[18] Unhappily they were not everywhere recognized as calumnies. Among the bitterest of Basil's trials was the failure to credit him with honour and orthodoxy on the part of those

---

Grégoire de Nazianze. Formée dans les écoles, entretenue par l'amour des lettres, elle avait pour but unique, non plus la patrie, mais Dieu. L'amitié de Grégoire et plus tendre et plus humaine. . . . Il a voué sa vie à son ami, mais il en attend la même condescendance, le même denouement à ses propres désirs. Basile au contraire, semble prendre à la lettre ce qu'il a lu dans Plutarque et dans Xénophon de l'amitié antique." E. Fialon, Et. Hist. In other words, Gregory's idea of friendship was to sacrifice one's self: Basil's to sacrifice one's friend. This is an interesting vindication of Basil, but the cause of God was hardly identical with the humiliation of Anthimus.

[1] Ep. xcvii.   [3] Greg. Naz., Ep. clii.   [5] Epp. cii., ciii.   [7] Ep. ccx.
[2] Ep. xcviii.   [4] Ep. xcix.   [6] Epp. cxx., cxxi., cxxii.
[8] Ep. ccxiii. § 3. He had been in early days a disciple of Arius at Alexandria.   [9] Id. § 5.
[10] Ep. cxxx. § 1.   [13] Ep. ccxliv. § 9.   [16] Ep. cxxviii.
[11] cf. Ep. ccxliv. § 9. Fialon, Et. Hist. 128.   [14] Epp. cxxi., ccxliv.   [17] Ep. ccxxxvii.
[12] Ep. ccxii. § 2. cf. Newman, Hist. Sketches, iii. 20.   [15] Ep. ccxliv.   [18] Epp. ccxxiii., ccxliv., cclxiii.

from whom he might have expected sympathy and support. An earlier instance of this is the feeling shewn at the banquet at Nazianzus already referred to.[1] In later days he was cruelly troubled by the unfriendliness of his old neighbours at Neocæsarea,[2] and this alienation would be the more distressing inasmuch as Atarbius, the bishop of that see, appears to have been Basil's kinsman.[3] He was under the suspicion of Sabellian unsoundness. He slighted and slandered Basil on several apparently trivial pretexts, and on one occasion hastened from Nicopolis for fear of meeting him.[4] He expressed objection to supposed novelties introduced into the Church of Cæsarea, to the mode of psalmody practised there, and to the encouragement of ascetic life.[5] Basil did his utmost to win back the Neocæsareans from their heretical tendencies and to their old kindly sentiments towards himself.

The clergy of Pisidia and Pontus, where Eustathius had been specially successful in alienating the district of Dazimon, were personally visited and won back to communion.[6] But Atarbius and the Neocæsareans were deaf to all appeal, and remained persistently irreconcilable.[7] On his visiting the old home at Annesi, where his youngest brother Petrus was now residing, in 375, the Neocæsareans were thrown into a state of almost ludicrous panic. They fled as from a pursuing enemy.[8] They accused Basil of seeking to win their regard and support from motives of the pettiest ambition, and twitted him with travelling into their neighbourhood uninvited.[9]

IX. — Unbroken Friendships.

Brighter and happier intimacies were those formed with the older bishop of Samosata, the Eusebius who, of all the many bearers of the name, most nearly realised its meaning,[10] and with Basil's junior, Amphilochius of Iconium. With the former, Basil's relations were those of an affectionate son and of an enthusiastic admirer. The many miles that stretched between Cæsarea and Samosata did not prevent these personal as well as epistolary communications.[11] In 372 they were closely associated in the eager efforts of the orthodox bishops of the East to win the sympathy and active support of the West.[12] In 374 Eusebius was exiled, with all the picturesque incidents so vividly described by Theodoret.[13] He travelled slowly from Samosata into Thrace, but does not seem to have met either Gregory or Basil on his way. Basil contrived to continue a correspondence with him in his banishment. It was more like that of young lovers than of elderly bishops.[14] The friends deplore the hindrances to conveyance, and are eager to assure one another that neither is guilty of forgetfulness.[15]

The friendship with Amphilochius seems to have begun at the time when the young advocate accepted the invitation conveyed in the name of Heracleidas,[16] his friend, and repaired from Ozizala to Cæsarea. The consequences were prompt and remarkable. Amphilochius, at this time between thirty and forty years of age, was soon ordained and consecrated, perhaps, like Ambrose of Milan and Eusebius of Cæsarea, *per saltum*, to the important see of Iconium, recently vacated by the death of Faustinus. Henceforward the intercourse between the spiritual father and the spiritual son, both by letters and by visits, was constant. The first visit of Amphilochius to Basil, as bishop, probably at Easter 374, not only gratified the older prelate, but made a deep impression on the Church of Cæsarea.[17] But his visits were usually paid in September, at the time of the services in commemoration of the martyr Eupsychius. On the occasion of the first of them, in 374, the friends conversed together on the doctrine of the Holy Spirit, now impugned by the Macedonians, and the result was the composition of the treatise *De Spiritu Sancto*. This was closely followed by the three famous canonical epistles,[18] also addressed to Amphilochius. Indeed, so great was the affectionate confidence of the great administrator and theologian[19] in his younger brother, that, when infirmities were closing round him, he asked Amphilochius to aid him in the administration of the archdiocese.[20]

If we accept the explanation given of Letter CLXIX. in a note on a previous page,[21] Gregory the elder, bishop of Nazianzus, must be numbered among those of Basil's correspondents letters to whom have been preserved. The whole episode referred to in that and in the two following letters is curiously illustrative of outbursts of fanaticism and folly which might

1 § vi. 3 *Ep.* ccx. § 4. 5 *Ep.* ccvii. 7 *Epp.* lxv., xxvi., ccx.
2 *Epp.* cciv., ccvii. 4 *Ep.* cxxvi. 6 *Epp.* cciii. and ccxvi. 8 *Ep.* ccxvi.
9 *Ib.* 10 Bp. in 361. *cf.* Greg. Naz., *Ep.* xxviii. and xxix., and Theod., *Ecc. Hist.* xxvii.
11 In 369, it is to the prayers of Eusebius, under the divine grace, that Basil refers his partial recovery from sickness (*Ep.* xxvii.), and sends Hypatius to Samosata in hope of similar blessing. (*Ep.* xxxi.)
12 *Ep.* xcii. 13 *Ecc. Hist.* iv. 14. 14 *cf.* Principal Reynolds in *D.C.B.* i. 372.
15 *Epp.* clvii., clviii., clxii., clxvii., clxviii., cxcviii., ccxxxvii., ccxxxix., ccxli., cclxvii. 16 *Ep.* cl.
17 *Epp.* clxiii., clxxvi. 19 "Pace Eunomii," whom Greg. of Nyssa quotes. *C. Eunom.* i.
18 *Epp.* clxxxviii., cxcix., ccxvii. 20 *Ep.* cc., cci. 21 § viii.

have been expected to occur in Cappadocia in the fourth century, as well as in soberer regions in several other centuries when they have occurred. It has been clothed with fresh interest by the very vivid narrative of Professor Ramsay, and by the skill with which he uses the scanty morsels of evidence available to construct the theory which he holds about it.[1] This theory is that the correspondence indicates a determined attempt on the part of the rigidly orthodox archbishop to crush proceedings which were really " only keeping up the customary ceremonial of a great religious meeting," and, as such, were winked at, if not approved of, by the bishop to whom the letter of remonstrance is addressed, and the presbyter who was Glycerius' superior. Valuable information is furnished by Professor Ramsay concerning the great annual festival in honour of Zeus of Venasa (or Venese), whose shrine was richly endowed, and the inscription discovered on a Cappadocian hill-top, " Great Zeus in heaven, be propitious to me." But the " evident sympathy " of the bishop and the presbyter is rather a strained inference from the extant letters; and the fact that in the days when paganism prevailed in Cappadocia Venasa was a great religious centre, and the scene of rites in which women played an important part, is no conclusive proof that wild dances performed by an insubordinate deacon were tolerated, perhaps encouraged, because they represented a popular old pagan observance. Glycerius may have played the patriarch, without meaning to adopt, or travesty, the style of the former high priest of Zeus. Cappadocia was one of the most Christian districts of the empire long before Basil was appointed to the exarchate of Cæsarea, and Basil is not likely to have been the first occupant of the see who would strongly disapprove of, and endeavour to repress, any such manifestations as those which are described.[2] That the bishop whom Basil addresses and the presbyter served by Glycerius should have desired to deal leniently with the offender individually does not convict them of accepting the unseemly proceedings of Glycerius and his troupe as a pardonable, if not desirable, survival of a picturesque national custom.[3]

Among other bishops of the period with whom Basil communicated by letter are Abramius, or Abraham, of Batnæ in Osrhoene,[4] the illustrious Athanasius,[5] and Ambrose,[6] Athanasius of Ancyra;[7] Barses of Edessa,[8] who died in exile in Egypt; Elpidius,[9] of some unknown see on the Levantine seaboard, who supported Basil in the controversy with Eustathius; the learned Epiphanius of Salamis;[10] Meletius,[11] the exiled bishop of Antioch; Patrophilus of Ægæ;[12] Petrus of Alexandria;[13] Theodotus of Nicopolis,[14] and Ascholius of Thessalonica.[15]

Basil's correspondence was not, however, confined within the limits of clerical clanship. His extant letters to laymen, both distinguished and undistinguished, shew that he was in touch with the men of mark of his time and neighbourhood, and that he found time to express an affectionate interest in the fortunes of his intimate friends.

Towards the later years of his life the archbishop's days were darkened not only by ill-health and anxiety, but by the death of some of his chief friends and allies. Athanasius died in 373, and so far as personal living influence went, there was an extinction of the Pharos not of Alexandria only, but of the world.[16] It was no longer " *Athanasius contra mundum*,"[17] but " *Mundus sine Athanasio*." In 374 Gregory the elder died at Nazianzus, and the same year saw the banishment of Eusebius of Samosata to Thrace. In 375 died Theodotus of Nicopolis, and the succession of Fronto was a cause of deep sorrow.

---

[1] Ramsay's *Church of the Roman Empire*, chap. xviii.
[2] The description of Cæsarea, as being " Christian to a man " (πανδημεὶ χριστιανίζοντας. Soz. v. 4), would apply pretty generally to all the province.
[3] In the chapter in which Professor Ramsay discusses the story of Glycerius he asks how it was that, while Phrygia was heretical, Cappadocia, in the fourth century, was orthodox: "Can any reason be suggested why this great Cappadocian leader followed the Roman Church, whereas all the most striking figures in Phrygian ecclesiastical history opposed it?" In Phrygia was the great centre of Montanism, a form of religionism not unfavourable to excesses such as those of Glycerius. But in *Letter* cciv., placed in 375, Basil claims both the Phrygias, *i.e.* Pacatiana and Salutaris, as being in communion with him. By the "Roman Church," followed by Cappadocia and opposed by Phrygia, must be meant either the ecclesiastical system of the Roman Empire, or the Church at Rome regarded as holding a kind of hegemony of Churches. If the former, it will be remembered that Cappadocia boldly withstood the creed patronized and pressed by imperial authority, when the influence of Valens made Arianism the official religion of Rome. If the latter, the phrase seems a misleading anachronism. In the fourth century there was no following or opposing the Church of Rome as we understand the phrase. To the bishop of Rome was conceded a certain personal precedence, as bishop of the capital, and he was beginning to claim more. In the West there was the dignity of the only western apostolic see, and the Church of Rome, as a society, was eminently orthodox and respectable. But, as important ecclesiastical centres, Antioch and Alexandria were far ahead of Rome, and the pope of Alexandria occupied a greater place than the pope of Rome. What Basil was eager to follow was not any local church, but the Faith which he understood to be the true and Catholic Faith, *i.e.*, the Faith of Nicæa. There was no church of Rome in the sense of an organized œcumenical society governed by a central Italian authority. Basil has no idea of any such thing as a Roman supremacy. *cf. Letter* ccxiv. and note. [4] *Ep.* cxxxii.
[5] *Epp.* lxi., lxvi., lxvii., lxix., lxxx., lxxxii. [9] *Epp.* ccli., ccv., ccvi. [12] *Epp.* ccxliv., ccl.
[6] *Ep.* cxcvii. [10] *Ep.* cclviii. [13] *Epp.* cxxxiii., cclxvi.
[7] *Ep.* xxiv. [11] *Epp.* lvii., lxviii., lxxxix., cxx., cxxix., ccxvi.
[8] *Epp.* cclxiv., cclxvii. [14] *Epp.* cxxi., cxxx. [15] *Epp.* cliv., clxiv., clxv. [16] *cf. Epp.* lxxxii. and note.
[17] The proverbial expression is conjectured by Dean Stanley to be derived from the Latin version of the famous passage concerning Athanasius in Hooker, *Ecc. Pol.* v. 42. *Vide* Stanley, *Grk. Church*, lect. vii.

At this time [1] some short solace would come to the Catholics in the East in the synodical letter addressed to the Orientals of the important synod held in Illyria, under the authority of Valentinian.   The letter which is extant [2] is directed against the Macedonian heresy.   The charge of conveying it to the East was given to the presbyter Elpidius.[3] Valentinian sent with it a letter to the bishops of Asia in which persecution is forbidden, and the excuse of submission to the reigning sovereign anticipated and condemned.   Although the letter runs in the names of Valentinian, Valens, and Gratian, the western brother appears to condemn the eastern.[4]

X. — TROUBLES OF THE CLOSING YEARS.

The relief to the Catholic East was brief.   The paroxysm of passion which caused Valentinian to break a blood-vessel, and ended his life,[5] ended also the force of the imperial rescript.   The Arians lifted their heads again.   A council was held at Ancyra,[6] in which the homoousion was condemned, and frivolous and vexatious charges were brought against Gregory of Nyssa.[7]   At Cyzicus a Semiarian synod blasphemed the Holy Spirit.[8] Similar proceedings characterized a synod of Antioch at about the same time.[9]   Gregory of Nyssa having been prevented by illness from appearing before the synod of Ancyra, Eustathius and Demosthenes persisted in their efforts to wound Basil through his brother, and summoned a synod at Nyssa itself, where Gregory was condemned in his absence and deposed.[10]   He was not long afterwards banished.[11]   On the other hand the Catholic bishops were not inactive.   Synods were held on their part, and at Iconium Amphilochius presided over a gathering at which Basil was perhaps present himself, and where his treatise on the Holy Spirit was read and approved.[12]   The Illyrian Council was a result incommensurate with Basil's passionate entreaties for the help of the westerns. From the midst of the troubles which beset the Eastern Church Basil appealed,[13] as he had appealed before,[14] for the sympathy and active aid of the other half of the empire.   He was bitterly chagrined at the failure of his entreaties for support, and began to suspect that the neglect he complained of was due to coldness and to pride.[15]   It has seemed to some that this coldness in the West was largely due to resentment at Basil's non-recognition of the supremacy of the Roman see.[16]   In truth the supremacy of the Roman see, as it has been understood in later times, was hardly in the horizon.[17]   No bishop of Rome had even been present at Nicæa, or at Sardica, where a certain right of appeal to his see was conceded. A bishop of Rome signed the Sirmian blasphemy.   No bishop of Rome was present to save 'the world' from the lapse of Ariminum.   Julian " might seem to have forgotten that there was such a city as Rome. " [18]   The great intellectual Arian war was fought out without any claim of Rome to speak.   Half a century after Basil's death great orientals were quite unconscious of this supremacy.[19]   At Chalcedon the measure of the growing claim is aptly typified by the wish of Paschasinus of Lilybæum, one of the representatives of Leo, to be regarded as presiding, though he did not preside.   The supremacy is hardly in view even at the last of the four great Councils.

In fact the appeal of Basil seems to have failed to elicit the response he desired, not so much from the independent tone of his letters, which was only in accordance with the recognised facts of the age,[20] as from occidental suspicions of Basil's orthodoxy,[21] and from the failure of men, who thought and wrote in Latin, to enter fully into the controversies conducted in a more subtle tongue.[22]   Basil had taken every precaution to ensure the conveyance of his letters by messengers of tact and discretion.   He had deprecated the advocacy of so simple-minded and undiplomatic an ambassador as his brother Gregory.[23]   He

---

[1] The date of the Council is, however, disputed. Pagi is for 373, Cave for 367. Hefele and Ceillier are satisfied of the correctness of 375. cf. D.C.A. i. 813.   [2] Theod., Ecc. Hist. iv. 8.   [3] Mansi, iii. 386. Hefele, § 90.
[4] Theod., H.E. iv. 7.   [7] Ep. ccxxv.   [10] Ep. ccxxxvii.
[5] Nov. 17, 375. Amm. Marc. xxx. 6. Soc. iv. 31.   [8] Ep. ccxliv.   [11] Greg., Vit. Mac. ii. 192.
[6] Mansi, iii. 499. Hefele, § 90.   [9] Soc. v. 4.
[12] Ep. ccii., cclxxii. Hefele, § 90. Mansi, iii. 502-506. There is some doubt as to the exact date of this synod. cf. D.C.A. i. 807.   [13] Ep. ccxliii.   [14] Ep. lxx., addressed in 371 to Damasus.   [15] Ep. ccxxxix.
[16] cf. D.C.B. i. 294: " C'est esprit, conciliant aux les orientaux jusqu'à soulever l'intolérance orientale, est aussi inflexible avec les occidentaux qu'avec le pouvoir impérial.   On sent dans ses lettres la révolte de l'orient qui réclame ses prérogatives, ses droits d'ancienneté ; l'esprit d'indépendance de la Grèce, qui, si elle supporte le joug matériel de Rome, refuse de reconnaître sa suprématie spirituelle." Fialon, Ét. Hist. 133.
[17] cf. note on § ix.   [18] Milman, Lat. Christ. i. 85.   [19] cf. Proleg. to Theodoret in this series, p. 9, note.
[20] A ses yeux, l'Orient et l'Occident ne sont ils pas, deux frères, dont les droits sont égaux, sans suprématie, sans aînesse ? " Fialon, Ét. Hist. p. 134. This is exactly what East and West were to most eyes, and what they were asserted to be in the person of the two imperial capitals by the Twenty-Eighth Canon of Chalcedon. cf. Bright, Canons of the First Four General Councils, pp. 93, 192, and note on Theodoret in this series, p. 293.
[21] Ep. cclxvi. § 2.   [22] cf. Ep. ccxiv. § 4, p. 254.   [23] Ep. ccxv.

had poured out his very soul in entreaty.[1]   But all was unavailing.   He suffered, and he had to suffer unsupported by a human sympathy on which he thought he had a just claim.[2]

It is of a piece with Basil's habitual silence on the general affairs of the empire that he should seem to be insensible of the shock caused by the approach of the Goths in 378. A letter to Eusebius in exile in Thrace does shew at least a consciousness of a disturbed state of the country, and he is afraid of exposing his courier to needless danger by entrusting him with a present for his friend.   But this is all.[3]   He may have written letters shewing an interest in the fortunes of the empire which have not been preserved.   But his whole soul was absorbed in the cause of Catholic truth, and in the fate of the Church.   His youth had been steeped in culture, but the work of his ripe manhood left no time for the literary amusement of the dilettante.   So it may be that the intense earnestness with which he said to himself, " This one thing I do," of his work as a shepherd of souls, and a fighter for the truth, and his knowledge that for the doing of this work his time was short, accounts for the absence from his correspondence of many a topic of more than contemporary interest.   At all events, it is not difficult to descry that the turn in the stream of civil history was of vital moment to the cause which Basil held dear.   The approach of the enemy was fraught with important consequences to the Church.   The imperial attention was diverted from persecution of the Catholics to defence of the realm.   Then came the disaster of Adrianople,[4] and the terrible end of the unfortunate Valens.[5]   Gratian, a sensible lad, of Catholic sympathies, restored the exiled bishops, and Basil, in the few months of life yet left him, may have once more embraced his faithful friend Eusebius.   The end drew rapidly near.   Basil was only fifty, but he was an old man.   Work, sickness, and trouble had worn him out.   His health had never been good.   A chronic liver complaint was a constant cause of distress and depression.

In 373 he had been at death's door.   Indeed, the news of his death was actually circulated, and bishops arrived at Cæsarea with the probable object of arranging the succession.[6] He had submitted to the treatment of a course of natural hot baths, but with small beneficial result.[7]   By 376, as he playfully reminds Amphilochius, he had lost all his teeth.[8]   At last the powerful mind and the fiery enthusiasm of duty were no longer able to stimulate the energies of the feeble frame.

The winter of 378–9 dealt the last blow, and with the first day of what, to us, is now the new year, the great spirit fled.   Gregory, alas! was not at the bedside.   But he has left us a narrative which bears the stamp of truth.   For some time the bystanders thought that the dying bishop had ceased to breathe.   Then the old strength blazed out at the last. He spoke with vigour, and even ordained some of the faithful who were with him.   Then he lay once more feeble and evidently passing away.   Crowds surrounded his residence, praying eagerly for his restoration to them, and willing to give their lives for his.   With a few final words of advice and exhortation, he said: " Into thy hands I commend my spirit," and so ended.

The funeral was a scene of intense excitement and rapturous reverence.   Crowds filled every open space, and every gallery and window; Jews and Pagans joined with Christians in lamentation, and the cries and groans of the agitated oriental multitude drowned the music of the hymns which were sung.   The press was so great that several fatal accidents added to the universal gloom.   Basil was buried in the " sepulchre of his fathers" — a phrase which may possibly mean in the ancestral tomb of his family at Cæsarea.

So passed away a leader of men in whose case the epithet ' great' is no conventional compliment.   He shared with his illustrious brother primate of Alexandria the honour of rallying the Catholic forces in the darkest days of the Arian depression.   He was great as foremost champion of a great cause, great in contemporary and posthumous influence, great in industry and self-denial, great as a literary controversialist.   The estimate formed of him by his contemporaries is expressed in the generous, if somewhat turgid, eloquence of the laudatory oration of the slighted Gregory of Nazianzus.   Yet nothing in Gregory's

---

[1] See specially *Ep.* ccxlii.

[2] " Foiled in all his repeated demands; a deaf ear turned to his most earnest entreaties; the council he had begged for not summoned; the deputation he had repeatedly solicited unsent; Basil's span of life drew to its end amid blasted hopes and apparently fruitless labours for the unity of the faith.   It was not permitted him to live to see the Eastern Churches, for the purity of whose faith he had devoted all his powers, restored to peace and unanimity." Canon Venables, *D.C.B.* i. 295.

" He had to fare on as best he might, — admiring, courting, but coldly treated by the Latin world, desiring the friendship of Rome, yet wounded by her superciliousness, suspected of heresy by Damasus, and accused by Jerome of pride." Newman, *Church of the Fathers,* p. 115.

[3] *Ep.* cclxviii.   So Fialon, *Ét. Hist.* p. 149: " *On n'y trouve pas un mot sur la désastreuse expédition de Julien, sur le honteux traité de Jovien, sur la révolte de Procope.*"   At the same time the argument from silence is always dangerous.   It may be unfair to charge Basil with indifference to great events, because we do not possess his letters about them.

[4] Aug. 9, 378.   [5] Theod. iv. 32.   Amm. Marc. xxxi. 13.   [6] *Ep.* cxli.   [7] *Ep.* cxxxvii.   [8] *Ep.* ccxxxii.

eulogy goes beyond the expressions of the prelate who has seemed to some to be "the wisest and holiest man in the East in the succeeding century."[1] Basil is described by the saintly and learned Theodoret[2] in terms that might seem exaggerated when applied to any but his master, as the light not of Cappadocia only, but of the world.[3] To Sophronius[4] he is the "glory of the Church." To Isidore of Pelusium,[5] he seems to speak as one inspired. To the Council of Chalcedon he is emphatically a minister of grace;[6] to the second council of Nicæa a layer of the foundations of orthodoxy.[7] His death lacks the splendid triumph of the martyrdoms of Polycarp and Cyprian. His life lacks the vivid incidents which make the adventures of Athanasius an enthralling romance. He does not attract the sympathy evoked by the unsophisticated simplicity of Gregory his friend or of Gregory his brother. There does not linger about his memory the close personal interest that binds humanity to Augustine, or the winning loyalty and tenderness that charm far off centuries into affection for Theodoret. Sometimes he seems a hard, almost a sour man.[8] Sometimes there is a jarring reminder of his jealousy for his own dignity.[9] Evidently he was not a man who could be thwarted without a rupture of pleasant relations, or slighted with impunity. In any subordinate position he was not easy to get on with.[10] But a man of strong will, convinced that he is championing a righteous cause, will not hesitate to sacrifice, among other things, the amenities that come of amiable absence of self-assertion. To Basil, to assert himself was to assert the truth of Christ and of His Church. And in the main the identification was a true one. Basil was human, and occasionally, as in the famous dispute with Anthimus, so disastrously fatal to the typical friendship of the earlier manhood, he may have failed to perceive that the Catholic cause would not suffer from the existence of two metropolitans in Cappadocia. But the great archbishop could be an affectionate friend, thirsty for sympathy.[11] And he was right in his estimate of his position. Broadly speaking, Basil, more powerfully than any contemporary official, worker, or writer in the Church, did represent and defend through all the populous provinces of the empire which stretched from the Balkans to the Mediterranean, from the Ægean to the Euphrates, the cause whose failure or success has been discerned, even by thinkers of no favourable predisposition, to have meant death or life to the Church.[12] St. Basil is duly canonized in the grateful memory, no less than in the official bead-roll, of Christendom, and we may be permitted to regret that the existing Kalendar of the Anglican liturgy has not found room for so illustrious a Doctor in its somewhat niggard list.[13] For the omission some amends have lately[14] been made in the erection of a statue of the great archbishop of Cæsarea under the dome of the Cathedral of St. Paul in London.[15]

II. WORKS.

The extant works of St. Basil may be conveniently classified as follows:

I. DOGMATIC.	(i)	*Adversus Eunomium.*	Πρὸς Εὐνόμιον.
	(ii)	*De Spiritu Sancto.*	Περὶ τοῦ Πνεύματος.
II. EXEGETIC.[16]	(i)	*In Hexaemeron.*	Εἰς τὴν Ἑξαήμερον.
	(ii)	*Homiliæ on Pss.* i., vii., xiv., xxviii., xxix., xxxii., xxxiii., xliv., xlv., xlviii., lix., lxi., cxiv.	
	(iii)	*Commentary on Isaiah* i.–xvi.	

---

1 Kingsley, *Hypatia*, chap. xxx.
2 *cf.* Gibbon, chap. xxi.
3 Theod., *H.E.* iv 16, and *Ep.* cxlvi.
4 *Apud Photium* Cod. 231.
5 *Ep.* lxi.
6 *cf.* Ceillier, vi. 8, 1.
7 *Ib.*
8 *cf. Ep.* xxv.
9 *cf.* xcviii.
10 *e.g.* his relations with his predecessor.
11 *Ep.* xci.

12 *e.g.* T. Carlyle. " He perceived Christianity itself to have been at stake. If the Arians had won, it would have dwindled away into a legend." [A. Froude, *Life of Carlyle in London*, ii. 462.
13 In the Greek Kalendar January 1, the day of the death, is observed in honour of the saint. In the West St. Basil's day is June 14, the traditional date of the consecration. The martyrologies of Jerome and Bede do not contain the name. The first mention is ascribed by the Bollandists to Usuard. (Usuard's martyrology was composed for Charles the Bold at Paris.) In the tenth century a third day was consecrated in the East to the common commemoration of SS. Basil, Gregory of Nazianzus, and John Chrysostom.   14 1894.
15 Basil lived at the period when the relics of martyrs and saints were beginning to be collected and honoured. (*e g. Ep.* cxcvii.) To Damasus, the bishop of Rome, whose active sympathy he vainly strove to win, is mainly due the reverent rearrangement of the Roman catacombs. (*Roma Sotteranea*, Northcote and Brownlow, p. 97.) It was not to be expected that Basil's own remains should be allowed to rest in peace; but the gap between the burial at Cæsarea and the earliest record of their supposed reappearance is wide. There was a Church of St. Basil at Bruges founded in 1187, which was believed to possess some of the archbishop's bones. These were solemnly translated in 1463 to the Church of St. Donatian, which disappeared at the time of the French revolution. Pancirola (d. 1599) mentions a head, an arm, and a rib, said to be Basil's, among the treasures of Rome.
16 According to Cassiodorus (*Instit. Divin. Litt. Præfat.*) St. Basil wrote in interpretation of the whole of Scripture, but this statement lacks confirmation. *cf.* Maran, *Vit. Bas.* xli.

		(i)	*Tractatus prævii.*	
III.	ASCETIC.	(ii)	*Procemium de Judicio Dei* and *De Fide.*	
		(iii)	*Moralia.*	Τὰ Ἠθικά.
		(iv)	*Regulæ fusius tractatæ.*	Ὅροι κατὰ πλάτος.
		and	*Regulæ brevius tractatæ.*	Ὅροι κατ' ἐπιτόμην.

IV.	HOMILETIC.	XXIV. HOMILIES.	(i) Dogmatic.
			(ii) Moral.
			(iii) Panegyric.

		(i)	Historic.
		(ii)	Dogmatic.
		(iii)	Moral.
V.	LETTERS.	(iv)	Disciplinary.
		(v)	Consolatory.
		(vi)	Commendatory.
		(vii)	Familiar.

VI. LITURGIC.

I. (i) *Against Eunomius.* The work under this title comprises five books, the first three generally accepted as genuine, the last two sometimes regarded as doubtful. Gregory of Nazianzus,[1] Jerome,[2] and Theodoret[3] all testify to Basil's having written against Eunomius, but do not specify the number of books. Books IV. and V. are accepted by Bellarmine, Du Pin, Tillemont, and Ceillier, mainly on the authority of the edict of Justinian against the Three Chapters (Mansi ix., 552), the Council of Seville (Mansi x., 566) and the Council of Florence (Hardouin ix., 200). Maran (*Vit. Bas.* xliii.) speaks rather doubtfully. Böhringer describes them as of suspicious character, alike on grounds of style, and of their absence from some MSS. They may possibly be notes on the controversy in general, and not immediately directed against Eunomius. Fessler's conclusion is "*Major tamen eruditorum pars eos etiam genuinos esse censet.*"

The year 364 is assigned for the date of the publication of the three books.[4] At that time Basil sent them with a few words of half ironical depreciation to Leontius the sophist.[5] He was now about thirty-four years of age, and describes himself as hitherto inexperienced in such a kind of composition.[6] Eunomius, like his illustrious opponent, was a Cappadocian. Emulous of the notoriety achieved by Aetius the Anomœan, and urged on by Secundus of Ptolemais, an intimate associate of Aetius, he went to Alexandria about 356, and resided there for two years as Aetius' admiring pupil and secretary. In 358 he accompanied Aetius to Antioch, and took a prominent part in the assertion of the extreme doctrines which revolted the more moderate Semiarians. He was selected as the champion of the advanced blasphemers, made himself consequently obnoxious to Constantius, and was apprehended and relegated to Migde in Phrygia. At the same time Eudoxius withdrew for a while into Armenia, his native province, but ere long was restored to the favour of the fickle Constantius, and was appointed to the see of Constantinople in 359. Eunomius now was for overthrowing Aetius, and removing whatever obstacles stood between him and promotion, and, by the influence of Eudoxius, was nominated to the see of Cyzicus, vacant by the deposition of Eleusius. Here for a while he temporized, but ere long displayed his true sentiments. To answer for this he was summoned to Constantinople by Constantius, and, in his absence, condemned and deposed. Now he became more marked than ever in his assertion of the most extreme Arianism, and the advanced party were henceforward known under his name. The accession of Julian brought him back with the rest of the banished bishops, and he made Constantinople the centre for the dissemination of his views.[7]

Somewhere about this period he wrote the work entitled *Apologeticus*, in twenty-eight chapters, to which Basil replies. The title was at once a parody on the *Apologies* of defenders of the Faith, and, at the same time, a suggestion that his utterances were not spontaneous, but forced from him by attack. The work is printed in Fabricius, *Bibl. Græc.* viii. 262, and in the appendix to Migne's *Basil. Pat. Gr.* xxx. 837.[8] It is a brief treatise, and occupies only about fifteen columns of Migne's edition. It professes to be a defence of the " simpler creed which is common to all Christians."[9]

---

[1] *Or.* xliii. § 67.
[2] *De Script. Eccl.* 116.
[3] Theod., *H E.* ii. 25; and *Hær. Fab.* iv. 3. Philost., *H.E.* vi. 1.
[3] *Dial.* ii. p. 207 in the ed. of this series.
[4] Maran, *Vit. Bas.* viii.
[5] cf. *Ep.* xx.
[6] i Eunom. i.
[8] cf. also Basnage in *Canisii Lectiones antt.* i. 172; Fessler, *Inst. Pat.* 1. 507. Dorner, *Christologie*, 1. 853, and Böhringer, *Kirchengeschichte*, vii. 62. [9] ἁπλουστέρα καὶ κοινῇ πάντων πίστις. § 5.

This creed is as follows: "We believe in one God, Father Almighty, of Whom are all things: and in one only-begotten Son of God, God the Word, our Lord Jesus Christ, through Whom are all things: and in one Holy Spirit, the Comforter."[1] But it is in reality like the extant *Exposition of the Creed*,[2] a reading into this "simpler" creed, in itself orthodox and unobjectionable, of explanations which ran distinctly counter to the traditional and instinctive faith of the Church, and inevitably demanded corrective explanations and definitions.

In the creed of Eunomius the Son is *God*, and it is not in terms denied that He is of one substance with the Father. But in his doctrinal system there is a practical denial of the Creed; the Son may be styled God, but He is a creature, and therefore, in the strict sense of the term, not God at all, and, at best, a hero or demigod. The Father, unbegotten, stood alone and supreme; the very idea of "begotten" implied posteriority, inferiority, and unlikeness. Against this position Basil[3] protests. The arguments of Eunomius, he urges, are tantamount to an adoption of what was probably an Arian formula, "We believe that ingenerateness is the essence of God,"[4] *i.e.*, we believe that the Only-begotten is essentially unlike the Father.[5] This word "unbegotten," of which Eunomius and his supporters make so much, what is its real value? Basil admits that it is apparently a convenient term for human intelligence to use; but, he urges, "It is nowhere to be found in Scripture; it is one of the main elements in the Arian blasphemy; it had better be left alone. The word 'Father' implies all that is meant by 'Unbegotten,' and has moreover the advantage of suggesting at the same time the idea of the Son. He Who is essentially Father is alone of no other. In this being of no other is involved the sense of 'Unbegotten.' The title 'unbegotten' will not be preferred by us to that of Father, unless we wish to make ourselves wiser than the Saviour, Who said, 'Go and baptize in the name' not of the Unbegotten, but ' of the Father.' "[6] To the Eunomian contention that the word "Unbegotten" is no mere complimentary title, but required by the strictest necessity, in that it involves the confession of what He is,[7] Basil rejoins that it is only one of many negative terms applied to the Deity, none of which completely expresses the Divine Essence. "There exists no name which embraces the whole nature of God, and is sufficient to declare it; more names than one, and these of very various kinds, each in accordance with its own proper connotation, give a collective idea which may be dim indeed and poor when compared with the whole, but is enough for us."[8] The word "unbegotten," like "immortal," "invisible," and the like, expresses only negation. "Yet essence[9] is not one of the qualities which are absent, but signifies the very being of God; to reckon this in the same category as the non-existent is to the last degree unreasonable."[10] Basil "would be quite ready to admit that the essence of God is unbegotten," but he objects to the statement that the essence and the unbegotten are identical.[11] It is sometimes supposed that the Catholic theologians have been hair-splitters in the sphere of the inconceivable, and that heresy is the exponent of an amiable and reverent vagueness. In the Arian controversy it was Arius himself who dogmatically defined with his negative "There was when He was not," and Eunomius with his "The essence is the unbegotten." "What pride! What conceit!" exclaims Basil. "The idea of imagining that one has discovered the very essence of God most high! Assuredly in their magniloquence they quite throw into the shade even Him who said, 'I will exalt my throne above the stars.'[12] It is not stars, it is not heaven, that they dare to assail. It is in the very essence of the God of

---

[1] THE CREED OF EUNOMIUS.

(*Adv. Eunom.* i. 4.) .

Πιστεύομεν εἰς ἕνα Θεὸν, Πατέρα παντοκράτορα, ἐξ οὗ τὰ πάντα· καὶ εἰς ἕνα Μονογενῆ Ὑιὸν τοῦ Θεοῦ, Θεὸν Λόγον, τὸν Κύριον ἡμῶν Ἰησοῦν Χριστὸν, δι' οὗ τὰ πάντα· καὶ εἰς ἓν Πνεῦμα ἅγιον, τὸ παράκλητον. Eunom., *Apol.* § 5.

THE CREED OF ARIUS AND EUZOIUS.

(Soc. *H.E.* i. 26.)

Πιστεύομεν εἰς ἕνα Θεὸν Πατέρα παντοκράτορα, καὶ εἰς Κύριον Ἰησοῦν Χριστὸν, τὸν Ὑιὸν αὐτοῦ, τὸν ἐξ αὐτοῦ πρὸ πάντων τῶν αἰώνων γεγεννημένον, Θεὸν Λόγον, δι' οὗ τὰ πάντα ἐγένετο τά τε ἐν τοῖς οὐρανοῖς καὶ τὰ ἐπὶ τῆς γῆς, τὸν κατελθόντα, καὶ σαρκωθέντα, καὶ παθόντα, καὶ ἀναστάντα, καὶ ἀνελθόντα εἰς τοὺς οὐρανοὺς καὶ πάλιν ἐρχόμενον κρῖναι ζῶντας καὶ νεκρούς· καὶ εἰς τὸ ἅγιον Πνεῦμα· καὶ εἰς σαρκὸς ἀναστάσιν· καὶ εἰς ζωὴν τοῦ μέλλοντος αἰῶνος· καὶ εἰς Βασιλείαν οὐρανῶν· καὶ εἰς μίαν καθολικὴν ἐκκλησίαν τοῦ Θεοῦ τὴν ἀπὸ περάτων ἕως περάτων.

[2] Ἔκθεσις τῆς πίστεως, published in the notes of Valesius to Soc., *Ecc. Hist.* v. 12. This was offered to Theodosius after the Council of Constantinople. The Son is πρωτότοκον πάσης κτίσεως, and πρὸ πάσης κτίσεως γενόμενον, but οὐκ ἄκτιστον. The Holy Ghost is γενόμενον ὑπὸ τοῦ Μονογενοῦς καὶ . . . καθάπαξ ὑποτεταγμένον, οὔτε κατὰ τὸν Πατέρα οὔτε τῷ Πατρὶ συναριθμούμενον· οὔτε τῷ Υἱῷ συνεξισούμενον οὔτε μὴν ἄλλῳ τινὶ συντασσόμενον . . . πρῶτον ἔργον καὶ κράτιστον τοῦ Μονογενοῦς. *cf.* St. Aug.. *De Hær.* liv., "Eunomius asserted that the Son was altogether dissimilar to the Father and the Spirit to the Son," and Philostrius, *De Hær.* lxviii., who represents the Eunomians as believing in three essences descending in value like gold, silver, and copper. *Vide* Swete, *Doctrine of the Holy Ghost*, p. 61. [3] *Adv. Eunom.* i. 5.

[4] πιστεύομεν τὴν ἀγεννησίαν οὐσίαν εἶναι τοῦ Θεοῦ. For the word ἀγεννησία *cf. Letter* ccxxxiv., p. 274.

[5] *Adv. Eunom.* i. 4. [6] Matt. xxviii. 19. *Adv. Eun.* i. 5. [7] ἐν τῇ τοῦ εἶναι ὁ ἐστιν ὁμολογία. *Adv. Eunom.* i. 8. [8] *Id.* i. 10. [9] οὐσία. [10] *Id.* [11] *Id.* ii. [12] *i.e.* Lucifer, *cf.* Is. xiv. 13.

all the world that they boast that they make their haunt. Let us question him as to where he acquired comprehension of this essence. Was it from the common notion that all men share?[1] This does indeed suggest to us that there is a God, but not what God is. Was it from the teaching of the Spirit? What teaching? Where found? What says great David, to whom God revealed the hidden secrets of His wisdom? He distinctly asserts the unapproachableness of knowledge of Him in the words, ' Such knowledge is too wonderful for me ; it is high, I cannot attain unto it.'[2] And Isaiah, who saw the glory of God, what does he tell us concerning the Divine Essence? In his prophecy about the Christ he says, ' Who shall declare His generation?'[3] And what of Paul, the chosen vessel, in whom Christ spake, who was caught up into the third heaven, who heard unspeakable words, which it is not lawful to man to utter? What teaching has he given us of the essence of God? When Paul is investigating the special methods of the work of redemption[4] he seems to grow dizzy before the mysterious maze which he is contemplating, and utters the well-known words, ' O the depth of the riches both of the wisdom and knowledge of God ! How unsearchable are His judgments, and His ways past finding out!'[5] These things are beyond the reach even of those who have attained the measure of Paul's knowledge. What then is the conceit of those who announce that they know the essence of God! I should very much like to ask them what they have to say about the earth whereon they stand, and whereof they are born. What can they tell us of its 'essence'? If they can discourse without hesitation of the nature of lowly subjects which lie beneath our feet, we will believe them when they proffer opinions about things which transcend all human intelligence. What is the essence of the earth? How can it be comprehended? Let them tell us whether reason or sense has reached this point! If they say sense, by which of the senses is it comprehended? Sight? Sight perceives colour. Touch? Touch distinguishes hard and soft, hot and cold, and the like; but no idiot would call any of these essence. I need not mention taste or smell, which apprehend respectively savour and scent. Hearing perceives sounds and voices, which have no affinity with earth. They must then say that they have found out the earth's essence by reason. What? In what part of Scripture? A tradition from what saint?[6]

" In a word, if any one wishes to realise the truth of what I am urging, let him ask himself this question; when he wishes to understand anything about God, does he approach the meaning of ' the unbegotten ' ? I for my part see that, just as when we extend our thought over the ages that are yet to come, we say that the life bounded by no limit is without end, so is it when we contemplate in thought the ages of the past, and gaze on the infinity of the life of God as we might into some unfathomable ocean. We can conceive of no beginning from which He originated : we perceive that the life of God always transcends the bounds of our intelligence ; and so we call that in His life which is without origin, unbegotten.[7] The meaning of the unbegotten is the having no origin from without."[8] As Eunomius made ingenerateness the essence of the Divine, so, with the object of establishing the contrast between Father and Son, he represented the *being begotten* to indicate the essence of the Son.[9] God, said Eunomius, being ingenerate, could never admit of generation. This statement, Basil points out, may be understood in either of two ways. It may mean that ingenerate nature cannot be subjected to generation. It may mean that ingenerate nature cannot generate. Eunomius, he says, really means the latter, while he makes converts of the multitude on the lines of the former. Eunomius makes his real meaning evident by what he adds to his dictum, for, after saying " could never admit of generation," he goes on, " so as to impart His own proper nature to the begotten."[10] As in relation to the Father, so now in relation to the Son, Basil objects to the term. Why " begotten " ?[11] Where did he get this word? From what teaching? From what prophet? Basil nowhere finds the Son called " begotten " in Scripture.[12] We read that the Father begat, but nowhere that the Son was a *begotten thing*. " Unto us a child is born,[13] unto us a Son is given."[14] But His name is not *begotten thing*, but " angel of great counsel."[15] If this word had indicated the essence of the Son, no other word would have been revealed by the Spirit.[16] Why, if God begat, may we not call that which was begotten a thing begotten? It is a terrible thing for us to coin names for Him to Whom

---

¹ On κοινὴ ἔννοια, *cf.* Origen, *C. Cels.* i. 4.   ⁴ τοὺς μερικοὺς τῆς οἰκονομίας λόγους.   ⁸ *Id.* i. 16.
² Ps. cxxxix. 6.   ⁵ Rom. xi. 33.   ⁶ *Id.* i. 13.   ⁹ τὸ γέννημα. *Id.* ii. 6.
³ Is. liii. S.   ⁷ τοῦτο τὸ ἄναρχον τῆς ζωῆς ἀγέννητον προσειρήκαμεν.   ¹⁰ *Id.* i. 16.
¹¹ γέννημα, *i.e.,* " *thing begotten ;*" the distinction between this substantive and the scriptural adjective μονογενής must be borne in mind.
¹² *Id.* ii. 6.   ¹³ LXX., ἐγεννήθη.   ¹⁴ Is. ix. 6.   ¹⁵ *Id.* LXX.   ¹⁶ *Id.* ii. 7.

God has given a "name which is above every name."[1] We must not add to or take from what is delivered to us by the Spirit.[2] Things are not made for names, but names for things.[3] Eunomius unhappily was led by distinction of name into distinction of being.[4] If the Son is begotten in the sense in which Eunomius uses the word, He is neither begotten of the essence of God nor begotten from eternity. Eunomius represents the Son as not of the essence of the Father, because begetting is only to be thought of as a sensual act and idea, and therefore is entirely unthinkable in connexion with the being of God. " The essence of God does not admit of begetting; no other essence exists for the Son's begetting; therefore I say that the Son was begotten when non-existent."[5] Basil rejoins that no analogy can hold between divine generation or begetting and human generation or begetting. "Living beings which are subject to death generate through the operation of the senses: but we must not on this account conceive of God in the same manner; nay, rather shall we be hence guided to the truth that, because corruptible beings operate in this manner, the Incorruptible will operate in an opposite manner."[6] " All who have even a limited loyalty to truth ought to dismiss all corporeal similitudes. They must be very careful not to sully their conceptions of God by material notions. They must follow the theologies[7] delivered to us by the Holy Ghost. They must shun questions which are little better than conundrums, and admit of a dangerous double meaning. Led by the ray that shines forth from light to the contemplation of the divine generation, they must think of a generation worthy of God, without passion, partition, division, or time. They must conceive of the image of the invisible God not after the analogy of images which are subsequently fashioned by craft to match their archetype, but as of one nature and subsistence with the originating prototype.[8] . . .[9] This image is not produced by imitation, for the whole nature of the Father is expressed in the Son as on a seal."[10] "Do not press me with the questions: What is the generation? Of what kind was it? In what manner could it be effected? The manner is ineffable, and wholly beyond the scope of our intelligence; but we shall not on this account throw away the foundation of our faith in Father and Son. If we try to measure everything by our comprehension, and to suppose that what we cannot comprehend by our reasoning is wholly non-existent, farewell to the reward of faith; farewell to the reward of hope! If we only follow what is clear to our reason, how can we be deemed worthy of the blessings in store for the reward of faith in things not seen"?[11]

If not of the essence of God, the Son could not be held to be eternal. " How utterly absurd," exclaims Basil, "to deny the glory of God to have had brightness;[12] to deny the wisdom of God to have been ever with God! . . . The Father is of eternity. So also is the Son of eternity, united by generation to the unbegotten nature of the Father. This is not my own statement. I shall prove it by quoting the words of Scripture. Let me cite from the Gospel 'In the beginning was the Word.'[13] and from the Psalm, other words spoken as in the person of the Father, 'From the womb before the morning I have begotten them.'[14] Let us put both together, and say, He was, and He was begotten. . . . How absurd to seek for something higher in the case of the unoriginate and the unbegotten! Just as absurd is it to start questions as to time, about priority in the case of Him Who was with the Father from eternity, and between Whom and Him that begat Him there is no interval."[15]

A dilemma put by Eunomius was the following: When God begat the Son, the Son either was or was not.[16] If He was not, no argument could lie against Eunomius and the Arians. If He was, the position is blasphemous and absurd, for that which is needs no begetting.[17]

To meet this dilemma, Basil drew a distinction between eternity and the being unoriginate.[18] The Eunomians, from the fact of the unoriginateness of the Father being called eternity, maintained that unoriginateness and eternity are identical.[19] Because the Son is not unbegotten they do not even allow Him to be eternal. But there is a wide distinction to be observed in the meaning of the terms. The word *unbegotten* is

1 Phil. ii. 9.　　2 *Id.* ii. 8.　　3 *Id.* ii. 4.　　4 *Id.* ii. 3.　　5 *Id.* ii. 18.　　6 *Id.* ii. 23.
7 On the distinction between θεολογία and οἰκονομία, *cf.* p. 7, n.
8 συνυπάρχουσαν καὶ παρυφεστηκυίαν τῷ πρωτοτύπῳ ὑποστήσαντι. Expressions of this kind, used even by Basil, may help to explain the earlier Nicene sense of ὑπόστασις. The Son has, as it were, a *parallel* hypostasis to that of the Father, Who eternally furnishes this hypostasis. *cf.* p. 195, n.
9 Here the MSS. vary, but the main sense is not affected by the omission of the variant phrase.
10 *Id.* ii. 16.　*cf. De Sp. Scto.* § 15, p. 9, and § 84, p. 40, and notes.　　11 *Id.* ii. 24.
12 ἀπαύγασμα.　*cf.* Heb. i. 13.　　15 *Id.* ii. 17.　　18 *cf. De Sp. Scto.* pp. 27, 30, and notes.
13 John i. 1.　　16 Ἤτοι ὄντα ἐγέννησεν ὁ Θεὸς τὸν Υἱόν, ἢ οὐκ ὄντα.
14 Ps. cx, 3, LXX.　　17 *Id.* ii. 14.　　19 ταυτὸν τῷ ἀνάρχῳ τὸ ἀΐδιον.

predicated of that which has origin of itself, and no cause of its being : the word *eternal* is predicated of that which is in being beyond all time and age.[1] Wherefore the Son is both not unbegotten and eternal.[2] Eunomius was ready to give great dignity to the Son as a supreme creature. He did not hold the essence of the Son to be common to that of the things created out of nothing.[3] He would give Him as great a preëminence as the Creator has over His own created works.[4] Basil attributes little importance to this concession, and thinks it only leads to confusion and contradiction. If the God of the universe, being unbegotten, necessarily differs from things begotten, and all things begotten have their common hypostasis of the non-existent, what alternative is there to a natural conjunction of all such things ? Just as in the one case the unapproachable effects a distinction between the natures, so in the other equality of condition brings them into mutual contact. They say that the Son and all things that came into being under Him are of the non-existent, and so far they make those natures common, and yet they deny that they give Him a nature of the non-existent. For again, as though Eunomius were Lord himself, and able to give to the Only Begotten what rank and dignity he chooses, he goes on to argue, — We attribute to Him so much supereminence as the Creator must of necessity have over His own creature. He does not say, "We conceive," or "We are of opinion," as would be befitting when treating of God, but he says "We attribute," as though he himself could control the measure of the attribution. And how much supereminence does he give ? As much as the Creator must necessarily have over His own creatures. This has not yet reached a statement of difference of substance. Human beings in art surpass their own works, and yet are consubstantial with them, as the potter with his clay, and the shipwright with his timber. For both are alike bodies, subject to sense, and earthy.[5] Eunomius explained the title "Only Begotten" to mean that the Son alone was begotten and created by the Father alone, and therefore was made the most perfect minister. "If," rejoins Basil, "He does not possess His glory in being perfect God, if it lies only in His being an exact and obedient subordinate, in what does He differ from the ministering spirits who perform the work of their service without blame?[6] Indeed Eunomius joins 'created' to 'begotten' with the express object of shewing that there is no distinction between the Son and a creature![7] And how unworthy a conception of the Father that He should need a servant to do His work ! 'He commanded and they were created.'[8] What service was needed by Him Who creates by His will alone ? But in what sense are all things said by us to be 'through the Son'? In that the divine will, starting from the prime cause, as it were from a source, proceeds to operation through its own image, God the Word."[9] Basil sees that if the Son is a creature mankind is still without a revelation of the Divine. He sees that Eunomius, "by alienating the Only Begotten from the Father, and altogether cutting Him off from communion with Him, as far as he can, deprives us of the ascent of knowledge which is made through the Son. Our Lord says that all that is the Father's is His.[10] Eunomius states that there is no fellowship between the Father and Him Who is of Him."[11] If so there is no "brightness" of glory; no "express image of hypostasis."[12] So Dorner,[13] who freely uses the latter portion of the treatise, "The main point of Basil's opposition to Eunomius is that the word unbegotten is not a name indicative of the essence of God, but only of a condition of existence.[14] The divine essence has other predicates. If every peculiar mode of existence causes a distinction in essence also, then the Son cannot be of the same essence with the Father, because He has a peculiar mode of existence, and the Father another; and men cannot be of the same essence, because each of them represents a different mode of existence. By the names of Father, Son, and Spirit, we do not understand different essences, (οὐσίας), but they are names which distinguish the ὕπαρξις of each. All are God, and the Father is no more God than the Son, as one man is no more man than another. Quantitative differences are not reckoned in respect of essence ; the question is only of being or non-being. But this does not exclude the idea of a variety in condition in the

---

[1] ἀΐδιον δὲ τὸ χρόνου παντὸς καὶ αἰῶνος κατὰ τὸ εἶναι πρεσβύτερον.   [2] *Id.* ii. 18.
[3] Eunomius is therefore not to be ranked with the extreme "Exucontians." *cf.* Soc. *H.E.* ii. 45.
[4] *Id.* ii. 19.   [5] *Id.* ii. 19.
[6] So R.V. distinguishes between the words λειτουργικὰ and διακονίαν which are confused in A.V.
[7] *Id.* i. 21.   [8] Ps. cxlviii. 5.   [9] *Id.* i. 21.   [10] *cf.* John xvii. 10.   [11] *Id.* i. 18.
[12] On this brief summary of Basil's controversy with Eunomius, *cf.* Böhringer, *Kirchengeschichte,* vii. 62, *seqq.*
[13] *Christologie,* i. 906.   [14] τὸ ἀγέννητος ὑπάρξεως τρόπος καὶ οὐκ οὐσίας ὄνομα. *Adv. Eunom.* iv.

Father and the Son (ἑτέρως ἔχειν), — the generation of the Latter. The dignity of both is equal. The essence of Begetter and Begotten is identical."[1]

The Fourth Book contains notes on the chief passages of Scripture which were relied on by Arian disputants. Among these are

1 Cor. xv. 28. On the Subjection of the Son.

"If the Son is subjected to the Father in the Godhead, then He must have been subjected from the beginning, from whence He was God. But if He was not subjected, but shall be subjected, it is in the manhood, as for us, not in the Godhead, as for Himself."

Philipp. ii. 9. On the Name above every Name.

"If the name above every name was given by the Father to the Son, Who was God, and every tongue owned Him Lord, after the incarnation, because of His obedience, then before the incarnation He neither had the name above every name nor was owned by all to be Lord. It follows then that after the incarnation He was greater than before the incarnation, which is absurd." So of Matt. xxviii. 18. "We must understand this of the incarnation, and not of the Godhead."

John xiv. 28. "My Father is Greater than I."

"'Greater' is predicated in bulk, in time, in dignity, in power, or as cause. The Father cannot be called greater than the Son in bulk, for He is incorporeal: nor yet in time, for the Son is Creator of times: nor yet in dignity, for He was not made what He had once not been: nor yet in power, for 'what things soever the Father doeth, these also doeth the son likewise':[2] nor as cause, since (the Father) would be similarly greater than He and than we, if He is cause of Him and of us. The words express rather the honour given by the Son to the Father than any depreciation by the speaker; moreover what is greater is not necessarily of a different essence. Man is called greater than man, and horse than horse. If the Father is called greater, it does not immediately follow that He is of another substance. In a word, the comparison lies between beings of one substance, not between those of different substances.[3]

"A man is not properly said to be greater than a brute, than an inanimate thing, but man than man, and brute than brute. The Father is therefore of one substance with the Son, even though He be called greater."[4]

On Matt. xxiv. 36. Of Knowledge of that Day and of that Hour.[5]

"If the Son is the Creator of the world, and does not know the time of the judgment, then He does not know what He created. For He said that He was ignorant not of the judgment, but of the time. How can this be otherwise than absurd?

"If the Son has not knowledge of all things whereof the Father has knowledge, then He spake untruly when He said 'All things that the Father hath are mine'[6] and 'As the Father knoweth me so know I the Father.'[7] If there is a distinction between knowing the Father and knowing the things that the Father hath, and if, in proportion as every one is greater than what is his, it is greater to know the Father than to know what is His, then the Son, though He knew the greater (for no man knoweth the Father save the Son),[8] did not know the less.

"This is impossible. He was silent concerning the season of the judgment, because it was not expedient for men to hear. Constant expectation kindles a warmer zeal for true religion. The knowledge that a long interval of time was to elapse would have made men more careless about true religion, from the hope of being saved by a subsequent change of

---

[1] cf. *De Sp. Scto.* pp. 13, 39, and notes; Thomasius, *Dogmengeschichte*, i. 245; Herzog, *Real-Encycl.* "*Eunomius und Eunomianer.*"
[2] John v. 19.   [3] ἐπὶ τῶν ὁμοουσίων οὐκ ἐπὶ τῶν ἑτεροουσίων.
[4] It will be noted that Basil explains this passage on different grounds from those suggested by the Clause in the Athanasian Creed, on which Waterland's remark is that it "needs no comment." St. Athanasius himself interpreted the "minority" not of the humanity, or of the special subordination of th time when the words were uttered. *cf.* Ath., *Orat. c. Ar.* i. § 58: "The Son says not 'my Father is better than I,' lest we should conceive Him to be foreign to His nature, but 'greater,' not indeed in size, nor in time, but because of His generation from the Father Himself; nay, in saying 'greater,' He again shews that He is proper to His essence" (Newman's transl.). The explanation given in *Letter* viii., p. 118, does include the inferiority as touching His manhood.
[5] cf. *Letter* viii. p. 118.   [6] John xv. 16.   [7] John x. 15.   [8] Matt. xi. 27.

life. How could He who had known everything up to this time (for so He said) not know that hour also? If so, the Apostle vainly said ' In whom are hid all the treasures of wisdom and knowledge.'[1]

" If the Holy Spirit, who ' searcheth the deep things of God,'[2] cannot be ignorant of anything that is God's, then, as they who will not even allow Him to be equal must contend, the Holy Ghost is greater than the Son."[3]

On Matt. xxvi. 39. Father, if it be Possible, let this Cup pass from Me.

" If the Son really said, ' Father, if it be possible, let this cup pass from me,' He not only shewed His own cowardice and weakness, but implied that there might be something impossible to the Father. The words ' if it be possible ' are those of one in doubt, and not thoroughly assured that the Father could save Him. How could not He who gave the boon of life to corpses much rather be able to preserve life in the living? Wherefore then did not He Who had raised Lazarus and many of the dead supply life to Himself? Why did He ask life from the Father, saying, in His fear, ' Father, if it be possible, let this cup pass away from me'? If He was dying unwillingly, He had not yet humbled Himself; He had not yet been made obedient to the Father unto death;[4] He had not given Himself, as the Apostle says, ' who gave Himself for our sins,[5] a ransom.'[6] If He was dying willingly, what need of the words ' Father, if it be possible, let this cup pass away'? No: this must not be understood of Himself; it must be understood of those who were on the point of sinning against Him, to prevent them from sinning; when crucified in their behalf He said, ' Father, forgive them, for they know not what they do.'[7] We must not understand words spoken in accordance with the œconomy[8] to be spoken simply."

On John vi. 57. I live by the Father.[9]

" If the Son lives on account of[10] the Father, He lives on account of another, and not of Himself. But He who lives on account of another cannot be Self-life.[11] So He who is holy of grace is not holy of himself.[12] Then the Son did not speak truly when He said, ' I am the life,'[13] and again, ' the Son quickeneth whom He will.'[14] We must therefore understand the words to be spoken in reference to the incarnation, and not to the Godhead."

On John v. 19. The Son can do Nothing of Himself.

" If freedom of action[15] is better than subjection to control,[16] and a man is free, while the Son of God is subject to control, then the man is better than the Son. This is absurd. And if he who is subject to control cannot create free beings (for he cannot of his own will confer on others what he does not possess himself), then the Saviour, since He made us free, cannot Himself be under the control of any."

" If the Son could do nothing of Himself, and could only act at the bidding of the Father, He is neither good nor bad. He was not responsible for anything that was done. Consider the absurdity of the position that men should be free agents both of good and evil, while the Son, who is God, should be able to do nothing of His own authority!"

On John xv. 1. I am the Vine.

" If, say they, the Saviour is a vine, and we are branches, but the Father is husbandman; and if the branches are of one nature with the vine, and the vine is not of one nature with the husbandman; then the Son is of one nature with us, and we are a part of Him, but the Son is not of one nature with, but in all respects of a nature foreign to, the Father, I shall reply to them that He called us branches not of His Godhead, but of His flesh, as the Apostle says, we are ' the body of Christ, and members in particular,'[17] and again, ' know ye not that your bodies are the members of Christ?'[18] and in other places, ' as is

---

[1] Col. ii. 3.   [2] 1 Cor. ii. 10.
[3] cf. this passage more fully treated of in Letter ccxxxvi. p. 276. The above is rather a tentative memorandum than an explanation.
[4] cf. Phil. ii. 8.   [5] Gal. i. 4.   [6] Matt. xxi. 28.   [7] Luke xxiii. 34.
[8] cf. pp. 7 and 12. Most commentators that I am acquainted with write on the lines of Bengel. "poculum a patre oblatum, tota passionis massa plenum." cf. Athanasius, "the terror was of the flesh." C. Arian. Orat. III., § xxxix., Amphilochius, Apud Theod. Dial. iii., and Chrysost., Hom. in Matt. lxxxiii.
[9] cf. Ep. viii. and note on p. 117.   [12] αὐτοάγιος.   [15] τὸ αὐτεξούσιον.   [18] 1 Cor. vi. 15.
[10] διά. Vide note referred to.   [13] John xi. 25.   [16] τὸ ὑπεξούσιον.
[11] Or underived life. αὐτοζωή.   [14] John v. 21.   [17] 1 Cor. xii. 27.

the earthy, such are they that are earthy ; and as is the heavenly, such are they also that are heavenly.   And as we have borne the image of the earthy, let us all bear the image of the heavenly.' ¹   If the head of the ' man is Christ, and the head of Christ is God,' ² and man is not of one substance with Christ, Who is God (for man is not God), but Christ is of one substance with God (for He is God), therefore God is not the head of Christ in the same sense as Christ is the head of man.   The natures of the creature and the creative Godhead do not exactly coincide.   God is head of Christ, as Father; Christ is head of us, as Maker.   If the will of the Father is that we should believe in His Son (for this is the will of Him that sent me, that every one which seeth the Son, and believeth on Him, may have everlasting life),³ the Son is not a Son of will.   That we should believe in Him is (an injunction) found with Him, or before Him." ⁴

On Mark x. 18.   There is none Good, etc.

" If the Saviour is not good, He is necessarily bad.   For He is simple, and His character does not admit of any intermediate quality.   How can it be otherwise than absurd that the Creator of good should be bad?   And if life is good, and the words of the Son are life, as He Himself said, ' the words which I speak unto you, they are spirit, and they are life,' ⁵ in what sense, when He hears one of the Pharisees address Him as good Master, does He rejoin, ' There is none good but One, that is God'?   It was not when He had heard no more than good that he said, ' there is none good,' but when He had heard good Master.   He answered as to one tempting Him, as the gospel expresses it, or to one ignorant, that God is good, and not simply a good master."

On John xvii. 5.   Father, glorify Me.

" If when the Son asked to be glorified of the Father He was asking in respect of His Godhead, and not of His manhood, He asked for what He did not possess.   Therefore the evangelist speaks falsely when he says ' we beheld His glory '; ⁶ and the apostle, in the words ' They would not have crucified the Lord of glory,' ⁷ and David in the words ' And the King of glory shall come in.' ⁸   It is not therefore an increase of glory which he asks.   He asks that there may be a manifestation of the œconomy.⁹   Again, if He really asked that the glory which He had before the world might be given Him of the Father, He asked it because He had lost it.   He would never have sought to receive that of which He was in possession.   But if this was the case, He had lost not only the glory, but also the Godhead.   For the glory is inseparable from the Godhead.   Therefore, according to Photinus,¹⁰ He was mere man.   It is then clear that He spoke these words in accordance with the œconomy of the manhood, and not through failure in the Godhead."

On Coloss. i. 15.   Firstborn of every Creature.

" If before the creation the Son was not a generated being but a created being,¹¹ He would have been called first created and not firstborn.¹²   If, because He is called first

---

¹ 1 Cor. xv. 48, 49: in the last clause Basil reads φορέσωμεν, instead of the φορέσομεν of A.V., with ℵ, A, C, D, E, F, G, K, L, P.   ² 1 Cor. xi. 3.   ³ John vi. 40.
⁴ *i.e.* simultaneous with, or even anterior to, His advent. Maran hesitates as to the meaning of the phrase, and writes : " *Suspicor tamen intelligi sic posse.   Quanquam voluntas patris est ut in Filium credamus, non tamen propterea sequitur, Filium ex voluntate esse.   Nam credere nos oportet in Filium, ut primum in hunc mundum venit, imo antequam etiam naturam humanam assumeret, cum patriarchæ et Judæi prisci ad salutem consequendam in Christum venturum credere necesse habuerint.   Itaque cum debeamus necessario credere in Filium omni ætate et tempore; hinc efficitur, Filium esse natura, non voluntate, neque adoptione.   Si voluntas est Patris ut nos in ejus Filium credamus, non est ex voluntate Filius, quippe nostra in ipsum fides aut cum ipso aut ante ipsum invenitur.   Subtilis hæc ratiocinatio illustratur ex alia simili, quæ reperitur (i.e. at the beginning of Book IV.).   Si fides in Filium nostra opus est Dei, ipse Dei opus esse non potest.   Nam fides in ipsum et ipse non idem.*"
⁵ John vi. 64.   ⁶ John i. 14.   ⁷ 1 Cor. ii. 8.   ⁸ Ps. xxiv. 7.   ⁹ *i.e.* of the incarnation, *cf.* pp. 7, 12.
¹⁰ On Photinus *cf.* Socrates, *Ecc. Hist.* ii. 29, and Theodoret, *Hær. Fab.* iii. 1, and Epiphanius, *Hær.* lxxi. § 2. The question as to what Synod condemned and deposed him has been thought to have been settled in favour of that of Sirmium in 349. (*D:C.B.* iv. 394.)   *cf.* Hefele's *Councils,* tr. Oxenham, ii. 188.
¹¹ οὐ γέννημα ἀλλὰ κτίσμα.   The use of the word γέννημα in this book is one of the arguments alleged against its genuineness, for in Book II., Capp. 6, 7, and 8. Basil objects to it; but in the same Book II., Cap. 32, he uses it apparently without objection in the sentence ἐκ τοῦ γεννήματος νοῆσαι ῥάδιον τοῦ γεγεννηκότος τὴν φύσιν. Maran, *Vit. Bas.* xliii. 7.
¹² The English word *firstborn* is not an exact rendering of the Greek πρωτότοκος, and in its theological use it may lead to confusion. " Bear " and its correlatives in English are only used of the mother. τίκτω (√TEK. *cf.* Ger. *Zeug.*) is used indifferently of both father and mother. πρωτότοκος is exactly rendered *firstborn* in Luke ii. 7; but *first begotten,* as in A.V. Heb. i. 6, and Rev. i. 5, more precisely renders the word in the text, and in such passages as Ex. xiii. 2, and Psalm lxxxix. 28, which are Messianically applied to the divine Word.   So early as Clemens Alexandrinus the *only begotten* and *first begotten* had been contrasted with the *first created,* the highest order of created beings. With him may be compared Tertullian, *Adv. Prax.* 7, *Adv. Marc.* v. 19, Hippolytus, *Hær.* x. 33, Origen, *C. Cels.* vi. 47, 63, 64, *In Ioann.* 1, § 22 (iv. p. 21), xix. § 5 (p. 305), xxviii. § 14 (p. 392), Cyprian, *Test.* ii. 1, Novatian, *De Trin.* 16.   On the history and uses of the word, see the exhaustive note of Bp. Lightfoot on Col. i. 15.

begotten of creation He is first created, then because He is called first begotten of the dead [1] He would be the first of the dead who died. If on the other hand He is called first begotten of the dead because of His being the cause of the resurrection from the dead, He is in the same manner called first begotten of creation, because He is the cause of the bringing of the creature from the non-existent into being. If His being called first begotten of creation indicates that He came first into being, then the Apostle, when he said, 'all things were created by Him and for Him,'[2] ought to have added, 'And He came into being first of all.' But in saying ' He is before all things,'[3] he indicated that He exists eternally, while the creature came into being. ' Is ' in the passage in question is in harmony with the words ' In the beginning was the Word.'[4] It is urged that if the Son is first begotten, He cannot be only begotten, and that there must needs be some other, in comparison with whom He is styled first begotten. Yet, O wise objector, though He is the only Son born of the Virgin Mary, He is called her first born. For it is said, ' Till she brought forth her first born Son.'[5] There is therefore no need of any brother in comparison with whom He is styled first begotten.[6]

'' It might also be said that one who was before all generation was called first begotten, and moreover in respect of them who are begotten of God through the adoption of the Holy Ghost, as Paul says, ' For whom He did foreknow, He also did predestinate to be conformed to the image of His Son, that He might be the first born among many brethren.' ''[7]

On Prov. vii. 22. The Lord created Me (LXX.).[8]

'' If it is the incarnate Lord who says ' I am the way,'[9] and ' No man cometh unto the Father but by me,'[10] it is He Himself Who said, ' The Lord created me beginning of ways.' The word is also used of the creation and making of a begotten being,[11] as ' I have created a man through the Lord,'[12] and again ' He begat sons and daughters,'[13] and so David, ' Create in me a clean heart, O God,'[14] not asking for another, but for the cleansing of the heart he had. And a new creature is spoken of, not as though another creation came into being, but because the enlightened are established in better works. If the Father created the Son for works, He created Him not on account of Himself, but on account of the works. But that which comes into being on account of something else, and not on its own account, is either a part of that on account of which it came into being, or is inferior. The Saviour will then be either a part of the creature, or inferior to the creature. We must understand the passage of the manhood. And it might be said that Solomon uttered these words of the same wisdom whereof the Apostle makes mention in the passage ' For after that in the wisdom of God, the world by wisdom knew not God.'[15] It must moreover be borne in mind that the speaker is not a prophet, but a writer of proverbs. Now proverbs are figures of other things, not the actual things which are uttered. If it was God the Son Who said, ' The Lord created me,' He would rather have said, ' The Father created me.' Nowhere did He call Him Lord, but always Father. The word ' begot,' then, must be understood in reference to God the Son, and the word created, in reference to Him who took on Him the form of a servant. In all these cases we do not mention two, God apart and man apart (for He was One), but in thought we take into account the nature of each. Peter had not two in his mind when he said, ' Christ hath suffered for us in the flesh.'[16] If, they argue, the Son is a thing begotten and not a thing made, how does Scripture say, ' Therefore let all the house of Israel know assuredly that God hath made that same Jesus, Whom ye have crucified, both Lord and Christ'?[17] We must also say here that

---

[1] Rev. i. 5. [2] Col. i. 16. [3] Col. i. 17. [4] John i. 1. [5] Matt. i. 25.
[6] Jerome's *Tract on the Perpetual Virginity of the Blessed Virgin* appeared about 383, and was written at Rome in the episcopate of Damasus (363-384). The work of Helvidius which Jerome controverted was not published till about 380, and there can be no reference to him in the passage in the text. Basil is contending against the general Arian inference, rather than against any individual statement as to who the " Brethren of the Lord" were. *cf.* also dub. *Hom. in Sanct. Christ. Gen.* p. 600. Ed. Garn. On the whole subject see Bp. Lightfoot, in his *Ep. to the Galatians*, E. S. Ffoulkes in *D.C.B. s.v.* Helvidius, and Archdeacon Farrar in his *Life of Chrrst*, chap. vii., who warmly supports the Helvidian theory in opposition to the almost universal belief of the early Church. Basil evidently has no more idea that the ἕως οὗ of Matt. i. 25 implies any thing as to events subsequent to the τόκος than had when he said that Michal had no child till (LXX. ἕως) the day of her death, or St. Paul had that Christ's reigning *till* (ἄχρις οὗ) He had put all enemies under His feet implied that He would not reign afterwards. Too much importance must not be given to niceties of usage in Hellenistic Greek, but it is a well-known distinction in Attic Greek that ποίν with the infinitive is employed where the action is not asserted to take place, while it is used with the indicative of a *past fact*. Had St. Matthew written πρὶν συνῆλθον, the Helvidians might have laid still greater stress than they did on the argument from Matt. i. 18, which St. Jerome ridicules. His writing πρὶν ἢ συνελθεῖν is what might have been expected if he wished simply to assert that the conception was not preceded by any cohabitation.
[7] Rom. viii. 29. [8] The LXX. version is Κύριος ἔκτισέ με ἀρχὴν ὁδῶν αὐτοῦ. [9] John xiv. 6. [10] *Id.*
[11] γέννημα. [12] The Heb. verb here is the same as in Prov. viii. 22, though rendered ἐκτησάμην in the LXX.
[13] Gen. v. 4. Here Basil has ἐποίησεν for the LXX. ἐγέννησεν, representing another Hebrew verb.
[14] Ps. li. 10 καρδίαν καθαρὰν κτίσον. [15] 1 Cor. i. 21. [16] 1 Pet. iv. 1. [17] Acts ii. 36.

this was spoken according to the flesh about the Son of Man; just as the angel who announced the glad tidings to the shepherds says, 'To you is born to-day a Saviour, Who is Christ the Lord.'[1] The word 'to-day' could never be understood of Him Who was before the ages. This is more clearly shewn by what comes afterwards where it is said, 'That same Jesus whom ye have crucified.'[2] If when the Son was born[3] He was then made wisdom, it is untrue that He was 'the power of God and the wisdom of God.'[4] His wisdom did not come into being, but existed always. And so, as though of the Father, it is said by David, 'Be thou, God, my defender,'[5] and again, 'Thou art become my salvation,'[6] and so Paul, 'Let God be true, but every man a liar.'[7] Thus the Lord 'of God is made unto us wisdom and sanctification and redemption.'[8] Now when the Father was made defender and true, He was not a thing made; and similarly when the Son was made wisdom and sanctification, He was not a thing made. If it is true that there is one God the Father, it is assuredly also true that there is one Lord Jesus Christ the Saviour. According to them the Saviour is not God nor the Father Lord, and it is written in vain, 'the Lord said unto my Lord.'[9] False is the statement, 'Therefore God, thy God, hath anointed thee.'[10] False too, 'The Lord rained from the Lord.'[11] False, 'God created in the image of God,'[12] and 'Who is God save the Lord?'[13] and 'Who is a God save our God.'[14] False the statement of John that 'the Word was God and the Word was with God;'[15] and the words of Thomas of the Son, 'my Lord and my God.'[16] The distinctions, then, ought to be referred to creatures and to those who are falsely and not properly called gods, and not to the Father and to the Son."

On John xvii. 3. That they may know Thee, the only true God.

" The *true* (sing.) is spoken of in contradistinction to the false (pl.). But He is incomparable, because in comparison with all He is in all things superexcellent. When Jeremiah said of the Son, 'This is our God, and there shall none other be accounted of in comparison with Him,'[17] did he describe Him as greater even than the Father? That the Son also is true God, John himself declares in the Epistle, 'That we may know the only true God, and we are (in Him that is true, even) in His (true) Son Jesus Christ. This is the true God, and eternal life.'[18] It would be wrong, on account of the words 'There shall none other be accounted of in comparison of Him,' to understand the Son to be greater than the Father; nor must we suppose the Father to be the only true God. Both expressions must be used in connexion with those who are falsely styled, but are not really, gods. In the same way it is said in Deuteronomy, 'So the Lord alone did lead him, and there was no strange God with him.'[19] If God is alone invisible and wise, it does not at once follow that He is greater than all in all things. But the God Who is *over* all is necessarily superior to all.. Did the Apostle, when he styled the Saviour God *over all*, describe Him as greater than the Father? The idea is absurd. The passage in question must be viewed in the same manner. The great God cannot be less than a different God. When the Apostle said of the Son, we look for 'that blessed hope, and the glorious appearing of the great God and our Saviour Jesus Christ,'[20] did he think of Him as greater than the Father?[21] It is the Son, not the Father, Whose appearance and advent we are waiting for. These terms are thus used without distinction of both the Father and the Son, and no exact nicety is observed in their employment. 'Being equally with God'[22] is identical with being equal with God.[23] Since the Son 'thought it not robbery' to be equal with God, how can He be unlike and unequal to God? Jews are nearer true religion than Eunomius. Whenever the Saviour called Himself no more than Son of God, as though it were due to the Son, if He be really Son, to be Himself equal to the Father, they wished, it is said, to stone Him, not only because He was breaking the Sabbath, but because, by saying that God was His own Father, He made Himself equal with God.[24] Therefore, even though

1 Luke ii. 11.   2 Acts ii. 36.   3 ἐγεννήθη. But it seems to refer to the birth from Mary.   4 1 Cor. i. 24.
5 Ps. xxxi. 2, LXX.   6 1 Cor. i. 30.   11 Gen. xix. 24.   14 *Id.* LXX.
6 Ps. cxviii. 21.   9 Ps. cx. 1.   12 Gen. i. 27.   15 John i. 1.
7 Rom. iii. 4.   10 Ps. xlv. 8.   13 Ps. xviii. 31.   16 John xx. 28.
17 Baruch iii. 35.   The quoting of Baruch under the name of Jeremiah has been explained by the fact that in the LXX. Baruch was placed with the Lamentations, and was regarded in the early Church as of equal authority with Jeremiah. It was commonly so quoted, *e.g.* by Irenæus, Clemens Alexandrinus, and Tertullian. So Theodoret, *Dial.* i. (in this edition, p. 165, where *cf.* note).
18 1 John v. 20.   There is some MS. authority for the insertion of " God " in the first clause, but none for the omission of the former ἐν τῷ.   19 Deut. xxxii. 12.   20 Tit. ii. 13.
21 St. Basil, with the mass of the Greek orthodox Fathers, has no idea of any such interpretation of Tit. ii. 13, as Alford endeavours to support.   *cf.* Theodoret, pp. 391 and 321, and notes.
22 τὸ εἶναι ἴσα Θεῷ, as in Phil. ii. 6, tr. in A.V. to be equal with God; R.V. has to be on an equality with God.
23 τῷ εἶναι ἴσον Θεῷ.   24 John v. 18.

Eunomius is unwilling that it should be so, according both to the Apostle and to the Saviour's own words, the Son is equal with the Father."

On Matt. xx. 23. Is not Mine to give, save for whom it is prepared.[1]

" If the Son has not authority over the judgment, and power to benefit some and chastise others, how could He say, ' The Father judgeth no man, but hath committed all judgment unto the Son '?[2] And in another place, ' The Son of man hath power on earth to forgive sins; '[3] and again, ' All power is given unto me in heaven and in earth ; '[4] and to Peter, ' I will give thee the keys of the kingdom of heaven; '[5] and to the disciples, ' Verily, I say unto you that ye which have followed me, in the regeneration, . . . shall sit upon twelve thrones, judging the twelve tribes of Israel.'[6] The explanation is clear from the Scripture, since the Saviour said, ' Then will I reward every man according to his work ; '[7] and in another place, 'They that have done good shall come forth unto the resurrection of life, and they that have done evil unto the resurrection of damnation.'[8] And the Apostle says, ' We must all appear before the judgment seat of Christ, that every one may receive the things done in his body, according to what he hath done, whether it be good or bad.'[9] It is therefore the part of the recipients to make themselves worthy of a seat on the left and on the right of the Lord : it is not the part of Him Who is able to give it, even though the request be unjust."[10]

On Ps. xviii. 31, LXX. Who is God, save the Lord? Who is God save our God?

" It has already been sufficiently demonstrated that the Scriptures employ these expressions and others of a similar character not of the Son, but of the so-called gods who were not really so. I have shewn this from the fact that in both the Old and the New Testament the Son is frequently styled both God and Lord. David makes this still clearer when he says, ' Who is like unto Thee?'[11] and adds, ' among the gods, O Lord,' and Moses, in the words, ' So the Lord alone did lead him, and there was no strange god with him.'[12] And yet although, as the Apostle says, the Saviour was with them, ' They drank of that spiritual rock that followed them, and that rock was Christ,'[13] and Jeremiah, ' The gods that have not made the heavens and the earth, . . . let them perish under the heavens.'[14] The Son is not meant among these, for He is Himself Creator of all. It is then the idols and images of the heathen who are meant alike by the preceding passage and by the words, ' I am the first God and I am the last, and beside me there is no God,'[15] and also, ' Before me there was no God formed, neither shall there be after me,'[16] and ' Hear, O Israel, the Lord our God is one Lord.'[17] None of these passages must be understood as referring to the Son."

The Fifth Book against Eunomius is on the Holy Spirit, and therefore, even if it were of indubitable genuineness, it would be of comparatively little importance. as the subject is fully discussed in the treatise of his maturer life. A reason advanced against its genuineness has been the use concerning the Holy Ghost of the term God. (§ 3.) But it has been replied that the reserve which St. Basil practised after his elevation to the episcopate was but for a special and temporary purpose. He calls the Spirit God in Ep. VIII. § 11. At the time of the publication of the Books against Eunomius there would be no such reason for any " economy "[18] as in 374.

(ii) *De Spiritu Sancto.* To the illustration and elucidation of this work I have little to add to what is furnished, however inadequately, by the translation and notes in the following pages. The famous treatise of St. Basil was one of several put out about the same time by the champions of the Catholic cause. Amphilochius, to whom it was

---

[1] I do not here render with the Arian gloss of A.V., infelicitously reproduced in the equally inexact translation of R.V. The insertion of the words "it shall be given" and " it is" is apparently due to a pedantic prejudice against translating ἀλλά by " save " or "except," a rendering which is supported in classical Greek by such a passage as Soph., *O.T.* 1331, and in Hellenistic Greek by Mark ix. 8. The Vulgate has, quite correctly, " *non est meum dare vobis, sed quibus paratum est a patre meo,*" so far as the preservation of the Son as the giver is concerned. A similar error is to be found in both the French and German (Luther's) of Bagster's polyglot edition. Wiclif has correctly, "is not myn to geve to you but to whiche it is made redi of my fadir." So Tyndale, "is not myne to geve but to them for whom it is prepared of my father." The gloss begins with Cranmer (1539), "it shall chance unto them that it is prepared for," and first appears in the Geneva of 1557 as the A.V. has perpetuated it. The Rheims follows the *vobis* of the Vulgate, but is otherwise correct. *cf.* note on Theodoret in this edition, p. 169. [2] John v. 22. [3] Mark ii. 10. [4] Matt. xxviii. 18. [5] Matt. xvi. 19. [6] Matt. xix. 28. [7] *cf.* Matt. xvi. 27. [8] John v. 29. [9] 2 Cor. v. 10. [10] These last words are explained by a Scholium to the MS. Reg. II. to be a reference to the unreasonable petition of James and John. It will be seen how totally opposed Basil's interpretation is to that required by the gloss of A.V. [11] Ps. lxxxvi. 8. [12] Deut. xxxii. 12. [13] 1 Cor. x. 4. [14] Jer. x. 2, LXX. [15] Is. xliv. 6, "God" inserted. [16] Is. xliii. 10. [17] Deut. vi. 4. [18] *cf.* remarks in § vi. p. xxiii. of Prolegomena.

addressed, was the author of a work which Jerome describes (*De Vir. Ill.*, cxxxiii.) as arguing that He is God Almighty, and to be worshipped. The *Ancoratus* of Epiphanius was issued in 373 in support of the same doctrine. At about the same time Didymus, the blind master of the catechetical school at Alexandria, wrote a treatise which is extant in St. Jerome's Latin; and of which the work of St. Ambrose, composed in 381, for the Emperor Gratian, is " to a considerable extent an echo." [1]

So in East and West a vigorous defence was maintained against the Macedonian assault. The Catholic position is exactly defined in the Synodical Letter sent by Damasus to Paulinus of Tyre in 378.[2] Basil died at the crisis of the campaign, and with no bright Pisgah view of the ultimate passage into peace. The generalship was to pass into other hands. There is something of the irony of fate, or of the mystery of Providence, in the fact that the voice condemned by Basil to struggle against the mean din and rattle of Sasima should be the vehicle for impressing on the empire the truths which Basil held dear. Gregory of Sasima was no archiepiscopal success at Constantinople. He was not an administrator or a man of the world. But he was a great divine and orator, and the imperial basilica of the Athanasia rang with outspoken declarations of the same doctrines, which Basil had more cautiously suggested to inevitable inference. The triumph was assured, Gregory was enthroned in St. Sophia, and under Theodosius the Catholic Faith was safe from molestation.

II. EXEGETIC.

(i) As of the *De Spiritu Sancto*, so of the *Hexaemeron*, no further account need be given here. It may, however, be noted that the Ninth Homily ends abruptly, and the latter, and apparently more important, portion of the subject is treated of at less length than the former. Jerome [3] and Cassiodorus [4] speak of nine homilies only on the creation. Socrates [5] says the Hexaemeron was completed by Gregory of Nyssa. Three orations are published among Basil's works, two on the creation of men and one on Paradise, which are attributed to Basil by Combefis and Du Pin, but not considered genuine by Tillemont, Maran, Garnier, Ceillier, and Fessler. They appear to be compositions which some editor thought congruous to the popular work of Basil, and so appended them to it.

The nine discourses in the Hexaemeron all shew signs of having been delivered extempore, and the sequence of argument and illustration is not such as to lead to the conclusion that they were ever redacted by the author into exact literary form. We probably owe their preservation to the skilled shorthand writers of the day.[6]

(ii) The Homilies on the Psalms as published are seventeen in number; it has however been commonly held that the second Homily on Ps. xxviii. is not genuine, but the composition of some plagiarist. The Homily also on Ps. xxxvii. has been generally objected to. These are omitted from the group of the Ben. Ed., together with the first on Ps. cxiv., and that on cxv. Maran [7] thinks that none of these orations shew signs of having been delivered in the episcopate, or of having reference to the heresy of the Pneumatomachi; two apparently point directly to the presbyterate. In that on Ps. xiv. he speaks of an ἀμεριμνία which would better befit the priest than the primate; on Ps. cxiv. he describes himself as serving a particular church. Both arguments seem a little far-fetched, and might be opposed on plausible grounds. Both literal and allegorical interpretations are given. If Basil is found expressing himself in terms similar to those of Eusebius, it is no doubt because both were inspired by Origen.[8] The Homily on Psalm i. begins with a partial quotation from 2 Tim. iii. 16, " All Scripture is given by inspiration of God, and is profitable," and goes on, " and was composed by the Spirit to the end that all of us men, as in a general hospital for souls, may choose each what is best for his own cure." For him, Scripture is supreme.[9] As is noticed on Hom. IX.[10] of the Hexaemeron, Basil is on the whole for the simpler sense. But he was a student of Origen, and he well knows

[1] Swete, *Doctrine of the Holy Spirit*, p. 71, who further notes : " St. Jerome is severe upon St. Ambrose for copying Didymus, and says that the Archbishop of Milan had produced '*ex Græcis bonis Latina non bona*.' The work of the Latin Father is, however, by no means a mere copy; and other writers besides Didymus are laid under contribution in the argument; *e.g.* St. Basil and perhaps St. Athanasius."
[2] Theod. v. 11 in this edition, p. 139; Mansi iii. 486.
[3] *De Vir. Illust.* cxvi.　　　　[4] *Instit. Div.* i.　　　　[5] *Ecc. Hist.* iv. 26.
[6] *cf. Letter* ccxxiii. § 5, p. 264. It is believed that tachygraphy was known from very early times, and Xenophon is said to have " reported " Socrates by its aid. The first plain mention of a tachygraphist is in a letter of Flavius Philostratus (A.D. 195). It has been thought that the systems in use in the earlier centuries of our era were modifications of a cryptographic method employed by the Christians to circulate documents in the Church. No examples are extant of an earlier date than the tenth century, and of these an interesting specimen is the Paris MS. of Hermogenes described by Montfaucon, *Pal. Gr.* p. 351. The exact minutes of some of the Councils —*e.g.* Chalcedon — seem to be due to very successful tachygraphy.
[7] *Vit. Bas.* xli. 4.　　[8] *cf.* Fessler, p. 512.　　[9] *cf. Epp.* cv., clx. § 2, cxcviii. § 3, and cclxiv. § 4.　　[10] See p. 101.

how to use allegory when he thinks fit.[1] An example may be observed in Letter VIII.,[2] where there is an elaborate allegorisation of the " times and the seasons " of Acts i. 7. An instance of the application of both systems is to be found in the Homily on Psalm xxviii. (*i.e.* in A.V. xxix.). The LXX. Title is Ψαλμὸς τῷ Δαυὶδ ἐξοδίου σκηνῆς, "*Psalmus David in exitu e tabernaculo.*" Primarily this is a charge delivered to the priests and Levites on leaving their sacred cffices. They are to remember all that it is their duty to prepare for the holy service. As they go out of the Tabernacle the psalm tells them all that it behoves them to have in readiness for the morrow, young rams (Ps. xxix. 1, LXX.), glory and honour, glory for His name. " But to our minds, as they contemplate high and lofty things, and by the aid of an interpretation dignified and worthy of Holy Scripture make the Law our own, the meaning is different. There is no question of ram in flock, nor tabernacle fashioned of lifeless material, nor departure from the temple. The tabernacle for us is this body of ours, as the Apostle has told us in the words, ' For we that are in this tabernacle do groan.' [3] The departure from the temple is our quitting this life. For this these words bid us be prepared, bringing such and such things to the Lord, if the deeds done here are to be a means to help us on our journey to the life to come."

This is in the style of exegesis hitherto popular. To hearers familiar with exegesis of the school of Origen, it is an innovation for Basil to adopt such an exclusively literal system of exposition as he does,— *e.g.* in Hom. IX. on the Hexaemeron,— the system which is one of his distinguishing characteristics.[4] In his common-sense literalism he is thus a link with the historical school of Antioch, whose principles were in contrast with those of Origen and the Alexandrians, a school represented by Theodore of Mopsuestia, Diodorus of Tarsus, and later by Theodoret.[5]

It is remarked by Gregory of Nazianzus in his memorial oration[6] that Basil used a threefold method of enforcing Scripture on his hearers and readers. This may be understood to be the literal, moral, and allegorical. Ceillier points out that this description, so far as we know, applies only to the Homilies on the Psalms.

The praise of the Psalms, prefixed to Psalm i., is a passage of noticeable rhetorical power and of considerable beauty. Its popularity is shewn by the fact of its being found in some manuscripts of St. Augustine, and also in the commentary of Rufinus. The latter probably translated it; portions of it were transcribed by St. Ambrose.[7]

" The prophets," says St. Basil, " the historians, the law, give each a special kind of teaching, and the exhortation of the proverbs furnishes yet another. But the use and profit of all are included in the book of Psalms. There is prediction of thing to come. There our memories are reminded of the past. There laws are laid down for the guidance of life. There are directions as to conduct. The book, in a word, is a treasury of sound teaching, and provides for every individual need. It heals the old hurts of souls, and brings about recovery where the wound is fresh. It wins the part that is sick and preserves that which is sound. As far as lies within its power, it destroys the passions which lord it in this life in the souls of men. And all this it effects with a musical persuasiveness and with a gratification that induces wise and wholesome reflexion. The Holy Spirit saw that mankind was hard to draw to goodness, that our life's scale inclined to pleasure, and that so we were neglectful of the right. What plan did He adopt? He combined the delight of melody with His teaching, to the end that by the sweetness and softness of what we heard we might, all unawares, imbibe the blessing of the words. He acted like wise leeches, who, when they would give sour draughts to sickly patients, put honey round about the cup. So the melodious music of the Psalms has been designed for us, that those who are boys in years, or at least but lads in ways of life, while they seem to be singing, may in reality be carrying on the education of the soul. It is not easy for the inattentive to retain in their memory, when they go home, an injunction of an apostle or prophet; but the sayings of the Psalms are sung in our houses and travel with us through the streets.

---

[1] " *Origène sacrifiait tout au sens mystique Eusèbe le faisait aller de pair avec le sens historique. Comme lui St. Basile respecte scrupuleusement la lettre ; mais comme lui aussi, il voit sous la lettre tous les mystères du Nouveau Testament et surtout des enseignements moraux. Les différents caractères que présente son interprétation sont un moyen presque infaillible de connaitre la date des ses grands travaux exégétiques. Aussi ne doit-on pas hésiter à assigner aux premières années de sa retraite la composition du commentaire d'Isaie, dans lequel domine à peu près exclusivement l'interprétation morale ; à sa prêtrese celle des homilies sur les Psaumes, où il donne une égale importance au sens moral et au sens mystique, mais en leur sacrifiant sans cesse le sens littéral : à son épiscopat, enfin. J'Hexaméron, qui, sans négliger les sens figurés, s'attache surtout à donner une explication exacte de la lettre.*" Fialon, *Ét Hist.* p. 291. The theory is suggestive, but I am not sure that the prevalence of the literal or of the allegorical is not due less to the period of the composition than to the objects the writer has in view. [2] p. 118. [3] 2 Cor. v. 4.

[4] *Im Allgemeinen und im Grundsatze aber ist Basil gegen die allegorische Erklärungsweise, so oft er sie dann auch im Einzelnen anwendet.* Böhringer, *Basil,* p. 116.

[5] *cf.* Gieseler i. p. 109. [6] *Or.* xliii. § 67. [7] Ceillier.

Let a man begin even to grow savage as some wild beast, and no sooner is he soothed by psalm-singing than straightway he goes home with passions lulled to calm and quiet by the music of the song.[1]

" A psalm is souls' calm, herald of peace, hushing the swell and agitation of thoughts. It soothes the passions of the soul; it brings her license under law. A psalm is welder of friendship, atonement of adversaries, reconciliation of haters. Who can regard a man as his enemy, when they have lifted up one voice to God together? So Psalmody gives us the best of all boons, love. Psalmody has bethought her of concerted singing as a mighty bond of union, and links the people together in a symphony of one song. A psalm puts fiends to flight, and brings the aid of angels to our side; it is armour in the terrors of the night; in the toils of the day it is refreshment; to infants it is a protection, to men in life's prime a pride, to elders a consolation, to women an adornment. It turns wastes into homes. It brings wisdom into marts and meetings. To beginners it is an alphabet, to all who are advancing an improvement, to the perfect a confirmation. It is the voice of the church. It gladdens feasts. It produces godly sorrow. It brings a tear even from a heart of stone. A psalm is angels' work, the heavenly conversation, the spiritual sacrifice. Oh, the thoughtful wisdom of the Instructor Who designed that we should at one and the same time sing and learn to our profit! It is thus that His precepts are imprinted on our souls. A lesson that is learned unwillingly is not likely to last, but all that is learned with pleasure and delight effects a permanent settlement in our souls. What can you not learn from this source? You may learn magnificent manliness, scrupulous righteousness, dignified self-control, perfect wisdom. You may learn how to repent, and how far to endure. What good thing can you not learn? There is a complete theology;[2] a foretelling of the advent of Christ in the flesh; threatening of judgment; hope of resurrection; fear of chastisement; promise of glory; revelation of mysteries. Everything is stored in the book of the Psalms as in some vast treasury open to all the world. There are many instruments of music, but the prophet has fitted it to the instrument called Psaltery. I think the reason is that he wished to indicate the grace sounding in him from on high by the gift of the Spirit, because of all instruments the Psaltery is the only one which has the source of its sounds above.[3] In the case of the cithara and the lyre the metal gives forth its sound at the stroke of the plectrum from below. The Psaltery has the source of its melodious strains above. So are we taught to be diligent in seeking the things which are above, and not to allow ourselves to be degraded by our pleasure in the music to the lusts of the flesh. And what I think the word of the Prophet profoundly and wisely teaches by means of the fashion of the instrument is this, — that those whose souls are musical and harmonious find their road to the things that are above most easy."

On Psalm xiv. (in A. V. xv.) the commentary begins:

" Scripture, with the desire to describe to us the perfect man, the man who is ordained to be the recipient of blessings, observes a certain order and method in the treatment of points in him which we may contemplate, and begins from the simplest and most obvious, ' Lord, who shall sojourn[4] in thy tabernacle?' A sojourning is a transitory dwelling. It indicates a life not settled, but passing, in hope of our removal to the better things. It is the part of a saint to pass through this world, and to hasten to another life. In this sense David says of himself, ' I am a stranger with thee and a sojourner, as all my fathers were.'[5] Abraham was a sojourner, who did not possess even so much land as to set his foot on, and, when he needed a tomb, bought one for money.[6] The word teaches us that so long as he lives in the flesh he is a sojourner, and, when he removes from this life, rests in his own home. In this life he sojourns with strangers, but the land which he bought in the tomb to receive his body is his own. And truly blessed is it, not to rot with things of earth as though they were one's own, nor cling to all that is about us here as though here were our natural fatherland, but to be conscious of the fall from nobler things, and of our passing our time in heaviness because of the punishment that is laid upon us, just like exiles who for some crimes' sake have been banished by the magistrates into regions far from the land that gave them birth. Hard it is to find a man who will not heed present things as though they were his own; who knows that he has the use of wealth but for a season; who

---

[1] The English reader is reminded of Congreve's " music" charming " the savage breast."   [2] cf. p. 7, note.
[3] Cassiodorus (*Præf. in P's.* iv.) describes a psaltery shaped like the Greek Δ, with *the sounding board above the strings* which were struck downwards. cf. St. Aug. on Ps. xxxii. and *Dict. Bib. s.v.*
[4] A.V. marg. and R.V. The LXX. is παροικήσει.   [5] Ps. xxxix. 12.   [6] cf. Gen. xxiii. 16, and Acts vii. 16.

reckons on the brief duration of his health; who remembers that the bloom of human glory fades away.

"'Who shall sojourn in thy tabernacle?' The flesh that is given to man's soul for it to dwell in is called God's tabernacle. Who will be found to treat this flesh as though it were not his own? Sojourners, when they hire land that is not their own, till the estate at the will of the owner. So, too, to us the care of the flesh has been entrusted by bond, for us to toil with diligence therein, and make it fruitful for the use of Him Who gave it. And if the flesh is worthy of God, it becomes verily a tabernacle of God, accordingly as He makes His dwelling in the saints. Such is the flesh of the sojourner. 'Lord, who shall sojourn in Thy tabernacle?' Then there come progress and advance to that which is more perfect. 'And who shall dwell in thy holy hill?' A Jew, in earthly sense, when he hears of the 'hill,' turns his thoughts to Sion. 'Who shall dwell in thy holy hill?' The sojourner in the flesh shall dwell in the holy hill, he shall dwell in that hill, that heavenly country, bright and splendid, whereof the Apostle says, 'Ye are come unto Mount Sion, and unto the city of the living God, the heavenly Jerusalem,' where is the general assembly of 'angels, and church of the first-born, which are written in heaven.'" [1]

The Second Homily on Psalm xiv. (xv.) has a special interest in view of the denunciation of usury alike in Scripture and in the early Church. The matter had been treated of at Nicæa. With it may be compared Homily VII., *De Avaritia*.[2]

After a few words of introduction and reference to the former Homily on the same Psalm, St. Basil proceeds; — "In depicting the character of the perfect man, of him, that is, who is ordained to ascend to the life of everlasting peace, the prophet reckons among his noble deeds his never having given his money upon usury. This particular sin is condemned in many passages of Scripture. Ezekiel [3] reckons taking usury and increase among the greatest of crimes. The law distinctly utters the prohibition 'Thou shalt not lend upon usury to thy brother' [4] and to thy neighbour. Again it is said, 'Usury upon usury; guile upon guile.' [5] And of the city abounding in a multitude of wickednesses, what does the Psalm say? 'Usury and guile depart not from her streets.' [6] Now the prophet instances precisely the same point as characteristic of the perfect man, saying, 'He that putteth not out his money to usury.' [7] For in truth it is the last pitch of inhumanity that one man, in need of the bare necessities of life, should be compelled to borrow, and another, not satisfied with the principal, should seek to make gain and profit for himself out of the calamities of the poor. The Lord gave His own injunction quite plainly in the words, 'from him that would borrow of thee turn not thou away.' [8] But what of the money lover? He sees before him a man under stress of necessity bent to the ground in supplication. He sees him hesitating at no act, no words, of humiliation. He sees him suffering undeserved misfortune, but he is merciless. He does not reckon that he is a fellow-creature. He does not give in to his entreaties. He stands stiff and sour. He is moved by no prayers; his resolution is broken by no tears. He persists in refusal, invoking curses on his own head if he has any money about him, and swearing that he is himself on the lookout for a friend to furnish him a loan. He backs lies with oaths, and makes a poor addition to his stock in trade by supplementing inhumanity with perjury. Then the suppliant mentions interest, and utters the word security. All is changed. The frown is relaxed; with a genial smile he recalls old family connexion. Now it is 'my friend.' 'I will see,' says he, 'if I have any money by me. Yes; there is that sum which a man I know has left in my hands on deposit for profit. He named very heavy interest. However, I shall certainly take something off, and give it you on better terms.' With pretences of this kind and talk like this he fawns on the wretched victim, and induces him to swallow the bait. Then he binds him with written security, adds loss of liberty to the trouble of his pressing poverty, and is off. The man who has made himself responsible for interest which he cannot pay has accepted voluntary slavery for life. Tell me; do you expect to get money and profit out of the pauper? If he were in a position to add to your wealth, why should he come begging at your door? He came seeking an ally, and he found a foe. He was looking for medicine, and he lighted on poison. You ought to have comforted him in his distress, but in your attempt to grow fruit on the waste you are aggravating his necessity. Just as well might a physician go in to his patients, and instead of restoring them to health, rob them of the little strength they might have left. This is the way in which you try to profit by the misery of the wretched. Just as farmers pray for rain to make their fields fatter, so you are anxious for men's need and indigence, that your money may make more. You forget that the addition which you are making to your sins is larger than the increase to your wealth which you are reckoning on getting for your usury. The seeker of the loan is helpless either way: he bethinks him of his poverty, he gives up all idea of payment as hopeless when at the need of the moment he risks the loan. The borrower bends to necessity and is beaten. The lender goes off secured by bills and bonds.

"After he has got his money, at first a man is bright and joyous; he shines with another's splendour, and is conspicuous by his altered mode of life. His table is lavish; his dress is most expensive. His servants appear in finer liveries; he has flatterers and boon companions; his rooms are full of drones innumerable. But the money slips away. Time as it runs on adds the interest to its tale. Now night brings him no rest; no day is joyous; no sun is bright; he is weary of his life; he hates the days that are hurrying on to the appointed period; he is afraid of the months, for they are parents of interest. Even if he sleeps, he sees the lender in his slumbers — a bad dream — standing by his pillow. If he wakes up, there is the anxiety and dread of the interest. 'The poor and the usurer,' he exclaims, 'meet together: the Lord lighteneth both their eyes.'[1] The lender runs like a hound after the game. The borrower like a ready prey crouches at the coming catastrophe, for his penury robs him of the power of speech. Both have their ready-reckoner in their hands, the one congratulating himself as the interest mounts up, the other groaning at the growth of his calamities. 'Drink waters out of thine own cistern.'[2] Look, that is to say, at your own resources; do not approach other men's springs; provide your comforts from your own reservoirs. Have you household vessels, clothes, beast of burden, all kinds of furniture? Sell these. Rather surrender all than lose your liberty. Ah, but — he rejoins — I am ashamed to put them up for sale. What then do you think of another's bringing them out a little later on, and crying your goods, and getting rid of them for next to nothing before your very eyes? Do not go to another man's door. Verily 'another man's well is narrow.'[3] Better is it to relieve your necessity gradually by one contrivance after another than after being all in a moment elated by another man's means, afterwards to be stripped at once of everything. If you have anything wherewith to pay, why do you not relieve your immediate difficulties out of these resources? If you are insolvent, you are only trying to cure ill with ill. Decline to be blockaded by an usurer. Do not suffer yourself to be sought out and tracked down like another man's game.[4] Usury is the origin of lying; the beginning of ingratitude, unfairness, perjury. . . .

. . . .

"But, you ask, how am I to live? You have hands. You have a craft. Work for wages. Go into service. There are many ways of getting a living, many kinds of resources. You are helpless? Ask those who have means. It is discreditable to ask? It will be much more discreditable to rob your creditor. I do not speak thus to lay down the law. I only wish to point out that any course is more advantageous to you than borrowing.

. . . .

"Listen, you rich men, to the kind of advice I am giving to the poor because of your inhumanity. Far better endure under their dire straits than undergo the troubles that are bred of usury! But if you were obedient to the Lord, what need of these words? What is the advice of the Master? Lend to those from whom ye do not hope to receive.[5] And what kind of loan is this, it is asked, from which all idea of the expectation of repayment is withdrawn? Consider the force of the expression, and you will be amazed at the loving kindness of the legislator. When you mean to supply the need of a poor man for the Lord's sake, the transaction is at once a gift and a loan. Because there is no expectation of reimbursement, it is a gift. Yet because of the munificence of the Master, Who repays on the recipient's behalf, it is a loan. 'He that hath pity on the poor lendeth unto the Lord.'[6] Do you not wish the Master of the universe to be responsible for your repayment? If any wealthy man in the town promises you repayment on behalf of others, do you admit his suretyship? But you do not accept God, Who more than repays on behalf of the poor. Give the money lying useless, without weighting it with increase, and both shall be benefited. To you will accrue the security of its safe keeping. The recipients will have the advantage of its use. And if it is increase which you seek,

---

[1] Prov. xxix. 13, A.V. marg. R.V. has "oppressor."   [2] Prov. v. 15.   [3] Prov. xxiii. 27, LXX.
[4] ὥσπερ ἀλλότριον θήραμα. Ed. Par. Vulg. ὥσπερ ἄλλο τι θήραμα.   [5] cf. Luke vi. 34, 35.   [6] Prov. xix. 17.

be satisfied with that which is given by the Lord. He will pay the interest for the poor. Await the loving-kindness of Him Who is in truth most kind.

"What you are taking involves the last extremity of inhumanity. You are making your profit out of misfortune; you are levying a tax upon tears. You are strangling the naked. You are dealing blows on the starving. There is no pity anywhere, no sense of your kinship to the hungry; and you call the profit you get from these sources kindly and humane! Wo unto them that 'put bitter for sweet, and sweet for bitter,'[1] and call inhumanity humanity! This surpasses even the riddle which Samson proposed to his boon companions: — 'Out of the eater came forth meat, and out of the strong came forth sweetness.'[2] Out of the inhuman came forth humanity! Men do not gather grapes of thorns, nor figs of thistles,[3] nor humanity of usury. A corrupt tree bringeth forth evil fruit.[4] There are such people as twelve-per-cent-men and ten-per-cent-men: I shudder to mention their names. They are exactors by the month, like the demons who produce epilepsy, attacking the poor as the changes of the moon come round.[5]

"Here there is an evil grant to either, to giver and to recipient. To the latter, it brings ruin on his property; to the former, on his soul. The husbandman, when he has the ear in store, does not search also for the seed beneath the root; you both possess the fruit and cannot keep your hands from the principal. You plant where there is no ground. You reap where there has been no sowing. For whom you are gathering you cannot tell. The man from whom usury wrings tears is manifest enough; but it is doubtful who is destined to enjoy the results of the superfluity. You have laid up in store for yourself the trouble that results from your iniquity, but it is uncertain whether you will not leave the use of your wealth to others. Therefore, 'from him that would borrow of thee, turn not thou away;'[6] and do not give your money upon usury. Learn from both Old and New Testament what is profitable for you, and so depart hence with good hope to your Lord; in Him you will receive the interest of your good deeds, — in Jesus Christ our Lord to Whom be glory and might for ever and ever, Amen."

(iii.) *The Commentary on Isaiah.* The Commentary on Isaiah is placed by the Benedictine Editors in the appendix of doubtful composition, mainly on the ground of inferiority of style. Ceillier is strongly in favour of the genuineness of this work, and calls attention to the fact that it is attested by strong manuscript authority, and by the recognition of St. Maximus, of John of Damascus, of Simeon Logothetes, of Antony Melissa of Tarasius, and of the Greek scholiast on the Epistles of St. Paul, who is supposed to be Œcumenius. Fessler[7] ranks the work among those of doubtful authority on the ground of the silence of earlier Fathers and of the inferiority of style, as well as of apparent citations from the Commentary of Eusebius, and of some eccentricity of opinion. He conjectures that we may possibly have here the rough material of a proposed work on Isaiah, based mainly on Origen, which was never completed. Garnier regards it as totally unworthy of St. Basil. Maran (*Vit. Bas.* 42) would accept it, and refutes objections.

Among the remarks which have seemed frivolous is the comment on Is. xi. 12, that the actual cross of the Passion was prefigured by the four parts of the universe joining in the midst.[8] Similar objections have been taken to the statement that the devils like rich fare, and crowd the idols' temples to enjoy the sacrificial feasts.[9] On the other hand it has been pointed out that this ingenuity in finding symbols of the cross is of a piece with that of Justin Martyr,[10] who cites the yard on the mast, the plough, and the Roman trophies, and that Gregory of Nazianzus[11] instances the same characteristic of the devils. While dwelling on the holiness of character required for the prophetic offices, the Commentary points out[12] that sometimes it has pleased God to grant it to Pharaoh and Nebuchadnezzar for the sake of their great empires; to Caiaphas as the high priest; to Balaam, because of the exigencies of the crisis at which he appeared. The unchaste lad[13] who has some great sin upon his conscience shrinks from taking his place among the faithful, and is ashamed to rank himself with the weepers. So he tries to avoid the examination of those whose duty it is to enquire into sins[14] and he invents excuses for leaving the church before the celebration of the mysteries. The Commentary urges[15] that without penitence the best conduct is unavailing for salvation; that God requires of the sinner not merely the abandonment

---

[1] Is. v. 20. [2] Judges xiv. 14. [3] Matt. vii. 16. [4] cf. Matt. vii. 18.
[5] On the connexion between σεληνιασμός and ἐπιληψία, cf. Origen iii. 575–577, and Cæsarius, Quæst. 50. On the special attribution of epilepsy to dæmoniacal influence illustrated by the name ιερὰ νοσος, see Hippocrates, *De Morbo Sacro.*
[6] Matt. v. 42. [7] *Patr.* i. 522. [8] § 249. [9] § 236. [10] *Apol.* i. § 72.
[11] *Carm.* 11, *Epig.* 28: Δαίμοσιν εἰλαπίναζον, ὅσοις τοπάροιθε μέμηλει
Δαίμοσιν ἦρα φέρειν, οὐ καθαρὰς θυσίας.
[12] § 4. cf. § 199. [13] § 19. [14] id. ὄκνος εἰς προφάσεις πεπλασμένας ἐπινοῶν πρὸς τοὺς ἐπιζητοῦντας. [15] § 34, 278.

of the sinful part, but also the amends of penance, and warns men [1] that they must not dream that the grace of baptism will free them from the obligation to live a godly life. The value of tradition is insisted on.[2] Every nation, as well as every church, is said to have its own guardian angel.[3]

The excommunication reserved for certain gross sins is represented [4] as a necessary means enjoined by St. Paul to prevent the spread of wickedness. It is said [5] to be an old tradition that on leaving Paradise Adam went to live in Jewry, and there died; that after his death, his skull appearing bare, it was carried to a certain place hence named " place of a skull," and that for this reason Jesus Christ, Who came to destroy death's kingdom, willed to die on the spot where the first fruits of mortality were interred.[6]

On Is. v. 14, " Hell hath enlarged herself, and opened her mouth without measure," [7] it is remarked that these are figurative expressions to denote the multitude of souls that perish. At the same time an alternative literal meaning is admitted, the mouth being the opening through which the souls of the damned are precipitated into a dark region beneath the earth.

It is noted in some MSS. that the Commentary was given to the world by an anonymous presbyter after St. Basil's death, who may have abstained from publishing it because it was in an unfinished state. Erasmus was the first to undertake to print it, and to translate it into Latin, but he went no further than the preface. It was printed in Paris in 1556 by Tilmann, with a lengthy refutation of the objections of Erasmus.[8]

III. Ascetic.

(i) Of the works comprised under this head, the first are the three compositions entitled *Tractatus Prævii*. The first, *Prævia Institutio ascetica* (᾽Ασκητικὴ προδιατύπωσις), is an exhortation to enlistment in the sacred warfare; the second, on renunciation of the world and spiritual perfection, is the *Sermo asceticus* (λόγος ἀσκητικός). The third, *Sermo de ascetica disciplina* (λόγος περὶ ἀσκήσεως, πῶς δεῖ κοσμεῖσθαι τὸν μοναχόν), treats of the virtues to be exhibited in the life of the solitary.

The first of the three is a commendation less of monasticism than of general Christian endurance. It has been supposed to have been written in times of special oppression and persecution.

The second discourse is an exhortation to renunciation of the world. Riches are to be abandoned to the poor. The highest life is the monastic. But this is not to be hastily and inconsiderately embraced. To renounce monasticism and return to the world is derogatory to a noble profession. The idea of pleasing God in the world as well as out of it is, for those who have once quitted it, a delusion. God has given mankind the choice of two holy estates, marriage or virginity. The law which bids us love God more than father, mother, or self, more than wife and children, is as binding in wedlock as in celibacy. Marriage indeed demands the greater watchfulness, for it offers the greater temptations. Monks are to be firm against all attempts to shake their resolves. They will do well to put themselves under the guidance of some good man of experience and pious life, learned in the Scriptures, loving the poor more than money, superior to the seductions of flattery, and loving God above all things. Specific directions are given for the monastic life, and monks are urged to retirement, silence, and the study of the Scriptures.

The third discourse, which is brief, is a summary of similar recommendations. The monk ought moreover to labour with his hands, to reflect upon the day of judgment, to succour the sick, to practise hospitality, to read books of recognized genuineness, not to dispute about the doctrine of Father, Son, and Holy Ghost, but to believe in and confess an uncreate and consubstantial Trinity.

(ii) Next in order come the *Proœmium de Judicio Dei* (προοίμιον περὶ κρίματος Θεοῦ) and the *De Fide* (περὶ πίστεως). These treatises were prefixed by Basil to the *Moralia*. He

---

[1] § 39.   [2] cf. De Sp. S. p.   .   [3] § 240.   [4] § 55.   [5] § 141.
[6] The tradition that Adam's skull was found at the foot of the cross gave rise to the frequent representation of a skull in Christian art. Instances are given by Mr. Jameson, *Hist. of our Lord*, i. 22. Jeremy Taylor, (*Life of our Lord*, Part iii. § xv.) quotes Nonnus (*In Joann.* xix. 17):

Εἰσόκε χῶρον ἵκανε φατιζομένοιο κρανίου
Ἀδὰμ πρωτογόνοιο φερώνυμον ἄντυγι κόρσης.

cf. Origen, *In Matt. Tract.* 35, and Athan, *De Pass. et Cruc.* Jerome speaks of the tradition in reference to its association with the words "As in Adam all die, so in Christ shall all be made alive," as " smooth to the ear, but not true." One version of the tale was that Noah took Adam's bones with him in the ark; that on Ararat they were divided, and the head fell to Seth's share. This he buried at Golgotha. cf. Fabricius i. 61.
[7] LXX. ἐπλάτυνεν ὁ ῾Αδης τὴν ψυχὴν αὐτοῦ καὶ διήνοιξε τὸ στόμα αὐτοῦ.   [8] cf. Ceillier VI. viii. 2.

states that, when he enquired into the true causes of the troubles which weighed heavily on the Church, he could only refer them to breaches of the commandments of God. Hence the divine punishment, and the need of observing the Divine Law. The apostle says that what is needed is faith working by love. So St. Basil thought it necessary to append an exposition of the sound faith concerning the Father, the Son, and the Holy Ghost, and so pass in order to morals.[1] It has, however, been supposed by some [2] that the composition published in the plan as the *De Fide* is not the original tract so entitled, but a letter on the same subject written, if not during the episcopate, at least in the presbyterate. This view has been supported by the statement " Thus we believe and baptize." [3]

This, however, might be said generally of the custom obtaining in the Church, without reference to the writer's own practice. Certainly the document appears to have no connexion with those among which it stands, and to be an answer to some particular request for a convenient summary couched in scriptural terms.[4] Hence it does not contain the Homoousion, and the author gives his reason for the omission — an omission which, he points out, is in contrast with his other writings against heretics.[5] Obviously, therefore, this composition is to be placed in his later life. Yet he describes the *De Fide* as being anterior to the *Moralia.*

It will be remembered that this objection to the title and date of the extant *De Fide* implies nothing against its being the genuine work of the archbishop.

While carefully confining himself to the language of Scripture, the author points out that even with this aid, Faith, which he defines as an impartial assent to what has been revealed to us by the gift of God,[6] must necessarily be dark and incomplete. God can only be clearly known in heaven, when we shall see Him face to face.[7] The statement that had been requested is as follows:

" We believe and confess one true and good God, Father Almighty, of Whom are all things, the God and Father of our Lord Jesus Christ: and His one Only-begotten Son, our Lord and God, Jesus Christ, only true, through Whom all things were made, both visible and invisible, and by Whom all things consist: Who was in the beginning with God and was God, and, after this, according to the Scriptures, was seen on earth and had His conversation with men: Who being in the form of God thought it not robbery to be equal with God, but emptied Himself, and by means of the birth from a virgin took a servant's form, and was formed in fashion as a man, and fulfilled all things written with reference to Him and about Him, according to His Father's commandment, and became obedient unto death, even the death of the Cross. And on the third day He rose from the dead, according to the Scriptures, and was seen by His holy disciples, and the rest, as it is written: And He ascended into heaven, and sitteth on the right hand of His Father, whence He is coming at the end of this world, to raise all men, and to give to every man according to his conduct. Then the just shall be taken up into life eternal and the kingdom of heaven, but the sinner shall be condemned to eternal punishment, where their worm dieth not and the fire is not quenched: And in one Holy Ghost, the Comforter, in Whom we were sealed to the day of redemption: The Spirit of truth, the Spirit of adoption, in Whom we cry, Abba, Father; Who divideth and worketh the gifts that come of God, to each one for our good, as He will; Who teaches and calls to remembrance all things that He has heard from the Son; Who is good; Who guides us into all truth, and confirms all that believe, both in sure knowledge and accurate confession, and in pious service and spiritual and true worship of God the Father, and of His only begotten Son our Lord, and of Himself." [8]

(iii) The *Moralia* (τὰ ἠθικά) is placed in 361, in the earlier days of the Anomœan heresy. Shortly before this time the extreme Arians began to receive this name,[9] and it is on the rise of the Anomœans that Basil is moved to write. The work comprises eighty Rules of Life, expressed in the words of the New Testament, with special reference to the needs of bishops, priests, and deacons, and of all persons occupied in education.

Penitence consists not only in ceasing to sin, but in expiating sin by tears and mortification.[10] Sins of ignorance are not free from peril of judgment.[11]

Sins into which we feel ourselves drawn against our will are the results of sins to which we have consented.[12] Blasphemy against the Holy Ghost consists in attributing

---

[1] *De Jud. Dei.* § 8.　　[2] *cf.* Ceillier VI. viii. 3.
[3] οὕτως φρονοῦμεν καὶ οὕτως Βαπτίζομεν εἰς Τριάδα ὁμοούσιον, κατὰ τὴν ἐντολὴν αὐτοῦ τοῦ κυρίου ἡμῶν Ἰησοῦ Χριστοῦ εἰπόντος πορευθέντες μαθητεύσατε κ.τ.λ. §; the co-essential Trinity being described as involved in the baptismal formula.
[4] § 1.　　[5] § 1.
[6] συγκατάθεσις ἀδιάκριτος τῶν ἀκουσθέντων ἐν πληροφορίᾳ τῆς ἀληθείας τῶν κηρυχθέντων Θεοῦ χάριτι. § 1.　　[7] § 2.
[8] The rest of the clause seems to be rather in the way of explanation and assertion, and here he explains, as cited before, that the baptismal formula involves the homoousion.
[9] Ath., *De Syn.* § 31, in this series, p. 467.　　[10] *Reg.* i.　　[11] *Reg.* ix.　　[12] *Reg.* xi.

to the devil the good works which the Spirit of God works in our brethren. We ought carefully to examine whether the doctrine offered us is conformable to Scripture, and if not, to reject it.[2] Nothing must be added to the inspired words of God; all that is outside Scripture is not of faith, but is sin.[3]

(iv) The *Regulæ fusius tractatæ* (ὅροι κατὰ πλάτος), 55 in number, and the *Regulæ brevius tractatæ* (ὅροι κατ᾽ ἐπιτομήν), in number 313, are a series of precepts for the guidance of religious life put in the form of question and answer. The former are invariably supported by scriptural authority.

Their genuineness is confirmed by strong external evidence.[4] Gregory of Nazianzus (*Or.* xliii. § 34) speaks of Basil's composing rules for monastic life, and in *Ep.* vi. intimates that he helped his friend in their composition.[5] Rufinus (*H.E.* ii. 9) mentions Basil's *Instituta Monachorum*. St. Jerome (*De Vir. illust.* cxvi.) says that Basil wrote τὸ ἀσκητικόν, and Photius (*Cod.* 191) describes the *Asceticum* as including the *Regulæ*. Sozomen (*H.E.* iii. 14) remarks that the *Regulæ* were sometimes attributed to Eustathius of Sebaste, but speaks of them as generally recognised as St. Basil's.

The monk who relinquishes his status after solemn profession and adoption is to be regarded as guilty of sacrilege, and the faithful are warned against all intercourse with him, with a reference to 2 Thess. iii. 14.[6]

Children are not to be received from their parents except with full security for publicity in their reception. They are to be carefully instructed in the Scriptures. They are not to be allowed to make any profession till they come to years of discretion (XV.). Temperance is a virtue, but the servants of God are not to condemn any of God's creatures as unclean, and are to eat what is given them. (XVIII.) Hospitality is to be exercised with the utmost frugality and moderation, and the charge to Martha in Luke x. 41, is quoted with the reading ὀλίγων δέ ἐστι χρεία ἢ ἑνός [7] and the interpretation "few," namely for provision, and "one," namely the object in view,—enough for necessity. It would be as absurd for monks to change the simplicity of their fare on the arrival of a distinguished guest as it would be for them to change their dress (XX.). Rule XXI. is against unevangelical contention for places at table, and Rule XXII. regulates the monastic habit. The primary object of dress is said to be shewn by the words of Genesis,[8] where God is said to have made Adam and Eve "coats of skins," or, as in the LXX., χιτῶνας δερματίνους, *i.e.* tunics of hides. This use of tunics was enough for covering what was unseemly. But later another object was added — that of securing warmth by clothing. So we must keep both ends in view — decency, and protection against the weather. Among articles of dress some are very serviceable; some are less so. It is better to select what is most useful, so as to observe the rule of poverty, and

---

[1] *Reg.* xxxv.   [2] *Reg.* xxviii.

[3] *Reg.* lxxx. § 22. Fessler (*De Pat. Sæc.* iv. p. 514) notes the similarity of a Homily, *De perfectione vitæ Monachorum*, published under the name of St. Basil in a book published by C. F. Matthæi at Moscow in 1775, entitled *Joannis Xiphilini et Basilii M. aliquot orationes*. He describes it as quite unworthy in style of St. Basil.

[4] Combefis, however, refused to accept them.   [5] In this series, p. 448.

[6] With this may be compared the uncompromising denunciation in *Letter* cclxxxviii., and what is said in the first of the three *Tractatus Prævii*. It has been represented that St. Basil introduced the practice of irrevocable vows. *cf.* Dr. Travers Smith, *St. Basil*, p. 223. De Broglie, *L'Eglise et l'empire*, v. 180: "*Avant lui, c'était, aux yeux de beaucoup de ceux même qui s'y destinaient, une vocation libre, affaire de goût et de zèle, pouvant être dilaissée à volonté, comme elle avait été embrassée par choix. Le sceau de la perpetuité obligatoire, ce fut Basile qui l'imprima; c'est à lui réellement que remonte, comme règle commune, et comme habitude générale, l'institution des vœux perpétuels.* Helvot, *Hist. des ordres monastiques*, i. § 3, Bulteau, *Hist. des moines d'orient*, p. 402, Montalembert, *Hist. des moines d'occident*, i. 105, *s'accordent à reconnaître que l'usage général des vœux perpétuels remonte à St. Basil.*" To St. Basil's posthumous influence the system may be due. But it seems questionable whether St. Basil's *Rule* included formal vows of perpetual obligation in the more modern sense. I am not quite sure that the passages cited fully bear this out. Is the earnest exhortation not to quit the holier life consistent with a binding pledge? Would not a more distinctly authoritative tone be adopted? *cf. Letters* xlv. and xlvi. It is plain that a reminder was needed, and that the plea was possible that the profession had not the binding force of matrimony. The line taken is rather that a monk or nun *ought* to remain in his or her profession, and that it is a grievous sin to abandon it, than that there is an irrevocable contract. So in the *Sermo asceticus* (it is not universally accepted), printed by Garnier between the *Moralia* and the *Regulæ*, it is said: "Before the profession of the religious life, any one is at liberty to get the good of this life, in accordance with law and custom, and to give himself to the yoke of wedlock. But when he has been enlisted, of his own consent, it is fitting (προσήκει) that he keep himself for God, as one of the sacred offerings, so that he may not risk incurring the damnation of sacrilege, by defiling in the service of this world the body consecrated by promise to God." This προσήκει is repeated in the *Regulæ*. Basil's monk, says Fialon (*Et. Hist.*, p. 49) was irrevocably bound by the laws of the Church, by public opinion, and, *still more*, by his *conscience*. It is to the last that the founder of the organisation seems to appeal. In *Letter* xlvi. the reproach is not addressed merely to a "*religieuse échappée de son cloitre*," as De Broglie has it, but to a nun guilty of unchastity. Vows of virginity were among the earliest of religious obligations. (*cf.* J. Martyr, *Apol.* i. 15, Athenvaras, *Legat.* 32, Origen, *C. Celsum.* vii. 48.)

Basil (*Can.* xviii.) punishes a breach of the vow of virginity as he does adultery, but it was not till the Benedictine rule was established in Europe that it was generally regarded as absolutely irrevocable. (*cf. D.C.A. s.v.* "Nun," ii. p. 1411, and H. C. Lea's *History of Celibacy*, Philadelphia, 1867.) As a matter of fact, Basil's cœnobitic monasticism, in comparison with the "wilder and more dreamy asceticism which prevailed in Egypt and Syria" (Milman, *Hist. Christ.* iii. 109). was "far more moderate and practical." It was a community of self-denying practical beneficence. Work and worship were to aid one another. This was the highest life, and to quit it was desertion of and disloyalty to neighbour and God. To Basil. is it not rather the violation of holiness than the technical breach of a formal vow which is sacrilege? Lea (p. 101) quotes Epiphanius (*Panar.* 61) as saying that it was better for a lapsed monk to take a lawful wife and be reconciled to the church through Penance. Basil in Can. lx. (p. 256) contemplates a similar reconciliation.

[7] Supported by א, B, C, and L.   [8] iii. 21.

to avoid a variety of vestments, some for show, others for use; some for day, some for night. A single garment must be devised to serve for all purposes, and for night as well as day. As the soldier is known by his uniform, and the senator by his robe, so the Christian ought to have his own dress. Shoes are to be provided on the same principle, they are to be simple and cheap. The girdle (XXIII.) is regarded as a necessary article of dress, not only because of its practical utility, but because of the example of the Lord Who girded Himself. In Rule XXVI. all secrets are ordered to be confided to the superintendent or bishop.[1] If the superintendent himself is in error (XXVII.) he is to be corrected by other brothers. Vicious brethren (XXVIII.) are to be cut off like rotten limbs. Self-exaltation and discontent are equally to be avoided (XXIX.). XXXVII. orders that devotional exercise is to be no excuse for idleness and shirking work. Work is to be done not only as a chastisement of the body, but for the sake of love to our neighbour and supplying weak and sick brethren with the necessaries of life. The apostle [2] says that if a man will not work he must not eat. Daily work is as necessary as daily bread. The services of the day are thus marked out. The first movements of heart and mind ought to be consecrated to God. Therefore early in the morning nothing ought to be planned or purposed before we have been gladdened by the thought of God; as it is written, " I remembered God, and was gladdened; " [3] the body is not to be set to work before we have obeyed the command, " O Lord, in the morning shalt thou hear my voice; in the morning will I order my prayer unto thee." [4] Again at the third hour there is to be a rising up to prayer, and the brotherhood is to be called together, even though they happen to have been dispersed to various works. The sixth hour is also to be marked by prayer, in obedience to the words of the Psalmist,[5] " Evening, and morning, and at noon will I pray, and cry aloud: and He shall hear my voice." To ensure deliverance from the demon of noon-day,[6] the XCIst Psalm is to be recited. The ninth hour is consecrated to prayer by the example of the Apostles[7] Peter and John, who at that hour went up into the Temple to pray. Now the day is done. For all the boons of the day, and the good deeds of the day, we must give thanks. For omissions there must be confession. For sins voluntary or involuntary, or unknown, we must appease God in prayer.[8] At nightfall the XCIst Psalm is to be recited again, midnight is to be observed in obedience to the example of Paul and Silas,[9] and the injunction of the Psalmist.[10] Before dawn we should rise and pray again, as it is written, " Mine eyes prevent the night watches." [11] Here the canonical hours are marked, but no details are given as to the forms of prayer.

XL. deals with the abuse of holy places and solemn assemblies. Christians ought not to appear in places sacred to martyrs or in their neighbourhood for any other reason than to pray and commemorate the sacred dead. Anything like a worldly festival or common-mart at such times is like the sacrilege of the money changers in the Temple precincts.[12]

LI. gives directions for monastic discipline. " Let the superintendent exert discipline after the manner of a physician treating his patients. He is not angry with the sick, but fights with the disease, and sets himself to combat their bad symptoms. If need be, he must heal the sickness of the soul by severer treatment; for example, love of vain glory, by the imposition of lowly tasks; foolish talking, by silence; immoderate sleep, by watching and prayer; idleness, by toil; gluttony, by fasting; murmuring, by seclusion, so that no brothers may work with the offender, nor admit him to participation in their works, till by his penitence that needeth not to be ashamed he appear to be rid of his complaint."

LV. expounds at some length the doctrine of original sin, to which disease and death are traced.

The 313 *Regulæ brevius tractatæ* are, like the *Regulæ fusius tractatæ*, in the form of questions and answers. Fessler singles out as a striking specimen XXXIV.

Q. " How is any one to avoid the sin of man-pleasing, and looking to the praises of men?"

A. " There must be a full conviction of the presence of God, an earnest intention to

---

[1] τῷ προεστῶτι. *cf.* Just. Mart. *Apol.* i. § 87.   [2] 2 Thess. iii. 10.   [3] Ps. lxxvii. 3, LXX.   [4] Ps. v. 3.   [5] Ps. lv. 17.
[6] Ps. xci. 6, LXX. δαιμόνιον μεσημβρινόν. *cf.* Jer. Taylor, *Serm.* ii. pt. 2: " Suidas " (Col. 1227) " tells of certain empusæ that used to appear a noon, at such times as the Greeks did celebrate the funerals of the dead; and at this time some of the Russians do fear the noon-day devil, which appeareth like a mourning widow to reapers of hay and corn, and uses to break their arms and legs unless they worship her."   [7] Acts iii. 1.
[8] *cf.* Pythag. *Aur. Carm.* 40 (quoted by Jer. Taylor in *Holy Living and Holy Dying*): μηδ᾽ ὕπνον μαλακοῖσιν ἐπ᾽ ὄμμασι προσδέξασθαι, πρὶν τῶν ἡμερινῶν ἔργων τρὶς ἕκαστον ἐπελθεῖν, πῆ παρέβην ; τί δ᾽ ἔρεξα ; τί μοι δέον οὐκ ἐτελέσθη.
[9] Acts xvi. 25.   [10] Ps. cxix. 62.   [11] Ps. cxix. 148.
[12] *cf. Letter* clxix. and notes on this case in the *Prolegomena*. It is curious to notice in the Oriental church a survival of something akin to the irreverence deprecated by St. Basil. A modern traveller in Russia has told me that on visiting a great cemetery on the day which the Greek church observes, like November 2 in the Latin, in memory of the dead, he found a vast and cheerful picnic going on.

please Him, and a burning desire for the blessings promised by the Lord. No one before his Master's very eyes is excited into dishonouring his Master and bringing condemnation on himself, to please a fellow servant."

XLVII. points out that it is a grave error to be silent when a brother sins.

XLIX. tells us that vain gloriousness (τὸ περπερεύεσθαι. *Cf.* 1 Cor. xiii. 4) consists in taking things not for use, but for ostentation; and L. illustrates this principle in the case of dress.

Q. " When a man has abandoned all more expensive clothing, does he sin, and, if so, how, if he wishes his cheap upper garment or shoes to be becoming to him?"

A. " If he so wishes in order to gratify men, he is obviously guilty of the sin of man-pleasing. He is alienated from God, and is guilty of vain glory even in these cheap belongings."

LXIV. is a somewhat lengthy comment on Matt. xviii. 6. To "make to offend," or " to scandalize," is to induce another to break the law, as the serpent Eve, and Eve Adam.

LXXXIII. is pithy.

Q. " If a man is generally in the right, and falls into one sin. how are we to treat him?"

A. " As the Lord treated Peter."

CXXVIII. is on fasting.

Q. " Ought any one to be allowed to exercise abstinence beyond his strength, so that he is hindered in the performance of his duty?"

A. " This question does not seem to me to be properly worded. Temperance[1] does not consist in abstinence from earthly food,[2] wherein lies the 'neglecting of the body'[3] condemned by the Apostles, but in complete departure from one's own wishes. And how great is the danger of our falling away from the Lord's commandment on account of our own wishes is clear from the words of the Apostle, 'fulfilling the desires of the flesh, and of the mind. and were by nature the children of wrath.' "[4] The numbers in the Cœnobium are not to fall below ten, the number of the eaters of the Paschal supper.[5] Nothing is to be considered individual and personal property.[6] Even a man's thoughts are not his own.[7] Private friendships are harmful to the general interests of the community.[8] At meals there is to be a reading, which is to be thought more of than mere material food.[9] The cultivation of the ground is the most suitable occupation for the ascetic life.[10] No fees are to be taken for the charge of children entrusted to the monks.[11] Such children are not to be pledged to join the community till they are old enough to understand what they are about.[12]

---

[1] ἐγκράτεια. Gal. v. 23.
[2] ἄλογα βρώματα. Combefis translates " *terreni cibi*." Garnier " *nihil ad rem pertinentium*." [3] Col. ii. 23.
[4] Eph. ii. 3. [5] *Sermo Asceticus*, 3. [6] *Reg. brev. tract.* lxxxv., but see note on p.
[7] *Proœm. in Reg. fus. tract.*
[8] *Sermo Asceticus.* 5. The sacrifice of Gregory of Nazianzus may have been due to the idea that all private interests must be subordinated to those of the Church.
[9] *Reg. brev. tract.* clxxx. [10] *Reg. fus. tract.* xxxviii. [11] *Reg. brev. tract.* ccciv.
[12] *Reg. fus. tract.* xv. After the *Regulæ* are printed, in Garnier's Ed. 34, *Constitutiones Monasticæ*, with the note that their genuineness is more suspicious than that of any of the ascetic writings. They treat of the details of monastic life, of the virtues to be cultivated in it and the vices to be avoided. Sozomen (*H.E.* iii. 14) has been supposed to refer to them. All later criticism has been unfavourable to them. *cf.* Maran, *Vit. Bas.* xliii. 7; Ceillier VI. viii. 3; Fessler, p. 524. It may be remarked generally that the asceticism of St. Basil is eminently practical. He has no notion of mortification for mortification's sake, — no praise for the self-advertising and vain-glorious rigour of the Stylites. Neglecting the body, or " not sparing the body " by exaggerated mortification, is in cclviii. condemned as Manichæism. It is of course always an objection to exclusive exaltation of the ascetic life that it is a kind of moral docetism, and ignores the fact that Christianity has not repudiated all concern with the body, but is designed to elevate and to purify it. (*cf.* Böhringer vii. p. 150.) Basil may be not unjustly criticised from this point of view, and accused of the very Manichæism which he distinctly condemns. But it will be remembered that he recognises the holiness of marriage and family life, and if he thinks virginity and cœnobitism a higher life, has no mercy for the dilettante asceticism of a morbid or indolent "*incivisme*." Valens, from the point of view of a master of legions, might deplore monastic celibacy, and press Egyptian monks by thousands into the ranks of his army. (*cf.* Milman, *Hist. Christ.* iii. 47.) Basil from his point of view was equally positive that he was making useful citizens, and that his industrious associates, of clean and frugal lives, were doing good service.
" En effet, le moine basilien, n'est pas, comme le cénobite d'Égypte, séparé du monde par un mur infranchissable. ' Les poissons meurent,' disait Saint Antoine, ' quand on les tire de l'eau, et les moines s'énervent dans les villes ; rentrons vite dans les montagnes, comme les poissons dans l'eau.' (Montalembert, Moines d'Occident, i. 61.) Les moines basiliens vivent aussi dans la solitude pour gagner le ciel, mais ils ne veulent pas le gagner seuls. . . . Les principaux, au moins, doivent se mêler à la société pour l'instruire. Cet homme à la chevelure négligée. à la démarche posée, dont l'œil nes s'égare jamais, ouvre son monastère à ses semblables, ou va les trouver, du moment qu'il s'agit de leur édification. Son contact fortifie le clergé; il entre lui-même dans les ordres, et devient collaborateur de l'évêque. Il va aux fêtes des martyrs et prêche dans les églises. Il entre dans les maisons, prend part aux conversations, aux repas, et, tout en évitant les longs entretiens et les liaisons aux les femmes, et le directeur et le compagnon de piété des âmes. . . . Le moine ne doit pas seulement soulager les mœux de l'âme. Les maisons des pauvres, dont se couvrait une partie de l'Asie Mineure, étaient des asiles ouverts à toutes les souffrances physiques. . . . Pour Basile, ces deux institutions, le monastère et la maisons des pauvres, quoique séparées et distinctes, n'en formaient qu'une. A ses yeux, les secours corporels n'étaient qu'un moyen d'arriver à l'âme. Pendant que la main du moine servait les voyageurs, nourissait les pauvres. pausait les malades. ses lèvres leur distribuaient une aumône plus précieuse, celle de la parole de Dieu." Fialon, Ét Historique, pp. 51-53. A high ideal! Perhaps never more nearly realized than in the Cappadocian cœnobia of the fourth century.

IV. Homiletical.

Twenty-four homilies on miscellaneous subjects, published under St. Basil's name, are generally accepted as genuine. They are conveniently classified as (i) Dogmatic and Exegetic, (ii) Moral, and (iii) Panegyric. To Class (i) will be referred

III. *In Illud, Attende tibi ipsi.*
VI. *In Illud, Destruam horrea, etc.*
IX. *In Illud. Quod Deus non est auctor malorum.*
XII. *In principium Proverbiorum.*
XV. *De Fide.*
XVI. *In Illud, In principio erat Verbum.*
XXIV. *Contra Sabellianos et Arium et Anomœos.*

Class (ii) will include

I. and II. *De Jejunio.*
IV. *De gratiarum actione.*
VII. *In Divites.*
VIII. *In famem et siccitatem.*
X. *Adversus beatos.*
XI. *De invidia.*
XIII. *In Sanctum Baptismum.*
XIV. *In Ebriosos.*
XX. *De humilitate.*
XXI. *Quod rebus mundanis adhærendum non sit, et de incendio extra ecclesiam facto.*
XXII. *Ad adolescentes, de legendis libris Gentilium.*

The Panegyric (iii) are

V. *In martyrem Julittam.*
XVII. *In Barlaam martyrem.*
XVIII. *In Gordium martyrem.*
XIX. *In sanctos quadraginta martyres.*
XXIII. *In Mamantem martyrem.*

Homily III. on Deut. xv. 9,[1] is one of the eight translated by Rufinus. Section 2 begins:

" ' Take heed,' it is written, ' to thyself.' Every living creature possesses within himself, by the gift of God, the Ordainer of all things, certain resources for self protection. Investigate nature with attention, and you will find that the majority of brutes have an instinctive aversion from what is injurious; while, on the other hand, by a kind of natural attraction, they are impelled to the enjoyment of what is beneficial to them. Wherefore also God our Teacher has given us this grand injunction, in order that what brutes possess by nature may accrue to us by the aid of reason, and that what is performed by brutes unwittingly may be done by us through careful attention and constant exercise of our reasoning faculty. We are to be diligent guardians of the resources given to us by God, ever shunning sin, as brutes shun poisons, and ever hunting after righteousness, as they seek for the herbage that is good for food. Take heed to thyself, that thou mayest be able to discern between the noxious and the wholesome. This taking heed is to be understood in a twofold sense. Gaze with the eyes of the body at visible objects. Contemplate incorporeal objects with the intellectual faculty of the soul. If we say that obedience to the charge of the text lies in the action of our eyes, we shall see at once that this is impossible. How can there be apprehension of the whole self through the eye? The eye cannot turn its sight upon ttself; the head is beyond it; it is ignorant of the back, the countenance, the disposition of the intestines. Yet it were impious to argue that the charge of the Spirit cannot be obeyed. It follows then that it must be understood of intellectual action. ' Take heed to thyself.' Look at thyself round about from every point of view.

---

[1] LXX. πρόσεχε σεαυτῷ.

Keep thy soul's eye sleepless[1] in ceaseless watch over thyself. 'Thou goest in the midst of snares.'[2] Hidden nets are set for thee in all directions by the enemy. Look well around thee, that thou mayest be delivered 'as a gazelle from the net and a bird from the snare.'[3] It is because of her keen sight that the gazelle cannot be caught in the net. It is her keen sight that gives her her name.[4] And the bird, if only she take heed, mounts on her light wing far above the wiles of the hunter.

"Beware lest in self protection thou prove inferior to brutes, lest haply thou be caught in the gins and be made the devil's prey, and be taken alive by him to do with thee as he will."

A striking passage from the same Homily is thus rendered by Rufinus: " *Considera ergo primo omnium quod homo es, id est solum in terres animal ipsis divinis manibus formatum. Nonne sufficeret hoc solum recte atque integre sapienti ad magnum sum- mumque solutium, quod ipsius Dei manibus qui omnia reliqua præcepti solius fecit auctoritate subsistere, homo fictus es et formatus? Tum deinde quod cum ad imaginem Creatoris et similitudinem sis, potes sponte etiam ad angelorum dignitatem culmenque remeare. Animam namque accepisti intellectualem, et rationalem, per quam Deum possis agnoscere, et naturam rerum conspicabili rationis intelligentia contemplari: sapientiæ dulcissimis fructibus perfrui præsto est. Tibi omnium cedit animantium genus, quæ per connexa montium vel prærupta rupium aut opaca silvarum feruntur; omne quod vel aquis tegitur, vel præpetibus pennis in acre suspenditur. Omne, inquam, quod hujus mundi est, servitis et subjectioni tuæ liberalis munificentia conditoris in- dulsit. Nonne tu, sensu tibi rationabili suggerente, diversitates artium reperisti? Nonne tu urbes condere, omnemque earum reliquum usum pernecessarium viventibus in- venisti? Nonne tibi per rationem quæ in te est mare pervium fit? Terra, flumina, fontesque tuis vel usibus vel voluptatibus famulantur. Nonne aer hic et cœlum ipsum atque omnes stellarum chori vitæ mortalium ministerio cursus suos atque ordines servant? Quid ergo deficis animo, et deesse tibi aliquid putas, si non tibi equus pro- ducitur phaleris exornatus et·spumanti ore frena mandens argentea? Sed sol tibi producitur, veloci rapidoque cursu ardentes tibi faces caloris simul ac luminis portans. Non habes aureos et argenteos discos: sed habes lunæ discum purissimo et blandissimo splendore radiantem. Non ascendis currum, nec rotarum lupsibus veheris, sed habes pedum tuorum vehiculum tecum natum. Quid ergo beatos censes eos qui aurum quidem possisent, alienis autem pedibus indigent, ad necessarios commeatus? Non recubas eburneis thoris, sed adjacent fecundi cespites viridantes et herbidi thori, florum varietate melius quam fucatis coloribus Tyrii muricis picti, in quibus dulces et salubres somni nullis curarum morsibus effugantur. Non te contegunt aurata laquearia : sed cœlum te contegit ineffabili fulgore stellarum depictum. Hæc quidem quantum ad communem humanitatis attinet vitam. Accipe vero majora. Propter te Deus in hom- inibus, Spiritus sancti distributio, mortis ablatio, resurrectionis spes. Propter te divina præcepta hominibus delata, quæ te perfectam doceant vitam, et iter tuum ad Deum per mandatorum tramitem dirigant. Tibi panduntur regna cœlorum, tibi coronæ justitiæ præparantur ; si tamen labores et ærumnas· pro justitia ferre non refugis.*"[5]

Homily VI., on Luke xii. 18, is on selfish wealth and greed.

Beware, says the preacher,[6] lest the fate of the fool of the text be thine. "These things are written that we may shun their imitation. Imitate the earth, O man. Bear fruit, as she does, lest thou prove inferior to that which is without life. She produces her fruits, not that she may enjoy them, but for thy service. Thou dost gather for thyself whatever fruit of good works thou hast shewn, because the grace of good works returns to the giver. Thou hast given to the poor, and the gift becomes thine own, and comes back with in- crease. Just as grain that has fallen on the earth becomes a gain to the sower, so the loaf thrown to the hungry man renders abundant fruit thereafter. Be the end of thy husbandry the beginning of the heavenly sowing. 'Sow,' it is written, 'to yourselves in righteous- ness.'[7] Why then art thou distressed? Why dost thou harass thyself in thy efforts to shut up thy riches in clay and bricks? 'A good name is rather to be chosen than great riches.'[8] If thou admire riches because of the honour that comes from them, bethink thee how very much more it tends to thine honour that thou shouldst be called the father of

1 ἀκοίμητον. On the later existence of an order of sleepless monks, known as the Accœmetæ. *cf.* Theodoret, *Ep.* cxli. p. 309, in this series, and note.
2 Ecclus. ix. 13.   3 Prov. v. 5, LXX.   4 δορκάς, from δέρκομαι, = *seer*. So Tabitha (*Syr.*) = keen-sighted.
5 § 6.   6 § 3.   7 Hos. x. 12.   8 Prov. ii. 1.

innumerable children than that thou shouldst possess innumerable staters in a purse. Thy wealth thou wilt leave behind thee here, even though thou like it not. The honour won by thy good deeds thou shalt convey with thee to the Master. Then all people standing round about thee in the presence of the universal Judge shall hail thee as feeder and benefactor, and give thee all the names that tell of loving kindness. Dost thou not see theatregoers flinging away their wealth on boxers and buffoons and beast-fighters, fellows whom it is disgusting even to see, for the sake of the honour of a moment, and the cheers and clapping of the crowd? And art thou a niggard in thy expenses, when thou art destined to attain glory so great? God will welcome thee, angels will laud thee, mankind from the very beginning will call thee blessed. For thy stewardship of these corruptible things thy reward shall be glory everlasting, a crown of righteousness, the heavenly kingdom. Thou thinkest nothing of all this. Thy heart is so fixed on the present that thou despisest what is waited for in hope. Come then; dispose of thy wealth in various directions. Be generous and liberal in thy expenditure on the poor. Let it be said of thee, ' He hath dispersed, he hath given to the poor ; his righteousness endureth for ever.' [1] Do not press heavily on necessity and sell for great prices. Do not wait for a famine before thou openest thy barns. ' He that withholdeth corn, the people shall curse him.' [2] Watch not for a time of want for gold's sake — for public scarcity to promote thy private profit. Drive not a huckster's bargains out of the troubles of mankind. Make not God's wrathful visitation an opportunity for abundance. Wound not the sores of men smitten by the scourge. Thou keepest thine eye on thy gold, and wilt not look at thy brother. Thou knowest the marks on the money, and canst distinguish good from bad. Thou canst not tell who is thy brother in the day of distress."

The conclusion is [3] " 'Ah !' — it is said — ' words are all very fine : gold is finer.' I make the same impression as I do when I am preaching to libertines against their unchastity. Their mistress is blamed, and the mere mention of her serves but to enkindle their passions. How can I bring before your eyes the poor man's sufferings that thou mayest know out of what deep groanings thou art accumulating thy treasures, and of what high value will seem to thee in the day of judgment the famous words, ' Come, ye blessed of my Father, inherit the kingdom prepared for you from the foundation of the world : for I was an hungred and ye gave me meat : I was thirsty and ye gave me drink : . . . I was naked and ye clothed me.' [4] What shuddering, what sweat, what darkness will be shed round thee, as thou hearest the words of condemnation ! — ' Depart from me, ye cursed, into outer darkness prepared for the devil and his angels : for I was an hungred and ye gave me no meat : I was thirsty and ye gave me no drink : . . . I was naked and ye clothed me not.' [5] I have told thee what I have thought profitable To thee now it is clear and plain what are the good things promised for thee if thou obey. If thou disobey, for thee the threat is written. I pray that thou mayest change to a better mind and thus escape its peril. In this way thy own wealth will be thy redemption. Thus thou mayest advance to the heavenly blessings prepared for thee by the grave of Him who hath called us all into His own kingdom, to Whom be glory and might for ever and ever. Amen."

Homily IX. is a demonstration that *God is not the Author of Evil*. It has been conjectured that it was delivered shortly after some such public calamity as the destruction of Nicæa in 368. St. Basil naturally touches on passages which have from time to time caused some perplexity on this subject. He asks [6] if God is not the Author of evil, how is it said " I form the light and create darkness, I make peace and create evil," [7] and again, " The evil came down from the Lord unto the gate of Jerusalem, " [8] and again, " Shall there be evil in a city and the Lord hath not done it," [9] and in the great song of Moses, " See now that I, even I, am he and there is no god with me : I kill and I make alive, I wound and I heal " ? [10] But to any one who understands the meaning of Scripture no one of these passages accuses God of being the Cause and Creator of evil. He who uses the words, " I form the light and create darkness," describes Himself not as Creator of any evil, but as Demiurge of creation. " It is lest thou shouldst suppose that there is one cause of light and another of darkness that He described Himself as being Creator and Artificer of parts of creation which seem to be mutually opposed. It is to prevent thy seeking one Demiurge of fire, another of water, one of air and another of earth, these seeming to have a kind of mutual opposition and contrariety of qualities. By adopting these views many

---

[1] Ps. cxii. 9.   [2] Prov. xi. 26.   [3] § 8.   [4] Matt. xxv. 34.
[5] Matt. xxv. 41. With the variation of " outer darkness " for " everlasting fire " and the omission of the clause about strangers. In this passage, it is not a robber who is accused ; the condemnation falls upon him who has not shared what he has.   [6] § 4.   [7] Is. xlv. 7.   [8] Micah i. 12.   [9] Amos iii. 6.   [10] Deut. xxxii. 39.

have ere now fallen into polytheism, but He makes peace and creates evil. Unquestionably
He makes peace in thee when He brings peace into thy mind by His good teaching, and
calms the rebel passions of thy soul.   And He creates evil, that is to say, He reduces
those evil passions to order, and brings them to a better state so that they may cease to be
evil and may adopt the nature of good. ' Create in me a clean heart, O God.'[1]   This
does not mean *Make now for the first time;*[2] it means *Renew the heart that had become old
from wickedness.*   The object is that He may make both one.[3]   The word create is used
not to imply the bringing out of nothing, but the bringing into order those which already
existed.   So it is said, ' If any man be in Christ he is a new creature.'[4]   Again, Moses
says, ' Is not He thy Father that hath bought thee?   Hath He not made thee and created
thee?'[5]   Now, the creation put in order after the making evidently teaches us that the
word creation, as is commonly the case, is used with the idea of improvement.   And so it
is thus that He makes peace out of creating evil; that is, by transforming and bringing to
improvement.   Furthermore, even if you understand peace to be freedom from war, and
evil to mean the troubles which are the lot of those who make war; marches into far
regions, labours, vigils, terrors, sweatings, wounds, slaughters, taking of towns, slavery,
exile, piteous spectacles of captives; and, in a word, all the evils that follow upon war,
all these things, I say, happen by the just judgment of God, Who brings vengeance
through war on those who deserve punishment.   Should you have wished that Sodom had
not been burnt after her notorious wickedness?   Or that Jerusalem had not been overturned,
nor her temple made desolate after the horrible wickedness of the Jews against the Lord?
How otherwise was it right for these things to come to pass than by the hands of the
Romans to whom our Lord had been delivered by the enemies of His life, the Jews?
Wherefore it does sometimes come to pass that the calamities of war are righteously inflicted on those who deserve them — if you like to understand the words ' I kill and I
make alive' in their obvious sense.   Fear edifies the simple. ' I wound and I heal' is at
once perceived to be salutary.   The blow strikes terror; the cure attracts to love.   But it
is permissible to thee to find a higher meaning in the words, ' I kill '— by sin; ' I make
alive ' — by righteousness. ' Though our outward man perish, yet the inward man is renewed day by day.'[6]   He does not kill one and make another alive, but He makes the
same man alive by the very means by which He kills him; He heals him by the blows
which He inflicts upon him.   As the proverb has it, ' Thou shalt beat him with the rod
and shalt deliver his soul from hell.'[7]   The flesh is smitten that the soul may be healed;
sin is put to death that righteousness may live.   In another passage[8] it is argued that death
is not an evil.   Deaths come from God.   Yet death is not absolutely an evil, except in the
case of the death of the sinner, in which case departure from this world is a beginning of
the punishments of hell.   On the other hand, of the evils of hell the cause is not God, but
ourselves.   The origin and root of sin is what is in our own control and our free will."
     Homily XII. is " on the beginning of the proverbs." " The proverbs of Solomon, the
son of David, king of Israel."[9]
     " The name proverbs (παροιμίαι) has been by heathen writers used of common ex-
pressions, and of those which are generally used in the streets.   Among them a way is
called οἶμος, whence they define a παροιμία to be a common expression, which has become trite through vulgar usage, and which it is possible to transfer from a limited number
of subjects to many analogous subjects.[10]   With Christians the παροιμία is a serviceable utterance, conveyed with a certain amount of obscurity, containing an obvious meaning of much
utility, and at the same time involving a depth of meaning in its inner sense.   Whence the
Lord says : ' These things have I spoken unto you in proverbs, but the time cometh when I
shall no more speak unto you in proverbs, but I shall shew you plainly of the Father.' "[11]
     On the " wisdom and instruction " of verse 2, it is said: Wisdom is the science of
things both human and divine, and of their causes.   He, therefore, who is an effective
theologian[12] knows wisdom.   The quotation of 1 Cor. ii. 6, follows.
     On general education it is said,[13] " The acquisition of sciences is termed education,[14]
as it is written of Moses, that he was learned[15] in all the wisdom of the Egyptians.[16]   But
it is of no small importance, with a view to man's sound condition,[17] that he should not

---

[1] Ps. li. 10.   [2] δημιούργησον.   [3] *cf.* Eph. ii. 14.   [4] 2 Cor. v. 17.   [5] Deut. xxxii. 6, LXX.
[6] 2 Cor. iv. 16.   [7] Prov. xxiii. 14.   [8] § 3.   [9] Prov. 1.
[10] παροιμία is defined by Hesychius the Alexandrian grammarian, who was nearly contemporary with Basil, as a βιωφελὴς
λόγος, παρὰ τὴν ὁδὸν λεγόμενος.
[11] John xvi. 25.   [12] ἐπιτετευγμένως θεολογεῖ.   [13] § 6.   [14] ἡ τῶν μαθημάτων ἀνάληψις παιδεία λέγεται.
[15] ἐπαιδεύθη.   [16] Acts vii. 22.   [17] σωτηρία.

devote himself to any sciences whatsoever, but should become acquainted with the education which is most profitable. It has ere now happened that men who have spent their time in the study of geometry, the discovery of the Egyptians, or of astrology, the favourite pursuit of the Chaldæans, or have been addicted to the loftier natural philosophy [1] which is concerned with figures and shadows, have looked with contempt on the education which is based upon the divine oracles. Numbers of students have been occupied with paltry rhetoric, and the solution of sophisms, the subject matter of all of which is the false and unreal. Even poetry is dependent for its existence on its myths.[2] Rhetoric would not be but for craft in speech. Sophistics must have their fallacies. Many men for the sake of these pursuits have disregarded the knowledge of God, and have grown old in the search for the unreal. It is therefore necessary that we should have a full knowledge of education, in order to choose the profitable, and to reject the unintelligent and the injurious. Words of wisdom will be discerned by the attentive reader of the Proverbs, who thence patiently extracts what is for his good."

The Homily concludes with an exhortation to rule life by the highest standard.

" Hold fast, then, to the rudder of life. Guide thine eye, lest haply at any time through thine eyes there beat upon thee the vehement wave of lust. Guide ear and tongue, lest the one receive aught harmful, or the other speak forbidden words. Let not the tempest of passion overwhelm thee. Let no blows of despondency beat thee down; no weight of sorrow drown thee in its depths. Our feelings are waves. Rise above them, and thou wilt be a safe steersman of life. Fail to avoid each and all of them skilfully and steadily, and, like some untrimmed boat, with life's dangers all round about thee, thou wilt be sunk in the deep sea of sin. Hear then how thou mayest acquire the steersman's skill. Men at sea are wont to lift up their eyes to heaven. It is from heaven that they get guidance for their cruise; by day from the sun, and by night from the Bear, or from some of the ever-shining stars. By these they reckon their right course. Do thou too keep thine eye fixed on heaven, as the Psalmist did who said, ' Unto thee lift I up mine eye, O thou that dwellest in the heavens.' [3] Keep thine eyes on the Sun of righteousness. Directed by the commandments of the Lord, as by some bright constellations, keep thine eye ever sleepless. Give not sleep to thine eyes or slumber to thine eyelids,[4] that the guidance of the commandments may be unceasing. ' Thy word,' it is said, ' is a lamp unto my feet, and a light unto my paths.' [5] Never slumber at the tiller, so long as thou livest here, amid the unstable circumstances of this world, and thou shalt receive the help of the Spirit. He shall conduct thee ever onward. He shall waft thee securely by gentle winds of peace, till thou come one day safe and sound to you calm and waveless haven of the will of God, to Whom be glory and majesty for ever and ever, Amen."

Homilies XV. and XVI. are more distinctly dogmatic. They do not present the doctrines of which they treat in any special way. XV., *De Fide*, is concerned rather with the frame of mind of the holder and expounder of the Faith than with any dogmatic formula.

XVI., on John i. 1, begins by asserting that every utterance of the gospels is grander than the rest of the lessons of the Spirit, inasmuch as, while in the latter He has spoken to us through His servants the prophets, in the gospels the Master has conversed with us face to face. " The most mighty voiced herald of the actual gospel proclamation, who uttered words loud beyond all hearing and lofty beyond all understanding, is John, the son of thunder, the prelude of whose gospel is the text." After repeating the words the preacher goes on to say that he has known many who are not within the limits of the word of truth, many of the heathen, that is, " who have prided themselves upon the wisdom of this world, who in their admiration for these words have ventured to insert them among their own writings. For the devil is a thief, and carries off our property for the use of his own prophets." [6]

---

[1] μετεωρολογία. The word had already been used by Plato in a certain contemptuous sense. *cf. Pal.* 299 B.: μετεωρόλογον ἀδολέσχην τινὰ σοφιστήν. But not always, *e.g. Crat.* 401, B.: κωδυνεύουσι γοῦν οἱ πρῶτοι τὰ ὀνόματα τιθέμενοι οὐ φαῦλοι εἶναι, ἀλλὰ μετεωρολόγοι τινὲς καὶ ἀδολέσχαι.

[2] Gregory of Nazianzus was publishing verses which formed no unworthy early link in the *Catena Poetarum Christianorum*, in our sense of the word poet. Basil may have in his mind the general idea that the Poetics of the heathen schools were all concerned with mythical inventions.

[3] Ps. xxiii. 1.   [4] *cf.* Ps. cxxxii. 4.   [5] Ps. cxix. 105.

[6] There are instances of high admiration of the passage: I have not found one of appropriation. Augustine (*De Civ. Dei* x. 29), says: " *Quod initium Sancti Evangelii, cui nomen est secundum Johannem, quidam Platonicus, sicut a sancto sene Simpliciano, qui postea ecclesiæ Mediolanensi præsedit episcopus, solebamus audire, aureis litteris conscribendum et per omnes ecclesias in locis eminentissimis proponendum esse dicebat.*" Eusebius (*Præp. Evang.* xi. 17 and 18) refers to the statements of Plotinus and Numerius on the δεύτερος αἴτιος, and (19) mentions Aurelius (on Aurelius *vide* Mosheim's note on Cudworth's *Int. System*, vol. i. cap. iv. 17), as quoting the passage in question. *Vide* also Theodoret, *Græc. Aff.* 33, and Bentley's *Remarks on Freethinking*, § xlvi.

"If the wisdom of the flesh has been so smitten with admiration for the force of the words, what are we to do, who are disciples of the Spirit? . . . Hold fast to the text, and you will suffer no harm from men of evil arts. Suppose your opponent to argue, 'If He was begotten, He was not,' do you retort, 'In the beginning He was.' But, he will go on, 'Before He was begotten, in what way was He?' Do not give up the words 'He was.' Do not abandon the words 'In the beginning.' The highest point of beginning is beyond comprehension; what is outside beginning is beyond discovery. Do not let any one deceive you by the fact that the phrase has more than one meaning. There are in this world many beginnings of many things, yet there is one beginning which is beyond them all. 'Beginning of good way,' says the Proverb. But the beginning of a way is the first movement whereby we begin the journey of which the earlier part can be discovered. And, 'The fear of the Lord is the beginning of wisdom.'[1] To this beginning is prefixed something else, for elementary instruction is the beginning of the comprehension of arts. The fear of the Lord is then a primary element of wisdom, but there is something anterior to this beginning — the condition of the soul, before it has been taught wisdom and apprehended the fear of the Lord. . . . The point is the beginning of the line, and the line is the beginning of the surface, and the surface is the beginning of the body, and the parts of speech are the beginnings of grammatical utterance. But the beginning in the text is like none of these. . . . *In the beginning was the Word!* Marvellous utterance! How all the words are found to be combined in mutual equality of force! 'Was' has the same force as 'In the beginning.' Where is the blasphemer? Where is the tongue that fights against Christ? Where is the tongue that said, 'There was when He was not'? Hear the gospel: '*In the beginning was.*' If He was in the beginning, when was He not? Shall I bewail their impiety or execrate their want of instruction? But, it is argued, before He was begotten, He was not. Do you know when He was begotten, that you may introduce the idea of priority to the time? For the word 'before' is a word of time, placing one thing before another in antiquity. In what way is it reasonable that the Creator of time should have a generation subjected to terms of time? '*In the beginning was—*' Never give up the *was*, and you never give any room for the vile blasphemy to slip in. Mariners laugh at the storm, when they are riding upon two anchors. So will you laugh to scorn this vile agitation which is being driven on the world by the blasts of wickedness, and tosses the faith of many to and fro, if only you will keep your soul moored safely in the security of these words."

In § 4 on the force of *with God.*[2] "Note with admiration the exact appropriateness of every single word. It is not said 'The Word was *in* God.' It runs 'was *with* God.' This is to set forth the proper character of the hypostasis. The Evangelist did not say '*in* God,' to avoid giving any pretext for the confusion of the hypostasis. That is the vile blasphemy of men who are endeavouring to confound all things together, asserting that Father, Son, and Holy Ghost, form one subject matter, and that different appellations are applied to one thing. The impiety is vile, and no less to be shunned than that of those who blasphemously maintain that the Son is in essence unlike God the Father. *The Word was with God.* Immediately after using the term Word to demonstrate the impassibility of the generation, he forthwith gives an explanation to do away with the mischief arising in us from the term Word. As though suddenly rescuing Him from the blasphemers' calumny, he asks, what is the Word? *The Word was God.* Do not put before me any ingenious distinctions of phrase; do not with your wily cleverness blaspheme the teachings of the Spirit. You have the definitive statement. Submit to the Lord. *The Word was God.*"

Homily XXIV., against the Sabellians, Arians, and Anomœans, repeats points which are brought out again and again in the *De Spiritu Sancto*, in the work *Against Eunomius*, and in some of the *Letters.*

Arianism is practical paganism, for to make the Son a creature, and at the same time to offer Him worship, is to reintroduce polytheism. Sabellianism is practical Judaism, — a denial of the Son.[3] John i. 1, xiv. 9, 7, xvi. 28, and viii. 16 are quoted against both extremes. There may be a note of time in the admitted impatience of the auditory at hearing of every other subject than the Holy Spirit. The preacher is constrained to speak upon this topic, and he speaks with the combined caution and completeness which characterize the *De Spiritu Sancto*. "Your ears," he says, "are all eager to hear something concerning the Holy Ghost. My wish would be, as I have received in all simplicity, as I

---

[1] Prov. i. 7.   [2] πρὸς τὸν Θεόν.   [3] cf. ccx. p. 249.

have assented with guileless agreement, so to deliver the doctrine to you my hearers. I would if I could avoid being constantly questioned on the same point. I would have my disciples convinced of one consent. But you stand round me rather as judges than as learners. Your desire is rather to test and try me than to acquire anything for yourselves. I must therefore, as it were, make my defence before the court, again and again giving answer, and again and again saying what I have received. And you I exhort not to be specially anxious to hear from me what is pleasing to yourselves, but rather what is pleasing to the Lord, what is in harmony with the Scriptures, what is not in opposition to the Fathers. What, then, I asserted concerning the Son, that we ought to acknowledge His proper Person, this I have also to say concerning the Holy Spirit. The Spirit is not identical with the Father, because of its being written 'God is a Spirit.'[1] Nor on the other hand is there one Person of Son and of Spirit, because it is said, 'If any man have not the spirit of Christ he is none of his. . . . Christ is in you.'[2] From this passage some persons have been deceived into the opinion that the Spirit and Christ are identical. But what do we assert? That in this passage is declared the intimate relation of nature and not a confusion of persons. For there exists the Father having His existence perfect and independent, root and fountain of the Son and of the Holy Ghost. There exists also the Son living in full Godhead, Word and begotten offspring of the Father, independent. Full too is the Spirit, not part of another, but contemplated whole and perfect in Himself. The Son is inseparably conjoined with the Father and the Spirit with the Son. For there is nothing to divide nor to cut asunder the eternal conjunction. No age intervenes, nor yet can our soul entertain a thought of separation as though the Only-begotten were not ever with the Father, or the Holy Ghost not co-existent with the Son. Whenever then we conjoin the Trinity, be careful not to imagine the Three as parts of one undivided thing, but receive the idea of the undivided and common essence of three perfect incorporeal [existences]. Wherever is the presence of the Holy Spirit, there is the indwelling of Christ: wherever Christ is, there the Father is present. 'Know ye not that your body is the temple of the Holy Ghost which is in you?' "[3]

First of the Homilies on moral topics come I. and II. on Fasting. The former is of uncontested genuineness. Erasmus rejected the latter, but it is accepted without hesitation by Garnier, Maran and Ceillier, and is said by the last named to be quoted as Basil's by John of Damascus and Symeon Logothetes. From Homily I. two passages are cited by St. Augustine against the Pelagians.[4] The text is Ps. lxxx. 3. "Reverence," says one passage,[5] "the hoary head of fasting. It is coæval with mankind. Fasting was ordained in Paradise. The first injunction was delivered to Adam, 'Of the tree of the knowledge of good and evil thou shalt not eat.'[6] 'Thou shalt not eat' is a law of fasting and abstinence." The general argument is rather against excess than in support of ceremonial abstinence. In Paradise there was no wine, no butchery of beasts, no eating of flesh. Wine came in after the flood. Noah became drunk because wine was new to him. So fasting is older than drunkenness. Esau was defiled, and made his brother's slave, for the sake of a single meal. It was fasting and prayer which gave Samuel to Hannah. Fasting brought forth Samson. Fasting begets prophets, strengthens strong men. Fasting makes lawgivers wise, is the soul's safeguard, the body's trusty comrade, the armour of the champion, the training of the athlete.

The conclusion is a warning against mere carnal abstinence.[7] "Beware of limiting the good of fasting to mere abstinence from meats. Real fasting is alienation from evil. 'Loose the bands of wickedness.'[8] Forgive your neighbour the mischief he has done you. Forgive him his trespasses against you. Do not 'fast for strife and debate.'[9] You do not devour flesh, but you devour your brother. You abstain from wine, but you indulge in outrages. You wait for evening before you take food, but you spend the day in the law courts. Wo to those who are 'drunken, but not with wine.'[10] Anger is the intoxication of the soul, and makes it out of its wits like wine. Drunkenness, too, is sorrow, and drowns our intelligence. Another drunkenness is needless fear. In a word, whatever passion makes the soul beside herself may be called drunkenness. . . . Dost thou know Whom thou art ordained to receive as thy guest? He Who has promised that He and His Father will come and make their abode with thee.[11] Why do you allow drunkenness to enter in, and shut the door on the Lord? Why allow the foe to come in and occupy your strongholds? Drunkenness dare not receive the Lord; it drives away the

1 John iv. 24.   3 1 Cor. vi. 19.   5 § 3.   7 § 10.   9 Is. lviii. 4.   11 cf. John xiv. 23.
2 Rom. viii. 9 and 10.   4 August. in *Julian.* i. 18.   6 Gen. iii. 17.   8 Is. lviii. 6.   10 Is. li. 21.

Spirit. Smoke drives away bees, and debauch drives away the gifts of the Spirit. . . .
Wilt thou see the nobility of fasting? Compare this evening with to-morrow evening:
thou wilt see the town turned from riot and disturbance to profound calm. Would that
to-day might be like to-morrow in solemnity, and the morrow no less cheerful than to-day.
May the Lord Who has brought us to this period of time grant to us, as to gladiators and
wrestlers, that we may shew firmness and constancy in the beginning of contests, and may
reach that day which is the Queen of Crowns; that we may remember now the passion of
salvation, and in the age to come enjoy the requital of our deeds in this life, in the just
judgment of Christ." [1]

Homily IV. on the giving of thanks (περὶ εὐχαριστίας), is on text 1 Thess. v. 16.
Our Lord, it is remarked, wept over Lazarus, and He called them that mourn
blessed. How [2] is this to be reconciled with the charge " Rejoice alway"? " Tears and
joy have not a common origin. On the one hand, while the breath is held in round the
heart, tears spontaneously gush forth, as at some blow, when an unforeseen calamity smites
upon the soul. Joy on the other hand is like a leaping up of the soul rejoicing when things
go well. Hence come different appearances of the body. The sorrowful are pale, livid,
chilly. The habit of the joyous and cheerful is blooming and ruddy; their soul all but leaps
out of their body for gladness. On all this I shall say that the lamentations and tears of the
saints were caused by their love to God. So, with their eyes ever fixed on the object of
their love, and from hence gathering greater joy for themselves, they devoted themselves
to the interests of their fellow-servants. Weeping over sinners, they brought them to better
ways by their tears. But just as men standing safe on the seashore, while they feel for
those who are drowning in the deep, do not lose their own safety in their anxiety for those
in peril, so those who groan over the sins of their neighbours do not destroy their own
proper cheerfulness. Nay, they rather increase it, in that, through their tears over their
brother, they are made worthy of the joy of the Lord. Wherefore, blessed are they that
weep; blessed are they that mourn; for they shall themselves be comforted; they themselves shall laugh. But by laughter is meant not the noise that comes out through the
cheeks from the boiling of the blood, but cheerfulness pure and untainted with despondency.
The Apostle allows us to weep with weepers, for this tear is made, as it were, a seed and
loan to be repaid with everlasting joy. Mount in mind with me, and contemplate the condition of the angels; see if any other condition becomes them but one of joy and gladness.
It is for that they are counted worthy to stand beside God, and to enjoy the ineffable beauty
and glory of our Creator. It is in urging us on to that life that the Apostle bids us always
rejoice."

The Homily contains an eloquent exhortation to Christian fortitude in calamity, and
concludes with the charge to look beyond present grief to future felicity. " Hast thou
suffered dishonour? Look to the glory which through patience is laid up for thee in
heaven. Hast thou suffered loss? Fix thine eyes on the heavenly riches, and on the treasure
which thou hast put by for thyself through thy good works. Hast thou suffered exile?
Thy fatherland is the heavenly Jerusalem. Hast thou lost a child? Thou hast angels,
with whom thou shalt dance about the throne of God, and shalt be glad with everlasting
joy. Set expected joys over against present griefs, and thus thou wilt preserve for thyself
that calm and quiet of the soul whither the injunction of the Apostle calls us. Let not the
brightness of human success fill thy soul with immoderate joy; let not grief bring low thy
soul's high and lofty exaltation through sadness and anguish. Thou must be trained in the
lessons of this life before thou canst live the calm and quiet life to come. Thou wilt
achieve this without difficulty, if thou keep ever with thee the charge to rejoice alway.
Dismiss the worries of the flesh. Gather together the joys of the soul. Rise above the
sensible perception of present things. Fix thy mind on the hope of things eternal. Of
these the mere thought suffices to fill the soul with gladness, and to plant in our hearts the
happiness of angels."

Homily VII., against the rich, follows much the same line of argument as VI. Two
main considerations are urged against the love of worldly wealth; firstly, the thought of
the day of judgment; secondly, the fleeting and unstable nature of the riches themselves.
The luxury of the fourth century, as represented by Basil, is much the same as the
luxury of the nineteenth.

" I am filled with amazement," says the preacher, " at the invention of superfluities.

---

[1] The sermon seems to have been preached at the beginning of Lent, when Cæsarea was still suffering from Carnival
indulgences. *Homily* 11. may be placed at a similar season in another year.   [2] § 4.

The vehicles are countless, some for conveying goods, others for carrying their owners; all covered with brass and with silver. There are a vast number of horses, whose pedigrees are kept like men's, and their descent from noble sires recorded. Some are for carrying their haughty owners about the town, some are hunters, some are hacks. Bits, girths, collars, are all of silver, all decked with gold. Scarlet cloths make the horses as gay as bridegrooms. There is a host of mules, distinguished by their colours, and their muleteers with them, one after another, some before and some behind. Of other household servants the number is endless, who satisfy all the requirements of men's extravagance; agents, stewards, gardeners, and craftsmen, skilled in every art that can minister to necessity or to enjoyment and luxury; cooks, confectioners, butlers, huntsmen, sculptors, painters, devisers and creators of pleasure of every kind. Look at the herds of camels, some for carriage, some for pasture; troops of horses, droves of oxen, flocks of sheep, herds of swine, with their keepers, land to feed all these, and to increase men's riches by its produce; baths in town, baths in the country; houses shining all over with every variety of marble,— some with stone of Phrygia, others with slabs of Spartan or Thessalian.[1] There must be some houses warm in winter,[2] and others cool in summer. The pavement is of mosaic, the ceiling gilded. If any part of the wall escapes the slabs, it is embellished with painted flowers. . . . You who dress your walls, and let your fellow-creatures go bare, what will you answer to the Judge? You who harness your horses with splendour, and despise your brother if he is ill-dressed; who let your wheat rot, and will not feed the hungry; who hide your gold, and despise the distressed? And, if you have a wealth-loving wife, the plague is twice as bad. She keeps your luxury ablaze; she increases your love of pleasure; she gives the goad to your superfluous appetites; her heart is set on stones, — pearls, emeralds, and sapphires.[3] Gold she works and gold she weaves,[4] and increases the mischief with never-ending frivolities. And her interest in all these things is no mere by-play: it is the care of night and day. Then what innumerable flatterers wait upon their idle wants! They must have their dyers of bright colours, their goldsmiths, their perfumers, their weavers, their embroiderers. With all their behests they do not leave their husbands breathing time. No fortune is vast enough to satisfy a woman's wants, — no, not if it were to flow like a river! They are as eager for foreign perfumes as for oil from the market. They must have the treasures of the sea, shells and pinnas,[5] and more of them than wool from the sheep's back. Gold encircling precious stones serves now for an ornament for their foreheads, now for their necks. There is more gold in their girdles; more gold fastens hands and feet. These gold-loving ladies are delighted to be bound by golden fetters, — only let the chain be gold! When will the man have time to care for his soul, who has to serve a woman's fancies?"

Homily VIII., on the Famine and Drought, belongs to the disastrous year 368. The circumstances of its delivery have already been referred to.[6] The text is Amos iii. 8, "The lion hath roared: who will not fear?" National calamity is traced to national sin, specially to neglect of the poor. Children, it appears,[7] were allowed a holiday from school to attend the public services held to deprecate the divine wrath. Crowds of men, to whose sins the distress was more due than to the innocent children, wandered cheerfully about the town instead of coming to church.

Homily X. is against the angry. Section 2 contains a description of the outward appearance of the angry men. "About the heart of those who are eager to requite evil for evil, the blood boils as though it were stirred and sputtering by the force of fire. On the surface it breaks out and shews the angry man in other form, familiar and well known to all, as though it were changing a mask upon the stage. The proper and usual eyes of the angry man are recognized no more; his gaze is unsteady, and fires up in a moment. He whets his teeth like boars joining battle. His countenance is livid and suffused with blood. His body seems to swell. His veins are ruptured, as his breath struggles under the storm within. His voice is rough and strained. His speech — broken and falling from him at random — proceeds without distinction, without arrangement. and without meaning. When he is roused by those who are irritating him, like a flame with plenty of fuel, to an inextinguishable pitch, then, ah! then indeed the spectacle is indescribable and unendurable. See the hands lifted against his fellows, and attacking every part of their bodies;

---

[1] A precious, red-streaked marble was quarried in Phrygia. The Spartan or Tænarian was the kind known as *verde antico*. cf. Bekker, *Gallus*. p. 16, n. The taste for the "Phrygian stone" was an old one. cf. Hor., *Carm*. III. i. 41.
[2] The Cappadocian winters were severe. cf. *Ep*. cxxi., cxcviii., cccxlix.
[3] ὑακίνθους. See L. and S., *s.v.*, and King's *Antique Gems*, 46.
[4] *i.e.* she must have ornaments of wrought gold and stuff embroidered with gold.
[5] cf. *Hexaemeron*, p. 94.   [6] p. xxi.   [7] § 3.

see the feet jumping without restraint on dangerous parts. See whatever comes to hand turned into a weapon for his mad frenzy. The record of the progress from words to wounds recalls familiar lines which probably Basil never read.[1] Rage rouses strife ; strife begets abuse ; abuse, blows ; blows, wounds ; and from wounds often comes death."

St. Basil, however, does not omit to notice [2] that there is such a thing as righteous indignation, and that we may " be angry and sin not." " God forbid that we should turn into occasions for sin gifts given to us by the Creator for our salvation ! Anger, stirred at the proper time and in the proper manner, is an efficient cause of manliness, patience, and endurance. . . . Anger is to be used as a weapon. So Moses, meekest of men, armed the hands of the Levites for the slaughter of their brethren, to punish idolatry. The wrath of Phinehas was justifiable. So was the wrath of Samuel against Agag. Thus, anger very often is made the minister of good deeds."

Homily XI., against Envy, adduces the instances of Saul's envy of David, and that of the patriarchs against Joseph. It is pointed out that envy grows out of familiarity and proximity. " A man is envied of his neighbour." [3] The Scythian does not envy the Egyptian. Envy arises among fellow-countrymen. The remedy for this vice is to recognise the pettiness of the common objects of human ambition, and to aspire to eternal joys. If riches are a mere means to unrighteousness,[4] wo be to the rich man ! If they are a ministering to virtue, there is no room for envy, since the common advantages proceeding from them are open to all, — unless any one out of superfluity of wickedness envies himself his own good things !

In Homily XIII., on Holy Baptism, St. Basil combats an error which had naturally arisen out of the practice of postponing baptism. The delay was made an occasion of license and indulgence. St. Augustine [5] cites the homily as St. Chrysostom's, but the quotation has not weakened the general acceptance of the composition as Basil's, and as one of those referred to by Amphilochius.[6] Ceillier mentions its citation by the emperor Justinian.[7] It was apparently delivered at Easter. Baptism is good at all times.[8] "Art thou a young man? Secure thy youth by the bridle of baptism. Has thy prime passed by? Do not be deprived of thy viaticum. Do not lose thy safeguard. Do not think of the eleventh hour as of the first. It is fitting that even at the beginning of life we should have the end in view.'

" Imitate [9] the eunuch.[10] He found one to teach him. He did not despise instruction. The rich man made the poor man mount into his chariot. The illustrious and the great welcomed the undistinguished and the small. When he had been taught the gospel of the kingdom, he received the faith in his heart, and did not put off the seal of the Spirit."

Homily XIV., against Drunkards, has the special interest of being originated by a painful incident which it narrates. The circumstances may well be compared with those of the scandal caused by the deacon Glycerius.[11] Easter day, remarks St. Basil, is a day when decent women ought to have been sitting in their homes, piously reflecting on future judgment. Instead of this, certain wanton women, forgetful of the fear of God, flung their coverings from their heads, despising God, and in contempt of His angels, lost to all shame before the gaze of men, shaking their hair, trailing their tunics, sporting with their feet, with immodest glances and unrestrained laughter, went off into a wild dance. They invited all the riotous youth to follow them, and kept up their dances in the Basilica of the Martyrs, before the walls of Cæsarea, turning hallowed places into the workshop of their unseemliness. They sang indecent songs, and befouled the ground with their unhallowed tread. They got a crowd of lads to stare at them, and left no madness undone. On this St. Basil builds a stirring temperance sermon. Section 6 contains a vivid picture of a drinking bout, and Section 7 describes the sequel. The details are evidently not imaginary.

" Sorrowful sight for Christian eyes ! A man in the prime of life, of powerful frame, of high rank in the army, is carried furtively home, because he cannot stand upright, and travel on his own feet. A man who ought to be a terror to our enemies is a laughing stock to the lads in the streets. He is smitten down by no sword — slain by no foe. A military man, in the bloom of manhood, the prey of wine, and ready to suffer any fate his foes may choose ! Drunkenness is the ruin of reason, the destruction of strength ; it is untimely old age ; it is, for a short time, death.

" What are drunkards but the idols of the heathen ? They have eyes and see not, ears and

---

[1] *Jurgia proludunt ; sed mox et pocula torques*
Saucius, et rubra deterges vulnera mappa.   Juv., Sat. v. 26.
[2] § 6.   [3] Ecc. iv. 4.   [4] § 5.   [5] *In Julian.* vi.   [6] *Orat.* ii.   [7] *Conc.* v. p. 668.   [8] § 5.   [9] § 6.
[10] Acts viii. 27.   [11] cf. *Letter* clxix. and observations in *Prolegomena*, p. xxix.

hear not.[1] Their hands are helpless ; their feet dead." The whole Homily is forcible. It is quoted by Isidore of Pelusium,[2] and St. Ambrose seems to have been acquainted with it.[3]

Homily XX., on Humility, urges the folly of Adam, in sacrificing eternal blessings to his ambition, and the example of St. Paul in glorying only in the Lord.[4]

Pharaoh, Goliath, and Abimelech are instanced. St. Peter is cited for lack of humility in being sure that he of all men will be true to the death.

" No detail can be neglected [5] as too insignificant to help us in ridding ourselves of pride. The soul grows like its practices, and is formed and fashioned in accordance with its conduct. Your appearance, your dress, your gait, your chair, your style of meals, your bed and bedding, your house and its contents, should be all arranged with a view to cheapness. Your talk, your songs, your mode of greeting your neighbour, should look rather to moderation than to ostentation. Give me, I beg, no elaborate arguments in your talk, no surpassing sweetness in your singing, no vaunting and wearisome discussions. In all things try to avoid *bigness*. Be kind to your friend, gentle to your servant, patient with the impudent, amiable to the lowly. Console the afflicted, visit the distressed, despise none. Be agreeable in address, cheerful in reply, ready, accessible to all. Never sing your own praises, nor get other people to sing them. Never allowing any uncivil communication, conceal as far as possible your own superiority." [6]

Homily XXI., on disregard of the things of this world. was preached out of St. Basil's diocese, very probably at Satala in 372.[7] The second part [8] is in reference to a fire which occurred in the near neighbourhood of the church on the previous evening.

"Once more the fiend has shewn his fury against us, has armed himself with flame .of fire, and has attacked the precincts of the church. Once more our common mother has won the day, and turned back his devices on himself. He has done nothing but advertise his hatred. . . . How do you not suppose the devil must be groaning to-day at the failure of his projected attempt? Our enemy lighted his fire close to the church that he might wreck our prosperity. The flames raised on every side by his furious blasts were streaming over all they could reach ; they fed on the air round about; they were being driven to touch the shrine, and to involve us in the common ruin ; but our Saviour turned them back on him who had kindled them, and ordered his madness to fall on himself. The congregation who have happily escaped are urged to live worthily of their preservation, shining like pure gold out of the furnace."

Homily XXII., which is of considerable interest, on the study of pagan literature, is really not a homily at all.[9] It is a short treatise addressed to the young on their education. It would seem to have been written in the Archbishop's later years, unless the experience of which he speaks may refer rather to his earlier experience, alike as a student and a teacher.

No source of instruction can be overlooked in the preparation for the great battle of life,[10] and there is a certain advantage to be derived from the right use of heathen writers. The illustrious Moses is described as training his intellect in the science of the Egyptians, and so arriving at the contemplation of Him Who is.[11] So in later days Daniel at Babylon was wise in the Chaldean philosophy, and ultimately apprehended the divine instruction. But granted that such heathen learning is not useless, the question remains how you are to participate in it. To begin with the poets. Their utterances are of very various kinds, and it will not be well to give attention to all without exception. When they narrate to you the deeds and the words of good men, admire and copy them, and strive diligently to be like them. When they come to bad men, shut your ears, and avoid imitating them, like Ulysses fleeing from the sirens' songs.[12] Familiarity with evil words is a sure road to evil deeds, wherefore every possible precaution must be taken to prevent our souls from unconsciously imbibing evil influences through literary gratification, like men who take poison in honey. We shall not therefore praise the poets when they revile and mock, or when they describe licentious, intoxicated characters, when they define happiness as consisting in a laden table and dissolute ditties. Least of all shall we attend to the

[1] Ps. cxv. 5. [2] 1 *Ep.* lxi. [3] *De Eb. et Jejunio.* c. 18. [4] 1 Cor. i. 30, 31. [5] § 7.
[6] Here several touches remind us of Theophrastus. cf. *Char.* xxiii. and xxiv.
[7] Ceillier, VI. viii. 2. [8] § 9.
[9] It has often been separately published. In 1600 it was included by Martin Haynoccius in an *Enchiridion Ethicum*, containing also Plutarch's two tracts on the education of boys and the study of the poets, with which it is interesting to compare it. Grotius published it with Plutarch's *De Legendis Poetis* at Paris in 1623. They were also published together by Archbishop Potter at Oxford in 1691. [10] § 2.
[11] τοῦ ὄντος. The highest heathen philosophy strove to reach the neuter τὸ ὄν. The revelation of Jehovah is of the masculine ὁ ὤν, who communicates with his creatures, and says ἐγώ εἰμί.
[12] Hom., *Od.* xii. 158. cf. *Letter* i. p. 109.

poets when they are talking about the gods, specially when their talk is of many gods, and those in mutual disagreement. For among them brother is at variance with brother, parent against children, and children wage a truceless war against parents. The gods' adulteries and amours and unabashed embraces, and specially those of Zeus, whom they describe as the chief and highest of them all, — things which could not be told without a blush of brutes, — all this let us leave to actors on the stage.[1]

I must make the same remark about historians, specially when they write merely to please. And we certainly shall not follow rhetoricians in the art of lying. . . . I have been taught by one well able to understand a poet's mind that with Homer all his poetry is praise of virtue, and that in him all that is not mere accessory tends to this end. A marked instance of this is his description of the prince of the Kephallenians saved naked from shipwreck. No sooner did he appear than the princess viewed him with reverence; so far was she from feeling anything like shame at seeing him naked and alone, since his virtue stood him in the stead of clothes.[2] Afterwards he was of so much estimation among the rest of the Phæacians that they abandoned the pleasures amid which they lived, all looked up to him and imitated him, and not a man of the Phæacians prayed for anything more eagerly than that he might be Ulysses, — a mere waif saved from shipwreck. Herein my friend said that he was the interpreter of the poet's mind; that Homer all but said aloud, Virtue, O men, is what you have to care for. Virtue swims out with the shipwrecked sailor, and when he is cast naked on the coast, virtue makes him more noble than the happy Phæacians. And truly this is so. Other belongings are not more the property of their possessors than of any one else. They are like dice flung hither and thither in a game. Virtue is the one possession which cannot be taken away, and remains with us alike alive and dead.

It is in this sense that I think Solon said to the rich,

'Αλλ' ἡμεῖς αὐτοῖς οὐ διαμειψόμεθα
Τῆς ἀρετῆς τὸν πλοῦτον· ἐπεὶ τὸ μὲν ἔμπεδον αἰεί,
Χρήματα δ' ἀνθρώπων ἄλλοτε ἄλλος ἔχει.[3]

Similar to these are the lines of Theognis,[4] in which he says that God (whatever he means by " God ") inclines the scale to men now one way and now another, and so at one moment they are rich, and at another penniless. Somewhere too in his writings Prodicus, the Sophist of Chios, has made similar reflexions on vice and virtue, to whom attention may well be paid, for he is a man by no means to be despised. So far as I recollect his sentiments, they are something to this effect. I do not remember the exact words, but the sense, in plain prose, was as follows:[5]

Once upon a time, when Hercules was quite young, and of just about the same age as yourselves, he was debating within himself which of the two ways he should choose, the one leading through toil to virtue, the other which is the easiest of all. There approached him two women. They were Virtue and Vice, and though they said not a word they straightway shewed by their appearance what was the difference between them. One was tricked out to present a fair appearance with every beautifying art. Pleasure and delights were shed around her and she led close after her innumerable enjoyments like a swarm of bees. She showed them to Hercules, and, promising him yet more and more, endeavoured to attract him to her side. The other, all emaciated and squalid, looked earnestly at the lad, and spoke in quite another tone. She promised him no ease, no pleasure, but toils, labours, and perils without number, in every land and sea. She told him that the reward of all this would be that he should become a god (so the narrator tells it). This latter Hercules followed even to the death. Perhaps all those who have written anything about wisdom, less or more, each according to his ability, have praised Virtue in their writings.

---

[1] This shews that the shameless and cruel exhibitions of earlier days had not died out even in the fourth century. *cf.* Suetonius, *Nero* xi., xii., Tertullian, *Apol.* 15. On the whole subject, see Bp. Lightfoot's note on St. Clem. Rom., *Ep. ad Cor.* vi., where Δαναΐδες καὶ Δίρκαι is probably a misreading for νεάνιδες παιδίσκαι. He refers for illustrations to Friedländer, *Sittengeschichte Roms*, ii. 234.   [2] *Od.* vi. 135 κ.τ.λ.
[3] These lines are attributed to Solon by Plutarch, in the tract πῶς ἄν τις ὑπ' ἐχθρῶν ὠφελοῖτο, but they occur among the elegiac "*gnomæ*" of Theognis, lines 316–318. Fronton du Duc in his notes on the *Homilies* points out that they are also quoted in Plutarch's life of Solon. Basil was well acquainted with Plutarch. (*cf.* references in the notes to the *Hexaemeron*.)
[4] The lines are:

Ζεὺς γάρ τοι τὸ τάλαντον ἐπιρρέπει ἄλλοτε ἄλλως
'Άλλοτε μὲν πλουτεῖν, ἄλλοτε δ' οὐδὲν ἔχειν.   Theog. 157.

[5] The story of *The Choice of Hercules* used to be called, from Prodicus (of Ceos, not Chios) *Hercules Prodicius.* Suidas says that the title of the work quoted was Ὧραι. The allegory is given at length in Xenophon's *Memorabilia* (II. i. 21) in Dion Chrysostom's *Regnum*, and in Cicero (*De Officiis* i. 32), who refers to Xenophon. It is imitated in the *Somnium* of Lucian.

These must be obeyed, and the effort made to show forth their teaching in the conduct of life. For he alone is wise who confirms in act the philosophy which in the rest goes no farther than words. They do but flit like shadows [1]

It is as though some painter had represented a sitter as a marvel of manly beauty, and then he were to be in reality what the artist had painted on the panel. But to utter glorious eulogies on virtue in public, and make long speeches about it, while in private putting pleasure before continence and giving gain higher honour than righteousness, is conduct which seems to me illustrated by actors on the stage : they enter as monarchs and magnates, when they are neither monarchs nor magnates, and perhaps even are only slaves. A singer could never tolerate a lyre that did not match his voice, nor a coryphæus a chorus that did not chant in tune. Yet every one will be inconsistent with himself, and will fail to make his conduct agree with his words. The tongue has sworn, but the heart has never sworn, as Euripides [2] has it ; and a man will aim at seeming, rather than at being, good. Nevertheless, if we may believe Plato, the last extreme of iniquity is for one to seem just without being just.[3] This then is the way in which we are to receive writings which contain suggestions of good deeds. And since the noble deeds of men of old are preserved for our benefit either by tradition, or in the works of poets and historians, do not let us miss the good we may get from them. For instance : a man in the street once pursued Pericles with abuse, and persisted in it all day. Pericles took not the slightest notice. Evening fell, and darkness came on, and even then he could hardly be persuaded to give over. Pericles lighted him home, for fear this exercise in philosophy might be lost.[4] Again : once upon a time a fellow who was angry with Euclid of Megara threatened him with death, and swore at him. Euclid swore back that he would appease him, and calm him in spite of his rage.[5] A man once attacked Socrates the son of Sophroniscus and struck him again and again in the face. Socrates made no resistance, but allowed the drunken fellow to take his fill of frenzy, so that his face was all swollen and bloody from the blows. When the assault was done, Socrates, according to the story, did nothing besides writing on his forehead, as a sculptor might on a statue, " This is so and so's doing." [6]

This was his revenge. Where conduct, as in this case, is so much on a par with Christian conduct,[7] I maintain that it is well worth our while to copy these great men. The behaviour of Socrates on this occasion is akin to the precept that we are by no means to take revenge, but to turn the other cheek to the smiter. So the conduct of Pericles and Euclid matches the commands to put up with persecutors, and to bear their wrath with meekness, and to invoke not cursing but blessing on our enemies. He who has been previously instructed in these examples will no longer regard the precepts as impracticable. I should like, too, to instance the conduct of Alexander, when he had captured the daughters of Darius.[8] Their beauty is described as extraordinary, and Alexander would not so much as look at them, for he thought it shameful that a conqueror of men should be vanquished by women. This is of a piece with the statement that he who looks at a woman impurely, even though he do not actually commit the act of adultery with her, is not free from its guilt, because he has allowed lust to enter his heart. Then there is the case of Clinias, the follower of Pythagoras ; it is difficult to believe this is a case of accidental, and not intentional, imitation of our principles.[9] What of him? He might have escaped a fine of three talents by taking an oath, but he preferred to pay rather than swear, and this when he would have sworn truly. He appears to me to have heard of the precept which orders us to swear not at all.[10] To return to the point with which I began. We must not take everything indiscriminately, but only what is profitable. It would be

---

[1] *cf.* Hom., *Od.* x. 494, where it is said of Teiresias :

Τῷ καὶ τεθνηῶτι νόον πόρε Περσεφόνεια,
Οἴῳ πεπνῦσθαι· τοὶ δὲ σκιαὶ ἀίσσουσι.

[2] Eur., *Hippolytus*, 612: ἡ γλῶσσ' ὀμώμοχ' ἡ δὲ φρὴν ἀνώμοτος, the famous line which Aristophanes made fun of in *Thesmophoriazusæ*, 275.

[3] Fronton du Duc notes that Basil has taken this allusion to Plato from Plutarch's tract, *How to distinguish between Flatterer and Friend*, p. 50: ὡς γαο ὁ Πλάτων φησὶν ἐσχάτης ἀδικίας εἶναι δοκεῖν δίκαιον μὴ ὄντα. [4] Plut., *Pericles*.

[5] Plut., *De Ira Cohibenda*, where the story is told of a brother. The aggressor says ἀπολοίμην εἰ μή σε τιμωρησαίμην. The rejoinder is ἐγὼ δὲ ἀπολο μην εἰ μή σε πείσαιμι.

[6] ἐποίει in Greek will of course stand for "made it," like our " *hoc fecit*," or " did it." Du Duc gives authority for the use of the Imp. from Politian.

[7] τοῖς ἡμετέροις. [8] *cf.* Plutarch, *Alex.* and Arrian. II. xii.

[9] Clinias was a contemporary of Plato (Diog. Laert. ix. 40).

[10] St. Basil can hardly imagine that Clinias lived after Christ; yet Old Testament prohibitions are against false swearing only. Possibly the third commandment and such a passage as Lev. xix. 12, may have been in his mind. If Clinias had lived some half a millennium later there seems no reason why he should not have saved himself three talents by using the words of the Apostle in 2 Cor. xi. 31.

shameful for us in the case of food to reject the injurious, and at the same time, in the case of lessons, to take no account of what keeps the soul alive, but, like *mountain streams*, to sweep in everything that happens to be in our way. The sailor does not trust himself to the mercy of the winds, but steers his boat to the port; the archer aims at his mark; the smith and the carpenter keep the end of the crafts in view. What sense is there in our shewing ourselves inferior to these craftsmen, though we are quite able to understand our own affairs? In mere handicrafts is there some object and end in labour, and is there no aim in the life of man, to which any one ought to look who means to live a life better than the brutes'? Were no intelligence to be sitting at the tiller of our souls, we should be dashed up and down in the voyage of life like boats that have no ballast. It is just as with competitions in athletics, or, if you like, in music. In competitions mere crowns are offered for prizes, there is always training, and no one in training for wrestling or the pancration [1] practises the harp or flute. Certainly not Polydamas, who before his contests at the Olympic games used to make chariots at full speed stand still, and so kept up his strength.[2] Milo, too, could not be pushed off his greased shield, but, pushed as he was, held on as tightly as statues fastened by lead.[3] In one word, training was the preparation for these feats. Suppose they had neglected the dust and the gymnasia, and had given their minds to the strains of Marsyas or Olympus, the Phrygians,[4] they would never have won crowns or glory, nor escaped ridicule for their bodily incapacity. On the other hand Timotheus did not neglect harmony and spend his time in the wrestling schools. Had he done so it would never have been his lot to surpass all the world in music, and to have attained such extraordinary skill in his art as to be able to rouse the soul by his sustained and serious melody, and then again relieve and sooth it by his softer strains at his good pleasure. By this skill, when once he sang in Phrygian strains to Alexander, he is said to have roused the king to arms in the middle of a banquet, and then by gentler music to have restored him to his boon companions.[5] So great is the importance, alike in music and in athletics, in view of the object to be attained, of training. . . .

. . . .

To us are held out prizes whereof the marvellous number and splendour are beyond the power of words to tell. Will it be possible for those who are fast asleep, and live a life of indulgence, to seize them without an effort?[6] If so, sloth would have been of great price, and Sardanapalus would have been esteemed especially happy, or even Margites, if you like, who is said by Homer to have neither ploughed nor dug, nor done any useful work, — if indeed Homer wrote this. Is there not rather truth in the saying of Pittacus,[7] who said that "It is hard to be good?" . . .

. . . .

We must not be the slaves of our bodies, except where we are compelled. Our best provision must be for the soul. We ought by means of philosophy to release her from fellowship with all bodily appetites as we might from a dungeon, and at the same time make our bodies superior to our appetites. We should, for instance, supply our bellies with necessaries, not with dainties like men whose minds are set on cooks and table arrangers, and who search through every land and sea, like the tributaries of some stern despot, much to be pitied for their toil. Such men are really suffering pains as intolerable as the torments of hell, carding into a fire,[8] fetching water in a sieve, pouring into a tub with holes in it, and getting nothing for their pains. To pay more than necessary attention to our hair and dress is, as Diogenes phrases it, the part either of the unfortunate or of the wicked. To be finely dressed, and to have the reputation of being so, is to my mind quite as disgraceful as to play the harlot or to plot against a neighbour's wedlock. What does it matter to a man with any sense, whether he wears a grand state robe, or a common cloak,

---

[1] *i.e.* wrestling and boxing together. [2] Paus. VI. v. *cf.* Pers., *Sat.* i. 4. [3] Paus. VI. xiv.

[4] Marsyas, the unhappy rival of Apollo, was said to be a native of Celænæ in Phrygia. Olympus was a pupil of Marsyas (*Schol. in Aristoph. Eq.* 9). By Plutarch (*Mus.* xi.) he is called ἀρχηγὸς τῆς Ἑλληνικῆς καὶ καλῆς μουσικῆς. *cf.* Arist., *Pol.* VIII. v. 16.

[5] *cf.* Cic., *Legg.* ii. 15, Plutarch, *De Mus.* There are two Timothei of musical fame, one anterior to Alexander. It will be remembered that in Dryden's *Alexander's Feast* "the king seized a flambeau with zeal to destroy," *after* the "Lydian measures" had "*soothed his soul to pleasures.*"

[6] Lit., who sleep with both ears, to seize with one hand (idiom for sleeping soundly. *cf.* Aul. Gell. ii. 23, who quotes ἐπ' ἀμφοτέραν καθεύδειν from Menander).

[7] Of Mitylene, *cf.* Arist., *Pol.* III. xiv. 9, and Diog. Laert. I. iv., who mentions Simonides' quotation of the maxim of the text Ἄνδρα ἀγαθὸν ἀλαθέως γενέσθαι χαλεπὸν, τὸ Πιττάκειον.

[8] εἰς πῦρ ξαίνοντες, *i.e.* labouring in vain. *cf.* Plat., *Legg.* 780 c. The ordinary rendering to "flog fire," adopted by Erasmus (*Adag. Chil.* i., *Centur.* iv.), seems wrong. *cf.* Bekker on the phrase in Plato.

so long as it serves to keep off heat and cold? In other matters necessity is to be the rule, and the body is only to be so far regarded as is good for the soul."

.   .   .   .

Similar precepts are urged, with further references and allusions to Pythagoras, the Corybantes, Solon, Diogenes, Pythius, the rich man who feasted Xerxes on his way to Greece, Pheidias, Bias, Polycletus, Archilochus, and Tithonus.[1]

It is suggestive to compare the wealth of literary illustration in this little tract with the severe restrictions which Basil imposes on himself in his homilies for delivery in church, where nothing but Scripture is allowed to appear. In studying the sermons, it might be supposed that Basil read nothing but the Bible. In reading the treatise on heathen authors, but for an incidental allusion to David and Methuselah, it might be supposed that he spent all his spare time over his old school and college authors.

(iii)   The Panegyrical Homilies are five in number.

Homily V. is on Julitta, a lady of Cæsarea martyred in 306, and commemorated on July 30. (In the Basilian menology, July 31.) Her property being seized by an iniquitous magistrate, she was refused permission to proceed with a suit for restitution unless she abjured Christianity. On her refusal to do this she was arraigned and burned. She is described as having said that women no less than men were made after the image of God; that women as well as men were made by their Creator capable of manly virtue; that it took bone as well as flesh to make the woman, and that constancy, fortitude, and endurance are as womanly as they are manly.

The homily, which recommends patience and cheerfulness in adversity, contains a passage of great beauty upon prayer. "Ought we to pray without ceasing? Is it possible to obey such a command? These are questions which I see you are ready to ask. I will endeavour, to the best of my ability, to defend the charge. Prayer is a petition for good addressed by the pious to God. But we do not rigidly confine our petition to words. Nor yet do we imagine that God requires to be reminded by speech. He knows our needs even though we ask Him not. What do I say then? I say that we must not think to make our prayer complete by syllables. The strength of prayer lies rather in the purpose of our soul and in deeds of virtue reaching every part and moment of our life. 'Whether ye eat,' it is said, 'or drink, or whatever ye do, do all to the glory of God.'[2] As thou takest thy seat at table, pray. As thou liftest the loaf, offer thanks to the Giver. When thou sustainest thy bodily weakness with wine, remember Him Who supplies thee with this gift, to make thy heart glad and to comfort thy infirmity. Has thy need for taking food passed away? Let not the thought of thy Benefactor pass away too. As thou art putting on thy tunic, thank the Giver of it. As thou wrappest thy cloak about thee, feel yet greater love to God, Who alike in summer and in winter has given us coverings convenient for us, at once to preserve our life, and to cover what is unseemly. Is the day done? Give thanks to Him Who has given us the sun for our daily work, and has provided for us a fire to light up the night, and to serve the rest of the needs of life. Let night give the other occasions of prayer. When thou lookest up to heaven and gazest at the beauty of the stars, pray to the Lord of the visible world; pray to God the Arch-artificer of the universe, Who in wisdom hath made them all. When thou seest all nature sunk in sleep, then again worship Him Who gives us even against our wills release from the continuous strain of toil, and by a short refreshment restores us once again to the vigour of our strength. Let not night herself be all, as it were, the special and peculiar property of sleep. Let not half thy life be useless through the senselessness of slumber. Divide the time of night between sleep and prayer. Nay, let thy slumbers be themselves experiences in piety; for it is only natural that our sleeping dreams should be for the most part echoes of the anxieties of the day. As have been our conduct and pursuits, so will inevitably be our dreams. Thus wilt thou pray without ceasing; if thou prayest not only in words, but unitest thyself to God through all the course of life and so thy life be made one ceaseless and uninterrupted prayer."

Barlaam, the subject of Homily XVII.,[3] was martyred under Diocletian, either at Antioch or at Cæsarea. The ingenuity of his tormentors conceived the idea of compelling him to fling the pinch of incense to the gods by putting it, while burning, into his hand, and forcing him to hold it over the altar. The fire fought with the right hand, and the fire proved the weaker. The fire burned through the hand, but the hand was firm. The martyr might say, " Thou hast holden me by my right hand. Thou shalt guide me

---

[1] Herod. vii. 21.   [2] 1 Cor. x. 31.
[3] Supposed by some to be not Basil's, but Chrysostom's. cf. Ceillier, iv. p. 53.

with thy counsel, and afterward receive me to glory." [1]   The homily concludes with an apostrophe to the painters of such scenes.   " Up, I charge you, ye famous painters of the martyrs' struggles!   Adorn by your art the mutilated figure of this officer of our army!   I have made but a sorry picture of the crowned hero.   Use all your skill and all your colours in his honour."

This was taken at the second Council of Nicæa as proof of an actual painting.[2]

Homily XVIII. is on the martyr Gordius, who was a native of Cæsarea, and was degraded from his rank of centurion when Licinius removed Christians from the army. Gordius retired into the wilderness, and led the life of an anchorite.   One day there was a great festival at Cæsarea in honour of Mars.   There were to be races in the theatre, and thither the whole population trooped.   Not a Jew, not a heathen, was wanting.   No small company of Christians had joined the crowd, men of careless life, sitting in the assembly of folly, and not shunning the counsel of the evil-doers, to see the speed of the horses and the skill of the charioteers.   Masters had given their slaves a holiday.   Even boys ran from their schools to the show.   There was a multitude of common women of the lower ranks. The stadium was packed, and every one was gazing intently on the races.   Then that noble man, great of heart and great of courage, came down from the uplands into the theatre.   He took no thought of the mob.   He did not heed how many hostile hands he met. . . .   In a moment the whole theatre turned to stare at the extraordinary sight. The man looked wild and savage.   From his long sojourn in the mountains his head was squalid, his beard long, his dress filthy.   His body was like a skeleton.   He carried a stick and a wallet.   Yet there was a certain grace about him, shining from the unseen all around him.   He was recognised.   A great shout arose.   Those who shared his faith clapped for joy, but the enemies of the truth urged the magistrate to put in force the penalty he had incurred, and condemned him beforehand to die.   Then an universal shouting arose all round.   Nobody looked at the horses — nobody at the charioteers.   The exhibition of the chariots was mere idle noise.   Not an eye but was wholly occupied with looking at Gordius, not an ear wanted to hear anything but his words.   Then a confused murmur, running like a wind through all the theatre, sounded above the din of the course. Heralds were told to proclaim silence.   The pipes were hushed, and all the band stopped in a moment.   Gordius was being listened to ; Gordius was the centre of all eyes, and in a moment he was dragged before the magistrate who presided over the games.   With a mild and gentle voice the magistrate asked him his name, and whence he came.   He told his country, his family, the rank he had held, the reason for his flight, and his return. " Here I am," he cried ; " ready to testify by deed to the contempt in which I hold your orders, and my faith in the God in whom I have trusted.   For I have heard that you are inferior to few in cruelty.   This is why I have chosen this time in order to carry out my wishes."   With these words he kindled the wrath of the governor like a fire, and roused all his fury against himself.   The order was given, " Call the lictors ; where are the plates of lead?   Where are the scourges?   Let him be stretched upon a wheel ; let him be wrenched upon the rack ; let the instruments of torture be brought in ; make ready the beasts, the fire, the sword, the cross.   What a good thing for the villain that he can die only once!"[3]   " Nay," replied Gordius, " what a bad thing for me that I cannot die for Christ again and again!"   .   .   .

All the town crowded to the spot where the martyrdom was to be consummated. Gordius uttered his last words.   Death is the common lot of man.   As we must all die, let us through death win life.   Make the necessary voluntary.   Exchange the earthly for the heavenly.   He then crossed himself, he stepped forward for the fatal blow, without changing colour or losing his cheerful mien.   It seemed as though he were not going to meet an executioner, but to yield himself into the hands of angels.[4]

Homily XIX. is on the Forty Soldier Martyrs of Sebaste, who were ordered by the officers of Licinius, A.D. 320, to offer sacrifice to the heathen idols, and, at their refusal, were plunged for a whole night into a frozen pond in the city, in sight of a hot bath on the brink.   One man's faith and fortitude failed him.   He rushed to the relief of the shore,

---

[1] Ps. lxxiii. 23, 24.   [2] Labbe vii. 272.   *cf.* Chrys. *Hom.* lxxiii.
[3] ἀλλὰ γὰρ οἷα κερδαίνει, φησίν, ἅπαξ μόνον ἀποθνῄσκων. Garnier seems to have completely missed the force of this exclamation in the explanation in a note, " *Judex hoc dicere volebat, quem fructum referet ex sua pertinacia, si semel mortuus fuerit; neque enim in hanc vitam rursus redibit, ejus ut gaudiis perfruatur, neque tamen ulla alia vita est.*"
[4] For the tortures and modes of execution enumerated, Du Duc compares Aristoph., *Pax.* 452, Chrysost., *De Luciano Martyre*, and Nicephorus vi. 14.

plunged into the hot water, and died on the spot. One of the executioners had stood warming himself and watching the strange scene. He had seemed to see angels coming down from heaven and distributing gifts to all the band but one. When the sacred number of forty was for the moment broken the officer flung off his clothes, and sprang into the freezing pond with the cry, "I am a Christian." Judas departed. Matthias took his place. . . .

. . . .

What trouble wouldst thou not have taken to find one to pray for thee to the Lord! Here are forty, praying with one voice. Where two or three are gathered together in the name of the Lord, there is He in the midst. Who doubts His presence in the midst of forty? The afflicted flees to the Forty; the joyous hurries to them; the former, that he may find relief from his troubles; the latter, that his blessings may be preserved. Here a pious woman is found beseeching for her children; she begs for the return of her absent husband, or for his health if he be sick. Let your supplications be made with the martyrs. Let young men imitate their fellows. Let fathers pray to be fathers of like sons. Let mothers learn from a good mother. The mother of one of these saints saw the rest overcome by the cold, and her son, from his strength or his constancy, yet alive. The executioners had left him, on the chance of his having changed his mind. She herself lifted him in her arms, and placed him on the car in which the rest were being drawn to the pyre, a veritable martyr's mother.[1]

The last of the Panegyrical Homilies (XXIII.) is on Saint Mamas, commemorated on September 2 by the Greeks, and on August 17 by the Latins. He is said to have been a shepherd martyred at Cæsarea in 274 in the persecution of Aurelian. Sozomen (v. 2) relates that when the young princes Julian and Gallus were at the castle of Macellum [2] they were engaged in building a church in the martyr's honour, and that Julian's share in the work never prospered.[3] The homily narrates no details concerning the saint, and none seem to be known. It does contain a more direct mention of a practice of invocation. There is a charge to all who have enjoyed the martyr in dreams to remember him; to all who have met with him in the church, and have found him a helper in their prayers; to all those whom he has aided in their doings, *when called on by name*.[4] The conclusion contains a summary of the Catholic doctrine concerning the Son. "You have been told before, and now you are being told again, ' In the beginning was the Word,'[5] to prevent your supposing that the Son was a being generated after the manner of men,[6] from His having come forth out of the non-existent. 'Word' is said to you, because of His impassibility. 'Was' is said because of His being beyond time. He says 'beginning' to conjoin the Begotten with His Father. You have seen how the obedient sheep hears a master's voice. 'In the beginning,' and 'was,' and 'Word.' Do not go on to say,

---

[1] The name of this youngest of the Forty is given as Melito (*D.C.B.* s.v.). They are commemorated on March 9 in the Roman Kalendar of Gregory XIII. and the Menology of Basil; on March 10 in the old Roman Mart. of Bened. XIV.; on the 11th in the old Roman Kal., and on March 16 in the Armenian. The legend of the discovery of some of their relics is given in Sozomen ix. 2. Others were obtained for the church built in their honour at Annesi. (*cf.* p. xiv.) Two doctrinal points come out in this homily, (*a*) The officer who took the place of Melito is said to have been baptized, not in water but in his own blood (§ 7). Here is martyrdom represented as the equivalent of baptism. (*b*) The stage arrived at in the progress of Christian sentiment towards the invocation of departed saints is indicated. Garnier, the Jesuit, writes in the margin of the passage quoted above, *Invocantur martyres;* and Ceillier notes, *Il reconnait que les prieres des martyrs peuvent beaucoup nous aider auprès de Dieu*. But in this particular passage the idea of " fleeing to the Forty" seems to be not fleeing to them to ask for their prayers, but fleeing to the shrine to pray in company with them. It is rather the fellowship than the intercession of the saints which is sought. μετὰ μαρτύρων γιγνέσθω τὰ αἰτήματα ὑμῶν. Let your requests be made not *to* but *with* the martyrs. In the Homily on St. Mamas, the next in order, the expressions are less equivocal. At the same time it must be remarked that with St. Basil the invocation and the intercession are *local*. In the *De Sp. Scto.* (chap. xxiii. p. 34) a significant contrast is drawn between the ubiquity of the Holy Ghost and the limited and local action of angels. And if of angels, so of saints. The saints who have departed this life are thought of as accessible at the shrines where their relics rest, but, if we apply the analogy of the *De Sp. Scto.*, not everywhere. It has been said that this is the period when requests for the prayers of the holy dead begin to appear, and Archbishop Ussher (*Address to a Jesuit*, chap. ix.) cites Gregory of Nazianzus for the earliest instance within his knowledge of a plain invocation of the departed. But, as bishop Harold Browne points out, his invocation is rather rhetorical than supplicatory. Gregory " had even a pious persuasion that they still continued as much as ever to aid with their prayers those for whom they had been wont to pray on earth (*Orat.* xxiv. p. 425). And he ventures to think, if it be not too bold to say so (εἰ μὴ τολμηρὸν τοῦτο εἰπεῖν), that the saints, being nearer to God and having put off the fetters of the flesh, have more avail with Him than when on earth (*Orat.* xix. p. 228). In all these he does not appear to have gone further than some who preceded him, nor is there anything in such speculations beyond what might be consistent with the most Protestant abhorrence of saint worship and Mariolatry" (Bp. Harold Browne in Art. xxii.). Romish authorities in support of a yet earlier development, point to Irenæus (*Adv. Hær.* v. 19), where in a highly rhetorical passage the Virgin Mary is said to have become the " advocate " of the Virgin Eve, and to Origen, who "invoked" his guardian angel (*Hom. i. in Ezek.* 7). The later mediæval invocation Bp. Jeremy Taylor (vol. vi. Eden's ed. p. 489) ingeniously shews to be of a piece rather with early heresy than with early Catholicity: " It pretends to know their present state, which is hid from our eyes; and it proceeds upon the very reason upon which the Gnostics and Valentinians went; that is, that it is fit to have mediators between God and us; that we may present our prayers to them, and they to God. To which add that the Church of Rome presenting candles and other donaries to the Virgin Mary as to the Queen of heaven, do that which the Collyridians did (Epiphan. *Hær.* lxxix. vol. i. p. 1057). The gift is only differing, as candle and cake, gold and garments, this vow or that vow."

[2] *cf.* p. xv., n.   [3] *cf.* Greg. Naz., *Or.* iv. § 25.

[4] ὅσοις, ὀνόματι, κληθεὶς, ἐπὶ τῶν ἔργων παρέστη. On the reverence for relics *cf. Letters* cxcvii., cclii., and cclvii.

[5] John i. 1.   [6] γέννημα ἀνθρώπινον.

'How was He?' and 'If He was, He was not begotten;' and 'If He was begotten, He was not.' It is not a sheep who says these things. The skin is a sheep's; but the speaker within is a wolf. Let him be recognised as an enemy. 'My sheep hear my voice.'[1] You have heard the Son. Understand His likeness to His Father. I say *likeness* because of the weakness of the stronger bodies: In truth, and I am not afraid of approaching the truth, I am no ready deceiver: I say *identity*, always preserving the distinct existence of Son and Father. In the hypostasis of Son understand the Father's Form, that you may hold the exact doctrine of this Image, — that you may understand consistently with true religion the words, 'I am in the Father and the Father in me.'[2] Understand not confusion of essences, but identity of characters."

V. Letters.

Under this head I will add nothing to the notes, however inadequate, appended to the text.

VI. Liturgical.

It is beyond the scope of the present work to discuss at length the history and relation of the extant Liturgies, which go by the name of St. Basil. St. Basil's precise share in their composition, as we possess them, must be conjectural.

(i) The Liturgy, which St. Basil himself used and gave to his clergy and monks, preserved the traditional form in use in the archdiocese of Cæsarea.[3] It is mentioned in the xxxii[nd] canon of the council "in Trullo" of 692. This is no doubt the basis of the Greek Liturgy known as St. Basil's, and used in the East as well as the Liturgy of St. Chrysostom. The form in use is contained in Neale's *Primitive Liturgies* (1875). Dr. Swainson (*Greek Liturgies chiefly from Oriental Sources*, p. 75) printed an edition of it from the Barberini MS. in 1884.

(ii) There is an Alexandrine Liturgy in Coptic, Arabic, and Greek form, called St. Basil's, and used on fast days by the Monophysites (Renaudot, *Lit. Orient. Collectio*, i. 154). This differs entirely from the first named.

(iii) Yet again there is a Syriac Liturgy called St. Basil's, translated by Masius, and given by Renaudot in his second volume.[4]

VII. Writings Spurious and Dubious.

Under this head will be ranked, besides writings objections against which have been already noticed:

1. Constitutiones monasticæ ('Ασκητικαὶ διατάξεις), in number thirty-four.
2. Pœnæ in monachos delinquentes, and Pœnæ in Canonicas (ἐπιτίμια).
3. Libri duo de Baptismo.
4. Sermones duo ascetici.
5. Various Homilies:
    Adversus Calumniatores SS. Trinitatis,
    Altera de Sp. Scto.,
    In Sanctam Christi Generationem,
    De Libero Arbitrio,
    In aliquot Scripturæ locis, dicta in Lacizis.
    III. De Jejunio.
    De Pœnitentia.
6. A book On True Virginity.
7. A treatise On consolation in adversity.

---

[1] cf. John x. 16.   [2] John xiv. 10. cf. *De Sp. Scto.* § 45, p. 28.
[3] cf. *De Sp. Scto.* chap. xxvii. p. 41.
[4] cf. *Dict. Christ. Ant. s.v.* "Liturgy," and C. Hole, *Manual of the Book of Common Prayer*, chap. ii. Fessler notes: "*Extat Liturgia S. Basilii tam fusior quam brevior gr. et lat. in Eucholog. Gr. ed. J. Goar Venetiis* 1730 *et alia gr. et lat. in E. Renaudot Coll. Lit. Or. Paris,* 1716, *item alia latine tantum conversa ex Coptico Jacobitarum in eadem collect., ac rursus alia latine tantum ex Syriaco conversa. . . . De formæ varietate hæc optime monet Renaudot:* 'Liturgia illa, quod extra dubium est, usurpatur in Græca ecclesia ab annis plus mille ducentis; atque inde originem habuerunt leves aliquot discrepantiæ in precibus præparatoriis aut in aliis orationibus. Quædam exemplaria cæremoniales rubricas habent, quæ in aliis non reperiuntur; at alicujus momenti discrimen in illis partibus quæ canonem sacræ Actionis constituunt, non reperitur. . . . Varietates in codicibus omnes prope ad ritus spectant, qui enucleatius in aliquibus, in aliis brevius explicantur, in nonnullis omittuntur, quia aliunde peti debebant' Eo autem sensu Liturgiæ hujus auctor dicitur Basilius, non quod proprio ingenio eam excogitaverit, sed quod preces publicas, eisque contiguos ritus, quoad rei essentiam ex communi traditionis Apostolicæ fonte manantes, ordinaverit et in scriptis codicibus ad certam formam redegerit.*"

8. A treatise De laude solitariæ vitæ.
9. Admonitio ad filium spiritualem (extant only in Latin).
10. Sermones de moribus XXIV. (ἠθικοὶ λόγοι), a cento of extracts made by Simeon Metaphrastes.

VIII. Writings Mentioned, but Lost.

A book against the Manichæans (Augustine, c. Julian. i. 16–17). Tillemont (Art. cxlv. p. 303) mentions authors in which lost fragments of St. Basil are to be found, and (Art. cxxxvii. p. 290) refers to the lost Commentary on the Book of Job.

IX. Additional Notes on some Points in St. Basil's Doctrinal and Ecclesiastical Position.

It has been claimed with reason that the doctrinal standpoint of St. Basil is identical with that of the English Church, with the one exception of the veneration of relics and the invocation of saints.[1]

In confirmation of this view, the following points may be noted:

1. *The Holy Eucharist.* The remarkable passage on the spiritual manducation of the elements in Letter VIII. is commented on on p. 118. His custom as to frequent communion and his opinion as to the reserved sacrament are remarked on on p. 179.

A significant passage is to be found in the *Moralia*, Rule XXI., that participation in the Body and Blood of Christ is necessary to eternal life. John vi. 54, is then quoted. That no benefit is derived by him who comes to communion without consideration of the method whereby participation of the Body and Blood of Christ is given; and that he who receives unworthily is condemned. On this John vi. 54 and 62, and 1 Cor. xiii. 27, are quoted. By what method (ποίῳ λόγῳ) we must eat the Body and drink the Blood of the Lord, in remembrance of the Lord's obedience unto death, that they who live may no longer live unto themselves, but to Him who died and rose again for them. In answer, the quotations are Luke xxii. 29, 1 Cor. xi. 23, 2 Cor. v. 14, and 1 Cor. x. 16.

2. *Mariolatry.* Even Letter CCCLX., which bears obvious marks of spuriousness, and of proceeding from a later age, does not go beyond a recognition of the Blessed Virgin as Θεοτόκος, in which the Catholic Church is agreed, and a general invocation of apostles, prophets, and martyrs, the Virgin not being set above these. The argument of Letter CCLXI. (p. 300) that " if the Godbearing flesh was not ordained to be assumed of the lump of Adam, what need was there of the Blessed Virgin?" seems quite inconsistent with the modern doctrine of the Immaculate Conception. Of any cultus of the Virgin, St. Basil's writings shew no trace.

3. *Relations to the Roman Church.*
In order to say something under this head, Ceillier, the Benedictine, is driven to such straits as to quote the application of the term "Coryphæus" to Damasus in Letter CCXXXIX. Certainly St. Basil saw no reason to congratulate the Westerns on their "Coryphæus," so far as intelligent interest in the East was involved. Fialon[2] sees the position more clearly, so far as Basil is concerned, though he assumes the Councils to have given more authority to the patriarch of the ancient capital than was in fact conceded. "*Si Basile ne va pas, comme la majorité du Concile de Constantinople, jusqu'à traiter l'Occident comme étranger; s'il ne pretend pas que l'empire appartienne à l'Orient, parce que l'Orient voit naitre le Soleil, et que c'est en Orient que Dieu brilla dans une enveloppe charnelle,[3] ne voudrait il pas, dans l'ordre religieux, l'union indépendante, qui, depuis Constantin, rattache, dans l'ordre politique, ces deux parties du monde Romain? A ses yeux l'Orient et l'Occident ne sont ils pas deux frères, dont les droit sont égaux, sans suprématie, sans ainesse?*"

In truth Basil appealed to Damasus as Theodoret to Leo, and as Chrysostom to Innocent, not as vassal to liege lord, but as brother to brother. In Basil's case, even the brotherhood was barely recognised, if recognised at all, by the western prelate.

---

[1] *cf.* Dr. Travers Smith, *St. Basil,* p. 125.　　　　　　[2] *Etude Hist.* p. 133.

[3] Ξένον γάρ ἐστιν, ὡς ὁρῶ, νῦν ἡ δύσις,
Καὶ τὸν λογισμὸν, ὡς ἐπαίνετος σκόπει,
Δεῖν γὰρ συνάλλεσθαι ἡλίῳ τὰ πράγματα,
Ἐντεῦθεν ἀρχὴν λαμβάνοντ' ὅθεν Θεὸς
Ἐλαμψεν ἡμῖν σαρκικῷ προβλήματι.　　　Greg. Naz., *Carm.*

X. Editions and Manuscripts.

Among the chief editions and MSS. the following may be mentioned:

The Editio Princeps of the complete extant works of Basil in the original Greek is that which Froben published for Janus Cornarius at Bale in 1551. But Froben had already published in 1532, under the editorship of Erasmus, an edition containing the *De Spiritu Sancto*, the *Hexaemeron*, the *Homilies on the Psalms*, twenty-nine different *Homilies* and some *Letters*.

A Venetian edition, published by Fabius in 1535, comprised the *Moralia*, as well as the dubious book on Virginity, three books against Eunomius, and the tract against the Sabellians, Arians, and Anomœans.

The Greek editions had been preceded by a Latin version at Rome, by Raphael Volateranus in 1515, of which the autograph manuscript is in the British Museum, and by another at Paris in 1525, and by a third Latin edition issued at Cologne in 1531. These were followed by other editions printed at Paris, Antwerp, and Cologne. In 1618 Fronton du Duc, commonly known as Ducæus, published, in conjunction with Frederic Morel, an edition in two folio volumes containing a Latin version as well as the Greek. The edition of the French Dominican Father, Francis Combefis, was published shortly after his death in 1679. The most important step in the direction of accuracy and completeness was taken by Julian Garnier, a Benedictine Father of the Congregation of St. Maur. He revised and corrected the Greek text of earlier editions on the authority of a number of manuscripts in Paris, Italy, and England, and issued the first of his three folio volumes at Paris, at the press of John Baptist Coignard, in 1721. The third volume did not appear till 1730, five years after Garnier's death. In the meanwhile the editorial work had been taken up by Prudent Maran, another Benedictine, to whom are due a careful and voluminous biographical notice, many notes, and a chronological arrangement of the Letters. This was reissued in three 4° volumes in Paris in 1889, and is the basis of the edition published, with additions, by the Abbé Jacques Paul Migne, in the *Patrologia Græca*, in 1857.

An important edition of a separate work is the revised text, with notes and introduction, of the *De Spiritu Sancto*, by the Rev. C. F. H. Johnston, published at the Clarendon Press in 1892.

German translations were published by Count Schweikhard at Ingolstadt in 1591 (Ceillier VI. viii. 8), and by J. von Wendel at Vienna in 1776–78. There have also been issued *Basilius des Grossen auserlesenes Homilien, übersetzt und mit Ammerkungen versehen von J. G. Krabinger*, Landshut, 1839, and *Auserlesene Schriften, übersetzt von Gröne*, Kempten, 1875.

Homilies and Orations were published in Italian in 1711 by Gio. Maria Lucchini. *Omelie Scelte*, translated by A. M. Ricci, were published in Florence in 1732.

Many important extracts are translated into French in the *Histoire Générale des Auteurs Sacrés* of the Benedictine Remy Ceillier (Paris, 1737).

E. Fialon, in his *Ét. Hist.* (1869) has translated the *Hexaemeron;* and in 1889 the *Panégyrique du Martyr Gordius* was published in French by J. Genouille.

A complete account of the bibliography of St. Basil is given in the *Notitia ex Bibliotheca Fabricii* (Ed. Harles, tom. ix. 1804), in Migne's ed. vol. i., *Prolegomena* p. ccxli.

In 1888 a translation of the *De Spiritu Sancto*, by G. Lewis, was included in the Christian Classic Series.

Of all the smaller works a great popularity, as far as popularity can be gauged by the number of editions and translations, has belonged to the *Advice to the Young* and the *Homily on the Forty Martyrs.*

The MSS. collated by the Ben. Edd. for their edition of the *De Spiritu Sancto* are five entitled *Regii*, and a sixth known as *Colbertinus*, now in the national library at Paris. The Ben. *Regius Secundus* (2293) is described by Omont (*Inventaire Sommaire des MSS. Grecs*) as of the Xth c., the *Colbertinus* (4529) and the *Regius Tertius* (2893) as of the XIth c., and the *Regius Primus* (2286), *Regius Quartus* (2896), and *Regius Quintus* (3430) as of the XIVth c.

For his edition, Mr. C. F. H. Johnston also collated or had collated 22,509 Add. MSS., Xth c., in the British Museum; Codd. Misc. xxxvii., XIth c., in the Bodleian Library at Oxford; Cod. Theol. 142, XIIth c., in the Imperial Library at Vienna; Cod. Theol. 18, XIVth c., also at Vienna; Cod. xxiii., XIth c., in the Library of the Holy Synod at Moscow;

500 (Reg. 1824, 3) G, XIth c., at Paris; Cod. lviii., Xth c., at St. Mark's, Venice; Cod. lxvi., XIIth c., also at St. Mark's, Venice; Codd. Regin. Suaecor. 35, XIVth c., in the Vatican at Rome.

For the *Hexaemeron* the Ben. Edd. used eight MSS. styled *Regii*, and numbered respectively 1824, 2286 (originally in the collection of Henry II. at Fontainebleau, the *Regius Primus* of the enumeration for the *De Spiritu Sancto*, but the *Secundus* for that of the *Hexaemeron*), 2287 (1°), 2287 (2°), 2349, 2892, 2896 (the *Regius Quartus* of the *De Spiritu Sancto*), and 2989; two MSS. entitled *Colbertinus*, 3069 and 4721 ; two Coistiniani, 229, IXth c., and 235; and a MS. in the Bodleian, " a doctissimo viro Joanne Wolf collatus."

The sources of the Ben. Ed. of the *Letters* were Coislinianus 237, XIth c., a Codex Harlæanus of the Xth or XIth c., and a Codex Medicæus, Codex Regius 2293, Codex Regius 2897, Codex Regius 2896, Codex Regius 2502, Codex Regius 1824, Codex Regius 1906, and Codex Regius 1908.

The following MSS. of St. Basil are in the library of the Bodleian at Oxford :

Homiliæ et Epistolæ. Codex membranaceus, in 4to majori ff. 250, sec. xii. Epistola ad Optimum, episcopum, in septem ultiones. Cain. fol. iii.
Epistola ad virginem lapsam, fol. 211b.
Ejusdem Basilii epistola ad monachum lapsum, fol. 215b.
Epistolæ canonicæ. Barocciani. xxvi. 285b (*i.e.* pt. 1, p. 36).
Codex membranaceus, in 4to minori, ff. 370, sec. xi. fol. 285b.
Epist canon. Baroc. xxxvi. 121 (*i.e.* pt. 1, p. 147).
Codex membranaceus, in 4to minori, ff. 12 et 161, sec. xii. exeuntis.
Ejusdem epistolæ canonicæ tertiæ prologus, fol. 125b.
CLVIII. 202 (*i.e.* pt. 1, p. 268). Codex chartaceus, in 4to majori, ff. 374, sec. xv.
S. Basilii ad Amphilochium, Iconii episcopum, et alias epistolæ quinque canonicæ, fol. 202.
CLXXXV. 129b (*i.e.* pt. 1, p. 307). Membranaceus, in folio, ff. 83 et 312, sec. xi. exeuntis, bene exaratus et servatus.
S. Basilii magni epistolæ canonicæ, cum scholius nonnullis, fol. 129b.
Ejusdem epistolæ septem aliæ, fol. 141.
Epist. Canon. Baroc. cxcvi. 184b (*i.e.* pt. 1, p. 336). Membranaceus, in 4to majori, ff. 313, sec. xi. anno scilicet 1043 exaratus.
S. Basilii expositio de jejunio quadragesimali, f. 6b.
CCV. 400b (*i.e.* pt. 1, p. 361). Codex chartaceus, in folio, ff. 520, sec. xiv. mutilus et madore corruptus.
Dionysii Alexandrini, Petri Alexandrini, Gregorii Thaumaturgi, Athanasii, Basilii, Gregorii Nysseni, Timothei Alexandrini, Theophili Alexandrini, Cyrilli Alexandrini, et Gennadii epistolæ encyclicæ ; interpretatione Balsamonis illustratæ, fol. 378b.
Epistolæ canonicæ. Laudiani. xxxix. 200 (*i.e.* pt. 1, p. 519). Codex membranaceus in 4to maj. ff. 347, sec. forsan. xi. ineuntis, etc.
S. Basilii Cæsareensis octo, subnexis capitulis duobus ex opere de S. Spiritu, fol. 200.
Seld. xlviii. 151 (*i.e.* pt. 1, p. 611). Codex membranaceus, in 4to ff. 189, sec. xiii. nitide exaratus ; quandam monasterii S. Trinitatis apud Chalcem insulam [ol. 3385].
S. Basilii ad Amphilochium, Diodorum et Gregorium canones, fol. 151.
Misc. clxx. 181, 263, 284b (*i.e.* pt. 1, p. 717). Codex membranaceus, in 4to majori, ff. 363, secc. si tabulam sec. xi. excipiamus, xiv. et xv.; initio et fine mutilus. Rawl. Auct. G. 158.
S. Basilii, archiep. Cæsareensis, ad Amphilochium epistolæ tres canonicæ, fol. 181.
S. Basilii epistolæ duæ, scilicet, ad chorepiscopos, ad episcopos sibi subjectos, cum excerptis duobus ex capp. xxvii. et xxix. ad Amphilochium de S. Spiritu, fol. 263.
S. Basilii epistolæ duæ, ad Diodorum et ad Gregorium, fol. 284b.
Epist. Canon. misc. ccvi. 171 (*i.e.* pt. 1, p. 763). Codex membranaceus, in folio minori, ff. 242. sec. forsan xi. exeuntis ; bene exaratus et servatus. Meerm. Auct. T. 2. 6.
S. Basilii, archiep. Cæsareensis, ad Amphilochium ep. Icon. epistolæ tres canonicæ cum scholiis hic illic margini adpositis, fol. 171.

Epistolæ cccxxxiv. Misc. xxxviii. 1 (*i.e.* pt. 1, p. 642). Codex chartaceus, in folio, ff. 196, sec. xvi. anno 1547 scriptus [ol. 3091]. Auct. E. 2. 10.

S. Basilii epistolæ, ut e numeris marginalibus apparet, cccxxxiv. fol. 1.

Ult. est ad eundem Eusebium, et exstat in ed. cit. tom. iii. p. 257.

Epistola ccxlv. Baroc cxxi. [*i.e.* pt. 1, p. 199]. Membranaceus, in 4to ff. 226, sec. xii. exeuntis, bene exaratus; in calce mutilus.

S. Basilii, archiepiscopi Cæsareensis, epistolæ ad diversos, numero ducentæ quadraginta quinque.

Epist. clxxvii. Roc. xviii. 314 (*i.e.* pt. 1, p. 471). Codex chartaceus, in folio, ff. 475, hodie in duo volumina distinctus, anno 1349 manu Constantini Sapientis binis columnis scriptus; olim ecclesiæ S. Trinitatis apud insulam Chalcem [ol. 264].

S. Basilii Cæsareensis epistolæ circiter centum septuaginta septem, fol. 314.

Epistolæ variæ. Baroc. lvi. 28b et passim (*i.e.* pt. 1, p. 83). Codex bombycinus, ff. 175, sec. xiv. exeuntis; initio mutilus, et madore corruptus.

S. Basilii adversus Eunomium epistola, fol. 28b.

Epist. xiii. ad diversos. Baroc. ccxxviii 118b (*i.e.* pt. 1, p. 393). Membranaceus, in folio, ff. 206, sec. forsan xii. ineuntis; foliis aliquot chartaceis a manu recentiori hic illic suppletis. S. Basilii et Libanii epistolæ septem mutuæ, f. 126.

Ibid. epp. 341, 342, 337–340, 356.

Epist. tres. Misc. clxxix. 423 (*i.e.* pt. 1, p. 724). Codex chartaceus, in folio marjori, ff. 262, sec. xvii.; olim peculium coll. soc. Jesu Clarom. Paris, postea Joh. Meerman. Auct. T. 1. 1.

S. Basilii, archiep. Cæsareensis, epistola ad Optimum episcopum in illud, πᾶς ὁ ἀποκτείνας καίν, p. 423.

Epistola ad Chilonem. Laud. xvii. 352 (*i.e.* pt. 1, p. 500). Codex chartaceus, et lævigatus, in 4° ff. 358, sec. xv. [ol. 692].

S. Basilii Magni epistola ad Chilonem, fol. 352.

Epist. ad Coloneos. Baroc. cxlii. 264b (*i.e.* pt 1, p. 242). Codex chartaceus, in 4° ff. 292, sec. xiv. ineuntis.

S. Basilii Magni epistola ad Coloneos, fol. 264b.

Ejus et Libanii epistolæ. Baroc. xix. 191 (*i.e.* pt. 1, p. 27). Codex chartaceus in 4° minori, ff. 200, sec. xv. manibus tamen diversis scriptus.

S. Basilii et Libanii sophistæ epistolæ decem amœbœæ, fol. 191.

Ejus et Libanii epistolæ. Baroc. cxxxi. 296 (*i.e.* pt. 1, p. 211). Codex bombycinus, in 4° maj. ff. 4 et 536, sec. xiv. haud eadem manu scriptus; madore aliquantum corruptus.

S. Basilii et Libanii epistolæ tres mutuæ, f. 299b.

Epistolæ ad Libanium et Modestum. Baroc. ccxvi. 301 (*i.e.* pt. 1, p. 376). Codex, fragmentis constans pluribus, in 4° ff. 379 quorum 43 priora membranacea, cætera chartacea sunt.

S. Basilii epistola ad Libanium, fol. 301b.

Ejusdem ad Modestum epistola, imperf. fol. 301b.

Basilii et Libanii epistolæ quinque mutuæ, fol. 302.

Ibid. epp. cccxxxv. seq., cccxlii., ccxli., ccclix.

The following MSS. of St. Basil are in the British Museum:

Harleian Collection:

1801. Codex membranaceus (Newton's arms in spare leaf). Doctrina Beati Basilii.

2580. Liber chartaceus. S. Basilii sermo de parentum honore, Latine redditus per Guarinum.

2678. Codex membranaceus. S. Basilii de institutis juvenum liber ex versione et cum præfatione Leonardi Aretini.

5576.	XIVth c.	40 Homilies.
5639.	XVth c.	Homilies.
5576.	XIVth c.	Hexaemeron.
5622.	XIVth c.	Com. on Isaiah.
5541.	XVth c.	Ad juvenes.
5609.	XVth c.	"
5660.	XVth c.	"
5657.	XIVth c.	Extracts.

5689.   XIIth c.   De V. Virg.
5624.   XIVth c.   Ep. ad Greg. Frat.
6827.   XVIIth c. Epp.
3651.   XVth c.   De Cons. in Adv.
4987.   XVth c.   Admon.

Burney Collection :
  70.   XVth c.   Ad juvenes.
  75.   XVth c.   Epp. ad Liban.

Additional :
22509.   Vellum curs. Xth c.   De Sp. Scto.
34060.   XVth c.   The doubtful work De Sp. Scto.
14066.   XIIth c.   Homilies.
34060.   XVth c.   Against Drunkards.
25881.   XVIth c.   The Forty Martyrs.
10014.   XVIIth c. Ad juvenes.
10069.   XIIth c.   Reg. fus. tract.
 9347.   XIVth c.   Ascetic.
18492.   XVIth c.   De Frugalitate.
17474.   XVth c.   Epp. can.
23771.   c. 1500.   Sermones Tractatus.
         Autograph of Raph. Volterrano (translation).

Arundel :
 535.   XIVth c.   Excerp. ex adv. Eunom. v.
 532.   Xth c.   Hexaemeron.
 528.   XVth c.   Against Drunkards.
 520.   XVth c.   De tranqu. an.
 583.   XIVth c.   Epp. can. ad Amph.
 181.   XIIth c.   Adm. ad Fil.

ΤΟΥ ΑΓΙΟΥ ΒΑCΙΛΕΙΟΥ ΠΕΡΙ ΤΟΥ ΠΝΕΥΜΑΤΟC ΒΙΒΛΙΟΝ.

THE BOOK OF SAINT BASIL ON THE SPIRIT.

DE SPIRITU SANCTO.

PREFACE.

THE heresy of Arius lowered the dignity of the Holy Ghost as well as that of the Son. He taught that the Three Persons of the Holy Trinity are wholly unlike one another both in essence and in glory. " There is a triad, not in equal glories ; " "one more glorious than the other in their glories to an infinite degree." So says the *Thalia*, quoted in Ath. de Syn. § 15. But the Nicene definition, while it was precise in regard to the Son, left the doctrine of the Holy Ghost comparatively open, (Πιστεύομεν εἰς τὸ Ἅγιον Πνεῦμα,) not from hesitation or doubt, but because this side of Arian speculation was not prominent. (*Cf.* Basil, Letters cxxv. and ccxxvi. and Dr. Swete in D.C.B. iii. 121.) It was the expulsion of Macedonius from the see of Constantinople in 360 which brought " Macedonianism" to a head. He was put there by Arians as an Arian. Theodoret (Ecc. Hist. ii. 5) explains how disagreement arose. He was an upholder, if not the author, of the watchword ὁμοιούσιον (Soc. ii. 45), but many supporters of the ὁμοιούσιον (*e.g.*, Eustathius of Sebasteia) shrank from calling the Holy Ghost a creature. So the Pneumatomachi began to be clearly marked off. The various creeds of the Arians and semi-Arians did not directly attack the Godhead of the Holy Ghost, though they did not accept the doctrine of the essential unity of the Three Persons. (*Cf.* Hahn, *Bibliothek der Symbole*, pp. 148–174, quoted by Swete.) But their individual teaching went far beyond their confessions. The Catholic theologians were roused to the danger, and on the return of Athanasius from his third exile, a council was held at Alexandria which resulted in the first formal ecclesiastical condemnation of the depravers of the Holy Ghost, in the *Tomus ad Antiochenos* (*q.v.* with the preface on p. 481 of Ath. in the edition of this series. *Cf.* also Ath. ad Serap. i. 2, 10). In the next ten years the Pneumatomachi, Macedonians, or Marathonians, so called from Marathonius, bishop of Nicomedia, whose support to the party was perhaps rather pecuniary than intellectual (Nicephorus H.E. ix. 47), made head, and were largely identified with the Homoiousians. In 374 was published the *Ancoratus* of St. Epiphanius, bishop of Salamis in Cyprus, written in 373, and containing two creeds (*vide* Heurtley de F. et Symb. pp. 14–18), the former of which is nearly identical with the Confession of Constantinople. It expresses belief in τὸ Πνεῦμα τὸ Ἅγιον, Κύριον, καὶ Ζωοποιόν, τὸ ἐκ τοῦ Πατρὸς ἐκπορευόμενον, τὸ σὺν Πατρὶ καὶ Υἱῷ συμπροσκυνοίμενον καὶ συνδοξαζόμενον, τὸ λαλῆσαν διὰ τῶν προφητῶν. It is in this same year, 374, that Amphilochius, the first cousin of Gregory of Nazianzus and friend and spiritual son of Basil, paid the first of his annual autumn visits to Cæsarea (Bishop Lightfoot, D.C.B. i. 105) and there urged St. Basil to clear up all doubt as to the true doctrine of the Holy Spirit by writing a treatise on the subject. St. Basil complied, and, on the completion of the work, had it engrossed on parchment (Letter ccxxxi.) and sent it to Amphilochius, to whom he dedicated it.

CHAPTER I.

Prefatory remarks on the need of exact investigation of the most minute portions of theology.

1. YOUR desire for information, my right well-beloved and most deeply respected brother Amphilochius, I highly commend, and not less your industrious energy. I have been exceedingly delighted at the care and watchfulness shewn in the expression of your opinion that of all the terms concerning God in every mode of speech, not one ought to be left without exact investigation. You have turned to good account your reading of the exhortation of the Lord, " Every one that asketh receiveth, and he that seeketh findeth," [1] and by your diligence in asking might, I ween, stir even the most reluctant to give you a share of what they possess. And this in you yet further moves my admiration, that you do not, according to the manners of the most part of the men of our time, propose your questions by way of mere test, but with the honest desire to arrive at the actual truth. There is no lack in these days of captious listeners and questioners; but to find a character desirous of information, and seeking the truth as a remedy for ignorance, is very difficult. Just as in the hunter's snare, or in the soldier's ambush, the trick is generally ingeniously concealed, so it is with the inquiries of the majority of the questioners who advance arguments, not so much with the view of getting any good out of them, as in order that, in the event of their failing to elicit answers which chime in with their own desires, they may seem to have fair ground for controversy.

2. If " To the fool on his asking for wisdom, wisdom shall be reckoned," [2] at how high a price shall we value " the wise hearer" who is quoted by the Prophet in the same verse with " the admirable counsellor"? [3] It is right, I ween, to hold him worthy of all approbation, and to urge him on to further progress, sharing his enthusiasm, and in all things toiling at his side as he presses onwards to perfection. To count the terms used in theology as of primary importance, and to endeavour to trace out the hidden meaning in every phrase and in every syllable, is a characteristic wanting in those who are idle in the pursuit of true religion, but distinguishing all who get knowledge of " the mark " " of our calling;" [4] for what is set before us is, so far as is possible with human nature, to be made like unto God. Now without knowledge there can be no making like; and knowledge is not got without lessons. The beginning of teaching is speech, and syllables and words are parts of speech. It follows then that to investigate syllables is not to shoot wide of the mark, nor, because the questions raised are what might seem to some insignificant, are they on that account to be held unworthy of heed. Truth is always a quarry hard to hunt, and therefore we must look everywhere for its tracks. The acquisition of true religion is just like that of crafts; both grow bit by bit; apprentices must despise nothing. If a man despise the first elements as small and insignificant, he will never reach the perfection of wisdom.

Yea and Nay are but two syllables, yet there is often involved in these little words at once the best of all good things, Truth, and that beyond which wickedness cannot go, a Lie. But why mention Yea and Nay? Before now, a martyr bearing witness for Christ has been judged to have paid in full the claim of true religion by merely nodding his head.[1] If, then, this be so, what term in theology is so small but that the effect of its weight in the scales according as it be rightly or wrongly used is not great? Of the law we are told " not one jot nor one tittle shall pass away ; " [2] how then could it be safe for us to leave even the least unnoticed? The very points which you yourself have sought to have thoroughly sifted by us are at the same time both small and great. Their use is the matter of a moment, and peradventure they are therefore made of small account; but, when we reckon the force of their meaning, they are great. They may be likened to the mustard plant which, though it be the least of shrubseeds, yet when properly cultivated and the forces latent in its germs unfolded, rises to its own sufficient height.

If any one laughs when he sees our subtilty, to use the Psalmist's [3] words, about syllables, let him know that he reaps laughter's fruitless fruit; and let us, neither giving in to men's reproaches, nor yet vanquished

---

[1] *i.e.,* confessed or denied himself a Christian. The Benedictine Editors and their followers seem to have missed the force of the original, both grammatically and historically, in referring it to the time when St. Basil is writing; ἤδη ἐκρίθη does not mean " at the present day is judged," but " ere now has been judged." And in A.D. 374 there was no persecution of Christians such as seems to be referred to, although Valens tried to crush the Catholics.
[2] Matt. v. 18.
[3] Ps. cxix. 85, lxx. " The lawless have described subtilties for me, but not according to thy law, O Lord;" for A.V. & R.V., " The proud have digged pits for me which are not after thy law." The word ἀδολεσχία is used in a bad sense to mean garrulity; in a good sense, keenness, subtilty.

---

[1] Luke xi. 10.
[2] Prov. xvii. 28, lxx.
[3] Is. iii. 3, lxx.
[4] Phil. iii. 14.

by their disparagement, continue our investigation. So far, indeed, am I from feeling ashamed of these things because they are small, that, even if I could attain to ever so minute a fraction of their dignity, I should both congratulate myself on having won high honour, and should tell my brother and fellow-investigator that no small gain had accrued to him therefrom.

While, then, I am aware that the controversy contained in little words is a very great one, in hope of the prize I do not shrink from toil, with the conviction that the discussion will both prove profitable to myself, and that my hearers will be rewarded with no small benefit. Wherefore now with the help, if I may so say, of the Holy Spirit Himself, I will approach the exposition of the subject, and, if you will, that I may be put in the way of the discussion, I will for a moment revert to the origin of the question before us.

3. Lately when praying with the people, and using the full doxology to God the Father in both forms, at one time " *with* the Son *together with* the Holy Ghost," and at another " *through* the Son *in* the Holy Ghost," I was attacked by some of those present on the ground that I was introducing novel and at the same time mutually contradictory terms.[1]

You, however, chiefly with the view of benefiting them, or, if they are wholly incurable, for the security of such as may fall in with them, have expressed the opinion that some clear instruction ought to be published concerning the force underlying the syllables employed. I will therefore write as concisely as possible, in the endeavour to lay down some admitted principle for the discussion.

CHAPTER II.

The origin of the heretics' close observation of syllables.

4. The petty exactitude of these men about syllables and words is not, as might be supposed, simple and straightforward; nor is the mischief to which it tends a small one. There is involved a deep and covert design against true religion. Their pertinacious contention is to show that the mention

---

[1] It is impossible to convey in English the precise force of the prepositions used. " *With* " represents μετά, of which the original meaning is " amid; " " *together* with," σύν, of which the original meaning is " at the same time as." The Latin of the Benedictine edition translates the first by " *cum*," and the second by " *una cum*." " *Through* " stands for διά, which, with the genitive, is used of the instrument; " *in* " for ἐν, " *in*," but also commonly used of the instrument or means. In the well known passage in 1 Cor. viii. 6, A.V. renders δι' οὖ τὰ πάντα by " *through* whom are all things; " R.V., by " *by* whom."

of Father, Son, and Holy Ghost is unlike, as though they will thence find it easy to demonstrate that there is a variation in nature. They have an old sophism, invented by Aetius, the champion of this heresy, in one of whose Letters there is a passage to the effect that things naturally unlike are expressed in unlike terms, and, conversely, that things expressed in unlike terms are naturally unlike. In proof of this statement he drags in the words of the Apostle, " One God and Father OF whom are all things, . . . and one Lord Jesus Christ BY whom are all things." [1] " Whatever, then," he goes on, " is the relation of these terms to one another, such will be the relation of the natures indicated by them; and as the term ' of whom ' is unlike the term ' by whom,' so is the Father unlike the Son." [2] On this heresy depends the idle subtilty of these men about the phrases in question. They accordingly assign to God the Father, as though it were His distinctive portion and lot, the phrase " of Whom ; " to God the Son they confine the phrase " by Whom ; " to the Holy Spirit that of " in Whom," and say that this use of the syllables is never in-

---

[1] 1. Cor. viii. 6.

[2] The story as told by Theodoret (Ecc. Hist. ii. 23) is as follows : " Constantius, on his return from the west, passed some time at Constantinople " (*i.e.*, in 360, when the synod at Constantinople was held, shortly after that of the Isaurian Seleucia, " substance " and " hypostasis " being declared inadmissible terms, and the Son pronounced like the Father according to the Scriptures). The Emperor was urged that " Eudoxius should be convicted of blasphemy and lawlessness. Constantius however . . . replied that a decision must first be come to on matters concerning the faith, and that afterwards the case of Eudoxius should be enquired into. Basilius (of Ancyra), relying on his former intimacy, ventured boldly to object to the Emperor that he was attacking the apostolic decrees; but Constantius took this ill, and told Basilius to hold his tongue, for to you, said he, the disturbance of the churches is due. When Basilius was silenced, Eustathius (of Sebasteia) intervened and said, Since, sir, you wish a decision to be come to on what concerns the faith, consider the blasphemies uttered against the Only Begotten by Eudoxius; and, as he spoke, he produced the exposition of faith, wherein, besides many other impieties, were found the following expressions : Things that are spoken of in unlike terms are unlike in substance; there is one God the Father of Whom are all things, and one Lord Jesus Christ by Whom are all things. Now the term ' of Whom ' is unlike the term ' by Whom ; ' so the Son is unlike God the Father. Constantius ordered this exposition of the faith to be read, and was displeased with the blasphemy which it involved. He therefore asked Eudoxius if he had drawn it up. Eudoxius instantly repudiated the authorship, and said that it was written by Aetius. Now Aetius . . . at the present time was associated with Eunomius and Eudoxius, and, as he found Eudoxius to be, like himself, a sybarite in luxury as well as a heretic in faith, he chose Antioch as the most congenial place of abode, and both he and Eunomius were fast fixtures at the couches of Eudoxius. . . . The Emperor had been told all this, and now ordered Aetius to be brought before him. On his appearance, Constantius shewed him the document in question, and proceeded to enquire if he was the author of its language. Aetius, totally ignorant of what had taken place, and unaware of the drift of the enquiry, expected that he should win praise by confession, and owned that he was the author of the phrases in question. Then the Emperor perceived the greatness of his iniquity, and forthwith condemned him to exile and to be deported to a place in Phrygia." St. Basil accompanied Eustathius and his namesake to Constantinople on this occasion, being then only in deacon's orders. (Philost. iv. 12.) Basil of Ancyra and Eustathius in their turn suffered banishment. Basil, the deacon, returned to the Cappadocian Cæsarea.

terchanged, in order that, as I have already said, the variation of language may indicate the variation of nature.[1] Verily it is sufficiently obvious that in their quibbling about the words they are endeavouring to maintain the force of their impious argument.

By the term " *of* whom " they wish to indicate the Creator ; by the term " *through* whom," the subordinate agent[2] or instrument ;[3] by the term " *in* whom," or " *in* which," they mean to shew the time or place. The object of all this is that the Creator of the universe[4] may be regarded as of no higher dignity than an instrument, and that the Holy Spirit may appear to be adding to existing things nothing more than the contribution derived from place or time.

CHAPTER III.

5. The systematic discussion of syllables is derived from heathen philosophy.

THEY have, however, been led into this error by their close study of heathen writers, who have respectively applied the terms " *of* whom " and " *through* whom " to things which are by nature distinct. These writers suppose that by the term " *of* whom " or " *of* which " the matter is indicated, while the term " *through* whom " or " *through* which "[5] represents the instrument, or, generally speaking, subordinate agency.[6] Or rather — for there seems no reason why we

---

[1] *cf.* the form of the Arian Creed as given by Eunomius in his Ἀπολογία (Migne, xxx. 840. "We believe in one God, Father Almighty, of whom are all things; and in one only begotten Son of God, God the word, our Lord Jesus Christ, through whom are all things ; and in one Holy Ghost, the Comforter, in whom distribution of all grace in proportion as may be most expedient is made to each of the Saints."

[2] *cf.* Eunomius, Liber. Apol. § 27, where of the Son he says ὑπουργός.

[3] On the word ὄργανον, a tool, as used of the Word of God, *cf.* Nestorius in Marius Merc. Migne, p. 761 & Cyr. Alex. Ep. 1. Migne, x. 37. "The creature did not give birth to the uncreated, but gave birth to man, organ of Godhead." *cf.* Thomasius, Christ. Dog. i. 336.
    Mr. Johnston quotes Philo (de Cher. § 35; i. 162, n.) as speaking of ὄργανον δὲ λόγον Θεοῦ δι' οὗ κατεσκευάσθη (sc. ὁ κόσμος).

[4] Here of course the Son is meant.

[5] The ambiguity of gender in ἐξ οὗ and δι' οὗ can only be expressed by giving the alternatives in English.

[6] There are four causes or varieties of cause.
1. The essence or quiddity (Form) : τὸ τί ἦν εἶναι.
2. The necessitating conditions (Matter) : τὸ τίνων ὄντων ἀνάγκη τοῦτ' εἶναι.
3. The proximate mover or stimulator of change (Efficient) : ἡ τί πρῶτον ἐκίνησε.
4. That for the sake of which (Final Cause or End) : τὸ τίνος ἕνεκα. Grote's *Aristotle*, i. 354.
    The four Aristotelian causes are thus : 1. Formal. 2. Material. 3. Efficient. 4. Final. *cf.* Arist. Analyt. Post. II. xi., Metaph. I. iii., and Phys. II. iii. The six causes of Basil may be referred to the four of Aristotle as follows :

Aristotle.	Basil.
1. τὸ τί ἦν εἶναι.	καθ' ὅ : *i.e.*, the form or idea *according to which* a thing is made.
2. τὸ ἐξ οὗ γίνεταί τι.	ἐξ οὗ : *i.e.*, the matter *out of which* it is made.
3. ἡ ἀρχὴ τῆς μεταβολῆς ἡ πρώτη.	ὑφ' οὗ : *i.e.*, the agent, using means. δι' οὗ : *i.e.*, the means.
4. τὸ οὗ ἕνεκα.	δι' ὅ : *i.e.*, the end. ἐν ᾧ, or *sine quâ non*, applying to all.

---

should not take up their whole argument, and briefly expose at once its incompatibility with the truth and its inconsistency with their own teaching — the students of vain philosophy, while expounding the manifold nature of cause and distinguishing its peculiar significations, define some causes as principal,[1] some as coöperative or con-causal, while others are of the character of " *sine qua non*," or indispensable.[2]

For every one of these they have a distinct and peculiar use of terms, so that the maker is indicated in a different way from the instrument. For the maker they think the proper expression is " *by* whom," maintaining that the bench is produced " *by* " the carpenter ; and for the instrument " *through* which," in that it is produced " through " or by means of adze and gimlet and the rest. Similarly they appropriate " *of* which " to the material, in that the thing made is " of" wood, while " according to which " shews the design, or pattern put before the craftsman. For he either first makes a mental sketch, and so brings his fancy to bear upon what he is about, or else he looks at a pattern previously put before him, and arranges his work accordingly. The phrase " *on account of* which " they wish to be confined to the end or purpose, the bench, as they say, being produced for, or on account of, the use of man. " *In* which " is supposed to indicate time and place. When was it produced? In this time. And where? In this place. And though place and time contribute nothing to what is being produced, yet without these the production of anything is impossible, for efficient agents must have both place and time. It is these careful distinctions, derived from unpractical philosophy and vain delusion,[3] which our opponents have first studied and admired, and then transferred to the simple and unsophisticated doctrine of the Spirit, to the belittling of God the Word, and the setting at naught of the Divine Spirit. Even the phrase set apart by non-Christian writers for the case of lifeless instruments[4] or of manual

---

[1] προκαταρκτική. *cf.* Plut. 2, 1056. B.D. προκαταρκτικὴ αἰτία ἡ εἱμαρμένη.

[2] *cf.* Clem. Alex. Strom. viii. 9. "Of causes some are principal, some preservative, some coöperative, some indispensable; *e.g.*, of education the principal cause is the father ; the preservative, the schoolmaster ; the coöperative, the disposition of the pupil ; the indispensable, time."

[3] ἐκ τῆς ματαιότητος καὶ κενῆς ἀπάτης.
    cf. ματαιότης ματαιοτήτων, "vanity of vanities," Ecc. i. 2, lxx. In Arist. Eth. i. 2, a desire is said to be κενὴ καὶ ματαία, which goes into infinity, — everything being desired for the sake of something else, — *i e.*, κενή, void, like a desire for the moon, and ματαία, unpractical, like a desire for the empire of China. In the text ματαιότης seems to mean heathen philosophy, a vain delusion as distinguished from Christian philosophy.

[4] ἄψυχα ὄργανα. A slave, according to Aristotle, Eth. Nich. viii. 7, 6, is ἔμψυχον ὄργανον.

service of the meanest kind, I mean the expression "*through* or *by means of* which," they do not shrink from transferring to the Lord of all, and Christians feel no shame in applying to the Creator of the universe language belonging to a hammer or a saw.

CHAPTER IV.

That there is no distinction in the scriptural use of these syllables.

6. WE acknowledge that the word of truth has in many places made use of these expressions; yet we absolutely deny that the freedom of the Spirit is in bondage to the pettiness of Paganism. On the contrary, we maintain that Scripture varies its expressions as occasion requires, according to the circumstances of the case. For instance, the phrase "*of* which" does not always and absolutely, as they suppose, indicate the material,[1] but it is more in accordance with the usage of Scripture to apply this term in the case of the Supreme Cause, as in the words "One God, of whom are all things,"[2] and again, "All things of God."[3] The word of truth has, however, frequently used this term in the case of the material, as when it says "Thou shalt make an ark of incorruptible wood;"[4] and "Thou shalt make the candlestick of pure gold;"[5] and "The first man is of the earth, earthy;"[6] and "Thou art formed out of clay as I am."[7] But these men, to the end, as we have already remarked, that they may establish the difference of nature, have laid down the law that this phrase befits the Father alone. This distinction they have originally derived from heathen authorities, but here they have shewn no faithful accuracy of imitation. To the Son they have in conformity with the teaching of their masters given the title of instrument, and to the Spirit that of place, for they say *in* the Spirit, and *through* the Son. But when they apply "of whom" to God they no longer follow heathen example,

but go over, as they say, to apostolic usage, as it is said, "But of him are ye in Christ Jesus,"[1] and "All things of God."[2] What, then, is the result of this systematic discussion? There is one nature of Cause; another of Instrument; another of Place. So the Son is by nature distinct from the Father, as the tool from the craftsman; and the Spirit is distinct in so far as place or time is distinguished from the nature of tools or from that of them that handle them.

CHAPTER V.

That "through whom" is said also in the case of the Father, and "of whom" in the case of the Son and of the Spirit.

7. AFTER thus describing the outcome of our adversaries' arguments, we shall now proceed to shew, as we have proposed, that the Father does not first take "of whom" and then abandon "through whom" to the Son; and that there is no truth in these men's ruling that the Son refuses to admit the Holy Spirit to a share in "of whom" or in "through whom," according to the limitation of their new-fangled allotment of phrases. "There is one God and Father of whom are all things, and one Lord Jesus Christ through whom are all things."[3]

Yes; but these are the words of a writer not laying down a rule, but carefully distinguishing the hypostases.[4]

The object of the apostle in thus writing was not to introduce the diversity of nature, but to exhibit the notion of Father and of Son as unconfounded. That the phrases are not opposed to one another and do not, like squadrons in war marshalled one against another, bring the natures to which they are applied into mutual conflict, is perfectly plain from the passage in question. The blessed Paul brings both phrases to bear upon one and the same subject, in the words "of him and through him and to him are all things."[5] That this plainly refers to the Lord will be admitted even by a reader paying but small attention to the meaning of the words. The apostle has just quoted from the prophecy of Isaiah, "Who hath known the mind of the Lord, or who hath

---

[1] ὕλη = Lat. *materies*, from the same root as *mater*, whence Eng. *material* and *matter*. (ὕλη, ὕλϜα, is the same word as *sylva* = wood. With *materies* cf. Madeira, from the Portuguese "*madera*" = timber.)
"The word ὕλη in Plato bears the same signification as in ordinary speech: it means wood, timber, and sometimes generally material. The later philosophic application of the word to signify the abstract conception of material substratum is expressed by Plato, so far as he has that concept at all, in other ways." Ed. Zeller. *Plato and the older Academy*, ii. 296. Similarly Basil uses ὕλη. As a technical philosophic term for abstract matter, it is first used by Aristotle.
[2] 1 Cor. viii. 6.   [3] 1 Cor. xi. 12.
[4] Ex. xxv. 10, lxx. A.V. "shittim." R.V. "acacia." St. Ambrose (*de Spiritu Sancto*, ii. 9) seems, say the Benedictine Editors, to have here misunderstood St. Basil's argument. St. Basil is accusing the Pneumatomachi not of tracing all things to God as the material "of which," but of unduly limiting the use of the term "of which" to the Father alone
[5] Ex. xxv. 31.   [6] 1 Cor. xv. 47.   [7] Job xxxiii. 6, lxx.

[1] 1 Cor. i. 30.   [2] 1 Cor. xi. 12.   [3] 1 Cor. viii. 6.
[4] If Catholic Theology does not owe to St. Basil the distinction between the connotations of οὐσία and ὑπόστασις which soon prevailed over the identification obtaining at the time of the Nicene Council, at all events his is the first and most famous assertion and defence of it. At Nicæa, in 325, to have spoken of St. Paul as "distinguishing the hypostases" would have been held impious. Some forty-five years later St. Basil writes to his brother, Gregory of Nyssa (Ep. xxxviii.), in fear lest Gregory should fall into the error of failing to distinguish between hypostasis and ousia, between person and essence. cf. Theodoret Dial. i. 7, and my note on his Ecc. Hist. i. 3.
[5] Rom. xi. 36.

been his counsellor,[1] and then goes on, "For of him and from him and to him are all things." That the prophet is speaking about God the Word, the Maker of all creation, may be learnt from what immediately precedes: "Who hath measured the waters in the hollow of his hand, and meted out heaven with the span, and comprehended the dust of the earth in a measure, and weighed the mountains in scales, and the hills in a balance? Who hath directed the Spirit of the Lord, or being his counsellor hath taught him?"[2] Now the word "who" in this passage does not mean absolute impossibility, but rarity, as in the passage "Who will rise up for me against the evil doers?"[3] and "What man is he that desireth life?"[4] and "Who shall ascend into the hill of the Lord?"[5] So is it in the passage in question, "Who hath directed [lxx., known] the Spirit of the Lord, or being his counsellor hath known him?" "For the Father loveth the Son and sheweth him all things."[6] This is He who holds the earth, and hath grasped it with His hand, who brought all things to order and adornment, who poised[7] the hills in their places, and measured the waters, and gave to all things in the universe their proper rank, who encompasseth the whole of heaven with but a small portion of His power, which, in a figure, the prophet calls a span. Well then did the apostle add "Of him and through him and to him are all things."[8] For of Him, to all things that are, comes the cause of their being, according to the will of God the Father. Through Him all things have their continuance[9] and constitution,[10] for He created all things, and metes out to each severally what is necessary for its health and preservation. Wherefore to Him all things are turned, looking with irresistible longing and unspeakable affection to "the author"[11] and maintainer "of" their "life," as it is written "The eyes of all wait upon thee,"[12] and again, "These wait all upon thee,"[13] and "Thou openest thine hand, and satisfiest the desire of every living thing."[14]

8. But if our adversaries oppose this our interpretation, what argument will save them from being caught in their own trap?

For if they will not grant that the three expressions "of him" and "through him" and "to him" are spoken of the Lord, they cannot but be applied to God the Father. Then without question their rule will fall through, for we find not only "of whom," but also "through whom" applied to the Father. And if this latter phrase indicates nothing derogatory, why in the world should it be confined, as though conveying the sense of inferiority, to the Son? If it always and everywhere implies ministry, let them tell us to what superior the God of glory[1] and Father of the Christ is subordinate.

They are thus overthrown by their own selves, while our position will be on both sides made sure. Suppose it proved that the passage refers to the Son, "of whom" will be found applicable to the Son. Suppose on the other hand it be insisted that the prophet's words relate to God, then it will be granted that "through whom" is properly used of God, and both phrases have equal value, in that both are used with equal force of God. Under either alternative both terms, being employed of one and the same Person, will be shewn to be equivalent. But let us revert to our subject.

9. In his Epistle to the Ephesians the apostle says, "But speaking the truth in love, may grow up into him in all things, which is the head, even Christ; from whom the whole body fitly joined together and compacted by that which every joint supplieth, according to the effectual working in the measure of every part, maketh increase of the body."[2] And again in the Epistle to the Colossians, to them that have not the knowledge of the Only Begotten, there is mention of him that holdeth "the head," that is, Christ, "from which all the body by joints and bands having nourishment ministered increaseth with the increase of God."[3] And that Christ is the head of the Church we have learned in another passage, when the apostle says "gave him to be the head over all things to the Church,"[4] and "of his fulness have all we received."[5] And the Lord Himself says "He shall take of mine, and shall shew it unto you."[6] In a word, the diligent reader will perceive that "of whom" is used in diverse manners.[7] For instance, the Lord says, "I perceive that virtue is gone out of me."[8] Similarly we have frequently observed "of whom" used of the Spirit. "He that soweth to the spirit," it is said,

1 Rom. xi. 34, and Is. xl. 13.
2 Is. xl. 12, 13.
3 Ps. xciv. 16.
4 Ps. xxxiv. 12.
5 Ps. xxiv 3.
6 John v. 20.
7 ἰσορροπία. cf. Plat. Phæd. 109, A.
8 Rom. xi. 3S.
9 διαμονή. cf. Arist. de Sp. i. 1.
10 cf. Col. i. 16, 17.
11 Acts iii. 15.
12 Ps. cxlv. 15.
13 Ps. civ. 27.
14 Ps. cxlv. 16.

1 Ps. xxix. 3; Acts vii. 2.
2 Eph. iv. 15, 16.
3 Col. ii. 19.
4 Eph. i. 22.
t John i. 16.
6 1 John xvi. 15.
7 πολύτροποι. cf. the cognate adverb in Heb. i. 1.
8 "ἐξ ἐμοῦ." The reading in St. Luke (viii. 46) is ἀπ' ἐμοῦ. In the parallel passage, Mark v. 30, the words are, "Jesus knowing in himself that virtue had gone out of him," ἐξ αὐτοῦ which D. inserts in Luke viii. 45.

" shall of the spirit reap life everlasting." [1] John too .writes, " Hereby we know that he abideth in us by (ἐκ) the spirit which he hath given us." [2] " That which is conceived in her," says the angel, " is of the Holy Ghost," [3] and the Lord says " that which is born of the spirit is spirit." [4] Such then is the case so far.

10. It must now be pointed out that the phrase " through whom " is admitted by Scripture in the case of the Father and of the Son and of the Holy Ghost alike. It would indeed be tedious to bring forward evidence of this in the case of the Son, not only because it is perfectly well known, but because this very point is made by our opponents. We now show that " through whom " is used also in the case of the Father. " God is faithful," it is said, " by whom (δι' οὖ) ye were called unto the fellowship of his Son," [5] and " Paul an apostle of Jesus Christ by (διά) the will of God ; " and again, " Wherefore thou art no more a servant, but a son; and if a son, then an heir through God." [6] And " like as Christ was raised up from the dead by (διά) the glory of God the Father." [7] Isaiah, moreover, says, " Woe unto them that make deep counsel and not through the Lord ; " [8] and many proofs of the use of this phrase in the case of the Spirit might be adduced. " God hath revealed him to us," it is said, " by (διά) the spirit ; " [9] and in another place, " That good thing which was committed unto thee keep by (διά) the Holy Ghost ; " [10] and again, " To one is given by (διά) the spirit the word of wisdom." [11]

11. In the same manner it may also be said of the word " in," that Scripture admits its use in the case of God the Father. In the Old Testament it is said through (ἐν) God we shall do valiantly, [12] and, " My praise shall be continually of (ἐν) thee ; " [13] and again, " In thy name will I rejoice." [14] In Paul we read, " In God who created all things," [15] and, " Paul and Silvanus and Timotheus unto the church of the Thessalonians in God our Father ; " [16] and " if now at length I might have a prosperous journey by (ἐν) the will of God to come to you ; " [17] and, " Thou makest thy boast of God." [1] Instances are indeed too numerous to reckon ; but what we want is not so much to exhibit an abundance of evidence as to prove that the conclusions of our opponents are unsound. I shall, therefore, omit any proof of this usage in the case of our Lord and of the Holy Ghost, in that it is notorious. But I cannot forbear to remark that " the wise hearer " will find sufficient proof of the proposition before him by following the method of contraries. For if the difference of language indicates, as we are told, that the nature has been changed, then let identity of language compel our adversaries to confess with shame that the essence is unchanged.

12. And it is not only in the case of the theology that the use of the terms varies, [2] but whenever one of the terms takes the meaning of the other we find them frequently transferred from the one subject to the other. As, for instance, Adam says, " I have gotten a man through God," [3] meaning to say the same as from God ; and in another passage " Moses commanded . . . Israel through the word of the Lord," [4] and, again, " Is not the interpretation through God ? " [5] Joseph, discoursing about dreams to the prisoners, instead of saying " from God," says plainly " through God." Inversely Paul uses the term " from whom " instead of " through whom," when he says " made from a woman " (A.V., " of " instead of " through a woman "). [6] And this he has plainly distinguished in another passage, where he says that it is proper to a woman to be made of the man, and to a man to be made through the woman, in the words " For as the woman is from [A.V., of] the man, even so is the man also through [A.V., by] the woman." [7] Nevertheless in the passage in question the apostle, while illustrating the variety of usage, at the same time corrects *obiter* the error of those who supposed that the body of the Lord was a spiritual body, [8] and, to shew that the God-bearing [9] flesh was formed out of the com-

[1] Gal. vi. 8.   [3] Matt. i. 20.   [5] 1 Cor. i. 9.
[2] 1 John iii. 24.   [4] John iii. 6.
[6] Gal. iv. 7. A.V. rends " an heir of God through Christ ; " so ℵCD. R.V. with the copy used by Basil agrees with A.B.
[7] Rom. vi. 4. It is pointed out by the Rev. C.F. H. Johnston in his edition of the *De Spiritu* that among quotations from the New Testament on the point in question, St. Basil has omitted Heb. ii. 10, " It became him for whom (δι' ὄν) are all things and through whom (δι' οὖ) are all things," " where the Father is described as being the final Cause and efficient Cause of all things."
[8] Is. xxix. 15, lxx.   [10] 2 Tim. i. 14.   [12] Ps. cvii. 13.
[9] 1 Cor. ii. 10.   [11] 1 Cor. xii. 8.   [13] Ps. lxxi. 6.
[14] For " shall they rejoice," Ps. lxxxix. 16.
[15] Eph. iii. 9.   [16] 2 Thess. i. 1.   [17] Rom. 1. 10.

[1] Rom. ii. 17.
[2] According to patristic usage the word " theology " is concerned with all that relates to the divine and eternal nature of Christ, as distinguished from the οἰκονομία, which relates to the incarnation, and consequent redemption of mankind. *cf.* Bishop Lightfoot's *Apostolic Fathers*, Part II. Vol. ii. p. 75, and Newman's *Arians*, Chapter I. Section iii.
[3] Gen. iv. 1, lxx. A.V. renders " she conceived and bare Cain and said," and here St. Basil has been accused of quoting from memory. But in the Greek of the lxx. the subject to εἶπεν is not expressed, and a possible construction of the sentence is to refer it to Adam. In his work adv. Eunom. ii. 20, St. Basil again refers the exclamation to Adam.
[4] Num. xxxvi. 5, lxx.   [6] Gal. iv. 4.
[5] Gen. xl. 8, lxx.   [7] 1 Cor. xi. 12.
[8] The allusion is to the Docetæ. *cf.* Luke xxiv. 39.
[9] The note of the Benedictine Editors remarks that the French theologian Fronton du Duc (Ducæus) accuses Theodoret (on Cyril's Anath. vii.) of misquoting St. Basil as writing here " God-bearing man " instead of " God-bearing

mon lump[1] of human nature, gave precedence to the more emphatic preposition.

The phrase " through a woman " would be likely to give rise to the suspicion of mere transit in the generation, while the phrase " of the woman " would satisfactorily indicate that the nature was shared by the mother and the offspring. The apostle was in no wise contradicting himself, but he shewed that the words can without difficulty be interchanged. Since, therefore, the term " from whom " is transferred to the identical subjects in the case of which " through whom " is decided to be properly used, with what consistency can these phrases be invariably distinguished one from the other, in order that fault may be falsely found with true religion?

CHAPTER VI.

Issue joined with those who assert that the Son is not with the Father, but after the Father. Also concerning the equal glory.

13. OUR opponents, while they thus artfully and perversely encounter our argument, cannot even have recourse to the plea of ignorance. It is obvious that they are annoyed with us for completing the doxology to the Only Begotten together with the Father, and for not separating the Holy Spirit from the Son. On this account they style us innovators, revolutionizers, phrase-coiners, and every other possible name of insult. But so far am I from being irritated at their abuse, that, were it not for the fact that their loss causes me " heaviness and continual sorrow,"[2] I could almost have said that I was grateful to them for the blasphemy, as though they were agents for providing me with blessing. For " blessed are ye," it is said, " when men shall revile you for my sake."[3] The grounds of their indignation are these: The Son, according to them, is not together with the Father, but after the Father. Hence it follows that glory should be ascribed to the Father " *through* him," but not " *with* him; " inasmuch as " *with* him " expresses equality of dignity, while " *through* him " denotes subordination. They further assert that the Spirit is not to be ranked along with the Father and the Son, but under the Son and the Father; not co-

ordinated, but subordinated; not connumerated, but subnumerated.[1]

With technical terminology of this kind they pervert the simplicity and artlessness of the faith, and thus by their ingenuity, suffering no one else to remain in ignorance, they cut off from themselves the plea that ignorance might demand.

14. Let us first ask them this question: In what sense do they say that the Son is " after the Father; " later in time, or in order, or in dignity? But in time no one is so devoid of sense as to assert that the Maker of the ages[2] holds a second place, when no interval intervenes in the natural conjunction of the Father with the Son.[3] And indeed so far as our conception of human relations goes,[4] it is impossible to think of the Son as being later than the Father, not only from the fact that Father and Son are mutually conceived of in accordance with the relationship subsisting between them, but because posteriority in time is predicated of subjects separated by a less interval from the present, and priority of subjects farther off. For instance, what happened in Noah's time is prior to what happened to the men of Sodom, inasmuch as Noah is more remote from our own day; and, again, the events of the history of the men of Sodom are posterior, because they seem in a sense to approach nearer to our own day. But, in addition to its being a breach of true religion, is it not really the extremest folly to measure the existence of the life which transcends all time and all the ages by its distance from the present? Is it not as though God the Father could be compared with, and be made superior to, God the Son, who exists before the ages, precisely in the same way in which things liable to beginning and corruption are described as prior to one another?

The superior remoteness of the Father is really inconceivable, in that thought and intelligence are wholly impotent to go beyond the generation of the Lord; and St. John has admirably confined the conception within circumscribed boundaries by two words, " In the *beginning was* the Word." For thought cannot travel outside " *was*," nor imagination[5] beyond " *beginning*." Let

[1] ὑποτάσσω. *cf.* 1 Cor. xv. 27, and *inf. cf.* chapter xvii. ὑποτεταγμένος is applied to the Son in the Macrostich or Lengthy Creed, brought by Eudoxius of Germanicia to Milan in 344. *Vide* Soc. ii. 19.
[2] ποιητὴς τῶν αἰώνων.
[3] Yet the great watchword of the Arians was ἦν ποτε ὅτε οὐκ ἦν.
[4] τῇ ἐννοίᾳ τῶν ἀνθρωπίνων is here the reading of five MSS. The Benedictines prefer τῶν ἀνθρώπων, with the sense of " in human thought."
[5] Φαντασία is the philosophic term for imagination or presentation, the mental faculty by which the object made apparent, φάντασμα, becomes apparent, φαίνεται. Aristotle, de An. III.

flesh," a term of different signification and less open as a Nestorian interpretation. " God-bearing," θεοφόρος, was an epithet applied to mere men, as, for instance, St. Ignatius. So Clement of Alexandria, 1. Strom. p. 318, and Gregory of Nazianzus, Or. xxxvii. p. 609. St. Basil does use the expression Jesus Christ ἄνθρωπον Θεόν in Hom. on Ps. xlix.
[1] φύραμα. *cf.* Rom. ix. 21.
[2] *cf.* Rom. ix. 2.　　[3] Matt. v. 11.

your thought travel ever so far backward, you cannot get beyond the "*was*," and however you may strain and strive to see what is beyond the Son, you will find it impossible to get further than the "*beginning*." True religion, therefore, thus teaches us to think of the Son together with the Father.

15. If they really conceive of a kind of degradation of the Son in relation to the Father, as though He were in a lower place, so that the Father sits above, and the Son is thrust off to the next seat below, let them confess what they mean. We shall have no more to say. A plain statement of the view will at once expose its absurdity. They who refuse to allow that the Father pervades all things do not so much as maintain the logical sequence of thought in their argument. The faith of the sound is that God fills all things;[1] but they who divide their up and down between the Father and the Son do not remember even the word of the Prophet: "If I climb up into heaven thou art there; if I go down to hell thou art there also."[2] Now, to omit all proof of the ignorance of those who predicate place of incorporeal things, what excuse can be found for their attack upon Scripture, shameless as their antagonism is, in the passages "Sit thou on my right hand"[3] and "Sat down on the right hand of the majesty of God"?[4] The expression "right hand" does not, as they contend, indicate the lower place, but equality of relation; it is not understood physically, in which case there might be something sinister about God,[5] but Scripture puts before us the magnificence of the dignity of the Son by the use of dignified language indicating the seat of honour. It is left then for our opponents to allege that this expression signifies inferiority of rank. Let them learn that "Christ is the power of God and wisdom of God,"[6] and that "He is the image of the invisible God"[7] and "brightness of his glory,"[8] and that "Him hath God the Father sealed,"[9] by engraving Himself on Him.[10]

Now are we to call these passages, and others like them, throughout the whole of Holy Scripture, proofs of humiliation, or rather public proclamations of the majesty of the Only Begotten, and of the equality of His glory with the Father? We ask them to listen to the Lord Himself, distinctly setting forth the equal dignity of His glory with the Father, in His words, "He that hath seen me hath seen the Father;"[1] and again, "When the Son cometh in the glory of his Father;"[2] that they "should honour the Son even as they honour the Father;"[3] and, "We beheld his glory, the glory as of the only begotten of the Father;"[4] and "the only begotten God which is in the bosom of the Father."[5] Of all these passages they take no account, and then assign to the Son the place set apart for His foes. A father's bosom is a fit and becoming seat for a son, but the place of the footstool is for them that have to be forced to fall.[6]

We have only touched cursorily on these proofs, because our object is to pass on to other points. You at your leisure can put together the items of the evidence, and then contemplate the height of the glory and the preëminence of the power of the Only Begotten. However, to the well-disposed hearer, even these are not insignificant, unless the terms "right hand" and "bosom" be accepted in a physical and derogatory sense, so as at once to circumscribe God in local limits, and invent form, mould, and bodily position, all of which are totally distinct from the idea of the absolute, the infinite, and the incorporeal. There is moreover the fact that what is derogatory in the idea of it is the same in the case both of the Father and the Son; so that whoever repeats these arguments does not take away the dignity of the Son, but does incur the charge of blaspheming the Father; for whatever audacity a man be guilty of against the Son he cannot but transfer to the Father. If he assigns to the Father the upper place

---

iii. 20, defines it as "a movement of the mind generated by sensation." Fancy, which is derived from φαντασία (φαίνω, √BHA = shine) has acquired a slightly different meaning in some usages of modern speech.
[1] Eph. iv. 10. [2] Ps. cxxxix. 7, P.B. [3] Ps. cx. 1.
[4] Heb. i. 3, with the variation of "of God" for "on high."
[5] I know of no better way of conveying the sense of the original σκαιὸς than by thus introducing the Latin *sinister*, which has the double meaning of left and ill-omened. It is to the credit of the unsuperstitious character of English-speaking people that while the Greek σκαιὸς and ἀοιστεʴός, the Latin *sinister* and *lævus*, the French *gauche*, and the German *link*, all have the meaning of awkward and unlucky as well as simply on the left hand, the English *left* (though probably derived from lift = weak) has lost all connotation but the local one.
[6] 1 Cor. i. 24. [7] Col. i. 15. [8] Heb. i. 3. [9] John vi. 27.
[10] The more obvious interpretation of ἐσφράγισεν in John vi. 27, would be sealed with a mark of approval, as in the miracle just performed. *cf.* Bengel, "*sigillo id quod genuinum est*

commendatur, et omne quod non genuinum est excluditur." But St. Basil explains "sealed" by "stamped with the image of His Person," an interpretation which Alford rejects. St. Basil, at the end of Chapter xxvi. of this work, calls our Lord the χαρακτὴρ καὶ ἰσότυπος σφραγίς, i.e., "express image and seal graven to the like" of the Father. St. Athanasius (Ep. i. ad Serap. xxiii.) writes, "The seal has the form of Christ the sealer, and in this the sealed participate, being formed according to it." *cf.* Gal. iv. 19, and 2 Pet. i. 4.
[1] John xiv. 9. [2] Mark viii. 38. [3] John v. 23. [4] John i. 14.
[5] John i. 18. "Only begotten God" is here the reading of five MSS. of Basil. The words are wanting in one codex. In Chapter viii. of this work St. Basil distinctly quotes Scripture as calling the Son "only begotten God." (Chapter viii. Section 17.) But in Chapter xi. Section 27, where he has been alleged to quote John i. 18, with the reading "Only begotten SON" (e.g., Alford), the MS. authority for his text is in favour of "Only begotten GOD." ΘΣ is the reading of א. B.C. ΘΣ of A. On the comparative weight of the textual and patristic evidence *vide* Bp. Westcott *in loc*.
[6] *cf.* Ps. cx. 1.

by way of precedence, and asserts that the only begotten Son sits below, he will find that to the creature of his imagination attach all the consequent conditions of body. And if these are the imaginations of drunken delusion and phrensied insanity, can it be consistent with true religion for men taught by the Lord himself that " He that honoureth not the Son honoureth not the Father " [1] to refuse to worship and glorify with the Father him who in nature, in glory, and in dignity is conjoined with him? What shall we say? What just defence shall we have in the day of the awful universal judgment of all creation, if, when the Lord clearly announces that He will come " in the glory of his Father; " [2] when Stephen beheld Jesus standing at the right hand of God; [3] when Paul testified in the spirit concerning Christ " that he is at the right hand of God; " [4] when the Father says, " Sit thou on my right hand; " [5] when the Holy Spirit bears witness that he has sat down on " the right hand of the majesty " [6] of God; we attempt to degrade him who shares the honour and the throne, from his condition of equality, to a lower state? [7] Standing and sitting, I apprehend, indicate the fixity and entire stability of the nature, as Baruch, when he wishes to exhibit the immutability and immobility of the Divine mode of existence, says, " For thou sittest for ever and we perish utterly." [8] Moreover, the place on the right hand indicates in my judgment equality of honour. Rash, then, is the attempt to deprive the Son of participation in the doxology, as though worthy only to be ranked in a lower place of honour.

CHAPTER VII.

Against those who assert that it is not proper for " with whom " to be said of the Son, and that the proper phrase is " through whom."

16. BUT their contention is that to use the phrase " with him " is altogether strange and unusual, while " through him " is at once most familiar in Holy Scripture, and very common in the language of the brotherhood. [9] What is our answer to this? We say, Blessed are the ears that have not heard you and the hearts that have been kept from the wounds of your words. To you, on the

other hand, who are lovers of Christ, [1] I say that the Church recognizes both uses, and deprecates neither as subversive of the other. For whenever we are contemplating the majesty of the nature of the Only Begotten, and the excellence of His dignity, we bear witness that the glory is *with* the Father; while on the other hand, whenever we bethink us of His bestowal [2] on us of good gifts, and of our access [3] to, and admission into, the household of God, [4] we confess that this grace is effected for us *through* Him and *by* [5] Him.

It follows that the one phrase " *with* whom " is the proper one to be used in the ascription of glory, while the other, " *through* whom," is specially appropriate in giving of thanks. It is also quite untrue to allege that the phrase " *with* whom " is unfamiliar in the usage of the devout. All those whose soundness of character leads them to hold the dignity of antiquity to be more honourable than mere new-fangled novelty, and who have preserved the tradition of their fathers [6] unadulterated, alike in town and in country, have employed this phrase. It is, on the contrary, they who are surfeited with the familiar and the customary, and arrogantly assail the old as stale, who welcome innovation, just as in dress your lovers of display always prefer some utter novelty to what is generally worn. So you may even still see that the language of country folk preserves the ancient fashion, while of these, our cunning experts [7] in logomachy, the language bears the brand of the new philosophy.

What our fathers said, the same say we, that the glory of the Father and of the Son is common; wherefore we offer the doxology to the Father *with* the Son. But we do not rest only on the fact that such is the tradition of the Fathers; for they too followed the sense of Scripture, and started from the evidence which, a few sentences back, I deduced from Scripture and laid before you. For " the brightness " is always thought of

---

[1] Φιλόχριστοι. The word is not common, but occurs in inscriptions. *cf.* Anth. Pal. I. x. 13.
  ὀρθὴν πίστιν ἔχουσα φιλοχρίστοιο μενοινῆς.
[2] χορηγία. *cf.* the use of the cognate verb in 1 Pet. iv. 11. ἐξ ἰσχύος ἧς χορηγεῖ ὁ θεός.
[3] προσαγωγή. *cf.* Eph. ii. 18.
[4] οἰκείωσιν πρὸς τὸν Θεόν. *cf.* οἰκεῖοι τοῦ Θεοῦ in Eph. ii. 19.
[5] ἐν.   [6] *cf.* Gal. i. 14.
[7] The verb, ἐντετρίμμαι, appears to be used by St. Basil, if he wrote ἐντετριμμένων in the sense of to be ἐντριβής or versed in a thing (*cf.* Soph. Ant. 177) — a sense not illustrated by classical usage. But the reading of the Moscow MS. (ι) ἐντεθραμμένων, " trained in," " nurtured in," is *per se* much more probable. The idea of the country folk preserving the good old traditions shews the change of circumstances in St. Basil's day from those of the 2d c., when the " pagani " or villagers were mostly still heathen, and the last to adopt the novelty of Christianity. *cf.* Pliny's Letter to Trajan (Ep. 96), " *neque civitates tantum sed vicos etiam atque agros super-stitionis istius contagio pervagata est.*"

---

[1] John v. 23.   [3] Acts vii. 55.   [5] Ps. cx. 1.
[2] Matt. xvi. 27.   [4] Rom. viii. 34.   [6] Heb. viii. 1.
[7] Mr. Johnston well points out that these five testimonies are not cited fortuitously, but " in an order which carries the reader from the future second coming, through the present session at the right hand, back to the ascension in the past."
[8] Baruch iii. 3, lxx.
[9] The word ἀδελφότης is in the New Testament peculiar to S. Peter (1 Peter ii. 17, and v. 9); it occurs in the Epistle of St. Clement to the Corinthians, Chap. ii.

with "the glory,"[1] "the image" with the archetype,[2] and the Son always and everywhere together with the Father; nor does even the close connexion of the names, much less the nature of the things, admit of separation.

CHAPTER VIII.

In how many ways " THROUGH *whom" is used; and in what sense "* WITH *whom" is more suitable. Explanation of how the Son receives a commandment, and how He is sent.*

17. WHEN, then, the apostle "thanks God through Jesus Christ,"[3] and again says that "through Him" we have "received grace and apostleship for obedience to the faith among all nations,"[4] or "through Him have access unto this grace wherein we stand and rejoice,"[5] he sets forth the boons conferred on us by the Son, at one time making the grace of the good gifts pass through from the Father to us, and at another bringing us to the Father through Himself. For by saying "through whom we have received grace and apostleship,"[6] he declares the supply of the good gifts to proceed from that source; and again in saying "through whom we have had access,"[7] he sets forth our acceptance and being made "of the household of God"[8] through Christ. Is then the confession of the grace wrought by Him to usward a detraction from His glory? Is it not truer to say that the recital of His benefits is a proper argument for glorifying Him? It is on this account that we have not found Scripture describing the Lord to us by one name, nor even by such terms alone as are indicative of His godhead and majesty. At one time it uses terms descriptive of His nature, for it recognises the "name which is above every name,"[9] the name of Son,[10] and speaks of true Son,[11] and only begotten God,[12] and Power of God,[13] and Wisdom,[14] and Word.[15] Then again, on account of the divers manners[16] wherein grace is given to us, which, because of the riches of His goodness,[17] according to his manifold[18] wisdom, he bestows on

them that need, Scripture designates Him by innumerable other titles, calling Him Shepherd,[1] King,[2] Physician,[3] Bridegroom,[4] Way,[5] Door,[6] Fountain,[7] Bread,[8] Axe,[9] and Rock.[10] And these titles do not set forth His nature, but, as I have remarked, the variety of the effectual working which, out of His tenderheartedness to His own creation, according to the peculiar necessity of each, He bestows upon them that need. Them that have fled for refuge to His ruling care, and through patient endurance have mended their wayward ways,[11] He calls "sheep," and confesses Himself to be, to them that hear His voice and refuse to give heed to strange teaching, a "shepherd." For "my sheep," He says, "hear my voice." To them that have now reached a higher stage and stand in need of righteous royalty,[12] He is a King.

And in that, through the straight way of His commandments, He leads men to good actions, and again because He safely shuts in all who through faith in Him betake themselves for shelter to the blessing of the higher wisdom,[13] He is a Door.

So He says, "By me if any man enter in, . . . he shall go in and out and shall find pasture."[14] Again, because to the faithful He is a defence strong, unshaken, and harder to break than any bulwark, He is a Rock. Among these titles, it is when He is styled Door, or Way, that the phrase "through Him" is very appropriate and plain. As, however, God and Son, He is glorified with and together with[15] the Father, in that "at the name of Jesus every knee should bow, of things in heaven, and things in earth, and things under the earth; and that every tongue should confess that Jesus Christ is Lord, to

---

[1] Heb. i. 1. *cf.* Aug. *Ep.* ii. ad Serap.: "The Father is Light, and the Son brightness and true light."
[2] 2 Cor. iv. 4.   [5] Rom. v. 2.   [8] *cf.* Eph. ii. 19.
[3] Rom. i. 8.   [6] Rom. i. 5.   [9] Phil. ii. 9.
[4] Rom. i. 5.   [7] Rom. v. 2.
[10] Two πολύτροπον. *cf.* Heb. i. 1.
[10] Two MSS., those in the B. Museum and at Vienna, read here Ἰησοῦ. In *Ep.* 210. 4, St. Basil writes that the name above every name is αὐτὸ τὸ καλεῖσθαι αὐτὸν Υἱὸν τοῦ Θεοῦ.
[11] *cf.* Matt. xiv. 33, and xxvii. 54.
[12] John i. 18. *cf.* note on p. .
[13] 1 Cor. i. 24, and possibly Rom. i. 16, if with D. we read gospel *of Christ*.
[14] 1 Cor. i. 24.
[15] *e.g.*, John i. 1. *cf.* Ps. cvii. 20; Wisdom ix. 1, xviii. 15; Ecclesiasticus xliii. 20.
[16] Τὸ πολύτροπον. *cf.* Heb. i. 1.
[17] Τὸν πλοῦτον τῆς ἀγαθότητος. *cf.* Rom ii. 4, τοῦ πλούτου τῆς χρηστότητος.
[18] Eph. iii. 10.

[1] *e.g.*, John x. 12.   [6] *e.g.*, John x. 9.
[2] *e.g.*, Matt. xxi. 5.   [7] *cf.* Rev. xxi. 6.
[3] *e.g.*, Matt. ix. 12.   [8] *e.g.*, John vi. 21.
[4] *e.g.*, Matt. ix. 15.   [9] *cf.* Matt. iii. 10.
[5] John xiv. 6.   [10] *e.g.*, 1 Cor. x. 4.
[11] I translate here the reading of the Parisian Codex, called by the Benedictine Editors *Regius Secundus*, τὸ εὐμετάβολον κατωρθωκότας. The harder reading, τὸ εὐμετάδοτον, which may be rendered "have perfected their readiness to distribute," has the best manuscript authority, but it is barely intelligible; and the Benedictine Editors are quite right in calling attention to the fact that the point in question here is not the readiness of the flock to distribute (*cf.* 1 Tim. vi. 18), but their patient following of their Master. The Benedictine Editors boldly propose to introduce a word of no authority τὸ ἀμετάβολον, rendering *qui per patientiam animam immutabilem præbuerunt.* The reading adopted above is supported by a passage in *Ep.* 244, where St. Basil is speaking of the waywardness of Eustathius, and seems to fit in best with the application of the passage to the words of our Lord, "have fled for refuge to his ruling care," corresponding with "the sheep follow him, for they know his voice" (St. John x. 4), and "have mended their wayward ways," with "a stranger will they not follow," v. 5. Mr. Johnston, in his valuable note, compares Origen's teaching on the Names of our Lord.
[12] So three MSS. Others repeat ἐπιστασία, translated "ruling care" above. ἔννομος is used by Plato for "lawful" and "law-abiding." (Legg. 921 C. and Rep. 424 E.) In 1 Cor. ix. 21, A.V. renders "under the law."
[13] Τὸ τῆς γνώσεως ἀγαθόν: possibly "the good of knowledge of him."
[14] John x. 9.   [15] *cf.* note on page 3, on μετά and σύν.

the glory of God the Father."[1] Wherefore we use both terms, expressing by the one His own proper dignity, and by the other His grace to usward.

18. For "through Him" comes every succour to our souls, and it is in accordance with each kind of care that an appropriate title has been devised. So when He presents to Himself the blameless soul, not having spot or wrinkle,[2] like a pure maiden, He is called Bridegroom, but whenever He receives one in sore plight from the devil's evil strokes, healing it in the heavy infirmity of its sins, He is named Physician. And shall this His care for us degrade to meanness our thoughts of Him? Or, on the contrary, shall it smite us with amazement at once at the mighty power and love to man[3] of the Saviour, in that He both endured to suffer with us[4] in our infirmities, and was able to come down to our weakness? For not heaven and earth and the great seas, not the creatures that live in the water and on dry land, not plants, and stars, and air, and seasons, not the vast variety in the order of the universe,[5] so well sets forth the excellency of His might as that God, being incomprehensible, should have been able, impassibly, through flesh, to have come into close conflict with death, to the end that by His own suffering He might give us the boon of freedom from suffering.[6] The apostle, it is true, says, "In all these things we are more than conquerors through him that loved us."[7] But in a phrase of this kind there is no suggestion of any lowly and subordinate ministry,[8] but rather of the succour rendered "in the power of his might."[9] For He Him-

self has bound the strong man and spoiled his goods,[1] that is, us men, whom our enemy had abused in every evil activity, and made "vessels meet for the Master's use"[2] us who have been perfected for every work through the making ready of that part of us which is in our own control.[3] Thus we have had our approach to the Father through Him, being translated from "the power of darkness to be partakers of the inheritance of the saints in light."[4] We must not, however, regard the œconomy[5] through the Son as a compulsory and subordinate ministration resulting from the low estate of a slave, but rather the voluntary solicitude working effectually for His own creation in goodness and in pity, according to the will of God the Father. For we shall be consistent with true religion if in all that was and is from time to time perfected by Him, we both bear witness to the perfection of His power, and in no case put it asunder from the Father's will. For instance, whenever the Lord is called the Way, we are carried on to a higher meaning, and not to that which is derived from the vulgar sense of the word. We understand by Way that advance[6] to perfection which is made stage by stage, and in regular order, through the works of righteousness and "the illumination of knowledge;"[7] ever longing after what is before, and reaching forth unto those things which remain,[8] until we shall have reached the blessed end, the knowledge of God, which the Lord through Himself bestows on them that have trusted in Him. For our Lord is an essentially good Way, where erring and straying are unknown, to that which is essentially good, to the Father. For "no one," He says, "cometh to the Father but ["by," A.V.] through me."[9] Such is our way up to God "through the Son."

19. It will follow that we should next in order point out the character of the provision of blessings bestowed on us by the

---

[1] Phil. ii. 10, 11.   [2] Eph. v. 29.

[3] φιλανθρωπία occurs twice in the N.T. (Acts xxviii. 2, and Titus iii. 4) and is in the former passage rendered by A.V. "*kindness*," in the latter by "love to man." The φιλανθρωπία of the Maltese barbarians corresponds with the lower classical sense of kindliness and courtesy. The love of God in Christ to man introduces practically a new connotation to the word and its cognates.

[4] Or to sympathize with our infirmities.

[5] ποικίλη διακόσμησις. διακόσμησις was the technical term of the Pythagorean philosophy for the orderly arrangement of the universe (cf. Arist. *Metaph.* I. v. 2, "ἡ ὅλη διακόσμησις"); Pythagoras being credited with the first application of the word κόσμος to the universe. (Plut. 2, 886 c.) So *mundus* in Latin, whence Augustine's oxymoron, "*O munde immunde !*" On the scriptural use of κόσμος; and αἰών *vide* Archbp. Trench's *New Testament Synonyms*, p. 204.

[6] In Hom. on Ps. lxv. Section 5, St. Basil describes the power of God the Word being most distinctly shewn in the œconomy of the incarnation and His descent to the lowliness and the infirmity of the manhood. *cf.* Ath. on the Incarnation, sect. 54, "He was made man that we might be made God; and He manifested Himself by a body that we might receive the idea of the unseen Father; and He endured the insolence of men that we might inherit immortality. For while He Himself was in no way injured, being impassible and incorruptible and very Word and God, men who were suffering, and for whose sakes He endured all this, He maintained and preserved in His own impassibility." [7] Rom. viii. 37.

[8] ὑπηρεσία. Lit. "under-rowing." The cognate ὑπηρέτης is the word used in Acts xxvi. 16, in the words of the Saviour to St. Paul, "to make thee a minister," and in 1 Cor. iv. 1, "Let a man so account of us as of the ministers of Christ."

[9] Eph. vi. 10.

[1] *cf.* Matt. xii. 29.   [2] 2 Tim. ii. 21.

[3] This passage is difficult to render alike from the variety of readings and the obscurity of each. I have endeavoured to represent the force of the Greek ἐκ τῆς ἑτοιμασίας τοῦ ἐφ' ἡμῖν. understanding by "τὸ ἐφ' ἡμῖν," practically, "our free will." *cf.* the enumeration of what is ἐφ' ἡμῖν, within our own control, in the Enchiridion of Epictetus, Chap. I. "Within our own control are impulse, desire, inclination." On Is. vi. 8, "Here am I; send me," St. Basil writes, "He did not add 'I will go;' for the acceptance of the message is within our control (ἐφ' ἡμῖν), but to be made capable of going is of Him that gives the grace, of the enabling God." The Benedictine translation of the text is "*per liberi arbitrii nostri præparationem.*" But other readings are (i) τῆς ἐφ' ἡμῖν, "the preparation which is in our own control;" (ii) τῆς ἑτοιμασίας αὐτοῦ, "His preparation;" and (iii) the Syriac represented by "*arbitrio suo.*"

[4] Col. i. 12, 13.   [5] *cf.* note on page 7.

[6] προκοπή: *cf.* Luke ii. 52, where it is said that our Lord προέκοπτε, *i.e.*, "continued to cut His way forward."

[7] 1 Cor. iv. 6, R.V. marg.

[8] There seems to be here a recollection, though not a quotation, of Phil. iii. 13.   [9] John xiv. 6.

Father "through him." Inasmuch as all created nature, both this visible world and all that is conceived of in the mind, cannot hold together without the care and providence of God, the Creator Word, the Only begotten God, apportioning His succour according to the measure of the needs of each, distributes mercies various and manifold on account of the many kinds and characters of the recipients of His bounty, but appropriate to the necessities of individual requirements. Those that are confined in the darkness of ignorance He enlightens: for this reason He is true Light.[1] Portioning requital in accordance with the desert of deeds, He judges: for this reason He is righteous Judge.[2] "For the Father judgeth no man, but hath committed all judgment to the Son."[3] Those that have lapsed from the lofty height of life into sin He raises from their fall: for this reason He is Resurrection.[4] Effectually working by the touch of His power and the will of His goodness He does all things. He shepherds; He enlightens; He nourishes; He heals; He guides; He raises up; He calls into being things that were not; He upholds what has been created. Thus the good things that come from God reach us "through the Son," who works in each case with greater speed than speech can utter. For not lightnings, not light's course in air, is so swift; not eyes' sharp turn, not the movements of our very thought. Nay, by the divine energy is each one of these in speed further surpassed than is the slowest of all living creatures outdone in motion by birds, or even winds, or the rush of the heavenly bodies; or, not to mention these, by our very thought itself. For what extent of time is needed by Him who "upholds all things by the word of His power,"[5] and works not by bodily agency, nor requires the help of hands to form and fashion, but holds in obedient following and unforced consent the nature of all things that are? So as Judith says, "Thou hast thought, and what things thou didst determine were ready at hand."[6] On the other hand, and lest we should ever be drawn away by the greatness of the works wrought to imagine that the Lord is without beginning,[7] what saith

the Self-Existent?[1] "I live through [by, A.V.] the Father,"[2] and the power of God; "The Son hath power [can, A.V.] to do nothing of himself."[3] And the self-complete Wisdom? I received "a commandment what I should say and what I should speak."[4] Through all these words He is guiding us to the knowledge of the Father, and referring our wonder at all that is brought into existence to Him, to the end that "through Him" we may know the Father. For the Father is not regarded from the difference of the operations, by the exhibition of a separate and peculiar energy; for whatsoever things He sees the Father doing, "these also doeth the Son likewise;"[5] but He enjoys our wonder at all that comes to pass out of the glory which comes to Him from the Only Begotten, rejoicing in the Doer Himself as well as in the greatness of the deeds, and exalted by all who acknowledge Him as Father of our Lord Jesus Christ, "through whom [by whom, A.V.] are all things, and for whom are all things."[6] Wherefore, saith the Lord, "All mine are thine,"[7] as though the sovereignty over created things were conferred on Him, and "Thine are mine," as though the creating Cause came thence to Him. We are not to suppose that He used assistance in His action, or yet was entrusted with the ministry of each individual work by detailed commission, a condition distinctly menial and quite inadequate to the divine dignity. Rather was the Word full of His Father's excellences; He shines forth from the Father, and does all things according to the likeness of Him that begat Him. For if in essence He is without variation, so also is He without

---

[1] John i. 9. [3] John v. 22. [5] Heb. i. 3.
[2] 2 Tim. iv. 8. [4] John xi. 25. [6] Judith ix. 5 and 6.
[7] ἄναρχος. This word is used in two senses by the Fathers. (i) In the sense of ἀΐδιος or eternal, it is applied (a) to the Trinity in unity. e.g., Quæst. Misc. v.442 (Migne Ath. iv. 783), attributed to Athanasius, κοινὸν ἡ οὐσία· κοινὸν τὸ ἄναρχον. (b) To the Son. e.g., Greg. Naz. Orat. xxix. 490, ἐὰν τὴν ἀπὸ χρόνον νοῆς ἀρχὴν καὶ ἄναρχος ὁ υἱός, οὐκ ἄρχεται γὰρ ἀπὸ χρόνου ὁ χρόνων δεσπότης. (ii) In the sense of ἀναίτιος, "causeless," "originis principio carens," it is applied to the Father alone, and not to the Son. So Gregory of Nazianzus, in the oration quoted above, ὁ υἱὸς, ἐὰν ὡς αἴτιον τὸν πατέρα λαμβάνῃς, οὐκ

ἄναρχος, "the Son, if you understand the Father as cause, is not without beginning." ἀρχὴ γὰρ υἱοῦ πατὴρ ὡς αἴτιος. "For the Father, as cause, is Beginning of the Son." But, though the Son in this sense was not ἄναρχος; He was said to be begotten ἀνάρχως. So Greg. Naz. (Hom. xxxvii. 590) τὸ ἴδιον ὄνομα τοῦ ἀνάρχως γεννηθέντος, υἱός. Cf. the Letter of Alexander of Alexandria to Alexander of Constantinople. Theod. Ecc. Hist. i. 3. τὴν ἄναρχον αὐτῷ παρὰ τοῦ πατρὸς γέννησιν ἀνατίθεντας. cf. Hooker, Ecc. Pol. v. 54. "By the gift of eternal generation Christ hath received of the Father one and in number the self-same substance which the Father hath of himself unreceived from any other. For every beginning is a father unto that which cometh of it; and every offspring is a son unto that out of which it groweth. Seeing, therefore, the Father alone is originally that Deity which Christ originally is not (for Christ is God by being of God, light by issuing out of light), it followeth hereupon that whatsoever Christ hath common unto him with his heavenly Father, the same of necessity must be given him, but naturally and eternally given." So Hilary De Trin. xii. 21. "Ubi auctor eternus est, ibi et nativatis æternitas est: quia sicut nativitas ab auctore est, ita et ab æterno auctore æterna nativitas est." And Augustine De Trin. v. 15, "Naturam præstat filio SINE INITIO generatio."
[1] ἡ αὐτοζωή. [3] John v. 19. [5] John v. 19.
[2] John vi. 57. [4] John xii. 49.
[6] Heb. ii. 10. cf. Rom. xi. 36, to which the reading of two manuscripts more distinctly assimilates the citation. The majority of commentators refer Heb. ii. 10, to the Father, but Theodoret understands it of the Son, and the argument of St. Basil necessitates the same application.
[7] John xvii. 10.

variation in power.[1] And of those whose power is equal, the operation also is in all ways equal. And Christ is the power of God, and the wisdom of God.[2] And so "all things are made through [by, A.V.] him," [3] and "all things were created through [by, A.V.] him and for him," [4] not in the discharge of any slavish service, but in the fulfilment of the Father's will as Creator.

20. When then He says, "I have not spoken of myself," [5] and again, "As the Father said unto me, so I speak," [6] and "The word which ye hear is not mine, but [the Father's] which sent me," [7] and in another place, "As the Father gave me commandment, even so I do," [8] it is not because He lacks deliberate purpose or power of initiation, nor yet because He has to wait for the preconcerted key-note, that he employs language of this kind. His object is to make it plain that His own will is connected in indissoluble union with the Father. Do not then let us understand by what is called a "commandment" a peremptory mandate delivered by organs of speech, and giving orders to the Son, as to a subordinate, concerning what He ought to do. Let us rather, in a sense befitting the Godhead, perceive a transmission of will, like the reflexion of an object in a mirror, passing without note of time from Father to Son. "For the Father loveth the Son and sheweth him all things," [9] so that "all things that the Father hath" belong to the Son, not gradually accruing to Him little by little, but with Him all together and at once. Among men, the workman who has been thoroughly taught his craft, and, through long training, has sure and established experience in it, is able, in accordance with the scientific methods which now he has in store, to work for the future by himself. And are we to suppose that the wisdom of God, the Maker of all creation, He who is eternally perfect, who is wise without a teacher, the Power of God, "in whom are hid all the treasures of wisdom and knowledge," [10] needs piecemeal instruction to mark out the manner and measure of His operations? I presume that in the vanity of your calculations, you mean to open a school; you will make the one take His seat in the teacher's place, and the other stand by in a scholar's ignorance, gradually learning wisdom and advancing to perfection, by lessons given Him bit by bit. Hence, if you have sense to abide by what logically follows, you will find the Son being eternally taught, nor yet ever able to reach the end of perfection, inasmuch as the wisdom of the Father is infinite, and the end of the infinite is beyond apprehension. It results that whoever refuses to grant that the Son has all things from the beginning will never grant that He will reach perfection. But I am ashamed at the degraded conception to which, by the course of the argument, I have been brought down. Let us therefore revert to the loftier themes of our discussion.

21. "He that hath seen me hath seen the Father;" [1] not the express image, nor yet the form, for the divine nature does not admit of combination; but the goodness of the will, which, being concurrent with the essence, is beheld as like and equal, or rather the same, in the Father as in the Son.[2]

What then is meant by "became subject"?[3] What by "delivered him up for us all"?[4] It is meant that the Son has it of the Father that He works in goodness on behalf of men. But you must hear too the words, "Christ hath redeemed us from the curse of the law;" [5] and "while we were yet sinners, Christ died for us." [6]

Give careful heed, too, to the words of the Lord, and note how, whenever He instructs us about His Father, He is in the habit of using terms of personal authority, saying, "I will; be thou clean;" [7] and "Peace, be still;" [8] and "But I say unto you;" [9] and "Thou dumb and deaf spirit, I charge thee;" [10] and all other expressions of the same kind, in order that by these we may recognise our Master and Maker, and by the former may be taught the Father of our Master and Creator.[11]

---

[1] John xiv. 9.
[2] The argument appears to be not that Christ is not the "express image," or impress of the Father, as He is described in Heb. i. 3, or form, as in Phil. ii. 6, but that this is not the sense in which our Lord's words in St. John xiv. 9, must be understood to describe "seeing the Father." Χαρακτήρ and μορφή are equivalent to ἡ θεία φύσις, and μορφή is used by St. Basil as it is used by St. Paul,—coinciding with, if not following, the usage of the older Greek philosophy,—to mean essential attributes which the Divine Word had before the incarnation (cf. Eustathius in Theod. Dial. II. [Wace and Schaff Ed., p. 203]; "the express image made man,"—ὁ τῷ πνεύματι σωματοποιηθεὶς ἄνθρωπος χαρακτήρ.)
The divine nature does not admit of combination, in the sense of confusion (cf. the protests of Theodoret in his Dialogues against the confusion of the Godhead and manhood in the Christ), with the human nature in our Lord, and remains invisible. On the word χαρακτήρ vide Suicer, and on μορφή Archbp. Trench's New Testament Synonyms and Bp. Lightfoot on Philippians ii. 6.
[3] Phil. ii. 8.   [6] Rom. v. 8.   [9] Matt. v. 22, etc.
[4] Rom. viii. 32. [7] Matt. viii. 3. [10] Mark ix. 25.
[5] Gal. iii. 13.   [8] Mark iv. 39.
[11] There is a difficulty in following the argument in the foregoing quotations. F. Combefis, the French Dominican editor of Basil, would boldly interpose a "not," and read 'whenever he does not instruct us concerning the Father.' But there is no MS. authority for this violent remedy. The Benedictine

---

[1] ἀπαραλλάκτως ἔχει. cf. Jas. i. 17. παρ' ᾧ οὐκ ἔνι παραλλαγή. The word ἀπαράλλακτος was at first used by the Catholic bishops at Nicæa, as implying ὁμοούσιος. Vide Athan. De Decretis, § 20, in Wace and Schaff's ed., p. 163.
[2] 1 Cor. i. 24.   [5] John xii. 49.   [8] John xiv. 31.
[3] John i. 3.   [6] John xii. 50.   [9] John v. 20.
[4] Col. i. 16.   [7] John xiv. 24.
[10] Col. ii. 3, A.V. cf. the amendment of R.V., "all the treasures of wisdom and knowledge hidden," and Bp. Lightfoot on St. Paul's use of the gnostic term ἀπόκρυφος.

Thus on all sides is demonstrated the true doctrine that the fact that the Father creates through the Son neither constitutes the creation of the Father imperfect nor exhibits the active energy of the Son as feeble, but indicates the unity of the will; so the expression "through whom" contains a confession of an antecedent Cause, and is not adopted in objection to the efficient Cause.

CHAPTER IX.

Definitive conceptions about the Spirit which conform to the teaching of the Scriptures.

22. LET us now investigate what are our common conceptions concerning the Spirit, as well those which have been gathered by us from Holy Scripture concerning It as those which we have received from the unwritten tradition of the Fathers. First of all we ask, who on hearing the titles of the Spirit is not lifted up in soul, who does not raise his conception to the supreme nature? It is called "Spirit of God,"[1] "Spirit of truth which proceedeth from the Father,"[2] "right Spirit,"[3] "a leading Spirit."[4] Its[5] proper and peculiar title is "Holy Spirit;" which is a name specially appropriate to everything that is incorporeal, purely immaterial, and indivisible. So our Lord, when teaching the woman who thought God to be an object of local worship that the incorporeal is incomprehensible, said "God is a spirit."[6] On our hearing, then, of a spirit, it is impossible to form the idea of a nature circumscribed, subject to change and variation, or at all like the creature. We are compelled to advance in our conceptions to the highest, and to think of an intelligent essence, in power infinite, in magnitude unlimited, unmeasured by times or ages, generous of It's good gifts, to whom turn all things needing sanctification, after whom reach all things that live in virtue, as being watered by It's inspiration and helped on toward their natural and proper end; perfecting all other things, but Itself in nothing lacking; living not as needing restoration, but as Supplier of life; not growing by additions, but straightway full, self-established, omnipresent, origin of sanctification, light perceptible to the mind, supplying, as it were, through Itself, illumination to every faculty in the search for truth; by nature un-

approachable, apprehended by reason of goodness, filling all things with Its power,[1] but communicated only to the worthy; not shared in one measure, but distributing Its energy according to "the proportion of faith;"[2] in essence simple, in powers various, wholly present in each and being wholly everywhere; impassively divided, shared without loss of ceasing to be entire, after the likeness of the sunbeam, whose kindly light falls on him who enjoys it as though it shone for him alone, yet illumines land and sea and mingles with the air. So, too, is the Spirit to every one who receives It, as though given to him alone, and yet It sends forth grace sufficient and full for all mankind, and is enjoyed by all who share It, according to the capacity, not of Its power, but of their nature.

23. Now the Spirit is not brought into intimate association with the soul by local approximation. How indeed could there be a corporeal approach to the incorporeal? This association results from the withdrawal of the passions which, coming afterwards gradually on the soul from its friendship to the flesh, have alienated it from its close relationship with God. Only then after a man is purified from the shame whose stain he took through his wickedness, and has come back again to his natural beauty, and as it were cleaning the Royal Image and restoring its ancient form, only thus is it possible for him to draw near to the Paraclete.[3] And He, like the sun, will by the aid of thy purified eye show thee in Himself the image of the invisible, and in the blessed spectacle of the image thou shalt behold the unspeakable beauty of the archetype.[4] Through His aid hearts are lifted up, the weak are held by the hand, and they who are advancing are brought to perfection.[5] Shining upon those that are cleansed from every spot, He makes them spiritual by fellowship with Himself. Just as when a sunbeam falls on bright and transparent bodies, they themselves become brilliant too, and shed forth a fresh brightness from themselves, so souls wherein the Spirit dwells, illuminated by the Spirit, themselves become spiritual, and send forth their grace to others.

---

[1] *cf.* Wisdom i. 7.   [2] Rom. xii. 6.

[3] *cf.* Theodoret, *Dial.* i. p. 164, Schaff and Wace's ed. "Sin is not of nature, but of corrupt will." So the ninth article of the English Church describes it as not the nature, but the "fault and corruption of the nature, of every man." On the figure of the restored picture *cf.* Ath. *de Incar.* § 14, and Theod. *Dial.* ii. p. 183.

[4] *cf.* Ep. 236. "Our mind, enlightened by the Spirit, looks toward the Son, and in Him, as in an image, contemplates the Father." There seems at first sight some confusion in the text between the "Royal Image" in us and Christ as the image of God; but it is in proportion as we are like Christ that we see God in Christ. It is the "pure in heart" who "see God."

[5] "*Proficientes perficiuntur.*" Ben. Ed.

Editors say all is plain if we render "*postquam nos de patre erudivit.*" But the Greek will not admit of this.
[1] Matt. xii. 28, etc.   [2] John xv. 26.   [3] Ps. li. 10.
[4] Ps. li. 12, lxx. R.V. and A.V., "free spirit."
[5] It will be remembered that in the Nicene Creed "the Lord and Giver of life" is τὸ κύριον τὸ ζωοποιόν. In A.V. we have both *he* (John xv. 26, ἐκεῖνος) and *it* (Rom. viii. 16, αὐτὸ τὸ πνεῦμα).
[6] John iv. 24.

Hence comes foreknowledge of the future, understanding of mysteries, apprehension of what is hidden, distribution of good gifts, the heavenly citizenship, a place in the chorus of angels, joy without end, abiding in God, the being made like to God, and, highest of all, the being made God.[1] Such, then, to instance a few out of many, are the conceptions concerning the Holy Spirit, which we have been taught to hold concerning His greatness, His dignity, and His operations, by the oracles [2] of the Spirit themselves.

CHAPTER X.

Against those who say that it is not right to rank the Holy Spirit with the Father and the Son.

24. BUT we must proceed to attack our opponents, in the endeavour to confute those " oppositions " advanced against us which are derived from " knowledge falsely so-called." [3]

It is not permissible, they assert, for the Holy Spirit to be ranked with the Father and Son, on account of the difference of His nature and the inferiority of His dignity. Against them it is right to reply in the words of the apostles, " We ought to obey God rather than men." [4]

For if our Lord, when enjoining the baptism of salvation, charged His disciples to baptize all nations in the name " of the Father and of the Son and of the Holy Ghost," [5]

not disdaining fellowship with Him, and these men allege that we must not rank Him with the Father and the Son, is it not clear that they openly withstand the commandment of God? If they deny that coördination of this kind is declaratory of any fellowship and conjunction, let them tell us why it behoves us to hold this opinion, and what more intimate mode of conjunction [1] they have.

If the Lord did not indeed conjoin the Spirit with the Father and Himself in baptism, do not [2] let them lay the blame of conjunction upon us, for we neither hold nor say anything different. If on the contrary the Spirit is there conjoined with the Father and the Son, and no one is so shameless as to say anything else, then let them not lay blame on us for following the words of Scripture.

25. But all the apparatus of war has been got ready against us; every intellectual missile is aimed at us; and now blasphemers' tongues shoot and hit and hit again, yet harder than Stephen of old was smitten by the killers of the Christ.[3] And do not let them succeed in concealing the fact that, while an attack on us serves for a pretext for the war, the real aim of these proceedings is higher. It is against us, they say, that they are preparing their engines and their snares; against us that they are shouting to one another, according to each one's strength or cunning, to come on. But the object of attack is faith. The one aim of the whole band of opponents and enemies of " sound doctrine " [4] is to shake down the foundation of the faith of Christ by levelling apostolic tradition with the ground, and utterly destroying it. So like the debtors, — of course *bona fide* debtors, — they clamour for written proof, and reject as worthless the unwritten tradition of the Fathers.[5] But we will not slacken in our de

---

[1] Θεὸν γενεσθαι. The thought has its most famous expression in Ath. *de Incar.* § 54. He was made man that we might be made God — Θεοποιηθῶμεν. cf. *De Decretis*, § 14, and other passages of Ath. Irenæus (*Adv. Hær.* iv. 38 [lxxv.]) writes " *non ab initio dii facti sumus, sed primo quidem homines, tunc demum dii.*" " *Secundum enim benignitatem suam bene dedit bonum, et similes sibi suæ potestatis homines fecit ;*" and Origen (*contra Celsum*, iii. 28), " That the human nature by fellowship with the more divine might be made divine, not in Jesus only, but also in all those who with faith take up the life which Jesus taught;" and Greg. Naz. *Or.* xxx. § 14, " Till by the power of the incarnation he make me God."
    In Basil *adv. Eunom.* ii. 4, we have, " They who are perfect in virtue are deemed worthy of the title of God."
    cf. 2 Pet. i. 4: " That ye might be partakers of the divine nature."

[2] ὑπ' αὐτῶν τῶν λογίων τοῦ πνεύματος. St. Basil is as unconscious as other early Fathers of the limitation of the word λόγια to " discourses." *Vide* Salmon's *Int. to the N.T. Ed.* iv. p. 95.

[3] 1 Tim. vi. 20. The intellectual championship of Basil was chiefly asserted in the vindication of the consubstantiality of the Spirit, against the Arians and Semi-Arians, of whom Eunomius and Macedonius were leaders, the latter giving his name to the party who were unsound on the third Person of the Trinity, and were known as Macedonians as well as Pneumatomachi. But even among the maintainers of the Nicene confession there was much less clear apprehension of the nature and work of the Spirit than of the Son. Even so late as 380, the year after St. Basil's death, Gregory of Nazianzus, *Orat.* xxxi. *de Spiritu Sancto*, Cap. 5, wrote " of the wise on our side some held it to be an energy, some a creature, some God. Others, from respect, they say, to Holy Scripture, which lays down no law on the subject, neither worship nor dishonour the Holy Spirit." cf. Schaff's *Hist. of Christian Ch.* III. Period, Sec. 128. In Letter cxxv. of St. Basil will be found a summary of the heresies with which he credited the Arians, submitted to Eustathius of Sebaste in 373, shortly before the composition of the present treatise for Amphilochius.

[4] Acts v. 29.   [5] Matt. xxviii. 19.

---

[1] The word used is συνάφεια, a crucial word in the controversy concerning the union of the divine and human natures in our Lord, cf. the third Anathema of Cyril against Nestorius and the use of this word, and Theodoret's counter statement (Theod. pp. 25, 27). Theodore of Mopsuestia had preferred συνάφεια to ἕνωσις; Andrew of Samosata saw no difference between them. Athanasius (*de Sent. Dionys.* § 17) employs it for the mutual relationship of the Persons in the Holy Trinity : " προκαταρκτικὸν γάρ ἐστι τῆς συναφείας τὸ ὄνομα."

[2] μηδέ. The note of the Ben. Eds. is, " This reading, followed by Erasmus, stirs the wrath of Combefis, who would read, as is found in four MSS., τότε ἡμῖν, ' then let them lay the blame on us.' But he is quite unfair to Erasmus, who has more clearly apprehended the drift of the argument. Basil brings his opponents to the dilemma that the words ' In the name of the Father and of the Son and of the Holy Ghost ' either do or do not assert a conjunction with the Father and the Son. If not, Basil ought not to be found fault with on the score of ' conjunction,' for he abides by the words of Scripture, and conjunction no more follows from his words than from those of our Lord. If they do, he cannot be found fault with for following the words of Scripture. The attentive reader will see this to be the meaning of Basil, and the received reading ought to be retained."

[3] Χριστοφόνοι. The compound occurs in Ps. Ignat. *ad Philad.* vi.

[4] 1 Tim. i. 10.

[5] Mr. Johnston sees here a reference to the parable of the unjust steward, and appositely quotes Greg. Naz. *Orat.* xxxi.

fence of the truth. We will not cowardly abandon the cause. The Lord has delivered to us as a necessary and saving doctrine that the Holy Spirit is to be ranked with the Father. Our opponents think differently, and see fit to divide and rend [1] asunder, and relegate Him to the nature of a ministering spirit. Is it not then indisputable that they make their own blasphemy more authoritative than the law prescribed by the Lord? Come, then, set aside mere contention. Let us consider the points before us, as follows:

26. Whence is it that we are Christians? Through our faith, would be the universal answer. And in what way are we saved? Plainly because we were regenerate through the grace given in our baptism. How else could we be? And after recognising that this salvation is established through the Father and the Son and the Holy Ghost, shall we fling away "that form of doctrine" [2] which we received? Would it not rather be ground for great groaning if we are found now further off from our salvation " than when we first believed," [3] and deny now what we then received? Whether a man have departed this life without baptism, or have received a baptism lacking in some of the requirements of the tradition, his loss is equal.[4] And whoever does not always and everywhere keep to and hold fast as a sure protection the confession which we recorded at our first admission, when, being delivered "from the idols," we came "to the living God," [5] constitutes himself a "stranger" from the "promises" [6] of God, fighting against his own handwriting,[7] which he put

§ 3, on the heretics' use of Scripture, "They find a cloak for their impiety in their affection for Scripture." The Arians at Nicæa objected to the ὁμοούσιον as unscriptural.
[1] cf. Ep. cxx. 5.   [2] Rom. vi. 17.   [3] Rom. xiii. 11. R.V.
[4] The question is whether the baptism has been solemnized, according to the divine command, in the name of the Father, and of the Son, and of the Holy Ghost. St. Cyprian in his controversy with Stephen, Bp. of Rome, represented the sterner view that heretical baptism was invalid. But, with some exceptions in the East, the position ultimately prevailed that baptism with water, and *in the prescribed words*, by whomsoever administered, was valid. So St. Augustine, " *Si evangelicis verbis in nomine Patris et Filii et Spiritus Sancti Marcion baptismum consecrabat, integrum erat Sacramentum, quamvis ejus fides sub eisdem verbis aliud opinantis quam catholica veritas docet non esset integra.*" (*Cont. Petil. de unico bapt.* § 3.) So the *VIII. Canon of Arles* (314), " *De Afris, quod propria lege sua utuntur ut rebaptizent, placuit, ut, si ad ecclesiam aliquis de hæresi venerit, interrogent eum symbolum; et si perviderint eum in Patre, et Filio et Spiritu Sancto, esse baptizatum, manus ei tantum imponantur, ut accipiat spiritum sanctum. Quod si interrogatus non responderit hanc Trinitatem, baptizetur.*" So the VII. Canon of Constantinople (381) by which the Eunomians who only baptized with one immersion, and the Montanists, here called Phrygians, and the Sabellians, who taught the doctrine of the Fatherhood of the Son, were counted as heathen. Vide Bright's notes on the *Canons of the Councils*, p. 106. Socrates, v. 24, describes how the Eunomi-Eutychians baptized not in the name of the Trinity, but into the death of Christ.
[5] 1 Thess. i. 9.   [6] Eph. ii. 12.
[7] The word χειρόγραφον, more common in Latin than in Greek, is used generally for a bond. cf. Juv. Sat. xvi. 41, "*Debitor aut sumptos pergit non reddere nummos, vana supervacui dicens chirographa ligni.*" On the use of the word, vide Bp. Lightfoot on Col. ii. 14. The names of the catechu-

on record when he professed the faith. For if to me my baptism was the beginning of life, and that day of regeneration the first of days, it is plain that the utterance uttered in the grace of adoption was the most honourable of all. Can I then, perverted by these men's seductive words, abandon the tradition which guided me to the light, which bestowed on me the boon of the knowledge of God, whereby I, so long a foe by reason of sin, was made a child of God? But, for myself, I pray that with this confession I may depart hence to the Lord, and them I charge to preserve the faith secure until the day of Christ, and to keep the Spirit undivided from the Father and the Son, preserving, both in the confession of faith and in the doxology, the doctrine taught them at their baptism.

CHAPTER XI.

That they who deny the Spirit are transgressors.

27. "Who hath woe? Who hath sorrow?" [1] For whom is distress and darkness? For whom eternal doom? Is it not for the transgressors? For them that deny the faith? And what is the proof of their denial? Is it not that they have set at naught their own confessions? And when and what did they confess? Belief in the Father and in the Son and in the Holy Ghost, when they renounced the devil and his angels, and uttered those saving words. What fit title then for them has been discovered, for the children of light to use? Are they not addressed as transgressors, as having violated the covenant of their salvation? What am I to call the denial of God? What the denial of Christ? What but transgressions? And to him who denies the Spirit, what title do you wish me to apply? Must it not be the same, inasmuch as he has broken his covenant with God? And when the confession of faith in Him secures the blessing of true religion, and its denial subjects men to the doom of godlessness, is it not a fearful thing for them to set the confession at naught, not through fear of fire, or sword, or cross, or scourge, or wheel, or rack, but merely led astray by the sophistry and seductions of the pneumatomachi? I testify to every man who is confessing Christ and denying God, that Christ will profit him nothing; [2] to every man that calls upon God but rejects the Son, that his faith is vain; [3] to every man that sets aside the Spirit, that

mens were registered, and the Renunciation and Profession of Faith (*Interrogationes et Responsa; ἐπερωτήσεις καὶ ἀποκρίσεις*) may have been signed.
[1] Prov. xxiii. 29.   [2] cf. Gal. v. 2.   [3] cf. 1 Cor. xv. 17.

his faith in the Father and the Son will be useless, for he cannot even hold it without the presence of the Spirit. For he who does not believe the Spirit does not believe in the Son, and he who has not believed in the Son does not believe in the Father. For none "can say that Jesus is the Lord but by the Holy Ghost,"[1] and " No man hath seen God at any time, but the only begotten God which is in the bosom of the Father, he hath declared him."[2]

Such an one hath neither part nor lot in the true worship; for it is impossible to worship the Son, save by the Holy Ghost; impossible to call upon the Father, save by the Spirit of adoption.

CHAPTER XII.

Against those who assert that the baptism in the name of the Father alone is sufficient.

28. LET no one be misled by the fact of the apostle's frequently omitting the name of the Father and of the Holy Spirit when making mention of baptism, or on this account imagine that the invocation of the names is not observed. " As many of you," he says, " as were baptized into Christ have put on Christ; "[3] and again, " As many of you as were baptized into Christ were baptized into his death."[4] For the naming of Christ is the confession of the whole,[5] shewing forth as it does the God who gave, the Son who received, and the Spirit who is, the unction.[6] So we have learned from Peter, in the Acts, of " Jesus of Nazareth whom God anointed with the Holy Ghost;"[7] and in Isaiah, "The Spirit of the Lord is upon me, because the Lord hath anointed me;"[8] and the Psalmist, " Therefore God, even thy God, hath anointed thee with the oil of gladness above thy fellows."[9] Scripture, however, in the case of baptism, sometimes plainly mentions the Spirit alone.[10]

" For into one Spirit,"[11] it says, " we were all baptized in[12] one body."[13] And in har-

mony with this are the passages: "You shall be baptized with the Holy Ghost,"[1] and " He shall baptize you with the Holy Ghost."[2] But no one on this account would be justified in calling that baptism a perfect baptism wherein only the name of the Spirit was invoked. For the tradition that has been given us by the quickening grace must remain for ever inviolate. He who redeemed our life from destruction[3] gave us power of renewal, whereof the cause is ineffable and hidden in mystery, but bringing great salvation to our souls, so that to add or to take away anything[4] involves manifestly a falling away from the life everlasting. If then in baptism the separation of the Spirit from the Father and the Son is perilous to the baptizer, and of no advantage to the baptized, how can the rending asunder of the Spirit from Father and from Son be safe for us?[5] Faith and baptism are two kindred and inseparable ways of salvation: faith is perfected through baptism, baptism is established through faith, and both are completed by the same names. For as we believe in the Father and the Son and the Holy Ghost, so are we also baptized in the name of the Father and of the Son and of the Holy Ghost: first comes the confession, introducing us to salvation, and baptism follows, setting the seal upon our assent.

CHAPTER XIII.

Statement of the reason why in the writings of Paul the angels are associated with the Father and the Son.

29. IT is, however, objected that other beings which are enumerated with the Father and the Son are certainly not always glorified together with them. The apostle, for instance, in his charge to Timothy, associates the angels with them in the words, " I charge thee before God and the Lord Jesus Christ and the elect angels."[6] We are not for alienating the angels from the rest of creation, and yet, it is argued, we do not allow of their being reckoned with the Father and the Son. To this I reply, although the argument, so obviously absurd is it, does not really deserve a reply, that possibly before a mild and gentle judge, and especially before One who by His leniency to those arraigned before Him demonstrates the unimpeachable equity of His decisions, one might be willing to offer as witness even a fellow-slave; but for a slave to be made free and called a son

---

[1] 1 Cor. xii. 3.
[2] John i. 18. On the reading "only begotten God" cf. note on p. 9. In this passage in St. Basil "God" is the reading of three MSS. at Paris, that at Moscow, that at the Bodleian, and that at Vienna. "Son" is read by Regius III., Regius I., Regius IV., and Regius V. in Paris, the three last being all of the 14th century, the one in the British Museum, and another in the Imperial Library at Vienna, which generally agrees with our own in the Museum.
[3] Gal. iii. 27, R.V.
[4] Rom. vi. 3, with change to 2d person.
[5] cf. note on p. 17
[6] " ἡ τοῦ Χριστοῦ προσηγορία . . . δηλοῖ τόν τε Χρίσαντα Θεὸν καὶ τὸν Χρισθέντα Υἱὸν καὶ τὸ Χρίσμα τὸ Πνεῦμα."
[7] Acts x. 38.   [8] Is. lx. 1.   [9] Ps. xlv. 7.
[10] No subject occurs in the original, but " Scripture " seems better than " the Apostle " of the Bened. Tr. " *Videtur fecisse mentionem,*" moreover, is not the Latin for φαίνεται μνημονεύσας, but for φαίνεται μνημονεῦσαι.
[11] *Sic.*   [12] *Sic.*   [13] 1 Cor. xii. 13, loosely quoted.

[1] Acts i. 5.   [2] Luke iii. 16.   [3] cf. Ps. ciii. 4.
[4] cf. Deut. iv. 2, and Rev. xxi. 18, 19.
[5] cf. note on p. 17.   [6] 1 Tim. v. 21.

of God and quickened from death can only be brought about by Him who has acquired natural kinship with us, and has been changed from the rank of a slave. For how can we be made kin with God by one who is an alien? How can we be freed by one who is himself under the yoke of slavery? It follows that the mention of the Spirit and that of angels are not made under like conditions. The Spirit is called on as Lord of life, and the angels as allies of their fellow-slaves and faithful witnesses of the truth. It is customary for the saints to deliver the commandments of God in the presence of witnesses, as also the apostle himself says to Timothy, " The things which thou hast heard of me among many witnesses, the same commit thou to faithful men;"[1] and now he calls the angels to witness, for he knows that angels shall be present with the Lord when He shall come in the glory of His Father to judge the world in righteousness. For He says, " Whoever shall confess me before men, him shall the Son of Man also confess before the angels of God, but he that denieth Me before men shall be denied before the angels of God;"[2] and Paul in another place says, " When the Lord Jesus shall be revealed from heaven with his angels."[3] Thus he already testifies before the angels, preparing good proofs for himself at the great tribunal.

30. And not only Paul, but generally all those to whom is committed any ministry of the word, never cease from testifying, but call heaven and earth to witness on the ground that now every deed that is done is done within them, and that in the examination of all the actions of life they will be present with the judged. So it is said, " He shall call to the heavens above and to earth, that he may judge his people."[4] And so Moses when about to deliver his oracles to the people says, " I call heaven and earth to witness this day;"[5] and again in his song he says, " Give ear, O ye heavens, and I will speak, and hear, O earth, the words of my mouth;"[6] and Isaiah, " Hear, O heavens, and give ear, O earth;"[7] and Jeremiah describes astonishment in heaven at the tidings of the unholy deeds of the people: "The heaven was astonished at this, and was horribly afraid, because my people committed two evils."[8] And so the apostle, knowing the angels to be set over men as tutors and guardians, calls them to witness. Moreover, Joshua, the son of Nun, even

set up a stone as witness of his words (already a heap somewhere had been called a witness by Jacob),[1] for he says, " Behold this stone shall be a witness unto you this day to the end of days, when ye lie to the Lord our God," [2] perhaps believing that by God's power even the stones would speak to the conviction of the transgressors; or, if not, that at least each man's conscience would be wounded by the force of the reminder. In this manner they who have been entrusted with the stewardship of souls provide witnesses, whatever they may be, so as to produce them at some future day. But the Spirit is ranked together with God, not on account of the emergency of the moment, but on account of the natural fellowship; is not dragged in by us, but invited by the Lord.

CHAPTER XIV.

Objection that some were baptized unto Moses and believed in him, and an answer to it; with remarks upon types.

31. But even if some are baptized unto the Spirit, it is not, it is urged, on this account right for the Spirit to be ranked with God. Some "were baptized unto Moses in the cloud and in the sea." [3] And it is admitted that faith even before now has been put in men; for " The people believed God and his servant Moses." [4] Why then, it is asked, do we, on account of faith and of baptism, exalt and magnify the Holy Spirit so far above creation, when there is evidence that the same things have before now been said of men? What, then, shall we reply? Our answer is that the faith in the Spirit is the same as the faith in the Father and the Son ; and in like manner, too, the baptism. But the faith in Moses and in the cloud is, as it were, in a shadow and type. The nature of the divine is very frequently represented by the rough and shadowy outlines [5] of the types ; but because divine things are prefigured by small and human things, it is obvious that we must not therefore conclude the divine nature to be small. The type is an exhibition of things expected, and gives an imitative anticipation of the future. So Adam was a type of " Him that was to come." [6] Typically, " That rock was Christ; " [7] and the water a type of the living power of the word; as He says, " If any

1 2 Tim. ii. 2.   5 Deut. iv. 26.
2 Luke xii. 8, 9.   6 Deut. xxxii. 1.
3 2 Thess. i. 7.   7 Isa. i. 2.
4 Ps. l. 4.   8 Jer. ii. 12, 13, lxx.

1 Gen. xxxi. 47.   3 1 Cor. x. 2.
2 Josh. xxiv. 27, lxx.   4 Ex. xiv. 31, lxx.
5 σκιαγραφία, or shade-painting, is illusory scene-painting. Plato (*Crit.* 107 c.) calls it "indistinct and deceptive." *cf.* Ar. *Eth. Nic.* i. 3, 4, "παχυλῶς καὶ ἐν τύπῳ." The τύπος gives the general design, not an exact anticipation.
6 Rom. v. 14.   7 1 Cor. x. 4.

man thirst, let him come unto me and drink." [1] The manna is a type of the living bread that came down from heaven; [2] and the serpent on the standard, [3] of the passion of salvation accomplished by means of the cross, wherefore they who even looked thereon were preserved. So in like manner, the history of the exodus of Israel is recorded to shew forth those who are being saved through baptism. For the firstborn of the Israelites were preserved, like the bodies of the baptized, by the giving of grace to them that were marked with blood. For the blood of the sheep is a type of the blood of Christ; and the firstborn, a type of the first-formed. And inasmuch as the first-formed of necessity exists in us, and, in sequence of succession, is transmitted till the end, it follows that " in Adam" we " all die," [4] and that " death reigned" [5] until the fulfilling of the law and the coming of Christ. And the firstborn were preserved by God from being touched by the destroyer, to show that we who were made alive in Christ no longer die in Adam. The sea and the cloud for the time being led on through amazement to faith, but for the time to come they typically prefigured the grace to be. " Who is wise and he shall understand these things?" [6] — how the sea is typically a baptism bringing about the departure of Pharaoh, in like manner as this washing causes the departure of the tyranny of the devil. The sea slew the enemy in itself: and in baptism too dies our enmity towards God. From the sea the people came out unharmed: we too, as it were, alive from the dead, step up from the water " saved " by the " grace " of Him who called us. [7] And the cloud is a shadow of the gift of the Spirit, who cools the flame of our passions by the " mortification " of our " members." [8]

32. What then? Because they were typically baptized unto Moses, is the grace of baptism therefore small? Were it so, and if we were in each case to prejudice the dignity of our privileges by comparing them with their types, not even one of these privileges could be reckoned great; then not the love of God, who gave His only begotten Son for our sins, would be great and extraordinary, because Abraham did not spare his own son; [9] then even the passion of the Lord would not be glorious, because a sheep typified the offering instead of Isaac; then the descent into hell was not fearful, because Jonah

had previously typified the death in three days and three nights. The same prejudicial comparison is made also in the case of baptism by all who judge of the reality by the shadow, and, comparing the typified with the type, attempt by means of Moses and the sea to disparage at once the whole dispensation of the Gospel. What remission of sins, what renewal of life, is there in the sea? What spiritual gift is there through Moses? What dying [1] of sins is there? Those men did not die with Christ; wherefore they were not raised with Him. [2] They did not " bear the image of the heavenly; " [3] they did not " bear about in the body the dying of Jesus; " [4] they did not " put off the old man; " they did not " put on the new man which is renewed in knowledge after the image of Him which created him." [5] Why then do you compare baptisms which have only the name in common, while the distinction between the things themselves is as great as might be that of dream and reality, that of shadow and figures with substantial existence?

33. But belief in Moses not only does not show our belief in the Spirit to be worthless, but, if we adopt our opponents' line of argument, it rather weakens our confession in the God of the universe. " The people," it is written, " believed the Lord and his servant Moses." [6] Moses then is joined with God, not with the Spirit; and he was a type not of the Spirit, but of Christ. For at that time in the ministry of the law, he by means of himself typified " the Mediator between God and men." [7] Moses, when mediating for the people in things pertaining to God, was not a minister of the Spirit; for the law was given, " ordained by angels in the hand of a mediator," [8] namely Moses, in accordance with the summons of the people, " Speak thou with us, . . . but let not God speak with us." [9] Thus faith in Moses is referred to the Lord, the Mediator between God and men, who said, " Had ye believed Moses, ye would have believed me." [10] Is then our faith in the Lord a trifle, because it was signified beforehand through Moses? So then, even if men were baptized unto Moses, it does not follow that the grace given of the Spirit in baptism is small. I may point out, too, that it is usual in Scripture to say Moses and the law, [11] as in the passage, " They have Moses and the prophets." [12] When therefore it is meant to speak of the baptism of the law,

---

[1] John vii. 37.   [2] John vi. 49, 51.
[3] σημεῖον, as in the LXX. cf. Numb. xxi. 9 and John iii. 14.
[4] 1 Cor. xv. 22.   [7] Eph. ii. 5.
[5] Rom. v. 17.   [8] Col. iii. 5. .
[6] Hos. xiv. 9.   [9] cf. Rom. viii. 32.

[1] νέκρωσις. A.V. in 2 Cor. iv. 10, "dying," Rom. iv. 19, "deadness."
[2] cf. Rom. vi. 8.   [5] Col. iii. 9, 10.   [8] Gal. iii. 19.
[3] 1 Cor. xv. 49.   [6] Ex. xiv. 31.   [9] Ex. xx. 19.
[4] 2 Cor. iv. 10.   [7] 1 Tim. ii. 5.   [10] John v. 46.
[11] i.e., to mean by " Moses," the law.   [12] Luke xvi. 29.

the words are, " They were baptized unto Moses." [1] Why then do these calumniators of the truth, by means of the shadow and the types, endeavour to bring contempt and ridicule on the " rejoicing" of our " hope," [2] and the rich gift of our God and Saviour, who through regeneration renews our youth like the eagle's? [3] Surely it is altogether childish, and like a babe who must needs be fed on milk, [4] to be ignorant of the great mystery of our salvation; inasmuch as, in accordance with the gradual progress of our education, while being brought to perfection in our training for godliness, [5] we were first taught elementary and easier lessons, suited to our intelligence, while the Dispenser of our lots was ever leading us up, by gradually accustoming us, like eyes brought up in the dark, to the great light of truth. For He spares our weakness, and in the depth of the riches [6] of His wisdom, and the inscrutable judgments of His intelligence, used this gentle treatment, fitted for our needs, gradually accustoming us to see first the shadows of objects, and to look at the sun in water, to save us from dashing against the spectacle of pure unadulterated light, and being blinded. Just so the Law, having a shadow of things to come, and the typical teaching of the prophets, which is a dark utterance of the truth, have been devised as means to train the eyes of the heart, in that hence the transition to the wisdom hidden in mystery [7] will be made easy. Enough so far concerning types; nor indeed would it be possible to linger longer on this topic, or the incidental discussion would become many times bulkier than the main argument.

CHAPTER XV.

Reply to the suggested objection that we are baptized " into water." Also concerning baptism.

34. WHAT more? Verily, our opponents are well equipped with arguments. We are baptized, they urge, into water, and of course we shall not honour the water above all creation, or give it a share of the honour of the Father and of the Son. The arguments of these men are such as might be expected from angry disputants, leaving no means untried in their attack on him who has offended them, because their reason is clouded over by their feelings. We will not, however, shrink from the discussion even

of these points. If we do not teach the ignorant, at least we shall not turn away before evil doers. But let us for a moment retrace our steps.

35. The dispensation of our God and Saviour concerning man is a recall from the fall, and a return from the alienation caused by disobedience to close communion with God. This is the reason for the sojourn of Christ in the flesh, the pattern life described in the Gospels, the sufferings, the cross, the tomb, the resurrection; so that the man who is being saved through imitation of Christ receives that old adoption. For perfection of life the imitation of Christ is necessary, not only in the example of gentleness, [1] lowliness, and long suffering set us in His life, but also of His actual death. So Paul, the imitator of Christ, [2] says, " being made conformable unto his death; if by any means I might attain unto the resurrection of the dead." [3] How then are we made in the likeness of His death? [4] In that we were buried [5] with Him by baptism. What then is the manner of the burial? And what is the advantage resulting from the imitation? First of all, it is necessary that the continuity of the old life be cut. And this is impossible unless a man be born again, according to the Lord's word; [6] for the regeneration, as indeed the name shews, is a beginning of a second life. So before beginning the second, it is necessary to put an end to the first. For just as in the case of runners who turn and take the second course, [7] a kind of halt and pause intervenes between the movements in the opposite direction, so also in making a change in lives it seemed necessary for death to come as mediator between the two, ending all that goes before, and beginning all that comes after. How then do we achieve the descent into hell? By imitating, through baptism, the burial of Christ. For the bodies of the baptized are, as it were, buried in the water. Baptism then symbolically signifies the putting off of the works of the flesh; as the apostle says, ye were " circumcised with the circumcision made without hands, in putting off the body of the sins of the flesh by the circumcision of Christ; buried with him in baptism." [8]

---

[1] 1 Cor. x. 2.
[2] Heb. iii. 6.
[3] *cf.* Ps. ciii. 5.
[4] *cf.* Heb. v. 12.
[5] *cf.* 1 Tim. iv. 7.
[6] Rom. xi. 33.
[7] 1 Cor. ii. 7.

---

[1] ἀοργησία in Arist. *Eth.* iv. 5, 5, is the defect where meekness (πραότης) is the mean. In Plutarch, who wrote a short treatise on it, it is a virtue. In Mark iii. 5, Jesus looked round on them " with anger, " μετ᾽ ὀργῆς, but in Matt. xi. 29, He calls Himself πρᾷος.
[2] *cf.* 1 Cor. xi. 1.   [3] Phil. iii. 10, 11.   [4] Rom. vi. 4, 5.
[5] A.V., " are buried." Grk. and R.V., " were buried."
[6] John iii. 3.
[7] In the double course (δίαυλος) the runner turned (κάμπτω) the post at the end of the stadium. So " κάμψαι διαύλου θάτερον κῶλον πάλιν " in Æsch. *Ag.* 335, for retracing one's steps another way.
[8] Col. ii. 11, 12.

And there is, as it were, a cleansing of the soul from the filth [1] that has grown on it from the carnal mind,[2] as it is written, " Thou shalt wash me, and I shall be whiter than snow." [3] On this account we do not, as is the fashion of the Jews, wash ourselves at each defilement, but own the baptism of salvation [4] to be one.[5] For there the death on behalf of the world is one, and one the resurrection of the dead, whereof baptism is a type. For this cause the Lord, who is the Dispenser of our life, gave us the covenant of baptism, containing a type of life and death, for the water fulfils the image of death, and the Spirit gives us the earnest of life. Hence it follows that the answer to our question why the water was associated with the Spirit [6] is clear: the reason is because in baptism two ends were proposed; on the one hand, the destroying of the body of sin,[7] that it may never bear fruit unto death; [8] on the other hand, our living unto the Spirit,[9] and having our fruit in holiness; [10] the water receiving the body as in a tomb figures death, while the Spirit pours in the quickening power, renewing our souls from the deadness of sin unto their original life. This then is what it is to be born again of water and of the Spirit, the being made dead being effected in the water, while our life is wrought in us through the Spirit. In three immersions,[11] then, and with three invocations, the great mystery of baptism is performed, to the end that the type of death may be fully figured, and that by the tradition of the divine knowledge the baptized may have their souls enlightened. It follows that if there is any grace in the water, it is not of the nature of the water, but of the presence of the Spirit. For baptism is " not the putting away of the filth of the flesh, but the answer of a good conscience towards God." [1] So in training us for the life that follows on the resurrection the Lord sets out all the manner of life required by the Gospel, laying down for us the law of gentleness, of endurance of wrong, of freedom from the defilement that comes of the love of pleasure, and from covetousness, to the end that we may of set purpose win beforehand and achieve all that the life to come of its inherent nature possesses. If therefore any one in attempting a definition were to describe the gospel as a forecast of the life that follows on the resurrection, he would not seem to me to go beyond what is meet and right. Let us now return to our main topic.

36. Through the Holy Spirit comes our restoration to paradise, our ascension into the kingdom of heaven, our return to the adoption of sons, our liberty to call God our Father, our being made partakers of the grace of Christ, our being called children of light, our sharing in eternal glory, and, in a word, our being brought into a state of all " fulness of blessing," [2] both in this world and in the world to come, of all the good gifts that are in store for us, by promise whereof, through faith, beholding the reflection of their grace as though they were already present, we await the full enjoyment. If such is the earnest, what the perfection? If such the first fruits, what the complete fulfilment? Furthermore, from this too may be apprehended the difference between the grace that comes from the Spirit and the baptism by water: in that John indeed baptized with water, but our Lord Jesus Christ by the Holy Ghost. " I indeed," he says, " baptize you with water unto repentance; but he that cometh after me is mightier than I, whose shoes I am not worthy to bear: he shall baptize you with the Holy Ghost and with fire." [3] Here He calls the trial at the judgment the baptism of fire, as the apostle says, " The fire shall try every man's work, of what sort it is." [4] And again, " The day shall declare it, because it shall be revealed by fire." [5] And ere now there have been some who in their championship of true religion have undergone the death for Christ's sake, not in mere similitude, but in actual fact, and so have needed none of the outward signs of water for their salvation, because they were baptized in their own blood.[6] Thus I write

---

[1] cf. 1 Pet. iii. 21.
[2] τὸ σαρκικὸν φρόνημα. cf. the φρόνημα τῆς σαρκός of Rom. viii. 6. cf. Article ix.
[3] Ps. li. 9.
[4] cf. 1 Pet. iii. 21.
[5] cf. Eph. iv. 5.
[6] cf. John iii. 5.
[7] cf. Rom. vi. 6.
[8] cf. Rom. vii. 5.
[9] cf. Gal v. 25.
[10] cf. Rom. vi. 22.
[11] Trine immersion was the universal rule of the Catholic Church. cf. Greg. Nyss. The Great Catechism, p. 502 of this edition. So Tertull. de Cor. Mil. c. iii., Aquam adituri, ibidem, sed et aliquanto prius in ecclesia, sub antistitis manu contestamur, nos renuntiare diabolo et pompæ et angelis ejus. Dehinc ter mergitamur. Sozomen (vi. 26) says that Eunomius was alleged to be the first to maintain that baptism ought to be performed in one immersion and to corrupt in this manner the tradition of the apostles, and Theodoret (Hæret. fab. iv. 3) describes Eunomius as abandoning the trine immersion, and also the invocation of the Trinity as baptizing into the death of Christ. Jeremy Taylor (Ductor dubitantium, iii. 4, Sect. 13) says, " In England we have a custom of sprinkling, and that but once. . . . As to the number, though the Church of England hath made no law, and therefore the custom of doing it once is the more indifferent and at liberty, yet if the trine immersion be agreeable to the analogy of the mystery, and the other be not, the custom ought not to prevail, and is not to be complied with, if the case be evident or declared."

[1] 1 Pet. iii. 21.
[2] Rom. xv. 29.
[3] Matt. iii. 11.
[4] 1 Cor. iii. 13.
[5] id.
[6] On the martyrs' baptism of blood, cf. Eus. vi. 4, on the martyrdom of the Catechumen Herais. So St. Cyril. of Jerusalem (Cat. Lect. iii. 10), " If a man receive not baptism, he has not salvation; excepting only the martyrs, even who without the water receive the kingdom. For when the Saviour was ransoming the world through the cross, and was pierced

not to disparage the baptism by water, but to overthrow the arguments [1] of those who exalt themselves against the Spirit; who confound things that are distinct from one another, and compare those which admit of no comparison.

CHAPTER XVI.

That the Holy Spirit is in every conception inseparable from the Father and the Son, alike in the creation of perceptible objects, in the dispensation of human affairs, and in the judgment to come.

37. LET us then revert to the point raised from the outset, that in all things the Holy Spirit is inseparable and wholly incapable of being parted from the Father and the Son. St. Paul, in the passage about the gift of tongues, writes to the Corinthians, " If ye all prophesy and there come in one that believeth not, or one unlearned, he is convinced of all, he is judged of all; and thus are the secrets of the heart made manifest; and so falling down on his face he will worship God and report that God is in you of a truth." [2] If then God is known to be in the prophets by the prophesying that is acting according to the distribution of the gifts of the Spirit, let our adversaries consider what kind of place they will attribute to the Holy Spirit. Let them say whether it is more proper to rank Him with God or to thrust Him forth to the place of the creature. Peter's words to Sapphira, " How is it that ye have agreed together to tempt the Spirit of the Lord? Ye have not lied unto men, but unto God," [3] show that sins against the Holy Spirit and against God are the same; and thus you might learn that in every operation the Spirit is closely conjoined with, and inseparable from, the Father and the Son. God works the differences of operations, and the Lord the diversities of administrations, but all the while the Holy Spirit is present too of His own will, dispensing distribution of the gifts according to each recipient's worth. For, it is said, " there are diversities of gifts, but the same Spirit; and differences of administrations, but the same Lord; and there are diversities of operations, but it is the same God which worketh all in all." [4] " But all these," it is

said, " worketh that one and the self-same Spirit, dividing to every man severally as He will." [1] It must not however be supposed because in this passage the apostle names in the first place the Spirit, in the second the Son, and in the third God the Father, that therefore their rank is reversed. The apostle has only started in accordance with our habits of thought; for when we receive gifts, the first that occurs to us is the distributer, next we think of the sender, and then we lift our thoughts to the fountain and cause of the boons.

38. Moreover, from the things created at the beginning may be learnt the fellowship of the Spirit with the Father and the Son. The pure, intelligent, and supermundane powers are and are styled holy, because they have their holiness of the grace given by the Holy Spirit. Accordingly the mode of the creation of the heavenly powers is passed over in silence, for the historian of the cosmogony has revealed to us only the creation of things perceptible by sense. But do thou, who hast power from the things that are seen to form an analogy of the unseen, glorify the Maker by whom all things were made, visible and invisible, principalities and powers, authorities, thrones, and dominions, and all other reasonable natures whom we cannot name.[2] And in the creation bethink thee first, I pray thee, of the original cause of all things that are made, the Father; of the creative cause, the Son; of the perfecting cause, the Spirit; so that the ministering spirits subsist by the will of the Father, are brought into being by the operation of the Son, and perfected by the presence of the Spirit. Moreover, the perfection of angels is sanctification and continuance in it. And let no one imagine me either to affirm that there are three original hypostases [3] or to allege the operation of the Son to be imperfect. For the first principle of existing things is One, creating through the Son and perfecting through the Spirit.[4] The operation of the Father who worketh all in all is not imperfect, neither is the creating work of the Son incomplete if not perfected by the Spirit. The Father, who creates by His sole will, could not stand in any need of the Son, but nevertheless He wills through the Son; nor could the Son, who works according to the likeness of the Father, need co-operation, but the Son too wills to make perfect through the Spirit. "For by the word of the Lord were the

---

in the side, He gave forth blood and water, that some in times of peace should be baptized in water; others in time of persecution, in their own blood." So Tertullian (*In Valentin.* ii.) of the Holy Innocents, "baptized in blood for Jesus' sake" (Keble), "*testimonium Christi sanguine litavere.*"
[1] Τοὺς λογισμοὺς καθαιρῶν. *cf.* 2 Cor. x. 4.
[2] 1 Cor. xiv. 24, 25.
[3] Acts v. 9 and 4. " Thou hast not lied," said to Ananias, interpolated into the rebuke of Sapphira.
[4] 1 Cor. xii. 4, 5, 6.

[1] 1 Cor. xii. 11.   [2] *cf.* Col. i. 16.
[3] ὑποστάσεις, apparently used here as the equivalent of οὐσίαι, unless the negation only extends to ἀρχικάς. *cf.* note on p. 5.
[4] Contrast the neuter τὸ ὄν of Pagan philosophy with the ὁ ὤν or ἐγώ εἰμι of Christian revelation.

heavens made, and all the host of them by the breath [the Spirit] of His mouth."[1] The Word then is not a mere significant impression on the air, borne by the organs of speech; nor is the Spirit of His mouth a vapour, emitted by the organs of respiration; but the Word is He who "was with God in the beginning" and "was God,"[2] and the Spirit of the mouth of God is "the Spirit of truth which proceedeth from the Father."[3] You are therefore to perceive three, the Lord who gives the order, the Word who creates, and the Spirit who confirms.[4] And what other thing could confirmation be than the perfecting according to holiness? This perfecting expresses the confirmation's firmness, unchangeableness, and fixity in good. But there is no sanctification without the Spirit. The powers of the heavens are not holy by nature; were it so there would in this respect be no difference between them and the Holy Spirit. It is in proportion to their relative excellence that they have their meed of holiness from the Spirit. The branding-iron is conceived of together with the fire; and yet the material and the fire are distinct. Thus too in the case of the heavenly powers; their substance is, peradventure, an aërial spirit, or an immaterial fire, as it is written, "Who maketh his angels spirits and his ministers a flame of fire;"[5] wherefore they exist in space and become visible, and appear in their proper bodily form to them that are worthy. But their sanctification, being external to their substance, superinduces their perfection through the communion of the Spirit. They keep their rank by their abiding in the good and true, and while they retain their freedom of will, never fall away from their patient attendance on Him who is truly good. It results that, if by your argument you do away with the Spirit, the hosts of the angels are disbanded, the dominions of archangels are destroyed, all is thrown into confusion, and their life loses law, order, and distinctness. For how are angels to cry "Glory to God in the highest"[6] without being empowered by the Spirit? For "No man can say that Jesus is the Lord but by the Holy Ghost, and no man speaking by the Spirit of God calleth Jesus accursed;"[7] as might be said by wicked and hostile spirits, whose fall establishes our statement of the freedom of the will of the invisible powers; being, as they are, in a condition of equipoise between virtue and vice, and on this account needing the succour of the Spirit. I indeed maintain that even Gabriel[1] in no other way foretells events to come than by the foreknowledge of the Spirit, by reason of the fact that one of the boons distributed by the Spirit is prophecy. And whence did he who was ordained to announce the mysteries of the vision to the Man of Desires[2] derive the wisdom whereby he was enabled to teach hidden things, if not from the Holy Spirit? The revelation of mysteries is indeed the peculiar function of the Spirit, as it is written, "God hath revealed them unto us by His Spirit."[3] And how could "thrones, dominions, principalities and powers"[4] live their blessed life, did they not "behold the face of the Father which is in heaven"?[5] But to behold it is impossible without the Spirit! Just as at night, if you withdraw the light from the house, the eyes fall blind and their faculties become inactive, and the worth of objects cannot be discerned, and gold is trodden on in ignorance as though it were iron, so in the order of the intellectual world it is impossible for the high life of Law to abide without the Spirit. For it so to abide were as likely as that an army should maintain its discipline in the absence of its commander, or a chorus its harmony without the guidance of the coryphæus. How could the Seraphim cry "Holy, Holy, Holy,"[6] were they not taught by the Spirit how often true religion requires them to lift their voice in this ascription of glory? Do "all His angels" and "all His hosts"[7] praise God? It is through the co-operation of the Spirit. Do "thousand thousand" of angels stand before Him, and "ten thousand times ten thousand" ministering spirits?[8] They are blamelessly doing their proper work by the power of the Spirit. All the glorious and unspeakable harmony[9] of the highest heavens both in the service of God, and in the mutual concord of the celestial powers, can therefore only be preserved by the direction of the Spirit. Thus with those beings who are not gradually perfected by increase and advance,[10] but are perfect from the moment of the creation, there is in creation the presence of the

---

[1] Ps. xxxiii. 6. [2] John i. 1. [3] John xv. 26.
[4] τὸν στερεοῦντα τὸ πνεῦμα. It is to be noticed here that St. Basil uses the masculine and more personal form in apposition with the neuter πνεῦμα, and not the neuter as in the creed of Constantinople, τὸ κύριον καὶ τὸ Ζωοποιὸν τὸ ἐκ τοῦ πατρὸς ἐκπορευόμενον, etc. There is scriptural authority for the masculine in the "ὅταν δὲ ἔλθῃ ἐκεῖνος, τὸ πνεῦμα τῆς ἀληθείας" of John xvi. 13. cf. p. 15–17.
[b] Ps. xiv. 4.   [6] Luke ii. 14.   [7] 1 Cor. xii. 3.

[1] Luke i. 11.
[2] "Man greatly beloved." A.V. and R.V. Dan. x. 11.
[3] 1 Cor. ii. 10.   [6] Is. vi. 3.
[4] Col. i. 16.   [7] Ps. cxlviii. 2.
[5] Matt. xviii. 10.   [8] Dan. vii. 10.
[9] cf. Job xxxviii. 7, though for the first clause the lxx. reads ὅτε ἐγενήθη ἄστρα. On the Pythagorean theory of the harmony of the spheres vide Arist. De Cœl. ii. 9, 1.
[10] προκοπή. cf. προέκοπτε of the boy Jesus in Luke ii. 52.

Holy Spirit, who confers on them the grace that flows from Him for the completion and perfection of their essence.[1]

39. But when we speak of the dispensations made for man by our great God and Saviour Jesus Christ,[2] who will gainsay their having been accomplished through the grace of the Spirit? Whether you wish to examine ancient evidence ; — the blessings of the partriarchs, the succour given through the legislation, the types, the prophecies, the valorous feats in war, the signs wrought through just men ; — or on the other hand the things done in the dispensation of the coming of our Lord in the flesh ; — all is through the Spirit. In the first place He was made an unction, and being inseparably present was with the very flesh of the Lord, according to that which is written, " Upon whom thou shalt see the Spirit descending and remaining on Him, the same is " [3] " my beloved Son ; " [4] and " Jesus of Nazareth " whom " God anointed with the Holy Ghost." [5] After this every operation was wrought with the co-operation of the Spirit. He was present when the Lord was being tempted by the devil ; for, it is said, " Jesus was led up of the Spirit into the wilderness to be tempted." [6] He was inseparably with Him while working His wonderful works ; [7] for, it is said, " If I by the Spirit of God cast out devils." [8] And He did not leave Him when He had risen from the dead ; for when renewing man, and, by breathing on the face of the disciples,[9] restoring the grace, that came of the inbreathing of God, which man had lost, what did the Lord say ? " Receive ye the Holy Ghost : whose soever sins ye remit, they are remitted unto them ; and whose soever ye retain, they are retained." [10] And is it not plain and incontestable that the ordering of the Church is effected through the Spirit ? For He gave, it is said, " in the church, first Apostles, secondarily prophets,

thirdly teachers, after that miracles, then gifts of healing, helps, governments, diversities of tongues," [1] for this order is ordained in accordance with the division of the gifts that are of the Spirit.[2]

40. Moreover by any one who carefully uses his reason it will be found that even at the moment of the expected appearance of the Lord from heaven the Holy Spirit will not, as some suppose, have no functions to discharge : on the contrary, even in the day of His revelation, in which the blessed and only potentate [3] will judge the world in righteousness,[4] the Holy Spirit will be present with Him. For who is so ignorant of the good things prepared by God for them that are worthy, as not to know that the crown of the righteous is the grace of the Spirit, bestowed in more abundant and perfect measure in that day, when spiritual glory shall be distributed to each in proportion as he shall have nobly played the man ? For among the glories of the saints are " many mansions " in the Father's house,[5] that is differences of dignities : for as " star differeth from star in glory, so also is the resurrection of the dead." [6] They, then, that were sealed by the Spirit unto the day of redemption,[7] and preserve pure and undiminished the first fruits which they received of the Spirit, are they that shall hear the words " well done thou good and faithful servant ; thou hast been faithful over a few things, I will make thee ruler over many things." [8] In like manner they which have grieved the Holy Spirit by the wickedness of their ways, or have not wrought for Him that gave to them, shall be deprived of what they have received, their grace being transferred to others ; or, according to one of the evangelists, they shall even be wholly cut asunder,[9] — the cutting asunder meaning complete separation from the Spirit. The body is not divided, part being delivered to chastisement, and part let off ; for when a whole has sinned it were like the old fables, and unworthy of a righteous judge, for only the half to suffer chastisement. Nor is the soul cut in two, — that soul the whole of which possesses the sinful affection throughout, and works the wickedness in co-operation with the body. The cutting asunder, as I have observed, is the separation for aye of the soul from the Spirit. For now, although the Spirit does not suffer admixture with the unworthy, He

---

1 ὑπόστασις, apparently again used in its earlier identification with οὐσία.
2 Titus ii. 13, R.V. The A.V. favours the view, opposed to that of the Greek Fathers, that " the great God " means the Father. cf. Theodoret in this edition, pp. 319 and 321 and notes.
3 John i. 33.   5 Acts x. 38.
4 Matt. iii. 17.   6 Matt. iv. 1.
7 δυνάμεις, rendered " wonderful works " in Matt. vii. 22; " mighty works " in Matt. xi. 20, Mark vi. 14, and Luke x. 13; and " miracles " in Acts ii. 22, xix. 11, and Gal. iii. v.
8 Matt. xii. 28.
9 Gen. ii. 7, lxx. is ἐνεφύσησεν εἰς τὸ πρόσωπον αὐτοῦ. " εἰς τὸ πρόσωπον " is thence imported into John xx. 22. Mr. C. F. H. Johnston notes, " This addition . . . is found in the Prayer at the Little Entrance in the Liturgy of St. Mark. Didymus, in his treatise on the Holy Spirit, which we have only in St. Jerome's Latin Version, twice uses 'insufflans in faciem eorum,' §§ 6, 33. The text is quoted in this form by Epiphanius Adv. Hær. lxxiv. 13, and by St. Aug. De Trin. iv. 20." To these instances may be added Athan. Ep. i. § 8, and the versions of Upper and Lower Egypt, the Thebaic, known as the Sahidic, and the Memphitic, or Coptic, both ascribed to the 3d century.   10 John xx. 22, 23.

1 1 Cor. xii. 28.   3 1 Tim. vi. 15.
2 cf. 1 Cor. xii. 11.   4 Acts xvii. 31.
5 παρὰ τῷ πατρί, (= chez le Père,) with little or no change of meaning, for ἐν τῇ οἰκίᾳ τοῦ πατρός μου. John xiv. 2.
6 1 Cor. xv. 41, 42.   8 Matt. xxv. 21.
7 cf. Eph. iv. 30.   9 Matt. xxiv. 51.

nevertheless does seem in a manner to be present with them that have once been sealed, awaiting the salvation which follows on their conversion; but then He will be wholly cut off from the soul that has defiled His grace. For this reason " In Hell there is none that maketh confession; in death none that remembereth God," [1] because the succour of the Spirit is no longer present. How then is it possible to conceive that the judgment is accomplished without the Holy Spirit, wherein the word points out that He is Himself the prize [2] of the righteous, when instead of the earnest [3] is given that which is perfect, and the first condemnation of sinners, when they are deprived of that which they seem to have? But the greatest proof of the conjunction of the Spirit with the Father and the Son is that He is said to have the same relation to God which the spirit in us has to each of us. " For what man " it is said, " knoweth the things of a man, save the spirit of man which is in him? even so the things of God knoweth no man but the Spirit of God." [4]

On this point I have said enough.

CHAPTER XVII.

Against those who say that the Holy Ghost is not to be numbered with, but numbered under, the Father and the Son. Wherein moreover there is a summary notice of the faith concerning right sub-numeration.

41. WHAT, however, they call subnumeration, [5] and in what sense they use this word, cannot even be imagined without difficulty. It is well known that it was imported into our language from the " wisdom of the world; " [6] but a point for our present consideration will be whether it has any immediate relation to the subject under discussion. Those who are adepts in vain investigations tell us that, while some nouns are common and of widely extended denotation, others are more specific, and that the force of some is more limited than that of others. Essence, for instance, is a common noun, predicable of all things both animate and inanimate; while animal is more specific, being predicated of fewer subjects than the former, though of more than those which are considered under it, as it embraces both rational and irrational nature. Again, human is more specific than animal, and man than human, and than man the individual Peter, Paul or John. [1] Do they then mean by subnumeration the division of the common into its subordinate parts? But I should hesitate to believe they have reached such a pitch of infatuation as to assert that the God of the universe, like some common quality conceivable only by reason and without actual existence in any hypostasis, is divided into subordinate divisions, and that then this subdivision is called subnumeration. This would hardly be said even by men melancholy mad, for, besides its impiety, they are establishing the very opposite argument to their own contention. For the subdivisions are of the same essence as that from which they have been divided. The very obviousness of the absurdity makes it difficult for us to find arguments to confute their unreasonableness; so that really their folly looks like an advantage to them; just as soft and yielding bodies offer no resistance, and therefore cannot be struck a stout blow. It is impossible to bring a vigorous confutation to bear on a palpable absurdity. The only course open to us is to pass by their abominable impiety in silence. Yet our love for the brethren and the importunity of our opponents makes silence impossible.

42. What is it that they maintain? Look at the terms of their imposture. " We assert that connumeration is appropriate to subjects of equal dignity, and subnumeration to those which vary in the direction of inferiority." " Why," I rejoined, " do you say this? I fail to understand your extraordinary wisdom. Do you mean that gold is numbered with gold, and that lead is unworthy of the connumeration, but, because of the cheapness of the material, is subnumerated to gold? And do you attribute so much importance to number as that it can

---

[1] Ps. vi. 5, lxx. ὅτι οὐκ ἔστιν ἐν τῷ θανάτῳ ὁ μνημονεύων σου, ἐν δὲ τῷ ἅδῃ τίς ἐξομολογήσεταί σοι; Vulg. " *In inferno autem quis confitebitur tibi ?* "

[2] Phil. iii. 14.   [3] 2 Cor. i. 22, v. 5.   [4] 1 Cor. ii. 11.

[5] " The word was used as a quasi philosophical term to express the doctrine quoted by St. Basil, in § 13: it does not occur in the confession of Eunomius, which was prepared after this book, A.D. 382; but it was used by him in his *Liber Apologeticus* (before A.D. 365) against which St. Basil wrote." Rev. C. F. H. Johnston. For " ὑπαρίθμησις " the only authorities given by the lexicons are " ecclesiastical." But the importation from the " wisdom of the world " implies use in heathen philosophy.

[6] *cf.* 1 Cor. i. 20.

[1] " This portion of the theory of general language is the subject of what is termed the doctrine of the Predicables; a set of distinctions handed down from Aristotle, and his follower Porphyry, many of which have taken a firm root in scientific, and some of them even in popular, phraseology. The predicables are a five-fold division of General Names, not grounded as usual on a difference in their meaning, that is, in the attribute which they connote, but on a difference in the kind of class which they denote. We may predicate of a thing five different varieties of class-name:

A *genus* of the thing (γένος).
A *species* (εἶδος).
A *differentia* (διαφορά).
A *proprium* (ἴδιον).
An *accidens* (συμβεβηκός).

It is to be remarked of these distinctions, that they express, not what the predicate is in its own meaning, but what relation it bears to the subject of which it happens on the particular occasion to be predicated." *J. S. Mill, System of Logic*, i. 133.

either exalt the value of what is cheap, or destroy the dignity of what is valuable? Therefore, again, you will number gold under precious stones, and such precious stones as are smaller and without lustre under those which are larger and brighter in colour. But what will not be said by men who spend their time in nothing else but either ' to tell or to hear some new thing'?[1] Let these supporters of impiety be classed for the future with Stoics and Epicureans. What subnumeration is even possible of things less valuable in relation to things very valuable? How is a brass obol to be numbered under a golden stater? "Because," they reply, "we do not speak of possessing two coins, but one and one." But which of these is subnumerated to the other? Each is similarly mentioned. If then you number each by itself, you cause an equality of value by numbering them in the same way; but, if you join them, you make their value one by numbering them one with the other. But if the subnumeration belongs to the one which is numbered second, then it is in the power of the counter to begin by counting the brass coin. Let us, however, pass over the confutation of their ignorance, and turn our argument to the main topic.

43. Do you maintain that the Son is numbered under the Father, and the Spirit under the Son, or do you confine your subnumeration to the Spirit alone? If, on the other hand, you apply this subnumeration also to the Son, you revive what is the same impious doctrine, the unlikeness of the substance, the lowliness of rank, the coming into being in later time, and once for all, by this one term, you will plainly again set circling all the blasphemies against the Only-begotten. To controvert these blasphemies would be a longer task than my present purpose admits of; and I am the less bound to undertake it because the impiety has been refuted elsewhere to the best of my ability.[2] If on the other hand they suppose the subnumeration to benefit the Spirit alone, they must be taught that the Spirit is spoken of together with the Lord in precisely the same manner in which the Son is spoken of with the Father. "The name of the Father and of the Son and of the Holy Ghost"[3] is delivered in like manner, and, according to the co-ordination of words delivered in baptism, the relation of the Spirit to the Son is the same as that of the Son to the Father. And if the Spirit is co-ordinate with the

Son, and the Son with the Father, it is obvious that the Spirit is also co-ordinate with the Father. When then the names are ranked in one and the same co-ordinate series,[1] what room is there for speaking on the one hand of connumeration, and on the other of subnumeration? Nay, without exception, what thing ever lost its own nature by being numbered? Is it not the fact that things when numbered remain what they naturally and originally were, while number is adopted among us as a sign indicative of the plurality of subjects? For some bodies we count, some we measure, and some we weigh;[2] those which are by nature continuous we apprehend by measure; to those which are divided we apply number (with the exception of those which on account of their fineness are measured); while heavy objects are distinguished by the inclination of the balance. It does not however follow that, because we have invented for our convenience symbols to help us to arrive at the knowledge of quantity, we have therefore changed the nature of the things signified. We do not speak of " weighing under " one another things which are weighed, even though one be gold and the other tin; nor yet do we " measure under " things that are measured; and so in the same way we will not " number under " things which are numbered. And if none of the rest of things admits of subnumeration how can they allege that the Spirit ought to be subnumerated? Labouring as they do under heathen unsoundness, they imagine that things which are inferior, either by grade of rank or subjection of substance, ought to be subnumerated.

CHAPTER XVIII.

In what manner in the confession of the three hypostases we preserve the pious dogma of the Monarchia. Wherein also is the refutation of them that allege that the Spirit is subnumerated.[3]

44. In delivering the formula of the Fa-

---

[1] Acts xvii. 21.
[2] *i e.*, in the second book of his work against Eunomius.
[3] Matt. xxviii. 19.

[1] συστοιχία, a series of similar things, as in Arist. *An. Pr.* ii. 21, 2. In the Pythagorean philosophy, a co-ordinate or parallel series. Arist. *Met.* i. 5, 6, and *Eth. Nic.* i. 6, 7.
[2] *cf.* Wis. xi. 20. "Thou hast ordered all things in measure and number and weight."
[3] The term Μοναρχία first acquired importance in patristic literature in Justin's work *De monarchia*, against Polytheism. Of the lost letter of Irenæus to the Roman Presbyter Florinus, who was deposed for heresy, presumably gnostic, the title, according to Eusebius (*H. E.* v. 20), was περὶ Μοναρχίας, ἢ περὶ τοῦ μὴ εἶναι τὸν θεὸν ποιητὴν κακῶν. Later it came to be used to express not the Divine unity as opposed to Polytheism or Oriental Dualism, but the Divine unity as opposed to Tritheism. *Vide* the words of Dionysius of Rome, as quoted by Athan. *De Decretis*, § 26, "Next let me turn to those who cut in pieces, divide, and destroy that most sacred doctrine of the church of God, the divine Monarchy, making it, as it were, three powers and divided subsistences and three godheads." So St. Basil *Cont. Eunom.* ii. Ἀρχὴ μὲν οὖν πατρὸς οὐδεμία,

ther, the Son, and the Holy Ghost,[1] our Lord did not connect the gift with number. He did not say " into First, Second, and Third,"[2] nor yet " into one, two, and three, but He gave us the boon of the knowledge of the faith which leads to salvation, by means of holy names. So that what saves us is our faith. Number has been devised as a symbol indicative of the quantity of objects. But these men, who bring ruin on themselves from every possible source, have turned even the capacity for counting against the faith. Nothing else undergoes any change in consequence of the addition of number, and yet these men in the case of the divine nature pay reverence to number, lest they should exceed the limits of the honour due to the Paraclete. But, O wisest sirs, let the unapproachable be altogether above and beyond number, as the ancient reverence of the Hebrews wrote the unutterable name of God in peculiar characters, thus endeavouring to set forth its infinite excellence. Count, if you must; but you must not by counting do damage to the faith. Either let the ineffable be honoured by silence ; or let holy things be counted consistently with true religion. There is one God and Father, one Only-begotten, and one Holy Ghost. We proclaim each of the hypostases singly; and, when count we must, we do not let an ignorant arithmetic carry us away to the idea of a plurality of Gods.

45. For we do not count by way of addition, gradually making increase from unity

to multitude, and saying one, two, and three, — nor yet first, second, and third. For " I," God, " am the first, and I am the last."[1] And hitherto we have never, even at the present time, heard of a second God. Worshipping as we do God of God, we both confess the distinction of the Persons, and at the same time abide by the Monarchy. We do not fritter away the theology[2] in a divided plurality, because one Form, so to say, united[3] in the invariableness of the Godhead, is beheld in God the Father, and in God the Only begotten. For the Son is in the Father and the Father in the Son; since such as is the latter, such is the former, and such as is the former, such is the latter ; and herein is the Unity. So that according to the distinction of Persons, both are one and one, and according to the community of Nature, one. How, then, if one and one, are there not two Gods? Because we speak of a king, and of the king's image, and not of two kings. The majesty is not cloven in two, nor the glory divided. The sovereignty and authority over us is one, and so the doxology ascribed by us is not plural but one;[4] because the honour paid to the image passes on to the prototype. Now what in the one case the image is by reason of imitation, that in the other case the Son is by nature ; and as in works of art the likeness is dependent on the form, so in the case of the divine and uncompounded nature the union consists in the communion of the Godhead.[5] One, moreover, is the Holy Spirit, and we speak of Him singly, conjoined as He is to the one Father through the one Son, and through Himself completing the adorable and blessed Trinity. Of Him the intimate relationship to the Father and the Son is sufficiently declared by the fact of His not being ranked in the plurality of the creation, but being spoken of singly ; for he is not one of many, but One. For as there is one Father and one Son, so is there one Holy Ghost. He is consequently as far removed from created Nature as reason requires the singular to be removed from compound and plural bodies ; and He is in such wise united to the Father and to the Son as unit has affinity with unit.

ἀρχὴ δὲ τοῦ υἱοῦ ὁ πατήρ. And in *Ep.* xxxviii. Ἀλλά τίς ἐστι δύναμις ἀγεννήτως καὶ ἀνάρχως ὑφεοτῶσα ἥτις ἐστὶν αἰτία τῆς ἁπάντων τῶν ὄντων αἰτίας, ἐκ γὰρ τοῦ πατρὸς ὁ υἱὸς δι' οὗ τα πάντα. And in *Ep.* cxxv. Ἕνα γὰρ οἴδαμεν ἀγέννητον καὶ μίαν τῶν πάντων ἀρχήν, τὴν πατέρα τοῦ κυρίου ἡμῶν Ἰησοῦ Χριστοῦ. On the doctrine and its exponents compare § 72 of the *De Sp. S.*
   On the other hand " Monarchians " was a name connoting heresy when applied to those who pushed the doctrine of the Unity to an extreme, involving denial of a Trinity. Of these, among the more noteworthy were Paul of Samosata, bp. of Antioch, who was deposed in 269, a representative of thinkers who have been called dynamical monarchians, and Praxeas (supposed by some to be a nickname), who taught at Rome in the reign of Marcus Aurelius, and of whom Tertullian, the originator of the term patripassians, as applied to Monarchians, wrote " *Paracletum fugavit et patrem crucifixit.*" This heretical Monarchianism culminated in Sabellius, the "most original, ingenious, and profound of the Monarchians." Schaff. *Hist. Chr. Church*, i. 293. *cf.* Gisseler, i. p. 127, Harnack's *Monarchianismus* in Herzog's *Real Encyclopædie*, Vol. x. Thomasius *Dog. Gesch.* i. p. 179, and Fialon *Et. Hist.* p. 241.
   [1] Matt. xxviii. 19.
   [2] Mr. C. F. H. Johnston quotes as instances of the application of the word "third" to the Holy Ghost; Justin Martyr (*Apol.* i. 13) " We honour the Spirit of prophecy in the third rank." Tertullian (*In Prax.* 8) " As the fruit from the tree is third from the root, and the rivulet from the river third from the source, and the flame from the ray third from the sun." Eunomius (*Lib. Apol.* § 25) " observing the teaching of Saints, we have learned from them that the Holy Spirit is third in dignity and order, and so have believed him to be third in nature also." On the last St. Basil (*Adv. Eunom.* ii.) rejoins " Perhaps the word of piety allows Him to come in rank second to the Son . . . although He is inferior to the Son in rank and dignity (that we may make the utmost possible concession) it does not reasonably follow thence that he is of a different nature." On the word " perhaps " a dispute arose at the Council of Florence, the Latins denying its genuineness.

   [1] Is. xliv. 6.
   [2] According to patristic usage θεολογία proper is concerned with all that relates to the Divine and Eternal nature of our Lord. *cf.* Bp. Lightfoot. *Ap. Fathers*, Part II. vol. ii. p. 75.
   [3] ἐνιζομένην. Var. lectiones are ἐνιζομένῃ, " seated in," and ἐνεικονιζομένην, " imaged in."
   [4] *cf.* the embolismus, or intercalated prayer in the *Liturgy of St. James*, as cited by Mr. C. F. H. Johnston, " For of thee is the kingdom and the power and the glory, of Father, of Son, and of Holy Ghost, now and ever."
   [5] On the right use of the illustration of εἰκών, *cf.* Basil *Ep.* xxxviii., and Bp. Lightfoot's note on Col. i. 15. *cf.* also John i. 18 and xiv. 9, 10.

46. And it is not from this source alone that our proofs of the natural communion are derived, but from the fact that He is moreover said to be " of God ; "[1] not indeed in the sense in which " all things are of God," [2] but in the sense of proceeding out of God, not by generation, like the Son, but as Breath of His mouth. But in no way is the " mouth " a member, nor the Spirit breath that is dissolved ; but the word " mouth " is used so far as it can be appropriate to God, and the Spirit is a Substance having life, gifted with supreme power of sanctification. Thus the close relation is made plain, while the mode of the ineffable existence is safeguarded. He is moreover styled ' Spirit of Christ,' as being by nature closely related to Him. Wherefore " If any man have not the Spirit of Christ, he is none of His." [3] Hence He alone worthily glorifies the Lord, for, it is said, " He shall glorify me," [4] not as the creature, but as " Spirit of truth," [5] clearly shewing forth the truth in Himself, and, as Spirit of wisdom, in His own greatness revealing " Christ the Power of God and the wisdom of God." [6] And as Paraclete [7] He expresses in Himself the goodness of the Paraclete who sent Him, and in His own dignity manifests the majesty of Him from whom He proceeded. There is then on the one hand a natural glory, as light is the glory of the sun; and on the other a glory bestowed judicially and of free will ' ab extra ' on them that are worthy. The latter is twofold. " A son," it is said, " honoureth his father, and a servant his master." [1] Of these two the one, the servile, is given by the creature ; the other, which may be called the intimate, is fulfilled by the Spirit. For, as our Lord said of Himself, " I have glorified Thee on the earth : I have finished the work which thou gavest me to do ; " [2] so of the Paraclete He says " He shall glorify me : for He shall receive of mine, and shall show it unto you." [3] And as the Son is glorified of the Father when He says " I have both glorified it and will glorify it [4] again," [5] so is the Spirit glorified through His communion with both Father and Son, and through the testimony of the Only-begotten when He says " All manner of sin and blasphemy shall be forgiven unto men : but the blasphemy against the Holy Ghost shall not be forgiven unto men." [6]

47. And when, by means of the power that enlightens us, we fix our eyes on the beauty of the image of the invisible God, and through the image are led up to the supreme beauty of the spectacle of the archetype, then, I ween, is with us inseparably the Spirit of knowledge, in Himself bestowing on them that love the vision of the truth the power of beholding the Image, not making the exhibition from without, but in Himself leading on to the full knowledge. " No man knoweth the Father save the Son." [7] And so " no man can say that Jesus is the Lord but by the Holy Ghost." [8] For it is not said through the Spirit, but by the Spirit, and " God is a spirit, and they that worship Him must worship Him in spirit and in truth," [9] as it is written " in thy light shall we see light," [10] namely by the illumination of the Spirit, " the true light which lighteth every man that cometh into the world." [11] It results that in Himself He shows the glory of the Only begotten, and on true worshippers He in Himself bestows the knowledge of God. Thus the way of the knowledge of God lies from One Spirit through the One Son to the One Father, and conversely the natural Goodness and the inherent Holiness and the royal Dignity extend from the Father through the Only-begotten to the Spirit. Thus there is both acknowledgment of the hypostases and the true

[1] 2 Cor. i. 12.
[2] 1 Cor. xi. 12. George of Laodicea applied this passage to the Son, and wrote to the Arians: " Why complain of Pope Alexander (i.e. of Alexandria) for saying that the Son is from the Father. . . . For if the apostle wrote All things are from God . . . He may be said to be from God in that sense in which all things are from God." Athan., De Syn. 17.
[3] Rom. viii. 9. [5] John xiv. 17. [6] 1 Cor. i. 24.
[4] John xvi. 14.
[7] παράκλητος occurs five times in the N.T., and is rendered in A.V. in John xiv. 16 and 26, xv. 26 and xvi. 7, Comforter; in 1 John ii. 1, Advocate, as applied to the Son. In the text the Son, the Paraclete, is described as sending the Spirit, the Paraclete; in the second clause of the sentence it can hardly be positively determined whether the words τοῦ οθεν προηλθεν refer to the Father or to the Son. The former view is adopted by Mr. C. F. H. Johnston, the latter by the editor of Keble's Studia Sacra, p. 176. The sequence of the sentences in John xv. 26 might lead one to regard οθεν προηλθεν as equivalent to παρα τοῦ Πατρὸς εκπορεύεται. On the other hand, St. Basil's avoidance of direct citation of the verb εκπορεύεται, his close connexion of τοῦ ἀποστείλαντος with οθεν προηλθεν, and the close of the verse in St. John's gospel εκεῖνος μαρτυρήσει περι εμοῦ, suggest that the μεγαλωσύνη in St. Basil's mind may be the μεγαλωσύνη of the Son. At the same time, while the Western Church was in the main unanimous as to the double procession, this passage from St. Basil is not quoted as an exception to the general current of the teaching of the Greek Fathers, who, as Bp. Pearson expresses it, " stuck more closely to the phrase and language of the Scriptures, saying that the spirit proceedeth from the Father." (Pearson On the Creed, Art. viii. where vide quotations.) Vide also Thomasius, Christ. Dogm., i. 270, Namentlich auf letzere Bestimmung legten die griechischen Väter grosses Gewicht. Im Gegensatz gegen den macedonischen Irrtum, der den Geist für ein Geschöpf des Sohnes ansah, führte man die Subsistenz desselben ebenso auf den Vater zurück wie die des Sohnes. Man lehrte, also, der heilige Geist geht vom Vater aus, der Vater ist die ἀρχη wie des Sohnes so auch des Geistes; aber mit der dem herkömmlichen Zuge des Dogma entsprechenden Näherbestimmung: nicht ἀμέσως, sondern ἐμμέσως, interventu filii geht der Geist vom Vater aus, also " durch den Sohn vom Vater." So die bedeutendsten Kirchenlehrer, während andere einfach bei der Formel stehen blieben; er gehe vom Vater aus.

[1] Mal. i. 6. [2] John xvii. 4. [3] John xvi. 14.
[4] Four MSS. of the De S.S. read ἐδόξασά σε, a variation not appearing in MSS. of the Gospel.
[5] John xii. 28. [6] Matt. xii. 31.
[7] Matt. xi. 27, " οὐδεὶς οἶδε τὸν πατέρα εἰ μὴ ὁ Υἱός " substituted for " οὐ δὲ τὸν πατέρα τὶς ἐπιγνώσκει εἰ μὴ ὁ Υἱός."
[8] 1 Cor. xii. 3. [10] Ps. xxxvi. 9.
[9] John iv. 24. [11] John i. 9.

dogma of the Monarchy is not lost.[1] They on the other hand who support their sub-numeration by talking of first and second and third ought to be informed that into the undefiled theology of Christians they are importing the polytheism of heathen error. No other result can be achieved by the fell device of subnumeration than the confession of a first, a second, and a third God. For us is sufficient the order prescribed by the Lord. He who confuses this order will be no less guilty of transgressing the law than are the impious heathen.

Enough has been now said to prove, in contravention of their error, that the communion of Nature is in no wise dissolved by the manner of subnumeration. Let us, however, make a concession to our contentious and feeble minded adversary, and grant that what is second to anything is spoken of in subnumeration to it. Now let us see what follows. " The first man " it is said " is of the earth earthy, the second man is the Lord from heaven."[2] Again "that was not first which is spiritual but that which is natural and afterward that which is spiritual."[3] If then the second is subnumerated to the first, and the subnumerated is inferior in dignity to that to which it was subnumerated, according to you the spiritual is inferior in honour to the natural, and the heavenly man to the earthy.

CHAPTER XIX.

Against those who assert that the Spirit ought not to be glorified.

48. " Be it so," it is rejoined, " but glory is by no means so absolutely due to the Spirit as to require His exaltation by us in doxologies." Whence then could we get our demonstrations of the dignity of the Spirit, " passing all understanding,"[4] if His communion with the Father and the Son were not reckoned by our opponents as good for testimony of His rank? It is, at all events, possible for us to arrive to a certain extent at intelligent apprehension of the sublimity of His nature and of His unapproachable power, by looking at the mean-ing of His title, and at the magnitude of His operations, and by His good gifts bestowed on us or rather on all creation. He is called Spirit, as " God is a Spirit,"[1] and " the breath of our nostrils, the anointed of the Lord."[2] He is called holy,[3] as the Father is holy, and the Son is holy, for to the creature holiness was brought in from without, but to the Spirit holiness is the fulfilment of nature, and it is for this reason that He is described not as being sanctified, but as sanctifying. He is called good,[4] as the Father is good, and He who was begotten of the Good is good, and to the Spirit His goodness is essence. He is called upright,[5] as " the Lord is upright,"[6] in that He is Himself truth,[7] and is Himself Righteousness,[8] having no divergence nor leaning to one side or to the other, on account of the immutability of His substance. He is called Paraclete, like the Only begotten, as He Himself says, " I will ask the Father, and He will give you another comforter."[9] Thus names are borne by the Spirit in common with the Father and the Son, and He gets these titles from His natural and close relationship. From what other source could they be derived? Again He is called royal,[10] Spirit of truth,[11] and Spirit of wisdom.[12] " The Spirit of God," it is said " hath made me,"[13] and God filled Bezaleel with " the divine Spirit of wisdom and understanding and knowledge."[14] Such names as these are su-per-eminent and mighty, but they do not transcend His glory.

49. And His operations, what are they? For majesty ineffable, and for numbers innumerable. How shall we form a conception of what extends beyond the ages? What were His operations before that creation whereof we can conceive? How great the grace which He conferred on creation? What the power exercised by Him over the ages to come? He existed; He pre-existed; He co-existed with the Father and the Son before the ages. It follows that, even if you can conceive of anything beyond the ages, you will find the Spirit yet further above and beyond. And if you think of the creation, the powers of the heavens were estab-

---

[1] *cf.* note on p. 27 and the distinction between δόγμα and κήρυγμα in § 66. "The great objection which the Eastern Church makes to the *Filioque*, is, that it implies the existence of two ἀρχαὶ in the godhead; and if we believe in δυο ἄναρχοι; we, in effect, believe in two Gods. The unity of the Godhead can only be maintained by acknowledging the Father to be the sole Ἀρχὴ or πηγὴ Θεότητος, who from all eternity has communicated His own Godhead to His co-eternal and consubstantial Son and Spirit. This reasoning is generally true. But, as the doctrine of the Procession of the Spirit from the Father and the Son presupposes the eternal generation of the Son from the Father; it does not follow, that that doctrine impugns the Catholic belief in the Μία Ἀρχή." Bp. Harold Browne, *Exp. xxxix Art.*, Note on Art v.
[2] 1 Cor. xv. 47. [3] 1 Cor. xv. 46. [4] Phil. iv. 7.

[1] John iv. 24.
[2] Lam. iv. 20. *Sic* in A.V. and R.V., the reference being to Zedekiah. *cf.* Jer. xxxix. 5. The Vulgate reads, "*Spiritus oris nostri Christus Dominus*," from the Greek of the LXX. quoted by St. Basil, " Πνεῦμα προσώπου ἡμῶν χριστὸς κύριος."
[3] 1 John i. 20. [5] Ps. li. 10.
[4] Ps. cxliii. 10. [6] Ps. xcii. 15.
[7] John xiv. 17; xv. 26; xvi. 13; 1 John v. 6.
[8] 2 Cor. iii. 8, 9.
[9] John xiv. 16, παράκλητον. *cf.* Note on p. 29.
[10] Ps. li. 12, lxx. πνεῦμα ἡγεμονικόν. Vulg. *spiritus principalis.*
[11] John xv. 26, etc. [13] Job xxxiii. 4.
[12] Is. xi. 2. [14] Ex. xxxi. 3, LXX.

lished by the Spirit,[1] the establishment being understood to refer to disability to fall away from good. For it is from the Spirit that the powers derive their close relationship to God, their inability to change to evil, and their continuance in blessedness. Is it Christ's advent? The Spirit is forerunner. Is there the incarnate presence? The Spirit is inseparable. Working of miracles, and gifts of healing are through the Holy Spirit. Demons were driven out by the Spirit of God. The devil was brought to naught by the presence of the Spirit. Remission of sins was by the gift of the Spirit, for "ye were washed, ye were sanctified, . . . in the name of the Lord Jesus Christ, and in the holy Spirit of our God."[2] There is close relationship with God through the Spirit, for " God hath sent forth the Spirit of His Son into your hearts, crying Abba, Father."[3] The resurrection from the dead is effected by the operation of the Spirit, for " Thou sendest forth thy spirit, they are created; and Thou renewest the face of the earth."[4] If here creation may be taken to mean the bringing of the departed to life again, how mighty is not the operation of the Spirit, Who is to us the dispenser of the life that follows on the resurrection, and attunes our souls to the spiritual life beyond? Or if here by creation is meant the change to a better condition of those who in this life have fallen into sin, (for it is so understood according to the usage of Scripture, as in the words of Paul " if any man be in Christ he is a new creature"[5]), the renewal which takes place in this life, and the transmutation from our earthly and sensuous life to the heavenly conversation which takes place in us through the Spirit, then our souls are exalted to the highest pitch of admiration. With these thoughts before us are we to be afraid of going beyond due bounds in the extravagance of the honour we pay? Shall we not rather fear lest, even though we seem to give Him the highest names which the thoughts of man can conceive or man's tongue utter, we let our thoughts about Him fall too low?

It is the Spirit which says, as the Lord says, " Get thee down, and go with them, doubting nothing: for I have sent them."[6] Are these the words of an inferior, or of one in dread? " Separate me Barnabas and Saul for the work whereunto I have called them."[7] Does a slave speak thus? And Isaiah, " The Lord God and His Spirit hath sent me,"[1] and " the Spirit came down from the Lord and guided them."[2] And pray do not again understand by this guidance some humble service, for the Word witnesses that it was the work of God; — " Thou leddest thy people," it is said " like a flock,"[3] and " Thou that leadest Joseph like a flock,"[4] and " He led them on safely, so that they feared not."[5] Thus when you hear that when the Comforter is come, He will put you in remembrance, and " guide you into all truth."[6] do not misrepresent the meaning.

50. But, it is said that " He maketh intercession for us."[7] It follows then that, as the suppliant is inferior to the benefactor, so far is the Spirit inferior in dignity to God. But have you never heard concerning the Only-begotten that He " is at the right hand of God, who also maketh intercession for us"?[8] Do not, then, because the Spirit is in you, — if indeed He is at all in you, — nor yet because He teaches us who were blinded, and guides us to the choice of what profits us, — do not for this reason allow yourself to be deprived of the right and holy opinion concerning Him. For to make the loving kindness of your benefactor a ground of ingratitude were indeed a very extravagance of unfairness. " Grieve not the Holy Spirit;"[9] hear the words of Stephen, the first fruits of the martyrs, when he reproaches the people for their rebellion and disobedience; " you do always," he says, " resist the Holy Ghost; "[10] and again Isaiah, — " They vexed His Holy Spirit, therefore He was turned to be their enemy; "[11] and in another passage, " the house of Jacob angered the Spirit of the Lord."[12] Are not these pas-

---

[1] Isa. xlviii. 16. Mr. C. F. Johnston remarks: " In Isaiah xlviii. 16 St. Didymus, as translated by St. Jerome, gives *Spiritum suum*. The Targum has the same. St. Ambrose writes: ' *Quis est qui dicit; misit me Dominus Deus et Spiritus Ejus; nisi Qui venit a Patre. ut salvos faceret peccatores? Quem ut audis, et Spiritus misit; ne cum legis quia Filius Spiritum mittit, inferioris esse Spiritum createres potestatis,*' (*De Sp. S.* iii. 1, § 7.) The passage is quoted by St. Athanasius, St. Basil, St. Cyril Hieros., and, as far as the editor is aware, without any comment which would help to determine their way of understanding the case of τὸ πνεῦμα; but Origen, on the words ' Whosoever shall humble himself as this little child' (*Comm. in Evang.*, Matt. xiii. 18) says, — quoting the original, which may be rendered, " ' humbling himself as this little child is imitating the Holy Spirit, who humbled Himself for men's salvation. That the Saviour and the Holy Ghost were sent by the Father for the salvation of men is made plain by Isaiah saying, in the person of the Saviour, 'the Lord sent me, and His Spirit.' It must be observed, however, that the phrase is ambiguous, for either God sent and the Holy Ghost also sent, the Saviour; or, as I understand, the Father sent both, the Saviour and the Holy Ghost.'" The Vulgate and Beza both render " *Spiritus.*" The order of the Hebrew is in favour of the nominative, as in the Vulgate and lxx. *cf.* Note A on Chap. xlviii. of Isaiah in the *Speaker's Commentary*.

[2] Is. lxii. 14, LXX. [8] Rom. viii. 34.
[3] Ps. lxxvii. 20. [9] Eph. iv. 30.
[4] Ps. lxxx. 1. [10] Acts vii. 51.
[5] Ps. lxxviii. 53. [11] Is. lxiii. 10.
[6] John xvi. 13. *cf.* xiv. 26. [12] Ps. cvi. 32; Micah ii. 7.
[7] Rom. viii. 26; 27.

---

[1] *cf.* Ps. xxxiii. 6. [5] 2 Cor. v. 17.
[2] 1 Cor. vi. 11 R.V. [6] Acts x. 20.
[3] Gal. iv. 6. [7] Acts xiii. 2.
[4] Ps. civ. 30.

sages indicative of authoritative power? I leave it to the judgment of my readers to determine what opinions we ought to hold when we hear these passages; whether we are to regard the Spirit as an instrument, a subject, of equal rank with the creature, and a fellow servant of ourselves, or whether, on the contrary, to the ears of the pious the mere whisper of this blasphemy is not most grievous. Do you call the Spirit a servant? But, it is said, "the servant knoweth not what his Lord doeth," [1] and yet the Spirit knoweth the things of God, as "the spirit of man that is in him." [2]

CHAPTER XX.

Against those who maintain that the Spirit is in the rank neither of a servant nor of a master, but in that of the free.

51. He is not a slave, it is said; not a master, but free. Oh the terrible insensibility, the pitiable audacity, of them that maintain this! Shall I rather lament in them their ignorance or their blasphemy? They try to insult the doctrines that concern the divine nature [3] by comparing them with the human, and endeavour to apply to the ineffable nature of God that common custom of human life whereby the difference of degrees is variable, not perceiving that among men no one is a slave by nature. For men are either brought under a yoke of slavery by conquest, as when prisoners are taken in war; or they are enslaved on account of poverty, as the Egyptians were oppressed by Pharaoh; or, by a wise and mysterious dispensation, the worst children are by their fathers' order condemned to serve the wiser and the better; [4] and this any righteous enquirer into the circumstances would declare to be not a sentence of condemnation but a benefit. For it is more profitable that the man who, through lack of intelligence, has no natural principle of rule within himself, should become the chattel of another, to the end that, being guided by the reason of his master, he may be like a chariot with a charioteer, or a boat with a steersman seated at the tiller. For this reason Jacob by his father's blessing became lord of Esau, [5] in order that the foolish son, who had not intelligence, his proper guardian, might, even though he wished it not, be benefited by his prudent brother. So Canaan shall be "a servant unto his brethren" [6] because, since his father Ham was unwise, he was

uninstructed in virtue. In this world, then, it is thus that men are made slaves, but they who have escaped poverty or war, or do not require the tutelage of others, are free. It follows that even though one man be called master and another servant, nevertheless, both in view of our mutual equality of rank and as chattels of our Creator, we are all fellow slaves. But in that other world what can you bring out of bondage? For no sooner were they created than bondage was commenced. The heavenly bodies exercise no rule over one another, for they are unmoved by ambition, but all bow down to God, and render to Him alike the awe which is due to Him as Master and the glory which falls to Him as Creator. For "a son honoureth his father and a servant his master," [1] and from all God asks one of these two things; for "if I then be a Father where is my honour? and if I be a Master where is my fear?" [2] Otherwise the life of all men, if it were not under the oversight of a master, would be most pitiable; as is the condition of the apostate powers who, because they stiffen their neck against God Almighty, fling off the reins of their bondage, — not that their natural constitution is different, but the cause is in their disobedient disposition to their Creator. Whom then do you call free? Him who has no King? Him who has neither power to rule another nor willingness to be ruled? Among all existent beings no such nature is to be found. To entertain such a conception of the Spirit is obvious blasphemy. If He is a creature of course He serves with all the rest, for "all things," it is said "are thy servants," [3] but if He is above Creation, then He shares in royalty. [4]

---

[1] Mal. i. 6.   [2] Mal. i. 6.   [3] Ps. cxix. 91.

[4] St. Basil's view of slavery is that (a) as regards our relation to God, all created beings are naturally in a condition of subservience to the Creator; (b) as regards our relationship to one another, slavery is not of nature, but of convention and circumstance. How far he is here at variance with the well known account of slavery given by Aristotle in the first Book of the *Politics* will depend upon the interpretation we put upon the word "nature." "Is there," asks Aristotle, "any one intended by nature to be a slave, and for whom such a condition is expedient and right, or rather is not all slavery a violation of nature? There is no difficulty in answering this question, on grounds both of reason and fact. For that some should rule, and others be ruled, is a thing not only necessary, but expedient; from the hour of their birth some are marked out for subjection, others for rule. . . . Where, then, there is such a difference as that between soul and body, or between men and animals (as in the case of those whose business it is to use their body, and who can do nothing better), the lower sort are by nature slaves, and it is better for them, as for all inferiors, that they should be under the rule of a master. . . . It is clear, then, that some men are by nature free and others slaves, and that for these latter slavery is both expedient and right." *Politics*, Bk. i, Sec. 5. Here by *Nature* seems to be meant something like Basil's "lack of intelligence," and of the τὸ κατὰ φύσιν ἄρχον, which makes it "profitable" for one man to be the chattel of another (κτῆμα is livestock, especially *mancipium*. *cf.* Shakspere's K. and Pet., "She is my goods, my chattels." "Chattel" is a doublet of "cattle"). St. Basil and Aristotle are at one as to the advantage to the weak slave of his having a powerful protector; and this, no doubt, is the point of view from which slavery can be best apologized for.

---

[1] John xv. 15.   [2] 1 Cor. ii. 11.
[3] τὰ τῆς θεολογίας δόγματα. *cf.* note on § 66.
[4] *cf.* Gen. ix. 25.   [5] Gen. xxvii. 29.   [6] Gen. ix. 25.

CHAPTER XXI.

Proof from Scripture that the Spirit is called Lord.

52. BUT why get an unfair victory for our argument by fighting over these undignified questions, when it is within our power to prove that the excellence of the glory is beyond dispute by adducing more lofty considerations? If, indeed, we repeat what we have been taught by Scripture, every one of the Pneumatomachi will peradventure raise a loud and vehement outcry, stop their ears, pick up stones or anything else that comes to hand for a weapon, and charge against us. But our own security must not be regarded by us before the truth. We have learnt from the Apostle, "the Lord direct your hearts into the love of God and into the patient waiting for Christ" [1] *for our tribulations.* Who is the Lord that directs into the love of God and into the patient waiting for Christ for tribulations? Let those men answer us who are for making a slave of the Holy Spirit. For if the argument had been about God the Father, it would certainly have said, 'the Lord direct you into His own love,' or if about the Son, it would have added 'into His own patience.' Let them then seek what other Person there is who is

worthy to be honoured with the title of Lord. And parallel with this is that other passage, " and the Lord make you to increase and abound in love one toward another, and toward all men, even as we do towards you; to the end He may establish your hearts unblamable in holiness before God, even our Father, at the coming of our Lord Jesus Christ with all His saints." [1] Now what Lord does he entreat to stablish the hearts of the faithful at Thessalonica, unblamable in holiness before God even our Father, at the coming of our Lord? Let those answer who place the Holy Ghost among the ministering spirits that are sent forth on service. They cannot. Wherefore let them hear yet another testimony which distinctly calls the Spirit Lord. " The Lord," it is said, " is that Spirit;" and again "even as from the Lord the Spirit." [2] But to leave no ground for objection, I will quote the actual words of the Apostle;—" For even unto this day remaineth the same veil untaken away in the reading of the Old Testament, which veil is done away in Christ. . . . Nevertheless, when it shall turn to the Lord, the veil shall be taken away. Now the Lord is that Spirit." [3] Why does he speak thus? Because he who abides in the bare sense of the letter, and in it busies himself with the observances of the Law, has, as it were, got his own heart enveloped in the Jewish acceptance of the letter, like a veil; and this befalls him because of his ignorance that the bodily observance of the Law is done away by the presence of Christ, in that for the future the types are transferred to the reality. Lamps are made needless by the advent of the sun; and, on the appearance of the truth, the occupation of the Law is gone, and prophecy is hushed into silence. He, on the contrary, who has been empowered to look down into the depth of the meaning of the Law, and, after passing through the obscurity of the letter, as through a veil, to arrive within things unspeakable, is like Moses taking off the veil when he spoke with God. He, too, turns from the letter to the Spirit. So with the veil on the face of Moses corresponds the obscurity of the teaching of the Law, and spiritual contemplation with the turning to the Lord. He, then, who in the reading of the Law takes away the letter and turns to the Lord, — and the Lord is now called the

---

Christianity did indeed do much to better the condition of the slave by asserting his spiritual freedom, but at first it did little more than emphasize the later philosophy of heathendom, εἰ σῶμα δοῦλον, ἀλλ᾽ ὁ νοῦς ἐλεύθερος (Soph., *frag. incert.* xxii.), and gave the highest meaning to such thoughts as those expressed in the late *Epigram* of Damascius (c. 530) on a dead slave:

Ζωσίμη ἡ πρὶν ἐοῦσα μόνῳ τῷ σώματι δούλη,
Καὶ τῷ σώματι νῦν εὗρεν ἐλευθερίην.

It thought less of a slave's servitude to fellow man than of the slavery of bond and free alike to evil. *cf.* Aug., *De Civit. Dei.* iv. cap. iii. " *Bonus etiamsi serviat liber est : malus autem si regnat servus est : nec est unius hominis, sed quod gravius est tot dominorum quot vitiorum.*" Chrysostom even explains St. Paul's non-condemnation of slavery on the ground that its existence, with that of Christian liberty, was a greater moral triumph than its abolition. (*In Genes. Serm.* v. I.) Even so late as the sixth century the legislation of Justinian, though protective, supposed no natural liberty. " *Expedit enim respublicæ ne quis re suâ utatur male.*" *Instit.* i. viii. quoted by Milman, *Lat. Christ.* ii. 14. We must not therefore be surprised at not finding in a Father of the fourth century an anticipation of a later development of Christian sentiment. At the same time it was in the age of St. Basil that " the language of the Fathers assumes a bolder tone" (*cf. Dict. Christ. Ant.* ii. 1905), and "in the correspondence of Gregory Nazianzen we find him referring to a case where a slave had been made bishop over a small community in the desert. The Christian lady to whom he belonged endeavoured to assert her right of ownership, for which she was severely rebuked by St. Basil. (*cf. Letter* CXV.) After St. Basil's death she again claimed the slave, whereupon Gregory addressed her a letter of grave remonstrance at her unchristian desire to recall his brother bishop from his sphere of duty. *Ep.* 79," *id.*

[1] 2 Thess. iii. 5. A note of the Benedictine Editors on this passage says: " It must be admitted that these words are not found in the sacred text and are wanting in three manuscripts of this work. Moreover, in the *Regis Quintus* they are only inserted by a second hand, but since they are shortly afterwards repeated by Basil, as though taken from the sacred context, I am unwilling to delete them, and it is more probable that they were withdrawn from the manuscripts from which they are wanting because they were not found in the apostle, than added, without any reason at all, to the manuscripts in which they occur."

[1] 1 Thess. iii. 12, 13.
[2] 2 Cor. iii. 17, 18, R.V. In *Adv. Eunom.* iii. 3 St. Basil had quoted v. 17 of the Son, making πνεῦμα descriptive of our Lord. "This was written." adds Mr. C. F. H. Johnston, "during St. Basil's presbyterate, at least ten years earlier."
[3] 2 Cor. iii. 14, 16, 17.

Spirit, — becomes moreover like Moses, who had his face glorified by the manifestation of God. For just as objects which lie near brilliant colours are themselves tinted by the brightness which is shed around, so is he who fixes his gaze firmly on the Spirit by the Spirit's glory somehow transfigured into greater splendour, having his heart lighted up, as it were, by some light streaming from the truth of the Spirit.[1] And this is "being changed from[2] the glory" of the Spirit "into" His own "glory," not in niggard degree, nor dimly and indistinctly, but as we might expect any one to be who is enlightened by[3] the Spirit. Do you not, O man, fear the Apostle when he says "Ye are the temple of God, and the Spirit of God dwelleth in you"?[4] Could he ever have brooked to honour with the title of "temple" the quarters of a slave? How can he who calls Scripture "God-inspired,"[5] because it was written through the inspiration of the Spirit, use the language of one who insults and belittles Him?

CHAPTER XXII.

Establishment of the natural communion of the Spirit from His being, equally with the Father and the Son, unapproachable in thought.[6]

53. MOREOVER the surpassing excellence of the nature of the Spirit is to be learned not only from His having the same title as the Father and the Son, and sharing in their operations, but also from His being, like the Father and the Son, unapproachable in thought. For what our Lord says of the Father as being above and beyond human conception, and what He says of the Son, this same language He uses also of the Holy Ghost. "O righteous Father," He says, "the world hath not known Thee,"[7] meaning here by the world not the complex whole compounded of heaven and earth, but this life of ours subject to death,[8] and exposed to innumerable vicissitudes. And when discoursing of Himself He says, "Yet a little while and the world seeth me no more, but

ye see me;"[1] again in this passage, applying the word *world* to those who being bound down by this material and carnal life, and beholding[2] the truth by material sight alone,[3] were ordained, through their unbelief in the resurrection, to see our Lord no more with the eyes of the heart. And He said the same concerning the Spirit. "The Spirit of truth," He says, "whom the world cannot receive, because it seeth Him not, neither knoweth Him: but ye know Him, for He dwelleth with you."[4] For the carnal man, who has never trained his mind to contemplation,[5] but rather keeps it buried deep in the lust of the flesh,[6] as in mud, is powerless to look up to the spiritual light of the truth. And so the world, that is life enslaved by the affections of the flesh, can no more receive the grace of the Spirit than a weak eye the light of a sunbeam. But the Lord, who by His teaching bore witness to purity of life, gives to His disciples the power of now both beholding and contemplating the Spirit. For "now," He says, "Ye are clean through the word which I have spoken unto you,"[7] wherefore "the world cannot receive Him, because it seeth Him not, . . . but ye know Him; for he dwelleth with you."[8] And so says Isaiah; — "He that spread forth the earth and that which cometh out of it; he that giveth breath unto the people upon it, and Spirit to them that trample on it"[9]; for they that trample down earthly things and rise above them are borne witness to as worthy of the gift of the Holy Ghost. What then ought to be thought of Him whom the world cannot receive, and Whom saints alone can contemplate through pureness of heart? What kind of honours can be deemed adequate to Him?

CHAPTER XXIII.

The glorifying of the Spirit is the enumeration of His attributes.

54. [10] Now of the rest of the Powers each

---

[1] cf. 2 Cor. iii. 18.
[2] St. Basil gives ἀπό the sense of "*by*." So Theodoret, Œcum., Theophylact, Bengel. *cf.* Alford *in loc.* The German is able to repeat the prep., as in Greek and Latin, "*von einer Klarheit zu der andern, als vom Herrn.*"
[3] ἀπό.   [4] 1 Cor. iii. 16.   [5] 2 Tim. iii. 16.
[6] πρὸς θεωρίαν δυσέφικτον. The Benedictine Latin is "*incomprehensibilis*," but this is rather ἀκατάληπτος. The "incomprehensible" of the Ath. Creed is "*immensus.*"
[7] John xvii. 25.
[8] ἐπίκηρος. The force of the word as applied to this life is illustrated by the 61st Epigram of Callimachus:

Τίς ξένος, ὦ ναυηγέ; Λεόντιχος ἐνθάδε νεκρὸν
    εὗρεν ἐπ' αἰγιαλοῖς, χῶσε δὲ τῷδε τάφῳ
δακρύσας ἐπίκηρον ἑὸν βίον· οὐδὲ γὰρ αὐτὸς
    ἥσυχος, αἰθυίῃς δ' ἴσα θαλασσοπορεῖ.

[1] John xiv. 19.
[2] ἐπιβλέποντας, the reading of the Viennese MS. vulgo ἐπιτρέποντας.
[3] μόνοις ὀφθαλμοῖς.   [4] John xiv. 17.
[5] ἀγύμναστον ἔχων τὸν νοῦν. *cf.* Heb. v. 14.
[6] τῷ φρονήματι τῆς σαρκός. *cf.* Rom. viii. 6 τὸ γὰρ φρόνημα τῆς σαρκὸς θάνατος.
[7] John xv. 3.   [8] John xiv. 17.
[9] Is. xlii. 5, LXX. πατοῦσιν αὐτήν. So St. Basil's argument requires us to translate the lxx. The "walk therein" of A.V. would not bear out his meaning. For this use of πατεῖν. *cf.* Soph., *Ant.* 745, οὐ γὰρ σέβεις τιμάς γε τὰς θεῶν πατῶν. So in the vulgate we read "*et spiritum calcantibus eam.*"—*calcare* bearing the sense of "trample on," as in Juvenal, *Sat.* x 86, "*calcemus Cæsaris hostem.*" The Hebrew bears no such meaning.
[10] Here the Benedictine Editors begin Chapter xxiii., remarking that they do so "*cum plures MSS. codices. tum ipsam sermonis seriem et continuationem secuti. Liquet enim hic Basilium ad aliud argumentum transire.*" Another

is believed to be in a circumscribed place. The angel who stood by Cornelius[1] was not at one and the same moment with Philip ;[2] nor yet did the angel who spoke with Zacharias from the altar at the same time occupy his own post in heaven. But the Spirit is believed to have been operating at the same time in Habakkuk and in Daniel at Babylon,[3] and to have been at the prison with Jeremiah,[4] and with Ezekiel at the Chebar.[5] For the Spirit of the Lord filleth the world,[6] and " whither shall I go from thy spirit? or whither shall I flee from thy presence?"[7] And, in the words of the Prophet, " For I am with you, saith the Lord . . . and my spirit remaineth among you."[8] But what nature is it becoming to assign to Him who is omnipresent, and exists together with God? The nature which is all-embracing, or one which is confined to particular places, like that which our argument shews the nature of angels to be? No one would so say. Shall we not then highly exalt Him who is in His nature divine, in His greatness infinite, in His operations powerful, in the blessings He confers, good? Shall we not give Him glory? And I understand glory to mean nothing else than the enumeration of the wonders which are His own. It follows then that either we are forbidden by our antagonists even to· mention the good things which flow to us from Him, or on the other hand that the mere recapitulation of His attributes is the fullest possible attribution of glory. For not even in the case of the God and Father of our Lord Jesus Christ and of the Only begotten Son, are we capable of giving Them glory otherwise than by recounting, to the extent of our powers, all the wonders that belong to Them.

CHAPTER XXIV.

Proof of the absurdity of the refusal to glorify the Spirit, from the comparison of things glorified in creation.

55. FURTHERMORE man is " crowned with glory and honour,"[9] and " glory, honour and peace " are laid up by promise " to every man that worketh good."[10] There is more-

over a special and peculiar glory for Israelites " to whom," it is said " pertaineth the adoption and the glory . . and the service,"[1] and the Psalmist speaks of a certain glory of his own, " that my glory may sing praise to Thee[2] ; " and again " Awake up my glory "[3] and according to the Apostle there is a certain glory of sun and moon and stars,[4] and " the ministration of condemnation is glorious."[5] While then so many things are glorified, do you wish the Spirit alone of all things to be unglorified? Yet the Apostle says " the ministration of the Spirit is glorious."[6] How then can He Himself be unworthy of glory? How according to the Psalmist can the glory of the just man be great[7] and according to you the glory of the Spirit none? How is there not a plain peril from such arguments of our bringing on ourselves the sin from which there is no escape? If the man who is being saved by works of righteousness glorifies even them that fear the Lord[8] much less would he deprive the Spirit of the glory which is His due.

Grant, they say, that He is to be glorified, but not with the Father and the Son. But what reason is there in giving up the place appointed by the Lord for the Spirit, and inventing some other? What reason is there for robbing of His share of glory Him Who is everywhere associated with the Godhead ; in the confession of the Faith, in the baptism of redemption, in the working of miracles, in the indwelling of the saints, in the graces bestowed on obedience? For there is not even one single gift which reaches creation without the Holy Ghost ;[9] when not even a single word can be spoken in defence of Christ except by them that are aided by the Spirit, as we have learnt in the Gospels from our Lord and Saviour.[10] And I know not whether any one who has been partaker of the Holy Spirit will consent that we should overlook all this, forget His fellowship in all things, and tear the Spirit asunder from the Father and the Son. Where then are we to take Him and rank Him? With the creature? Yet all the creature is in bondage, but the Spirit maketh free. " And where the Spirit of the Lord is, there is liberty."[11] Many arguments might be adduced to them that it is unseemly to coordinate the Holy Spirit with created nature, but for the present I will pass them by. Were I indeed to bring forward, in a manner befitting the

division of the text makes Chapter XXIII. begin with the words " But I do not mean by glory."
[1] Acts x. 3.   [2] Acts viii. 26.   [3] Bel and the Dragon, 34.
[4] Jer. xx. 2, LXX. εἰς τὸν καταρἡάκτην ὃς ἦν ἐν πύλῃ. Καταρἡάκτης τῶν πυλῶν occurs in Dion. Halic. viii. 67, in the same sense as the Latin *cataracta* (Livy xxvii. 27) *a portcullis*. The Vulgate has *in nervum*, which may either be *gyve* or *gaol*. The Hebrew =stocks, as in A.V. and R.V. καταρἡάκτης in the text of Basil and the lxx. may be assumed to mean *prison*, from the notion of the barred grating over the door. *cf.* Ducange s.v. *cataracta*.
[5] Ez. i. 1.   [7] Ps. xxxix. 7.   [9] Ps. viii. 5.
[6] Wis. i. 7.   [8] Hag. ii. 4, 5.   [10] Rom. ii. 10.

[1] Rom. ix. 4.   [5] 2 Cor. iii. 9.
[2] Ps. xxix. 12.   [6] 2 Cor. iii. 8.
[3] Ps. lvii. 8.   [7] cf. Ps. xxi. 5.
[4] cf. 1 Cor. xv. 41.   [8] cf. Ps. xv.
[9] cf. Matt. xxviii. 19; 1 Cor. xii. 11; Rom. viii. 11; 1 Pet. i. 2.
[10] Matt. x. 19, 20.   [11] 2 Cor. iii. 17.

dignity of the discussion, all the proofs always available on our side, and so overthrow the objections of our opponents, a lengthy dissertation would be required, and my readers might be worn out by my prolixity. I therefore propose to reserve this matter for a special treatise,[1] and to apply myself to the points now more immediately before us.

56. Let us then examine the points one by one. He is good by nature, in the same way as the Father is good, and the Son is good; the creature on the other hand shares in goodness by choosing the good. He knows "The deep things of God;"[2] the creature receives the manifestation of ineffable things through the Spirit. He quickens together with God, who produces and preserves all things alive,[3] and together with the Son, who gives life. "He that raised up Christ from the dead," it is said, "shall also quicken your mortal bodies by the spirit that dwelleth in you;"[4] and again "my sheep hear my voice, . . . and I give unto them eternal life;"[5] but "the Spirit" also, it is said, "giveth life,"[6] and again "the Spirit," it is said, "is life, because of righteousness."[7] And the Lord bears witness that "it is the Spirit that quickeneth; the flesh profiteth nothing."[8] How then shall we alienate the Spirit from His quickening power, and make Him belong to lifeless nature? Who is so contentious, who is so utterly without the heavenly gift,[9] and unfed by God's good words, who is so devoid of part and lot in eternal hopes, as to sever the Spirit from the Godhead and rank Him with the creature?

57. Now it is urged that the Spirit is in us as a gift from God, and that the gift is not reverenced with the same honour as that which is attributed to the giver. The Spirit is a gift of God, but a gift of life, for the law of "the Spirit of life," it is said, "hath made" us "free;"[10] and a gift of power, for "ye shall receive power after that the Holy Ghost is come upon you."[11] Is He on this account to be lightly esteemed? Did not God also bestow His Son as a free gift to mankind?

"He that spared not His own Son," it is said, "but delivered Him up for us all, how shall He not with Him also freely give us all things?"[1] And in another place, "that we might truly know the things that are freely given us of God,"[2] in reference to the mystery of the Incarnation. It follows then that the maintainers of such arguments, in making the greatness of God's loving kindness an occasion of blasphemy, have really surpassed the ingratitude of the Jews. They find fault with the Spirit because He gives us freedom to call God our Father. "For God hath sent forth the Spirit of His Son into" our "hearts crying Abba, Father,"[3] that the voice of the Spirit may become the very voice of them that have received him.

CHAPTER XXV.

That Scripture uses the words "in" or "by," ἐν, cf. note on p. 3, in place of "with." Wherein also it is proved that the word "and" has the same force as "with."

58. It is, however, asked by our opponents, how it is that Scripture nowhere describes the Spirit as glorified together with the Father and the Son, but carefully avoids the use of the expression "with the Spirit," while it everywhere prefers to ascribe glory "in Him" as being the fitter phrase. I should, for my own part, deny that the word in [or by] implies lower dignity than the word "with;" I should maintain on the contrary that, rightly understood, it leads us up to the highest possible meaning. This is the case where, as we have observed, it often stands instead of *with;* as for instance, "I will go into thy house *in* burnt offerings,"[4] instead of *with* burnt offerings and "he brought them forth also *by* silver and gold,"[5] that is to say *with* silver and gold and "thou goest not forth *in* our armies"[6] instead of *with* our armies, and innumerable similar passages. In short I should very much like to learn from this newfangled philosophy what kind of glory the Apostle ascribed by the word *in*, according to the interpretation which our opponents proffer as derived from Scripture, for I have nowhere found the formula "To Thee, O Father, be honour and glory, through Thy only begotten Son, *by* [or *in*] the Holy Ghost," — a form which to our opponents comes, so to say, as naturally as the air they breathe. You may indeed find each of these clauses

---

[1] Mr. C. F. H. Johnston conjectures the allusion to be to *Hom.* xxiv. "*Contra Sabellianos et Arium et Anomœos.*"
[2] 1 Cor. ii. 10, 11.
[3] In 1 Tim. vi. 13, St. Paul writes τοῦ θεοῦ τοῦ ζωοποιοῦντος πάντα. In the text St. Basil writes τὰ πάντα ζωογονοῦντος. The latter word is properly distinguished from the former as meaning not to make alive after death, but to engender alive. In Luke xvii. 33, it is rendered in A.V. "preserve." In Acts vii. 19, it is "to the end they might not *live*." On the meaning of ζωογονεῖν in the lxx. and the Socinian arguments based on its use in Luke xvii. 33, *cf.* Pearson, *On the Creed*, Art. V. note to p. 257 Ed. 1676.
[4] Rom. viii. 11.
[5] John x. 27-28.
[6] 2 Cor. iii. 6.
[7] Rom. viii. 10.
[8] John vi. 63.
[9] *cf.* Heb. vi. 4.
[10] Rom. viii. 2.
[11] Acts i. 8.

[1] Rom. viii. 32.　　[2] 1. Cor. ii. 12.　　[3] Gal. iv. 6.
[4] Ps. lxvi. 13. LXX.
[5] Ps. cv. 37.　　[6] Ps. xliv. 9.

separately,[1] but they will nowhere be able to show them to us arranged in this conjunction. If, then, they want exact conformity to what is written, let them give us exact references. If, on the other hand, they make concession to custom, they must not make us an exception to such a privilege.

59. As we find both expressions in use among the faithful, we use both; in the belief that full glory is equally given to the Spirit by both. The mouths, however, of revilers of the truth may best be stopped by the preposition which, while it has the same meaning as that of the Scriptures, is not so wieldy a weapon for our opponents, (indeed it is now an object of their attack) and is used instead of the conjunction *and*. For to say "Paul and Silvanus and Timothy"[2] is precisely the same thing as to say Paul *with* Timothy and Silvanus; for the connexion of the names is preserved by either mode of expression. The Lord says "The Father, the Son and the Holy Ghost."[3] If I say the Father and the Son *with* the Holy Ghost shall I make any difference in the sense? Of the connexion of names by means of the conjunction *and* the instances are many. We read "The grace of our Lord Jesus Christ and the love of God and the fellowship of the Holy Ghost,"[4] and again "I beseech you for the Lord Jesus Christ's sake, and for the love of the Spirit."[5] Now if we wish to use *with* instead of *and*, what difference shall we have made? I do not see; unless any one according to hard and fast grammatical rules might prefer the conjunction as copulative and making the union stronger, and reject the preposition as of inferior force. But if we had to defend ourselves on these points I do not suppose we should require a defence of many words. As it is, their argument is not about syllables nor yet about this or that sound of a word, but about things differing most widely in power and in truth. It is for this reason that, while the use of the syllables is really a matter of no importance whatever, our opponents are making the endeavour to authorise some syllables, and hunt out others from the Church. For my own part, although the usefulness of the word is obvious as soon as it is heard, I will nevertheless set forth the arguments which led our fathers to adopt the reasonable course of employing the preposition "*with*."[6] It does indeed,

equally well with the preposition "*and*," confute the mischief of Sabellius;[1] and it sets forth quite as well as "*and*" the distinction of the hypostases, as in the words "I and my Father will come,"[2] and "I and my Father are one."[3] In addition to this the proof it contains of the eternal fellowship and uninterrupted conjunction is excellent. For to say that the Son is *with* the Father is to exhibit at once the distinction of the hypostases, and the inseparability of the fellowship. The same thing is observable even in mere human matters, for the conjunction "*and*" intimates that there is a common element in an action, while the preposition "*with*" declares in some sense as well the communion in action. As, for instance; — Paul and Timothy sailed to Macedonia, but both Tychicus and Onesimus were sent to the Colossians. Hence we learn that they did the same thing. But suppose we are told that they sailed *with*, and were sent *with?* Then we are informed in addition that they carried out the action in company with one another. Thus while the word "with" upsets the error of Sabellius as no other word can, it routs also sinners who err in the very opposite direction; those, I mean, who separate the Son from the Father and the Spirit from the Son, by intervals of time.[4]

60. As compared with "*in*," there is this difference, that while "*with*" sets forth the mutual conjunction of the parties associated, —as, for example, of those who sail with, or dwell with, or do anything else in common, "*in*" shews their relation to that matter in which they happen to be acting. For we no sooner hear the words "sail in" or "dwell in" than we form the idea of the boat or the house. Such is the distinction

---

temporary writer, as far as the editor is aware, nor is it contradicted." Rev. C. F. H. Johnston.

[1] "Sabellius has been usually assigned to the middle of third century, Mr. Clinton giving A.D. 256-270 as his active period. The discovery of the *Philosophumena* of Hippolytus has proved this to be a mistake, and thrown his period back to the close of the second and beginning of the third century. . . . He was in full activity in Rome during the Episcopate of Zephyrinus, A.D. 198-217." Professor Stokes in *D.C. Biog.* iv. 569. For Basil's views of Sabellianism *vide* Epp. CCX., CCXIV., CCXXXV. In his *Hær. Fab. Conf.* ii. 9 Theodoret writes: "Sabellius said that Father, Son, and Holy Ghost were one Hypostasis; one Person under three names; and he describes the same now as Father, now as Son, now as Holy Ghost. He says that in the old Testament He gave laws as Father, was incarnate in the new as Son, and visited the Apostles as Holy Ghost." So in the Ἔκθεσις τῆς κατὰ μέρος πίστεως, a work falsely attributed to Gregory Thaumaturgus, and possibly due to Apollinaris, (*cf.* Theod., *Dial.* iii.) "We shun Sabellius, who says that Father and Son are the same, calling Him who speaks Father, and the Word, remaining in the Father and at the time of creation manifested, and, on the completion of things returning to the Father, Son. He says the same of the Holy Ghost."

[2] Apparently an inexact reference to John xiv. 23.

[3] John x. 30.

[4] *i.e.*, The Arians, who said of the Son, "There was when he was not;" and the Pneumatomachi, who made the Spirit a created being.

---

[1] In Eph. ii. 18 they are combined, but no Scriptural doxology uses ἐν of the Spirit.

[2] 1 Thess. i. 1. [4] 2 Cor. xiii. 13.

[3] Matt. xxviii. 19. [5] Rom. xv. 30.

[6] "St. Basil's statement of the reason of the use of μετά, σύν, in the Doxology, is not confirmed by any earlier or con-

between these words in ordinary usage; and laborious investigation might discover further illustrations. I have no time to examine into the nature of the syllables. Since then it has been shewn that " *with* " most clearly gives the sense of conjunction, let it be declared, if you will, to be under safe-conduct, and cease to wage your savage and truceless war against it. Nevertheless, though the word is naturally thus auspicious, yet if any one likes, in the ascription of praise, to couple the names by the syllable " and," and to give glory, as we have taught in the Gospel, in the formula of baptism, Father and Son and Holy Ghost,[1] be it so: no one will make any objection. On these conditions, if you will, let us come to terms. But our foes would• rather surrender their tongues than accept this word. It is this that rouses against us their implacable and truceless war. We must offer the ascription of glory to God, it is contended, *in* the Holy Ghost, and not *and* to the Holy Ghost, and they passionately cling to this word *in*, as though it lowered the Spirit. It will therefore be not unprofitable to speak at greater length about it; and I shall be astonished if they do not, when they have heard what we have to urge, reject the *in* as itself a traitor to their cause, and a deserter to the side of the glory of the Spirit.

CHAPTER XXVI.

That the word "in," in as many senses as it bears, is understood of the Spirit.

61. Now, short and simple as this utterance is, it appears to me, as I consider it, that its meanings are many and various. For of the senses in which " *in* " is used, we find that all help our conceptions of the Spirit. *Form* is said to be *in Matter; Power* to be *in* what is capable of it; *Habit* to be *in* him who is affected by it; and so on.[2] Therefore, inasmuch as the Holy Spirit perfects rational beings, completing their excellence, He is analogous to Form. For he, who no longer " lives after the flesh," [3] but, being " led by the Spirit of God," [4] is called a Son of God, being " conformed to the image of the Son of God," [5] is described as spiritual. And as is the power of seeing in the healthy eye, so is the operation of the Spirit in the purified

soul. Wherefore also Paul prays for the Ephesians that they may have their " eyes enlightened " by " the Spirit of wisdom." [1] And as the art in him who has acquired it, so is the grace of the Spirit in the recipient ever present, though not continuously in operation. For as the art is potentially in the artist, but only in operation when he is working in accordance with it, so also the Spirit is ever present with those that are worthy, but works, as need requires, in prophecies, or in healings, or in some other actual carrying into effect of His potential action.[2] Furthermore as in our bodies is health, or heat, or, generally, their variable conditions, so, very frequently is the Spirit in the soul; since He does not abide with those who, on account of the instability of their will, easily reject the grace which they have received. An instance of this is seen in Saul,[3] and the seventy elders of the children of Israel, except Eldad and Medad, with whom alone the Spirit appears to have remained,[4] and, generally, any one similar to these in character. And like reason in the soul, which is at one time the thought in the heart, and at another speech uttered by the tongue,[5] so is the Holy Spirit, as when He " beareth witness with our spirit," [6] and when He " cries in our hearts, Abba, Father," [7] or when He speaks on our behalf, as it is said, " It is not ye that speak, but the Spirit of your Father which speaketh in you." [8] Again, the Spirit is conceived of, in relation to the distribution of gifts, as a whole in parts. For we all are " members one of another, having gifts differing according to the grace that is given us." [9] Wherefore " the eye cannot say to the hand, I have no need of thee; nor again the head to the feet, I have no need of you," [10] but all together complete the Body of Christ in the Unity of the Spirit, and render to one another the needful aid that comes of the gifts. " But God hath set the members in the body,

---

[1] Matt. xxviii. 19.
[2] *cf.* Note on Chap i. p. 4. In the Aristotelian philosophy, εἶδος, or Form, is the τὸ τί ἦν εἶναι, the essence or formal cause. *cf.* Ar., *Met.* vi. 7, 4. εἶδος δὲ λέγω τὸ τί ἦν εἶναι ἑκάστου καὶ τὴν πρώτην οὐσίαν. Δύναμις, or Potentia, is potential action or existence, as opposed to ἐνέργεια, *actus*, actual action or existence, or ἐντελέχεια. *cf.* Ar., *Met.* viii. 3, 9, and viii. 8, 11. Sir W. Hamilton, *Metaph.* i. 178–180.
[3] Rom. viii. 12.   [4] Rom. viii. 14.   [5] Rom. viii. 29.

[1] Eph. i. 17, 18.
[2] ἐν ἄλλοις τισὶ δυνάμεων ἐνεργήμασι. The Benedictine translation is *in aliis miraculorum operationibus*." It is of course quite true that δύναμις is one of the four words used in the New Testament for miracle, and often has that sense, but here the context suggests the antithesis between potential and actual operation. and moreover non-miraculous (in the ordinary sense) operations of the Spirit need not be excluded; in a deep sense all His operations are miraculous. ἐνέργημα is an uncommon word, meaning the work wrought by ἐνέργεια or operation.
[3] 1 Sam. xvi. 14.
[4] Numb. xi. 25, 26. LXX. and R.V. " did so no more " for " did not cease " of A.V.
[5] The distinction between the λόγος ἐνδιάθετος, thought, and the λόγος προφορικός, speech, appears first in Philo. II. 154. On the use of the term in Catholic Theology *cf.* Dr. Robertson's note on Ath., *De Syn.* § xxvi. p. 463 of the Ed. in this series. Also, Dorner, Div. I. i. p. 338, note.
[6] Rom. viii. 16.   [8] Matt. x. 20.   [10] 1 Cor. xii. 21.
[7] Gal. vi. 4.   [9] Rom. xii. 5, 6.

every one of them, as it hath pleased Him." [1] But " the members have the same care for one another," [2] according to the inborn spiritual communion of their sympathy. Wherefore, " whether one member suffer, all the members suffer with it ; or one member be honoured, all the members rejoice with it." [3] And as parts in the whole so are we individually in the Spirit, because we all " were baptized in one body into one spirit." [4]

62. It is an extraordinary statement, but it is none the less true, that the Spirit is frequently spoken of as the *place* of them that are being sanctified, and it will become evident that even by this figure the Spirit, so far from being degraded, is rather glorified. For words applicable to the body are, for the sake of clearness, frequently transferred in scripture to spiritual conceptions. Accordingly we find the Psalmist, even in reference to God, saying " Be Thou to me a champion God and a strong place to save me " [5] and concerning the Spirit " behold there is a place by me, and stand upon a rock." [6] Plainly meaning the place or contemplation in the Spirit wherein, after Moses had entered thither, he was able to see God intelligibly manifested to him. This is the special and peculiar place of true worship ; for it is said " Take heed to thyself that thou offer not thy burnt offerings in every place . . . but in the place the Lord thy God shall choose." [7] Now what is a spiritual burnt offering? " The sacrifice of praise." [8] And in what place do we offer it? In the Holy Spirit. Where have we learnt this? From the Lord himself in the words " The true worshippers shall worship the Father in spirit and in truth." [9] This place Jacob saw and said " The Lord is in this place." [10] It follows that the Spirit is verily the place of the saints and the saint is the proper place for the Spirit, offering himself as he does for the indwelling of God, and called God's Temple. [11] So Paul speaks in Christ, saying " In the sight of God we speak in Christ," [12] and Christ in Paul, as he himself says " Since ye seek a proof of Christ speaking in me." [13] So also in the Spirit he speaketh mysteries, [14] and again the Spirit speaks in him. [15]

63. In relation to the originate,[1] then, the Spirit is said to *be in* them " in divers portions and in divers manners," [2] while in relation to the Father and the Son it is more consistent with true religion to assert Him not to *be in* but to *be with*. For the grace flowing from Him when He dwells in those that are worthy, and carries out His own operations, is well described as existing in those that are able to receive Him. On the other hand His essential existence before the ages, and His ceaseless abiding with Son and Father, cannot be contemplated without requiring titles expressive of eternal conjunction. For absolute and real co-existence is predicated in the case of things which are mutually inseparable. We say, for instance, that heat exists in the hot iron, but in the case of the actual fire it co-exists ; and, similarly, that health exists in the body, but that life co-exists with the soul. It follows that wherever the fellowship is intimate, congenital,[3] and inseparable, the word *with* is more expressive, suggesting, as it does, the idea of inseparable fellowship. Where on the other hand the grace flowing from the Spirit naturally comes and goes, it is properly and truly said to exist *in*, even if on account of the firmness of the recipients' disposition to good the grace abides with them continually. Thus whenever we have in mind the Spirit's proper rank, we contemplate Him as being *with* the Father and the Son, but when we think of the grace that

---

1 1 Cor. xii. 18, slightly varied in order.
2 1 Cor. xii. 25.
3 1 Cor. xii. 26.
4 An inversion of 1 Cor. xii. 13.
5 Ps. lxxi. 3, LXX.
6 Ex. xxxiii. 21, LXX.
7 Deut. xii. 13, 14.
8 Ps. l. 14, LXX.
9 John iv. 23. With this interpretation, *cf.* Athan., *Epist.* i. *Ad Serap.* § 33, " Hence it is shewn that the Truth is the Son Himself . . . for they worship the Father, but in Spirit and in Truth, confessing the Son and the Spirit in him ; for the Spirit is inseparable from the Son as the Son is inseparable from the Father."
10 Gen. xxviii. 16.
11 1 Cor. vi. 19.
12 2 Cor. ii. 17.
13 2 Cor. xiii. 3.
14 1 Cor. xiv. 2.
15 1 Peter i. 11.

---

1 ἐν τοῖς γεννητοῖς, as in the Bodleian MS. The Benedictine text adopts the common reading γεννητοις, with the note, " *Sed discrimen illud parvi momenti.*" If St. Basil wrote γεννητοις, he used it in the looser sense of mortal : in its strict sense of " begotten " it would be singularly out of place here, as the antithesis of the reference to the Son, who is γεννητός, would be spoilt. In the terminology of theology, so far from being " *parvi momenti*," the distinction is vital. In the earlier Greek philosophy ἀγένητος and ἀγέννητος are both used as nearly synonymous to express unoriginate or eternal. *cf.* Plat., *Phæd.* 245 D., ἀρχὴ δὲ ἀγένητόν, with Plat , *Tim.* 52 A., Τουτων δὲ οὕτως ἐχόντων ὁμολογητέον ἐν μὲν εἶναι τὸ κατὰ ταυτὰ εἶδος ἔχον ἀγέννητον καὶ ἀνώλεθρον. And the earliest patristic use similarly meant by γεννητός and ἀγέννητος created and uncreated, as in Ign., *Ad Eph.* vii., where our Lord is called γεννητὸς καὶ ἀγέννητος, ἐν ἀνθρώπῳ Θεὸς, ἐν θανάτῳ ζωὴ ἀληθινή. *cf.* Bp. Lightfoot's note. But " such language is not in accordance with later theological definitions, which carefully distinguished between γενητός and γεννητός, between ἀγένητος and ἀγέννητος; so that γενητός, ἀγένητος, respectively denied and affirmed the eternal existence, being equivalent to κτιστός, ἄκτιστος, while γεννητός, ἀγέννητος; described certain ontological relations, whether in time or in eternity. In the later theological language, therefore, the Son was γεννητός even in His Godhead. See esp. Joann. Damasc., *De Fid. Orth.* i. S (I. p. 135, Lequien), χρὴ γὰρ εἰδέναι ὅτι τὸ ἀγένητον, διὰ τοῦ ἑνὸς ν γραφόμενον, τὸ ἀκτιστον ἢ τὸ μὴ γενόμενον σημαίνει, τὸ δὲ ἀγέννητον, διὰ τῶν δύο νν γραφόμενον, δηλοῖ τὸ μὴ γεννηθέν; whence he draws the conclusion that μόνος ὁ πατὴρ ἀγέννητος and μόνος ὁ υἱὸς γεννητός." Bp. Lightfoot, *Ap. Fathers*, Pt. II. Vol. II. p. 90, where the history of the words is exhaustively discussed. At the time of the Arian controversy the Catholic disputants were chary of employing these terms, because of the base uses to which their opponents put them ; so St. Basil, *Contra Eunom.* iv. protests against the Arian argument εἰ ἀγέννητος ὁ πατὴρ γεννητὸς δὲ ὁ υἱός, οὐ τῆς αὐτῆς οὐσιος.
cf. Ath., *De Syn.* in this series, p. 475, and *De Decretis*, on Newman's confusion of the terms, p. 149 and 169.
2 Heb. i. 1.   3 συμφυής.

flows from Him operating on those who participate in it, we say that the Spirit is *in* us. And the doxology which we offer " in the Spirit " is not an acknowledgment of His rank ; it is rather a confession of our own weakness, while we shew that we are not sufficient to glorify Him of ourselves, but our sufficiency [1] is in the Holy Spirit. Enabled in, [or by,] Him we render thanks to our God for the benefits we have received, according to the measure of our purification from evil, as we receive one a larger and another a smaller share of the aid of the Spirit, that we may offer " the sacrifice of praise to God." [2] According to one use, then, it is thus that we offer our thanksgiving, as the true religion requires, *in* the Spirit ; although it is not quite unobjectionable that any one should testify of himself " the Spirit of God is in me, and I offer glory after being made wise through the grace that flows from Him." For to a Paul it is becoming to say " I think also that I have the Spirit of God," [3] and again, " that good thing which was committed to thee keep by the Holy Ghost which dwelleth in us." [4] And of Daniel it is fitting to say that " the Holy Spirit of God is in him," [5] and similarly of men who are like these in virtue.

64. Another sense may however be given to the phrase, that just as the Father is seen in the Son, so is the Son in the Spirit. The " worship in the Spirit " suggests the idea of the operation of our intelligence being carried on in the light, as may be learned from the words spoken to the woman of Samaria. Deceived as she was by the customs of her country into the belief that worship was local, our Lord, with the object of giving her better instruction, said that worship ought to be offered " in Spirit and in Truth," [6] plainly meaning by the Truth, Himself. As then we speak of the worship offered in the Image of God the Father as worship in the Son, so too do we speak of worship in the Spirit as shewing in Himself the Godhead of the Lord. Wherefore even in our worship the Holy Spirit is inseparable from the Father and the Son. If you remain outside the Spirit you will not be able even to worship at all ; and on your becoming in Him you will in no wise be able to dissever Him from God ; —any more than you will divorce light from visible objects. For it is impossible to behold the Image of the invisible God except by the enlightenment of the Spirit, and impracticable for

him to fix his gaze on the Image to dissever the light from the Image, because the cause of vision is of necessity seen at the same time as the visible objects. Thus fitly and consistently do we behold the " Brightness of the glory " of God by means of the illumination of the Spirit, and by means of the " Express Image " we are led up to Him of whom He is the Express Image and Seal, graven to the like.[1]

CHAPTER XXVII.

Of the origin of the word " with," and what force it has. Also concerning the unwritten laws of the church.

65. THE word " *in*," say our opponents, " is exactly appropriate to the Spirit, and sufficient for every thought concerning Him. Why then, they ask, have we introduced this new phrase, saying, " *with* the Spirit " instead of " *in* the Holy Spirit," thus employing an expression which is quite unnecessary, and sanctioned by no usage in the churches? Now it has been asserted in the previous portion of this treatise that the word " *in* " has not been specially allotted to the Holy Spirit, but is common to the Father and the Son. It has also been, in my opinion, sufficiently demonstrated that, so far from detracting anything from the dignity of the Spirit, it leads all, but those whose thoughts are wholly perverted, to the sublimest height. It remains for me to trace the origin of the word " *with ;* " to explain what force it has, and to shew that it is in harmony with Scripture.

66. [2] Of the beliefs and practices whether

---

[1] *cf.* note on § 15. So Athan. *in Matt.* xi. 22. Σφραγὶς γάρ ἐστιν ἰσότυπος ἐν ἑαυτῷ δεικνὺς τὸν πατέρα. *cf.* Athan., *De Dec.* § 20, and note 9 in this series, p. 163. *cf.* also Greg. Nyss., *In Eunom.* ii. 12.

[2] The genuineness of this latter portion of the Treatise was objected to by Erasmus on the ground that the style is unlike that of Basil's soberer writings. Bp. Jeremy Taylor follows Erasmus (Vol. vi. ed. 1852, p. 427). It was vindicated by Casaubon, who recalls St. John Damascene's quotation of the *Thirty Chapters to Amphilochius.* Mr. C. F. H. Johnston remarks, " The later discovery of the Syriac Paraphrases of the whole book pushes back this argument to about one hundred years from the date of St. Basil's writing. The peculiar care taken by St. Basil for the writing out of the treatise, and for its safe arrival in Amphilochius' hands, and the value set upon it by the friends of both, make the forgery of half the present book, and the substitution of it for the original within that period, almost incredible." Section 66 is quoted as an authoritative statement on the right use of Tradition " as a guide to the right understanding of Holy Scripture, for the right ministration of the Sacraments, and the preservation of sacred rights and ceremonies in the purity of their original institution," in Philaret's *Longer Catechism of the Eastern Church.*
St. Basil is, however, strong on the supremacy of Holy Scripture, as in the passages quoted in Bp. H. Browne, *On the xxxix Articles:* " Believe those things which are written; the things which are not written seek not." (*Hom. xxix. adv. Calum. S. Trin.*) " It is a manifest defection from the faith, and a proof of arrogance, either to reject anything of what is written, or to introduce anything that is not." (*De Fide.* i.) *cf.* also Letters CV. and CLIX. On the right use of Tradition *cf.* Hooker, *Ecc. Pol.* lxv. 2, " Lest, therefore, the name of tradition should be offensive to any, considering how far by

---

[1] *cf.* 2 Cor. iii. 5.
[2] Heb. xiii. 15.
[3] 1 Cor. vii. 40.
[4] 2 Tim. i. 14.
[5] Dan. iv. 8, lxx.
[6] John iv. 24.

generally accepted or publicly enjoined which are preserved in the Church[1] some we possess derived from written teaching; others we have received delivered to us " in a mystery "[1] by the tradition of the apostles; and both of these in relation to true religion have the same force. And these no one will gainsay; — no one, at all events, who is even moderately versed in the institutions of the Church. For were we to attempt to reject such customs as have no written authority, on the ground that the importance they possess is small, we should unintentionally injure the Gospel in its very vitals; or, rather, should make our public definition a mere phrase and nothing more.[2] For instance, to take the first and most general example, who is there who has taught us in writing to sign with the sign of the cross those who have trusted in the name of our Lord Jesus Christ? What writing has taught us to turn to the East at the prayer? Which of the saints has left us in writing the words of the invocation at the displaying[3] of the bread of the Eucharist and the cup of blessing? For we are not, as is well known, content with what the apostle or the Gospel has recorded, but both in preface and conclusion we add other words as being of great importance to the validity of the ministry, and these we derive from unwritten teaching.

---

some it hath been and is abused, we mean by traditions ordinances made in the prime of Christian Religion, established with that authority which Christ hath left to His Church for matters indifferent, and in that consideration requisite to be observed, till like authority see just and reasonable cause to alter them. So that traditions ecclesiastical are not rudely and in gross to be shaken off, because the inventors of them were men."
cf. Tert., *De Præsc.* 36, 20, 21, "*Constat omnem doctrinam quæ cum illis ecclesiis apostolicis matricibus et originalibus fidei conspiret veritati deputandam, id sine dubio tenentem quod ecclesiæ ab apostolis, apostoli a Christo, Christus a Deo accepit.*" *Vide* Thomasius, *Christ. Dogm.* i. 10§.

[1] "τῶν ἐν τῇ Ἐκκλησίᾳ πεφυλαγμένων δογμάτων καὶ κηρυγμάτων." To give the apparent meaning of the original seems impossible except by some such paraphrase as the above. In Scripture δόγμα, which occurs five times (Luke ii. 1, Acts xvi. 4, xvii. 7, Eph. ii. 15, and Col. ii. 14), always has its proper sense of decree or ordinances. cf. Bp. Lightfoot, on Col. ii. 14, and his contention that the Greek Fathers generally have mistaken the force of the passage in understanding δόγματα in both Col. and Eph. to mean the doctrines and precepts of the Gospel. Κήρυγμα occurs eight times (Matt. xii. 41, Luke xi. 32, Rom. xvi. 25, 1 Cor. i. 21, ii. 4, xv. 14, 2 Tim. iv. 17, and Tit. i. 3), always in the sense of preaching or proclamation.
"The later Christian sense of δόγμα, meaning *doctrine*, came from its secondary classical use, where it was applied to the authoritative and categorical 'sentences' of the philosophers: cf. Just. Mart., *Apol.* i. 7. οἱ ἐν Ἕλλησι τὰ αὐτοῖς ἀρεστὰ δογματίσαντες ἐκ παντὸς τῷ ἑνὶ ὀνόματι φιλοσοφίας προσαγορεύοντα, καίπερ τῶν δογμάτων ἐναντίων ὄντων." [All the sects in general among the Greeks are known by the common name of philosophy, though their doctrines are different.] Cic., *Acad.* ii. 19, '*De suis decretis quæ philosophi vocant δόγματα.*' . . . There is an approach towards the ecclesiastical meaning in Ignat., *Mag.* 13, βεβαιωθῆναι ἐν το ς δόγμασι τοῦ κυρίου καὶ τῶν ἀποστόλων." Bp. Lightfoot in Col. ii. 14. The "doctrines" of heretics are also called δόγματα, as in Basil, *Ep. CCLXI.* and Socr., *E. H.* iii. 10. cf. Bp. Bull, in *Serm.* 2, "The dogmata or tenets of the Sadducees." In Orig., *c. Cels.* iii. p. 135, Ed. Spencer, 165S, δόγμα is used of the gospel or teaching of our Lord.
The special point about St. Basil's use of δόγματα is that he uses the word of doctrines and practices privately and tacitly sanctioned in the Church (like ἀπόρρητα, which is used of the esoteric doctrine of the Pythagoreans, Plat., *Phæd.* 62. B.), while he reserves κηρύγματα for what is now often understood by δόγματι, *i.e.* "*legitima synodo decreta.*" cf. *Ep. LII.*, where he speaks of the great κήρυγμα of the Fathers at Nicæa. In this he is supported by Eulogius, Patriarch of Alexandria, 579–607, of whom Photius (*Cod.* ccxxx. Migne Pat. Gr. ciii. p. 1027) writes, "In this work," *i.e.* Or. II. "he says that of the doctrines (διδαγμάτων) handed down in the church by the ministers of the word, some are δόγματα, and others κηρύγματα. The distinction is that δόγματα are announced with concealment and prudence, and are often designedly compassed with obscurity, in order that holy things may not be exposed to profane persons nor pearls cast before swine. Κηρύγματα, on the other hand, are announced without any concealment." So the Benedictine Editors speak of Origen (*c. Cels.* i. 7) as replying to Celsus, "*prædicationem Christianorum toti orbi notiorem esse quam placita philosophorum: sed tamen fatetur, ut apud philosophos, ita etiam apud Christianos nonulla esse veluti interiora, quæ post exteriorem et propositam omnibus doctrinam tradantur.*" Of which they note, "*Videntur hoc nomine designari leges ecclesiasticæ et canonum decreta quæ promulgari in ecclesia mos erat, ut neminem laterent.*" Mr. C. F. H. Johnston remarks: "The οὐσιῶσιον, which many now-a-days would call the Nicene dogma (τὸ τοῦ ὁμοουσίου δόγματα, Soc., *E. H.* iii. 10) because it was set forth in the Council of Nicæa, was for that reason called not δόγμα, but κήρυγμα, by St. Basil, who would have said that it became the κήρυγμα (definition) of that Council, because it had always been the δόγμα of the Church."
In extra theological philosophy a dogma has all along meant a certainly expressed opinion whether formally decreed or not. So Shaftesbury, *Misc. Ref.* ii. 2, "He who is certain, or presumes to say he knows, is in that particular, whether he be mistaken or in the right, a dogmatist." cf. Littré, *S. V.* for a similar use in French. In theology the modern Roman limitation of dogma to decreed doctrine is illustrated by the statement of Abbé Bergier (*Dict. de Théol.* Ed. 1844) of the Immaculate Conception of the Blessed Virgin. "Or, *nous convenons que ce n'est pas un dogme de foi,*" because, though a common opinion among Romanists, it had not been so asserted at the Council of Trent. Since the publication of Pius IX's Edict of 1854 it has become, to ultramontanists, a "dogma of faith."

[1] 1 Cor. ii. 7. Whether there is or is not here a conscious reference to St. Paul's words, there seems to be both in the text and in the passage cited an employment of μυστήριον in its proper sense of a secret revealed to the initiated.
[2] *i.e.* if nothing were of weight but what was written, what need of any authorisation at all? There is no need of κήρυγμα for a δόγμα expressly written in Scripture.
[3] ἐπὶ τῇ ἀναδείξει. The Benedictine note is: "*Non respicit Basilius ad ritum ostensionis Eucharistiæ, ut multi existimarunt, sed potius ad verba Liturgiæ ipsi ascriptæ, cum petit sacerdos, ut veniat Spiritus sanctus* ἁγιάσαι καὶ ἀναδεῖξαι τὸν μὲν ἄρτον τοῦτον αὐτὸ τὸ τίμιον σῶμα τοῦ κυρίου. *Haec autem verba* ἐπὶ τῇ ἀναδείξει, *sic reddit Erasmus, cum ostendit. Vituperat eum Ducaeus, sicque ipse vertit, cum conficitur, atque hanc interpretationem multis exemplis confirmat. Videtur tamen nihil prorsus vitii habitura haec interpretatio, Invocationis verba cum ostenditur panis Eucharistiæ, id est, cum panis non jam panis sed panis Eucharistiæ, sive corpus Christi ostenditur; et in liturgia, ut sanctificet et ostendat hunc quidem panem, ipsum pretiosum corpus Domini. Nam 10 Cur eam vocem reformidemus, qua Latini uti non dubitant, ubi de Eucharistia ioquuntur? Quale est illud Cypriani in epistola 63 ad Cæcilium: Vino Christi sanguis ostenditur. Sic etiam Tertullianus I. Marc. c. 14: Panem quo ipsum corpus suum repraesentat 20 Ut Græce,* ἀναδεῖξαι, ἀποφαίνειν, *ita etiam Latine, ostendere, corpus Christi præsens in Eucharistia significatione quodam modo exprimit. Hoc enim verbum non solum panem fieri corpus Domini significat, sed etiam fidem nostram excitat, ut illud corpus sub specie panis videndum, tegendum, adorandum ostendi credamus. Quemadmodum Irenæus, cum ait lib. iv. cap. 33: Accipiens panem suum corpus esse confitebatur, et temperamentum calicis suum sanguinem conformavit, non solum mutationem panis et vini in corpus et sanguinem Christi exprimit, sed ipsam etiam Christi asseverationem, quæ hanc nobis mutationem persuadet: sic qui corpus Christi in Eucharistia ostendi et repræsentari dicunt, non modo jejuno et exiliter loqui non videntur, sed etiam acriores Christi præsentis adorandi stimulos subjicere. Poterat ergo retineri interpretatio Erasmi; sed quia viris eruditis displicuit, satius visum est quid sentirem in hac nota exponere.*"
This view of the meaning of ἀναδεικνύσθαι and ἀνάδειξις as being equivalent to ποιεῖν and ποίησις is borne out and illustrated by Suicer, *S. V.* "*Ex his jam satis liquere arbitror* ἀναδεῖξαι *apud Basilium id esse quod alii Græci patres dicunt* ποιεῖν *vel* ἀποφαίνειν σῶμα χριστοῦ."
It is somewhat curious to find Bellarmine (*De Sacr. Euch.* iv. § 14) interpreting the prayer to God εὐλογῆσαι καὶ ἁγιάσαι καὶ ἀναδεῖξαι to mean "*ostende per effectum salutarem in mentibus nostris istum panem salutificatum non esse panem vulgarem sed cælestem.*"

Moreover we bless the water of baptism and the oil of the chrism, and besides this the catechumen who is being baptized. On what written authority do we do this? Is not our authority silent and mystical tradition? Nay, by what written word is the anointing of oil[1] itself taught? And whence comes the custom of baptizing thrice?[2] And as to the other customs of baptism from what Scripture do we derive the renunciation of Satan and his angels? Does not this come from that unpublished and secret teaching which our fathers guarded in a silence out of the reach of curious meddling and inquisitive investigation? Well had they learnt the lesson that the awful dignity of the mysteries is best preserved by silence. What the uninitiated are not even allowed to look at was hardly likely to be publicly paraded about in written documents. What was the meaning of the mighty Moses in not making all the parts of the tabernacle open to every one? The profane he stationed without the sacred barriers; the first courts he conceded to the purer; the Levites alone he judged worthy of being servants of the Deity; sacrifices and burnt offerings and the rest of the priestly functions he allotted to the priests; one chosen out of all he admitted to the shrine, and even this one not always but on only one day in the year, and of this one day a time was fixed for his entry so that he might gaze on the Holy of Holies amazed at the strangeness and novelty of the sight. Moses was wise enough to know that contempt attaches to the trite and to the obvious, while a keen interest is naturally associated with the unusual and the unfamiliar. In the same manner the Apostles and Fathers who laid down laws for the Church from the beginning thus guarded the awful dignity of the mysteries in secrecy and silence, for what is bruited abroad at random among the common folk is no mystery at all. This is the reason for our tradition of unwritten precepts and practices, that the knowledge of our dogmas may not become neglected and contemned by the multitude through familiarity. "Dogma" and "Kerugma" are two distinct things; the former is observed in silence; the latter is proclaimed to all the world. One form of this silence is the obscurity employed in Scripture, which makes the meaning of "dogmas" difficult to be understood for

the very advantage of the reader: Thus we all look to the East[1] at our prayers, but few of us know that we are seeking our own old country,[2] Paradise, which God planted in Eden in the East.[3] We pray standing,[4] on the first day of the week, but we do not all know the reason. On the day of the resurrection (or "standing again" Grk. ἀνάστασις) we remind ourselves of the grace given to us by standing at prayer, not only because we rose with Christ,[5] and are bound to "seek those things which are above,"[6] but because the day seems to us to be in some sense an image of the age which we expect, wherefore, though it is the beginning of days, it is not called by Moses *first*, but *one*.[7] For he says "There was evening, and there was morning, one day," as though the same day often recurred. Now "one" and "eighth" are the same, in itself distinctly indicating that really "one" and "eighth" of which the Psalmist makes mention in certain titles of the Psalms, the state which follows after this present time, the day which knows no waning or eventide, and no successor, that age which endeth not or groweth old.[8] Of necessity, then, the church teaches her own foster children to offer their prayers on that day standing, to the end that through continual reminder of the endless life we may not neglect to make provision for our removal thither. Moreover all Pentecost is a reminder of the resurrection expected in the age to come. For that one and first day, if seven times multiplied by seven, completes the seven weeks of the holy Pentecost; for, beginning at the first, Pentecost ends with the same, making fifty revolutions through the like intervening days. And so it is a likeness of eternity, beginning as it does and ending, as in a circling course, at the same point. On this day the rules of the church have educated us to prefer the upright attitude of prayer, for by their plain reminder they, as it were, make our mind to dwell no longer in the present but in the future. Moreover every time we fall upon our knees and rise

---

[1] For the unction of catechumens *cf. Ap. Const.* vii. 22; of the baptized, Tertullian, *De Bapt.* vii.; of the confirmed, *id.* viii.; of the sick *vide* Plumptre on St. James v. 14, in *Cambridge Bible for Schools. cf. Letter* clxxxviii.
[2] For trine immersion an early authority is Tertullian, *c. Praxeam* xxvi. *cf.* Greg. Nyss., *De Bapt.* ὕδατι ἑαυτοὺς ἐγκρύπτομεν . . . καὶ τρίτον τοῦτο ποιήσαντες. *Dict. Ch. Ant.* i. 161.

---

[1] *cf.* my note on Theodoret in this series, p. 112.
[2] Heb. xi. 14, R.V.   [3] Gen. ii. 8.
[4] The earliest posture of prayer was standing, with the hands extended and raised towards heaven, and with the face turned to the East. *cf.* early art, and specially the figures of "oranti." Their rich dress indicates less their actual station in this life than the expected felicity of Paradise. *Vide, Dict. Christ. Ant.* ii. 1684.
[5] "Stood again with"—συναναστάντες.
[6] Col. iii. 1.
[7] Gen. i. 5. Heb. LXX. Vulg. R.V. *cf.* p. 64.
[8] *Vide* Titles to Pss. vi. and xii. in A.V. "upon Sheminith," marg. "the eighth." LXX. ὑπὲρ τῆς ὀγδόης. Vulg. *pro octava.* On various explanations of the Hebrew word *vide* Dict. Bib. S. V. where Dr. Aldis Wright inclines to the view that it is a tune or key, and that the Hebrews were not acquainted with the octave.

from off them we shew by the very deed that by our sin we fell down to earth, and by the loving kindness of our Creator were called back to heaven.

67. Time will fail me if I attempt to recount the unwritten mysteries of the Church. Of the rest I say nothing; but of the very confession of our faith in Father, Son, and Holy Ghost, what is the written source? If it be granted that, as we are baptized, so also under the obligation to believe, we make our confession in like terms as our baptism, in accordance with the tradition of our baptism and in conformity with the principles of true religion, let our opponents grant us too the right to be as consistent in our ascription of glory as in our confession of faith. If they deprecate our doxology on the ground that it lacks written authority, let them give us the written evidence for the confession of our faith and the other matters which we have enumerated. While the unwritten traditions are so many, and their bearing on "the mystery of godliness [1] is so important, can they refuse to allow us a single word which has come down to us from the Fathers; — which we found, derived from untutored custom, abiding in unperverted churches; — a word for which the arguments are strong, and which contributes in no small degree to the completeness of the force of the mystery?

68. The force of both expressions has now been explained. I will proceed to state once more wherein they agree and wherein they differ from one another; — not that they are opposed in mutual antagonism, but that each contributes its own meaning to true religion. The preposition "*in*" states the truth rather relatively to ourselves; while "*with*" proclaims the fellowship of the Spirit with God. Wherefore we use both words, by the one expressing the dignity of the Spirit; by the other announcing the grace that is with us. Thus we ascribe glory to God both "in" the Spirit, and "with" the Spirit; and herein it is not our word that we use, but we follow the teaching of the Lord as we might a fixed rule, and transfer His word to things connected and closely related, and of which the conjunction in the mysteries is necessary. We have deemed ourselves under a necessary obligation to combine in our confession of the faith Him who is numbered with Them at Baptism, and we have treated the confession of the faith as the origin and parent of the doxology. What, then, is to be done? They must now instruct us either not to

baptize as we have received, or not to believe as we were baptized, or not to ascribe glory as we have believed. Let any man prove if he can that the relation of sequence in these acts is not necessary and unbroken; or let any man deny if he can that innovation here must mean ruin everywhere. Yet they never stop dinning in our ears that the ascription of glory "*with*" the Holy Spirit is unauthorized and unscriptural and the like. We have stated that so far as the sense goes it is the same to say "glory be to the Father and to the Son *and* to the Holy Ghost," and glory be to the Father and to the Son *with* the Holy Ghost." It is impossible for any one to reject or cancel the syllable "and," which is derived from the very words of our Lord, and there is nothing to hinder the acceptance of its equivalent. What amount of difference and similarity there is between the two we have already shewn. And our argument is confirmed by the fact that the Apostle uses either word indifferently, — saying at one time "in the name of the Lord Jesus and by the Spirit of our God;" [1] at another "when ye are gathered together, and my Spirit, with the power of our Lord Jesus," [2] with no idea that it makes any difference to the connexion of the names whether he use the conjunction or the preposition.

CHAPTER XXVIII.

That our opponents refuse to concede in the case of the Spirit the terms which Scripture uses in the case of men, as reigning together with Christ.

69. BUT let us see if we can bethink us of any defence of this usage of our fathers; for they who first originated the expression are more open to blame than we ourselves. Paul in his Letter to the Colossians says, "And you, being dead in your sins and the uncircumcision . . . hath He quickened together with" [3] Christ. Did then God give to a whole people and to the Church the boon of the life with Christ, and yet the life with Christ does not belong to the Holy Spirit? But if this is impious even to think of, is it not rightly reverent so to make our confession, as They are by nature in close conjunction? Furthermore what boundless lack of sensibility does it not shew in these men to confess that the Saints are with Christ, (if, as we know is the case, Paul, on becoming absent from the body, is present with the

---

[1] 1 Tim. iii. 16.

[1] 1 Cor. vi. 11.
[2] 1 Cor. v. 4.
[3] Col. ii. 13.

Lord,[1] and, after departing, is with Christ[2])
and, so far as lies in their power, to refuse to
allow to the Spirit to be with Christ even to
the same extent as men? And Paul calls himself a " labourer together with God "[3] in the
dispensation of the Gospel; will they bring
an indictment for impiety against us, if we
apply the term " fellow-labourer " to the
Holy Spirit, through whom in every creature
under heaven the Gospel bringeth forth
fruit?[4] The life of them that have trusted in
the Lord " is hidden," it would seem, " with
Christ in God, and when Christ, who is our
life, shall appear, then shall " they themselves
also " appear with Him in glory; "[5] and is
the Spirit of life Himself, " Who made us
free from the law of sin,"[6] not with Christ,
both in the secret and hidden life with Him,
and in the manifestation of the glory which
we expect to be manifested in the saints?
We are " heirs of God and joint heirs with
Christ,"[7] and is the Spirit without part or lot
in the fellowship of God and of His Christ?
" The Spirit itself beareth witness with our
spirit that we are the children of God; "[8]
and are we not to allow to the Spirit even
that testimony of His fellowship with God
which we have learnt from the Lord? For
the height of folly is reached if we through
the faith in Christ which is in the Spirit[9]
hope that we shall be raised together with
Him and sit together in heavenly places,[10]
whenever He shall change our vile body
from the natural to the spiritual,[11] and yet
refuse to assign to the Spirit any share in the
sitting together, or in the glory, or anything
else which we have received from Him. Of
all the boons of which, in accordance with
the indefeasible grant of Him who has promised them, we have believed ourselves worthy,
are we to allow none to the Holy Spirit, as
though they were all above His dignity? It
is yours according to your merit to be " ever
with the Lord," and you expect to be caught
up " in the clouds to meet the Lord in the
air and to be ever with the Lord."[12] You
declare the man who numbers and ranks the
Spirit with the Father and the Son to be
guilty of intolerable impiety. Can you really
now deny that the Spirit is with Christ?

70. I am ashamed to add the rest. You
expect to be glorified together with Christ;
(" if so be that we suffer with him that we
may be also glorified together; "[13]) but you

do not glorify the " Spirit of holiness "[1] together with Christ, as though He were not
worthy to receive equal honour even with
you. You hope to " reign with "[2] Christ;
but you " do despite unto the Spirit of grace "[3]
by assigning Him the rank of a slave and a
subordinate. And I say this not to demonstrate that so much is due to the Spirit in the
ascription of glory, but to prove the unfairness of those who will not ever give so much
as this, and shrink from the fellowship of the
Spirit with Son and Father as from impiety.
Who could touch on these things without a
sigh?[4] Is it not so plain as to be within the
perception even of a child that this present
state of things preludes the threatened eclipse
of the faith? The undeniable has become
the uncertain. We profess belief in the
Spirit, and then we quarrel with our own
confessions. We are baptized, and begin to
fight again. We call upon Him as the
Prince of Life, and then despise Him as a
slave like ourselves. We received Him with
the Father and the Son, and we dishonour
Him as a part of creation. Those who
" know not what they ought to pray for,"[5]
even though they be induced to utter a word
of the Spirit with awe, as though coming
near His dignity, yet prune down all that
exceeds the exact proportion of their speech.
They ought rather to bewail their weakness,
in that we are powerless to express in words
our gratitude for the benefits which we are
actually receiving; for He " passes all understanding,"[6] and convicts speech of its natural
inability even to approach His dignity in the
least degree; as it is written in the Book of
Wisdom,[7] " Exalt Him as much as you
can, for even yet will He far exceed; and
when you exalt Him put forth all your
strength, and be not weary, for you can
never go far enough." Verily terrible is the
account to be given for words of this kind
by you who have heard from God who cannot lie that for blasphemy against the Holy
Ghost there is no forgiveness.[8]

CHAPTER XXIX.

*Enumeration of the illustrious men in the
Church who in their writings have used the
word " with."*

71. In answer to the objection that the doxology in the form " with the Spirit " has no
written authority, we maintain that if there is

---

[1] *cf.* 2 Cor. v. 8.   [4] *cf.* Col. i. 6.   [7] Rom. viii. 17.
[2] *cf.* Phil. i. 23.   [5] Col. iii. 3, 4.
[3] 1 Cor. iii. 9.   [6] Rom. viii. 2.
[8] Rom. viii. 16, 17. In this passage A.V. follows the neuter
of the Greek original. R.V. has substituted " himself." *cf.*
note on p. 15.
[9] *cf.* Gal. v. 5.   [10] *cf.* Eph. ii. 6.
[11] *cf.* Phil. iii. 21, and 1 Cor. xv. 44.
[12] 1 Thess. iv. 17.   [13] Rom. viii. 17.

[1] Rom. i. 4.   [2] 2 Tim. ii. 12.   [3] Heb. x. 29.
[4] *cf.* Verg., *Æn.* ii. *Quis talia fando . . . temperet a lacry-
mis ?*
[5] Rom. viii. 26.   [6] Phil. iv. 7.
[7] *i.e.* of Jesus the Son of Sirach, or Ecclus. xliii. 30.
[8] Luke xii. 10.

no other instance of that which is unwritten, then this must not be received. But if the greater number of our mysteries are admitted into our constitution without written authority, then, in company with the many others, let us receive this one. For I hold it apostolic to abide also by the unwritten traditions. " I praise you," it is said, " that ye remember me in all things, and keep the ordinances as I delivered them to you;"[1] and " Hold fast the traditions which ye have been taught whether by word, or our Epistle."[2] One of these traditions is the practice which is now before us, which they who ordained from the beginning, rooted firmly in the churches, delivering it to their successors, and its use through long custom advances pace by pace with time. If, as in a Court of Law, we were at a loss for documentary evidence, but were able to bring before you a large number of witnesses, would you not give your vote for our acquittal? I think so; for " at the mouth of two or three witnesses shall the matter be established."[3] And if we could prove clearly to you that a long period of time was in our favour, should we not have seemed to you to urge with reason that this suit ought not to be brought into court against us? For ancient dogmas inspire a certain sense of awe, venerable as they are with a hoary antiquity. I will therefore give you a list of the supporters of the word (and the time too must be taken into account in relation to what passes unquestioned). For it did not originate with us. How could it? We, in comparison with the time during which this word has been in vogue, are, to use the words of Job, " but of yesterday."[4] I myself, if I must speak of what concerns me individually, cherish this phrase as a legacy left me by my fathers. It was delivered to me by one[5] who spent a long life in the service of God, and by him I was both baptized, and admitted to the ministry of the church. While examining, so far as I could, if any of the blessed men of old used the words to which objection is now made, I found many worthy of credit both on account of their early date, and also — a characteristic in which they are unlike the men of to-day — because of the exactness of their knowledge. Of these some coupled the word in the doxology by the preposition, others by the conjunction, but were in no case supposed to be acting divergently, — at least so far as the right sense of true religion is concerned.

72. There is the famous Irenæus,[1] and Clement of Rome;[2] Dionysius of Rome,[3] and, strange to say, Dionysius of Alexandria, in his second Letter to his namesake, on " Conviction and Defence," so concludes. I will give you his very words. " Following all these, we, too, since we have received from the presbyters who were before us a form and rule, offering thanksgiving in the same terms with them, thus conclude our Letter to you. To God the Father and the Son our Lord Jesus Christ, with the Holy Ghost, glory and might for ever and ever; amen." And no one can say that this passage has been altered. He would not have so persistently stated that he had received a form and rule if he had said " *in* the Spirit." For of this phrase the use is abundant: it was the use of " *with* " which required defence. Dionysius moreover in the middle of his treatise thus writes in opposition to the Sabellians, " If by the hypostases being three they say that they are divided, there are three, though they like it not. Else let them destroy the divine Trinity altogether." And again: " most divine on this account after the Unity is the Trinity."[4] Clement, in more primitive fashion, writes, " God lives, and the Lord Jesus Christ, and the Holy Ghost."[5] And now let us hear how Irenæus, who lived near the times of the Apostles, mentions the Spirit in his work " Against the Heresies."[6] " The Apostle rightly calls *carnal* them that are unbridled and carried away to their own desires, having no desire for the Holy Spirit,"[7] and in another passage Irenæus says, " The Apostle exclaimed that flesh and blood cannot inherit the kingdom of the heavens lest we, being without share in the divine Spirit, fall short of the kingdom of the heavens." If any one thinks Eusebius of Palestine[8] worthy of credit on

---

[1] 1 Cor. xi. 2.   [3] Deut. xix. 15.
[2] 2 Thess. ii. 15.   [4] Job viii. 9.
[5] *i.e.* Dianius, bp. of the Cappadocian Cæsarea, who baptized St. Basil c. 357 on his return from Athens, and ordained him Reader. He was a waverer, and signed the creed of Ariminum in 359; Basil consequently left him, but speaks reverentially of him in Ep. 51.

[1] † c. 200.   [2] † 100.   [3] † 269.
[4] Dionysius was Patriarch of Alexandria A.D. 247-265. Basil's " strange to say" is of a piece with the view of Dionysius' heretical tendencies expressed in Letter ix. *q.v.* Athanasius, however, (*De Sent. Dionysii*) was satisfied as to the orthodoxy of his predecessor. Bp. Westcott (*Dict. C. Biog.* i. 851) quotes Lumper (*Hist. Pat.* xii. 86) as supposing that Basil's charge against Dionysius of sowing the seeds of the Anomœan heresy was due to imperfect acquaintance with his writings. In Letter clxxxviii. Basil calls him " the Great," which implies general approval.
[5] Clem. Rom., *Ep. ad Cor.* lviii. Bp. Lightfoot's *Ap. Fathers*, Pt. I. ii. 169.
[6] Irenæus is near the Apostles in close connexion, as well as in time, through his personal knowledge of Polycarp. *Vide his Ep. to Florinus* quoted in Euseb., *Ecc. Hist.* v. 20. In his work *On the Ogdoad*, quoted in the same chapter, Irenæus says of himself that he τὴν πρωτὴν τῶν Ἀποστολῶν κατειληφενικ τὴν διαδοχήν " had himself had the nearest succession of the Apostles."
[7] The reference is presumably to 1 Cor. ii. 11 and iii. 1.
[8] *i.e.* Eusebius of Cæsarea, the historian, so called to distinguish him from his namesake of Nicomedia. *cf.* Theodoret, *Ecc. Hist.* i. 1. The work is not extant. It may be that

account of his wide experience, I point further to the very words he uses in discussing questions concerning the polygamy of the ancients. Stirring up himself to his work, he writes " invoking the holy God of the Prophets, the Author of light, through our Saviour Jesus Christ, with the Holy Spirit."

73. Origen, too, in many of his expositions of the Psalms, we find using the form of doxology " *with* the Holy Ghost. The opinions which he held concerning the Spirit were not always and everywhere sound; nevertheless in many passages even he himself reverently recognises the force of established usage, and expresses himself concerning the Spirit in terms consistent with true religion. It is, if I am not mistaken, in the Sixth[1] Book of his *Commentary on the Gospel of St. John* that he distinctly makes the Spirit an object of worship. His words are : — " The washing of water is a symbol of the cleaning of the soul which is washed clean of all filth that comes of wickedness;[2] but none the less is it also by itself, to him who yields himself to the Godhead of the adorable Trinity, through the power of the invocations, the origin and source of blessings." And again, in his *Exposition of the Epistle to the Romans* " the holy powers," he says " are able to receive the Only-begotten, and the Godhead of the Holy Spirit." Thus I apprehend, the powerful influence of tradition frequently impels the men to express themselves in terms contradictory to their own opinions.[3] Moreover this form of the doxology was not unknown

even to Africanus the historian. In the Fifth Book of his *Epitome of the Times* he says " we who know the weight of those terms, and are not ignorant of the grace of faith, render thanks to the Father, who bestowed on us His own creatures, Jesus Christ, the Saviour of the world and our Lord, to whom be glory and majesty with the Holy Ghost, for ever."[1] The rest of the passages may peradventure be viewed with suspicion; or may really have been altered, and the fact of their having been tampered with will be difficult to detect because the difference consists in a single syllable. Those however which I have quoted at length are out of the reach of any dishonest manipulation, and can easily be verified from the actual works.

I will now adduce another piece of evidence which might perhaps seem insignificant, but because of its antiquity must in nowise be omitted by a defendant who is indicted on a charge of innovation. It seemed fitting to our fathers not to receive the gift of the light at eventide in silence, but, on its appearing, immediately to give thanks. Who was the author of these words of thanksgiving at the lighting of the lamps, we are not able to say. The people, however, utter the ancient form, and no one has ever reckoned guilty of impiety those who say " We praise Father, Son, and God's Holy Spirit."[2] And if any one knows the Hymn of Athenogenes,[3] which, as he was hurrying on to his perfecting by fire, he left as a kind of farewell gift[4] to his friends, he knows the mind of the martyrs as to the Spirit. On this head I shall say no more.

74. But where shall I rank the great Gregory,[5] and the words uttered by him? Shall we not place among Apostles and

mentioned by Eusebius in his Præp. Evang. vii. 8, 20 under the title of περὶ τῆς τῶν παλαιῶν ἀνδρῶν πολυπαιδίας.

[1] The quotation is from the *Eighth* Book.

[2] cf. 1 Pet. iii. 21.

[3] As to Origen's unorthodoxy concerning the Holy Spirit St. Basil may have had in his mind such a passage as the following from the First Book of the *De Principiis*, extant in the original in Justinian, *Ep. ad Mennam*. Migne, Pat. Gr. xi. p. 150. ὅτι ὁ μὲν θεὸς καὶ πατὴρ συνέχων τὰ πάντα φθάνει εἰς ἕκαστον τῶν ὄντων μεταδιδοὺς ἑκάστῳ ἀπὸ τοῦ ἰδίου τὸ εἶναι· ὧν γάρ ἐστιν· ἐλάττων δὲ παρὰ τὸν πατέρα ὁ Υἱὸς φθάνει ἐπὶ μόνα τὰ λογικά· δεύτερος γάρ ἐστι τοῦ πατρός· ἔτι δὲ ἥττον τὸ πνεῦμα τὸ ἅγιον ἐπὶ μόνους τοὺς ἁγίους διικνούμενον· ὥστε κατὰ τοῦτο μείζων ἡ δύναμις τοῦ Πατρὸς παρὰ τὸν Υἱὸν καὶ τὸ πνεῦμα τὸ ἅγιον πλείων δὲ ἡ τοῦ Υἱοῦ παρὰ τὸ πνεῦμα τὸ ἅγιον. The work does not even exist as a whole in the translation of Rufinus, who 'omitted portions, and St. Jerome thought that Rufinus had misrepresented it. Photius (*Biblioth. cod.* viii.) says that Origen, in asserting in this work that the Son was made by the Father, and the Spirit by the Son, is most blasphemous. Bp. Harold Browne, however (*Exposition of the xxxix. Art.* p. 113, n. 1), is of opinion that if Rufinus fairly translated the following passage, Origen cannot have been fairly charged with heresy concerning the Holy Ghost: " *Ne quis sane existimet nos ex eo quod diximus Spiritum sanctum solis sanctis præstari. Patris vero et Filii beneficia vel inoperationes pervenire ad bonos et malos, justos et injustos, prætulisse per hoc Patri et Filio Spiritum Sanctum, vel majorem ejus per hoc asserere dignitatem; quod utique valde inconsequens est. Proprietatem namque gratiæ ejus operisque descripsimus. Porro autem nihil in Trinitate majus minusve dicendum est, quum unius Divinitatis Fons verbo ac ratione sua teneat universa, spiritu vero oris sui quæ digna sunt, sanctificatione sanctificet, sicut in Psalmo scriptum est verbo domini cœli firmati sunt et spiritu oris ejus omnis virtus eorum.*" *De Princ.* I. iii. 7. On the obligations of both Basil and Gregory of Nazianzus to Origen, cf. Socrates iv. 26.

[1] Of the chief writings of Julius Africanus (called Sextus Africanus by Suidas), who wrote at Emmaus and Alexandria c. 220, only fragments remain. A *Letter to Origen* is complete. His principal work was a *Chronicon* from the Creation to A.D. 221, in Five Books. Of this Dr. Salmon (*D.C.B.* i. 56) thinks the doxology quoted by Basil was the conclusion.

[2] Ps. cxli. was called ὁ ἐπιλύχνιος ψαλμός (*Ap. Const.* viii. 35). In the Vespers of the Eastern Church an evening hymn is sung, translated in *D.C.A.* i. 634, " Joyful Light of the holy glory of the immortal Father, the heavenly, the holy, the blessed Jesus Christ, we having come to the setting of the sun and beholding the evening light, praise God, Father, Son, and Holy Ghost. It is meet at all times that thou shouldest be hymned with auspicious voices, Son of God, Giver of Life: wherefore the world glorifieth thee."

[3] Identified by some with two early hymns, Δόξα ἐν ὑψίστοις, and Φῶς ἱλαρόν.

[4] The MSS. vary between ἐξιτήριον and ἀλεξιτήριον, farewell gift and amulet or charm. In *Ep.* cciii. 299 Basil says that our Lord gave His disciples peace as an ἐξιτήριον δῶρον, using the word, but in conjunction with δῶρον. Greg.Naz., *Orat.* xiv. 223 speaks of our Lord leaving peace "ὥσπερ ἄλλο τι ἐξιτήριον."

[5] i.e. Gregory, bishop of Neocæsarea, known as Gregorius Thaumaturgus, or Gregory the Wonder-worker. To the modern reader " Gregory the Great" more naturally suggests Gregory of Nazianzus, but this he hardly was to his friend and contemporary, though the title had accrued to him by the time of the accepted Ephesine Council in 431 (*vide* Labbe, vol. iv. p. 1192) Gregory the Wonder-worker, † c. 270.

Prophets a man who walked by the same Spirit as they;[1] who never through all his days diverged from the footprints of the saints; who maintained, as long as he lived, the exact principles of evangelical citizenship? I am sure that we shall do the truth a wrong if we refuse to number that soul with the people of God, shining as it did like a beacon in the Church of God; for by the fellow-working of the Spirit the power which he had over demons was tremendous, and so gifted was he with the grace of the word " for obedience to the faith among . . . the nations,"[2] that, although only seventeen Christians were handed over to him, he brought the whole people alike in town and country through knowledge to God. He too by Christ's mighty name commanded even rivers to change their course,[3] and caused a lake, which afforded a ground of quarrel to some covetous brethren, to dry up.[4] Moreover his predictions of things to come were such as in no wise to fall short of those of the great prophets. To recount all his wonderful works in detail would be too long a task. By the superabundance of gifts, wrought in him by the Spirit in all power and in signs and in marvels, he was styled a second Moses by the very enemies of the Church. Thus in all that he through grace accomplished, alike by word and deed, a light seemed ever to be shining, token of the heavenly power from the unseen which followed him. To this day he is a great object of admiration to the people of his own neighbourhood, and his memory, established in the churches ever fresh and green, is not dulled by length of time. Thus not a practice, not a word, not a mystic rite has been added to the Church besides what he bequeathed to it. Hence truly on account of the antiquity of their institution many of their ceremonies appear to be defective.[5] For his successors in the administration of the Churches could not endure to accept any subsequent discovery in addition to what had had his sanction. Now one of the institutions of Gregory is the very form of the doxology to which objection is now made, preserved by the Church on the authority of his tradition; a statement which may be verified without much trouble by any one who likes to make a short journey. That our Firmilian held this belief is testified by the writings which he has left.[6] The

contemporaries also of the illustrious Meletius say that he was of this opinion. But why quote ancient authorities? Now in the East are not the maintainers of true religion known chiefly by this one term, and separated from their adversaries as by a watchword? I have heard from a certain Mesopotamian, a man at once well skilled in the language and of unperverted opinions, that by the usage of his country it is impossible for any one, even though he may wish to do so, to express himself in any other way, and that they are compelled by the idiom of their mother tongue to offer the doxology by the syllable " and," or, I should more accurately say, by their equivalent expressions. We Cappadocians, too, so speak in the dialect of our country, the Spirit having so early as the division of tongues foreseen the utility of the phrase. And what of the whole West, almost from Illyricum to the boundaries of our world? Does it not support this word?

75. How then can I be an innovator and creator of new terms, when I adduce as originators and champions of the word whole nations, cities, custom going back beyond the memory of man, men who were pillars of the church and conspicuous for all knowledge and spiritual power? For this cause this banded array of foes is set in motion against me, and town and village and remotest regions are full of my calumniators. Sad and painful are these things to them that seek for peace, but great is the reward of patience for sufferings endured for the Faith's sake. So besides these let sword flash, let axe be whetted, let fire burn fiercer than that of Babylon, let every instrument of torture be set in motion against me. To me nothing is more fearful than failure to fear the threats which the Lord has directed against them that blaspheme the Spirit.[1] Kindly readers will find a satisfactory defence in what I have said, that I accept a phrase so dear and so familiar to the saints, and confirmed by usage so long, inasmuch as, from the day when the Gospel was first preached up to our own time, it is shewn to have been admitted to all full rights within the churches, and, what is of greatest moment, to have been accepted as bearing a sense in accordance with holiness and true religion. But before the great tribunal what have I prepared to say in my defence? This; that I was in the first place led to the glory of the Spirit by the honour conferred by the Lord

---

[1] 2 Cor. xii. 18.   [2] Rom. i. 5.
[3] *e.g.* according to the legend, the Lycus. *cf.* Newman, *Essays on Miracles*, p. 267.
[4] The story is told by Gregory of Nyssa, Life of *Greg. Thaum.* Migne xlvi. 926–930.
[5] The Neocæsareans appear to have entertained a Puritan objection to the antiphonal psalmody becoming general in the Church in the time of Basil. *cf. Ep.* ccvii.
[6] Firmilian, like Gregory the Wonder-worker, a pupil of

Origen, was bishop of Cæsarea from before A.D. 232 (Euseb. vi. 26) to 272 (Euseb. vii. 30). By some his death at Tarsus is placed in 264 or 5.
[1] *cf.* Matt. xii. 31.

in associating Him with Himself and with His Father at baptism; [1] and secondly by the introduction of each of us to the knowledge of God by such an initiation; and above all by the fear of the threatened punishment shutting out the thought of all indignity and unworthy conception. But our opponents, what will they say? After shewing neither reverence for the Lord's honour [2] nor fear of His threats, what kind of defence will they have for their blasphemy? It is for them to make up their mind about their own action or even now to change it. For my own part I would pray most earnestly that the good God will make His peace rule in the hearts of all, [3] so that these men who are swollen with pride and set in battle array against us may be calmed by the Spirit of meekness and of love; and that if they have become utterly savage, and are in an untamable state, He will grant to us at least to bear with long suffering all that we have to bear at their hands. In short "to them that have in themselves the sentence of death," [4] it is not suffering for the sake of the Faith which is painful; what is hard to bear is to fail to fight its battle. The athlete does not so much complain of being wounded in the struggle as of not being able even to secure admission into the stadium. Or perhaps this was the time for silence spoken of by Solomon the wise. [5] For, when life is buffeted by so fierce a storm that all the intelligence of those who are instructed in the word is filled with the deceit of false reasoning and confounded, like an eye filled with dust, when men are stunned by strange and awful noises, when all the world is shaken and everything tottering to its fall, what profits it to cry, as I am really crying, to the wind?

CHAPTER XXX.

Exposition of the present state of the Churches.

76. To what then shall I liken our present condition? It may be compared, I think, to some naval battle which has arisen out of time old quarrels, and is fought by men who cherish a deadly hate against one another, of long experience in naval warfare, and eager for the fight. Look, I beg you, at the picture thus raised before your eyes. See the rival fleets rushing in dread array to the attack. With a burst of uncontrollable fury they engage and fight it out. Fancy, if you like, the ships driven to and fro by a raging tempest, while thick darkness falls from the clouds and blackens all the scene, so that watchwords are indistinguishable in the confusion, and all distinction between friend and foe is lost. To fill up the details of the imaginary picture, suppose the sea swollen with billows and whirled up from the deep, while a vehement torrent of rain pours down from the clouds and the terrible waves rise high. From every quarter of heaven the winds beat upon one point, where both the fleets are dashed one against the other. Of the combatants some are turning traitors; some are deserting in the very thick of the fight; some have at one and the same moment to urge on their boats, all beaten by the gale, and to advance against their assailants. Jealousy of authority and the lust of individual mastery splits the sailors into parties which deal mutual death to one another. Think, besides all this, of the confused and unmeaning roar sounding over all the sea, from howling winds, from crashing vessels, from boiling surf, from the yells of the combatants as they express their varying emotions in every kind of noise, so that not a word from admiral or pilot can be heard. The disorder and confusion is tremendous, for the extremity of misfortune, when life is despaired of, gives men license for every kind of wickedness. Suppose, too, that the men are all smitten with the incurable plague of mad love of glory, so that they do not cease from their struggle each to get the better of the other, while their ship is actually settling down into the deep.

77. Turn now I beg you from this figurative description to the unhappy reality. Did it not at one time [1] appear that the Arian schism, after its separation into a sect opposed to the Church of God, stood itself alone in hostile array? But when the attitude of our foes against us was changed from one of long standing and bitter strife to one of open warfare, then, as is well known, the war was split up in more ways than I can tell into many subdivisions, so that all men were stirred to a state of inveterate hatred alike by common party spirit and individual suspicion. [2] But what storm at sea was ever so

---

[1] Matt. xxviii. 19.
[2] The Benedictine version for τὰς τιμὰς τοῦ κυρίου is *honorem quem Dominus tribuit Spiritui.* The reading of one MS. is τὰς φωνάς. There is authority for either sense of the genitive with τιμή, *i.e.* the honours *due to the Lord* or *paid by the Lord.*
[3] *cf.* Col. iii. 15.   [4] 2 Cor. i. 9.   [5] Eccl. iii. 7.

[1] *i.e.* after the condemnation of Arius at Nicæa.
[2] In Ep. ccxlii. written in 376, St. Basil says: "This is the thirteenth year since the outbreak of the war of heretics against us." 363 is the date of the Acacian Council of Antioch; 364 of the accession of Valens and Valentian, of the Semi-Arian Synod of Lampsacus, and of St. Basil's ordination to the priesthood and book against Eunomius. On the propagation by scission and innumerable subdivisions of Arianism Canon Bright writes:
" The extraordinary versatility, the argumentative subtlety, and the too frequent profanity of Arianism are matters of which a few lines can give no idea. But it is necessary, in

fierce and wild as this tempest of the Churches? In it every landmark of the Fathers has been moved; every foundation, every bulwark of opinion has been shaken; everything buoyed up on the unsound is dashed about and shaken down. We attack one another. We are overthrown by one another. If our enemy is not the first to strike us, we are wounded by the comrade at our side. If a foeman is stricken and falls, his fellow soldier tramples him down. There is at least this bond of union between us that we hate our common foes, but no sooner have the enemy gone by than we find enemies in one another. And who could make a complete list of all the wrecks? Some have gone to the bottom on the attack of the enemy, some through the unsuspected treachery of their allies, some from the blundering of their own officers. We see, as it were, whole churches, crews and all, dashed and shattered upon the sunken reefs of disingenuous heresy, while others of the enemies of the Spirit[1] of Salvation have seized the helm and made shipwreck of the faith.[2] And then the disturbances wrought by the princes of the world[3] have caused the downfall of the people with a violence unmatched by that of hurricane or whirlwind. The luminaries of the world, which God set to give light to the souls of the people, have been driven from their homes, and a darkness verily gloomy and disheartening has settled

even the briefest notice of this long-lived heresy, to remark on the contrast between its changeable inventiveness and the simple steadfastness of Catholic doctrine. On the one side, some twenty different creeds (of which several, however, were rather negatively than positively heterodox) and three main sects, the Semi-Arians, with their formula of Homoiousion, *i.e.* the Son is like in essence to the Father; the Acacians, vaguely calling Him like (Homoion); the Aetians, boldly calling Him unlike, as much as to say He is in no sense Divine. On the other side, the Church with the Nicene Creed, confessing Him as Homoousion, 'of one essence with the Father,' meaning thereby, as her great champion repeatedly bore witness, to secure belief in the reality of the Divine Sonship, and therefore in the real Deity, as distinguished from the titular deity which was so freely conceded to Him by the Arians." Canon Bright, *St. Leo on the Incarnation*, p. 140.

Socrates (ii. 41), pausing at 360, enumerates, after Nicæa:
1. 1st of Antioch
2. 2d of Antioch } (omitted the ὁμοούσιον, A.D. 341).
3. The Creed brought to Constans in Gaul by Narcissus and other Arians in 342.
4. The Creed "sent by Eudoxius of Germanicia into Italy," *i.e.* the " Macrostich," or " Lengthy Creed," rejected at Milan in 346.
5. The 1st Creed of Sirmium; *i.e.* the Macrostich with 26 additional clauses, 351.
6. The 2d Sirmian Creed. The "manifesto;" called by Athanasius (*De Synod*. 28) " the blasphemy," 357.
7. The 3d Sirmian, or " dated Creed," in the consulship of Flavius Eusebius and Hypatius, May 22d, 359.
8. The Acacian Creed of Seleucia, 359.
9. The Creed of Ariminum adopted at Constantinople, as revised at Nike.
[1] On the authority of the MS. of the tenth century at Paris, called by the Ben. Editors *Regius Secundus*, they read for πνεύματος πάθους, denying πνεύματος to be consistent with the style and practice of Basil, who, they say, never uses the epithet σωτήριος of the Spirit. Mr. C. F. H. Johnston notes that St. Basil " always attributes the saving efficacy of Baptism to the presence of the Spirit, and here applies the word to Him." In § 35 we have τὸ σωτήριον βάπτισμα.
[2] 1 Tim. i. 19. [3] 1 Cor. ii. 6.

on the Churches.[1] The terror of universal ruin is already imminent, and yet their mutual rivalry is so unbounded as to blunt all sense of danger. Individual hatred is of more importance than the general and common warfare, for men by whom the immediate gratification of ambition is esteemed more highly than the rewards that await us in a time to come, prefer the glory of getting the better of their opponents to securing the common welfare of mankind. So all men alike, each as best he can, lift the hand of murder against one another. Harsh rises the cry of the combatants encountering one another in dispute; already all the Church is almost full of the inarticulate screams, the unintelligible noises, rising from the ceaseless agitations that divert the right rule of the doctrine of true religion, now in the direction of excess, now in that of defect. On the one hand are they who confound the Persons and are carried away into Judaism;[2] on the other hand are they that, through the opposition of the natures, pass into heathenism.[3] Between these opposite parties inspired Scripture is powerless to mediate; the traditions of the apostles cannot suggest terms of arbitration. Plain speaking is fatal to friendship, and disagreement in opinion all the ground that is wanted for a quarrel. No oaths of confederacy are so efficacious in keeping men true to sedition as their likeness in error. Every one is a theologue though he have his soul branded with more spots than can be counted. The result is that innovators find a plentiful supply of men ripe for faction, while self-appointed scions of the house of place-hunters[4] reject the government[5] of the Holy Spirit and divide the chief dignities of the Churches. The institutions of the Gospel have now everywhere been thrown into confusion by want of discipline; there is an indescribable pushing for the chief places while every self-advertiser

[1] Among the bishops exiled during the persecution of Valens were Meletius of Antioch, Eusebius of Samosata, Pelagius of Laodicea, and Barses of Edessa. *cf.* Theodoret, *Hist. Ecc.* iv. 12 *sq. cf.* Ep. 195.
[2] The identification of an unsound Monarchianism with Judaism is illustrated in the *1st Apology of Justin Martyr. e.g.* in § lxxxiii. (Reeves' Trans.). " The Jews, therefore, for maintaining that it was the Father of the Universe who had the conference with Moses, when it was the very Son of God who had it, and who is styled both Angel and Apostle, are justly accused by the prophetic spirit and Christ Himself, for knowing neither the Father nor the Son; for they who affirm the Son to be the Father are guilty of not knowing the Father, and likewise of being ignorant that the Father of the Universe has a Son, who, being the Logos and First-begotten of God, is God."
[3] *i.e.* the Arians, whose various ramifications all originated in a probably well-meant attempt to reconcile the principles of Christianity with what was best in the old philosophy, and a failure to see that the ditheism of Arianism was of a piece with polytheism.
[4] The word σπουδαρχίδης is a comic patronymic of σπου-δάρχης, a place-hunter, occurring in *the Acharnians* of Aristophanes, 595. [5] οἰκονομία.

tries to force himself into high office. The result of this lust for ordering is that our people are in a state of wild confusion for lack of being ordered; [1] the exhortations of those in authority are rendered wholly purposeless and void, because there is not a man but, out of his ignorant impudence, thinks that it is just as much his duty to give orders to other people, as it is to obey any one else.

78. So, since no human voice is strong enough to be heard in such a disturbance, I reckon silence more profitable than speech, for if there is any truth in the words of the Preacher, "The words of wise men are heard in quiet," [2] in the present condition of things any discussion of them must be anything but becoming. I am moreover restrained by the Prophet's saying, "Therefore the prudent shall keep silence in that time, for it is an evil time," [3] a time when some trip up their neighbours' heels, some stamp on a man when he is down, and others clap their hands with joy, but there is not one to feel for the fallen and hold out a helping hand, although according to the ancient law he is not uncondemned, who passes by even his enemy's beast of burden fallen under his load. [4] This is not the state of things now. Why not? The love of many has waxed cold; [5] brotherly concord is destroyed, the very name of unity is ignored, brotherly admonitions are heard no more, nowhere is there Christian pity, nowhere falls the tear of sympathy. Now there is no one to receive "the weak in faith," [6] but mutual hatred has blazed so high among fellow clansmen that they are more delighted at a neighbour's fall than at their own success. Just as in a plague, men of the most regular lives suffer from the same sickness as the rest, because they catch the disease by communication with the infected, so nowadays by the evil rivalry which possesses our souls we are carried away to an emulation in wickedness, and are all of us each as bad as the others. Hence merciless and sour sit the judges of the erring; unfeeling and hostile are the critics of the well disposed. And to such a depth is this evil rooted among us that we have become more brutish than the brutes; they do at least herd with their fellows, but our most savage warfare is with our own people.

79. For all these reasons I ought to have kept silence, but I was drawn in the other direction by love, which "seeketh not her own," [1] and desires to overcome every difficulty put in her way by time and circumstance. I was taught too by the children at Babylon, [2] that, when there is no one to support the cause of true religion, we ought alone and all unaided to do our duty. They from out of the midst of the flame lifted up their voices in hymns and praise to God, recking not of the host that set the truth at naught, but sufficient, three only that they were, with one another. Wherefore we too are undismayed at the cloud of our enemies, and, resting our hope on the aid of the Spirit, have, with all boldness, proclaimed the truth. Had I not so done, it would truly have been terrible that the blasphemers of the Spirit should so easily be emboldened in their attack upon true religion, and that we, with so mighty an ally and supporter at our side, should shrink from the service of that doctrine, which by the tradition of the Fathers has been preserved by an unbroken sequence of memory to our own day. A further powerful incentive to my undertaking was the warm fervour of your "love unfeigned," [3] and the seriousness and taciturnity of your disposition; a guarantee that you would not publish what I was about to say to all the world, — not because it would not be worth making known, but to avoid casting pearls before swine. [4] My task is now done. If you find what I have said satisfactory, let this make an end to our discussion of these matters. If you think any point requires further elucidation, pray do not hesitate to pursue the investigation with all diligence, and to add to your information by putting any uncontroversial question. Either through me or through others the Lord will grant full explanation on matters which have yet to be made clear, according to the knowledge supplied to the worthy by the Holy Spirit. Amen.

---

[1] ἀναρχία ἀπὸ φιλαρχίας.
[2] Eccl. ix. 17.
[3] Amos v. 13.
[4] Ezek. xxiii. 5.
[5] Matt. xxiv. 12.
[6] Rom. xiv. 1.

[1] 1 Cor. xiii. 5.
[2] Dan. iii. 12 seqq.
[3] Rom. xii. 9 and 2 Cor. vi. 6.
[4] Matt. vii. 6.

INTRODUCTION TO THE HEXAEMERON.

The *Hexaemeron* is the title of nine homilies delivered by St. Basil on the cosmogony of the opening chapters of Genesis. When and where they were delivered is quite uncertain. They are Lenten sermons, delivered at both the morning and evening services, and appear to have been listened to by working men. (*Hom.* iii. 1). Some words in *Hom.* viii. have confirmed the opinion that they were preached extempore, in accordance with what is believed to have been Basil's ordinary practice.[1] Internal evidence points in the same direction, for though a marked contrast might be expected between the style of a work intended to be read, like the *De Spiritu Sancto*, and that of orations to be spoken in public, the *Hexaemeron* shews signs of being an unwritten composition.

In earlier ages it was the most celebrated and admired of Basil's works. Photius (Migne, Pat. Gr. cxli) puts it first of all, and speaks warmly of its eloquence and force. As an example of oratory he would rank it with the works of Plato and Demosthenes.

Suidas singles it out for special praise. Jerome (*De Viris Illust.*) among Basil's works names only the *Hexaemeron*, the *De Sp. Scto*, and the treatise *Contra Eunomium*.

That Basil's friends should think highly of it is only what might be expected. "Whenever I take his *Hexaemeron* in hand," says Gregory of Nazianzus, (*Orat.* xliii. 67) "and quote its words, I am brought face to face with my Creator: I begin to understand the method of creation: I feel more awe than ever I did before, when I only looked at God's work with my eyes."

Basil's brother Gregory, in the *Procemium* to his own *Hexaemeron*, speaks in exaggerated terms of Basil's work as inspired, and as being, in his opinion, as admirable as that of Moses.

The *Hexaemeron* of Ambrose is rather an imitation than a translation or adaptation of that of Basil. Basil's *Hexaemeron* was translated into Latin by Eustathius Afer (c. A.D. 440) and is said to have been also translated by Dionysius Exiguus, the Scythian monk of the 6th C. to whom is due our custom of dating from the Saviour's birth.

More immediately interesting to English readers is the Anglo-Saxon abbreviation attributed to Ælfric, Abbot of St. Albans in 969, and by some identified with the Ælfric who was Archbishop of Canterbury from 996 to 1006. This is extant in a MS. numbered Junius 23 in the Bodleian Library, and was collated with the MS. Jun. 47 in the same, a transcript of a MS. in the Hatton Collection, by the Rev. Henry W. Norman for his edition and translation published in 1848. It is nowhere a literal translation, but combines with the thoughts of St. Basil extracts from the *Commentary upon Genesis* of the Venerable Bede, as well as original matter. It is entitled

STI BASILII EXAMERON, ꝺᴇᴛ Is Be Godes Six Daga Weorcvm.

"L'Hexaméron," writes Fialon, "est l'explication de l'œuvre des six jours, explication souvent tentée avant et après Saint Basile. 'Il n'est personne parmi les hommes, disait Théophile d'Antioche au deuxième siècle, qui puisse dignement faire le récit et exposer toute l'ecomomie de l'œuvre des six jours; eût il mille bouches et mille langues. . . . Beaucoup d'écrivains ont tenté ce récit; ils ont pris pour sujet, les uns la création du monde, les autres l'origine de l'homme, et peut-être n'ont ils pas fait jaillir une étincelle qui fût digne de la vérité.'[2] Nous ne pouvons savoir ce que fut l'Hexaméron de Saint Hippolyte et nous ne savons guère qu'une chose de celui d'Origène: c'est qu'il dénaturait complètement le récit mosaïque et n'y voyait que des allégories. L'Hexaméron de Saint Basile, par la pureté de la doctrine et la beauté du style, fit disparaitre tous ceux qui l'avaient précédé."[3] So, too, bishop Fessler. "Sapienter, pie, et admodum eloquenter

---

[1] *cf.* Rufinus ii. 9. [2] Theophilus of Antioch, *ii. Ad Autolycum.* [3] *Étude sur St. Basile*, 296.

istæ homiliæ confectæ sunt; quædam explicationes physicæ profecto juxta placita scientiæ illius ætatis dijudicandæ sunt." [1]   On the other hand the prominence of the " scientiæ illius ætatis " is probably the reason why the Hexaemeron has received from adverse critics less favour than it deserves.   " Diese letztern," *i.e.* the Homilies in question, says Böhringer, " erlangten im Alterthum eine ganz unverdiente Berühmtheit.   . . .   Die Art, wie Basil seine Aufgabe löste, ist diese ; er nimmt die mosaische Erzählung von der Schöpfung Vers für Vers vor, erklärt sie von dem naturhistorischen Standpunkt seiner Zeit aus, wobei er Gelegenheit nimmt, die Ansichten der griechischen Philosophen von der Weltschöpfung u. s. w. zu widerlegen, und schliesst dann mit moralischer und religiöser Nutzandwendung, um den Stoff auch für Geist und Herz seiner Zuhörer fruchtbar zu machen.   Es braucht indess kaum bemerkt zu werden, dass vom naturwissenschaftlichen wie exegetischen Standpunkt unserer Zeit diese Arbeit wenig Werth mehr hat." *The Three Cappadocians,* p. 61.   But in truth the fact that Basil is not ahead of the science of his time is not to his discredit.   It is to his credit that he is abreast with it ; and this, with the exception of his geography, he appears to be.   Of him we may say, as Bp. Lightfoot writes of St. Clement, in connexion with the crucial instance of the Phœnix, " it appears that he is not more credulous than the most learned and intelligent heathen writers of the preceding and following generations."   He reads the Book of Genesis in the light of the scientific knowledge of his age, and in the amplification and illustration of Holy Scripture by the supposed aid of this supposed knowledge, neither he nor his age stands alone.   Later centuries may possibly not accept all the science of the XIXth.

HOMILY I.

In the Beginning God made the Heaven and the Earth.

1.   IT is right that any one beginning to narrate the formation of the world should begin with the good order which reigns in visible things.   I am about to speak of the creation of heaven and earth, which was not spontaneous, as some have imagined, but drew its origin from God.   What ear is worthy to hear such a tale?   How earnestly the soul should prepare itself to receive such high lessons!   How pure it should be from carnal affections, how unclouded by worldly disquietudes, how active and ardent in its researches, how eager to find in its surroundings an idea of God which may be worthy of Him!

But before weighing the justice of these remarks, before examining all the sense contained in these few words, let us see who addresses them to us.   Because, if the weakness of our intelligence does not allow us to penetrate the depth of the thoughts of the writer, yet we shall be involuntarily drawn to give faith to his words by the force of his authority.   Now it is Moses who has composed this history ; Moses, who, when still at the breast, is described as exceeding fair ; [2] Moses, whom the daughter of Pharaoh adopted ; who received from her a royal education, and who had for his teachers the wise men of Egypt ; [3] Moses, who disdained the pomp of royalty, and, to share the humble condi-

tion of his compatriots, preferred to be persecuted with the people of God rather than to enjoy the fleeting delights of sin ; Moses, who received from nature such a love of justice that, even before the leadership of the people of God was committed to him, he was impelled, by a natural horror of evil, to pursue malefactors even to the point of punishing them by death ; Moses, who, banished by those whose benefactor he had been, hastened to escape from the tumults of Egypt and took refuge in Ethiopia, living there far from former pursuits, and passing forty years in the contemplation of nature ; Moses, finally, who, at the age of eighty, saw God, as far as it is possible for man to see Him ; or rather as it had not previously been granted to man to see Him, according to the testimony of God Himself, " If there be a prophet among you, I the Lord will make myself known unto him in a vision, and will speak unto him in a dream.   My servant Moses is not so, who is faithful in all mine house, with him will I speak mouth to mouth, even apparently and not in dark speeches." [4]   It is this man, whom God judged worthy to behold Him, face to face, like the angels, who imparts to us what he has learnt from God.   Let us listen then to these words of truth written without the help of the " enticing words of man's wisdom " [5] by the dictation of the Holy Spirit ; words destined to produce not the applause of those who hear them, but the salvation of those who are instructed by them.

---

[1] *Inst. Pat.*, Ed. B. Jungmann 1890.
[2] Acts vii. 20, A.V.
[3] *cf.* Joseph. ii. x. 2.   So Justin M., *Cohort. ad gent.*, Philo, *Vit. Moys*, and Clem. Al., *Strom.* i.   *Vide* Fialon, *Et. Hist.* 302.
[4] Num. xii. 6, 7, 8.
[5] 1 Cor. ii. 4.

2. "In the beginning God created the heaven and the earth."[1] I stop struck with admiration at this thought. What shall I first say? Where shall I begin my story? Shall I show forth the vanity of the Gentiles? Shall I exalt the truth of our faith? The philosophers of Greece have made much ado to explain nature, and not one of their systems has remained firm and unshaken, each being overturned by its successor. It is vain to refute them; they are sufficient in themselves to destroy one another. Those who were too ignorant to rise to a knowledge of a God, could not allow that an intelligent cause presided at the birth of the Universe; a primary error that involved them in sad consequences. Some had recourse to material principles and attributed the origin of the Universe[2] to the elements of the world. Others imagined that atoms,[3] and indivisible bodies, molecules and ducts, form, by their union, the nature of the visible world. Atoms reuniting or separating, produce births and deaths and the most durable bodies only owe their consistency to the strength of their mutual adhesion: a true spider's web woven by these writers who give to heaven, to earth, and to sea so weak an origin and so little consistency! It is because they knew not how to say " In the beginning God created the heaven and the earth." Deceived by their inherent atheism it appeared to them that nothing governed or ruled the universe, and that was all was given up to chance.[4] To guard us against this error the writer on the creation, from the very first words, enlightens our understanding with the name of God; " In the beginning God created." What a glorious order! He first establishes a beginning, so that it might not be supposed that the world never had a beginning. Then he adds " Created " to show that that which was made was a very small part of the power of the Creator. In the same way that the potter, after having made

with equal pains a great number of vessels, has not exhausted either his art or his talent; thus the Maker of the Universe, whose creative power, far from being bounded by one world, could extend to the infinite, needed only the impulse of His will to bring the immensities of the visible world into being. If then the world has a beginning, and if it has been created, enquire who gave it this beginning, and who was the Creator: or rather, in the fear that human reasonings may make you wander from the truth, Moses has anticipated enquiry by engraving in our hearts, as a seal and a safeguard, the awful name of God: " In the beginning God created "— It is He, beneficent Nature, Goodness without measure, a worthy object of love for all beings endowed with reason, the beauty the most to be desired, the origin of all that exists, the source of life, intellectual light, impenetrable wisdom, it is He who " in the beginning created heaven and earth."

3. Do not then imagine, O man! that the visible world is without a beginning; and because the celestial bodies move in a circular course, and it is difficult for our senses to define the point where the circle begins, do not believe that bodies impelled by a circular movement are, from their nature, without a beginning. Without doubt the circle (I mean the plane figure described by a single line) is beyond our perception, and it is impossible for us to find out where it begins or where it ends; but we ought not on this account to believe it to be without a beginning. Although we are not sensible of it, it really begins at some point where the draughtsman has begun to draw it at a certain radius from the centre.[1] Thus seeing that figures which move in a circle always return upon themselves, without for a single instant interrupting the regularity of their course, do not vainly imagine to yourselves that the world has neither beginning nor end. " For the fashion of this world passeth away "[2] and " Heaven and earth shall pass away."[3] The dogmas of the end, and of the renewing of the world, are announced beforehand in these short words put at the head of the inspired history. " In the beginning God made." That which was begun in time is condemned to come to an end in time. If there has been a beginning do not doubt of the end.[4] Of what use then are geometry — the calculations of arithmetic — the study of solids and

---

[1] Gen. i. 1.

[2] cf. note on Letter viii. on the στοιχεῖα or elements which the Ionian philosophers made the ἀρχαί of the universe. Vide Plato, Legg. x. § 4 and Arist., Met. i. 3.

[3] Posidonius the Stoic names Moschus, or Mochus of Sidon, as the originator of the atomic theory " before the Trojan period." Vide Strabo, xvi. 757. But the most famous Atomists, Leucippus and Democritus of Abdera, in the 5th c. B.C., arose in opposition to the Eleatic school, and were followed in the 3d by Epicurus. Vide Diog. Laert. ix. § 30. sq. and Cicero, De Nat. Deor. i. 24-26. Ista enim flagitia Democriti, sive etiam ante Leucippi, esse corpuscula quædam lævia, alia aspera, rotunda alia, partim autem angulata, curvata quædam, et quasi adunca; ex his effectum esse cœlum atque terram, nulla cogente natura, sed concursu quodam fortuito. Atqui, si hæc Democritea non audisset, quid audierat? quid est in physicis Epicuri non a Democrito? Nam, etsi quædam commodavit, ut, quod paulo ante de inclinatione atomorum dixi: tamen pleraque dixit eadem; atomos, inane, imagines, infinitatem locorum, innumerabilitatemque mundorum eorum ortus, interitus, omnia fere, quibus naturæ ratio continetur. [4] cf. the Fortuna gubernans of Lucretius (v. 108).

[1] Fialon refers to Aristotle (De Cælo. i. 5) on the non-infinitude of the circle. The conclusion is ῞Οτι μὲν οὖν τὸ κύκλῳ κινούμενον οὐκ ἔστιν ἀτελεύτητον οὐδ᾽ ἄπειρον, ἀλλ᾽ ἔχει τέλος, φανερόν.

[2] 1 Cor. vii. 31.　　[3] Matt. xxiv. 35.

[4] cf. Arist. De Cælo. i. 12, 10 Δῆλον δ᾽ ὅτι καὶ εἰ γενητὸν ἢ φθαρτόν, οὐκ ἀΐδιον.

far-famed astronomy, this laborious vanity, if those who pursue them imagine that this visible world is co-eternal with the Creator of all things, with God Himself; if they attribute to this limited world, which has a material body, the same glory as to the incomprehensible and invisible nature ; if they cannot conceive that a whole, of which the parts are subject to corruption and change, must of necessity end by itself submitting to the fate of its parts? But they have become " vain in their imaginations and their foolish heart was darkened. Professing themselves to be wise, they became fools." [1] Some have affirmed that heaven co-exists with God from all eternity ; [2] others that it is God Himself without beginning or end, and the cause of the particular arrangement of all things. [3]

4. One day, doubtless, their terrible condemnation will be the greater for all this worldly wisdom, since, seeing so clearly into vain sciences, they have wilfully shut their eyes to the knowledge of the truth. These men who measure the distances of the stars and describe them, both those of the North, always shining brilliantly in our view, and those of the southern pole visible to the inhabitants of the South, but unknown to us ; who divide the Northern zone and the circle of the Zodiac into an infinity of parts, who observe with exactitude the course of the stars, their fixed places, their declensions, their return and the time that each takes to make its revolution ; these men, I say, have discovered all except one thing : the fact that God is the Creator of the universe, and the just Judge who rewards all the actions of life according to their merit. They have not known how to raise themselves to the idea of the consummation of all things, the consequence of the doctrine of judgment, and to see that the world must change if souls pass from this life to a new life. In reality, as the nature of the present life presents an affinity to this world, so in the future life our souls will enjoy a lot conformable to their new condition. But they are so far from applying these truths, that they do but laugh when

we announce to them the end of all things and the regeneration of the age. Since the beginning naturally precedes that which is derived from it, the writer, of necessity, when speaking to us of things which had their origin in time, puts at the head of his narrative these words — " In the beginning God created."

5. It appears, indeed, that even before this world an order of things [1] existed of which our mind can form an idea, but of which we can say nothing, because it is too lofty a subject for men who are but beginners and are still babes in knowledge. The birth of the world was preceded by a condition of things suitable for the exercise of supernatural powers, outstripping the limits of time, eternal and infinite. The Creator and Demiurge of the universe perfected His works in it, spiritual light for the happiness of all who love the Lord, intellectual and invisible natures, all the orderly arrangement [2] of pure intelligences who are beyond the reach of our mind and of whom we cannot even discover the names. They fill the essence of this invisible world, as Paul teaches us. " For by him were all things created that are in heaven, and that are in earth, visible and invisible whether they be thrones or dominions or principalities or powers " [3] or virtues or hosts of angels or the dignities of archangels. To this world at last it was necessary to add a new world, both a school and training place where the souls of men should be taught and a home for beings destined to be born and to die. Thus was created, of a nature analogous to that of this world and the animals and plants which live thereon, the succession of time, for ever pressing on and passing away and never stopping in its course. Is not this the nature of time, where the past is no more, the future does not exist, and the present escapes before being recognised? And such also is the nature of the creature which lives in time, — condemned to grow or to perish without rest and without certain stability. It is therefore fit that the bodies of animals and plants, obliged to follow a sort of current, and carried away by the motion which leads them to birth or to death, should live in the midst of surroundings whose nature is in accord with beings subject to change. [4]

---

[1] Rom. i. 21, 22.
[2] Arist., *De Cœlo*. ii. 1. 1. calls it εἶς καὶ ἀίδιος. *cf.* the end of the *Timæus*.
[3] *cf.* Cic., *De nat. Deo*. i. 14, " *Cleanthes* " (of Assos, c. 264 B.C., a disciple of Zeno) " *autem tum ipsum mundum Deum dicit esse ; tum totius naturæ menti atque animo tribuit hoc nomen ; tum ultimum, et altissimum, atque undique circumfusum, et extremum, omnia cingentem atque complexum, ardorem, qui æther nominetur, certissimum Deum judicat*," and *id.* 15. " *Chrysippus* " (of Tarsus, † c. 212 B.C.) . . . " *ipsum mundum Deum dicit esse*." Yet the *Hymn of Cleanthes* (apud Stobæum) begins :
　Κύδιστ' ἀθανάτων, πολυώνυμε, παγκρατὲς αἰεί,
　Ζεὺς, φύσεως ἀρχηγέ, νόμου μέτα πάντα κυβερνῶν.
cf. Orig., *v. Celsum* V. σαφῶς δὴ τὸν ὅλον κόσμον (Ἕλληνες) λέγουσιν εἶναι θεόν, Στωικοὶ μὲν τὸν πρῶτον. οἱ δ' ἀπὸ Πλάτωνος τὸν δεύτερον, τινὲς δ' αὐτῶν τὸν τρίτον; and Athan., *De Incarn.*
§ 2.

[1] *cf.* Origen, *De Principiis*, ii. 1, 3.
[2] διακόσμησις. *cf.* Arist., *Met.* i. 5, 2.
[3] Col. i. 16.
[4] *cf.* Plato, *Timæus*, § 14. χρόνος δ' οὖν μετ' οὐρανοῦ γέγονεν ἵνα ἅμα γεννηθέντες ἅμα καὶ λυθῶσιν, ἄν ποτε λύσις τις αὐτῶν γίγνηται καὶ κατὰ τὸ παράδειγμα τῆς αἰωνίας φύσεως ἵν, ὡς ὁμοιότατος αὐτῷ κατὰ δύναμιν ᾖ. Fialon (p. 311) quotes Cousin's translation at greater length, and refers also to Plotinus, *Enn.* II. vii. 10–12. The parallel transitoriness of time and things has become the commonplace of poets. " *Immortalia ne*

Thus the writer who wisely tells us of the birth of the Universe does not fail to put these words at the head of the narrative. " In the beginning God created;" that is to say, in the beginning of time. Therefore, if he makes the world appear in the beginning, it is not a proof that its birth has preceded that of all other things that were made. He only wishes to tell us that, after the invisible and intellectual world, the visible world, the world of the senses, began to exist.

The first movement is called beginning. " To do right is the beginning of the good way." [1] Just actions are truly the first steps towards a happy life. Again, we call " beginning " the essential and first part from which a thing proceeds, such as the foundation of a house, the keel of a vessel; it is in this sense that it is said, " The fear of the Lord is the beginning of wisdom," [2] that is to say that piety is, as it were, the groundwork and foundation of perfection. Art is also the beginning of the works of artists, the skill of Bezaleel began the adornment of the tabernacle. [3] Often even the good which is the final cause is the beginning of actions. Thus the approbation of God is the beginning of almsgiving, and the end laid up for us in the promises the beginning of all virtuous efforts.

6. Such being the different senses of the word beginning, see if we have not all the meanings here. You may know the epoch when the formation of this world began, if, ascending into the past, you endeavour to discover the first day. You will thus find what was the first movement of time; then that the creation of the heavens and of the earth were like the foundation and the groundwork, and afterwards that an intelligent reason, as the word beginning indicates, presided in the order of visible things. [4] You will finally discover that the world was not conceived by chance and without reason, but for an useful end and for the great advantage of all beings, since it is really the school where reasonable souls exercise themselves, the training ground where they learn to know God; since by the sight of visible and sensible things the mind is led, as by a hand, to the contemplation of invisible things. " For," as the Apostle says, " the invisible things of him from the creation of the world are clearly seen, being understood by the things that are made." [1] Perhaps these words " In the beginning God created " signify the rapid and imperceptible moment of creation. The beginning, in effect, is indivisible and instantaneous. The beginning of the road is not yet the road, and that of the house is not yet the house; so the beginning of time is not yet time and not even the least particle of it. If some objector tell us that the beginning is a time, he ought then, as he knows well, to submit it to the division of time — a beginning, a middle and an end. Now it is ridiculous to imagine a beginning of a beginning. Further, if we divide the beginning into two, we make two instead of one, or rather make several, we really make an infinity, for all that which is divided is divisible to the infinite. [2] Thus then, if it is said, " In the beginning God created," it is to teach us that at the will of God the world arose in less than an instant, and it is to convey this meaning more clearly that other interpreters have said: " God made summarily " that is to say all at once and in a moment. [3] But enough concerning the beginning, if only to put a few points out of many.

7. Among arts, some have in view production, some practice, others theory. [4] The object of the last is the exercise of thought, that of the second, the motion of the body. Should it cease, all stops; nothing more is to be seen. Thus dancing and music have nothing behind; they have no object but themselves. In creative arts on the contrary the work lasts after the operation. Such is architecture — such are the arts which work in wood and brass and weaving, all those indeed which, even when the artisan has disappeared, serve to show an industrious intelligence and to cause the architect, the worker in brass or the weaver, to be admired on account of his work. Thus, then, to show that the world is a work of art displayed for the beholding of all people; to make them know Him who

---

speres monet annus et almum Quæ rapit hora diem." Hor., Carm. iv. 7.
[1] Prov. xvi. 5, LXX.   [2] Prov. ix. 10.
[3] cf. Arist., Met. iv. 1. Ἀρχη ἡ μὲν λέγεται ὅθεν ἄν τι τοῦ πράγματος κινηθείη πρῶτον· οἷον τοῦ μήκους, καὶ ὁδοῦ . . . ἡ δὲ ὅθεν ἄν κάλλιστα ἕκαστον γένοιτο · οἷον καὶ μαθήσεως, οὐκ ἀπὸ τοῦ πρώτου καὶ τῆς τοῦ πράγματος ἀρχῆς ἐνίοτε ἀρκτέον, ἀλλ' ὅθεν ῥᾷστ' ἄν μάθοι, ἡ δὲ, ὅθεν πρῶτον γίνεται ἐνυπάρχοντος · οἷον ὡς πλοίου τρόπις, καὶ οἰκίας θεμέλιος.
[4] In the Homily of Origen extant in the Latin of Rufinus (Migne Pat. Gr. xii. 146) ἀρχή is used of the Divine Word, " In principio. Quod est omnium principium nisi Dominus noster Christus Iesus ? . . . In hoc ergo principio, hoc est in Verbo suo, Deus cælum et terram fecit." An interpretation of John viii. 25, τὴν ἀρχὴν ὅτι καὶ λαλῶ ὑμιν widely prevalent at all events in the Latin church, was " Initium quod et loquor vobis ;" " I am the Beginning, that which I am even saying to you." See note to Sp. Comment. on John viii. ad fin.

[1] Rom. i. 20.
[2] On the inconceivability either of an absolute minimum of space or of its infinite divisibility, cf. Sir Wm. Hamilton, Met. ii. 371.
[3] Aquila's version in the Hexapla of Origen for ἐν ἀρχῇ has ἐν κεφαλαίῳ ἔκτισεν.
[4] ἡ ἅπασα διάνοια ἡ πρακτικὴ ἡ ποιητικὴ ἡ θεωρητική. Arist., Met. v. i.

created it, Moses does not use another word. "In the beginning," he says "God created." He does not say "God worked," "God formed," but "God created." Among those who have imagined that the world co-existed with God from all eternity, many have denied that it was created by God, but say that it exists spontaneously, as the shadow of this power. God, they say, is the cause of it, but an involuntary cause, as the body is the cause of the shadow and the flame is the cause of the brightness.[1] It is to correct this error that the prophet states, with so much precision, "In the beginning God created." He did not make the thing itself the cause of its existence.[2] Being good, He made it an useful work. Being wise, He made it everything that was most beautiful. Being powerful He made it very great.[3] Moses almost shows us the finger of the supreme artisan taking possession of the substance of the universe, forming the different parts in one perfect accord, and making a harmonious symphony result from the whole.[4]

"In the beginning God made heaven and earth." By naming the two extremes, he suggests the substance of the whole world, according to heaven the privilege of seniority, and putting earth in the second rank. All intermediate beings were created at the same time as the extremities. Thus, although there is no mention of the elements, fire, water and air,[5] imagine that they were all compounded together, and you will find water, air and fire, in the earth. For fire leaps out from stones; iron which is dug from the earth produces under friction fire in plentiful measure. A marvellous fact! Fire shut up in bodies lurks there hidden without harming them, but no sooner is it released than it consumes that which has hitherto preserved it. The earth contains water, as diggers of wells teach us. It contains

air too, as is shown by the vapours that it exhales under the sun's warmth [1] when it is damp. Now, as according to their nature, heaven occupies the higher and earth the lower position in space, (one sees, in fact, that all which is light ascends towards heaven, and heavy substances fall to the ground); as therefore height and depth are the points the most opposed to each other it is enough to mention the most distant parts to signify the inclusion of all which fills up intervening space. Do not ask, then, for an enumeration of all the elements; guess, from what Holy Scripture indicates, all that is passed over in silence.

8. "In the beginning God created the heaven and the earth." If we were to wish to discover the essence of each of the beings which are offered for our contemplation, or come under our senses, we should be drawn away into long digressions, and the solution of the problem would require more words than I possess, to examine fully the matter. To spend time on such points would not prove to be to the edification of the Church. Upon the essence of the heavens we are contented with what Isaiah says, for, in simple language, he gives us sufficient idea of their nature, "The heaven was made like smoke," [2] that is to say, He created a subtle substance, without solidity or density, from which to form the heavens. As to the form of them we also content ourselves with the language of the same prophet, when praising God "that stretcheth out the heavens as a curtain and spreadeth them out as a tent to dwell in." [3] In the same way, as concerns the earth, let us resolve not to torment ourselves by trying to find out its essence, not to tire our reason by seeking for the substance which it conceals. Do not let us seek for any nature devoid of qualities by the conditions of its existence, but let us know that all the phenomena with which we see it clothed regard the conditions of its existence and complete its essence. Try to take away by reason each of the qualities it possesses, and you will arrive at nothing. Take away black, cold, weight, density, the qualities which concern taste, in one word all these which we see in it, and the substance vanishes.[4]

---

[1] "The *one* and the *perfect* continually overflows, and from it Being, Reason, and Life are perpetually derived, without deducting anything from its substance, inasmuch as it is simple in its nature, and not, like matter, compound. (*Enn.* vi. ix. 9.) This derivation of all things from unity does not resemble creation, which has reference to time, but takes place purely in conformity with the principles of causality and order, without volition, because to will is to change. (*Enn.* iv. 5, i. 6.)" Tennemann on Plotinus, *Hist. Phil.* § 207.

[2] The Ben. note is "*neque idipsum in causa fuit cur esset, hoc est, non res cæca, non res coacta, non res invite et præter voluntatem agens in causa fuit cur mundus exstiterit. Hoc igitur dicit Basilius Deum aliter agere atque corpora opaca aut lucida. Nam corpus producit umbram vi atque necessi tate, nec liberius agit corpus lucidum: Deus vero omnia nutu conficit et voluntate. Illud ἐποίησεν, etc.. alio modo intellexit et interpretatus est Eustathius. Illius subjicimus verba: non causam præstitit ut esset solam, sed fecit ut bonus utilem.*"

[3] cf. Plat., *Tim.* § 10. Ἀγαθὸς ἦν, ἀγαθῷ δὲ οὐδεὶς περὶ οὐδενὸς οὐδέποτε ἐγγίγνεται φθόνος, τούτου δ' ἐκτὸς ὢν πάντα ὅτι μάλιστα γενέσθαι ἐβουλήθη παραπλήσια ἑαυτῷ.

[4] cf. Huxley, *Lay Sermons*, xii. p. 286, on the "delicate finger" of the "hidden artist" in the changes in an egg.

[5] cf. note on *Letter* viii.

---

[1] φαμὲν δὲ πῦρ καὶ ἀέρα καὶ ὕδωρ γίγνεσθαι ἐξ ἀλλήλων καὶ ἕκαστον ἐν ἑκάστῳ ὑπάρχειν τούτων δυνάμει. Arist., *Meteor.* i. 3.

[2] Isa. li. 6, LXX.   [3] Isa. xl. 22, LXX.

[4] Fialon points to the coincidence with Arist., *Met.* vii. 3. Ἀλλὰ μὴν ἀφαιρουμένου μήκους καὶ πλάτους καὶ βάθους, οὐδὲν ὁρῶμεν ὑπολειπόμενον πλὴν εἴ τι ἐστὶ τὸ ὁριζόμενον ὑπὸ τούτων, ὥστε τὴν ὕλην ἀνάγκη φαίνεσθαι μόνην οὐσίαν οὕτω σκοπουμένοις. Λέγω δ' ὕλην ἣ καθ' αὑτὴν μήτε τί, μήτε ποσὸν, μήτε ἄλλο μηδὲν λέγεται οἷς ὥρισται τὸ ὄν· ἔστι γάρ τι καθ' οὗ κατηγορεῖται τούτων ἕκαστον, ᾧ τὸ εἶναι ἕτερον, καὶ τῶν κατηγοριῶν ἑκάστῃ. Τὰ μὲν γὰρ ἄλλα τῆς οὐσίας κατηγορεῖται· αὕτη δὲ, τῆς ὕλης. Ὥστε τὸ ἔσχατον, καθ' αὑτὸ οὔτε τί, οὔτε ποσὸν, οὔτε ἄλλο οὐδέν ἐστιν· οὐδὲ δὴ αἱ ἀποφάσεις.

If I ask you to leave these vain questions, I will not expect you to try and find out the earth's point of support. The mind would reel on beholding its reasonings losing themselves without end. Do you say that the earth reposes on a bed of air?[1] How, then, can this soft substance, without consistency, resist the enormous weight which presses upon it? How is it that it does not slip away in all directions, to avoid the sinking weight, and to spread itself over the mass which overwhelms it? Do you suppose that water is the foundation of the earth?[2] You will then always have to ask yourself how it is that so heavy and opaque a body does not pass through the water; how a mass of such a weight is held up by a nature weaker than itself. Then you must seek a base for the waters, and you will be in much difficulty to say upon what the water itself rests.

9. Do you suppose that a heavier body prevents the earth from falling into the abyss? Then you must consider that this support needs itself a support to prevent it from falling. Can we imagine one? Our reason again demands yet another support, and thus we shall fall into the infinite, always imagining a base for the base which we have already found.[3] And the further we advance in this reasoning the greater force we are obliged to give to this base, so that it may be able to support all the mass weighing upon it. Put then a limit to your thought, so that your curiosity in investigating the incomprehensible may not incur the reproaches of Job, and you be not asked by him, "Whereupon are the foundations thereof fastened?"[4] If ever you hear in the Psalms, "I bear up the pillars of it;"[5] see in these pillars the power which sustains it. Because what means this other passage, "He hath founded it upon the sea,"[6] if not that the water is spread all around the earth? How then can water, the fluid element which flows down every declivity, remain suspended without ever flowing? You do not reflect that the idea of the earth suspended by itself throws your reason into a like but even greater difficulty, since from its nature it is heavier. But let us admit that the earth rests upon itself, or let us say that it rides on the waters, we must still remain faithful to thought of true religion and recognise that all is sustained by the Creator's power. Let us then reply to ourselves, and let us reply to those who ask us upon what support this enormous mass rests, "In His hands are the ends of the earth."[1] It is a doctrine as infallible for our own information as profitable for our hearers.

10. There are inquirers into nature[2] who with a great display of words give reasons for the immobility of the earth. Placed, they say, in the middle of the universe and not being able to incline more to one side than the other because its centre is everywhere the same distance from the surface, it necessarily rests upon itself; since a weight which is everywhere equal cannot lean to either side. It is not, they go on, without reason or by chance that the earth occupies the centre of the universe. It is its natural and necessary position. As the celestial body occupies the higher extremity of space all heavy bodies, they argue, that we may suppose to have fallen from these high regions, will be carried from all directions to the centre, and the point towards which the parts are tending will evidently be the one to which the whole mass will be thrust together. If stones, wood, all terrestrial bodies, fall from above downwards, this must be the proper and natural place of the whole earth. If, on the contrary, a light body is separated from the centre, it is evident that it will ascend towards the higher regions. Thus heavy bodies move from the top to the bottom, and following this reasoning, the bottom is none other than the centre of the world. Do not then be surprised that the world never falls: it occupies the centre of the universe, its natural place. By all necessity it is obliged to remain in its place, unless a movement contrary to nature should displace it.[3] If there is anything in this system which might appear probable to you, keep your admiration for the source of such perfect order, for the wisdom of God. Grand phenomena do not strike us the less when we have discovered something of their wonderful mechanism. Is it otherwise here? At all events let us prefer the simplicity of faith to the demonstrations of reason.

11. We might say the same thing of the

---

[1] cf. Arist., De Cælo. ii. 13, 16. Ἀναξιμένης δὲ καὶ Ἀναξάγορας καὶ Δημόκριτος τὸ πλάτος αἴτιον εἶναί φασι τοῦ μένειν αὐτήν· οὐ γὰρ τέμνειν ἀλλ' ἐπιπωματίζειν (covers like a lid) τὸν ἀέρα τὸν κάτωθεν, ὅπερ φαίνεται τὰ πλάτος ἔχοντα τῶν σωμάτων ποιεῖν.
[2] The theory of Thales. cf. note on Letter viii. 2 and Arist., De Cælo. ii. 13, 13, where he speaks of Thales describing the earth floating like wood on water.
[3] cf. Arist., De Cælo. ii. 13 (Grote's tr.): "The Kolophonian Xenophanes affirmed that the lower depths of the earth were rooted downwards to infinity, in order to escape the trouble-some obligation of looking for a reason why it remained sta-tionary." To this Empedokles objected, and suggested velocity of rotation for the cause of the earth's maintaining its position
[4] Job xxxviii. 6.   [5] Ps. lxxv. 3.   [6] Ps. xxiv. 2.

[1] Ps. xcv. 4, LXX.
[2] οἱ φυσικοὶ was the name given to the Ionic and other phi-losophers who preceded Socrates. Lucian (Ner. 4) calls Thales φυσικώτατος.
[3] cf. De Cælo. ii. 14, 4. Ἔτι δ' ἡ φορὰ τῶν μορίων καὶ ὅλης αὐτῆς ἡ κατὰ φύσιν ἐπὶ τὸ μέσον τοῦ παντός ἐστιν, διὰ τοῦτο γὰρ καὶ τυγχάνει κειμένη νῦν ἐπὶ τὸ κέντρου.

heavens. With what a noise of words the sages of this world have discussed their nature! Some have said that heaven is composed of four elements as being tangible and visible, and is made up of earth on account of its power of resistance, with fire because it is striking to the eye, with air and water on account of the mixture.[1] Others have rejected this system as improbable, and introduced into the world, to form the heavens, a fifth element after their own fashioning. There exists, they say, an æthereal body which is neither fire, air, earth, nor water, nor in one word any simple body. These simple bodies have their own natural motion in a straight line, light bodies upwards and heavy bodies downwards; now this motion upwards and downwards is not the same as circular motion; there is the greatest possible difference between straight and circular motion. It therefore follows that bodies whose motion is so various must vary also in their essence. But, it is not even possible to suppose that the heavens should be formed of primitive bodies which we call elements, because the reunion of contrary forces could not produce an even and spontaneous motion, when each of the simple bodies is receiving a different impulse from nature. Thus it is a labour to maintain composite bodies in continual movement, because it is impossible to put even a single one of their movements in accord and harmony with all those that are in discord; since what is proper to the light particle, is in warfare with that of a heavier one. If we attempt to rise we are stopped by the weight of the terrestrial element; if we throw ourselves down we violate the igneous part of our being in dragging it down contrary to its nature. Now this struggle of the elements effects their dissolution. A body to which violence is done and which is placed in opposition to nature, after a short but energetic resistance, is soon dissolved into as many parts as it had elements, each of the constituent parts returning to its natural place. It is the force of these reasons, say the inventors of the fifth kind of body for the genesis of heaven and the stars, which constrained them to reject the system of their predecessors and to have recourse to their own hypothesis.[2] But

yet another fine speaker arises and disperses and destroys this theory to give predominance to an idea of his own invention.

Do not let us undertake to follow them for fear of falling into like frivolities; let them refute each other, and, without disquieting ourselves about essence, let us say with Moses "God created the heavens and the earth." Let us glorify the supreme Artificer for all that was wisely and skillfully made; by the beauty of visible things let us raise ourselves to Him who is above all beauty; by the grandeur of bodies, sensible and limited in their nature, let us conceive of the infinite Being whose immensity and omnipotence surpass all the efforts of the imagination. Because, although we ignore the nature of created things, the objects which on all sides attract our notice are so marvellous, that the most penetrating mind cannot attain to the knowledge of the least of the phenomena of the world, either to give a suitable explanation of it or to render due praise to the Creator, to Whom belong all glory, all honour and all power world without end. Amen.

HOMILY II.

" The earth was invisible and unfinished." [1]

1. IN the few words which have occupied us this morning we have found such a depth of thought that we despair of penetrating further. If such is the fore court of the sanctuary, if the portico of the temple is so grand and magnificent, if the splendour of its beauty thus dazzles the eyes of the soul, what will be the holy of holies? Who will dare to try to gain access to the innermost shrine? Who will look into its secrets? To gaze into it is indeed forbidden us, and language is powerless to express what the mind conceives. However, since there are rewards, and most desirable ones, reserved by the just Judge for the intention alone of doing good, do not let us hesitate to continue our researches. Although we may not attain to the truth, if, with the help of the

---

[1] This is the doctrine of Plato *vide Tim.* The Combef. MSS. reads not μίξις, mixture, but μέθεξις, participation.

[2] Here appears to be a reference to Arist., *De Gen. Ann.* ii. 3, 11, πάσης μὲν οὖν ψυχῆς δύναμις ἑτέρου σώματος ἔοικε κεκοινωνηκέναι καὶ θειοτέρου τῶν καλουμένων στοιχείων· ὡς δὲ διαφέρουσι τιμιότητι αἱ ψυχαὶ καὶ ἀτιμίᾳ ἀλλήλων οὕτω καὶ ἡ τοιαύτη διαφέρει φύσις, and again. πνεῦμα . . . ἀνάλογον οὖσα τῷ τῶν ἄστρων στοιχείῳ. On the fifth element of Aristotle *cf.* Cic., *Tusc. Disp.* i. 10. *Aristoteles . . . cum quatuor illa genera principiorum erat complexus, equibus omnia orirentur, quintam quandam naturam censet esse, equa sit mens.* Aug., *De Civ. Dei* xxii. 11. 2, and Cudworth's *Int. Syst.* (Harrison's Ed. 1845) iii. p. 465.

Hence the word "quintessence," for which the Dictionaries quote Howard's *Translation of Plutarch,* "Aristoteles hath put . . . for elements foure; and for a fifth quintessence, the heavenly body which is immutable." Skeat s. v. points out that "the idea is older than Aristotle: *cf.* the five Skt. *bhútas,* or elements, which were earth, air, fire, and water, and again. The fifth essence is æther, the subtlest and highest." It is evident that Milton had these theories in mind when he wrote (*Par. Lost,* iii. 716):

" Swift to their several quarters hasted then
The cumbrous elements, earth, flood, air, fire;
And this ethereal quintessence of heaven
Flew upward, spirited with various forms,
That rolled orbicular, and turned to stars
Numberless."

[1] Gen. i. 2, LXX.

Spirit, we do not fall away from the meaning of Holy Scripture we shall not deserve to be rejected, and, with the help of grace, we shall contribute to the edification of the Church of God.

" The earth," says Holy Scripture, " was invisible and unfinished." The heavens and the earth were created without distinction. How then is it that the heavens are perfect whilst the earth is still unformed and incomplete? In one word, what was the unfinished condition of the earth? And for what reason was it invisible? The fertility of the earth is its perfect finishing; growth of all kinds of plants, the upspringing of tall trees, both productive and sterile, flowers' sweet scents and fair colours, and all that which, a little later, at the voice of God came forth from the earth to beautify her, their universal Mother. As nothing of all this yet existed, Scripture is right in calling the earth " without form." We could also say of the heavens that they were still imperfect and had not received their natural adornment, since at that time they did not shine with the glory of the sun and of the moon and were not crowned by the choirs of the stars.[1] These bodies were not yet created. Thus you will not diverge from the truth in saying that the heavens also were " without form." The earth was invisible for two reasons: it may be because man, the spectator, did not yet exist, or because being submerged under the waters which overflowed the surface, it could not be seen, since the waters had not yet been gathered together into their own places, where God afterwards collected them, and gave them the name of seas. What is invisible? First of all that which our fleshly eye cannot perceive; our mind, for example; then that which, visible in its nature, is hidden by some body which conceals it, like iron in the depths of the earth. It is in this sense, because it was hidden under the waters, that the earth was still invisible. However, as light did not yet exist, and as the earth lay in darkness, because of the obscurity of the air above it, it should not astonish us that for this reason Scripture calls it " invisible."

2. But the corrupters of the truth, who, incapable of submitting their reason to Holy Scripture, distort at will the meaning of the Holy Scriptures, pretend that these words mean matter. For it is matter, they say, which from its nature is without form and invisible, — being by the conditions of its existence without quality and without form

and figure.[1] The Artificer submitting it to the working of His wisdom clothed it with a form, organized it, and thus gave being to the visible world.

If matter is uncreated, it has a claim to the same honours as God, since it must be of equal rank with Him. Is this not the summit of wickedness, that an extreme deformity, without quality, without form, shape, ugliness without configuration, to use their own expression, should enjoy the same prerogatives with Him, Who is wisdom, power and beauty itself, the Creator and the Demiurge of the universe? This is not all. If matter is so great as to be capable of being acted on by the whole wisdom of God, it would in a way raise its hypostasis to an equality with the inaccessible power of God, since it would be able to measure by itself all the extent of the divine intelligence. If it is insufficient for the operations of God, then we fall into a more absurd blasphemy, since we condemn God for not being able, on account of the want of matter, to finish His own works. The poverty of human nature has deceived these reasoners. Each of our crafts is exercised upon some special matter — the art of the smith upon iron, that of the carpenter on wood. In all, there is the subject, the form and the work which results from the form. Matter is taken from without — art gives the form — and the work is composed at the same time of form and of matter.[2]

Such is the idea that they make for themselves of the divine work. The form of the world is due to the wisdom of the supreme Artificer; matter came to the Creator from without; and thus the world results from a double origin. It has received from outside its matter and its essence, and from God its form and figure.[3] They thus come to deny that the mighty God has presided at the formation of the universe, and pretend that He has only brought a crowning contribution to a common work, that He has only contributed some small portion to the genesis of beings: they are incapable from the debase-

---

[1] cf. Hom., *Il.* xviii. 485, ἐν δὲ τὰ τείρεα πάντα τά τ' οὐρανὸς ἐστεφάνωται, and Tennyson's "When young night divine crowned dying day with stars." (*Palace of Art.*)

[1] On prime matter and its being ἀσώματος and ἄμορφος *vide* Cudworth, *Int. Syst.* v. ii. § 27, and Mosheim's note. " *Ingens vero quondam summorum et inclytorum virorum numerus ab eorum semper stetit partibus, quibus ex qua dixi ratione, materiam placuit decernere ἀσώματον esse, sive corpore carere Cicero omnes post Platonem philosophos hoc dogma perhibet tenuisse, Acad. Quæst. i.7.* ' *sed subjectam putant omnibus sine ulla specie, atque carentem omni illa qualitate materiam quandam ex qua omnia expressa atque effecta sint.* ' *Sed jam diu ante Platonem Pythagoræorum multi ei addicti fuerunt, quod ex* Timæi Locri, *nobilis hujus scholæ et perantiqui philosophi, De Anima Mundi libello* (*Cap. i.p.544, Ed. Galei*) *intelligitur:* τὰν ὕλαν ἄμορφον δὲ καθ' αὑτὰν καὶ ἀχρημάτιστον δεχόμενον δὲ πᾶσαν μορφάν."

[2] cf. Arist., *Met.* vi. 7, πάντα δὲ τὰ γιγνόμενα ὑπό τέ τινος γίγνεται, καὶ ἔκ τινος, καὶ τί ... τὸ δὲ ἐξ οὗ γίγνεται, ἣν λέγομεν ὕλην ... τὸ δὲ ὑφ' οὗ, τῶν φύσει τι ὄντων ... εἶδος δὲ λέγω τὸ τί ἦν εἶναι ἑκάστου, καὶ τὴν πρώτην οὐσίαν.

[3] cf. Cudworth, *Int. Syst.* iv. 6, and remarks there on Cic., *Acad. Quæst.* i. 6. Arist. (*Metaph.* i. 2) says Θεὸς γὰρ δοκεῖ τὸ αἴτιον πᾶσιν εἶναι καὶ ἀρχή τις, but does this refer only to form?

ment of their reasonings of raising their glances to the height of truth. Here below arts are subsequent to matter — introduced into life by the indispensable need of them. Wool existed before weaving made it supply one of nature's imperfections. Wood existed before carpentering took possession of it, and transformed it each day to supply new wants, and made us see all the advantages derived from it, giving the oar to the sailor, the winnowing fan to the labourer, the lance to the soldier. But God, before all those things which now attract our notice existed, after casting about in His mind and determining to bring into being that which had no being, imagined the world such as it ought to be, and created matter in harmony with the form which He wished to give it.[1] He assigned to the heavens the nature adapted for the heavens, and gave to the earth an essence in accordance with its form. He formed, as He wished, fire, air and water, and gave to each the essence which the object of its existence required. Finally, He welded all the diverse parts of the universe by links of indissoluble attachment and established between them so perfect a fellowship and harmony that the most distant, in spite of their distance, appeared united in one universal sympathy. Let those men therefore renounce their fabulous imaginations, who, in spite of the weakness of their argument, pretend to measure a power as incomprehensible to man's reason as it is unutterable by man's voice.

3. God created the heavens and the earth, but not only half; — He created all the heavens and all the earth, creating the essence with the form. For He is not an inventor of figures, but the Creator even of the essence of beings. Further let them tell us how the efficient power of God could deal with the passive nature of matter, the latter furnishing the matter without form, the former possessing the science of the form without matter, both being in need of each other; the Creator in order to display His art, matter in order to cease to be without form and to receive a form.[2] But let us stop here and return to our subject.

"*The earth was invisible and unfinished.*" In saying "In the beginning God created the heavens and the earth," the sacred writer passed over many things in silence, water, air, fire and the results from them, which, all forming in reality the true complement of the world, were, without doubt, made at the same time as the universe. By this silence, history wishes to train the activity of our intelligence, giving it a weak point for starting, to impel it to the discovery of the truth. Thus, we are not told of the creation of water; but, as we are told that the earth was invisible, ask yourself what could have covered it, and prevented it from being seen? Fire could not conceal it. Fire brightens all about it, and spreads light rather than darkness around. No more was it air that enveloped the earth. Air by nature is of little density and transparent. It receives all kinds of visible object, and transmits them to the spectators. Only one supposition remains; that which floated on the surface of the earth was water — the fluid essence which had not yet been confined to its own place. Thus the earth was not only invisible; it was still incomplete. Even to-day excessive damp is a hindrance to the productiveness of the earth. The same cause at the same time prevents it from being seen, and from being complete, for the proper and natural adornment of the earth is its completion: corn waving in the valleys — meadows green with grass and rich with many coloured flowers — fertile glades and hill-tops shaded by forests. Of all this nothing was yet produced; the earth was in travail with it in virtue of the power that she had received from the Creator. But she was waiting for the appointed time and the divine order to bring forth.

4. "Darkness was upon the face of the deep."[1] A new source for fables and most impious imaginations if one distorts the sense of these words at the will of one's fancies. By "darkness" these wicked men do not understand what is meant in reality — air not illumined, the shadow produced by the inter-

---

[1] Gen. ii. 5, "every herb of the field *before it grew.*" There seems here an indication of the actual creation, ποίησις, being in the mind of God.

[2] Fialon quotes Bossuet: "*Je ne trouve point que Dieu, qui a créé toutes choses, ait eu besoin, comme un ouvrier vulgaire, de trouver une matière préparée sur laquelle il travaillât, et de laquelle il dît son ouvrage. Mais, n'ayant besoin pour agir que de lui-même et de sa propre puissance il a fait tout son ouvrage. Il n'est point un simple faiseur de formes et de figures dans une matière préexistante; il a fait et la matière et la forme, c'est-à-dire son ouvrage dans son tout; autrement son ouvrage ne lui doit pas tout, et dans son fond il est indépendamment de son ouvrier. . . .*

"*O Dieu quelle a été l'ignorance des sages du monde, qu'on a appelés philosophes d'avoir cru que vous, parfait architecte et absolu formateur de tout ce qui est, vous aviez trouvé sous vos mains une matière qui vous était co-éternelle, informe* néamoins, et qui attendait de vous sa perfection! Aveugles, qui n'entendaient pas que d'être capable de forme, c'est deja quelque forme; c'est quelque perfection. que d'être capable de perfection; et si la matière avait d'elle-même ce commencement de perfection et de forme, elle en pouvait aussitôt avoir d'ellemème l'entier accomplissement.

"*Aveugles, conducteurs d'aveugles, qui tombez dans le précipice, et y jetez ceux qui vous suivent (St. Matthieu xv. 14), dites-moi qui a assujeti à Dieu ce qu'il n'a pas fait, ce qui est de soi aussi bien que Dieu, ce qui est indépendamment de Dieu même? Par où a-t-il trouvé prise sur ce qui lui est étranger et independant et sa puissance; et par quel art ou quel pouvoir se l'est-il soumis? . . . Mais qu'est-ce après tout que cette matière si parfaite, qu'elle ait elle-même ce fond de son être; et si imparfaite, qu'elle attende sa perfection d'un autre? Dieu aura fait l'accident et n'aura pas fait la substance?* (Bossuet, Elévations sur les mystères, 3e semaine, 2e elevat.)

[1] Gen. i. 2.

position of a body, or finally a place for some reason deprived of light. For them "darkness" is an evil power, or rather the personification of evil, having his origin in himself in opposition to, and in perpetual struggle with, the goodness of God. If God is light, they say, without any doubt the power which struggles against Him must be darkness, "Darkness" not owing its existence to a foreign origin, but an evil existing by itself. "Darkness" is the enemy of souls, the primary cause of death, the adversary of virtue. The words of the Prophet, they say in their error, show that it exists and that it does not proceed from God. From this what perverse and impious dogmas have been imagined! What grievous wolves,[1] tearing the flock of the Lord, have sprung from these words to cast themselves upon souls! Is it not from hence that have come forth Marcions and Valentini,[2] and the detestable heresy of the Manicheans,[3] which you may without going far wrong call the putrid humour of the churches.

O man, why wander thus from the truth, and imagine for thyself that which will cause thy perdition? The word is simple and within the comprehension of all. "The earth was invisible." Why? Because the " deep " was spread over its surface. What is " the deep "? A mass of water of extreme depth. But we know that we can see many bodies through clear and transparent water. How then was it that no part of the earth appeared through the water? Because the air which surrounded it was still without light and in darkness. The rays of the sun, penetrating the water, often allow us to see the pebbles which form the bed of the river, but in a dark night it is impossible for our glance to penetrate under the water. Thus, these words "the earth was invisible" are explained by those that follow; "the deep" covered it and itself was in darkness. Thus, the deep is not a multitude of hostile powers, as has been imagined;[4] nor "darkness" an

evil sovereign force in enmity with good. In reality two rival principles of equal power, if engaged without ceasing in a war o mutual attacks, will end in self destruction. But if one should gain the mastery it would completely annihilate the conquered. Thus, to maintain the balance in the struggle between good and evil is to represent them as engaged in a war without end and in perpetual destruction, where the opponents are at the same time conquerors and conquered. If good is the stronger, what is there to prevent evil being completely annihilated? But if that be the case, the very utterance of which is impious, I ask myself how it is that they themselves are not filled with horror to think that they have imagined such abominable blasphemies.

It is equally impious to say that evil has its origin from God;[1] because the contrary cannot proceed from its contrary. Life does not engender death; darkness is not the origin of light; sickness is not the maker of health.[2] In the changes of conditions there are transitions from one condition to the contrary; but in genesis each being proceeds from its like, and not from its contrary. If then evil is neither uncreate nor created by God, from whence comes its nature? Certainly that evil exists, no one living in the world will deny. What shall we say then? Evil is not a living animated essence; it is the condition of the soul opposed to virtue, developed in the careless on account of their falling away from good.[3]

5. Do not then go beyond yourself to seek for evil, and imagine that there is an original nature of wickedness. Each of us,

---

[1] Acts xx. 29.

[2] Marcion and Valentinus are roughly lumped together as types of gnostic dualism. On the distinction between their systems see Dr. Salmon in *D.C.B.* iii. S2o. Marcion, said to have been the son of a bishop of Sinope, is the most Christian of the gnostics, and " tries to fit in his dualism with the Christian creed and with the scriptures." But he expressly " asserted the existence of two Gods." The Valentinian ideas and emanations travelled farther afield.

[3] On Manicheism, *vide* Beausobre's *Critical History of Manicheism*, and Walch, *Hist. Ketz.* i. 770. With its theory of two principles it spread widely over the empire in the 4th c., was vigorous in Armenia in the 9th, and is said to have appeared in France in the 12th. (*cf.* Bayle, *Dict. s.v.*) On the view taken of the heresy in Basil's time *cf.* Gregory of Nyssa, *Against Eunomius* i. § 35.

[4] *i.e.* by those who would identify the ἄβυσσος (Tehōm) of Gen. i. 2 with that of Luke i. 31, and understand it to mean the abode in prison of evil spirits. The Hebrew word occurs in Job xxviii. 14 and Deut. xxxiii. 13 for the depth of waters.

[1] With this view Plutarch charges the Stoics. Αὐτοὶ τῶν κακῶν ἀρχὴν ἀγαθὸν ὄντα τὸν Θεον ποιοῦσι. (*c. Stoicos*, 1970.) But it is his deduction from their statements — not their own statement. *cf.* Mosheim's note on Cudworth iv. § 13. Origen (*c. Celsum* vi.) distinguishes between τὴν κακίαν καὶ τὰς ἀπ' αὐτῆς πράξεις, and κακόν as punitive and remedial; if the latter can rightly be called evil in any sense, God is the author of it. *cf.* Amos iii. 6. *Vide*, also, Basil's treatment of this question in his Treatise ὅτι οὐκ ἔστιν αἴτιος τῶν κακῶν ὁ θεος. *cf.* Schroeck. *Kirchengeschichte* xiii. 194.

[2] Fialon points out the correspondence with Plat. *Phæd.* § 119, καὶ τις εἶπε τῶν παρόντων ἀκούσας . . . πρὸς Θεν, οὐκ ἐν τοῖς πρόσθεν ἡμῖν λόγοις αὐτὸ τὸ ἐναντίον τῶν νυνὶ λεγομένων ὡμολογεῖτο, ἐκ τοῦ ἐλάττονος τὸ μεῖζον γίγνεσθαι, καὶ ἐκ τοῦ μείζονος τὸ ἔλαττον, καὶ ἀτεχνῶς αὕτη εἶναι ἡ γένεσις τοῖς ἐναντίοις ἐκ τῶν ἐναντίων; νῦν δέ μοι δοκεῖ λέγεσθαι ὅτι τοῦτο οὐκ ἄν ποτε γένοιτο. καὶ ὁ Σωκράτης ... ἔφη ... οὐκ ἐννοεῖς τὸ διαφέρον τοῦ τι νῦν λεγομένου καὶ τοῦ τότε· τότε μὲν γὰρ ἐλέγετο ἐκ τοῦ ἐναντίου πράγματος τὸ ἐναντίον πρᾶγμα γίγνεσθαι, νῦν δὲ ὅτι αὐτὸ τὸ ἐναντίον ἑαυτῷ ἐναντίον οὐκ ἄν ποτε γένοιτο, οὔτε τὸ ἐν ἡμῖν οὔτε τὸ ἐν φύσει· τότε μὲν γὰρ περὶ τῶν ἐχόντων τῶν ἐναντίων ἐλέγομεν, ἐπονομάζοντες αὐτὰ τῇ ἐκείνων ἐπωνυμίᾳ, νῦν δὲ περὶ ἐκείνων αὐτῶν ὧν ἐνόντων, ἔχει τὴν ἐπωνυμίαν τὰ ὀνομαζόμενα, αὐτὰ δ' ἐκεῖνα οὐκ ἄν ποτε φαμεν ἐθελῆσαι γένεσιν ἀλλήλων δέξασθαι.

[3] " *Cette phrase est prise textuellement dans Denys l'Aréopagite, ou du moins dans l'ouvrage qui lui est attribué.* (*De Div. Nom. iv* 18. *Laur. Lyd. de mensib. ed. Ræth.* 186, 28.)." Fialon. In the Treatise referred to, περὶ Θείων Ὀνομάτων, " evil " is said to be " nothing real and positive, but a defect, a negation only. Στέρησις ἄρα ἐστὶ τὸ κακὸν, καὶ ἔλλειψις, καὶ ἀσθένεια, καὶ ἀσυμμετρία." *D.C.B.* i. 846. *cf.* "Evil is null, is nought, is silence implying sound." Browning. Abt Vogler.

let us acknowledge it, is the first author of his own vice. Among the ordinary events of life, some come naturally, like old age and sickness, others by chance like unforeseen occurrences, of which the origin is beyond ourselves, often sad, sometimes fortunate, as for instance the discovery of a treasure when digging a well, or the meeting of a mad dog when going to the market place. Others depend upon ourselves, such as ruling one's passions, or not putting a bridle on one's pleasures, to be master of our anger, or to raise the hand against him who irritates us, to tell the truth, or to lie, to have a sweet and well-regulated disposition, or to be fierce and swollen and exalted with pride.[1] Here you are the master of your actions. Do not look for the guiding cause beyond yourself, but recognise that evil, rightly so called, has no other origin than our voluntary falls. If it were involuntary, and did not depend upon ourselves, the laws would not have so much terror for the guilty, and the tribunals would not be so without pity when they condemn wretches according to the measure of their crimes. But enough concerning evil rightly so called. Sickness, poverty, obscurity, death, finally all human afflictions, ought not to be ranked as evils; since we do not count among the greatest boons things which are their opposites.[2] Among these afflictions, some are the effect of nature, others have obviously been for many a source of advantage. Let us then be silent for the moment about these metaphors and allegories, and, simply following without vain curiosity the words of Holy Scripture, let us take from darkness the idea which it gives us.

But reason asks, was darkness created with the world? Is it older than light? Why in spite of its inferiority has it preceded it? Darkness, we reply, did not exist in essence; it is a condition produced in the air by the withdrawal of light. What then is that light which disappeared suddenly from the world, so that darkness should cover the face of the deep? If anything had existed before the formation of this sensible and perishable world, no doubt we conclude it would have been in light. The orders of angels, the heavenly hosts, all intellectual natures named or unnamed, all the ministering spirits,[1] did not live in darkness, but enjoyed a condition fitted for them in light and spiritual joy.[2]

No one will contradict this; least of all he who looks for celestial light as one of the rewards promised to virtue, the light which, as Solomon says, is always a light to the righteous,[3] the light which made the Apostle say "Giving thanks unto the Father, which hath made us meet to be partakers of the inheritance of the saints in light."[4] Finally, if the condemned are sent into outer darkness[5] evidently those who are made worthy of God's approval, are at rest in heavenly light. When then, according to the order of God, the heaven appeared, enveloping all that its circumference included, a vast and unbroken body separating outer things from those which it enclosed, it necessarily kept the space inside in darkness for want of communication with the outer light. Three things are, indeed, needed to form a shadow, light, a body, a dark place. The shadow of heaven forms the darkness of the world. Understand, I pray you, what I mean, by a simple example; by raising for yourself at mid-day a tent of some compact and impenetrable material, and shutting yourself up in it in sudden darkness. Suppose that original darkness was like this, not subsisting directly by itself, but resulting from some external causes. If it is said that it rested upon the deep, it is because the extremity of air naturally touches the surface of bodies; and as at that time the water covered everything, we are obliged to say that darkness was upon the face of the deep.

6. *And the Spirit of God was borne upon the face of the waters.*[6] Does this spirit mean the diffusion of air? The sacred writer wishes to enumerate to you the elements of the world, to tell you that God created the heavens, the earth, water, and air and that the last was now diffused and in motion; or rather, that which is truer and confirmed by the authority of the ancients, by the Spirit of God, he means the Holy Spirit. It is, as has been remarked, the special name, the name above all others that Scripture delights to give to the Holy Spirit, and always by the spirit of God the Holy Spirit is meant,

---

[1] cf. Epictetus, *Ench.* i. ἐφ' ἡμῖν μὲν ὑπόληψις, ὁρμὴ, ὄρεξις, ἔκκλισις, καὶ ἑνὶ λόγῳ, ὅσα ἡμέτερα ἔργα.

[2] cf. M. Aurelius II. xi. ὁ γὰρ χείρω μὴ ποιεῖ ἄνθρωπον, πῶς δὴ τοῦτο βίον ἀνθρώπου χείρω ποιήσειεν; . . . θάνατος δέ γε καὶ ζωὴ, δόξα καὶ ἀδοξία, πόνος καὶ ἡδονὴ, πλοῦτος καὶ πενία, πάντα ταῦτα ἐπίσης συμβαίνει ἀνθρώπων τοῖς τε ἀγαθοῖς καὶ τοῖς κακοῖς, οὔτε καλὰ ὄντα οὔτε αἰσχρά · οὔτ' ἀο' ἀγαθὰ οὔτε κακά ἐστι. Also Greg. Nyss., *Orat. Cat.* viii. and Aug., *De Civ. Dei.* i. 8. *Ista vero temporalia bona et mala utrisque voluit esse communia, ut nec bona cupidius appetantur, quæ mali quoque habere cernuntur, nec mala turpiter evitentur, quibus et boni plerumque afficiuntur.*

[1] cf. Heb. i. 14.

[2] cf. Theod. (*Quæst. in Gen. vi.*) who is ready to accept the creation of angels before the creation of the world. Origen, *Hom. i. in Gen. Hom. iv.* in Is. taught the existence of angels "before the æons." Greg. Naz., *Orat.* xxxviii. The lxx. Trans. of Job xxxviii. 7, ἠνεσάν με πάντες ἄγγελοί μου may have aided in the formation of the general opinion of the Greek Fathers. The systematization of the hierarchies is due to the pseudo. Dionysius, and was transmitted to the west through John Erigena. cf. Milman, *Lat. Christ.* ix. 59.

[3] Prov. xiii. 9, lxx.   [5] cf. Matt. xxii. 13.
[4] Col. i. 12.   [6] Gen. i. 2, lxxx.

the Spirit which completes the divine and blessed Trinity. You will find it better therefore to take it in this sense. How then did the Spirit of God move upon the waters? The explanation that I am about to give you is not an original one, but that of a Syrian,[1] who was as ignorant in the wisdom of this world as he was versed in the knowledge of the Truth. He said, then, that the Syriac word was more expressive, and that being more analogous to the Hebrew term it was a nearer approach to the scriptural sense. This is the meaning of the word; by "was borne" the Syrians, he says, understand: it cherished[2] the nature of the waters as one sees a bird cover the eggs with her body and impart to them vital force from her own warmth. Such is, as nearly as possible, the meaning of these words — the Spirit was borne: let us understand, that is, prepared the nature of water to produce living beings:[3] a sufficient proof for those who ask if the Holy Spirit took an active part in the creation of the world.

7. *And God said, Let there be light:*[4] The first word of God created the nature of light; it made darkness vanish, dispelled gloom, illuminated the world, and gave to all beings at the same time a sweet and gracious aspect. The heavens, until then enveloped in darkness, appeared with that beauty which they still present to our eyes. The air was lighted up, or rather made the light circulate mixed with its substance, and, distributing its splendour rapidly in every direction, so dispersed itself to its extreme limits. Up it sprang to the very æther and heaven. In an instant it lighted up the whole extent of the world, the North and the South, the East and the West. For the æther also is such a subtle substance and so transparent that it needs not the space of a moment for light to pass through it. Just as it carries our sight instantaneously to the object of vision,[1] so without the least interval, with a rapidity that thought cannot conceive, it receives these rays of light in its uttermost limits. With light the æther becomes more pleasing and the waters more limpid. These last, not content with receiving its splendour, return it by the reflection of light and in all directions send forth quivering flashes. The divine word gives every object a more cheerful and a more attractive appearance, just as when men in deep sea pour in oil they make the place about them clear. So, with a single word and in one instant, the Creator of all things gave the boon of light to the world.[2]

Let there be light. The order was itself an operation, and a state of things was brought into being, than which man's mind cannot even imagine a pleasanter one for our enjoyment. It must be well understood that when we speak of the voice, of the word, of the command of God, this divine language does not mean to us a sound which escapes from the organs of speech, a collision of air[3] struck by the tongue; it is a simple sign of the will of God, and, if we give it the form of an order, it is only the better to impress the souls whom we instruct.[4]

And God saw the light, that it was good.[5] How can we worthily praise light after the testimony given by the Creator to its goodness? The word, even among us, refers the judgment to the eyes, incapable of raising itself to the idea that the senses have already received.[6] But, if beauty in bodies results from symmetry of parts, and the harmonious

---

[1] Tillemont understands Eusebius of Samosata. The Ben. note prefers Ephrem Syrus, and compares Jerome, *Quæst. Heb.* Col. 508.

[2] Gen. i. 2. *Vide* R.V. margin. The word *rachaph*, "brood," is not used of wind, and itself appears to fix the meaning of the Spirit in the place. An old interpretation of the Orphic Poem *Argonautica* would identify the brooding Spirit of Genesis with the All-Wise Love of the Greek poet:

πρῶτα μὲν ἀρχαίου χάεος μεγαλήφατον ὕμνον,
ὡς ἐπάμειψε φύσεις, ὥς τ' οὐρανὸς ἐς πέρας ἦλθεν,
γῆς τ' εὐρυστέρνου γένεσιν, πυθμένας τε θαλάσσης,
πρεσβύτατόν τε καὶ αὐτοτελῆ πολύμητιν Ἔρωτα,
ὅσσα τ' ἔφυσεν ἅπαντα, τὰ δ' ἔκριθεν ἄλλου ἀπ' ἄλλο.

Orph., *Argon.* 423-427.

On the translation of *rachaph* by "brooding," *cf.* Milton, *P. Lost*, vii.:

"darkness profound
Covered the abyss; but on the watery calm
His brooding wings the Spirit of God outspread,
And vital virtue infused, and vital warmth,
Throughout the fluid mass."

[3] ζωογονία. cf. *De Sp. S.* § 56, and Bp. Pearson, *on the Creed.* Art. V.

[4] Gen. i. 3.

[1] Light is said to travel straight at the rate of about 195,000 English miles a second; a velocity estimated by observations on the eclipses of Jupiter's satellites. The modern undulatory theory of light, of which Huyghens († 1695) is generally regarded as the author, describes light as propagated by the vibrations of the imponderable matter termed *Ether* or *Æther.*

[2] The simile seems hardly worthy of the topic. The practice is referred to by Plutarch, *Symp. Quæst.* i. 9, and by Pliny, *Hist. Nat.* ii. 106. "*Omne oleo tranquillari; et ob id urinantes ore spargere, quoniam mitiget naturam asperam lucemque deportet.*" "*gerere*" says the Delph. note, "*tum credas oleum vicem conspiciliorum.*"

[3] A statement not unlike the "Vibrations of the elastic medium," to which sound might now be referred. "*Sed vocem Stoici corpus esse contendunt: eamque esse dicunt ictum aera: Plato autem non esse vocem corpus esse putat. Non enim percussus, inquit, aer, sed plaga ipsa atque percussio, vox est: οὐκ ἁπλῶς πληγὴ ἀέρος ἐστὶν ἡ φωνή· πλήττει γὰρ τὸν ἀέρα καὶ δάκτυλος παραγόμενος, καὶ οὐδέπω ποιεῖ φωνήν· ἀλλ' ἡ πόση πληγή, καὶ σφοδρά, καὶ τότη δὲ ὥστε ἀκουστὴν γενέσθαι.*" Aul. Gell., *N.A.* v. 15. So Diog. Laert. in *Vita Zenonis; ἔστι φωνὴ ἀὴρ πεπληγμένος.*

[4] Fialon quotes Bossuet 4me élev. 3me sem.: "*Le roi dit Qu'on marche; et l'armée marche; qu'on fasse telle évolution, et elle se fait; toute une armée se remue au seul commandement d'un prince, c'est à dire, à un seul petit mouvement de ces lèvres, c'est, parmi les choses humaines, l'image la plus excellente de la puissance de Dieu; mais au fond que c'est image est défectueuse! Dieu n'a point de lèvres à remuer; Dieu ne frappe point l'air pour en tirer quelque son; Dieu n'a qu'à vouloir en lui même; et tout ce qu'il veut éternellement s'accomplit comme il l'a voulu, et au temps qu'il a marqué.*"

[5] Gen. i. 4.

[6] St. Basil dwells rather on the sense of "beautiful" in the lxx. καλόν. The Vulgate has *pulchra.*

appearance of colours, how in a simple and homogeneous essence like light, can this idea of beauty be preserved? Would not the symmetry in light be less shown in its parts than in the pleasure and delight at the sight of it? Such is also the beauty of gold, which it owes not to the happy mingling of its parts, but only to its beautiful colour which has a charm attractive to the eyes.

Thus again, the evening star is the most beautiful of the stars :[1] not that the parts of which it is composed form a harmonious whole; but thanks to the unalloyed and beautiful brightness which meets our eyes. And further, when God proclaimed the goodness of light, it was not in regard to the charm of the eye but as a provision for future advantage, because at that time there were as yet no eyes to judge of its beauty. "*And God divided the light from the darkness ;*[2] that is to say, God gave them natures incapable of mixing, perpetually in opposition to each other, and put between them the widest space and distance.

8. "*And God called the light Day and the darkness he called Night.*"[3] Since the birth of the sun, the light that it diffuses in the air, when shining on our hemisphere, is day ; and the shadow produced by its disappearance is night. But at that time it was not after the movement of the sun, but following this primitive light spread abroad in the air or withdrawn in a measure determined by God, that day came and was followed by night.

"*And the evening and the morning were the first day.*"[4] Evening is then the boundary common to day and night ; and in the same way morning constitutes the approach of night to day. It was to give day the privileges of seniority that Scripture put the end of the first day before that of the first night, because night follows day : for, before the creation of light, the world was not in night, but in darkness. It is the opposite of day which was called night, and it did not receive its name until after day. Thus were created the evening and the morning.[5] Scripture means the space of a day and a night, and afterwards no more says day and night, but calls them both under the name of the more important : a custom which you will find throughout Scripture. Everywhere the measure of time is counted by days, without mention of nights. "The days of our years,"[1] says the Psalmist. "Few and evil have the days of the years of my life been,"[2] said Jacob, and elsewhere "all the days of my life."[3] Thus under the form of history the law is laid down for what is to follow.

And the evening and the morning were one day.[4] Why does Scripture say "one day" not "the first day"? Before speaking to us of the second, the third, and the fourth days, would it not have been more natural to call that one the first which began the series? If it therefore says "one day," it is from a wish to determine the measure of day and night, and to combine the time that they contain. Now twenty-four hours fill up the space of one day — we mean of a day and of a night ; and if, at the time of the solstices, they have not both an equal length, the time marked by Scripture does not the less circumscribe their duration. It is as though it said : twenty-four hours measure the space of a day, or that, in reality a day is the time that the heavens starting from one point take to return there. Thus, every time that, in the revolution of the sun, evening and morning occupy the world, their periodical succession never exceeds the space of one day.

But must we believe in a mysterious reason for this? God who made the nature of time measured it out and determined it by intervals of days ; and, wishing to give it a week as a measure, he ordered the week to revolve from period to period upon itself, to count the movement of time, forming the week of one day revolving seven times upon itself : a proper circle begins and ends with itself. Such is also the character of eternity, to revolve upon itself and to end nowhere. If then the beginning of time is called "one day" rather than "the first day," it is because Scripture wishes to establish its relationship with eternity. It was, in reality, fit and natural to call "one" the day whose character is to be one wholly separated and isolated from all the others. If Scripture speaks to us of many ages, saying everywhere, "age of age, and ages of ages," we do not see it enumerate them as first, second, and third. It follows that we are hereby shown not so much limits, ends and succession of ages, as distinctions between various states and modes of action. "The day of the Lord," Scripture says, "is great and very terrible,"[5] and elsewhere "Woe unto you

---

[1] cf. Bion. xvi. 1 :

Ἕσπερε, κυανέας ἱερὸν, φίλε, νυκτὸς ἄγαλμα,
Τόσσον ἀφαυρότερος μήνας ὅσον ἔξοχος ἀστρων,

and Milton, *P.L.* iv. 605:

"Hesperus, that led
The starry host, rode brightest."

[2] Gen. i. 4.   [3] Gen. i. 5.   [4] Gen. i. 5.
[5] lxx. The Heb. = literally "And evening happened and morning happened, one day." On the unique reckoning of the day from evening to morning, see the late Dr. McCaul in *Replies to Essays and Reviews.*

[1] Ps. xc. 10.   [3] Ps. xxiii. 6, LXX.   [5] Joel ii. 11.
[2] Gen. xlvii. 9.   [4] Gen. i. 5, LXX. and Heb.

THE HEXAEMERON.

that desire the day of the Lord: to what end is it for you? The day of the Lord is darkness and not light."[1] A day of darkness for those who are worthy of darkness. No; this day without evening, without succession, and without end is not unknown to Scripture, and it is the day that the Psalmist calls the eighth day, because it is outside this time of weeks.[2] Thus whether you call it day, or whether you call it eternity, you express the same idea. Give this state the name of day; there are not several, but only one. If you call it eternity still it is unique and not manifold. Thus it is in order that you may carry your thoughts forward towards a future life, that Scripture marks by the word "one" the day which is the type of eternity, the first fruits of days, the contemporary of light, the holy Lord's day, honoured by the Resurrection of our Lord. *And the evening and the morning were one day.*"

But, whilst I am conversing with you about the first evening of the world, evening takes me by surprise, and puts an end to my discourse. May the Father of the true light, Who has adorned day with celestial light, Who has made the fire to shine which illuminates us during the night, Who reserves for us in the peace of a future age a spiritual and everlasting light, enlighten your hearts in the knowledge of truth, keep you from stumbling, and grant that " you may walk honestly as in the day."[3] Thus shall you shine as the sun in the midst of the glory of the saints, and I shall glory in you in the day of Christ, to Whom belong all glory and power for ever and ever. Amen.

HOMILY III.

On the Firmament.

1. WE have now recounted the works of the first day, or rather of one day. Far be it from me indeed, to take from it the privilege it enjoys of having been for the Creator a day apart, a day which is not counted in the same order as the others. Our discussion yesterday treated of the works of this day, and divided the narrative so as to give you food for your souls in the morning, and joy in the evening. To-day we pass on to the wonders of the second day. And here I do not wish to speak of the narrator's talent, but of the grace of Scripture, for the narrative is so naturally told that it pleases and delights all

the friends of truth. It is this charm of truth which the Psalmist expresses so emphatically when he says, "How sweet are thy words unto my taste. yea, sweeter than honey to my mouth."[1] Yesterday then, as far as we were able, we delighted our souls by conversing about the oracles of God, and now to-day we are met together again on the second day to contemplate the wonders of the second day.

I know that many artisans, belonging to mechanical trades, are crowding around me. A day's labour hardly suffices to maintain them; therefore I am compelled to abridge my discourse, so as not to keep them too long from their work. What shall I say to them? The time which you lend to God is not lost: he will return it to you with large interest. Whatever difficulties may trouble you the Lord will disperse them. To those who have preferred spiritual welfare, He will give health of body, keenness of mind, success in business, and unbroken prosperity. And, even if in this life our efforts should not realise our hopes, the teachings of the Holy Spirit are none the less a rich treasure for the ages to come Deliver your heart, then, from the cares of this life and give close heed to my words. Of what avail will it be to you if you are here in the body, and your heart is anxious about your earthly treasure?

2. And God said "Let there be a firmament in the midst of the waters, and let it divide the waters from the waters."[2] Yesterday we heard God's decree, "Let there be light." To-day it is, "Let there be a firmament." There appears to be something more in this. The word is not limited to a simple command. It lays down the reason necessitating the structure of the firmament: it is, it is said, to separate the waters from the waters. And first let us ask how God speaks? Is it in our manner? Does His intelligence receive an impression from objects, and, after having conceived them, make them known by particular signs appropriate to each of them? Has He consequently recourse to the organs of voice to convey His thoughts? Is He obliged to strike the air by the articulate movements of the voice, to unveil the thought hidden in His heart? Would it not seem like an idle fable to say that God should need such a circuitous method to manifest His thoughts? And is it not more conformable with true religion to say, that the divine will and the first impetus of divine intelligence are the Word of God? It is He whom Scripture vaguely represents, to show us that God has not only

---

[1] Amos v. 18.
[2] The argument here is due to a misapprehension of the meaning of the term *eighth* in Psalm vi. and xi. title. *cf.* n. on *De Sp. S.* § 66.
[3] Rom. xiii. 13.

[1] Ps. cxix. 103.   [2] Gen. i. 6.

wished to create the world, but to create it with the help of a co-operator. Scripture might continue the history as it is begun: In the beginning God created the heaven and the earth; afterwards He created light, then He created the firmament. But, by making God command and speak, the Scripture tacitly shows us Him to Whom this order and these words are addressed.[1] It is not that it grudges us the knowledge of the truth, but that it may kindle our desire by showing us some trace and indication of the mystery. We seize with delight, and carefully keep, the fruit of laborious efforts, whilst a possession easily attained is despised.[2] Such is the road and the course which Scripture follows to lead us to the idea of the Only begotten. And certainly, God's immaterial nature had no need of the material language of voice, since His very thoughts could be transmitted to His fellow-worker. What need then of speech, for those Who by thought alone could communicate their counsels to each other? Voice was made for hearing, and hearing for voice. Where there is neither air, nor tongue, nor ear, nor that winding canal which carries sounds to the seat of sensation in the head, there is no need for words: thoughts of the soul are sufficient to transmit the will. As I said then, this language is only a wise and ingenious contrivance to set our minds seeking the Person to whom the words are addressed.

3. In the second place, does the firmament that is called heaven differ from the firmament that God made in the beginning? Are there two heavens? The philosophers, who discuss heaven, would rather lose their tongues than grant this. There is only one heaven,[3] they pretend; and it is of a nature neither to admit of a second, nor of a third, nor of several others. The essence of the celestial body quite complete constitutes its vast unity. Because, they say, every body which has a circular motion is one and finite. And if this body is used in the construction of the first heaven, there will be

nothing left for the creation of a second or a third. Here we see what those imagine who put under the Creator's hand uncreated matter; a lie that follows from the first fable. But we ask the Greek sages not to mock us before they are agreed among themselves. Because there are among them some who say there are infinite heavens and worlds.[1] When grave demonstrations shall have upset their foolish system, when the laws of geometry shall have established that, according to the nature of heaven, it is impossible that there should be two, we shall only laugh the more at this elaborate scientific trifling. These learned men see not merely one bubble but several bubbles formed by the same cause, and they doubt the power of creative wisdom to bring several heavens into being! We find, however, if we raise our eyes towards the omnipotence of God, that the strength and grandeur of the heavens differ from the drops of water bubbling on the surface of a fountain. How ridiculous, then, is their argument of impossibility! As for myself, far from not believing in a second, I seek for the third whereon the blessed Paul was found worthy to gaze.[2] And does not the Psalmist in saying "heaven of heavens"[3] give us an idea of their plurality? Is the plurality of heaven stranger than the seven circles through which nearly all the philosophers agree that the seven planets pass, — circles which they represent to us as placed in connection with each other like casks fitting the one into the other? These circles, they say, carried away in a direction contrary to that of the world, and striking the æther, make sweet and harmonious sounds, unequalled by the sweetest melody.[4] And if we ask them for the wit-

---

[1] Origen, c. Cels. vi. says τὸν μὲν προσεχεῖς δημιουργὸν εἶναι τὸν υἱὸν τοῦ Θεοῦ λόγον, καὶ ὡσπερεὶ αὐτουργὸν τοῦ κόσμου, τὸν δὲ πατέρα τοῦ λόγου, τῷ προστετάχέναι τῷ υἱῷ ἑαυτοῦ λόγῳ ποιῆσαι τὸν κόσμον, εἶναι πρώτως δημιουργόν. cf. Athan., c. gentes § 48. sq.
[2] Solon is credited with the saving, δύσκολα τὰ καλά. cf. the German proverb, Gut ding wil weile haben, and Virgil in Georg. i. 121:

"Pater ipse colendi
Haud facilem esse viam voluit."

[3] Plato said one. πότερον οὖν ὀρθῶς ἕνα οὐρανὸν προειρήκαμεν; ἢ πολλοὺς ἢ ἀπείρους λέγειν ἦν ὀρθότερον; εἴπερ κατὰ τὸ παράδειγμα δεδημιουργημένος ἔσται, τὸ γὰρ περιέχον πάντα ὁπόσα νοητὰ ζῷα, μεθ' ἑτέρου δεύτερον οὐκ ἂν ποτ' εἴη... εἷς ὅδε μονογενὴς οὐρανὸς γεγονὼς ἔστι τε καὶ ἔσται. Plat., Tim. § 11. On the other hand was the Epicurean doctrine of the ἀπειρία κόσμων, referred to in Luc. i. 73:

Ergo vivida vis animi pervicit, et extra
Processit longe flammantia mœnia mundi.

[1] So Anaximander (Diog. Laert. ii. 1, 2) and Democritus (Diog. Laert. ix. 44).
But, as Fialon points out, the Greek philosophers used κόσμος and οὐρανός as convertible terms: Basil uses οὐρανός of the firmament or sky.
[2] cf. 2. Cor. xii. 2.　　　　[3] Ps. cxlvii. 4.
[4] "You must conceive it" (the whirl) "to be of such a kind as this: as if in some great hollow whirl, carved throughout, there was such another, but lesser, within it, adapted to it, like casks fitted one within another; and in the same manner a third, and a fourth, and four others, for that the whirls were eight in all, as circles one within another . . . and that in each of its circles there was seated a siren on the upper side, carried round, and uttering one voice variegated by diverse modulations; but that the whole of them, being eight, composed one harmony." (Plat., Rep. x. 14, Davies' Trans.) Plato describes the Fates "singing to the harmony of the Sirens." Id. On the Pythagorean Music of the Spheres, cf. also Cic., De Divin. i. 3, and Macrobius In Somn: Scip.
cf. Shaksp., M. of Ven. v. 1:

"There's not the smallest orb which thou behold'st
But in his motion like an angel sings,
Still quiring to the young-eyed cherubim."

And Milton, Arcades:

"Then listen I
To the celestial Sirens' harmony,
That sit upon the nine infolded spheres,
And sing to those that hold the vital sheres,
And turn the adamantine spindle round
On which the fate of gods and men is wound."

ness of the senses, what do they say? That we, accustomed to this noise from our birth, on account of hearing it always, have lost the sense of it; like men in smithies with their ears incessantly dinned. If I refuted this ingenious frivolity, the untruth of which is evident from the first word, it would seem as though I did not know the value of time, and mistrusted the intelligence of such an audience.

But let me leave the vanity of outsiders to those who are without, and return to the theme proper to the Church. If we believe some of those who have preceded us, we have not here the creation of a new heaven, but a new account of the first. The reason they give is, that the earlier narrative briefly described the creation of heaven and earth; while here scripture relates in greater detail the manner in which each was created. I, however, since Scripture gives to this second heaven another name and its own function, maintain that it is different from the heaven which was made at the beginning; that it is of a stronger nature and of an especial use to the universe.

4. "*And God said, let there be a firmament in the midst of the waters, and let it divide the waters from the waters. And God made the firmament, and divided the waters which were under the firmament from the waters which were above the firmament.*"[1] Before laying hold of the meaning of Scripture let us try to meet objections from other quarters. We are asked how, if the firmament is a spherical body, as it appears to the eye, its convex circumference can contain the water which flows and circulates in higher regions? What shall we answer? One thing only : because the interior of a body presents a perfect concavity it does not necessarily follow that its exterior surface is spherical and smoothly rounded. Look at the stone vaults of baths, and the structure of buildings of cave form; the dome, which forms the interior, does not prevent the roof from having ordinarily a flat surface. Let these unfortunate men cease, then, from tormenting us and themselves about the impossibility of our retaining water in the higher regions.

Now we must say something about the nature of the firmament, and why it received the order to hold the middle place between the waters. Scripture constantly makes use of the word firmament to express extraordinary strength. "The Lord my firmament and refuge".[2] "I have strengthened the pillars of it"[3] "Praise him in the firmament of his

power."[1] The heathen writers thus call a strong body one which is compact and full,[2] to distinguish it from the mathematical body. A mathematical body is a body which exists only in the three dimensions, breadth, depth, and height. A firm body, on the contrary, adds resistance to the dimensions. It is the custom of Scripture to call firmament all that is strong and unyielding. It even uses the word to denote the condensation of the air : He, it says, who strengthens the thunder.[3] Scripture means by the strengthening of the thunder, the strength and resistance of the wind, which, enclosed in the hollows of the clouds, produces the noise of thunder when it breaks through with violence.[4] Here then, according to me, is a firm substance, capable of retaining the fluid and unstable element water ; and as, according to the common acceptation, it appears that the firmament owes its origin to water, we must not believe that it resembles frozen water or any other matter produced by the filtration of water ; as, for example, rock crystal, which is said to owe its metamorphosis to excessive congelation,[5] or the transparent stone [6] which forms in mines.[7] This pellucid stone, if one finds it in its natural perfection, without cracks inside, or the least spot of corruption, almost rivals the air in clearness. We cannot compare the firmament to one of these substances. To hold such an opinion about celestial bodies would be childish and foolish; and although everything may be in everything, fire in earth, air in water, and of the other elements the one in the other ; although none of those which come under our senses are pure and without mixture, either with the element which serves as a medium for it, or with that which is contrary to it; I, nevertheless, dare not affirm that the firmament was formed of one of these simple substances, or of a mixture of them, for I am taught by Scripture not to allow my imagination to wander too far afield. But do not

[1] Ps. cl. 1, LXX.
[2] ναστός (fr. νάσσω, press or knead) = close, firm. Democritus used it as opposed to κενόν, void. Arist. fr. 202.
[3] Amos iv. 13, LXX.
[4] Pliny (*Hist. Nat.* ii. 43) writes : " *Si in nube luctetur flatus aut vapor, tonitrua edi : si erumpat ardens, fulmina ; si longiore tractu nitatur, fulgetra. His findi nubem, illis perrumpi. Etesse tonitrua impactorum ignium plagas.*" *cf.* Sen., *Quæst. Nat.* ii. 12.
[5] Ἐμπεδοκλῆς στερέμνιον εἶναι τὸν οὐρανὸν ἐξ ἀέρος συμπαγέντος ὑπὸ πυρὸς κρυσταλλοειδῶς, τὸ πυρῶδες καὶ ἀερῶδες ἐν ἑκατέρῳ τῶν ἡμισφαιρίων περιέχοντα. (Plutarch περὶ τῶν ἀρεσκόντων τοῖς φιλοσόφοις, ii. 11) Pliny (*Hist. Nat.* xxxvii. 9) says that crystal is made "*gelu* (*vide* Sir T. Browne, *Vulgar Errors,* ii. 1) *vehementiore concreto . . . glaciem que esso certum est; unde et nomen græci dedere.*" So Seneca, *Quæst. Nat.* iii. 25. Diodorus Siculus, however, asserts it "*coalescere non a frigore sed divini ignis potentia.*" (*Bibl.* ii. 134.)
[6] *i.e.* the " *Lapis Specularis.*" or mica, which was used for glazing windows. *cf.* Plin., *Ep.* ii. 17, and Juv., *Sat.* iv. 21.
[7] Mica is found in large plates in Siberia, Peru, and Mexico, as well as in Sweden and Norway.

[1] Gen. i. 6, 7.
[2] Ps. xviii. 2, LXX.
[3] Ps. lxxv. 3, LXX.

let us forget to remark that, after these divine words " let there be a firmament," it is not said " and the firmament was made," but, " and God made the firmament, and divided the waters ." [1] Hear, O ye deaf! See, O ye blind! — who, then, is deaf? He who does not hear this startling voice of the Holy Spirit. Who is blind? He who does not see such clear proofs of the Only begotten.[2] " Let there be a firmament." It is the voice of the primary and principal Cause. " And God made the firmament." Here is a witness to the active and creative power of God.

5. But let us continue our explanation: "*Let it divide the waters from the waters.*" [3] The mass of waters, which from all directions flowed over the earth, and was suspended in the air, was infinite, so that there was no proportion between it and the other elements. Thus, as it has been already said, the abyss covered the earth. We will give the reason for this abundance of water. None of you assuredly will attack our opinion; not even those who have the most cultivated minds, and whose piercing eye can penetrate this perishable and fleeting nature; you will not accuse me of advancing impossible or imaginary theories, nor will you ask me upon what foundation the fluid element rests. By the same reason which makes them attract the earth, heavier than water, from the extremities of the world to suspend it in the centre, they will grant us without doubt that it is due both to its natural attraction downwards and its general equilibrium, that this immense quantity of water rests motionless upon the earth.[4] Therefore the prodigious mass of waters was spread around the earth; not in proportion with it and infinitely larger, thanks to the foresight of the supreme Artificer, Who, from the beginning, foresaw what was to come, and at the first provided all for the future needs of the world. But what need was there for this superabundance of water? The essence of fire is necessary for the world, not only in the œconomy of earthly produce, but for the completion of the universe; for it would be imperfect [5] if the most powerful and the most vital of its elements were lacking.[1] Now fire and water are hostile to and destructive of each other. Fire, if it is the stronger, destroys water, and water, if in greater abundance, destroys fire. As, therefore, it was necessary to avoid an open struggle between these elements, so as not to bring about the dissolution of the universe by the total disappearance of one or the other, the sovereign Disposer created such a quantity of water that in spite of constant diminution from the effects of fire, it could last until the time fixed for the destruction of the world. He who planned all with weight and measure, He who, according to the word of Job,[2] knows the number of the drops of rain, knew how long His work would last, and for how much consumption of fire He ought to allow. This is the reason of the abundance of water at the creation. Further, there is no one so strange to life as to need to learn the reason why fire is essential to the world. Not only all the arts which support life, the art of weaving, that of shoemaking, of architecture, of agriculture, have need of the help of fire, but the vegetation of trees, the ripening of fruits, the breeding of land and water animals, and their nourishment, all existed from heat from the beginning, and have been since maintained by the action of heat. The creation of heat was then indispensable for the formation and the preservation of beings, and the abundance of waters was no less so in the presence of the constant and inevitable consumption by fire.

6. Survey creation; you will see the power of heat reigning over all that is born and perishes. On account of it comes all the water spread over the earth, as well as that which is beyond our sight and is dispersed in the depths of the earth. On account of it are abundance of fountains, springs or wells, courses of rivers, both mountain torrents and ever flowing streams, for the storing of moisture in many and various reservoirs. From the East, from the winter solstice flows the Indus, the greatest river of the earth, according to geographers. From the middle of the East proceed the Bactrus,[3] the Choaspes,[4] and the Araxes,[5] from which the Tanais [6] detaches itself to fall into the Palus-Mæotis.[7] Add to these the Phasis [8] which descends from Mount Caucasus, and countless other rivers, which, from northern regions, flow into the Euxine Sea. From

---

[1] Gen. i. 7.
[2] With Christian associations it is startling to read at the end of the Timæus that the Cosmos is the εἰκὼν τοῦ Θεοῦ, or, according to another reading, itself Θεός, . . . μονογενὴς ὤν.
[3] Gen. i. 6.
[4] According to Plutarch (περὶ τῶν ἀρέσκ: etc. iii. 10) Thales and the Stoics affirmed the earth to be spherical, Thales (*id.* 11) placing it " in the middle." Pliny, *Hist. Nat.* ii. 4, says that the earth " *universi cardine stare pendentem librantem per quæ pendeat ; ita solam immobilem circa eam volubili universitate, eandem ex omnibus necti, eidemque omnia in nti.*"
[5] On κολοβός, docked, curtailed, cf. Matt. xxiv. 22.

---

[1] The supremacy of fire was the idea of Heraclitus. Τὸ πῦρ Θεὸν ὑπειλήφασιν Ἵππασος . . . καὶ Ἡράκλειτος. Clem. Alex., *Protrep.* v. 55. Plutarch has an essay on the comparative usefulness of fire and water.
[2] Job xxxvi. 27, LXX.   [5] Probably the Volga is meant.
[3] Balkh.   [6] Don.   [8] Phaz.
[4] Kerak.   [7] Sea of Asov.

the warm countries of the West, from the foot of the Pyrenees, arise the Tartessus [1] and the Ister,[2] of which the one discharges itself into the sea beyond the Pillars and the other, after flowing through Europe, falls into the Euxine Sea. Is there any need to enumerate those which the Ripæan mountains [3] pour forth in the heart of Scythia, the Rhone,[4] and so many other rivers, all navigable, which after having watered the countries of the western Gauls and of Celts and of the neighbouring barbarians, flow into the Western sea? And others from the higher regions of the South flow through Ethiopia to discharge themselves some into our sea, others into inaccessible seas, the Ægon [5] the Nyses, the Chremetes,[6] and above all the Nile, which is not of the character of a river when, like a sea, it inundates Egypt. Thus the habitable part of our earth is surrounded by water, linked together by vast seas and irrigated by countless perennial rivers, thanks to the ineffable wisdom of Him Who ordered all to prevent this rival element to fire from being entirely destroyed.

However, a time will come, when all shall be consumed by fire; as Isaiah says of the God of the universe in these words, "That saith to the deep, Be dry, and I will dry up thy rivers." [7] Reject then the foolish wisdom of this world,[8] and receive with me the more simple but infallible doctrine of truth.

7. Therefore we read: "*Let there be a firmament in the midst of the waters, and let it divide the waters from the waters.*" I have said what the word firmament in Scripture means. It is not in reality a firm and solid substance which has weight and resistance; this name would otherwise have better suited the earth. But, as the substance of superincumbent bodies is light, without consistency, and cannot be grasped by any one of our senses, it is in comparison with these pure and imperceptible substances that the firmament has received its name. Imagine a place fit to divide the moisture, sending it, if pure and filtered, into higher regions, and making it fall, if it is dense and earthy; to

the end that by the gradual withdrawal of the moist particles the same temperature may be preserved from the beginning to the end. You do not believe in this prodigious quantity of water; but you do not take into account the prodigious quantity of heat, less considerable no doubt in bulk, but exceedingly powerful nevertheless, if you consider it as destructive of moisture. It attracts surrounding moisture, as the melon shows us, and consumes it as quickly when attracted, as the flame of the lamp draws to it the fuel supplied by the wick and burns it up. Who doubts that the æther is an ardent fire?[1] If an impassable limit had not been assigned to it by the Creator, what would prevent it from setting on fire and consuming all that is near it, and absorbing all the moisture from existing things? The aerial waters which veil the heavens with vapours that are sent forth by rivers, fountains, marshes, lakes, and seas, prevent the æther from invading and burning up the universe. Thus we see even this sun, in the summer season, dry up in a moment a damp and marshy country, and make it perfectly arid. What has become of all the water? Let these masters of omniscience tell us. Is it not plain to every one that it has risen in vapour, and has been consumed by the heat of the sun? They say, none the less, that even the sun is without heat. What time they lose in words! And see what proof they lean upon to resist what is perfectly plain. Its colour is white, and neither reddish nor yellow. It is not then fiery by nature, and its heat results, they say, from the velocity of its rotation.[2] What do they gain? That the sun does not seem to absorb moisture? I do not, however, reject this statement, although it is false, because it helps my argument. I said that the consumption of heat required this prodigious quantity of water. That the sun owes its heat to its nature, or that heat results from its action, makes no difference, provided that it produces the same effects upon the same matter. If you kindle fire by rubbing two pieces of wood together, or if you light them by holding them to a flame, you will have absolutely the same effect. Besides, we see that the great wisdom of Him who governs all, makes the sun travel

---

[1] Ebro. [2] The Danube.
[3] Used vaguely for any mountains in the north of Europe and Asia. Strabo (vii. pp. 295, 299) considers them fabulous.
[4] A *varia lectio* is Eridanus.
[5] Αἰγών is properly the Ægean Sea.
[6] Basil's geography is bad. He might have improved it by consulting Strabo or Ptolemæus, but has been content to go for his facts to Aristotle (*Met.* i. 13), whose errors he repeats. Fialon remarks "*nouvelle preuve de l'indifférence des cités grecques de l'Asie pour cet Occident lointain dont elles se séparèrent si facilement.*" If this refers to the theological separation it is hardly fair. The East in the 4th c. and 5th c. shewed no indifference to the sympathy of the W., and when the split came the "separation" was not taken "easily."
[7] Isa. xliv. 27.
[8] Schools of "the wisdom of the world" did, however, teach that the world was a world γενόμενον καὶ φθαρτόν. cf. Lucretius v. 322, "*totum nativum mortali corpore constat.*"

[1] So the "*liquidissimus æther*" of the Epicurean Lucretius (v. 501), "Suos ignes fert;" i.e. the fiery stars are of the nature of the element in which they move. cf. the Stoic Manilius i. 149, "*Ignis in æthereas volucer se sustulit oras summaque complexus stellantis culmina cæli, Flammarum vallo naturæ mænia fecit.*"
[2] So Aristotle, *Meteor.* i. 3, 30. Ὁρῶμεν δὴ τὴν κίνησιν ὅτι δύναται διακρίνειν τὸν ἀέρα καὶ ἐκπυροῦν ὥστε καὶ τὰ φερόμενα τηκόμενα φαίνεσθαι πολλάκις. Τὸ μὲν οὖν γίγνεσθαι τὴν ἀλέαν καὶ τὴν θερμότητα ἱκανή ἐστι παρασκευάζειν καὶ ἡ τοῦ ἡλίου φορὰ μόνον.

from one region to another, for fear that, if it remained always in the same place, its excessive heat would destroy the order of the universe. Now it passes into southern regions about the time of the winter solstice, now it returns to the sign of the equinox; from thence it betakes itself to northern regions during the summer solstice, and keeps up by this imperceptible passage a pleasant temperature throughout all the world.

Let the learned people see if they do not disagree among themselves. The water which the sun consumes is, they say, what prevents the sea from rising and flooding the rivers; the warmth of the sun leaves behind the salts and the bitterness of the waters, and absorbs from them the pure and drinkable particles,[1] thanks to the singular virtue of this planet in attracting all that is light and in allowing to fall, like mud and sediment, all which is thick and earthy. From thence come the bitterness, the salt taste, and the power of withering and drying up, which are characteristic of the sea. While, as is notorious, they hold these views, they shift their ground and say that moisture cannot be lessened by the sun.[2]

8. "*And God called the firmament heaven.*"[3] The nature of right belongs to another, and the firmament only shares it on account of its resemblance to heaven. We often find the visible region called heaven, on account of the density and continuity of the air within our ken, and deriving its name "heaven" from the word which means to see.[4] It is of it that Scripture says, "The fowl of the air,"[5] "Fowl that may fly . . . in the open firmament of heaven;"[6] and, elsewhere, "They mount up to heaven."[7] Moses, blessing the tribe of Joseph, desires for it the fruits and the dews of heaven, of the suns of summer and the conjunctions of the moon, and blessings from the tops of the mountains and from the everlasting hills,"[8]

in one word, from all which fertilises the earth. In the curses on Israel it is said, "And thy heaven that is over thy head shall be brass."[1] What does this mean? It threatens him with a complete drought, with an absence of the aerial waters which cause the fruits of the earth to be brought forth and to grow.

Since, then, Scripture says that the dew or the rain falls from heaven, we understand that it is from those waters which have been ordered to occupy the higher regions. When the exhalations from the earth, gathered together in the heights of the air, are condensed under the pressure of the wind, this aerial moisture diffuses itself in vaporous and light clouds; then mingling again, it forms drops which fall, dragged down by their own weight; and this is the origin of rain. When water beaten by the violence of the wind, changes into foam, and passing through excessive cold quite freezes, it breaks the cloud, and falls as snow.[2] You can thus account for all the moist substances that the air suspends over our heads.

And do not let any one compare with the inquisitive discussions of philosophers upon the heavens, the simple and inartificial character of the utterances of the Spirit; as the beauty of chaste women surpasses that of a harlot,[3] so our arguments are superior to those of our opponents. They only seek to persuade by forced reasoning. With us truth presents itself naked and without artifice. But why torment ourselves to refute the errors of philosophers, when it is sufficient to produce their mutually contradictory books, and, as quiet spectators, to watch the war?[4] For those thinkers are not less numerous, nor less celebrated, nor more sober in speech in fighting their adversaries, who say that the universe is being consumed by fire, and that from the seeds which remain in the ashes of the burnt world all is being brought to life again. Hence in the world there is destruction and palingenesis to infinity.[5] All, equally far from the truth, find each on their side by-ways which lead them to error.

9. But as far as concerns the separation of the waters I am obliged to contest the

---

[1] cf. Diog. Laert. vii. on Zeno. Τρέπεσθαι δὲ τὰ ἔμπυρα ταῦτι ἀλλὰ τι ἄλλι ἄστρα, τὸν μὴν ἥλιον ἐκ τῆς μεγάλης θαλάττης. So Zeno, Chrysippus, and Posidonius.

[2] Pliny (ii. 103, 104) writes: "*Itaque solis ardore siccatur liquor; . . . sic mari late patenti saporem incoqui salis, aut quia exhausto inde dulci tenuique, quod facillime trahat vis ignea, omne asperius crassiusque linquatur: ideo summa æquarum aqua dulciorem profundam: hanc esse veriorem causam asperi saporis, quam quod mare terræ sudor sit æternus: aut quia plurimum ex arido misceatur illi vapore, aut quia terræ natura sicut medicatas aquas inficiat.*" The first of these three theories was that of Hippocrates (*De Aere, Locis, et Aquis*, iv. 197) and of Anaximander (Plutarch περὶ τῶν ἀρέσκ, etc. ii. 552). On the second *vide* Arist., *Prob.* xxiii. 3ο. The idea of the sea being the earth's sweat was that of Empedocles. *cf.* Arist., *Meteor.* ii. 1.

[3] Gen. i. 8.

[4] The derivation of οὐοανός from ὁράω is imaginary. Aristotle (*De Cæl.* i. 19, 9) derives it from ὅρος, a boundarv. *cf.* Ὁοίζων. The real root is the Skt. *var* = cover. M. Müller, *Oxford Essays*, 1856.

[5] Ps. viii. 8.　　　　[7] Ps. cvii. 26.
[6] Gen. i. 20.　　　　[8] cf. Deut. xxxiii. 13-15, LXX.

[1] Deut. xxviii. 23.

[2] cf. Arist., *Meteor.* i. 9-12, and Plutarch περὶ τῶν ἀρέσκ. etc. iii. 4.

[3] Fialon quotes Hor., *Ep.* i. 18: "*Ut matrona meretrici dispar erit atque Discolor.*"

[4] The well known "*Per campos instructa, tua sine parte pericli suave etiam belli certamina magna tueri*" (Lucr. ii. 5) may be an echo of some Greek lines in the preacher's mind, just as the preceding "*suave mari magno*" is of Menander.

[5] "These Stoical atheists did also agree with the generality of the other Stoical theists in supposing a successive infinity of worlds generated and corrupted" (ἀπειρία κόσμων) "by reason of intervening periodical conflagrations." Cudworth, l. iii. 23.

opinion of certain writers in the Church [1] who, under the shadow of high and sublime conceptions, have launched out into metaphor, and have only seen in the waters a figure to denote spiritual and incorporeal powers. In the higher regions, above the firmament, dwell the better; in the lower regions, earth and matter are the dwelling place of the malignant. So, say they, God is praised by the waters that are above the heaven, that is to say, by the good powers, the purity of whose soul makes them worthy to sing the praises of God. And the waters which are under the heaven represent the wicked spirits, who from their natural height have fallen into the abyss of evil. Turbulent, seditious, agitated by the tumultuous waves of passion, they have received the name of sea, because of the instability and the inconstancy of their movements.[2] Let us reject these theories as dreams and old women's tales. Let us understand that by water water is meant; for the dividing of the waters by the firmament let us accept the reason which has been given us. Although, however, waters above the heaven are invited to give glory to the Lord of the Universe, do not let us think of them as intelligent beings; the heavens are not alive because they " declare the glory of God," nor the firmament a sensible being because it " sheweth His handiwork."[3] And if they tell you that the heavens mean contemplative powers, and the firmament active powers which produce good, we admire the theory as ingenious without being able to acknowledge the truth of it. For thus dew, the frost, cold and heat, which in Daniel are ordered to praise the Creator of all things,[4] will be intelligent and invisible natures. But this is only a figure, accepted as such by enlightened minds, to complete the glory of the Creator. Besides, the waters above the heavens, these waters privileged by the virtue which they possess in themselves, are not the only waters to celebrate the praises of God. " Praise the Lord from the earth, ye dragons and all deeps."[5] Thus the singer of the Psalms does not reject the deeps which our inventors of allegories rank in the divisions of evil; he admits them to the universal choir of creation, and the deeps sing in their language a harmonious hymn to the glory of the Creator.

10. *" And God saw that it was good."* God does not judge of the beauty of His work by the charm of the eyes, and He does not form the same idea of beauty that we do. What He esteems beautiful is that which presents in its perfection all the fitness [1] of art, and that which tends to the usefulness of its end. He, then, who proposed to Himself a manifest design in His works, approved each one of them, as fulfilling its end in accordance with His creative purpose. A hand, an eye, or any portion of a statue lying apart from the rest, would look beautiful to no one. But if each be restored to its own place, the beauty of proportion, until now almost unperceived, would strike even the most uncultivated. But the artist, before uniting the parts of his work, distinguishes and recognises the beauty of each of them, thinking of the object that he has in view. It is thus that Scripture depicts to us the Supreme Artist, praising each one of His works; soon, when His work is complete, He will accord well deserved praise to the whole together. Let me here end my discourse on the second day, to allow my industrious hearers to examine what they have just heard. May their memory retain it for the profit of their soul; may they by careful meditation inwardly digest and benefit by what I say. As for those who live by their work, let me allow them to attend all day to their business, so that they may come, with a soul free from anxiety, to the banquet of my discourse in the evening. May God who, after having made such great things, put such weak words in my mouth, grant you the intelligence of His truth, so that you may raise yourselves from visible things to the invisible Being, and that the grandeur and beauty of creatures may give you a just idea of the Creator. For the visible things of Him from the creation of the world are clearly seen, and His power and divinity are eternal.[2] Thus earth, air, sky, water, day, night, all visible things, remind us of who is our Benefactor. We shall not therefore give occasion to sin, we shall not give place to the enemy within us, if by unbroken recollection we keep God ever dwelling in our hearts, to Whom be all glory and all adoration, now and for ever, world without end. Amen.

[1] *i.e.* Origen.
[2] *cf.* Jerome to Pammachius against John of Jerusalem, § 7 (in this edition vol. vi. p. 428) and Origen's *Homily on Genesis,* preserved in the Translation of Rufinus.
[3] Ps. xviii. 1.   [4] Bened.   [5] Ps. cxlviii. 7.

[1] καλον μὲν οὖν ἐστιν ὃ ἂν δ' αὐτὸ αἱρετὸν ὂν ἐπαινετὸν ῇ, ἢ ὃ ἂν ἀγαθὸν ὂν ἡδὺ ῇ ὅτι ἀγαθόν. Arist., *Rhet.* i. 9.
cf. E. Burke (*On the Sublime and Beautiful,* iii. § 6): " It is true that the infinitely wise and good creator has, of his bounty, frequently joined beauty to those things which he has made useful to us. But this does not prove that our idea of use and beauty are the same thing, or that they are in any way dependent on each other." Dr. Johnson instances a painting on a coffee-cup as beautiful, but not useful. " Boswell," Ann. 1772. St. Basil's idea is in accord with that of Ruskin (*Mod. P.* chap. vi.). " In all high ideas of beauty it is more than probable that much of the pleasure depends on delicate and untraceable perception of fitness, propriety, and relation, which are purely intellectual, and through which we arrive at our noblest ideas of what is commonly and rightly called ' intellectual beauty.' "   [2] *cf.* Rom. i. 20.

HOMILY IV.

Upon the gathering together of the waters.

1. THERE are towns where the inhabitants, from dawn to eve, feast their eyes on the tricks of innumerable conjurors. They are never tired of hearing dissolute songs which cause much impurity to spring up in their souls, and they are often called happy, because they neglect the cares of business and trades useful to life, and pass the time, which is assigned to them on this earth, in idleness and pleasure. They do not know that a theatre full of impure sights is, for those who sit there, a common school of vice; that these melodious and meretricious songs insinuate themselves into men's souls, and all who hear them, eager to imitate the notes [1] of harpers and pipers, are filled with filthiness.[2] Some others, who are wild after horses, think they are backing their horses in their dreams; they harness their chariots, change their drivers, and even in sleep are not free from the folly of the day.[3] And shall we, whom the Lord, the great worker of marvels, calls to the contemplation of His own works, tire of looking at them, or be slow to hear the words of the Holy Spirit? Shall we not rather stand around the vast and varied workshop of divine creation and, carried back in mind to the times of old, shall we not view all the order of creation? Heaven, poised like a dome, to quote the words of the prophet;[4] earth, this immense mass which rests upon itself; the air around it, of a soft and fluid nature, a true and continual nourishment for all who breathe it, of such tenuity that it yields and opens at the least movement of the body, opposing no resistance to our motions, while, in a moment, it streams back to its place, behind those who cleave it; water, finally, that supplies drink for man, or may be designed for our other needs, and the marvellous gathering together of it into definite places which have been assigned to it: such is the spectacle which the words which I have just read will show you.

2. "*And God said, Let the waters under the heaven be gathered together unto one place, and let the dry land appear, and it was so.*" And the water which was under the heaven gathered together unto one place; " And God called the dry land earth and the gathering together of the waters called He seas."[1] What trouble you have given me in my previous discourses by asking me why the earth was invisible, why all bodies are naturally endued with colour, and why all colour comes under the sense of sight. And, perhaps, my reason did not appear sufficient to you, when I said that the earth, without being naturally invisible, was so to us, because of the mass of water that entirely covered it. Hear then how Scripture explains itself. " Let the waters be gathered together, and let the dry land appear." The veil is lifted and allows the earth, hitherto invisible, to be seen. Perhaps you will ask me new questions. And first, is it not a law of nature that water flows downwards? Why, then, does Scripture refer this to the fiat of the Creator? As long as water is spread over a level surface, it does not flow; it is immovable. But when it finds any slope, immediately the foremost portion falls, then the one that follows takes its place, and that one is itself replaced by a third. Thus incessantly they flow, pressing the one on the other, and the rapidity of their course is in proportion to the mass of water that is being carried, and the declivity down which it is borne. If such is the nature of water, it was supererogatory to command it to gather into one place. It was bound, on account of its natural instability, to fall into the most hollow part of the earth and not to stop until the levelling of its surface. We see how there is nothing so level as the surface of water. Besides, they add, how did the waters receive an order to gather into one place, when we see several seas, separated from each other by the greatest distances? To the first question I reply: Since God's command, you know perfectly well the motion of water; you know that it is unsteady and unstable and falls naturally over declivities and into hollow places. But what was its nature before this command made it take its course? You do not know yourself, and you have heard from no eyewitness. Think, in reality, that a word of God makes the nature, and that this order is for the creature a direction for its future course. There was only one creation of day and night, and since that moment they have incessantly succeeded each other and divided time into equal parts.

3. " Let the waters be gathered to-

---

[1] κρούμα, properly " beat," " stroke," is used of the blow of the plectrum on the string, and hence of the note produced.

[2] *cf.* Plato, *Rep.* iii. 18, *ad init.*, and his reference to the ―αλθακὸς αἰχμητῆς of Homer, *Il.* xvii. 586. The same subject is treated of the *Laws* ii. § 3 and 5 and vii.

[3] *cf.* Ar., *Nub.* 16, ὀνειροπολεῖ ἵππους and 27, ὀνειροπολεῖ καὶ καθεύδων ἱππικήν. So Claudian, *De vi. Cons. Hon.* 1, sq.:

> Omnia quæ sensu volvuntur vota diurno,
> Pectore sopito reddit amica quies.
> Venator defessa toro cum membra reponit,
> Mens tamen ad sylvas et sua lustra redit.
> Judicibus lites, aurigæ somnia currus,
> Vanaque nocturnis meta cavetur equis.

[4] Isa. xl. 22, LXX.

[1] Gen. i. 9, 10.

gether." It was ordered that it should be the natural property of water to flow, and in obedience to this order, the waters are never weary in their course. In speaking thus, I have only in view the flowing property of waters. Some flow of their own accord like springs and rivers, others are collected and stationary. But I speak now of flowing waters. "Let the waters be gathered together unto one place." Have you never thought, when standing near a spring which is sending forth water abundantly, Who makes this water spring from the bowels of the earth? Who forced it up? Where are the store-houses which send it forth? To what place is it hastening? How is it that it is never exhausted here, and never overflows there? All this comes from that first command; it was for the waters a signal for their course.

In all the story of the waters remember this first order, "let the waters be gathered together." To take their assigned places they were obliged to flow, and, once arrived there, to remain in their place and not to go farther. Thus in the language of Ecclesiastes, "All the waters run into the sea; yet the sea is not full."[1] Waters flow in virtue of God's order, and the sea is enclosed in limits according to this first law, "Let the waters be gathered together unto one place." For fear the water should spread beyond its bed, and in its successive invasions cover one by one all countries, and end by flooding the whole earth, it received the order to gather unto one place. Thus we often see the furious sea raising mighty waves to the heaven, and, when once it has touched the shore, break its impetuosity in foam and retire. "Fear ye not me, saith the Lord. . . . which have placed the sand for the bound of the sea."[2] A grain of sand, the weakest thing possible, curbs the violence of the ocean. For what would prevent the Red Sea from invading the whole of Egypt, which lies lower, and uniting itself to the other sea which bathes its shores, were it not fettered by the fiat of the Creator? And if I say that Egypt is lower than the Red Sea, it is because experience has convinced us of it every time that an attempt has been made to join the sea of Egypt[3] to the Indian Ocean, of which the Red Sea is a part.[4] Thus we have renounced this enterprise, as also have the Egyptian Sesostris, who conceived the idea, and Darius the Mede who afterwards wished to carry it out.[5]

I report this fact to make you understand the full force of the command, "Let the waters be gathered unto one place"; that is to say, let there be no other gathering, and, once gathered, let them not disperse.

4. To say that the waters were gathered in one place indicates that previously they were scattered in many places. The mountains, intersected by deep ravines, accumulated water in their valleys, when from every direction the waters betook themselves to the one gathering place. What vast plains, in their extent resembling wide seas, what valleys, what cavities hollowed in many different ways, at that time full of water, must have been emptied by the command of God! But we must not therefore say, that if the water covered the face of the earth, all the basins which have since received the sea were originally full. Where can the gathering of the waters have come from if the basins were already full? These basins, we reply, were only prepared at the moment when the water had to unite in a single mass. At that time the sea which is beyond Gadeira[1] and the vast ocean, so dreaded by navigators, which surrounds the isle of Britain and western Spain, did not exist. But, all of a sudden, God created this vast space, and the mass of waters flowed in.

Now if our explanation of the creation of the world may appear contrary to experience, (because it is evident that all the waters did not flow together in one place,) many answers may be made, all obvious as soon as they are stated. Perhaps it is even ridiculous to reply to such objections. Ought they to bring forward in opposition ponds and accumulations of rain water, and think that this is enough to upset our reasonings? Evidently the chief and most complete affluence of the waters was what received the name of gathering unto one place. For wells are also gathering places for water, made by the hand of man to receive the moisture diffused in the hollow of the earth. This name of gathering does not mean any chance massing of water, but the greatest and most important one, wherein the ele-

---

[1] Eccl. i. 6, 7. [2] Jer. v. 22. [3] *i.e.* the Mediterranean.
[4] *Geminum mare . . . quod Rubrum dixere nostri . . . in duos dividitur sinus. Is qui ab oriente Persicus est . . . altero sinu Arabico nominato.* Plin. vi. 28.
[5] This illustration is taken from the work on which Basil

has been so largely dependent, the *Meteorology* of Aristotle (i. 14, 548). Pliny (vi. 33) writes: " *Daneos Fortus, ex quo navigabilem alveum perducere in Nilum, qua parte ad Delta dictum decurrit lxii. mill. D. Pass. intervallo, quod inter flumen et Rubrum mare inter est, primus omnium Sesostris Ægypti rex cogitavit; mox Darius Persarum; deinde Ptolemæus sequens*" (*i.e.* Ptolemy II.) " *. . . deterruit inundationis metus, excelsiore tribus cubitis Rubro mari comperto quam terra Ægypti.*" Herodotus (ii. 158) attributes the canal to Necho. Strabo (xvii. 804) says Darius, in supposing Egypt to lie lower than the sea, was ψευδει πεισθεις. The early canal, choked by sand, was reopened by Trajan, and choked again. Amron, Omar's general, again cleared it, but it was blocked A.D. 767. The present Suez Canal, opened in 1869, follows a new course.
[1] *i.e.* Cadiz, a corruption of Gadeira, which, like Geder and Gadara, is connected with the Phœnician *Gadir*, an enclosure.

ment is shewn collected together. In the same way that fire, in spite of its being divided into minute particles which are sufficient for our needs here, is spread in a mass in the æther; in the same way that air, in spite of a like minute division, has occupied the region round the earth; so also water, in spite of the small amount spread abroad everywhere, only forms one gathering together, that which separates the whole element from the rest. Without doubt the lakes as well those of the northern regions and those that are to be found in Greece, in Macedonia, in Bithynia and in Palestine, are gatherings together of waters; but here it means the greatest of all, that gathering the extent of which equals that of the earth. The first contain a great quantity of water; no one will deny this. Nevertheless no one could reasonably give them the name of seas, not even if they are like the great sea, charged with salt and sand. They instance for example, the Lacus Asphaltitis in Judæa, and the Serbonian lake which extends between Egypt and Palestine in the Arabian desert. These are lakes, and there is only one sea, as those affirm who have travelled round the earth. Although some authorities think the Hyrcanian and Caspian Seas are enclosed in their own boundaries, if we are to believe the geographers, they communicate with each other and together discharge themselves into the Great Sea.[1] It is thus that, according to their account, the Red Sea and that beyond Gadeira only form one. Then why did God call the different masses of water seas? This is the reason; the waters flowed into one place, and their different accumulations, that is to say, the gulfs that the earth embraced in her folds, received from the Lord the name of seas: North Sea, South Sea, Eastern Sea, and Western Sea. The seas have even their own names, the Euxine, the Propontis, the Hellespont, the Ægean, the Ionian, the Sardinian, the Sicilian, the Tyrrhene, and many other names of which an exact enumeration would now be too long, and quite out of place. See why God calls the gathering together of waters seas. But let us return to the point from which the course of my argument has diverted me.

5. And God said: "*Let the waters be gathered together unto one place and let the dry land appear.*" He did not say let the earth appear, so as not to show itself again without form, mud-like, and in combination with the water, nor yet endued with proper form and virtue. At the same time, lest we should attribute the drying of the earth to the sun, the Creator shows it to us dried before the creation of the sun. Let us follow the thought Scripture gives us. Not only the water which was covering the earth flowed off from it, but all that which had filtered into its depths withdrew in obedience to the irresistible order of the sovereign Master. And it was so. This is quite enough to show that the Creator's voice had effect: however, in several editions, there is added "And the water which was under the heavens gathered itself unto one place and the dry land was seen;" words that other interpreters have not given, and which do not appear conformable to Hebrew usage. In fact, after the assertion, "and it was so," it is superfluous to repeat exactly the same thing. In accurate copies these words are marked with an obelus,[1] which is the sign of rejection.

"*And God called the dry land earth; and the gathering together of the waters called He seas.*"[2] Why does Scripture say above that the waters were gathered together unto one place, and that the dry earth appeared? Why does it add here the dry land appeared, and God gave it the name of earth? It is that dryness is the property which appears to characterize the nature of the subject, whilst the word earth is only its simple name. Just as reason is the distinctive faculty of man, and the word man serves to designate the being gifted with this faculty, so dryness is the special and peculiar quality of the earth. The element essentially dry receives therefore the name of earth, as the animal who has a neigh for a characteristic cry is called a horse. The other elements, like the earth, have received some peculiar property which distinguishes them from the rest, and makes them known for what they are. Thus water has cold for its distinguishing property; air, moisture; fire, heat. But this theory really applies only to the primitive elements of the world. The elements which contribute to the formation of bodies, and come under our senses, show us these qualities in combination, and in the whole of nature our eyes and senses can find nothing which is completely singular, simple and pure. Earth is at the same time dry and cold;

---

[1] Pliny (vi. 15) shared a common error that the Caspian flowed into a Northern Sea. The eastern part was known as the Hyrcanian, the western as the Caspian. Strabo xi. 507, *et sq.*

[1] The obelus (†) is used by Jerome to mark superfluous matter in the lxx. *cf.* Jer. p. 494, in Canon Fremantle's Translation. The addition in question appears neither in the Vulgate, nor in Aquila, or Symmachus, or Theodotion. Ambrose, however, in *Hexaem.* iii. 5 approves of it.

[2] Gen. i. 10

water, cold and moist; air, moist and warm; fire, warm and dry. It is by the combination of their qualities that the different elements can mingle. Thanks to a common quality each of them mixes with a neighbouring element, and this natural alliance attaches it to the contrary element. For example, earth, which is at the same time dry and cold, finds in cold a relationship which unites it to water, and by the means of water unites itself to air. Water placed between the two, appears to give each a hand, and, on account of its double quality, allies itself to earth by cold and to air by moisture. Air, in its turn, takes the middle place and plays the part of a mediator between the inimical natures of water and fire, united to the first by moisture, and to the second by heat. Finally, fire, of a nature at the same time warm and dry, is linked to air by warmth, and by its dryness reunites itself to the earth. And from this accord and from this mutual mixture of elements, results a circle and an harmonious choir whence each of the elements deserves its name. I have said this in order to explain why God has given to the dry land the name of earth, without however calling the earth dry. It is because dryness is not one of those qualities which the earth acquired afterwards, but one of those which constituted its essence from the beginning. Now that which causes a body to exist, is naturally antecedent to its posterior qualities and has a pre-eminence over them. It is then with reason that God chose the most ancient characteristic of the earth whereby to designate it.

6. "*And God saw that it was good.*"[1] Scripture does not merely wish to say that a pleasing aspect of the sea presented itself to God. It is not with eyes that the Creator views the beauty of His works. He contemplates them in His ineffable wisdom. A fair sight is the sea all bright in a settled calm; fair too, when, ruffled by a light breeze of wind, its surface shows tints of purple and azure, — when, instead of lashing with violence the neighbouring shores, it seems to kiss them with peaceful caresses. However, it is not in this that Scripture makes God find the goodness and charm of the sea. Here it is the purpose of the work which makes the goodness.

In the first place sea water is the source of all the moisture of the earth. It filters through imperceptible conduits, as is proved by the subterranean openings and caves whither its waves penetrate; it is received in oblique and sinuous canals; then, driven out by the wind, it rises to the surface of the earth, and breaks it, having become drinkable and free from its bitterness by this long percolation. Often, moved by the same cause, it springs even from mines that it has crossed, deriving warmth from them, and rises boiling, and bursts forth of a burning heat, as may be seen in islands and on the sea coast; even inland in certain places, in the neighbourhood of rivers, to compare little things with great, almost the same phenomena occur. To what do these words tend? To prove that the earth is all undermined with invisible conduits, where the water travels everywhere underground from the sources of the sea.

7. Thus, in the eyes of God, the sea is good, because it makes the under current of moisture in the depths of the earth. It is good again, because from all sides it receives the rivers without exceeding its limits. It is good, because it is the origin and source of the waters in the air. Warmed by the rays of the sun, it escapes in vapour, is attracted into the high regions of the air, and is there cooled on account of its rising high above the refraction of the rays from the ground, and, the shade of the clouds adding to this refrigeration, it is changed into rain and fattens the earth. If people are incredulous, let them look at caldrons on the fire, which, though full of water, are often left empty because all the water is boiled and resolved into vapour. Sailors, too, boil even sea water, collecting the vapour in sponges, to quench their thirst in pressing need.

Finally the sea is good in the eyes of God, because it girdles the isles, of which it forms at the same time the rampart and the beauty, because it brings together the most distant parts of the earth, and facilitates the intercommunication of mariners. By this means it gives us the boon of general information, supplies the merchant with his wealth, and easily provides for the necessities of life, allowing the rich to export their superfluities, and blessing the poor with the supply of what they lack.

But whence do I perceive the goodness of the Ocean, as it appeared in the eyes of the Creator? If the Ocean is good and worthy of praise before God, how much more beautiful is the assembly of a Church like this, where the voices of men, of children, and of women, arise in our prayers to God mingling and re-sounding like the waves which beat upon the shore. This Church also enjoys a profound calm, and malicious spirits cannot trouble it with the breath of heresy. Deserve, then, the approbation of the Lord by remain-

---

[1] Gen. i. 10.

ing faithful to such good guidance, in our Lord Jesus Christ, to whom be glory and power for ever and ever. Amen.

HOMILY V.

The Germination of the Earth.

1. "*And God said Let the earth bring forth grass, the herb yielding seed, and the fruit tree yielding fruit after his kind, whose seed is in itself.*" [1] It was deep wisdom that commanded the earth, when it rested after discharging the weight of the waters, first to bring forth grass, then wood, as we see it doing still at this time. For the voice that was then heard and this command were as a natural and permanent law for it; it gave fertility and the power to produce fruit for all ages to come; "Let the earth bring forth." The production of vegetables shows first germination. When the germs begin to sprout they form grass; this develops and becomes a plant, which insensibly receives its different articulations, and reaches its maturity in the seed. Thus all things which sprout and are green are developed. "Let the earth bring forth green grass." Let the earth bring forth by itself without having any need of help from without. Some consider the sun as the source of all productiveness on the earth. It is, they say, the action of the sun's heat which attracts the vital force from the centre of the earth to the surface. The reason why the adornment of the earth was before the sun is the following; that those who worship the sun, as the source of life, may renounce their error. If they be well persuaded that the earth was adorned before the genesis of the sun, they will retract their unbounded admiration for it, because they see grass and plants vegetate before it rose. [2] If then the food for the flocks was prepared, did our race appear less worthy of a like solicitude? He, who provided pasture for horses and cattle, thought before all of your riches and pleasures. If he fed your cattle, it was to provide for all the needs of your life. And what object was there in the bringing forth of grain, if not for your subsistence? Moreover, many grasses and vegetables serve for the food of man.

2. "*Let the earth bring forth grass yielding seed after his kind.*" So that although some kind of grass is of service to animals, even their gain is our gain too, and seeds are especially designed for our use. Such

is the true meaning of the words that I have quoted. "Let the earth bring forth grass, the herb yielding seed after his kind." In this manner we can re-establish the order of the words, of which the construction seems faulty in the actual version, and the economy of nature will be rigorously observed. In fact, first comes germination, then verdure, then the growth of the plant, which after having attained its full growth arrives at perfection in seed.

How then, they say, can Scripture describe all the plants of the earth as seed-bearing, when the reed, couch-grass,[1] mint, crocus, garlic, and the flowering rush and countless other species, produce no seed? To this we reply that many vegetables have their seminal virtue in the lower part and in the roots. The reed, for example, after its annual growth sends forth a protuberance from its roots, which takes the place of seed for future trees. Numbers of other vegetables are the same and all over the earth reproduce by the roots. Nothing then is truer than that each plant produces its seed or contains some seminal virtue; this is what is meant by "after its kind." So that the shoot of a reed does not produce an olive tree, but from a reed grows another reed, and from one sort of seed a plant of the same sort always germinates. Thus, all which sprang from the earth, in its first bringing forth, is kept the same to our time, thanks to the constant reproduction of kind.[2]

"Let the earth bring forth." See how, at this short word, at this brief command, the cold and sterile earth travailed and hastened to bring forth its fruit, as it cast away its sad and dismal covering to clothe itself in a more brilliant robe, proud of its proper adornment and displaying the infinite variety of plants.

I want creation to penetrate you with so much admiration that everywhere, wherever you may be, the least plant may bring to you the clear remembrance of the Creator. If you see the grass of the fields, think of human nature, and remember the comparison of the wise Isaiah. "All flesh is grass, and all the goodliness thereof is as the flower of the field." Truly the rapid flow of life, the short gratification and pleasure that an instant of happiness gives a man, all wonderfully suit the comparison of the prophet. To-day he is vigorous in body, fattened by luxury, and in the prime of life, with complexion fair like the flowers, strong and pow-

[1] Gen. i. 11.
[2] Empedocles, according to Plutarch (περὶ τῶν ἀρέσκ, etc. v. 342) πρῶτα τῶν ζώων τὰ δένδρα ἐκ γῆς ἀναδῦναί φησι, πρὶν τὸν ἥλιον περιαπλωθῆναι καὶ πρὶν ἡμέραν καὶ νύκτα διακριθῆναι.

[1] *Triticum repens.*
[2] On the history of this doctrine, of which Linnæus was the latest great exponent, and its contradiction in Darwin, see Haeckel's *Schöpfungsgeschichte*, vol. i. ch. 2.

erful and of irresistible energy; tomorrow and he will be an object of pity, withered by age or exhausted by sickness. Another shines in all the splendour of a brilliant fortune, and around him are a multitude of flatterers, an escort of false friends on the track of his good graces; a crowd of kinsfolk, but of no true kin; a swarm of servants who crowd after him to provide for his food and for all his needs; and in his comings and goings this innumerable suite, which he drags after him, excites the envy of all whom he meets. To fortune may be added power in the State, honours bestowed by the imperial throne, the government of a province, or the command of armies; a herald who precedes him is crying in a loud voice; lictors right and left also fill his subjects with awe, blows, confiscations, banishments, imprisonments, and all the means by which he strikes intolerable terror into all whom he has to rule. And what then? One night, a fever, a pleurisy, or an inflammation of the lungs, snatches away this man from the midst of men, stripped in a moment of all his stage accessories, and all this, his glory, is proved a mere dream. Therefore the Prophet has compared human glory to the weakest flower.

3. Up to this point, the order in which plants shoot bears witness to their first arrangement. Every herb, every plant proceeds from a germ. If, like the couch-grass and the crocus, it throws out a shoot from its root and from this lower protuberance, it must always germinate and start outwards. If it proceeds from a seed, there is still, by necessity, first a germ, then the sprout, then green foliage, and finally the fruit which ripens upon a stalk hitherto dry and thick. "Let the earth bring forth grass." When the seed falls into the earth, which contains the right combination of heat and moisture, it swells and becomes porous, and, grasping the surrounding earth, attracts to itself all that is suitable for it and that has affinity to it. These particles of earth, however small they may be, as they fall and insinuate themselves into all the pores of the seed, broaden its bulk and make it send forth roots below, and shoot upwards, sending forth stalks no less numerous than the roots. As the germ is always growing warm, the moisture, pumped up through the roots, and helped by the attraction of heat, draws a proper amount of nourishment from the soil, and distributes it to the stem, to the bark, to the husk, to the seed itself and to the beards with which it is armed. It is owing to these successive accretions that each plant attains its natural development, as well corn as vegetables,

herbs or brushwood. A single plant, a blade of grass is sufficient to occupy all your intelligence in the contemplation of the skill which produced it.[1] Why is the wheat stalk better with joints?[2] Are they not like fastenings, which help it to bear easily the weight of the ear, when it is swollen with fruit and bends towards the earth? Thus, whilst oats, which have no weight to bear at the top, are without these supports, nature has provided them for wheat. It has hidden the grain in a case, so that it may not be exposed to birds' pillage, and has furnished it with a rampart of barbs, which, like darts, protect it against the attacks of tiny creatures.

4. What shall I say? What shall I leave unsaid? In the rich treasures of creation it is difficult to select what is most precious; the loss of what is omitted is too severe. "Let the earth bring forth grass;" and instantly, with useful plants, appear noxious plants; with corn, hemlock; with the other nutritious plants, hellebore, monkshood, mandrake and the juice of the poppy. What then? Shall we show no gratitude for so many beneficial gifts, and reproach the Creator for those which may be harmful to our life? And shall we not reflect that all has not been created in view of the wants of our bellies? The nourishing plants, which are destined for our use, are close at hand, and known by all the world. But in creation nothing exists without a reason. The blood of the bull is a poison:[3] ought this animal then, whose strength is so serviceable to man, not to have been created, or, if created, to have been bloodless? But you have sense enough in yourself to keep you free from deadly things. What! Sheep and goats know how to turn away from what threatens their life, discerning danger by instinct alone: and you, who have reason and the art of medicine to supply what you need, and the experience of your forebears to tell you to avoid all that is dangerous, you tell me that you find it difficult to keep yourself from poisons! But not a single thing has been created without reason, not a single thing is useless. One serves as food to some animal; medicine has found in another a relief for one of our maladies. Thus the starling eats hemlock, its constitution rendering it insusceptible to the action of the poison.

---

[1] " To me the meanest flower that blows can give
   Thoughts that do often lie too deep for tears."
              Wordsworth, *Ode on Immortality.*

[2] Literally, knee—Latin *geniculum.* cf. Xen., *Anab.* iv 5, 26, and Theoph. viii. 2, 4. "Knee-jointed" is a recognised English term for certain grasses.

[3] " *Taurorum (sanguis) pestifer potu maxime.*" Plin. xi. 90. *Taurinus recens inter venena est.* 2d. xxviii. 41. cf. Dioscorid. in *Alexiph.* 25.

Thanks to the tenuity of the pores of its heart, the malignant juice is no sooner swallowed than it is digested, before its chill can attack the vital parts.[1] The quail, thanks to its peculiar temperament, whereby it escapes the dangerous effects, feeds on hellebore. There are even circumstances where poisons are useful to men; with mandrake[2] doctors give us sleep; with opium they lull violent pain. Hemlock has ere now been used to appease the rage of unruly diseases;[3] and many times hellebore has taken away long standing disease.[4] These plants, then, instead of making you accuse the Creator, give you a new subject for gratitude.

5. "*Let the earth bring forth grass.*" What spontaneous provision is included in these words, — that which is present in the root, in the plant itself, and in the fruit, as well as that which our labour and husbandry add! God did not command the earth immediately to give forth seed and fruit, but to produce germs, to grow green, and to arrive at maturity in the seed; so that this first command teaches nature what she has to do in the course of ages. But, they ask, is it true that the earth produces seed after his kind, when often, after having sown wheat, we gather black grain? This is not a change of kind, but an alteration, a disease of the grain. It has not ceased to be wheat; it is on account of having been burnt that it is black, as one can learn from its name.[5] If a severe frost had burnt it,[6] it would have had another colour and a different flavour. They even pretend that, if it could find suitable earth and moderate temperature, it might return to its first form. Thus, you find nothing in nature contrary to the divine command. As to the darnel and all those bastard grains which mix themselves with the harvest, the tares of Scripture, far from being a variety of corn, have their own origin and their own kind; image of those who alter the doctrine of the Lord and, not being rightly instructed in the word, but, corrupted by the teaching of the evil one, mix themselves with the sound body of the Church to spread their pernicious errors secretly among purer souls. The Lord thus compares the perfection of those who believe in Him to the growth of seed, "as if a man should cast seed into the ground; and should sleep and rise, night and day, and the seed should spring and grow up, he knoweth not how. For the earth bringeth forth fruit of herself; first the blade, then the ear, after that the full corn in the ear."[1] "Let the earth bring forth grass." In a moment earth began by germination to obey the laws of the Creator, completed every stage of growth, and brought germs to perfection. The meadows were covered with deep grass, the fertile plains quivered[2] with harvests, and the movement of the corn was like the waving of the sea. Every plant, every herb, the smallest shrub, the least vegetable, arose from the earth in all its luxuriance. There was no failure in this first vegetation: no husbandman's inexperience, no inclemency of the weather, nothing could injure it; then the sentence of condemnation was not fettering the earth's fertility. All this was before the sin which condemned us to eat our bread by the sweat of our brow.

6. "*Let the earth,*" the Creator adds, "*bring forth the fruit tree yielding fruit after his kind, whose seed is in itself.*"[3] At this command every copse was thickly planted; all the trees, fir, cedar, cypress, pine, rose to their greatest height, the shrubs were straightway clothed with thick foliage.[4] The plants called crown-plants, roses, myrtles, laurels, did not exist; in one moment they came into being, each one with its distinctive peculiarities. Most marked differences separated them from other plants, and each one was distinguished by a character of its own. But then the rose was without thorns; since then the thorn has been added to its beauty, to make us feel that sorrow is very near to pleasure, and to remind us of our sin, which condemned the earth to produce thorns[5] and caltrops. But, they say, the earth has received the command to produce trees "yielding fruit whose seed was in itself," and we see many trees which have neither fruit, nor seed. What shall we reply? First, that only the more important trees are mentioned; and then, that a careful examination will show us that every tree has seed, or some property which takes the place of it. The black poplar, the willow, the elm, the white poplar, all the trees of this family, do not produce any apparent fruit; however, an attentive observer finds

---

[1] cf. Galen. *De Simp. Fac.* iii.
[2] ὁ μανδραγόρας τοὺς ἀνθρώπους κοιμίζει. Xen., *Symp.* ii. 24.
[3] cf. Aretæus, *De Morb. Aent.* ii. 11.
[4] The Black Hellebore, or Christmas Rose, is a recognised alterative. Whether this is the plant of Anticyra is doubtful.
[5] πυρός=wheat. The root, which has nothing to do with πῦρ, is found by Curtius in the Slavonic *pyro*=rye, the Bohemian *pyr*=quitch grass, the Lettish *purji*=wheat, and the Lithuanian *pyragas*=wheaten bread. (L. & S. *in loc.*)
[6] cf. Virg., *Georg.* i. 93: "*Aut Borea penetrabile frigus adurat.*" Ov. *M.* xiv. 763, *Frigus adurat poma,* and in Greek Arist., *Meteor.* iv. 5.

[1] Matt. iv. 26–28.
[2] cf. *Horrescunt segetes.* Virg., *Georg.* iii. 39.
[3] Gen. i. 11.
[4] ἀμφίκομοι καὶ δασεῖς. cf. Milton, "With frizzled hair implicit." *P. L.* vii.
[5] cf. Milton, *P.L.,* B. iv., "Flowers of all hue and without thorn the rose," and August. *De Genesi contra Manichæos.* i. 13.

seed in each of them. This grain which is at the base of the leaf, and which those who busy themselves with inventing words call mischos, has the property of seed. And there are trees which reproduce by their branches, throwing out roots from them. Perhaps we ought even to consider as seeds the saplings which spring from the roots of a tree : for cultivators tear them out to multiply the species. But, we have already said, it is chiefly a question of the trees which contribute most to our life ; which offer their various fruits to man and provide him with plentiful nourishment. Such is the vine, which produces wine to make glad the heart of man ; such is the olive tree, whose fruit brightens his face with oil. How many things in nature are combined in the same plant ! In a vine, roots, green and flexible branches, which spread themselves far over the earth, buds, tendrils, bunches of sour grapes and ripe grapes. The sight of a vine, when observed by an intelligent eye, serves to remind you of your nature. Without doubt you remember the parable where the Lord calls Himself a vine and His Father the husbandman, and every one of us who are grafted by faith into the Church the branches. He invites us to produce fruits in abundance, for fear lest our sterility should condemn us to the fire.[1] He constantly compares our souls to vines. " My well beloved," says He, " hath a vineyard in a very fruitful hill," [2] and elsewhere, I have " planted a vineyard and hedged it round about." [3] Evidently He calls human souls His vine, those souls whom He has surrounded with the authority of His precepts and a guard of angels. " The angel of the Lord encampeth round about them that fear him." [4] And further : He has planted for us, so to say, props, in establishing in His Church apostles, prophets, teachers ; [5] and raising our thoughts by the example of the blessed in olden times, He has not allowed them to drag on the earth and be crushed under foot. He wishes that the claspings of love, like the tendrils of the vine, should attach us to our neighbours and make us rest on them, so that, in our continual aspirations towards heaven, we may imitate these vines, which raise themselves to the tops of the tallest trees. He also asks us to allow ourselves to be dug about ; and that is what the soul does when it disembarrasses itself from the cares of the world, which are a weight on our hearts. He, then, who is

freed from carnal affections and from the love of riches, and, far from being dazzled by them, disdains and despises this miserable vain glory, is, so to say, dug about and at length breathes, free from the useless weight of earthly thoughts. Nor must we, in the spirit of the parable, put forth too much wood, that is to say, live with ostentation, and gain the applause of the world ; we must bring forth fruits, keeping the proof of our works for the husbandman. Be " like a green olive tree in the house of God," [1] never destitute of hope, but decked through faith with the bloom of salvation. Thus you will resemble the eternal verdure of this plant and will rival it in fruitfulness, if each day sees you giving abundantly in alms.

7. But let us return to the examination of the ingenious contrivances of creation. How many trees then arose, some to give us their fruits, others to roof our houses, others to build our ships, others to feed our fires ! What a variety in the disposition of their several parts ! And yet, how difficult is it to find the distinctive property of each of them, and to grasp the difference which separates them from other species. Some strike deep roots, others do not ; some shoot straight up and have only one stem, others appear to love the earth and, from their root upwards, divide into several shoots. Those whose long branches stretch up afar into the air, have also deep roots which spread within a large circumference, a true foundation placed by nature to support the weight of the tree. What variety there is in bark ! Some plants have smooth bark, others rough, some have only one layer, others several. What a marvellous thing ! You may find in the youth and age of plants resemblances to those of man. Young and vigorous, their bark is distended ; when they grow old, it is rough and wrinkled. Cut one, it sends forth new buds ; the other remains henceforward sterile and as if struck with a mortal wound. But further, it has been observed that pines, cut down, or even submitted to the action of fire, are changed into a forest of oaks.[2] We know besides that the industry of agriculturists remedies the natural defects

---

[1] Ps. lii. 8.

[2] The phenomenon has been observed in later days, though Basil may be at fault in his account of the cause. When pines have been cleared away in North American forests young oaklings have sprung up. The acorn lay long hid, unable to contend against the pine, but, when once the ground was clear, it sprouted. This upgrowth of a new kind of tree has been accounted for partly by the burial of germs by jays, rooks, and some quadrupeds ; partly by the theory of De Candolle and Liebig that roots expel certain substances which, though unfavourable to the vitality of the plant excreting them, are capable of supporting others. So, on the pine pressure being removed, the hidden seeds sprout in a kind of vegetable manure. cf. Sir Charles Lyell's *Travels in the United States* and Rough's *Elements of Forestry*, p. 19.

---

[1] cf. S. John xv. 1-6. [4] Ps. xxxiv. 7.
[2] Isa. v. 1. [5] cf. 1 Cor. xii. 28.
[3] Matt. xxi. 33.

of certain trees. Thus the sharp pomegranate and bitter almonds, if the trunk of the tree is pierced near the root to introduce into the middle of the pith a fat plug of pine, lose the acidity of their juice, and become delicious fruits.[1] Let not the sinner then despair of himself, when he thinks, if agriculture can change the juices of plants, the efforts of the soul to arrive at virtue, can certainly triumph over all infirmities.

Now there is such a variety of fruits in fruit trees that it is beyond all expression; a variety not only in the fruits of trees of different families, but even in those of the same species, if it be true, as gardeners say, that the sex of a tree influences the character of its fruits. They distinguish male from female in palms; sometimes we see those which they call female lower their branches, as though with passionate desire, and invite the embraces of the male. Then, those who take care of these plants shake over these palms the fertilizing dust from the male palm-tree, the *psen* as they call it: the tree appears to share the pleasures of enjoyment; then it raises its branches, and its foliage resumes its usual form. The same is said of the fig tree. Some plant wild fig trees near cultivated fig trees, and there are others who, to remedy the weakness of the productive fig tree of our gardens, attach to the branches unripe figs and so retain the fruit which had already begun to drop and to be lost. What lesson does nature here give us? That we must often borrow, even from those who are strangers to the faith, a certain vigour to show forth good works. If you see outside the Church, in pagan life, or in the midst of a pernicious heresy, the example of virtue and fidelity to moral laws, redouble your efforts to resemble the productive fig tree, who by the side of the wild fig tree, gains strength, prevents the fruit from being shed, and nourishes it with more care.

8. Plants reproduce themselves in so many different ways, that we can only touch upon the chief among them. As to fruits themselves, who could review their varieties, their forms, their colours, the peculiar flavour, and the use of each of them? Why do some fruits ripen when exposed bare to the rays of the sun, while others fill out while encased in shells? Trees of which the fruit is tender have, like the fig tree, a thick shade of leaves; those, on the contrary, of which the

fruits are stouter, like the nut, are only covered by a light shade. The delicacy of the first requires more care; if the latter had a thicker case, the shade of the leaves would be harmful. Why is the vine leaf serrated, if not that the bunches of grapes may at the same time resist the injuries of the air and receive through the openings all the rays of the sun? Nothing has been done without motive, nothing by chance. All shows ineffable wisdom.[1]

What discourse can touch all? Can the human mind make an exact review, remark every distinctive property, exhibit all the differences, unveil with certainty so many mysterious causes? The same water, pumped up through the root, nourishes in a different way the root itself, the bark of the trunk, the wood and the pith. It becomes leaf, it distributes itself among the branches and twigs and makes the fruits swell — it gives to the plant its gum and its sap. Who will explain to us the difference between all these? There is a difference between the gum of the mastich and the juice of the balsam, a difference between that which distils in Egypt and Libya from the fennel. Amber is, they say, the crystallized sap of plants. And for a proof, see the bits of straws and little insects which have been caught in the sap while still liquid and imprisoned there. In one word, no one without long experience could find terms to express the virtue of it. How, again, does this water become wine in the vine, and oil in the olive tree? Yet what is marvellous is, not to see it become sweet in one fruit, fat and unctuous in another, but to see in sweet fruits an inexpressible variety of flavour. There is one sweetness of the grape, another of the apple, another of the fig, another of the date. I shall willingly give you the gratification of continuing this research. How is it that this same water has sometimes a sweet taste, softened by its remaining in certain plants, and at other times stings the palate because it has become acid by passing through others? How is it, again, that it attains extreme bitterness, and makes the mouth rough when it is found in wormwood and in scammony? That it has in acorns

---

[1] Ambrose, *Hexaem.* iii. 13, writes: *Amygdalis quoque hoc genere medicari feruntur agricolæ, ut ex amaris dulces fiant fructus, ut et terebrent ejus radicem arboris, et in medium inserant surculum ejus arboris quam Græci πεύχην, nos piceam dicimus: quo facto succi amaritudo deponitur.*

[1] On the argument from design, *cf.* Aristotle, *De Part. Anim.* iii. 1, as quoted and translated by Cudworth, III. xxxvii. 3 : " A carpenter would give a better account than so, for he would not think it sufficient to say that the fabric came to be of such a form because the instruments happened to fall so and so, but he will tell you that it is because himself made such strokes, and that he directed the instruments and determined their motion after such a manner, to this end that he might make the whole a fabric fit and useful for such purposes." On the strength and weakness of the argument from design, in view of modern speculation, suggestive matter is contained in Dr. Eagar's *Butler's Analogy and Modern Thought*, p. 49 *et sq.*

and dogwood a sharp and rough flavour? That in the turpentine tree and the walnut tree it is changed into a soft and oily matter?

9. But what need is there to continue, when in the same fig tree we have the most opposite flavours, as bitter in the sap as it is sweet in the fruit? And in the vine, is it not as sweet in the grapes as it is astringent in the branches? And what a variety of colour! Look how in a meadow this same water becomes red in one flower, purple in another, blue in this one, white in that. And this diversity of colours, is it to be compared to that of scents? But I perceive that an insatiable curiosity is drawing out my discourse beyond its limits. If I do not stop and recall it to the law of creation, day will fail me whilst making you see great wisdom in small things.

" *Let the earth bring forth the fruit tree yielding fruit.*" Immediately the tops of the mountains were covered with foliage; paradises were artfully laid out, and an infinitude of plants embellished the banks of the rivers. Some were for the adornment of man's table; some to nourish animals with their fruits and their leaves; some to provide medicinal help by giving us their sap, their juice, their chips, their bark or their fruit. In a word, the experience of ages, profiting from every chance, has not been able to discover anything useful, which the penetrating foresight of the Creator did not first perceive and call into existence. Therefore, when you see the trees in our gardens, or those of the forest, those which love the water or the land, those which bear flowers, or those which do not flower, I should like to see you recognising grandeur even in small objects, adding incessantly to your admiration of, and redoubling your love for the Creator. Ask yourself why He has made some trees evergreen and others deciduous; why, among the first, some lose their leaves, and others always keep them. Thus the olive and the pine shed their leaves, although they renew them insensibly and never appear to be despoiled of their verdure. The palm tree, on the contrary, from its birth to its death, is always adorned with the same foliage. Think again of the double life of the tamarisk; it is an aquatic plant, and yet it covers the desert. Thus, Jeremiah compares it to the worst of characters — the double character.[1]

10. " *Let the earth bring forth.*" This short command was in a moment a vast nature, an elaborate system. Swifter than

thought it produced the countless qualities of plants. It is this command which, still at this day, is imposed on the earth, and in the course of each year displays all the strength of its power to produce herbs, seeds and trees. Like tops, which after the first impulse, continue their evolutions, turning upon themselves when once fixed in their centre; thus nature, receiving the impulse of this first command, follows without interruption the course of ages, until the consummation of all things.[1] Let us all hasten to attain to it, full of fruit and of good works; and thus, planted in the house of the Lord we shall flourish in the court of our God,[2] in our Lord Jesus Christ, to whom be glory and power for ever and ever. Amen.

HOMILY VI.

The creation of luminous bodies.

· 1. At the shows in the circus the spectator must join in the efforts of the athletes. This the laws of the show indicate, for they prescribe that all should have the head uncovered when present at the stadium. The object of this, in my opinion, is that each one there should not only be a spectator of the athletes, but be, in a certain measure, a true athlete himself.[3] Thus, to investigate the great and prodigious show of creation, to understand supreme and ineffable wisdom, you must bring personal light for the contemplation of the wonders which I spread before your eyes, and help me, according to your power, in this struggle, where you are not so much judges as fellow combatants,[4] for fear lest the truth might escape you, and lest my error might turn to your common prejudice. Why these words? It is because we propose to study the world as a whole, and to consider the universe, not by the light of worldly wisdom, but by that with which

---

[1] cf. Jer. xvii. 6, LXX.

---

[1] " *Ac mihi quidem videtur, cum duæ sententiæ fuissent veterum philosophorum, una eorum qui censerent omnia ita fato fieri, ut id fatum vim necessitatis afferret, in qua sententia Democritus, Heraclitus, Empedocles, Aristoteles fuit; altera eorum, quibus viderentur sine ullo fato esse animorum motus voluntarii: Chrysippus tanquam arbiter honorarius, medium ferire voluisse . . . quanquam assensio non possit fieri nisi commota visa, tamen cum id visum proximam causam habeat, non principalem hanc habet rationem, ut Chrysippus vult, quam dudum diximus, non, ut illa quidem fieri possit, nulla vi extrinsecus excitata, necesse est enim assensionem viso commoveri, sed revertitur ad cylindrum, et ad turbinem suum, quæ moveri incipere, nisi pulsa non possunt: id autem cum accidit suapte natura, quod superest et cylindrum volvi, et versari turbinem putat.*" (Cic., *De fato*. xviii.)

[2] cf. Ps. xcii. 13.

[3] In the Theatrum spectators might be covered. cf. Mart. xiv. 29:
" *In Pompeiano tectus spectabo theatro ;
Nam ventus populo vela negare solet.*"
cf. Dion Cassius lix. 7. These passages may, however, indicate exceptional cases.

[4] cf. Greg., *In Ez.*: *Propter bonos auditores malis doctoribus sermo datur: et propter malos auditores bonis doctoribus sermo subtrahitur.*

God wills to enlighten His servant, when He speaks to him in person and without enigmas. It is because it is absolutely necessary that all lovers of great and grand shows should bring a mind well prepared to study them. If sometimes, on a bright night,[1] whilst gazing with watchful eyes on the inexpressible beauty of the stars, you have thought of the Creator of all things; if you have asked yourself who it is that has dotted heaven with such flowers, and why visible things are even more useful than beautiful; if sometimes, in the day, you have studied the marvels of light, if you have raised yourself by visible things to the invisible Being, then you are a well prepared auditor, and you can take your place in this august and blessed amphitheatre. Come in the same way that any one not knowing a town is taken by the hand and led through it; thus I am going to lead you, like strangers, through the mysterious marvels of this great city of the universe.[2] Our first country was in this great city, whence the murderous dæmon whose enticements seduced man to slavery expelled us. There you will see man's first origin and his immediate seizure by death, brought forth by sin, the first born of the evil spirit. You will know that you are formed of earth, but the work of God's hands; much weaker than the brute, but ordained to command beings without reason and soul; inferior as regards natural advantages, but, thanks to the privilege of reason, capable of raising yourself to heaven. If we are penetrated by these truths, we shall know ourselves, we shall know God, we shall adore our Creator, we shall serve our Master, we shall glorify our Father, we shall love our Sustainer, we shall bless our Benefactor, we shall not cease to honour the Prince[3] of present and future life, Who, by the riches that He showers upon us in this world, makes us believe in His promises and uses present good things to strengthen our expectation of the future. Truly, if such are the good things of time, what will be those of eternity? If such is the beauty of visible things, what shall we think of invisible

things? If the grandeur of heaven exceeds the measure of human intelligence, what mind shall be able to trace the nature of the everlasting? If the sun, subject to corruption, is so beautiful, so grand, so rapid in its movement, so invariable in its course; if its grandeur is in such perfect harmony with and due proportion to the universe: if, by the beauty of its nature, it shines like a brilliant eye in the middle of creation; if finally, one cannot tire of contemplating it, what will be the beauty of the Sun of Righteousness?[1] If the blind man suffers from not seeing the material sun, what a deprivation is it for the sinner not to enjoy the true light!

2. "*And God said, Let there be lights in the firmament of the heaven to give light upon the earth, and to divide the day from the night.*"[2] Heaven and earth were the first; after them was created light; the day had been distinguished from the night, then had appeared the firmament and the dry element. The water had been gathered into the reservoir assigned to it, the earth displayed its productions, it had caused many kinds of herbs to germinate and it was adorned with all kinds of plants. However, the sun and the moon did not yet exist, in order that those who live in ignorance of God may not consider the sun as the origin and the father of light, or as the maker of all that grows out of the earth.[3] That is why there was a fourth day, and then God said: " Let there be lights in the firmament of the heaven."

When once you have learnt Who spoke, think immediately of the hearer. God said, " Let there be lights . . . and God made two great lights." Who spoke? and Who made? Do you not see a double person? Everywhere, in mystic language, history is sown with the dogmas of theology.

The motive follows which caused the lights to be created. It was to illuminate the earth. Already light was created; why therefore say that the sun was created to give light? And, first, do not laugh at the strangeness of this expression. We do not follow your nicety about words, and we trouble ourselves but little to give them a harmonious turn. Our writers do not amuse

---

1 " By night an atheist half believes in God." Young, *N.T.* v. 177. *cf.* also Cic., *De nat. Deor.* ii. 38: *Quis enim hunc hominem dixerit, qui tam certos cœli motus, tam ratos astrorum ordines, tamque omnia ister se connexa et apta viderit, neget in his ullam inesse rationem, eaque casu fieri dicat, quæ quanto consilio gerantur, nullo consilio assequi possumus*

2 *cf.* Cic., *De Nat. Deor.* ii. 62. *Est enim mundus quasi communis deorum atque hominum domus, aut urbs utrorumque. Soli etiam ratione utentes, jure ac lege vivunt.* Bp. Lightfoot quotes in illustration of Phil. iii. 20, Philo, *De Conf.* i. 416, M. πατρίδα μὲν τὸν οὐράνιον χῶρον ἐν ᾧ πολιτεύονται ξένον δὲ τὸν περίγειον ἐν ᾧ παρῴκησαν νομίζουσαι. So Clem. Alex., *Strom.* iv. 26, λέγουσι γὰρ οἱ Στωϊκοὶ τὸν μὲν οὐρανὸν κυρίως πόλιν τὰ δὲ ἐπὶ γῆς ἐνταῦθα οὐκ ἔτι πόλεις, λέγεσθαι γὰρ, οὐκ εἶναι δέ, and Plato, *Rep.* ix. 592, B. ἐν οὐρανῷ ἴσως παράδειγμα (τῆς πόλεως) ἀνάκειται τῷ βουλομένῳ ὁρᾶν καὶ ὁρῶντι ἑαυτὸν κατοικίζειν.

3 *cf.* Acts iii. 15.

1 *cf.* Mal. iv. 2.   2 Gen. i. 14, LXX.
3 Fialon quotes Bossuet (5th elev. 3d week) : " *Ainsi il a fait la lumière avant que de faire les grands luminaires où il a voulu la ramasser : et il a fait la distinction des jours avant que d'avoir créé les astres dont il s'est servi pour les régler parfaitement : et le soir et le matin ont été distingués, avant que leur distinction et la division parfaite du jour et de la nuit fût bien marquée; et les arbres, et les arbustes, et les herbes ont germé sur la terre par ordre de Dieu, avant qu'il eût fait le soleil, qui devait être le père de toutes ces plantes ; et il a détaché exprès les effets d'avec leurs causes naturelles, pour montrer que naturellement tout ne tient qu'à lui seul, et ne dépend que de sa seule volonté.*"

themselves by polishing their periods, and everywhere we prefer clearness of words to sonorous expressions. See then if, by this expression " to light up," the sacred writer sufficiently made his thought understood. He has put " to give light "[1] instead of " illumination."[2] Now there is nothing here contradictory to what has been said of light. Then the actual nature of light was produced: now the sun's body is constructed to be a vehicle for that original light. A lamp is not fire. Fire has the property of illuminating, and we have invented the lamp to light us in darkness. In the same way, the luminous bodies have been fashioned as a vehicle for that pure, clear, and immaterial light. The Apostle speaks to us of certain lights which shine in the world[3] without being confounded with the true light of the world, the possession of which made the saints luminaries of the souls which they instructed and drew from the darkness of ignorance. This is why the Creator of all things, made the sun in addition to that glorious light, and placed it shining in the heavens.

3. And let no one suppose it to be a thing incredible that the brightness of the light is one thing, and the body which is its material vehicle is another. First, in all composite things, we distinguish substance susceptible of quality, and the quality which it receives. The nature of whiteness is one thing, another is that of the body which is whitened; thus the natures differ which we have just seen reunited by the power of the Creator. And do not tell me that it is impossible to separate them. Even I do not pretend to be able to separate light from the body of the sun ; but I maintain that that which we separate in thought, may be separated in reality by the Creator of nature. You cannot, moreover, separate the brightness of fire from the virtue of burning which it possesses ; but God, who wished to attract His servant by a wonderful sight, set a fire in the burning bush, which displayed all the brilliancy of flame while its devouring property was dormant. It is that which the Psalmist affirms in saying " The voice of the Lord divideth the flames of fire."[4] Thus, in the requital which awaits us after this life, a mysterious voice seems to tell us that the double nature of fire will be divided; the just will enjoy its light, and the torment of its heat will be the torture of the wicked.

In the revolutions of the moon we find a new proof of what we have advanced. When it stops and grows less it does not consume itself in all its body, but in the measure that it deposits or absorbs the light which surrounds it, it presents to us the image of its decrease or of its increase. If we wish an evident proof that the moon does not consume its body when at rest, we have only to open our eyes. If you look at it in a cloudless and clear sky, you observe, when it has taken the complete form of a crescent, that the part, which is dark and not lighted up, describes a circle equal to that which the full moon forms. Thus the eye can take in the whole circle, if it adds to the illuminated part this obscure and dark curve. And do not tell me that the light of the moon is borrowed, diminishing or increasing in proportion as it approaches or recedes from the sun. That is not now the object of our research ; we only wish to prove that its body differs from the light which makes it shine. I wish you to have the same idea of the sun ; except however that the one, after having once received light and having mixed it with its substance, does not lay it down again, whilst the other, turn by turn, putting off and reclothing itself again with light, proves by that which takes place in itself what we have said of the sun.

The sun and moon thus received the command to divide the day from the night. God had already separated light from darkness; then He placed their natures in opposition, so that they could never mingle, and that there could never be anything in common between darkness and light. You see what a shadow is during the day ; that is precisely the nature of darkness during the night. If, at the appearance of a light, the shadow always falls on the opposite side ; if in the morning it extends towards the setting sun ; if in the evening it inclines towards the rising sun, and at mid-day turns towards the north ; night retires into the regions opposed to the rays of the sun, since it is by nature only the shadow of the earth. Because, in the same way that, during the day, shadow is produced by a body which intercepts the light, night comes naturally when the air which surrounds the earth is in shadow. And this is precisely what Scripture says, " God divided the light from the darkness." Thus darkness fled at the approach of light, the two being at their first creation divided by a natural antipathy. Now God commanded the sun to measure the day, and the moon, whenever she rounds her disc, to rule the night. For then these two luminaries are almost diametrically opposed ; when the sun

[1] φαῦσις, the act of giving light, LXX.
[2] φωτισμός, the condition produced by φαῦσις.
[3] cf. Phil. ii. 15.   [4] Ps. xxix. 7.

rises, the full moon disappears from the horizon, to re-appear in the east at the moment the sun sets. It matters little to our subject if in other phases the light of the moon does not correspond exactly with night. It is none the less true, that when at its perfection it makes the stars to turn pale and lightens up the earth with the splendour of its light, it reigns over the night, and in concert with the sun divides the duration of it in equal parts.

4. "*And let them be for signs, and for seasons, and for days and years.*"[1] The signs which the luminaries give are necessary to human life. In fact what useful observations will long experience make us discover, if we ask without undue curiosity! What signs of rain, of drought, or of the rising of the wind, partial or general, violent or moderate! Our Lord indicates to us one of the signs given by the sun when He says, "It will be foul weather to-day; for the sky is red and lowering."[2] In fact, when the sun rises through a fog, its rays are darkened, but the disc appears burning like a coal and of a bloody red colour. It is the thickness of the air which causes this appearance; as the rays of the sun do not disperse such amassed and condensed air, it cannot certainly be retained by the waves of vapour which exhale from the earth, and it will cause from superabundance of moisture a storm in the countries over which it accumulates. In the same way, when the moon is surrounded with moisture, or when the sun is encircled with what is called a halo, it is the sign of heavy rain or of a violent storm; again, in the same way, if mock suns accompany the sun in its course they foretell certain celestial phenomena. Finally, those straight lines, like the colours of the rainbow, which are seen on the clouds, announce rain, extraordinary tempests, or, in one word, a complete change in the weather.

Those who devote themselves to the observation of these bodies find signs in the different phases of the moon, as if the air, by which the earth is enveloped, were obliged to vary to correspond with its change of form. Towards the third day of the new moon, if it is sharp and clear, it is a sign of fixed fine weather. If its horns appear thick and reddish it threatens us either with heavy rain or with a gale from the South.[3] Who does not know how useful[4] are these signs in

life? Thanks to them, the sailor keeps back his vessel in the harbour, foreseeing the perils with which the winds threaten him, and the traveller beforehand takes shelter from harm, waiting until the weather has become fairer. Thanks to them, husbandmen, busy with sowing seed or cultivating plants, are able to know which seasons are favourable to their labours. Further, the Lord has announced to us that at the dissolution of the universe, signs will appear in the sun, in the moon and in the stars. The sun shall be turned into blood and the moon shall not give her light,[1] signs of the consummation of all things.

5. But those who overstep the borders,[2] making the words of Scripture their apology for the art of casting nativities, pretend that our lives depend upon the motion of the heavenly bodies, and that thus the Chaldæans read in the planets that which will happen to us.[3] By these very simple words "let them be for signs," they understand neither the variations of the weather, nor the change of seasons; they only see in them, at the will of their imagination, the distribution of human destinies. What do they say in reality? When the planets cross in the signs of the Zodiac, certain figures formed by their meeting give birth to certain destinies, and others produce different destinies.

Perhaps for clearness sake it is not useless to enter into more detail about this vain science. I will say nothing of my own to refute them; I will use their words, bringing a remedy for the infected, and for others a preservative from falling. The inventors of astrology seeing that in the extent of time many signs escaped them, divided it and enclosed each part in narrow limits, as if in the least and shortest interval, in a moment, in the twinkling of an eye,[4] to speak with the Apostle, the greatest difference should be found between one birth and another. Such an one is born in this moment; he will be a prince over cities and will govern the people,

---

[1] Gen. i. 14.   [2] St. Matt. xvi. 3.

[3] πάντη γὰρ καθαρῇ κε μάλ' εὐδια τεκμήραιο, πάντα δ' ἐρευθομένη δοκέειν ἀνέμοιο κελεύθους, ἀλλοθι δ' ἄλλο μελαινομένη δοκέειν ὕετοιο. Aratus 70.   [4] cf. Verg., *Georg.* i. 424:
Si vero solem ad rapidum lunasque sequentes
Ordine respicies, nunquam te crastina fallet
Hora, neque insidiis noctis capiere serenæ.

[1] Basil seems to be confusing Joel ii. 31 and Matt. xxiv. 29.

[2] ὑπὲρ τὰ ἐσκαμμένα πηδᾶν is a proverbial phrase for going beyond bounds. *cf.* Lucian., *Gall.* vi. and Plat., *Crat.* 413, a.

[3] "*On doit d'autant plus louer le grand sens de Saint Basile qui s'inspire presqu' entièrement d'Origène et de Plotin, sans tomber dans leur erreur. En riant toute espèce de relation entre les astres et les actes de l'homme, il conserve intacte notre liberté.*" Fialon, p. 425. "*Quale deinde judicium de hominum factis Deo relinquitur, quibus cælestis necessitas adhibetur quum Dominus ille sit et siderum et hominum. Aut si non dicunt stellas accepta quidam potestate a summo Deo, arbitrio suo ista decernere, sed in talibus necessitatibus ingerendis illius omnino jussa complere, ita ne de ipso Deo sentiendum est, quod indignissimum visum est de stellarum voluntate sentire. Quod si dicuntur stellæ significare potius ista quam facere, ut quasi locutio sit quædam illa positio prædicens futura, non agens (non enim mediocriter doctorum hominum fuit ista sententia) non quidem ita solent loqui mathematici, ut verbi gratia dicunt, Mars ita positus homicidam significat, sed homicidam non facit.*" August., *De C. Dei.* v. i.

[4] 1 Cor. xv. 52.

in the fulness of riches and power. Another is born the instant after; he will be poor, miserable, and will wander daily from door to door begging his bread. Consequently they divide the Zodiac into twelve parts, and, as the sun takes thirty days to traverse each of the twelve divisions of this unerring circle, they divide them into thirty more. Each of them forms sixty new ones, and these last are again divided into sixty. Let us see then if, in determining the birth of an infant, it will be possible to observe this rigorous division of time. The child is born. The nurse ascertains the sex; then she awaits the wail which is a sign of its life. Until then how many moments have passed do you think? The nurse announces the birth of the child to the Chaldæan: how many minutes would you count before she opens her mouth, especially if he who records the hour is outside the women's apartments? And we know that he who consults the dial, ought, whether by day or by night, to mark the hour with the most precise exactitude. What a swarm of seconds passes during this time! For the planet of nativity ought to be found, not only in one of the twelve divisions of the Zodiac, and even in one of its first sub-divisions, but again in one of the sixtieth parts which divide this last, and even, to arrive at the exact truth, in one of the sixtieth sub-divisions that this contains in its turn. And, to obtain such minute knowledge, so impossible to grasp from this moment, each planet must be questioned to find its position as regards the signs of the Zodiac and the figures that the planets form at the moment of the child's birth. Thus, if it is impossible to find exactly the hour of birth, and if the least change can upset all, then both those who give themselves up to this imaginary science and those who listen to them open-mouthed, as if they could learn from them the future, are supremely ridiculous.

6. But what effects are produced? Such an one will have curly hair and bright eyes, because he is born under the Ram; such is the appearance of a ram. He will have noble feelings; because the Ram is born to command. He will be liberal and fertile in resources, because this animal gets rid of its fleece without trouble, and nature immediately hastens to reclothe it. Another is born under the Bull: he will be enured to hardship and of a slavish character, because the bull bows under the yoke. Another is born under the Scorpion; like to this venomous reptile he will be a striker. He who is born under the Balance will be just, thanks to the justness of our balances. Is not this the height of folly? This Ram, from whence you draw the nativity of man, is the twelfth part of the heaven, and in entering into it the sun reaches the spring. The Balance and the Bull are likewise twelfth parts of the Zodiac. How can you see there the principal causes which influence the life of man? And why do you take animals to characterize the manners of men who enter this world? He who is born under the Ram will be liberal, not because this part of heaven gives this characteristic, but because such is the nature of the beast. Why then should we frighten ourselves by the names of these stars and undertake to persuade ourselves with these bleatings? If heaven has different characteristics derived from these animals, it is then itself subject to external influences since its causes depend on the brutes who graze in our fields. A ridiculous assertion; but how much more ridiculous the pretence of arriving at the influence on each other of things which have not the least connexion! This pretended science is a true spider's web; if a gnat or a fly, or some insect equally feeble falls into it it is held entangled; if a stronger animal approaches, it passes through without trouble, carrying the weak tissue away with it.[1]

7. They do not, however, stop here; even our acts, where each one feels his will ruling, I mean, the practice of virtue or of vice, depend, according to them, on the influence of celestial bodies. It would be ridiculous seriously to refute such an error, but, as it holds a great many in its nets, perhaps it is better not to pass it over in silence. I would first ask them if the figures which the stars describe do not change a thousand times a day. In the perpetual motion of planets, some meet in a more rapid course, others make slower revolutions, and often in an hour we see them look at each other and then hide themselves. Now, at the hour of birth, it is very important whether one is looked upon by a beneficent star or by an evil one, to speak their language. Often then the astrologers do not seize the moment when a good star shows itself, and, on account of having let this fugitive moment escape, they enrol the new-born under the influence of a bad genius. I am compelled to use their own words. What madness! But, above all, what impiety! For the evil stars throw the blame of their wickedness upon Him Who made them. If evil is inherent in their nature, the

1 Ἔλεγε δὲ . . . τοὺς νόμους τοῖς ἀραχνίοις ὁμοίους · καὶ γὰρ ἐκεῖνα ἐὰν μὲν ἐμπέσῃ τι κοῦφον καὶ ἀσθενὲς στέγειν, ἐὰν δὲ μεῖζον, διακόψαν οἴχεσθαι. Solon, in Diog. Laert. ii. 1.

Creator is the author of evil. If they make it themselves, they are animals endowed with the power of choice, whose acts will be free and voluntary. Is it not the height of folly to tell these lies about beings without souls? Again, what a want of sense does it show to distribute good and evil without regard to personal merit; to say that a star is beneficent because it occupies a certain place; that it becomes evil, because it is viewed by another star; and that if it moves ever so little from this figure it loses its malign influence.

But let us pass on. If, at every instant of duration, the stars vary their figures, then in these thousand changes, many times a day, there ought to be reproduced the configuration of royal births. Why then does not every day see the birth of a king? Why is there a succession on the throne from father to son? Without doubt there has never been a king who has taken measures to have his son born under the star of royalty. For what man possesses such a power? How then did Uzziah beget Jotham, Jotham Ahaz, Ahaz Hezekiah? And by what chance did the birth of none of them happen in an hour of slavery? If the origin of our virtues and of our vices is not in ourselves, but is the fatal consequence of our birth, it is useless for legislators to prescribe for us what we ought to do, and what we ought to avoid; it is useless for judges to honour virtue and to punish vice. The guilt is not in the robber, not in the assassin: it was willed for him; it was impossible for him to hold back his hand, urged to evil by inevitable necessity. Those who laboriously cultivate the arts are the maddest of men. The labourer will make an abundant harvest without sowing seed and without sharpening his sickle. Whether he wishes it or not, the merchant will make his fortune, and will be flooded with riches by fate. As for us Christians, we shall see our great hopes vanish, since from the moment that man does not act with freedom, there is neither reward for justice, nor punishment for sin. Under the reign of necessity and of fatality there is no place for merit, the first condition of all righteous judgment. But let us stop. You who are sound in yourselves have no need to hear more, and time does not allow us to make attacks without limit against these unhappy men.

8. Let us return to the words which follow. "Let them be for signs and for seasons and for days and years."[1] We have

spoken about signs. By times, we understand the succession of seasons, winter, spring, summer and autumn, which we see follow each other in so regular a course, thanks to the regularity of the movement of the luminaries. It is winter when the sun sojourns in the south and produces in abundance the shades of night in our region. The air spread over the earth is chilly, and the damp exhalations, which gather over our heads, give rise to rains, to frosts, to innumerable flakes of snow. When, returning from the southern regions, the sun is in the middle of the heavens and divides day and night into equal parts, the more it sojourns above the earth the more it brings back a mild temperature to us. Then comes spring, which makes all the plants germinate, and gives to the greater part of the trees their new life, and, by successive generation, perpetuates all the land and water animals. From thence the sun, returning to the summer solstice, in the direction of the North, gives us the longest days. And, as it travels farther in the air, it burns that which is over our heads, dries up the earth, ripens the grains and hastens the maturity of the fruits of the trees. At the epoch of its greatest heat, the shadows which the sun makes at mid-day are short, because it shines from above, from the air over our heads. Thus the longest days are those when the shadows are shortest, in the same way that the shortest days are those when the shadows are longest. It is this which happens to all of us " Hetero-skii "[1] (shadowed-on-one-side) who inhabit the northern regions of the earth. But there are people who, two days in the year, are completely without shade at mid-day, because the sun, being perpendicularly over their heads, lights them so equally from all sides, that it could through a narrow opening shine at the bottom of a well. Thus there are some who call them " askii " (shadowless). For those who live beyond the land of spices[2] see their shadow now on one side, now on another, the only inhabitants of this land of which the shade falls at mid-day; thus they are given the name of " amphiskii,"[3] (shadowed-on-both-

---

[1] *i.e.* throwing a shadow only one way at noon,— said of those who live north and south of the tropics, while those who live in the tropics cast a shadow sometimes north, sometimes south, *vide* Strabo ii. 5, § 43. It was "incredible" to Herodotus that Necho's Phœnician mariners, in their circumnavigation of Africa, had "the sun on their right hand." Her. iv. 42.

[2] *i.e.* Arabia. *cf.* Lucan., *Phars.* iii. 247:

Ignotum vobis Arabes venistis in orbem,
Umbras mirati nemorum non ire sinistras.

[3] " *Simili modo tradunt in Syene oppido, quod est super Alexandriam quinque millibus stadiorum, solstitii die medio nullam umbram jaci; puteumque ejus experimenti gratia*

sides). All these phenomena happen whilst the sun is passing into northern regions: they give us an idea of the heat thrown on the air, by the rays of the sun and of the effects that they produce. Next we pass to autumn, which breaks up the excessive heat, lessening the warmth little by little, and by a moderate temperature brings us back without suffering to winter, to the time when the sun returns from the northern regions to the southern. It is thus that seasons, following the course of the sun, succeed each other to rule our life.

"Let them be for days"[1] says Scripture, not to produce them but to rule them; because day and night are older than the creation of the luminaries and it is this that the psalm declares to us. "The sun to rule by day . . . the moon and stars to rule by night."[2] How does the sun rule by day? Because carrying everywhere light with it, it is no sooner risen above the horizon than it drives away darkness and brings us day. Thus we might, without self deception, define day as air lighted by the sun, or as the space of time that the sun passes in our hemisphere. The functions of the sun and moon serve further to mark years. The moon, after having twelve times run her course, forms a year which sometimes needs an intercalary month to make it exactly agree with the seasons. Such was formerly the year of the Hebrews and of the early Greeks.[3] As to the solar year, it is the time that the sun, having started from a certain sign, takes to return to it in its normal progress.

9. "*And God made two great lights.*"[4] The word "great," if, for example we say it of the heaven of the earth or of the sea, may have an absolute sense; but ordinarily it has only a relative meaning, as a great horse, or a great ox. It is not that these animals are of an immoderate size, but that in comparison with their like they deserve the title of great. What idea shall we ourselves form here of greatness? Shall it be the idea that we have of it in the ant and in all the little creatures of nature, which we call great in comparison with those like themselves, and to show their superiority over them? Or shall we predicate greatness of the luminaries, as of the natural greatness inherent in them? As for me, I think so. If the sun and moon are great, it is not in comparison

with the smaller stars, but because they have such a circumference that the splendour which they diffuse lights up the heavens and the air, embracing at the same time earth and sea. In whatever part of heaven they may be, whether rising, or setting, or in mid heaven, they appear always the same in the eyes of men, a manifest proof of their prodigious size. For the whole extent of heaven cannot make them appear greater in one place and smaller in another. Objects which we see afar off appear dwarfed to our eyes, and in measure as they approach us we can form a juster idea of their size. But there is no one who can be nearer or more distant from the sun. All the inhabitants of the earth see it at the same distance. Indians and Britons see it of the same size. The people of the East do not see it decrease in magnitude when it sets; those of the West do not find it smaller when it rises. If it is in the middle of the heavens it does not vary in either aspect. Do not be deceived by mere appearance, and because it looks a cubit's breadth, imagine it to be no bigger.[1] At a very great distance objects always lose size in our eyes; sight, not being able to clear the intermediary space, is as it were exhausted in the middle of its course, and only a small part of it reaches the visible object.[2] Our power of sight is small and makes all we see seem small, affecting what it sees by its own condition. Thus, then, if sight is mistaken its testimony is fallible. Recall your own impressions and you will find in yourself the proof of my words. If you have ever from the top of a high mountain looked at a large and level plain, how big did the yokes of oxen appear to you? How big were the ploughmen themselves? Did they not look like ants?[3] If from the top of a commanding rock, looking over the wide sea, you cast your eyes over the vast extent how big did the greatest islands appear to

---

factum, totum illuminari." Pliny ii. 75. *cf.* Lucan., *Phars.* 507, "atque umbras nunquam flectente Syene."
[1] Gen. i. 14.   [2] Ps. cxxxvi. 8, 9.
[3] The Syrians and Macedonians had also an intercalary thirteenth month to accommodate the lunar to the solar cycle. Solon is credited with the introduction of the system into Greece about 594 B.C. But the Julian calendar improved upon this mode of adjustment.
[4] Gen. i. 16.

[1] "*Tertia ex utroque vastitas solis aperitur, ut non sit necesse amplitudinem ejus oculorum argumentis, atque conjectura animi scrutari: immensum esse quia arborum in limitibus porrectarum in quotlibet passuum millia umbras paribus jaciat intervallis, tanquam toto spatio medius: et quia per æquinoctium omnibus in meridiana plaga habitantibus, simul fiat a vertice: ita quia circa solstitialem circulum habitantium meridie ad Septemtrionem umbræ cadant, ortu vero ad occasum. Quæ fieri nullo modo possent nisi multo quam terra major esset.*" Plin. ii. 8.
[2] Πλάτων κατὰ συναύγειαν, τοῦ μὲν ἐκ τῶν ὀφθαλμῶν φωτὸς ἐπὶ ποσὸν ἀπορρέοντος εἰς τὸν ὁμογενῆ ἀέρα, τοῦ δὲ ἀπὸ τοῦ σώματος φερομένου ἀπορρεῖν· τὸν δὲ μεταξὺ ἀέρα εὐδιάχυτον ὄντα καὶ εὔτρεπτον, συνεκτεινοντος τῷ πυρώδει τῆς ὄψεως, αὕτη, λέγεται πλατωνικὴ συναύγεια. Plut. περὶ τῶν ἀρεσκ. iv. 13. The Platonic theory of sight is explained in the *Timæus*, Chap. xix.
[3] Plato (*Phæd.* § 133) makes the same comparison. Ἔτι τοίνυν, ἔφη, πάμμεγά τι εἶναι αὐτό, καὶ ἡμᾶς οἰκεῖν τοὺς μέχρι Ἡρακλείων στηλῶν ἀπὸ Φάσιδος ἐν σμικρῷ τινι μορίῳ, ὥσπερ περὶ τέλμα μύρμηκας ἢ βατράχους περὶ τὴν θάλατταν οἰκοῦντας. Fialon names Seneca (*Quæst. Nat.* i. præf. 505) and Lucian (Hermotimus v. and Icaromenippus xix.) as following him. To these may be added Celsus "καταγελῶν τὸ Ἰουδαίων καὶ Χριστιανῶν γένος" in Origen, *C. Cels.* iv. 517, B.

you? How large did one of those barks of great tonnage, which unfurl their white sails to the blue sea, appear to you. Did it not look smaller than a dove? It is because sight, as I have just told you, loses itself in the air, becomes weak and cannot seize with exactness the object which it sees. And further : your sight shows you high mountains intersected by valleys as rounded and smooth, because it reaches only to the salient parts, and is not able, on account of its weakness, to penetrate into the valleys which separate them. It does not even preserve the form of objects, and thinks that all square towers are round. Thus all proves that at a great distance sight only presents to us obscure and confused objects. The luminary is then great, according to the witness of Scripture, and infinitely greater than it appears.

10. See again another evident proof of its greatness. Although the heaven may be full of stars without number, the light contributed by them all could not disperse the gloom of night. The sun alone, from the time that it appeared on the horizon, while it was still expected and had not yet risen completely above the earth, dispersed the darkness, outshone the stars, dissolved and diffused the air, which was hitherto thick and condensed over our heads, and produced thus the morning breeze and the dew which in fine weather streams over the earth. Could the earth with such a wide extent be lighted up entirely in one moment if an immense disc were not pouring forth its light over it? Recognise here the wisdom of the Artificer. See how He made the heat of the sun proportionate to this distance. Its heat is so regulated that it neither consumes the earth by excess, nor lets it grow cold and sterile by defect.

To all this the properties of the moon are near akin; she, too, has an immense body, whose splendour only yields to that of the sun. Our eyes, however, do not always see her in her full size. Now she presents a perfectly rounded disc, now when diminished and lessened she shows a deficiency on one side. When waxing she is shadowed on one side, and when she is waning another side is hidden. Now it is not without a secret reason of the divine Maker of the universe, that the moon appears from time to time under such different forms. It presents a striking example of our nature. Nothing is stable in man ; here from nothingness he raises himself to perfection ; there after having hasted to put forth his strength to attain his full greatness he suddenly is subject to gradual deterioration, and is destroyed by diminution. Thus, the sight of the moon, making us think of the

rapid vicissitudes of human things, ought to teach us not to pride ourselves on the good things of this life, and not to glory in our power, not to be carried away by uncertain riches, to despise our flesh which is subject to change, and to take care of the soul, for its good is unmoved. If you cannot behold without sadness the moon losing its splendour by gradual and imperceptible decrease, how much more distressed should you be at the sight of a soul, who, after having possessed virtue, loses its beauty by neglect, and does not remain constant to its affections, but is agitated and constantly changes because its purposes are unstable. What Scripture says is very true, " As for a fool he changeth as the moon." [1]

I believe also that the variations of the moon do not take place without exerting great influence upon the organization of animals and of all living things. This is because bodies are differently disposed at its waxing and waning. When she wanes they lose their density and become void. When she waxes and is approaching her fulness they appear to fill themselves at the same time with her, thanks to an imperceptible moisture that she emits mixed with heat, which penetrates everywhere. [2] For proof, see how those who sleep under the moon feel abundant moisture filling their heads ; [3] see how fresh meat is quickly turned under the action of the moon ; [4] see the brain of animals, the moistest part of marine animals, the pith of trees. Evidently the moon must be, as Scripture says, of enormous size and power to make all nature thus participate in her changes.

11. On its variations depends also the condition of the air, as is proved by sudden dis-

---

[1] Ecclus. xxvii. 11.

[2] cf. Alcman (ap. Plut., Sympos. iii. 10), who calls the dew Διὸς θυγάτηρ καὶ Σελάνας ; and Plutarch himself in loc. Virg., Georg. iii. 337, " Roscida Luna," and Statius, Theb. i. 336 :
" Iamque per emeriti surgens confinia Phœbi
Titanis, late mundo subvecta silenti
Rorifera gelidum tenuaverat aera biga."

[3] The baleful influence of " iracunda Diana" (Hor., De Art. Poet. 454) is an early belief, not yet extinct. cf. the term σεληνιασμός for epilepsy, and " lunaticus " for the " moonstruck " madman. Vide Cass., Quæst. Med. xxv. 1. Perowne on Ps. cxxi. 6 notes, " De Wette refers to Andersen's Eastern Travels in proof that this opinion is commonly entertained. Delitzsch mentions having heard from Texas that the consequence of sleeping in the open air, when the moon was shining, was mental aberration, dizziness, and even death."
" Dass auch der Mond in heller Nacht dem ohne gehörigen Schutz Schlafenden schaden könne ist allgemeine Meinung des Orients und der köhlen Nächte wegen leicht möglich. Vgl. Carne 'Leben und Sitten im Morgenl.'" Ewald, Dichter des A.B. ii. 266.

[4] A fact, however explained. Plutarch (Sympos. Prob. iii. 10) discusses the question Διὰ τί τὰ κρέα σήπεται μᾶλλον ὑπὸ τὴν σελήνην ἢ τὸν ἥλιον, and refers the decomposition to the moistening influence of the moon. " Air, moisture, and a certain degree of warmth, are necessary to the decay of animal bodies . . . where moisture continues present—even though warmth and air be in a great measure excluded—decay still slowly takes place." J. F. W. Johnston, Chemistry of Common Life, ii. 273.

turbances which often come after the new moon, in the midst of a calm and of a stillness in the winds, to agitate the clouds and to hurl them against each other ; as the flux and reflux in straits, and the ebb and flow of the ocean prove, so that those who live on its shores see it regularly following the revolutions of the moon. The waters of straits approach and retreat from one shore to the other during the different phases of the moon ; but, when she is new, they have not an instant of rest, and move in perpetual swaying to and fro, until the moon, reappearing, regulates their reflux. As to the Western sea,[1] we see it in its ebb and flow now return into its bed, and now overflow, as the moon draws it back by her respiration and then, by her expiration, urges it to its own boundaries.[2]

I have entered into these details, to show you the grandeur of the luminaries, and to make you see that, in the inspired words, there is not one idle syllable. And yet my sermon has scarcely touched on any important point ; there are many other discoveries about the size and distance of the sun and moon to which any one who will make a serious study of their action and of their characteristics may arrive by the aid of reason. Let me then ingenuously make an avowal of my weakness, for fear that you should measure the mighty works of the Creator by my words. The little that I have said ought the rather to make you conjecture the marvels on which I have omitted to dwell. We must not then measure the moon with the eye, but with the reason. Reason, for the discovery of truth, is much surer than the eye.

Everywhere ridiculous old women's tales, imagined in the delirium of drunkenness, have been circulated ; such as that enchantments can remove the moon from its place and make it descend to the earth. How could a magician's charm shake that of which the Most High has laid the foundations? And if once torn out what place could hold it?[3]

Do you wish from slight indications to have a proof of the moon's size? All the towns in the world, however distant from each other,

equally receive the light from the moon in those streets that are turned towards its rising If she did not look on all face to face, those only would be entirely lighted up which were exactly opposite ; as to those beyond the extremities of her disc, they would only receive diverted and oblique rays. It is this effect which the light of lamps produces in houses ; if a lamp is surrounded by several persons, only the shadow of the person who is directly opposite to it is cast in a straight line, the others follow inclined lines on each side. In the same way, if the body of the moon were not of an immense and prodigious size she could not extend herself alike to all. In reality, when the moon rises in the equinoctial regions, all equally enjoy her light, both those who inhabit the icy zone, under the revolutions of the Bear, and those who dwell in the extreme south in the neighbourhood of the torrid zone. She gives us an idea of her size by appearing to be face to face with all people. Who then can deny the immensity of a body which divides itself equally over such a wide extent?

But enough on the greatness of the sun and moon. May He who has given us intelligence to recognise in the smallest objects of creation the great wisdom of the Contriver make us find in great bodies a still higher idea of their Creator. However, compared with their Author, the sun and moon are but a fly and an ant. The whole universe cannot give us a right idea of the greatness of God ; and it is only by signs, weak and slight in themselves, often by the help of the smallest insects and of the least plants, that we raise ourselves to Him. Content with these words let us offer our thanks, I to Him who has given me the ministry of the Word, you to Him who feeds you with spiritual food ; Who, even at this moment, makes you find in my weak voice the strength of barley bread. May He feed you for ever, and in proportion to your faith grant you the manifestation of the Spirit[1] in Jesus Christ our Lord, to whom be glory and power for ever and ever. Amen.

HOMILY VII.

The creation of moving creatures.[2]

1. " *And God said, Let the waters bring forth abundantly the moving creature that hath life*" after their kind, " *and fowl that may fly above the earth*" *after their kind.*[3] After the creation of the luminaries the waters are now filled with living beings and

---

[1] *i.e.* the Atlantic. *cf.* Ovid., *Met.* xi. 258, "*Hesperium fretum.*"
[2] Pytheas, of Marseilles, is first named as attributing the tides to the moon. Plut. περὶ ἀρεσκ. κ.τ.λ. iii. 17. On the ancient belief generally *vide* Plin. ii. 99.
[3] "*Inventa jam pridem ratio est prænuntians horas, non modo dies ac noctes, Solis Lunæque defectuum. Durat tamen tradita persuasio in magna parte vulgi, veneficiis et herbis id cogi, eamque num fæminarum scientiam prævalere.*" Plin. xxv. v. So it was a custom to avert the spells of sorceresses, which might bring the eclipsed moon to the ground, by beating brass and shouting. *cf.* Juv., *Sat.* vi. 443,
"*Tam nemo tubas, nemo æra fatigat,
Una laboranti poterit succurrere lunæ,*"
and the "*æra auxiliaria lunæ*" of Ov., *Met.* iv. 333.

[1] *cf.* 1 Cor. xii. 7. [3] Gen. i. 20.
[2] LXX. creeping things.

its own adornment is given to this part of the world. Earth had received hers from her own plants, the heavens had received the flowers of the stars, and, like two eyes, the great luminaries beautified them in concert. It still remained for the waters to receive their adornment. The command was given, and immediately the rivers and lakes becoming fruitful brought forth their natural broods; the sea travailed with all kinds of swimming creatures; not even in mud and marshes did the water remain idle; it took its part in creation. Everywhere from its ebullition frogs, gnats and flies came forth. For that which we see to-day is the sign of the past. Thus everywhere the water hastened to obey the Creator's command. Who could count the species which the great and ineffable power of God caused to be suddenly seen living and moving, when this command had empowered the waters to bring forth life? Let the waters bring forth moving creatures that have life. Then for the first time is made a being with life and feeling. For though plants and trees be said to live, seeing that they share the power of being nourished and growing; nevertheless they are neither living beings, nor have they life.[1] To create these last God said, "Let the water produce moving creatures."

Every creature that swims, whether it skims on the surface of the waters, or cleaves the depths, is of the nature of a moving creature,[2] since it drags itself on the body of the water. Certain aquatic animals have feet and walk; especially amphibia, such as seals, crabs, crocodiles, river horses[3] and frogs; but they are above all gifted with the power of swimming. Thus it is said, Let the waters produce moving creatures. In these few words what species is omitted? Which is not included in the command of the Creator? Do we not see viviparous animals, seals, dolphins, rays and all cartilaginous animals? Do we not see oviparous animals comprising every sort of fish, those which have a skin and those which have scales, those which have fins and those which have not? This command has only required one word, even less than a word, a sign, a motion of the divine will, and it has such a wide sense that it includes all the varieties and all the families of fish. To review them all would be to undertake to count the waves of the ocean or to measure its waters in the hollow of the hand. "Let the waters pro-

duce moving creatures." That is to say, those which people the high seas and those which love the shores; those which inhabit the depths and those which attach themselves to rocks; those which are gregarious and those which live dispersed, the cetaceous, the huge, and the tiny. It is from the same power, the same command, that all, small and great receive their existence. "Let the waters bring forth." These words show you the natural affinity of animals which swim in the water; thus, fish, when drawn out of the water, quickly die, because they have no respiration such as could attract our air and water is their element, as air is that of terrestrial animals. The reason for it is clear. With us the lung, that porous and spongy portion of the inward parts which receives air by the dilatation of the chest, disperses and cools interior warmth; in fish the motion of the gills, which open and shut by turns to take in and to eject the water, takes the place of respiration.[1] Fish have a peculiar lot, a special nature, a nourishment of their own, a life apart. Thus they cannot be tamed and cannot bear the touch of a man's hand.[2]

2. "Let the waters bring forth moving creatures after their kind." God caused to be born the firstlings of each species to serve as seeds for nature. Their multitudinous numbers are kept up in subsequent succession, when it is necessary for them to grow and multiply. Of another kind is the species of testacea, as muscles, scallops, sea snails, conches, and the infinite variety of oysters. Another kind is that of the crustacea, as crabs and lobsters; another of fish without shells, with soft and tender flesh, like polypi and cuttle fish. And amidst these last what an innumerable variety! There are weevers, lampreys and eels, produced in the mud of rivers and ponds, which more resemble venomous reptiles than fish in their nature. Of another kind is the species of the ovipara; of another, that of the vivipara. Among the latter are sword-fish, cod, in one word, all cartilaginous fish, and even the greater part of the cetacea, as dolphins, seals, which, it is said, if they see their little ones,

---

[1] Plants are neither ζῶα nor ἔμψυχα.

[2] LXX. creeping.

[3] Basil uses the classical Greek form οἱ ποτάμιοι ἵπποι, as in Herod. and Arist. The dog-Greek hippopotamus, properly a horse-river, is first found in Galen.

---

[1] cf. Arist., De Part. Anim. iii. 6. διόπερ τῶν μὲν ἰχθύων οὐδεὶς ἔχει πνεύμονα ἀλλ᾽ ἀντὶ τούτου βράγχια καθάπερ εἴρηται ἐν τοῖς περὶ ἀναπνοῆς· ὕδατι γὰρ ποιεῖται τὴν κατάψυξιν, τὰ δ᾽ ἀναπνέοντα ἔχει πνεύμονα ἀναπνεῖ δὲ τὰ πεζὰ πάντα.

[2] Here Basil is curiously in contradiction to ancient as well as modern experience. Martial's epigram on Domitian's tame fish, "qui norunt dominum, manumque lambunt illam qua nihil est in orbe majus" (iv. 30), is illustrated by the same author's "natat ad magistrum delicata muræna" (x. 30), as well as by Ælian (De animal. viii.4). "Apud Baulos in parte Baiana piscinam habuit Hortensius orator, in qua murænam adeo dilexit ut exanimatam flesse credatur: in eadem villa Antonia Drusi muræna quam diligebat inaures addidit." Plin. ix. 71. So Lucian οὗτοι δε (ἰχθύες) καὶ ὀνόματα ἔχουσι καὶ ἔρχονται καλούμενοι. (De Syr. Dea. 45.) John Evelyn (Diary 1644) writes of Fontainebleau: "The carps come familiarly to hand." There was recently a tame carp at Azay le Rideau.

still quite young, frightened, take them back into their belly to protect them.[1]

Let the waters bring forth after their kind. The species of the cetacean is one; another is that of small fish. What infinite variety in the different kinds! All have their own names, different food, different form, shape, and quality of flesh. All present infinite variety, and are divided into innumerable classes. Is there a tunny fisher who can enumerate to us the different varieties of that fish? And yet they tell us that at the sight of great swarms of fish they can almost tell the number of the individual ones which compose it. What man is there of all that have spent their long lives by coasts and shores, who can inform us with exactness of the history of all fish?

Some are known to the fishermen of the Indian ocean, others to the toilers of the Egyptian gulf, others to the islanders, others to the men of Mauretania.[2] Great and small were all alike created by this first command, by this ineffable power. What a difference in their food! What a variety in the manner in which each species reproduces itself! Most fish do not hatch eggs like birds; they do not build nests; they do not feed their young with toil; it is the water which receives and vivifies the egg dropped into it. With them the reproduction of each species is invariable, and natures are not mixed. There are none of those unions which, on the earth, produce mules and certain birds contrary to the nature of their species. With fish there is no variety which, like the ox and the sheep, is armed with a half-equipment of teeth, none which ruminates except, according to certain writers, the scar.[3] All have serried and very sharp teeth, for fear their food should escape them if they masticate it for too long a time. In fact, if it were not crushed and swallowed as soon as divided, it would be carried away by the water.

3. The food of fish differs according to their species. Some feed on mud; others eat sea weed; others content themselves with the herbs that grow in water. But the greater part devour each other, and the smaller is food for the larger, and if one which has possessed itself of a fish weaker than itself becomes a prey to another, the conqueror and the conquered are both swallowed up in the belly of the last. And we mortals, do we act otherwise when we oppress our inferiors?[1] What difference is there between the last fish and the man who, impelled by devouring greed, swallows the weak in the folds of his insatiable avarice? Yon fellow possessed the goods of the poor; you caught him and made him a part of your abundance. You have shown yourself more unjust than the unjust, and more miserly than the miser. Look to it lest you end like the fish, by hook, by weel, or by net. Surely we too, when we have done the deeds of the wicked, shall not escape punishment at the last.

Now see what tricks, what cunning, are to be found in a weak animal, and learn not to imitate wicked doers. The crab loves the flesh of the oyster; but, sheltered by its shell, a solid rampart with which nature has furnished its soft and delicate flesh, it is a difficult prey to seize. Thus they call the oyster " sherd-hide." [2] Thanks to the two shells with which it is enveloped, and which adapt themselves perfectly the one to the other, the claws of the crab are quite powerless. What does he do? When he sees it, sheltered from the wind, warming itself with pleasure, and half opening its shells to the sun,[3] he secretly throws in a pebble, prevents them from closing, and takes by cunning what force had lost.[4] Such is the malice of these animals, deprived as they are of reason and of speech. But I would that you should at once rival the crab in cunning and industry, and abstain from harming your neighbour; this animal is the image of him who craftily approaches his brother, takes advantage of his neighbour's misfortunes, and finds his delight in other men's troubles. O copy not the damned! Content yourself with your own lot. Poverty, with what is necessary, is of more value in the eyes of the wise than all pleasures.

I will not pass in silence the cunning and trickery of the squid, which takes the colour of the rock to which it attaches itself. Most fish swim idly up to the squid as they might to a rock, and become themselves the prey of the crafty creature.[5] Such are men who

---

[1] Narrated by Ælian (*Anim.* i. 16) of the "glaucus," a fish apparently unknown.
[2] Μαυρούσιοι. *cf.* Strabo, ii. 33.
[3] *e.g.* Arist., *De Anim.* viii. 2 and Ælian, ii. 54.

[1] *cf.* Pericles ii. i.
[3] *Fish.* Master, I marvel how the fishes live in the sea.
1 Fish. Why, as men do a-land; the great ones eat up the little ones. [2] ὀστρακόδερμος.
[3] Fialon quotes La Fontaine *Le Rat et l'Huître:*
Parmi tant d'huitres toutes closes,
Une s'était ouverte, et baillant au soleil,
Par un doux Zéphyr réjouie,
Humait l'air, respirait, était épanouie,
Blanche, grasse, et d'un goût, à la voir, sans pareil.
[4] Pliny ix. 48, says of the octopus : " imposito lapillo extra corpus ne palpitatu ejiciatur : ita securi grassantur, extrahuntque carnes."
[5] *cf.* Theog. 215:
πούλυπου ὀργὴν ἴσχε πολυπλόκου, ὃς ποτὶ πέτρῃ
τῇ προσομιλήσει τοῖος ἰδεῖν ἐφάνη.
Νῦν μὲν τῆς ἐφέπου, ποτὲ δ'ἀλλοῖος χρόα γίγνου,
κραιπνόν τοι σοφίη γίγνεται εὐτροπίης.

court ruling powers, bending themselves to all circumstances and not remaining for a moment in the same purpose; who praise self-restraint in the company of the self-restrained, and license in that of the licentious, accommodating their feelings to the pleasure of each. It is difficult to escape them and to put ourselves on guard against their mischief; because it is under the mask of friendship that they hide their clever wickedness. Men like this are ravening wolves covered with sheep's clothing, as the Lord calls them.[1] Flee then fickleness and pliability; seek truth, sincerity, simplicity. The serpent is shifty; so he has been condemned to crawl. The just is an honest man, like Job.[2] Wherefore God setteth the solitary in families.[3] So is this great and wide sea, wherein are things creeping innumerable, both small and great beasts.[4] Yet a wise and marvellous order reigns among these animals. Fish do not always deserve our reproaches; often they offer us useful examples. How is it that each sort of fish, content with the region that has been assigned to it, never travels over its own limits to pass into foreign seas? No surveyor has ever distributed to them their habitations, nor enclosed them in walls, nor assigned limits to them; each kind has been naturally assigned its own home. One gulf nourishes one kind of fish, another other sorts; those which swarm here are absent elsewhere. No mountain raises its sharp peaks between them; no rivers bar the passage to them; it is a law of nature, which according to the needs of each kind, has allotted to them their dwelling places with equality and justice.[5]

4. It is not thus with us. Why? Because we incessantly move the ancient landmarks which our fathers have set.[1] We encroach, we add house to house, field to field, to enrich ourselves at the expense of our neighbour. The great fish know the sojourning place that nature has assigned to them; they occupy the sea far from the haunts of men, where no islands lie, and where are no continents rising to confront them, because it has never been crossed and neither curiosity nor need has persuaded sailors to tempt it. The monsters that dwell in this sea are in size like high mountains, so witnesses who have seen tell us, and never cross their boundaries to ravage islands and seaboard towns. Thus each kind is as if it were stationed in towns, in villages, in an ancient country, and has for its dwelling place the regions of the sea which have been assigned to it.

Instances have, however, been known of migratory fish, who, as if common deliberation transported them into strange regions, all start on their march at a given sign. When the time marked for breeding arrives, they, as if awakened by a common law of nature, migrate from gulf to gulf, directing their course toward the North Sea. And at the epoch of their return you may see all these fish streaming like a torrent across the Propontis towards the Euxine Sea. Who puts them in marching array? Where is the prince's order? Has an edict affixed in the public place indicated to them their day of departure? Who serves them as a guide? See how the divine order embraces all and extends to the smallest object. A fish does not resist God's law, and we men cannot endure His precepts of salvation! Do not despise fish because they are dumb and quite unreasoning; rather fear lest, in your resistance to the disposition of the Creator, you have even less reason than they. Listen to the fish, who by their actions all but speak and say: it is for the perpetuation of our race that we undertake this long voyage.

Greg. Naz., *Or.* xxxvi.: πολλὰς μεταλαμβάνων χρόας ὥσπερ τὰ τῶν πετρῶν εἰ πολύποδες αἷς ἂν ὁμιλήσωσι, and Arist., *Hist. An.* ix. 37: καὶ θηρεύει τοὺς ἰχθῦς τὸ χρῶμα μεταβάλλων καὶ ποιῶν ὅμοιον οἷς δὴ πλησιάζῃ λίθοις.

[1] *cf.* Matt. vii. 15.

[2] So the *Cod. Colb.* and Eustathius, who renders *Justus nihil habet fictum sicut Job.* The Ben. Ed. suspect that Basil wrote Jacob and Job. Four MSS. support Jacob alone, who, whatever may be the meaning of the Hebrew in Gen. xxv. 27, is certainly ἄπλαστος only in the LXX., and a bad instance of guilelessness.

[3] Ps. lxviii. 6.   [4] Ps. civ. 25.

[5] *cf.* Cudworth, *Int. Syst.* iii. 37, 23: " Besides this plastick Nature which is in animals, forming their several bodies artificially, as so many microcosms or little worlds, there must also be a general plastick Nature in the macrocosm, the whole corporeal universe, that which makes all things thus to conspire everywhere, and agree together into one harmony. Concerning which plastick nature of the universe, the Author *De Mundo* writes after this manner, καὶ τὸν ὅλον κόσμον, διεκόσμησε μία ἡ διὰ πάντων διήκουσα δύναμις, one power, passing through all things, ordered and formed the whole world. Again he calls the same πνεῦμα καὶ ἔμψυχον καὶ γόνιμον οὐσίαν, a spirit, and a living and Generative Nature, and plainly declares it to be a thing distinct from the Deity, but subordinate to it and dependent on it. But Aristotle himself, in that genuine work of his before mentioned, speaks clearly and positively concerning this Plastick Nature of the Universe, as well as that of animals, in these words: 'It seemeth that as there is Art in Artificial things, so in the things of Nature, there is another such like Principle or Cause, which we ourselves partake of; in the same manner as we do of Heat and Cold, from the Universe. Wherefore it is more probable that the whole world was at first made by such a cause as this (if at least it were made) and that it is still conserved by the same, than that mortal animals should be so: for there is much more of order and determinate Regularity in the Heavenly Bodies than in ourselves; but more of Fortuitousness and inconstant Regularity among these mortal things. Notwithstanding which, some there are, who, though they cannot but acknowledge that the Bodies of Animals were all framed by an Artificial Nature, yet they will need contend that the System of the Heavens sprung merely from Fortune and Chance; although there be not the least appearance of Fortuitousness or Temerity in it.' And then he sums up all into this conclusion: ὥστε εἶναι φανερὸν ὅτι ἔστι τι τοιοῦτον ὃ δὴ καὶ καλοῦμεν φύσιν. 'Wherefore it is manifest that there is some such thing as that which we call Nature,' that is, that there is not only an 'Artificial,' 'Methodical,' and Plastick Nature in Animals, by which their respective Bodies are Framed and Conserved, but also that there is such a General Plastick Nature likewise in the Universe, by which the Heavens and whole World are thus Artificially Ordered and Disposed."

[1] *cf.* Prov. xxii. 28.

They have not the gift of reason, but they have the law of nature firmly seated within them, to show them what they have to do. Let us go, they say, to the North Sea. Its water is sweeter than that of the rest of the sea ; for the sun does not remain long there, and its rays do not draw up all the drinkable portions.[1] Even sea creatures love fresh water.[2] Thus one often sees them enter into rivers and swim far up them from the sea. This is the reason which makes them prefer the Euxine Sea to other gulfs, as the most fit for breeding and for bringing up their young. When they have obtained their object the whole tribe returns home. Let us hear these dumb creatures tell us the reason. The Northern sea, they say, is shallow and its surface is exposed to the violence of the wind, and it has few shores and retreats. Thus the winds easily agitate it to its bottom and mingle the sands of its bed with its waves. Besides, it is cold in winter, filled as it is from all directions by large rivers. Wherefore after a moderate enjoyment of its waters, during the summer, when the winter comes they hasten to reach warmer depths and places heated by the sun, and after fleeing from the stormy tracts of the North, they seek a haven in less agitated seas.

5. I myself have seen these marvels, and I have admired the wisdom of God in all things. If beings deprived of reason are capable of thinking and of providing for their own preservation ; if a fish knows what it ought to seek and what to shun, what shall we say, who are honoured with reason, instructed by law, encouraged by the promises, made wise by the Spirit, and are nevertheless less reasonable about our own affairs than the fish? They know how to provide for the future, but we renounce our hope of the future and spend our life in brutal indulgence. A fish traverses the extent of the sea to find what is good for it ; what will you say then— you who live in idleness, the mother of all vices?[3] Do not let any one make his ignorance an excuse. There has been implanted in us natural reason which tells us to identify ourselves with good, and to avoid all that is harmful. I need not go far from the sea to find examples, as that is the object of our researches. I have heard it said by one living near the sea, that the sea urchin, a little contemptible creature, often foretells calm and tempest to sailors. When it foresees a disturbance of the winds, it gets under

a great pebble, and clinging to it as to an anchor, it tosses about in safety, retained by the weight which prevents it from becoming the plaything of the waves.[1] It is a certain sign for sailors that they are threatened with a violent agitation of the winds. No astrologer, no Chaldæan, reading in the rising of the stars the disturbances of the air, has ever communicated his secret to the urchin : it is the Lord of the sea and of the winds who has impressed on this little animal a manifest proof of His great wisdom. God has foreseen all, He has neglected nothing. His eye, which never sleeps, watches over all.[2] He is present everywhere and gives to each being the means of preservation. If God has not left the sea urchin outside His providence, is He without care for you?

" *Husbands love your wives.*"[3] Although formed of two bodies you are united to live in the communion of wedlock. May this natural link, may this yoke imposed by the blessing, reunite those who are divided. The viper, the cruelest of reptiles, unites itself with the sea lamprey, and, announcing its presence by a hiss, it calls it from the depths to conjugal union. The lamprey obeys, and is united to this venomous animal.[4] What does this mean? However hard, however fierce a husband may be, the wife ought to bear with him, and not wish to find any pretext for breaking the union. He strikes you, but he is your husband. He is a drunkard, but he is united to you by nature. He is brutal and cross, but he is henceforth one of your members, and the most precious of all.

6. Let husbands listen as well : here is a lesson for them. The viper vomits forth its venom in respect for marriage ; and you, will you not put aside the barbarity and the inhumanity of your soul, out of respect for your union? Perhaps the example of the viper contains another meaning. The union of the viper and of the lamprey is an adulterous violation of nature. You, who are plotting against other men's wedlock, learn what creeping creature you are like. I have only one object, to make all I say turn to the edification of the Church. Let then liber-

---

1 " *Tradunt sævitiam maris præsagire eos, correptisque opperiri lapillis, mobilitatem pondere stabilientes : nolunt volutatione spinas atterere, quod ubi videre nautici, statim pluribus ancoris navigia infrænant.*" Plin. ix. 5. *cf.* Plut., *De Solert. An.* 979, Oppian, *Halieut.* ii. 225, and Ælian, *Hist. An.* vii. 33.
2 *cf.* Prov. xv. 3 : " The eyes of the Lord are in every place," and Ps. cxxi. 3. So Hesiod, πάντα ἰδῶν Διὸς ὀφθαλμὸς καὶ πάντα νοήσας. Hes. *Works und Days*, 265.
3 Eph. v. 25.
4 The fable is in Ælian, *Hist. An.* ix. 66, and is contradicted by Athenæus, who says (vii. p. 312) : Ἀνδρέας δὲ ἐν τῷ περὶ τῶν ψευδῶς πεπιστευμένων ψευδῶς φησιν εἶναι τὸ Μύραιναν ἔχει μίγνυσθαι προσερχομένην ἐπὶ τὸ τεναγῶδες, οὐδὲ γὰρ ἐπὶ τενάγους ἔχεις νέμεσθαι, φιληδοῦντας λιμώδεσιν ἐρημίαις. Σώστρατος δὲ ἐν τοῖς περὶ Ζώων συγκατατίθεται τῇ μίξει.

---

1 *cf.* Arist., *Hist. Animal.* viii. 12 and 13, and note on p. 70.
2 *cf.* Arist. and Theophrastus.
3 *Otiosa mater est nugarum noverca omnium virtutum.* St. Bernard.

tines put a restraint on their passions, for they are taught by the examples set by creatures of earth and sea.

My bodily infirmity and the lateness of the hour force me to end my discourse. However, I have still many observations to make on the products of the sea, for the admiration of my attentive audience. To speak of the sea itself, how does its water change into salt? How is it that coral, a stone so much esteemed, is a plant in the midst of the sea, and when once exposed to the air becomes hard as a rock? Why has nature enclosed in the meanest of animals, in an oyster, so precious an object as a pearl? For these pearls, which are coveted by the caskets of kings, are cast upon the shores, upon the coasts, upon sharp rocks, and enclosed in oyster shells. How can the sea pinna produce her fleece of gold, which no dye has ever imitated?[1] How can shells give kings purple of a brilliancy not surpassed by the flowers of the field?

"*Let the waters bring forth.*" What necessary object was there that did not immediately appear? What object of luxury was not given to man? Some to supply his needs, some to make him contemplate the marvels of creation. Some are terrible, so as to take our idleness to school. "God created great whales."[2] Scripture gives them the name of "great" not because they are greater than a shrimp and a sprat, but because the size of their bodies equals that of great hills. Thus when they swim on the surface of the waters one often sees them appear like islands. But these monstrous creatures do not frequent our coasts and shores; they inhabit the Atlantic ocean. Such are these animals created to strike us with terror and awe. If now you hear say that the greatest vessels, sailing with full sails, are easily stopped by a very small fish, by the remora, and so forcibly that the ship remains motionless for a long time, as if it had taken root in the middle of the sea,[3] do you not see in this little creature a like proof of the power of the Creator? Sword fish, saw

---

[1] The Pinna is a bivalve with a silky beard, of which several species are found in the Mediterranean. The beard is called by modern naturalists byssus. The shell of the giant pinna is sometimes two feet long.
[2] Gen. i. 21.
[3] "*Tamen omnia hæc, pariterque eodem impellentia unus ac parvus admodum pisciculus, echeneis appellatus, in se tenet. Ruant venti licet, et sæviant procellæ, imperat furori, viresque tantas compescit, et cogit stare navigia: quod non vincula ulla, non anchoræ pondere irrevocabili jactæ . . . Fertur Actiaco marte tenuisse navim Antonii properantis circumire et exhortare suos donec transiret in aliam. . . . Tenuit et nostra memoria Caii principis ab Astura Antium renavigantes.*" Plin. xxxii. 1. The popular error was long lived.
"Life is a voyage, and, in our life's ways,
Countries, courts, towns, are rocks or *remoras.*"
Donne, *To Sir Henry Wotton.*

---

fish, dog fish, whales, and sharks, are not therefore the only things to be dreaded; we have to fear no less the spike of the stingray even after its death,[1] and the sea-hare,[2] whose mortal blows are as rapid as they are inevitable. Thus the Creator wishes that all may keep you awake, so that full of hope in Him you may avoid the evils with which all these creatures threaten you.

But let us come out of the depths of the sea and take refuge upon the shore. For the marvels of creation, coming one after the other in constant succession like the waves, have submerged my discourse. However, I should not be surprised if, after finding greater wonders upon the earth, my spirit seeks like Jonah's to flee to the sea. But it seems to me, that meeting with these innumerable marvels has made me forget all measure, and experience the fate of those who navigate the high seas without a fixed point to mark their progress, and are often ignorant of the space which they have traversed. This is what has happened to me; whilst my words glanced at creation, I have not been sensible of the multitude of beings of which I spoke to you. But although this honourable assembly is pleased by my speech, and the recital of the marvels of the Master is grateful to the ears of His servants, let me here bring the ship of my discourse to anchor, and await the day to deliver you the rest. Let us, therefore, all arise, and, giving thanks for what has been said, let us ask for strength to hear the rest. Whilst taking your food may the conversation at your table turn upon what has occupied us this morning and this evening. Filled with these thoughts may you, even in sleep, enjoy the pleasure of the day, so that you may be permitted to say, "I sleep but my heart waketh,"[3] meditating day and night upon the law of the Lord, to Whom be glory and power world without end. Amen.

HOMILY VIII.

The creation of fowl and water animals.[4]

1. AND God said "*Let the earth bring forth the living creature after his kind, cattle and creeping things, and beast of the earth after his kind; and it was so.*"[5] The command of God advanced step by step and earth thus received her adornment.

---

[1] Pliny (ix.72) says it is sometimes five inches long. Ælian (*Hist. An.* i. 56) calls the wound incurable.
[2] Pliny (ix. 72) calls it *tactu pestilens*, and says (xxxii. 3) that no other fish eats it, except the mullet.
[3] Cant. v. 2.
[4] *Codex Colb.* 1 has the title "about creeping things and beasts."
[5] Gen. i. 24.

Yesterday it was said, " Let the waters produce moving things," and to-day " let the earth bring forth the living creature." Is the earth then alive? And are the mad-minded Manichæans right in giving it a soul? At these words " Let the earth bring forth," it did not produce a germ contained in it, but He who gave the order at the same time gifted it with the grace and power to bring forth. When the earth had heard this command " Let the earth bring forth grass and the tree yielding fruit," it was not grass that it had hidden in it that it caused to spring forth, it did not bring to the surface a palm tree, an oak, a cypress, hitherto kept back in its depths. It is the word of God which forms the nature of things created. " Let the earth bring forth ; " that is to say not that she may bring forth that which she has but that she may acquire that which she lacks, when God gives her the power. Even so now, " Let the earth bring forth the living creature," not the living creature that is contained in herself, but that which the command of God gives her. Further, the Manichæans contradict themselves, because if the earth has brought forth the life, she has left herself despoiled of life. Their execrable doctrine needs no demonstration.

But why did the waters receive the command to bring forth the moving creature that hath life and the earth to bring forth the living creature? We conclude that, by their nature, swimming creatures appear only to have an imperfect life, because they live in the thick element of water. They are hard of hearing, and their sight is dull because they see through the water ; they have no memory, no imagination, no idea of social intercourse. Thus divine language appears to indicate that, in aquatic animals, the carnal life originates their psychic movements, whilst in terrestrial animals, gifted with a more perfect life,[1] the soul[2] enjoys supreme authority. In fact the greater part of quadrupeds have more power of penetration in their senses ; their apprehension of present objects is keen, and they keep an exact remembrance of the past. It seems therefore, that God, after the command given to the waters to bring forth moving creatures that have life, created simply living bodies for aquatic animals, whilst for terrestrial animals He commanded the soul to exist and to direct the body, showing thus that the inhabitants of the earth are gifted with greater vital force. Without doubt terrestrial animals are devoid of reason. At the same time how

many affections of the soul each one of them expresses by the voice of nature! They express by cries their joy and sadness, recognition of what is familiar to them, the need of food, regret at being separated from their companions, and numberless emotions. Aquatic animals, on the contrary, are not only dumb ; it is impossible to tame them, to teach them, to train them for man's society.[1] " The ox knoweth his owner, and the ass his master's crib." [2] But the fish does not know who feeds him. The ass knows a familiar voice, he knows the road which he has often trodden, and even, if man loses his way, he sometimes serves him as a guide. His hearing is more acute than that of any other terrestrial animal. What animal of the sea can show so much rancour and resentment as the camel? The camel conceals its resentment for a long time after it has been struck, until it finds an opportunity, and then repays the wrong. Listen, you whose heart does not pardon, you who practise vengeance as a virtue ; see what you resemble when you keep your anger for so long against your neighbour like a spark, hidden in the ashes, and only waiting for fuel to set your heart ablaze !

2. " *Let the earth bring forth a living soul.*" Why did the earth produce a living soul? so that you may make a difference between the soul of cattle and that of man. You will soon learn how the human soul was formed ; hear now about the soul of creatures devoid of reason. Since, according to Scripture, " the life of every creature is in the blood," [3] as the blood when thickened changes into flesh, and flesh when corrupted decomposes into earth, so the soul of beasts is naturally an earthy substance. " Let the earth bring forth a living soul." See the affinity of the soul with blood, of blood with flesh, of flesh with earth ; and remounting in an inverse sense from the earth to the flesh, from the flesh to the blood, from the blood to the soul, you will find that the soul of beasts is earth. Do not suppose that it is older than the essence [4] of their body, nor that it survives the dissolution of the flesh ; [5] avoid the non-

---

[1] ζωή. [2] ψυχή.

[1] See note on p. 90. [3] *cf.* Lev. xvii. 11.
[2] Isa. i. 3. [4] ὑπόστασις.
[5] It may be supposed " that the souls of brutes, being but so many eradiations or effluxes from that source of life above, are, as soon as ever those organized bodies of theirs, by reason of their indisposition, become uncapable of being further acted upon by them, then to be resumed again and retracted back to their original head and fountain. Since it cannot be doubted but what creates anything out of nothing, or sends it forth from itself, by free and voluntary emanation, may be able either to retract the same back again to its original source, or else to annihilate it at pleasure. And I find that there have not wanted some among the Gentile philosophers themselves who have entertained this opinion, whereof Porphyry is one, λύεται ἑκάστη δύναμις ἄλογος εἰς τὴν ὅλην ζωὴν τοῦ παντός." Cudworth, i. 35.

sense of those arrogant philosophers who do not blush to liken their soul to that of a dog ; who say that they have been formerly themselves women, shrubs, fish.[1] Have they ever been fish? I do not know; but I do not fear to affirm that in their writings they show less sense than fish. "Let the earth bring forth the living creature." Perhaps many of you ask why there is such a long silence in the middle of the rapid rush of my discourse. The more studious among my auditors will not be ignorant of the reason why words fail me. What! Have I not seen them look at each other, and make signs to make me look at them, and to remind me of what I have passed over? I have forgotten a part of the creation, and that one of the most considerable, and my discourse was almost finished without touching upon it. "Let the waters bring forth abundantly the moving creature that hath life and fowl that may fly above the earth in the open firmament of heaven."[2] I spoke of fish as long as eventide allowed : to-day we have passed to the examination of terrestrial animals; between the two, birds have escaped us. We are forgetful like travellers who, unmindful of some important object, are obliged, although they be far on their road, to retrace their steps, punished for their negligence by the weariness of the journey. So we have to turn back. That which we have omitted is not to be despised. It is the third part of the animal creation, if indeed there are three kinds of animals, land, winged and water.

"*Let the waters*" it is said "*bring forth abundantly moving creature that hath life and fowl that may fly above the earth in the open firmament of heaven.*" Why do the waters give birth also to birds? Because there is, so to say, a family link between the creatures that fly and those that swim. In the same way that fish cut the waters, using their fins to carry them forward and their tails to direct their movements round and round and straightforward, so we see birds float in the air by the help of their wings. Both endowed with the property of swimming, their common derivation from the waters has made them of one family.[3]

At the same time no bird is without feet, because finding all its food upon the earth it cannot do without their service. Rapacious birds have pointed claws to enable them to close on their prey ; to the rest has been given the indispensable ministry of feet to seek their food and to provide for the other needs of life. There are a few who walk badly, whose feet are neither suitable for walking nor for preying. Among this number are swallows, incapable of walking and seeking their prey, and the birds called swifts[1] who live on little insects carried about by the air. As to the swallow, its flight, which grazes the earth, fulfils the function of feet.

3. There are also innumerable kinds of birds. If we review them all, as we have partly done the fish, we shall find that under one name, the creatures which fly differ infinitely in size, form and colour ; that in their life, their actions and their manners, they present a variety equally beyond the power of description. Thus some have tried to imagine names for them of which the singularity and the strangeness might, like brands, mark the distinctive character of each kind known. Some, as eagles, have been called Schizoptera, others Dermoptera, as the bats, others Ptilota, as wasps, others Coleoptera, as beetles and all those insects which brought forth in cases and coverings, break their prison to fly away in liberty.[2] But we have enough words of common usage to characterise each species and to mark the distinction which Scripture sets up between clean and unclean birds. Thus the species of carnivora is of one sort and of one constitution which suits their manner of living, sharp talons, curved beak, swift wings, allowing them to swoop easily upon their prey and to tear it up after having seized it.[3] The constitution of those who pick up seeds is different, and again that of those who live on all they come across. What a variety in all these creatures ! Some are gregarious, except the birds of prey who know no other society than conjugal union; but innumerable kinds, doves, cranes, starlings, jackdaws, like a common life.[4] Among them some live without a chief and in a sort of independence ; others, as cranes, do not refuse to submit themselves to a leader. And a fresh difference between

---

[1] Empedocles is named as author of the lines :

ἤδη γὰρ ποτ' ἐγὼ γενόμην κούρητε κόρος τε,
Θάμνος τ' οἰωνός τε καὶ εἰν ἁλὶ ἔλλοπος ἰχθύς.

cf. Diog. Laert. viii. 78. and Plutarch, *D Solert. An.* ii. 964. Whether the " faba Pythagoræ cognata " of Hor., *Sat.* ii. 6, 63, implies the transmigration of the soul into it is doubtful. *cf.* Juv., *Sat.* xv. 153. Anaximander thought that human beings were originally generated from fish. Plut., *Symp.* viii. 8.

[2] Gen. i. 20.

[3] Fialon quotes Bossuet, 1st Elev. 5th week : " *Qui a donné aux oiseaux et aux poissons ces rames naturelles, qui leur font fendre les eaux et les airs ? Ce qui peut être a donné lieu à leur Créateur de les produire ensemble, comme animaux d'un*

dessin à peu près semblable : le vol des oiseaux semblant, être une espèce de faculté de nager dans une liqueur plus subtile, comme la faculté de nager dans les poissons est une espèce de vol dans une liqueur plus épaisse."

The theory of evolutionists is, as is well known, that birds developed out of reptiles and reptiles from fish. *Vide* E. Haeckel's monophyletic pedigree in his *History of Creation.*

[1] δοσπανίς, *i.e.* sickle-bird.

[2] These are the terms of Aristotle, *Hist. An.* i. 5.

[3] *cf.* Arist., *Hist. An.* viii. 3.

[4] Whence the proverb κολοιὸς ποτὶ κολοιόν. Arist., *Eth. Nic.* I. viii. 6.

them is that some are stationary and non-migratory; others undertake long voyages and the greater part of them, migrate at the approach of winter. Nearly all birds can be tamed and are capable of training, except the weakest, who through fear and timidity cannot bear the constant and annoying contact of the hand. Some like the society of man and inhabit our dwellings; others delight in mountains and in desert places. There is a great difference too in their peculiar notes. Some twitter and chatter, others are silent, some have a melodious and sonorous voice, some are wholly inharmonious and incapable of song; some imitate the voice of man, taught their mimicry either by nature or training;[1] others always give forth the same monotonous cry. The cock is proud; the peacock is vain of his beauty; doves and fowls are amorous, always seeking each other's society. The partridge is deceitful and jealous, lending perfidious help to the huntsmen to seize their prey.[2]

4. What a variety, I have said, in the actions and lives of flying creatures! Some of these unreasoning creatures even have a government, if the feature of government is to make the activity of all the individuals centre in one common end. This may be observed in bees. They have a common dwelling place; they fly in the air together, they work at the same work together; and what is still more extraordinary is that they give themselves to these labours under the guidance of a king and superintendent, and that they do not allow themselves to fly to the meadows without seeing if the king is flying at their head. As to this king, it is not election that gives him this authority; ignorance on the part of the people often puts the worst man in power; it is not fate; the blind decisions of fate often give authority to the most unworthy. It is not heredity that places him on the throne; it is only too common to see the children of kings, corrupted by luxury and flattery, living in ignorance of all virtue. It is nature which makes the king of the bees, for nature gives him superior size, beauty, and sweetness of character. He has a sting like the others, but he does not use it to revenge himself.[3] It is a principle of natural and unwritten law, that those who are raised to high office, ought to be lenient in punishing. Even bees who do not follow

the example of their king, repent without delay of their imprudence, since they lose their lives with their sting. Listen, Christians, you to whom it is forbidden to "recompense evil for evil" and commanded "to overcome evil with good."[1] Take the bee for your model, which constructs its cells without injuring any one and without interfering with the goods of others. It gathers openly wax from the flowers with its mouth, drawing in the honey scattered over them like dew, and injects it into the hollow of its cells. Thus at first honey is liquid; time thickens it and gives it its sweetness.[2] The book of Proverbs has given the bee the most honourable and the best praise by calling her wise and industrious.[3] How much activity she exerts in gathering this precious nourishment, by which both kings and men of low degree are brought to health! How great is the art and cunning she displays in the construction of the store houses which are destined to receive the honey! After having spread the wax like a thin membrane, she distributes it in contiguous compartments which, weak though they are, by their number and by their mass, sustain the whole edifice. Each cell in fact holds to the one next to it, and is separated by a thin partition; we thus see two or three galleries of cells built one upon the other. The bee takes care not to make one vast cavity, for fear it might break under the weight of the liquid, and allow it to escape. See how the discoveries of geometry are mere by-works to the wise bee![4]

The rows of honey-comb are all hexagonal with equal sides. They do not bear on each other in straight lines, lest the supports should press on empty spaces between and give way; but the angles of the lower hexagons serve as foundations and bases to those which rise above, so as to furnish a sure support to the lower mass, and so that each cell may securely keep the liquid honey.[5]

[1] Rom. xii. 17, 21.

[2] The ancient belief was that honey fell from heaven, in the shape of dew, and the bee only gathered it from leaves. So Verg., Ec. iv. 30, "roscida mella," and Georg. iv. 1, "aerii mellis cœlestia dona." cf. Arist., H. A. v. 22, μελὶ δὲ τὸ πίπτον ἐκ τοῦ ἀέρος, καὶ μάλιστα τῶν ἄστρων ἀνατολαῖς, καὶ ὅταν κατασκήψῃ ἡ ἶρις, and Plin. xi. 12. "Sive ille est cœli sudor, sive quædam siderum saliva, sine purgantis se aeris succus, . . . magnam tamen cœlestis naturæ voluptatem affert." So Coleridge (Kubla Khan):
"For he on honey dew hath fed
And drunk the milk of Paradise."

[3] Prov. vi. 8, lxx. The reference to the bee is not in the Hebrew.

[4] cf. Ælian. v. 13. γεωμετρίαν δὲ καὶ κάλλη σχημάτων καὶ ὡραίας πλάσεις αὐτῶν ἄνευ τέχνης τε καὶ κανόνων καὶ τοῦ καλουμένου ὑπὸ τῶν σοφῶν διαβήτου, τὸ κάλλιστον σχημάτων ἐξαγωνόν τε καὶ ἐξάπλευρον καὶ ἰσογώνιον ἀποδείκνυνται αἱ μέλιτται.

[5] The mathematical exactness of the bee is described by Darwin in terms which make it even more marvellous than it appeared to Basil. "The most wonderful of all known instincts, that of the hive bee, may be explained by natural selection having taken advantage of numerous slight modifications of simpler instincts; natural selection having by slow degrees more and more perfectly led the bees to sweep equal spheres

[1] "Super omnia humanas voces reddunt, posittaci quidem sermocinantes." Plin. x. 53.

[2] Arist., Hist. An. ix. 10.

[3] Arist., Hist. An. v. 21, and Plin. xi. 17. "Ecce in re parva, villisque nostra annexa, cujus assidua copia est, non constat inter auctores, rex nullumne solus habeat aculeum, majestate tantum armatus; an dederit eum quidem natura, sed usum ejus illi tantum negaverit. Illud constat imperatorem aculeo non uti."

5. How shall we make an exact review of all the peculiarities of the life of birds? During the night cranes keep watch in turn; some sleep, others make the rounds and procure a quiet slumber for their companions. After having finished his duty, the sentry utters a cry, and goes to sleep, and the one who awakes, in his turn, repays the security which he has enjoyed.[1] You will see the same order reign in their flight. One leads the way, and when it has guided the flight of the flock for a certain time, it passes to the rear, leaving to the one who comes after the care of directing the march.

The conduct of storks comes very near intelligent reason. In these regions the same season sees them all migrate. They all start at one given signal. And it seems to me that our crows, serving them as escort, go to bring them back, and to help them against the attacks of hostile birds. The proof is that in this season not a single crow appears, and that they return with wounds, evident marks of the help and of the assistance that they have lent. Who has explained to them the laws of hospitality? Who has threatened them with the penalties of desertion? For not one is missing from the company. Listen, all inhospitable hearts, ye who shut your doors, whose house is never open either in the winter or in the night to travellers. The solicitude of storks for their old would be sufficient, if our children would reflect upon it, to make them love their parents; because there is no one so failing in good sense, as not to deem it a shame to be surpassed in virtue by birds devoid of reason. The storks surround their father, when old age makes his feathers drop off, warm him with their wings, and provide abundantly for his support, and even in their flight they help him as much as they are able, raising him gently on each side upon their wings, a conduct so notorious that it has given to gratitude the name of "antipelargosis."[2] Let no one lament poverty; let not the man whose house is bare despair of his life, when he considers the industry of the swallow. To build her nest, she brings bits of straw

in her beak; and, as she cannot raise the mud in her claws, she moistens the end of her wings in water and.then rolls in very fine dust and thus procures mud.[1] After having united, little by little, the bits of straw with this mud, as with glue, she feeds her young; and if any one of them has its eyes injured, she has a natural remedy to heal the sight of her little ones.[2]

This sight ought to warn you not to take to evil ways on account of poverty; and, even if you are reduced to the last extremity, not to lose all hope; not to abandon yourself to inaction and idleness, but to have recourse to God. If He is so bountiful to the swallow, what will He not do for those who call upon Him with all their heart?

The halcyon is a sea bird, which lays its eggs along the shore, or deposits them in the sand. And it lays in the middle of winter, when the violence of the winds dashes the sea against the land. Yet all winds are hushed, and the wave of the sea grows calm, during the seven days that the halcyon sits.[3]

For it only takes seven days to hatch the young. Then, as they are in need of food so that they may grow, God, in His munificence, grants another seven days to this tiny animal. All sailors know this, and call these days halcyon days. If divine Providence has established these marvellous laws in favour of creatures devoid of reason, it is to induce you to ask for your salvation from God. Is there a wonder which He will not perform for you — you have been made in His image, when for so little a bird, the great, the fearful sea is held in check and is commanded in the midst of winter to be calm.

6. It is said that the turtle-dove, once separated from her mate, does not contract a new union, but remains in widowhood, in remembrance of her first alliance.[4] Listen, O women! What veneration for widowhood, even in these creatures devoid of reason, how they prefer it to an unbecoming multiplicity of marriages. The eagle shows the greatest injustice in the edu-

at a given distance from each other in a double layer, and to build up and excavate the wax along the planes of intersection." *Origin of Species*, ii. 255, ed. 1861 According to this view the beings from whom have bees, as we know them, are descended were gifted with certain simple instincts capable of a kind of hereditary unconscious education, resulting in a complex instinct which constructs with exact precision the hexagonal chamber best fitted for the purpose it is designed to fulfil, and then packs it. And it is interesting to note how the great apostle of abstract selection personifies it as a "taker" of "advantage," and a "leader."

[1] Arist., *Hist. An.* ix. 10.
[2] From πελαργός. On the pious affection of the stork, *cf.* Plato, *Alc.* i. 135 (§ 61), Arist., *H.A.* ix. 13, 20, Ælian, *H.A.* iii. 23, and x. 16, and Plin. x. 32. From πελαργὸς was supposed to be derived the Pythagorean word πελαργᾶν (Diog. Laert. viii. 20), but this is now regarded as a corruption of πεδαρτᾶν.

[1] "*Hirundines luto construunt, stramine roborant: si quando inopia est luti, madefactæ multa aqua pennis pulverem spargunt.*" Plin. x. 49. *cf.* Arist., *Hist. An.* ix. 10.
[2] "*Chelidoniam visui saluberrimam hirundines monstravere. vexatis pullorum oculis illa medentes.*" Plin. viii. 41. *cf.* Ælian, *H.A.* iii. 25. Chelidonia is swallowwort or celandine.
[3] "*Fœtificant bruma, qui dies halcyonides vocantur. placido mari per eos et navigabili, Siculo maxime.*" Plin. x. 47. *cf.* Arist., *H.A.* v. 8, 9, and Ælian, *H.N.* i. 36. So Theoc. vii. 57:

X' ἀλκυόνες στορεσεῦντι τὰ κύματα, τάν τε θάλασσαν
Τόν τε νότον τόντ' εὑρον ὃς ἔσχατα φυκία κινεῖ.

Sir Thomas Browne (*Vulgar Errors*) denies the use of a kingfisher as a weather-gauge, but says nothing as to the "halcyon days." Kingfishers are rarely seen in the open sea, but haunt estuaries which are calm without any special miracle. Possibly the halcyon was a tern or sea-swallow, which resembles a kingfisher, but they brood on land.
[4] Arist., *H.A.* ix. 7.

cation which she gives to her young. When she has hatched two little ones, she throws one on the ground, thrusting it out with blows from her wings, and only acknowledges the remaining one. It is the difficulty of finding food which has made her repulse the offspring she has brought forth. But the osprey, it is said, will not allow it to perish, she carries it away and brings it up with her young ones.[1] Such are parents who, under the plea of poverty, expose their children; such are again those who, in the distribution of their inheritance, make unequal divisions. Since they have given existence equally to each of their children, it is just that they should equally and without preference furnish them with the means of livelihood. Beware of imitating the cruelty of birds with hooked talons. When they see their young are from henceforth capable of encountering the air in their flight, they throw them out of the nest, striking them and pushing them with their wings, and do not take the least care of them. The love of the crow for its young is laudable! When they begin to fly, she follows them, gives them food, and for a very long time provides for their nourishment. Many birds have no need of union with males to conceive. But their eggs are unfruitful, except those of vultures, who more often, it is said, bring forth without coupling:[2] and this although they have a very long life, which often reaches its hundredth year. Note and retain, I pray you, this point in the history of birds; and if ever you see any one laugh at our mystery, as if it were impossible and contrary to nature that a virgin should become a mother without losing the purity of her virginity, bethink you that He who would save the faithful by the foolishness of preaching, has given us beforehand in nature a thousand reasons for believing in the marvellous.[3]

7. "*Let the waters bring forth the moving creatures that have life, and fowl that may fly above the earth in the open firmament of heaven.*" They received the command to fly above the earth because earth provides them with nourishment. "In the firmament of heaven," that is to say, as we have said before, in that part of the air called οὐρανός, heaven,[1] from the word ὁρᾶν, which means to see;[2] called firmament, because the air which extends over our heads, compared to the æther, has greater density, and is thickened by the vapours which exhale from the earth. You have then heaven adorned, earth beautified, the sea peopled with its own creatures, the air filled with birds which scour it in every direction. Studious listener, think of all these creations which God has drawn out of nothing, think of all those which my speech has left out, to avoid tediousness, and not to exceed my limits; recognise everywhere the wisdom of God; never cease to wonder, and, through every creature, to glorify the Creator.

There are some kinds of birds which live by night in the midst of darkness; others which fly by day in full light. Bats, owls, nightravens are birds of night: if by chance you cannot sleep, reflect on these nocturnal birds and their peculiarities and glorify their Maker. How is it that the nightingale is always awake when sitting on her eggs, passing the night in a continual melody?[3] How is it that one animal, the bat, is at the same time quadruped and fowl? That it is the only one of the birds to have teeth? That it is viviparous like quadrupeds, and traverses the air, raising itself not upon wings, but upon a kind of membrane?[4] What natural love bats have for each other! How they interlace like a chain and hang the one upon the other! A very rare spectacle among men, who for the greater part prefer individual and private life to the union of common life. Have not those who give themselves up to vain science the eyes of owls? The sight of the owl, piercing during the night time, is dazzled by the splendour of the sun; thus the intelligence of these men, so keen to contemplate vanities, is blind in presence of the true light.

During the day, also, how easy it is for you to admire the Creator everywhere! See how

---

[1] Ar. vi. 6 and ix. 34. "*Melanaetos . . . sola aquilarum fœtus suos alit; ceteræ . . . fugant.*" Plin. x. 3. "*Pariunt ova terna: excludunt pullos binos: visi sunt et tres aliquando.*" id. 4, following Musæus (*apud* Plutarch, *In Mario*, p. 426). ὡς τρία μὲν τίκτει, δύο δ' ἐκλέπει, ἓν δ' ἀλεγίζει. On the osprey, see Arist., *H.A.* ix. 44 and Pliny *loc.* "*Sed ejectos ab his cognatum genus ossifragi excipiunt, et educant cum suis.*"
[2] Arist., *Hist. An.* vi. 6 and ix. 15. So Pliny x. vii. "*Nidos nemo attigit: ideo etiam fuere qui putarent illos ex adverso orbe advolare, nidificant enim in excelsissimis rupibus.*" cf. also Ælian, ii. 46: γύπα δὲ ἄρρενα οὔ φασι γίγνεσθαί ποτε ἀλλὰ θηλείας ἁπάσας.
[3] This analogy is repeated almost in identical words in Basil's Hom. xxii. *De Providentia.* cf. also his *Com. on Isaiah.* St. Ambrose repeats the illustration (*Hex.* v. 20). The analogy, even if the facts were true, would be false and misleading. But it is curious to note that were any modern divine desirous of here following in Basil's track, he might find the alleged facts in the latest modern science,—*e.g.* in the so-called Parthenogenesis, or virginal reproduction, among insects, as said to be demonstrated by Siebold. Haeckel (*Hist. of Creation,* Lankester's ed. ii. p. 198) represents sexual reproduction as quite a recent development of non-sexual reproduction.

[1] cf. note on p. 70.
[2] The Greek word στερέωμα, from στερεός, strong, is traceable to the root STAR, to spread out, and so indirectly associated with the connotation of the Hebrew *rakia*.
[3] Arist., *H.A.* viii. 75. Pliny x. 43. "*Luscinus diebus ac noctibus continuis quindecim garrulus sine intermissu cantus, densante se frondium germine, non in novissima digna miratu ave.*"
[4] So also Basil in *Hom. on Isaiah* iii. 447. cf. Pliny x. 81, "*cui et membranaceæ pinnæ uni.*"

the domestic cock calls you to work with his shrill cry, and how, forerunner of the sun, and early as the traveller, he sends forth labourers to the harvest! What vigilance in geese! With what sagacity they divine secret dangers! Did they not once upon a time save the imperial city? When enemies were advancing by subterranean passages to possess themselves of the capitol of Rome, did not geese announce the danger?[1] Is there any kind of bird whose nature offers nothing for our admiration? Who announces to the vultures that there will be carnage when men march in battle array against one another? You may see flocks of vultures following armies and calculating the result of warlike preparations;[2] a calculation very nearly approaching to human reasoning. How can I describe to you the fearful invasions of locusts, which rise everwhere at a given signal, and pitch their camps all over a country? They do not attack crops until they have received the divine command. Or shall I describe how the remedy for this curse, the thrush, follows them with its insatiable appetite, and the devouring nature that the loving God has given it in His kindness for men?[3] How does the grasshopper modulate its song?[4] Why is it more melodious at midday owing to the air that it breathes in dilating its chest?

But it appears to me that in wishing to describe the marvels of winged creatures, I remain further behind than I should if my feet had tried to match the rapidity of their flight. When you see bees, wasps, in short all those flying creatures called insects, because they have an incision all around, reflect that they have neither respiration nor lungs, and that they are supported by air through all parts of their bodies.[5] Thus they perish, if they are covered with oil, because it stops up their pores. Wash them with vinegar, the pores reopen and the animal returns to life. Our God has created

nothing unnecessarily and has omitted nothing that is necessary. If now you cast your eyes upon aquatic creatures, you will find that their organization is quite different. Their feet are not split like those of the crow, nor hooked like those of the carnivora, but large and membraneous; therefore they can easily swim, pushing the water with the membranes of their feet as with oars. Notice how the swan plunges his neck into the depths of the water to draw his food from it, and you will understand the wisdom of the Creator in giving this creature a neck longer than his feet, so that he may throw it like a line, and take the food hidden at the bottom of the water.[1]

8. If we simply read the words of Scripture we find only a few short syllables. "Let the waters bring forth fowl that may fly above the earth in the open firmament of heaven," but if we enquire into the meaning of these words, then the great wonder of the wisdom of the Creator appears. What a difference He has foreseen among winged creatures! How He has divided them by kinds! How He has characterized each one of them by distinct qualities! But the day will not suffice me to recount the wonders of the air. Earth is calling me to describe wild beasts, reptiles and cattle, ready to show us in her turn sights rivalling those of plants, fish, and birds. "Let the earth bring forth the living soul" of domestic animals, of wild beasts, and of reptiles after their kind. What have you to say, you who do not believe in the change that Paul promises you in the resurrection, when you see so many metamorphoses among creatures of the air? What are we not told of the horned worm of India! First it changes into a caterpillar,[2] then becomes a buzzing insect, and not content with this form, it clothes itself, instead of wings, with loose, broad plates. Thus, O women, when you are seated busy with your weaving, I mean of the silk which is sent you by the Chinese to make your delicate dresses,[3] remember the metamorphoses of this creature, conceive a clear idea of the resurrection, and do not refuse to believe in the change that Paul announces for all men.

But I am ashamed to see that my discourse oversteps the accustomed limits; if I consider the abundance of matters on which I have just discoursed to you, I feel that I am being borne beyond bounds; but when I reflect upon the inexhaustible wisdom which

[1] cf. Livy v. 47 and Plutarch, Camillus, or Verg. viii. 655. The alternative tradition of the mine is preserved by Servius.

[2] cf. Ælian, H.A. ii. 46. καὶ μέντοι καὶ ταῖς ἐκδήμοις στρατιαῖς ἕπονται γῦπες καὶ μάλα γε μαντικῶς ὅτι εἰς πόλεμον χωροῦσιν εἰδότες καὶ ὅτι μάχη πᾶσα ἐργάζεται νεκροὺς καὶ τοῦτο ἐγνωκότες. cf. Pliny x. 88: "vultures sagacius odorantur."

[3] cf. Galen. vi. 3.

[4] Fialon, quoting the well known ode of Anakreon, "μακαρίζομέν σε τέττιξ," and Plato's theory of the affection of grasshoppers and the muses in the Phædrus, contrasts the "cantu querulæ rumpent arbusta cicadæ" of Vergil (Georg. iii. 328), and points out that the Romans did not share the Greek admiration for the grasshopper's song.

[5] "Insecta multi negarunt spirare, idque ratione persuadentes, quoniam in viscera interiora nexus spirabilis non inesset. Itaque vivere ut fruges, arboresque: sed plurimum interesse spiret aliquid an vivat. Eadem de causa nec sanguinem iis esse qui sit nullis carentibus corde atque jecore. Sic nec spirare ea quibus pulmo desit unde numerosa series quæstionum exoritur. Iidem enim et vocem esse his negant, in tanto murmure apium, cicadarum sono . . . nec video cur magis possint non trahere animam talia, et vivere, quam spirare sine visceribus." Plin. xi. 2.

[1] Arist., De Part. An. iv. 12.

[2] This word is curiously rendered by Eustathius verucæ, and by Ambrose caulis. Garnier (Præf. in Bas. 28) thinks that the latter perhaps found in some corrupt MS. κράμβην for κάμπην.

[3] Arist., H.A. v. 19.

is displayed in the works of creation, I seem to be but at the beginning of my story. Nevertheless, I have not detained you so long without profit. For what would you have done until the evening? You are not pressed by guests, nor expected at banquets. Let me then employ this bodily fast to rejoice your souls. You have often served the flesh for pleasure, to-day persevere in the ministry of the soul. "Delight thyself also in the Lord and he shall give thee the desire of thine heart." [1] Do you love riches? Here are spiritual riches. "The judgments of the Lord are true and righteous altogether. More to be desired are they than gold and precious stones." [2] Do you love enjoyment and pleasures? Behold the oracles of the Lord, which, for a healthy soul, are "sweeter than honey and the honey-comb." [3] If I let you go, and if I dismiss this assembly, some will run to the dice, where they will find bad language, sad quarrels and the pangs of avarice. There stands the devil, inflaming the fury of the players with the dotted bones,[4] transporting the same sums of money from one side of the table to the other, now exalting one with victory and throwing the other into despair, now swelling the first with boasting and covering his rival with confusion.[5] Of what use is bodily fasting and filling the soul with innumerable evils? He who does not play spends his leisure elsewhere. What frivolities come from his mouth! What follies strike his ears! Leisure without the fear of the Lord is, for those who do not know the value of time, a school of vice.[6] I hope that my words will be profitable; at least by occupying you here they have prevented you from sinning. Thus the longer I keep you, the longer you are out of the way of evil.

An equitable judge will deem that I have said enough, not if he considers the riches of creation, but if he thinks of our weakness and of the measure one ought to keep in that which tends to pleasure. Earth has welcomed you with its own plants, water with its fish, air with its birds; the continent in its turn is ready to offer you as rich treasures.

But let us put an end to this morning banquet, for fear satiety may blunt your taste for the evening one. May He who has filled all with the works of His creation and has left everywhere visible memorials of His wonders, fill your hearts with all spiritual joys in Jesus Christ, our Lord, to whom belong glory and power, world without end. Amen.

HOMILY IX.

The creation of terrestrial animals.

1. How did you like the fare of my morning's discourse? It seemed to me that I had the good intentions of a poor giver of a feast, who, ambitious of having the credit of keeping a good table saddens his guests by the poor supply of the more expensive dishes. In vain he lavishly covers his table with his mean fare; his ambition only shows his folly. It is for you to judge if I have shared the same fate. Yet, whatever my discourse may have been, take care lest you disregard it. No one refused to sit at the table of Elisha; and yet he only gave his friends wild vegetables.[1] I know the laws of allegory, though less by myself than from the works of others. There are those truly, who do not admit the common sense of the Scriptures, for whom water is not water, but some other nature, who see in a plant, in a fish, what their fancy wishes, who change the nature of reptiles and of wild beasts to suit their allegories, like the interpreters of dreams who explain visions in sleep to make them serve their own ends. For me grass is grass; plant, fish, wild beast, domestic animal, I take all in the literal sense.[2] "For I am not ashamed of the gospel." [3] Those who have written about the nature of the universe have discussed at length the shape of the earth. If it be spherical or cylindrical, if it resemble a disc and is equally rounded in all parts, or if it has the form of a winnowing basket and is hollow in the middle;[4] all these conjectures have been suggested by cosmographers, each one upsetting that of his predecessor. It will not lead me to give less importance to the creation of the universe, that the servant of God, Moses, is silent as to shapes;

---

[1] Ps. xxxvii. 4.   [2] Ps. xix. 9 and 10, LXX.
[3] Ps. xix. 10.
[4] The κύβοι were marked on all six sides, the ἀστράγαλοι on only four, the ends being rounded.
[5] With Basil's description of the gaming tables, presumably of Cæsarea, cf. Ovid's of those of Rome:

    "Ira subit, deforme malum, lucrique cupido ;
     Jurgiaque et rixæ, sollicitusque dolor.
     Crimina dicuntur, resonat clamoribus æther,
     Invocat iratos et sibi quisque deos,
     Nulla fides : tabulæque novæ per vota petuntur,
     Et lacrymis vidi sæpe madere genis."
                         De A.A. iii. 373 seqq.
[6] "Cernis ut ignavum corrumpant otia corpus." Ovid, I. Pont. 6. "Facito aliquid operis ut semper Diabolus inveniat te occupatum." Jerome, In R. Monach.

---

[1] 2 Kings iv. 39.
[2] Fialon thinks that this plain reference to Origen may have been evoked by some criticisms on the IIIrd Homily. (cf. p. 71.) St. Basil's literalism and bold departure from the allegorizing of Origen and from the milder mysticism of Eusebius are remarked on in the Prolegomena.
[3] Rom. i. 16.
[4] θαλῆς καὶ οἱ Στωϊκοὶ καὶ οἱ ἀπ' αὐτῶν σφαιροειδῆ τὴν γῆν. Ἀναξίμανδρος λίθῳ κίονι τὴν γῆν προσφερῆ τῶν ἐπιπέδων. Ἀναξιμένης, τραπεζοειδῆ. Λεύκιππος, τυμπανοειδῆ. Δημόκριτος, δισκοειδῆ μὲν τῷ πλάτει, κοίλην δὲ τὸ μέσον. Plut. περὶ τῶν ἀρεσκ. iii. 10. Arist. (De . Cœlo ii. 14) follows Thales. So Manilius i. 235:
    "Ex quo colligitur terrarum forma rotunda."

he has not said that the earth is a hundred and eighty thousand furlongs in circumference; he has not measured into what extent of air its shadow projects itself whilst the sun revolves around it, nor stated how this shadow, casting itself upon the moon, produces eclipses. He has passed over in silence, as useless, all that is unimportant for us. Shall I then prefer foolish wisdom to the oracles of the Holy Spirit? Shall I not rather exalt Him who, not wishing to fill our minds with these vanities, has regulated all the economy of Scripture in view of the edification and the making perfect of our souls? It is this which those seem to me not to have understood, who, giving themselves up to the distorted meaning of allegory, have undertaken to give a majesty of their own invention to Scripture. It is to believe themselves wiser than the Holy Spirit, and to bring forth their own ideas under a pretext of exegesis. Let us hear Scripture as it has been written.

2. "*Let the earth bring forth the living creature.*" [1] Behold the word of God pervading creation, beginning even then the efficacy which is seen displayed to-day, and will be displayed to the end of the world! As a ball, which one pushes, if it meet a declivity, descends, carried by its form and the nature of the ground and does not stop until it has reached a level surface; so nature, once put in motion by the Divine command, traverses creation with an equal step, through birth and death, and keeps up the succession of kinds through resemblance, to the last.[2] Nature always makes a horse succeed to a horse, a lion to a lion, an eagle to an eagle, and preserving each animal by these uninterrupted successions she transmits it to the end of all things. .Animals do not see their peculiarities destroyed or effaced by any length of time; their nature, as though it had been just constituted, follows the course of ages, for ever young.[3] "Let the earth bring forth the living creature." This command has continued and earth does not cease to obey the Creator. For, if there are creatures which are successively produced by their predecessors, there are others that even to-day we see born from the earth itself. In wet weather she brings forth grasshoppers and an immense number of insects which fly in the air and have no names because they are so small; she also produces mice and frogs. In the environs of Thebes in Egypt, after abundant rain in hot weather,

the country is covered with field mice.[1] We see mud alone produce eels; they do not proceed from an egg, nor in any other manner; it is the earth alone which gives them birth.[2] Let the earth produce a living creature."

Cattle are terrestrial and bent towards the earth. Man, a celestial growth, rises superior to them as much by the mould of his bodily conformation as by the dignity of his soul. What is the form of quadrupeds? Their head is bent towards the earth and looks towards their belly, and only pursues their belly's good. Thy head, O man! is turned towards heaven; thy eyes look up.[3] When therefore thou degradest thyself by the passions of the flesh, slave of thy belly, and thy lowest parts, thou approachest animals without reason and becomest like one of them.[4] Thou art called to more noble cares; "seek those things which are above where Christ sitteth."[5] Raise thy soul above the earth; draw from its natural conformation the rule of thy conduct; fix thy conversation in heaven. Thy true country is the heavenly Jerusalem;[6] thy fellow-citizens and thy compatriots are "the first-born which are written in heaven."[7]

3. "*Let the earth bring forth the living creature.*" Thus when the soul of brutes appeared it was not concealed in the earth, but it was born by the command of God. Brutes have one and the same soul of which the common characteristic is absence of reason. But each animal is distinguished by peculiar qualities. The ox is steady, the ass is lazy, the horse has strong passions, the wolf cannot be tamed, the fox is deceitful, the stag timid, the ant industrious, the dog grateful and faithful in his friendships. As each animal was created the distinctive character of his nature appeared in him in due measure; in the lion spirit, taste for solitary life, an unsociable character. True tyrant of animals, he, in his natural arrogance, admits but few to share his honours. He disdains his yesterday's food and never re-

---

[1] Gen. i. 24.   [2] *cf.* note on *Hom.* v. p. 76.
[3] " *Sed, si quæque suo ritu procedit, et omnes*
    Fædere naturæ certo discrimina servant."
                   Luc. v. 921.

[1] *cf.* Plin. ix. 84: " *Verum omnibus his fidem Nili inundatio affert omnia excedente miraculo : quippe detegente eo musculi reperiuntur inchoato opere genitalis aquæ terræque, jam parte corporis viventes, novissima effigie etiamnum terrena.*" So Mela *De Nilo* i. 9, " *Glebis etiam infundit animas, ex ipsoque humo vitalia effingit,*" and Ovid, *Met.* i. 42:
   " *Sic ubi deseruit madidos septemfluus agros*
    Nilus, et antiquo sua flumina reddidit alveo,
    Æthereoque recens exarsit sidere limus,
    Plurima cultores versis animalia glebis
    Inveniunt."
[2] Arist., *H.A.* vi. 16. Αἱ ἐγχέλυς γίγνονται εκ τῶν καλουμενων γῆς ἐντέρων ἃ αὐτόματα συνίστσται εν τῷ πηλῷ καὶ ἐν τῇ γῇ ἐνίκμῳ. Καὶ ἤδη εἰσιν ὠμμέναι αἱ μὲν ἐκδὺνουσαι ἐκ τούτων, αἱ δὲ ἐν διακνιζομένοις καὶ διαιρουμένοις γίγνονται φανεραί.
[3] Arist., *Part. An.* iv. 10, 18. μόνον ὀρθόν ἐστι τῶν ζῴων ὁ ἄνθρωπος.
[4] *cf.* Ps. xlix. 12.   [6] *cf.* Phil. iii. 20.
[5] Col. iii. 1.   [7] Heb. xii. 23.

turns to the remains of the prey. Nature has provided his organs of voice with such great force that often much swifter animals are caught by his roaring alone. The panther, violent and impetuous in his leaps, has a body fitted for his activity and lightness, in accord with the movements of his soul. The bear has a sluggish nature, ways of its own, a sly character, and is very secret; therefore it has an analogous body, heavy, thick, without articulations such as are necessary for a cold dweller in dens.

When we consider the natural and innate care that these creatures without reason take of their lives we shall be induced to watch over ourselves and to think of the salvation of our souls; or rather we shall be the more condemned when we are found falling short even of the imitation of brutes. The bear, which often gets severely wounded, cares for himself and cleverly fills the wounds with mullein, a plant whose nature is very astringent. You will also see the fox heal his wounds with droppings from the pine tree; the tortoise, gorged with the flesh of the viper, finds in the virtue of marjoram a specific against this venomous animal[1] and the serpent heals sore eyes by eating fennel.[2]

And is not reasoning intelligence eclipsed by animals in their provision for atmospheric changes? Do we not see sheep, when winter is approaching, devouring grass with avidity as if to make provision for future scarcity? Do we not also see oxen, long confined in the winter season, recognise the return of spring by a natural sensation, and look to the end of their stables towards the doors, all turning their heads there by common consent? Studious observers have remarked that the hedgehog makes an opening at the two extremities of his hole. If the wind from the north is going to blow he shuts up the aperture which looks towards the north; if the south wind succeeds it the animal passes to the northern door.[3] What lesson do these animals teach man? They not only show us in our Creator a care which extends to all beings, but a certain presentiment of future even in brutes. Then we ought not to attach ourselves to this present life and ought to give all heed to that which is to come. Will you not be industrious for yourself, O man? And will you

not lay up in the present age rest in that which is to come, after having seen the example of the ant? The ant during summer collects treasures for winter. Far from giving itself up to idleness, before this season has made it feel its severity, it hastens to work with an invincible zeal until it has abundantly filled its storehouses. Here again, how far it is from being negligent! With what wise foresight it manages so as to keep its provisions as long as possible! With its pincers it cuts the grains in half, for fear lest they should germinate and not serve for its food. If they are damp it dries them; and it does not spread them out in all weathers, but when it feels that the air will keep of a mild temperature. Be sure that you will never see rain fall from the clouds so long as the ant has left the grain out.[1]

What language can attain to the marvels of the Creator? What ear could understand them? And what time would be sufficient to relate them? Let us say, then, with the prophet, "O Lord, how manifold are thy works! in wisdom hast thou made them all."[2] We shall not be able to say in self-justification, that we have learnt useful knowledge in books, since the untaught law of nature makes us choose that which is advantageous to us. Do you know what good you ought to do your neighbour? The good that you expect from him yourself. Do you know what is evil? That which you would not wish another to do to you. Neither botanical researches nor the experience of simples have made animals discover those which are useful to them; but each knows naturally what is salutary and marvellously appropriates what suits its nature.

4. Virtues exist in us also by nature, and the soul has affinity with them not by education, but by nature herself. We do not need lessons to hate illness, but by ourselves we repel what afflicts us, the soul has no need of a master to teach us to avoid vice. Now all vice is a sickness of the soul as virtue is its health. Thus those have defined health well who have called it a regularity in the discharge of natural functions; a definition that can be applied without fear to the good condition of the soul. Thus, without having need of lessons, the soul can attain by herself to what is fit and conformable to nature.[3] Hence it

---

[1] Plut. πότ. τῶν. ζ. κ.τ.λ. χελῶναι μὲν ὀρίγανον, γαλαῖ δὲ πήγανον, ὅταν ὄφεως φάγωσιν, ἐπεσθίουσαι.
cf. Pliny xx. 68: "Tragoriganum contra viperae ictum efficacissimum."
[2] ὁ δράκων ὁ τῷ μαράθρῳ τὸν ὀφθαλμὸν ἀμβλυώπτοντα λεπτύνων καὶ διαναράττων. Plut. πότερα τῶν ζ. κ.τ.λ. 731.
[3] Ar., Hist. An. ix. 6. περὶ δὲ τῆς τῶν ἐχίνων αἰσθήσεως συμβέβηκε πολλαχοῦ τεθεωρῆσθαι ὅτι μεταβαλλόντων βορέων καὶ νότων οἱ μὲν ἐν τῇ γῇ τὰς ὀπὰς αὐτῶν μεταμείβουσι οἱ δ' ἐν ταῖς οἰκίαις τρεφόμενοι μεταβάλλουσι πρὸς τοὺς τοίχους.

[1] ὑετοῦ ποιεῖται σημεῖον ὁ Ἄρατος
' ἢ κοίλης μύρμηκες ὀχῆς ἐξ ὤεα πάντα
θᾶσσον ἀνηνέγκαντο.'
καίτινες οὐκ ὠὰ γράφουσιν, ἀλλὰ ἵνα τοὺς ἀποκειμένους καρποὺς ὅταν εὑρῶτα συναγόντας αἰσθῶνται καὶ φοβηθῶσι φθορὰν καὶ σῆψιν ἀναφερόντων, ὑπερβάλλει δὲ πᾶσαν ἐπίνοιαν συνέσεως ἡ τοῦ πυροῦ τῆς βλαστήσεως προκατάληψις. Plut. ποτ. τῶν. ζ. κ.τ.λ. 725.
[2] Ps. civ. 24.
[3] This is the Stoic doctrine. " Stoicorum quidem facilis conclusio est; qui cum finem bonorum esse senserint, con-

comes that temperance everywhere is praised, justice is in honour, courage admired, and prudence the object of all aims; virtues which concern the soul more than health concerns the body. Children love[1] your parents, and you, " parents provoke not your children to wrath."[2] Does not nature say the same? Paul teaches us nothing new; he only tightens the links of nature. If the lioness loves her cubs, if the she wolf fights to defend her little ones, what shall man say who is unfaithful to the precept and violates nature herself; or the son who insults the old age of his father; or the father whose second marriage has made him forget his first children?

With animals invincible affection unites parents with children. It is the Creator, God Himself, who substitutes the strength of feeling for reason in them. From whence it comes that a lamb as it bounds from the fold, in the midst of a thousand sheep recognises the colour and the voice of its mother, runs to her, and seeks its own sources of milk. If its mother's udders are dry, it is content, and, without stopping, passes by more abundant ones. And how does the mother recognise it among the many lambs? All have the same voice, the same colour, the same smell, as far at least as regards our sense of smell. Yet there is in these animals a more subtle sense than our perception which makes them recognise their own.[1] The little dog has as yet no teeth, nevertheless he defends himself with his mouth against any one who teases him. The calf has as yet no horns, nevertheless he already knows where his weapons will grow.[2] Here we have evident proof that the instinct of animals is innate, and that in all beings there is nothing disorderly, nothing unforeseen. All bear the marks of the wisdom of the Creator, and show that they have come to life with the means of assuring their preservation.

The dog is not gifted with a share of reason; but with him instinct has the power of reason. The dog has learnt by nature the secret of elaborate inferences, which sages of the world, after long years of study, have hardly been able to disentangle. When the dog is on the track of game, if he sees it divide in different directions, he examines these different paths, and speech alone fails him to announce his reasoning. The creature, he says, is gone here or there or in another direction. It is neither here nor there; it is therefore in the third direction. And thus, neglecting the false tracks, he discovers the true one. What more is done by those who, gravely occupied in demonstrating theories, trace lines upon the dust and reject two propositions to show that the third is the true one?[3]

Does not the gratitude of the dog shame all who are ungrateful to their benefactors? Many are said to have fallen dead by their murdered masters in lonely places.[4] Others, when a crime has just been committed, have led those who were searching for the murderers, and have caused the criminals to be brought to justice. What will those say who, not content with not loving the Master who has created them and nourished them, have for their friends men whose mouth attacks the Lord, sitting at the same table with them, and, whilst partaking of their food, blaspheme Him who has given it to them?

---

gruere naturæ, cumque ea convenienter vivere." cf. Cic., De Fin. iii. 7, 26, and De Nat. D. i. 14, and Hor., Ep., i. x. 12. " Vivere naturæ si convenienter oportet." So the Stoics' main rule of life is ὁμολογουμένως τῇ φύσει ζῆν. But with Basil this apparent disregard of the doctrine of original sin and the need of grace for redemption must be understood in the light of the catholic doctrine that sin is the corruption of human nature (cf. Art. ix. of Original or Birth Sin), which nature, though corrupt and prone to evil, retains capacities for good. But these capacities do need grace and training. cf. Basil's Homily on Ps. xlv. 166. " What is said about the Saviour has a double sense on account of the nature of the Godhead and the Economy of the incarnation. So, looking to the humanity of God, it is said 'thou hast loved righteousness and hated iniquity,' instead of saying ' the rest of men by toil and discipline and careful attention mostly attain a disposition towards good and an aversion from vice. But thou hast a kind of natural relationship to good and alienation from iniquity.' And so to us, if we will, it is not hard to acquire a love of righteousness and a hatred of iniquity." i.e. In Christ, redeemed humanity loves good, and all men ' naturally' do need toil and discipline. The heredity of sin is recognised by Basil. (e.g. in Hom. in Famem. 7.) Man fell from grace given, and must return to it. (Serm. Ascet. in init.) It must always be remembered that questions of original sin, the will, and grace never had the same importance in the Greek as they had in the Latin church. cf. Dr. Travers Smith on St. Basil (c. ix. p. 108) and Böhringer (Das Vierte Jahrhundert. Rasil, p. 102) who remarks: Wenn er auch noch von einer "Wieder herstellung des freien Willens, den wir zu brauchbaren Gefässen für den Herrn und zu jedem guten Werke fähig Werden" (De spir. sanct. 18), spricht, so hat er dies doch nirgends begründet, obschon er bei der Besprechung der Folgen des Falls zuweilen sich äussert, es sei der Mensch der von dem Schöpfer erhaltenen Freiheit beraubt worden. Im Allgemeinen setzt er den freien Willen auch nach dem Fall im Menschen so gut wieder Voraus, wie vor dem Fall, so dass jene Aeusserungen kaum mehr als den Werth einer Redensart haben. Im Ganzen erinnert seine Darstellung wieder an diejenige des Athanasius, dessen Einfluss Man nicht verkennen kann.

[1] In Eph. vi. the word is " obey."
[2] cf. Eph. vi. 4.

[1] Fialon quotes Luc. ii. 367-370:
" Præterea teneri tremulis cum vocibus hædi
Cornigeras norunt matres, agnique petulci
Balantum pecudes : ita, quod natura reposcit,
Ad sua quisque fere decurrunt ubera lactis."
[2] cf. Ovid (Halieut. ad init.) :
" Accepit mundus legem ; dedit arma per omnes,
Admonuitque sui. Vitulus sic namque minatur,
Qui nondum gerit in tenera jam cornua fronte."
[3] cf. Plutarch (ποτ. των. ς. φρ. κ.τ.λ. 726). οἱ δὲ διαλεκτικοί φασι τὸν κύνα τῷ διὰ πλειόνων διεζευγμένῳ χρώμενον ἐν τοῖς πολυσχιδέσιν ἀτραποῖς συλλογίζεσθαι πρὸς ἑαυτὸν ἤτοι τήνδε τὸ θηρίον ὥρμηκεν ἢ τήνδε ἢ τήνδε· ἀλλὰ μὴν οὔτε τήνδε οὔτε τήνδε, τήνδε λοιπὸν. ἄρα. But the dog is said to smell the first, the second, and the third. If he started off on the third without smelling, he would reason. As it is, there is no " syllogism."
[4] Also taken from Plutarch (πότεοα τῶν ς. 726), who tells stories of a dog found by King Pyrrhus on a journey, and of Hesiod's dog.

5. But let us return to the spectacle of creation. The easiest animals to catch are the most productive. It is on account of this that hares and wild goats produce many little ones, and that wild sheep have twins, for fear lest these species should disappear, consumed by carnivorous animals. Beasts of prey, on the contrary, produce only a few and a lioness with difficulty gives birth to one lion;[1] because, if they say truly, the cub issues from its mother by tearing her with its claws; and vipers are only born by gnawing through the womb, inflicting a proper punishment on their mother.[2] Thus in nature all has been foreseen, all is the object of continual care. If you examine the members even of animals, you will find that the Creator has given them nothing superfluous, that He has omitted nothing that is necessary. To carnivorous animals He is given pointed teeth which their nature requires for their support. Those that are only half furnished with teeth have received several distinct receptacles for their food. As it is not broken up enough in the first, they are gifted with the power of returning it after it has been swallowed, and it does not assimilate until it has been crushed by rumination. The first, second, third, and fourth stomachs of ruminating animals do not remain idle; each one of them fulfils a necessary function.[3] The neck of the camel is long so that it may lower it to its feet and reach the grass on which it feeds. Bears, lions, tigers, all animals of this sort, have short necks buried in their shoulders; it is because they do not live upon grass and have no need to bend down to the earth; they are carnivorous and eat the animals upon whom they prey.

Why has the elephant a trunk? This enormous creature, the greatest of terrestrial animals, created for the terror of those who meet it, is naturally huge and fleshy. If its neck was large and in proportion to its feet it would be difficult to direct, and would be of such an excessive weight that it would make it lean towards the earth. As it is, its head is attached to the spine of the back by short vertebræ and it has its trunk to take the place of a neck, and with it it picks up its food and draws up its drink. Its feet, without joints,[1] like united columns, support the weight of its body. If it were supported on lax and flexible legs, its joints would constantly give way, equally incapable of supporting its weight, should it wish either to kneel or rise. But it has under the foot a little ankle joint which takes the place of the leg and knee joints whose mobility would never have resisted this enormous and swaying mass. Thus it had need of this nose which nearly touches its feet. Have you seen them in war marching at the head of the phalanx, like living towers, or breaking the enemies' battalions like mountains of flesh with their irresistible charge? If their lower parts were not in accordance with their size they would never have been able to hold their own. Now we are told that the elephant lives three hundred years and more,[2] another reason for him to have solid and unjointed feet. But, as we have said, his trunk, which has the form and the flexibility of a serpent, takes its food from the earth and raises it up. Thus we are right in saying that it is impossible to find anything superfluous or wanting in creation. Well! God has subdued this monstrous animal to us to such a point that he understands the lessons and endures the blows we give him; a manifest proof that the Creator has submitted all to our rule, because we have been made in His image. It is not in great animals only that we see unapproachable wisdom; no less wonders are seen in the smallest. The high tops of the mountains which, near to the clouds and continually beaten by the winds, keep up a perpetual winter, do not arouse more admiration in me than the hollow valleys, which escape the · storms of lofty peaks and preserve a constant mild temperature. In the same way in the constitution of animals I am not more astonished at the size of the elephant, than at the mouse, who is feared by the elephant, or at the scorpion's delicate sting, which has been hollowed like a pipe by the supreme artificer to throw venom into the wounds it makes. And let nobody accuse the Creator of having produced venomous animals, destroyers and enemies of our life. Else let them consider it a crime in the schoolmaster when he disciplines the restlessness of youth by the use of the rod and whip to maintain order.[3]

6. Beasts bear witness to the faith. Hast thou confidence in the Lord? " Thou

---

[1] cf. Herod. iii. 108. Aristotle (*Hist. An.* vi. 31) refutes this.

[2] cf. Pliny (x. 72) : " *Tertia die intra uterum catulos excludit, deinde singulos singulis diebus parit, viginti fere numero. Itaque ceteræ, tarditatis impatientes, perrumpunt latera, occisa parente.* cf. Herod. iii. 109.
So Prudentius (*Hamartigenia* 583) :
" *Sic vipera, ut aiunt,*
Dentibus emoritur fusæ per viscera prolis."
See Sir T. Browne's *Vulgar Errors,* iii. 16.

[3] Pliny (xi. 78) says *ruminantibus* geminus, but this is supposed to be a misreading for *quadrigeminus,* or a mistaken interpretation of Aristotle (*H.A.* ii. 19), whom Basil is no doubt following.

---

[1] See Sir T. Browne, *Vulgar Errors,* iii. 1.
[2] Arist. *H.A.* viii. 12 and ix. 72. Pliny vii. 10.
[3] cf. *Hom.* v. 4.

shalt walk upon the asp and the basilisk and thou shalt trample under feet the lion and the dragon." [1] With faith thou hast the power to walk upon serpents and scorpions. Do you not see that the viper which attached itself to the hand of Paul, whilst he gathered sticks, did not injure him, because it found the saint full of faith? If you have not faith, do not fear beasts so much as your faithlessness, which renders you susceptible of all corruption. But I see that for a long time you have been asking me for an account of the creation of man, and I think I can hear you all cry in your hearts, We are being taught the nature of our belongings, but we are ignorant of ourselves. Let me then speak of it, since it is necessary, and let me put an end to my hesitation. In truth the most difficult of sciences is to know one's self. Not only our eye, from which nothing outside us escapes, cannot see itself ; but our mind, so piercing to discover the sins of others, is slow to recognise its own faults.[2] Thus my speech, after eagerly investigating what is external to myself, is slow and hesitating in exploring my own nature. Yet the beholding of heaven and earth does not make us know God better than the attentive study of our being does ; I am, says the Prophet, fearfully and wonderfully made ;[3] that is to say, in observing myself I have known Thy infinite wisdom.[4] And God said " Let us make man." [5] Does not the light of theology shine, in these words, as through windows ; and does not the second Person show Himself in a mystical way, without yet manifesting Himself until the great day? Where is the Jew who resisted the truth and pretended that God was speaking to Himself? It is He who spoke, it is said, and it is He who made. " Let there be light and there was light." But then their words contain a manifest absurdity. Where is the smith, the carpenter, the shoemaker, who, without help and alone before the instruments of his trade, would say to himself ; let us make the sword, let us put together the plough, let us make the boot? Does he not perform the work of his craft in silence? Strange folly, to say that any one has seated himself to command himself, to watch over himself, to constrain himself, to hurry him-

self, with the tones of a master ! But the unhappy creatures are not afraid to calumniate the Lord Himself. What will they not say with a tongue so well practised in lying? Here, however, words stop their mouth ; " And God said let us make man." Tell me ; is there then only one Person? It is not written " Let man be made," but, " Let us make man." The preaching of theology remains enveloped in shadow before the appearance of him who was to be instructed, but, now, the creation of man is expected, that faith unveils herself and the dogma of truth appears in all its light. " Let us make man." O enemy of Christ, hear God speaking to His Co-operator, to Him by Whom also He made the worlds, Who upholds all things by the word of His power.[1] But He does not leave the voice of true religion without answer. Thus the Jews, race hostile to truth, when they find themselves pressed, act like beasts enraged against man, who roar at the bars of their cage and show the cruelty and the ferocity of their nature, without being able to assuage their fury. God, they say, addresses Himself to several persons ; it is to the angels before Him that He says, " Let us make man." Jewish fiction ! a fable whose frivolity shows whence it has come. To reject one person, they admit many. To reject the Son, they raise servants to the dignity of counsellors ; they make of our fellow slaves the agents in our creation. The perfect man attains the dignity of an angel ; but what creature can be like the Creator ? Listen to the continuation, " In our image." What have you to reply ? Is there one image of God and the angels? Father and Son have by absolute necessity the same form, but the form is here understood as becomes the divine, not in bodily shape, but in the proper qualities of Godhead. Hear also, you who belong to the new concision,[2] and who, under the appearance of Christianity, strengthen the error of the Jews.[3] To Whom does He say, " in our image," to whom if it is not to Him who is " the brightness of His glory and the express image of His person," [4] " the image of the invisible God " ? [5] It is then to His living image, to Him Who has said " I and my Father are one," [6] " He that hath seen me hath seen the Father," [7] that God says " Let us make man in our image." Where is the unlikeness [8] in these Beings who have only one image ? " So God created man," [9]

---

[1] cf. Ps. xci. 13. [2] cf. St. Matt. vii. 3.
[3] cf. Ps. cxxxix. 14.
[4] " E cœlo descendit γνῶθι σεαυτόν " (Juv. xi. 27). Socrates, Chilo, Thales, Cleobulus, Bias, Pythagoras, have all been credited with the saying. " On reconnaît ici le précepte fécond de l'école socratique. L'église chrétienne s'en empara comme de tout ce qu'elle trouvait de grand et de bon dans l'ancienne Grèce. Fialon.
St. Basil has a Homily on the text πρόσεχε σεαυτῷ (Deut. xv. 9, lxx.)
[5] Gen. i. 26.

[1] cf. Heb. i. 2, 3.   [4] Heb. i. 3.   [6] John x. 30.
[2] Phil. iii. 2.   [5] Col. i. 15.   [7] John xiv. 9.
[3] The Arians.
[8] τὸ ἀνόμοιον. Arius had taught that the Persons are ἀνόμοιοι πάμπαν ἀλλήλων.   [9] Gen. i. 27.

It is not " They made." Here Scripture avoids the plurality of the Persons. After having enlightened the Jew, it dissipates the error of the Gentiles in putting itself under the shelter of unity, to make you understand that the Son is with the Father, and guarding you from the danger of polytheism. He created him in the image of God. God still shows us His co-operator, because He does not say, in His image, but in the image of God.

If God permits, we will say later in what way man was created in the image of God, and how he shares this resemblance. To-day we say but only one word. If there is one image, from whence comes the intolerable blasphemy of pretending that the Son is unlike the Father? What ingratitude! You have yourself received this likeness and you refuse it to your Benefactor! You pretend to keep personally that which is in you a gift of grace, and you do not wish that the Son should keep His natural likeness to Him who begat Him.

But evening, which long ago sent the sun to the west, imposes silence upon me. Here, then, let me be content with what I have said, and put my discourse to bed. I have told you enough up to this point to excite your zeal; with the help of the Holy Spirit I will make for you a deeper investigation into the truths which follow. Retire, then, I beg you, with joy, O Christ-loving congregation, and, instead of sumptuous dishes of various delicacies, adorn and sanctify your tables with the remembrance of my words. May the Anomœan be confounded, the Jew covered with shame, the faithful exultant in the dogmas of truth, and the Lord glorified, the Lord to Whom be glory and power, world without end. Amen.

INTRODUCTION TO THE LETTERS.

Of Saint Basil the extant letters, according to popular ascription, number three hundred and sixty-six. Of these three hundred and twenty-five, or, according to some, only three hundred and nineteen are genuine. They are published in three chronological divisions, the 1st, (Letters 1–46) comprising those written by Basil before his elevation to the episcopate; the second (47–291) the Letters of the Episcopate; the third (292–366) those which have no note of time, together with some that are of doubtful genuineness, and a few certainly spurious.[1] They may be classified as (a) historical, (b) dogmatic, (c) moral and ascetic, (d) disciplinary, (e) consolatory, (f) commendatory, and (g) familiar. In the historic we have a vivid picture of his age. The doctrinal are of special value as expressing and defending the Nicene theology. The moral and ascetic indicate the growing importance of the monastic institution which Athanasius at about the same time was instrumental in recommending to the Latin Church. The disciplinary, (notably 188, 199, and 217), to Amphilochius, illustrate the earlier phases of ecclesiastical law. The consolatory, commendatory, and familiar, have an immediate biographical value as indicating the character and faith of the writer, and may not be without use alike as models of Christian feeling and good breeding, and as bringing comfort in trouble to readers remote in time and place. The text in the following translation is that of Migne's edition, except where it is stated to the contrary. Of the inadequacy of the notes to illustrate the letters as they deserve no one can be more vividly conscious than myself. But the letters tell their own story.

LETTER I.[2]

To Eustathius the Philosopher.[3]

MUCH distressed as I was by the flouts of what is called fortune, who always seems to be hindering my meeting you, I was wonderfully cheered and comforted by your letter, for I had already been turning over in my mind whether what so many people say is really true, that there is a certain Necessity or Fate which rules all the events of our lives both great and small, and that we human beings have control over nothing; or, that at all events, all human life is driven by a kind of luck.[4] You will be very ready to forgive me for these reflexions, when you learn by what causes I was led to make them.

On hearing of your philosophy, I entertained a feeling of contempt for the teachers of Athens, and left it. The city on the Hellespont I passed by, more unmoved than any Ulysses, passing Sirens' songs.[5] Asia[6] I admired; but I hurried on to the capital of all that is best in it. When I arrived home, and did not find you, — the prize which I had sought so eagerly, — there began many and various unexpected hindrances. First I must miss you because I fell ill; then when you were setting out for the East I could not start with you; then, after endless trouble, I reached Syria, but I missed the philosopher, who had set out for Egypt. Then I must set out for Egypt, a long and weary way, and even there I did not gain my end. But so passionate was my longing that I must either set out for Persia, and proceed with you to the farthest lands of barbarism, (you had got there; what an obstinate devil possessed me!) or settle here at Alexandria. This last I did. I really think that unless, like some tame beast, I had followed a bough held out

[1] Fessler, *Inst. Pat.* i. 518.   [2] Placed in 357.
[3] Another MS. reading is "To Eustathius, Presbyter of Antioch." The Benedictine note is "Eustathius was not a Presbyter, but a heathen, as is indicated by Basil's words, 'Are not these things work of fate, — of necessity, as you would say?'"   [4] The word τύχη does not occur in the N.T.
[5] ὡς οὐδεὶς Ὀδυσσεύς. The Ben. translation is "citius *quam quisquam Ulysses.*" But the reason of the escape of Ulysses was not his speed, but his stopping the ears of his crew with wax and tying himself to the mast. *cf.* Hom. *Od.* xii. 158. The "city on the Hellespont," is, according to the Ben. note, Constantinople; but Constantinople is more than 100 m. from the Dardanelles, and Basil could hardly write so loosely.
[6] Apparently not the Roman Province of Asia, but what we call Asia Minor, a name which came into use in Basil's century. The "metropolis" is supposed to mean Cæsarea.

to me till I was quite worn out, you would have been driven on and on beyond Indian Nyssa,[1] or any more remote region, and wandered about out there. Why say more?

On returning home, I cannot meet you, hindered by lingering ailments. If these do not get better I shall not be able to meet you even in the winter. Is not all this, as you yourself say, due to Fate? Is not this Necessity? Does not my case nearly outdo poets' tales of Tantalus? But, as I said, I feel better after getting your letter, and am now no longer of the same mind. When God gives good things I think we must thank Him, and not be angry with Him while He is controlling their distribution. So if He grant me to join you, I shall think it best and most delightful; if He put me off, I will gently endure the loss. For He always rules our lives better than we could choose for ourselves.

LETTER II.[2]

Basil to Gregory.

1. [I recognised your letter, as one recognises one's friends' children from their obvious likeness to their parents. Your saying that to describe the kind of place I live in, before letting you hear anything about how I live, would not go far towards persuading you to share my life, was just like you; it was worthy of a soul like yours, which makes nothing of all that concerns this life here, in comparison with the blessedness which is promised us hereafter. What I do myself, day and night, in this remote spot, I am ashamed to write. I have abandoned my life in town, as one sure to lead to countless ills; but I have not yet been able to get quit of myself. I am like travellers at sea, who have never gone a voyage before, and are distressed and seasick, who quarrel with the ship because it is so big and makes such a tossing, and, when they get out of it into the pinnace or dingey, are everywhere and always seasick and distressed. Wherever they go their nausea and misery go with them. My state is something like this. I carry my own troubles with me, and so everywhere I am in the midst of similar discomforts. So in the end I have not got much good out of my solitude. What I ought to have done; what would have enabled me to keep close to the footprints of

Him who has led the way to salvation — for He says, "If any one will come after me, let him deny himself and take up his cross, and follow me"[1] — is this.]

2. We must strive after a quiet mind. As well might the eye ascertain an object put before it while it is wandering restless up and down and sideways, without fixing a steady gaze upon it, as a mind, distracted by a thousand worldly cares, be able clearly to apprehend the truth. He who is not yet yoked in the bonds of matrimony is harassed by frenzied cravings, and rebellious impulses, and hopeless attachments; he who has found his mate is encompassed with his own tumult of cares; if he is childless, there is desire for children; has he children? anxiety about their education, attention to his wife,[2] care of his house, oversight of his servants,[3] misfortunes in trade, quarrels with his neighbours, lawsuits, the risks of the merchant, the toil of the farmer. Each day, as it comes, darkens the soul in its own way; and night after night takes up the day's anxieties, and cheats the mind with illusions in accordance. Now one way of escaping all this is separation from the whole world; that is, not bodily separation, but the severance of the soul's sympathy with the body, and to live so without city, home, goods, society, possessions, means of life, business, engagements, human learning, that the heart may readily receive every impress of divine doctrine. Preparation of heart is the unlearning the prejudices of evil converse. It is the smoothing the waxen tablet before attempting to write on it.[4]

Now solitude is of the greatest use for this purpose, inasmuch as it stills our passions, and gives room for principle to cut them out of the soul.[5] [For just as animals are more easily controlled when they are stroked, lust and anger, fear and sorrow, the soul's deadly foes, are better brought under the control of reason, after being calmed by inaction, and where there is no continuous stimulation.] Let there then be such a place as ours, separate from intercourse with men, that the tenour of our exercises be not interrupted from without. Pious exercises nourish the soul with divine thoughts. What state can be more blessed than to imitate on earth the choruses of angels? to begin the day with

---

[1] Matt. xvi. 24.
[2] γυναικὸς φυλακή, rather " guardianship of his wife."
[3] οἰκετῶν προστασίαι, rather " protection of his servants."
[4] Rather " for just as it is impossible to write on the wax without previously erasing the marks on it, so is it impossible to communicate divine doctrines to the soul without removing from it its preconceived and habitual notions."
[5] The following paragraph is altogether omitted by Newman.

---

[1] Νύσιος = 'Ινδικός. cf. Soph. Aj. 707. Nyssa was in the Punjab.
[2] Placed circa 358, on Basil's retiring to Pontus. Translated in part by Newman, The Church of the Fathers, p. 131, ed. 1840. With the exception of the passages in brackets [ ], the version in the text is that of Newman.

prayer, and honour our Maker with hymns and songs? As the day brightens, to betake ourselves, with prayer attending on it throughout, to our labours, and to sweeten[1] our work with hymns, as if with salt? Soothing hymns compose the mind to a cheerful and calm state. Quiet, then, as I have said, is the first step in our sanctification; the tongue purified from the gossip of the world; the eyes unexcited by fair colour or comely shape; the ear not relaxing the tone of mind by voluptuous songs, nor by that especial mischief, the talk of light men and jesters. Thus the mind, saved from dissipation from without, and not through the senses thrown upon the world, falls back upon itself, and thereby ascends to the contemplation of God. [When[2] that beauty shines about it, it even forgets its very nature; it is dragged down no more by thought of food nor anxiety concerning dress; it keeps holiday from earthly cares, and devotes all its energies to the acquisition of the good things which are eternal, and asks only how may be made to flourish in it self-control and manly courage, righteousness and wisdom, and all the other virtues, which, distributed under these heads, properly enable the good man to discharge all the duties of life.]

3. The study of inspired Scripture is the chief way of finding our duty, for in it we find both instruction about conduct and the lives of blessed men, delivered in writing, as some breathing images of godly living, for the imitation of their good works. Hence, in whatever respect each one feels himself deficient, devoting himself to this imitation, he finds, as from some dispensary, the due medicine for his ailment. He who is enamoured of chastity dwells upon the history of Joseph, and from him learns chaste actions, finding him not only possessed of self-command over pleasure, but virtuously-minded in habit. He is taught endurance by Job [who,[3] not only when the circumstances of life began to turn against him, and in one moment he was plunged from wealth into penury, and from being the father of fair children into childlessness, remained the same, keeping the disposition of his soul all through uncrushed, but was not even stirred to anger against the friends who came to comfort him, and trampled on him, and aggravated his troubles.] Or should he be enquiring how to be at once meek and great-hearted, hearty against sin, meek towards men, he will find David noble in warlike exploits, meek and unruf-

fled as regards revenge on enemies. Such, too, was Moses, rising up with great heart upon sinners against God, but with meek soul bearing their evil-speaking against himself. [Thus,[1] generally, as painters, when they are painting from other pictures, constantly look at the model, and do their best to transfer its lineaments to their own work, so too must he who is desirous of rendering himself perfect in all branches of excellency, keep his eyes turned to the lives of the saints as though to living and moving statues, and make their virtue his own by imitation.

4. Prayers, too, after reading, find the soul fresher, and more vigorously stirred by love towards God. And that prayer is good which imprints a clear idea of God in the soul; and the having God established in self by means of memory is God's indwelling. Thus we become God's temple, when the continuity of our recollection is not severed by earthly cares; when the mind is harassed by no sudden sensations; when the worshipper flees from all things and retreats to God, drawing away all the feelings that invite him to self-indulgence, and passes his time in the pursuits that lead to virtue.]

5. This, too, is a very important point to attend to, — knowledge how to converse; to interrogate without over-earnestness; to answer without desire of display; not to interrupt a profitable speaker, or to desire ambitiously to put in a word of one's own; to be measured in speaking and hearing; not to be ashamed of receiving, or to be grudging in giving information, nor to pass another's knowledge for one's own, as depraved women their supposititious children, but to refer it candidly to the true parent. The middle tone of voice is best, neither so low as to be inaudible, nor to be ill-bred from its high pitch. One should reflect first what one is going to say, and then give it utterance: be courteous when addressed; amiable in social intercourse; not aiming to be pleasant by facetiousness, but cultivating gentleness in kind admonitions. Harshness is ever to be put aside, even in censuring.[2] [The more you shew modesty and humility yourself, the more likely are you to be acceptable to the patient who needs your treatment. There are however many occasions when we shall do well to employ the kind of rebuke used by the prophet who did not in his own person utter the sentence of condemnation on David after his sin, but by suggesting an imaginary character made the

---

[1] Rather "season."   [2] Omitted by Newman.
[3] Clause omitted by Newman.

[1] Omitted by Newman.
[2] Here Newman notes that Basil seems sometimes to have fallen short of his own ideal. His translation ends at this point.

sinner judge of his own sin, so that, after passing his own sentence, he could not find fault with the seer who had convicted him.[1]

6. From the humble and submissive spirit comes an eye sorrowful and downcast, appearance neglected, hair rough, dress dirty;[2] so that the appearance which mourners take pains to present may appear our natural condition. The tunic should be fastened to the body by a girdle, the belt not going above the flank, like a woman's, nor left slack, so that the tunic flows loose, like an idler's. The gait ought not to be sluggish, which shews a character without energy, nor on the other hand pushing and pompous, as though our impulses were rash and wild. The one end of dress is that it should be a sufficient covering alike in winter and summer. As to colour, avoid brightness; in material, the soft and delicate. To aim at bright colours in dress is like women's beautifying when they colour cheeks and hair with hues other than their own. The tunic ought to be thick enough not to want other help to keep the wearer warm. The shoes should be cheap but serviceable. In a word, what one has to regard in dress is the necessary. So too as to food; for a man in good health bread will suffice, and water will quench thirst; such dishes of vegetables may be added as conduce to strengthening the body for the discharge of its functions. One ought not to eat with any exhibition of savage gluttony, but in everything that concerns our pleasures to maintain moderation, quiet, and self-control; and, all through, not to let the mind forget to think of God, but to make even the nature of our food, and the constitution of the body that takes it, a ground and means for offering Him the glory, bethinking us how the various kinds of food, suitable to the needs of our bodies, are due to the provision of the great Steward of the Universe. Before meat let grace be said, in recognition alike of the gifts which God gives now, and which He keeps in store for time to come. Say grace after meat in gratitude for gifts given and petition for gifts promised. Let there be one fixed hour for taking food, always the same in regular course, that of all the four and twenty of the day and night barely this one may be spent upon the body. The rest the ascetic[1] ought to spend in mental exercise. Let sleep be light and easily interrupted, as naturally happens after a light diet; it should be purposely broken by thoughts about great themes. To be overcome by heavy torpor, with limbs unstrung, so that a way is readily opened to wild fancies, is to be plunged in daily death. What dawn is to some this midnight is to athletes of piety; then the silence of night gives leisure to their soul; no noxious sounds or sights obtrude upon their hearts; the mind is alone with itself and God, correcting itself by the recollection of its sins, giving itself precepts to help it to shun evil, and imploring aid from God for the perfecting of what it longs for.]

LETTER III.[2]

To Candidianus.[3]

1. WHEN I took your letter into my hand, I underwent an experience worth telling. I looked at it with the awe due to a document making some state announcement, and as I was breaking the wax, I felt a dread greater than ever guilty Spartan felt at sight of the Laconian scytale.[4]

When, however, I had opened the letter, and read it through, I could not help laughing, partly for joy at finding nothing alarming in it; partly because I likened your state of affairs to that of Demosthenes. Demosthenes, you remember, when he was providing for a certain little company of chorus dancers and musicians, requested to be styled no longer Demosthenes, but "choragus."[5] You are always the same, whether playing the "choragus" or not. "Choragus" you are indeed to soldiers myriads more in number than the individuals to whom De-

---

[1] Basil's admirable little summary of the main principles of conversation may have been suggested by the recollection of many well known writers. On such a subject no wide reader could be original. cf. *inter alios*, the ἄκουε πολλὰ λάλει δ' ὀλίγα of Bias; the γλῶττα μὴ προτρεχέτω τοῦ νοῦ of Pittacus. Aulus Gellius (*Noct. Att.* i. 15), referring to the

Γλώσσης τοι θησαυρὸς ἐν ἀνθρώποισιν ἄριστος
Φειδωλῆς πλείστη δὲ χάρις κατὰ μέτρον ἰούσης

of Hesiod, says: "*Hesiodus poetarum prudentissimus linguam non vulgandam sed recondendam esse dicit, perinde ut thesaurum. Ejusque esse in promendo gratiam plurimam, si modesta et parca et modulata sit.*"

On the desirability of gentleness in blame, cf. Ambrose, *In Lucam.*: "*Plus proficit amica correctio quam accusatio turbulenta: illa pudorem incutit, hæc indignationem movet.*"

[2] This was the mark of the old heathen philosophers. cf. Aristoph., *Birds* 1282, ἐρρύπων ἐσωκράτων.

[1] ἀσκητής, firstly an artisan, came to = ἀθλητής, and by ecclesiastical writers is used for hermit or monk. The ἐρημίτης, or desert dweller, lives either in retreat as an anchoret, or solitary, μοναχός, whence "monk;" or in common with others, in a κοινόβιον, as a "cœnobite." All would be ἀσκηταί.

[2] Placed at the beginning of the retreat in Pontus.

[3] A governor of Cappadocia, friendly to Basil and to Gregory of Nazianzus. (cf. Greg., *Ep.* cxciv.)

[4] *i.e.* the staff or baton used at Sparta for dispatches. The strip of leather on which the communication was to be made is said to have been rolled slantwise round it, and the message was then written lengthwise. The correspondent was said to have a staff of a size exactly corresponding, and so by rewinding the strip could read what was written. *Vide* Aulus Gellius xvii. 9.

[5] Plutarch πολ. παραγγ. xxii. ἤ τὸ τοῦ Δημοσθένους ὅτι νῦν οὐκ ἔστι Δημοσθένης ἀλλὰ καὶ θεσμοθέτης ἤ χορηγὸς ἤ στεφανηφόρος.

mosthenes supplied necessaries; and yet you do not when you write to me stand on your dignity, but keep up the old style. You do not give up the study of literature, but, as Plato [1] has it, in the midst of the storm and tempest of affairs, you stand aloof, as it were, under some strong wall, and keep your mind clear of all disturbance; nay, more, as far as in you lies, you do not even let others be disturbed. Such is your life; great and wonderful to all who have eyes to see; and yet not wonderful to any one who judges by the whole purpose of your life.

Now let me tell my own story, extraordinary indeed, but only what might have been expected.

2. One of the hinds who live with us here at Annesi,[2] on the death of my servant, without alleging any breach of contract with him, without approaching me, without making any complaint, without asking me to make him any voluntary payment, without any threat of violence should he fail to get it, all on a sudden, with certain mad fellows like himself, attacked my house, brutally assaulted the women who were in charge of it, broke in the doors, and after appropriating some of the contents himself, and promising the rest to any one who liked, carried off everything. I do not wish to be regarded as the *ne plus ultra* of helplessness, and a suitable object for the violence of any one who likes to attack me. Shew me, then, now, I beg you, that kindly interest which you have always shewn in my affairs. Only on one condition can my tranquillity be secured, — that I be assured of having your energy on my side. It would be quite punishment enough, from my point of view, if the man were apprehended by the district magistrate and locked up for a short period in the gaol. It is not only that I am indignant at the treatment I have suffered, but I want security for the future.

LETTER IV.[3]

To Olympius.[4]

WHAT do you mean, my dear Sir, by evicting from our retreat my dear friend and nurse of philosophy, Poverty? Were she but gifted with speech, I take it you would have to appear as defendant in an action for unlawful ejectment. She might plead " I chose to live with this man Basil, an admirer of Zeno,[5] who, when he had lost everything

in a shipwreck, cried, with great fortitude, ' well done, Fortune! you are reducing me to the old cloak; '[1] a great admirer of Cleanthes, who by drawing water from the well got enough to live on and pay his tutors' fees as well;[2] an immense admirer of Diogenes, who prided himself on requiring no more than was absolutely necessary, and flung away his bowl after he had learned from some lad to stoop down and drink from the hollow of his hand." In some such terms as these you might be chidden by my dear mate Poverty, whom your presents have driven from house and home. She might too add a threat; " if I catch you here again, I shall shew that what went before was Sicilian or Italian luxury: so I shall exactly requite you out of my own store."

But enough of this. I am very glad that you have already begun a course of medicine, and pray that you may be benefited by it. A condition of body fit for painless activity would well become so pious a soul.

LETTER V.[3]

To Nectarius.[4]

1. I HEARD of your unendurable loss, and was much distressed. Three or four days went by, and I was still in some doubt because my informant was not able to give me any clear details of the melancholy event. While I was incredulous about what was noised abroad, because I prayed that it might not be true, I received a letter from the Bishop fully confirming the unhappy tidings. I need not tell you how I sighed and wept. Who could be so stony-hearted, so truly inhuman, as to be insensible to what has occurred, or be affected by merely moderate grief? He is gone; heir of a noble house, prop of a family, a father's hope, offspring of pious parents, nursed with innumerable prayers, in the very bloom of manhood, torn from his father's hands. These things are enough to break a heart of adamant and make it feel. It is only natural then that I am deeply touched at this trouble; I who have been intimately connected with you from the beginning and have made your joys and sorrows mine. But yesterday it seemed that you had only little to trouble

---

[1] *Rep.* vi. 10. οἷον ἐν χειμῶνι κονιορτοῦ καὶ ζάλης ὑπὸ πνεύματος φερομένου ὑπὸ τειχίον ἀποστάς.

[2] *Vide Prolegomena.*

[3] Placed about 358. Olympius sends Basil a present in his retreat, and he playfully remonstrates.

[4] *cf. Letters* xii., xiii., lxiii., lxiv., and ccxi.

[5] The founder of the Stoic school.

---

[1] The τρίβων, dim. τριβώνιον, or worn cloak, was emblematic of the philosopher and later of the monk, as now the cowl. *cf.* Lucian, *Pereg.* 15, and Synesius, *Ep.* 147.

[2] Cleanthes, the Lydian Stoic, was hence called φρέαντλος, or well drawer. On him *vide* Val. Max. viii. 7 and Sen., *Ep.* 44.

[3] Placed about 358.

[4] *cf. Letter* 290. The identification of the two Nectarii is conjectural. " Tillemont is inclined to identify Basil's correspondent with the future bishop of Constantinople, but without sufficient grounds." *D.C.B.* see.

you, and that your life's stream was flowing prosperously on. In a moment, by a demon's malice,[1] all the happiness of the house, all the brightness of life, is destroyed, and our lives are made a doleful story. If we wish to lament and weep over what has happened, a life time will not be enough; and if all mankind mourns with us they will be powerless to make their lamentation match our loss. Yes, if all the streams run tears[2] they will not adequately weep our woe.

2. But we mean,— do we not? — to bring out the gift which God has stored in our hearts; I mean that sober reason which in our happy days is wont to draw lines of limitation round our souls, and when troubles come about us to recall to our minds that we are but men, and to suggest to us, what indeed we have seen and heard, that life is full of similar misfortunes, and that the examples of human sufferings are not a few. Above all, this will tell us that it is God's command that we who trust in Christ should not grieve over them who are fallen asleep, because we hope in the resurrection; and that in reward for great patience great crowns of glory are kept in store by the Master of life's course. Only let us allow our wiser thoughts to speak to us in this strain of music, and we may peradventure discover some slight alleviation of our trouble. Play the man, then, I implore you; the blow is a heavy one, but stand firm; do not fall under the weight of your grief; do not lose heart. Be perfectly assured of this, that though the reasons for what is ordained by God are beyond us, yet always what is arranged for us by Him Who is wise and Who loves us is to be accepted, be it ever so grievous to endure. He Himself knows how He is appointing what is best for each and why the terms of life that He fixes for us are unequal. There exists some reason incomprehensible to man why some are sooner carried far away from us, and some are left a longer while behind to bear the burdens of this painful life. So we ought always to adore His loving kindness, and not to repine, remembering those great and famous words of the great athlete Job, when he had seen ten children at one table, in one short moment, crushed to death, "The Lord gave and the Lord hath taken away."[3] As the Lord thought good so it came to pass. Let us adopt those marvellous words. At the hands of the righteous

Judge, they who show like good deeds shall receive a like reward. We have not lost the lad; we have restored him to the Lender. His life is not destroyed; it is changed for the better. He whom we love is not hidden in the ground; he is received into heaven. Let us wait a little while, and we shall be once more with him. The time of our separation is not long, for in this life we are all like travellers on a journey, hastening on to the same shelter. While one has reached his rest another arrives, another hurries on, but one and the same end awaits them all. He has outstripped us on the way, but we shall all travel the same road, and the same hostelry awaits us all. God only grant that we through goodness may be likened to his purity, to the end that for the sake of our guilelessness of life we may attain the rest which is granted to them that are children in Christ.

LETTER VI.[1]

To the wife of Nectarius.

1. I HESITATED to address your excellency, from the idea that, just as to the eye when inflamed even the mildest of remedies causes pain, so to a soul distressed by heavy sorrow, words offered in the moment of agony, even though they do bring much comfort, seem to be somewhat out of place. But I bethought me that I should be speaking to a Christian woman, who has long ago learned godly lessons, and is not inexperienced in the vicissitudes of human life, and I judged it right not to neglect the duty laid upon me. I know what a mother's heart is,[2] and when I remember how good and gentle you are to all, I can reckon the probable extent of your misery at this present time. You have lost a son whom, while he was alive, all mothers called happy, with prayers that their own might be like him, and on his death bewailed, as though each had hidden her own in the grave. His death is a blow to two provinces, both to mine and to Cilicia. With him has fallen a great and illustrious race, dashed to the ground as by the withdrawal of a prop. Alas for the mighty mischief that the contact with an evil demon was able to wreak! Earth, what a calamity thou hast been compelled to sustain! If the sun had any feeling one would think he might have

---

[1] cf. Luke xiii. 16 and 2 Cor. xii. 7.
[2] cf. Lam. ii. 18.   [3] Job i. 21.

[1] To be placed with *Letter* V.
[2] *i.e.* from his knowledge of what Emmelia had been to him. Yet to the celibate the wife of Nectarius might have anticipated the well known retort of Constance to Pandulph in *King John.*

shuddered at so sad a sight. Who could utter all that the spirit in its helplessness would have said?

2. But our lives are not without a Providence. So we have learnt in the Gospel, for not a sparrow falls to the ground without the will of our Father.[1] Whatever has come to pass has come to pass by the will of our Creator. And who can resist God's will? Let us accept what has befallen us; for if we take it ill we do not mend the past and we work our own ruin. Do not let us arraign the righteous judgment of God. We are all too untaught to assail His ineffable sentences. The Lord is now making trial of your love for Him. Now there is an opportunity for you, through your patience, to take the martyr's lot. The mother of the Maccabees[2] saw the death of seven sons without a sigh, without even shedding one unworthy tear. She gave thanks to God for seeing them freed from the fetters of the flesh by fire and steel and cruel blows, and she won praise from God, and fame among men. The loss is great, as I can say myself; but great too are the rewards laid up by the Lord for the patient. When first you were made a mother, and saw your boy, and thanked God, you knew all the while that, a mortal yourself, you had given birth to a mortal. What is there astonishing in the death of a mortal? But we are grieved at his dying before his time. Are we sure that this was not his time? We do not know how to pick and choose what is good for our souls, or how to fix the limits of the life of man. Look round at all the world in which you live; remember that everything you see is mortal, and all subject to corruption. Look up to heaven; even it shall be dissolved; look at the sun, not even the sun will last for ever. All the stars together, all living things of land and sea, all that is fair on earth, aye, earth itself, all are subject to decay; yet a little while and all shall be no more. Let these considerations be some comfort to you in your trouble. Do not measure your loss by itself; if you do it will seem intolerable; but if you take all human affairs into account you will find that some comfort is to be derived from them. Above all, one thing I would strongly urge; spare your husband. Be a comfort to others. Do not make his trouble harder to bear by wearing yourself away with sorrow. Mere words I know cannot give comfort. Just now what is wanted is prayer; and I do pray the

Lord Himself to touch your heart by His unspeakable power, and through good thoughts to cause light to shine upon your soul, that you may have a source of consolation in yourself.

LETTER VII.

To Gregory my friend.[2]

WHEN I wrote to you, I was perfectly well aware that no theological term is adequate to the thought of the speaker, or the want of the questioner, because language is of natural necessity too weak to act in the service of objects of thought. If then our thought is weak, and our tongue weaker than our thought, what was to be expected of me in what I said but that I should be charged with poverty of expression? Still, it was not possible to let your question pass unnoticed. It looks like a betrayal, if we do not readily give an answer about God to them that love the Lord. What has been said, however, whether it seems satisfactory, or requires some further and more careful addition, needs a fit season for correction. For the present I implore you, as I have implored you before, to devote yourself entirely to the advocacy of the truth, and to the intellectual energies God gives you for the establishment of what is good. With this be content, and ask nothing more from me. I am really much less capable than is supposed, and am more likely to do harm to the word by my weakness than to add strength to the truth by my advocacy.

LETTER VIII.[3]

To the Cæsareans.

A defence of his withdrawal, and concerning the faith.

1. I HAVE often been astonished at your feeling towards me as you do, and how it comes about that an individual so small and insignificant, and having, may be, very little that is lovable about him, should have so won your allegiance. You remind me of the claims of friendship and of fatherland,[4] and

---

1 Matt. x. 29.   2 2 Mac. vii.

1 Written from the retirement in Pontus.
2 i.e. Gregory of Nazianzus.
3 This important letter was written A.D. 360, when Basil, shocked at the discovery that Dianius, the bishop who had baptized him, had subscribed the Arian creed of Ariminum, as revised at Nike (Theod., *Hist. Ecc.* II. xvi.), left Cæsarea, and withdrew to his friend Gregory at Nazianzus. The Benedictine note considers the traditional title an error, and concludes the letter to have been really addressed to the monks of the Cœnobium over which Basil had presided. But it may have been written to monks in or near Cæsarea, so that title and sense will agree.
4 πατρίς seems to be used of the city or neighbourhood of Cæsarea, and so far to be in favour of Basil's birth there.

press me urgently in your attempt to make me come back to you, as though I were a runaway from a father's heart and home. That I am a runaway I confess. I should be sorry to deny it; since you are already regretting me, you shall be told the cause. I was astounded like a man stunned by some sudden noise. I did not crush my thoughts, but dwelt upon them as I fled, and now I have been absent from you a considerable time. Then I began to yearn for the divine doctrines, and the philosophy that is concerned with them. How, said I, could I overcome the mischief dwelling with us? Who is to be my Laban, setting me free from Esau, and leading me to the supreme philosophy? By God's help, I have, so far as in me lies, attained my object; I have found a chosen vessel, a deep well; I mean Gregory, Christ's mouth. Give me, therefore, I beg you, a little time. I am not embracing a city life.[1] I am quite well aware how the evil one by such means devises deceit for mankind, but I do hold the society of the saints most useful. For in the more constant change of ideas about the divine dogmas I am acquiring a lasting habit of contemplation. Such is my present situation.

2. Friends godly and well beloved, do, I implore you, beware of the shepherds of the Philistines; let them not choke your wills unawares; let them not befoul the purity of your knowledge of the faith. This is ever their object, not to teach simple souls lessons drawn from Holy Scripture, but to mar the harmony of the truth by heathen philosophy. Is not he an open Philistine who is introducing the terms " *unbegotten* " and " *begotten* " into our faith, and asserts that there was once a time when the Everlasting was not;[2] that He who is by nature and eternally a Father became a Father; that the Holy Ghost is not eternal? He bewitches our Patriarch's sheep that they may not drink " of the well of water springing up into everlasting life,"[3] but may rather bring upon themselves the words of the prophet, " They have forsaken me, the fountain of living waters, and hewed them out cisterns, broken cisterns, that can hold no water;"[4] when all the while they ought to confess that the Father is God, the Son God, and the Holy Ghost God,[5] as they have been taught by the divine words, and by those who have understood them in their highest sense. Against

those who cast it in our teeth that we are Tritheists, let it be answered that we confess one God not in number but in nature. For everything which is called one in number is not one absolutely, nor yet simple in nature; but God is universally confessed to be simple and not composite. God therefore is not one in number. What I mean is this. We say that the world is one in number, but not one by nature nor yet simple; for we divide it into its constituent elements, fire, water, air, and earth.[1] Again, man is called one in number. We frequently speak of one man, but man who is composed of body and soul is not simple. Similarly we say one angel in number, but not one by nature nor yet simple, for we conceive of the hypostasis of the angel as essence with sanctification. If therefore everything which is one in number is not one in nature, and that which is one and simple in nature is not one in number; and if we call God one in nature how can number be charged against us, when we utterly exclude it from that blessed and spiritual nature? Number relates to quantity; and quantity is conjoined with bodily nature, for number is of bodily nature. We believe our Lord to be Creator of bodies. Wherefore every number indicates those things which have received a material and circumscribed nature. Monad and Unity on the other hand signify the nature which is simple and incomprehensible. Whoever therefore confesses either the Son of God or the Holy Ghost to be number or creature introduces unawares a material and circumscribed nature. And by circumscribed I mean not only locally limited, but a nature which is comprehended in foreknowledge by Him who is about to educe it from the non-existent into the existent and which can be comprehended by science. Every holy thing then of which the nature is circumscribed and of which the holiness is acquired is not insusceptible of evil. But the Son and the Holy Ghost are the source of sanctification by which every reasonable creature is hallowed in proportion to its virtue.

3. We in accordance with the true doctrine speak of the Son as neither like,[2] nor unlike[3] the Father. Each of these terms is equally

---

[1] *i.e.* the life of the city, presumably Nazianzus, from which he is writing.
[2] *cf.* the Arian formula ἦν ποτὲ ὅτε οὐκ ἦν.
[3] John iv. 14.   [4] Jer. ii. 13.
[5] *cf* p. 16, note. This is one of the few instances of St. Basil's use of the word θεός of the Holy Ghost.

[1] For the four elements of ancient philosophy modern chemistry now catalogues at least sixty-seven. Of these, earth generally contains eight; air is a mixture of two; water is a compound of two; and fire is the visible evidence of a combination between elements which produces light and heat. On the "elements" of the Greek philosophers *vide* Arist., *Met.* i. 3. Thales (†c. 550 B.C.) said *water ;* Anaximenes (†c. B.C. 480) *air ;* and Heraclitus (†c. B.C. 500) *fire.* To these Empedocles (who " *ardentem frigidus Ætnam insiluit,* c. B.C. 440) added a fourth, *earth.*
[2] Asserted at Seleucia and Ariminum.
[3] *cf.* D. Sp. S. § 4 on Aetius' responsibility for the Anomœan formula.

impossible, for like and unlike are predicated in relation to quality, and the divine is free from quality. We, on the contrary, confess identity of nature and accepting the consubstantiality, and rejecting the composition of the Father, God in substance, Who begat the Son, God in substance. From this the consubstantiality [1] is proved. For God in essence or substance is co-essential or consubstantial with God in essence or substance. But when even man is called "god" as in the words, " I have said ye are gods," [2] and " dæmon " as in the words, " The gods of the nations are dæmons," [3] in the former case the name is given by favour, in the latter untruly. God alone is substantially and essentially God. When I say " alone " I set forth the holy and uncreated essence and substance of God. For the word " alone " is used in the case of any individual and generally of human nature. In the case of an individual, as for instance of Paul, that he alone was caught into the third heaven and " heard unspeakable words which it is not lawful for a man to utter," [4] and of human nature, as when David says, "as for man his days are as grass," [5] not meaning any particular man, but human nature generally; for every man is short-lived and mortal. So we understand these words to be said of the nature, "who alone hath immortality " [6] and " to God only wise," [7] and " none is good save one, that is God," [8] for here " one " means the same as alone. So also, " which alone spreadest out the heavens," [9] and again " Thou shalt worship the Lord thy God and Him only shalt thou serve." [10] " There is no God beside me." [11] In Scripture " one " and " only " are not predicated of God to mark distinction from the Son and the Holy Ghost, but to except the unreal gods falsely so called. As for instance, " The Lord alone did lead them and there was no strange god with them," [12] and " then the children of Israel did put away Baalim and Ashtaroth, and did serve the Lord only." [13] And so St. Paul, "For as there be gods many and lords many, but to us there is but one god, the Father, of whom are all things; and one Lord Jesus Christ by Whom are all things." [14] Here we enquire why when he had said " one God " he was not content, for we have said that " one " and " only " when applied to God, indicate nature. Why did he add the

word Father and make mention of Christ? Paul, a chosen vessel, did not, I imagine, think it sufficient only to preach that the Son is God and the Holy Ghost God, which he had expressed by the phrase " one God," without, by the further addition of " the Father," expressing Him of Whom are all things; and, by mentioning the Lord, signifying the Word by Whom are all things; and yet further, by adding the words Jesus Christ, announcing the incarnation, setting forth the passion and publishing the resurrection. For the word Jesus Christ suggests all these ideas to us. For this reason too before His passion our Lord deprecates the designation of " Jesus Christ," and charges His disciples to " tell no man that He was Jesus, the Christ." [1] For His purpose was, after the completion of the œconomy,[2] after His resurrection from the dead, and His assumption into heaven, to commit to them the preaching of Him as Jesus, the Christ. Such is the force of the words " That they may know Thee the only true God and Jesus Christ whom thou hast sent," [3] and again " Ye believe in God, believe also in me." [4] Everywhere the Holy Ghost secures our conception of Him to save us from falling in one direction while we advance in the other, heeding the theology but neglecting the œconomy,[5] and so by omission falling into impiety.

4. Now let us examine, and to the best of our ability explain, the meaning of the words of Holy Scripture, which our opponents seize and wrest to their own sense, and urge against us for the destruction of the glory of the Only-begotten. First of all take the words " I live because of the Father," [6] for this is one of the shafts hurled heavenward by those who impiously use it. These words I do not understand to refer to the eternal life; for whatever lives because of something else cannot be self-existent, just as that which is warmed by another cannot be warmth itself; but He Who is our Christ and God says, " I am the life." [7] I understand the life lived because of the Father to be this life in the flesh, and in this time. Of His own will He came to live the life of men. He did not say " I have lived

---

[1] Matt. xvi. 19.
[2] i.e. of His work on earth as God manifest in the flesh. *Vide* note, p. 7.
[3] John xvii. 3.   [4] John xiv. 1.   [5] *cf.* note, p. 7.
[6] John vi. 57, R.V. The Greek is ἐγὼ ζῶ διὰ τὸν πατέρα, *i.e.* not through or by the Father, but " because of " or " on account of " the Father. " The preposition (Vulg. *propter Patrem*) describes the ground or object, not the instrument or agent (by, through, διὰ τοῦ π.). Complete devotion to the Father is the essence of the life of the Son; and so complete devotion to the Son is the life of the believer. It seems better to give this full sense to the word than to take it as equivalent to ' *by reason of :*' that is, ' I live because the Father lives.' " Westcott, *St. John* ad loc.
[7] John xi. 25.

---

[1] τὸ ὁμοούσιον.   [4] 2 Cor. xii. 4.   [7] Rom. xvi. 27.
[2] Ps. lxxxii. 6.   [5] Ps. cii. 15.   [8] Luke xviii. 19.
[3] Ps. xcvi. 5, LXX.   [6] 1 Tim. vi. 16.   [9] Job. ix. 8.
[10] Deut. vi. 13, LXX., where the text runs κύριον τὸν θεόν σου φοβηθήτη. St. Basil may quote the version in Matt. iv. 10 and Luke iv. 8, προσκυνήσεις. The Hebrew = fear.
[11] Deut. xxxii. 39, LXX.   [13] 1 Sam. vii. 4.
[12] Deut. xxxii. 12, LXX.   [14] 1 Cor. viii. 5, 6.

because of the Father," but "I live because of the Father," clearly indicating the present time, and the Christ, having the word of God in Himself, is able to call the life which He leads, life, and that this is His meaning we shall learn from what follows. "He that eateth me," He says, "he also shall live because of me;"[1] for we eat His flesh, and drink His blood, being made through His incarnation and His visible life partakers of His Word and of His Wisdom. For all His mystic sojourn among us He called flesh and blood, and set forth the teaching consisting of practical science, of physics, and of theology, whereby our soul is nourished and is meanwhile trained for the contemplation of actual realities. This is perhaps the intended meaning of what He says.[2]

5. And again, "My Father is greater than I."[3] This passage is also employed by the ungrateful creatures, the brood of the evil one. I believe that even from this passage the consubstantiality of the Son with the Father is set forth. For I know that comparisons may properly be made between things which are of the same nature. We speak of angel as greater than angel, of man as juster than man, of bird as fleeter than bird. If then comparisons are made between things of the same species, and the Father by comparison is said to be greater than the Son, then the Son is of the same substance as the Father. But there is another sense underlying the expression. In what is it extraordinary that He who "is the Word and was made flesh"[4] confesses His Father to be greater than Himself, when He was seen in glory inferior to the angels, and in form to men? For "Thou hast made him a little lower than the angels,"[5] and again "Who was made a little lower than the angels,"[6] and "we saw Him and He had neither form nor comeliness, his form was deficient beyond all men."[7] All this He endured on account of His abundant loving kindness towards His work, that He might save the lost sheep and bring it home when He had saved it, and bring back safe and sound to his own land the man who went down from Jerusalem to Jericho and so fell among thieves.[8] Will the heretic cast in His teeth the manger out of which he in his un-

reasonableness was fed by the Word of reason? Will he, because the carpenter's son had no bed to lie on, complain of His being poor? This is why the Son is less than the Father; for your sakes He was made dead to free you from death and make you sharer in heavenly life. It is just as though any one were to find fault with the physician for stooping to sickness, and breathing its foul breath, that he may heal the sick.

6. It is on thy account that He knows not the hour and the day of judgment. Yet nothing is beyond the ken of the real Wisdom, for "all things were made by Him;"[1] and even among men no one is ignorant of what he has made. But this is His dispensation[2] because of thine own infirmity, that sinners be not plunged into despair by the narrow limits of the appointed period,[3] no opportunity for repentance being left them; and that, on the other hand, those who are waging a long war with the forces of the enemy may not desert their post on account of the protracted time. For both of these classes He arranges[4] by means of His assumed ignorance; for the former cutting the time short for their glorious struggle's sake; for the latter providing an opportunity for repentance because of their sins. In the gospels He numbered Himself among the ignorant, on account, as I have said, of the infirmity of the greater part of mankind. In the Acts of the Apostles, speaking, as it were, to the perfect apart, He says, "It is not for you to know the times or the seasons which the Father hath put in His own power."[5] Here He implicitly excepts Himself. So much for a rough statement by way of preliminary attack. Now let us enquire into the meaning of the text from a higher point of view. Let me knock at the door of knowledge, if haply I may wake the Master of the house, Who gives the spiritual bread to them who ask Him, since they whom we are eager to entertain are friends and brothers.

7. Our Saviour's holy disciples, after getting beyond the limits of human thought, and then being purified by the word,[6] are enquiring about the end, and longing to know the ultimate blessedness which our Lord declared to be unknown to His angels and to Himself. He calls all the exact comprehension of the purposes of God, a day; and the contemplation of the One-ness and Unity, knowledge of which He attributes to

---

[1] John vi. 57, R.V
[2] With this striking exposition of Basil's view of the spiritual meaning of eating the flesh and drinking the blood, *cf.* the passage from Athanasius quoted by Bp. Harold Browne in his *Exposition of the XXXIX. Articles*, p. 693. It is not easy for Roman commentators to cite passages even apparently in support of the less spiritual view of the manducation, *e.g.* Fessler, *Inst. Pat.* i. 530, and the quotations under the word "*Eucharistia*," in the *Index* of Basil ed. Migne. Contrast Gregory of Nyssa, in chap. xxxvii. of the *Greater Catechism*.
[3] John xiv. 28.   [5] Ps. viii. 5.   [7] Isa liii. 2, 3, LXX.
[4] John i. 14.   [6] Heb. ii. 9.   [8] *cf.* Luke x. 30.

[1] John i. 3.   [2] τοῦτο οἰκονομεῖ.
[3] τῷ στενῷ τῆς προθεσμίας. ἡ προθεσμία sc. ἡμέρα was in Attic Law a day fixed beforehand before which money must be paid, actions brought, etc. *cf.* Plat., *Legg.* 954, D. It is the "time appointed" of the Father in Gal. iv. 2.
[4] οἰκονομεῖ.   [5] Acts i. 7.
[6] *cf.* John xv. 3, "Now ye are clean through the word."

the Father alone, an hour. I apprehend, therefore, that God is said to know of Himself what is; and not to know what is not; God, Who is, of His own nature, very righteousness and wisdom, is said to know righteousness and wisdom; but to be ignorant of unrighteousness and wickedness; for God who created us is not unrighteousness and wickedness. If, then, God is said to know about Himself that which is, and not to know that which is not; and if our Lord, according to the purpose of the Incarnation and the denser doctrine, is not the ultimate object of desire; then our Saviour does not know the end and the ultimate blessedness. But He says the angels do not know;[1] that is to say, not even the contemplation which is in them, nor the methods of their ministries are the ultimate object of desire. For even their knowledge, when compared with the knowledge which is face to face, is dense.[2] Only the Father, He says, knows, since He is Himself the end and the ultimate blessedness, for when we no longer know God in mirrors and not immediately,[3] but approach Him as one and alone, then we shall know even the ultimate end. For all material knowledge is said to be the kingdom of Christ; while immaterial knowledge, and so to say the knowledge of actual Godhead, is that of God the Father. But our Lord is also Himself the end and the ultimate blessedness according to the purpose of the Word; for what does He say in the Gospel? "I will raise him up at the last day."[4] He calls the transition from material knowledge to immaterial contemplation a resurrection, speaking of that knowledge after which there is no other, as the last day: for our intelligence is raised up and roused to a height of blessedness at the time when it contemplates the One-ness and Unity of the Word. But since our intelligence is made dense and bound to earth, it is both commingled with clay and incapable of gazing intently in pure contemplation, being led through adornments[5]

cognate to its own body. It considers the operations of the Creator, and judges of them meanwhile by their effects, to the end that growing little by little it may one day wax strong enough to approach even the actual unveiled Godhead. This is the meaning, I think, of the words "my Father is greater than I,"[1] and also of the statement, "It is not mine to give save to those for whom it is prepared by my Father."[2] This too is what is meant by Christ's "delivering up the kingdom to God even the Father;"[3] inasmuch as according to the denser doctrine which, as I said, is regarded relatively to us and not to the Son Himself, He is not the end but the first fruits. It is in accordance with this view that when His disciples asked Him again in the Acts of the Apostles, "When wilt thou restore the kingdom of Israel?" He replied, "It is not for you to know the times or the seasons which the Father hath put in His own power."[4] That is to say, the knowledge of such a kingdom is not for them that are bound in flesh and blood. This contemplation the Father hath put away in His own power, meaning by "power" those that are empowered, and by "His own" those who are not held down by the ignorance of things below. Do not, I beg you, have in mind times and seasons of sense but certain distinctions of knowledge made by the sun apprehended by mental perception. For our Lord's prayer must be carried out. It is Jesus Who prayed "Grant that they may be one in us as I and Thou are one, Father."[5] For when God, Who is one, is in each, He makes all one; and number is lost in the indwelling of Unity.

This is my second attempt to attack the text. If any one has a better interpretation to give, and can consistently with true religion amend what I say, let him speak and let him amend, and the Lord will reward him for me. There is no jealousy in my heart. I have not approached this investigation of these passages for strife and vain glory. I have done so to help my brothers, lest the earthen vessels which hold the treasure of God should seem to be deceived by stony-hearted and uncircumcised men, whose weapons are the wisdom of folly.[6]

[1] Mark xiii. 32.
[2] The Ben. note is *Tota hæc explicandi ratio non sua sponte deducta, sed vi pertracta multis videbitur. Sed illud ad excusandum difficilius, quod ait Basilius angelorum scientiam crassam esse, si comparetur cum ea quæ est facie ad faciem. Videtur subtilis explicatio, quam hic sequitur, necessitatem ei imposuisse ita de angelis sentiendi. Nam cum diem et horam idem esse statueret, ac extremam beatitudinem; illud Scriptura, sed neque angeli sciunt, cogebat illis visionem illam, quæ fit facie ad faciem, denegare; quia idem de illis non poterat dici ac de Filio, eos de se ipsis scire id quod sunt, nescire quod non sunt. Quod si hanc hausit opinionem ex origenis fontibus, qui pluribus locis eam insinuat, certe cito deposuit. Ait enim tom* II. p 320. *Angelos in divinum faciem continenter intentos oculos habere. Idem docet in Com. Is.* p.515, n. 185, *et De Sp. S. cap.* XVI.
[3] δἱα τῶν ἀλλοτρίων. cf. 1 Cor. xiii. 12, where St. Paul's word is ἔσοπτρον. St. Basil's κάτοπτρον may rather be suggested by 2 Cor. iii. 18, where the original is κατοπτριζόμενοι.
[4] John vi. 40.
[5] κόσμων. The Ben. note quotes Combefis as saying, "*Dura*

mihi hic vox: sit pro στοιχείων, *per cognata corpori elementa,*" and then goes on, "*sed hac in re minus vidit vir eruditus; non enim idem sonat illa vox ac* mundi, *quasi plures ejusmodi mundos admittat Basilius; sed idem ac ornatus, sive ut ait Basilius in Epist.* vi. τὰ περὶ γῆν κάλλη, *pulchritudines quæ sunt circa terram. In Com. in* Is. n. 58, p. 422. *Ecclesia dicitur* πρέπουσιν ἑαυτῇ κοσμίοις κεκοσμημένη, *convenientibus sibi ornamentis instructa eadem voce utitur Gregorius Nazianz. Ep.* cvii.
[1] John xiv. 28.　　　　　　[3] 1 Cor. xv. 24.
[2] Matt. xx. 23. cf. n. *Theodoret*, p. 28.　[4] Acts i. 6, 7.
[5] John xvii. 21 and 22, slightly varied.
[6] Basil also refers to this passage in the treatise, *C. Euno-*

8. Again, as is said through Solomon the Wise in the Proverbs, " He was created ; "[1] and He is named " Beginning of ways "[1] of good news, which lead us to the kingdom of heaven. He is not in essence and substance a creature, but is made a " way " according to the œconomy. Being made and being created signify the same thing. As He was made a way, so was He made a door, a shepherd, an angel, a sheep, and again a High Priest and an Apostle,[2] the names being used in other senses. What again would the heretics say about God unsubjected, and about His being made sin for us ?[3] For it is written " But when all things shall be subdued unto Him, then shall the Son also Himself be subject unto Him that put all things under Him."[4] Are you not afraid, sir, of God called unsubjected ? For He makes thy subjection His own ; and because of thy struggling against goodness He calls Himself unsubjected. In this sense too He once spoke of Himself as persecuted — " Saul, Saul," He says, " why persecutest thou me ? "[5] on the occasion when Saul was hurrying to Damascus with a desire to imprison the disciples. Again He calls Himself naked, when any one of his brethren is naked.

" I was naked," He says, " and ye clothed me ; "[1] and so when another is in prison He speaks of Himself as imprisoned, for He Himself took away our sins and bare our sicknesses.[2] Now one of our infirmities is not being subject, and He bare this. So all the things which happen to us to our hurt He makes His own, taking upon Him our sufferings in His fellowship with us.

9. But another passage is also seized by those who are fighting against God to the perversion of their hearers : I mean the words " The Son can do nothing of Himself."[3] To me this saying too seems distinctly declaratory of the Son's being of the same nature as the Father. For if every rational creature is able to do anything of himself, and the inclination which each has to the worse and to the better is in his own power, but the Son can do nothing of Himself, then the Son is not a creature. And if He is not a creature, then He is of one essence and substance with the Father. Again ; no creature can do what he likes. But the Son does what He wills in heaven and in earth. Therefore the Son is not a creature. Again ; all creatures are either constituted of contraries or receptive of contraries. But the Son is very righteousness, and immaterial. Therefore the Son is not a creature, and if He is not a creature, He is of one essence and substance with the Father.

10. This examination of the passages before us is, so far as my ability goes, sufficient. Now let us turn the discussion on those who attack the Holy Spirit, and cast down every high thing of their intellect that exalts itself against the knowledge of God.[4] You say that the Holy Ghost is a creature. And every creature is a servant of the Creator, for " all are thy servants."[5] If then He is a servant, His holiness is acquired ; and everything of which the holiness is acquired is receptive of evil ; but the Holy Ghost being holy in essence is called " fount of holiness."[6] Therefore the Holy Ghost is not a creature. If He is not a creature, He is of one essence and substance with the Father. How, tell me, can you give the name of servant to Him Who through your baptism frees you from your servitude ? " The law," it is said, " of the Spirit of life hath made me free from the law of sin."[7] But you will never venture to call His nature even variable, so long as you have regard to the nature of the opposing power of the enemy,

---

mium i. 20: " Since the Son's origin (ἀρχή) is from (ἀπό) the Father, in this respect the Father is greater, as cause and origin (ὡς αἴτιος καὶ ἀρχή). Whence also the Lord said thus *my Father is greater than I*, clearly inasmuch as He is Father (καθὸ πατήρ). Yea ; what else does the word Father signify unless the being cause and origin of that which is begotten by Him?" And in iii. 1: " The Son is second in order (τάξει) to the Father, because He is from Him (ἀπό) and in dignity (ἀξιώματι) because the Father is the origin and cause of His being." Quoted by Bp. Westcott in his *St. John* in the additional notes on xiv. 16, 28, pp. 211 *seqq.*, where also will be found quotations from other Fathers on this passage.

[1] The text of Prov. viii. 22 in the LXX. is κύριος ἔκτισέ με ἀρχην ὁδῶν αὐτοῦ εἰς ἐργα αὐτοῦ. The rendering of A.V. is " possessed me in the beginning of His way ; " of R.V., " possessed," with " formed " in the margin.
 The Hebrew verb occurs some eighty times in the Old Testament, and in only four passages is translated by possess, viz., Gen. xiv. 19, 22, Ps. cxxxix. 13, Jer. xxxii. 15, and Zec. xi. 5. In the two former, though the LXX. renders the word in the Psalms ἐκτήσω, it would have borne the sense of " create." In the passage under discussion the Syriac agrees with the LXX., and among critics adopting the same view Bishop Wordsworth cites Ewald, Hitzig, and Gesenius. The ordinary meaning of the Hebrew is " get " or " acquire," and hence it is easy to see how the idea of getting or possessing passed in relation to the Creator into that of creation. The Greek translators were not unanimous, and Aquila wrote ἐκτήσατο. The passage inevitably became the Jezreel or Low Countries of the Arian war, and many a battle was fought on it. The depreciators of the Son found in it Scriptural authority for calling Him a κτίσμα, *e.g.* Arius in the *Thalia*, as quoted by Athanasius in *Or. c. Ar.* I. iii. § 9, and such writings of his followers as the Letter of Eusebius of Nicomedia to Paulinus of Tyre cited in Theod., *Ecc. Hist.* I. v., and Eunomius as quoted by Greg. Nyss., *c. Eunom.* II. 10 ; but as Dr. Liddon observes in his *Bampton Lect.* (p. 60, ed. 1868), " They did not doubt that this created Wisdom was a real being or person."
 ἔκτισε was accepted by the Catholic writers, but explained to refer to the manhood only, *cf.* Eustathius of Antioch, quoted in Theod., *Dial.* I. The view of Athanasius will be found in his dissertation on the subject in the *Second Discourse against the Arians*, pp. 357-385 of Schaff & Wace's edition. *cf.* Bull, *Def. Fid. Nic.* II. vi. 8.
[2] Heb. iii. 1.   [3] *cf.* 2 Cor. v. 21.
[4] 1 Cor. xv. 28. *i.e.* Because the Son *then* shall be subjected, He is previously ἀνυπότακτος, not as being " *disobedient* " (1 Tim. i. 9), or " *unruly* " (Tit. i. 6, 10), but as being made man, and humanity, though subject unto Him, is not yet seen to be " put under Him " (Heb. ii. 8).   [5] Acts ix. 4.

---

[1] Matt xxv. 36.   [4] 2 Cor. xi. 5.
[2] *cf.* Isa. liii. 4 and Matt. viii. 17.   [5] Ps. xix. 91.
[3] John v. 19.   [6] Rom. i. 4.   [7] Rom. viii. 2.

which, like lightning, is fallen from heaven, and fell out of the true life because its holiness was acquired, and its evil counsels were followed by its change. So when it had fallen away from the Unity and had cast from it its angelic dignity, it was named after its character " Devil,"[1] its former and blessed condition being extinct and this hostile power being kindled.

Furthermore if he calls the Holy Ghost a creature he describes His nature as limited. How then can the two following passages stand? " The Spirit of the Lord filleth the world;"[2] and " Whither shall I go from thy Spirit?"[3] But he does not, it would seem, confess Him to be simple in nature; for he describes Him as one in number. And, as I have already said, everything that is one in number is not simple. And if the Holy Spirit is not simple, He consists of essence and sanctification, and is therefore composite. But who is mad enough to describe the Holy Spirit as composite, and not simple, and consubstantial with the Father and the Son?

11. If we ought to advance our argument yet further, and turn our inspection to higher themes, let us contemplate the divine nature of the Holy Spirit specially from the following point of view. In Scripture we find mention of three creations. The first is the evolution from non-being into being.[4] The second is change from the worse to the better. The third is the resurrection of the dead. In these you will find the Holy Ghost co-operating with the Father and the Son. There is a bringing into existence of the heavens; and what says David? " By the word of the Lord were the heavens made and all the host of them by the breath of His mouth."[5] Again, man is created through baptism, for " if any man be in Christ he is a new creature."[6] And why does the Saviour say to the disciples, " Go ye therefore and teach all nations, baptizing them in the name of the Father and of the Son and of the Holy Ghost"? Here too you see the Holy Ghost present with the Father and the Son. And what would you say also as to the resurrection of the dead when we shall have failed and returned to our dust? Dust we are and unto dust we shall return.[1] And He will send the Holy Ghost and create us and renew the face of the earth.[2] For what the holy Paul calls resurrection David describes as renewal. Let us hear, once more, him who was caught into the third heaven. What does he say? " You are the temple of the Holy Ghost which is in you."[3] Now every temple[4] is a temple of God, and if we are a temple of the Holy Ghost, then the Holy Ghost is God. It is also called Solomon's temple, but this is in the sense of his being its builder. And if we are a temple of the Holy Ghost in this sense, then the Holy Ghost is God, for " He that built all things is God."[5] If we are a temple of one who is worshipped, and who dwells in us, let us confess Him to be God, for thou shalt worship the Lord thy God, and Him only shalt thou serve.[6] Supposing them to object to the word " God," let them learn what this word means. God is called Θεὸς either because He placed (τεθεικέναι) all things or because He beholds (Θεᾶσθαι) all things. If He is called Θεὸς because He " placed " or " beholds " all things, and the Spirit knoweth all the things of God, as the Spirit in us knoweth our things, then the Holy Ghost is God.[7] Again, if the sword of the spirit is the word of God,[8] then the Holy Ghost is God, inasmuch as the sword belongs to Him of whom it is also called the word. Is He named the right hand of the Father? For " the right hand of the Lord bringeth mighty things to pass;"[9] and " thy right hand, O Lord, hath dashed in pieces the enemy."[10] But the Holy Ghost is the finger of God, as it is said " if I by the finger of God cast out devils,"[11] of which the version in another Gospel is " if I by the Spirit of God cast out devils."[12] So the Holy Ghost is of the same nature as the Father and the Son.

12. So much must suffice for the present on the subject of the adorable and holy Trinity. It is not now possible to extend the enquiry about it further. Do ye take seeds from a humble person like me, and cultivate the ripe ear for yourselves, for, as you

---

[1] In *Letter* cciv. The name of Διάβολος is more immediately connected with Διαβάλλειν, to calumniate. It is curious that the occasional spelling (*e.g.* in Burton) Divell, which is nearer to the original, and keeps up the association with Diable, Diavolo, etc., should have given place to the less correct and misleading " Devil."

[2] Wisdom i. 7.   [3] Ps. cxxxix. 7.

[4] παραγωγὴ ἀπὸ τοῦ μὴ ὄντος εἰς τὸ εἶναι. For παραγωγὴ is not easy to give an equivalent; it is leading or bringing with a notion of change, sometimes a change into error, as when it means a quibble. It is not quite the Ben. Latin "*productio.*" It is not used intransitively; if there is a παραγωγή, there must be ὁ παράγων, and similarly if there is evolution or development, there must be an evolver or developer.

[5] Ps. xxxiii. 6. τῷ πνεύματι τοῦ στόματος αὐτοῦ, LXX.

[6] 2 Cor. v. 17.

---

[1] *cf.* Gen. iii. 19.   [2] *cf.* Ps. ciii. 30.   [3] 1 Cor. vi. 19.
[4] The Greek word ναός (ναίω) = dwelling-place. The Hebrew probably indicates capacity.

Our " temple," from the Latin *Templum* (τέμενος — √ TAM) is derivatively *a place cut off.*

[5] Heb. iii. 4.   [6] Matt. iv. 10. *cf.* note on p. .
[7] 1 Cor. ii. 10, 11. On the derivation of Θεός from θέω (τίθημι) or θεάομαι, *cf.* Greg. Naz.

Skeat rejects the theory of connexion with the Latin *Deus*, and thinks that the root of τίθημι may be the origin.

[8] Eph. vi. 17.
[9] Ps. cxviii. 16. P.B. " doeth valiantly," A.V. ἐποίησε δύναμιν, LXX.
[10] Ex. xv. 6.   [11] Luke xi. 20.   [12] Matt. xii. 28.

know, in such cases we look for interest. But I trust in God that you, because of your pure lives, will bring forth fruit thirty, sixty. and a hundred fold. For, it is said, Blessed are the pure in heart, for they shall see God.[1] And, my brethren, entertain no other conception of the kingdom of the heavens than that it is the very contemplation of realities. This the divine Scriptures call blessedness. For " the kingdom of heaven is within you." [2]

The inner man consists of nothing but contemplation. The kingdom of the heavens, then, must be contemplation. Now we behold their shadows as in a glass; hereafter, set free from this earthly body, clad in the incorruptible and the immortal, we shall behold their archetypes, we shall see them, that is, if we have steered our own life's course aright, and if we have heeded the right faith, for otherwise none shall see the Lord. For, it is said, into a malicious soul Wisdom shall not enter, nor dwell in the body that is subject unto sin.[3] And let no one urge in objection that, while I am ignoring what is before our eyes, I am philosophizing to them about bodiless and immaterial being. It seems to me perfectly absurd, while the senses are allowed free action in relation to their proper matter, to exclude mind alone from its peculiar operation. Precisely in the same manner in which sense touches sensible objects, so mind apprehends the objects of mental perception. This too must be said that God our Creator has not included natural faculties among things which can be taught. No one teaches sight to apprehend colour or form, nor hearing to apprehend sound and speech, nor smell, pleasant and unpleasant scents, nor taste, flavours and savours, nor touch, soft and hard, hot and cold. Nor would any one teach the mind to reach objects of mental perception; and just as the senses in the case of their being in any way diseased, or injured, require only proper treatment and then readily fulfil their own functions; just so the mind, imprisoned in flesh, and full of the thoughts that arise thence, requires faith and right conversation which make " its feet like hinds' feet. and set it on its high places." [4]

The same advice is given us by Solomon the wise, who in one passage offers us the example of the diligent worker the ant,[1] and recommends her active life; and in another the work of the wise bee in forming its cells,[2] and thereby suggests a natural contemplation wherein also the doctrine of the Holy Trinity is contained, if at least the Creator is considered in proportion to the beauty of the things created.

But with thanks to the Father, the Son and the Holy Ghost let me make an end to my letter, for, as the proverb has it, πᾶν μέτρον ἄριστον.[3]

LETTER IX.[4]

To Maximus the Philosopher.

1. SPEECH is really an image of mind; so I have learned to know you from your letters, just as the proverb tells us we may know " the lion from his claws." [5]

I am delighted to find that your strong inclinations lie in the direction of the first and greatest of good things — love both to God and to your neighbour. Of the latter I find proof in your kindness to myself; of the former, in your zeal for knowledge. It is well known to every disciple of Christ that in these two all is contained.

2. You ask for the writings of Dionysius;[6] they did indeed reach me, and a great many they were; but I have not the books with me, and so have not sent them. My opinion is, however, as follows. I do not admire everything that is written; indeed of some things I totally disapprove. For it may be, that of the impiety of which we are now hearing so much, I mean the Anomœan, it is he, as far as I know, who first gave men the seeds. I do not trace his so doing to any mental depravity, but only to his earnest desire to resist Sabellius. I often compare him to a woodman trying to straighten some ill-grown sapling, pulling so immoderately in the opposite direction as to exceed the mean, and so dragging the plant awry on the other side. This is very much what we find to be the case with Dionysius. While vehe-

---

[1] Matt. v. 8.
[2] Luke xvii. 21, ἐντὸς ὑμῶν. Many modern commentators interpret "in your midst," "among you." So Alford, who quotes Xen., *Anab.* I. x. 3 for the Greek, Bp. Walsham How, Bornemann. Meyer. The older view coincided with that of Basil; so Theophylact, Chrysostom, and with them Olshausen and Godet.
To the objection that the words were said to the *Pharisees*, and that the kingdom was not in their hearts, it may be answered that our Lord might use "you" of humanity, even when addressing Pharisees. He never, like a merely human preacher, says "we."
[3] Wisdom i. 4.　　　　[4] Ps. xviii. 33.

[1] *cf.* Prov. vi. 6.
[2] Ecclus. xi. 3. The ascription of this book to Solomon is said by Rufinus to be confined to the Latin church, while the Greeks know it as the Wisdom of Jesus son of Sirach (vers. Orig., *Hom. in Num.* xvii.).
[3] Attributed to Cleobulus of Lindos. Thales is credited with the injunction μέτρῳ χρῶ. *cf.* my note on Theodoret, *Ep.* cli. p. 329.
[4] To be ascribed to the same period as the preceding.
[5] In Lucian (*Hermot.* 54) the proverb is traced to a story of Pheidias, who, " after a look at a claw, could tell how big the whole lion, formed in proportion, would be." A parallel Greek adage was ἐκτοῦ κρασπέδου τὸ πᾶν ὕφασμα. *Vide* Leutsch., *Corp. Paræmiog. Græc.* I. 252.
[6] *i.e.* of Alexandria.

mently opposing the impiety of the Libyan,[1] he is carried away unawares by his zeal into the opposite error. It would have been quite sufficient for him to have pointed out that the Father and the Son are not identical in substance,[2] and thus to score against the blasphemer. But, in order to win an unmistakable and superabundant victory, he is not satisfied with laying down a difference of hypostases, but must needs assert also difference of substance, diminution of power, and variableness of glory. So he exchanges one mischief for another, and diverges from the right line of doctrine. In his writings he exhibits a miscellaneous inconsistency, and is at one time to be found disloyal to the homoousion, because of his opponent[3] who made a bad use of it to the destruction of the hypostases, and at another admitting it in his Apology to his namesake.[4] Besides this he uttered very unbecoming words about the Spirit, separating Him from the Godhead, the object of worship, and assigning Him an inferior rank with created and subordinate nature. Such is the man's character.

3. If I must give my own view, it is this. The phrase " like in essence," [5] if it be read with the addition " without any difference," [6] I accept as conveying the same sense as the homoousion, in accordance with the sound meaning of the homoousion. Being of this mind the Fathers at Nicæa spoke of the Only-begotten as " Light of Light," " Very God of very God," and so on, and then consistently added the homoousion. It is impossible for any one to entertain the idea of variableness of light in relation to light, of truth in relation to truth, nor of the essence of the Only begotten in relation to that of the Father. If, then, the phrase be accepted in this sense, I have no objection to it. But if any one cuts off the qualification " without any difference " from the word " like," as was done at Constantinople,[7] then I regard

the phrase with suspicion, as derogatory to the dignity of the Only-begotten. We are frequently accustomed to entertain the idea of " likeness " in the case of indistinct resemblances, coming anything but close to the originals. I am myself for the homoousion, as being less open to improper interpretation. But why, my dear sir, should you not pay me a visit, that we may talk of these high topics face to face, instead of committing them to lifeless letters, — especially when I have determined not to publish my views? And pray do not adopt, to me, the words of Diogenes to Alexander, that " it is as far from you to me as from me to you." I am almost obliged by ill-health to remain like the plants, in one place ; moreover I hold " the living unknown" [1] to be one of the chief goods. You, I am told, are in good health ; you have made yourself a citizen of the world, and you might consider in coming to see me that you are coming home. It is quite right for you, a man of action, to have crowds and towns in which to show your good deeds. For me, quiet is the best aid for the contemplation and mental exercise whereby I cling to God. This quiet I cultivate in abundance in my retreat, with the aid of its giver, God. Yet if you cannot but court the great, and despise me who lie low upon the ground, then write, and in this way make my life a happier one.

LETTER X.[2]

To a widow.[3]

THE art of snaring pigeons is as follows. When the men who devote themselves to this craft have caught one, they tame it, and make it feed with them. Then they smear its wings with sweet oil, and let it go and join the rest outside. Then the scent of that sweet oil makes the free flock the possession of the owner of the tame bird, for all the rest are attracted by the fragrance, and settle

[1] i.e. Sabellius. Basil is the first writer who asserts his African birth. In Ep. ccvii. he is " Sabellius the Libyan." His active life was Roman; his views popular in the Pentapolis.
[2] οὐ ταυτὸν τῷ ὑποκειμένῳ. Aristotle, Metaph. vi. 3, 1, says, μάλιστα δοκεῖ εἶναι οὐσία τὸ ὑποκείμενον τὸ πρῶτον. On the distinction between ὁμοούσιος and ταυτὸν τῷ ὑποκειμένῳ, cf. Athan., Exp. Fid. ii., where the Sabellians are accused of holding an υἱοπατώρ, and Greg. Nyss. answer to Eunomius. Second Book, p. 254 in Schaff and Wace's ed. Vide also Prolegg. to Athan., p. xxxi. in this series. Epiphanius says of Noetus, μονοτύπως τὸν αὐτὸν πατέρα καὶ Υἱὸν καὶ ἅγιον πνεῦμα . . . ἡγησάμενος (Hæres. lvii. 2) and of Sabellius, Δογματίζει οὗτος καὶ οἱ ἀπ' αὐτοῦ Σαβελλιανοὶ τὸν αὐτὸν εἶναι Πατέρα τὸν αὐτὸν Υἱὸν τὸν αὐτὸν εἶναι ἅγιον πνεῦμα, ὡς εἶναι ἐν μιᾷ ὑποστάσει τρεῖς ὀνομασίας. (Hæres. lxii. 1.)
[3] Sabellius.
[4] Dionysius of Rome.
[5] ὅμοιον κατ' οὐσίαν.
[6] ἀπαραλλάκτως.
[7] i.e. at the Acacian council of Constantinople in 360, at which fifty bishops accepted the creed of Ariminum as revised at Nike, proscribing οὐσία and ὑπόστασις, and pronounced the Son to be " like the Father, as say the Holy Scriptures." cf. Theod. II. xvi. and Soc. II. xli. In 366 Semiarian deputies

from the Council of Lampsacus represented to Liberius at Rome that κατὰ πάντα ὅμοιος and ὁμοούσιος were equivalent.
[1] λάθε βιώσας is quoted by Theodoret in Ep. lxii. as a saying of " one of the men once called wise." It is attributed to Epicurus. Horace imitates it in Ep. I. xvii. 10: " Nec vixit male qui natus moriensque fefellit." So Ovid, Tristia III. iv. 25 : " crede mihi ; bene qui latuit, bene vixit," and Eurip., Iph. in Aul. 17:

Ζηλῶ σὲ, γέρον,
Ζηλῶ δ' ἀνδρῶν ὃς ἀκίνδυνον
Βίον ἐξεπέρασ' ἀγνὼς ἀκλεής.

Plutarch has an essay on the question, εἰ καλῶς εἴρηται τὸ λάθε βιώσας.
[2] Placed during the retreat.
[3] πρὸς ἐλευθέραν. The Benedictine note, after giving reasons why the name Julitta should not be introduced into the address, continues : " neque etiam in hac et pluribus aliis Basilii epistolis ἐλευθέρα nomen proprium est, sed viduam matronam designat. Sic Gregorius Naz. in Epist. cxlvii., ἐλευθέραν Alypii, id est viduam, apellat Simpliciam quam ipsius quondam conjugem fuisse dixerat in Epist. cxlvi." The usage may be traceable to Rom. vii. 3.

in the house. But why do I begin my letter thus? Because I have taken your son Dionysius, once Diomedes,[1] and anointed the wings of his soul with the sweet oil of God, and sent him to you that you may take flight with him, and make for the nest which he has built under my roof. If I live to see this, and you, my honoured friend, translated to our lofty life, I shall require many persons worthy of God to pay Him all the honour that is His due.

LETTER XI.[2]

Without address. To some friends.[3]

AFTER by God's grace I had passed the sacred day with our sons, and had kept a really perfect feast to the Lord because of their exceeding love to God, I sent them in good health to your excellency, with a prayer to our loving God to give them an angel of peace to help and accompany them, and to grant them to find you in good health and assured tranquillity, to the end that wherever your lot may be cast, I to the end of my days, whenever I hear news of you, may be gladdened to think of you as serving and giving thanks to the Lord. If God should grant you to be quickly freed from these cares I beg you to let nothing stand in the way of your coming to stay with me. I think you will find none to love you so well, or to make more of your friendship. So long, then, as the Holy One ordains this separation, be sure that you never lose an opportunity of comforting me by a letter.

LETTER XII.[4]

To Olympius.[5]

BEFORE you did write me a few words: now not even a few. Your brevity will soon become silence. Return to your old ways, and do not let me have to scold you for your laconic behaviour. But I shall be glad even of a little letter in token of your great love. Only write to me.

LETTER XIII.[1]

To Olympius.

As all the fruits of the season come to us in their proper time, flowers in spring, corn in summer, and apples[2] in autumn, so the fruit for winter is talk.

LETTER XIV.[3]

To Gregory his friend.

MY brother Gregory writes me word that he has long been wishing to be with me, and adds that you are of the same mind; however, I could not wait, partly as being hard of belief, considering I have been so often disappointed, and partly because I find myself pulled all ways by business. I must at once make for Pontus, where, perhaps, God willing, I may make an end of wandering. After renouncing, with trouble, the idle hopes which I once had, [about you][4] or rather the dreams, (for it is well said that hopes are waking dreams), I departed into Pontus in quest of a place to live in. There God has opened on me a spot exactly answering to my taste, so that I actually see before my eyes what I have often pictured to my mind in idle fancy. There is a lofty mountain covered with thick woods, watered towards the north with cool and transparent streams. A plain lies beneath, enriched by the waters which are ever draining off from it; and skirted by a spontaneous profusion of trees almost thick enough to be a fence; so as even to surpass Calypso's Island, which Homer seems to have considered the most beautiful spot on the earth. Indeed it is like an island, enclosed as it is on all sides; for deep hollows cut off two sides of it; the river, which has lately fallen down a precipice, runs all along the front, and is impassable as a wall; while the mountain extending itself behind, and meeting the hollows in a crescent, stops up the path at its roots. There is but one pass, and I am master of it. Behind my abode there is another gorge, rising into a ledge up above, so as to command the extent of the plains and the stream

---

[1] A second name was given at baptism, or assumed with some religious motive. In the first three centuries considerations of prudence would prevent an advertisement of Christianity through a name of peculiar' meaning, and even baptismal names were not biblical or of pious meaning and association. Later the early indifference of Christians as to the character of their names ceased, and after the fourth century heathen names were discouraged. *cf.* D.C.A. ii. 1368. "Dionysius," though of pagan origin, is biblical; but "martyrs often encountered death bearing the names of these very divinities to whom they refuse to offer sacrifice." So we have Apollinarius, Hermias, Demetrius, Origenes (sprung from Horus), Arius, Athenodorus, Aphrodisius, and many more.
[2] Of the same period as X.
[3] Possibly to Olympius, the recipient of XII. *cf. Letter* ccxi.
[4] Of the same date as the preceding.
[5] Olympius was an influential friend of Basil's, and sympathized with him in his later troubles, and under the attacks of Eustathius. *cf. Letters* ccxi., lxiii., lxiv.

[1] Placed with the preceding.
[2] μῆλον. But, like the Latin *malum*, this word served for more than we mean by "apple." So the *malum Cydonium* was quince, the *malum Persicum*, peach, etc.
[3] Placed after Basil's choice of his Pontic retreat. Translated by Newman, whose version is here given (*Church of the Fathers*, 126). On the topography, *cf. Letters* iii., x., ccxxiii., and remarks in the *Prolegomena*.
[4] Omitted by Newman.

which bounds it, which is not less beautiful, to my taste, than the Strymon as seen from Amphipolis.[1] For while the latter flows leisurely, and swells into a lake almost, and is too still to be a river, the former is the most rapid stream I know, and somewhat turbid, too, from the rocks just above; from which, shooting down, and eddying in a deep pool, it forms a most pleasant scene for myself or any one else; and is an inexhaustible resource to the country people, in the countless fish which its depths contain. What need to tell of the exhalations from the earth, or the breezes from the river? Another might admire the multitude of flowers, and singing birds; but leisure I have none for such thoughts. However, the chief praise of the place is, that being happily disposed for produce of every kind, it nurtures what to me is the sweetest produce of all, quietness; indeed, it is not only rid of the bustle of the city, but is even unfrequented by travellers, except a chance hunter. It abounds indeed in game, as well as other things, but not, I am glad to say, in bears or wolves, such as you have, but in deer, and wild goats, and hares, and the like. Does it not strike you what a foolish mistake I was near making when I was eager to change this spot for your Tiberina,[2] the very pit of the whole earth?

Pardon me, then, if I am now set upon it; for not Alcmæon himself, I suppose, could endure to wander further when he had found the Echinades.[3]

LETTER XV.[4]

To Arcadius, Imperial Treasurer.[5]

THE townsmen of our metropolis have conferred on me a greater favour than they have received, in giving me an opportunity of writing to your excellency. The kindness, to win which they have received this letter from me, was assured them even before I wrote, on account of your wonted and inborn courtesy to all. But I have considered it a very great advantage to have the opportunity of addressing your excellency, praying to the holy God that I may continue to rejoice, and share in the pleasure of the recipients of your bounty, while you please Him more and more, and while the splendour of your high place continues to increase. I pray that in due time I may with joy once more welcome those who are delivering this my letter into your hands,[1] and send them forth praising, as do many, your considerate treatment of them, and I trust that they will have found my recommendation of them not without use in approaching your exalted excellency.

LETTER XVI.[2]

Against Eunomius the heretic.[3]

HE who maintains that it is possible to arrive at the discovery of things actually existing, has no doubt by some orderly method advanced his intelligence by means of the knowledge of actually existing things. It is after first training himself by the apprehension of small and easily comprehensible objects, that he brings his apprehensive faculty to bear on what is beyond all intelligence. He makes his boast that he has really arrived at the comprehension of actual existences; let him then explain to us the nature of the least of visible beings; let him tell us all about the ant. Does its life depend on breath and breathing? Has it a skeleton? Is its body connected by sinews and ligaments? Are its sinews surrounded with muscles and glands? Does its marrow go with dorsal vertebræ from brow to tail? Does it give impulse to its moving members by the enveloping nervous membrane? Has it a liver, with a gall bladder near the liver?

---

[1] The hill, of which the western half is covered by the ruins of Amphipolis, is insulated by the Strymon on the north-west and south, and a valley on the east. To the north-west the Strymon widens into a lake, compared by Dr. Arnold to that formed by the Mincio at Mantua. *cf.* Thucyd. iv. 108 and v. 7.

[2] Tiberina was a district in the neighbourhood of Gregory's home at Arianzus. *cf.* Greg. Naz., *Ep.* vi. and vii.

[3] "Alcmæon slew his mother; but the awful Erinnys, the avenger of matricide, inflicted on him a long and terrible punishment, depriving him of his reason, and chasing him about from place to place without the possibility of repose or peace of mind. He craved protection and cure from the god at Delphi, who required him to dedicate at the temple, as an offering, the precious necklace of Kadmus, that irresistible bribe which had originally corrupted Eriphyle. He further intimated to the unhappy sufferer that, though the whole earth was tainted with his crime and had become uninhabitable for him, yet there was a spot of ground which was not under the eye of the sun at the time when the matricide was committed, and where, therefore, Alcmæon might yet find a tranquil shelter. The promise was realised at the mouth of the river Achelous, whose turbid stream was perpetually depositing new earth and forming additional islands. Upon one of these Alcmæon settled permanently and in peace." Grote, *Hist. Gr.* i. 381. [4] Written from the Pontic retreat.

[5] *Comes rei privatæ,* " who managed the enormous revenues of the fiscus and kept account of the privileges granted by the Emperor (*liber beneficiorum.* Hyginus, *De Const. Limit.* p. 203, ed. Lachm. and Du Cange *s.v.*)." D.C.B. i. 634.

---

[1] There is confusion here in the text, and the Benedictines think it unmanageable as it stands. But the matter is of no importance.

[2] Placed by the Ben. Ed. in the reign of Julian 361-363.

[3] Eunomius the Anomœan, bp. of Cyzicus, against whose *Liber Apologeticus* Basil wrote his counter-work. The first appearance of the αἱρετικὸς ἄνθρωπος, the "chooser" of his own way rather than the common sense of the Church, is in Tit. iii. 10. αἱρετίζειν is a common word in the LXX., but does not occur in 1s. xlii. 1, though it is introduced into the quotation in Matt. xii. 18. αἱρεσις is used six times by St. Luke for "sect;" twice by St. Paul and once by St. Peter for "heresy." Augustine, *C. Manich.* writes: "*Qui in ecclesia Christi morbidum aliquid pravumque quid sapiunt, si, correcti ut sanum rectumque sapiant, resistunt contumaciter suaque pestifera et mortifera dogmata emendare nolunt, sed defensare persistunt hæretici sunt.*"

Has it kidneys, heart, arteries, veins, membranes, cartilages? Is it hairy or hairless? Has it an uncloven hoof, or are its feet divided? How long does it live? What is its mode of reproduction? What is its period of gestation? How is it that ants neither all walk nor all fly, but some belong to creeping things, and some travel through the air? The man who glories in his knowledge of the really-existing ought to tell us in the meanwhile about the nature of the ant. Next let him give us a similar physiological account of the power that transcends all human intelligence. But if your knowledge has not yet been able to apprehend the nature of the insignificant ant, how can you boast yourself able to form a conception of the power of the incomprehensible God? [1]

LETTER XVII.[2]

To Origenes.[3]

It is delightful to listen to you, and delightful to read you; and I think you give me the greater pleasure by your writings. All thanks to our good God Who has not suffered the truth to suffer in consequence of its betrayal by the chief powers in the State, but by your means has made the defence of the doctrine of true religion full and satisfactory. Like hemlock, monkshood, and other poisonous herbs, after they have bloomed for a little while, they will quickly wither away. But the reward which the Lord will give you in requital of all that you have said in defence of His name blooms afresh for ever. Wherefore I pray God grant you all happiness in your home, and make His blessing descend to your sons. I was delighted to see and embrace those noble boys, express images of your excellent goodness, and my prayers for them ask all that their father can ask.

LETTER XVIII.[4]

To Macarius [5] and John.

The labours of the field come as no novelty to tillers of the land; sailors are not aston-

ished if they meet a storm at sea; sweats in the summer heat are the common experience of the hired hind; and to them that have chosen to live a holy life the afflictions of this present world cannot come unforeseen. Each and all of these have the known and proper labour of their callings, not chosen for its own sake, but for the sake of the enjoyment of the good things to which they look forward. What in each of these cases acts as a consolation in trouble is that which really forms the bond and link of all human life, — hope. Now of them that labour for the fruits of the earth, or for earthly things, some enjoy only in imagination what they have looked for, and are altogether disappointed; and even in the case of others, where the issue has answered expectation, another hope is soon needed, so quickly has the first fled and faded out of sight. Only of them that labour for holiness and truth are the hopes destroyed by no deception; no issue can destroy their labours, for the kingdom of the heavens that awaits them is firm and sure. So long then as the word of truth is on our side, never be in any wise distressed at the calumny of a lie; let no imperial threats scare you; do not be grieved at the laughter and mockery of your intimates, nor at the condemnation of those who pretend to care for you, and who put forward, as their most attractive bait to deceive, a pretence of giving good advice. Against them all let sound reason do battle, invoking the championship and succour of our Lord Jesus Christ, the teacher of true religion, for Whom to suffer is sweet, and " to die is gain." [1]

LETTER XIX.[2]

To Gregory my friend.[3]

I received a letter from you the day before yesterday. It is shewn to be yours not so much by the handwriting as by the peculiar style. Much meaning is expressed in few words. I did not reply on the spot, because I was away from home, and the letter-carrier, after he had delivered the packet to one of my friends, went away. Now, however, I am able to address you through Peter, and at the same time both to return your greeting, and give you an opportunity for another letter. There is certainly no trouble in writing a laconic dispatch like those which reach me from you.

[1] As an argument against Eunomius this Letter has no particular force, inasmuch as a man may be a good divine though a very poor entomologist, and might tell us all about the ant without being better able to decide between Basil and Eunomius. It is interesting, however, as shewing how far Basil was abreast of the physiology of his time, and how far that physiology was correct.
[2] Placed during the reign of Julian.
[3] Nothing is known of this Origen beyond what is suggested in this letter. He is conjectured to have been a layman, who, alike as a rhetorician and a writer, was popularly known as a Christian apologist.
[4] Placed in the reign of Julian.
[5] MS. variations are Macrinus and Machrinus.

[1] Phil. i. 21.
[2] Placed by the Ben. Ed. shortly after Basil's ordination as priest.
[3] i.e. Gregory of Nazianzus, and so Letter xiv.

LETTER XX.[1]

To Leontius the Sophist.[2]

I TOO do not write often to you, but not more seldom than you do to me, though many have travelled hitherward from your part of the world. If you had sent a letter by every one of them, one after the other, there would have been nothing to prevent my seeming to be actually in your company, and enjoying it as though we had been together, so uninterrupted has been the stream of arrivals. But why do you not write? It is no trouble to a Sophist to write. Nay, if your hand is tired, you need not even write; another will do that for you. Only your tongue is needed. And though it does not speak to me, it may assuredly speak to one of your companions. If nobody is with you, it will talk by itself. Certainly the tongue of a Sophist and of an Athenian is as little likely to be quiet as the nightingales when the spring stirs them to song. In my own case, the mass of business in which I am now engaged may perhaps afford some excuse for my lack of letters. And peradventure the fact of my style having been spoilt by constant familiarity with common speech may make me somewhat hesitate to address Sophists like you, who are certain to be annoyed and unmerciful, unless you hear something worthy of your wisdom. You, on the other hand, ought assuredly to use every opportunity of making your voice heard abroad, for you are the best speaker of all the Hellenes that I know; and I think I know the most renowned among you; so that there really is no excuse for your silence. But enough on this point.

I have sent you my writings against Eunomius. Whether they are to be called child's play, or something a little more serious, I leave you to judge. So far as concerns yourself, I do not think you stand any longer in need of them; but I hope they will be no unworthy weapon against any perverse men with whom you may fall in. I do not say this so much because I have confidence in the force of my treatise, as because I know well that you are a man likely to make a little go a long way. If anything strikes you as weaker than it ought to be, pray have no hesitation in showing me the error. The chief difference between a friend and a flatterer is this; the flatterer speaks to please, the friend will not leave out even what is disagreeable.

LETTER XXI.[1]

To Leontius the Sophist.

THE excellent Julianus[2] seems to get some good for his private affairs out of the general condition of things. Everything nowadays is full of taxes demanded and called in, and he too is vehemently dunned and indicted. Only it is a question not of arrears of rates and taxes, but of letters. But how he comes to be a defaulter I do not know. He has always paid a letter, and received a letter — as he has this. But possibly you have a preference for the famous "four-times-as-much."[3] For even the Pythagoreans were not so fond of their Tetractys,[4] as these modern tax-collectors of their "four-times-as-much." Yet perhaps the fairer thing would have been just the opposite, that a Sophist like you, so very well furnished with words, should be bound in pledge to me for "four-times-as-much." But do not suppose for a moment that I am writing all this out of ill-humour. I am only too pleased to get even a scolding from you. The good and beautiful do everything, it is said, with the addition of goodness and beauty.[5] Even grief and anger in them are becoming. At all events any one would rather see his friend angry with him than any one else flattering him. Do not then cease preferring charges like the last! The very charge will mean a letter; and nothing can be more precious or delightful to me.

LETTER XXII.[6]

Without address. On the Perfection of the Life of Solitaries.

1. MANY things are set forth by inspired Scripture as binding upon all who are anxious to please God. But, for the present, I have only deemed it necessary to speak by

---

[1] Of about the same date as the preceding.
[2] cf. Ep. ccxciii.
[3] The Ben. note quotes Ammianus Marcellinus xxvi. 6, where it is said of Petronius, father-in-law of Valens: "ad nudandos sine discretione cunctos immaniter flagrans nocentes pariter et insontes post exquisita tormenta quadrupli nexibus vinciebat, debita jam inde a temporibus principio Aureliani perscrutans, et impendio mærens si quemquam absolvisset indemnem ;" and adds : " Est ergo quadruplum hoc loco non quadrimenstrua pensio, non superexactio, sed debitorum, quæ soluta non fuerant, crudelis inquisitio et quadrupli pæna his qui non solverant imposita."
[4] τετρακτύς was the Pythagorean name for the sum of the first four numbers (1+2+3+4 = 10), held by them to be the root of all creation. cf. the Pythagorean oath:

Ναὶ μὰ τὸν ἁμετέρᾳ ψύχᾳ παραδόντα τετρακτύν,
Παγὰν ἀενάου φύσεως ῥιζώματ᾽ ἔχουσαν.

cf. my note on Theodoret, Ep. cxxx. for the use of τετρακτύς for the Four Gospels.
[5] Τοῖς καλοῖς πάντα μετὰ τῆς τοῦ καλοῦ προσθήκης γίνεσθαι. The pregnant sense of καλός makes translation difficult.
[6] Placed in 364.

---

way of brief reminder concerning the questions which have recently been stirred among you, so far as I have learnt from the study of inspired Scripture itself. I shall thus leave behind me detailed evidence, easy of apprehension, for the information of industrious students, who in their turn will be able to inform others. The Christian ought to be so minded as becomes his heavenly calling,[1] and his life and conversation ought to be worthy of the Gospel of Christ.[2] The Christian ought not to be of doubtful mind,[3] nor by anything drawn away from the recollection of God and of His purposes and judgments. The Christian ought in all things to become superior to the righteousness existing under the law, and neither swear nor lie.[4] He ought not to speak evil;[5] to do violence;[6] to fight;[7] to avenge himself;[8] to return evil for evil;[9] to be angry.[10] The Christian ought to be patient,[11] whatever he have to suffer, and to convict the wrong-doer in season,[12] not with the desire of his own vindication, but of his brother's reformation,[13] according to the commandment of the Lord. The Christian ought not to say anything behind his brother's back with the object of calumniating him, for this is slander, even if what is said is true.[14] He ought to turn away from the brother who speaks evil against him;[15] he ought not to indulge in jesting.[16] he ought not to laugh nor even to suffer laugh makers.[17] He must not talk idly, saying things which are of no service to the hearers nor to such usage as is necessary and permitted us by God;[18] so that workers may do their best as far as possible to work in silence; and that good words be suggested to them by those who are entrusted with the duty of carefully dispensing the word to the building up of the faith, lest God's Holy Spirit be grieved. Any one who comes in ought not to be able, of his own free will, to accost or speak to any of the brothers, before those to whom the responsibility of general discipline is committed have approved of it as pleasing to God, with a view to the common good.[19] The Christian

ought not to be enslaved by wine;[1] nor to be eager for flesh meat,[2] and as a general rule ought not to be a lover of pleasure in eating or drinking,[3] " for every man that striveth for the mastery is temperate in all things."[4] The Christian ought to regard all the things that are given him for his use, not as his to hold as his own or to lay up;[5] and, giving careful heed to all things as the Lord's, not to overlook any of the things that are being thrown aside and disregarded, should this be the case. No Christian ought to think of himself as his own master, but each should rather so think and act as though given by God to be slave to his like minded brethren;[6] but " every man in his own order."[7]

2. The Christian ought never to murmur[8] either in scarcity of necessities, or in toil or labour, for the responsibility in these matters lies with such as have authority in them. There never ought to be any clamour, or any behaviour or agitation by which anger is expressed,[9] or diversion of mind from the full assurance of the presence of God.[10] The voice should be modulated; no one ought to answer another, or do anything, roughly or contemptuously,[11] but in all things moderation[12] and respect should be shewn to every one.[13] No wily glances of the eye are to be allowed, nor any behaviour or gestures which grieve a brother and shew contempt.[14] Any display in cloak or shoes is to be avoided; it is idle ostentation.[15] Cheap things ought to be used for bodily necessity; and nothing ought to be spent beyond what is necessary, or for mere extravagance; this is a misuse of our property. The Christian ought not to seek for honour, or claim precedence.[16] Every one ought to put all others before himself.[17] The Christian ought not to be unruly.[18] He who is able to work ought not to eat the bread of idleness,[19] but even he who is busied in deeds well done for the glory of Christ ought to force himself to the active discharge of such work as he can do.[20] Every Christian, with the approval of his superiors, ought so to do everything with reason and assurance, even down to actual eating and drinking, as done to the glory of God.[21] The Christian ought not to change over from one work to another without the approval of those who are appointed for the

---

1 cf. Heb. iii.
2 cf. Phil. i. 27.
3 cf. Luke xii. 29.
4 cf. Matt. v. 20.
6 Tit. iii. 2.
6 1 Tim. ii. 13.
7 2 Tim. ii. 24.
8 Rom. xii. 19.
9 Rom. xii. 17.
10 Matt. v. 22.
11 James v. 8.
12 Tit. ii. 15.
13 Matt. xv. 18.
14 cf. 2 Cor. xii. 20 and 1 Peter ii. 1.
15 cf. 1 Peter iii. 16, 17, and James iv. 11.
16 Eph. v. 4.
17 This charge is probably founded on Luke vi. 21 and 25, and James iv.9. Yet our Lord's promise that they who hunger and weep " shall laugh," admits of fulfilment in the kingdom of God on earth. Cheerfulness is a note of the Church, whose members, " if sorrowful," are yet " alway rejoicing." (2 Cor. vi. 10.)
18 Eph. v. 4.
19 It is less easy to find explicit Scriptural sanction even for such a modified rule of silence as is here given by St. Basil. St. Paul can only be quoted for the " silence " of the woman. But even St. Basil's " silence," with a view to preserving his cœnobium from vain conversation, is a long way off the " silence " of St. Bruno's Carthusians.

1 1 Pet. iv. 3.
2 Rom. xiv. 21.
3 2 Tim. iii.4.
4 1 Cor. ix. 25.
5 cf. Acts iv. 32.
6 cf. 1 Cor. ix. 19.
7 cf. 1 Cor. xv. 23.
8 cf. 1 Cor. x. 10.
9 cf. Eph. iv. 31.
10 cf. Heb. iv. 13.
11 cf. Tit. iii. 2.
12 Phil. iv. 5, τὸ ἐπιεικές. In 1 Tim. iii. 3, " patient " is ἐπιεικής.
13 Rom. xii. 10 and 1 Pet. ii. 17.
14 Rom. xiv. 10.
15 Matt. vi. 29, Luke xii. 27.
16 Mark ix. 37.
17 Phil. ii. 3.
18 Tit. i. 10.
19 2 Thess. iii. 10.
20 1 Thess. iv. 11.
21 1 Cor. x. 31.

arrangement of such matters; unless some unavoidable necessity suddenly summon any one to the relief of the helpless. Every one ought to remain in his appointed post, not to go beyond his own bounds and intrude into what is not commanded him, unless the responsible authorities judge any one to be in need of aid. No one ought to be found going from one workshop to another. Nothing ought to be done in rivalry or strife with any one.

3. The Christian ought not to grudge another's reputation, nor rejoice over any man's faults;[1] he ought in Christ's love to grieve and be afflicted at his brother's faults, and rejoice over his brother's good deeds.[2] He ought not to be indifferent or silent before sinners.[3] He who shows another to be wrong ought to do so with all tenderness,[4] in the fear of God, and with the object of converting the sinner.[5] He who is proved wrong or rebuked ought to take it willingly, recognizing his own gain in being set right. When any one is being accused, it is not right for another, before him or any one else, to contradict the accuser; but if at any time the charge seems groundless to any one, he ought privately to enter into discussion with the accuser, and either produce, or acquire, conviction. Every one ought, as far as he is able, to conciliate one who has ground of complaint against him. No one ought to cherish a grudge against the sinner who repents, but heartily to forgive him.[6] He who says that he has repented of a sin ought not only to be pricked with compunction for his sin, but also to bring forth fruits worthy of repentance.[7] He who has been corrected in first faults, and received pardon, if he sins again prepares for himself a judgment of wrath worse than the former.[8] He, who after the first and second admonition[9] abides in his fault, ought to be brought before the person in authority,[10] if haply after being rebuked by more he may be ashamed.[11] If even thus he fail to be set right he is to be cut off from the rest as one that maketh to offend, and regarded as a heathen and a publican,[12] for the security of them that are obedient, according to the saying, When the impious fall the righteous tremble.[13] He should be grieved over as a limb cut from the body. The sun ought not to go down upon a brother's wrath,[14] lest haply night come between brother and brother, and

make the charge stand in the day of judgment. A Christian ought not to wait for an opportunity for his own amendment,[1] because there is no certainty about the morrow; for many after many devices have not reached the morrow. He ought not to be beguiled by over eating, whence come dreams in the night. He ought not to be distracted by immoderate toil, nor overstep the bounds of sufficiency, as the apostle says, "Having food and raiment let us be therewith content;"[2] unnecessary abundance gives appearance of covetousness, and covetousness is condemned as idolatry.[3] A Christian ought not to be a lover of money,[4] nor lay up treasure for unprofitable ends. He who comes to God ought to embrace poverty in all things, and to be riveted in the fear of God, according to the words, "Rivet my flesh in thy fear, for I am afraid of thy judgments."[5] The Lord grant that you may receive what I have said with full conviction and shew forth fruits worthy of the Spirit to the glory of God, by God's good pleasure, and the coöperation of our Lord Jesus Christ.

LETTER XXIII.[6]

To a Solitary.

A CERTAIN man, as he says, on condemning the vanity of this life, and perceiving that its joys are ended here, since they only provide material for eternal fire and then quickly pass away, has come to me with the desire of separating from this wicked and miserable life, of abandoning the pleasures of the flesh, and of treading for the future a road which leads to the mansions of the Lord. Now if he is sincerely firm in his truly blessed purpose, and has in his soul the glorious and laudable passion, loving the Lord his God with all his heart, with all his strength, and with all his mind, it is necessary for your reverence to show him the difficulties and distresses of the strait and narrow way, and establish him in the hope of the good things which are as yet unseen, but are laid up in promise for all that are worthy of the Lord. I therefore write to entreat your incomparable perfection in Christ, if it be possible to mould his character, and, without me, to bring about his renunciation according to what is pleasing to God, and to see that he receive elementary instruction in accordance with what has been decided by the Holy Fathers, and

---

[1] 1 Cor. xiii. 6.
[2] 1 Cor. xii. 26.
[3] 1 Tim. v. 20.
[4] 2 Tim. iv. 2.
[5] 2 Tim. iv. 2.
[6] 2 Cor. ii. 7.
[7] Luke iii. 8.
[8] Heb. x. 26, 27.
[9] Tit. iii. 10.
[10] τῷ προεστῶτι. ὁ προεστὼς is the "president" in Justin Martyr's description of the Christian service in *Apol. Maj.* i.
[11] *cf.* Tit. ii. 8.
[12] Matt. xviii. 17.
[13] Prov. xxix. 16, LXX.
[14] Eph. iv. 26.

---

[1] *cf.* Matt. xxiv. 14; Luke xii. 40.
[2] 1 Tim. vi. 8.
[3] Col. iii. 5.
[4] *cf.* Mark x. 23, 24; Luke xviii. 24.
[5] Ps. cxix. 120, LXX.
[6] Written at Cæsarea during his presbyterate.

put forth by them in writing. See too that he have put before him all things that are essential to ascetic discipline, and that so he may be introduced to the life, after having accepted, of his own accord, the labours undergone for religion's sake, subjected himself to the Lord's easy yoke, adopted a conversation in imitation of Him Who for our sakes became poor [1] and took flesh, and may run without fail to the prize of his high calling, and receive the approbation of the Lord. He is wishful to receive here the crown of God's love, but I have put him off, because I wish, in conjunction with your reverence, to anoint him for such struggles, and to appoint over him one of your number whom he may select to be his trainer, training him nobly, and making him by his constant and blessed care a tried wrestler, wounding and overthrowing the prince of the darkness of this world, and the spiritual powers of iniquity, with whom, as the blessed Apostle says, is "our wrestling." [2] What I wish to do in conjunction with you, let your love in Christ do without me.

LETTER XXIV.[3]

To Athanasius, father of Athanasius bishop of Ancyra.[4]

THAT one of the things hardest to achieve, if indeed it be not impossible, is to rise superior to calumny, I am myself fully persuaded, and so too, I presume, is your excellency. Yet not to give a handle by one's own conduct, either to inquisitive critics of society, or to mischief makers who lie in wait to catch us tripping, is not only possible, but is the special characteristic of all who order their lives wisely and according to the rule of true religion. And do not think me so simple and credulous as to accept depreciatory remarks from any one without due investigation. I bear in mind the admonition of the Spirit, "Thou shalt not receive a false report." [5] But you, learned men, yourselves say that "The seen is significant of the unseen." I therefore beg ; — (and pray do not take it ill if I seem to be speaking as though I were giving a lesson ; for "God has chosen the weak" and "despised things of the world," [6] and often by their means brings about the salvation of such as are being saved) ;

what I say and urge is this ; that by word and deed we act with scrupulous attention to propriety, and, in accordance with the apostolic precept, "give no offence in anything." [1] The life of one who has toiled hard in the acquisition of knowledge, who has governed cities and states, and who is jealous of the high character of his forefathers, ought to be an example of high character itself. You ought not now to be exhibiting your disposition towards your children in word only, as you have long exhibited it, ever since you became a father ; you ought not only to shew that natural affection which is shewn by brutes, as you yourself have said, and as experience shews. You ought to make your love go further, and be a love all the more personal and voluntary in that you see your children worthy of a father's prayers. On this point I do not need to be convinced. The evidence of facts is enough. One thing, however, I will say for truth's sake, that it is not our brother Timotheus, the Chorepiscopus, who has brought me word of what is noised abroad. For neither by word of mouth nor by letter has he ever conveyed anything in the shape of slander, be it small or great. That I have heard something I do not deny, but it is not Timotheus who, accuses you. Yet while I hear whatever I do, at least I will follow the example of Alexander, and will keep one ear clear for the accused. [2]

LETTER XXV.[3]

To Athanasius, bishop of Ancyra.[4]

1. I HAVE received intelligence from those who come to me from Ancyra, and they are many and more than I can count, but they all agree in what they say, that you, a man very dear to me, (how can I speak so as to give no offence?) do not mention me in very pleasant terms, nor yet in such as your character would lead me to expect. I, however, learned long ago the weakness of human nature, and its readiness to turn from one extreme to another ; and so, be well assured, nothing connected with it can astonish me, nor does any change come quite unexpected. Therefore that my lot should have changed

---

[1] 2 Cor. viii. 9.
[2] Eph. vi. 12.
[3] Placed before Basil's episcopate.
[4] *Vide* note on *Letter* xxv. Nothing more is known of the elder of these two Athanasii than is to be gathered from this letter.
[5] Ex. xxiii. 1, LXX. and marg.
[6] 1 Cor. i. 27, 28.

[1] 2 Cor. vi. 3.
[2] *cf.* Plut., *Vit. Alex.*
[3] Placed, like the former, before the episcopate.
[4] This Athanasius was appointed to the see of Ancyra (Angora) by the influence of Acacius the one-eyed, bp. of Cæsarea, the inveterate opponent of Cyril of Jerusalem, and leader of the Homœans. He therefore started his episcopate under unfavorable auspices, but acquired a reputation for orthodoxy. *cf.* Greg. Nyss., *Contra Eunom.* I. ii. 292. On Basil's high opinion of him, *cf. Letter* xxix.

for the worse, and that reproaches and insults should have arisen in the place of former respect, I do not make much ado. But one thing does really strike me as astonishing and monstrous, and that is that it should be you who have this mind about me, and go so far as to feel anger and indignation against me, and, if the report of your hearers is to be believed, have already proceeded to such extremities as to utter threats. At these threats, I will not deny, I really have laughed. Truly I should have been but a boy to be frightened at such bugbears. But it does seém to me alarming and distressing that you, who, as I have trusted, are preserved for the comfort of the churches, a buttress of the truth where many fall away, and a seed of the ancient and true love, should so far fall in with the present course of events as to be more influenced by the calumny of the first man you come across than by your long knowledge of me, and, without any proof, should be seduced into suspecting absurdities.

2. But, as I said, for the present I postpone the case. Would it have been too hard a task, my dear sir, to discuss in a short letter, as between friend and friend, points which you wish to raise; or, if you objected to entrusting such things to writing, to get me to come to you? But if you could not help speaking out, and your uncontrollable anger allowed no time for delay, at least you might have employed one of those about you who are naturally adapted for dealing with confidential matters, as a means of communication with me. But now, of all those who for one reason or another approach you, into whose ears has it not been dinned that I am a writer and composer of certain "pests"? For this is the word which those, who quote you word for word, say that you have used. The more I bring my mind to bear upon the matter the more hopeless is my puzzle. This idea has struck me. Can any heretic have grieved your orthodoxy, and driven you to the utterance of that word by malevolently putting my name to his own writings? For you, a man who has sustained great and famous contests on behalf of the truth, could never have endured to inflict such an outrage on what I am well known to have written against those who dare to say that God the Son is in essence unlike God the Father, or who blasphemously describe the Holy Ghost as created and made. You might relieve me from my difficulty yourself, if you would tell me plainly what it is that has stirred you to be thus offended with me.

LETTER XXVI.[1]

To Cæsarius, brother of Gregory.[2]

THANKS to God for shewing forth His wonderful power in your person, and for preserving you to your country and to us your friends, from so terrible a death. It remains for us not to be ungrateful, nor unworthy of so great a kindness, but, to the best of our ability, to narrate the marvellous works of God, to celebrate by deed the kindness which we have experienced, and not return thanks by word only. We ought to become in very deed what I, grounding my belief on the miracles wrought in you, am persuaded that you now are. We exhort you still more to serve God, éver increasing your fear more and more, and advancing on to perfection, that we may be made wise stewards of our life, for which the goodness of God has reserved us. For if it is a command to all of us " to yield ourselves unto God as those that are alive from the dead," [3] how much more strongly is not this commanded them who have been lifted up from the gates of death? And this, I believe, would be best effected, did we but desire ever to keep the same mind in which we were at the moment of our perils. For, I ween, the vanity of our life came before us, and we felt that all that belongs to man, exposed as it is to vicissitudes, has about it nothing sure, nothing firm. We felt, as was likely, repentance for the past; and we gave a promise for the future, if we were saved, to serve God and give careful heed to ourselves. If the imminent peril of death gave me any cause for reflection, I think that you must have been moved by the same or nearly the same thoughts. We are therefore bound to pay a binding debt, at once joyous at God's good gift to us, and, at the same time, anxious about the future. I have ventured to make these suggestions to you. It is yours to receive what I say well and kindly, as you were wont to do when we talked together face to face.

LETTER XXVII.[4]

To Eusebius, bishop of Samosata.[5]

WHEN by God's grace, and the aid of

1 Placed in 368.
2 Cæsarius was the youngest brother of Gregory of Nazianzus. After a life of distinguished service under Julian, Valens, and Valentinian, he was led, shortly after the escape narrated in this letter, to retire from the world. A work entitled Πεύσεις, or Quæstiones (sive Dialogi) de Rebus Divinis, attributed to him, is of doubtful genuineness. Vide D.C.B. s.v. The earthquake, from the effects of which Cæsarius was preserved, took place on the tenth of October, 368. cf. Greg. Naz. Orat. x. 3 Rom. vii. 13. 4 Placed in 368. 5 This, the first of the twenty-two letters addressed by Basil to Eusebius of Samosata, has no particular interest. Euse-

your prayers, I had seemed to be somewhat recovering from my sickness, and had got my strength again, then came winter, keeping me a prisoner at home, and compelling me to remain where I was. True, its severity was much less than usual, but this was quite enough to keep me not merely from travelling while it lasted, but even from so much as venturing to put my head out of doors. But to me it is no slight thing to be permitted, if only by letter, to communicate with your reverence, and to rest tranquil in the hope of your reply. However, should the season permit, and further length of life be allowed me, and should the dearth not prevent me from undertaking the journey,[1] peradventure through the aid of your prayers I may be able to fulfil my earnest wish, may find you at your own fireside, and, with abundant leisure, may take my fill of your vast treasures of wisdom.

LETTER XXVIII.[2]

To the Church of Neocæsarea. Consolatory.[3]

1. WHAT has befallen you strongly moved me to visit you, with the double object of joining with you, who are near and dear to me, in paying all respect to the blessed dead, and of being more closely associated with you in your trouble by seeing your sorrow with my own eyes, and so being able to take counsel with you as to what is to be done. But many causes hinder my being able to approach you in person, and it remains for me to communicate with you in writing. The admirable qualities of the departed, on account of which we chiefly estimate the greatness of our loss, are indeed too many to be enumerated in a letter; and it is, besides, no time to be discussing the multitude of his good deeds, when our spirits are thus prostrated with grief. For of all that he did, what can we ever forget? What could we deem deserving of silence? To tell all at once were impossible; to tell a part would, I fear, involve dis-

loyalty to the truth. A man has passed away who surpassed all his contemporaries in all the good things that are within man's reach; a prop of his country; an ornament of the churches; a pillar and support of the truth; a stay of the faith of Christ; a protector of his friends; a stout foe of his opponents; a guardian of the principles of his fathers; an enemy of innovation; exhibiting in himself the ancient fashion of the Church, and making the state of the Church put under him conform to the ancient constitution, as to a sacred model, so that all who lived with him seemed to live in the society of them that used to shine like lights in the world two hundred years ago and more. So your bishop put forth nothing of his own, no novel invention; but, as the blessing of Moses has it, he knew how to bring out of the secret and good stores of his heart, " old store, and the old because of the new." [1] Thus it came about that in meetings of his fellow bishops he was not ranked according to his age, but, by reason of the old age of his wisdom, he was unanimously conceded precedence over all the rest. And no one who looks at your condition need go far to seek the advantages of such a course of training. For, so far as I know, you alone, or, at all events, you and but very few others, in the midst of such a storm and whirlwind of affairs, were able under his good guidance to live your lives unshaken by the waves. You were never reached by heretics' buffeting blasts, which bring shipwreck and drowning on unstable souls; and that you may for ever live beyond their reach I pray the Lord who ruleth over all, and who granted long tranquillity to Gregory His servant, the first founder of your church.[2]

Do not lose that tranquillity now; do not, by extravagant lamentation, and by entirely giving yourself up to grief, put the opportunity for action into the hands of those who are plotting your bane. If lament you must, (which I do not allow, lest you be in this respect like " them which have no hope,")[3] do you, if so it seem good to you, like some wailing chorus, choose your leader, and raise with him a chant of tears.

2. And yet, if he whom you mourn had not reached extreme old age, certainly, as regards his government of your church, he was allowed no narrow limit of life. He had as much strength of body as enabled him to show strength of mind in his distresses. Perhaps some of you may suppose

bius, the friend of Basil, Gregory of Nazianzus, and of Meletius, was bishop of Samosata (in Commagene on the Euphrates, now Samsat) from 360 to 373, and was of high character and sound opinions. Theodoret (*Ecc. Hist.* iv. 15), in mentioning his exile to Thrace in the persecution under Valens, calls him "that unflagging labourer in apostolic work," and speaks warmly of his zeal. Concerning the singular and touching circumstances of his death, *vide* Theodoret, *E.H.* v. 4, and my note in the edition of this series, p. 134.
[1] Samosata was about two hundred miles distant from Cæsarea, as the crow flies.
[2] Placed in 368.
[3] *i.e.* on the death of Musonius, bp. of Neocæsarea. Musonius is not named, but he is inferred to be the bishop referred to in *Ep.* ccx., in which Basil asserts that sound doctrine prevailed in Neocæsarea up to the time of "the blessed Musonius, whose teaching still rings in your ears."

[1] Lev. xxvi. 10.   [3] 1 Thess. iv. 13.
[2] *i.e.* Gregory Thaumaturgus.

that time increases sympathy and adds affection, and is no cause of satiety, so that, the longer you have experienced kind treatment, the more sensible you are of its loss. You may think that of a righteous person the good hold even the shadow in honour. Would that many of you did feel so! Far be it from me to suggest anything like disregard of our friend! But I do counsel you to bear your pain with manly endurance. I myself am by no means insensible of all that may be said by those who are weeping for their loss. Hushed is a tongue whose words flooded our ears like a mighty stream: a depth of heart, never fathomed before, has fled, humanly speaking, like an unsubstantial dream. Whose glance so keen as his to look into the future? Who with like fixity and strength of mind able to dart like lightning into the midst of action? O Neocaearea, already a prey to many troubles, never before smitten with so deadly a loss! Now withered is the bloom of your beauty; your church is dumb; your assemblies are full of mournful faces; your sacred synod craves for its leader; your holy utterances wait for an expounder; your boys have lost a father, your elders a brother, your nobles one first among them, your people a champion, your poor a supporter. All, calling him by the name that comes most nearly home to each, lift up the wailing cry which to each man's own sorrow seems most appropriate and fit. But whither are my words carried away by my tearful joy? Shall we not watch? Shall we not meet together? Shall we not look to our common Lord, Who suffers each of his saints to serve his own generation, and summons him back to Himself at His own appointed time? Now in season remember the voice of him who when preaching to you used always to say "Beware of dogs, beware of evil workers." [1] The dogs are many. Why do I say dogs? Rather grievous wolves, hiding their guile under the guise of sheep, are all over the world, tearing Christ's flock. Of these you must beware, under the protection of some wakeful bishop. Such an one it is yours to ask, purging your souls of all rivalry and ambition: such an one it is the Lord's to show you. That Lord, from the time of Gregory the great champion of your church down to that of the blessed departed, setting over you one after another, and from time to time fitting one to another like gem set close to gem, has bestowed on you glorious ornaments for your church. You have, then, no need to despair of them that are to come. The Lord knoweth who are His. He may bring into our midst those for whom peradventure we are not looking.

3. I meant to have come to an end long before this, but the pain at my heart does not allow me. Now I charge you by the Fathers, by the true faith, by our blessed friend, lift up your souls, each man making what is being done his own immediate business, each reckoning that he will be the first to reap the consequences of the issue, whichever way it turn out, lest your fate be that which so very frequently befalls, every one leaving to his neighbour the common interests of all; and then, while each one makes little in his own mind of what is going on, all of you unwittingly draw your own proper misfortunes on yourselves by your neglect. Take, I beg you, what I say with all kindliness, whether it be regarded as an expression of the sympathy of a neighbour, or as fellowship between fellow believers, or, which is really nearer the truth, of one who obeys the law of love, and shrinks from the risk of silence. I am persuaded that you are my boasting, as I am yours, till the day of the Lord, and that it depends upon the pastor who will be granted you whether I shall be more closely united to you by the bond of love, or wholly severed from you. This latter God forbid. By God's grace it will not so be; and I should be sorry now to say one ungracious word. But this I do wish you to know, that though I had not that blessed man always at my side, in my efforts for the peace of the churches, because, as he himself affirmed, of certain prejudices, yet, nevertheless, at no time did I fail in unity of opinion with him, and I have always invoked his aid in my struggles against the heretics. Of this I call to witness God and all who know me best.

LETTER XXIX.[1]

To the Church of Ancyra. Consolatory.[2]

My amazement at the most distressing news of the calamity which has befallen you for a long time kept me silent. I felt like a man whose ears are stunned by a loud clap of thunder. Then I somehow recovered a little from my state of speechlessness. Now I have mourned, as none could help mourning, over the event, and, in the midst of my lamentations, have sent you this letter. I write not so much to console you, — for who could find words to cure a calamity so great?

---

[1] Phil. iii. 2.

— as to signify to you, as well as I can by these means, the agony of my own heart. I need now the lamentations of Jeremiah, or of any other of the Saints who has feelingly lamented a great woe. A man has fallen who was really a pillar and stay of the Church; or rather he himself has been taken from us and is gone to the blessed life, and there is no small danger lest many at the removal of this prop from under them fall too, and lest some men's unsoundness be brought to light. A mouth is sealed gushing with righteous eloquence and words of grace to the edification of the brotherhood. Gone are the counsels of a mind which truly moved in God. Ah! how often, for I must accuse myself, was it my lot to feel indignation against him, because, wholly desiring to depart and be with Christ, he did not prefer for our sakes to remain in the flesh![1] To whom for the future shall I commit the cares of the Churches? Whom shall I take to share my troubles? Whom to participate in my gladness? O loneliness terrible and sad! How am I not like to a pelican of the wilderness?[2] Yet of a truth the members of the Church, united by his leadership as by one soul, and fitted together into close union of feeling and fellowship, are both preserved and shall ever be preserved by the bond of peace for spiritual communion. God grants us the boon, that all the works of that blessed soul, which he did nobly in the churches of God, abide firm and immovable. But the struggle is no slight one, lest, once more strifes and divisions arising over the choice of the bishop, all your work be upset by some quarrel.

LETTER XXX.[3]

To Eusebius of Samosata.

IF I were to write at length all the causes which, up to the present time, have kept me at home, eager as I have been to set out to see your reverence, I should tell an interminable story. I say nothing of illnesses coming one upon another, hard winter weather, and press of work, for all this has been already made known to you. Now, for my sins, I have lost my Mother,[4] the only comfort I had in life. Do not smile, if, old as I am, I lament my orphanhood. Forgive me if I cannot endure separation from a soul, to compare with whom I see nothing in the future that lies before me. So once more my complaints have come back to me; once more I

am confined to my bed, tossing about in my weakness, and every hour all but looking for the end of life; and the Churches are in somewhat the same condition as my body, no good hope shining on them, and their state always changing for the worse. In the meantime Neocæsarea and Ancyra have decided to have successors of the dead, and so far they are at peace. Those who are plotting against me have not yet been permitted to do anything worthy of their bitterness and wrath. This we make no secret of attributing to your prayers on behalf of the Churches. Weary not then in praying for the Churches and in entreating God. Pray give all salutations to those who are privileged to minister to your Holiness.

LETTER XXXI.[1]

To Eusebius, bishop of Samosata.

THE dearth is still with us, and I am therefore compelled to remain where I am, partly by the duty of distribution, and partly out of sympathy for the distressed. Even now, therefore, I have not been able to accompany our reverend brother Hypatius,[2] whom I am able to style brother, not in mere conventional language, but on account of relationship, for we are of one blood. You know how ill he is. It distresses me to think that all hope of comfort is cut off for him, as those who have the gifts of healing have not been allowed to apply their usual remedies in his case. Wherefore again he implores the aid of your prayers. Receive my entreaty that you will give him the usual protection alike for your own sake, for you are always kind to the sick, and for mine who am petitioning on his behalf. If possible, summon to your side the very holy brethren that he may be treated under your own eyes. If this be impossible, be so good as to send him on with a letter, and recommend him to friends further on.

LETTER XXXII.[3]

To Sophronius the Master.[4]

1. OUR God — beloved brother, Gregory

---

[1] cf. Phil. i. 23, 24.　　[2] cf. Ps. cii. 6.　　[3] Placed in 369.
[4] Emmelia. Vide account of Basil's family in the prolegomena.

[1] Placed in 369. cf. note on Letter ccxxxvi.
[2] Nothing more is known of this Hypatius. Gregory of Nazianzus (Ep. 192) writes to a correspondent of the same name. [3] Placed in 369.
[4] i.e. Magister officiorum. Sophronius was a fellow student with Basil at Athens, and a friend of Gregory of Nazianzus. He secured the favour of Valens, who was staying at Cæsarea in 365, by conveying him intelligence of the usurpation of Procopius at Constantinople. (Amm. Marc. xxv. 9.) On the circumstances which gave rise to this letter, cf. Greg. Naz., Ep. xviii. Letters lxxvi., xcvi., clxxvii., clxxx., cxcii., and cclxxii. are addressed to the same correspondent, the last, as it will be seen, indicating a breach in their long friendship.

the bishop,[1] shares the troubles of the times, for he too, like everybody else, is distressed at successive outrages, and resembles a man buffeted by unexpected blows. For men who have no fear of God, possibly forced by the greatness of their troubles, are reviling him, on the ground that they have lent Cæsarius[2] money. It is not indeed the question of any loss which is serious, for he has long learnt to despise riches. The matter rather is that those who have so freely distributed all the effects of Cæsarius that were worth anything, after really getting very little, because his property was in the hands of slaves, and of men of no better character than slaves, did not leave much for the executors.[3] This little they supposed to be pledged to no one, and straightway spent it on the poor, not only from their own preference, but because of the injunctions of the dead. For on his death bed Cæsarius is declared to have said "I wish my goods to belong to the poor." In obedience then to the wishes of Cæsarius they made a proper distribution of them. Now, with the poverty of a Christian, Gregory is immersed in the bustle of a chafferer. So I bethought me of reporting the matter to your excellency, in order that you may state what you think proper about Gregory to the Comes Thesaurorum, and so may honour a man whom you have known for many years, glorify the Lord who takes as done to Himself what is done to His servants, and honour me who am specially bound to you. You will, I hope, of your great sagacity devise a means of relief from these outrageous people and intolerable annoyances.

2. No one is so ignorant of Gregory as to have any unworthy suspicion of his giving an inexact account of the circumstances because he is fond of money. We have not to go far to find a proof of his liberality. What is left of the property of Cæsarius he gladly abandons to the Treasury, so that the property may be kept there, and the Treasurer may give answer to those who attack it and demand their proofs ; for we are not adapted for such business. Your excellency may be informed that, so long as it was possible, no one went away without getting what he wanted, and each one carried off what he demanded without any difficulty. The con-sequence indeed was that a good many were sorry that they had not asked for more at first ; and this made still more objectors, for with the example of the earlier successful applicants before them, one false claimant starts up after another. I do then entreat your excellency to make a stand against all this and to come in, like some intervening stream, and solve the continuity of these troubles. You know how best you will help matters, and need not wait to be instructed by me. I am inexperienced in the affairs of this life, and cannot see my way out of our difficulties. Of your great wisdom discover some means of help. Be our counsellor. Be our champion.

LETTER XXXIII.[1]

To Aburgius.[2]

WHO knows so well as you do how to respect an old friendship, to pay reverence to virtue, and to sympathise with the sick? Now my God-beloved brother Gregory the bishop has become involved in matters which would be under any circumstances disagreeable, and are quite foreign to his bent of mind. I have therefore thought it best to throw myself on your protection, and to endeavour to obtain from you some solution of our difficulties. It is really an intolerable state of things that one who is neither by nature nor inclination adapted for anything of the kind should be compelled to be thus responsible; that demands for money should be made on a poor man; and that one who has long determined to pass his life in retirement should be dragged into publicity. It would depend upon your wise counsel whether you think it of any use to address the Comes Thesaurorum or any other persons.

LETTER XXXIV.[3]

To Eusebius, bishop of Samosata.

How could I be silent at the present juncture? And if I cannot be silent, how am I to find utterance adequate to the circumstances, so as to make my voice not like a mere groan but rather a lamentation intelligibly indicating the greatness of the misfort-

---

[1] The word Episcopus in this and in the following letter is supposed by Maran to have crept into the text from the margin. Gregory of Nazianzus is referred to, who was not then a bishop. Gregory the Elder, bishop of Nazianzus, was in good circumstances, and had not adopted the monastic life.
[2] *cf. Letter* xxvi. Cæsarius died in 368, leaving his brother Gregory as executor.
[3] τούτοις. So the MSS., but the editors here substituted τούτῳ, *i.e.* Gregory, and similarly the singular in the following words.

[1] Placed in 369.
[2] *cf. Ep.* xxxiii., lxxv., cxlvii., clxxviii., ccciv., and also cxcvi., though the last is also attributed to Greg. Naz. He was an important lay compatriot of Basil. Tillemont was of opinion that the dear brother Gregory referred to in this letter is Gregory of Nyssa; but Maran points out that the events referred to are the same as those described in *Letter* xxxii., and supposes the word *episcopus* to have been inserted by a commentator. [3] Placed in 369.

une? Ah me! Tarsus is undone.[1] This is a trouble grievous to be borne, but it does not come alone. It is still harder to think that a city so placed as to be united with Cilicia, Cappadocia, and Assyria, should be lightly thrown away by the madness of two or three individuals, while you are all the while hesitating, settling what to do, and looking at one another's faces. It would have been far better to do like the doctors. (I have been so long an invalid that I have no lack of illustrations of this kind.) When their patients' pain becomes excessive they produce insensibility; so should we pray that our souls may be made insensible to the pain of our troubles, that we be not put under unendurable agony. In these hard straits I do not fail to use one means of consolation. I look to your kindness; I try to make my troubles milder by my thought and recollection of you.[2] When the eyes have looked intently on any brilliant objects it relieves them to turn again to what is blue and green; the recollection of your kindness and attention has just the same effect on my soul; it is a mild treatment that takes away my pain. I feel this the more when I reflect that you individually have done all that man could do. You have satisfactorily shewn us, men, if we judge things fairly, that the catastrophe is in no way due to you personally. The reward which you have won at God's hand for your zeal for right is no small one. May the Lord grant you to me and to His churches to the improvement of life and the guidance of souls, and may He once more allow me the privilege of meeting you.

LETTER XXXV.[3]

Without address.

I HAVE written to you about many people as belonging to myself; now I mean to write about more. The poor can never fail, and I can never say, no. There is no one more intimately associated with me, nor better able to do me kindnesses wherever he has the ability, than the reverend brother Leontius. So treat his house as if you had found me, not in that poverty in which now by God's help I am living, but endowed with wealth and landed property. There is no doubt that you would not have made me poor, but would have taken care of what I had, or even added to my possessions. This is the way I ask you to behave in the house of Leontius. You will get your accustomed reward from me; my prayers to the holy God for the trouble you are taking in shewing yourself a good man and true, and in anticipating the supplication of the needy.

LETTER XXXVI.[1]

Without address.

IT has, I think, been long known to your excellency that the presbyter of this place is a foster brother of my own. What more can I say to induce you, in your kindness, to view him with a friendly eye, and give him help in his affairs? If you love me, as I know you do, I am sure that you will endeavour, to the best of your power, to relieve any one whom I look upon as a second self. What then do I ask? That he do not lose his old rating. Really he takes no little trouble in ministering to my necessities, because I, as you know, have nothing of my own, but depend upon the means of my friends and relatives. Look, then, upon my brother's house as you would on mine, or let me rather say, on your own. In return for your kindness to him God will not cease to help alike yourself, your house, and your family. Be sure that I am specially anxious lest any injury should be done to him by the equalization of rates.

LETTER XXXVII.[2]

Without address.

I LOOK with suspicion on the multiplication of letters. Against my will, and because I cannot resist the importunity of petitioners, I am compelled to speak. I write because I can think of no other means of relieving myself than by assenting to the supplications of those who are always asking letters from me. I am really afraid lest, since many are carrying letters off, one of the many be reckoned to be that brother. I have, I own, many friends and relatives in my own country, and I am placed *in loco parentis* by the position [3] which the Lord has given me. Among them is this my foster

---

[1] Silvanus, Metropolitan of Tarsus, one of the best of the Semi-Arians (Ath., *De Synod.* 41), died, according to Tillemont, in 373, according to Maran four years earlier, and was succeeded by an Arian; but events did not turn out so disastrously as Basil had anticipated. The majority of the presbyters were true to the Catholic cause, and Basil maintained friendship and intercourse with them. *cf. Letters* lxvii., cxiii., cxiv.

[2] Basil is supposed to have in the meanwhile carried out his previously-expressed intention of paying Eusebius a visit.

[3] Placed before 370.

[1] Placed before 370.
[2] Of the same time as the preceding.
[3] By some supposed to be that of a bishop; but Maran, who dates the letter before the episcopate, thinks the use of the phrase is justified by our understanding the presbyterate to be meant. *Vide* Prolegomena.

brother, son of my nurse, and I pray that the house in which I was brought up may remain at its old assessment, so that the sojourn among us of your excellency, so beneficial to us all, may turn out no occasion of trouble to him. Now too I am supported from the same house, because I have nothing of my own, but depend upon those who love me. I do then entreat you to spare the house in which I was nursed as though you were keeping up the supply of support for me. May God in return grant you His everlasting rest. One thing however, and it is most true, I think your excellency ought to know, and that is that the greater number of the slaves were given him from the outset by us, as an equivalent for my sustenance, by the gift of my father and mother. At the same time this was not to be regarded as an absolute gift; he was only to have the use for life, so that, if anything serious happen to him on their account, he is at liberty to send them back to me, and I shall thus in another way be responsible for rates and to collectors.

LETTER XXXVIII.[1]

To his Brother Gregory, concerning the difference between οὐσία and ὑπόστασις.

1. MANY persons, in their study of the sacred dogmas, failing to distinguish between what is common in the essence or substance, and the meaning of the hypostases, arrive at the same notions, and think that it makes no difference whether οὐσία or hypostasis be spoken of. The result is that some of those who accept statements on these subjects without any enquiry, are pleased to speak of "one hypostasis," just as they do of one "essence" or "substance;" while on the other hand those who accept three hypostases are under the idea that they are bound in accordance with this confession, to assert also, by numerical analogy, three essences or substances. Under these circumstances, lest you fall into similar error, I have composed a short treatise for you by way of memorandum. The meaning of the words, to put it shortly, is as follows:

2. Of all nouns the sense of some, which are predicated of subjects plural and numerically various, is more general; as for instance *man*. When we so say, we employ the noun to indicate the common nature, and do not confine our meaning to any one man in particular who is known by that name. Peter, for instance is no more *man*, than Andrew, John, or James. The predicate therefore being common, and extending to all the individuals ranked under the same name, requires some note of distinction whereby we may understand not man in general, but Peter or John in particular.

Of some nouns on the other hand the denotation is more limited; and by the aid of the limitation we have before our minds not the common nature, but a limitation of anything, having, so far as the peculiarity extends, nothing in common with what is of the same kind; as for instance, Paul or Timothy. For, in a word, of this kind there is no extension to what is common in the nature; there is a separation of certain circumscribed conceptions from the general idea, and expression of them by means of their names. Suppose then that two or more are set together, as, for instance, Paul, Silvanus, and Timothy, and that an enquiry is made into the essence or substance of humanity; no one will give one definition of essence or substance in the case of Paul, a second in that of Silvanus, and a third in that of Timothy; but the same words which have been employed in setting forth the essence or substance of Paul will apply to the others also. Those who are described by the same definition of essence or substance are of the same essence or substance[1] when the enquirer has learned what is common, and turns his attention to the differentiating properties whereby one is distinguished from another, the definition by which each is known will no longer tally in all particulars with the definition of another, even though in some points it be found to agree.

3. My statement, then, is this. That which is spoken of in a special and peculiar manner is indicated by the name of the hypostasis. Suppose we say "a man." The indefinite meaning of the word strikes a certain vague sense upon the ears. The nature is indicated, but what subsists and is specially and peculiarly indicated by the name is not made plain. Suppose we say "Paul." We set forth, by what is indicated by the name, the nature subsisting.[2]

This then is the hypostasis, or "*understanding;*" not the indefinite conception of the essence or substance, which, because what is signified is general, finds no "*standing,*" but the conception which by means of

---

[1] This important letter is included also among the works of Gregory of Nyssa, as addressed to Peter, bp. of Sebaste, brother of Basil and Gregory. The Ben. note says: "*Stylus Basilii fetum esse clamitat.*" It was, moreover, referred to at Chalcedon as Basil's. [Mansi, *T.* vii. *col.* 464.]

[1] ὁμοούσιοι.
[2] ὑφεστῶσαν. ὑπόστασις is derivatively that which "*stands under*" or subsists, ὃ ὑφέστηκε. *cf.* my note on Theodoret, p. 36.

the expressed peculiarities gives *standing* and circumscription to the general and un-circumscribed. It is customary in Scripture to make a distinction of this kind, as well in many other passages as in the History of Job. When purposing to narrate the events of his life, Job first mentions the common, and says "a man;" then he straightway particularizes by adding "a certain."[1] As to the description of the essence, as having no bearing on the scope of his work, he is silent, but by means of particular notes of identity, mentioning the place and points of character, and such external qualifications as would individualize, and separate from the common and general idea, he specifies the "certain man," in such a way that from name, place, mental qualities, and outside circumstances, the description of the man whose life is being narrated is made in all particulars perfectly clear. If he had been giving an account of the essence, there would not in his explanation of the nature have been any mention of these matters. The same moreover would have been the account that there is in the case of Bildad the Shuhite, and Zophar the Naamathite, and each of the men there mentioned.[2] Transfer, then, to the divine dogmas the same standard of difference which you recognise in the case both of essence and of hypostasis in human affairs, and you will not go wrong. Whatever your thought suggests to you as to the mode of the existence of the Father, you will think also in the case of the Son, and in like manner too of the Holy Ghost. For it is idle to halt the mind at any detached conception from the conviction that it is beyond all conception.[3] For the account of the uncreate and of the incomprehensible is one and the same in the case of the Father and of the Son and of the Holy Ghost. For one is not more incomprehensible and uncreate than another. And since it is necessary, by means of the notes of differentiation, in the case of the Trinity, to keep the distinction unconfounded, we shall not take into consideration, in order to estimate that which differentiates, what is contemplated in common, as the uncreate, or what is beyond all comprehension, or any quality of this nature; we shall only direct our attention to the enquiry by what means each particular conception will be lucidly and distinctly separated from that which is conceived of in common.

4. Now the proper way to direct our investigation seems to me to be as follows. We say that every good thing, which by God's providence befalls us, is an operation, of the Grace which worketh in us all things, as the apostle says, "But all these worketh that one and the self same Spirit dividing to every man severally as he will."[1] If we ask, if the supply of good things which thus comes to the saints has its origin in the Holy Ghost alone, we are on the other hand guided by Scripture to the belief that of the supply of the good things which are wrought in us through the Holy Ghost, the Originator and Cause is the Only-begotten God;[2] for we are taught by Holy Scripture that "All things were made by Him,"[3] and "by Him consist."[4] When we are exalted to this conception, again, led by God-inspired guidance, we are taught that by that power all things are brought from non-being into being, but yet not by that power to the exclusion of origination.[5] On the other hand there is a certain power subsisting without generation and without origination,[6] which is the cause of the cause of all things. For the Son, by whom are all things, and with whom the Holy Ghost is inseparably conceived of, is of the Father.[7] For it is not possible for any one to conceive of the Son if he be not previously enlightened by the Spirit. Since, then, the Holy Ghost, from Whom all the supply of good things for creation has its source, is attached to the Son, and with Him is inseparably apprehended, and has Its[8] being attached to the Father, as cause, from Whom also It proceeds; It has this note of Its peculiar hypostatic nature, that It is known after the Son[9] and together with the Son, and that It has Its subsistence of the Father. The Son, Who declares the Spirit proceeding from the Father through Himself and with Himself, shining forth alone and by only-begetting from the unbegotten light, so far as the peculiar notes are concerned, has nothing in common either with the Father or with

---

[1] Job i. 1, LXX. [2] Job ii. 11.
[3] The MSS. vary as to this parenthetical clause, and are apparently corrupt. The rendering above is conjectural, but not satisfactory.

[1] 1 Cor. xii. 11.
[2] ὁ μονογενὴς θεός is the reading of the Sinaitic and Vatican MSS. in John i. 18. The insertion f the words οὐδὲ ὁ υἱος, adopted by R.V. in Matt. xxiv. 36, but of which St. Basil knows nothing, as appears from his argument on the difference between the statements of St. Matthew and St. Mark on this subject in *Letter* ccxxxvi., is supported by these same two MSS.
[3] John i. 3. [4] Col. i. 17. [5] ἀνάρχως.
[6] ἀγεννήτως καὶ ἀνάρχως ὑφεστῶσα.
[7] For similar statements by St. Basil, *cf. De Sp. S.* p. *cf.* also *Cont. Eunom.* i: ἐπειδὴ γὰρ ἀπὸ τοῦ πατρὸς ἡ ἀρχὴ τῷ υἱῷ, κατὰ τοῦτο μείζων ὁ πατὴρ ὡς αἴτιος καὶ ἀρχή.
[8] *cf.* notes, pp. 15, 24.
[9] μετὰ τὸν υἱόν. So the Benedictine text with four MSS. in the Paris Library, and the note. "μετὰ τοῦ υἱοῦ" is a reading which is inadmissible, repeating as it does the sense of the following clause καὶ σὺν αὐτῷ. The sense in which the Son is both "after the Son" and "with the Son" is explained further on by St. Basil, where he says that the three Persons are known in consecution of order but in conjunction of nature.

the Holy Ghost. He alone is known by the stated signs. But God, Who is over all, alone has, as one special mark of His own hypostasis, His being Father, and His deriving His hypostasis[1] from no cause; and through this mark He is peculiarly known. Wherefore in the communion of the substance we maintain that there is no mutual approach or intercommunion of those notes of indication perceived in the Trinity, whereby is set forth the proper peculiarity of the Persons delivered in the faith, each of these being distinctively apprehended by His own notes. Hence, in accordance with the stated signs of indication, discovery is made of the separation of the hypostases; while so far as relates to the infinite, the incomprehensible, the uncreate, the uncircumscribed, and similar attributes, there is no variableness in the life-giving nature; in that, I mean, of Father, Son, and Holy Ghost, but in Them is seen a certain communion indissoluble and continuous. And by the same considerations, whereby a reflective student could perceive the greatness of any one of the (Persons) believed in in the Holy Trinity, he will proceed without variation. Beholding the glory in Father, Son, and Holy Ghost, his mind all the while recognises no void interval wherein it may travel between Father, Son, and Holy Ghost, for there is nothing inserted between Them; nor beyond the divine nature is there anything so subsisting as to be able to divide that nature from itself by the interposition of any foreign matter. Neither is there any vacuum of interval, void of subsistence, which can make a break in the mutual harmony of the divine essence, and solve the continuity by the interjection of emptiness. He who perceives the Father, and perceives Him by Himself, has at the same time mental perception of the Son; and he who receives the Son does not divide Him from the Spirit, but, in consecution so far as order is concerned, in conjunction so far as nature is concerned, expresses the faith commingled in himself in the three together. He who makes mention of the Spirit alone, embraces also in this confession Him of whom He is the Spirit. And since the Spirit is Christ's and of God,[2] as says Paul, then just as he who lays hold on one end of the chain pulls the other to him, so he who "draws the Spirit,"[3] as says the prophet, by His means draws to him at the same time both the Son and the Father. And if any one verily receives the Son, he will hold Him on both sides, the Son drawing towards him on the one His own Father, and on the other His own Spirit. For He who eternally exists in the Father can never be cut off from the Father, nor can He who worketh all things by the Spirit ever be disjoined from His own Spirit. Likewise moreover he who receives the Father virtually receives at the same time both the Son and the Spirit; for it is in no wise possible to entertain the idea of severance or division, in such a way as that the Son should be thought of apart from the Father, or the Spirit be disjoined from the Son. But the communion and the distinction apprehended in Them are, in a certain sense, ineffable and inconceivable, the continuity of nature being never rent asunder by the distinction of the hypostases, nor the notes of proper distinction confounded in the community of essence. Marvel not then at my speaking of the same thing as being both conjoined and parted, and thinking as it were darkly in a riddle, of a certain[1] new and strange conjoined separation and separated conjunction. Indeed, even in objects perceptible to the senses, any one who approaches the subject in a candid and uncontentious spirit, may find similar conditions of things.

5. Yet receive what I say as at best a token and reflexion of the truth; not as the actual truth itself. For it is not possible that there should be complete correspondence between what is seen in the tokens and the objects in reference to which the use of tokens is adopted. Why then do I say that an analogy of the separate and the conjoined is found in objects perceptible to the senses? You have before now, in springtime, beheld the brightness of the bow in the cloud; the bow, I mean, which, in our common parlance, is called Iris, and is said by persons skilled in such matters to be formed when a certain moisture is mingled with the air, and the force of the winds expresses what is dense and moist in the vapour, after it has become cloudy, into rain. The bow is said to be formed as follows. When the sunbeam, after traversing obliquely the dense and darkened portion of the cloud-formation, has directly cast its own orb on some cloud, the radiance is then reflected back from what is moist and shining, and the result is a bending and return, as it were, of the light upon itself. For flame-like flashings are so constituted that if they

---

[1] ὑποστῆναι. [2] Rom. viii. 9; 1 Cor. ii. 12.
[3] Apparently a mistaken interpretation of the LXX. version of Ps. cxix. 131, εἵλκυσα πνεῦμα = "I drew breath." A.V. and R.V., "I panted." Vulg., attraxi spiritum.

[1] ὥσπερ ἐκ αἰνίγματι. cf. 1 Cor. xiii. 12. ἐν αἰνίγματι or ἐξ αἰνιγμάτων, as in Æsch., Ag. 1113 = by dark hints. The bold oxymoron concluding this sentence is illustrated by Ovid's "impietate pia" (Met. viii. 477), Lucan's "concordia discors" (Phars. i. 98), or Tennyson's "faith unfaithful."

fall on any smooth surface they are refracted on themselves; and the shape of the sun, which by means of the beam is formed on the moist and smooth part of the air, is round. The necessary consequence therefore is that the air adjacent to the cloud is marked out by means of the radiant brilliance in conformity with the shape of the sun's disc. Now this brilliance is both continuous and divided. It is of many colours; it is of many forms; it is insensibly steeped in the variegated bright tints of its dye; imperceptibly abstracting from our vision the combination of many coloured things, with the result that no space, mixing or parting within itself the difference of colour, can be discerned either between blue and flame-coloured, or between flame-coloured and red, or between red and amber. For all the rays, seen at the same time, are far shining, and while they give no signs of their mutual combination, are incapable of being tested, so that it is impossible to discover the limits of the flame-coloured or of the emerald portion of the light, and at what point each originates before it appears as it does in glory. As then in the token we clearly distinguish the difference of the colours, and yet it is impossible for us to apprehend by our senses any interval between them; so in like manner conclude, I pray you, that you may reason concerning the divine dogmas; that the peculiar properties of the hypostases, like colours seen in the Iris, flash their brightness on each of the Persons Whom we believe to exist in the Holy Trinity; but that of the proper nature no difference can be conceived as existing between one and the other, the peculiar characteristics shining, in community of essence, upon each. Even in our example, the essence emitting the many-coloured radiance, and refracted by the sunbeam, was one essence; it is the colour of the phænomenon which is multiform. My argument thus teaches us, even by the aid of the visible creation, not to feel distressed at points of doctrine whenever we meet with questions difficult of solution, and when at the thought of accepting what is proposed to us, our brains begin to reel. In regard to visible objects experience appears better than theories of causation, and so in matters transcending all knowledge, the apprehension of argument is inferior to the faith which teaches us at once the distinction in hypostasis and the conjunction in essence. Since then our discussion has included both what is common and what is distinctive in the Holy Trinity, the common is to be understood as referring to the essence; the hypostasis on the other hand is the several distinctive sign.[1]

6. It may however be thought that the account here given of the hypostasis does not tally with the sense of the Apostle's words, where he says concerning the Lord that He is " the brightness of His glory, and the express image of His person,"[2] for if we have taught hypostasis to be the conflux of the several properties; and if it is confessed that, as in the case of the Father something is contemplated as proper and peculiar, whereby He alone is known, so in the same way is it believed about the Only-begotten; how then does Scripture in this place ascribe the name of the hypostasis to the Father alone, and describes the Son as form of the hypostasis, and designated not by His own proper notes, but by those of the Father? For if the hypostasis is the sign of several existence, and the property of the Father is confined to the unbegotten being, and the Son is fashioned according to His Father's properties, then the term unbegotten can no longer be predicated exclusively of the Father, the existence of the Only-begotten being denoted by the distinctive note of the Father.

7. My opinion is, however, that in this passage the Apostle's argument is directed to a different end; and it is looking to this that he uses the terms "brightness of glory," and " express image of person." Whoever keeps this carefully in view will find nothing that clashes with what I have said, but that the argument is conducted in a special and peculiar sense. For the object of the apostolic argument is not the distinction of the hypostases from one another by means of the apparent notes; it is rather the apprehension of the natural, inseparable, and close relationship of the Son to the Father. He does not say " Who being the glory of the Father " (although in truth He is); he omits this as admitted, and then in the endeavour to teach that we must not think of one form of glory in the case of the Father and of another in that of the Son, He defines the glory of the Only-begotten as the brightness of the glory of the Father, and, by the use of the example of the light, causes the Son to be thought of in indisso-

---

[1] The scientific part of the analogy of the rainbow is of course obsolete and valueless. The general principle holds good that what is beyond comprehension in theology finds its parallel in what is beyond comprehension in the visible world. We are not to be staggered and turn dizzy in either sphere of thought at the discovery that we have reached a limit beyond which thought cannot go. We may live in a finite world, though infinite space is beyond our powers of thought; we may trust in God revealed in the Trinity, though we cannot analyse or define Him.   [2] Heb. i. 3.

luble association with the Father. For just as the brightness is emitted by the flame, and the brightness is not after the flame, but at one and the same moment the flame shines and the light beams brightly, so does the Apostle mean the Son to be thought of as deriving existence from the Father, and yet the Only-begotten not to be divided from the existence of the Father by any intervening extension in space, but the caused to be always conceived of together with the cause. Precisely in the same manner, as though by way of interpretation of the meaning of the preceding cause, and with the object of guiding us to the conception of the invisible by means of material examples, he speaks also of " express image of person." For as the body is wholly in form, and yet the definition of the body and the definition of the form are distinct, and no one wishing to give the definition of the one would be found in agreement with that of the other ; and yet, even if in theory you separate the form from the body, nature does not admit of the distinction, and both are inseparably apprehended ; just so the Apostle thinks that even if the doctrine of the faith represents the difference of the hypostases as unconfounded and distinct, he is bound by his language to set forth also the continuous and as it were concrete relation of the Only-begotten to the Father. And this he states, not as though the Only-begotten had not also a hypostatic being, but in that the union does not admit of anything intervening between the Son and the Father, with the result that he, who with his soul's eyes fixes his gaze earnestly on the express image of the Only-begotten, is made perceptive also of the hypostasis of the Father. Yet the proper quality contemplated in them is not subject to change, nor yet to commixture, in such wise as that we should attribute either an origin of generation to the Father or an origin without generation to the Son, but so that if we could compass the impossibility of detaching one from the other, that one might be apprehended severally and alone, for, since the mere name implies the Father, it is not possible that any one should even name the Son without apprehending the Father.[1]

8. Since then, as says the Lord in the Gospels,[2] he that hath seen the Son sees the Father also ; on this account he says that the Only-begotten is the express image

of His Father's person. That this may be made still plainer I will quote also other passages of the apostle in which he calls the Son " the image of the invisible God,"[1] and again " image of His goodness ; "[2] not because the image differs from the Archetype according to the definition of indivisibility and goodness, but that it may be shewn that it is the same as the prototype, even though it be different. For the idea of the image would be lost were it not to preserve throughout the plain and invariable likeness. He therefore that has perception of the beauty of the image is made perceptive of the Archetype. So he, who has, as it were mental apprehension of the form of the Son, prints the express image of the Father's hypostasis, beholding the latter in the former, not beholding in the reflection the unbegotten being of the Father (for thus there would be complete identity and no distinction), but gazing at the unbegotten beauty in the Begotten. Just as he who in a polished mirror beholds the reflection of the form as plain knowledge of the represented face, so he, who has knowledge of the Son, through his knowledge of the Son receives in his heart the express image of the Father's Person. For all things that are the Father's are beheld in the Son, and all things that are the Son's are the Father's ; because the whole Son is in the Father and has all the Father in Himself.[3] Thus the hypostasis of the Son becomes as it were form and face of the knowledge of the Father, and the hypostasis of the Father is known in the form of the Son, while the proper quality which is contemplated therein remains for the plain distinction of the hypostases.

LETTER XXXIX.[4]

Julian[5] *to Basil.*

THE proverb says " You are not pro-

---

[1] Col. i. 15.

[2] This phrase is not in the Epistles, nor indeed does the substantive ἀγαθότης occur in the N.T. at all. "Image of his goodness" is taken from Wisdom vii. 26, and erroneously included among the "words of the Apostle."

[3] *cf.* John xiv. 11.

[4] To be placed probably in 362, if genuine.

[5] These Letters are placed in this order by the Ben. Editors as being written, if genuine, before Basil's episcopate. Maran (*Vita S. Bas. Cap.* ii.) is puzzled as to prevent all intercourse that he learned the Bible with Julian, and points out that at Athens they devoted themselves to profane literature. But this may have allowed intervals for other work. In 344, when Basil was at Cæsarea, Julian was relegated by Constantius to the neighbouring fortress of Macellum, and there, with his elder half-brother Gallus, spent six years in compulsory retirement. Sozomen tells us that the brothers studied the Scriptures and became Readers (Soz. v. 2; Amm. Marc. xv. 2, 7). Their seclusion, in which they were reduced to the society of their own household (Greg. Naz., *Or.* iii., Julian, *Ad Ath.* 271 c.), may not have been so complete as to prevent all intercourse with a harmless schoolboy like Basil. "*Malgré l'authorité de dom Maran, nous croyons avec Tillemont, Dupont et M. Albert de Broglie, que cette lettre a été réellement adressée par*

---

[1] The simpler explanation of the use of the word hypostasis in the passage under discussion is that it has the earlier sense, equivalent to οὐσία. *cf.* Athan., *Or. c. Ar.* iii. 65, iv. 33, and *Ad. Apos.* 4.   [2] John xiv. 9.

claiming war," [1] and, let me add, out of the comedy, " O messenger of golden words." [2] Come then; prove this in act, and hasten to me. You will come as friend to friend. Conspicuous and unremitting devotion to business seems, to those that treat it as of secondary importance, a heavy burden; yet the diligent are modest, as I persuade myself, sensible, and ready for any emergency. I allow myself relaxation, so that even rest may be permitted to one who neglects nothing. Our mode of life is not marked by the court hypocrisy, of which I think you have had some experience, and in accordance with which compliments mean deadlier hatred than is felt to our worst foes; but, with becoming freedom, while we blame and rebuke where blame is due, we love with the love of the dearest friends. I may therefore, let me say, with all sincerity, both be diligent in relaxation and, when at work, not get worn out, and sleep secure; since when awake I do not wake more for myself, than, as is fit, for every one else. I am afraid this is rather silly and trifling, as I feel rather lazy, (I praise myself like Astydamas [3]) but I am writing to prove to you that to have the pleasure of seeing you, wise man as you are, will be more likely to do me good than to cause any difficulty. Therefore, as I have said, lose no time; travel post haste. After you have paid me as long a visit as you like, you shall go on your journey, whithersoever you will, with my best wishes.

LETTER XL. [4]

Julian to Basil.

WHILE showing up to the present time the gentleness and benevolence which have been natural to me from my boyhood, I have reduced all who dwell beneath the sun to obedience. For lo! every tribe of barbarians to the shores of ocean has come to lay its gifts before my feet. So too the Sagadares who dwell beyond the Danube, wondrous with their bright tattooing, and hardly like human beings, so wild and strange are they, now grovel at my feet, and pledge themselves to obey all the behests my sovereignty imposes on them. I have a

further object. I must as soon as possible march to Persia and rout and make a tributary of that Sapor, descendant of Darius. I mean too to devastate the country of the Indians and the Saracens until they all acknowledge my superiority and become my tributaries. You, however, profess a wisdom above and beyond these things; you call yourself clad with piety, but your clothing is really impudence, and everywhere you slander me as one unworthy of the imperial dignity. Do you not know that I am the grandson of the illustrious Constantius? [1] I know this of you, and yet I do not change the old feelings which I had to you, and you to me in the days when we were both young. [2] But of my merciful will I command that a thousand pounds of gold be sent me from you, when I pass by Cæsarea; for I am still on the march, and with all possible dispatch am hurrying to the Persian campaign. If you refuse I am prepared to destroy Cæsarea, to overthrow the buildings that have long adorned it; to erect in their place temples and statues; and so to induce all men to submit to the Emperor of the Romans and not exalt themselves. Wherefore I charge you to send me without fail by the hands of some trusty messenger the stipulated gold, after duly counting and weighing it, and sealing it with your ring. In this way I may show mercy to you for your errors, if you acknowledge, however late, that no excuses will avail. I have learned to know, and to condemn, what once I read. [3]

LETTER XLI. [4]

Basil to Julian.

1. THE heroic deeds of your present splendour are small, and your grand attack against me, or rather against yourself, is paltry. When I think of you robed in purple, a crown on your dishonoured head, which, so long as true religion is absent, rather disgraces than graces your empire, I tremble. And you yourself who have risen to be so high and great, now that vile and honour-hating demons have brought you to this

<hr>

Julien, non a un homonyme de St. Basile mais à St. Basile lui-même." Étude historique et littéraire sur St. Basile. Fialon.
[1] "your words are friendly." cf. Plat., *Legg.* 702 D. οὐ πόλεμόν γε ἐπαγγέλλεις, ὦ Κλεινία.
[2] ὦ χρυσοῦ ἀγγελίας ἐπῶν. Aristoph., *Plut.* 268.
[3] A playwright of Athens, who put a boastful epigram on his own statue, and became a byword for self-praise. *Vide* Suidas *s.v.*, σαυτὸν ἐπαινεῖς.
[4] If genuine, which is exceedingly doubtful, this letter would be placed in the June or July of 362.

<hr>

[1] *i.e.* of Constantius Chlorus. *Vide* pedigree prefixed to Theodoret in this edition, p. 32. Julian was the youngest son of Julius Constantius, half-brother of Constantine the Great.
[2] The fact of the early acquaintance of Basil and Julian does not rest wholly on the authority of this doubtful letter. *cf* Greg. Naz., *Orat.* iv.
[3] A strong argument against the genuineness of this letter is the silence of Gregory of Nazianzus as to this demand on Basil (*Or.* v. 39). For Julian's treatment of Cæsarea, *vide* Sozomen v. 4. Maran (*Vita S. Bas.* viii.) remarks that when Julian approached Cæsarea Basil was in his Pontic retreat. On the punning conclusion, *vide* note on *Letter* xli. (ἃ ἀνέγνων ἔγνων καὶ κατέγνων.)
[4] If genuine, of the same date as xl.

pass, have begun not only to exalt yourself above all human nature, but even to uplift yourself against God, and insult His Church, mother and nurse of all, by sending to me, most insignificant of men, orders to forward you a thousand pounds of gold. I am not so much astonished at the weight of the gold, although it is very serious; but it has made me shed bitter tears over your so rapid ruin. I bethink me how you and I have learned together the lessons of the best and holiest books. Each of us went through the sacred and God-inspired Scriptures. Then nothing was hid from you. Nowadays you have become lost to proper feeling, beleaguered as you are with pride. Your serene Highness did not find out for the first time yesterday that I do not live in the midst of superabundant wealth. To-day you have demanded a thousand pounds of gold of me. I hope your serenity will deign to spare me. My property amounts to so much, that I really shall not have enough to eat as much as I shall like to-day. Under my roof the art of cookery is dead. My servants' knife never touches blood. The most important viands, in which lies our abundance, are leaves of herbs with very coarse bread and sour wine, so that our senses are not dulled by gluttony, and do not indulge in excess.

2. Your excellent tribune Lausus, trusty minister of your orders, has also reported to me that a certain woman came as a suppliant to your serenity on the occasion of the death of her son by poison; that it has been judged by you that poisoners are not allowed to exist;[1] if any there be, that they are to be destroyed, or, only those are reserved, who are to fight with beasts. And, this rightly decided by you, seems strange to me, for your efforts to cure the pain of great wounds by petty remedies are to the last degree ridiculous. After insulting God, it is useless for you to give heed to widows and orphans. The former is mad and dangerous; the latter the part of a merciful and kindly man. It is a serious thing for a private individual like myself to speak to an emperor; it will be more serious for you to speak to God. No one will appear to mediate between God and man. What you read you did not understand. If you had understood, you would not have condemned.[2]

LETTER XLII.[1]

To Chilo, his disciple.

1. IF, my true brother, you gladly suffer yourself to be advised by me as to what course of action you should pursue, specially in the points in which you have referred to me for advice, you will owe me your salvation. Many men have had the courage to enter upon the solitary life; but to live it out to the end is a task which perhaps has been achieved by few. The end is not necessarily involved in the intention; yet in the end is the guerdon of the toil. No advantage, therefore, accrues to men who fail to press on to the end of what they have in view and only adopt the solitary's life in its inception. Nay, they make their profession ridiculous, and are charged by outsiders with unmanliness and instability of purpose. Of these, moreover, the Lord says, who wishing to build a house "sitteth not down first and counteth the cost whether he have sufficient to finish it? lest haply after he hath laid the foundation and is not able to finish it," the passers-by "begin to mock him saying," this man laid a foundation "and was not able to finish."[2] Let the start, then, mean that you heartily advance in virtue. The right noble athlete Paul, wishing us not to rest in easy security on so much of our life as may have been lived well in the past, but, every day to attain further progress, says "Forgetting those things which are behind, and reaching forth unto those things which are before, I press toward the mark for the prize of the high calling."[3] So truly stands the whole of human life, not contented with what has gone before and fed not so much on the past as on the future. For how is a man the better for having his belly filled yesterday, if his natural hunger fails to find its proper satisfaction in food to-day? In the same way the soul gains nothing by yesterday's virtue unless it be followed by the right conduct of to-day. For it is said "I shall judge thee as I shall find thee."

2. Vain then is the labour of the righteous man, and free from blame is the way of the sinner, if a change befall, and the former turn from the better to the worse, and the latter from the worse to the better. So we hear from Ezekiel teaching as it were in

---

[1] φαρμακοὺς μηδαμοῦ εἶναι. The Ben. Ed. compares with the form of expression the phrase of St. Cyprian: "legibus vestris bene atque utiliter censuistis delatores non esse." cf. Letter lv.

[2] Ἀ ἀνέγνως οὐκ ἔγνως· εἰγὰρ ἔγνως, οὐκ ἂν κατέγνως. In Soz. v. 18, Julian's words, ἃ ἀνέγνων ἔγνων καὶ κατέγνων, are stated to have been written to 'the bishops' in reference to Apologies by the younger Apollinarius, bp. of the Syrian Laodicea (afterwards the heresiarch) and others. The reply is credited to 'the bishops,' with the remark that some attribute it to Basil.

---

[1] This and the four succeeding letters must be placed before the episcopate. Their genuineness has been contested, but apparently without much reason. In one of the Parisian Codices the title of xlii. is given with the note: "Some attribute this work to the holy Nilus." Ceillier (iv. 435-437) is of opinion that, so far as style goes, they must stand or fall together, and points out that xlvii. is cited entire as Basil's by Metaphrastes.

[2] Luke xiv. 28, 30.   [3] Phil. iii. 13, 14.

the name of the Lord, when he says, " if the righteous turneth away and committeth iniquity, I will not remember the righteousness which he committed before; in his sin he shall die," [1] and so too about the sinner; if he turn away from his wickedness, and do that which is right, he shall live. Where were all the labours of God's servant Moses, when the gainsaying of one moment shut him out from entering into the promised land? What became of the companionship of Gehazi with Elissæus, when he brought leprosy on himself by his covetousness? What availed all Solomon's vast wisdom, and his previous regard for God, when afterwards from his mad love of women he fell into idolatry? Not even the blessed David was blameless, when his thoughts went astray and he sinned against the wife of Uriah. One example were surely enough for keeping safe one who is living a godly life, the fall from the better to the worse of Judas, who, after being so long Christ's disciple, for a mean gain sold his Master and got a halter for himself. Learn then, brother, that it is not he who begins well who is perfect. It is he who ends well who is approved in God's sight. Give then no sleep to your eyes or slumber to your eyelids [2] that you may be delivered " as a roe from the net and a bird from the snare." [3] For, behold, you are passing through the midst of snares; you are treading on the top of a high wall whence a fall is perilous to the faller; wherefore do not straightway attempt extreme discipline; above all things beware of confidence in yourself, lest you fall from a height of discipline through want of training. It is better to advance a little at a time. Withdraw then by degrees from the pleasures of life, gradually destroying all your wonted habits, lest you bring on yourself a crowd of temptations by irritating all your passions at once. When you have mastered one passion, then begin to wage war against another, and in this manner you will in good time get the better of all. Indulgence, so far as the name goes, is one, but its practical workings are diverse. First then, brother, meet every temptation with patient endurance. And by what various temptations the faithful man is proved; by worldly loss, by accusations, by lies, by opposition, by calumny, by persecution! These and the like are the tests of the faithful. Further, be quiet, not rash in speech, not quarrelsome, not disputatious, not covetous of vain glory, not more anxious

to get than to give knowledge,[1] not a ma[n] of many words, but always more ready t[o] learn than to teach. Do not trouble yoursel[f] about worldly life; from it no good can com[e] to you. It is said, " That my mouth spea[k] not the works of men." [2] The man who [is] fond of talking about sinners' doings, soo[n] rouses the desire for self indulgence; muc[h] better busy yourself about the lives of goo[d] men for so you will get some profit for your[-] self. Do not be anxious to go travellin[g] about [3] from village to village and house t[o] house; rather avoid them as traps for soul[s.] If any one, for true pity's sake, invite yo[u] with many pleas to enter his house, let hi[m] be told to follow the faith of the centurio[n,] who, when Jesus was hastening to him t[o] perform an act of healing, besought him no[t] to do so in the words, " Lord I am n[ot] worthy that thou shouldest come under m[y] roof, but speak the word only and my serva[nt] shall be healed," [4] and when Jesus had said [to] him " Go thy way; as thou hast believed, s[o] be it done unto thee," [5] his servant wa[s] healed from that hour. Learn then, brothe[r,] that it was the faith of the suppliant, not th[e] presence of Christ, which delivered the sic[k] man. So too now, if you pray, in whateve[r] place you be, and the sick man believes th[is,] he will be aided by your prayers, all wi[ll] fall out as he desires.

3. You will not love your kinsfolk mo[re] than the Lord. " He that loveth," He say[s,] " father, or mother, or brother, more tha[n] me, is not worthy of me." [6] What is th[e] meaning of the Lord's commandment? " H[e] that taketh not up his cross and followe[th] after me, cannot be my disciple?" [7] If, t[o]gether with Christ, you died to your kinsfo[lk] according to the flesh, why do you wish to liv[e] with them again? If for your kinsfolk's sak[e] you are building up again what you de[-]stroyed for Christ's sake, you make yoursel[f] a transgressor. Do not then for your kin[s]folk's sake abandon your place: if yo[u] abandon your place, perhaps you wi[ll] abandon your mode of life. Love not th[e] crowd, nor the country, nor the town; lov[e] the desert, ever abiding by yourself with [a] wandering mind,[8] regarding prayer an[d] praise as your life's work. Never negle[ct] reading, especially of the New Testamen[t,] because very frequently mischief comes o[ut]

---

1 cf. Ezek. xviii. 24.
2 cf. Ps. cxxxii. 4.
3 Prov. vi. 5, LXX.

1 μὴ ἐξηγητικὸς ἀλλα φιλόπευστος, as suggested by Combe[s] for φιλόπιστος.
2 Ps. xvi. 4, LXX.   4 Matt. viii. 8
3 Another reading is (exhibiting yourself). 5 Matt. viii. [13]
6 Matt. x. 37, with ἀδελφούς added perhaps from Luke xi[v.] 26.
7 Luke xiv. 27 and Matt. x. 38.
8 For the contrary view of life, cf. Seneca, Ep. 61: " Omn[ia] nobis mala solitudo persuadet; nemo est cui non sanctius s[it] cum quolibet esse quam secum."

reading the Old; not because what is written is harmful, but because the minds of the injured are weak. All bread is nutritious, but it may be injurious to the sick. Just so all Scripture is God inspired and profitable,[1] and there is nothing in it unclean: only to him who thinks it is unclean, to him it is unclean. " Prove all things; hold fast that which is good; abstain from every form of evil."[2] " All things are lawful but all things are not expedient."[3] Among all, with whom you come in contact, be in all things a giver of no offence,[4] cheerful, " loving as a brother,"[5] pleasant, humble-minded, never missing the mark of hospitality through extravagance of meats, but always content with what is at hand. Take no more from any one than the daily necessaries of the solitary life. Above all things shun gold as the soul's foe, the father of sin and the agent of the devil. Do not expose yourself to the charge of covetousness on the pretence of ministering to the poor; but, if any one brings you money for the poor and you know of any who are in need, advise the owner himself to convey it to his needy brothers, lest haply your conscience may be defiled by the acceptance of money.

4. Shun pleasures; seek after continence; train your body to hard work; accustom your soul to trials. Regarding the dissolution of soul and body as release from every evil, await that enjoyment of everlasting good things in which all the saints have part. Ever, as it were, holding the balance, against every suggestion of the devil throw in a holy thought, and, as the scale inclines, do thou go with it. Above all when the evil thought starts up and says, " What is the good of your passing your life in this place? What do you gain by withdrawing yourself from the society of men? Do you not know that those, who are ordained by God to be bishops of God's churches, constantly associate with their fellows, and indefatigably attend spiritual gatherings at which those who are present derive very great advantage? There are to be enjoyed explanations of hard sayings, expositions of the teachings of the apostles, interpretations of the thoughts of the gospels, lessons in theology and the intercourse of spiritual brethren, who do great good to all they meet if only by the sight of their faces. You, however, who have decided to be a stranger to all these good things, are sitting here in a wild state like the beasts. You see round you a wide desert with scarcely a fellow creature in it, lack

of all instruction, estrangement from your brothers, and your spirit inactive in carrying out the commandments of God." Now, when the evil thought rises against you, with all these ingenious pretexts and wishes to destroy you, oppose to it in pious reflection your own practical experience, and say, You tell me that the things in the world are good; the reason why I came here is because I judged myself unfit for the good things of the world. With the world's good things are mingled evil things, and the evil things distinctly have the upper hand. Once when I attended the spiritual assemblies I did with difficulty find one brother, who, so far as I could see, feared God, but he was a victim of the devil, and I heard from him amusing stories and tales made up to deceive those whom he met. After him I fell in with many thieves, plunderers, tyrants. I saw disgraceful drunkards; I saw the blood of the oppressed; I saw women's beauty, which tortured my chastity. From actual fornication I fled, but I defiled my virginity by the thoughts of my heart. I heard many discourses which were good for the soul, but I could not discover in the case of any one of the teachers that his life was worthy of his words. After this, again, I heard a great number of plays, which were made attractive by wanton songs. Then I heard a lyre sweetly played, the applause of tumblers, the talk of clowns, all kinds of jests and follies and all the noises of a crowd. I saw the tears of the robbed, the agony of the victims of tyranny, the shrieks of the tortured. I looked and lo, there was no spiritual assembly, but only a sea, wind-tossed and agitated, and trying to drown every one at once under its waves.[1] Tell me, O evil thought, tell me, dæmon of short lived pleasure and vain glory, what is the good of my seeing and hearing all these things, when I am powerless to succour any of those who are thus wronged; when I am allowed neither to defend the helpless nor correct the fallen; when I am perhaps doomed to destroy myself too. For just as a very little fresh water is blown away by a storm of wind and dust, in like manner the good deeds, that we think we do in this life, are overwhelmed by the multitude of evils. Pieces acted for men in this life are driven through joy and merriment, like stakes into their hearts, so that the brightness of their worship is bedimmed. But the wails and lamentations of

---

[1] cf. 2 Tim. iii. 16.
[2] 1 Thess. v. 21, R.V.
[3] 1 Cor. vi. 12.
[4] cf. 1 Cor. x. 32.
[5] 1 Pet. iii. 8.

[1] The Ben. note on this painful picture suggests that the description applies to Palestine, and compares the account of Jerusalem to be found in Gregory of Nyssa's letter on Pilgrimages in this edition, p. 382. On Basil's visit to the Holy Land, cf. Ep. ccxxiii. § 2.

men wronged by their fellows are introduced to make a show of the patience of the poor.

5. What good then do I get except the loss of my soul? For this reason I migrate to the hills like a bird. "I am escaped as a bird out of the snare of the fowlers."[1] I am living, O evil thought, in the desert in which the Lord lived. Here is the oak of Mamre; here is the ladder going up to heaven, and the stronghold of the angels which Jacob saw; here is the wilderness in which the people purified received the law, and so came into the land of promise and saw God. Here is Mount Carmel where Elias sojourned and pleased God. Here is the plain whither Esdras withdrew, and at God's bidding uttered all the God inspired books.[2] Here is the wilderness in which the blessed John ate locusts and preached repentance to men. Here is the Mount of Olives, whither Christ came and prayed, and taught us to pray. Here is Christ the lover of the wilderness, for He says "Where two or three are gathered together in my name there am I in the midst of them."[3] "Here is the strait and narrow way which leadeth unto life."[4] Here are the teachers and prophets "wandering in deserts and in mountains and in dens and caves of the earth."[5] Here are apostles and evangelists and solitaries' life remote from cities. This I have embraced with all my heart, that I may win what has been promised to Christ's martyrs and all His other saints, and so I may truly say, "Because of the words of thy lips I have kept hard ways."[6] I have heard of Abraham, God's friend, who obeyed the divine voice and went into the wilderness; of Isaac who submitted to authority; of Jacob, the patriarch, who left his home; of Joseph, the chaste, who was sold; of the three children, who learnt how to fast, and fought with the fire; of Daniel thrown twice into the lion's den;[7] of Jeremiah speaking boldly and thrown into a pit of mud; of Isaiah, who saw unspeakable things, cut asunder with a saw; of Israel led away captive; of John the rebuker of adultery, beheaded; of Christ's martyrs slain. But why say more? Here our Saviour Himself was crucified for our sakes that by His death He might give us life, and train and attract us all to endurance. To Him I press on, and to the Father and to the Holy Ghost. I strive to be found true, judging myself unworthy of this world's goods.

And yet not I because of the world, but the world because of me. Think of all these things in your heart; follow them with zeal fight, as you have been commanded, for the truth to the death. For Christ was made "obedient" even "unto death."[1] The Apostle says, "Take heed lest there be in any of you an evil heart . . . in departing from the living God. But exhort one another . . . (and edify one another) while it is called to-day."[3] To-day means the whole time of our life. Thus living brother, you will save yourself, you will make me glad, and you will glorify God from everlasting to everlasting. Amen.

LETTER XLIII.[4]

Admonition to the Young.

O FAITHFUL man of solitary life, and practiser of true religion, learn the lessons of the evangelic conversation, of mastery over the body, of a meek spirit, of purity of mind, of destruction of pride. Pressed into the service,[5] add to your gifts, for the Lord's sake; robbed, never go to law; hated, love; persecuted, endure; slandered, entreat. Be dead to sin; be crucified to God. Cast all your care upon the Lord, that you may be found where are tens of thousands of angels, assemblies of the first-born, the thrones of prophets, sceptres of patriarchs, crowns of martyrs, praises of righteous men. Earnestly desire to be numbered with those righteous men in Christ Jesus our Lord. To Him be glory for ever. Amen.

LETTER XLIV.[6]

To a lapsed Monk.[7]

1. I DO not wish you joy, for there is no joy for the wicked. Even now I cannot believe it; my heart cannot conceive iniquity so great as the crime which you have committed; if, that is, the truth really is what is generally understood. I am at a loss to think how wisdom so deep can have been made to disappear; how such exact discipline can have been undone; whence blindness so profound can have been shed round you; how with utter inconsiderateness you have wrought such destruction of souls. If this

---

[1] Ps. cxxiv. 7.
[2] *cf.* Esdras ii. 14; Irenæus, *Adv. Hær.* iii, 21, 2; Tertullian, *De Cult. Fam.* i. 3; Clem. Alex., *Strom.* i. 22.
[3] Matt. xviii. 20; a curious misapplication of the text.
[4] Matt. vii. 14.　　[6] Ps. xvii. 4, LXX.
[5] Heb. xi. 38.　　[7] *Vide* Bel and the dragon.

[1] Phil. ii. 8.　　[2] 1 Thess. v. 11.　　[3] Heb. iii. 12, 13.
[4] Ranked with the preceding, and of dubious genuineness.
[5] ἀγγαρευόμενος. *cf.* Matt. v. 41.
[6] To be ranked with the former letter.
[7] One MS. adds, in a later hand, Alexius.

be true, you have given over your own soul to the pit, and have slackened the earnestness of all who have heard of your impiety. You have set at nought the faith; you have missed the glorious fight. I grieve over you. What cleric[1] does not lament as he hears? What ecclesiastic does not beat the breast? What layman is not downcast? What ascetic is not sad? Haply, even the sun has grown dark at your fall, and the powers of heaven have been shaken at your destruction. Even senseless stones have shed tears at your madness; even your enemies have wept at the greatness of your iniquity. Oh hardness of heart! Oh cruelty! You did not fear God; you did not reverence men; you cared nothing for your friends; you made shipwreck of all at once; at once you were stripped of all. Once more I grieve over you, unhappy man. You were proclaiming to all the power of the kingdom, and you fell from it. You were making all stand in fear of your teaching, and there was no fear of God before your eyes. You were preaching purity, and you are found polluted. You were priding yourself on your poverty, and you are convicted of covetousness; you were demonstrating and explaining the chastisement of God, and you yourself brought chastisement on your own head. How am I to lament you, how grieve for you? How is Lucifer that was rising in the morning fallen and dashed on the ground? Both the ears of every hearer will tingle. How is the Nazarite, brighter than gold, become dark above pitch? How has the glorious son of Sion become an unprofitable vessel! Of him, whose memory of the sacred Scriptures was in all men's mouths, the memory to-day has perished with the sound. The man of quick intelligence has quickly perished. The man of manifold wit has wrought manifold iniquity. All who profited by your teaching have been injured by your fall. All who came to listen to your conversation have stopped their ears at your fall. I, sorrowful and downcast, weakened in every way, eating ashes for bread and with sackcloth on my wound, am thus recounting your praises; or rather, with none to comfort and none to cure, am making an inscription for a tomb. For comfort is hid from my eyes. I have no salve, no oil, no bandage to put on. My wound is sore, how shall I be healed?

2. If you have any hope of salvation; if you have the least thought of God, or any desire for good things to come; if you have any fear of the chastisements reserved for the impenitent, awake without delay, lift up your eyes to heaven, come to your senses, cease from your wickedness, shake off the stupor that enwraps you, make a stand against the foe who has struck you down. Make an effort to rise from the ground. Remember the good Shepherd who will follow and rescue you. Though it be but two legs or a lobe of an ear,[1] spring back from the beast that has wounded you. Remember the mercies of God and how He cures with oil and wine. Do not despair of salvation. Recall your recollection of how it is written in the Scriptures that he who is falling rises and he who turns away returns;[2] the wounded is healed, the prey of beasts escapes; he who owns his sin is not rejected. The Lord willeth not the death of a sinner but rather that he should turn and live.[3] Do not despise, like the wicked in the pit of evil.[4] There is a time of endurance, a time of long suffering, a time of healing, a time of correction. Have you stumbled? Arise. Have you sinned? Cease. Do not stand in the way of sinners,[5] but spring away. When you are converted and groan you shall be saved. Out of labour comes health, out of sweat salvation. Beware lest, from your wish to keep certain obligations, you break the obligations to God which you professed before many witnesses.[6] Pray do not hesitate to come to me for any earthly considerations. When I have recovered my dead I shall lament, I shall tend him, I will weep " because of the spoiling of the daughter of my people." [7] All are ready to welcome you, all will share your efforts. Do not sink back. Remember the days of old. There is salvation; there is amendment. Be of good cheer; do not despair. It is not a law condemning to death without pity, but mercy remitting punishment and awaiting improvement. The doors are not yet shut; the bridegroom hears; sin is not the master. Make another effort, do not hesitate, have pity on yourself and on all of us in Jesus Christ our Lord, to Whom be glory and might now and for ever and ever. Amen.

LETTER XLV.[8]

To a lapsed Monk.

1. I AM doubly alarmed to the very bottom of my heart, and you are the cause. I am

---

1 ἱερεύς. When first this word and its correlatives came to be used of the Christian ministry it was applied generally to the clergy. cf. Letter of the Council of Illyricum in Theod., *Ecc. Hist.* iv. 8, and note on *Letter* liv. p. 157.

1 cf. Amos iii. 12.
2 cf. Jer. viii. 4.
3 cf. Ezek. xviii. 32.
4 Prov. xviii. 3, LXX.
5 cf. Ps. i. 1.
6 cf. 1 Tim. vi. 12.
7 Is. xxii. 4.
8 To be ranked with the preceding.

either the victim of some unkindly prepossession, and so am driven to make an unbrotherly charge; or, with every wish to feel for you, and to deal gently with your troubles, I am forced to take a different and an unfriendly attitude. Wherefore, even as I take my pen to write, I have nerved my unwilling hand by reflection; but my face, downcast as it is, because of my sorrow over you, I have had no power to change. I am so covered with shame, for your sake, that my lips are turned to mourning and my mouth straightway falls. Ah me! What am I to write? What shall I think in my perplexity?

If I call to mind your former empty mode of life, when you were rolling in riches and had abundance of petty mundane reputation, I shudder; then you were followed by a mob of flatterers, and had the short enjoyment of luxury, with obvious peril and unfair gain; on the one hand, fear of the magistrates scattered your care for your salvation, on the other the agitations of public affairs disturbed your home, and the continuance of troubles directed your mind to Him Who is able to help you. Then, little by little, you took to seeking for the Saviour, Who brings you fears for your good, Who delivers you and protects you, though you mocked Him in your security. Then you began to train yourself for a change to a worthy life, treating all your perilous property as mere dung, and abandoning the care of your household, and the society of your wife. All abroad, like a stranger and a vagabond, wandering through town and country, you betook yourself to Jerusalem.[1] There I myself lived with you, and, for the toil of your ascetic discipline, called you blessed, when fasting for weeks you continued in contemplation before God, shunning the society of your fellows, like a routed runaway. Then you arranged for yourself a quiet and solitary life, and refused all the disquiets of society. You pricked your body with rough sackcloth; you tightened a hard belt round your loins; you bravely put wearing pressure on your bones; you made your sides hang loose from front to back, and all hollow with fasting; you would wear no soft bandage, and drawing in your stomach, like a gourd, made it adhere to the parts about your kidneys. You emptied out all fat from your flesh; all the channels below your belly you dried

up; your belly itself you folded up for want of food; your ribs, like the eaves of a house, you made to overshadow all the parts about your middle, and, with all your body contracted, you spent the long hours of the night in pouring out confession to God, and made your beard wet with channels of tears. Why particularize? Remember how many mouths of saints you saluted with a kiss, how many holy bodies you embraced, how many held your hands as undefiled, how many servants of God, as though in worship, ran and clasped you by the knees.

2. And what is the end of all this? My ears are wounded by a charge of adultery, flying swifter than an arrow, and piercing my heart with a sharper sting. What crafty wiliness of wizard has driven you into so deadly a trap? What many-meshed devil's nets have entangled you and disabled all the powers of your virtue? What has become of the story of your labours? Or must we disbelieve them? How can we avoid giving credit to what has long been hid when we see what is plain? What shall we say of your having by tremendous oaths bound souls which fled for refuge to God, when what is more than yea and nay is carefully attributed to the devil?[1] You have made yourself security for fatal perjury; and, by setting the ascetic character at nought, you have cast blame even upon the Apostles and the very Lord Himself. You have shamed the boast of purity. You have disgraced the promise of chastity; we have been made a tragedy of captives, and our story is made a play of before Jews and Greeks. You have made a split in the solitaries' spirit, driving those of exacter discipline into fear and cowardice, while they still wonder at the power of the devil, and seducing the careless into imitation of your incontinence. So far as you have been able, you have destroyed the boast of Christ, Who said, " Be of good cheer I have overcome the world," [2] and its Prince. You have mixed for your country a bowl of ill repute. Verily you have proved the truth of the proverb, " Like a hart stricken through the liver." [3]

But what now? The tower of strength has not fallen, my brother. The remedies of correction are not mocked; the city of refuge is not shut. Do not abide in the depths of evil. Do not deliver yourself to the slayer of souls. The Lord knows how to set up them that are dashed down. Do not try to flee afar off, but hasten to me. Resume once more the labours of your youth,

---

[1] cf. note on *Letter* xlii. p. 145. Maran, *Vit. S. Bas. cap.* xii., regards this implied sojourn at Jerusalem as unfavourable to the genuineness of the letter; but supposing the letter to be genuine, and grounds to exist for doubting Basil to have spent any long time in the Holy Land, there seems no reason why " Jerusalem " may not be taken in a figurative sense for the companionship of the saints. See also *Proleg.* on Basil's baptism.

[1] cf. Matt. v. 37.   [2] John xvi. 33.   [3] cf. Prov. vii. 22, 23, LXX.

and by a fresh course of good deeds destroy the indulgence that creeps foully along the ground. Look to the end, that has come so near to our life. See how now the sons of Jews and Greeks are being driven to the worship of God, and do not altogether deny the Saviour of the World. Never let that most awful sentence apply to you, "Depart from me, I never knew you."[1]

LETTER XLVI.[2]

To a fallen virgin.

1. Now is the time to quote the words of the prophet and to say, "Oh that my head were waters, and mine eyes a fountain of tears, that I might weep day and night for the slain of the daughter of my people."[3] Though they are wrapped in profound silence and lie stunned by their misfortune, robbed of all sense of feeling by the fatal blow, I at all events must not let such a fall go unlamented. If, to Jeremiah, it seemed that those whose bodies had been wounded in war, were worthy of innumerable lamentations, what shall be said of such a disaster of souls? " My slain men," it is said, " are not slain with the sword, nor dead in battle."[4] But I am bewailing the sting of the real death, the grievousness of sin and the fiery darts of the wicked one, which have savagely set on fire souls as well as bodies. Truly God's laws would groan aloud on seeing so great a pollution on the earth. They have pronounced their prohibition of old " Thou shalt not covet thy neighbour's wife ";[5] and through the holy gospels they say that " Whosoever looketh on a woman to lust after her, hath committed adultery already with her in his heart."[6] Now they see the bride of the Lord herself, whose head is Christ, boldly committing adultery.[7] So too would groan the companies[8] of the Saints. Phinehas, the zealous, because he can now no more take his spear into his hands and avenge the outrage on the bodies; and John the Baptist, because he cannot quit the realms above, as in his life he left the wilderness, to hasten to convict iniquity, and if he must suffer for the deed, rather lose his head than his freedom to speak. But, peradventure, like the blessed Abel, he too though dead yet speaks to us,[9] and now exclaims, more loudly than John of

old concerning Herodias, " It is not lawful for thee to have her."[1] For even if the body of John in obedience to the law of nature has received the sentence of God, and his tongue is silent, yet " the word of God is not bound."[2] John, when he saw the wedlock of a fellow servant set at nought, was bold to rebuke even to the death: how would he feel on seeing such an outrage wreaked on the marriage chamber of the Lord?

2. You have flung away the yoke of that divine union; you have fled from the undefiled chamber of the true King; you have shamefully fallen into this disgraceful and impious corruption; and now that you cannot avoid this painful charge, and have no means or device to conceal your trouble, you rush into insolence. The wicked man after falling into a pit of iniquity always begins to despise, and you are denying your actual covenant with the true bridegroom; you say that you are not a virgin, and made no promise, although you have undertaken and publicly professed many pledges of virginity. Remember the good profession which you witnessed[3] before God, angels, and men. Remember the hallowed intercourse, the sacred company of virgins, the assembly of the Lord, the Church of the holy. Remember your grandmother, grown old in Christ, still youthful and vigorous in virtue; and your mother vying with her in the Lord, and striving to break with ordinary life in strange and unwonted toils; remember your sister, who copies their doings, nay, endeavours to surpass them, and goes beyond the good deeds of her fathers in her virgin graces, and earnestly challenges by word and deed you her sister, as she thinks, to like efforts, while she earnestly prays that your virginity be preserved.[4] All these call to mind, and your holy service of God with them, your life spiritual, though in the flesh; your conversation heavenly, though on earth. Remember days of calm, nights lighted up, spiritual songs, sweet music of psalms, saintly prayers, a bed pure and undefiled, procession of virgins, and moderate fare.[5] What has become of your grave appearance, your gracious demeanour, your plain dress, meet for a virgin, the beautiful blush of modesty, the comely and bright pallor due to temperance and vigils, shining fairer than any brilliance of complexion? How often have you not prayed, perhaps with tears,

[1] Luke xiii. 27.
[2] Placed with the preceding.
[3] Jer. ix. 1.
[4] Is. xxii. 2.
[8] Τάγματα, with two MSS. The alternative reading is πνεύματα.
[5] Deut. v. 21.
[6] Matt. v. 28.
[7] cf. Letter ccxvii. § 60.
[9] cf. Heb. xi. 4.

[1] Matt xiv. 4. [2] 2 Tim. ii. 9. [3] cf. 1 Tim. vi. 12.
[4] These words occur in the MSS. after "moderate fare," below, where they make no sense. The Ben. Ed. conjectures that they may belong here.
[5] Vide note above.

that you might preserve your virginity without spot! How often have you not written to the holy men, imploring them to offer up prayers in your behalf, not that it should be your lot to marry, still less to be involved in this shameful corruption, but that you should not fall away from the Lord Jesus? How often have you received gifts from the Bridegroom? Why enumerate the honours given you for His sake by them that are His? Why tell of your fellowship with virgins, your progress with them, your being greeted by them with praises on account of virginity, eulogies of virgins, letters written as to a virgin? Now, nevertheless, at a little blast from the spirit of the air, "that now worketh in the children of disobedience,"[1] you have abjured all these; you have changed the honourable treasure, worth fighting for at all costs, for short-lived indulgence which does for the moment gratify the appetite; one day you will find it more bitter than gall.

3. Who would not grieve over such things and say, "How is the faithful city become an harlot?"[2] How would not the Lord Himself say to some of those who are now walking in the spirit of Jeremiah, "Hast thou seen what the virgin of Israel has done to me?"[3] I betrothed her to me in trust, in purity, in righteousness, in judgment, in pity, and in mercy;[4] as I promised her through Hosea the prophet. But she loved strangers, and while I, her husband, was yet alive, she is called adulteress, and is not afraid to belong to another husband. What then says the conductor of the bride,[5] the divine and blessed Paul, both that one of old, and the later one of to-day under whose mediation and instruction you left your father's house and were united to the Lord? Might not either, in sorrow for such a trouble, say, "The thing which I greatly feared is come upon me, and that which I was afraid of is come unto me."[6] "I have espoused you to one husband that I may present you as a chaste virgin to Christ."[7] I was indeed ever afraid "lest by any means as the serpent beguiled Eve through his subtilty, so your mind should be corrupted;"[8] wherefore by countless counter-charms I strove to control the agitation of your senses, and by countless safeguards to preserve the bride of the Lord. So I continually set forth the life of the unmarried maid, and described how

"the unmarried" alone "careth for the things of the Lord, that she may be holy both in body and spirit."[1] I used to describe the high dignity of virginity, and, addressing you as a temple of God, used as it were to give wings to your zeal as I strove to lift you to Jesus. Yet through fear of evil I helped you not to fall by the words "if any man defile the temple of God, him shall God destroy"[2] So by my prayers I tried to make you more secure, if by any means "your body, soul, and spirit might be preserved blameless unto the coming of our Lord Jesus Christ."[3] Yet all my toil on your behalf has been in vain. Bitter to me has been the end of those sweet labours. Now I needs must groan again at that over which I ought to have rejoiced. You have been deceived by the serpent more bitterly than Eve; and not only your mind but also your body has been defiled. Even that last horror has come to pass which I shrink from saying, and yet cannot leave unsaid, for it is as a burning and blazing fire in my bones, and I am undone and cannot endure. You have taken the members of Christ and made them the members of a harlot.[4] This is an evil with which no other can be matched. This outrage in life is new. "For pass over the Isles of Chittim and see; and send unto Chedar and consider diligently, and see if there be such a thing. Hath a nation changed their gods which are yet no gods."[5] But the virgin has changed her glory, and her glory is in her shame. The heavens are astonished at this, and the earth is horribly afraid, saith the Lord, for the virgin has committed two evils; she has forsaken[6] Me, the true and holy Bridegroom of holy souls, and has betaken herself to an impious and lawless destroyer of body and soul alike. She has revolted from God, her Saviour, and yielded her members servants to uncleanness and to iniquity.[7] She forgot me and went after her lover[8] from whom she will get no good.

4. It were better for him that a mill-stone had been hanged about his neck, and that he had been cast into the sea, than that he should have offended the virgin of the Lord.[9] What slave ever reached such a pitch of mad audacity as to fling himself upon his master's bed? What robber ever attained such a height of folly as to lay hands upon the very offerings of God, not

1 Eph. ii. 2.
2 Is. i. 21.
3 cf. Jer. xviii. 13.
4 cf. Hosea ii. 19.
5 The νυμφαγωγός was the friend who conducted the bride from her parents' or her own house to the bridegroom's. cf. Luc.. Dial. Deor. 20, 16.
6 Job iii. 25.   7 2 Cor. xi. 2.   8 2 Cor. xi. 3.

1 1 Cor. vii. 34.   6 cf. Jer. ii. 12, 13, LXX.
2 1 Cor. iii. 17.   7 cf. Rom. vi. 19.
3 1 Thess. v. 23.   8 cf. Hosea ii. 13.
4 1 Cor. vi. 15.   9 cf. Luke xvii. 2.
5 Jer. ii. 10, 11.

dead vessels, but bodies living and enshrining a soul made after the image of God?[1] Who was ever known to have the hardihood, in the heart of a city and at high noon, to mark figures of filthy swine upon a royal statue? He who has set at naught a marriage of man, with no mercy shewn him, in the presence of two or three witnesses, dies.[2] Of how much sorer punishment, suppose you, shall he be thought worthy who hath trodden under foot the Son of God, and defiled His pledged bride and done despite unto the spirit of virginity?[3] But the woman, he urges, consented, and I did no violence to her against her will. So, that unchaste lady of Egypt raged with love for comely Joseph, but the chaste youth's virtue was not overcome by the frenzy of the wicked woman, and, even when she laid her hand upon him, he was not forced into iniquity. But still, he urges, this was no new thing in her case; she was no longer a maid; if I had been unwilling, she would have been corrupted by some one else. Yes; and it is written, the Son of Man was ordained to be betrayed, but woe unto that man by whom He was betrayed.[4] It must needs be that offences come, but woe to that man by whom they come.[5]

5. In such a state of things as this, "Shall they fall and not arise? Shall he turn away and not return?"[6] Why did the virgin turn shamefully away, though she had heard Christ her bridegroom saying through the mouth of Jeremiah, "And I said, after she had done all these things (committed all these fornications, LXX.), turn thou unto me, but she returned not?"[7] "Is there no balm in Gilead; is there no physician there? Why then is not the health of the daughter of my people recovered?"[8] You might indeed find many remedies for evil in Scripture, many medicines to save from destruction and lead to health; the mysteries of death and resurrection, the sentences of terrible judgment and everlasting punishment; the doctrines of repentance and of remission of sins; all the countless illustrations of conversion, the piece of money, the sheep, the son who wasted his substance with harlots, who was lost and was found, who was dead and alive again. Let us not use these remedies for ill; by these means let us heal our soul. Bethink you of your last

day, for you will surely not, unlike all other women, live for ever. The distress, the gasping for breath, the hour of death, the imminent sentence of God, the angels hastening on their way, the soul fearfully dismayed, and lashed to agony by the consciousness of sin, turning itself piteously to things of this life and to the inevitable necessity of that long life to be lived elsewhere. Picture to me, as it rises in your imagination, the conclusion of all human life, when the Son of God shall come in His glory with His angels, "For he shall come and shall not keep silence;"[1] when He shall come to judge the quick and dead, to render to every one according to his work; when that terrible trumpet with its mighty voice shall wake those that have slept through the ages, and they that have done good shall come forth unto the resurrection of life, and they that have done evil unto the resurrection of damnation.[2] Remember the vision of Daniel, and how he brings the judgment before us: "I beheld till the thrones were cast down, and the Ancient of days did sit, whose garment was white as snow, and the hair of His head like the pure wool; . . . and His wheels as burning fire. A fiery stream issued and came forth before Him; thousand thousands ministered unto Him, and ten thousand times ten thousand stood before Him: the judgment was set, and the books were opened,"[3] clearly disclosing in the hearing of all, angels and men, things good and evil, things done openly and in secret, deeds, words, and thoughts all at once. What then must those men be who have lived wicked lives? Where then shall that soul hide which in the sight of all these spectators shall suddenly be revealed in its fulness of shame? With what kind of body shall it sustain those endless and unbearable pangs in the place of fire unquenched, and of the worm that perishes and never dies, and of depth of Hades, dark and horrible; bitter wailings, loud lamenting, weeping and gnashing of teeth and anguish without end? From all these woes there is no release after death; no device, no means of coming forth from the chastisement of pain.

6. We can escape now. While we can, let us lift ourselves from the fall: let us never despair of ourselves, if only we depart from evil. Jesus Christ came into the world to save sinners. "O come, let us worship and fall down; let us weep before Him."[4] The Word

---

[1] St. Basil has no idea of the image and likeness of God being a bodily likeness, as in the lines of Xenophanes.
[2] i.e. by the old Jewish law. Deut. xvii. 6. Adultery was not capital under the Lex Julia, but was made so by Constantine.
[3] cf. Heb. x. 29.
[4] cf. Mark xiv. 21.
[5] cf. Matt. xviii. 7.
[6] Jer. viii. 4.
[7] Jer. iii. 7.
[8] Jer. viii. 22.

[1] Ps. l. 3.
[2] cf. John v. 29.
[3] Dan. vii. 9, 10.
[4] Ps. xcv. 6, LXX.

Who invited us to repentance calls aloud, "Come unto me all ye that labour and are heavy laden, and I will give you rest."[1] There is, then, a way of salvation, if we will. "Death in his might has swallowed up, but again the Lord hath wiped away tears from off all faces"[2] of them that repent. The Lord is faithful in all His words.[3] He does not lie when He says, "Though your sins be as scarlet they shall be as white as snow. Though they be red like crimson they shall be as wool."[4] The great Physician of souls, Who is the ready liberator, not of you alone, but of all who are enslaved by sin, is ready to heal your sickness. From Him come the words, it was His sweet and saving lips that said, "They that be whole need not a physician but they that are sick. . . . I am not come to call the righteous but sinners to repentance."[5] What excuse have you, what excuse has any one, when He speaks thus? The Lord wishes to cleanse you from the trouble of your sickness and to show you light after darkness. The good Shepherd, Who left them that had not wandered away, is seeking after you. If you give yourself to Him He will not hold back. He, in His love, will not disdain even to carry you on His own shoulders, rejoicing that He has found His sheep which was lost. The Father stands and awaits your return from your wandering. Only come back, and while you are yet afar off, He will run and fall upon your neck, and, now that you are cleansed by repentance, will enwrap you in embraces of love. He will clothe with the chief robe the soul that has put off the old man with all his works; He will put a ring on hands that have washed off the blood of death, and will put shoes on feet that have turned from the evil way to the path of the Gospel of peace. He will announce the day of joy and gladness to them that are His own, both angels and men, and will celebrate your salvation far and wide. For "verily I say unto you," says He, "there is joy in heaven before God over one sinner that repenteth."[6] If any of those who think they stand find fault because of your quick reception, the good Father will Himself make answer for you in the words, "It was meet that we should make merry and be glad for this" my daughter "was dead and is alive again, was lost and is found."[7]

[1] Matt. xi. 28.
[2] Is. xxv. 8, LXX.
[3] Ps. cxlv. 13, LXX.
[4] Is. i. 18.
[5] Matt. ix. 12, 13.
[6] cf. Luke xv. 7.
[7] Luke xv. 32.

LETTER XLVII.[1]

To Gregory.[2]

"Who will give me wings like a dove? Or how can my old age be so renewe that I can travel to your affection, satisfy m deep longing to see you, tell you all th troubles of my soul, and get from you som comfort in my affliction? For when th blessed bishop Eusebius[4] fell asleep, w were under no small alarm lest plotters again the Church of our Metropolis, wishful to fil it with their heretical tares, should seize th present opportunity, root out by their wicke teaching the true faith sown by much la bour in men's souls, and destroy its unity This has been the result of their action i many churches.[5] When however I receive the letters of the clergy exhorting me not t let their needs be overlooked at such a crisis as I ranged my eyes in all directions I be thought me of your loving spirit, your righ faith, and your unceasing zeal on behalf o the churches of God. I have therefore sen the well beloved Eustathius,[6] the deacon, t invite your reverence, and implore you t

[1] Placed in 370. The letters numbered 47 to 291, inclusive are placed by the Benedictine editors during St. Basil's epi copate.
[2] On this title the Benedictine editors remark that no careful reader can fail to note that the letter is written not by Bas but about Basil. "Hodie," they write, "inter eruditos fer conveniit eam a Gregorio patre, filii manu, ad Eusebium Samosatensem scriptam fuisse. Nam senem se esse declarat auctor Epistolæ et in Cappadocia Episcopum, ut qui litter cleri ad electionem Episcopi, et Ecclesiæ Cæsariensis defe sionem invitatus fuerit. Is autem ad quem scribit et eadem dignitate præditus erat, et laboribus pro Ecclesia susceptis clarus, et amicus Basilio, nec Cappadociæ vicinus. Omni in Eusebium Samosatensem mirificè conveniunt, quem Basili ordinationi scimus interfuisse," and they give, moreover, a their descriptive heading: " Gregorius Theologi pater Euse bium Samosatensem, misso Eustathio diacono, invitat a electionem Episcopi Cæsariensis ut eo adjuvante Basilius elig possit." Fialon, however, apparently forgetting the referenc to old age, writes (Étude Hist. p. 87, n.) : " Cette lettre es évidemment de Grégoire de Nazianze," meaning the younger The election of St. Basil, who probably " voluit episcopari" to the archiepiscopal throne, was indeed mainly due to th intervention of the elder Gregory. Basil's unfortunate an indefensible disingenuousness in summoning the younge Gregory to Cæsarea on the plea of his own severe illnes defeated its object. But for the prompt and practical in tervention of Gregory the elder, and this appeal to Eusebiu of Samosata, the archbishopric might have fallen into un worthy, or at least inferior, hands. Vide Biog. Notice i Proleg.,
[3] cf. Ps. lv. 6, LXX.
[4] Eusebius, at the time of his election an unbaptized lay man, was elevated to the throne of Cæsarea on the death o Dianius in 362. In this case too it was due to the counsel of the elder Gregory that the objections both of Eusebius an of the bishops, forced by the opposing party to consecrate him were finally overcome. It was he who ordained Basil to th presbyterate and chafed against the ascendancy of his mor able and brilliant subordinate.
[5] In 365 Valens came to Cæsarea with Arian bishops, an endeavoured to put down the Catholics. Basil returned from his retreat in order to aid Eusebius in resisting the attack, an seems to have shown much tact and good feeling as well a vigour and ability. cf. Greg. Naz., Or. xx. 340.
[6] cf. Letter cxxxvi., where it appears that Basil kindl nursed a deacon Eustathius. The fact of an Eustathius being one of Basil's deacons is so far in favour of Basil's havin written the letter. But Eustathius was a common name, an Eustathius, a monk, is mentioned in the will of Gregory o Nazianzus.

add this one more to all your labours on behalf of the Church. I entreat you also to refresh my old age by a sight of you; and to maintain for the true Church its famous orthodoxy, by uniting with me, if I may be deemed worthy of uniting with you, in the good work, to give it a shepherd in accordance with the will of the Lord, able to guide His people aright. I have before my eyes a man not unknown even to yourself. If only we be found worthy to secure him, I am sure that we shall acquire a confident access to God and confer a very great benefit on the people who have invoked our aid. Now once again, aye, many times I call on you, all hesitation put aside, to come to meet me, and to set out before the difficulties of winter intervene.

LETTER XLVIII.[1]

To Eusebius, Bishop of Samosata.[2]

I HAVE had considerable difficulty in finding a messenger to convey a letter to your reverence, for our men are so afraid of the winter that they can hardly bear even to put their heads outside their houses. We have suffered from such a very heavy fall of snow that we have been buried, houses and all, beneath it, and now for two months have been living in dens and caves. You know the Cappadocian character and how hard it is to get us to move.[3] Forgive me then for not writing sooner and bringing to the knowledge of your excellency the latest news from Antioch. To tell you all this now, when it is probable that you learnt it long ago, is stale and uninteresting. But as I do not reckon it any trouble to tell you even what you know, I have sent you the letters conveyed by the reader. On this point I shall say no more. Constantinople has now for some time had Demophilus,[4] as the bearers of this letter will themselves tell you, and as has doubtless been reported to your holiness. From all who come to us from that city there is unanimously reported about him a certain counterfeit of orthodoxy and sound religion, to such an extent that even the divided portions of

the city have been brought to agreement, and some of the neighbouring bishops have accepted the reconciliation. Our men here have not turned out better than I expected. They came directly you were gone,[1] said and did many painful things, and at last went home again, after making their separation from me wider.[2] Whether anything better will happen in the future, and whether they will give up their evil ways, is unknown to all but God. So much for our present condition. The rest of the Church, by God's grace, stands sound, and prays that in the spring we may have you with us again, and be renewed by your good counsel. My health is no better than it ever is.

LETTER XLIX.[3]

To Arcadius the Bishop.

I THANKED the Holy God when I read your letter, most pious brother. I pray that I may not be unworthy of the expectations you have formed of me, and that you will enjoy a full reward for the honour which you pay me in the name of our Lord Jesus Christ. I was exceedingly pleased to hear that you have been occupied in a matter eminently becoming a Christian, have raised a house to the glory of God, and have in practical earnest loved, as it is written, " the beauty of the house of the Lord."[4] and have so provided for yourself that heavenly mansion which is prepared in His rest for them that love the Lord. If I am able to find any relics of martyrs, I pray that I may take part in your earnest endeavour. If " the righteous shall be had in everlasting remembrance,"[5] I shall without doubt have a share in the good fame which the Holy One will give you.

LETTER L.[6]

To Bishop Innocentius.[7]

WHOM, indeed, could it better befit to

---

[1] Placed at the beginning of the episcopate.
[2] cf. Letters xxxi., xxxiv.
[3] The Cappadocians were of notoriously bad character, and shared with the Cretans and Cilicians the discredit of illustrating τρία κάππα κάκιστα. cf. note on Theodoret, Ecc. Hist. II. xi. p. 75. It was Phrygians, however, who were specially notorious for cowardice. cf. the proverb : " More cowardly than a Phrygian hare." cf. Lightfoot, Coloss., etc., p. 378 n. But Cappadocia may claim the counter credit of having given birth to three of the most famous divines, Basil and the two Gregorys.
[4] On the death of Eudoxius, in 370, Demophilus was elected by the Arians to fill the vacant see. Eustathius, the deposed bishop of Antioch, ordained Evagrius. Eustathius and Evagrius were both banished by Valens, and their adherents cruelly treated. Soc., Ecc. Hist. iv. 14, 16; Soz., Ecc. Hist. vi. 13, 14, and Philost., Ecc. Hist. ix. 10.

[1] After the departure of Eusebius at the close of the visit which he had undertaken, in accordance with the request of the previous letter, in order to secure Basil's consecration to the vacant see.
[2] On the difficulties thrown in Basil's way by the bishops who had opposed his election, cf. Letters xcviii., cxli., and cclxxxii.
[3] Of about the same date as the preceding.
[4] Ps. xxvi. 8, LXX.   [5] Ps. cxii. 6.
[6] Placed at the beginning of the Episcopate.
[7] The Benedictine title runs, Basilius gratias agit Episcopo cuidam, and a Ben. note points out that the common addition of " of Rome " to the title must be an error, because Damasus, not Innocent, was Bishop of Rome at the time. Combefis supposed that the letter was written to Innocent, then a presbyter, and that the allusion at the end of the letter is to Damasus ; the Ben. note says absurde. Innocent did not become Bishop of Rome till 402, three years after Basil's death. Whatever was the see of the recipient of this letter, it was one of importance. cf. Letter lxxxi.

encourage the timid, and rouse the slumbering, than you, my godly lord, who have shewn your general excellence in this, too, that you have consented to come down among us, your lowly inferiors, like a true disciple of Him Who said, " I am among you," not as a fellow guest, but "as he that serveth." [1] For you have condescended to minister to us your spiritual gladness, to refresh our souls by your honoured letter, and, as it were, to fling the arms of your greatness round the infancy of children. We, therefore, implore your good soul to pray, that we may be worthy to receive aid from the great, such as yourself, and to have a mouth and wisdom wherewith to chime in with the strain of all, who like you are led by the Holy Spirit. Of Him I hear that you are a friend and true worshipper, and I am deeply thankful for your strong and unshaken love to God. I pray that my lot may be found with the true worshippers, among whom we are sure your excellency is to be ranked, as well as that great and true bishop who has filled all the world with his wonderful work.

LETTER LI. [2]

To Bishop Bosporius. [3]

How do you think my heart was pained at hearing of the slanders heaped on me by some of those that feel no fear of the Judge, who "shall destroy them that speak leasing"? [4] I spent nearly the whole night sleepless, thinking of your words of love; so did grief lay hold upon my heart of hearts. For verily, in the words of Solomon, slander humbleth a man. [5] And no man is so void of feeling as not to be touched at heart, and bowed down to the ground, if he falls in with lips prone to lying. But we must needs put up with all things and endure all things, after committing our vindication to the Lord. He will not despise us ; for " he that oppresseth the poor reproacheth his Maker." [6] They, however, who have patched up this new tragedy of blasphemy seem to have lost all belief in the Lord, Who has declared that we must give account at the day of judgment even for an idle word. [7] And I, tell me, I anathema-

tized the right blessed Dianius? For this is what they have said against me. Where? When? In whose presence? On what pretext? In mere spoken words, or in writing? Following others, or myself the author and originator of the deed? Alas for the impudence of men who make no difficulty at saying anything! Alas for their contempt of the judgment of God! Unless, indeed, they add this further to their fiction, that they make me out to have been once upon a time so far out of my mind as not to know what I was saying. For so long as I have been in my senses I know that I never did anything of the kind, or had the least wish to do so. What I am, indeed, conscious of is this; that from my earliest childhood I was brought up in love for him, thought as I gazed at him how venerable he looked, how dignified, how truly reverend. Then when I grew older I began to know him by the good qualities of his soul, and took delight in his society, gradually learning to perceive the simplicity, nobility, and liberality of his character, and all his most distinctive qualities, his gentleness of soul, his mingled magnanimity and meekness, the seemliness of his conduct, his control of temper, the beaming cheerfulness and affability which he combined with majesty of demeanour. From all this I counted him among men most illustrious for high character.

However, towards the close of his life (I will not conceal the truth) I, together with many of them that in our country [1] feared the Lord, sorrowed over him with sorrow unendurable, because he signed the creed brought from Constantinople by George. [2] Afterwards, full of kindness and gentleness as he was, and willing out of the fulness of his fatherly heart to give satisfaction to everyone, when he had already fallen sick of the disease of which he died, he sent for me, and, calling the Lord to witness, said that in the simplicity of his heart he had agreed to the document sent from Constantinople, but had had no idea of rejecting the creed put forth by the holy Fathers at Nicæa, nor had had any other disposition of heart than from the beginning he had always had. He prayed, moreover, that he might not be cut off from the lot of those

---

[1] Luke xxii. 27.
[2] Placed at the beginning of Basil's episcopate, c. 370.
[3] Bosporius, an intimate friend of Basil and of Gregory of Nazianzus, was bishop of Colonia, in Cappadocia Secunda. Basil left Cæsarea in 360 in distress at hearing that Dianius had subscribed the creed of Ariminum, but was hurt at the charge that he had anathematized his friend and bishop. Dianius died in Basil's arms in 362.
[4] Ps. v. 6.
[5] συκοφαντία ἄνδρα ταπεινοῖ, for Eccles. vii. 7, LXX. συκοφαντία περιδέρει σοφῖν : oppression maketh a wise man mad, A.V.; extortion maketh a wise man foolish, R.V.
[6] Prov. xiv. 31.   [7] Matt. xii. 36.

[1] Here Cæsarea appears to be called πατρίς. cf. Ep. viii. Vide Proleg.
[2] i.e. the Homœan creed of Ariminum, as revised at Nike and accepted at the Acacian Synod of Constantinople in 360. George is presumably the George bp. of Laodicea, who at Seleucia opposed the Acacians, but appears afterwards to have become reconciled to that party, and to have joined them in persecuting the Catholics at Constantinople. cf. Basil, Ep. ccli.

blessed three hundred and eighteen bishops who had announced the pious decree[1] to the world. In consequence of this satisfactory statement I dismissed all anxiety and doubt, and, as you are aware, communicated with him, and gave over grieving. Such have been my relations with Dianius. If anyone avers that he is privy to any vile slander on my part against Dianius, do not let him buzz it slave-wise in a corner; let him come boldly out and convict me in the light of day.

LETTER LII.[2]

To the Canonicæ.

1. I HAVE been very much distressed by a painful report which reached my ears; but I have been equally delighted by my brother, beloved of God, bishop Bosporius,[4] who has brought a more satisfactory account of you. He avers by God's grace that all those stories spread abroad about you are inventions of men who are not exactly informed as to the truth about you. He added, moreover, that he found among you impious calumnies about me, of a kind likely to be uttered by those who do not expect to have to give the Judge in the day of His righteous retribution an account of even an idle word. I thank God, then, both because I am cured of my damaging opinion of you, an opinion which I have derived from the calumnies of men, and because I have heard of your abandonment of those baseless notions about me, on hearing the assurances of my brother. He, in all that he has said as coming from himself, has also completely expressed my own feeling. For in us both there is one mind about the faith, as being heirs of the same Fathers who once at Nicæa promulgated their great decree[5] concerning the faith. Of this, some portions are universally accepted without cavil, but the term homoousion, ill received in certain quarters, is still rejected by some. These objectors we may very properly blame, and yet on the contrary deem them deserving of pardon. To refuse to follow the Fathers, not holding their declaration of more authority than one's own opinion, is conduct worthy of blame, as being

brimful of self-sufficiency. On the other hand the fact that they view with suspicion a phrase which is misrepresented by an opposite party does seem to a small extent to relieve them from blame. Moreover, as a matter of fact, the members of the synods which met to discuss the case of Paul of Samosata[1] did find fault with the term as an unfortunate one.

For they maintained that the homoousion set forth the idea both of essence and of what is derived from it, so that the essence, when divided, confers the title of co-essential on the parts into which it is divided. This explanation has some reason in the case of bronze and coins made therefrom, but in the case of God the Father and God the Son there is no question of substance anterior or even underlying both; the mere thought and utterance of such a thing is the last extravagance of impiety. What can be conceived of as anterior to the Unbegotten? By this blasphemy faith in the Father and the Son is destroyed, for things, constituted out of one, have to one another the relation of brothers.

2. Because even at that time there were men who asserted the Son to have been brought into being out of the non-existent, the term homoousion was adopted, to extirpate this impiety. For the conjunction of the Son with the Father is without time and without interval. The preceding words shew this to have been the intended meaning. For after saying that the Son was light of light, and begotten of the substance of the Father, but was not made, they went on to add the homoousion, thereby showing that whatever proportion of light any one would attribute in the case of the Father will obtain also in that of the Son. For very light in relation to very light, according to the actual sense of light, will have no variation. Since then the Father is light without

---

[1] κήρυγμα. cf. p. 41.

[2] Placed at the beginning of St. Basil's episcopate, c. 370.

[3] Canonicæ, in the early church, were women enrolled in a list in the churches, devoted to works of charity, and living apart from men, though not under vows, nor always in a cœnobium. In Soc., H.E. i. 17 they are described as the recipients of St. Helena's hospitality. St. Basil is supposed to refuse to recognise marriage with them as legitimate in Ep. cclxxxviii. The word κανονικῶν may stand for either gender, but the marriage of Canonici was commonly allowed. Letter clxxiii. is addressed to the canonica Theodora.

[4] Vide the Letter li.

[5] κήρυγμα. On Basil's use of this word and of dogma, vide note on p. 41.

[1] i.e. the two remarkable Antiochene synods of 264 and 269, to enforce the ultimate decisions of which against Paul of Samosata appeal was made to the pagan Aurelian. On the explanation of how the Homoousion came to be condemned in one sense by the Origenist bishops at Antioch in 264, and asserted in another by the 318 at Nicæa in 325, see prolegomena to Athanasius in Schaff and Wace's ed. p. xxxi. cf. Ath., De Syn. § 45, Hil., De Trin. iv. 4, and Basil, Cont. Eunom. i. 19. "Wurde seiner Lehre: 'Gott sey mit dem Logos zugleich Eine Person, ἓν πρόσωπον wie der Mensch mit seiner Vernunft Eines sey.' entgegengehalten, die Kirchenlehre verlange Einen Gott, aber mehrere πρόσωπα desselben, so sagte er, da auch ihm Christus eine Person (nämlich als Mensch) sey, so habe auch sein Glaube mehrere πρόσωπα, Gott und Christus stehen sich als ὁμοιούσιοι, d.h. wahrscheinlich gleich persönliche gegenüber, Diese veratorische Dialektik konnte zwar nicht täuschen; wohl aber wurde das Wort ὁμοούσιος, so gebraucht und auf die Person überhaupt bezogen, dadurch eine Weile verdächtig (man fürchtete nach Athan. De Syn. Ar. et Sel. c. 45. eine menschliche Person nach Paul in die Trinität einlassen zu müssen), bis das vierte Jahrhundert jenem Wort bestimmten kirchlichen Stempel gab." Dorner, Christologie. B. i. 513.

Vide also Thomasius, Christliche Dogmengeschichte, B. 1, p. 188.

beginning, and the Son begotten light, but each of Them light and light; they rightly said "of one substance," in order to set forth the equal dignity of the nature. Things, that have a relation of brotherhood, are not, as some persons have supposed, of one substance; but when both the cause and that which derives its natural existence from the cause are of the same nature, then they are called "of one substance."

3. This term also corrects the error of Sabellius, for it removes the idea of the identity of the hypostases, and introduces in perfection the idea of the Persons. For nothing can be of one substance with itself, but one thing is of one substance with another. The word has therefore an excellent and orthodox use, defining as it does both the proper character of the hypostases, and setting forth the invariability of the nature. And when we are taught that the Son is of the substance of the Father, begotten and not made, let us not fall into the material sense of the relations. For the substance was not separated from the Father and bestowed on the Son; neither did the substance engender by fluxion, nor yet by shooting forth[1] as plants their fruits. The mode of the divine begetting is ineffable and inconceivable by human thought. It is indeed characteristic of poor and carnal intelligence to compare the things that are eternal with the perishing things of time, and to imagine, that as corporeal things beget, so does God in like manner; it is rather our duty to rise to the truth by arguments of the contrary, and to say, that since thus is the mortal, not thus is He who is immortal. We must neither then deny the divine generation, nor contaminate our intelligence with corporeal senses.

4. The Holy Spirit, too, is numbered with the Father and the Son, because He is above creation, and is ranked as we are taught by the words of the Lord in the Gospel, "Go and baptize in the name of the Father and of the Son and of the Holy Ghost."[2] He who, on the contrary, places the Spirit before the Son, or alleges Him to be older than the Father, resists the ordinance of God, and is a stranger to the sound faith, since he fails to preserve the form of doxology which he has received, but adopts some new fangled device in order to be pleasing to men. It is written "The Spirit is of God,"[3] and if He is of God, how can He be older than that of which He is? And what folly is it not, when there is one Unbegotten, to speak of

something else as superior to the Unbegotten. He is not even anterior, for nothing intervenes between Son and Father. If, however, He is not of God but is through Christ He does not even exist at all. It follows that this new invention about the order really involves the destruction of the actual existence, and is a denial of the whole faith. is equally impious to reduce Him to the level of a creature, and to subordinate Him either to Son or to Father, either in time or in rank. These are the points on which have heard that you are making enquiry. I the Lord grant that we meet I may possibly have more to say on these subjects, and may myself, concerning points which I am investigating, receive satisfactory information from you.

LETTER LIII.[1]

To the Chorepiscopi.[2]

1. My soul is deeply pained at the enormity of the matter on which I write, if for this only, that it has caused general suspicion and talk. But so far it has seemed to me incredible. I hope then that what I am writing about it may be taken by the guilty as medicine, by the innocent as a warning, by the indifferent, in which class I trust none of you may be found, as a testimony. And what is it of which I speak? There is a report that some of you take money from candidates for ordination,[3] and excuse it on grounds of religion. This is indeed worse. If any one does evil under the guise of good he deserves double punishment; because he not only does what is in itself not good, but so to say, makes good an accomplice in the commission of sin. If the allegation be true let it be so no more. Let a better state of things begin. To the recipient of the bribe it must be said, as was said by the Apostle to him who was willing to give money t

[1] Placed in the beginning of the episcopate.

[2] "A class of ministers between bishops proper and presbyters, defined in the Arabic version of the Nicene canons be ' *loco episcopi super villas et monasteria et sacerdotes v. larum ;* ' called into existence in the latter part of the thi century, and first in Asia Minor, in order to meet the wants episcopal supervision in the country parts of the now enlarg dioceses without subdivision : first mentioned in the Counci of Ancyra and Neo-Cæsarea A.D. 314." D.C.A. i. 354. Thr MSS. give the title "to the bishops under him." The Be Ed. remarks : " *Liquet Basilium agere de episcopis sibi su ditis. Nam qui proprie dicebantur chorepiscopi, manus n ponebant, sed clero inferiores ministros ascribebant, ut vide est in epist. sequenti. Sed tamen ipsi etiam episcopi, q Ecclesias metropoli subjectas regebant, interdum vocabant chorepiscopi. Queritur enim Gregorius Naz. in carmine vita sua, quod a Basilio, qui quinquaginta chorepiscopos s se habebat, vilissimi oppiduli constitutus episcopus fuisset.*

τούτοις μ' ὁ πεντήκοντα χωρεπισκόποις στενούμενος δέδωκεν.

Hoc exemplo confirmatur vetustissimorum codicum scriptu quam secuti sumus.

[3] *cf.* note on Theodoret, iv. 20, p. 125.

[1] *cf.* Luke xxi. 30. [3] 1 Cor. ii. 12.
[2] Matt. xxviii. 19.

buy the fellowship of the Holy Ghost, "Thy money perish with thee.[1] It is a lighter sin to wish in ignorance to buy, than it is to sell, the gift of God. A sale it was; and if you sell what you received as a free gift you will be deprived of the boon, as though you were yourself sold to Satan. You are obtruding the traffic of the huckster into spiritual things and into the Church where we are entrusted with the body and blood of Christ. These things must not be. And I will mention wherein lies an ingenious contrivance. They think that there is no sin because they take the money not before but after the ordination; but to take is to take at whatever time.

2. I exhort you, then, abandon this gain, or, I would rather say, this approach to Hell. Do not, by defiling your hands with such bribes, render yourselves unfit to celebrate holy mysteries. But forgive me. I began by discrediting; and now I am threatening as though I were convinced. If, after this letter of mine, any one do anything of the kind, he will depart from the altars here and will seek a place where he is able to buy and to sell God's gift. We and the Churches of God have no such custom.[2] One word more, and I have done. These things come of covetousness. Now covetousness is the root of all evil and is called idolatry.[3] Do not then price idols above Christ for the sake of a little money. Do not imitate Judas and once more betray for a bribe Him who was crucified for us. For alike the lands and the hands of all that make such gain shall be called Aceldama.[4]

LETTER LIV.[5]

To the Chorepiscopi.

I AM much distressed that the canons of the Fathers have fallen through, and that the exact discipline of the Church has been banished from among you. I am apprehensive lest, as this indifference grows, the affairs of the Church should, little by little, fall into confusion. According to the ancient custom observed in the Churches of God, ministers in the Church were received after careful examination; the whole of their life was investigated; an enquiry was made as to their being neither railers nor drunkards, not quick to quarrel, keeping their youth in subjection, so as to be able to maintain "the holiness without which no man shall see the Lord."[6] This examination was made by

presbyters and deacons living with them. Then they brought them to the Chorepiscopi; and the Chorepiscopi, after receiving the suffrages of the witnesses as to the truth and giving information to the Bishop, so admitted the minister to the sacerdotal order.[1] Now, however, you have quite passed me over; you have not even had the grace to refer to me, and have transferred the whole authority to yourselves. Furthermore, with complete indifference, you have allowed presbyters and deacons to introduce unworthy persons into the Church, just any one they choose, without any previous examination of life and character, by mere favoritism, on the score of relationship or some other tie. The consequence is, that in every village, there are reckoned many ministers, but not one single man worthy of the service of the altars. Of this you yourselves supply proof from your difficulty in finding suitable candidates for election. As, then, I perceive that the evil is gradually reaching a point at which it would be incurable, and especially at this moment when a large number of persons are presenting themselves for the ministry through fear of the conscription, I am constrained to have recourse to the restitution of the canons of the Fathers. I thus order you in writing to send me the roll of the ministers in every village, stating by whom each has been introduced, and what is his mode of life. You have the roll in your own keeping, so that your version can be compared with the documents which are in mine, and no one can insert his own name when he likes. So if any have been introduced by presbyters after the first appointment,[2] let

---

[1] Acts viii. 20.
[2] cf. 1 Cor. xi. 16.
[3] Placed at the same time as the foregoing.
[4] Heb. xii. 14.
[3] cf. Col. iii. 5.
[4] cf. Acts i. 19.

[1] The Ben. note runs, "*Ministros, sive subdiaconos, sacratorum ordini ascribit Basilius. Synodus Laodicena inferiores clericos sacratorum numero non comprehendit, sed numerat sacratos a presbyteris usque ad diaconos,* ἀπο πρεσβυτέρων ἔως διακόνων, *can. 24, distinguit canone 27,* ἱερατικοὺς, ἢ κληρικοὺς ἢ λαικούς, *sive sacratos, sive clericos, sive laicos. Et can. 30.* Ὅτι οὐ δεῖ ἱερατικὸν ἢ κληρικὸν ἢ ἀσκητὴν ἐν βαλανείῳ μετὰ γυναικῶν ἀπολούεσθαι, μηδὲ πάντα Χιστιανὶν ἢ λαικόν. *Non oportet sacratum vel clericum aut ascetam in balneo cum mulieribus lavari. sed nec ullum Christianum aut laïcum. Non sequuntur hujus synodi morem ecclesiastici scriptores. Basilius, epist. 287, excommunicato omne cum sacratis commercium intercludit. Et in epist. 198,* ἱ·ρατ·ιου *intelligit cœtum clericorum, eique ascribit clericos qui epistolas episcopi perferebant. Athanasius ad Rufinianum scribens, rogat eum ut epistolam legat* ἱεpατείῳ *et populo. Gregorius Nazianzenus lectores sacri ordinis,* ἱεροῦ ταγματος, *partem esse agnoscit in epist. 45. Notandus etiam canon 8 apostolicus,* ἐι τις ἐπίσκοπος ἢ *etc.* πρεσβύτερος ἢ διάκονος ἢ ἐκ τοῦ ἱεραρικου καταλόγου, *etc. Si quis episcopus vel presbyter vel diaconus, vel ex sacro ordine. Hæc visa sunt observanda, quia pluribus Basilii locis, quae deinceps occurrent, non parum afferent lucis.*" The letter of the Council in Illyricum uses ἱερατικον τάγμα in precisely the same way. Theod., *Ecc. Hist.* iv. 8, where see note on p. 113. So Sozomen, *On the Council of Nicæa*, i. 23. *Ordo*, the nearest Latin equivalent to the Greek τάγμα, was originally used of any estate in the church, *e.g.* St. Jerome, *On Isaiah* v. 19, 18.
On the testing of qualifications for orders, *cf.* St. Cyprian, *Ep.* lxviii.

[2] μετὰ τὴν πρώτην ἐπινέμησιν. Ἐπινέμησις is in later Greek the recognised equivalent for "*indictio*" in the sense of a period of fifteen years (*Cod. Theod.* xi. 28, 3). I have had some hesitation as to whether it could possibly in this passage

them be rejected, and take their place among the laity. Their examination must then be begun by you over again, and, if they prove worthy, let them be received by your decision. Drive out unworthy men from the Church, and so purge it. For the future, test by examination those who are worthy, and then receive them; but do not reckon them of the number before you have reported to me. Otherwise, distinctly understand that he who is admitted to the ministry without my authority will remain a layman.

LETTER LV.[1]

To Paregorius the presbyter.

I HAVE given patient attention to your letter, and I am astonished that when you are perfectly well able to furnish me with a short and easy defence by taking action at once, you should choose to persist in what is my ground of complaint, and endeavour to cure the incurable by writing a long story about it. I am not the first, Paregorius, nor the only man, to lay down the law that women are not to live with men. Read the canon put forth by our holy Fathers at the Council of Nicæa, which distinctly forbids subintroducts. Unmarried life is honourably distinguished by its being cut off from all female society. If, then, any one, who is known by the outward profession, in reality follows the example of those who live with wives, it is obvious that he only affects the distinction of virginity in name, and does not hold aloof from unbecoming indulgence. You ought to have been all the more ready to submit yourself without difficulty to my demands, in that you allege that you are .free from all bodily appetite. I do not suppose that a man of three score years and ten lives with a woman from any such feelings, and I have not decided, as I have decided, on the ground of any crime having been committed. But we have learnt from the Apostle, not to put a stumbling block or an occasion to fall in a brother's way;"[2] and I know that what is done very properly by some, naturally becomes to others an occasion for sin. I have therefore given my order, in obedience to the injunction of the holy Fathers, that you are to separate from the woman. Why then, do you find fault with the Chorepiscopus? What

is the good of mentioning ancient ill-will? Why do you blame me for lending an easy ear to slander? Why do you not rather lay the blame on yourself, for not consenting to break off your connexion with the woman? Expel her from your house, and establish her in a monastery. Let her live with virgins, and do you be served by men, that the name of God be not blasphemed in you. Till you have so done, the innumerable arguments, which you use in your letters, will not do you the slightest service. You will die useless, and you will have to give an account to God for your uselessness. If you persist in clinging to your clerical position without correcting your ways, you will be accursed before all the people, and all, who receive you, will be excommunicate throughout the Church.[1]

LETTER LVI.[2]

To Pergamius.[3]

I NATURALLY forget very easily, and I have had lately many things to do, and so my natural infirmity is increased. I have no doubt, therefore, that you have written to me, although I have no recollection of having received any letter from your excellency; for I am sure you would not state what is not the case. But for there having been no reply, it is not I that am in fault; the guilt lies with him who did not ask for one. Now, however, you have this letter, containing my defence for the past and affording ground for a second greeting. So, when you write to me, do not suppose that you are taking the initiative in another correspondence. You are only discharging your proper obligation in this. For really, although this letter of mine is a return for a previous one of yours, as it is more than twice as bulky, it will fulfil a double purpose. You see to what sophisms my idleness drives me. But, my dear Sir, do not in a few words bring serious charges, indeed the most serious of all. Forgetfulness of one's friends, and neglect of them arising from high place, are faults which involve every kind of wrong. Do we fail to love

---

indicate a date. But ἐπινέμησις does not appear to have been used in its chronological sense before Evagrius, and his expression (iv. 29) τοὺς περιόδους τῶν κύκλων καλουμένων ἐπινεμήσεων looks as though the term were not yet common; ἐπινέμησις here I take to refer to the assignment of presbyters to different places on ordination. I am indebted to Mr. J. W. Parker for valuable information and suggestions on this question.

[1] Placed at the beginning of the Episcopate.
[2] Rom. xiv. 13.

[1] On the subject of the *subintroductæ* or συνείσακτοι, one of the greatest difficulties and scandals of the early church, *vide* the article of Can. Venables in D.C.A. ii. 1937. The earliest prohibitive canon against the custom is that of the Council of Elvira, A.D. 305. (Labbe i. 973.) The Canon of Nicæa, to which Basil refers, only allowed the introduction of a mother, sister, or aunt. The still more extraordinary and perilous custom of ladies of professed celibacy entertaining male συνείσακτοι, referred to by Gregory of Nazianzus in his advice to virgins, ἄρσενα πάντ' ἀλέεινε συνείσακτον δὲ μάλιστα, may he traced even so far back as "the Shepherd of Hermas" (iii. Simil. ix. 11). On the charges against Paul of Samosata under this head, *vide* Eusebius, vii. 30.
[2] Placed at the beginning of the Episcopate.
[3] A layman, of whom nothing more is known.

according to the commandment of the Lord? Then we lose the distinctive mark imprinted on us. Are we puffed to repletion with empty pride and arrogance? Then we fall into the inevitable condemnation of the devil. If, then, you use these words because you held such sentiments about me, pray that I may flee from the wickedness which you have found in my ways; if, however, your tongue shaped itself to these words, in a kind of inconsiderate conventionality, I shall console myself, and ask you to be good enough to adduce some tangible proof of your allegations. Be well assured of this, that my present anxiety is an occasion to me of humility. I shall begin to forget you, when I cease to know myself. Never, then, think that because a man is a very busy man he is a man of faulty character.

LETTER LVII.[1]

To Meletius, Bishop of Antioch.[2]

IF your holiness only knew the greatness of the happiness you cause me whenever you write to me, I know that you would never have let slip any opportunity of sending me a letter; nay, you would have written me many letters on each occasion, knowing the reward that is kept in store by our loving Lord for the consolation of the afflicted. Everything here is still in a very painful condition, and the thought of your holiness is the only thing that recalls me from my own troubles; a thought made more distinct to me by my communication with you through that letter of yours which is so full of wisdom and grace. When, therefore, I take your letter into my hand, first of all, I look at its size, and I love it all the more for being so big; then, as I read it, I rejoice over every word I find in it; as I draw near the end I begin to feel sad; so good is every word that I read, in what you write. The overflowing of a good heart is good. Should I, however, be permitted, in answer to your prayers, while I live on this earth, to meet you face to face, and to enjoy the profitable instruction of your living voice, or any aids to help me in the life that now is, or that which is to come, I should count this indeed the best of blessings, a prelude to the mercy of God. I should, ere

now, have adhered to this intention, had I not been prevented by true and loving brothers. I have told my brother Theophrastus [1] to make a detailed report to you of matters, as to which I do not commit my intentions to writing.

LETTER LVIII.[2]

To Gregory my brother.[3]

How am I to dispute with you in writing? How can I lay hold of you satisfactorily, with all your simplicity? Tell me; who ever falls a third time into the same nets? Who ever gets a third time into the same snare? Even a brute beast would find it difficult to do so. You forged one letter, and brought it me as though it came from our right reverend uncle the bishop, trying to deceive me, I have no idea why. I received it as a letter written by the bishop and delivered by you. Why should I not? I was delighted; I shewed it to many of my friends; I thanked God. The forgery was found out, on the bishop's repudiating it in person. I was thoroughly ashamed; covered as I was with the disgrace of cunning trickery and lies, I prayed that the earth might open for me. Then they gave me a second letter, as sent by the bishop himself by the hands of your servant Asterius. Even this second had not really been sent by the bishop, as my very reverend brother Anthimus [4] has told me. Now Adamantius has come bringing me a third. How ought I to receive a letter carried by you or yours? I might have prayed to have a heart of stone, so as neither to remember the past, nor to feel the present; so as to bear every blow, like cattle, with bowed head. But what am I to think, now that, after my first and second experience, I can admit nothing without positive proof? Thus I write attacking your simplicity, which I see plainly to be neither what generally becomes a Christian man, nor is appropriate to the present emergency; I write

[1] Placed in the year 371.
[2] This letter, the first of six to Meletius of Antioch, is supposed to be assigned to this date, because of Basil's statement that the state of the Church at Cæsarea was still full of pain to him. Basil had not yet overcome the opposition of his suffragans, or won the position secured to him after his famous intercourse with Valens in 372. Meletius had now been for seven years exiled from Antioch, and was suffering for the sake of orthodoxy, while not in full communion with the Catholics, because of the unhappy Eustathian schism.

[1] This Theophrastus may be identified with the deacon Theophrastus who died shortly after Easter A.D. 372. (cf. Letter xcv.) The secret instructions given him "seem to refer to Basil's design for giving peace to the Church, which Basil did not attempt to carry out before his tranquilization of Cappadocia, but may have had in mind long before." Maran, Vit. Bas. chap. xvi.
[2] Placed in 371.
[3] Three MSS. give the title Γρηγορίῳ ἐπισκόπῳ καὶ ἀδελφῷ, but, as is pointed out by the Ben. Ed., the letter itself is hardly one which would be written to one with the responsibilities of a bishop. Basil seems to regard his brother as at liberty to come and help him at Cæsarea. Gregory's consecration to the see of Nyssa is placed in 372, when his reluctance had to be overcome by force. cf. Letter ccxxv. On the extraordinary circumstance of his well meant but futile forgery of the name of his namesake and uncle, bishop of an unknown see, vide Prolegom.
[4] Bishop of Tyana, estranged from Basil, cf. Letters cxx., cxxi., cxxii., and ccx.

that, at least for the future, you may take care of yourself and spare me. I must speak to you with all freedom, and I tell you that you are an unworthy minister of things so great. However, whoever be the writer of the letter, I have answered as is fit. Whether, then, you yourself are experimenting on me, or whether really the letter which you have sent is one which you have received from the bishops, you have my answer. At such a time as this you ought to have borne in mind that you are my brother, and have not yet forgotten the ties of nature, and do not regard me in the light of an enemy, for I have entered on a life which is wearing out my strength, and is so far beyond my powers that it is injuring even my soul. Yet for all this, as you have determined to declare war against me, you ought to have come to me and shared my troubles. For it is said, "Brethren and help are against time of trouble."[1] If the right reverend bishops are really willing to meet me, let them make known to me a place and time, and let them invite me by their own men. I do not refuse to meet my own uncle, but I shall not do so unless the invitation reaches me in due and proper form.[2]

LETTER LIX.[3]

To Gregory, his uncle.[4]

1. "I HAVE long time holden my peace. Am I to hold my peace for ever?"[5] Shall I still further endure to enforce against myself the hardest punishment of silence, by neither writing myself, nor receiving any statement from another? By holding fast to this stern determination up to the present time I am able to apply to myself the prophet's words, "I endure patiently like a travailing woman."[6] Yet I am ever longing for communication either in person or by letter, and ever, for my own sins' sake, missing it. For I cannot imagine any reason for what is happening, other than what I am convinced is the true one, that by being cut off from your love I am expiating old sins; if indeed I am not wrong in using such a phrase as "cut off"

in your case, from any one, much less from me, to whom you have always been as a father. Now my sin, like some dense cloud overshadowing me, has made me forget all this. When I reflect that the only result to me of what is going on is sorrow, how can I attribute it to anything but to my own wickedness? But if events are to be traced to sins, be this the end of my troubles; if there was any intended discipline in it, then your object has been very completely attained, for the punishment has been going on for a long time; so I groan no longer, but am the first to break silence, and beseech you to remember both me and yourself who, to a greater degree than our relationship might have demanded, have shewn me strong affection all my life. Now, I implore you, show kindness to the city for my sake. Do not on my account alienate yourself from it.

2. If, then, there is any consolation in Christ, any fellowship of the Spirit, any mercy and pity, fulfil my prayer. Put a stop to my depression. Let there be a beginning of brighter things for the future. Be yourself a leader to others in the road to all that is best, and follow no one else in the way to what is wrong. Never was any feature so characteristic of any one's body as gentleness and peace are of your soul. It were well becoming such a one as you are to draw all others to yourself, and to cause all who come near you to be permeated with the goodness of your nature, as with the fragrance of myrrh. For though there be a certain amount of opposition now, nevertheless ere long there will be a recognition of the blessings of peace. So long, however, as room is found for the calumnies that are bred of dissension, suspicion is sure to grow from worse to worse. It is most certainly unbecoming for the rest to take no notice of me, but it is especially unbecoming in your excellency. If I am wrong I shall be all the better for being rebuked. This is impossible if we never meet. But, if I am doing no wrong, for what am I disliked? So much I offer in my own defence.

3. As to what the Churches might say in their own behalf, perhaps it is better for me to be silent: they reap the result of our disagreement, and it is not to their gain. I am not speaking to indulge my grief but to put a stop to it. And your intelligence, I am sure, has suffered nothing to escape you. You will yourself be better able to discern and to tell to others points of far greater importance than I can conceive. You saw the mischief done to the Churches before I did; and you are grieving more than I am, for you

[1] Eccles. xl. 24.
[2] *Negat Basilius se adfuturum, nisi decenter advocetur, id est, nisi mittantur qui eum in indictum locum deducant. Erat Basilius. ut in ejus modi officiis exhibendis diligentissimus, ita etiam in reposcendis attentus. Meletius Antiochenus et Theodorus Nicopolitanus, cum Basilium ad celebritatem quamdam obiter advocassent per Hellenium Nazianzi Peraequatorem, nec iterum misissent qui de iisdem admoneret ac deduceret; displicuit Basilio perfunctoria invitandi ratio, ac veritus ne suspectus illis esset, adesse noluit."* Note by Ben. Ed.
[3] Placed in 361, at about the same time as the preceding.
[4] *Vide* n. on preceding page.
[5] Isa. xlii. 14, LXX.   [6] Isa. xlii. 14, LXX.

have long learnt from the Lord not to despise even the least.[1] And now the mischief is not confined to one or two, but whole cities and peoples are sharers in my calamities. What need to tell what kind of report will spread about me even beyond our borders? It were well for you, large hearted as you are, to leave the love of strife to others; nay rather, if it be possible, to root it from their hearts, while you yourself vanquish what is grievous by endurance. Any angry man can defend himself, but to rise above the actual anger belongs only to you, and any one as good as you, if such there be. One thing I will not say, that he who has a grudge against me is letting his anger fall on the innocent. Do then comfort my soul by coming to me, or by a letter, or by inviting me to come to you, or by some means or other. My prayer is that your piety may be seen in the Church and that you may heal at once me and the people, both by the sight of you and by the words of your good grace. If this be possible it is best; if you determine on any other course I shall willingly accept it. Only accede to my entreaty that you will give me distinct information as to what your wisdom decides.

LETTER LX.[2]

To Gregory his uncle.

FORMERLY I was glad to see my brother. Why not, since he is my brother and such a brother? Now I have received him on his coming to visit me with the same feelings, and have lost none of my affection. God forbid that I should ever so feel as to forget the ties of nature and be at war with those who are near and dear to me. I have found his presence a comfort in my bodily sickness and the other troubles of my soul, and I have been especially delighted at the letter which he has brought me from your excellency. For a long time I have been hoping that it would come, for this only reason, that I need not add to my life any doleful episode of quarrel between kith and kin, sure to give pleasure to foes and sorrow to friends, and to be displeasing to God, Who has laid down perfect love as the distinctive characteristic of His disciples. So I reply, as I am indeed bound, with an earnest request for your prayers for me, and your care for me in all things, as your relative. Since I, from want of information, cannot clearly understand the meaning of what is going on, I have judged

it right to accept the truth of the account which you are so good as to give me. It is for you of your wisdom to settle the rest, our meeting with one another, the fitting time and a convenient place. If your reverence really does not disdain to come down to my lowliness and to have speech with me, whether you wish the interview to take place in the presence of others or in private, I shall make no objection, for I have once for all made up my mind to submit to you in love, and to carry out, without exception, what your reverence enjoins on me for the glory of God.

I have not laid my reverend brother under the necessity of reporting anything to you by word of mouth, because on the former occasion what he said was not borne out by facts.

LETTER LXI.[1]

To Athanasius, Bishop of Alexandria.[2]

I HAVE read the letter of your holiness, in which you have expressed your distress at the unhappy governor of Libya. I am grieved that my own country should have given birth to and nurtured such vices. I am grieved too that Libya, a neighbouring country, should suffer from our evils, and should have been delivered to the inhumanity of a man whose life is marked at once by cruelty and crime. This however is only in accordance with the wisdom of the Preacher, "Woe to thee O land when thy King is a child;"[3] (a still further touch of trouble) and whose "Princes" do not "eat" after night but revel at mid-day, raging after other men's wives with less understanding than brute beasts. This man must surely look for the scourges of the righteous Judge, repaid him in exact requital for those which he himself has previously inflicted on the saints. Notice has been given to my Church in accordance with the letter of your reverence, and he shall be held by all as abominable, cut off from fire, water and shelter, if indeed in the case of men so possessed there is any use in general and unanimous condemnation. Notoriety is enough for him, and your own letter, which has been read in all directions, for I shall not fail to show it to all his friends and relatives. Assuredly, even if retribution

---

[1] cf. Matt. xviii. 10.
[2] Of the same time as the preceding.

[1] Placed in 370 or 371.
[2] This, the first of Basil's six extant letters to Athanasius, is placed by the Ben. Ed. in 371. It has no certain indication of date. Athanasius, in the few years of comparative calm which preceded his death in May, 373, had excommunicated a vicious governor in Libya, a native of Cappadocia, and announced his act to Basil. The intercourse opened by this official communication led to a more important correspondence.
[3] Eccles. x. 16.

does not reach him at once, as it did Pharaoh, certainly it will bring on him hereafter a heavy and hard requital.

LETTER LXII.[1]

To the Church of Parnassus.[2]

FOLLOWING an ancient custom, which has obtained for many years, and at the same time shewing you love in God, which is the fruit of the Spirit, I now, my pious friends, address this letter to you. I feel with you at once in your grief at the event which has befallen you, and in your anxiety at the matter which you have in hand. Concerning all these troubles I can only say, that an occasion is given us to look to the injunctions of the Apostle, and not to sorrow "even as others which have no hope."[3] I do not mean that we should be insensible to the loss we have suffered, but that we should not succumb to our sorrow, while we count the Pastor happy in his end. He has died in a ripe old age, and has found his rest in the great honour given him by his Lord.

As to the future I have this recommendation to give you. You must now lay aside all mourning; you must come to yourselves; you must rise to the necessary management of the Church; to the end that the holy God may give heed to His own little flock, and may grant you a shepherd in accordance with His own will, who may wisely feed you.

LETTER LXIII.[4]

To the Governor of Neocæsarea.

THE wise man, even if he dwells far away, even if I never set eyes on him, I count a friend. So says the tragedian Euripides. And so, if, though I have never had the pleasure of meeting your excellency in person, I speak of myself as a familiar friend, pray do not set this down to mere empty compliment. Common report, which loudly proclaims your universal benevolence, is, in this instance, the promoter of friendship. Indeed since I met the highly respectable Elpidius,[5] I have known you as

well, and I have been as completely captured by you, as though I had long lived with you and had practical experience of your excellent qualities. For he did not cease telling me about you, mentioning one by one your magnanimity, your exalted sentiments, your mild manners, your skill in business, intelligence, dignity tempered by cheerfulness, and eloquence. All the other points that he enumerated in his long conversation with me it is impossible for me to write to you, without extending my letter beyond all reasonable bounds. How can I fail to love such a man? How could I put such restraint upon myself as not loudly to proclaim what I feel? Accept then, most excellent Sir, the greeting which I send you, for it is inspired by true and unfeigned friendship. I abhor all servile compliment. Pray keep me enrolled in the list of your friends, and, by frequently writing to me, bring yourself before me and comfort me in your absence.

LETTER LXIV.[1]

To Hesychius.[2]

FROM the beginning I have had many points in common with your excellency, your love of letters, everywhere reported by all who have experienced it, and our old friendship with the admirable Terentius. But since that most excellent man, who is to me all that friendship could require, my worthy brother Elpidius, has met me, and told me all your good qualities, (and who more capable than he at once to perceive a man's virtue and to describe it?) he has kindled in me such a desire to see you, that I pray that you may one day visit me in my old home, that I may enjoy your good qualities not merely by hearing of them, but by actual experience.

LETTER LXV.[3]

To Atarbius.[4]

IF I continue to insist on the privileges to which my superior age entitles me, and wait for you to take the initiative in communica-

---

[1] Placed about 371.

[2] A town in Northern Cappadocia, on the right bank of the Halys, on or near a hill whence it was named, on the road between Ancyra and Archelais. The letter appears to Maran (*Vita S. Bas.* xvi.) to have been written before the encouragement given to the Arians by the visit of Valens in 372. The result of Basil's appeal to the Parnassenes was the election of an orthodox bishop, expelled by the Arians in 375, and named Hypsis or Hypsinus. *cf. Letter* ccxxxvii., where Ecdicius is said to have succeeded Hypsis; and ccxxxviii., where Ecdicius is called Παρνασσηνός. [3] 1 Thess. iv. 13.

[4] Of about the same date as the preceding.

[5] Another reading is Helladius. *cf. Letters* lxiv., lxxvii., and lxxviii. The identification of these Elpidii is conjectural. The name was common.

[1] Of about the same date as the preceding.

[2] *cf. Letter* lxii.

[3] Placed about 371, or, at all events, according to Maran before the year 373, when the ill will of Atarbius towards Basil was violently manifested.

[4] Atarbius is recognised as bishop of Neocæsarea, partly on the evidence of the Codices Coislinanus and Medicæus, which describe him as of Neocæsarea, partly on a comparison of *Letters* lxv. and cxxvi., addressed to him, with the circumstances of the unnamed bishop of Neocæsarea referred to in *Letter* ccx. Moreover (*cf.* Bp. Lightfoot, D.C.B. i. 179) at the Council of Constantinople he represented the province of Pontus Polemoniacus, of which Neocæsarea was metropolis. On the authority of an allusion in *Letter* ccx. sec. 4, Atarbius is supposed to be a kinsman of Basil.

tion, and if you, my friend, wish to adhere more persistently to your evil counsel of inaction, what end will there be to our silence? However, where friendship is involved, to be defeated is in my opinion to win, and so I am quite ready to give you precedence, and retire from the contest as to which should maintain his own opinion. I have been the first to betake myself to writing, because I know that "charity beareth all things, . . . endureth all things . . . seeketh not her own" and so "never faileth." [1] He who subjects himself to his neighbour in love can never be humiliated. I do beg you, then, at all events for the future, show the first and greatest fruit of the Spirit, Love; [2] away with the angry man's sullenness which you are showing me by your silence, and recover joy in your heart, peace with the brothers who are of one mind with you, and zeal and anxiety for the continued safety of the Churches of the Lord. If I were not to make as strenuous efforts on behalf of the Churches as the opponents of sound doctrine make to subvert and utterly destroy them, you may be quite sure that there is nothing to prevent the truth from being swept away and destroyed by its enemies, and my being involved in the condemnation, for not shewing all possible anxiety for the unity of the Churches, with all zeal and eagerness in mutual unanimity and godly agreement. I exhort you, then, drive out of your mind the idea that you need communion with no one else. To cut one's self off from connexion with the brethren is not the mark of one who is walking by love, nor yet the fulfilling of the commandment of Christ. At the same time I do wish you, with all your good intentions, to take into account that the calamities of the war which are now all round about us [3] may one day be at our own doors, and if we too, like all the rest, have our share of outrage, we shall not find any even to sympathise with us, because in the hour of our prosperity we refused to give our share of sympathy to the wronged.

LETTER LXVI.[4]

To Athanasius, bishop of Alexandria.

No one, I feel sure, is more distressed at the present condition, or, rather to speak more truly, ill condition of the Churches than your excellency; for you compare the

present with the past, and take into account how great a change has come about. You are well aware that if no check is put to the swift deterioration which we are witnessing, there will soon be nothing to prevent the complete transformation of the Churches. And if the decay of the Churches seems so pitiful to me, what must — so I have often in my lonely musings reflected — be the feelings of one who has known, by experience, the old tranquillity of the Churches of the Lord, and their one mind about the faith? But as your excellency feels most deeply this distress, it seems to me only becoming that your wisdom should be more strongly moved to interest itself in the Church's behalf. I for my part have long been aware, so far as my moderate intelligence has been able to judge of current events, that the one way of safety for the Churches of the East lies in their having the sympathy of the bishops of the West. For if only those bishops liked to show the same energy on behalf of the Christians sojourning in our part of the world [1] which they have shewn in the case of one or two of the men convicted of breaches of orthodoxy in the West, our common interests would probably reap no small benefit, our sovereigns treating the authority of the people with respect, and the laity in all quarters unhesitatingly following them. [2] But, to carry out these objects, who has more capacity than yourself, with your intelligence and prudence? Who is keener to see the needful course to be taken? Who has more practical experience in working a profitable policy? Who feels more deeply the troubles of the brethren? What through all the West is more honoured than your venerable gray hairs? [3] O most honoured father, leave behind you some memorial worthy of your life and character. By this one act crown your innumerable efforts on behalf of true religion. Despatch from the holy Church placed under your care men of ability in sound doctrine to the bishops in the West. Recount to them the troubles whereby we are beset. Suggest some mode of relief. Be a Samuel to the Churches. Share the grief of the beleaguered people. Offer prayers for peace. Ask favour from

---

[1] 1 Cor. xiii. 7 and 8.   [2] *cf.* Gal. v. 22.
[3] *i.e.* the attacks of Valens on the Church.
[4] Placed in 371. *cf. Letter* lxii.

[1] ὑπὲρ τῆς παροικίας τῶν καθ' ἡμᾶς μεοῶν. On the use of παροικία in this sense, *cf.* Bp. Lightfoot, *Ap. Fathers* I. ii. 5. So Apollon. in *Eus., H.E.* v. 18. ἡ ἰδία παροικία, of the Christians society. Thus the meaning passes to parochia and parish.
[2] "Them" is referred by the Ben. Ed. not to the sovereigns (τῶν κρατούντων they understand to mean Valens) but to the Western bishops.
[3] A various reading ("*Tres MSS. et secunda manu Medicæus*," Ben. Ed.) for πολιᾶς reads πολιτείας, "the life and conversation of your Holiness." — Athanasius was now about 75. His death is placed in 373.

the Lord, that He will send some memorial of peace to the Churches. I know how weak letters are to move men in matters of such importance; but you yourself no more need exhortation from others than the noblest athletes need the children's cheers. It is not as though I were instructing one in ignorance; I am only giving a new impulse to one whose energies are already roused. For the rest of the affairs of the East perhaps you may need the aid of more, and we must wait for the Westerns. But plainly the discipline of the Church of Antioch depends upon your reverence's being able to control some, to reduce others to silence, and to restore strength to the Church by concord.[1] No one knows better than you do, that, like all wise physicians, you ought to begin your treatment in the most vital parts, and what part is more vital to the Churches throughout the world than Antioch? Only let Antioch be restored to harmony, and nothing will stand in the way of her supplying, as a healthy head, soundness to all the body. Truly the diseases of that city, which has not only been cut asunder by heretics, but is torn in pieces by men who say that they are of one mind with one another, stand in need of your wisdom and evangelic sympathy. To unite the sundered parts again, and bring about the harmony of one body, belongs to Him alone Who by His ineffable power grants even to the dry bones to come back again to sinews and flesh. But the Lord always works His mighty works by means of them that are worthy of Him. Once again, in this case too, we trust that the ministry of matters so important may beseem your excellency, with the result that you will lay the tempest of the people, do away with the party superiorities, and subject all to one another in love, and give back to the Church her ancient strength.

LETTER LXVII.[2]

To Athanasius, bishop of Alexandria.

In my former letter it seemed to me sufficient to point out to your excellency, that all that portion of the people of the holy Church of Antioch who are sound in the faith, ought to be brought to concord and

unity. My object was to make it plain that the sections, now divided into several parts, ought to be united under the God-beloved bishop Meletius. Now the same beloved deacon, Dorotheus, has requested a more distinct statement on these subjects, and I am therefore constrained to point out that it is the prayer of the whole East, and the earnest desire of one who, like myself, is so wholly united to him, to see him in authority over the Churches of the Lord. He is a man of unimpeachable faith; his manner of life is incomparably excellent, he stands at the head, so to say, of the whole body of the Church, and all else are mere disjointed members. On every ground, then, it is necessary as well as advantageous, that the rest should be united with him, just as smaller streams with great ones. About the rest,[1] however, a certain amount of management is needed, befitting their position, and likely to pacify the people. This is in keeping with your own wisdom, and with your famous readiness and energy. It has however by no means escaped your intelligence, that this same course of procedure has already recommended itself to the Westerns who are in agreement with you, as I learn from the letters brought to me by the blessed Silvanus.

LETTER LXVIII.[2]

To Meletius, bishop of Antioch.

I wished to detain the reverend brother Dorotheus, the deacon, so long at my side, with the object of keeping him until the end of the negociations, and so by him acquainting your excellency with every detail. But day after day went by; the delay was becoming protracted; now, the moment that some plan, so far as is possible in my difficulties, has occurred to me concerning the course to be taken, I send him to approach your holiness, to make a personal report to you on all the circumstances, and show you my memorandum, to the end that, if what has occurred to me seems to you to be likely to be of service, your excellency may urge on its accomplishment. To be brief, the opinion has prevailed that it is best for this our brother Dorotheus to travel to Rome, to move some of the Italians to undertake a voyage by sea to visit us, that they may avoid all who would put difficulties in their way. My reason for this course is that I see that those, who are all powerful with the Emperor, are neither willing nor able to make any suggestion to him about the

[1] To end the schism caused by the refusal of the Eustathian or old Catholic party to recognise Meletius as bishop of the whole orthodox body. The churches of the West and of Egypt, on the whole, supported Paulinus, who had been ordained by Lucifer of Cagliari, bishop of the old Catholics. The Ben. Ed. supposes the word οἰκονομῆσαι, which I have rendered "control," to refer to Paulinus. The East supported Meletius, and if the οἰκονομία in Basil's mind does refer to Paulinus, the "management" meant may be management to get rid of him.
[2] Of the same year as the preceding.
[1] i.e. Paulinus and his adherents. [2] Of the same time.

exiled, but only count it so much to the good that they see no worse thing befalling the Churches. If, then, my plan seems good also to your prudence, you will be good enough both to indite letters and dictate memoranda as to the points on which he must enlarge, and as to whom he had better address himself. And so that your despatches may have weight and authority, you will add all those who share your sentiments, even though they are not on the spot. Here all is uncertain; Euippius[1] has arrived, but so far has made no sign. However, he and those who think with him from the Armenian Tetrapolis and Cilicia are threatening a tumultuous meeting.

LETTER LXIX.[2]

To Athanasius, bishop of Alexandria.

1. As time moves on, it continually confirms the opinion which I have long held of your holiness; or rather that opinion is strengthened by the daily course of events. Most men are indeed satisfied with observing, each one, what lies especially within his own province; not thus is it with you, but your anxiety for all the Churches is no less than that which you feel for the Church that has been especially entrusted to you by our common Lord; inasmuch as you leave no interval in speaking, exhorting, writing, and despatching emissaries, who from time to time give the best advice in each emergency as it arises. Now, from the sacred ranks of your clergy, you have sent forth the venerable brother Peter, whom I have welcomed with great joy. I have also approved of the good object of his journey, which he manifests in accordance with the commands of your excellency, in effecting reconciliation where he finds opposition, and bringing about union instead of division. With the object of offering some contribution to the action which is being taken in this matter, I have thought that I could not make a more fitting beginning than by having recourse to your excellency, as to the head and chief of all, and treating you as alike adviser and commander in the enterprise. I have therefore determined to send to your reverence our brother Dorotheus the deacon, of the Church under the right honourable bishop Meletius, being one who at once is an energetic supporter of the orthodox faith, and is earnestly desirous of seeing the peace of the Churches. The results, I hope, will be, that, following

your suggestions (which you are able to make with the less likelihood of failure, both from your age and your experience in affairs, and because you have a greater measure than all others of the aid of the Spirit), he may thus attempt the achievement of our objects. You will welcome him, I am sure, and will look upon him with friendly eyes. You will strengthen him by the help of your prayers; you will give him a letter as provision by the way; you will grant him, as companions, some of the good men and true that you have about you; so you will speed him on the road to what is before him. It has seemed to me to be desirable to send a letter to the bishop of Rome, begging him to examine our condition, and since there are difficulties in the way of representatives being sent from the West by a general synodical decree, to advise him to exercise his own personal authority in the matter by choosing suitable persons to sustain the labours of a journey, — suitable, too, by gentleness and firmness of character, to correct the unruly among us here; able to speak with proper reserve and appropriateness, and thoroughly well acquainted with all that has been effected after Ariminum to undo the violent measures adopted there. I should advise that, without any one knowing anything about it, they should travel hither, attracting as little attention as possible, by the sea, with the object of escaping the notice of the enemies of peace. 2. A point also that is insisted upon by some of those in these parts, very necessarily, as is plain even to myself, is that they[1] should drive away the heresy of Marcellus,[2] as grievous and injurious and opposed to the sound faith. For up to this time, in all the letters which they write, they are constant in thoroughly anathematizing the ill-famed Arius and in repudiating him from the Churches. But they attach no blame to Marcellus, who propounded a heresy diametrically opposite to that of Arius, and impiously attacked the very existence of the Only begotten Godhead, and erroneously understood the term "Word."[3] He grants indeed that the Only begotten was called "Word," on coming forth at need and in season, but states that He re-

---

1 i.e. the Romans; specially the proposed commissioners. It was a sore point with Basil that Marcellus, whom he regarded as a trimmer, should have been "received into communion by Julius and Athanasius, popes of Rome and Alexandria." Jer., De Vir. Illust. c. 86.
2 On the heretical opinions attributed to Marcellus of Ancyra, cf. Letters cxxv. and cclxiii.
3 Although he strongly espoused the Catholic cause of Nicæa later in attacking the errors of Asterius, he was supposed to teach that the Son had no real personality, but was merely an external manifestation of the Father.

---

1 cf. Letter ccli. 2 Of the same period as the preceding.

turned again to Him whence He had come forth, and had no existence before His coming forth, nor hypostasis[1] after His return. The books in my possession which contain his unrighteous writings exist as a proof of what I say. Nevertheless they nowhere openly condemned him, and are to this extent culpable that, being from the first in ignorance of the truth, they received him into the communion of the Church. The present state of affairs makes it specially necessary that attention should be called to him, so that those who seek for their opportunity, may be prevented from geting it, from the fact of sound men being united to your holiness, and all who are lame in the true faith may be openly known; that so we may know who are on our side, and may not struggle, as in a night battle, without being able to distinguish between friends and foes. Only I do beseech you that the deacon, whom I have mentioned, be despatched by the earliest possible packet, that at least some of the ends which we pray for may be accomplished during the ensuing year. One thing, however, even before I mention it, you quite understand and I am sure will give heed to, that, when they come, if God will, they must not let loose schisms among the Churches; and, even though they find some who have personal reasons for mutual differences, they must leave no means untried to unite all who are of the same way of thinking. For we are bound to regard the interests of peace as paramount, and that first of all attention be paid to the Church at Antioch, lest the sound portion of it grow diseased through division on personal grounds. But you will yourself give more complete attention to all these matters, so soon as, by the blessing of God, you find every one entrusting to you the responsibility of securing the peace of the Church.

LETTER LXX.[2]

Without address.[3]

To renew laws of ancient love, and once again to restore to vigorous life that heavenly and saving gift of Christ which in course of time has withered away, the peace, I mean, of the Fathers, is a labour necessary indeed and profitable to me, but pleasant too, as I am sure it will seem to your Christ-loving disposition. For what could be more delightful than to behold all,

who are separated by distances so vast, bound together by the union effected by love into one harmony of members in Christ's body? Nearly all the East (I include under this name all the regions from Illyricum to Egypt) is being agitated, right honourable father, by a terrible storm and tempest. The old heresy, sown by Arius the enemy of the truth, has now boldly and unblushingly reappeared. Like some sour root, it is producing its deadly fruit and is prevailing. The reason of this is, that in every district the champions of right doctrine have been exiled from their Churches by calumny and outrage, and the control of affairs has been handed over to men who are leading captive the souls of the simpler brethren. I have looked upon the visit of your mercifulness as the only possible solution of our difficulties. Ever in the past I have been consoled by your extraordinary affection; and for a short time my heart was cheered by the gratifying report that we shall be visited by you. But, as I was disappointed, I have been constrained to beseech you by letter to be moved to help us, and to send some of those, who are like minded with us, either to conciliate the dissentient and bring back the Churches of God into friendly union, or at all events to make you see more plainly who are responsible for the unsettled state in which we are, that it may be obvious to you for the future with whom it befits you to be in communion. In this I am by no means making any novel request, but am only asking what has been customary in the case of men who, before our own day, were blessed and dear to God, and conspicuously in your own case. For I well remember learning from the answers made by our fathers when asked, and from documents still preserved among us, that the illustrious and blessed bishop Dionysius, conspicuous in your see as well for soundness of faith as for all other virtues, visited by letter my Church of Cæsarea, and by letter exhorted our fathers, and sent men to ransom our brethren from captivity.[1] But now our condition is yet more painful and gloomy and needs more careful treatment. We are lamenting no mere overthrow of earthly buildings, but the capture of Churches; what we see

---

[1] ὑφεστάναι.　　[2] Of the same period as the preceding.
[3] "This letter is obviously addressed to Pope Damasus." — Be Ed. n.

[1] The Ben. Ed. points out that what is related by Basil, of the kindness of the bishops of Rome to other churches, is confirmed by the evidence both of Dionysius, bishop of Corinth (*cf.* Eusebius, *Hist. Ecc.* iv. 23), of Dionysius of Alexandria (Dionysius to Sixtus II. *Apud Euseb.*, *Ecc. Hist.* vii. 5), and of Eusebius himself who in his history speaks of this practice having been continued down to the persecution in his own day. The troubles referred to by Basil took place in the time of Gallienus, when the Scythians ravaged Cappadocia and the neighbouring countries. (*cf.* Sozomen, ii. 6.) Dionysius succeeded Sixtus II. at Rome in 259.

before us is no mere bodily slavery, but a carrying away of souls into captivity, perpetrated day by day by the champions of heresy. Should you not, even now, be moved to succour us, ere long all will have fallen under the dominion of the heresy, and you will find none left to whom you may hold out your hand.

LETTER LXXI.[1]

Basil to Gregory.[2]

1. I HAVE received the letter of your holiness, by the most reverend brother Helenius, and what you have intimated he has told me in plain terms. How I felt on hearing it, you cannot doubt at all. However, since I have determined that my affection for you shall outweigh my pain, whatever it is, I have accepted it as I ought to do, and I pray the holy God, that my remaining days or hours may be as carefully conducted in their disposition towards you as they have been in past time, during which, my conscience tells me, I have been wanting to you in nothing small or great. [But that the man who boasts that he is now just beginning to take a look at the life of Christians, and thinks he will get some credit by having something to do with me, should invent what he has not heard, and narrate what he has never experienced, is not at all surprising. What is surprising and extraordinary is that he has got my best friends among the brethren at Nazianzus to listen to him; and not only to listen to him, but as it seems, to take in what he says. On most grounds it might be surprising that the slanderer is of such a character, and that I am the victim, but these troublous times have taught us to bear everything with patience. Slights greater than this have, for my sins, long been things of common occurrence with me. I have never yet given this man's brethren any evidence of my sentiments[3] about God, and I have no answer to make now. Men who are not convinced by long experience are not likely to be convinced by a short letter. If the former is enough let the charges of the slanderers be counted as idle tales. But if I give license to unbridled mouths, and uninstructed hearts,

to talk about whom they will, all the while keeping my ears ready to listen, I shall not be alone in hearing what is said by other people; they will have to hear what I have to say.]

2. I know what has led to all this, and have urged every topic to hinder it; but now I am sick of the subject, and will say no more about it, I mean our little intercourse. For had we kept our old promise to each other, and had due regard to the claims which the Churches have on us, we should have been the greater part of the year together; and then there would have been no opening for these calumniators. Pray have nothing to say to them; let me persuade you to come here and assist me in my labours, particularly in my contest with the individual who is now assailing me. Your very appearance will have the effect of stopping him; directly you show these disturbers of our home that you will, by God's blessing, place yourself at the head of our party, you will break up their cabal, and you will shut every unjust mouth that speaketh unrighteousness against God. And thus facts will show who are your followers in good, and who are the halters and cowardly betrayers of the word of truth. If, however, the Church be betrayed, why then I shall care little to set men right about myself, by means of words, who account of me as men would naturally account who have not yet learned to measure themselves. Perhaps, in a short time, by God's grace, I shall be able to refute their slanders by very deed, for it seems likely that I shall have soon to suffer somewhat for the truth's sake more than usual; the best I can expect is banishment, or, if this hope fails, after all Christ's judgment-seat is not far distant. [If then you ask for a meeting for the Churches' sake, I am ready to betake myself whithersoever you invite me. But if it is only a question of refuting these slanders, I really have no time to reply to them.]

LETTER LXXII.[1]

To Hesychius.[2]

I KNOW your affection for me, and your zeal for all that is good. I am exceedingly anxious to pacify my very dear son Callisthenes, and I thought that if I could associate you with me in this I might more easily achieve my object. Callisthenes is very much annoyed at the conduct of Eustochius, and he has

---

1 Placed in the same period.
2 When Gregory, on the elevation of Basil to the Episcopate, was at last induced to visit his old friend, he declined the dignities which Basil pressed upon him (τήνδε τῆς καθέδρας τιμήν, *i.e.* the position of chief presbyter or coadjutor bishop, *Orat.* xliii. 30), and made no long stay. Some Nazianzene scandal-mongers had charged Basil with heterodoxy. Gregory asked him for explanations, and Basil, somewhat wounded, rejoins that no explanations are needed. The translation in the text, with the exception of the passages in brackets, is that of Newman. *cf. Proleg.* and reff. to Greg. Naz.
3 προαιρέσεως, as in three MSS.

1 Placed at about the same period as the preceding.
2 *cf. Letter* lxiv. *Letters* lxxii. and lxxiii. illustrate the efforts made by Basil to mitigate the troubles caused by slavery, and to regulate domestic as well as ecclesiastical matters.

very good ground for being so. He charges the household of Eustochius with impudence and violence against himself. I am begging him to be propitiated, satisfied with the fright which he has given the impudent fellows and their master, and to forgive, and end the quarrel. Thus two results will follow; he will win the respect of men, and praise with God, if only he will combine forbearance with threats. If you have any friendship and intimacy with him, pray ask this favour of him, and, if you know any in the town likely to be able to move him, get them to act with you, and tell them that it will be specially gratifying to me. Send back the deacon so soon as his commission is performed. After men have fled for refuge to me, I should be ashamed not to be able to be of any use to them.

LETTER LXXIII.[1]

To Callisthenes.

1. WHEN I had read your letter I thanked God; first, that I been greeted by a man desirous of doing me honour, for truly I highly estimate any intercourse with persons of high merit; secondly, with pleasure at the thought of being remembered. For a letter is a sign of remembrance; and when I had received yours and learnt its contents I was astonished to find how, as all were agreed, it paid me the respect due to a father from a son. That a man in the heat of anger and indignation, eager to punish those who had annoyed him, should drop more than half his vehemence and give me authority to decide the matter, caused me to feel such joy as I might over a son in the spirit. In return, what remains for me but to pray for all blessings for you? May you be a delight to your friends, a terror to your foes, an object of respect to all, to the end that any who fall short in their duty to you may, when they learn how gentle you are, only blame themselves for having wronged one of such a character as yourself!

2. I should be very glad to know the object which your goodness has in view, in ordering the servants to be conveyed to the spot where they were guilty of their disorderly conduct. If you come yourself, and exact in person the punishment due for the offence, the slaves shall be there. What other course is possible if you have made up your mind? Only that I do not know what further favour I shall have received, if I shall have failed to get the boys off their punishment.

But if business detain you on the way, who is to receive the fellows there? Who is to punish them in your stead? But if you have made up your mind to meet them yourself, and this is quite determined on, tell them to halt at Sasima, and there show the extent of your gentleness and magnanimity. After having your assailants in your own power, and so showing them that your dignity is not to be lightly esteemed, let them go scot free, as I urged you in my former letter. So you will confer a favour on me, and will receive the requital of your good deed from God.

3. I speak in this way, not because the business ought so to be ended, but as a concession to your agitated feelings, and in fear lest somewhat of your wrath may remain still raw. When a man's eyes are inflamed the softest application seems painful, and I am afraid lest what I say may rather irritate than calm you. What would really be most becoming, bringing great credit to you, and no little cause of honour to me with my friends and contemporaries, would be for you to leave the punishment to me. And although you have sworn to deliver them to execution as the law enjoins, my rebuke is still of no less value as a punishment, nor is the divine law of less account than the laws current in the world. But it will be possible for them, by being punished here by our laws, wherein too lies your own hope of salvation, both to release you from your oath and to undergo a penalty commensurate with their faults.

But once more I am making my letter too long. In the very earnest desire to persuade you I cannot bear to leave unsaid any of the pleas which occur to me, and I am much afraid lest my entreaty should prove ineffectual from my failing to say all that may convey my meaning. Now, true and honoured son of the Church, confirm the hopes which I have of you; prove true all the testimony unanimously given to your placability and gentleness. Give orders to the soldier to leave me without delay; he is now as tiresome and rude as he can well be; he evidently prefers giving no cause of annoyance to you to making all of us here his close friends.

LETTER LXXIV.[1]

To Martinianus.[2]

1. How high do you suppose one to prize the pleasure of our meeting one another once

again? How delightful to spend longer time with you so as to enjoy all your good qualities! If powerful proof is given of culture in seeing many men's cities and knowing many men's ways,[1] such I am sure is quickly given in your society. For what is the difference between seeing many men singly or one who has gained experience of all together? I should say that there is an immense superiority in that which gives us the knowledge of good and beautiful things without trouble, and puts within our reach instruction in virtue, pure from all admixture of evil. Is there question of noble deed ; of words worth handing down ; of institutions of men of superhuman excellence? All are treasured in the store house of your mind. Not then, would I pray, that I might listen to you, like Alcinous to Ulysses, only for a year, but throughout all my life ; and to this end I would pray that my life might be long, even though my state were no easy one. Why, then, am I now writing when I ought to be coming to see you? Because my country in her troubles calls me irresistibly to her side. You know, my friend, how she suffers. She is torn in pieces like Pentheus by veritable Mænads, dæmons. They are dividing her, and dividing her again, like bad surgeons who, in their ignorance, make wounds worse. Suffering as she is from this dissection, it remains for me to tend her like a sick patient. So the Cæsareans have urgently appealed to me by letter, and I must go, not as though I could be of any help, but to avoid any blame of neglect. You know how ready men in difficulties are to hope ; and ready too, I ween, to find fault, always charging their troubles on what has been left undone.

2. Yet for this very reason I ought to have come to see you, and to have told you my mind, or rather to implore you to bethink you of some strong measure worthy of your wisdom ; not to turn aside from my country falling on her knees, but to betake yourself to the Court, and, with the boldness which is all your own, not to let them suppose that they own two provinces instead of one. They have not imported the second from some other part of the world, but have acted somewhat in the same way in which some owner of horse or ox might act, who should cut it in two, and then think that he had two instead of one, instead of failing to make two and destroying the one he had. Tell the Emperor and his ministers that they are not after this fashion increasing the empire, for power lies not in number but in condition. I am sure that now men are neglecting the course of events, some, possibly, from ignorance of the truth, some from their being unwilling to say anything offensive, some because it does not immediately concern them. The course likely to be most beneficial, and worthy of your high principles, would be for you, if possible, to approach the Emperor in person. If this is difficult both on account of the season of the year and of your age, of which, as you say, inactivity is the foster brother, at all events you need have no difficulty in writing. If you thus give our country the aid of a letter, you will first of all have the satisfaction of knowing that you have left nothing undone that was in your power, and further, by showing sympathy, if only in appearance, you will give the patient much comfort. Would only that it were possible for you to come yourself among us and actually see our deplorable condition! Thus, perhaps, stirred by the plain evidence before you, you might have spoken in terms worthy alike of your own magnanimity and of the affliction of Cæsarea. But do not withhold belief from what I am telling you. Verily we want some Simonides, or other like poet, to lament our troubles from actual experience. But why name Simonides? I should rather mention Æschylus, or any other who has set forth a great calamity in words like his, and uttered lamentation with a mighty voice.

3. Now we have no more meetings, no more debates, no more gatherings of wise men in the Forum, nothing more of all that made our city famous. In our Forum nowadays it would be stranger for a learned or eloquent man to put in an appearance, than it would for men, shewing a brand of iniquity or unclean hands, to have presented themselves in Athens of old. Instead of them we have the imported boorishness of Massagetæ and Scythians. And only one noise is heard of drivers of bargains, and losers of bargains, and of fellows under the lash. On either hand the porticoes resound with doleful echoes, as though they were uttering a natural and proper sound in groaning at what is going on. Our distress prevents our paying any attention to locked gymnasia and nights when no torch is lighted. There is no small danger lest, our magistrates being removed, everything crash down together as with fallen props. What words can adequately describe our calamities? Some have

---

of visitation, or to consecrate his brother bishop of Nyssa (Maran, *Vit. Bas. Cap.* xix.), and returned to Cæsarea at the appeal of his people there.

[1] *cf.* the opening of the *Odyssey*, and the imitation of Horace, *De Arte Poet.* 142:

" *Qui mores hominum multorum vidit et urbes.*"

fled into exile, a considerable portion of our senate, and that not the least valuable, prefering perpetual banishment to Podandus.[1] When I mention Podandus, suppose me to mean the Spartan Ceadas[2] or any natural pit that you may have seen, spots breathing a noxious vapour, to which some have involuntarily given the name Charonian. Picture to yourself that the evils of Podandus are a match for such a place. So, of three parts, some have left their homes and are in exile, wives and hearth and all; some are being led away like captives, the majority of the best men in the city, a piteous spectacle to their friends, fulfilling their enemies' prayers; if, that is, any one has ever been found to call down so dire a curse upon our heads. A third division yet remains: these, unable to endure abandonment by their old companions, and at the same time unable to provide for themselves, have to hate their very lives.

This is what I implore you to make known everywhere with an eloquence all your own, and that righteous boldness of speech which your manner of life gives you. One thing distinctly state; that, unless the authorities soon change their counsels, they will find none left on whom to exercise their clemency. You will either prove some help to the state, or at least you will have done as Solon did, who, when he was unable to defend his abandoned fellow citizens on the capture of the Acropolis, put on his armour, and sat down before the gates, thus making it plain by this guise that he was no party to what was going on.[3] Of one thing I am assured, even though at the present moment there may be some who do not approve of your advice, the day is not far distant when they will give you the greatest credit for benevolence and sagacity, because they see events corresponding with your prediction.

LETTER LXXV.[4]

To Aburgius.[5]

You have many qualities which raise you above the common run of men, but nothing is more distinctly characteristic of you than your zeal for your country. Thus you, who have risen to such a height as to become illustrious throughout all the world, pay a righteous recompense to the land that gave you birth. Yet she, your mother city, who bore you and nursed you, has fallen into the incredible condition of ancient story; and no one visiting Cæsarea, not even those most familiar with her, would recognise her as she is; to such complete abandonment has she been suddenly transformed, many of her magistrates having been previously removed, and now nearly all of them transferred to Podandus. The remainder, torn from these like mutilated extremities, have themselves fallen into complete despair, and have caused such a general weight of despondency, that the population of the city is now but scanty; the place looks like a desert, a piteous spectacle to all who love it, and a cause for delight and encouragement to all who have long been plotting for our fall. Who then will reach out a hand to help us? Who will drop a tear of pity over our faith? You have sympathised with a stranger city in like distress; will not your kindly excellency feel for her who gave you birth? If you have any influence, show it in our present need. Certainly you have great help from God, Who has never abandoned you, and has given you many proofs of His kindness. Only be willing to exert yourself in our behalf, and use all the influence you have for the succour of your fellow citizens.

LETTER LXXVI.[1]

To Sophronius the Master.[2]

THE greatness of the calamities, which have befallen our native city, did seem likely to compel me to travel in person to the court, and there to relate, both to your excellency and to all those who are most influential in affairs, the dejected state in which Cæsarea is lying. But I am kept here alike by ill-health and by the care of the Churches. In the meantime, therefore, I hasten to tell your lordship our troubles by letter, and to acquaint you that never ship, drowned in sea by furious winds, so suddenly disappeared, never city shattered by earthquake or overwhelmed by flood, so swiftly vanished out of sight, as our city, engulfed by this new constitution, has gone utterly to ruin. Our misfortunes have passed into a tale. Our institutions are a thing of the past; and all

---

[1] Now Podando, in Southern Cappadocia, made by Valens the chief town of the new division of the province.
[2] So the Spartans named the pit into which condemned criminals were thrown. Pausanias, Book IV. 18, 4. Thucyd., i. 134. Strabo, viii. 367.
[3] i.e. on the seizure of the Acropolis by Pisistratus, Solon, resisting the instances of his friends that he should flee, returned them for answer, when they asked him on what he relied for protection, "On my old age." Plutarch, Solon 30. The senate being of the faction of Pisistratus, said that he was mad. Solon replied:

Δείξει δὴ μανίην μὲν ἐμὴν Βαιὸς χρόνος ἀστοῖς,
Δείξει ἀληθείης ἐς μέσον ἐρχομένης. Diog. Lært. 1-49.

[4] About the same date as the preceding.
[5] cf. Letters xxxiii. cxlvii. clxxviii. cxcvi. and cciv.

[1] Of the same date as the preceding.
[2] i.e. magister officiorum. cf. Letters xxxii., xcvi., clxxvii., clxxx., cxciii., cclxxii.

our men of high civil rank, in despair at what has happened to our magistrates, have left their homes in the city and are wandering about the country. There is a break therefore in the necessary conduct of affairs, and the city, which ere now gloried both in men of learning and in others who abound in opulent towns, has become a most unseemly spectacle. One only consolation have we left in our troubles, and that is to groan over our misfortunes to your excellency and to implore you, if you can, to reach out the helping hand to Cæsarea who falls on her knees before you. How indeed you may be able to aid us I am not myself able to explain; but I am sure that to you, with all your intelligence, it will be easy to discover the means, and not difficult, through the power given you by God, to use them when they are found.

LETTER LXXVII.[1]

Without inscription: about Therasius.[2]

ONE good thing we have certainly gained from the government of the great Therasius, and that is that you have frequently paid us a visit. Now, alas! we have lost our governor, and we are deprived of this good thing too. But since the boons once given us by God remain immovable, and, although we are parted in body, abide fixed by memory in the souls of each of us, let us constantly write, and communicate our needs to one another. And this we may well do at the present moment, when the storm for a brief space has cried a truce. I trust that you will not part from the admirable Therasius, for I think that it is very becoming to share his great anxieties, and I am delighted at the opportunity given you both of seeing your friends and of being seen by them.[3] I have much to say about many things, but I put it off till we meet, for it is, I think, hardly safe to entrust matters of such importance to letters.

LETTER LXXVIII.[4]

Without inscription, on behalf of Elpidius.

I HAVE not failed to observe the interest you have shown in our venerable friend Elpidius; and how with your usual intelligence you have given the prefect an opportunity of showing his kindness. What I am

now writing to ask you is to make this favour complete and suggest to the prefect that he should by a particular order set over our city the man who is full of all possible care for the public interests. You will therefore have many admirable reasons to urge upon the prefect for his ordering Elpidius to remain at Cæsarea. There is at all events no need for you to be taught by me, since you yourself know only too well, what is the position of affairs, and how capable Elpidius is in administration.

LETTER LXXIX.[1]

To Eustathius bishop of Sebastia.[2]

EVEN before receiving your letter I knew what trouble you are ready to undergo for every one, and specially for my humble self because I am exposed in this struggle. So when I received your letter from the reverend Eleusinius, and saw him actually before my face, I praised God for bestowing on me such a champion and comrade, in my struggles on behalf of true religion by the aid of the Spirit. Be it known to your exalted reverence that I have hitherto sustained some attacks from high magistrates, and these no light ones; while both the prefect and the high chamberlain pleaded with sympathy for my opponents. But, so far, I have sustained every assault unmoved, by that mercy of God which supplies to me the aid of the Spirit, and strengthens my weakness through Him.

LETTER LXXX.[3]

To Athanasius, bishop of Alexandria.

THE worse the diseases of the Churches grow, the more do we all turn to your excellency, in the belief that your championship is the one consolation left to us in our troubles. By the power of your prayers, and your knowledge of what is the best course to suggest in the emergency, you are believed to be able to save us from this terrible tempest by all alike who know your excellency even to a small extent, whether by hearsay or by personal experience. Wherefore, cease not, I implore, to pray for our souls and to rouse us by your letters. Did you but know of what service these are

---

[1] Of the same date as the preceding.
[2] Perhaps to Elpidius. Therasius is probably the governor referred to in *Letter* xcvi. to Sophronius.
[3] The text is here corrupt. The Ben. Ed. say "*corruptissimus.*" [4] Of the same date.

[1] Also of the year 371.
[2] *cf. Letter* cxix. Sebaste is Siwas on the Halys. On Eustathius to Basil a type at once of the unwashable Ethiopian for persistent heresy (*Letter* cxxx. 1) and of the wind-driven cloud for shiftiness and time-serving, (*Letter* ccxliv. 9.) Vide proleg.
[3] Placed in 371 or early in 372.

to us you would never have lost a single opportunity of writing. Could I only, by the aid of your prayers, be deemed worthy of seeing you, and of enjoying your good qualities, and of adding to the story of my life a meeting with your truly great and apostolical soul, then I should indeed believe that I had received from God's mercy a consolation equivalent to all the afflictions of my life.

LETTER LXXXI.[1]

To Bishop Innocent.[2]

I was delighted to receive the letter your affection sent me; but I am equally grieved at your having laid on me the load of a responsibility which is more than I can carry. How can I, so far removed as I am, undertake so great a charge? As long as the Church possesses you, it rests as it were on its proper buttress. Should the Lord be pleased to make some dispensation in the matter of your life, whom, from among us here can I send to take the charge of the brethren, who will be in like esteem with yourself? That is a very wise and proper wish which you express in your letter, that while you are yet alive you may see the successor destined after you to guide the chosen flock of the Lord (like the blessed Moses, who both wished and saw). As the place is great and famous, and your work has great and wide renown, and the times are difficult, needing no insignificant guide on account of the continuous storms and tempests which are attacking the Church, I have not thought it safe for my own soul to treat the matter perfunctorily, specially when I bear in mind the terms in which you write. For you s.y that, accusing me of disregard of the Churches, you mean to withstand me before the Lord. Not then to be at issue with you, but rather to have you on my side in my defence which I make in the presence of Christ I have, after looking round in the assembly of the presbyters of the city, chosen the very honourable vessel, the offspring[3] of the blessed Hermogenes, who wrote the great and invincible creed in the great Synod.[4] He is a presbyter of the Church, of many

years standing, of steadfast character, skilled in canons, accurate in the faith, who has lived up to this time in continence and ascetic discipline, although the severity of his austere life has now subdued the flesh; a man of poverty, with no resources in this world, so that he is not even provided with bare bread, but by the labour of his hands gets a living with the brethren who dwell with him. It is my intention to send him. If, then, this is the kind of man you want, and not some younger man fit only to be sent and to discharge the common duties of this world, be so good as to write to me at the first opportunity, that I may send you this man, who is elect of God, adapted for the present work, respected by all who meet him, and who instructs with meekness all who differ from him. I might have sent him at once, but since you yourself had anticipated me in asking for a man of honourable character, and beloved by myself, but far inferior to the one whom I have indicated, I wished my mind in the matter to be made known to you. If therefore this is the kind of man you want, either send one of the brethren to fetch him at the time of the fast, or, if you have no one able to undertake the journey to me, let me know by letter.

LETTER LXXXII.[1]

To Athanasius, bishop of Alexandria.

When I turn my gaze upon the world, and perceive the difficulties by which every effort after good is obstructed, like those of a man walking in fetters, I am brought to despair of myself. But then I direct my gaze in the direction of your reverence; I remember that our Lord has appointed you to be physician of the diseases in the Churches; and I recover my spirits, and rise from the depression of despair to the hope of better things. As your wisdom well knows, the whole Church is undone. And you see everything in all directions in your mind's eye like a man looking from some tall watch tower,[2] as when at sea many ships sailing together are all dashed one against the other by the violence of the waves, and shipwreck arises in some cases from the sea being furiously agitated from without, in others from the disorder of the sailors hindering and crowding one another. It is enough to present this picture, and to say

---

[1] Placed in 372.
[2] cf. Letter 1. The see of this Innocent is unknown. cf. *Letter* lxxxi. and note. To the title of this letter one manuscript adds "of Rome," as the Ben. Ed. note "*prorsus absurde.*"
[3] ἔκγονος. *i.e.* the spiritual offspring of Hermogenes, by whom he had been ordained.
[4] Bishop of Cæsarea, in which see he preceded Dianius. cf. *Letters* ccxliv. 9 and cclxiii. 3. "The great Synod" is Nicæa. Baronius on the year 325 remarks that Basil's memory must have failed him, inasmuch as not Hermogenes but Leontius was present at Nicæa as Bishop of Cæsarea. But Hermogenes may have been present in lower orders. cf. Stanley, *East. Ch.* pp. 105, 140.

[1] Placed at the end of 371 or the beginning of 372.
[2] The fitness of this figure in a letter to the bishop of Alexandria will not escape notice. At the eastern extremity of the island of Pharos still stood the marble lighthouse erected more than 600 years before by Ptolemy II., and not destroyed till after the thirteenth century.

no more.[1] Your wisdom requires nothing farther, and the present state of affairs does not allow me freedom of speech. What capable pilot can be found in such a storm? Who is worthy to rouse the Lord to rebuke the wind and the sea? Who but he who from his boyhood[2] fought a good fight on behalf of true religion? Since now truly all that is sound among us is moving in the direction of fellowship and unity with those who are of the same opinion, we have come confidently to implore you to send us a single letter, advising us what is to be done. In this way they wish that they may have a beginning of communication which may promote unity. They may, peradventure, be suspected by you, when you remember the past, and therefore, most God-beloved Father, do as follows; send me the letters to the bishops, either by the hand of some one in whom you place trust in Alexandria, or by the hand of our brother Dorotheus the deacon: when I have received these letters I will not deliver them till I have got the bishops' answers; if not, let me " bear the blame for ever." [3] Truly this ought not to have struck more awe into him who first uttered it to his father, than into me who now say it to my spiritual father. If however you altogether renounce this hope, at least free me from all blame in acting as I have, for I have undertaken this message and mediation in all sincerity and simplicity, from desire for peace and the mutual intercourse of all who think alike about the Lord.

LETTER LXXXIII.[4]

To a Magistrate.[5]

I HAVE had only a short acquaintance and intercourse with your lordship, but I have no small or contemptible knowledge of you from the reports through which I am brought into communication with many men of position and importance. You yourself are better able to say whether I, by report, am of any account with you. At all events your reputation with me is such as I have said. But since God has called you to an occupation which gives you opportunity of showing kindness, and in the exercise of which it

lies in your power to bring about the restoration of my own city, now level with the ground, it is, I think, only my duty to remind your excellency that in the hope of the requital God will give, you should show yourself of such a character as to win a memory that cannot die, and be made an inheritor of everlasting rest, in consequence of your making the afflictions of the distressed less hard to bear. I have a property at Chamanene, and I beg you to look after its interests as though they were your own. And pray do not be surprised at my calling my friend's property my own, for among other virtues I have been taught that of friendship, and I remember the author of the wise saying a friend is another self.[1] I therefore commend to your excellency this property belonging to my friend, as though it were my own. I beg you to consider the misfortunes of the house, and both to grant them consolation for the past, and for the future to make the place more comfortable for them; for it is now left and abandoned on account of the weight of the rates imposed upon it. I will do my best to meet your excellency and converse with you on points of detail.

LETTER LXXXIV.[2]

To the President.[3]

1. You will hardly believe what I am about to write, but it must be written for truth's sake. I have been very anxious to communicate as often as possible with your excellency, but when I got this opportunity of writing a letter I did not at once seize the lucky chance. I hesitated and hung back. What is astonishing is, that when I got what I had been praying for, I did not take it. The reason of this is that I am really ashamed to write to you every time, not out of pure friendship, but with the object of getting something. But then I bethought me (and when you consider it, I do hope you will not think that I communicate with you more for the sake of a bargain than of friendship) that there must be a difference between the way in which one approaches a magistrate and a private man. We do not accost a physician as we do any mere nobody; nor a magistrate as we do a private individual. We try to get some advantage from the skill of the one and the position of the other.

---

[1] On Basil's use of this nautical metaphor, cf. De Spiritu Sancto, chap. xxx. It is of course a literary commonplace, but Basil's associations all lay inland.

[2] The story of " the boy bishop " will be remembered, whose serious game of baptism attracted the notice of Alexander and led to the education of Athanasius in the Episcopal palace. Soc., Ecc. Hist. i. 15. Rufinus i. 14. cf. Keble, Lyra Innocentium, " Enacting holy rites."

[3] Gen. xliii. 9.   [4] Placed in 372.

[5] Censitor, i.e. the magistrate responsible for rating and taxation in the provinces.

[1] cf. Aristotle Eth. Nic. viii. 12, 3; and Cic. Læl. xxi. So, amicus est tanquam alter idem.

[2] Placed in the year 372.

[3] Probably Elias. cf. Letters xciv. and xcvi. The orphan grandson of the aged man in whose behalf Basil writes had been placed on the Senatorial roll, and the old man in consequence was compelled to serve again.

Walk in the sun, and your shadow will follow you, whether you will or not. Just so intercourse with the great is followed by an inevitable gain, the succour of the distressed. The first object of my letter is fulfilled in my being able to greet your excellency. Really, if I had no other cause for writing at all, this must be regarded as an excellent topic. Be greeted then, my dear Sir; may you be preserved by all the world while you fill office after office, and succour now some now others by your authority. Such greeting I am wont to make; such greeting is only due to you from all who have had the least experience of your goodness in your administration.

2. Now, after this prayer, hear my supplication on behalf of the poor old man whom the imperial order had exempted from serving in any public capacity; though really I might say that old age anticipated the Emperor in giving him his discharge. You have yourself satisfied the boon conferred on him by the higher authority, at once from respect to natural infirmity, and, I think, from regard to the public interest, lest any harm should come to the state from a man growing imbecile through age. But how, my dear Sir, have you unwittingly dragged him into public life, by ordering his grandson, a child not yet four years old, to be on the roll of the senate? You have done the very same thing as to drag the old man, through his descendant, again into public business. But now, I do implore you, have mercy on both ages, and free both on the ground of what in each case is pitiable. The one never saw father or mother, never knew them, but from his very cradle was deprived of both, and has entered into life by the help of strangers: the other has been preserved so long as to have suffered every kind of calamity. He saw a son's untimely death; he saw a house without successors; now, unless you devise some remedy commensurate with your kindness, he will see the very consolation of his bereavement made an occasion of innumerable troubles, for, I suppose, the little lad will never act as senator, collect tribute, or pay troops; but once again the old man's white hairs must be shamed. Concede a favour in accordance with the law and agreeable to nature; order the boy to be allowed to wait till he come to man's estate, and the old man to await death quietly on his bed. Let others, if they will, urge the pretext of press of business and inevitable necessity. But, even if you are under a press of business, it would not be like you to despise the distressed, to slight

the law, or to refuse to yield to the prayers of your friends.

LETTER LXXXV.[1]

That the oath ought not to be taken.[2]

It is my invariable custom to protest at every synod and to urge privately in conversation, that oaths about the taxes ought not to be imposed on husbandmen by the collectors. It remains for me to bear witness, on the same matters, in writing, before God and men, that it behoves you to cease from inflicting death upon men's souls, and to devise some other means of exaction, while you let men keep their souls unwounded. I write thus to you, not as though you needed any spoken exhortation (for you have your own immediate inducements to fear the Lord), but that all your dependents may learn from you not to provoke the Holy One, nor let a forbidden sin become a matter of indifference, through faulty familiarity. No possible good can be done them by oaths, with a view to their paying what is exacted from them, and they suffer an undeniable wrong to the soul. For when men become practised in perjury, they no longer put any pressure on themselves to pay, but they think that they have discovered in the oath a means of trickery and an opportunity for delay. If, then, the Lord brings a sharp retribution on the perjured, when the debtors are destroyed by punishment there will be none to answer when summoned. If on the other hand the Lord endures with long suffering, then, as I said before, those who have tried the patience of the Lord despise His goodness. Let them not break the law in vain; let them not whet the wrath of God against them. I have said what I ought. The disobedient will see.

LETTER LXXXVI.[3]

To the Governor.[4]

I know that a first and foremost object of your excellency is in every way to support the right; and after that to benefit your friends, and to exert yourself in behalf of those who have fled to your lordship's protection. Both these pleas are combined in the matter before us. The cause is right for

[1] Placed in the year 372.
[2] The distress of the Cappadocians under the load of taxes is described in *Letter* lxxiv. An objectionable custom arose, or was extended, of putting the country people on oath as to their inability to pay.
[3] Of the same date as the preceding.
[4] Probably to Elias. Three manuscripts add " of recommendation on behalf of presbyters about the carrying off of corn."

which we are pleading; it is dear to me who am numbered among your friends; it is due to those who are invoking the aid of your constancy in their sufferings. The corn, which was all my very dear brother Dorotheus had for the necessaries of life, has been carried off by some of the authorities at Berisi, entrusted with the management of affairs, driven to this violence of their own accord or by others' instigation. Either way it is an indictable offence. For how does the man whose wickedness is his own do less wrong than he who is the mere minister of other men's wickedness? To the sufferers the loss is the same. I implore you, therefore, that Dorotheus may have his corn returned by the men by whom he has been robbed, and that they may not be allowed to lay the guilt of their outrage on other men's shoulders. If you grant me my request I shall reckon the value of the boon conferred by your excellency in proportion to the necessity of providing one's self with food.

LETTER LXXXVII.[1]

Without address on the same subject.[2]

I AM astonished that, with you to appeal to, so grave an offence should have been committed against the presbyter as that he should have been deprived of his only means of livelihood. The most serious part of the business is that the perpetrators transfer the guilt of their proceedings to you; while all the while it was your duty not only not to suffer such deeds to be done, but to use all your authority to prevent them in the case of any one, but specially in the case of presbyters, and such presbyters as are in agreement with me, and are walking in the same way of true religion. If then you have any care to give me gratification, see that these matters are set right without delay. For, God helping you, you are able to do this, and greater things than this to whom you will. I have written to the governor of my own country,[3] that, if they refuse to do what is right of their own accord, they may be compelled to do so on pressure from the courts.

LETTER LXXXVIII.[4]

Without address on the subject of the exaction of taxes.

YOUR excellency knows better than any one else the difficulty of getting together the gold furnished by contribution.[1] We have no better witness to our poverty than yourself, for with your great kindness you have felt for us, and, up to the present time, so far as has lain within your power, have borne with us, never departing from your own natural forbearance from any alarm caused by superior authority. Now of the whole sum there is still something wanting, and that must be got in from the contribution which we have recommended to all the town. What I ask is, that you will grant us a little delay, that a reminder may be sent to dwellers in the country, and most of our magistrates are in the country. If it is possible for it to be sent in short of as many pounds as those in which we are still behindhand, I should be glad if you would so arrange, and the amount shall be sent later. If, however, it is absolutely necessary that the whole sum should be sent in at once, then I repeat my first request that we may be allowed a longer time of grace.

LETTER LXXXIX.[2]

To Meletius, bishop of Antioch.

1. THE eagerness of my longing is soothed by the opportunities which the merciful God gives me of saluting your reverence. He Himself is witness of the earnest desire which I have to see your face, and to enjoy your good and soul-refreshing instruction. Now by my reverend and excellent brother Dorotheus, the deacon, who is setting out, first of all I beg you to pray for me that I be no stumbling block to the people, nor hindrance to your petitions to propitiate the Lord. In the second place I would suggest that you would be so good as to make all arrangements through the afore-mentioned brother; and, if it seems well that a letter should be sent to the Westerns, because it is only right that communication should be made in writing even through our own messenger, that you will dictate the letter. I have met Sabinus the deacon, sent by them, and have written to the bishops in Illyria, Italy, and Gaul, and to some of those who have written privately to myself. For it is right that some one should be sent in the common interests of the Synod, conveying a second letter which I beg you to have written.

---

[1] χρυσίον πραγματευτικόν, Lat. *aurum comparatitium*. The gold collected for the equipment of troops. *Cod. Theod.* vii. 6. 3. The provinces of the East, with the exception of Osroene and Isauria, contributed gold instead of actual equipment. The Ben. note quotes a law of Valens that this was to be paid between Sept. 1 and April 1, and argues thence that this letter may be definitely dated in March, 372, and not long before Easter, which fell on April 8.

[2] Placed in the year 372.

---

[1] Of the same date as the preceding.   [2] Probably to Elias.
[3] Πατρίς. The Ben. Ed suppose the reference to be here to Annesi. *cf. Letters* viii. and li.   [4] Of the same date.

2. As to what concerns the right reverend bishop Athanasius, your intelligence is already aware of what I will mention, that it is impossible for anything to be advanced by my letters, or for any desirable objects to be carried out, unless by some means or other he receives communion from you, who at that time postponed it. He is described as being very anxious to unite with me, and to be willing to contribute all he can, but to be sorry that he was sent away without communion, and that the promise still remains unfulfilled.[1]

What is going on in the East cannot have failed to reach your reverence's ears, but the afore mentioned brother will give you more accurate information by word of mouth. Be so good as to dispatch him directly after Easter, because of his waiting for the answer from Samosata. Look kindly on his zeal; strengthen him by your prayers and so dispatch him on this commission.

LETTER XC.[2]

To the holy brethren the bishops of the West.[3]

1. THE good God Who ever mixes consolation with affliction has, even now in the midst of my pangs, granted me a certain amount of comfort in the letters which our right honourable father bishop Athanasius has received from you and sent on to me. For they contain evidence of sound faith and proof of your inviolable agreement and concord, showing thus that the shepherds are following in the footsteps of the Fathers and feeding the people of the Lord with knowledge. All this has so much gladdened my heart as to dispel my despondency and to create something like a smile in my soul in the midst of the distressing state of affairs in which we are now placed. The Lord has also extended His consolation to me by means of the reverend deacon Sabinus, my son, who has cheered my soul by giving me an exact narrative of your condition; and from personal experience of his own, will give you clear tidings of ours, that you may,

in the first place, aid me in my trouble by earnest and constant prayer to God; and next that you may consent to give such consolation as lies in your power to our afflicted Churches. For here, very honourable brethren, all is in a weak state; the Church has given way before the continuous attacks of her foes, like some bark in mid-ocean buffeted by successive blows of the waves; unless haply there be some quick visitation of the divine mercy. As then we reckon your mutual sympathy and unity an important blessing to ourselves, so do we implore you to pity our dissensions; and not, because we are separated by a great extent of country, to part us from you, but to admit us to the concord of one body, because we are united in the fellowship of the Spirit.

2. Our distresses are notorious, even though we leave them untold, for now their sound has gone out into all the world. The doctrines of the Fathers are despised; apostolic traditions are set at nought; the devices of innovators are in vogue in the Churches; now 'men are rather contrivers of cunning systems than theologians; the wisdom of this world wins the highest prizes and has rejected the glory of the cross. Shepherds are banished, and in their places are introduced grievous wolves harrying the flock of Christ. Houses of prayer have none to assemble in them; desert places are full of lamenting crowds. The elders lament when they compare the present with the past. The younger are yet more to be compassionated, for they do not know of what they have been deprived. All this is enough to stir the pity of men who have learnt the love of Christ; but, compared with the actual state of things, words fall very far short. If then there be any consolation of love, any fellowship of the Spirit, any bowels of mercy, be stirred to help us. Be zealous for true religion, and rescue us from this storm. Ever be spoken among us with boldness that famous dogma[1] of the Fathers, which destroys the ill-famed heresy of Arius, and builds up the Churches in the sound doctrine wherein the Son is confessed to be of one substance with the Father, and the Holy Ghost is ranked and worshipped as of equal honour, to the end that through your prayers and co-operation the Lord may grant to us that same boldness for the truth and glorying in the confession of the divine and saving Trinity which He has given you. But the aforenamed deacon will tell you every thing in detail. We have welcomed your apostolic zeal for orthodoxy

---

[1] It is the contention of Tillemont that this cannot apply to the great Athanasius, to whom Meletius is not likely to have refused communion, but is more probably to be referred to some other unknown Athanasius. Maran, however, points out (*Vit. Bas.* xxii.) not only how the circumstances fit in, but how the statement that communion was refused by Meletius is borne out by *Letter* cclviii. § 3. *q.v.* Athanasius was in fact so far committed to the other side in the unhappy Antiochene dispute that it was impossible for him to recognise Meletius. *cf.* Newman, *Church of the Fathers*, chap. vii.

[2] Placed in 372.

[3] By Newman, who translates the first paragraphs, this letter, as well as xcii., is viewed in close connection with *Letter* lxx., addressed to Damasus.

---

[1] κήρυγμα. *cf.* note on the *De Sp. Sancto.* p. 41.

and have agreed to all that has been canonically done by your reverences.

LETTER XCI.

To Valerianus, Bishop of Illyricum.[2]

THANKS be to the Lord, Who has permitted me to see in your unstained life the fruit of primitive love. Far apart as you are in body, you have united yourself to me by writing; you have embraced me with spiritual and holy longing; you have implanted unspeakable affection in my soul. Now I have realized the force of the proverb, "As cold water is to a thirsty soul so is good news from a far country."[3] Honoured brother, I really hunger for affection. The cause is not far to seek, for iniquity is multiplied and the love of many has grown cold.[4] For this reason your letter is precious to me, and I am replying by our reverend brother Sabinus. By him I make myself known to you, and beseech you to be watchful in prayers on our behalf, that God may one day grant calm and quiet to the Church here, and rebuke this wind and sea, that so we may be freed from the storm and agitation in which we are now every moment expecting to be submerged. But in these our troubles one great boon has God given us in hearing that you are in exact agreement and unity with one another, and that the doctrines of true religion are preached among you without let or hindrance. For at some time or other, unless the period of this world is not already concluded, and if there yet remain days of human life, it must needs be that by your means the faith must be renewed in the East, and that in due season you recompense her for the blessings which she has given you. The sound part among us here, which preserves the true religion of the Fathers, is sore stricken, and the devil in his wiliness has shattered it by many and various subtle assaults. But, by the help of the prayers of you who love the Lord, may the wicked and deceitful heresy of the Arian error be quenched; may the good teaching of the Fathers, who met at Nicæa, shine forth; so that the ascription of glory may be rendered to the blessed Trinity in the terms of the baptism of salvation.

LETTER XCII.[1]

To the Italians and Gauls.

1. To our right godly and holy brethren who are ministering in Italy and Gaul, bishops of like mind with us, we, Meletius,[2] Eusebius,[3] Basil,[4] Bassus,[5] Gregory,[6] Pelagius,[7] Paul, Anthimus,[8] Theodotus,[9] Bithus,[10] Abraamius,[11] Jobinus, Zeno,[12] Theodoretus, Marcianus, Barachus, Abraamius,[13] Libanius, Thalassius, Joseph, Boethus, Iatrius,[14] Theodotus, Eustathius,[15] Barsumas, John, Chosroes, Iosaces,[16] Narses, Maris, Gregory,[17] and Daphnus, send greeting in the Lord. Souls in anguish find some consolation in sending sigh after sigh from the bottom of the heart, and even a tear shed breaks the force of affliction. But sighs and tears give us less consolation than the opportunity of telling our troubles to your love. We are moreover cheered by the better hope that, peradventure, if we announce our troubles to you, we may move you to give us that succour which we have long hoped you would give the Churches in the East, but which we have not yet received; God, Who in His wisdom arranges all things, must have ordained according to the hidden judgments of His righteousness, that we should be tried for a longer time in these temptations. The fame of our condition has travelled to the ends of the earth, and you are not ignorant of it; nor are you without sympathy with brethren of like mind with yourselves, for you are disciples of the apostle, who teaches us that love for our neighbour is the fulfilling of the law.[18] But, as we have said, the just judgment of God, which has ordained that the affliction due to our sins must be fulfilled, has held you back. But when you have learnt all, specially what has not hitherto reached your ears, from our reverend brother the deacon Sabinus, who will be able to narrate in person what is omitted in our letter, we do beseech you to be roused both to zeal for the truth and sympathy for us. We implore you to put on bowels of mercy, to lay aside all hesitation, and to undertake the labour of love, without counting length of way, your own occupations, or any other human interests.

---

[1] Placed in 372.
[2] Or, in some MSS., the Illyrians. Valerianus, bishop of Aquileia, was present at the Synod held in Rome in 371 (Theodoret, *Hist. Ecc.* ii. 2). and also at the Synod in the same city in 382. (Theod. *Ecc. Hist.* v. 9, where see note.) Dorotheus or Sabinus had brought letters from Athanasius and at the same time a letter from Valerianus. Basil takes the opportunity to reply.
[3] Prov. v. 25.　　[4] *cf.* Matt. xxiv. 12.

[1] Placed in 372.　　[8] Of Tyana.
[2] Of Antioch.　　[9] Of Nicopolis.
[3] Of Samosata.　　[10] Vitus of Carrhæ.
[4] Of Cæsarea.　　[11] Of Batnæ. *cf. Letter* cxxxii.
[5] Tillemont conjectures Barses of Edessa.
[6] Of Nazianzus, the elder.　　[12] Of Tyre.
[7] Of Laodicea.　　[13] Of Urimi in Syria.
[14] For Iatrius, Maran would read Otreius of Melitine.
[15] Of Sebasteia.
[16] Maran would read Isaaces, and identify him with the the Isacoces of Armenia Major.
[17] Probably of Nyssa, lately consecrated.
[18] *cf.* Rom. xiii. 10.

2. It is not only one Church which is in peril, nor yet two or three which have fallen under this terrible storm. The mischief of this heresy spreads almost from the borders of Illyricum to the Thebaid. Its bad seeds were first sown by the infamous Arius; they then took deep root through the labours of many who vigorously cultivated the impiety between his time and ours. Now they have produced their deadly fruit. The doctrines of true religion are overthrown. The laws of the Church are in confusion. The ambition of men, who have no fear of God, rushes into high posts, and exalted office is now publicly known as the prize of impiety. The result is, that the worse a man blasphemes, the fitter the people think him to be a bishop. Clerical dignity is a thing of the past. There is a complete lack of men shepherding the Lord's flock with knowledge. Ambitious men are constantly throwing away the provision for the poor on their own enjoyment and the distribution of gifts. There is no precise knowledge of canons. There is complete immunity in sinning; for when men have been placed in office by the favour of men, they are obliged to return the favour by continually showing indulgence to offenders. Just judgment is a thing of the past; and everyone walks according to his heart's desire. Vice knows no bounds; the people know no restraint. Men in authority are afraid to speak, for those who have reached power by human interest are the slaves of those to whom they owe their advancement. And now the very vindication of orthodoxy is looked upon in some quarters as an opportunity for mutual attack,; and men conceal their private ill-will and pretend that their hostility is all for the sake of the truth. Others, afraid of being convicted of disgraceful crimes, madden the people into fratricidal quarrels, that their own doings may be unnoticed in the general distress. Hence the war admits of no truce, for the doers of ill deeds are afraid of a peace, as being likely to lift the veil from their secret infamy. All the while unbelievers laugh; men of weak faith are shaken; faith is uncertain; souls are drenched in ignorance, because adulterators of the word imitate the truth. The mouths of true believers are dumb, while every blasphemous tongue wags free; holy things are trodden under foot; the better laity shun the churches as schools of impiety; and lift their hands in the deserts with sighs and tears to their Lord in heaven. Even you must have heard what is going on in most of our cities, how

our people with wives and children and even our old men stream out before the walls, and offer their prayers in the open air, putting up with all the inconvenience of the weather with great patience, and waiting for help from the Lord.

3. What lamentation can match these woes? What springs of tears are sufficient for them? While, then, some men do seem to stand, while yet a trace of the old state of things is left, before utter shipwreck comes upon the Churches, hasten to us, hasten to us now, true brothers, we implore you; on our knees we implore you, hold out a helping hand. May your brotherly bowels be moved toward us; may tears of sympathy flow; do not see, unmoved, half the empire swallowed up by error; do not let the light of the faith be put out in the place where it shone first.

By what action you can then help matters, and how you are to show sympathy for the afflicted, you do not want to be told by us; the Holy Ghost will suggest to you. But unquestionably, if the survivors are to be saved, there is need of prompt action, and of the arrival of a considerable number of brethren, that those who visit us may complete the number of the synod, in order that they may have weight in effecting a reform, not merely from the dignity of those whose emissaries they are, but also from their own number: thus they will restore the creed drawn up by our fathers at Nicæa, proscribe the heresy, and, by bringing into agreement all who are of one mind, speak peace to the Churches. For the saddest thing about it all is that the sound part is divided against itself, and the troubles we are suffering are like those which once befel Jerusalem when Vespasian was besieging it. The Jews of that time were at once beset by foes without and consumed by the internal sedition of their own people. In our case, too, in addition to the open attack of the heretics, the Churches are reduced to utter helplessness by the war raging among those who are supposed to be orthodox. For all these reasons we do indeed desire your help, that, for the future all who confess the apostolic faith may put an end to the schisms which they have unhappily devised, and be reduced for the future to the authority of the Church; that so, once more, the body of Christ may be complete, restored to integrity with all its members. Thus we shall not only praise the blessings of others, which is all we can do now, but see our own Churches once more restored to their pristine boast of orthodoxy. For, truly, the boon given you by the Lord is fit subject for the highest congratulation, your power of discernment between the spurious and the genuine and pure, and your preaching the faith of the Fathers without any dissimulation. That faith we have received; that faith we know is stamped with the marks of the Apostles; to that faith we assent, as well as to all that was canonically and lawfully promulgated in the Synodical Letter.[1]

LETTER XCIII.[2]

To the Patrician Cæsaria,[3] concerning Communion.

It is good and beneficial to communicate every day, and to partake of the holy body and blood of Christ. For He distinctly says, " He that eateth my flesh and drinketh my blood hath eternal life." [4] And who doubts that to share frequently in life, is the same thing as to have manifold life. I, indeed, communicate four times a week, on the Lord's day, on Wednesday, on Friday, and on the Sabbath, and on the other days if there is a commemoration of any Saint.[5] It is needless to point out that for anyone in times of persecution to be compelled to take the communion in his own hand without the presence of a priest or minister is not a serious offence, as long custom sanctions this practice from the facts themselves. All the solitaries in the desert, where there is no priest, take the communion themselves, keeping communion at home. And at Alexandria and in Egypt, each one of the laity, for the most part, keeps the communion at his own house, and participates in it when he likes. For when once the priest has completed the offering, and given it, the

recipient, participating in it each time as entire, is bound to believe that he properly takes and receives it from the giver. And even in the church, when the priest gives the portion, the recipient takes it with complete power over it, and so lifts it to his lips with his own hand. It has the same validity whether one portion or several portions are received from the priest at the same time.[1]

LETTER XCIV.[2]

To Elias, Governor of the Province.

I too have been very anxious to meet your excellency, lest by my failure to do so I might come off worse than my accusers; but bodily sickness has prevented me, attacking me even more seriously than usual, and so I am perforce reduced to address you by letter. When, not long ago, most excellent sir, I had the pleasure of meeting your excellency, I was anxious to communicate with your wisdom about all my affairs; and I was also anxious to address you on behalf of the Churches, that no ground might be left for future calumnies. But I restrained myself, thinking it altogether superfluous and importunate to add troubles outside his own necessary business to a man charged with so many responsibilities. At the same time (for the truth shall be told) I did shrink from being driven to wound your soul by our mutual recriminations, when it ought in pure devotion to God to reap the perfect reward of piety. For really, if I attract your attention to me, I shall leave you but scant leisure for your public duties; shall act something like a man overloading with additional luggage some boatmen managing a new boat in very rough water, when all the while he ought to lessen the cargo and do his best to lighten the craft. For this very reason, I think, our great Emperor, after seeing how fully occupied I am, leaves me to manage the Churches by myself. Now I should like

---

[1] After noting that the Synodical Letter is to be found in Theodoret and in Sozomen (i.e. is in Theodoret I. viii. and in Socrates I. ix.) the Ben. Ed. express surprise that Basil should indicate concurrence with the Synodical Letter, which defines the Son to be τῆς αὐτῆς ὑποστάσεως καὶ οὐσίας, while he is known to have taught the distinction between ὑπόστασις and οὐσία. As a matter of fact, it is not in the Synodical Letter, but in the anathemas originally appended to the creed, that it is, not asserted that the Son is of the same, but, denied that He is of a different οὐσία or ὑπόστασις. On the distinction between οὐσία and ὑπόστασις see Letters xxxviii., cxxv., and ccxxxvi. and the De Sp. Sancto. §7. On the difficulty of expressing the terms in Latin, cf. Letter ccxiv. As ὑπόστασις was in 325 understood to be equivalent to οὐσία, and in 370 had acquired a different connotation, it would be no more difficult for Basil than for the Church now, to assent to what is called the Nicene position, while confessing three hypostases. In Letter cxxv. Basil does indeed try to shew, but apparently without success, that to condemn the statement that He is of a different hypostasis is not equivalent to asserting Him to be of the same hypostasis.

[2] Placed in 372.

[3] Two MSS. read Cæsarius.   [4] John vi. 54.

[5] A various reading is " martyr." In Letter cxcvii. to S. Ambrose, S. Basil, states that the same honour was paid to S. Dionysius of Milan in his place of sepulture as to a martyr. So Gregory Thaumaturgus was honoured at Neocæsarea, and Athanasius and Basil received like distinction soon after their death.

---

[1] The custom of the reservation of the Sacrament is, as is well known, of great antiquity. cf. Justin Martyr, Apol. i. 85; Tertull., De Orat. xix. and Ad Ux. ii. 5; S. Cyprian, De Lapsis cxxxii.; Jerome, Ep. cxxv. Abuses of the practice soon led to prohibition. So an Armenian Canon of the fourth century (Canones Isaaci, in Mai, Script. Vet. Nov. Coll. x. 280) and the Council of Saragossa, 380; though in these cases there seems an idea of surreptitious reservation. On the doctrine of the English Church on this subject reference may be made to the Report of a Committee of the Upper House of the Convocation of Canterbury in 1885.

The Rubric of 1549 allowed reservation, and it does not seem to have been prohibited until 1661. Bishop A. P. Forbes on Article xxviii. points out that in the Article reservation is not forbidden, but declared not to be of Christ's institution, and consequently not binding on the Church. The distinction will not be forgotten between reservation and worship of the reserved Sacrament.

[2] Placed in 372, at the departure of Valens.

those who are besieging your impartial ears to be asked what harm the government suffers from me? What depreciation is suffered by any public interests, be they small or great, by my administration of the Churches? Still, possibly, it might be urged that I have done damage to the government by erecting a magnificently appointed church to God, and round it a dwelling house, one liberally assigned to the bishop, and others underneath, allotted to the officers of the Church in order, the use of both being open to you of the magistracy and your escort. But to whom do we do any harm by building a place of entertainment for strangers, both for those who are on a journey and for those who require medical treatment on account of sickness, and so establishing a means of giving these men the comfort they want, physicians, doctors, means of conveyance, and escort?[1] All these men must learn such occupations as are necessary to life and have been found essential to a respectable career; they must also have buildings suitable for their employments, all of which are an honour to the place, and, as their reputation is credited to our governor, confer glory on him. Not indeed that for this reason you were unwillingly induced to accept the responsibility of ruling us, for you alone are sufficient by your high qualities to restore our ruins, to people deserted districts and turn wildernesses into towns. Would it be better to harrass and annoy, or to honour and reverence an associate in the discharge of these duties? Do not think, most excellent sir, that what I say is mere words. We have already, in the meanwhile, begun providing material. So much for our defence, before our ruler. As to what is to be said in answer to the charges of our accusers, to a Christian and to a friend who cares for my opinion, I must now say no more; the subject is too long for a letter, and cannot, besides, be safely committed to writing. But lest, before we have an opportunity of meeting, you are driven by the inducement of some men's calumnies to give up any of your good will towards me, do as Alexander did. The story is, as you remember, that, when one of his friends was being calumniated, he left one ear open to the slanderer, and carefully closed the other with his hand, with the object of showing that he whose duty is to judge ought not to be easily and wholly given over to the first

occupants of his attention, but should keep half his hearing open for the defence of the absent.[1]

LETTER XCV.[2]

To Eusebius, bishop of Samosata.

I HAD written some while since to your reverence about our meeting one another and other subjects, but I was disappointed at my letter not reaching your excellency, for after the blessed deacon Theophrastus had taken charge of the letter, on my setting out on an unavoidable journey, he did not convey it to your reverence, because he was seized by the sickness of which he died. Hence it happened that I was so late in writing, that, the time being now so exceedingly short, I did not look for there being much use in this letter. The godly bishop Meletius and Theodotus had strongly urged me to visit them, representing that a meeting would be a proof of affection, and being wishful of remedying the troubles which are at present a cause of anxiety.[3] They had appointed, as a time for our meeting, the middle of the approaching month of June, and for the place, Phargamus, a spot famous for martyr's glory and for the large number of people attending the synod there every year. Directly I returned and heard of the death of the blessed deacon, and that my letter was lying useless at home, I felt that I must not be idle, because thirty-three days were still remaining up to the appointed time, and so I hurriedly sent the letter to the very reverend Eustathius, my fellow minister, with the object of its being sent on by him to your reverence and of getting an answer without delay. If, then, it is possible and agreeable to you to come, I will come too. If not, I, God willing, will pay the debt of meeting due from last year: unless haply some hindrance for my sins comes in the way again, in which case I must put off my meeting with the bishops to another time.

LETTER XCVI.[4]

To Sophronius, the master.[5]

WHO ever loved his city, honouring with filial love the place which gave him birth

1 Among the honourable functions of the clergy was that of acting as guides and escort, παραπέμποντες. cf. Letters xcviii. and ccxliii.

1 The church and hospital, of which mention is here made, were built in the suburbs of Cæsarea. Gregory of Nazianzus calls it a new town. cf. Greg. Naz., Or. xx. and Theodoret, Ecc. Hist. iv. 19, and Sozomen, vi. 34. On Alexander's ear, cf. Letter xxiv.   2 Placed in 372.
3 Theodotus of Nicopolis was distressed at Basil's being in communion with Eustathius.
4 Placed in 372.   5 On the removal of Elias.

and nurture, as you do; praying for the whole city together, and for every one in it individually, and not merely praying but confirming your prayers by your own means? For this you are able to effect by God's help, and long, good man that you are, may you be able so to do. Nevertheless in your time our city has enjoyed but a brief dream of prosperity, in being committed to the charge of one the like of whom, according to the students of our oldest annals, never sat in the præfectorial chair. But now the city has suddenly lost his services, through the wickedness of men who have found a ground of attack in his very liberality and impartiality, and, without the knowledge of your excellency, have made up calumnies against him. There is therefore universal depression among us at the loss of a governor with unique capacity for raising our dejected community, a true guardian of justice, accessible to the wronged, a terror to law breakers, of like behaviour to rich and poor, and, what is most important, one who has restored the interests of Christians to their old place of honour. That he was, of all men that I know, the most incapable of being bribed, and never did any one an unfair favour, I have passed by as a small point in comparison with his other virtues. I am indeed testifying to all this too late, like men who sing dirges to console themselves when they can get no practical relief. Yet, it is not useless that his memory should remain in your generous heart, and that you should be grateful to him as a benefactor of your native place. Should any of those who feel a grudge against him, for not sacrificing justice to their interests, attack him, it will be well for you to defend and protect him. Thus you will make it clear to all that you count his interests yours, and think it quite a sufficient reason for this your close association with him that his record should be so unimpeachable, and his administration so remarkable in view of the time. For what any other man would not be able to affect in many years has been quickly accomplished by him. It will be a great favour to me, and a comfort under the circumstances, if you will recommend him to the Emperor, and dispel the calumnious charges brought against him. Believe me that I am speaking here not for myself alone, but for the whole community, and that it is our unanimous prayer that he may reap some benefit from your excellency's aid.

LETTER XCVII.[1]

To the Senate of Tyana.[2]

THE Lord, Who reveals hidden things, and makes manifest the counsels of men's hearts, has given even to the lowly knowledge of devices apparently hard to be understood. Nothing has escaped my notice, nor has any single action been unknown. Nevertheless I neither see nor hear anything but the peace of God and all that pertains to it. Others may be great and powerful and self-confident, but I am nothing and worth nothing, and so I could never take upon myself so much as to think myself able to manage matters without support. I know perfectly well that I stand more in need of the succour of each of the brethren than one hand does of the other. Truly, from our own bodily constitution, the Lord has taught us the necessity of fellowship. When I look to these my limbs and see that no one of them is self-sufficient, how can I reckon myself competent to discharge the duties of life? One foot could not walk securely without the support of the other; one eye could not see well, were it not for the alliance of the other and for its being able to look at objects in conjunction with it. Hearing is more exact when sound is received through both channels, and the grasp is made firmer by the fellowship of the fingers. In a word, of all that is done by nature and by the will, I see nothing done without the concord of fellow forces. Even prayer, when it is not united prayer, loses its natural strength and the Lord has told us that He will be in the midst where two or three call on Him in concord. The Lord Himself undertook the economy,[3] that by the blood of His cross He might make peace between things in earth and things in heaven. For all these reasons then, I pray that I may for my remaining days remain in peace; in peace I ask that it may be my lot to fall asleep. For peace's sake there is no trouble that I will not undertake, no act, no word of humility, that I will shrink from; I will reckon no length of journey, I will undergo any inconvenience, if only I may be rewarded by being able to make peace. If I am followed by any one in this direction, it is well, and my prayers are answered;

---

[1] Placed in 372.
[2] On the whole circumstances of the difficulties which arose in consequence of the civil division of Cappadocia, and the claim put forward in consequence by Anthimus, bp. of Tyana, to exercise metropolitan jurisdiction, see the biographical notice in the *Prolegomena.*
[3] *i.e.* of the Incarnation. *cf.* note on p. 7, and on Theodoret, p. 72.

but if the result is different I shall not recede from my determination. Every one will receive the fruit of his own works in the day of retribution.

LETTER XCVIII.[1]

To Eusebius, bishop of Samosata.

1. AFTER receiving the letter of your holiness, in which you said you would not come, I was most anxious to set out for Nicopolis, but I have grown weaker in my wish and have remembered all my infirmity. I bethought me, too, of the lack of seriousness in the conduct of those who invited me. They gave me a casual invitation by the hands of our reverend brother Hellenius, the surveyor of customs at Nazianzus, but they never took the trouble to send a messenger to remind me, or any one to escort me. As, for my sins, I was an object of suspicion to them, I shrank from sullying the brightness of their meeting by my presence. In company with your excellency I do not shrink from stripping for even serious trials of strength; but apart from you I feel myself hardly equal even to looking at every day troubles. Since, then, my meeting with them was intended to be about Church affairs, I let the time of the festival go by, and put off the meeting to a period of rest and freedom from distraction, and have decided to go to Nicopolis to discuss the needs of the Churches with the godly bishop Meletius, in case he should decline to go to Samosata. If he agrees, I shall hasten to meet him, provided this is made clear to me by both of you, by him in reply to me (for I have written), and by your reverence.

2. We were to have met the bishops of Cappadocia Secunda, who, directly they were ranked under another prefecture, suddenly got the idea that they were made foreigners and strangers to me. They ignored me, as though they had never been under my jurisdiction, and had nothing to do with me. I was expecting too a second meeting with the reverend bishop Eustathius, which actually took place. For on account of the cry raised by many against him that he was injuring the faith, I met him, and found, by God's grace, that he was heartily following all orthodoxy. By the fault of the very men who ought to have conveyed my letter, that of the bishop was not transmitted to your excellency, and, harassed as I was by a multitude of cares, it escaped my memory.

I, too, was anxious that our brother Gregory[1] should have the government of a Church commensurate with his abilities; and that would have been the whole Church under the sun gathered into one place. But, as this is impossible, let him be a bishop, not deriving dignity from his see, but conferring dignity on his see by himself. For it is the part of a really great man not only to be sufficient for great things, but by his own influence to make small things great.

But what is to be done to Palmatius,[2] who, after so many exhortations of the brethren, still helps Maximus in his persecutions? Even now they do not hesitate to write to him. They are prevented from coming themselves by bodily weakness and their own occupations. Believe me, very godly Father, our own affairs are much in need of your presence, and yet once more you must put your honourable old age in motion, that you may give your support to Cappadocia, which is now tottering and in danger of falling.

LETTER XCIX.[3]

To Count Terentius.[4]

I HAVE had every desire and have really done my best to obey, if only in part, the imperial order and the friendly letter of your excellency. I am sure that your every word and every thought are full of good intentions and right sentiments. But I have not been permitted to show my ready concurrence by practical action. The truest cause is my sins, which always rise before me and always hamper my steps. Then, again, there is the alienation of the bishop who had been appointed to coöperate with me, why, I know

---

[1] Tillemont supposes the reference to be to Gregory of Nyssa. Maran, however (*Vit. Bas.* xxiv.), regards this as an error, partly caused by the introduction into the text of the word ἐμόν, which he has eliminated; and he points out that Gregory of Nyssa, however unwilling to accept consecration, never objected after it had taken place, and was indeed sent to Nazianzus to console the younger Gregory of that place in his distress under like circumstances. Moreover, Gregory of Nyssa was consecrated in the ordinary manner on the demand of the people and clergy with the assent of the bishops of the province. (*cf. Letter* ccxxv.) Gregory the younger, however, was consecrated to Sasima without these formalities.
[2] Maran (*Vit. Bas.* xxiv.) notes that he knows nothing about Palmatius, and supposes that by "persecutions" are meant not persecutions in the ecclesiastical sense, but severities in the exaction of tribute. In *Letter* cxlvii. Basil calls Maximus "a very good man," praise which he is not likely to have given to a persecutor. Maximus succeeded Elias, and probably inaugurated a new régime of strict exaction.
[3] Placed in 372.
[4] *cf. Letter* ccxiv. On Terentius *vide* Amm. Marcellinus, xxvii. 12 and xxxi. He was an orthodox Christian, though in favour with Valens. In 372 he was in command of twelve legions in Georgia, and Basil communicates with him about providing bishops for the Armenian Church. According to some manuscripts of *Letter* cv., *q.v.*, his three daughters were deaconesses.

---

[1] Placed in 372.
[2] On a proposed meeting of bishops, with an allusion to the consecration of the younger Gregory.

not; but my right reverend brother Theodotus, who promised from the beginning to act with me, had cordially invited[1] me from Getasa to Nicopolis.[2] When however he saw me in the town, he was so shocked at me, and so afraid of my sins, that he could not bear to take me either to morning or evening prayer. In this he acted quite justly so far as my deserts go, and quite as befits my course of life, but not in a manner likely to promote the interests of the Churches. His alleged reason was that I had admitted the very reverend brother Eustathius to communion. What I have done is as follows. When invited to a meeting held by our brother Theodotus, and wishful, for love's sake, to obey the summons, that I might not make the gathering fruitless and vain, I was anxious to hold communication with the aforementioned brother Eustathius. I put before him the accusations concerning the faith, advanced against him by our brother Theodotus, and I asked him, if he followed the right faith, to make it plain to me, that I might communicate with him; if he were of another mind, he must know plainly that I should be separated, from him. We had much conversation on the subject, and all that day was spent in its examination; when evening came on we separated without arriving at any definite conclusion. On the morrow, we had another sitting in the morning and discussed the same points, with the addition of our brother Pœmenius, the presbyter of Sebasteia, who vehemently pressed the argument against me. Point by point I cleared up the questions on which he seemed to be accusing me, and brought them to agree to my propositions. The result was, that, by the grace of the Lord, we were found to be in mutual agreement, even on the most minute particulars. So about the ninth hour, after thanking God for granting us to think and say the same thing, we rose up to go to prayer. In addition to this I ought to have got some written statement from him, so that his assent might be made known to his opponents and the proof of his opinion might be sufficient for the rest. But I was myself anxious, with the desire for great exactitude, to meet my brother Theodotus, to get a written statement of the faith from him, and to propose it to Eustathius; that so both objects might be obtained at once, the confession of the right faith by Eustathius and the complete satisfaction of Theodotus and

his friends, and they would have no ground for objection after the acceptance of their own propositions. But Theodotus, before learning why we were met and what had been the result of our intercourse, decided not to allow us to take part in the meeting. So midway on our journey we set out back again, disappointed that our efforts for the peace of the Churches had been counteracted.

3. After this, when I was compelled to undertake a journey into Armenia, knowing the man's character, and with the view both of making my own defence before a competent witness, for what had taken place and of satisfying him, I travelled to Getasa, into the territory of the very godly bishop Meletius, the aforementioned Theodotus being with me; and while there, on being accused by him of my communication with Eustathius, I told him that the result of our intercourse was my finding Eustathius to be in all things in agreement with myself. Then he persisted that Eustathius, after leaving me, had denied this and asseverated to his own disciples that he had never come to any agreement with me about the faith. I, therefore, combated this statement; and see, O most excellent man, if the answer I made was not most fair and most complete. I am convinced, I said, judging from the character of Eustathius, that he cannot thus lightly be turning from one direction to another, now confessing now denying what he said; that a man, shunning a lie, even in any little matter, as an awful sin, is not likely to choose to run counter to the truth in matters of such vast importance and so generally notorious: but if what is reported among you turns out to be true, he must be confronted with a written statement containing the complete exposition of the right faith; then, if I find him ready to agree in writing, I shall continue in communion with him; but, if I find that he shrinks from the test, I shall renounce all intercourse with him. The bishop Meletius agreed to these arguments, and the brother Diodorus the presbyter, who was present, and then the right reverend brother Theodotus, assented, and invited me to go to Nicopolis, both to visit the Church there, and to keep him company as far as Satala. But he left me at Getasa, and, when I reached Nicopolis, forgetting all that he heard from me, and the agreement he had made with me, dismissed me, disgraced by the insults and dishonours which I have mentioned.

4. How, then, right honourable sir, was it possible for me to perform any of the in-

---

[1] καταγαγών. So six MSS., but the Ben. Ed. seem rightly to point out that the invitation never resulted in actual "conducting."

[2] *i.e.* The Armenian Nicopolis.

junctions laid on me, and to provide bishops for Armenia? How could I act, when the sharer of my responsibilities was thus disposed towards me, — the very man by whose aid I was expecting to be able to find suitable persons, because of his having in his district reverend and learned men, skilled in speech, and acquainted with the other peculiarities of the nation? I know their names, but I shall refrain from mentioning them, lest there arise any hindrance to the interests of Armenia being served at some future time.

Now, after getting as far as Satala in such a state of health, I seemed to settle the rest by the grace of God. I made peace between the Armenian bishops, and made them a suitable address, urging them to put away their customary indifference, and resume their ancient zeal in the Lord's cause. Moreover, I delivered them rules as to how it behoved them to give heed to iniquities generally practised in Armenia. I further accepted a decision of the Church of Satala, asking that a bishop might be given them through me. I was also careful to inquire into the calumnies promulgated against our brother Cyril, the Armenian bishop, and by God's grace I have found them to be started by the lying slanders of his enemies. This they confessed to me. And I seemed to some extent to reconcile the people to him, so that they avoid communion with him no more. Small achievements these, maybe, and not worth much, but in consequence of the mutual discord caused by the wiles of the devil, it was impossible for me to effect more. Even this much I ought not to have said, so as not to seem to be publishing my own disgrace. But as I could not plead my cause before your excellency in any other way, I was under the necessity of telling you the entire truth.

LETTER C.[1]

To Eusebius, Bishop of Samosata.

WHEN I saw your affectionate letter, in the country bordering on Armenia, it was like a lighted torch held up at a distance to mariners at sea, especially if the sea happen to be agitated by the wind. Your reverence's letter was of itself a pleasant one, and full of comfort; but its natural charm was very much enhanced by the time of its arrival, a time so painful to me, that I hardly know how to describe it, after once making up my mind to forget its troubles. However, my deacon will give you a full account. My

bodily strength completely failed me, so that I was not even able to bear the slightest movement without pain. Nevertheless I do pray that, by the aid of your prayers, my own longing may be fulfilled; although my journey has caused me great difficulties, in consequence of the affairs of my own Church having been neglected through its occupying such a long time. But if, while I yet live, God grants me to see your reverence in my Church, then truly I shall have good hope, even for the future, that I am not wholly excluded from the gifts of God. If it be possible, I beg that this meeting between us may take place at the Synod which we hold every year, in memory of the blessed martyr Eupsychius,[1] now about to be held on the 7th of September. I am compassed with anxieties which demand your help and sympathy, both in the matter of the appointment of bishops and in the consideration of the trouble caused me by the simplicity of Gregory of Nyssa,[2] who is summoning a Synod at Ancyra and leaving nothing undone to counteract me.

LETTER CI.[3]

Consolatory.[4]

THIS is my first letter to you, and I could have prayed that its subject were a brighter one. Had it been so, things would have fallen out as I desire, for it is my wish that the life of all those who are purposed to live in true religion should be happily spent. But the Lord, Who ordains our course in accordance with His ineffable wisdom, has arranged that all these things should come about for the advantage of our souls, whereby He has, on the one hand, made your life sorrowful, and on the other, roused the sympathy of one who, like myself, is united to you in godly love. Therefore on my learning from my brothers what has befallen you it has seemed to me that I could not but give you such comfort as I can. Had it indeed been possible to me to travel to the place in which you are now living I would have made every effort to do so. But my bad health and the present business which occupies me have caused this very journey, which I have

---

[1] cf. Letters clxxvi. and cclii. Eupsychius suffered for the part he took in demolishing the Temple of Fortune at Cæsarea. cf. Sozomen, Ecc. Hist. v. 11. An Eupsychius appears in the Bollandist acts under April 9th. Vide Prolegomena.

[2] The Ben. note, in answer to the suggested unlikelihood of Basil's being plotted against by his brother, calls attention to the fact that this opposition was due not to want of affection but to want of tact, and compares Letter lviii. on Gregory's foolish falsehood about their uncle.

[3] Placed in 372.

[4] To the title has been added "to the wife of Arinthæus," but no manuscript known to the Ben. Ed. contained it.

undertaken, to be injurious to the interests of my Church. I have, therefore, determined to address your excellency in writing, to remind you that these afflictions are not sent by the Lord, Who rules us, to the servants of God to no purpose, but as a test of the genuineness of our love to the divine Creator. Just as athletes win crowns by their struggles in the arena, so are Christians brought to perfection by the trial of their temptations, if only we learn to accept what is sent us by the Lord with becoming patience, with all thanksgiving. All things are ordained by the Lord's love. We must not accept anything that befalls us as grievous, even if, for the present, it affects our weakness. We are ignorant, peradventure, of the reasons why each thing that happens to us is sent to us as a blessing by the Lord; but we ought to be convinced that all that happens to us is for our good, either for the reward of our patience, or for the soul which we have received, lest, by lingering too long in this life, it be filled with the wickedness to be found in this world. If the hope of Christians is limited to this life, it might rightly have been reckoned a bitter lot to be prematurely parted from the body; but if, to them that love God, the sundering of the soul from these bodily fetters is the beginning of our real life, why do we grieve like them which have no hope?[1] Be comforted then, and do not fall under your troubles, but show that you are superior to them and can rise above them.

LETTER CII.[2]

To the citizens of Satala.[3]

MOVED by your importunity and that of all your people, I have undertaken the charge of your Church, and have promised before the Lord that I will be wanting to you in nothing which is within my power. So I have been compelled, as it is written, to touch as it were the apple of my eye.[4] Thus the high honour in which I hold you has suffered me to remember neither relationship, nor the intimacy which I have had from my boyhood with the person in question, as making a stronger demand on me than your request. I have forgotten all the private considerations which made him near and dear to me, making no account of the sighs which will be heaved by all my people on being deprived of his rule, none of the tears of all his kindred; nor have I taken to heart the affliction of his aged mother, who is supported by his aid alone. All these considerations, great and many as they are, I have put aside, keeping only in view the one object of giving your Church the blessing of the rule of such a man, and of aiding her, now distressed as she is, at being so long without a head, and needing great and powerful support to be enabled to rise again. So much for what concerns myself. Now, on the other hand, I ask you not to fall short of the hope which I have entertained and of the promises which I have made him, that I have sent him to close friends. I ask every one of you to try to surpass the rest in love and affection to him. I entreat you to show this laudable rivalry, and to comfort his heart by the greatness of your attentions to him, that he may forget his own home, forget his kinsfolk, and forget a people so dependent on his rule, like a child weaned from his mother's breast.

I have despatched Nicias beforehand to explain everything to your excellencies, and that you may fix a day to keep the feast and give thanks to the Lord, Who has granted the fulfilment of your prayer.[1]

LETTER CIII.[2]

To the people of Satala.

THE Lord has answered the prayer of His people and has given them, by my humble instrumentality, a shepherd worthy of the name; not one making traffic of the word, as many do, but competent to give full satisfaction to you, who love orthodoxy of doctrine, and have accepted a life agreeable to the Lord's commands, in the name of the Lord, Who has filled him with His own spiritual graces.

LETTER CIV.[3]

To the prefect Modestus.[4]

MERELY to write to so great a man, even though there be no other reason, must be esteemed a great honour. For communication with personages of high distinction confers glory upon all to whom it is permitted. My supplication, however, is one which I am driven by necessity to make to your excellency, in my great distress at the condition of my whole country. Bear with me, I beg you, kindly and in accordance with your own character, and reach a helping hand to my

1 1 Thess. iv. 12.   2 Placed in 372.
3 On the appointment of a bishop for that see in the North East of Armenia Minor.   4 cf. Zech. ii. 8.

1 The relative referred to is Pœmenius. cf. Letter cxxii.
2 Of the same date as the preceding.
3 Placed in 372.   4 On the rating of the clergy.

country, now beaten to the knee. The immediate object of my entreaty is as follows. By the old census, the clergy of God, presbyters and deacons,[1] were left exempt. The recent registrars, however, without any authority from your lordship, have enrolled them, except that in some cases a few were granted immunity on the score of age. I ask, then, that you will leave us this memorial of your beneficence, to preserve through all coming time your good fame; that in accordance with the old law the clergy be exempt from contribution. I do not ask the remission to be conceded personally and individually to those who are now included, in which case the grace will pass to their successors, who may not always be worthy of the sacred ministry. I would suggest that some general concession be made to the clergy, according to the form in the open register, so that the exemption may be given in each place to ministers by the rulers of the Church. This boon is sure to bring undying glory to your excellency for your good deeds, and will cause many to pray for the imperial house. It will also really be profitable to the government, if we afford the relief of exemption, not generally to all the clergy, but to those who from time to time are in distress. This, as any one who chooses may know, is the course we actually pursue when we are at liberty.

LETTER CV.[2]

To the deaconesses, the daughters of Count Terentius.[3]

On coming to Samosata I expected to have the pleasure of meeting your excellencies, and when I was disappointed I could not easily bear it. When, I said, will it be possible for me to be in your neighbourhood again? When will it be agreeable to you to come into mine? All this, however, must be left to the Lord's will. As to the present, when I found that my son Sophronius was setting out to you, I gladly delivered him this letter, to convey you my salutation, and to tell you how, by God's grace, I do not cease to remember you, and to thank the Lord on your behalf, in that you are goodly scions of a goodly stock, fruitful in good works, and verily like lilies among thorns. Surrounded as you are by

the terrible perversity of them that are corrupting the word of truth, you do not give in to their wiles; you have not abandoned the apostolic proclamation of faith, you have not gone over to the successful novelty of the day. Is not this cause of deep thankfulness to God? Shall not this rightly bring you great renown? You have professed your faith in Father, Son and Holy Ghost. Do not abandon this deposit; the Father — origin of all; the Son — Only begotten, begotten of Him, very God, Perfect of Perfect, living image, shewing the whole Father in Himself; the Holy Ghost, having His subsistence of God, the fount of holiness, power that gives life, grace that maketh perfect, through Whom man is adopted, and the mortal made immortal, conjoined with Father and Son in all things in glory and eternity, in power and kingdom, in sovereignty and godhead; as is testified by the tradition of the baptism of salvation.

But all who maintain that either Son or Spirit is a creature, or absolutely reduce the Spirit to ministerial and servile rank, are far removed from the truth. Flee their communion. Turn away from their teaching. They are destructive to souls. If ever the Lord grant us to meet, I will discourse to you further concerning the faith, to the end that you may perceive at once the power of the truth and the rottenness of heresy by Scriptural proof.

LETTER CVI.[1]

To a soldier.

I have many reasons for thanking God for mercies vouchsafed to me in my journey, but I count no blessing greater than the knowledge of your excellency, which has been permitted me by our good Lord's mercy. I have learnt to know one who proves that even in a soldier's life it is possible to preserve the perfection of love to God,[2] and that we must mark a Christian not by the style of his dress, but by the disposition of his soul. It was a great delight to me to meet you; and now, whenever I remember you, I feel very glad. Play the man; be strong; strive to nourish and multiply love to God, that there may be given you by Him yet greater boons of blessing. I need no further proof that you remember me; I have evidence in what you have done.

---

[1] τοὺς τοῦ θεοῦ ἱερωμένους, πρεσβυτέρους καὶ διακόνους. The Ben. note points out that the words priests and deacons probably crept into the MSS., in all of which it is found, from the margin, inasmuch as by ἱερωμένους and cognate words Basil means the whole clergy. cf. Letter liv. and note on p. 157.
[2] Placed in 372.   [3] cf. Letter xcix. and note.

[1] Placed in 372.
[2] Among others, conspicuous instances of the statement in the text are Cornelius, St. Martin, John de Joinville, Peter du Terreil, Sieur de Bayard, Henry Havelock, and Charles Gordon.

LETTER CVII.[1]

To the Widow Julitta.[2]

I was grieved to find on reading your ladyship's letter that you are involved in the same difficulties. What is to be done to men who show such a shifty character, saying now one thing now another and never abiding in the same pledges? If, after the promises made in my presence, and in that of the ex-prefect, he now tries to shorten the time of grace as though nothing had been said, he does seem to have lost, as far as I am concerned, all sense of shame. Nevertheless I wrote to him, rebuking him, and reminding him of his promises. I wrote also to Helladius, who is of the household of the prefect, that information might be given through him about your affairs. I hesitated myself to make so free with an officer of such importance, on account of my never having yet written to him about my own private affairs and my fearing some adverse decision from him, great men, as you know, being easily annoyed about such matters. If, however, any good is to be done in the matter, it will be through Helladius, an excellent man, well disposed towards me, fearing God, and having perfectly free access to the prefect. The Holy One is able to deliver you from all affliction, if only truly and sincerely we fix all our hope on Him.

LETTER CVIII.[3]

To the guardian of the heirs of Julitta.

I am very much astonished to hear that, after the kind promises which you made and which were only such as might be expected from your generous character, you have now forgotten them and are putting violent and stern pressure on our sister. What to think, under the circumstances, I really do not know. I know from many who have experienced your liberality, and bear testimony to it, how great it is; and I remember the promises which you made before me and the ex-prefect. You said that you were naming a shorter time in writing, but that you would grant a longer term of grace, from your wish to meet the necessities of the case, and do a favour to the widow, who is now compelled to pay out of her substance such a large sum of money at once. What is the cause of this change I cannot imagine. However, whatever it is, I beg you to be mindful of your own generous character, and to look to the Lord Who requites good deeds. I beg you to grant the time of remission, which you promised at the outset, that they may be able to sell their property and discharge the debt. I perfectly well remember that you promised, if you received the sum agreed on, to restore to the widow all the stipulated documents, as well those which had been executed before the magistrates as the private papers. I do beg you then, honour me and win great blessing for yourself from the Lord. Remember your own promises, recognizing that you are human and must yourself look for that time when you will need God's help. Do not shut yourself off from that help by your present severity; but, by showing all kindness and clemency to the afflicted, attract God's pity to yourself.

LETTER CIX.[1]

To the Count Helladius.

I shrink from troubling your good nature, on account of the greatness of your influence, for fear of seeming to make an unwarrantable use of your friendship; however, the necessity of the case prevents my holding my peace. Our sister, who is a relative of mine, and now in the sorrowful position of a widow, has to look after the affairs of her orphan boy. On seeing her above measure oppressed by intolerable responsibilities, I felt great compassion for her, and, feeling deeply on the subject, I have hastened to invoke your aid, in order that you may, if possible, deign to support the messenger whom she has sent, to the end that when she has paid what she promised in person in my presence, she may be freed from any further pressure. She had agreed that she should be relieved from the interest on payment of the capital. Now, however, those who are looking after the affairs of her heirs are trying to exact the payment of the interest as well as that of the capital. The Lord, you know, makes the care of widows and orphans His own, and so do you strive to use your best endeavours in this matter, in the hope of the recompense which God Himself will give you. I cannot help thinking that, when our admirable and kindly prefect has heard of the discharge of the capital, he will feel for this afflicted and unhappy house now stricken to the knee, and no longer able to cope with the injuries inflicted upon it. Pardon, then, the necessity which compels me to intrude upon you; and give your help

---

[1] Placed in 372.
[2] On the pressure put upon her by the guardian of her heirs.
[3] Placed in 372.

[1] Of the same date as the preceding.

in this matter, in proportion to the power which Christ has given you, good and true man as you are, and using your talents for the best.

LETTER CX.[1]

To the prefect Modestus.[2]

In kindly condescending to come down to me you give me great honour and allow me great freedom ; and these in like, aye and in greater, measure, I pray that your lordship may receive from our good Master during the whole of your life. I have long wanted to write to you and to receive honour at your hands, but respect for your great dignity has restrained me, and I have been careful lest I should ever seem to abuse the liberty conceded to me. Now, however, I am forced to take courage, not only by the fact of my having received permission from your incomparable excellency to write, but also by the necessity of the distressed. If, then, prayers of even the small are of any avail with the great, be moved, most excellent sir, of your good will to grant relief to a rural population now in pitiable case, and give orders that the tax of iron, paid by the inhabitants of iron-producing Taurus, may be made such as it is possible to pay. Grant this, lest they be crushed once for all, instead of being of lasting service to the state. I am sure that your admirable benevolence will see that this is done.

LETTER CXI.[3]

To Modestus, the prefect.

Under any ordinary circumstances I should have lacked courage to intrude upon your excellency, for I know how to gauge my own importance and to recognise dignities. But now that I have seen a friend in a distressing position at having been summoned before you, I have ventured to give him this letter. I hope that by using it, as a kind of propitiatory symbol, he may meet with merciful consideration. Truly, although I am of no account, moderation itself may be able to conciliate the most merciful of prefects, and to win pardon for me. Thus if my friend has done no wrong, he may be saved by the mere force of truth; if he has erred, he may be forgiven through my entreaty.

How we are situated here no one knows

better than yourself, for you discern the weak parts in each man and rule all with your admirable forethought.

LETTER CXII.[1]

To Andronicus, a general.[2]

1. Did but my health allow of my being able to undertake a journey without difficulty, and of putting up with the inclemency of the winter, I should, instead of writing, have travelled to your excellency in person, and this for two reasons. First to pay my old debt, for I know that I promised to come to Sebastia and to have the pleasure of seeing your excellency; I did indeed come, but I failed to meet you because I arrived a little later than your lordship; secondly, to be my own ambassador, because I have hitherto shrunk from sending, from the idea that I am too insignificant to win such a boon, and at the same time reckoning that no one by merely writing would be so likely to persuade any one of public or private rank, in behalf of any one, as by a personal interview, in which one might clear up some points in the charges, as to others make entreaty, and for others implore pardon; none of which ends can be easily achieved by a letter. Now against all this I can only set one thing, your most excellent self; and because it will suffice to tell you my mind in the matter, and all that is wanting you will add of yourself, I have ventured to write as I do.

2. But you see how from my hesitation, and because I put off explaining the reasons of my pleading, I write in roundabout phrase. This man Domitianus has been an intimate friend of my own and of my parents from the beginning, and is like a brother to me. Why should I not speak the truth? When I learnt the reasons for his being in his present troubles, I said that he had only got what he deserved. For I hoped that no one who has ever committed any offence be it small or great, will escape punishment. But when I saw him living a life of insecurity and disgrace, and felt that his only hope depends on your decision, I thought that he had been punished enough ; and so I implore you to be magnanimous and humane in the view you take of his case. To have one's opponents under one's power is right and proper for a man of spirit and authority ; but to be kind and gentle to

---

[1] Placed in 372.
[2] On the tribute of iron paid in Mount Taurus.
[3] Placed in 372.

[1] Placed in 372.
[2] Asking for the merciful consideration of Domitianus, a friend of Basil.

the fallen is the mark of the man super-eminent in greatness of soul, and in inclem-ency. So, if you will, it is in your power to exhibit your magnanimity in the case of the same man, both in punishing him and in saving him. Let the fear Domi-tian has of what he suspects, and of what he knows he deserves to suffer, be the extent of his chastisement. I entreat you to add noth-ing to his punishment, for consider this: many in former times, of whom no record has reached us, have had those who wronged them in their power. But those who sur-passed their fellows in philosophy did not persist in their wrath, and of these the memory has been handed down, immortal through all time. Let this glory be added to what history will say of you. Grant to us, who desire to celebrate your praises, to be able to go beyond the instances of kind-nesses sung of in days of old. In this manner Crœsus, it is said, ceased from his wrath against the slayer of his son, when he gave himself up for punishment,[1] and the great Cyrus was friendly to this very Crœsus after his victory.[2] We shall number you with these and shall proclaim this your glory, with all our power, unless we be counted too poor heralds of so great a man.

3. Yet another plea that I ought to urge is this, that we do not chastise transgressors for what is past and gone, (for what means can be devised for undoing the past?) but either that they may be reformed for the future, or may be an example of good be-haviour to others. Now, no one could say that either of these points is lacking in the present case; for Domitian will remember what has happened till the day of his death; and I think that all the rest, with his ex-ample before them, are dead with alarm. Under these circumstances any addition which we make to his punishment will only look like a satisfaction of our own anger. This I should say is far from being true in your case. I could not indeed be induced to speak of such a thing did I not see that a greater blessing comes to him that gives, than to him that receives. Nor will your magnanimity be known only to a few. All Cappadocia is looking to see what is to be done, and I pray that they may be able to number this among the rest of your good deeds. I shrink from concluding my letter for fear any omission may be to my hurt. But one thing I will add. Domitian has letters from many, who plead for him, but he thinks mine the most important of all,

because he has learnt, from whom I know not, that I have influence with your ex-cellency. Do not let the hopes he has placed in me be blasted; do not let me lose my credit among my people here; be entreated, illustrious sir, and grant my boon. You have viewed human life as clearly as ever philosopher viewed it, and you know how goodly is the treasure laid up for all those who give their help to the needy.

LETTER CXIII.[1]

To the presbyters of Tarsus.[2]

ON meeting this man, I heartily thanked God that by means of his visit He had com-forted me in many afflictions and had through him shewn me clearly your love. I seem to see in one man's disposition the zeal of all of you for the truth. He will tell you of our discourses with one another. What you ought to learn directly from me is as fol-lows.

We live in days when the overthrow of the Churches seems imminent; of this I have long been cognisant. There is no edification of the Church; no correction of error; no sympathy for the weak; no single defence of sound brethren; no remedy is found either to heal the disease which has already seized us, or as a preventive against that which we expect. Altogether the state of the Church (if I may use a plain figure though it may seem too humble an one) is like an old coat, which is always being torn and can never be restored to its original strength. At such a time, then, there is need of great effort and diligence that the Churches may in some way be benefited. It is an advantage that parts hitherto severed should be united. Union would be effected if we were willing to accommodate ourselves to the weaker, where we can do so without injury to souls; since, then, many mouths are open against the Holy Ghost, and many tongues whetted to blasphemy against Him, we implore you, as far as in you lies, to reduce the blasphemers to a small number, and to receive into com-munion all who do not assert the Holy Ghost to be a creature, that the blasphemers may be left alone, and may either be ashamed and return to the truth, or, if they abide in their error, may cease to have any importance from the smallness of their numbers. Let us then seek no more than this, but propose to all the brethren, who are willing to join

---

[1] Herod. i. 45.   [2] Herod. i. 88.

[1] Placed in 372.
[2] That the Nicene Creed alone is to be required of the brethren.

us, the Nicene Creed. If they assent to that, let us further require that the Holy Ghost ought not to be called a creature, nor any of those who say so be received into communion. I do not think that we ought to insist upon anything beyond this. For I am convinced that by longer communication and mutual experience without strife, if anything more requires to be added by way of explanation, the Lord Who worketh all things together for good for them that love Him,[1] will grant it.

LETTER CXIV.[2]

To Cyriacus, at Tarsus.[3]

I NEED hardly tell the sons of peace how great is the blessing of peace. But now this blessing, great, marvellous, and worthy as it is of being most strenuously sought by all that love the Lord, is in peril of being reduced to the bare name, because iniquity abounds, and the love of most men has waxed cold.[4] I think then that the one great end of all who are really and truly serving the Lord ought to be to bring back to union the Churches now "at sundry times and in divers manners"[5] divided from one another. In attempting myself to effect this, I cannot fairly be blamed as a busybody, for nothing is so characteristically Christian as the being a peacemaker, and for this reason our Lord has promised us peacemakers a very high reward.

When, therefore, I had met the brethren, and learnt how great was their brotherly love, their regard for you, and yet more their love for Christ, and their exactitude and firmness in all that concerns the faith, and moreover their earnestness in compassing two ends, the not being separated from your love, and the not abandoning their sound faith, I approved of their good disposition; and I now write to your reverence beseeching you with all love to retain them in true union, and associated with you in all your anxiety for the Church. I have moreover pledged myself to them for your orthodoxy, and that you too by God's grace are enrolled to fight with all vigour for the truth, whatever you may have to suffer for the true doctrine. My own opinion is that the following conditions are such as will not run counter to your own feeling and will be quite sufficient to satisfy the above mentioned

brethren; namely, that you should confess the faith put forth by our Fathers once assembled at Nicæa, that you should not omit any one of its propositions, but bear in mind that the three hundred and eighteen who met together without strife did not speak without the operation of the Holy Ghost, and not to add to that creed the statement that the Holy Ghost is a creature, nor hold communion with those who so say, to the end that the Church of God may be pure and without any evil admixture of any tare. If this full assurance is given them by your good feeling, they are prepared to offer proper submission to you. And I myself promise for the brethren that they will offer no opposition, but will show themselves entirely subordinate, if only your excellency shall have readily granted this one thing which they ask for.

LETTER CXV.[1]

To the heretic Simplicia.[2]

WE often ill advisedly hate our superiors and love our inferiors. So I, for my part, hold my tongue, and keep silence about the disgrace of the insults offered me. I wait for the Judge above, Who knows how to punish all wickedness in the end, even though a man pour out gold like sand; let him trample on the right, he does but hurt his own soul. God always asks for sacrifice, not, I think, because He needs it, but because He accepts a pious and right mind as a precious sacrifice. But when a man by his transgressions tramples on himself God reckons his prayers impure. Bethink thyself, then, of the last day, and pray do not try to teach me. I know more than you do, and am not so choked with thorns within. I do not mind tenfold wickedness with a few good qualities. You have stirred up against me lizards and toads,[3]

---

[1] Rom. viii. 28.
[2] Placed in 372.
[3] Like the preceding Letter, on the sufficiency of the Nicene Creed.
[4] cf. Matt. xxiv. 12.   [5] cf. Heb. i. 1.

[1] Placed in 372.
[2] The Ben. Ed. note that in the imperial codex No. lxvii. appears an argument of this letter wanting in the editions of St. Basil. It is as follows: "Letter of the same to Simplicia about her eunuchs. She was a heretic. The blessed Basil being ill and entering a bath to bathe, Simplicia told her eunuchs and maids to throw his towels out. Straightway the just judgment of God slew some of them, and Simplicia sent money to the blessed Basil to make amends for the injury. Basil refused to receive it, and wrote this letter." This extraordinary preface seems to have been written by some annotator ignorant of the circumstances, which may be learnt from Greg. Naz. Letter xxxviii. It appears that a certain Cappadocian church, long without a bishop, had elected a slave of Simplicia, a lady wealthy and munificent, but of suspected orthodoxy. Basil and Gregory injudiciously ordained the reluctant slave without waiting for his mistress's consent. The angry lady wrote in indignation, and threatened him with the vengeance of her slaves and eunuchs. After Basil's death she returned to the charge, and pressed Gregory to get the ordination annulled. cf. Maran, Vit. Bas. chap. xxv.
[3] Presumably the slaves and eunuchs mentioned below. If the letter is genuine it is wholly unworthy of the Archbishop of Cæsarea.

beasts, it is true, of Spring time, but nevertheless unclean. But a bird will come from above who will devour them. The account I have to render is not according to your ideas, but as God thinks fit to judge. If witnesses are wanted, there will not stand before the Judge slaves; nor yet a disgraceful and detestable set of eunuchs; neither woman nor man, lustful, envious, ill-bribed, passionate, effeminate, slaves of the belly, mad for gold, ruthless, grumbling about their dinner, inconstant, stingy, greedy, insatiable, savage, jealous. What more need I say? At their very birth they were condemned to the knife. How can their mind be right when their feet are awry? They are chaste because of the knife, and it is no credit to them. They are lecherous to no purpose, of their own natural vileness. These are not the witnesses who shall stand in the judgment, but rather the eyes of the just and the eyesight of the perfect, of all who are then to see with their eyes what they now see with their understanding.

LETTER CXVI.[1]

To Firminius.[2]

You write seldom, and your letters are short, either because you shrink from writing or from avoiding the satiety that comes from excess; or perhaps to train yourself to curt speech. I, indeed, am never satisfied, and however abundant be your communication, it is less than my desire, because I wish to know every detail about you. How are you as to health? How as to ascetic discipline? Do you persevere in your original purpose? Or have you formed some new plan, changing your mind according to circumstances? Had you remained the same, I should not have wanted a great number of letters. I should have been quite satisfied with " I am quite well and I hope you are quite well." But I hear what I am ashamed to say, that you have deserted the ranks of your blessed forefathers, and deserted to your paternal grandfather, and are anxious to be rather a Brettanius than a Firminius. I am very anxious to hear about this, and to learn the reasons which have induced you to take to this kind of life. You have yourself been silent; ashamed, I suppose, of your intentions, and therefore I must implore you

not to entertain any project, which can be associated with shame. If any such idea has entered into your mind, put it from you, come to yourself again, bid a long farewell to soldiering and arms and the toils of the camp. Return home thinking it, as your forefathers thought before you, quite enough for ease of life and all possible distinction to hold a high place in your city. This, I am sure, you will be able to achieve without difficulty, when I consider your natural gifts and the small number of your rivals. If, then, this was not your original intention, or if after forming it you have rejected it, let me know at once. If, on the other hand, which God forbid, you remain in the same mind, let the trouble come self announced. I do not want a letter.

LETTER CXVII.

Without address.[1]

For many reasons I know that I am a debtor to your reverence, and now the anxiety in which I find myself necessarily puts me in the way of services of this kind, although my advisers are mere chance comers, and not like yourself joined to me by many and different ties. There is no need to bring the past under review. I may say that I was the cause of my own difficulties, by determining to leave that good discipline which alone leads to salvation. The result was that in this trouble I soon fell into temptation. What happened has seemed worthy of mention, so that I may not again fall into similar distress. As to the future, I wish to give full assurance to your reverence, that, by God's grace, all will go well, since the proceeding is lawful, and there is no difficulty about it, as many of my friends about the court are ready to help me. I shall therefore have a petition drawn up, similar to the form presented to the Vicar; and, if no delay intervene, I shall promptly get my discharge, and shall be sure to give you relief by sending you the formal document. I feel sure that in this my own convictions have more force than the imperial orders. If I shew this fixed and firm in the highest life, by God's aid the keeping of my chastity will be inviolable and sure. I have been pleased to see the brother entrusted to me by you, and hold him among my intimate friends. I trust he may prove worthy of God and of your good word.

---

[1] Placed in 372.
[2] A young soldier whom Basil would win from the army to ascetic life.

[1] Answer of Firminius to the preceding.

LETTER CXVIII.[1]

To Jovinus, Bishop of Perrha.[2]

You owe me a good turn. For I lent you a kindness, which I ought to get back with interest ;— a kind of interest, this, which our Lord does not refuse. Pay me, then, my friend, by paying me a visit. So much for the capital ; what of the increment? It is the fact of the visit being paid by you, who are a man as much superior to me, as fathers are better than children.

LETTER CXIX.[3]

To Eustathius, Bishop of Sebasteia.[4]

I ADDRESS you by the very honourable and reverend brother Petrus, beseeching you now and ever to pray for me, that I may be changed from ways dangerous and to be shunned, and may be made one day worthy of the name of Christ. Though I say nothing, you will converse together about my affairs, and he will give you an exact account of what has taken place. But you admit, without due examination, the vile suspicions against me which will probably be raised by men who have insulted me, in violation of the fear of God and the regard of men. I am ashamed to tell you what treatment I have received from the illustrious Basilius, whom I had accepted at the hands of your reverence as a protection for my life. But, when you have heard what our brother has to say, you will know every detail. I do not thus speak to avenge myself upon him, for I pray that it may not be put to his account by the Lord, but in order that your affection to me may remain firm, and because I am afraid lest it be shaken by the monstrous slanders which these men are pretty sure to make up in defence of their fall. Whatever be the charges they adduce, I hope your intelligence will put these enquiries to them. Have they formally accused me? Have they sought for any correction of the error which they bring against me? Have they made their griev-ance against me plain? As matters are, by their ignoble flight they have made it evi-dent that under the cheerfulness of their countenance, and their counterfeit expres-sions of affection, they are all the while hiding in their heart an immense depth of guile and of gall. In all this, whether I

narrate it or not, your intelligence knows perfectly well what sorrow they have caused me, and what laughter to those who, always expressing their abomination for the pious life in this wretched city, affirm that the pretence of virtue is practised as a mere trick to get credit, a mere assumption to de-ceive. So in these days no mode of life is now so suspected of vice by people here as the pro-fession of asceticism. Your intelligence will consider what is the best cure for all this.

As to the charges patched up against me by Sophronius, far from being a prelude of blessings, they are a beginning of division and separation, and are likely to lead to even my love growing cold. I implore that by your merciful kindness he may be withheld from his injurious efforts, and that your affection may strive rather to tighten the bonds of what is falling asunder, and not to increase separation by joining with those who are eager for dissent.

LETTER CXX.[1]

To Meletius, bishop of Antioch.[2]

I HAVE received a letter from the very God-beloved bishop Eusebius, in which he enjoins that a second letter be written to the West-erns about certain Church matters. He has expressed a wish that the letter should be drawn up by me, and signed by all those who are in communion. Having no means of writing a letter about these wishes of his, I have sent on his minute to your holiness, in order that, when you have read it and can give heed to the information given by the very dear brother Sanctissimus, our fellow presbyter, you may yourself be so good as to indite a letter on these points as seems best to you. We are prepared to agree to it and to lose no time in having it conveyed to those in communion with us, so that, when all have signed it may be carried by the messenger, who is on the point of start-ing on his journey to visit the bishops of the West. Give orders for the decision of your holiness to be communicated to me as quickly as possible, that I may not be igno-rant of your intentions.

As to the intrigue which is now being devised, or has already been devised against

---

[1] Placed at the end of 372 or the beginning of 373.
[2] The MSS. vary between Jovinus and Jobinus. *cf.* Theod-oret, *Ecc. Hist.* iv. 13.
[3] Placed in the end of 372 or beginning of 373.
[4] On the misconduct of Basilius and Sophronius, two dis-ciples of Eustathius.

[1] Placed in 373.
[2] Basil keeps up his support of the claims of Meletius, now in exile in Armenia, to be recognised as Catholic bishop of Antioch, and complains of the irregular ordination of Faustus as bishop of an Armenian see by Basil's opponent, Anthimus of Tyana. Sanctissimus, the bearer of the letter, is supposed by Tillemont (vol. ix. p. 210) to be a Western on account of his Latin name. Maran (*Vit. Bas.* 26) points out that Orien-tals not infrequently bore Latin names, and supposes him to be a presbyter of Antioch.

me, in Antioch, the same brother will convey intimation to your holiness, unless indeed the report of what has been done does not anticipate him and make the position clear. There is ground for hope that the threats are coming to an end.

I wish your reverence to know that our brother Anthimus has ordained Faustus, who is living with the pope [1] as bishop, without having received the votes, and in place of our right reverend brother Cyril. Thus he has filled Armenia with schisms. I have thought it right to tell your reverence this, lest they should lie against me, and I be responsible for these disorderly proceedings. You will of course deem it right to make this known to the rest. I think such irregularity will distress many.

LETTER CXXI.[2]

To Theodotus, bishop of Nicopolis.[3]

THE winter is severe and protracted, so that it is difficult for me even to have the solace of letters. For this reason I have written seldom to your reverence and seldom heard from you, but now my beloved brother Sanctissimus, the co-presbyter, has undertaken a journey as far as your city. By him I salute your lordship, and ask you to pray for me, and to give ear to Sanctissimus, that from him you may learn in what situation the Churches are placed, and may give all possible heed to the points put before you. You must know that Faustus came with letters for me, from the pope, requesting that he might be ordained bishop. When however I asked him for some testimonial from yourself, and the rest of the bishops, he made light of me and betook himself to Anthimus. He came back, ordained by Anthimus, without any communication having been made to me on the subject.

LETTER CXXII.[4]

To Pœmenius,[5] *bishop of Satala.*

WHEN the Armenians returned by your way you no doubt asked for a letter from them, and you learnt why I had not given the letter to them. If they spoke as truth lovers should, you forgave me on the spot; if they kept anything back (which I do not suppose), at all events hear it from me.

The most illustrious Anthimus, who long ago made peace with me, when he found an opportunity of satisfying his own vain gloriousness, and of causing me some vexation, consecrated Faustus, by his own authority and with his own hand, without waiting for any election from you, and ridiculing my punctiliousness in such matters. Inasmuch, then, as he has confounded ancient order and has made light of you, for whose election I was waiting, and has acted in a manner, as I view it, displeasing to God, for these reasons I felt pained with them, and gave no letter for any of the Armenians, not even for your reverence. Faustus I would not even receive into communion, thereby plainly testifying that, unless he brought me a letter from you, I should be permanently alienated from him, and should influence those of the same mind with me to treat him in the same manner. If there is any remedy for these things, be sure to write to me yourself, giving your testimony to him, if you see that his life is good; and exhort the rest. If on the other hand the mischief is incurable, let me perfectly understand it to be so, that I may no longer take them into account; although really, as they have proved, they have agreed, for the future, to transfer their communion to Anthimus, in contempt of me and of my Church, as though my friendship were no longer worth having.

LETTER CXXIII.[1]

To Urbicius, the monk.[2]

YOU were to have come to see me (and the blessing was drawing near) to cool me, aflame in my temptations, with the tip of your finger. What then? My sins stood in the way and hindered your start, so that I am sick without a remedy. Just as when the waves are round us, one sinks and another rises, and another looms black and dreadful, so of my troubles: some have ceased, some are with me, some are before me. As is generally the case, the one remedy for these troubles is to yield to the crisis and withdraw from my persecutors. Yet come to me, to console, to advise, or even to travel with me; in any case you will make me better for the mere sight of you. Above all, pray, and pray again, that my reason be not whelmed by the waves of my troubles; pray that all through I may keep a heart pleasing to God, that I be not numbered with the wicked servants, who thank a master when he gives them good, and refuse to submit when he chastises them by adversity; but let me reap benefit from my very trials, trusting most in God when I need Him most.

LETTER CXXIV.[1]

To Theodorus.

It is sometimes said that slaves to the passion of love, when by some inevitable necessity they are separated from the object of their desire, are able to stay the violence of their passion by indulging the sense of sight, if haply they can look at the picture of the beloved object. Whether this be true or not I cannot say; but what has befallen me in your case, my friend, is not very different. I have felt a disposition towards your godly and guileless soul, somewhat, if I may so say, of the nature of love; but the gratification of my desire, like that of all other blessings, is made difficult to me by the opposition of my sins. However, I have seemed to see a very good likeness of you in the presence of my very reverend brothers. And if it had been my lot to fall in with you when far away from them, I should have fancied that I saw them in you. For the measure of love in each of you is so great, that in both of you there is a plain contest for the superiority. I have thanked God for this. If any longer life be left me, I pray that my life may be made sweet through you, just as now I look on life as a wretched thing to be avoided, because I am separated from the companionship of those I love best. For, in my judgment, there is nothing in which one can be cheerful when cut off from those who truly love us.

LETTER CXXV.[2]

A transcript of the faith as dictated by Saint Basil, and subscribed by Eustathius, bishop of Sebasteia.[3]

1. Both men whose minds have been preoccupied by a heterodox creed and now wish to change over to the congregation of the orthodox, and also those who are now for the first time desirous of being instructed

in the doctrine of truth, must be taught the creed drawn up by the blessed fathers in the Council which met at Nicæa. The same training would also be exceedingly useful in the case of all who are under suspicion of being in a state of hostility to sound doctrine, and who by ingenious and plausible excuses keep the depravity of their sentiments out of view. For these too this creed is all that is needed. They will either get cured of their concealed unsoundness, or, by continuing to keep it concealed, will themselves bear the load of the sentence due to their dishonesty, and will provide us with an easy defence in the day of judgment, when the Lord will lift the cover from the hidden things of darkness, and "make manifest the counsels of the hearts."[1] It is therefore desirable to receive them with the confession not only that they believe in the words put forth by our fathers at Nicæa, but also according to the sound meaning expressed by those words. For there are men who even in this creed pervert the word of truth, and wrest the meaning of the words in it to suit their own notions. So Marcellus, when expressing impious sentiments concerning the hypostasis of our Lord Jesus Christ, and describing Him as being Logos and nothing more,[2] had the hardihood to profess to find a pretext for his principles in that creed by affixing an improper sense upon the Homoousion. Some, moreover, of the impious following of the Libyan Sabellius, who understand hypostasis and substance to be identical, derive ground for the establishment of their blasphemy from the same source, because of its having been written in the creed "if any one says that the Son is of a different substance or hypostasis, the Catholic and Apostolic Church anathematizes him." But they did not there state hypostasis and substance to be identical. Had the words expressed one and the same meaning, what need of both? It is on the contrary clear that while by some it was denied that the Son was of the same substance with the Father, and some asserted that He was not of the substance and was of some other hypostasis, they thus condemned both opinions as outside that held by the Church. When they set forth their own view, they declared the Son to be of the substance of the Father, but they did not add the words "of the hypostasis." The

---

[1] Placed in 373.   [2] Placed in 373.
[3] On Basil's relations with Eustathius of Sebasteia (Siwas in Armenia Minor), the Vicar of Bray of the Arian controversies, who probably subscribed more creeds than any other prominent bishop of his age, see Letters cxxx. and ccxliv., and p. 171, n.

[1] 1 Cor. i. 5.
[2] Marcellus of Ancyra (Angora) was represented to teach that the Son had no real personality, but was only the outward manifestation (Προφορικὸς Λόγος) of the Father, but he could always defend himself on the ground that he was in communion with Julius and Athanasius, popes of Rome and Alexandria. cf. Jer., De Vir. Ill. chap. lxxxvi.

former clause stands for the condemnation of the faulty view; the latter plainly states the dogma of salvation. We are therefore bound to confess the Son to be of one substance with the Father, as it is written; but the Father to exist in His own proper hypostasis, the Son in His, and the Holy Ghost in His, as they themselves have clearly delivered the doctrine. They indeed clearly and satisfactorily declared in the words Light of Light, that the Light which begat and the Light which was begotten, are distinct, and yet Light and Light; so that the definition of the Substance is one and the same.[1] I will now subjoin the actual creed as it was drawn up at Nicæa.[2]

2. πιστεύομεν εἰς ἕνα Θεὸν Πατέρα παντοκράτορα, πάντων ὁρατῶν τε καὶ ἀοράτων ποιητήν · [ποιητὴν οὐρανοῦ καὶ γῆς ὁρατῶν τε καὶ πάντων καὶ ἀοράτων ·]

καὶ εἰς ἕνα Κύριον Ἰησοῦν Χριστόν, τὸν υἱὸν τοῦ Θεοῦ [τὸν μονογενῆ] γεννηθέντα ἐκ τοῦ Πατρὸς μονογενῆ. [τὸν ἐκ τοῦ Πατρὸς γεννηθέντα πρὸ πάντων τῶν αἰώνων.]

τουτέστιν ἐκ τῆς οὐσίας τοῦ Πατρός, Θεὸν ἐκ Θεοῦ [omit],[3] Φῶς ἐκ Φωτός, Θεὸν ἀληθινὸν ἐκ Θεοῦ ἀληθινοῦ, γεννηθέντα οὐ ποιηθέντα, ὁμοούσιον τῷ Πατρὶ, δι᾽ οὗ τὰ πάντα ἐγένετο, τά τε ἐν τῷ οὐρανῷ καὶ τὰ ἐν τῇ γῇ [omit].

τὸν δι᾽ ἡμᾶς τοὺς ἀνθρώπους καὶ διὰ τὴν ἡμετέραν σωτηρίαν, κατελθόντα [ἐκ τῶν οὐρανῶν] καὶ σαρκωθέντα. [ἐκ πνεύματος ἁγίου καὶ Μαρίας τῆς παρθένου.]

καὶ ἐνανθρωπήσαντα [σταυρωθέντα τε ὑπὲρ ἡμῶν ἐπὶ Ποντίου Πιλάτου, καὶ], παθόντα [καὶ ταφέντα], καί ἀναστάντα τῇ τρίτῃ ἡμέρα [κατὰ τὰς γραφὰς καὶ], ἀνελθόντα εἰς τοὺς οὐρανούς, [καὶ καθεζόμενον ἐκ δεξιῶν τοῦ Πατρός.]

καί πάλιν ἐρχόμενον [μετὰ δόξης] κρῖναι ζῶντας καὶ νεκρούς · [οὗ τῆς βασιλείας οὐκ ἔσται τέλος ·]

καὶ εἰς τὸ Πνεῦμα τὸ ἅγιον. [τὸ Κύριον καὶ τὸ ζωοποιὸν τὸ ἐκ τοῦ Πατρὸς ἐκπορευόμενον, τὸ σὺν Πατρὶ καὶ Υἱῷ συμπροσκυνούμενον καὶ συνδοξαζόμενον, τὸ λαλῆσαν διὰ τῶν προφητῶν · εἰς μίαν ἁγίαν καθολικὴν καὶ ἀποστολικὴν ἐκκλησίαν, ὁμολογοῦμεν ἓν βάπτισμα εἰς ἄφεσιν ἁμαρτιῶν, προσδοκῶμεν ἀνάστασιν νεκρῶν, καὶ ζωὴν τοῦ μέλλοντος αἰῶνος. Ἀμήν.]

τοὺς δὲ λέγοντας, ἦν ποτε ὅτε οὐκ ἦν, καὶ πρὶν γεννηθῆναι οὐκ ἦν, καὶ ὅτι ἐξ οὐκ ὄντων ἐγένετο, ἢ ἐξ ἑτέρας ὑποστάσεως ἢ οὐσίας φάσκοντας εἶναι, ἢ κτιστὸν ἢ τρεπτὸν ἢ ἀλλοιωτὸν τὸν Υἱὸν τοῦ Θεοῦ, τούτους ἀναθεματίζει ἡ καθολικὴ καὶ ἀποστολικὴ ἐκκλησια. [Omit all the Anathemas.]

3. Here then all points but one are satisfactorily and exactly defined, some for the correction of what had been corrupted, some as a precaution against errors expected to arise. The doctrine of the Spirit, however, is merely mentioned, as needing no elaboration, because at the time of the Council no question was mooted, and the opinion on this subject in the hearts of the faithful was exposed to no attack. Little by little, however, the growing poison-germs of impiety, first sown by Arius, the champion of the heresy, and then by those who succeeded to his inheritance of mischief, were nurtured to the plague of the Church, and the regular development of the impiety issued in blasphemy against the Holy Ghost. Under these circumstances we are under the necessity of putting before the men who have no pity for themselves, and shut their eyes to the inevitable threat directed by our Lord against blasphemers of the Holy Ghost, their bounden duty. They must anathematize all who call the Holy Ghost a creature, and all who so think; all who do not confess that He is holy by nature, as the Father is holy by nature, and the Son is holy by nature, and refuse Him His place in the blessed divine nature. Our not separating Him from Father and Son is a proof of our right mind, for we are bound to be baptized in the terms we have received and to profess belief in the terms in which we are baptized, and as we have professed belief in, so to give glory to Father, Son, and Holy Ghost; and to hold aloof from the communion of all who call Him creature, as from open blasphemers. One point must be regarded as settled; and the remark is necessary because of our slanderers; we do not speak of the Holy Ghost as unbegotten, for we recognise one Unbegotten and one Origin of all things,[1] the Father of our Lord Jesus Christ: nor do we speak of the Holy Ghost as begotten, for by the tradition of the faith we have been taught one Only-begotten: the Spirit of truth we have been taught to proceed from the Father, and we confess Him to be of God without creation. We are also bound to anathematize all who speak of the Holy Ghost as ministerial,[2] inasmuch as by this term they degrade Him to the rank of a creature. For that the ministering spirits are creatures we are told by Scripture in the words "they are all ministering spirits sent forth to minister."[3] But

---

[1] cf. *Letters* xxxviii. and xcii. Basil is anxious to show that his own view is identical with the Nicene, and does not admit a development and variation in the meaning of the word hypostasis; but on comparing such a passage as that in Athan. *c. Afros,* "hypostasis is substance, and means nothing else but very being" (ἡ δὲ ὑπόστασις οὐσία ἐστὶ καὶ οὐδὲν ἄλλο σημαινόμενον ἔχει ἢ αὐτὸ τὸ ὄν) with St. Basil's words in the text it appears plain that hypostasis is not used throughout in the same sense. An erroneous sense of "three hypostases" was understood to be condemned at Nicæa, though Athanasius, *e.g.* "*In illud omnia,*" etc., Schaff and Wace's ed., p. 90, does himself use the phrase, writing probably about ten years after Nicæa; but he more commonly treats οὐσία and ὑπόστασις as identical. See specially the *Tomus ad Antiochenos* of A.D. 362 on the possible use of either "three hypostases" or "one hypostasis." *cf.* also n. on p. 179.
[2] I give the creed in the original Greek. The passages in brackets indicate the alterations of the Constantinopolitan revision according to the text of Chalcedon.
[3] "*Deum de Deo*" is inserted in the Sarum Breviary.

[1] cf. pp. 27 and 39, notes.
[2] cf. *De Sp. S.* § 25, p. 17. On those who described the Spirit as merely a ministering spirit, *vide* Athan., Ad *Serap.* i. (λεγόντων αὐτὸ μὴ μόνον κτίσμα, ἀλλὰ καὶ τῶν λειτουργικῶν πνευμάτων ἐν αὐτὸ εἶναι). This new party arose in the Delta about 362, and was first known as "Tropici." They were condemned at the synod held at Alexandria on the return of Athanasius from his third exile. Its Synodical *Letter* is the *Tomus ad Antiochenos.* [3] Heb. i. 14.

because of men who make universal confusion, and do not keep the doctrine of the Gospels, it is necessary to add yet this further, that they are to be shunned, as plainly hostile to true religion, who invert the order left us by the Lord, and put the Son before the Father, and the Holy Spirit before the Son. For we must keep unaltered and inviolable that order which we have received from the very words of the Lord, "Go ye therefore and teach all nations, baptizing them in the name of the Father and of the Son, and of the Holy Ghost." [1]

I, Eustathius, bishop, have read to thee, Basil, and understood; and I assent to what is written above. I have signed in the presence of our Fronto, Severus, the chorepiscopus, and several other clerics.

LETTER CXXVI.[2]

To Atarbius.[3]

ON arriving at Nicopolis in the double hope of settling the disturbances which had arisen, and applying a remedy, as far as possible, to measures taken in a disorderly manner and in violation of the law of the Church, I was exceedingly disappointed at failing to meet you. I heard that you had hurriedly withdrawn, and actually from the very synod which was being held by you. I am, therefore, under the necessity of having recourse to writing, and by this letter I bid you present yourself before me, that you may in person apply some remedy to the pain which I felt, even unto death, on hearing that you had ventured on action, in the very middle of the church, of the like of which I hitherto have never heard. All this, although painful and serious, is endurable, as having happened to a man who has committed the punishment due for his sufferings to God, and is wholly devoted to peace and to preventing harm falling from any fault of his on God's people. Since, however, some honourable brethren, worthy of all credit, have told me that you have introduced certain innovations into the faith, and have spoken against sound doctrine, I am under the circumstances the more agitated, and above measure anxious, lest, in addition to the countless wounds which have been inflicted on the Church by traitors to the truth of the Gospel, yet a further calamity should spring up in the renewal of the ancient heresy of Sabellius, the enemy of the Church; for to this the brethren have reported your utter-

ances to be akin. I have, therefore, written to charge you not to shrink from undertaking a short journey to come to me, and, by giving me full assurance in the matter, at once to alleviate my pangs, and to solace the Churches of God, which are now pained to a grave, nay an unendurable extent, at your actions and your reported words.

LETTER CXXVII.[1]

To Eusebius, bishop of Samosata.[2]

OUR merciful God, Who makes comfort match trouble, and consoles the lowly, lest they be drowned unawares in exceeding grief, has sent a consolation, equivalent to the troubles I have suffered in Nicopolis, in seasonably bringing me the God-beloved bishop Jobinus. He must tell you himself how very opportune his visit was. I shrink from a long letter, and will hold my peace. And I am the more inclined to silence, lest I seem as it were to put a mark on men, who have turned round and begun to show regard to me, by mentioning their fall.

God grant that you may come to see me in my own home, so that I may embrace your reverence and tell you everything in detail. For we often find some comfort in telling what is painful in actual experience. However, for all that the very godly bishop has done, fully as far as regards his affection for me, and preëminently and stoutly as regards the exact observance of the canons, commend him. Moreover, thank God that your pupils everywhere exhibit your reverence's character.

LETTER CXXVIII.[3]

To Eusebius, bishop of Samosata.[4]

1. HITHERTO I have been unable to give any adequate and practical proof of my earnest desire to pacify the Churches of the Lord. But in my heart I affirm that I have so great a longing, that I would gladly give up even my life, if thereby the flame of hatred, kindled by the evil one, could be put out. If it was not for the sake of this longing for peace that I consented to come to Colonia,[5] may my life be unblessed by peace. The peace I seek is the true peace, left us by the Lord Himself; and what I have asked that I may have for my assurance belongs to one who desires nothing but the true peace,

---

[1] Matt. xxviii. 14. [2] Placed in 373.
[3] Bishop of Neocæsarea. *Vide Letter* lxv.

[1] Placed in 373.
[2] On Basil's difficulties while at Nicopolis, with a request for the sympathy of Eusebius.
[3] Placed in 373.
[4] On the difficulty of reconciliation with Eustathius.
[5] Maran supposes this to be the place referred to in *Letter* ccxliv. 2.

although some perversely interpret the truth into another sense. Let them use their tongues as they will, but assuredly they will one day be sorry for their words.

2. Now I beseech your holiness to remember the original propositions, and not to be led away by receiving answers that do not fit the questions, nor yet to give practical weight to the quibbles of men who, without any power of argument, very cleverly pervert the truth, from their own ideas alone. I set out propositions which were perfectly simple, clear and easy to remember; do we decline to receive into communion those who refuse to accept the Nicene Creed? Do we refuse to have part or lot with those who have the hardihood to assert that the Holy Ghost is a creature? He, however,[1] instead of answering my questions word for word, has concocted the statement which you have sent me : — and this not from simplemindedness, as might be imagined, nor yet from his inability to see the consequences. What he reckons is that, by repudiating my proposition, he will expose his true character to the people; while, if he agrees to it, he will depart from that *via media* which has hitherto seemed to him preferable to any other position. Let him not try to beguile me, nor, with the rest, deceive your intelligence. Let him send a concise answer to my question, whether he accepts or repudiates communion with the enemies of the faith. If you get him to do this and send me such a distinct answer as I pray for, I own myself in error in all that has gone before; I take all the blame upon myself; then ask from me a proof of humility. But, if nothing of the kind come to pass, pardon me, most God-beloved father, in my inability to approach God's altar with hypocrisy. Were it not for this dread, why should I separate myself from Euippius, so learned a man, so advanced in age, and bound to me by so many ties of affection? If, however, in this case I acted rightly, it would, I am sure, be absurd to appear united with those who maintain the same views as Euippius, through the mediation of these amiable and charming persons.

3. Not that I think it is absolutely our duty to cut ourselves off from those who do not receive the faith, but rather to have regard to them in accordance with the old law of love, and to write to them with one consent, giving them all exhortation with pity, and to propose to them the faith of the fathers, and invite them to union. If we succeed we should be united in communion with them; if we fail we must be content with one another and purge our conduct of this uncertain spirit, restoring the evangelical and simple conversation followed by those who accepted the Word from the beginning. " They," it is said, " were of one heart and of one soul."[1] If they obey you, this will be best; if not, recognise the real authors of the war, and, for the future do not write me any more letters about reconciliation.

LETTER CXXIX.[2]

To Meletius Bishop of Antioch.[3]

1. I KNEW that the charge which had lately sprung up against the loquacious Apollinarius would sound strange in the ears of your excellency. I did not know myself, till now, that he was accused; at the present time, however, the Sebastenes, after search in some quarter or another, have brought these things forward, and they are carrying about a document for which they are specially trying to condemn me on the ground that I hold the same sentiments. It contains the following phrases. " Wherefore it is everywhere necessary to understand the first identity in conjunction with, or rather in union with, the second, and to say that the second and the third are the same. For what the Father is firstly, the Son is secondly, and the Spirit thirdly. And, again, what the Spirit is firstly, the Son is secondly, in so far as the Spirit is the Lord; and the Father thirdly, in so far as the Spirit is God. And, to express the ineffable with greatest force, Father is Son in a paternal sense, and the Son Father in a filial sense, and so in the case of the Spirit, in so far as the Trinity is one God." This is what is being bruited about. I never can believe it to have been invented by those through whom it has been published, although, after their slanders against me, I can regard nothing as beyond their audacity. For writing to some of their party, they advanced their false accusation against me, and then added the words I have quoted, describing them as the work of heretics, but saying nothing as to the author of the document, in order that it might vulgarly be supposed to have come from my pen. Nevertheless, in my opinion, their intelligence would not have gone far enough in putting the phrases together. On this account, in order to repudiate the growing

---

[1] Acts iv. 32. [2] Placed in 373.
[3] A refutation of a charge that he was the author of an Apollinarian document.

blasphemy against myself, and shew to all the world that I have nothing in common with those who make such statements, I have been compelled to mention Apollinarius as approximating to the impiety of Sabellius. Of this subject I will say no more.

2. I have received a message from the court that, after the first impulse of the Emperor, to which he was impelled by my calumniators, a second decree has been passed, that I am not to be delivered to my accusers, nor given over to their will, as was ordered at the beginning; but that there has been in the meanwhile some delay. If then this obtains, or any gentler measure is determined on, I will let you know. If the former prevails, it shall not be so, without your knowledge.

3. Our brother Sanctissimus has certainly been with you a long time, and you have learnt the objects he has in view. If, then, the letter to the Westerns seems to you to contain at all what is requisite, be so good as to have it written out and conveyed to me, that I may get it signed by those who think with us, and may keep the subscription ready, and written out on a separate paper, which we can fasten on to the letter which is being carried about by our brother and fellow presbyter. As I did not find in the minute anything conclusive, I was in a difficulty on what point to write to the Westerns. Necessary points are anticipated, and it is useless to write what is superfluous, and on such points would it not be ridiculous to show feeling? One subject, however, did appear to me to be hitherto untouched, and to suggest a reason for writing, and that was an exhortation to them not indiscriminately to accept the communion of men coming from the East; but, after once choosing one side, to receive the rest on the testimony of their fellows, and not to assent to every one writing a form of creed on the pretext of orthodoxy. If they do so, they will be found in communion with men at war with one another, who often put forward the same formulæ, and yet battle vehemently against one another, as those who are most widely separated. To the end, then, that the heresy may not be the more widely kindled, while those who are at variance with one another mutually object to their own formulæ, they ought to be exhorted to make a distinction between the acts of communion which are brought them by chance comers, and those which are duly drawn up according to the rule of the Church.[1]

LETTER CXXX.[1]

To Theodotus bishop of Nicopolis.

1. You have very rightly and properly blamed me, right honourable and well beloved brother, in that ever since I departed from your reverence, conveying to Eustathius those propositions about the faith, I have told you neither much nor little about his business. This neglect is really not due to any contempt on my part for the way in which he has treated me, but simply to the fact that the story is now published abroad in all men's ears, and nobody needs any instructions from me in order to learn what his intentions are. For this he has had good heed, as though he were really afraid that he would have few witnesses of his opinion, and has sent to the ends of the earth the letter which he has written against me. He has therefore severed himself from communion with me. He did not consent to meet me at the appointed spot, and did not bring his disciples, as he had promised. On the contrary, he publicly stigmatized me in the public synods, with the Cilician Theophilus,[2] by the open and undisguised slander of sowing in the souls of the people doctrines at variance with his own teaching. This was quite enough to break up all union between us. Afterwards he came to Cilicia, and, on meeting with a certain Gelasius, showed him the creed which only an Arian, or a thorough disciple of Arius, could subscribe. Then, indeed, I was yet more confirmed in my alienation from him. I felt that the Ethiopian will never change his skin, nor the leopard his spots,[3] nor a man nurtured in doctrines of perversity ever be able to rub off the stain of his heresy.

2. In addition to all this he has had the impudence to write against me, or rather to compose long discourses full of all kinds of abuse and calumny. To these, up to this time, I have answered nothing, taught as we are by the Apostle, not to avenge ourselves, but to give place unto wrath.[4] Moreover, at the thought of the depth of the hypocrisy with which he has all along approached me, I have, in a way, become speechless with amazement. But, if all this had never happened, who would not feel horror and detestation of the fellow at this fresh piece of audacity? Now, as I hear, if the report is really true and not a slanderous invention, he has ventured to re-ordain

---

[1] The Ben. note adduces this letter and *Letter* ccxxiv. as shewing two kinds of communion, (1) Personal in the Eucharist and prayer, and (2) by letter.

[1] Placed in 373.
[2] Bishop of Castabala, whither he was translated from Eleutheropolis. *cf. Letters* ccxliv. and ccxlv.
[3] *cf.* Jer. xiii. 23.   [4] Rom. xii. 19.

certain men; a proceeding on which so far no heretic has ventured. How then can I quietly endure such treatment? How can I look upon the errors of the man as curable? Beware, then, of being led away by lies; do not be moved by the suspicions of men who are prone to look at everything in a bad light, as though I were making little of such things. For, be sure, my very dear and honourable friend, that I have never at any time been so grieved as I am now, on hearing of this confusion of the laws of the Church. Pray only that the Lord grant me to take no step in anger, but to maintain charity, which behaveth itself not unseemly and is not puffed up.[1] Only look how men without charity have been lifted up beyond all human bounds and conduct themselves in an unseemly manner, daring deeds which have no precedent in all the past.[2]

LETTER CXXXI.[3]

To Olympius.[4]

1. TRULY unexpected tidings make both ears tingle. This is my case. These compositions against me, which are being carried about, have fallen upon ears by this time pretty well seasoned, on account of my having formerly received the letter, appropriate enough to my sins, but which I should never have expected to be written by those who sent it. Nevertheless what followed did seem to me so extraordinarily cruel as to blot out all that had gone before. How could I fail to be driven almost out of my senses when I read the letter addressed to the reverend brother Dazinas, full of outrageous insults and calumnies and of attacks against me, as though I had been convicted of much pernicious designs against the Church? Moreover proofs were forthwith offered of the truth of the calumnies against me, from the document of whose authorship I am ignorant. Parts I recognise, I own, as having been written by Apollinarius of Laodicea. These I had purposely not even ever read, but I had heard of them from the report of others. Other portions I found included, which I had never either read or heard of from any one else; of the truth of this there is a faith-

ful witness in heaven. How then can men who shun lies, who have learnt that love is the fulfilling of the law, who profess to bear the burdens of the weak, have consented to bring these calumnies against me and to condemn me out of other men's writings? I have often asked myself this question, but I cannot imagine the reason, unless it be, as I have said from the beginning, that my pain in all this is a part of the punishment which is due to my sins.

2. First of all I sorrowed in soul that truths were lessened by the sons of men; in the second place I feared for my own self, lest in addition to my other sins, I should become a misanthrope, believing no truth and honour to be left in any man; if indeed those whom I have most greatly trusted are proved to be so disposed both to me and to the truth. Be sure then, my brother, and every one who is a friend of the truth, that the composition is not mine; I do not approve of it, for it is not drawn up according to my views. Even if I did write, a good many years ago, to Apollinarius or to any one else, I ought not to be blamed. I find no fault myself if any member of any society has been cut off into heresy (and you know perfectly well whom I mean though I mention nobody by name), because each man will die in his own sin.

This is my reply to the document sent me, that you may know the truth, and make it plain to all who wish not to hold the truth in unrighteousness. If it prove necessary to defend myself more at length on each separate count, I will do so, God being my helper. I, brother Olympius, neither maintain three Gods, nor communicate with Apollinarius.[1]

LETTER CXXXII.[2]

To Abramius, bishop of Batnæ.[3]

EVER since the autumn I have been quite ignorant of the whereabouts of your reverence; for I kept hearing uncertain rumours, some saying that you were stopping at Samosata, and some in the country, while others maintained that they had seen you at Batnæ. This is the reason of my not writing frequently. Now, on hearing that you are staying at Antioch, in the house of the honourable Count Saturninus, I have been glad to give this letter to our beloved and reverend brother Sanctissimus, our fellow presbyter,

---

[1] 1 Cor. xiii. 5 and 4.
[2] There is no other mention in Basil's letters of Eustathius being guilty of re-ordination. The Ben. note, however, states that Basil is not accurate in saying that there was no heretical precedent for such proceedings. The Arians are charged with it in the Book of the Prayers of Faustus and Marcellinus, Bib. Patr. v. 655. cf. also the letter of Constantius to the Ethiopians against Frumentius. Athan., Apol. ad Const. § 31.
[3] Placed in 373.   [4] cf. Letters xii. and xiii.

[1] cf. Letter cxxv. and Greg. Naz., Orat. i. and xxix.
[2] Placed in 373.
[3] cf. Letter xcii. He was present at the Council of Constantinople.

by whom I salute you, and exhort you, wherever you be, to remember firstly God, and secondly myself, whom you determined from the beginning to love and to reckon among your most intimate friends.

LETTER CXXXIII.

To Peter, bishop of Alexandria.[1]

THE sight of the eyes brings about bodily friendship, and long companionship strengthens it, but genuine regard is the gift of the Spirit, Who unites what is separated by long distances, and makes friends known to one another, not by bodily qualities, but by the characteristics of the soul. The grace of the Lord has granted me this favour, by permitting me to see you with the soul's eye, and to embrace you with genuine affection, and as it were, to be drawn very near to you, and to come into close union with you in the communion of faith. I am sure that you, disciple as you are of so great a man, and long associated with him, will walk in the same spirit and follow the same doctrines of true religion. Under these circumstances I address your excellency, and beseech you that among the other things in which you have succeeded that great man, you will succeed him in love to me, that you will frequently write me news of you, and will give heed to the brotherhood all over the world with the same affection and the same zeal which that most blessed man always showed to all that love God in truth.

LETTER CXXXIV.[2]

To the presbyter Pæonius.

YOU may conjecture from what it contains, what pleasure you have given me by your letter. The pureness of heart, from which such expressions sprang, was plainly signified by what you wrote. A streamlet tells of its own spring, and so the manner of speech marks the heart from which it came. I must confess that an extraordinary and improbable thing has happened to me. For deeply anxious as I always was to receive a letter from your excellency, when I had taken your letter into my hand and had read it, I was not so much pleased at what you had written, as annoyed at reckoning up the loss I had suffered in your long silence. Now that you have begun to write, pray do not leave off. You will give me greater

pleasure than men can give by sending much money to misers. I have had no writer with me, neither caligraphist, nor short-hand. Of all those whom I happen to employ, some have returned to their former mode of life, and others are unfit for work from long sickness.

LETTER CXXXV.[1]

To Diodorus, presbyter of Antioch.[2]

1. I HAVE read the books sent me by your excellency. With the second I was delighted, not only with its brevity, as was likely to be the case with a reader out of health and inclined to indolence, but, because it is at once full of thought, and so arranged that the objections of opponents, and the answers to them, stand out distinctly. Its simple and natural style seems to me to befit the profession of a Christian who writes less for self-advertisement than for the general good. The former work, which has practically the same force, but is much more elaborately adorned with rich diction, many figures, and niceties of dialogue, seems to me to require considerable time to read, and much mental labour, both to gather its meaning and retain it in the memory. The abuse of our opponents and the support of our own side, which are thrown in, although they may seem to add some charms of dialectic to the treatise, do yet break the continuity of the thought and weaken the strength of the argument, by causing interruption and delay. I know that your intelligence is perfectly well aware that the heathen philosophers who wrote dialogues, Aristotle and Theophrastus, went straight to the point, because they were aware of their not being gifted with the graces of Plato. Plato, on the other hand, with his great power of writing, at the same time attacks opinions and incidentally makes fun of his characters, assailing now the rashness and recklessness of a Thrasymachus, the levity and frivolity of a Hippias, and the arrogance and pomposity of a Protagoras. When, however, he introduces unmarked characters into his dialogues, he uses the interlocutors for making the point clear, but does not admit anything more belonging to the characters into his argument. An instance of this is in the Laws.

---

[1] Peter II. succeeded Athanasius in May, 373. Athanasius died May 2.   [2] Placed in 373.

[1] Placed in 373.
[2] cf. Letter clx. Theodoret, Hist. Ecc. iv. 24. He was a pupil of Silvanus, bishop of Tarsus Letter ccxliv. Theodoret, Ep. xvi., refers to his obligations to him as a teacher. In 378 he became bishop of Tarsus. Only some fragments of his works remain, the bulk having been destroyed, it is said, by the Arians.

2. It is well for us too, who betake ourselves to writing, not from any vain ambition, but from the design of bequeathing counsels of sound doctrine to the brethren, if we introduce some character well known to all the world for presumption of manners, to interweave into the argument some points in accordance with the quality of the character, unless indeed we have no right at all to leave our work and to accuse men. But if the subject of the dialogue be wide and general, digressions against persons interrupt its continuity and tend to no good end. So much I have written to prove that you did not send your work to a flatterer, but have shared your toil with a real brother. And I have spoken not for the correction of what is finished, but as a precaution for the future; for assuredly one who is so accustomed to write, and so diligent in writing, will not hesitate to do so; and the more so that there is no falling off in the number of those who give him subjects. Enough for me to read your books. I am as far from being able to write anything as, I had very nearly said, I am from being well, or from having the least leisure from my work. I have however now sent back the larger and earlier of the two volumes, after perusing it as far as I have been able. The second I have retained, with the wish to transcribe it, but, hitherto, without finding any quick writer. To such a pitch of poverty has come the enviable condition of the Cappadocians!

LETTER CXXXVI.[1]

To Eusebius, bishop of Samosata.[2]

1. In what state the good Isaaces has found me, he himself will best explain to you; though his tongue cannot be tragic enough to describe my sufferings, so great was my illness. However, any one who knows me ever so little, will be able to conjecture what it was. For, if when I am called well, I am weaker even than persons who are given over, you may fancy what I was when thus ill. Yet, since disease is my natural state, it would follow (let a fever have its jest) that in this change of habit, my health became especially flourishing. But it is the scourge of the Lord which goes on increasing my pain according to my deserts; therefore I have received illness upon illness, so that now even a child may see that this shell of mine must for certain fail, unless

perchance, God's mercy vouchsafe to me, in His long suffering, time for repentance, and now, as often before, extricate me from evils beyond human cure. This shall be, as it is pleasing to Him and good for myself.

2. I need hardly tell you how deplorable and hopeless is the condition of the Churches. Now, for the sake of our own safety, we neglect our neighbour's, and do not even seem able to see that general disaster involves individual ruin. Least of all need I say this to one who, like yourself, foresaw the future from afar, and has foretold and proclaimed it and has been among the first to be roused, and to rouse the rest, writing letters, coming yourself in person, leaving no deed undone, no word unspoken. I remember this in every instance, but yet we are none the better off. Now, indeed, were not my sins in the way, (first of all, my dear brother the reverend deacon Eustathius fell seriously ill and detained me two whole months, looking day by day for his restoration to health; and then all about me fell sick; brother Isaaces will tell you the rest; then last of all I myself was attacked by this complaint) I should long ago have been to see your excellency, not indeed thereby to try to improve the general state of affairs, but to get some good for myself from your society. I had made up my mind to get out of the reach of the ecclesiastical artillery, because I am quite unprepared to meet my enemies' attacks. May God's mighty hand preserve you for all of us, as a noble guardian of the faith, and a vigilant champion of the Churches; and grant me, before I die, to meet you for the comfort of my soul.

LETTER CXXXVII.[1]

To Antipater, on his assuming the governorship of Cappadocia.[2]

I do now really feel the loss which I suffer from being ill; so that, when such a man succeeds to the government of my country, my having to nurse myself compels me to be absent. For a whole month I have been undergoing the treatment of natural hot springs, in the hope of drawing some benefit from them. But I seem to be troubling myself to no purpose in my solitude, or indeed to be deservedly a laughing stock to mankind, for not heeding the proverb which says "warmth is no good to the dead." Even situated as I am, I am very anxious to put aside everything else, and betake myself to

---

[1] Placed in 373.
[2] On his own sickness and the troubles of the Church. On his bad health, cf. Letters ix., xxvii., cxcviii., ccii., cciii., and ccxvi. The translation of the first section is Newman's.

[1] Placed in 373.
[2] Compare Letters clxxxvi. and clxxxvii.

your excellency, that I may enjoy the benefit of all your high qualities, and through your goodness settle all my home affairs here in a proper manner. The house of our reverend mother Palladia is my own, for I am not only nearly related to her, but regard her as a mother on account of her character. Now, as some disturbance has been raised about her house, I ask your excellency to postpone the enquiry for a little while, and to wait till I come; not at all that justice may not be done, for I had rather die ten thousand times than ask a favour of that kind from a judge who is a friend of law and right, but that you may learn from me by word of mouth matters which it would be unbecoming for me to write. If you do so you will in no wise fail in fealty to the truth, and we shall suffer no harm. I beg you then to keep the individual in question[1] in safe custody under the charge of the troops, and not refuse to grant me this harmless favour.

LETTER CXXXVIII.[2]

To Eusebius, bishop of Samosata.[3]

1. WHAT was my state of mind, think you, when I received your piety's letter? When I thought of the feelings which its language expressed, I was eager to fly straight to Syria; but when I thought of the bodily illness, under which I lay bound, I saw myself unequal, not only to flying, but even to turning on my bed. This day, on which our beloved and excellent brother and deacon, Elpidius, has arrived, is the fiftieth of my illness. I am much reduced by the fever. For lack of what it might feed on, it lingers in this dry flesh as in an expiring wick, and so has brought on a wasting and tedious illness. Next my old plague, the liver, coming upon it, has kept me from taking nourishment, prevented sleep, and held me on the confines of life and death, granting just life enough to feel its inflictions. In consequence I have had recourse to the hot springs, and have availed myself of help from medical men.

But for all these the mischief has proved too strong. Perhaps another man might endure it, but, coming as it did unexpectedly, no one is so stout as to bear it. Long troubled by it as I have been, I have never been so distressed as now at being prevented by it from meeting you and enjoying your true friendship. I know of how much

pleasure I am deprived, although last year I did touch with the tip of my finger the sweet honey of your Church.

2. For many urgent reasons I felt bound to meet your reverence, both to discuss many things with you and to learn many things from you. Here it is not possible even to find genuine affection. And, could one even find a true friend, none can give counsel to me in the present emergency with anything like the wisdom and experience which you have acquired in your many labours on the Church's behalf. The rest I must not write. I may, however, safely say what follows. The presbyter Evagrius,[1] son of Pompeianus of Antioch, who set out some time ago to the West with the blessed Eusebius, has now returned from Rome. He demands from me a letter couched in the precise terms dictated by the Westerns. My own he has brought back again to me, and reports that it did not give satisfaction to the more precise authorities there. He also asks that a commission of men of repute may be promptly sent, that they may have a reasonable pretext for visiting me. My sympathisers in Sebasteia have stripped the covering from the secret sore of the unorthodoxy of Eustathius, and demand my ecclesiastical care.[2]

Iconium is a city of Pisidia, anciently the first after the greatest,[3] and now it is capital of a part, consisting of an union of different portions, and allowed the government of a distinct province. Iconium too calls me to visit her and to give her a bishop; for Faustinus[4] is dead. Whether I ought to shrink from consecrations over the border; what answer I ought to give to the Sebastenes; what attitude I should show to the propositions of Evagrius; all these are questions to which I was anxious to get answers in a personal interview with you, for here in my present weakness I am cut off from everything. If, then, you can find any one soon coming this way, be so good as to give me your answer on them all. If not, pray that what is pleasing to the Lord may come into my mind. In your synod also bid mention to be made of me, and pray for me yourself, and join your people with you

---

[1] Possibly the person to whom the disturbance at Palladia's house was due.　　　[2] Placed in 373.
[3] The translation of Sec. 1, down to "medical men," is partly Newman's.

[1] On Evagrius, known generally as Evagrius of Antioch, to distinguish him from Evagrius the historian, see especially Theodoret, *Ecc. Hist.* v. 23. He had travelled to Italy with Eusebius of Vercellæ. His communication to Basil from the Western bishops must have been disappointing and unsatisfactory. On his correspondence with Basil, after his return to Antioch, see *Letter* clvi. His consecration by the dying Paulinus in 388 inevitably prolonged the disastrous Meletian schism at Antioch.
[2] *i.e.* that Basil, as primate, should either consecrate them an orthodox bishop, or, if this was impossible under Valens, should take them under his own immediate episcopal protection.
[3] *i.e.* Antioch.
[4] He was succeeded by John I. *cf. Letter* clxi. and note.

in the prayer that it may be permitted me to continue my service through the remaining days or hours of my sojourning here in a manner pleasing to the Lord.

LETTER CXXXIX.[1]

To the Alexandrians.[2]

1. I HAVE already heard of the persecution in Alexandria and the rest of Egypt, and, as might be expected, I am deeply affected. I have observed the ingenuity of the devil's mode of warfare. When he saw that the Church increased under the persecution of enemies and flourished all the more, he changed his plan. He no longer carries on an open warfare, but lays secret snares against us, hiding his hostility under the name which they bear, in order that we may both suffer like our fathers, and, at the same time, seem not to suffer for Christ's sake, because our persecutors too bear the name of Christians. With these thoughts for a long time we sat still, dazed at the news of what had happened, for, in sober earnest, both our ears tingled on hearing of the shameless and inhuman heresy of your persecutors. They have reverenced neither age, nor services to society,[3] nor people's affection. They inflicted torture, ignominy, and exile; they plundered all the property they could find; they were careless alike of human condemnation and of the awful retribution to come at the hands of the righteous Judge. All this has amazed me and all but driven me out of my senses. To my reflections has been added this thought too; can the Lord have wholly abandoned His Churches? Has the last hour come, and is "the falling away" thus coming upon us, that now the lawless one "may be revealed, the son of perdition who opposeth and exalteth himself above all that is called God and is worshipped"?[4] But if the temptation is for a season, bear it, ye noble athletes of Christ. If the world is being delivered to complete, and final destruction, let us not lose heart for the present, but let us await the revelation from heaven, and the manifestation of our great God and Saviour Jesus Christ. If all creation is to be dissolved, and the fashion of this world transformed, why should we be surprised that we, who are a part of creation, should feel the general woe,

and be delivered to afflictions which our just God inflicts on us according to the measure of our strength, not letting us "be tempted above that we are able, but with the temptation giving us a way to escape that we may be able to bear it"?[1] Brothers, martyrs' crowns await you. The companies of the confessors are ready to reach out their hands to you and to welcome you into their own ranks. Remember how none of the saints of old won their crowns of patient endurance by living luxuriously and being courted; but all were tested by being put through the fire of great afflictions. "For some had trial of cruel mockings and scourgings, and others were sawn asunder and were slain with the sword."[2] These are the glories of saints. Blessed is he who is deemed worthy to suffer for Christ; more blessed is he whose sufferings are greater, since "the sufferings of this present time are not worthy to be compared with the glory that shall be revealed in us."[3]

2. Had it but been possible for me to travel to you I should have liked nothing better than to meet you, that I might see and embrace Christ's athletes, and share your prayers and spiritual graces. But now my body is wasted by long sickness, so that I can scarcely even leave my bed, and there are many who are lying in wait for me, like ravening wolves, watching the moment when they may be able to rend Christ's sheep. I have therefore been compelled to visit you by letter; and I exhort you first of all most earnestly to pray for me, that for the rest of my remaining days or hours I may be enabled to serve the Lord, in accordance with the gospel of His kingdom. Next I beg you to pardon me for my absence and for my delay in writing to you. I have only with great difficulty found a man able to carry out my wishes. I speak of my son, the monk Eugenius, by whom I beseech you to pray for me and for the whole Church, and to write back news of you so that, when I hear, I may be more cheerful.

LETTER CXL.[4]

To the Church of Antioch.

1. "OH that I had wings like a dove for then would I fly away"[5] to you, and satisfy my longing to meet you. But now it is not only wings that I want, but a whole body, for mine has suffered from long sickness, and now is quite worn away with continuous

---

[1] Placed in 373.
[2] On the cruel persecution roused by Valens in Alexandria shortly after the death of Athanasius in 373, and the horrors perpetrated there, see the letter of Peter, Athanasius' successor, in Theod. iv. 19.
[3] ἐν τῇ πολιτείᾳ καμάτους; or, possibly, labours in life, i.e. ascetic life. The Ben. ed. prefer the latter.
[4] 2 Thess. ii. 4.

[1] 1 Cor. x. 13.
[2] cf. Heb. xi. 36, 37.
[3] Rom. viii. 18.
[4] Placed in 373.
[5] Ps. lv. 6.

affliction. For no one can be so hard of heart, so wholly destitute of sympathy and kindness, as to hear the sigh that strikes my ear from every quarter, as though from some sad choir chanting a symphony of lamentation, without being grieved at heart, being bent to the ground, and wasting away with these irremediable troubles. But the holy God is able to provide a remedy for the irremediable, and to grant you a respite from your long toils. I should like you to feel this comfort and, rejoicing in the hope of consolation, to submit to the present pain of your afflictions. Are we paying the penalty of our sins? Then our plagues are such as to save us for the future from the wrath of God. Are we called upon through these temptations to fight for the truth? Then the righteous Giver of the prizes will not suffer us to be tried above that which we are able to bear, but, in return for our previous struggles, will give us the crown of patience and of hope in Him. Let us, therefore, not flinch from fighting a good fight on behalf of the truth, nor, in despair, fling away the labours we have already achieved. For the strength of the soul is not shewn by one brave deed, nor yet by effort only for a short time; but He Who tests our hearts wishes us to win crowns of righteousness after long and protracted trial. Only let our spirit be kept unbroken, the firmness of our faith in Christ be maintained unshaken, and ere long our Champion will appear; He will come and will not tarry. Expect tribulation after tribulation, hope upon hope; yet a little while; yet a little while. Thus the Holy Ghost knows how to comfort His nurslings by a promise of the future. After tribulations comes hope, and what we are hoping for is not far off, for let a man name the whole of human life, it is but a tiny interval compared with the endless age which is laid up in our hopes.

2. Now I accept no newer creed written for me by other men, nor do I venture to propound the outcome of my own intelligence, lest I make the words of true religion merely human words; but what I have been taught by the holy Fathers, that I announce to all who question me. In my Church the creed written by the holy Fathers in synod at Nicæa is in use. I believe that it is also repeated among you; but I do not refuse to write its exact terms in my letter, lest I be accused of taking too little trouble. It is as follows:[1] This is our faith. But no defini-

tion was given about the Holy Ghost, the Pneumatomachi not having at that date appeared. No mention was therefore made of the need of anathematizing those who say that the Holy Ghost is of a created and ministerial nature. For nothing in the divine and blessed Trinity is created.

LETTER CXLI.[1]

To Eusebius, bishop of Samosata.[2]

1. I HAVE now received two letters from your divine and most excellent wisdom, whereof the one told me clearly how I had been expected by the laity under the jurisdiction of your holiness, and what disappointment I had caused by failing to attend the sacred synod. The other, which from the writing I conjecture to be of the earlier date, though it was delivered later, gave me advice, at once honourable to yourself and necessary to me, not to neglect the interests of God's Churches, nor little by little to allow the guidance of affairs to pass to our opponents, whereby their interests must win, and ours lose. I think that I answered both. But, as I am uncertain whether my replies were preserved by those who were entrusted with the duty of conveying them, I will make my defence over again. As to my absence, I can put in an unimpeachable plea, as to which I think intelligence must have reached your holiness, that I have been detained by illness which has brought me to the very gates of death. Even now as I write about it, the remains of sickness are still upon me. And they are such as to another man might be unendurable.

2. As to the fact of its not being owing to my neglect that the interests of the Churches have been betrayed to our opponents, I wish your reverence to know that the bishops in communion with me, from lack of earnestness, or because they suspect me and are not open with me, or because the devil is always at hand to oppose good works, are unwilling to coöperate with me. Formerly, indeed, the majority of us were united with one another, including the excellent Bosporius.[3] In reality they give me no aid in what is most essential. The consequence of all this is, that to a great extent my recovery is hindered by my distress, and

Dianius, who next followed in the see, signed several Arian formulæ. The Nicene Creed, however, had been maintained at Cæsarea, and in *Letter* li. Dianius is described as supporting it.
[1] Placed in 373.
[2] On his being hindered from travelling by ill health, and on his difficulties with the bishops in communion with him.
[3] cf. *Letter* li.

[1] Here follows in the text the Nicene Creed with the anathemas. The Ben. note points out that the Nicene Creed was brought to Cæsarea by St. Leontius, and was vigorously defended by his successor Hermogenes. cf. *Letter* lxxxi.

the sorrow I feel brings back my worst symptoms. What, however, can I do alone and unaided, when the canons, as you yourself know, do not allow points of this kind to be settled by one man?[1] And yet what remedy have I not tried? Of what decision have I failed to remind them, some by letter and some in person? They even came to the city, when they heard a report of my death; when, by God's will, they found me yet alive I made them such a speech as was proper to the occasion. In my presence they respect me, and promise all that is fit, but no sooner have they got back again than they return to their own opinion. In all this I am a sufferer, like the rest, for the Lord has clearly abandoned us, whose love has grown cold because iniquity abounds. For all this may your great and powerful intercession with God be sufficient for me. Perhaps we shall either become of some use, or, even if we fail in our object, we may escape condemnation.

LETTER CXLII.[2]

To the prefects' accountant.[3]

I ASSEMBLED all my brethren the chorepiscopi at the synod of the blessed martyr Eupsychius[4] to introduce them to your excellency. On account of your absence they must be brought before you by letter. Know, therefore, this brother as being worthy to be trusted by your intelligence, because he fears the Lord. As to the matters on behalf of the poor, which he refers to your good-will, deign to believe him as one worthy of credit, and to give the afflicted all the aid in your power. I am sure you will consent to look favourably upon the hospital of the poor which is in his district, and exempt it altogether from taxation. It has already seemed good to your colleague to make the little property of the poor not liable to be rated.

LETTER CXLIII.[1]

To another accountant.[2]

HAD it been possible for me to meet your excellency I would have in person brought before you the points about which I am anxious, and would have pleaded the cause of the afflicted, but I am prevented by illness and by press of business. I have therefore sent to you in my stead this chorepiscopus, my brother, begging you to give him your aid and use him and to take him into counsel, for his truthfulness and sagacity qualify him to advise in such matters. If you are so good as to inspect the hospital for the poor, which is managed by him, (I am sure you will not pass it without a visit, experienced as you are in the work; for I have been told that you support one of the hospitals at Amasea out of the substance wherewith the Lord has blessed you), I am confident that, after seeing it, you will give him all he asks. Your colleague has already promised me some help towards the hospitals. I tell you this, not that you may imitate him, for you are likely to be a leader of others in good works, but that you may know that others have shown regard for me in this matter.

LETTER CXLIV.[3]

To the prefects' officer.[4]

YOU know the bearer from meeting him in the town. Nevertheless I write to commend him to you, that he may be useful to you in many matters in which you are interested, from his being able to give pious and sensible advice. Now is the time to carry out what you have said to me in private; I mean when this my brother has told you the state of the poor.

LETTER CXLV.[5]

To Eusebius, bishop of Samosata.[6]

I KNOW the countless labours which you have undergone for the Churches of God; I know your press of occupation, while you discharge your responsibilities, not as though they were of mere secondary importance, but in accordance with God's will. I know the man[7] who is, as it were, laying close siege to you and by whom you are forced, like

---

[1] The Ben. note is: " *Canones illos qui apostolis afficti fuere, nonnunquam citat Basilius in Epistolis canonicis. Videtur hoc loco respicere ad vigesimum (? xxxvii.) septimum, ubi præscribitur, ut in unaquaque provincia episcopi nihil majoris rei incipiant sine sententia illius, qui inter eos primus, ac unus quisque iis contentus sit, quæ ad parœciam suam pertinent: sed nec ille absque omnium voluntate quidquam faciat. Erat Basilius hujus canonis observandi studiosus, et quamvis nominis fama et sedis dignitate plurimum posset, nunquam ab eo communionis restitutionem impetrare potuerunt Marcelli discipuli, antequam Petri Alexandrini auctoritates accessisset: et cum ab Episcopis in Palæstina Exsulantibus non ex spectato aliorum Episcoporum consensu restituti fuissent, factum moleste tulit et libere reprehendit.*" *Epist.* cclxv.
[2] Placed in 373.
[3] On the exemption of hospitals from taxation.
[4] *cf. Letters* c. and cclii., and note on p. 184.

[1] Of the same date as the preceding.
[2] On the same subject. [4] On the same subject.
[3] Placed in 373. [5] Placed in 373.
[6] On a possible visit of Eusebius to Cæsarea.
[7] *i.e.* Valens.

birds crouching in cover under an eagle, not to go far from your shelter. I know all this. But longing is strong, both in hoping for the impracticable and attempting the impossible. Rather I should say, hope in God is the strongest of all things.[1] For it is not from unreasonable desire, but from strength of faith, that I expect a way out, even from the greatest difficulties, and that you will find a way to get over all hindrances, and to come to see the Church that loves you best of all, and to be seen by her. What she values most of all good things is to behold your face and to hear your voice. Beware then of making her hopes vain. When last year, on my return from Syria, I reported the promise which you had given me, you cannot think how elated with her hopes I made her. Do not, my friend, postpone your coming to another time. Even if it may be possible for you to see her one day, you may not see her and me too, for sickness is hurrying me on to quit this painful life.

LETTER CXLVI.[2]

To Antiochus.[3]

I CANNOT accuse you of carelessness and inattention, because, when an opportunity of writing occurred, you said nothing. For I count the greeting which you have sent me in your own honoured hand worth many letters. In return I salute you, and beg you earnestly to give heed to the salvation of your soul, disciplining all the lusts of the flesh by reason, and ever keeping the thought of God built up in your soul, as in a very holy temple. In every deed and every word hold before your eyes the judgment of Christ, so that every individual action, being referred to that exact and awful examination, may bring you glory in the day of retribution, when you win praise from all creation. If that great man[4] should be able to pay me a visit, it would be a pleasure to me to see you here with him.

LETTER CXLVII.[5]

To Aburgius.[6]

UP to this time I used to think Homer a fable, when I read the second part of his poem, in which he narrates the adventures of Ulysses. But the calamity which has befallen the most excellent Maximus has led me to look on what I used to think fabulous and incredible, as exceedingly probable. Maximus was governor of no insignificant people, just as Ulysses was chief of the Cephallenians. Ulysses had had great wealth, and returned stripped of everything. To such straits has calamity reduced Maximus, that he may have to present himself at home in borrowed rags. And perhaps he has suffered all this because he has irritated some Læstrygones against him, and has fallen in with some Scylla, hiding a dog's fierceness and fury under a woman's form. Since then he has barely been able to swim out of this inextricable whirlpool. He supplicates you by my means for humanity's sake to grieve for his undeserved misfortunes and not be silent about his needs, but make them known to the authorities. He hopes thus that he may find some aid against the slanders which have been got up against him : and if not, that at all events the intention of the enemy who has shewn such an intoxication of hostility against him may be made public. When a man has been wronged it is a considerable comfort to him if the wickedness of his enemies can be made plain.

LETTER CXLVIII.[1]

To Trajan.[2]

EVEN the ability to bewail their own calamities brings much comfort to the distressed; and this is specially the case when they meet with others capable, from their lofty character, of sympathizing with their sorrows. So my right honourable brother Maximus, after being prefect of my country, and then suffering what no other man ever yet suffered, stripped of all his belongings both inherited from his forefathers and collected by his own labours, afflicted in body in many and various ways, by his wanderings up and down the world, and not having been able to keep even his civil status free from attack, to preserve which freemen are wont to leave no labour undone, has made many complaints to me about all that has happened to him, and has begged me to give you a short description of the Iliad of woes in which he is involved.

---

[1] "*Vita vere mortalis spes est vitæ immortalis.*" St. Augustine in Ps. iii. "*Spes in æternitatem animum erigit, et idcirco nulla mala sentit.*" St. Greg., *Moral. cf.* Ovid. i. Pont. 7 :

　　Quamvis est igitur meritis indebita nostris,
　　Magna tamen spes est in bonitate Dei.

[2] Placed in 373.
[3] Nephew of Eusebius, who had written a salutation in his uncle's letter. *cf. Letter* clxviii.
[4] *i.e.* his uncle Eusebius.　　[5] Placed in 373.
[6] To commend Maximus, late prefect of Cappadocia and in great distress.

[1] Placed in 373.
[2] A Trajan was commander-in-chief under Valens. *cf.* Theod. iv. 30 and Amm. Marcellinus xxxi. He was killed at the battle of Adrianople in 378. This may have been the same officer.

And I, being quite unable to relieve him in any other way in his troubles, have readily done him the favour shortly to relate to your excellency a part of what I have heard from him. He, indeed, seemed to me to blush at the idea of making a plain tale of his own calamity. If what has happened shews that the inflicter of the wrong is a villain, at all events it proves the sufferer to be deserving of great pity; since the very fact of having fallen into troubles, inflicted by Divine Providence, seems in a manner to shew that a man has been devoted to suffering. But it would be a sufficient comfort to him if you will only look at him kindly, and extend also to him that abundant favour which all the recipients of it cannot exhaust, — I mean your clemency. We are all of us, convinced that before the tribunal your protection will be an immense step towards victory. He who has asked for my letter as likely to be of service is of all men most upright. May it be granted me to see him, with the rest, proclaiming aloud the praises of your lordship with all his power.

LETTER CXLIX.[1]

To Trajan.[2]

You yourself have seen with your own eyes the distressing condition of Maximus, once a man of high reputation, but now most of all to be pitied, formerly prefect of my country. Would that he had never been so! Many, I think, would be likely to shun provincial governorships, if their dignities are likely to issue in such an end. To a man, then, from the quickness of his intelligence, able from a few circumstances to conjecture the rest, I need hardly narrate in detail all that I have seen and all that I have heard. Perhaps, however, I shall not seem to be telling a superfluous story if I mention that, though many and terrible things were audaciously done against him before your coming, what went on afterwards was such as to cause the former proceedings to be reckoned as kindness; to such an excess of outrage and injury and actually of personal cruelty did the proceedings go which were afterwards taken against him by the person in authority. Now he is here with an escort to fill up the measure of his evil deeds unless

you are willing to stretch out your strong hand to protect the sufferer. In urging your goodness to an act of kindness I feel that I am undertaking an unnecessary task. Yet since I desire to be serviceable to Maximus I do beg your lordship to add something for my sake to your natural zeal for what is right, to the end that he may clearly perceive that my intervention on his behalf has been of service to him.

LETTER CL.[1]

To Amphilochius in the name of Heraclidas.[2]

1. I REMEMBER our old conversations with one another, and am forgetful neither of what I said, nor of what you said. And now public life has no hold upon me. For although I am the same in heart and have not yet put off the old man, nevertheless, outwardly and by withdrawing myself far from worldly life, I seem already to have begun to tread the way of Christian conversation. I sit apart, like men who are on the point of embarking on the deep, looking out at what is before me. Mariners, indeed, need winds to make their voyage prosperous; I on the other hand want a guide to take me by the hand and conduct me safely through life's bitter waves. I feel that I need first a curb for my young manhood, and then pricks to drive me to the course of piety. Both these seem to be provided by reason, which at one time disciplines my unruliness of soul, and at another time my sluggishness. Again I want other remedies that I may wash off the impurity of habit. You know how, long accustomed as I was to the Forum, I am lavish of words, and do not guard myself against the thoughts put into my mind by the evil one. I am the servant too of honour, and cannot easily give up thinking great things of myself. Against all this I feel that I need a great instructor. Then, further, I conclude that it is of no small importance, nor of benefit only for a little while, that the soul's eye should be so purged that, after being freed from all the darkness of ignorance, as though from some blinding humour, one can gaze intently

<hr>

[1] Placed in 373.
[2] The Ben. note points out that though in all the MSS. the inscription is τῷ αὐτῷ, to the same, that is to Trajan, the internal evidence points to its having been written to some one else. Trajan had had no personal knowledge of the troubles of Maximus.

<hr>

[1] Placed in 373.
[2] Amphilochius, not yet consecrated to Iconium, had abandoned his profession as an advocate, and was living in retirement at Ozizala, a place not far from Nazianzus, the see of his uncle Gregory, devoted to the care of his aged father, whose name he bore. Heraclidas, it appears, had also renounced the bar, and devoted himself to religious life; but did not join Amphilochius on the ground that he was living in Basil's hospital at Cæsarea. cf. the letters of Gregory, first cousin of Amphilochius. On the relationship, see Bp. Lightfoot in D.C.B. i. p. 104, and pedigree in prolegomena.

on the beauty of the glory of God. All this I know very well that your wisdom is aware of; I know that you would wish that I might have some one to give me such help, and if ever God grant me to meet you I am sure that I shall learn more about what I ought to heed. For now, in my great ignorance, I can hardly even form a judgment as to what I lack. Yet I do not repent of my first impulse; my soul does not hang back from the purpose of a godly life as you have feared for me, nobly and becomingly doing everything in your power, lest, like the woman of whom I have heard the story, I should turn back and become a pillar of salt.[1] I am still, however, under the restraint of external authority; for the magistrates are seeking me like a deserter. But I am chiefly influenced by my own heart, which testifies to itself of all that I have told you.

2. Since you have mentioned our bond, and have announced that you mean to prosecute, you have made me laugh in this my dejection, because you are still an advocate and do not give up your shrewdness. I hold, unless, indeed, like an ignorant man, I am quite missing the truth, that there is only one way to the Lord, and that all who are journeying to Him are travelling together and walking in accordance with one "bond" of life. If this be so, wherever I go how can I be separated from you? How can I cease to live with you, and with you serve God, to Whom we have both fled for refuge? Our bodies may be separated by distance, but God's eye still doubtless looks upon us both; if indeed a life like mine is fit to be beheld by the divine eyes; for I have read somewhere in the Psalms that the eyes of the Lord are upon the righteous.[2] I do indeed pray that with you and with all that are like minded with you, I may be associated, even in body, and that night and day with you and with any other true worshipper of God I may bow my knees to our Father which is in heaven; for I know that communion in prayer brings great gain. If, as often as it is my lot to lie and groan in a different corner, I am always to be accused of lying, I cannot contend against your argument, and already condemn myself as a liar, if with my own carelessness I have said anything which brings me under such a charge.

3. I was lately at Cæsarea, in order to learn what was going on there. I was unwilling to remain in the city itself, and betook myself to the neighbouring hospital, that I might get there what information I wanted. According to his custom the very godly bishop visited it, and I consulted him as to the points which you had urged upon me. It is not possible for me to remember all that he said in reply; it went far beyond the limits of a letter. In sum, however, what he said about poverty was this, that the rule ought to be that every one should limit his possessions to one garment. For one proof of this he quoted the words of John the Baptist " he that hath two coats let him impart to him that hath none;"[1] and for another our Lord's prohibition to His disciples to have two coats.[2] He further added "If thou wilt be perfect go and sell that thou hast and give to the poor."[3] He said too that the parable of the pearl bore on this point, because the merchant, who had found the pearl of great price, went away and sold all that he had and bought it; and he added too that no one ought even to permit himself the distribution of his own property, but should leave it in the hands of the person entrusted with the duty of managing the affairs of the poor; and he proved the point from the acts of the apostles,[4] because they sold their property and brought and laid it at the feet of the apostles, and by them it was distributed to each as every man had need.[5] For he said that experience was needed in order to distinguish between cases of genuine need and of mere greedy begging. For whoever gives to the afflicted gives to the Lord, and from the Lord shall have his reward; but he who gives to every vagabond casts to a dog, a nuisance indeed from his importunity, but deserving no pity on the ground of want.

4. He was moreover the first to speak shortly, as befits the importance of the subject, about some of the daily duties of life. As to this I should wish you to hear from himself, for it would not be right for me to weaken the force of his lessons. I would pray that we might visit him together, that so you might both accurately preserve in your memory what he said, and supply any omissions by your own intelligence. One thing that I do remember, out of the many which I heard, is this; that instruction how to lead the Christian life depends less on words, than on daily example. I know that, if you had not been detained by the duty of succouring your aged father, there is nothing that

---

[1] cf. Gen. xix. 26.   [2] Ps. xxxiv. 15.

[1] Luke iii. 11.   [3] Matt. xix. 21.
[2] Matt. x. 10.   [4] Acts iv. 35.
[5] It will be observed that St. Basil's quotation here does not quite bear out his point. There is no "by them " in Acts iv. 35. " Distribution was made unto every man according as he had need." In Acts ii. 45 the primitive communists are said themselves to have " parted to all men as every man had need," the responsibility of distribution being apparently retained.

you would have more greatly esteemed than a meeting with the bishop, and that you would not have advised me to leave him in order to wander in deserts. Caves and rocks are always ready for us, but the help we get from our fellow man is not always at hand. If, then, you will put up with my giving you advice, you will impress on your father the desirability of his allowing you to leave him for a little while in order to meet a man who, alike from his experience of others and from his own wisdom, knows much, and is able to impart it to all who approach him.

LETTER CLI.[1]

To Eustathius the Physician.

IF my letters are of any good, lose no time in writing to me and in rousing me to write. We are unquestionably made more cheerful when we read the letters of wise men who love the Lord. It is for you to say, who read it, whether you find anything worth attention in what I write. Were it not for the multitude of my engagements, I should not debar myself from the pleasure of writing frequently. Pray do you, whose cares are fewer, soothe me by your letters. Wells, it is said, are the better for being used. The exhortations which you derive from your profession are apparently beside the point, for it is not I who am applying the knife; it is men whose day is done, who are falling upon themselves.[3] The phrase of the Stoics runs, " since things do not happen as we like, we like what happens ; " but I cannot make my mind fall in with what is happening. That some men should do what they do not like because they cannot help it, I have no objection. You doctors do not cauterise a sick man, or make him suffer pain in some other way, because you like it ; but you often adopt this treatment in obedience to the necessity of the case. Mariners do not willingly throw their cargo overboard ; but in order to escape shipwreck they put up with the loss, preferring a life of penury to death. Be sure that I look with sorrow and with many groans upon the separation of those who are holding themselves aloof. But yet I endure it. To lovers of the truth nothing can be put before God and hope in Him.[4]

LETTER CLII.[1]

To Victor, the Commander.[2]

IF I were to fail to write to any one else I might possibly with justice incur the charge of carelessness or forgetfulness. But it is not possible to forget you, when your name is in all men's mouths. But I cannot be careless about one who is perhaps more distinguished than any one else in the empire. The cause of my silence is evident. I am afraid of troubling so great a man. If, however, to all your other virtues you add that of not only receiving what I send, but of actually asking after what is missing, lo! here I am writing to you with joyous heart, and I shall go on writing for the future, with prayers to God that you may be requited for the honour you pay me. For the Church, you have anticipated my supplications, by doing everything which I should have asked. And you act to please not man but God, Who has honoured you ; Who has given you some good things in this life, and will give you others in the life to come, because you have walked with truth in His way, and, from the beginning to the end, have kept your heart fixed in the right faith.

LETTER CLIII.[3]

To Victor the Ex-Consul.

As often as it falls to my lot to read your lordship's letters, so often do I thank God that you continue to remember me, and that you are not moved by any calumny to lessen the love which once you consented to entertain for me, either from your wise judgment or your kindly intercourse. I pray then the holy God that you may remain in this mind towards me, and that I may be worthy of the honour which you give me.

LETTER CLIV.[4]

To Ascholius, bishop of Thessalonica.[5]

YOU have done well, and in accordance with the law of spiritual love, in writing to me first, and by your good example challenging me to like energy. The friendship of the world, indeed, stands in need of actual sight and intercourse, that thence intimacy may begin. All, however, who know how to love in the spirit do not need the flesh to

---

1 Placed in 373.
2 cf. Letter clxxxix. On those who had renounced communion with Eustathius the bishop.
3 i.e. Eustathius, the bishop, is rushing upon the knife.
4 The view of the Ben. Ed. is that the bales thrown overboard represent the loss of unity incurred by the Sebastenes by leaving the communion of Eustathius for his own. cf. Letter ccxxxvii.

1 Placed in 373.
2 cf. Greg. Naz., Letters cxxxii. and cxxxiv. and Theodoret, Ecc. Hist. iv. 30 and Amm. Marc. xxxi. 7.
3 Placed in 373. 4 Placed in 373.
5 cf. Letters clxiv. and clxv. Ascholius baptized Theodosius at Thessalonica in 380, and was present at the Council of Constantinople in 381. Soc., Ecc. Hist. v. 6 and 8.

promote affection, but are led to spiritual communion in the fellowship of the faith. Thanks, then, to the Lord Who has comforted my heart by showing me that love has not grown cold in all, but that there are yet in the world men who show the evidence of the discipleship of Christ. The state of affairs with you seems to be something like that of the stars by night, shining some in one part of the sky and some in another, whereof the brightness is charming, and the more charming because it is unexpected. Such are you, luminaries of the Churches, a few at most and easily counted in this gloomy state of things, shining as in a moonless night, and, besides being welcome for your virtue, being all the more longed for because of its being so seldom that you are found. Your letter has made your disposition quite plain to me. Although small, as far as regards the number of its syllables, in the correctness of its sentiments it was quite enough to give me proof of your mind and purpose. Your zeal for the cause of the blessed Athanasius is plain proof of your being sound as to the most important matters. In return for my joy at your letter I am exceedingly grateful to my honourable son Euphemius, to whom I pray that all help may be given by the Holy One, and I beg you to join in my prayers that we may soon receive him back with his very honourable wife, my daughter in the Lord. As to yourself, I beg that you will not stay our joy at its beginning, but that you will write on every possible opportunity, and increase your good feeling towards me by constant communication. Give me news, I beg you, about your Churches and how they are situated as regards union. Pray for us here that our Lord may rebuke the winds and the sea, and that with us there may be a great calm.

LETTER CLV.[1]

Without address.[2] In the case of a trainer.

I am at a loss how to defend myself against all the complaints contained in the first and only letter which your lordship has been so good as to send me. It is not that there is any lack of right on my side, but because among so many charges it is hard to select the most vital, and fix on the point at which I ought to begin to apply a remedy. Perhaps, if I follow the order of your letter, I shall come upon each in turn. Up to to-day I

knew nothing about those who are setting out for Scythia; nor had any one told me even of those who came from your house, so that I might greet you by them, although I am anxious to seize every opportunity of greeting your lordship. To forget you in my prayers is impossible, unless first I forget the work to which God has called me, for assuredly, faithful as by God's grace you are, you remember all the prayers[1] of the Church; how we pray also for our brethren when on a journey and offer prayer in the holy church for those who are in the army, and for those who speak for the sake of the Lord's name, and for those who show the fruits of the Spirit. In most, or all of these, I reckon your lordship to be included. How could I ever forget you, as far as I am individually concerned, when I have so many reasons to stir me to recollection, such a sister, such nephews, such kinsfolk, so good, so fond of me, house, household, and friends? By all these, even against my will, I am perforce reminded of your good disposition. As to this, however, our brother has brought me no unpleasant news, nor has any decision been come to by me which could do him any injury. Free, then, the chorepiscopus and myself from all blame, and grieve rather over those who have made false reports. If our learned friend wishes to bring an action against me, he has law courts and laws. In this I beg you not to blame me. In all the good deeds that you do, you are laying up treasure for yourself; you are preparing for yourself in the day of retribution the same refreshment which you are providing for those who are persecuted for the sake of the name of the Lord. If you send the relics of the martyrs home you will do well; as you write that the persecution there is, even now, causing martyrs to the Lord.[2]

LETTER CLVI.[3]

To the Presbyter Evagrius.[4]

1. So far from being impatient at the length of your letter, I assure you I thought it even short, from the pleasure it gave me

---

[1] κηρύγματα. On St. Basil's use of this word for decree, *vide De Sp. S.* c. 66. Here it seems to have the force of an appointed liturgy. *cf.* the letter of Firmilianus to Cyprian. (*Ep. Cyp.* 75.)
[2] This is one of the earliest references to the preservation of relics. So late as the case of St. Fructuosus (*Acta SS. Fructuosi*, etc.), who died at Tarragona in 259, the friends are forbidden to keep the relics. On St. Basil's views on the subject, *cf. Hom. in Mart. Jul.* 2 and *Hom. de SS.* xl. *MM.* 8. So Gregory of Nyssa. *Hom.* i. *in* xl. *Mar.* ii. 935. As early as the time of St. Augustine (†430) a thriving trade in forged relics had already begun. (Aug., *De Opere Monach.* 28.) *cf.* Littledale's *Plain Reasons*, p. 51.
[3] Placed in 373.   [4] *cf. Letter* cxxxviii.

---

[1] Placed in 373.
[2] Supposed by Maran (*Vit. Bas.*) to be Julius Soranus, a relative of Basil, and dux of Scythia. Maran supposes that a copyist added these words to the title because Soranus was "a trainer" (αλείπτης) and encourager of martyrs; in *Letter* clxiv. Basil calls Ascholius "a trainer" of the martyr Sabas.

when reading it. For is there anything more pleasing than the idea of peace? Is anything more suitable to the sacred office, or more acceptable to the Lord, than to take measures for effecting it? May you have the reward of the peace-maker, since so blessed an office has been the object of your good desires and earnest efforts. At the same time, believe me, my revered friend, I will yield to none in my earnest wish and prayer to see the day when those who are one in sentiment shall all fill the same assembly. Indeed it would be monstrous to feel pleasure in the schisms and divisions of the Churches, and not to consider that the greatest of goods consists in the knitting together of the members of Christ's body. But, alas! my inability is as real as my desire. No one knows better than yourself, that time alone is the remedy of ills that time has matured. Besides, a strong and vigorous treatment is necessary to get at the root of the complaint. You will understand this hint, though there is no reason why I should not speak out.

2. Self-importance, when rooted by habit in the mind, cannot be destroyed by one man, by one single letter, or in a short time. Unless there be some arbiter in whom all parties have confidence, suspicions and collisions will never altogether cease. If, indeed, the influence of Divine grace were shed upon me, and I were given power in word and deed and spiritual gifts to prevail with these rival parties, then this daring experiment might be demanded of me; though, perhaps, even then, you would not advise me to attempt this adjustment of things by myself, without the co-operation of the bishop,[1] on whom principally falls the care of the church. But he cannot come hither, nor can I easily undertake a long journey while the winter lasts, or rather I cannot anyhow, for the Armenian mountains will be soon impassable, even to the young and vigorous, to say nothing of my continued bodily ailments. I have no objection to write to tell him of all this; but I have no expectation that writing will lead to anything, for I know his cautious character, and after all written words have little power to convince the mind. There are so many things to urge, and to hear, and to reply to, and to object, that a letter has no soul, and is in fact but waste paper. However, as I have said, I will write. Only give me credit, most religious and dear brother, for having no private feeling in the matter. Thank God, I have no such feeling towards any one. I have not busied myself in the in-

vestigation of the supposed or real complaints which are brought against this or that man; so my opinion has a claim on your attention as that of one who really cannot act from partiality or prejudice. I only desire, through the Lord's good will, that all things may be done with ecclesiastical propriety.

3. I was vexed to find from my dear son Dorotheus, our associate in the ministry, that you had been unwilling to communicate with him. This was not the kind of conversation which you had with me, as well as I recollect. As to my sending to the West it is quite out of the question. I have no one fit for the service. Indeed, when I look round, I seem to have no one on my side. I can but pray I may be found in the number of those seven thousand who have not bowed the knee to Baal. I know the present persecutors of us all seek my life; yet that shall not diminish ought of the zeal which I owe to the Churches of God.

LETTER CLVII.[1]

To Antiochus.[2]

You may well imagine how disappointed I was not to meet· you in the summer; not that our meeting in former years was enough to satisfy me, but even to see loved objects in a dream brings those who love some comfort. But you do not even write, so sluggish are you, and I think your absence can be referred to no other cause than that you are slow to undertake journeys for affection's sake. On this point I will say no more. Pray for me, and ask the Lord not to desert me, but as He has brought me out of bygone temptations so also to deliver me from those that I await, for the glory of the name of Him in Whom I put my trust.

LETTER CLVIII.[3]

To Antiochus.

My sins have prevented me from carrying out the wish to meet you, which I have long entertained. Let me apologise by letter for my absence, and beseech you not to omit to remember me in your prayers, that, if I live, I may be permitted to enjoy your

---

[1] Meletius of Antioch.

[1] Placed in 373.
[2] *cf. Letters* cxlvi. and ccxxxix. Maran. (*Vit. Bas.*) is of opinion that as these two letters, clvii. and clviii., written at the same time, are very much in the same terms, they cannot be to the same person, and thinks that the sluggishness, which Basil complains of, fits in with Eusebius much better than with Antiochus, who could not travel without his uncle's permission. [3] Placed in 373.

society. If not, by the aid of your prayers may I quit this world with good hope. I commend to you our brother the camel-master.

LETTER CLIX.[1]

To Eupaterius and his daughter.[2]

1. You may well imagine what pleasure the letter of your excellencies gave me, if only from its very contents. What, indeed, could give greater gratification to one who prays ever to be in communication with them who fear the Lord, and to share their blessings, than a letter of this kind, wherein questions are asked about the knowledge of God? For if, to me, "to live is Christ,"[3] truly my words ought to be about Christ, my every thought and deed ought to depend upon His commandments, and my soul to be fashioned after His. I rejoice, therefore, at being asked about such things, and congratulate the askers. By me, to speak shortly, the faith of the Fathers assembled at Nicæa is honoured before all later inventions. In it the Son is confessed to be con-substantial with the Father and to be naturally of the same nature with Him who begat Him, for He was confessed to be Light of Light, God of God, and Good of Good, and the like. Both by those holy men the same doctrine was declared, and by me now who pray that I may walk in their footsteps.

2. But since the question now raised by those who are always endeavouring to introduce novelties, but passed over in silence by the men of old, because the doctrine was never gainsaid, has remained without full explanation (I mean that which concerns the Holy Ghost) I will add a statement on this subject in conformity with the sense of Scripture. As we were baptized, so we profess our belief. As we profess our belief, so also we offer praise. As then baptism has been given us by the Saviour, in the name of the Father and of the Son and of the Holy Ghost, so, in accordance with our baptism, we make the confession of the creed, and our doxology in accordance with our creed. We glorify the Holy Ghost to-gether with the Father and the Son, from the conviction that He is not separated from the Divine Nature; for that which is foreign by nature does not share in the same honors. All who call the Holy Ghost a creature we pity, on the ground that, by this utterance, they are falling into the unpardonable sin of blasphemy against Him. I need use no argument to prove to those who are even slightly trained in Scripture, that the creature is separated from the Godhead. The creature is a slave; but the Spirit sets free.[1] The creature needs life; the Spirit is the Giver of life.[2] The creature requires teaching. It is the Spirit that teaches.[3] The creature is sanctified; it is the Spirit that sanctifies.[4] Whether you name angels, arch-angels, or all the heavenly powers, they receive their sanctification through the Spirit, but the Spirit Himself has His holiness by nature, not received by favour, but essentially His; whence He has received the distinctive name of Holy. What then is by nature holy, as the Father is by nature holy, and the Son by nature holy, we do not ourselves allow to be separated and severed from the divine and blessed Trinity, nor accept those who rashly reckon it as part of creation. Let this short summary be sufficient for you, my pious friends. From little seeds, with the co-operation of the Holy Ghost, you will reap the fuller crop of piety. "Give instruction to a wise man and he will be yet wiser."[5] I will put off fuller demonstration till we meet. When we do, it will be possible for me to answer objections, to give you fuller proofs from Scripture, and to confirm all the sound rule of faith. For the present pardon my brevity. I should not have written at all had I not thought it a greater injury to you to refuse your request altogether than to grant it in part.

LETTER CLX.[6]

To Diodorus.[7]

1. I HAVE received the letter which has raeched me under the name of Diodorus, but in what it contains creditable to any one rather than to Diodorus. Some ingenious person seems to have assumed your name, with the intention of getting credit with his hearers. It appears that he was asked by some one if it was lawful to contract marriage with his deceased wife's sister; and, instead of shuddering at such a question, he heard it unmoved, and quite boldly and bravely supported the unseemly desire. Had I his letter by me I would have sent it you, and you would have been able to defend both yourself and the truth. But the person who showed it me took it away

---

1 Placed about 373.
2 On the Nicene Creed and the Holy Ghost.
3 Phil. i. 21.

1 *cf.* Rom. viii. 2.　　　4 Rom. xv. 16.
2 John vi. 63.　　　　　5 Prov. ix. 9.
3 John xiv. 26.　　　　6 Placed in 373 or 374.
7 On marriage with a deceased wife's sister. *cf. Letter* cxxxv.

again, and carried it about as a kind of trophy of triumph against me who had forbidden it from the beginning, declaring that he had permission in writing. Now I have written to you that I may attack that spurious document with double strength, and leave it no force whereby it may injure its readers.

2. First of all I have to urge, what is of most importance in such matters, our own custom, which has the force of law, because the rules have been handed down to us by holy men. It is as follows: if any one, overcome by impurity, falls into unlawful intercourse with two sisters, this is not to be looked upon as marriage, nor are they to be admitted at all into the Church until they have separated from one another. Wherefore, although it were possible to say nothing further, the custom would be quite enough to safeguard what is right. But, since the writer of the letter has endeavoured to introduce this mischief into our practice by a false argument, I am under the necessity of not omitting the aid of reasoning; although in matters which are perfectly plain every man's instinctive sentiment is stronger than argument.

3. It is written, he says, in Leviticus, "Neither shalt thou take a wife to her sister, to vex her, to uncover her nakedness, beside the other *in her life time*."[1] From this it is plain, he argues, that it is lawful to take her when the wife is dead. To this my first answer shall be, that whatever the law says, it says to those who are under the law; otherwise we shall be subject to circumcision, the sabbath, abstinence from meats. For we certainly must not, when we find anything which falls in with our pleasures, subject ourselves to the yoke of slavery to the law; and then, if anything in the law seems hard, have recourse to the freedom which is in Christ. We have been asked if it is written that one may be taken to wife after her sister. Let us say what is safe and true, that it is not written. But to deduce by sequence of argument what is passed over in silence is the part of a legislator, not of one who quotes the articles of the law. Indeed, on these terms, any one who likes will be at liberty to take the sister, even in the lifetime of the wife. The same sophism fits in in this case also. It is written, he says, "Thou shalt not take a wife to vex her:" so that, apart from vexation, there is no prohibition to take her. The man who wants to indulge his desire will maintain that the re-

lationship of sisters is such that they cannot vex one another. Take away the reason given for the prohibition to live with both, and what is there to prevent a man's taking both sisters? This is not written, we shall say. Neither is the former distinctly stated. The deduction from the argument allows liberty in both cases. But a solution of the difficulty might be found by going a little back to what is behind the enactment. It appears that the legislator does not include every kind of sin, but particularly prohibits those of the Egyptians, from among whom Israel had gone forth, and of the Canaanites among whom they were going. The words are as follows, "After the doings of the land of Egypt, wherein ye dwelt, shall ye not do; and after the doings of the land of Canaan, whither I bring you, shall ye not do: neither shall ye walk in their ordinances."[1] It is probable that this kind of sin was not practised at that time among the Gentiles. Under these circumstances the lawgiver was, it may be supposed, under no necessity of guarding against it; the unwritten custom sufficed to condemn the crime. How then is it that while forbidding the greater he was silent about the less? Because the example of the patriarch seemed injurious to many who indulged their flesh so far as to live with sisters in their life time. What ought to be my course? To quote the Scriptures, or to work out what they leave unsaid? In these laws it is not written that a father and son ought not to have the same concubine, but, in the prophet, it is thought deserving of the most extreme condemnation, "A man and his father" it is said "will go in unto the same maid."[2] And how many other forms of unclean lust have been found out in the devils' school, while divine scripture is silent about them, not choosing to befoul its dignity with the names of filthy things and condemning their uncleanness in general terms! As the apostle Paul says, "Fornication and all uncleanness . . . let it not be once named among you as becometh saints,"[3] thus including the unspeakable doings of both males and females under the name of uncleanness. It follows that silence certainly does not give license to voluptuaries.

4. I, however, maintain that this point has not been left in silence, but that the lawgiver has made a distinct prohibition. The words "None of you shall approach to any one that is near of kin to him, to uncover their nakedness,"[4] embraces also this form

---

[1] Lev. xviii. 18.

[1] Lev. xviii. 3.
[2] Amos ii. 7.
[3] Eph. v. 3.
[4] Lev. xviii. 6.

of kinsmanship, for what could be more akin to a man than his own wife, or rather than his own flesh? " For they are no more twain but one flesh." [1] So, through the wife, the sister is made akin to the husband. For as he shall not take his wife's mother, nor yet his wife's daughter, because he may not take his own mother nor his own daughter, so he may not take his wife's sister, because he may not take his own sister. And, on the other hand, it will not be lawful for the wife to be joined with the husband's kin, for the rights of relationship hold good on both sides. But, for my part, to every one who is thinking about marriage I testify that, " the fashion of this world passeth away," [2] and the time is short: " it remaineth that both they that have wives be as though they had none." [3] If he improperly quotes the charge " Increase and multiply," [4] I laugh at him, for not discerning the signs of the times. Second marriage is a remedy against fornication, not a means of lasciviousness. " If they cannot contain," it is said " let them marry ; " [5] but if they marry they must not break the law.

5. But they whose souls are blinded by dishonourable lust do not regard even nature, which from old time distinguished the names of the family. For under what relationship will those who contract these unions name their sons? Will they call them brothers or cousins of one another? For, on account of the confusion, both names will apply. O man, do not make the aunt the little one's stepmother ; do not arm with implacable jealousy her who ought to cherish them with a mother's love. It is only stepmothers who extend their hatred even beyond death ; other enemies make a truce with the dead ; stepmothers begin their hatred after death. [6] The sum of what I say is this. If any one wants to contract a lawful marriage, the whole world is open to him : if he is only impelled by lust, let him be the more restricted, "that he may know how to possess his vessel in sanctification and honour, not in the lust of concupiscence." [7] I should like to say more, but the limits of my letter leave me no further room. I pray that my exhortation may prove stronger than lust, or at least that this pollution may not

be found in my own province. Where it has been ventured on there let it abide.

LETTER CLXI.[1]

To Amphilochius on his consecration as Bishop.

1. BLESSED be God Who from age to age chooses them that please Him, distinguishes vessels of election, and uses them for the ministry of the Saints. Though you were trying to flee, as you confess, not from me, but from the calling you expected through me, He has netted you in the sure meshes of grace, and has brought you into the midst of Pisidia to catch men for the Lord, and draw the devil's prey from the deep into the light. You, too, may say as the blessed David said, " Whither shall I go from thy Spirit? or whither shall I flee from thy presence." [2] Such is the wonderful work of our loving Master. " Asses are lost " [3] that there may be a king of Israel. David, however, being an Israelite was granted to Israel ; but the land which has nursed you and brought you to such a height of virtue, possesses you no longer, and sees her neighbour beautified by her own adornment. But all believers in Christ are one people ; all Christ's people, although He is hailed from many regions, are one Church ; and so our country is glad and rejoices at the dispensation of the Lord, and instead of thinking that she is one man the poorer, considers that through one man she has become possessed of whole Churches. Only may the Lord grant me both to see you in person, and, so long as I am parted from you, to hear of your progress in the gospel, and of the good order of your Churches.

2. Play the man, then, and be strong, and walk before the people whom the Most High has entrusted to your hand. Like a skilful pilot, rise in mind above every wave lifted by heretical blasts ; keep the boat from being whelmed by the salt and bitter billows of false doctrine ; and wait for the calm to be made by the Lord so soon as there shall have been found a voice worthy of rousing Him to rebuke the winds and the sea. If you wish to visit me, now hurried by long sickness towards the inevitable end, do not wait for an opportunity, or for the word from me. You know that to a father's heart every time is suitable to embrace a well-loved

---

[1] St. Matt. xix. 6. [3] 1 Cor. vii. 29. [5] 1 Cor. vii. 9.
[2] 1 Cor. vii. 31. [4] Gen. i. 28.
[6] On the ancient dislike of stepmothers, cf. Herod. iv. 154, and Eurip., *Alcestis* 309, where they are said to be as dangerous to the children as vipers. Menander writes δεινότερον οὐδὲν ἄλλο μητρυιᾶς κακόν.
[7] 1 Thess. iv. 4. So A.V., apparently taking σκεῦος for *body* with Chrys., Theodoret, and others. The Greek is, most simply, not " possess," but *get*, and is in favour of the interpretation of Theod. of Mops., Augustine, and others, " get his *wife*." See Ellicott, *Thess.* p. 53.

[1] Placed in 374. [2] Ps. cxxxix. 7.
[3] 1 Sam. ix. 3. So six MSS. Editors have substituted " enemies." The letter does not exist in the *Codex Harlæanus*. Ὄνοι is supposed to mean that Faustinus and John, the predecessors of Amphilochius in the see of Iconium, were not very wise bishops. ἐχθροί might mean that they were Arian. cf. Letter cxxxviii.

son, and that affection is stronger than words. Do not lament over a responsibility transcending your strength. If you had been destined to bear the burden unaided, it would have been not merely heavy ; it would have been intolerable. But if the Lord shares the load with you, " cast all your care upon the Lord " [1] and He will Himself act. Only be exhorted ever to give heed lest you be carried away by wicked customs. Rather change all previous evil ways into good by the help of the wisdom given you by God. For Christ has sent you not to follow others, but yourself to take the lead of all who are being saved. I charge you to pray for me, that, if I am still in this life, I may be permitted to see you with your Church. If, however, it is ordained that I now depart, may I see all of you hereafter with the Lord, your Church blooming like a vine with good works, and yourself like a wise husbandman and good servant giving meat in due season to his fellow-servants, and receiving the reward of a wise and trusty steward. All who are with me salute your reverence. May you be strong and joyful in the Lord. May you be preserved glorious in the graces of the Spirit and of wisdom.

LETTER CLXII.[2]

To Eusebius, bishop of Samosata.[3]

THE same cause seems to make me hesitate to write, and to prove that I must write. When I think of the visit which I owe, and reckon up the gain at meeting you, I cannot help despising letters, as being not even shadows in comparison with the reality. Then, again, when I reckon that my only consolation, deprived as I am of all that is best and most important, is to salute such a man and beg him, as I am wont, not to forget me in his prayers, I bethink me that letters are of no small value. I do not, myself, wish to give up all hope of my visit, nor to despair of seeing you. I should be ashamed not to seem to put so much confidence in your prayers as even to expect to be turned from an old man into a young one, if such a need were to arise, and not merely from a sick and emaciated one, as I am now, into one a little bit stronger. It is not easy to express in words the reason of my not being with you already, because I am not only prevented by actual illness, but have not even force of speech enough at any time to give you an account of such manifold and complex disease. I can only say that, ever

since Easter up to now, fever, diarrhœa, and intestinal disturbance, drowning me like waves, do not suffer me to lift my head above them. Brother Barachus may be able to tell you the character of my symptoms, if not as their severity deserves, at least clearly enough to make you understand the reason of my delay. If you join cordially in my prayers, I have no doubt that my troubles will easily pass away.

LETTER CLXIII.[1]

To Count Jovinus.

ONE can see your soul in your letter, for in reality no painter can so exactly catch an outward likeness, as uttered thoughts can image the secrets of the soul. As I read your letter, your words exactly characterized your steadfastness, your real dignity, your unfailing sincerity ; in all those things it comforted me greatly though I could not see you. Never fail, then, to seize every opportunity of writing to me, and to give me the pleasure of conversing with you at a distance ; for to see you face to face I am now forbidden by the distressing state of my health. How serious this is you will learn from the God-beloved bishop Amphilochius, who is both able to report to you from his having been constantly with me, and fully competent to tell you what he has seen. But the only reason why I wish you to know of my sufferings is, that you will forgive me for the future, and acquit me of lack of energy, if I fail to come and see you, though in truth my loss does not so much need defence from me as comfort from you. Had it been possible for me to come to you, I should have very much preferred a sight of your excellency to all the ends that other men count worth an effort.

LETTER CLXIV.[2]

To Ascholius.[3]

1. IT would not be easy for me to say how very much delighted I am with your holiness's letter. My words are too weak to express all that I feel ; you, however, ought to be able to conjecture it, from the beauty of what you have written. For what did not your letter contain? It contained love to God ; the marvellous description of the martyrs, which put the manner of their good fight so plainly before me that I seemed actually to see it ; love and kindness to myself ;

[1] *cf.* Ps. lv. 22 and 1 Pet. v. 7.   [2] Placed in 374.
[3] On Basil's hopes of visiting Eusebius.

[1] Placed in 374.   [2] Placed in 374.   [3] *cf. Letter* liv.

words of surpassing beauty. So when I had taken it into my hands, and read it many times, and perceived how abundantly full it was of the grace of the Spirit, I thought that I had gone back to the good old times, when God's Churches flourished, rooted in faith, united in love, all the members being in harmony, as though in one body. Then the persecutors were manifest, and manifest too the persecuted. Then the people grew more numerous by being attacked. Then the blood of the martyrs, watering the Churches, nourished many more champions of true religion, each generation stripping for the struggle with the zeal of those that had gone before. Then we Christians were in peace with one another, the peace which the Lord bequeathed us, of which, so cruelly have we driven it from among us, not a single trace is now left us. Yet my soul did go back to that blessedness of old, when a letter came from a long distance, bright with the beauty of love, and a martyr travelled to me from wild regions beyond the Danube, preaching in his own person the exactitude of the faith which is there observed. Who could tell the delight of my soul at all this? What power of speech could be devised competent to describe all that I felt in the bottom of my heart? However, when I saw the athlete, I blessed his trainer: he, too, before the just Judge, after strengthening many for the conflict on behalf of true religion, shall receive the crown of righteousness.

2. By bringing the blessed Eutyches[1] to my recollection, and honouring my country for having sown the seeds of true religion, you have at once delighted me by your reminder of the past, and distressed me by your conviction of the present. None of us now comes near Eutyches in goodness: so far are we from bringing barbarians under the softening power of the Spirit, and the operation of His graces, that by the greatness of our sins we turn gentle hearted men into barbarians, for to ourselves and to our sins I attribute it that the influence of the heretics is so widely diffused. Peradventure no part of the world has escaped the conflagration of heresy. You tell me of struggles of athletes, bodies lacerated for the truth's sake, savage fury despised by men of fearless heart, various tortures of persecutors, and constancy of the wrestlers through them all, the block and the water whereby the martyrs

died.[1] And what is our condition? Love is grown cold; the teaching of the Fathers is being laid waste; everywhere is shipwreck of the Faith; the mouths of the faithful are silent; the people, driven from the houses of prayer, lift up their hands in the open air to their Lord which is in heaven. Our afflictions are heavy, martyrdom is nowhere to be seen, because those who evilly entreat us are called by the same name as ourselves. Wherefore pray to the Lord yourself, and join all Christ's noble athletes with you in prayer for the Churches, to the end that, if any further time remains for this world, and all things are not being driven to destruction, God may be reconciled to his own Churches and restore them to their ancient peace.

LETTER CLXV.[2]

To Ascholius, bishop of Thessalonica.[3]

GOD has fulfilled my old prayer in deigning to allow me to receive the letter of your veritable holiness. What I most of all desire is to see you and to be seen by you, and to enjoy in actual intercourse all the graces of the Spirit with which you are endowed. This, however, is impossible, both on account of the distance which separates us, and the engrossing occupations of each of us. I therefore pray, in the second place, that my soul may be fed by frequent letters from your love in Christ. This has now been granted me on taking your epistle into my hands. I have been doubly delighted at the enjoyment of your communication. I felt as though I could really see your very soul shining in your words as in some mirror; and I was moved to exceeding joy, not only at your proving to be what all testimony says of you, but that your noble qualities are the ornament of my country. You have filled the country beyond our borders with spiritual fruits, like some vigorous branch sprung from a glorious root. Rightly, then, does our country rejoice in her own offshoots. When you were engaging in con-

---

[1] Eutyches was a Cappadocian, who was taken prisoner by the Goths, in the reign of Gallienus, in a raid into Cappadocia. It was through the teaching of these captives that the ancestors of Ulphilas became Christians. *cf.* Philost., *H.E.* ii. 5.

[1] The Ben. note illustrates these modes of martyrdom from the letter of the Gothic Church, supposed to have been written by Ascholius, sent to Cæsarea with the body of Saint Sabas, who suffered under Athanaricus, king of the Goths, in the end of the fourth century. "They bring him down to the water, giving thanks and glorifying God; then they flung him down, and put a block about his neck, and plunged him into the depth. So slain by wood and water, he kept the symbol of salvation undefiled, being 38 years old." *cf.* Ruinart., *Act. Sinc.* p. 670.

[2] Placed in 374.

[3] So all the MSS. But it is the opinion of Maran that there can be no doubt of the letter being addressed, not to Ascholius, but to Soranus, duke of Scythia. We have seen in letter 255 that Basil requested his relative Julius Soranus to send him some relics of the Gothic martyrs. This letter appears to refer to his prompt compliance with the request by sending relics of Saint Sabas.

flicts for the Faith she heard that the goodly heritage of the Fathers was preserved in you, and she glorified God. And now what are you about? You have honoured the land that gave you birth by sending her a martyr who has just fought a good fight in the barbarian country on your borders, just as a grateful gardener might send his first fruits to those who had given him the seeds. Verily the gift is worthy of Christ's athlete, a martyr of the truth just crowned with the crown of righteousness, whom we have gladly welcomed, glorifying God who has now fulfilled the gospel of His Christ in all the world. Let me ask you to remember in your prayers me who love you, and for my soul's sake earnestly to beseech the Lord that one day I, too, may be deemed worthy to begin to serve God, according to the way of His commandments which He has given us to salvation.

LETTER CLXVI.[1]

To Eusebius, bishop of Samosata.[2]

LETTER CLXVII.[3]

To Eusebius, bishop of Samosata.

I AM delighted at your remembering me and writing, and, what is yet more important, at your sending me your blessing in your letter. Had I been but worthy of your labours and of your struggles in Christ's cause, I should have been permitted to come to you and embrace you, and to take you as a model of patience. But since I am not worthy of this, and am detained by many afflictions and much occupation, I do what is next best. I salute your excellency, and beseech you not to grow weary of remembering me. For the honour and pleasure of receiving your letters is not only an advantage to me, but it is a ground of boasting and pride before the world that I should be held in honour by one whose virtue is so great, and who is in such close communion with God as to be able, alike by his teaching and example, to unite others with him in it.

LETTER CLXVIII.[4]

To Antiochus.[5]

I MOURN for the Church that is deprived of the guidance of such a shepherd.[6] But I

have so much the more ground for congratulating you on being worthy of the privilege of enjoying, at such a moment, the society of one who is fighting such a good fight in the cause of the truth, and I am sure that you, who nobly support and stimulate his zeal, will be thought worthy by the Lord of a lot like his. What a blessing, to enjoy in unbroken quiet the society of the man so rich in learning and experienced in life! Now, at least, you must, I am sure, know how wise he is. In days gone by his mind was necessarily given to many divided cares, and you were too busy a man to give your sole heed to the spiritual fountain which springs from his pure heart. God grant that you may be a comfort to him, and never yourself want consolation from others. I am sure of the disposition of your heart, alike from the experience which I, for a short time, have had of you, and from the exalted teaching of your illustrious instructor, with whom to pass one single day is a sufficient provision for the journey to salvation.

LETTER CLXIX.[1]

Basil to Gregory.[2]

YOU have undertaken a kindly and charitable task in getting together the captive troop of the insolent Glycerius (at present I must so write), and, so far as in you lay, covering our common shame. It is only right that your reverence should undo this dishonour with a full knowledge of the facts about him.

This grave and venerable Glycerius of yours was ordained by me deacon of the church of Venesa[3] to serve the presbyter, and look after the work of the Church, for, though the fellow is in other respects intractable, he is naturally clever at manual labour. No sooner was he appointed than he neglected his work, as though there had been absolutely nothing to do. But, of his own private power and authority, he got together some wretched virgins, some of whom came to him of their own accord (you know how young people are prone to anything of this

---

scene of his forced departure from his diocese, the agony of his flock at losing him, and his calm submission to the tyranny of Valens, see Theodoret iv. 12 and 13, pp. 115, 116, of this edition.

[1] Placed in 374, on the misconduct of Glycerius, a deacon.
[2] Tillemont says either of Nyssa or Nazianzus. In the MS. Coisl. I. it is preceded by lxxi., unquestionably addressed to Gregory of Nazianzus, and inscribed "to the same." In the *Codex Harl.* it is inscribed Γρηγορίῳ ἑταίρῳ. Garnier, however (*Vita S. Bas.* xxxi. § iv.) allows that there are arguments in favor of Gregory of Nyssa. Probably it is the elder Gregory who is addressed. See Prolegomena.
[3] Or Veësa, or Synnasa; the MSS. vary.

---

[1] Placed in 374.
[2] This letter is numbered lxv. among those of Gregory of Nazianzus, to whom it is to be attributed. It is only found in one MS. of the letters of Basil (Coisl. i.)
[3] Placed in 374.   [4] Placed in 374.
[5] Nephew of Eusebius. *cf. Letters* cxlvi., clvii., and clviii.
[6] Eusebius was now in exile in Thrace. On the picturesque

kind), and others were unwillingly forced to accept him as leader of their company. Then he assumed the style and title of patriarch, and began all of a sudden to play the man of dignity. He had not attained to this on any reasonable or pious ground ; his only object was to get a means of livelihood, just as some men start one trade and some another. He has all but upset the whole Church, scorning his own presbyter, a man venerable both by character and age ; scorning his chorepiscopus, and myself, as of no account at all, continually filling the town and all the clergy with disorder and disturbance. And now, on being mildly rebuked by me and his chorepiscopus, that he may not treat us with contempt (for he was trying to stir the younger men to like insubordination), he is meditating conduct most audacious and inhuman. After robbing as many of the virgins as he could, he has made off by night. I am sure all this will have seemed very sad to you. Think of the time too. The feast was being held there, and, as was natural, large numbers of people were gathered together. He, however, on his side, brought out his own troop, who followed young men and danced round them, causing all well-disposed persons to be most distressed, while loose chatterers laughed aloud. And even this was not enough, enormous as was the scandal. I am told that even the parents of the virgins, finding their bereavement unendurable, wishful to bring home the scattered company, and falling with not unnatural sighs and tears at their daughters' feet, have been insulted and outraged by this excellent young man and his troop of bandits. I am sure your reverence will think all this intolerable. The ridicule of it attaches to us all alike. First of all, order him to come back with the virgins. He might find some mercy, if he were to come back with a letter from you. If you do not adopt this course, at least send the virgins back to their mother the Church. If this cannot be done, at all events do not allow any violence to be done to those that are willing to return, but get them to return to me. Otherwise I call God and man to witness that all this is ill done, and a breach of the law of the Church. The best course would be for Glycerius to come back with a letter,[1] and in a becoming and proper frame of mind; if not, let him be deprived of his ministry.[2]

LETTER CLXX.[1]

To Glycerius.

How far will your mad folly go? How long will you counsel mischief against yourself? How long will you go on rousing me to wrath, and bringing shame on the common order of solitaries? Return. Put confidence in God, and in me, who imitate God's loving-kindness. If I rebuked you like a father, like a father I will forgive you. This is the treatment you shall receive from me, for many others are making supplication in your behalf, and before all the rest your own presbyter, for whose grey hairs and compassionate disposition I feel much respect. Continue longer to hold aloof from me and you have quite fallen from your degree.[2] You will also fall away from God, for with your songs and your garb[3] you are leading the young women not to God, but to the pit.

LETTER CLXXI.[4]

To Gregory.

I WROTE to you, not long ago, about Glycerius and the virgins. Even now they have not returned, but are still hesitating, how and why I know not. I should be sorry to charge this against you, as though you were acting thus to bring discredit on me, either because you have some ground of complaint against me, or to gratify others. Let them then come, fearing nothing. Do you be surety for their doing this. For it pains me to have my members cut off, although they have been rightly cut off. If they hold out the burden will rest on others. I wash my hands of it.

LETTER CLXXII.[5]

To Sophronius, the bishop.[6]

THERE is no need for me to say how much I was delighted by your letter. Your own

---

[1] ἐπιστολῆς is read in the version of this letter appearing in the works of Greg. Naz., and Combefis is no doubt right in thinking that it makes better sense than ἐπιστήμης, the reading of the chief MSS. here.
[2] cf. Prolegomena, and Ramsay's *Church and Roman Empire*, Cap. xviii.

[1] Placed with the preceding.
[2] τοῦ βαθμοῦ. cf. 1 Tim. iii. 13. οἱ καλῶς διακονήσαντες βαθμὸν ἑαυτοῖς καλὸν περιποιοῦνται. There seems an evident allusion to this passage, but not such as to enable Basil to be positively ranked with Chrysostom in his apparent interpretation of βαθμός objectively of preferment, or with Theodoret in his subjective idea of honour with God. Apparently the "degree" is the Diaconate.
[3] στολή. The technical use of this word for a "stole" is not earlier than the ninth century. It was indeed used for a sacred vestment, e.g. the sacred robe which Constantine presented to Macarius, Bishop of Jerusalem. (Theodoret ii. 27.) In Latin "stola" designated the distinctive dress of the matron, and it seems to be used with a suggestion of effeminacy.
[4] Placed with the preceding.   [5] Placed in 374.
[6] This Sophronius is distinguished by Maran from the Sophronius, *magister officiorum*, to whom *Letters* xxxii., lxxvi., and xcvi. have already been addressed, and who is also the recipient of clxxvi., clxxx., cxcii., cclxii. Nothing else is known of him.

words will enable you to conjecture what I felt on receiving it. You have exhibited to me in your letter, the first fruits of the Spirit, love. Than this what can be more precious to me in the present state of affairs, when, because iniquity abounds, the love of many has waxed cold?[1] Nothing is rarer now than spiritual intercourse with a brother, a word of peace, and such spiritual communion as I have found in you. For this I thank the Lord, beseeching Him that I may have part in the perfect joy that is found in you. If such be your letter, what must it be to meet you in person? If when you are far away you so affect me, what will you be to me when you are seen face to face? Be sure that if I had not been detained by innumerable occupations, and all the unavoidable anxieties which tie me down, I should have hurried to see your excellency. Although that old complaint of mine is a great hindrance to my moving about, nevertheless, in view of the good I expect, I would not have allowed this to stand in my way. To be permitted to meet a man holding the same views and reverencing the faith of the Fathers, as you are said to do by our honourable brethren and fellow presbyters, is in truth to go back to the ancient blessedness of the Churches, when the sufferers from unsound disputation were few, and all lived in peace, "workmen" obeying the commandments and not "needing to be ashamed,"[2] serving the Lord with simple and clear confession, and keeping plain and inviolate their faith in Father, Son and Holy Ghost.

LETTER CLXXIII.[3]

To Theodora the Canoness.[4]

I SHOULD be more diligent in writing to you but for my belief that my letters do not always, my friend, reach your own hands. I am afraid that through the naughtiness of those on whose service I depend, especially at a time like this when the whole world is in a state of confusion, a great many other people get hold of them. So I wait to be found fault with, and to be eagerly asked for my letters, that so I may have this proof of their delivery. Yet, whether I write or not, one thing I do without failing, and that is to keep in my heart the memory of your ex-

cellency, and to pray the Lord to grant that you may complete the course of good living which you have chosen. For in truth it is no light thing for one, who makes a profession, to follow up all that the promise entails. Any one may embrace the gospel life, but only a very few of those who have come within my knowledge have completely carried out their duty in its minutest details, and have overlooked nothing that is contained therein. Only a very few have been consistent in keeping the tongue in check and the eye under guidance, as the Gospel would have it; in working with the hands according to the mark of doing what is pleasing to God; in moving the feet, and using every member, as the Creator ordained from the beginning. Propriety in dress, watchfulness in the society of men, moderation in eating and drinking, the avoidance of superfluity in the acquisition of necessities; all these things seem small enough when they are thus merely mentioned, but, as I have found by experience, their consistent observance requires no light struggle. Further, such a perfection of humility as not even to remember nobility of family, nor to be elevated by any natural advantage of body or mind which we may have, nor to allow other people's opinion of us to be a ground of pride and exaltation, all this belongs to the evangelic life. There is also sustained self-control, industry in prayer, sympathy in brotherly love, generosity to the poor, lowliness of temper, contrition of heart, soundness of faith, calmness in depression, while we never forget the terrible and inevitable tribunal. To that judgment we are all hastening, but those who remember it, and are anxious about what is to follow after it, are very few.

LETTER CLXXIV.[1]

To a Widow.

I HAVE been most wishful to write constantly to your excellency, but I have from time to time denied myself, for fear of causing any temptation to beset you, because of those who are ill disposed toward me. As I am told, their hatred has even gone so far that they make a fuss if any one happens to receive a letter from me. But now that you have begun to write yourself, and very good it is of you to do so, sending me needful information about all that is in your mind, I am stirred to write back to you. Let me then set right what has been omitted in the past, and at the same time reply to what

[1] Matt. xxiv. 12. [2] 2 Tim. ii. 15. [3] Placed in 374.
[4] On the Canonicæ, pious women who devoted themselves to education, district visiting, funerals, and various charitable works, and living in a community apart from men, cf. Soc. i. 17, "virgins in the register," and Sozomen viii. 23, on Nicarete. They were distinguished from nuns as not being bound by vows, and from deaconesses as not so distinctly discharging ministerial duties.

[1] Placed in 374.

your excellency has written. Truly blessed is the soul, which by night and by day has no other anxiety than how, when the great day comes wherein all creation shall stand before the Judge and shall give an account for its deeds, she too may be able easily to get quit of the reckoning of life.

For he who keeps that day and that hour ever before him, and is ever meditating upon the defence to be made before the tribunal where no excuses will avail, will sin not at all, or not seriously, for we begin to sin when there is a lack of the fear of God in us. When men have a clear apprehension of what is threatened them, the awe inherent in them will never allow them to fall into inconsiderate action or thought. Be mindful therefore of God. Keep the fear of Him in your heart, and enlist all men to join with you in your prayers, for great is the aid of them that are able to move God by their importunity. Never cease to do this. Even while we are living this life in the flesh, prayer will be a mighty helper to us, and when we are departing hence it will be a sufficient provision for us on the journey to the world to come.[1]

Anxiety is a good thing; but, on the other hand, despondency, dejection, and despair of our salvation, are injurious to the soul. Trust therefore in the goodness of God, and look for His succour, knowing that if we turn to Him rightly and sincerely, not only will He not cast us off forever, but will say to us, even while we are in the act of uttering the words of our prayer, " Lo! I am with you."

LETTER CLXXV.[2]

To Count Magnenianus.[3]

YOUR excellency lately wrote to me, plainly charging me, besides other matters, to write concerning the Faith. I admire your zeal in the matter, and I pray God that your choice of good things may be persistent, and that, advancing in knowledge and good works, you may be made perfect. But I have no wish to leave behind me a treatise on the Faith, or to write various creeds, and so I have declined to send what you asked.[4] You seem to me to be surrounded by the din of your men there, idle fellows, who say certain things to calumniate me, with the idea that they will improve their own position by

lying disgracefully against me.[1] The past shews what they are, and future experience will shew them in still plainer colours. I, however, call on all who trust in Christ not to busy themselves in opposition to the ancient faith, but, as we believe, so to be baptized, and, as we are baptized, so to offer the doxology.[2] It is enough for us to confess those names which we have received from Holy Scripture. and to shun all innovation about them. Our salvation does not lie in the invention of modes of address, but in the sound confession of the Godhead in which we have professed our faith.

LETTER CLXXVI.[3]

To Amphilochius, Bishop of Iconium.[4]

GOD grant that when this letter is put into your hands, it may find you in good health, quite at leisure, and as you would wish to be. For then it will not be in vain that I send you this invitation to be present at our city, to add greater dignity to the annual festival which it is the custom of our Church to hold in honour of the martyrs.[5] For be sure my most honoured and dear friend, that our people here, though they have had experience of many, desire no one's presence so eagerly as they do yours; so affectionate an impression has your short intercourse with them left behind. So, then, that the Lord may be glorified, the people delighted, the martyrs honoured, and that I in my old age may receive the attention due to me from my true son, do not refuse to travel to me with all speed. I will beg you too to anticipate the day of assembly, that so we may converse at leisure and may comfort one another by the interchange of spiritual gifts. The day is the fifth of September.[6] Come then three days beforehand in order that you may also honour with your presence the Church[7] of the Hospital. May you by

---

1 " Prayer ardent opens heaven." Young, *N.T.* viii., 721.
2 Written probably early in 374.
3 One MS. reads Magninianus. On the identification of this officer with the recipient of cccxxv., see that letter.
4 But what Basil declined to do at the prompting of Magnenianus, he shortly afterwards did for Amphilochius, and wrote the *De Spiritu Sancto*.

1 Maran (*V. Basil* xxx.) thinks that the allusion is to Atarbius of Neocæsarea and to some of his presbyters. *cf. Letter* ccx.
2 *cf. De Sp. Scto.* p. 17.   3 Placed in 374.
4 An invitation to the feast of St. Eupsychius, with a request to arrive three days before the actual day of the festival, which was observed on the 7th of September. (*cf. Letter* c. and note, and the invitation to the Pontic bishops in cclii.)
5 *i.e.* Damas and Eupsychius.
6 So the date stands in eight MSS. However it arose, 5th is a mistake for 7th, the day of St. Eupsychius in the Greek Kalendar.
7 Μνήμη. The Ben. Ed. understand by this word the church erected by Basil in his hospital (*cf. Letter* xciv.) at Cæsarea. In illustration of the use of μνήμη in this sense Du Cange cites *Act. Conc. Chalced.* i. 144, and exp ains it as being equivalent to " *memoria*," *i e.* " æles sacra in qua extat sancti alicujus sepulcrum " *cf. Nomocan. Photii* v. § 1. For the similar use of " *memoria*," in Latin, *cf.* Aug., *De Civ. Dei.* xxii. 10: " *Nos aute*n *martyribus nostris non templa sicut diis sed* memorias *sicut hominibus mortuis fabricamus.*"

the grace of the Lord be kept in good health and spirits in the Lord, praying for me and for the Church of God.

LETTER CLXXVII.[1]

To Sophronius the Master.

To reckon up all those who have received kindness at your excellency's hand, for my sake, is no easy task ; so many are there whom I feel that I have benefited through your kind aid, a boon which the Lord has given me to help me in these very serious times. Worthiest of all is he who is now introduced to you by my letter, the reverend brother Eusebius, attacked by a ridiculous calumny which it depends upon you alone, in your uprightness, to destroy. I beseech you, therefore, both as respecting the right and as being humanely disposed, to grant me your accustomed favours, by adopting the cause of Eusebius as your own, and championing him, and, at the same time, truth. It is no small thing that he has the right on his side ; and this, if he be not stricken down by the present crisis, he will have no difficulty in proving plainly and without possibility of contradiction.

LETTER CLXXVIII.[2]

To Aburgius.[3]

I KNOW that I have often recommended many persons to your excellency, and so in serious emergencies have been very useful to friends in distress. But I do not think that I have ever sent to you one whom I regard with greater respect, or one engaged in contests of greater importance, than my very dear son Eusebius, who now places this letter in your hands. He will himself inform your excellency, if the opportunity is permitted him, in what difficulties he is involved. I ought to say, at least, as much as this. The man ought not to be misjudged, nor, because many have been convicted of disgraceful doings, ought he to come under common suspicion. He ought to have a fair trial, and his life must be enquired into. In this way the untruth of the charges against him will be made plain, and he, after enjoying your righteous protection, will ever proclaim what he owes to your kindness.[4]

---

[1] Placed in 374.   [2] Placed with the preceding.
[3] Also recommending the interests of Eusebius.
[4] The Ben. note considers the circumstances referred to are the cruelties of Valens to those who were accused of enquiring by divination as to who should succeed him on the throne. *cf.* Ammianus Marcellinus xxix. 1, 2.

LETTER CLXXIX.[1]

To Arinthæus.[2]

YOUR natural nobility of character and your general accessibility have taught me to regard you as a friend of freedom and of men. I have, therefore, no hesitation in approaching you in behalf of one who is rendered illustrious by a long line of ancestry, but is worthy of greater esteem and honour on his own account, because of his innate goodness of disposition. I beg you, on my entreaty, to give him your support under a legal charge, in reality, indeed, ridiculous, but difficult to meet on account of the seriousness of the accusation. It would be of great importance to his success if you would deign to say a kind word in his behalf. You would, in the first place, be helping the right ; but you would further be showing in this your wonted respect and kindness to myself, who am your friend.

LETTER CLXXX.[3]

To the Master Sophronius, on behalf of Eunathius.

I HAVE been much distressed on meeting a worthy man involved in very great trouble. Being human, how could I fail to sympathise with a man of high character afflicted beyond his deserts? On thinking in what way I could be useful to him, I did find one means of helping him out of his difficulties, and that is by making him known to your excellency. It is now for you to extend also to him the same good offices which, as I can testify, you have shown to many. You will learn all the facts of the case from the petition presented by him to the emperors. This document I beg you to take into your hands, and implore you to help him to the utmost of your power. You will be helping a Christian, a gentleman, and one whose deep learning ought to win respect. If I add that in helping him you will confer a great kindness upon me, though, indeed, my interests are matters of small moment, yet, since you are always so good as to make them of importance, your boon to me will be no small one.

---

[1] Placed in 374.
[2] Possibly commendatory of the same Eusebius.
[3] Of the same date.

LETTER CLXXXI.[1]

To Otreius, bishop of Melitene.[2]

YOUR reverence is, I know, no less distressed than myself at the removal of the very God-beloved bishop Eusebius. We both of us need comfort. Let us try to give it to one another. Do you write to me what you hear from Samosata, and I will report to you anything that I may learn from Thrace.[3]

It is to me no slight alleviation of our present distress to know the constancy of the people. It will be the same to you to have news of our common father. Of course I cannot now tell you this by letter, but I commend to you one who is fully informed, and will report to you in what condition he left him, and how he bears his troubles. Pray, then, for him and for me, that the Lord will grant him speedy release from his distress.

LETTER CLXXXII.[4]

To the presbyters of Samosata.

GRIEVED as I am at the desolation of the Church,[5] I none the less congratulate you on having been brought so soon to this extreme limit of your hard struggle. God grant that you may pass through it with patience, to the end that in return for your faithful stewardship, and the noble constancy which you have shewn in Christ's cause, you may receive the great reward.

LETTER CLXXXIII.[6]

To the Senate of Samosata.

SEEING, as I do, that temptation is now spread all over the world, and that the greater cities of Syria have been tried by the same sufferings as yourselves, (though, indeed, nowhere is the Senate so approved and renowned for good works, as your own, noted as you are for your righteous zeal,) I all but thank the troubles which have befallen you.[7]

For had not this affliction come to pass,

your proof under trial would never have been known. To all that earnestly strive for any good, the affliction they endure for the sake of their hope in God is like a furnace to gold.[1]

Rouse ye, then, most excellent sirs, that the labours you are about to undertake may not be unworthy of those which you have already sustained, and that on a firm foundation you may be seen putting a yet worthier finish. Rouse ye, that ye may stand round about the shepherd of the Church, when the Lord grants him to be seen on his own throne, telling each of you in his turn, some good deed done for the sake of the Church of God. On the great day of the Lord, each, according to the proportion of his labours, shall receive his recompense from the munificent Lord. By remembering me and writing to me as often as you can, you will be doing justice in sending me a reply, and will moreover give me very great pleasure, by sending me in writing a plain token of a voice which it is delightful to me to hear.

LETTER CLXXXIV.[2]

To Eustathius, bishop of Himmeria.[3]

ORPHANHOOD is, I know, very dismal, and entails a great deal of work, because it deprives us of those who are set over us. Whence I conclude that you do not write to me, because you are depressed at what has happened to you, and at the same time are now very much occupied in visiting the folds of Christ, because they are attacked on every side by foes. But every grief finds consolation in communication with sympathising friends. Do then, I beg you, as often as you can, write to me. You will both refresh yourself by speaking to me, and you will comfort me by letting me hear from you. I shall endeavour to do the same to you, as often as my work lets me. Pray yourself, and entreat all the brotherhood earnestly to importune the Lord, to grant us one day release from the present distress.

LETTER CLXXXV.[4]

To Theodotus, bishop of Berœa.[5]

ALTHOUGH you do not write to me, I know that there is recollection of me in your heart; and this I infer, not because I

---

[1] Placed in 374.
[2] In Armenia Minor, now Malatia. Basil asks him for and offers sympathy in the exile of Eusebius. Otreius was at Tyana in 367, and at Constantinople in 381 (Labbe ii. 99 and 955).
[3] Where Eusebius was in exile.   [4] Placed in 374.
[5] Specially the exile of Eusebius.   [6] Of the same date.
[7] χάριν ἔχειν τοῖς οἰκονομηθεῖσιν, with the *Cod. Med.*, instead of ἐπὶ τοῖς οἰκονομηθεῖσιν. The Ben. note points out that this expression of gratitude to the troubles themselves is of a piece with the expression of gratitude to enemies in the *De. Sp. S.* vi. § 13. (p. 8), and concludes: " *Sic etiam Machabæorum mater apud Gregorium Nazianzenum orat. xxii. ait se tyranno pene gratias agere.*"

[1] *cf.* Prov. xvii. 3 and xxvii. 21.   [2] Placed in 374.
[3] Nothing more is known of this Eustathius. Himmeria is in Osrhoene.   [4] Placed in 374.
[5] Nothing more is known of this Theodotus.

am worthy of any favourable recollection, but because your soul is rich in abundance of love. Yet, as far as in you lies, use whatever opportunities you have of writing to me, to the end that I may both be cheered by hearing news of you, and have occasion to send you tidings of myself. This is the only mode of communication for those who live far apart. Do not let us deprive one another of it, so far as our labours will permit. But I pray God that we may meet in person, that our love may be increased, and that we may multiply gratitude to our Master for His greater boons.

LETTER CLXXXVI.[1]

To Antipater, the governor.[2]

PHILOSOPHY is an excellent thing, if only for this, that it even heals its disciples at small cost; for, in philosophy, the same thing is both dainty and healthy fare. I am told that you have recovered your failing appetite by pickled cabbage. Formerly I used to dislike it, both on account of the proverb,[3] and because it reminded me of the poverty that went with it. Now, however, I am driven to change my mind. I laugh at the proverb when I see that cabbage is such a " good nursing mother of men,"[4] and has restored our governor to the vigour of youth. For the future I shall think nothing like cabbage, not even Homer's lotus,[5] not even that ambrosia,[6] whatever it was, which fed the Olympians.

LETTER CLXXXVII.

Antipater to Basil.

" TWICE cabbage is death," says the unkind proverb. I, however, though I have called for it often, shall die once. Yes: even though I had never called for it at all! If you do die anyhow, don't fear to eat a delicious relish, unjustly reviled by the proverb!

LETTER CLXXXVIII.[7]

(CANONICA PRIMA.)

To Amphilochius, concerning the Canons.[8]

" EVEN a fool," it is said, " when he asks

questions," is counted wise.[1] But when a wise man asks questions, he makes even a fool wise. And this, thank God, is my case, as often as I receive a letter from your industrious self. For we become more learned and wiser than we were before, merely by asking questions, because we are taught many things which we did not know; and our anxiety to answer them acts as a teacher to us. Assuredly at the present time, though I have never before paid attention to the points you raise, I have been forced to make accurate enquiry, and to turn over in my mind both whatever I have heard from the elders, and all that I have been taught in conformity with their lessons.

I. As to your enquiry about the Cathari,[2] a statement has already been made, and you have properly reminded me that it is right to follow the custom obtaining in each region, because those, who at the time gave decision on these points, held different opinions concerning their baptism. But the baptism of the Pepuzeni[3] seems to me to have no authority; and I am astonished how this can have escaped Dionysius,[4] acquainted as he was with the canons. The old authorities decided to accept that baptism which in nowise errs from the faith. Thus they used the names of heresies, of schisms, and of unlawful congregations.[5] By *heresies* they meant men who were altogether broken off and alienated in matters relating to the actual faith; by *schisms*[6] men who had separated for some ecclesiastical reasons and questions capable of mutual solution; by *unlawful congregations* gatherings held by disorderly presbyters or bishops or by unin-

---

structed laymen. As, for instance, if a man be convicted of crime, and prohibited from discharging ministerial functions, and then refuses to submit to the canons, but arrogates to himself episcopal and ministerial rights, and persons leave the Catholic Church and join him, this is unlawful assembly. To disagree with members of the Church about repentance, is *schism*. Instances of *heresy* are those of the Manichæans, of the Valentinians, of the Marcionites, and of these Pepuzenes; for with them there comes in at once their disagreement concerning the actual faith in God. So it seemed good to the ancient authorities to reject the baptism of heretics altogether, but to admit that of schismatics,[1] on the ground that they still belonged to the Church.

As to those who assembled in unlawful congregations, their decision was to join them again to the Church, after they had been brought to a better state by proper repentance and rebuke, and so, in many cases, when men in orders[2] had rebelled with the disorderly, to receive them on their repentance, into the same rank. Now the Pepuzeni are plainly heretical, for, by unlawfully and shamefully applying to Montanus and Priscilla the title of the Paraclete, they have blasphemed against the Holy Ghost. They are, therefore, to be condemned for ascribing divinity to men; and for outraging the Holy Ghost by comparing Him to men. They are thus also liable to eternal damnation, inasmuch as blasphemy against the Holy Ghost admits of no forgiveness. What ground is there, then, for the acceptance of the baptism of men who baptize into the Father and the Son and Montanus or Priscilla? For those who have not been baptized into the names delivered to us have not been baptized at all. So that, although this escaped the vigilance of the great Dionysius, we must by no means imitate his error. The absurdity of the position is obvious in a moment, and evident to all who are gifted with even a small share of reasoning capacity.

The Cathari are schismatics; but it seemed good to the ancient authorities, I mean Cyprian and our own[1] Firmilianus, to reject all these, Cathari, Encratites,[2] and Hydroparastatæ,[3] by one common condemnation, because the origin of separation arose through schism, and those who had apostatized from the Church had no longer on them the grace of the Holy Spirit, for it ceased to be imparted when the continuity was broken. The first separatists had received their ordination from the Fathers, and possessed the spiritual gift by the laying on of their hands. But they who were broken off had become laymen, and, because they are no longer able to confer on others that grace of the Holy Spirit from which they themselves are fallen away, they had no authority either to baptize or to ordain. And therefore those who were from time to time baptized by them, were ordered, as though baptized by laymen, to come to the church to be purified by the Church's true baptism. Nevertheless, since it has seemed to some of those of Asia that, for the sake of management of the majority, their baptism should be accepted, let it be accepted. We must, however, perceive the iniquitous action of the Encratites; who, in order to shut themselves out from being received back by the Church have endeavoured for the future to anticipate readmission by a peculiar baptism of their own, violating, in this manner even their own special practice.[4]

[1] τῶν ἀποσχισάντων, ὡς ἔτι ἐκ τῆς ἐκκλησίας ὄντων.

The Ben. note is: " *Quod autem addit Basilius*, ut adhuc ex Ecclesia exsistentium, *non idcirco addit quod schismaticos in Ecclesiæ membris numeraret. Illius verba si quis in deteriorem partem rapiat, facilis et expedita responsio, Nam sub finem hujus, canonis de Encratitis ipsis, id est, de hæreticis incarnationem et Dei singularitatem negantibus, ait sibi non jam integrum esse eos qui huic sectæ conjuncti sunt* ab Ecclesia *separare, quia duos eorum episcopos sine baptismo ac sine nova ordinatione receperat. Nemo autem suspicabitur Basilium ejusmodi hæreticos ab Ecclesia alienissimos non judicasse. Quare quidquid schismaticis tribuit, in sola baptismi societate positum est. Nam cum Cyprianus et Firmilianus schismaticos et hæreticos ita ab Ecclesia distractos crederent, ut nihil prorsus ad eos ex fontibus Ecclesiæ perflueret ; Basilius huic sententiæ non assentitur, et in schismaticis quia fidem Ecclesiæ retinent, vestigium quoddam agnoscit necessitudinis et societatis cum Ecclesia, ita ut valida sacramentorum administratio ab Ecclesia ad illos permanare possit. Hinc sibi integrum negat detestandos hæreticos* ab Ecclesia *separare, quorum baptisma ratum habuerat. Idem docent duo præstantissimi unitatis defensores. Optatus et Augustinus.* Quod enim scissum est, *inquit Optatus lib. iii. n. 9*, ex parte divisum est, non ex toto: cum constet merito, quia nobis et vobis ecclesiastica una est conversatio, et sic hominum litigant mentes, non litigant sacramenta. *Vid. lib. iv. n. 2. Sic etiam Augustinus lib. i* De baptismo n. 3: Itaque isti (*hæretici et schismatici*) in quibusdam rebus nobiscum sunt: in quibus autem nobiscum non sunt, ut veniendo accipiant, vel redeundo recipiant, adhortamur. *Vid. lib. iii. n. 26. Sic ex Basilio hæretici nobiscum sunt quoad baptisma.*"

[2] τοῖς ἐν βαθμῷ. *cf.* note on p. 218.

[1] As being one of Basil's predecessors in the see of Cæsarea.

[2] "*Hoc Encratitarum facinore non corrupta essentialis baptismi forma. Sed novæ quædam adjectæ cærimoniæ.*" Ben. Ed.

[3] *i.e.* those who used water instead of wine in the Eucharist, as Tatian and his followers. *cf.* Clem. Al., *Strom.* i. 19 and Cyprian. *Ep.* lxiii.

[4] The Ben. note points out that the improper proceeding of the Encratites consisted not in any corruption of the baptismal formula, but in the addition of certain novel ceremonies, and proceeds: " *Nam in canone 47 sic eos loquentes inducit.* In Patrem et Filium et Spiritum baptizati sumus. *Hinc eorum baptisma ratum habet, si qua inciderit magni momenti causa. Quod autem ait hoc facinus eos incipere*, ut reditum sibi in Ecclesiam intercludant, *videtur id prima specie in eam sententiam accipiendum, quasi Encratitæ baptisma suum ea mente immutassent, ut Catholicos ad illud rejiciendum incitarent, sicque plures in secta contineret odium et juga novi baptismatis. Abhorrebat enim ab omnium animis iteratus baptismus, ut pluribus exemplis probat Augustinus, lib. v.* De baptismo, n. 6. Videtur ergo prima specie Encratitis, ea, quam dixi, exstitisse causa, cur baptismum immutarent. Atque ita hunc locum interpretatur Tillemontius, tom. iv. p. 628. Sic etiam illius exemplo interpretatus sum in Præf. novæ Cypriani operum editioni præmissa cap. 4. p. 12. Sed huic interpretationi non convenit cum his quæ addit Basilius. Vereri enim se significat ne Catholici, dum Encratitas ab hac baptismi immutatione deterrere volunt, nimium restricti*

My opinion, therefore, is that nothing being distinctly laid down concerning them, it is our duty to reject their baptism, and that in the case of any one who has received baptism from them, we should, on his coming to the church, baptize him. If, however, there is any likelihood of this being detrimental to general discipline, we must fall back upon custom, and follow the fathers who have ordered what course we are to pursue. For I am under some apprehension lest, in our wish to discourage them from baptizing, we may, through the severity of our decision, be a hindrance to those who are being saved. If they accept our baptism, do not allow this to distress us. We are by no means bound to return them the same favour, but only strictly to obey canons. On every ground let it be enjoined that those who come to us from their baptism be anointed [1] in the presence of the faithful, and only on these terms approach the mysteries. I am aware that I have received into episcopal rank Izois and Saturninus from the Encratite following.[2] I am precluded therefore from separating from the Church those who have been united to their company, inasmuch as, through my acceptance of the bishops, I have promulgated a kind of canon of communion with them.

II. The woman who purposely destroys her unborn child is guilty of murder. With us there is no nice enquiry as to its being formed or unformed. In this case it is not only the being about to be born who is vindicated, but the woman in her attack upon herself; because in most cases women who make such attempts die. The destruction of the embryo is an additional crime, a second murder, at all events if we regard it as done with intent. The punishment, however, of these women should not be for life, but for the term of ten years. And let their treatment depend not on mere lapse of time, but on the character of their repentance.

III. A deacon who commits fornication after his appointment to the diaconate is to be deposed. But, after he has been rejected and ranked among the laity, he is not to be excluded from communion. For there is an ancient canon that those who have fallen from their degree are to be subjected to this kind of punishment alone.[1]

Herein, as I suppose, the ancient authorities followed the old rule " Thou shalt not avenge twice for the same thing."[2] There is this further reason too, that laymen, when expelled from the place of the faithful, are from time to time restored to the rank whence they have fallen; but the deacon undergoes once for all the lasting penalty of deposition. His deacon's orders not being restored to him, they rested at this one punishment. So far is this as regards what depends on law laid down. But generally a truer remedy is the departure from sin. Wherefore that man will give me full proof of his cure who, after rejecting grace for the sake of the indulgence of the flesh, has then, through bruising of the flesh [3] and the enslaving of it [4] by means of self control, abandoned the pleasures whereby he was subdued. We ought therefore to know both what is of exact prescription and what is of custom; and, in cases which do not admit of the highest treatment, to follow the traditional direction.

IV. In the case of trigamy and polygamy they laid down the same rule, in proportion, as in the case of digamy; namely one year for digamy (some authorities say two years); for trigamy men are separated for three and often for four years; but this is no longer described as marriage at all, but as polygamy; nay rather as limited fornication. It is for this reason that the Lord said to the woman of Samaria, who had had five husbands, " he whom thou now hast is not thy husband." [5] He does not reckon those who had exceeded the limits of a second marriage as worthy of the title of husband or wife. In cases of trigamy we have accepted a seclusion of five years, not by the canons, but following the precept of our predecessors. Such offenders ought not to be altogether prohibited from the privileges of the Church; they should be considered deserving of hearing after two or three years, and afterwards of being permitted to stand in their place; but they must be kept from the communion of the good gift, and only restored to the

---

sint et severi in eorum baptismo rejiciendo. Sperabant ergo Catholici tardiores ad ejus modi baptisma Encratitas futuros, si illud Catholici ratum habere nollent; nedum ipsi Encratitæ baptismatis immutationem eo consilio induxerint, ut ejusmodi baptisma a Catholicis rejiceretur. Quamobrem hæc verba, ut reditum sibi in Ecclesiam intercludant, *non consilium et propositum Encratitarum designant, sed incommodum quod ex eorum facinore consequebatur; velut si dicamus aliquem scelus admittere, ut æternam sibi damnationem accersat.*"

[1] *cf.* note on p. 42. St. Cyprian (*Ep.* lxx.) says that heretics who have no true altar cannot have oil sanctified by the altar. "Gregory of Nazianzus, *Orat.* (xlviii in Jul.) speaks of oil sanctified or consecrated on the spiritual or divine table; Optatus of Milevis (*c. Don.* vii. 102) says that this ointment is compounded (*conditur*) in the name of Christ; and the Pseudo-Dionysius (*De Hierarch. Eccles.* c. 4) mentions the use of the sign of the cross in the consecration of it." *D.C.A.* i. 355.

[2] This is the only known reference to these two bishops.

[1] " *Respicit, ni fallor, ad canonem* 25 *apostolorum, ad quem Balsamon et Zonaras observant nonnulla esse peccata, quibus excommunicatio, non solum depositio, infligitur; velut si quis pecunia, vel magistratus potentia, sacerdotium assequatur, ut sancitur Can.* 29 *et* 30." Ben note. [2] Nahum i. 9, LXX. [3] " *Duo veteres libri* συντριμμοῦ τῆς καρδίας." Ben. note. [4] *cf.* 1 Cor. ix. 27. [5] John iv. 18. For the more usual modern interpretation that the sixth union was an unlawful one, *cf.* Bengel. *Matrimonium hoc sextum non erat legitimum, vel non consummatum, aut desertio aliudve impedimentum intercesserat, ex altera utra parte.*

place of communion after showing some fruit of repentance.

V. Heretics repenting at death ought to be received; yet to be received, of course, not indiscriminately, but on trial of exhibition of true repentance and of producing fruit in evidence of their zeal for salvation.[1]

VI. The fornication of canonical persons is not to be reckoned as wedlock, and their union is to be completely dissolved, for this is both profitable for the security of the Church and will prevent the heretics from having a ground of attack against us, as though we induced men to join us by the attraction of liberty to sin.

VII. Abusers of themselves with mankind, and with beasts, as also murderers, wizards, adulterers, and idolaters, are deserving of the same punishment. Whatever rule you have in the case of the rest, observe also in their case. There can, however, be no doubt that we ought to receive those who have repented of impurity committed in ignorance for thirty years.[2] In this case there is ground for forgiveness in ignorance, in the spontaneity of confession, and the long extent of time. Perhaps they have been delivered to Satan for a whole age of man that they may learn not to behave unseemly;[3] wherefore order them to be received without delay, specially if they shed tears to move your mercy, and shew a manner of living worthy of compassion.[4]

VIII. The man who in a rage has taken

---

[1] τῶν κανονικῶν. The Greek is of either gender. The Ben. note is· *Clericos sive eos qui in canone recensentur hac voce designari hactenus existimarunt Basilii interpretes, ac ipsi etiam Zonaras et Balsamon. Sed ut canonicas sive sacras virgines interpreter, plurimis rationum momentis adducor: 1. Basilius hoc nomine clericos appellare non solet, sed sacras virgines, ut perspici potest ex epistolis 52 et 175; 2. præscriptum Basilii non convenit in clericos, quorum nonnullis, nempe lectoribus et aliis ejus modi venia dabatur ineundi matrimonii, quamvis in canone recenserentur: 3. prohibet Basilius ejusmodi stupra quæ honesto matrimonii nomine prætexi solebant. At id non inconcessum erat matrimonium, alios vero matrimonium post ordinationem inire nulla prorsus Ecclesia patiebatur, aut certe matrimonii pretium erat depositio. Contra virginibus nubentibus non longior pæna pluribus in locis imponebatur, quam digamis, ut perspicitur ex canone 18, ubi Basilius hance consuetudinem abrogat, ac virginum matrimonia instar adulterii existimat.*
[2] So the MSS. But the Ben. note points out that there must be some error, if a sin knowingly committed was punished by excommunication for fifteen years (Canons lviii., lxii., lxiii.), and one unwittingly committed by a punishment of twice the duration. [3] *cf.* 1 Tim. i. 20.
[4] The Ben. note continues: " *Deinde vero testatur Basilius eos fere hominis ætatem satanæ traditos fuisse. At ætas hominis* (γενεά) *sæpe annorum viginti spatio existimatur; velut cum ait Dionysius Alexandrinus apud Eusebium, lib. vii. cap. 21. Israëlitas in deserto fuisse duabus ætatibus. Ipse Basilius in Epistola 201, quæ scripta est anno 375, Neocæsarienses incusat quod sibi jam totam fere hominis ætatem succenseant; quos tamen non ita pridem amicos habuerat; ac anno 568, Musonii morte afflictos litteris amicissimis consolatus fuerat. Sæculum apud Latinos non semper stricte sumitur; velut cum ait Hieronymus in Epist. 27* ad Marcellum, *in Christi verbis explicandis per tanta jam sæcula tantorum ingenia sudasse; vel cum auctor libri* De rebaptismate *in Cyprianum tacito nomine invehitur, quod adversus prisca consulta post tot sæculorum tantam seriem nunc primum repente sine ratione insurgat, p. 357. De hoc ergo triginta annorum numero non paucos deducendos esse crediderim.*

---

up a hatchet against his own wife is a murderer. But it is what I should have expected from your intelligence that you should very properly remind me to speak on these points more fully, because a wide distinction must be drawn between cases where there is and where there is not intent. A case of an act purely unintentional, and widely removed from the purpose of the agent, is that of a man who throws a stone at a dog or a tree, and hits a man. The object was to drive off the beast or to shake down the fruit. The chance comer falls fortuitously in the way of the blow, and the act is unintentional. Unintentional too is the act of any one who strikes another with a strap or a flexible stick, for the purpose of chastising him, and the man who is being beaten dies. In this case it must be taken into consideration that the object was not to kill, but to improve, the offender. Further, among unintentional acts must be reckoned the case of a man in a fight who when warding off an enemy's attack with cudgel or hand, hits him without mercy in some vital part, so as to injure him, though not quite to kill him. This, however, comes very near to the intentional; for the man who employs such a weapon in self defence, or who strikes without mercy, evidently does not spare his opponent, because he is mastered by passion. In like manner the case of any one who uses a heavy cudgel, or a stone too big for a man to stand, is reckoned among the unintentional, because he does not do what he meant: in his rage he deals such a blow as to kill his victim, yet all he had in his mind was to give him a thrashing, not to do him to death. If, however, a man uses a sword, or anything of the kind, he has no excuse: certainly none if he throws his hatchet. For he does not strike with the hand, so that the force of the blow may be within his own control, but throws, so that from the weight and edge of the iron, and the force of the throw, the wound cannot fail to be fatal.

On the other hand acts done in the attacks of war or robbery are distinctly intentional, and admit of no doubt. Robbers kill for greed, and to avoid conviction. Soldiers who inflict death in war do so with the obvious purpose not of fighting, nor chastising, but of killing their opponents. And if any one has concocted some magic philtre for some other reason, and then causes death, I count this as intentional. Women frequently endeavour to draw men to love them by incantations and magic knots, and give them drugs which dull their intelligence. Such women, when they cause death, though the result of their action may not be what they intended, are nevertheless, on account of their proceedings being magical and prohibited, to be reckoned among intentional homicides. Women also who administer drugs to cause abortion, as well as those who take poisons to destroy unborn children, are murderesses. So much on this subject.

IX. The sentence of the Lord that it is unlawful to withdraw from wedlock, save on account of fornication,[1] applies, according to the argument, to men and women alike. Custom, however, does not so obtain. Yet, in relation with women, very strict expressions are to be found; as, for instance, the words of the apostle " He which is joined to a harlot is one body "[2] and of Jeremiah, If a wife " become another man's shall he return unto her again? shall not that land be greatly polluted?"[3] And again, " He that hath an adulteress is a fool and impious."[4] Yet custom ordains that men who commit adultery and are in fornication be retained by their wives. Consequently I do not know if the woman who lives with the man who has been dismissed can properly be called an adulteress; the charge in this case attaches to the woman who has put away her husband, and depends upon the cause for which she withdrew from wedlock.[5] In the case of her being beaten, and refusing to submit, it would be better for her to endure than to be separated from her husband; in the case of her objecting to pecuniary loss, even here she would not have sufficient ground. If her reason is his living in fornication we do not find this in the custom of the church; but from an unbelieving husband a wife is commanded not to depart, but to remain, on account of the uncertainty of the issue. " For what knowest thou, O wife, whether thou shalt save thy husband?"[6] Here then the wife, if she leaves her husband and goes to another, is an adulteress. But the man who has been abandoned is pardonable, and the woman who lives with such a man is not condemned. But if the man who

has deserted his wife goes to another, he is himself an adulterer because he makes her commit adultery ; and the woman who lives with him is an adulteress, because she has caused another woman's husband to come over to her.

X. Those who swear that they will not receive ordination, declining orders upon oath, must not be driven to perjure themselves, although there does seem to be a canon making concessions to such persons. Yet I have found by experience that perjurers never turn out well.[1] Account must however be taken of the form of the oath, its terms, the frame of mind in which it was taken, and the minutest additions made to the terms, since, if no ground of relief can anywhere be found, such persons must be dismissed. The case, however, of Severus, I mean of the presbyter ordained by him, does seem to me to allow of relief of this kind, if you will permit it. Give directions for the district placed under Mestia, to which the man was appointed, to be reckoned under Vasoda. Thus he will not forswear himself by not departing from the place, and Longinus, having Cyriacus with him, will not leave the Church unprovided for, nor himself be guilty of neglect of work.[2] I moreover shall not be held guilty of taking action in contravention of any canons by making a concession to Cyriacus who had sworn that he would remain at Mindana and yet accepted the transfer. His return will be in accordance with his oath, and his obedience to the arrangement will not be reckoned against him as perjury, because it was not added to his oath that he would not go, even a short time, from Mindana, but would remain there for the future. Severus, who pleads forgetfulness, I shall pardon, only telling him that One who knows what is secret will not overlook the ravaging of His Church by a man of such a character; a man who originally appoints uncanonically, then imposes oaths in violation of the Gospel, then tells a man to

---

1 Matt. v. 32.   3 Jer. iii. 1.
2 1 Cor. vi. 16.   4 Prov. xviii. 22, LXX.
5 The Ben. note is, *Sequitur in hoc canone Basilius Romanas leges, quas tamen fatetur cum evangelio minus consentire. Lex Constantini jubet in repudio mittendo a femina hæc sola crimina inquiri, si homicidam, vel medicamentarium, vel sepulcrorum dissolutorem maritum suum esse probaverit. At eadem lege viris conceditur, ut adulteras uxores dimittant. Aliud discrimen hoc in canone uxores inter et maritos ponitur, quod uxor injuste dimissa, si ab alia ducatur, adulterii notam non effugiat; dimissus autem injuste maritus nec adulter sit, si aliam ducat, nec quæ ab eo ducitur, adultera. Cæterum Basilius ante episcopatum eodem jure uxorem ac maritum esse censebat. Nam in Moral. reg. 73, statuit virum ab uxore, aut uxorem a viro non debere separari, nisi quis deprehendatur in adulterio. Utrique pariter interdicit novis nuptiis, sive repudiet, sive repudientur.*   6 1 Cor. vii. 16.

1 The Ben. note refers to the case of Dracontius, who had sworn that he would escape if he were ordained bishop, and so did; but was urged by Athanasius to discharge the duties of his diocese, notwithstanding his oath.
2 On this obscure passage the Ben. note is: *Longinus presbyter erat in agro Mestiæ subjecto. Sed cum is depositus esset ob aliquod delictum, ac forte honorem sacerdotii retineret, ut nonnumquam fiebat, Severus episcopus in ejus loco transtulit Cyriacum, quem antea Mindanis ordinaverat, ac jurare coegerat se Mindanis mansurum. Nihil hac in re statui posse videbatur, quod non in magnam aliquam difficultatem incurreret. Nam si in agro Mestiæ subjecto Cyriacus remaneret, perjurii culpam sustinebat. Si rediret Mindana, ager Mestiæ subjectus presbytero carebat, atque hujus incommodi culpa redundabat in caput Longini, qui ob delictum depositus fuerat. Quid igitur Basilius? Utrique occurrit incommodo; jubet agrum, qui Mestiæ subjectus erat Vasodis subjici, id est loco, cui subjecta erant Mindana. Hoc ex remedio duo consequebatur Basilius, ut et ager ille presbytero non careret, et Cyriacus ibi remanens Mindana tamen redire censeretur, cum jam hic locus eidem ac Mindana chorepiscopo pareret.*

perjure himself in the matter of his transfer, and last of all lies in pretended forgetfulness. I am no judge of hearts; I only judge by what I hear; let us leave vengeance to the Lord, and ourselves pardon the common human error of forgetfulness, and receive the man without question.

XI. The man who is guilty of unintentional homicide has given sufficient satisfaction in eleven years. We shall, without doubt, observe what is laid down by Moses in the case of wounded men, and shall not hold a murder to have been committed in the case of a man who lies down after he has been struck, and walks again leaning on his staff.[1] If, however, he does not rise again after he has been struck, nevertheless, from there being no intent to kill, the striker is a homicide, but an unintentional homicide.

XII. The canon absolutely excludes digamists from the ministry.[2]

XIII. Homicide in war is not reckoned by our Fathers as homicide; I presume from their wish to make concession to men fighting on behalf of chastity and true religion. Perhaps, however, it is well to counsel that those whose hands are not clean only abstain from communion for three years.[3]

XIV. A taker of usury, if he consent to spend his unjust gain on the poor, and to be rid for the future of the plague of covetousness, may be received into the ministry.[4]

XV. I am astonished at your requiring exactitude in Scripture, and arguing that there is something forced in the diction of the interpretation which gives the meaning of the original, but does not exactly render what is meant by the Hebrew word. Yet I must not carelessly pass by the question started by an enquiring mind. At the creation of the world, birds of the air and the fishes of the sea had the same origin;[1] for both kinds were produced from the water.[2] The reason is that both have the same characteristics. The latter swim in the water, the former in the air. They are therefore mentioned together. The form of expression is not used without distinction, but of all that lives in the water it is used very properly. The birds of the air and the fishes of the sea are subject to man; and not they alone, but all that passes through the paths of the sea. For every water-creature is not a fish, as for instance the sea monsters, whales, sharks, dolphins, seals, even sea-horses, sea-dogs, saw-fish, sword-fish, and sea-cows; and, if you like, sea nettles, cockles and all hard-shelled creatures of whom none are fish, and all pass through the paths of the sea; so that there are three kinds, birds of the air, fishes of the sea, and all water-creatures which are distinct from fish, and pass through the paths of the sea.

XVI. Naaman was not a great man with the Lord, but with his lord; that is, he was one of the chief princes of the King of the Syrians.[3] Read your Bible carefully, and you will find the answer to your question there.

LETTER CLXXXIX.[4]

To Eustathius the physician.[5]

HUMANITY is the regular business of all you who practise as physicians. And, in my opinion, to put your science at the head and front of life's pursuits is to decide reasonably and rightly. This at all events seems to be the case if man's most precious possession, life, is painful and not worth living, unless it be lived in health, and if for health we are dependent on your skill. In your own case medicine is seen, as it were, with two right hands; you enlarge the accepted limits of philanthropy by not confining the application of your skill to men's bodies, but by attending also to the cure of the diseases of their souls. It is not only in accordance with popular report that I thus write. I am moved by the personal experi-

---

[1] Exod. xxi. 19.
[2] *Ap.* Can. xiii. 14: "It is clear from the *Philosophumena* of Hippolytus (ix. 12) that by the beginning of the 3d century the rule of monogamy for the clergy was well established, since he complains that in the days of Callistus 'digamist and trigamist bishops, and priests and deacons, *began* to be admitted into the clergy.' Tertullian recognises the rule as to the clergy. Thus in his *De Exhortatione Castitatis* (c. 7) he asks scornfully; 'Being a digamist, dost thou baptize? Dost thou make the offering?'" *Dict. C.A.* i. 552.
Vide also Canon Bright, *Notes on the Canons of the first four General Councils.* On Can. Nic. viii. p. 27.
[3] The Ben. note quotes Balsamon, Zonaras, and Alexius Aristenus as remarking on this that Basil gives advice, not direction, and regards the hands, not the hearts, of soldiers as defiled; and as recalling that this canon was quoted in opposition to the Emperor Phocas when he wished to reckon soldiers as martyrs. The canon was little regarded, as being contrary to general Christian sentiment.
cf. Athan. *Ep.* xlviii. p. 557 of this edition: "In war it is lawful and praiseworthy to destroy the enemy; accordingly not only are they who have distinguished themselves in the field held worthy of great honours, but monuments are put up proclaiming their achievements."
[4] *cf.* Can. Nic. xvii. Canon Bright (*On the Canons*, etc., p. 56) remarks: "It must be remembered that interest, called τόκος and *fenus*, as the product of the principal, was associated in the early stages of society, — in Greece and Rome as well as in Palestine, — with the notion of undue profit extorted by a rich lender from the needy borrower (see Grote, *Hist. Gr.* ii. 311, H.; Arnold, *Hist. Rome* i. 282; Mommsen, *Hist. R.* i. 291). Hence Tacitus says, 'sane vetus urbi fenebre malum, et seditionum discordiarumque creberrima causa' (*Ann.* vi. 16), and Gibbon calls usury 'the inveterate grievance of the city, abolished by the clamours of the people, revived by their wants and idleness.'" (v. 314.)

[1] Ps. viii. 8.   [2] Gen. i. 20 and 21.   [3] 2 Kings v. 1.
[4] Placed in 374 or the beginning of 375.
[5] *cf. Letter* cli. This doctrinal statement is also found among the works of Gregory of Nyssa; but is more probably to be attributed to Basil. *Vide* Tillem. *Mém. Ecc.* ix. 678.

ence which I have had on many occasions, and to a remarkable degree at the present time, in the midst of the unspeakable wickedness of our enemies, which has flooded our life like a noxious torrent. You have most skilfully dispersed it and by pouring in your soothing words have allayed the inflammation of my heart. Having regard to the successive and diversified attacks of my enemies against me, I thought that I ought to keep silence and to bear their successive assaults without reply, and without attempting to contradict foes armed with a lie, that terrible weapon which too often drives its point through the heart of truth herself. You did well in urging me not to abandon the defence of truth, but rather to convict our calumniators, lest haply, by the success of lies, many be hurt.

2. In adopting an unexpected attitude of hatred against me my opponents seem to be repeating the old story in Æsop. He makes the wolf bring certain charges against the lamb, as being really ashamed to seem to kill a creature who had done him no harm without some reasonable pretext; then when the lamb easily rebuts the slander, the wolf, none the less, continues his attack, and, though defeated in equity, comes off winner in biting. Just so with those who seem to count hatred to me as a virtue. They will perhaps blush to hate me without a cause, and so invent pleas and charges against me, without abiding by any of their allegations, but urging as the ground of their detestation now this, now that, and now something else. In no single case is their malice consistent; but when they are baulked in one charge they cling to another and, foiled in this, have recourse to a third; and if all their accusations are scattered they do not drop their ill-will. They say that I preach three Gods, dinning the charge into the ears of the mob and pressing the calumny plausibly and persistently. Nevertheless, truth is fighting on my side; and both in public to all the world, and in private to all whom I meet, I prove that I anathematize every one who maintains three Gods and do not even allow him to be a Christian. No sooner do they hear this than Sabellius is handy for them to urge against me, and it is noised abroad that my teaching is tainted with his error. Once more I hold out in my defence my wonted weapon of truth, and demonstrate that I shudder at Sabellianism as much as at Judaism.

3. What then? After all these efforts were they tired? Did they leave off? Not at all. They are charging me with innova-

tion, and base their charge on my confession of three hypostases, and blame me for asserting one Goodness, one Power, one Godhead. In this they are not wide of the truth, for I do so assert. Their complaint is that their custom does not accept this, and that Scripture does not agree. What is my reply? I do not consider it fair that the custom which obtains among them should be regarded as a law and rule of orthodoxy. If custom is to be taken in proof of what is right, then it is certainly competent for me to put forward on my side the custom which obtains here. If they reject this, we are clearly not bound to follow them. Therefore let God-inspired Scripture decide between us; and on whichever side be found doctrines in harmony with the word of God, in favour of that side will be cast the vote of truth. What then is the charge? Two points are advanced at one and the same time in the accusations levelled against me. I am accused on the one hand of parting the hypostases asunder; on the other of never using in the plural any one of the nouns relating to the Divinity, but of always speaking in the singular number of one Goodness, as I have already said; of one Power; one Godhead; and so on. As to the parting of the hypostases, there ought to be no objection nor opposition on the part of those who assert in the case of the divine nature a distinction of essences. For it is unreasonable to maintain three essences and to object to three hypostases. Nothing, then, is left but the charge of using words of the divine nature in the singulars.

4. I have quite a little difficulty in meeting the second charge. Whoever condemns those who assert that the Godhead is one, must of necessity agree with all who maintain many godheads, or with those who maintain that there is none. No third position is conceivable. The teaching of inspired Scripture does not allow of our speaking of many godheads, but, wherever it mentions the Godhead, speaks of it in the singular number; as, for instance, "in him dwelleth all the fulness of the Godhead bodily."[1] And again; "for the invisible things of him from the creation of the world are clearly seen, being understood by the things that are made, even his eternal power and Godhead."[2] If, then, to multiply godheads is the special mark of the victims of polytheistic error, and to deny the Godhead altogether is to fall into atheism, what sense is there in this charge against me of con-

---

[1] Col. ii. 9.   [2] Rom. i. 20.

fessing one Godhead? But they make a plainer disclosure of the end they have in view; namely, in the case of the Father to agree that He is God, and consenting in like manner that the Son be honoured with the attribute of Godhead; but to refuse to comprehend the Spirit, though reckoned with Father and with Son in the idea of Godhead. They allow that the power of the Godhead extends from the Father to the Son, but they divide the nature of the Spirit from the divine glory. Against this view, to the best of my ability, I must enter a brief defence of my own position.

5. What, then, is my argument? In delivering the Faith of Salvation to those who are being made disciples in His doctrine, the Lord conjoins with Father and with Son the Holy Spirit also. That which is conjoined once I maintain to be conjoined everywhere and always. There is no question here of a ranking together in one respect and isolation in others. In the quickening power whereby our nature is transformed from the life of corruption to immortality, the power of the Spirit is comprehended with Father and with Son, and in many other instances, as in the conception of the good, the holy, the eternal, the wise, the right, the supreme, the efficient, and generally in all terms which have the higher meaning, He is inseparably united. Wherefrom I judge it right to hold that the Spirit, thus conjoined with Father and Son in so many sublime and divine senses, is never separated. Indeed I am unaware of any degrees of better or worse in the terms concerning the divine nature, nor can I imagine its being reverent and right to allow the Spirit a participation in those of lesser dignity, while He is judged unworthy of the higher. For all conceptions and terms which regard the divine are of equal dignity one with another, in that they do not vary in regard to the meaning of the subject matter to which they are applied. Our thought is not led to one subject by the attribution of good, and to another by that of wise, powerful, and just; mention any attributes you will, the thing signified is one and the same. And if you name God, you mean the same Being whom you understood by the rest of the terms. Granting, then, that all the terms applied to the divine nature are of equal force one with another in relation to that which they describe, one emphasizing one point and another another, but all bringing our intelligence to the contemplation of the same object; what ground is there for conceding to the Spirit fellowship with Father and Son in all other terms, and isolat-

ing Him from the Godhead alone? There is no escape from the position that we must either allow the fellowship here, or refuse it everywhere. If He is worthy in every other respect, He is certainly not unworthy in this. If, as our opponents argue, He is too insignificant to be allowed fellowship with Father and with Son in Godhead, He is not worthy to share any single one of the divine attributes: for when the terms are carefully considered, and compared with one another, by the help of the special meaning contemplated in each, they will be found to involve nothing less than the title of God. A proof of what I say lies in the fact that even many inferior objects are designated by this name. Nay, Holy Scripture does not even shrink from using this term in the case of things of a totally opposite character, as when it applies the title *god* to idols. " Let the gods," it is written, " who have not made heaven and earth, be taken away, and cast beneath the earth;"[1] and again, " the gods of the nations are idols."[2] And the witch, when she called up the required spirits for Saul, is said to have seen gods.[3] Balaam too, an augur and seer, with the oracles in his hand, as Scripture says, when he had got him the teaching of the demons by his divine ingenuity, is described by Scripture as taking counsel with God.[4] From many similar instances in Holy Scripture it may be proved that the name of God has no pre-eminence over other words which are applied to the divine, since, as has been said, we find it employed without distinction even in the case of things of quite opposite character. On the other hand we are taught by Scripture that the names holy, incorruptible, righteous, and good, are nowhere indiscriminately used of unworthy objects. It follows, then, that if they do not deny that the Holy Spirit is associated with the Son and with the Father, in the names which are specially applied, by the usage of true religion, to the divine nature alone, there is no reasonable ground for refusing to allow the same association in the case of that word alone which, as I have shown, is used as a recognised homonym even of demons and idols.

6. But they contend that this title sets forth the nature of that to which it is applied; that the nature of the Spirit is not a nature shared in common with that of Father and of Son; and that, for this reason, the Spirit ought not to be allowed the common use of the name. It is, therefore, for them to show by what means they have per-

[1] Jer. x. 11, LXX. [2] Ps. xcvi. 5. [3] 1 Sam. xxviii. 13.
[4] Num. xxii. 20. Contrast Bp. Butler, *Serm*. vii.

ceived this variation in the nature. If it were indeed possible for the divine nature to be contemplated in itself; could what is proper to it and what is foreign to it be discovered by means of visible things; we should then certainly stand in no need of words or other tokens to lead us to the apprehension of the object of the enquiry. But the divine nature is too exalted to be perceived as objects of enquiry are perceived, and about things which are beyond our knowledge we reason on probable evidence. We are therefore of necessity guided in the investigation of the divine nature by its operations. Suppose we observe the operations of the Father, of the Son, of the Holy Ghost, to be different from one another, we shall then conjecture, from the diversity of the operations, that the operating natures are also different. For it is impossible that things which are distinct, as regards their nature, should be associated as regards the form of their operations; fire does not freeze; ice does not warm; difference of natures implies difference of the operations proceeding from them. Grant, then, that we perceive the operation of Father, Son and Holy Ghost to be one and the same, in no respect showing difference or variation; from this identity of operation we necessarily infer the unity of the nature.

7. The Father, the Son and the Holy Ghost alike hallow, quicken, enlighten, and comfort. No one will attribute a special and peculiar operation of hallowing to the operation of the Spirit, after hearing the Saviour in the Gospel saying to the Father about His disciples, sanctify them in Thy name.[1] In like manner all other operations are equally performed, in all who are worthy of them, by the Father and by the Son and by the Holy Ghost; every grace and virtue, guidance, life, consolation, change into the immortal, the passage into freedom and all other good things which come down to man. Nay even the dispensation which is above us in relation to the creature considered both in regard to intelligence and sense, if indeed it is possible for any conjecture concerning what lies above us to be formed from what we know, is not constituted apart from the operation and power of the Holy Ghost, every individual sharing His help in proportion to the dignity and need of each. Truly the ordering and administration of beings above our nature is obscure to our perception; nevertheless any one, arguing from what is known to us, would find it more reasonable to conclude that the power of the Spirit operates even in those beings, than that He is excluded from the government of supramundane things. So to assert is to advance a blasphemy bare and unsupported; it is to support absurdity on fallacy. On the other hand to agree that even the world beyond us is governed by the power of the Spirit, as well as by that of the Father and of the Son, is to advance a contention, supported on the plain testimony of what is seen in human life. Identity of operation in the case of Father and of Son and of Holy Ghost clearly proves invariability of nature. It follows that, even if the name of Godhead does signify nature, the community of essence proves that this title is very properly applied to the Holy Spirit.

8. I am, however, at a loss to understand how our opponents with all their ingenuity can adduce the title of Godhead in proof of nature, as though they had never heard from Scripture that nature does not result from institution and appointment.[1] Moses was made[2] a god of the Egyptians when the divine voice said, "See I have made thee a god to Pharaoh.[3] The title therefore does give proof of a certain authority of oversight or of action. The divine nature, on the other hand, in all the words which are contrived, remains always inexplicable, as I always teach. We have learnt that it is beneficent, judicial, righteous, good, and so on; and so have been taught differences of operations. But we are, nevertheless, unable to understand the nature of the operator through our idea of the operations. Let any one give an account of each one of these names, and of the actual nature to which they are applied, and it will be found that the definition will not in both cases be the same. And where the definition is not identical the nature is different. There is, then, a distinction to be observed between the essence, of which no explanatory term has yet been discovered, and the meaning of the names applied to it in reference to some operation or dignity. That there should be no difference in the operations we infer from the community of terms. But, we derive no clear proof of variation in nature, because, as has been said, identity of operations indicates community of nature. If then Godhead be the name of an operation, we say that the Godhead is one, as there is one operation of Father, Son, and Holy Ghost; if, however, as is popularly supposed, the name of Godhead indicates nature, then,

---

[1] cf. St. John xvii. 11 and 17.

[1] χειροτονητή.   [2] ἐχειροτονήθη.   [3] Ex. vii. 1.

since we find no variation in the nature, we reasonably define the Holy Trinity to be of one Godhead.

LETTER CXC.[1]

To Amphilochius, bishop of Iconium.[2]

1. THE interest which you have shewn in the affairs of the Isaurian Church is only what might have been expected from that zeal and propriety of conduct which so continually rouses my admiration of you. The most careless observer must at once perceive that it is in all respects more advantageous for care and anxiety to be divided among several bishops. This has not escaped your observation, and you have done well in noting, and in acquainting me with, the position of affairs. But it is not easy to find fit men. While, then, we are desirous of having the credit that comes of numbers, and cause God's Church to be more effectively administered by more officers, let us be careful lest we unwittingly bring the word into contempt on account of the unsatisfactory character of the men who are called to office, and accustom the laity to indifference. You yourself know well that the conduct of the governed is commonly of a piece with that of those who are set over them. Perhaps therefore it might be better to appoint one well approved man, though even this may not be an easy matter, to the supervision of the whole city, and entrust him with the management of details on his own responsibility. Only let him be a servant of God, " a workman that needeth not to be ashamed," [3] not " looking on his own things," [4] but on the things of the most, " that they be saved." [5] If he finds himself overweighted with responsibility, he will associate other labourers for the harvest with himself. If only we can find such a man, I own that I think the one worth many, and the ordering of the cure of souls in this way likely to be attended at once with more advantage to the Churches and with less risk to us. If, however, this course prove difficult, let us first do our best to appoint superintendents [6] to the small townships or villages which have of old been episcopal

sees. Then afterwards we will appoint once more the [bishop] of the city. Unless we take this course the man appointed may prove a hindrance to subsequent administration, and from his wish to rule over a larger diocese, and his refusal to accept the ordination of the bishops, we may find ourselves suddenly involved in a domestic quarrel. If this course is difficult, and time does not allow, see to it that the Isaurian bishop is strictly kept within his own bounds by ordaining some of his immediate neighbours. In the future it will be reserved for us to give to the rest bishops at the proper season, after we have carefully examined those whom we ourselves may judge to be most fit.

2. I have asked George, as you requested. He replies as you reported. In all this we must remain quiet, casting the care of the house on the Lord. For I put my trust in the Holy God that He will by my aid [1] grant to him deliverance from his difficulties in some other way, and to me to live my life without trouble. If this cannot be, be so good as to send me word yourself as to what part I must look after, that I may begin to ask this favour of each of my friends in power, either for nothing, or for some moderate price, as the Lord may prosper me.[2]

I have, in accordance with your request, written to brother Valerius. Matters at Nyssa are going on as they were left by your reverence, and, by the aid of your holiness, are improving. Of those who were then separated from me some have gone off to the court, and some remain waiting for tidings from it. The Lord is able as well to frustrate the expectations of these latter as to make the return of the former useless.

3. Philo, on the authority of some Jewish tradition, explains the manna to have been of such a nature that it changed with the taste of the eater: that of itself it was like millet seed boiled in honey; it served sometimes for bread, sometimes for meat, either of birds or beasts; at other times for vegetables, ac-

---

[1] Placed by Maran in 374. After Easter 375 by Tillemont.
[2] Isauria, the district of Pisidia, forming the S. W. corner of the modern Karamania, was under the ecclesiastical jurisdiction of Iconium. " In the heart of the Roman monarchy, the Isaurians long continued a nation of wild barbarians. Succeeding powers, unable to reduce them to obedience either by arms or policy, were compelled to acknowledge their weakness by surrounding the hostile and independent spot with a strong chain of fortifications (*Hist. Aug.* 197) which often proved insufficient to restrain the invasions of these domestic foes." Gibbon. chap. X. Raids and Arian persecution had disorganised the Isaurian Episcopate. (Maran, *Vit. Bas.*)
[3] 2 Tim. ii. 15.   [5] 1 Thess. ii. 16.
[4] Phil. ii. 4.   [6] προϊσταμένους.

[1] Here the MSS. vary, and the sense is obscure. Ben. Ed. σὺν ἡμῖν. al. συνέσιν.
[2] "*Videtur illa dignitas, quam se amici causa alicujus petiturum promittit Basilius, non administratio aliqua fuisse, sed tantum codicillaria dignitas. Hoc enim consilio hanc dignitatem petere statuerat, ut amici domus magnum aliquod incommodum effugeret. Porro in hunc usum impetrari solebant codicilli, ut curia, vel saltem duumviratus et civitatis cura vitarentur. Pretio autem impetratos non modo nulla immunitas, sed etiam multa sequebatur ut perspicitur ex Cod. Theod. vi. 22. Sic enim habet lex secunda imperatoris Constantii: ' Ab honoribus mercandis per suffragia, vel qualibet ambitione quærendis, certa multa prohibuit: cui addimus et quicunque, fugientes obsequia curiarum, umbras et nomina affectaverint dignitatem, tricenas libras argenti inferre cogantur, manente illa præterita inlatione auri qua perpetua lege constructi sunt.' Unde miror Basilium ab hac via tentanda non omnino alienum fuisse. Sed forte hæ leges non admodum accurate servabuntur sub Valente.*" Ben. note.

cording to each man's liking; even for fish, so that the flavour of each separate kind was exactly reproduced in the eater's mouth.

Scripture recognises chariots containing three riders, because while other chariots contained two, the driver and the man-at-arms, Pharaoh's held three, two men-at-arms, and one to hold the reins.

Sympius has written me a letter expressive of respect and communion. The letter which I have written in reply I am sending to your holiness, that you may send it on to him if you quite approve of it, with the addition of some communication from yourself. May you, by the loving kindness of the Holy One, be preserved for me and for the Church of God, in good health, happy in the Lord, and ever praying for me.

LETTER CXCI.[1]

To Amphilochius, bishop of Iconium.[2]

ON reading the letter of your reverence I heartily thanked God. I did so because I found in your expressions traces of ancient affection. You are not like the majority. You did not persist in refusing to begin an affectionate correspondence. You have learned the greatness of the prize promised to the saints for humility, and so you have chosen, by taking the second place, to get before me. Among Christians such are the conditions of victory, and it is he who is content to take the second place who wins a crown. But I must not be behindhand in this virtuous rivalry, and so I thus salute your reverence in return; and inform you as to how I am minded, in that, since agreement in the faith is established among us,[3] there is nothing further to prevent our being one body and one spirit, as we have been called in one hope of our calling.[4] It is for you, then, of your charity to follow up a good beginning, to rally men of like mind to stand at your side, and to appoint both time and place for meeting. Thus, by God's grace, through mutual accommodation we may govern the Churches by the ancient kind of love; receiving as our own members brothers coming from the other side, sending as to our kin, and in turn receiving as from our own kin. Such, indeed, was once the boast of the Church. Brothers from each Church, travelling from one end of the world to the other, were provided with little tokens, and found all men fathers and brothers. This is a privilege whereof, like all the rest, the enemy of Christ's Churches has robbed us. We are confined each in his own city, and every one looks at his neighbour with distrust. What more is to be said but that our love has grown cold,[1] whereby alone our Lord has told us that His disciples are distinguished?[2] First of all, if you will, do you become known to one another, that I may know with whom I am to be in agreement. Thus by common consent we will fix on some place convenient to both, and, at a season suitable for travelling, we will hasten to meet one another; the Lord will direct us in the way. Farewell. Be of good cheer. Pray for me. May you be granted to me by the grace of the Holy One.[3]

LETTER CXCII.[4]

To Sophronius the Master.

WITH your extraordinary zeal in good deeds you have written to me to say that you yourself owe me double thanks; first, for getting a letter from me, and secondly, for doing me a service. What thanks, then, must not I owe you, both for reading your most delightful words, and for finding what I hoped for so quickly accomplished! The message was exceedingly gratifying on its own account, but it gave me much greater gratification from the fact that you were the friend to whom I owed the boon. God grant that ere long I may see you, and return you thanks in words, and enjoy the great pleasure of your society.

LETTER CXCIII.[5]

To Meletius the Physician.

I AM not able to flee from the discomforts of winter so well as cranes are, although for foreseeing the future I am quite as clever as a crane. But as to liberty of life the birds are almost as far ahead of me as they are in the being able to fly. In the first place I have been detained by certain worldly business; then I have been so wasted by constant and violent attacks of fever that there does seem something thinner even than I was, — I am

---

[1] Placed in 374.
[2] So the MSS. and Editors. The Ben. note would have it addressed to the recipient of the preceding. Tillemont thinks it written to one of the Lycian bishops referred to in *Letter* ccxviii.
[3] ἡμῖν. Some MSS. have ὑμῖν.   [4] cf. Eph. iv. 4.

[1] Matt. xxiv. 12.   [2] John xiii. 35.
[3] Whether the proposed meeting took place, and, indeed, what meeting is referred to, cannot be determined. Basil met Amphilochius and some neighbouring bishops in Pisidia in 375. But before this he counts the Isaurians as already in communion with him (*Letter* cciv.). Perhaps all that the meeting was desired to bring about was effected by correspondence. This is the explanation of the Ben. Ed.
[4] Placed in 374.   [5] Placed in 375.

thinner than ever. Besides all this, bouts of quartan ague have gone on for more than twenty turns. Now I do seem to be free from fever, but I am in such a feeble state that I am no stronger than a cobweb. Hence the shortest journey is too far for me, and every breath of wind is more dangerous to me than big waves to those at sea. I have no alternative but to hide in my hut and wait for spring, if only I can last out so long, and am not carried off beforehand[1] by the internal malady of which I am never rid. If the Lord saves me with His mighty hand, I shall gladly betake myself to your remote region, and gladly embrace a friend so dear. Only pray that my life may be ordered as may be best for my soul's good.

LETTER CXCIV.[2]

To Zoilus.

WHAT are you about, most excellent sir, in anticipating me in humility? Educated as you are, and able to write such a letter as you have sent, you nevertheless ask for forgiveness at my hands, as though you were engaged in some undertaking rash and beyond your position. But a truce to mockery. Continue to write to me on every occasion. Am I not wholly illiterate? It is delightful to read the letters of an eloquent writer. Have I learned from Scripture how good a thing is love? I count intercourse with a loving friend invaluable. And I do hope that you may tell me of all the good gifts which I pray for you; the best of health, and the prosperity of all your house. Now as to my own affairs, my condition is not more endurable than usual. It is enough to tell you this and you will understand the bad state of my health. It has indeed reached such extreme suffering as to be as difficult to describe as to experience, if indeed your own experience has fallen short of mine. But it is the work of the good God to give me power to bear in patience whatever trials are inflicted on me for my own good at the hands of our merciful Lord.

LETTER CXCV.[3]

To Euphronius, bishop of Colonia Armeniæ.

COLONIA, which the Lord has placed under your authority, is far out of the way of ordinary routes. The consequence is that,

although I am frequently writing to the rest of the brethren in Armenia Minor, I hesitate to write to your reverence, because I have no expectation of finding any one to convey my letter. Now, however, that I am hoping either for your presence, or that my letter will be sent on to you by some of the bishops to whom I have written, I thus write and salute you by letter. I wish to tell you that I seem to be still alive, and at the same time to exhort you to pray for me, that the Lord may lessen my afflictions, and lift from me the heavy load of pain which now presses like a cloud upon my heart. I shall have this relief if He will only grant a quick restoration to those godly bishops who are now punished for their faithfulness to true religion by being scattered all abroad.

LETTER CXCVI.[1]

To Aburgius.

RUMOUR, messenger of good news, is continually reporting how you dart across, like the stars, appearing now here, now there, in the barbarian regions; now supplying the troops with provisions, now appearing in gorgeous array before the emperor. I pray God that your doings may prosper as they deserve, and that you may achieve eminent success. I pray that, so long as I live and breathe this air, (for my life now is no more than drawing breath), our country may from time to time behold you.

LETTER CXCVII.[2]

To Ambrose, bishop of Milan.[3]

1. THE gifts of the Lord are ever great and many; in greatness beyond measure, in number incalculable. To those who are not insensible of His mercy one of the greatest of these gifts is that of which I am now availing myself, the opportunity allowed us, far apart in place though we be, of addressing one another by letter. He grants us two means of becoming acquainted; one by personal intercourse, another by epistolary correspondence. Now I have become acquainted with you through what you have said. I do not mean that my memory is impressed with your outward appearance, but that the beauty of the inner man has been brought home to me by the rich variety of your utterances, for

---

[1] προδιαρπασθῶμεν with two MSS. προδιαμάρτοιμεν has better authority, but is bad Greek, and makes worse sense.
[2] Placed in 375.   [3] Placed in 375.

[1] Placed in 375.   [2] Placed in 375.
[3] Ambrose was placed in the archiepiscopate of Milan in 374. The letter of Basil is in reply to a request the for restoration to his native city of the relics of St. Dionysius of Milan, who died in Cappadocia in 374. cf. Ath., *Ep. ad Sol.*; Amb. iii. 920.

each of us " speaketh out of the abundance of the heart." [1] I have given glory to God, Who in every generation selects those who are well-pleasing to Him; Who of old indeed chose from the sheepfold a prince for His people; [2] Who through the Spirit gifted Amos the herdman with power and raised him up to be a prophet; Who now has drawn forth for the care of Christ's flock a man from the imperial city, entrusted with the government of a whole nation, exalted in character, in lineage, in position, in eloquence, in all that this world admires. This same man has flung away all the advantages of the world, counting them all loss that he may gain Christ,[3] and has taken in his hand the helm of the ship, great and famous for its faith in God, the Church of Christ. Come, then, O man of God; not from men have you received or been taught the Gospel of Christ; it is the Lord Himself who has transferred you from the judges of the earth to the throne of the Apostles; fight the good fight; heal the infirmity of the people, if any are infected by the disease of Arian madness; renew the ancient footprints of the Fathers. You have laid the foundation of affection towards me; strive to build upon it by the frequency of your salutations. Thus shall we be able to be near one another in spirit, although our earthly homes are far apart.

2. By your earnestness and zeal in the matter of the blessed bishop Dionysius you testify all your love to the Lord, your honour for your predecessors, and your zeal for the faith. For our disposition towards our faithful fellow-servants is referred to the Lord Whom they have served. Whoever honours men that have contended for the faith proves that he has like zeal for it. One single action is proof of much virtue.

I wish to acquaint your love in Christ that the very zealous brethren who have been commissioned by your reverence to act for you in this good work have won praise for all the clergy by the amiability of their manners; for by their individual modesty and conciliatoriness they have shewn the sound condition of all. Moreover, with all zeal and diligence they have braved an inclement season; and with unbroken perseverance have persuaded the faithful guardians of the blessed body to transmit to them the custody of what they have regarded as the safeguard of their lives. And you must understand that they are men who would never have been forced by any human authority or sovereignty, had not the perseverance of these brethren moved them to compliance. No doubt a great aid to the attainment of the object desired was the presence of our well beloved and reverend son Therasius the presbyter. He voluntarily undertook all the toil of the journey; he moderated the energy of the faithful on the spot; he persuaded opponents by his arguments; in the presence of priests and deacons, and of many others who fear the Lord, he took up the relics with all becoming reverence, and has aided the brethren in their preservation. These relics do you receive with a joy equivalent to the distress with which their custodians have parted with them and sent them to you. Let none dispute; let none doubt. Here you have that unconquered athlete. These bones, which shared in the conflict with the blessed soul, are known to the Lord. These bones He will crown, together with that soul, in the righteous day of His requital, as it is written, " we must stand before the judgment seat of Christ, that each may give an account of the deeds he has done in the body." [1] One coffin held that honoured corpse. None other lay by his side. The burial was a noble one; the honours of a martyr were paid him. Christians who had welcomed him as a guest and then with their own hands laid him in the grave, have now disinterred him. They have wept as men bereaved of a father and a champion. But they have sent him to you, for they put your joy before their own consolation. Pious were the hands that gave; scrupulously careful were the hands that received. There has been no room for deceit; no room for guile. I bear witness to this. Let the untainted truth be accepted by you.

LETTER CXCVIII.[2]

To Eusebius, bishop of Samosata.

AFTER the letter conveyed to me by the officiales [3] I have received one other despatched to me later. I have not sent many myself, for I have not found any one travelling in your direction. But I have sent more than the four, among which also were those conveyed to me from Samosata after the first epistle of your holiness. These I have sealed and sent to our honourable brother Leontius, peræquator of Nicæa, urging that by his agency they may be delivered to the steward of the household of our honourable brother Sophronius, that he may see to their transmission to you.

[1] Matt. xii. 34.   [2] Ps. lxxviii. 70.   [3] Phil. iii. 8.

[1] cf. Rom. xiv. 10 and 2 Cor. v. 10.
[2] Placed in 375.   [3] Clergy engaged in crafts.

As my letters are going through many hands, it is likely enough that because one man is very busy or very careless, your reverence may never get them. Pardon me, then, I beseech you, if my letters are few. With your usual intelligence you have properly found fault with me for not sending, as I ought, a courier of my own when there was occasion for doing so; but you must understand that we have had a winter of such severity that all the roads were blocked till Easter, and I had no one disposed to brave the difficulties of the journey. For although our clergy do seem very numerous, they are men inexperienced in travelling because they never traffic, and prefer not to live far away from home, the majority of them plying sedentary crafts, whereby they get their daily bread. The brother whom I have now sent to your reverence I have summoned from the country, and employed in the conveyance of my letter to your holiness, that he may both give you clear intelligence as to me and my affairs, and, moreover, by God's grace, bring me back plain and prompt information about you and yours. Our dear brother Eusebius the reader has for some time been anxious to hasten to your holiness, but I have kept him here for the weather to improve. Even now I am under no little anxiety lest his inexperience in travelling may cause him trouble, and bring on some illness; for he is not robust.

2. I need say nothing to you by letter about the innovations of the East, for the brothers can themselves give you accurate information. You must know, my honoured friend, that, when I was writing these words, I was so ill that I had lost all hope of life. It is impossible for me to enumerate all my painful symptoms, my weakness, the violence of my attacks of fever, and my bad health in general. One point only may be selected. I have now completed the time of my sojourn in this miserable and painful life.

LETTER CXCIX.[1]

CANONICA SECUNDA.

To Amphilochius, concerning the Canons.

I WROTE some time ago in reply to the questions of your reverence, but I did not send the letter, partly because from my long and dangerous illness I had not time to do so; partly because I had no one to send with it. I have but few men with me who are experienced in travelling and fit for service

of this kind. When you thus learn the causes of my delay, forgive me. I have been quite astonished at your readiness to learn and at your humility. You are entrusted with the office of a teacher, and yet you condescend to learn, and to learn of me, who pretend to no great knowledge. Nevertheless, since you consent, on account of your fear of God, to do what another man might hesitate to do, I am bound for my part to go even beyond my strength in aiding your readiness and righteous zeal.

XVII. You asked me about the presbyter Bianor — can he be admitted among the clergy, because of his oath? I know that I have already given the clergy of Antioch a general sentence in the case of all those who had sworn with him; namely, that they should abstain from the public congregations, but might perform priestly functions in private.[1] Moreover, he has the further liberty for the performance of his ministerial functions, from the fact that his sacred duties lie not at Antioch, but at Iconium; for, as you have written to me yourself, he has chosen to live rather at the latter than at the former place. The man in question may, therefore, be received; but your reverence must require him to shew repentance for the rash readiness of the oath which he took before the unbeliever,[2] being unable to bear the trouble of that small peril.

XVIII. Concerning fallen virgins, who, after professing a chaste life before the Lord, make their vows vain, because they have fallen under the lusts of the flesh, our

1 The Ben. Ed. note: "Sæpe vituperantur apud sanctos Patres, qui sacra in privatis ædibus sive domesticis oratoriis celebrant. Hinc Irenæus, lib. iv. cap. 26, oportere ait eos, qui absistunt a principali successione et quocunque loco colligunt, suspectos habere, vel quasi hæreticos et malæ sententiæ, vel quasi scindentes et elatos et sibi placentes; aut rursus ut hypocritas quæstus gratia et vanæ gloriæ hoc operantes. Basilius, in Psalm xxvii. n. 3: Non igitur extra sanctam hanc aulam adorare oportet, sed intra ipsam, etc. Similia habet Eusebius in eundem psalmum, p. 313. Sic etiam Cyrillus Alexandrinus in libro adversus Anthropomorphitas, cap. 12, et in libro decimo De adorat., p. 356. Sed his in locis perspicuum est hæreticorum aut schismaticorum synagogas notari, vel quas vocat Basilius, can. 1. παρασυναγωγάς, sive illicitos conventus a presbyteris aut episcopis rebellibus habitos, aut a populis disciplinæ expertibus. At interdum graves causæ suberant, cur sacra in privatis ædibus impermissa non essent. Ipsa persecutio necessitatem hujus rei sæpe afferebat, cum catholici episcoporum hæreticorum communionem fugerent, ut Sebastiæ ecclesiarum aditu prohiberentur. Minime ergo mirum, si presbyteris Antiochenis eam sacerdotii perfunctionem Basilius reliquit, quæ et ad jurisjurandi religionem et ad temporum molestias accommodata videbatur. Synodus Laodicena vetat, can. 58, in domibus fieri oblationem ab episcopis vel presbyteris. Canon 31. Trullanus id clericis non interdicit, modo accedat episcopi consensus. Non inusitata fuisse ejusmodi sacra in domesticis oratoriis confirmat canon Basilii 27, ubi vetatur, ne presbyter illicitis nuptiis implicatus privatim aut publice sacerdotii munere fungatur. Eustathius Sebastenus Ancyræ cum Arianis in domibus communicavit, ut ex pluribus Basilii epistolis discimus, cum apertam ab eis communionem impetrare non posset."
2 Videtur infidelis ille vir unus aliquis fuisse ex potentioribus Arianis ejusque furor idcirco in presbyteros Antiochenos incitatus quod hi ecclesiam absente Meletio regerent, ac maximam civium partem in illius fide et communione retinerent.

fathers, tenderly [1] and meekly making allowance for the infirmities of them that fall, laid down that they might be received after a year, ranking them with the digamists. Since, however, by God's grace the Church grows mightier as she advances, and the order of virgins is becoming more numerous, it is my judgment that careful heed should be given both to the act as it appears upon consideration, and to the mind of Scripture, which may be discovered from the context. Widowhood is inferior to virginity; consequently the sin of the widows comes far behind that of the virgins. Let us see what Paul writes to Timothy. "The young widows refuse: for when they have begun to wax wanton against Christ, they will marry; having damnation because they have cast off their first faith." [2] If, therefore, a widow lies under a very heavy charge, as setting at naught her faith in Christ, what must we think of the virgin, who is the bride of Christ, and a chosen vessel dedicated to the Lord? It is a grave fault even on the part of a slave to give herself away in secret wedlock and fill the house with impurity, and, by her wicked life, to wrong her owner; but it is forsooth far more shocking for the bride to become an adulteress, and, dishonouring her union with the bridegroom, to yield herself to unchaste indulgence. The widow, as being a corrupted slave, is indeed condemned; but the virgin comes under the charge of adultery. We call the man who lives with another man's wife an adulterer, and do not receive him into communion until he has ceased from his sin; and so we shall ordain in the case of him who has the virgin. One point, however, must be determined beforehand, that the name *virgin* is given to a woman who voluntarily devotes herself to the Lord, renounces marriage, and embraces a life of holiness. And we admit professions dating from the age of full intelligence. [3] For it is not right in such cases to admit the words of mere children. But a girl of sixteen or seventeen years of age, in full possession of her faculties, who has been submitted to strict examination, and is then constant, and persists in her entreaty to be admitted, may then be ranked among the virgins, her profession ratified, and its violation rigorously punished. Many girls are brought forward by their parents and brothers, and other kinsfolk, before they are of full age, and

have no inner impulse towards a celibate life. The object of the friends is simply to provide for themselves. Such women as these must not be readily received, before we have made public investigation of their own sentiments.

XIX. I do not recognise the profession of men, except in the case of those who have enrolled themselves in the order of monks, and seem to have secretly adopted the celibate life. Yet in their case I think it becoming that there should be a previous examination, and that a distinct profession should be received from them, so that whenever they may revert to the life of the pleasures of the flesh, they may be subjected to the punishment of fornicators.

XX. I do not think that any condemnation ought to be passed on women who professed virginity while in heresy, and then afterwards preferred marriage. "What things soever the law saith, it saith to them who are under the law." [1] Those who have not yet put on Christ's yoke do not recognise the laws of the Lord. They are therefore to be received in the church, as having remission in the case of these sins too, as of all, from their faith in Christ. As a general rule, all sins formerly committed in the catechumenical state are not taken into account. [2] The Church does not receive these persons without baptism; and it is very necessary that in such cases the birthrights should be observed.

XXI. If a man living with a wife is not satisfied with his marriage and falls into fornication, I account him a fornicator, and prolong his period of punishment. Nevertheless, we have no canon subjecting him to the charge of adultery, if the sin be committed against an unmarried woman. For the adulteress, it is said, "being polluted shall be polluted," [3] and she shall not return to her husband: and "He that keepeth an adulteress is a fool and impious." [4] He, however, who has committed fornication is not to be cut off from the society of his own wife. So the wife will receive the husband on his return from fornication, but the husband will expel the polluted woman from his house. The argument here is not easy, but the custom has so obtained. [5]

---

[1] ἁπαλῶς, with four MSS., *al.* ἁπλῶς.   [2] 1 Tim. v. 11, 12.
[3] "*Hoc Basilii decretum de professionis ætate citatur in canone quadragesimo synodi in Trullo*" (A.D. 691) "*et decem et septem anni quos Basilius requirit, ad decem rediguntur.*"

[1] Rom. iii. 19.
[2] "*Male Angli in Pandectis et alii interpretes reddunt,* quæ in catechumenica vita fiunt. *Non enim dicit Basilius ea non puniri quæ in hoc statu peccantur, sed tantum peccata ante baptismum commissa baptismo expiari, nec jam esse judicio ecclesiastico obnoxia. Hinc observat Zonaras non pugnare hunc canonem cum canone quinto Neocæsariensi, in quo pœnæ catechumenis peccantibus decernuntur.*"
[3] Jer. iii. 1.   [4] Prov. xviii. 22, LXX.
[5] "*Non solus Basilius hanc consuetudinem secutus. Auctor constitutionum apostolicarum sic loquitur lib. vi. cap. 14: Qui corruptam retinet, naturæ legem violat: quando quidem*

XXII. Men who keep women carried off by violence, if they carried them off when betrothed to other men, must not be received before removal of the women and their restoration to those to whom they were first contracted, whether they wish to receive them, or to separate from them. In the case of a girl who has been taken when not betrothed, she ought first to be removed, and restored to her own people, and handed over to the will of her own people whether parents, or brothers, or any one having authority over her. If they choose to give her up, the cohabitation may stand; but, if they refuse, no violence should be used. In the case of a man having a wife by seduction, be it secret or by violence, he must be held guilty of fornication. The punishment of fornicators is fixed at four years. In the first year they must be expelled from prayer, and weep at the door of the church; in the second they may be received to sermon; in the third to penance; in the fourth to standing with the people, while they are withheld from the oblation. Finally, they may be admitted to the communion of the good gift.

XXIII. Concerning men who marry two sisters, or women who marry two brothers, a short letter of mine has been published, of which I have sent a copy to your reverence.[1] The man who has taken his own brother's wife is not to be received until he have separated from her.

XXIV. A widow whose name is in the list of widows, that is, who is supported[2] by the Church, is ordered by the Apostle to be supported no longer when she marries.[3]

There is no special rule for a widower. The punishment appointed for digamy may suffice. If a widow who is sixty years of age chooses again to live with a husband, she shall be held unworthy of the communion of the good gift until she be moved no longer by her impure desire. If we reckon her before sixty years, the blame rests with us, and not with the woman.

XXV. The man who retains as his wife the woman whom he has violated, shall be liable to the penalty of rape, but it shall be lawful for him to have her to wife.

XXVI. Fornication is not wedlock, nor yet the beginning of wedlock. Wherefore it is best, if possible, to put asunder those who are united in fornication. If they are set on cohabitation, let them admit the penalty of fornication. Let them be allowed to live together, lest a worse thing happen.

XXVII. As to the priest ignorantly involved in an illegal marriage,[1] I have made the fitting regulation, that he may hold his seat, but must abstain from other functions. For such a case pardon is enough. It is unreasonable that the man who has to treat his own wounds should be blessing another, for benediction is the imparting of holiness. How can he who through his fault, committed in ignorance, is without holiness, impart it to another? Let him bless neither in public nor in private, nor distribute the body of Christ to others, nor perform any other sacred function, but, content with his seat of honour, let him beseech the Lord with weeping, that his sin, committed in ignorance, may be forgiven.

XXVIII. It has seemed to me ridiculous that any one should make a vow to abstain from swine's flesh. Be so good as to teach men to abstain from foolish vows and promises. Represent the use to be quite indifferent. No creature of God, received with thanksgiving, is to be rejected.[2] The vow is ridiculous; the abstinence unnecessary.

XXIX. It is especially desirable that attention should be given to the case of persons in power who threaten on oath to do some hurt to those under their authority. The remedy is twofold. In the first place, let them be taught not to take oaths at random: secondly, not to persist in their wicked determinations. Any one who is arrested in the design of fulfilling an oath to injure another ought to shew repentance for the rashness of his oath, and must not confirm his wickedness under the pretext of piety. Herod was none the better for fulfilling his oath, when, of course only to save himself from perjury, he became the prophet's murderer.[3] Swearing is absolutely forbidden,[4] and it is only reasonable that the oath which tends to evil should be condemned. The swearer must therefore change his mind, and not persist in confirming his impiety. Consider the absurdity of the thing a little further. Suppose a man to swear that he will put his brother's eyes out: is it well for him to

---

qui retinet adulteram, stultus est et impius. Abscinde enim eam, inquit, a carnibus tuis. Nam adjutrix non est, sed insidiatrix, quæ mentem ad alium declinarit. *Canon* 8, *Neocæsariensis laicis, quorum uxores adulterii convictæ, aditum ad ministerium ecclesiasticum claudit; clericis depositionis pœnam irrogat, si adulteram nolint dimittere. Canon* 65 *Eliberitanus sic habet:* Si cujus clerici uxor fuerit mæchata, et scierit eam maritus suus mæchari, et non eam statim projecerit, nec in fine accipiat communionem. *Hermas lib.* 1, *c.* 2, *adulteram ejici jubet, sed tamen pœnitentem recipi. S. Augustinus adulterium legitimam esse dimittendi causam pronuntiat, sed non necessariam, lib.* ii. *De Adulter. nuptiis, cap.* 5, *n.* 13."

[1] Probably *Letter* clx. to Diodorus is referred to.
[2] Διακονουμένην. So the Ben. Ed. Another possible rendering is " received into the order of deaconesses."
[3] 1 Tim. v. 11, 12.

---

[1] " Ἀθέσμῳ γάμῳ." *Illicitas nuptias.*
[2] 1 Tim. iv. 4. [3] Matt. xiv. 10. [4] Matt. v. 34.

carry his oath into action? Or to commit murder? or to break any other commandment? "I have sworn, and I will perform it," [1] not to sin, but to "keep thy righteous judgments." It is no less our duty to undo and destroy sin, than it is to confirm the commandment by immutable counsels.

XXX. As to those guilty of abduction we have no ancient rule, but I have expressed my own judgment. The period is three years; [2] the culprits and their accomplices to be excluded from service. The act committed without violence is not liable to punishment, whenever it has not been preceded by violation or robbery. The widow is independent, and to follow or not is in her own power. We must, therefore, pay no heed to excuses.

XXXI. A woman whose husband has gone away and disappeared, and who marries another, before she has evidence of his death, commits adultery. Clerics who are guilty of the sin unto death [3] are degraded from their order, but not excluded from the communion of the laity. Thou shalt not punish twice for the same fault. [4]

XXXIII. Let an indictment for murder be preferred against the woman who gives birth to a child on the road and pays no attention to it.

XXXIV. Women who had committed adultery, and confessed their fault through piety, or were in any way convicted, were not allowed by our fathers to be publicly exposed, that we might not cause their death after conviction. But they ordered that they should be excluded from communion till they had fulfilled their term of penance.

XXXV. In the case of a man deserted by his wife, the cause of the desertion must be taken into account. If she appear to have abandoned him without reason, he is deserving of pardon, but the wife of punishment. Pardon will be given to him that he may communicate with the Church.

XXXVI. Soldiers' wives who have married in their husbands' absence will come under the same principle as wives who, when their husbands have been on a journey, have not waited their return. Their case, however, does admit of some concession on the ground of there being greater reason to suspect death.

XXXVII. The man who marries after abducting another man's wife will incur the charge of adultery for the first case; but for the second will go free.

XXXVIII. Girls who follow against their fathers' will commit fornication; but if their fathers are reconciled to them, the act seems to admit of a remedy. They are not however immediately restored to communion, but are to be punished for three years.

XXXIX. The woman who lives with an adulterer is an adulteress the whole time. [1]

XL. The woman who yields to a man against her master's will commits fornication; but if afterwards she accepts free marriage, she marries. The former case is fornication; the latter marriage. The covenants of persons who are not independent have no validity.

XLI. The woman in widowhood, who is independent, may dwell with a husband without blame, if there is no one to prevent their cohabitation; for the Apostle says; "but if her husband be dead, she is at liberty to be married to whom she will; only in the Lord." [2]

XLII. Marriages contracted without the permission of those in authority, are fornication. If neither father nor master be living the contracting parties are free from blame; just as if the authorities assent to the cohabitation, it assumes the fixity of marriage.

XLIII. He who smites his neighbour to death is a murderer, whether he struck first or in self defence.

XLIV. The deaconess who commits fornication with a heathen may be received into repentance and will be admitted to the oblation in the seventh year; of course if she be living in chastity. The heathen who, after he has believed, takes to idolatry, returns to his vomit. We do not, however, give up the body of the deaconess to the use of the flesh, as being consecrated.

XLV. If any one, after taking the name of Christianity, insults Christ, he gets no good from the name.

XLVI. The woman who unwillingly marries a man deserted at the time by his wife, and is afterwards repudiated, because of the return of the former to him, commits fornication, but involuntarily. She will, therefore, not be prohibited from marriage; but it is better if she remain as she is. [3]

XLVII. Encratitæ, [4] Saccophori, [5] and

---

[1] Ps. cxix. 106.

[2] The Ben. Ed. point out that in Canon xxii. four years is the allotted period, as in the case of fornicators.

[3] St. Basil on Isaiah iv. calls sins wilfully committed after full knowledge "sins unto death." But in the same commentary he applies the same designation to sins which lead to hell. The sense to be applied to the phrase in Canon xxxii. is to be learnt, according to the Ben. note, from Canons lxix. and lxx., where a less punishment is assigned to mere wilful sins unto death than in Canon xxxii.   [4] Nahum i. 9, LXX.

[1] Or, according to another reading, in every way.

[2] 1 Cor. vii. 39.

[3] This is Can. xciii. of the Council in Trullo.

[4] Generally reckoned rather as Manichæans than as here by Basil as Marcionites, but dualism was common to both systems.

[5] A Manichæan sect, who led a solitary life. Death is threatened against them in a law of Theodosius dated A.D.

Apotactitæ [1] are not regarded in the same manner as Novatians, since in their case a canon has been pronounced, although different; while of the former nothing has been said. All these I re-baptize on the same principle. If among you their re-baptism is forbidden, for the sake of some arrangement, nevertheless let my principle prevail. Their heresy is, as it were, an offshoot of the Marcionites, abominating, as they do, marriage, refusing wine, and calling God's creature polluted. We do not therefore receive them into the Church, unless they be baptized into our baptism. Let them not say that they have been baptized into Father, Son and Holy Ghost, inasmuch as they make God the author of evil, after the example of Marcion and the rest of the heresies. Wherefore, if this be determined on, more bishops ought to meet together in one place and publish the canon in these terms, that action may be taken without peril, and authority given to answers to questions of this kind.

XLVIII. The woman who has been abandoned by her husband, ought, in my judgment, to remain as she is. The Lord said, " If any one leave [2] his wife, saving for the cause of fornication, he causeth her to commit adultery;" [3] thus, by calling her adulteress, He excludes her from intercourse with another man. For how can the man being guilty, as having caused adultery, and the woman, go without blame, when she is called adulteress by the Lord for having intercourse with another man?

XLIX. Suffering violation should not be a cause of condemnation. So the slave girl, if she has been forced by her own master, is free from blame.

L. There is no law as to trigamy: a third marriage is not contracted by law. We look upon such things as the defilements of the Church. But we do not subject them to public condemnation, as being better than unrestrained fornication. [4]

LETTER CC. [5]

To Amphilochius, bishop of Iconium.

I am attacked by sickness after sickness, and all the work given me, not only by the affairs of the Church, but by those who are troubling the Church, has detained me during the whole winter, and up to the present time. It has been therefore quite impossible for me to send any one to you or to pay you a visit. I conjecture that you are similarly situated; not, indeed, as to sickness, God forbid; may the Lord grant you continued health for carrying out His commandments. But I know that the care of the Churches gives you the same distress as it does me. I was now about to send some one to get me accurate information about your condition. But when my well beloved son Meletius, who is moving the newly enlisted troops, reminded me of the opportunity of my saluting you by him, I gladly accepted the occasion to write and had recourse to the kind services of the conveyor of my letter. He is one who may himself serve instead of a letter, both because of his amiable disposition, and of his being well acquainted with all which concerns me. By him, then, I beseech your reverence especially to pray for me, that the Lord may grant to me a riddance from this troublesome body of mine; to His Churches, peace; and to you, rest; and, whenever you have settled the affairs of Lycaonia in apostolic fashion, as you have begun, an opportunity to visit also this place. Whether I be sojourning in the flesh, or shall have been already bidden to take my departure to the Lord, I hope that you will interest yourself in our part of the world, as your own, as indeed it is, strengthening all that is weak, rousing all that is slothful and, by the help of the Spirit Which abides in you, transforming everything into a condition well pleasing to the Lord. My very honourable sons, Meletius and Melitius, whom you have known for some time, and know to be devoted to yourself, keep in your good care and pray for them. This is enough to keep them in safety. Salute in my name, I beg you, all who are with your holiness, both the clergy, and all the laity under your pastoral care, and my very religious brothers and fellow ministers. Bear in mind the memory of the blessed martyr Eupsychius, and do not wait for me to mention him again. Do not take pains to come on the exact day, but anticipate it, and so give me joy, if I be yet living on this earth. Till then may you, by the grace of the Holy One, be preserved for me and for God's Churches, enjoying health and wealth in the Lord, and praying for me.

---

322 (Cod. Theod. lib. xvi. tit. 5, leg. 9), identified by the Ben. Ed. with the Hydroparastatæ.
[1] A Manichæan sect. cf. Epiphanius ii. 18. In the work of Macarius Magnes, published in Paris 1876, they are identified with the Encratites.
[2] καταλίπῃ for ἀπολύσῃ.   [3] Matt. v. 22.
[4] cf. however Canon iv., where trigamy is called polygamy or at best a limited fornication, and those guilty of it subjected to exclusion from the Eucharist.   [5] Placed in 375.

LETTER CCI.

To Amphilochius, bishop of Iconium.

I LONG to meet you for many reasons, that I may have the benefit of your advice in the matters I had in hand, and that on beholding you after a long interval I may have some comfort for your absence. But since both of us are prevented by the same reasons, you by the illness which has befallen you, and I by the malady of longer standing which has not yet left me, let us, if you will, each forgive the other, that both may free ourselves from blame.

LETTER CCII.

To Amphilochius, bishop of Iconium.

UNDER other circumstances I should think it a special privilege to meet with your reverence, but above all now, when the business which brings us together is of such great importance. But so much of my illness as still clings to me is enough to prevent my stirring ever so short a distance. I tried to drive as far as the martyrs[3] and had a relapse almost into my old state. You must therefore forgive me. If the matter can be put off for a few days, I will, by God's grace join you, and share your anxieties. If the business presses, do, by God's help, what has to be done; but reckon me as present with you and as participating in your worthy deeds. May you, by the grace of the Holy One, be preserved to God's Church, strong and joyous in the Lord, and praying for me.

LETTER CCIII.[4]

To the bishops of the sea coast.[5]

I HAVE had a strong desire to meet you, but from time to time some hindrance has

supervened and prevented my fulfilling my purpose. I have either been hindered by sickness, and you know well how, from my early manhood to my present old age, this ailment has been my constant companion, brought up with me, and chastising me, by the righteous judgment of God, Who ordains all things in wisdom; or by the cares of the Church, or by struggles with the opponents of the doctrines of truth. [Up to this day I live in much affliction and grief, having the feeling present before me, that you are wanting to me. For when God tells me, who took on Him His sojourn in the flesh for the very purpose that, by patterns of duty, He might regulate our life, and might by His own voice announce to us the Gospel of the kingdom, — when He says, 'By this shall all men know that ye are my disciples, if ye love one another,' and whereas the Lord left His own peace to His disciples as a farewell gift,[1] when about to complete the dispensation in the flesh, saying, 'Peace I leave with you, My peace I give you,' I cannot persuade myself that without love to others, and without, as far as rests with me, peaceableness towards all, I can be called a worthy servant of Jesus Christ. I have waited a long while for the chance of your love paying us a visit. For ye are not ignorant that we, being exposed to all, as rocks running out in the sea, sustain the fury of the heretical waves, which, in that they break around us, do not cover the district behind. I say " we " in order to refer it, not to human power, but to the grace of God, Who, by the weakness of men shows His power, as says the prophet in the person of the Lord, 'Will ye not fear Me, who have placed the sand as a boundary to the sea?' for by the weakest and most contemptible of all things, the sand, the Mighty One has bounded the great and full sea. Since, then, this is our position, it became your love to be frequent in sending true brothers to visit us who labour with the storm, and more frequently letters of love, partly to confirm our courage, partly to correct any mistake of ours. For we confess that we are liable to numberless mistakes, being men, and living in the flesh.]

2. But hitherto, very honourable brethren, you have not given me my due; and this for two reasons. Either you failed to perceive the proper course; or else, under the influence of some of the calumnies spread abroad about me, you did not think me deserving of being visited by you in love.

---

[1] Placed in 375.   [2] Placed in 375.
[3] Tillemont conjectures that the drive was to St. Eupsychius, but the day of St. Eupsychius fell in September, which the Ben. note thinks too late for the date of this letter. The memorials of St. Julitta and St. Gordius were also near Cæsarea, but their days fell in January, which the same note thinks too early. Gregory of Nyssa (Migne iii. p. 653) says that there were more altars in Cappadocia than in all the world, so that we need have no difficulty in supposing some saint whose date would synchronize with the letter. Basil, however, may have tried to drive to the shrine of some martyr on some other day than the anniversary of his death.
[4] Placed in 375.
[5] On this letter Newman notes that Eustathius brought about a separation of a portion of the coast of Pontus from the Church of Cæsarea, which for a time caused Basil great despondency, as if he were being left solitary in all Christendom, without communion with other places. With the advice of the bishops of Cappadocia, he addressed an expostulation with these separatists for not coming to him. (*Ch. of the Fathers*, p. 95.) The portion of the translation of this letter enclosed in brackets is Newman's.

[1] ἐξιτήριον δῶρον. cf. note on p. 46.

Now, therefore, I myself take the initiative. I beg to state that I am perfectly ready to rid myself, in your presence, of the charges urged against me, but only on condition that my revilers are admitted to stand face to face with me before your reverences. If I am convicted, I shall not deny my error. You, after the conviction, will receive pardon from the Lord for withdrawing yourselves from the communion of me a sinner. The successful accusers, too, will have their reward in the publication of my secret wickedness. If, however, you condemn me before you have the evidence before you, I shall be none the worse, barring the loss I shall sustain of a possession I hold most dear — your love: while you, for your part, will suffer the same loss in losing me, and will seem to be running counter to the words of the Gospel: " Doth our law judge any man before it hear him?" [1] The reviler, moreover, if he adduce no proof of what he says, will be shewn to have got nothing from his wicked language but a bad name for himself. For what name can be properly applied to the slanderer [2] except that which he professes to bear by the very conduct of which he is guilty? Let the reviler, therefore, appear not as slanderer, [3] but as accuser; nay, I will not call him accuser, I will rather regard him as a brother, admonishing in love, and producing conviction for my amendment. And you must not be hearers of calumny, but triers of proof. Nor must I be left uncured, because my sin is not being made manifest.

[3. Let not this consideration influence you. ' We dwell on the sea, we are exempt from the sufferings of the generality, we need no succour from others; so what is the good to us of foreign communion?' For the same Lord Who divided the islands from the continent by the sea, bound the island Christians to those of the continent by love. Nothing, brethren, separates us from each other, but deliberate estrangement. We have one Lord, one faith, the same hope. The hands need each other; the feet steady each other. The eyes possess their clear apprehension from agreement. We, for our part, confess our own weakness, and we seek your fellow feeling. For we are assured, that though ye are not present in body, yet by the aid of prayer, ye will do us much benefit in these most critical times. It is neither decorous before men, nor pleasing to God, that you should make avowals which not even the Gentiles adopt, which know not God.

Even they, as we hear, though the country they live in be sufficient for all things, yet, on account of the uncertainty of the future, make much of alliances with each other, and seek mutual intercourse as being advantageous to them. Yet we, the sons of fathers who have laid down the law that by brief notes the proofs of communion should be carried about from one end of the earth to the other, and that all should be citizens and familiars with all, now sever ourselves from the whole world, and are neither ashamed at our solitariness, nor shudder that on us is fallen the fearful prophecy of the Lord, ' Because of lawlessness abounding, the love of the many shall wax cold.']

4. Do not, most honourable brethren, do not suffer this. Rather, by letters of peace and by salutations of love, comfort me for the past. You have made a wound in my heart by your former neglect. Soothe its anguish, as it were, by a tender touch. Whether you wish to come to me, and examine for yourselves into the truth of what you hear of my infirmities, or whether by the addition of more lies my sins are reported to you to be yet more grievous, I must accept even this. I am ready to welcome you with open hands and to offer myself to the strictest test, only let love preside over the proceedings. Or if you prefer to indicate any spot in your own district to which I may come and pay you the visit which is due, submitting myself, as far as may be, to examination, for the healing of the past, and the prevention of slander for the future, I accept this. Although my flesh is weak, yet, as long as I breathe, I am responsible for the due discharge of every duty which may tend to the edification of the Churches of Christ. Do not, I beseech you, make light of my entreaty. Do not force me to disclose my distress to others. Hitherto, brethren, as you are well aware, I have kept my grief to myself, for I blush to speak of your alienation from me to those of our communion who are at a distance. I shrink at once from paining them and from gratifying those who hate me. I alone am writing this now; but I send in the name of all the brethren in Cappadocia, who have charged me not to employ any chance messenger, but some one who, in case I should, from my anxiety not to be too prolix, leave out any points of importance, might supply them with the intelligence wherewith God has gifted him. I refer to my beloved and reverend fellow presbyter Petrus. Welcome him in love, and send him forth to me in peace, that he may be a messenger to me of good things.

---

[1] John vii. 51.   [3] διάβολος.
[2] τὸν διαβάλλοντα.

LETTER CCIV.[1]

To the Neocæsarcans.[2]

1. [THERE has been a long silence on both sides, revered and well-beloved brethren, just as if there were angry feelings between us. Yet who is there so sullen and implacable towards the party which has injured him, as to lengthen out the resentment which has begun in disgust through almost a whole life of man?] This [is happening in our case, no just occasion of estrangement existing, as far as I myself know, but on the contrary, there being, from the first, many strong reasons for the closest friendship and unity. The greatest and first is this, our Lord's command, pointedly saying, "By this shall all men know that ye are my disciples if ye have love one to another."[3]] Again, the apostle clearly sets before us the good of charity where he tells us that love is the fulfilling of the law;[4] and again where he says that charity is a good thing to be preferred to all great and good things, in the words, "Though I speak with tongues of men and of angels and have not charity, I am become as sounding brass or a tinkling cymbal. And though I have the gift of prophecy and understand all mysteries, and all knowledge; and though I have all faith, so that I could remove mountains, and have not charity, I am nothing. And though I bestow all my goods to feed the poor and though I give my body to be burnt and have not charity, it profiteth me nothing."[5] Not that each of the points enumerated could be performed without love, but that the Holy One wishes, as He Himself has said, to attribute to the commandment super-eminent excellency by the figure of hyperbole.[6]

2. [Next, if it tend much towards intimacy to have the same teachers, there are to you and to me the same teachers of God's mysteries, and spiritual Fathers, who from the beginning were the founders of your Church. I mean the great Gregory, and all who succeeding in order to the throne of your episcopate, like stars rising one after another, have tracked the same course, so as to leave the tokens of the heavenly polity most clear to all who desire them.] And if natural relationships are not to be despised, but are greatly conducive to unbroken union and fellowship, these rights also exist naturally for you and me. [Why is it, then, O venerable among cities, for through you I address the whole city, that no civil writing comes from you, no welcome voice, but your ears are open to those who aim at slander?] I am therefore the more bound to groan, the more I perceive the end they have in view. There is no doubt as to who is the originator of the slander.[1] He is known by many evil deeds, but is best distinguished by this particular wickedness, and it is for this reason that the sin is made his name.[2] But you must put up with my plain speaking. You have opened both ears to my slanderers. You heartily welcome all you hear without any enquiry. Not one of you distinguishes between lies and truth. Who ever suffered for lack of wicked accusations when struggling all alone? Who was ever convicted of lying in the absence of his victim? What plea does not sound plausible to the hearers when the reviler persists that such and such is the case, and the reviled is neither present nor hears what is urged against him? Does not even the accepted custom of this world teach you, in reference to these matters, that if any one is to be a fair and impartial hearer, he must not be entirely led away by the first speaker, but must wait for the defence of the accused, that so truth may be demonstrated by a comparison of the arguments on both sides? "Judge righteous judgment."[3] This precept is one of those most necessary for salvation.

3. When I say this I am not forgetful of the words of the Apostle, who fled from human tribunals and reserved the defence of all his life for the unerring judgment seat, when he said, "With me it is a very small thing that I should be judged of you or of man's judgment."[4] Your ears have been preoccupied by lying slanders, slanders that have touched my conduct, slanders that have touched my faith in God. Nevertheless, knowing, as I do, that three persons at once are injured by the slanderer, his victim, his hearer, and himself; as to my own wrong, I would have held my tongue, be sure; not because I despise your good opinion, (how could I, writing now as I do and earnestly pleading as I do that I may not lose it?) but

---

[1] Placed in 375.
[2] Newman introduces his extracts from the following letter with the prefatory remark : " If Basil's Semi-Arian connexions brought suspicion upon himself in the eyes of Catholic believers, much more would they be obnoxious to persons attached, as certain Neocæsareans were, to the Sabellian party, who were in the opposite extreme to the Semi-Arians and their especial enemies in those times. It is not wonderful, then, that he had to write to the church in question in a strain like the following." (*Ch. of the Fathers.* p. 98.) The passages in brackets are Newman's version. The prime agent in the slandering of Basil was presumably Atarbius, bishop of Neocæsarea.
[3] John xiii. 35. [4] Rom. xiii. 10. [5] 1 Cor. xiii. 1-3.
[6] The allusion may be to Mark xi. 23, but St. Paul would probably reply to Basil that each of the points enumerated might proceed not from love, but from vanity, ambition, or fanaticism.

[1] τῆς διαβολῆς.
[2] *i.e.* ὁ διάβολος. The little paronomasia is untranslatable.
[3] John vii. 24. [4] 1 Cor. iv.

because I see that of the three sufferers the one who is least injured is myself. It is true that I shall be robbed of you, but you are being robbed of the truth, and he who is at the bottom of all this is parting me from you, but he is alienating himself from the Lord, inasmuch as no one can be brought near to the Lord by doing what is forbidden. Rather then for your sakes than for mine, rather to rescue you from unendurable wrong am I pleading. For who could suffer a worse calamity than the loss of the most precious of all things, the truth?

4. [What say I, brethren? Not that I am a sinless person; not that my life is not full of numberless faults. I know myself; and indeed I cease not my tears for my sins, if by any means I may be able to appease my God, and to escape the punishment threatened against them. But this I say: let him who judges me, hunt for motes in my eye, if he can say that his own is clear.] I own, brethren, that I need the care of the sound and healthy, and need much of it. If he cannot say that it is clear, and the clearer it is the less will he say so — (for it is the part of the perfect not to exalt themselves; if they do they will certainly come under the charge of the pride of the Pharisee, who, while justifying himself, condemned the publican), let him come with me to the physician; let him not "judge before the time until the Lord come, who both will bring to light the hidden things of darkness, and will make manifest the counsels of the hearts." [1] Let him remember the words. " Judge not, and ye shall not be judged; " [2] and " Condemn not, and ye shall not be condemned." [3] [In a word, brethren, if my offences admit of cure, why does not such an one obey the teacher of the Churches, " Reprove, exhort, rebuke"? [4] If, on the other hand, my iniquity be past cure, why does he not withstand me to the face, and, by publishing my transgressions, deliver the Churches from the mischief which I bring on them?] Do not put up with the calumny uttered against me within the teeth. [5] This is the abuse which any slave-girl from the grindstone might utter; this is the kind of fine shewing-off you might expect from any street vagabond; their tongues are whetted for any slander. But [there are bishops; let appeal be made to them. There is a clergy in each of God's dioceses; [6] let

the most eminent be assembled. Let whoso will, speak freely, that I may have to deal with a charge, not a slander.] Let my secret wickedness be brought into full view; let me no longer be hated, but admonished as a brother. It is more just that we sinners should be pitied by the blessed and the sinless, than that we should be treated angrily.

5. [If the fault be a point of faith, let the document be pointed out to me. Again, let a fair and impartial inquiry be appointed. Let the accusation be read; let it be brought to the test, whether it does not arise from ignorance in the accuser, not from blame in the matter of the writing. For right things often do not seem such to those who are deficient in accurate judgment. Equal weights seem unequal when the arms of the balance are of different sizes.] Men whose sense of taste is destroyed by sickness, sometimes think honey sour. A diseased eye does not see many things which do exist, and notes many things which do not exist. The same thing frequently takes place with regard to the force of words, when the critic is inferior to the writer. The critic ought really to set out with much the same training and equipment as the author. A man ignorant of agriculture is quite incapable of criticising husbandry, and the distinctions between harmony and discord can only be adequately judged by a trained musician. But any one who chooses will set up for a literary critic, though he cannot tell us where he went to school, or how much time was spent in his education, and knows nothing about letters at all. I see clearly that, even in the case of the words [1] of the Holy Spirit, the investigation of the terms is to be attempted not by every one, but by him who has the spirit of discernment, as the Apostle has taught us, in the differences of gifts; — " For to one is given by the Spirit the word of wisdom ; to another the word of knowledge by the same Spirit; to another faith by the same Spirit; to another the gift of healing by the same Spirit; to another the working of miracles; to another prophecy; to another discerning of spirits." [2] If, therefore, my gifts are spiritual, he who wishes to judge them must shew proof of his own possession of the gift of " discerning of spirits." If, on the contrary, as he calumniously contends, my gifts are of the wisdom of this world, let him shew that he is an adept in this world's wisdom, and I will submit myself to his verdict. And [let no one suppose that I am making excuses to

---

[1] 1 Cor. iv. 5. [3] Luke vi. 37.
[2] Matt. vii. 1. [4] 2 Tim. iv. 2.
[5] ὑπ' ὀδόντα. Ben. Lat., *intra dentes*.
[6] The Greek is παροικία which is used both for what is meant by the modern " diocese" and by the modern " parish." Of the sense of diocese instances are quoted among others in *D.C.A. s.v.* " Parish," from Iren. ad Florin. *apud Euseb. H.E.* v. 20; and Alexand. Alexandrin. *Ep. apud Theodoret, H.E.* i. 3.

---

[1] τοῖς λόγοις πνεύματος ἁγίου, the reading of the MSS. Bas. Sec. and Paris. The commoner reading is λογίοις.
[2] 1 Cor. xii. 8-10.

evade the charge. I put it into your hands, dearest brethren, to investigate for yourselves the points alleged against me.] Are you so slow of intelligence as to be wholly dependent upon advocates for the discovery of the truth? If the points in question seem to you to be quite plain of themselves, persuade the jesters to drop the dispute. [If there be anything you do not understand, put questions to me, through appointed persons who will do justice to me; or ask of me explanations in writing. And take all kinds of pains that nothing may be left unsifted.

6. What clearer evidence can there be of my faith, than that I was brought up by my grandmother, blessed woman, who came from you? I mean the celebrated Macrina who taught me the words of the blessed Gregory; which, as far as memory had preserved down to her day, she cherished herself, while she fashioned and formed me, while yet a child, upon the doctrines of piety. And when I gained the capacity of thought, my reason being matured by full age, I travelled over much sea and land, and whomsoever I found walking in the rule of godliness delivered, those I set down as fathers,] and made them my soul's guides in my journey to God. And up to this day, by the grace of Him who has called me in His holy calling to the knowledge of Himself, I know of no doctrine opposed to the sound teaching having sunk into my heart; nor was my soul ever polluted by the ill-famed blasphemy of Arius. If I have ever received into communion any who have come from that teacher, hiding their unsoundness deep within them, or speaking words of piety, or, at any rate, not opposing what has been said by me, it is on these terms that I have admitted them; and I have not allowed my judgment concerning them to rest wholly with myself, but have followed the decisions given about them by our Fathers. For after receiving the letter of the very blessed Father Athanasius, bishop of Alexandria, which I hold in my hand, and shew to any one who asks, wherein he has distinctly declared that any one expressing a wish to come over from the heresy of the Arians and accepting the Nicene Creed, is to be received without hesitation and difficulty, citing in support of his opinion the unanimous assent of the bishops of Macedonia and of Asia; I, considering myself bound to follow the high authority of such a man and of those who made the rule, and with every desire on my own part to win the reward promised to peacemakers, did enroll in the lists of communicants all who accepted that creed.

7. [The fair thing would be to judge of me, not from one or two who do not walk uprightly in the truth, but from the multitude of bishops throughout the world, connected with me by the grace of the Lord. Make enquiries of Pisidians, Lycaonians, Isaurians, Phrygians of both provinces, Armenians your neighbours, Macedonians, Achæans, Illyrians, Gauls, Spaniards, the whole of Italy, Sicilians, Africans, the healthy part of Egypt, whatever is left of Syria; all of whom send letters to me, and in turn receive them from me.] From these letters, alike from all which are despatched from them, and from all which go out from us to them, you may learn that we are all of one mind, and of one opinion. [Whoso shuns communion with me, it cannot escape your accuracy, cuts himself off from the whole Church. Look round about, brethren, with whom do you hold communion? If you will not receive it from me, who remains to acknowledge you? Do not reduce me to the necessity of counselling anything unpleasant concerning a Church so dear to me.] There are things now which I hide in the bottom of my heart, in secret groaning over and bewailing the evil days in which we live, in that the greatest Churches which have long been united to one another in brotherly love, now, without any reason, are in mutual opposition. Do not, oh! do not, drive me to complain of these things to all who are in communion with me. Do not force me to give utterance to words which hitherto I have kept in check by reflection and have hidden in my heart. Better were it for me to be removed and the Churches to be at one, than that God's people should suffer such evil through our childish ill-will. [Ask your fathers, and they will tell you that though our districts were divided in position, yet in mind they were one, and were governed by one sentiment. Intercourse of the people was frequent; frequent the visits of the clergy; the pastors, too, had such mutual affection, that each used the other as teacher and guide in things pertaining to the Lord.]

LETTER CCV.[1]

To Elpidius the bishop.[2]

ONCE again I have started the well-beloved presbyter Meletius to carry my greeting to you. I had positively determined to spare him, on account of the weakness which he

---

[1] Placed in 375.
[2] Of what see is uncertain. He was in friendly relations with Basil, and therefore was not in communion with Eustathius of Sebaste. (*Letter* ccli.)

has voluntarily brought upon himself, by bringing his body into subjection for the sake of the gospel of Christ. But I have judged it fitting to salute you by the ministry of such men as he is, able to supply of themselves all the shortcomings of my letter, and to become, alike to writer and recipient, a kind of living epistle. I am also carrying out the very strong wish, which he has always had, to see your excellency, ever since he has had experience of the high qualities you possess. So now I have besought him to travel to you, and through him I discharge the debt of the visit I owe you, and beseech you to pray for me and for the Church of God, that the Lord may grant me deliverance from the injuries of the enemies of the Gospel, and to pass my life in peace and quiet. Nevertheless, if you in your wisdom, think it needful that we should travel to the same spot, and meet the rest of our right honourable brother bishops of the sea board regions, do you yourself point out a suitable place and time where and when this meeting may take place. Write to our brethren to the end that each and all may, at the appointed time, leave the business they may have in hand, and may be able to effect something for the edification of the Churches of God, do away with the pain which we now suffer from our mutual suspicions, and establish love, without which the Lord Himself has ordained that obedience to every commandment must be of none effect.

LETTER CCVI.[1]

To Elpidius the bishop.   Consolatory.

Now, most of all, do I feel my bodily infirmity, when I see how it stands in the way of my soul's good. Had matters gone as I hoped, I should not now be speaking to you by letter or by messenger, but should in my own person have been paying the debt of affection and enjoying spiritual advantage face to face. Now, however, I am so situated that I am only too glad if I am able even to move about in my own country in the necessary visitation of parishes in my district. But may the Lord grant to you both strength and a ready will, and to me, in addition to my eager desire, ability to enjoy your society when I am in the country of Comana. I am afraid lest your domestic trouble may be some hindrance to you. For I have learnt of your affliction in the loss of your little boy. To a grandfather his death cannot but be grievous. On the other hand to a man who has attained to so high a degree of virtue, and alike from

his experience of this world and his spiritual training knows what human nature is, it is natural that the removal of those who are near and dear should not be wholly intolerable. The Lord requires from us what He does not require from every one. The common mass of mankind lives by habit, but the Christian's rule of life is the commandment of the Lord, and the example of holy men of old, whose greatness of soul was, above all, exhibited in adversity. To the end, then, that you may yourself leave to them that come after you an example of fortitude and of genuine trust in what we hope for, show that you are not vanquished by your grief, but are rising above your sorrows, patient in affliction, and rejoicing in hope. Pray let none of these things be a hindrance to our hoped for meeting. · Children, indeed, are held blameless on account of their tender age; but you and I are under the responsibility of serving the Lord, as He commands us, and in all things to be ready for the administration of the affairs of the Churches. For the due discharge of that duty the Lord has reserved great rewards for faithful and wise stewards.

LETTER CCVII.[1]

To the clergy of Neocæsarea.

You all concur in hating me. To a man you have followed the leader of the war against me.[2] I was therefore minded to say not a word to any one. I determined that I would write no friendly letter; that I would start no communication, but keep my sorrow in silence to myself. Yet it is wrong to keep silence in the face of calumny; not that by contradiction we may vindicate ourselves, but that we may not allow a lie to travel further and its victims to be harmed. I have therefore thought it necessary to put this matter also before you all, and to write a letter to you, although, when I recently wrote to all the presbyterate in common, you did not do me the honour to send me a reply. Do not, my brethren, gratify the vanity of those who are filling your minds with pernicious opinions. Do not consent to look lightly on, when, to your knowledge, God's people are being subverted by impious teaching. None but Sabellius the Libyan[3] and Marcellus the Galatian[4] have dared to teach and write what the leaders of your people are attempting to bring forward among you

---

[1] Placed in 375.   [2] i.e. Atarbius of Neocæsarea.
[3] Basil is described as the earliest authority for making Sabellius an African by birth. (D.C.B. iv. 569.) There is no contemporary authority for the statement.
[4] i.e. of Ancyra.

as their own private discovery. They are making a great talk about it, but they are perfectly powerless to give their sophisms and fallacies even any colour of truth. In their harangues against me they shrink from no wickedness, and persistently refuse to meet me. Why? Is it not because they are afraid of being convicted for their own wicked opinions? Yes; and in their attacks upon me they have become so lost to all sense of shame as to invent certain dreams to my discredit while they falsely accuse my teaching of being pernicious. Let them take upon their own heads all the visions of the autumn months; they can fix no blasphemy on me, for in every Church there are many to testify to the truth.

2. When they are asked the reason for this furious and truceless war, they allege psalms and a kind of music varying from the custom which has obtained among you, and similar pretexts of which they ought to be ashamed. We are, moreover, accused because we maintain men in the practice of true religion who have renounced the world and all those cares of this life, which the Lord likens to thorns that do not allow the word to bring forth fruit. Men of this kind carry about in the body the deadness of Jesus; they have taken up their own cross, and are followers of God. I would gladly give my life if these really were my faults, and if I had men with me owning me as teacher who had chosen this ascetic life. I hear that virtue of this kind is to be found now in Egypt, and there are, peradventure, some men in Palestine whose conversation follows the precepts of the Gospel. I am told too that some perfect and blessed men are to be found in Mesopotamia. We, in comparison with the perfect, are children. But if women also have chosen to live the Gospel life, preferring virginity to wedlock, leading captive the lust of the flesh, and living in the mourning which is called blessed, they are blessed in their profession wherever they are to be found. We, however, have few instances of this to show, for with us people are still in an elementary stage and are being gradually brought to piety. If any charges of disorder are brought against the life of our women I do not undertake to defend them. One thing, however, I do say and that is, that these bold hearts, these unbridled mouths are ever fearlessly uttering what Satan, the father of lies, has hitherto been unable to say. I wish you to know that we rejoice to have assemblies of both men and women, whose conversation is in heaven and who have crucified the flesh with

the affections and lusts thereof; they take no thought for food and raiment, but remain undisturbed beside their Lord, continuing night and day in prayer. Their lips speak not of the deeds of men : they sing hymns to God continually, working with their own hands that they may have to distribute to them that need.

3. Now as to the charge relating to the singing of psalms, whereby my calumniators specially scare the simpler folk, my reply is this. The customs which now obtain are agreeable to those of all the Churches of God. Among us the people go at night to the house of prayer, and, in distress, affliction, and continual tears, making confession to God, at last rise from their prayers and begin to sing psalms. And now, divided into two parts, they sing antiphonally with one another, thus at once confirming their study of the Gospels,[1] and at the same time producing for themselves a heedful temper and a heart free from distraction. Afterwards they again commit the prelude of the strain to one, and the rest take it up; and so after passing the night in various psalmody, praying at intervals as the day begins to dawn, all together, as with one voice and one heart, raise the psalm of confession to the Lord, each forming for himself his own expressions of penitence. If it is for these reasons that you renounce me, you will renounce the Egyptians; you will renounce both Libyans, Thebans, Palestinians, Arabians, Phœnicians, Syrians, the dwellers by the Euphrates; in a word all those among whom vigils, prayers, and common psalmody have been held in honour.

4. But, it is alleged, these practices were not observed in the time of the great Gregory. My rejoinder is that even the Litanies[2] which you now use were not used in his time. I do not say this to find fault with you; for my prayer would be that every one of you should live in tears and continual penitence. We, for our part, are always offering supplication for our sins, but we propitiate our God not as you do, in the words of mere man, but in the oracles of the Spirit. And what evidence have you that this custom was not followed in the time of the great Gregory? You have kept none of his customs up to the present time.[3] Gregory did not cover his head at prayer. How could

---

[1] τῶν λογίων. cf. note on Theodoret, p. 155.
[2] The Ben. note observes that in this passage Litanies do not mean processions or supplications, but penitential prayers. The intercessory prayers which occur in the liturgy of St. Basil, as in the introductory part of other Greek liturgies, are not confined to quotations from Scripture.
[3] This reproach appears to be in contradiction with the statement in the *De Spiritu Sancto*, § 74 (page 47), that the Church of Neocæsarea had rigidly preserved the traditions of Gregory. The Ben. note would remove the discrepancy by

he? He was a true disciple of the Apostle who says, "Every man praying or prophesying, having his head covered, dishonoureth his head." [1] And "a man indeed ought not to cover his head forasmuch as he is the image of God." [2] Oaths were shunned by Gregory, that pure soul, worthy of the fellowship of the Holy Ghost, content with yea and nay, in accordance with the commandment of the Lord Who said, "I say unto you swear not at all." [3] Gregory could not bear to call his brother a fool, [4] for he stood in awe of the threat of the Lord. Passion, wrath, and bitterness never proceeded out of his mouth. Railing he hated, because it leads not to the kingdom of heaven. Envy and arrogance had been shut out of that guileless soul. He would never have stood at the altar before being reconciled to his brother. A lie, or any word designed to slander any one, he abominated, as one who knew that lies come from the devil, and that the Lord will destroy all that utter a lie. [5] If you have none of these things, and are clear of all, then are you verily disciples of the disciple of the Lord. If not, beware lest, in your disputes about the mode of singing psalms, you are straining at the gnat and setting at naught the greatest of the commandments.

I have been driven to use these expressions by the urgency of my defence, that you may be taught to cast the beam out of your own eyes before you try to remove other men's motes. Nevertheless, I am conceding all, although there is nothing that is not searched into before God. Only let great matters prevail, and do not allow innovations in the faith to make themselves heard. Do not disregard the hypostases. Do not deny the name of Christ. Do not put a wrong meaning on the words of Gregory. If you do so, as long as I breathe and have the power of utterance, I cannot keep silence, when I see souls being thus destroyed.

LETTER CCVIII. [6]

To Eulancius.

You have been long silent, though you have very great power of speech, and are well trained in the art of conversation and of exhibiting yourself by your eloquence. Possibly it is Neocæsarea which is the cause of your not writing to me. I suppose I must take it as a kindness if those who are there do not remember me, for, as I am informed by those who report what they hear, the mention made of me is not kind. You, however, used to be one of those who were disliked for my sake, not one of those who dislike me for the sake of others. I hope this description will continue to fit you, that wherever you are you will write to me, and will have kindly thoughts of me, if you care at all for what is fair and right. It is certainly fair that those who have been first to show affection should be paid in their own coin.

LETTER CCIX. [1]

Without address.

It is your lot to share my distress, and to do battle on my behalf. Herein is proof of your manliness. God, who ordains our lives, grants to those who are capable of sustaining great fights greater opportunity of winning renown. You truly have risked your own life as a test of your valour in your friend's behalf, like gold in the furnace. I pray God that other men may be made better; that you may remain what you are, and that you will not cease to find fault with me, as you do, and to charge me with not writing often to you, as a wrong on my part which does you very great injury. This is an accusation only made by a friend. Persist in demanding the payment of such debts. I am not so very unreasonable in paying the claims of affection.

LETTER CCX. [2]

To the notables of Neocæsarea.

I am really under no obligation to publish my own mind to you, or to state the reasons for my present sojourn where I am; it is not my custom to indulge in self advertisement, nor is the matter worth publicity. I am not, I think, following my own inclinations; I am answering the challenge of your leaders. I have always striven to be ignored more earnestly than popularity hunters strive after notoriety. But, I am told, the ears of everybody in your town are set a thrilling, while

confining the rigid conservatism to matters of importance. In these the Neocæsareans would tolerate no change, and allowed no monasteries and no enrichment of their liturgies with new rites. "Litanies," however, are regarded as comparatively unimportant innovations. The note concludes: *Neque enim secum ipse pugnat Basilius, cum Neocæsarienses laudat in libro De Spiritu Sancto, quod Gregorii instituta arctissime teneant, hic autem vituperat quod ea omnino reliquerint. Illic enim respicit ad exteriora instituta, hic autem ad virtutum exemplar, convicii et iracundiæ fugam, odium juris jurandi et mendacii.*

[1] 1 Cor. xi. 4. [3] Matt. v. 34. [5] Ps. v. 6, LXX.
[2] 1 Cor. xi. 7. [4] cf. Matt. v. 22. [6] Placed in 375.

[1] Placed in 375.
[2] Placed in 375, the year after the composition of the *De Spiritu Sancto.* It apparently synchronizes with *Letter* ccxxiii., in which Basil more directly repels those calumnies of the versatile Eustathius of Sebaste which he had borne in silence for three years. On Annesi, from which he writes, and the occasion of the visit, see Prolegomena.

certain tale-mongers, creators of lies, hired for this very work, are giving you a history of me and my doings. I therefore do not think that I ought to overlook your being exposed to the teaching of vile intention and foul tongue; I think that I am bound to tell you myself in what position I am placed. From my childhood I have been familiar with this spot, for here I was brought up by my grandmother;[1] hither I have often retreated, and here I have spent many years, when endeavouring to escape from the hubbub of public affairs, for experience has taught me that the quiet and solitude of the spot are favourable to serious thought. Moreover as my brothers[2] are now living here, I have gladly retired to this retreat, and have taken a brief breathing time from the press of the labours that beset me, not as a centre from which I might give trouble to others, but to indulge my own longing.

2. Where then is the need of having recourse to dreams and of hiring their interpreters, and making me matter for talk over the cups at public entertainments? Had slander been launched against me in any other quarter, I should have called you to witness to prove what I think, and now I ask every one of you to remember those old days when I was invited by your city to take charge of the education of the young, and a deputation of the first men among you came to see me.[3] Afterwards, when you all crowded round me, what were you not ready to give? what not to promise? Nevertheless you were not able to keep me. How then could I, who at that time would not listen when you invited me, now attempt to thrust myself on you uninvited? How could I, who when you complimented and admired me, avoided you, have been intending to court you now that you calumniate me? Nothing of the kind, sirs; I am not quite so cheap. No man in his senses would go on board a boat without a steersman, or get alongside a Church where the men sitting at the helm

are themselves stirring up tempest and storm. Whose fault was it that the town was all full of tumult, when some were running away with no one after them, and others stealing off when no invader was near, and all the wizards and dream-tellers were flourishing their bogeys? Whose fault was it else? Does not every child know that it was the mob-leaders'? The reasons of their hatred to me it would be bad taste on my part to recount; but they are quite easy for you to apprehend. When bitterness and division have come to the last pitch of savagery, and the explanation of the cause is altogether groundless and ridiculous, then the mental disease is plain, dangerous indeed to other people's comfort, but greatly and personally calamitous to the patient. And there is one charming point about them. Torn and racked with inward agony as they are, they cannot yet for very shame speak out about it. The state they are in may be known not only from their behaviour to me, but from the rest of their conduct. If it were unknown, it would not much matter. But the veritable cause of their shunning communication with me may be unperceived by the majority among you. Listen; and I will tell you.

3. There is going on among you a movement ruinous to the faith, disloyal to the apostolical and evangelical dogmas, disloyal too to the tradition of Gregory the truly great,[1] and of his successors up to the blessed Musonius, whose teaching is still ringing in your ears.[2] For those men, who, from fear of confutation, are forging figments against me, are endeavouring to renew the old mischief of Sabellius, started long ago, and extinguished by the tradition of the great Gregory. But do you bid goodbye to those wine-laden heads, bemuddled by the swelling fumes that mount from their debauch, and from me who am wide awake and from fear of God cannot keep silence, hear what plague is rife among you. Sabellianism is Judaism[3] imported into the preaching of the Gospel under the guise of Christianity. For if a man calls Father Son and Holy Ghost one thing of many faces,[4] and makes the hypostasis of the three one,[5] what is this but to deny the ever-lasting pre-existence of the Only begotten? He denies too the Lord's sojourn among men in the incarnation,[6] the going down into hell, the resurrection, the judgment; he denies also the proper operations of the Spirit. And

---

[1] Macrina, at her residence at Annesi.

[2] cf. Ep. ccxvi., where he speaks of going to the house of his brother Peter near Neocæsarea. One of the five brothers apparently died young, as the property of the elder Basil was at his death, before 340, divided into nine portions, i.e. among the five daughters and four surviving sons, the youngest, Peter, being then an infant. (Greg. Nyss. Vita Mac. 186.) Naucratius, the second son, was killed by an accident while hunting, c. 357. Gregory of Nyssa must, therefore, be referred to in the text, if by "brothers" is meant brothers in blood. Was it to Peter's "cottage" or some neighbouring dwelling that Gregory fled when he escaped from the police of the Vicar Demosthenes, in order not to obey the summons of Valens to his synod at Ancyra? Is the cottage of Peter the "some quiet spot" of Ep. ccxxv.? The plural ἀδελφῶν might be used conventionally, or understood to include Peter and a sister or sisters.

[3] i.e. when he was resident at Cæsarea in his earlier manhood. If Letter ccclviii. (from Libanius to Basil) refers to this period. it would seem that for a time Basil did undertake school work.

[1] i.e. Gregory Thaumaturgus. cf. note on p. 247.

[2] Musonius, bp. of Neocæsarea, who died in 368. cf. Ep. xxviii.

[3] cf. De Sp. S. § 77, p. 49 and Ep. clxxxix. p. 229.

[4] ἐν πρᾶγμα πολύπροσωπον. Another MS. reading is πολυώνυμον, " of many names."

[5] cf. note on p. 195.   [6] οἰκονομικήν.

I hear that even rasher innovations than those of the foolish Sabellius are now ventured on among you. It is said, and that on the evidence of ear witnesses, that your clever men go to such an extreme as to say that there is no tradition of the name of the Onlybegotten, while of the name of the adversary there is; and at this they are highly delighted and elated, as though it were a discovery of their own. For it is said, "I came in my Father's name and ye received me not; if another shall come in his own name, him ye will receive." [1] And because it is said, "Go ye and teach all nations, baptizing them in the name of the Father, and of the Son, and of the Holy Ghost," [2] it is obvious, they urge, that the name is one, for it is not "in the *names*," but "in the *name*."

4. I blush so to write to you, for the men thus guilty are of my own blood; [3] and I groan for my own soul, in that, like boxers fighting two men at once, I can only give the truth its proper force by hitting with my proofs, and knocking down, the errors of doctrine on the right and on the left. On one side I am attacked by the Anomœan: on the other by the Sabellian. Do not, I implore you, pay any attention to these abominable and impotent sophisms. Know that the name of Christ which is above every name is His being called Son of God, as Peter says, "There is none other name under heaven given among men, whereby we must be saved." [4] And as to the words "I came in my Father's name," it is to be understood that He so says describing His Father as origin and cause of Himself. [5] And if it is said "Go and baptize in the name of the Father and of the Son and of the Holy Ghost," we must not suppose that here one name is delivered to us. For just as he who said Paul and Silvanus and Timothy mentioned three names, and coupled them one to the other by the word "and," so He who spoke of the name of Father, Son, and Holy Ghost," mentioned three, and united them by the conjunction, teaching that with each name must be understood its own proper meaning; for the names mean things. And no one gifted with even the smallest particle of intelligence doubts that the existence belonging to the things is peculiar and complete in itself. For of Father, Son, and Holy Ghost there is the same nature and one Godhead; but these are different names, setting forth to us the circumscription and exactitude of the meanings. For unless the meaning of the

distinctive qualities of each be unconfounded, it is impossible for the doxology to be adequately offered to Father, Son, and Holy Ghost.

If, however, they deny that they so say, and so teach, my object is attained. Yet I see that this denial is no easy matter, because of our having many witnesses who heard these things said. But let bygones be bygones; let them only be sound now. If they persist in the same old error I must proclaim your calamity even to other Churches, and get letters written to you from more bishops. In my efforts to break down this huge mass of impiety now gradually and secretly growing, I shall either effect something towards the object I have in view; or at least my present testimony will clear me of guilt in the judgment day.

5. They have already inserted these expressions in their own writings. They sent them first to the man of God, Meletius, [1] bishop, and after receiving from him a suitable reply, like mothers of monsters, ashamed of their natural deformities, these men themselves brought forth and bring up their disgusting offspring in appropriate darkness. They made an attempt too by letter on my dear friend Anthimus, bishop of Tyana, [2] on the ground that Gregory had said in his exposition of the faith [3] that Father and Son are in thought two, but in hypostasis one. [4] The men who congratulate themselves

[1] Meletius of Antioch.
[2] Tyana, at the north of Mount Taurus, is the city which gave a distinctive name to Apollonius the Thaumaturge. That Basil should speak in kindly and complimentary terms of Anthimus is remarkable, for from few contemporaries did he suffer more. It was the quarrel in which Anthimus attacked and plundered a train of Basil's sumpter mules, and Gregory of Nazianzus fought stoutly for his friend, that led to Basil's erecting Sasima into a bishopric, as a kind of buffer see against his rival metropolitan. (Greg. Naz., *Or.* xliii. 356, *Ep.* xxxi. and *Carm.* i. 8.) See *Prolegomena.*
[3] The ἔκθεσις τῆς πίστεως of Gregory Thaumaturgus. *cf. Ep.* cciv. and the *De Sp. Scto.* § 74. On the genuineness of the ἔκθεσις, *vide D.C. Biog.* i. 733; *cf.* Dorner's *Christologie* i. 737. It is given at length in the *Life of Greg. Thaumat.* by Gregory of Nyssa, and is found in the Latin Psalter, written in gold, which Charlemagne gave to Adrian I. Bp. Bull's translation is as follows:
"There is one God, Father of Him who is the living Word, subsisting Wisdom and Power and Eternal Impress, Perfect begotten of the Perfect, Father of the only begotten Son. There is one Lord, Alone of the Alone, God of God, Impress and Image of the Godhead, the operative Word; Wisdom comprehensive of the system of the universe, and Power productive of the whole creation; true Son of true Father, Invisible of Invisible and Incorruptible of Incorruptible, and Immortal of Immortal, and Eternal of Eternal. And there is one Holy Ghost, who hath His being of God, who hath appeared through the Son, Image of the Son, Perfect of the Perfect; Life, the cause of all them that live; Holy Fountain, Holiness, the Bestower of Sanctification, in whom is manifested God the Father, who is over all and in all, and God the Son, who is through all. A perfect Trinity, not divided nor alien in glory and eternity and dominion."
[4] The Ben. note refuses to believe that so Sabellian an expression can have been used by Gregory. Basil's explanation is that it was used in controversy with a heathen on another subject, loosely and not dogmatically. The words are said not to be found in any extant document attributed to Gregory, whether genuine or doubtful. But they may be matched in some of the expressions of Athanasius. *cf.* p. 195. Ath., *Tom. ad Af.* § 4 and *Hom. in Terem.* viii. 96.

[1] John v. 43. Slightly varied. [2] Matt. xxviii. 19. [3] The allusion is supposed to be to Atarbius. *cf. Letter* lxv. [4] Acts iv. 12. [5] *cf. De Sp. S.* § 44, p. 27.

on the subtilty of their intelligence could not perceive that this is said not in reference to dogmatic opinion, but in controversy with Ælian. And in this dispute there are not a few copyists' blunders, as, please God, I shall shew in the case of the actual expressions used. But in his endeavour to convince the heathen, he deemed it needless to be nice about the words he employed; he judged it wiser sometimes to make concessions to the character of the subject who was being persuaded, so as not to run counter to the opportunity given him. This explains how it is that you may find there many expressions which now give great support to the heretics, as for instance " creature " [1] and " thing made " [2] and the like. But those who ignorantly criticise these writings refer to the question of the Godhead much that is said in reference to the conjunction with man; as is the case with this passage which they are hawking about. For it is indispensable to have clear understanding that, as he who fails to confess the community of the essence or substance falls into polytheism, so he who refuses to grant the distinction of the hypostases is carried away into Judaism. For we must keep our mind stayed, so to say, on certain underlying subject matter, and, by forming a clear impression of its distinguishing lines, so arrive at the end desired. For suppose we do not bethink us of the Fatherhood, nor bear in mind Him of whom this distinctive quality is marked off, how can we take in the idea of God the Father? For merely to enumerate the differences of Persons [3] is insufficient; we must confess each Person [4] to have a natural existence in real hypostasis. Now Sabellius did not even deprecate the formation of the persons without hypostasis, saying as he did that the same God, being one in matter,[5] was metamorphosed as the need of the moment required, and spoken of now as Father, now as Son, and now as Holy Ghost. The inventors of this unnamed heresy are renewing the old long extinguished error; those, I mean, who are repudiating the hypostases, and denying the name of the Son of God. They must give over uttering iniquity against God,[6] or they will have to wail with them that deny the Christ.

6. I have felt compelled to write to you in these terms, that you may be on your guard against the mischief arising from bad teaching. If we may indeed liken pernicious teachings to poisonous drugs, as your dream-tellers have it, these doctrines are hemlock

and monkshood, or any other deadly to man. It is these that destroy souls; not my words, as this shrieking drunken scum, full of the fancies of their condition, make out. If they had any sense they ought to know that in souls, pure and cleansed from all defilement, the prophetic gift shines clear. In a foul mirror you cannot see what the reflexion is, neither can a soul preoccupied with cares of this life, and darkened with the passions of the lust of the flesh, receive the rays of the Holy Ghost. Every dream is not a prophecy, as says Zechariah, " The Lord shall make bright clouds, and give them showers of rain, . . . for the idols have spoken vanity and the diviners have told false dreams." [1] Those who, as Isaiah says, dream and love to sleep in their bed [2] forget that an operation of error is sent to "the children of disobedience." [3] And there is a lying spirit, which arose in false prophecies, and deceived Ahab.[4] Knowing this they ought not to have been so lifted up as to ascribe the gift of prophecy to themselves. They are shewn to fall far short even of the case of the seer Balaam; for Balaam when invited by the king of Moab with mighty bribes brooked not to utter a word beyond the will of God, nor to curse Israel whom the Lord cursed not.[5] If then their sleep-fancies do not tally with the commandments of the Lord, let them be content with the Gospels. The Gospels need no dreams to add to their credit. The Lord has sent His peace to us, and left us a new commandment, to love one another, but dreams bring strife and division and destruction of love. Let them therefore not give occasion to the devil to attack their souls in sleep; nor make their imaginations of more authority than the instruction of salvation.

LETTER CCXI.[6]

To Olympius.[7]

TRULY when I read your excellency's letter I felt unwonted pleasure and cheerfulness; and when I met your well-beloved sons, I seemed to behold yourself. They found me in the deepest affliction, but they so behaved as to make me forget the hemlock, which your dreamers and dream mongers are carrying about to my hurt, to please the people who have hired them. Some letters I have already sent; others, if you like, shall follow. I only hope that they may be of some advantage to the recipients.

[1] κτίσμα. [3] προσώπων. [5] τῷ ὑποκειμένῳ.
[2] ποίημα. [4] πρόσωπον. [6] Ps. lxxv. 5, LXX.

[1] Zech. x. 1, 2. [3] Eph. ii. 2. [5] Num. xxii. 11.
[2] cf. Is. lvi. 10. [4] 1 Kings xxii. 22. [6] Placed in 375.
[7] cf. Letters iv., xii., xiii., cxxxi.

LETTER CCXII.[1]

To Hilarius.[2]

1. You can imagine what I felt, and in what state of mind I was, when I came to Dazimon and found that you had left a few days before my arrival. From my boyhood I have held you in admiration, and, therefore, ever since our old school days, have placed a high value on intercourse with you. But another reason for my doing so is that nothing is so precious now as a soul that loves the truth, and is gifted with a sound judgment in practical affairs. This, I think, is to be found in you. I see most men, as in the hippodrome, divided into factions, some for one side and some for another, and shouting with their parties. But you are above fear, flattery, and every ignoble sentiment, and so naturally look at truth with an unprejudiced eye. And I see that you are deeply interested in the affairs of the Churches, about which you have sent me a letter, as you have said in your last. I should like to know who took charge of the conveyance of this earlier epistle, that I may know who has wronged me by its loss. No letter from you on this subject has yet reached me.

2. How much, then, would I not have given to meet you, that I might tell you all my troubles? When one is in pain it is, as you know, some alleviation, even to describe it. How gladly would I have answered your questions, not trusting to lifeless letters, but in my own person, narrating each particular. The persuasive force of living words is more efficient and they are not so susceptible as letters to attack and to mis-representation. For now no one has left anything untried, and the very men in whom I put the greatest confidence, men, who when I saw them among others, I used to think something more than human, have received documents written by some one, and have sent them on, whatever they are, as mine, and on their account are calumniating me to the brethren as though there is nothing now that pious and faithful men ought to hold in greater abhorrence than my name. From the beginning it has been my object to live unknown, to a degree not reached by any one who has considered human infirmity; but now, just as though on the other hand it had been my purpose to make myself notorious to the world, I have been talked about all over the earth, and I may add all over the sea too. For men, who go to the last limit of

impiety, and are introducing into the Churches the godless opinion of Unlikeness,[1] are waging war against me. Those too who hold the via media,[2] as they think, and, though they start from the same principles, do not follow out their logical consequences, because they are so opposed to the view of the majority, are equally hostile to me, overwhelming me to the utmost of their ability with their reproaches, and abstaining from no insidious attacks against me. But the Lord has made their endeavours vain.

Is not this a grievous state of things? Must it not make my life painful? I have at all events one consolation in my troubles, my bodily infirmity. This I am sure will not suffer me to remain much longer in this miserable life. No more on this point. You too I exhort, in your bodily infirmity, to bear yourself bravely and worthy of the God Who has called us. If He sees us accepting our present circumstances with thanksgiving, He will either put away our troubles as He did Job's, or will requite us with the glorious crowns of patience in the life to come.

LETTER CCXIII.[3]

Without address.

1. May the Lord, Who has brought me prompt help in my afflictions, grant you the help of the refreshment wherewith you have refreshed me by writing to me, rewarding you for your consolation of my humble self with the real and great gladness of the Spirit. For I was indeed downcast in soul when I saw in a great multitude the almost brutish and unreasonable insensibility of the people, and the inveterate and ineradicable unsatisfactoriness of their leaders. But I saw your letter; I saw the treasure of love which it contained; then I knew that He Who ordains all our lives had made some sweet, consolation shine on me in the bitterness of

---

[1] Placed in 375.
[2] An old schoolfellow of Basil's, of whom nothing seems to be known but what is gathered from this letter.

[1] i.e. the Anomœans. On the use of the word dogma for an heretical tenet, cf. note on p. 41.
[2] The Ben. note remarks that at first sight Eustathius of Sebasteia seems to be pointed at, for in Letter cxxviii. Basil speaks of him as occupying a contemptible half-and-half position. But, continues the note: Si res attentius consideretur, non Eustathium proprie hoc loco, sed generatim eosdem hæreticos, quos contra liber De Spiritu Sancto scriptus est, perspicuum erit notari. Nam medius ille Eustathii status in eo positus erat, quod nec catholicus potentioribus Arianis catholicis videri vellet. Nondum aperti cum Arianis conjunctus, nec probare quæ ipsi a Basilio proponebantur. At quos hic commemorat Basilius, hi catholicæ doctrinæ bellum apertum in dixerant, et quamvis dissimilitudinis impietatem fugere viderentur, iisdem tamen, ac Anomœi, principiis stabant. Hoc eis exprobat Basilius in libro De Spiritu Sancto, cap. 2, ubi impias eorum de Filio ac Spiritu sancto nugas ex principiis Actii deductas esse demonstrat, idem hæretici non desierunt nefarta Basillii expellendi consilia inire. Eorum convicia in Basilium, insidias et nefarias molitiones, furorem ac bellum inexpiabile, vide in libro De Spiritu Sancto, num. 13, 25, 34, 52, 60, 69, 75.
[3] Placed in 375.

my life. I therefore salute your holiness in return, and exhort you, as is my wont, not to cease to pray for my unhappy life, that I may never, drowned in the unrealities of this world, forget God, "who raiseth up the poor out of the dust;"[1] that I may never be lifted up with pride and fall into the condemnation of the devil;[2] that I may never be found by the Lord neglectful of my stewardship and asleep; never discharging it amiss, and wounding the conscience of my fellow-servants;[3] and, never companying with the drunken, suffer the pains threatened in God's just judgment against wicked stewards. I beseech you, therefore, in all your prayers to pray God that I may be watchful in all things; that I may be no shame or disgrace to the name of Christ, in the revelation of the secrets of my heart, in the great day of the appearing of our Saviour Jesus Christ.

2. Know then that I am expecting to be summoned by the wickedness of the heretics to the court, in the name of peace. Learn too that on being so informed, this bishop[4] wrote to me to hasten to Mesopotamia, and, after assembling together those who in that country are of like sentiments with us, and are strengthening the state of the Church, to travel in their company to the emperor. But perhaps my health will not be good enough to allow me to undertake a journey in the winter. Indeed, hitherto I have not thought the matter pressing, unless you advise it. I shall therefore await your counsel that my mind may be made up. Lose no time then, I beg you, in making known to me, by means of one of our trusty brethren, what course seems best to the divinely guided intelligence of your excellency.

LETTER CCXIV.[5]

To Count Terentius.[6]

1. WHEN I heard that your excellency had again been compelled to take part in public affairs, I was straightway distressed (for the truth must be told) at the thought of how contrary to your mind it must be that you, after once giving up the anxieties of official life, and allowing yourself leisure for the care of your soul, should again be forced back into your old career. But then I bethought me that peradventure the Lord has ordained that your lordship should again appear in public from this wish to

grant the boon of one alleviation for the countless pains which now beset the Church in our part of the world. I am, moreover, cheered by the thought that I am about to meet your excellency once again before I depart this life.

2. But a further rumour has reached me that you are in Antioch, and are transacting the business in hand with the chief authorities. And, besides this, I have heard that the brethren who are of the party of Paulinus are entering on some discussion with your excellency on the subject of union with us; and by "us" I mean those who are supporters of the blessed man of God, Meletius.[1] I hear, moreover, that the Paulinians are carrying about a letter of the Westerns,[2] assigning to them the episcopate of the Church in Antioch, but speaking under a false impression of Meletius, the admirable bishop of the true Church of God. I am not astonished at this. They[3] are totally ignorant of what is going on here; the others, though they might be supposed to know, give an account to them in which party is put before truth; and it is only what one might expect that they should either be ignorant of the truth, or should even endeavour to conceal the reasons which led the blessed Bishop Athanasius to write to Paulinus. But your excellency has on the spot those who are able to tell you accurately what passed between the bishops in the reign of Jovian, and from them I beseech you to get information.[4] I accuse no one; I pray that I may have love to all, and "especially unto them who are of the household of faith;"[5] and therefore I congratulate those who have received the letter from Rome. And, although it is a grand testimony in their favour, I only hope it is true and confirmed by facts. But I shall never be able to persuade myself on these grounds to ignore Meletius, or to forget the Church which is under him, or to treat as small, and of little importance to the true religion, the questions which originated the division. I shall never consent to give in, merely because somebody is very much elated at receiving a letter from

[1] On the divisions at Antioch, cf. Theod., H.E. iii. 2. Basil was no doubt taking the wise course in supporting Meletius, whose personal orthodoxy was unimpeachable. But the irreconcilable Eustathians could not forgive him his Arian nomination.
[2] This description might apply to either of the two letters written by Damasus to Paulinus on the subject of the admission to communion of Vitalius, bishop of the Apollinarian schism at Antioch. (Labbe, Conc. ii. 864 and 900, and Theod. H.E. v. 11.) The dates may necessitate its being referred to the former. [3] i.e. the Westerns.
[4] cf. Letter cclviii. and the Prolegomena to Athanasius in this edition, p. lxi. The events referred to took place in the winter of 363, when Athanasius was at Antioch, and in the early part of 364 on his return to Alexandria.
[5] Gal. vi. 10.

[1] Ps. cxiii. 7.   [2] cf. 1 Tim. iii. 6.   [3] cf. 1 Cor. viii. 12.
[4] Maran (Vit. Bas. vi.) conjectures this bishop to be Meletius, and refers to the beginning of Letter ccxvi. with an expression of astonishment that Tillemont should refer this letter to the year 373.
[5] Placed in 375.   [6] cf. Letters xcix. and cv.

men.[1] Even if it had come down from heaven itself, but he does not agree with the sound doctrine of the faith, I cannot look upon him as in communion with the saints.

3. Consider well, my excellent friend, that the falsifiers of the truth, who have introduced the Arian schism as an innovation on the sound faith of the Fathers, advance no other reason for refusing to accept the pious opinion of the Fathers than the meaning of the homoousion which they hold in their wickedness, and to the slander of the whole faith, alleging our contention to be that the Son is consubstantial in hypostasis. If we give them any opportunity by our being carried away by men who propound these sentiments and their like, rather from simplicity than from malevolence, there is nothing to prevent our giving them an unanswerable ground of argument against ourselves and confirming the heresy of those whose one end is in all their utterances about the Church, not so much to establish their own position as to calumniate mine. What more serious calumny could there be? What better calculated to disturb the faith of the majority than that some of us could be shewn to assert that there is one hypostasis of Father, Son, and Holy Ghost? We distinctly lay down that there is a difference of Persons; but this statement was anticipated by Sabellius, who affirms that God is one by hypostasis, but is described by Scripture in different Persons, according to the requirements of each individual case; sometimes under the name of Father, when there is occasion for this Person; sometimes under the name of Son when there is a descent to human interests or any of the operations of the œconomy;[2] and sometimes under the Person of Spirit when the occasion demands such phraseology. If, then, any among us are shewn to assert that Father, Son and Holy Ghost are one in substance,[3] while we maintain the three perfect Persons, how shall we escape giving clear and incontrovertible proof of the truth of what is being asserted about us?

4. The non-identity of hypostasis and ousia is, I take it, suggested even by our western brethren, where, from a suspicion of the inadequacy of their own language, they have given the word ousia in the Greek, to the end that any possible difference of meaning might be preserved in the clear and unconfounded distinction of terms. If you ask me to state shortly my own view, I shall state

that ousia has the same relation to hypostasis as the common has to the particular. Every one of us both shares in existence by the common term of essence (ousia) and by his own properties is such an one and such an one. In the same manner, in the matter in question, the term ousia is common, like goodness, or Godhead, or any similar attribute; while hypostasis is contemplated in the special property of Fatherhood, Sonship, or the power to sanctify. If then they describe the Persons as being without hypostasis,[1] the statement is per se absurd; but if they concede that the Persons exist in real hypostasis, as they acknowledge, let them so reckon them that the principle of the homoousion may be preserved in the unity of the Godhead, and that the doctrine preached may be the recognition of true religion, of Father, Son, and Holy Ghost, in the perfect and complete hypostasis of each of the Persons named. Nevertheless, there is one point which I should like to have pressed on your excellency, that you and all who like you care for the truth, and honour the combatant in the cause of true religion, ought to wait for the lead to be taken in bringing about this union and peace by the foremost authorities in the Church, whom I count as pillars and foundations of the truth and of the Church, and reverence all the more because they have been sent away for punishment, and have been exiled far from home. Keep yourself, I implore you, clear of prejudice, that in you, whom God has given me as a staff and support in all things, I may be able to find rest.[2]

LETTER CCXV.[3]

To the Presbyter Dorotheus.

I TOOK the earliest opportunity of writing to the most admirable Count Terentius, thinking it better to write to him on the subject in hand by means of strangers, and being anxious that our very dear brother Acacius shall not be inconvenienced by any delay. I have therefore given my letter to the government treasurer, who is travelling by the imperial post, and I have charged him to shew the letter to you first. I cannot understand how it is that no one has told you that the road to Rome is wholly impracticable in winter, the country between Constantinople and our own regions being full of enemies. If the route by sea must be taken, the season will be

---

[1] St. Basil seems quite unaware of any paramount authority in a letter from Rome. cf. *Prolegomena.*
[2] *Vide* notes, pp. 7 and 12. On Sabellius, cf. note on *Letter* ccxxxvi. [3] τὸ ὑποκείμενον.

[1] ἀνυπόστατα.
[2] On the point treated of in this letter, cf. note on p. 5 and *Letter* xxxviii. p. 137. But in the *De S.S. cap.* 38 (p. 23) St. Basil himself repudiates the assertion of three "*original hypostases,*" when he is apparently using ὑπόστασις in the Nicene sense. [3] Placed in 375.

favourable; if indeed my God-beloved brother Gregory [1] consents to the voyage and to the commission concerning these matters. For my own part, I do not know who can go with him, and am aware that he is quite inexperienced in ecclesiastical affairs. With a man of kindly character he may get on very well, and be treated with respect, but what possible good could accrue to the cause by communication between a man proud and exalted, and therefore quite unable to hear those who preach the truth to him from a lower standpoint, and a man like my brother, to whom anything like mean servility is unknown?

LETTER CCXVI.[2]

To Meletius, bishop of Antioch.

MANY other [3] journeys have taken me from home. I have been as far as Pisidia to settle the matters concerning the brethren in Isauria in concert with the Pisidian bishops. Thence I journeyed into Pontus, for Eustathius had caused no small disturbance at Dazimon, and had caused there a considerable secession from our church. I even went as far as the home of my brother Peter,[4] and, as this is not far from Neocæsarea, there was occasion of considerable trouble to the Neocæsareans, and of much rudeness to myself. Some men fled when no one was in pursuit. And I was supposed to be intruding uninvited, simply to get compliments from the folk there. As soon as I got home, after contracting a severe illness from the bad weather and my anxieties, I straightway received a letter from the East to tell me that Paulinus had had certain letters from the West addressed to him, in acknowledgement of a sort of higher claim; and that the Antiochene rebels were vastly elated by them, and were next preparing a form of creed, and offering to make its terms a condition of union with our Church. Besides all this it was reported to me that they had seduced to their faction that most excellent man Terentius. I wrote to him at once as forcibly as I could, to induce him to pause; and I tried to point out their disingenuousness.

LETTER CCXVII.

To Amphilochius, on the Canons.[1]

ON my return from a long journey (for I have been into Pontus on ecclesiastical business, and to visit my relations) with my body weak and ill, and my spirits considerably broken, I took your reverence's letter into my hand. No sooner did I receive the tokens of that voice which to me is of all voices the sweetest, and of that hand that I love so well, than I forgot all my troubles. And if I was made so much more cheerful by the receipt of your letter, you ought to be able to conjecture at what value I price your actual presence. May this be granted me by the Holy One, whenever it may be convenient to you and you yourself send me an invitation. And if you were to come to the house at Euphemias it would indeed be pleasant for me to meet you, escaping from my vexations here, and hastening to your unfeigned affection. Possibly also for other reasons I may be compelled to go as far as Nazianzus by the sudden departure of the very God-beloved bishop Gregory. How or why this has come to pass, so far I have no information.[2] The man about whom I had spoken to your excellency, and whom you expected to be ready by this time, has, you must know, fallen ill of a lingering disease, and is moreover now suffering from an affection of the eyes, arising from his old complaint and from the illness which has now befallen him, and he is quite unfit to do any work. I have no one else with me. It is consequently better, although the matter was left by them to me, for some one to be put forward by them. And indeed one cannot but think that the expressions were used merely as a necessary form, and that what they really wished was what they originally requested, that the person selected for the leadership should be one of themselves. If there is any one of the lately baptized,[3] whether Macedonius approve or not, let him be appointed. You will instruct him in his duties, the Lord,

---

[1] i.e. of Nyssa, an unsuitable envoy to Damascus.
[2] Placed in 375.
[3] On this word other the Ben. note grounds the argument that Meletius had proposed a journey which Basil had not undertaken, and hence that the unnamed bishop of Letter ccxiii. is Meletius; and further that the fact of the bishop not being named in ccxiii., and the obscurity of this and of other letters, may indicate the writer's hesitation to put particulars in his letters which might be more discreetly left to be conveyed by word of mouth.
[4] i.e. the settlement on the Iris, where Peter had succeeded Basil as Head.

[1] The third canonical letter, written on Basil's return from Pontus, in 375.
[2] This is the sudden disappearance of Gregory from Nazianzus at the end of 375, which was due at once to his craving for retirement and his anxiety not to complicate the appointment of a successor to his father (who died early in 374) in the see of Nazianzus. He found a refuge in the monastery of Thecla at the Isaurian Seleucia. (Carm. xi. 549.)
[3] The Ben. note appositely points out that any astonishment, such as expressed by Tillemont, at the consecration of a neophyte, is quite out of place, in view of the exigencies of the times and the practice of postponing baptism. St. Ambrose at Milan and Nectarius at Constantinople were not even "neophytes," but were actually unbaptized at the time of their appointment to their respective sees. "If there is any one among the lately baptized," argues the Ben. note, is tantamount to saying "If there is any one fit to be bishop."

Who in all things coöperates with you, granting you His grace for this work also.

LI. As to the clergy, the Canons have enjoined without making any distinction that one penalty is assigned for the lapsed,— ejection from the ministry, whether they be in orders[1] or remain in the ministry which is conferred without imposition of hands.

LII. The woman who has given birth to a child and abandoned it in the road, if she was able to save it and neglected it, or thought by this means to hide her sin, or was moved by some brutal and inhuman motive, is to be judged as in a case of murder. If, on the other hand, she was unable to provide for it, and the child perish from exposure and want of the necessities of life, the mother is to be pardoned.

LIII. The widowed slave is not guilty of a serious fall if she adopts a second marriage under colour of rape. She is not on this ground open to accusation. It is rather the object than the pretext which must be taken into account, but it is clear that she is exposed to the punishment of digamy.[2]

LIV. I know that I have already written to your reverence, so far as I can, on the distinctions to be observed in cases of involuntary homicide,[3] and on this point I can say no more. It rests with your intelligence to increase or lessen the severity of the punishment as each individual case may require.

LV. Assailants of robbers, if they are outside, are prohibited from the communion of the good thing.[4] If they are clerics they are degraded from their orders. For, it is said, "All they that take the sword shall perish with the sword."[5]

LVI. The intentional homicide, who has afterwards repented, will be excommunicated from the sacrament[6] for twenty years. The twenty years will be appointed for him as follows: for four he ought to weep, standing outside the door of the house of prayer, beseeching the faithful as they enter in to offer prayer in his behalf, and confessing his own sin. After four years he will be admitted among the hearers, and during five years will go out with them. During seven years he will go out with the kneelers,[1] praying. During four years he will only stand with the faithful, and will not take part in the oblation. On the completion of this period he will be admitted to participation of the sacrament.

LVII. The unintentional homicide will be excluded for ten years from the sacrament. The ten years will be arranged as follows: For two years he will weep, for three years he will continue among the hearers; for four he will be a kneeler; and for one he will only stand. Then he will be admitted to the holy rites.

LVIII. The adulterer will be excluded from the sacrament for fifteen years. During four he will be a weeper, and during five a hearer, during four a kneeler, and for two a stander without communion.

LIX. The fornicator will not be admitted to participation in the sacrament for seven years;[2] weeping two, hearing two, kneeling two, and standing one: in the eighth he will be received into communion.

LX. The woman who has professed virginity and broken her promise will complete the time appointed in the case of

---

[1] μετὰ τῶν ἐν ὑποπτώσει. The ὑποπίπτοντες or substrati constituted the third and chief station in the oriental system of penance, the first and second being the προσκλαίοντες, flentes or weepers, and the ἀκροώμενος, audientes, or hearers. In the Western Church it is the substrati who are commonly referred to as being in penitence, and the Latin versions of the Canons of Ancyra by Dionysius Exiguus and Martin of Braga render ὑποπίπτοντες and ὑποπτώσις by pœnitentes and pœnitentia. In Basil's Canon xxii. p. 238, this station is specially styled μετάνοια. cf. D.C.A. ii. 1593. "Μετάνοια notat pœnitentiam eorum qui ob delicta sua in ecclesia ἐπιτιμίοις ἐσωφρονίζοντο (Zonaras, Ad. Can. v. Conc. Antioch, p. 327), quique dicebantur οἱ ἐν μετανοίᾳ ὄντες. Chrysostom, Hom. iii. in Epist. ad Eph. in S. Cœnæ, communione clamabat κήρυξ, ὅσοι ἐν μετανοίᾳ ἀπέλθετε πάντες." Suicer s.v.

[2] cf. Can. xxii. p. 228. The Ben. note is "Laborant Balsamon et Zonaras in hoc canone conciliando cum vicesimo secundo, atque id causæ afferunt, cur in vicesimo secundo quatuor anni, septem in altero decernantur, quod Basilius in vicesimo secundo antiqua Patrum placita sequatur, suam in altero propriam sententiam exponat. Eundem hunc canonem Alexius Aristenus, ut clarum et perspicuum, negat explicatione indigere. Videbat nimirum doctissimus scriptor duplicem a Basilio distingui fornicationem, leviorem alteram, alteram graviorem levior dicitur, quæ inter personas matrimonio solutas committitur: gravior, cum conjugati hominis libido in mulierem solutam erumpit. Priori anni quatuor, septem alteri imponuntur. Manifesta res est ex canone 21, ubi conjugati peccatum cum soluta fornicationem appellat Basilius, ac longioribus pœnis coerceri, non tamen instar adulterii, testatur. In canone autem 77 eum qui legitimam uxorem dimittit, et aliam ducit, adulterum quidem esse ex Domini sententia testatur, sed tamen ex canonibus Patrum annos septem decernit, non quindecim, ut in adulterio cum aliena uxore commisso. Secum ergo non pugnat cum fornicationi nunc annos quatuor, nunc septem, adulterio nunc septem, nunc quindecim indicit. Eamdem in sententiam videtur accipiendus canon quartus epistolæ Sancti Gregorii Nysseni ad Letoium. Nam cum fornicationi novem annos, adulterio decem et octo imponit, gravior illa intelligenda fornicatio, quam conjugatur cum soluta committit. Hinc iliam adulterium videri fatetur his qui accuratius examinant.

---

[1] εἴτε ἐν βαθμῷ. This is understood by Balsamon and Zonaras to include Presbyters, Deacons, and sub-deacons; while the ministry conferred without imposition of hands refers to Readers, Singers, Sacristans, and the like. Alexius Aristenus ranks Singers and Readers with the higher orders, and understands by the lower, keepers of the sacred vessels, candle-lighters, and chancel door keepers. The Ben. note inclines to the latter view on the ground that the word "remain" indicates a category where there was no advance to a higher grade, as was the case with Readers and Singers.

[2] cf. Can. xxx. p. 239.

[3] i.e. in Canon viii. p. 226, and Canon xi. p. 228.

[4] Here reading, punctuation, and sense are obscure. The Ben. Ed. have ἔξω μὲν ὄντες, τῆς κοινωνίας εἴργονται, and render "Si sint quidem laici, a boni communione arcentur." But ἔξω ὄντες, standing alone, more naturally means non-Christians. Balsamon and Zonaras in the Pandects have ἔξω μὲν ὄντες τῆς Ἐκκλησίας εἴργονται τῆς κοινωνίας τοῦ ἀγαθοῦ.

[5] Matt. xxvi. 52.

[6] ἁγιάσματι. The Ben. Ed. render Sacramento. In the Sept. (e.g. Amos vii. 13) the word = sanctuary. In patristic usage both S. and P. are found for the Lord's Supper, or the consecrated elements; e.g. ἁγίασμα in Greg. Nyss., Ep. Canon. Can. v. The plural as in this place "frequentius." (Suicer s.v.)

adultery in her continence.[1] The same rule will be observed in the case of men who have professed a solitary life and who lapse.

LXI. The thief, if he have repented of his own accord and charged himself, shall only be prohibited from partaking of the sacrament for a year; if he be convicted, for two years. The period shall be divided between kneeling and standing. Then let him be held worthy of communion.

LXII. He who is guilty of unseemliness with males will be under discipline for the same time as adulterers.

LXIII. He who confesses his iniquity in the case of brutes shall observe the same time in penance.

LXIV. Perjurers shall be excommunicated for ten years; weeping for two, hearing for three, kneeling for four, and standing only during one year; then they shall be held worthy of communion.

LXV. He who confesses magic or sorcery shall do penance for the time of murder, and shall be treated in the same manner as he who convicts himself of this sin.

LXVI. The tomb breaker shall be excommunicated for ten years, weeping for two, hearing for three, kneeling for four, standing for one, then he shall be admitted.

LXVII. Incest with a sister shall incur penance for the same time as murder.

LXVIII. The union of kindred within the prohibited degrees of marriage, if detected as having taken place in acts of sin, shall receive the punishment of adultery.[2]

LXIX. The Reader who has intercourse with his betrothed before marriage, shall be allowed to read after a year's suspension, remaining without advancement. If he has had secret intercourse without betrothal, he shall be deposed from his ministry. So too the minister.[3]

LXX. The deacon who has been polluted in lips, and has confessed his commission of this sin, shall be removed from his ministry. But he shall be permitted to partake of the sacrament together with the deacons. The same holds good in the case of a priest.

---

[1] cf. Can. xviii. Augustine (De Bono Viduitatis, n. 14) represents breaches of the vows of chastity as graver offences than breaches of the vows of wedlock. The rendering of τῇ οἰκονομίᾳ τῆς καθ' ἑαυτὴν ζωῆς by continency is illustrated in the Ben. note by Hermas ii. 4 as well as by Basil, Canon xiv. and xlv.

[2] This Canon is thus interpreted by Aristenus, Matrimonium cum propinqua legibus prohibitum eadem ac adulterium pœna castigatur : et cum diversæ sint adulterorum pœnæ sic etiam pro ratione propinquitatis tota res temperabitur. Hinc duas sorores ducenti vii. anni pœnitentiæ irrogantur, ut in adulterio cum muliere libera commisso. non xv. ut in graviore adulterio, or does it mean that incestuous fornication shall be treated as adultery?

[3] By minister Balsamon and Zonaras understand the subdeacon. Aristenus understands all the clergy appointed without imposition of hands. The Ben. ed. approve the latter. cf. n. on Canon li. p. 256, and Letter liv. p. 157.

If any one be detected in a more serious sin, whatever be his degree, he shall be deposed.[1]

LXXI. Whoever is aware of the commission of any one of the aforementioned sins, and is convicted without having confessed, shall be under punishment for the same space of time as the actual perpetrator.

LXXII. He who has entrusted himself[2] to soothsayers, or any such persons, shall be under discipline for the same time as the homicide.

LXXIII. He who has denied Christ, and sinned against the mystery of salvation, ought to weep all his life long, and is bound to remain in penitence, being deemed worthy of the sacrament in the hour of death, through faith in the mercy of God.

LXXIV. If, however, each man who has committed the former sins is made good, through penitence,[3] he to whom is com-

---

[1] On the earlier part of this canon the Ben. note says: "Balsamon, Zonaras, et Aristenus varia commentantur in hunc canonem. sed a mente Basilii multum abludentia. Liquet enim hoc labiorum peccatum, cui remissior pœna infligitur ipsa actione, quam Basilius minime ignoscendam esse judicat, levius existimari debere. Simili ratione sanctus Pater in cap. vi. Isaiæ n. 185, p. 516, labiorum peccata actionibus, ut leviora, opponit, ac prophetæ delecta non ad actionem et operationem erupisse, sed labiis tenus constitisse observat. In eodem commentario n. 170. p. 501, impuritatis peccatum variis gradibus constare demonstrat, inter quos enumerat ῥήματα φθοροποιά, verba ad corruptelam apta, ὁμιλίας μαχράς, longas confabulationes, quibus ad stuprum pervenitur. Ex his perspici arbitror peccatum aliquod in hoc canone designari, quod ipsa actione levius sit : nedum ea suspicari liceat, quæ Basilii interpretibus in mentem venerunt. Sed tamen cum dico Basilium in puniendis labiorum peccatis leniorem esse, non quodlibet turpium sermonum genus, non immunda colloquia (quomodo enim presbyteris hoc vitio pollutis honorem cathedræ reliquisset?), sed ejusmodi intelligenda est peccandi voluntas, quæ foras quidem aliquo sermone prodit, sed tamen quominus in actum erumpat, subeunte meliori cogitatione, reprimitur. Quemadmodum enim peccata, quæ sola cogitatione committuntur, idcirco leviora esse pronuntiat Basilius, comment. in Isaiam n. 115, p. 459. et n. 243, p. 564, qui repressa est actionis turpitudo ; ita hoc loco non quælibet labiorum peccata ; non calumnias, non blasphemias, sed ea tantum lenius tractat, quæ adeo gravia non erant, vel etiam ob declinatam actionis turpitudinem, ut patet ex his verbis, seque eo usque peccasse confessus est, aliquid indulgentiæ merere videbantur."

On the word καθαιρεθήσεται it is remarked : "In his canonibus quos de clericorum peccatis edidit Basilius, duo videntur silentio prætermissa. Quæri enim possit 1° cur suspensionis pœnam soli lectori ac ministro, sive subdiacono, imponat, diaconis autem et presbyteris depositionem absque ulla prorsus exceptione infligat, nisi quod eis communionem cum diaconis et presbyteris relinquit, si peccatum non ita grave fuerit. Erat tamen suspensionis pœna in ipsos presbyteros non inusitata, ut patet ex plurimis apostolicis canonibus, in quibus presbyteri ac etiam ipsi episcopi segregantur, ac postea, si sese non emendaverint, deponuntur. Forte hæc reliquit Basilius episcopo dijudicanda quemadmodum ejusdem arbitrio permittet in canonibus 74 et 81, ut pœnitentiæ tempus imminuat, si bonus evasit is qui peccavit. 2° Hæc etiam possit institui quæstio, utrumne in gravissimis quidem criminibus pœnitentiam publicam depositioni adjecerit. Adhibita ratio in Canone 3, cur aliquid discriminis clericos inter et laicos ponendum sit, non solum ad gravia peccata, sed etiam ad gravissima pertinet. Ait enim æquum esse ut, cum laici post pœnitentiam in eumdem locum restituantur, clerici vero non restituantur, liberalius et mitius cum clericis agatur. Nolebat ergo clericos lapsos quadruplicem pœnitentiæ gradum percurrere. Sed quemadmodum lapso in fornicationem diacono non statim communionem reddit, sed ejus conversionem et morum emendationem probandam esse censit, et ad eumdem canonem tertium observavimus, ita dubium esse non potest quin ad criminis magnitudinem probandi modum et tempus accommodaverit."

[2] The Ben. ed. suppose for the purpose of learning sorcery. cf. Can. lxxxiii., where a lighter punishment is assigned to consulters of wizards.

[3] ἐξομολογούμενος. "The verb in St. Matt. xi. 25 expresses

mitted by the loving-kindness of God the power of loosing and binding [1] will not be deserving of condemnation, if he become less severe, as he beholds the exceeding greatness of the penitence of the sinner, so as to lessen the period of punishment, for the history in the Scriptures informs us that all who exercise penitence [2] with greater zeal quickly receive the loving-kindness of God.[3]

LXXV. The man who has been polluted with his own sister, either on the father's or the mother's side, must not be allowed to enter the house of prayer, until he has given up his iniquitous and unlawful conduct. And, after he has come to a sense of that fearful sin, let him weep for three years standing at the door of the house of prayer, and entreating the people as they go in to prayer that each and all will mercifully offer on his behalf their prayers with earnestness to the Lord. After this let him be received for another period of three years to hearing alone, and while hearing the Scriptures and the instruction, let him be expelled and not be admitted to prayer. Afterwards, if he has asked it with tears and has fallen before the Lord with contrition of heart and great humiliation, let kneeling be accorded to him during other three years. Thus, when he shall have worthily shewn the fruits of repentance, let him be received in the tenth year to ˌthe prayer of the faithful without oblation; and after standing with the faithful in prayer for two years, then, and not till then, let him be held worthy of the communion of the good thing.

LXXVI. The same rule applies to those who take their own daughters in law.

LXXVII. He who abandons the wife, lawfully united to him, is subject by the sentence of the Lord to the penalty of adultery. But it has been laid down as a canon by our Fathers that such sinners should weep for a year, be hearers for two years, in kneeling for three years, stand with the faithful in the

seventh; and thus be deemed worthy of the oblation, if they have repented with tears.[1]

LXXVIII. Let the same rule hold good in the case of those who marry two sisters, although at different times.[2]

LXXIX. Men who rage after their stepmothers are subject to the same canon as those who rage after their sisters.[3]

LXXX. On polygamy the Fathers are silent, as being brutish and altogether inhuman. The sin seems to me worse than fornication. It is therefore reasonable that such sinners should be subject to the canons; namely a year's weeping, three years kneeling and then reception.[4]

LXXXI. During the invasion of the barbarians many men have sworn heathen oaths, tasted things unlawfully offered them in magic temples and so have broken their faith in God. Let regulations be made in the case of these men in accordance with the canons laid down by our Fathers.[5] Those

---

[1] The Ben. note points out that St. Basil refers to the repudiation of a lawful wife for some other cause than adultery. It remarks that though Basil does not order it to be punished as severely as adultery there is no doubt that he would not allow communion before the dismissal of the unlawful wife. It proceeds " *illud autem difficilius est statuere, quid de matrimonio post ejectam uxorem adulteram contracto senserit. Ratum a Basilio habitum fuisse ejusmodi matrimonium pronuntiat Aristenus. Atque id quidem Basilius, conceptis verbis non declarat; sed tamen videtur hac in re a saniori ac meliori sententia discessisse. Nam 1° maritum injuste dimissum ab alio matrimonio non excludit, ut vidimus in canonibus 9 et 35. Porro non videtur jure dimittenti denegasse, quod injuste dimisso concedebat. 2° Cum jubeat uxorem adulteram ejici, vix dubium est quin matrimonium adulterio uxoris fuisset mariti, ac multo durior, quam uxoris conditio, si nec adulteram retinere, nec aliam ducere integrum fuisset.*

[2] cf. *Letter* clx. p. 212.

[3] The Ben. note is *Prima specie non omnino perspicuum est utrum sorores ex utroque parente intelligat, an tantum ex alterutro. Nam cum in canone 79 eos qui suas nurus accipiunt non severius puniat, quam cui cum sorore ex matre vel ex patre rem habent, forte videri posset idem statuere de iis qui in novercas insaniunt. Sed tamen multo probabilius est eamdem illis pœnam imponi, ac iis qui cum sorore ex utroque parente contaminantur. Non enim distinctione utitur Basilius ut in canone 75; nec mirum si peccatum cum noverca gravius quam cum nuru, ob factam patri injuriam, judicavit.*

[4] i.e. probably only into the place of standers. Zonaras and Balsamon understand by polygamy a fourth marriage; trigamy being permitted (cf. Canon l. p. 240) though discouraged. The Ben. annotator dissents, pointing out that in Canon iv. Basil calls trigamy, polygamy, and quoting Gregory of Nazianzus (*Orat.* 31) as calling a third marriage παρανομια. Maran confirms this opinion by the comparison of the imposition on polygamy of the same number of years of penance as are assigned to trigamy in Canon iv. " Theodore of Canterbury A.D. 687 imposes a penance of seven years on trigamists but pronounces the marriages valid (*Penitential, lib.* 1. c. xiv. § 3). Nicephorus of Constantinople, A.D. 814, suspends trigamists for five years. (*Hard. Concil. tom.* iv. p. 1052.) Herard of Tours, A.D. 858, declares any greater number of wives than two to be unlawful (*Cap* cxi. *ibid. tom.* v. p. 557). Leo the Wise, Emperor of Constantinople, was allowed to marry three wives without public remonstrance, but was suspended from communion by the patriarch Nicholas when he married a fourth. This led to a council being held at Constantinople, A.D. 920, which finally settled the Greek discipline on the subject of third and fourth marriages. It ruled that the penalty for a fourth marriage was to be excommunication and exclusion from the church; for a third marriage, if a man were forty years old, suspension for five years, and admission to communion thereafter only on Easter day. If he were thirty years old, suspension for four years, and admission to communion thereafter only three times a year." *Dict. Christ. Ant.* ii. p. 1104.

[5] The Ben. n. thinks that the Fathers of Ancyra are meant, whose authority seems to have been great in Cappadocia and the adjacent provinces.

---

thanksgiving and praise, and in this sense was used by many Christian writers (Suicer, *s.v.*). But more generally in the early Fathers it signifies the whole course of penitential discipline, the outward act and performance of penance. From this it came to mean that public acknowledgment of sin which formed so important a part of penitence. Irenæus (*c. Hær.* i. 13, § 5) speaks of an adulterer who, having been converted, passed her whole life in a state of penitence (ἐξομολογουμένη, in exomologesi); and (*ib.* iii. 4) of Cerdon often coming into the church and confessing his errors (ἐξομολογούμενος)." *D.C.A.* i. 644.

[1] Here we see "binding and loosing" passing from the Scriptural sense of declaring what acts are forbidden and committed (Matt. xvi. 19 and xxiii. 4. See note of Rev. A. Carr in *Cambridge Bible for Schools*) into the later ecclesiastical sense of imposing and remitting penalties for sin. The first regards rather moral obligation, and, as is implied in the force of the tenses alike in the passages of St. Matthew cited and in St. John xx. 23, the recognition and announcement of the divine judgment already passed on sins and sinners; the latter regards the imposition of disciplinary penalties.

[2] τοῖς ἐξομολογουμένους.

[3] e.g. according to the Ben. note, Manasseh and Hezekiah.

who have endured grievous tortures and have been forced to denial, through inability to sustain the anguish, may be excluded for three years, hearers for two, kneelers for three, and so be received into communion. Those who have abandoned their faith in God, laying hands on the tables of the demons and swearing heathen oaths, without undergoing great violence, should be excluded for three years, hearers for two. When they have prayed for three years as kneelers, and have stood other three with the faithful in supplication, then let them be received into the communion of the good thing.

LXXXII. As to perjurers, if they have broken their oaths under violent compulsion, they are under lighter penalties and may therefore be received after six years. If they break their faith without compulsion, let them be weepers for two years, hearers for three, pray as kneelers for five, during other two be received into the communion of prayer without oblation, and so at last, after giving proof of due repentance, they shall be restored to the communion of the body of Christ.

LXXXIII. Consulters of soothsayers and they who follow heathen customs, or bring persons into their houses to discover remedies and to effect purification, should fall under the canon of six years. After weeping a year, hearing a year, kneeling for three years and standing with the faithful for a year so let them be received.

LXXXIV. I write all this with a view to testing the fruits of repentance.[1] I do not decide such matters absolutely by time, but I give heed to the manner of penance. If men are in a state in which they find it hard to be weaned from their own ways and choose rather to serve the pleasures of the flesh than to serve the Lord, and refuse to accept the Gospel life, there is no common ground between me and them. In the midst of a disobedient and gainsaying people I have been taught to hear the words " Save thy own soul."[2] Do not then let us consent to perish together with such sinners. Let us fear the awful judgment. Let us keep before our eyes the terrible day of the retribution of the Lord. Let us not consent to perish in other men's sins, for if the terrors of the Lord have not taught us, if so great calamities have not brought us to feel that it is because of our iniquity that the Lord has abandoned us, and given us into the hands of barbarians, that the people have been led captive before our foes and given over to dispersion, because the bearers of Christ's

name have dared such deeds; if they have not known nor understood that it is for these reasons that the wrath of God has come upon us, what common ground of argument have I with them?

But we ought to testify to them day and night, alike in public and in private. Let us not consent to be drawn away with them in their wickedness. Let us above all pray that we may do them good, and rescue them from the snare of the evil one. If we cannot do this, let us at all events do our best to save our own souls from everlasting damnation.

LETTER CCXVIII.[1]

To Amphilochius, bishop of Iconium.

BROTHER ÆLIANUS has himself completed the business concerning which he came, and has stood in need of no aid from me. I owe him, however, double thanks, both for bringing me a letter from your reverence and for affording me an opportunity of writing to you. By him, therefore, I salute your true and unfeigned love, and beseech you to pray for me more than ever now, when I stand in such need of the aid of your prayers. My health has suffered terribly from the journey to Pontus and my sickness is unendurable. One thing I have long been anxious to make known to you. I do not mean to say that I have been so affected by any other cause as to forget it, but now I wish to put you in mind to send some good man into Lycia, to enquire who are of the right faith, for peradventure they ought not to be neglected, if indeed the report is true, which has been brought to me by a pious traveller from thence, that they have become altogether alienated from the opinion of the Asiani,[2] and wish to embrace communion with us. If any one is to go let him enquire at Corydala[3] for Alexander, the late monk, the bishop; at Limyra[4] for Diotimus, and at Myra[5] for Tatianus, Polemo,[6] and Macarius presbyters; at Patara[7] for Eudemus,[8] the bishop; at Telmessus[9] for Hilarius, the bishop; at Phelus for Lallianus, the bishop. Of these and of more besides I have been informed that they are sound in the faith, and

---

1 μετανοίας. cf. note on p. 256; here the word seems to include both repentance and penance. 2 Gen. xix. 17, lxx.

1 Placed in 375.
2 i.e. the inhabitants of the Roman province of Asia. cf. Acts xx. 4. Ἀσιανοὶ δὲ Τυχικὸς καὶ Τρόφιμος.
3 Corydalla, now Hadginella, is on the road between Lystra and Patara. There are ruins of a theatre. cf. Plin. v. 25.
4 Now Phineka.
5 So the Ben. ed. Other readings are ἐν Κύροις and ἐν Νύροις. On Myra cf. Acts xxvii. 5, on which Conybeare and Howson refer to Fellows' Asia Minor, p. 194 and Spratt and Forbes's Lycia.
6 Afterwards bishop of Myra, and as such at Constantinople 381, Labbe 1, 665.
7 cf. Acts xxi. 1. 8 At Constantinople in 381.
9 Now Macri, where the ruins are remarkable.

I have been grateful to God that even any in the Asian region should be clear of the heretic's pest. If, then, it be possible, let us in the meanwhile make personal enquiry about them. When we have obtained information. I am for writing a letter, and am anxious to invite one of them to meet me. God grant that all may go well with that Church at Iconium, which is so dear to me. Through you I salute all the honourable clergy and all who are associated with your reverence.

LETTER CCXIX.[1]

To the clergy of Samosata.

THE Lord ordereth "all things in measure and weight,"[2] and brings on us the temptations which do not exceed our power to endure them,[3] but tests all that fight in the cause of true religion by affliction, not suffering them to be tempted above that they are able to bear.[4] He gives tears to drink in great measure[5] to all who ought to show whether in their affections they are preserving their gratitude to Him. Especially in His dispensation concerning you has He shown His loving-kindness, not suffering such a persecution to be brought on you by your enemies as might turn some of you aside, or cause you to swerve from the faith of Christ. He has matched you with adversaries who are of small importance and easy to be repelled, and has prepared the prize for your patience in your victory over them. But the common enemy of our life, who, in his wiles, strives against the goodness of God, because he has seen that, like a strong wall, you are despising attack from without, has devised, as I hear, that there should arise among yourselves mutual offences and quarrels. These indeed, at the outset, are insignificant and easy of cure; as time goes on, however, they are increased by contention and are wont to result in irremediable mischief.[6] I have, therefore, undertaken to exhort you by this letter. Had it been possible, I would have come myself and supplicated you in person. But this is prevented by present circumstances, and so, in lieu of supplication, I hold out this letter to you, that you may respect my entreaty, may put a stop to your mutual rivalries, and may soon send me the good news that all cause of offence among you is at an end.

2. I am very anxious that you should

know that he is great before God who humbly submits to his neighbour and submits to charges against himself, without having cause for shame, even though they are not true, that he may bring the great blessing of peace upon God's Church.

I hope that there will arise among you a friendly rivalry, as to who shall first be worthy of being called God's son, after winning this rank for himself because of his being a peacemaker. A letter has also been written to you by your very God-beloved bishop as to the course which you ought to pursue. He will write again what it belongs to him to say. But I too, because of its having been already allowed me to be near you, cannot disregard your position. So on the arrival of the very devout brother Theodorus the sub-deacon, and his report that your Church is in distress and disturbance, being deeply grieved and much pained at heart, I could not endure to keep silence. I implore you to fling away all controversy with one another, and to make peace, that you may avoid giving pleasure to your opponents and destroying the boast of the Church, which is now noised abroad throughout the world, that you all, as you are ruled by one soul and heart, so live in one body. Through your reverences I salute all the people of God, both those in rank and office and the rest of the clergy. I exhort you to keep your old character. I can ask for nothing more than this because by the exhibition of your good works you have anticipated and made impossible any improvement on them.

LETTER CCXX.[1]

To the Berœans.[2]

THE Lord has given great consolation to all who are deprived of personal intercourse in allowing them to communicate by letter. By this means, it is true, we cannot learn the express image of the body, but we can learn the disposition of the very soul. Thus on the present occasion, when I had received the letter of your reverences, I at the same moment recognised you, and took your love towards me into my heart, and needed no long time to create intimacy with you. The disposition shewn in your letter was quite enough to enkindle in me affection for the beauty of your soul. And, besides your letter, excellent as it was, I had a yet plainer proof of how things are with you from

---

[1] Placed in 375.   [3] cf. Matt. vi. 13.   [5] cf. Ps. lxxx. 5.
[2] Wisd. xi. 20.   [4] cf. 1 Cor. x. 13.
[6] cf. Homer of Ἔρις, Il. iv. 442:

ἥ τ᾿ ὀλίγη μὲν πρῶτα κορύσσεται, αὐτὰρ ἔπειτα
οὐρανῷ ἐστήριξε κάρη καὶ ἐπὶ χθονὶ βαίνει.

---

[1] Placed in 375.
[2] The Syrian Berœa, Aleppo, or Haleb. cf. Letter clxxxv. p. 222.

the amiability of the brethren who have been the means of communication between us. The well-beloved and reverend presbyter Acacius, has told me much in addition to what you have written, and has brought before my eyes the conflict you have to keep up day by day, and the stoutness of the stand you are making for the true religion. He has thus so moved my admiration, and roused in me so earnest a desire of enjoying the good qualities in you, that I do pray the Lord that a time may come when I may know you and yours by personal experience. He has told me of the exactitude of those of you who are entrusted with the ministry of the altar, and moreover of the harmonious agreement of all the people, and the generous character and genuine love towards God of the magistrates and chief men of your city. I consequently congratulate the Church on consisting of such members, and pray that spiritual peace may be given to you in yet greater abundance, to the end that in quieter times you may derive enjoyment from your labours in the day of affliction. For sufferings that are painful while they are being experienced are naturally often remembered with pleasure. For the present I beseech you not to faint. Do not despair because your troubles follow so closely one upon another. Your crowns are near; the help of the Lord is near. Do not let all you have hitherto undergone go for nothing; do not nullify a struggle which has been famous over all the world. Human life is but of brief duration. " All flesh is grass, and all the goodliness thereof is as the flower of the field. . . . The grass withereth, the flower fadeth; but the word of our God shall stand for ever." [1] Let us hold fast to the commandment that abideth, and despise the unreality that passeth away. Many Churches have been cheered by your example. In calling new champions into the field you have won for yourselves a great reward, though you knew it not. The Giver of the prize is rich, and is able to reward you not unworthily for your brave deeds.

LETTER CCXXI.[2]

To the Berœans.

You were previously known to me, my dear friends, by your far-famed piety, and by the crown won by your confession in Christ. Peradventure one of you may ask in reply who can have carried these tidings of us so far? The Lord Himself; for He puts His worshippers like a lamp on a lamp-stand, and

makes them shine throughout the whole world. Are not winners in the games wont to be made famous by the prize of victory, and craftsmen by the skilful design of their work? Shall the memory of these and others like them abide for ever unforgotten, and shall not Christ's worshippers, concerning whom the Lord says Himself, Them that honour me I will honour, be made famous and glorious by Him before all? Shall He not display the brightness of their radiant splendour as He does the beams of the sun? But I have been moved to greater longing for you by the letter which you have been good enough to send me, a letter in which, above and beyond your former efforts on behalf of the truth you have been yet more lavish of your abounding and vigorous zeal for the true faith. In all this I rejoice with you, and I pray with you that the God of the universe, Whose is the struggle and the arena, and Who gives the crown, may fill you with enthusiasm, may make your souls strong, and make your work such as to meet with His divine approval.

LETTER CCXXII.[1]

To the people of Chalcis.[2]

THE letter of your reverences came upon me in an hour of affliction like water poured into the mouths of racehorses, inhaling dust with each eager breath at high noontide in the middle of the course. Beset by trial after trial, I breathed again, at once cheered by your words and invigorated by the thought of your struggles to meet that which is before me with unflinching courage. For the conflagration which has devoured a great part of the East is already advancing by slow degrees into our own neighbourhood, and after burning everything round about us is trying to reach even the Churches in Cappadocia, already moved to tears by the smoke that rises from the ruins of our neighbours' homes.[3] The flames have almost reached me. May the Lord divert them by the breath of His mouth, and stay this

---

[1] Is. xl. 6, 8.   [2] Placed in 375.

[1] Placed in 375.
[2] The Syrian Chaecis, now Kinesrin. Maran *Vit. Bas.* Chap. xxxiii. supposes this letter to have been probably carried with *Letter* ccxxi. by Acacius.
[3] Maran *Vit. Bas.* l. c. says that these words cannot refer to the persecution of Valens in Cappadocia in 371, for that persecution went on between Constantinople and Cappadocia, and did not start from the East. There need be no surprise, he thinks, at the two preceding letters containing no mention of this persecution, because Acacius, who was a native of Bera, would be sure to report all that he had observed in Cappadocia. I am not sure that the reference to a kind of prairie fire spreading from the East does not rather imply a prevalence of heresy than what is commonly meant by persecution. Meletius, however, was banished from Antioch in 374 and Eusebius from Samosata in the same year, as graphically described by Theodoret *H. E.* iv. 13.

wicked fire. Who is such a coward, so unmanly, so untried in the athlete's struggles, as not to be nerved to the fight by your cheers, and pray to be hailed victor at your side? You have been the first to step into the arena of true religion; you have beaten off many an attack in bouts with the heretics; you have borne the strong hot wind[1] of trial, both you who are leaders of the Church, to whom has been entrusted the ministry of the altar, and every individual of the laity, including those of higher rank. For this in you is specially admirable and worthy of all praise, that you are all one in the Lord, some of you leaders in the march to what is good, others willingly following. It is for this reason that you are too strong for the attack of your assailants, and allow no hold to your antagonists in any one of your members, wherefore day and night I pray the King of the ages to preserve the people in the integrity of their faith, and for them to preserve the clergy, like a head unharmed at the top, exercising its own watchful forethought for every portion of the body underneath. For while the eyes discharge their functions, the hands can do their work as they ought, the feet can move without tripping, and no part of the body is deprived of due care. I beseech you, then, to cling to one another, as you are doing and as you will do. I beseech you who are entrusted with the care of souls to keep each and all together, and to cherish them like beloved children. I beseech the people to continue to show you the respect and honour due to fathers, that in the goodly order of your Church you may keep your strength and the foundation of your faith in Christ; that God's name may be glorified and the good gift of love increase and abound. May I, as I hear of you, rejoice in your progress in God. If I am still bidden to sojourn in the flesh in this world, may I one day see you in the peace of God. If I be now summoned to depart this life, may I see you in the radiant glory of the saints, together with all them who are accounted worthy through patience and showing forth of good works, with crowns upon your heads.

LETTER CCXXIII.[2]

Against Eustathius of Sebasteia.[3]

1. THERE is a time to keep silence and a time to speak,[4] is the saying of the Preacher.

Time enough has been given to silence, and now the time has come to open my mouth for the publication of the truth concerning matters that are, up to now, unknown. The illustrious Job bore his calamities for a long time in silence, and ever showed his courage by holding out under the most intolerable sufferings, but when he had struggled long enough in silence, and had persisted in covering his anguish in the bottom of his heart, at last he opened his mouth and uttered his well-known words.[1] In my own case this is now the third year of my silence, and my boast has become like that of the Psalmist, "I was as a man that heareth not and in whose mouth are no reproofs."[2] Thus I shut up in the bottom of my heart the pangs which I suffered on account of the calumnies directed against me, for calumny humbles a man, and calumny makes a poor man giddy.[3] If, therefore, the mischief of calumny is so great as to cast down even the perfect man from his height, for this is what Scripture indicates by the word man, and by the poor man is meant he who lacks the great doctrines, as is the view also of the prophet when he says, "These are poor, therefore they shall not hear; . . . I will get me unto the great men,"[4] he means by poor those who are lacking in understanding; and here, too, he plainly means those who are not yet furnished in the inner man, and have not even come to the full measure of their age; it is these who are said by the proverb to be made giddy and tossed about. Nevertheless I thought that I ought to bear my troubles in silence, waiting for some indication to come out of them. I did not even think that what was said against me proceeded from ill will; I thought it was the result of ignorance of the truth. But now I see that hostility increases with time, and that my slanderers are not sorry for what they said at the beginning, and do not take any trouble to make amends for the past, but go on and on and rally themselves together to attain their original object. This was to make my life miserable and to devise means for sullying my reputation among the brethren. I, therefore, no longer see safety in silence. I have bethought me of the words of Isaiah: "I have long time holden my peace, shall I always be still and refrain myself? I have been patient like a travailing woman."[5] God grant that I may both receive the reward of silence, and gain some strength to confute my opponents, and that

---

[1] καύσωνα. cf. Matt. xx. 12. Luke xii. 55, and James i. 11.
[2] Placed in 375.
[3] On the mutual relations of Basil and Eustathius up to this time, cf. Prolegomena.   [4] Eccles. iii. 7.

[1] Job iii. 1, seqq.   [2] Ps. xxxviii. 14.
[3] cf. ἡ συκοφαντία περιφέρει σοφόν. Eccles. vii, 8, LXX. *Calumnia conturbat sapientem et perdet robur cordis illius.* Vulg.
[4] Jer. iv. 5, LXX.   [5] Isa. xlii. 14, LXX.

thus, by confuting them, I may dry up the bitter torrent of falsehood that has gushed out against me. So might I say, " My soul has passed over the torrent;" [1] and, " If it had not been the Lord who was on our side when men rose up against us, . . . then they had swallowed us up quick, the water had drowned us." [2]

2. Much time had I spent in vanity, and had wasted nearly all my youth in the vain labour which I underwent in acquiring the wisdom made foolish by God. Then once upon a time, like a man roused from deep sleep, I turned my eyes to the marvellous light of the truth of the Gospel, and I perceived the uselessness of " the wisdom of the princes of this world, that come to naught." [3] I wept many tears over my miserable life, and I prayed that guidance might be vouchsafed me to admit me to the doctrines of true religion. First of all was I minded to make some mending of my ways, long perverted as they were by my intimacy with wicked men. Then I read the Gospel, and I saw there that a great means of reaching perfection was the selling of one's goods, the sharing them with the poor, the giving up of all care for this life, and the refusal to allow the soul to be turned by any sympathy to things of earth. And I prayed that I might find some one of the brethren who had chosen this way of life, that with him I might cross life's short [4] and troubled strait. And many did I find in Alexandria, and many in the rest of Egypt, and others in Palestine, and in Cœle Syria, and in Mesopotamia. I admired their continence in living, and their endurance in toil; I was amazed at their persistency in prayer, and at their triumphing over sleep; subdued by no natural necessity, ever keeping their souls' purpose high and free, in hunger, in thirst, in cold, in nakedness, [5] they never yielded to the body; they were never willing to waste attention on it; always, as though living in a flesh that was not theirs, they shewed in very deed what it is to sojourn for a while in this life, [6] and what to have one's citizenship and home in heaven. [7] All this moved my admiration. I called these men's lives blessed, in that they did in deed shew that they " bear about in their body the dying of Jesus." [8] And I prayed that I, too, as far as in me lay, might imitate them.

3. So when I beheld certain men in my own country striving to copy their ways, I felt that I had found a help to my own salvation,

and I took the things seen for proof of things unseen. And since the secrets in the hearts of each of us are unknown, I held lowliness of dress to be a sufficient indication of lowliness of spirit; and there was enough to convince me in the coarse cloak, the girdle, and the shoes of untanned hide. [1] And though many were for withdrawing me from their society, I would not allow it, because I saw that they put a life of endurance before a life of pleasure ; and, because of the extraordinary excellence of their lives, I became an eager supporter of them. And so it came about that I would not hear of any fault being found with their doctrines, although many maintained that their conceptions about God were erroneous, and that they had become disciples of the champion of the present heresy, and were secretly propagating his teaching. But, as I had never at any time heard these things with my own ears, I concluded that those who reported them were calumniators. Then I was called to preside over the Church. Of the watchmen and spies, who were given me under the pretence of assistance and loving communion, I say nothing, lest I seem to injure my own cause by telling an incredible tale, or give believers an occasion for hating their fellows, if I am believed. This had almost been my own case, had I not been prevented by the mercy of God. For almost every one became an object of suspicion to me, and smitten at heart as I was by wounds treacherously inflicted, I seemed to find nothing in any man that I could trust. But so far there was, nevertheless, a kind of intimacy kept up between us. Once and again we held discussions on doctrinal points, and apparently we seemed to agree and keep together. But they began to find out that I made the same statements concerning my faith in God which they had always heard from me. For, if other things in me may move a sigh, this one boast at least I dare make in the Lord, that never for one moment have I held erroneous conceptions about God, or entertained heterodox opinions, which I have learnt later to change. The teaching about God which I had received as a boy from my blessed mother and my grandmother Macrina, I have ever held with increased conviction. On my coming to ripe years of reason I did not shift my opinions from one to another, but carried out the

---

[1] Ps. cxxiv. 5, LXX.
[2] Ps. cxxiv. 3, 4, LXX.
[3] 1 Cor. ii. 6.
[4] Al. deep.
[5] 2 Cor. xi. 27.
[6] cf. Heb. xi. 13.
[7] cf. Phil. iii. 20.
[8] 2 Cor. iv. 10.

[1] With St. Basil's too great readiness to believe in Eustathius because of his mean garb contrast Augustine De Serm. Dom. " Animadvertendum est non in solo rerum corporearum nitore atque pompa, sed etiam in ipsis sordibus lutosis esse posse jactantiam, et eo periculosiorem quo sub nomine servitutis Dei decipit."

principles delivered to me by my parents. Just as the seed when it grows is first tiny and then gets bigger but always preserves its identity, not changed in kind though gradually perfected in growth, so I reckon the same doctrine to have grown in my case through gradually advancing stages. What I hold now has not replaced what I held at the beginning. Let them search their own consciences. Let these men who have now made me the common talk on the charge of false doctrine, and deafened all men's ears with the defamatory letters which they have written against me, so that I am compelled thus to defend myself, ask themselves if they have ever heard anything from me, differing from what I now say, and let them remember the judgment seat of Christ.

4. I am charged with blasphemy against God. Yet it is impossible for me to be convicted on the ground of any treatise concerning the Faith, which they urge against me, nor can I be charged on the ground of the utterances which I have from time to time delivered by word of mouth, without their being committed to writing, in the churches of God. Not a single witness has been found to say that he has ever heard from me, when speaking in private, anything contrary to true religion. If then I am not an unorthodox writer, if no fault can be found with my preaching, if I do not lead astray those who converse with me in my own home, on what ground am I being judged? But there is a new invention! Somebody,[1] runs the charge, in Syria has written something inconsistent with true religion; and twenty years or more ago you wrote him a letter: so you are an accomplice of the fellow, and what is urged against him is urged against you. O truth-loving sir, I reply, you who have been taught that lies are the offspring of the devil; what has proved to you that I wrote that letter? You never sent; you never asked; you were never informed by me, who might have told you the truth. But if the letter was mine, how do you know that the document that has come into your hands now is of the same date as my letter? Who told you that it is twenty years old? How do you know that it is a composition of the man to whom my letter was sent? And if he was the composer, and I wrote to him, and my letter and his composition belong to the same date, what proof is there that I accepted it in my judgment, and that I hold those views?

5. Ask yourself. How often did you visit me in my monastery on the Iris, when my very God-beloved brother Gregory was with me, following the same course of life as myself? Did you ever hear anything of the kind? Was there any appearance of such a thing, small or great? How many days did we spend in the opposite village, at my mother's, living as friend with friend, and discoursing together night and day? Did you ever find me holding any opinion of the kind? And when we went together to visit the blessed Silvanus,[1] did we not talk of these things on the way? And at Eusinoe,[2] when you were about to set out with other bishops for Lampsacus,[3] was not our discourse about the faith? Were not your shorthand writers at my side the whole time while I was dictating my objections to the heresy? Were not your most faithful disciples there too? When I was visiting the brotherhood, and passing the night with them in their prayers, continually speaking and hearing of the things pertaining to God without dispute, was not the evidence which I gave of my sentiments exact and definite? How came you then to reckon this rotten and slender suspicion as of more importance than the experience of such a length of time? What evidence of my frame of mind ought you to have preferred to your own? Has there been the slightest want of harmony in my utterances about the faith at Chalcedon, again and again at Heraclea, and at an earlier period in the suburb of Cæsarea? Are they not all mutually consistent? I only except the increase in force of which I spoke just now, resulting from advance, and which is not to be regarded as a change from worse to better, but rather as a filling up of what was wanting in the addition of knowledge. How can you fail to bear in mind that the father shall not bear the iniquity of the son, nor the son bear the iniquity of the father, but each shall die in his own sin?[4] I have neither father nor son slandered by you; I have had neither teacher nor disciple. But if the sins of the parents must be made charges against their children, it is far fairer for the sins of Arius to be charged against his disciples; and, whoever begat the heretic Aetius,[5] for the charges against the son to be applied to the father. If on the other

---

[1] *i.e.* Apollinarius. *cf. Letters* cxxx. p. 198, and ccxxiv.

[1] *i.e.* Silvanus of Tarsus. *cf. Letters* xxxiv. p. 136, and lxvii. p. 164.
[2] I have not been able to identify Eusinoe. There was an Eusene on the north coast of Pontus.
[3] *i.e.* in 364, the year after St. Basil's ordination as presbyter, and the publication of his work against Eunomius. The Council of Lampsacus, at which Basil was not present, repudiated the Creeds of Ariminum and Constantinople (359 and 360), and reasserted the 2d Dedication Creed of Antioch of 341. Maran dates it 361 (*Vit. Bas.* x.).
[4] *cf.* Ezek. xviii. 20.   [5] *cf.* p. 3, n.

hand it is unjust for any one to be accused for their sakes, it is far more unjust that I should be held responsible for the sake of men with whom I have nothing to do, even if they were in every respect sinners, and something worthy of condemnation has been written by them. I must be pardoned if I do not believe all that is urged against them, since my own experience shows me how very easy it is for accusers to slip into slander.

6. Even if they did come forward to accuse me, because they had been deceived, and thought that I was associated with the writers of those words of Sabellius which they are carrying about, they were guilty of unpardonable conduct in straightway attacking and wounding me, when I had done them no wrong, before they had obtained plain proof. I do not like to speak of myself as bound to them in the closest intimacy; or of them as being evidently not led by the Holy Spirit, because of their cherishing false suspicions. Much anxious thought must be taken, and many sleepless nights must be passed, and with many tears must the truth be sought from God, by him who is on the point of cutting himself off from a brother's friendship. Even the rulers of this world, when they are on the point of sentencing some evil doer to death, draw the veil aside,[1] and call in experts for the examination of the case, and consume considerable time in weighing the severity of the law against the common fault of humanity, and with many a sigh and many a lament for the stern necessity of the case, proclaim before all the people that they are obeying the law from necessity, and not passing sentence to gratify their own wishes.[2] How much greater care and diligence, how much more counsel, ought to be taken by one who is on the point of breaking off from long established friendship with a brother! In this case there is only a single letter and that of doubtful genuineness. It would be quite impossible to argue that it is known by the signature, for they possess not the original, but only a copy. They depend on one single document and that an old one. It is now

twenty years since anything has been written to that person.[1] Of my opinions and conduct in the intervening time I can adduce no better witnesses than the very men who attack and accuse me.

7. But the real reason of separation is not this letter. There is another cause of alienation. I am ashamed to mention it; and I would have been for ever silent about it had not recent events compelled me to publish all their mind for the sake of the good of the mass of the people. Good men have thought that communion with me was a bar to the recovery of their authority. Some have been influenced by the signature of a certain creed which I proposed to them, not that I distrusted their sentiments, I confess, but because I wished to do away with the suspicions which the more part of the brethren who agree with me entertained of them. Accordingly, to avoid anything arising from that confession to prevent their being accepted by the present authorities,[2] they have renounced communion with me. This letter was devised by an after-thought as a pretext for the separation. A very plain proof of what I say is, that after they had denounced me, and composed such complaints against me as suited them, they sent round their letters in all directions before communicating with me. Their letter was in the possession of others who had received it in the course of transmission and who were on the point of sending it on seven days before it had reached my hands. The idea was that it would be handed from one to another and so would be quickly distributed over the whole country. This was reported to me at the time by those who were giving me clear information of all their proceedings. But I determined to hold my tongue until the Revealer of all secrets should publish their doings by plain and incontrovertible demonstration.

LETTER CCXXIV.[3]

To the presbyter Genethlius.

1. I HAVE received your reverence's letter and I am delighted at the title which you have felicitously applied to the writing which they have composed in calling it " a writing of divorcement."[4] What defence the writers will be able to make before the

---

1 ἀφέλκονται. So the Harl. MS. for ἐφέλκονται. On the sense which may be applied to either verb cf. Valesius on Am. Marcellinus xviii. 2, whom the Ben. Ed. point out to be in error in thinking that Basil's idea is of drawing a curtain or veil over the proceedings, and Chrysostom Hom. lvi. in Matt. 'Επὶ τοῖς δικασταῖς, ὅταν δημοσίᾳ κρίνωσι, τὰ παραπετάσματα συνελκύσαντες οἱ παρεστῶτες πᾶσιν αὐτοὺς δεικνύουσι. This meaning of drawing so as to disclose is confirmed by Basil's πάνδημοι πᾶσι γίγνονται in this passage and in Hom. in Ps. xxxii.

2 The Ben. note compares the praise bestowed on Candidianus by Gregory of Nazianzus for trying cases in the light of day (Ep. cxciv.) and Am. Marcellinus xvii. 1, who says of Julian, Numerium Narconensis paulo ante rectorem, accusatum ut furem, insitato censorio vigore pro tribunali palam admissis volentibus audiebat.

1 i.e. Apollinarius.
2 Though this phrase commonly means the reigning emperor, as in Letter lxvi., the Ben. note has no doubt that in this instance the reference is to Euzoius. In Letter ccxxvi. § 3. q v., Basil mentions reconciliation with Euzoius as the real object of Eustathius's hostility. Euzoius was now in high favour with Valens.
3 Placed in 375. 4 Matt. xix. 7.

tribunal of Christ, where no excuse will avail, I am quite unable to conceive. After accusing me, violently running me down, and telling tales in accordance not with the truth but with what they wished to be true, they have assumed a great show of humility, and have accused me of haughtiness for refusing to receive their envoys. They have written, as they have, what is all — or nearly all — for I do not wish to exaggerate, — lies, in the endeavour to persuade men rather than God, and to please men rather than God, with Whom nothing is more precious than truth. Moreover into the letter written against me they have introduced heretical expressions, and have concealed the author of the impiety, in order that most of the more unsophisticated might be deceived by the calumny got up against me, and suppose the portion introduced to be mine. For nothing is said by my ingenious slanderers as to the name of the author of these vile doctrines, and it is left for the simple to suspect that these inventions, if not their expression in writing, is due to me. Now that you know all this, I exhort you not to be perturbed yourselves, and to calm the excitement of those who are agitated. I say this although I know that it will not be easy for my defence to be received, because I have been anticipated by the vile calumnies uttered against me by persons of influence.

2. Now as to the point that the writings going the round as mine are not mine at all, the angry feeling felt against me so confuses their reason that they cannot see what is profitable. Nevertheless, if the question were put to them by yourselves, I do think that they would not reach such a pitch of obstinate perversity as to dare to utter the lie with their own lips, and allege the document in question to be mine. And if it is not mine, why am I being judged for other men's writings? But they will urge that I am in communion with Apollinarius, and cherish in my heart perverse doctrines of this kind. Let them be asked for proof. If they are able to search into a man's heart, let them say so; and do you admit the truth of all that they say about everything. If on the other hand, they are trying to prove my being in communion on plain and open grounds, let them produce either a canonical letter written by me to him, or by him to me. Let them shew that I have held intercourse with his clergy, or have ever received any one of them into the communion of prayer. If they adduce the letter written now five and twenty years ago, written by

layman to layman, and not even this as I wrote it, but altered (God knows by whom), then recognise their unfairness. No bishop is accused if, while he was a layman, he wrote something somewhat incautiously on an indifferent matter; not anything concerning the Faith, but a mere word of friendly greeting. Possibly even my opponents are known to have written to Jews and to Pagans, without incurring any blame. Hitherto no one has ever been judged for any such conduct as that on which I am being condemned by these strainers-out of gnats.[1] God, who knows men's hearts, knows that I never wrote these things, nor sanctioned them, but that I anathematize all who hold the vile opinion of the confusion of the hypostases, on which point the most impious heresy of Sabellius has been revived. And all the brethren who have been personally acquainted with my insignificant self know it equally well. Let those very men who now vehemently accuse me, search their own consciences, and they will own that from my boyhood I have been far removed from any doctrine of the kind.

3. If any one enquires what my opinion is, he will learn it from the actual little document, to which is appended their own autograph signature. This they wish to destroy, and they are anxious to conceal their own change of position in slandering me. For they do not like to own that they have repented of their subscription to the tract I gave them; while they charge me with impiety from the idea that no one perceives that their disruption from me is only a pretext, while in reality they have departed from that faith which they have over and over again owned in writing, before many witnesses, and have lastly received and subscribed when delivered to them by me. It is open to any one to read the signatures and to learn the truth from the document itself. Their intention will be obvious, if, after reading the subscription which they gave me, any one reads the creed which they gave Gelasius,[2] and observes what a vast difference there is between the two confessions. It would be better for men who so easily shift their own position, not to examine other men's motes but to cast out the beam in their own eye.[3] I am making a more complete defence on every point in another letter;[4] this will satisfy readers who want fuller assurance. Do you, now that you have received this letter, put away all despondency, and confirm the love to me,[5]

1 cf. Matt. xxiii. 24. 3 cf. Matt. vii. 4. 5 cf. 2 Cor. ii. 8.
2 cf. Letter cxxx. p. 198. 4 i.e. Letter ccxxiii.

which makes me eagerly long for union with you. Verily it is a great sorrow to me, and a pain in my heart that cannot be assuaged, if the slanders uttered against me so far prevail as to chill your love and to alienate us from one another. Farewell.

LETTER CCXXV.[1]

To Demosthenes,[2] as from the synod of bishops.

I AM always very thankful to God and to the emperor, under whose rule we live, when I see the government of my country put into the hands of one who is not only a Christian, but is moreover correct in life and a careful guardian of the laws according to which our life in this world is ordered. I have had special reason for offering this gratitude to God and to our God-beloved emperor on the occasion of your coming among us. I have been aware that some of the enemies of peace have been about to stir your august tribunal against me, and have been waiting to be summoned by your excellency that you might learn the truth from me; if indeed your high wisdom condescends to consider the examination of ecclesiastical matters to be within your province.[3] The tribunal overlooked me, but your excellency, moved by the reproaches of Philochares, ordered my brother and fellow-minister Gregory to be haled before your judgment seat. He obeyed your summons; how could he do otherwise? But he was attacked by pain in the side, and at the same time, in consequence of a chill, was attacked by his old kidney complaint. He has therefore been compelled, forcibly detained by your soldiers as he was, to be conveyed to some quiet spot, where he could have his maladies attended to, and get some comfort in his intolerable agony. Under these circumstances we have combined to approach your lordship with the entreaty that you will feel no anger at the postponement of the trial. The public interests have not in any way suffered through our delay, nor have those of the

Church been injured. If there is any question of the wasteful expenditure of money, the treasurers of the Church funds are there, ready to give an account to any one who likes, and to exhibit the injustice of the charges advanced by men who have braved the careful hearing of the case before you. For they can have no difficulty in making the truth clear to any one who seeks it from the actual writings of the blessed bishop himself. If there is any other point of canonical order which requires investigation, and your excellency deigns to undertake to hear and to judge it, it will be necessary for us all to be present, because, if there has been a failure in any point of canonical order, the responsibility lies with the consecrators and not with him who is forcibly compelled to undertake the ministry. We therefore petition you to reserve the hearing of the case for us in our own country, and not to compel us to travel beyond its borders, nor force us to a meeting with bishops with whom we have not yet come to agreement on ecclesiastical questions.[1] I beg you also to be merciful to my own old age and ill health. You will learn by actual investigation, if it please God, that no canonical rule be it small or great was omitted in the appointment of the bishop. I pray that under your administration unity and peace may be brought about with my brethren; but so long as this does not exist it is difficult for us even to meet, because many of our simpler brethren suffer from our mutual disputes.

LETTER CCXXVI.[2]

To the ascetics under him.

IT may be that the holy God will grant me the joy of a meeting with you, for I am ever longing to see you and hear about you, because in no other thing do I find rest for my soul than in your progress and perfection in the commandments of Christ. But so long as this hope remains unrealized I feel bound to visit you through the instrumentality of our dear and God-fearing brethren, and to address you, my beloved friends, by letter. Wherefore I have sent my reverend and dear brother and fellow-worker in the Gospel, Meletius the presbyter. He will tell you my yearning affection for you, and the anxiety of my soul, in that,

---

[1] Placed in 375.
[2] Vicar of Pontus. It is doubtful whether he is the same Demosthenes who was at Cæsarea with Valens in 371, of whom the amusing story is told in Theodoret *Hist. Ecc.* iv. 16, on which see note. If he is, it is not difficult to understand his looking with no friendly eye on Basil and his brother Gregory. He summoned a synod to Ancyra in the close of 375 to examine into alleged irregularities in Gregory's consecration and accusations of embezzlement. The above letter is to apologize for Gregory's failing to put in an appearance at Ancyra, and to rebut the charges made against him. Tillemont would refer *Letter* xxxiii. to this period. Maran *Vit. Bas.* xii. 5 connects it with the troubles following on the death of Cæsarius in 369.
[3] "*Sæpe vicario Basilius in hac epistola leniter insinuat, res ecclesiasticas illius judicii non esse.*" Ben. note.

[1] From *Letter* ccxxxvii. it would appear that Demosthenes was now in Galatia, where he had summoned a heretical synod. The Ben. note quotes a law of Valens of the year 373 (*Cod. Theod.* ix. tit. i. 10): *Ultra provinciæ terminos accusandi licentia non progrediatur. Oportet enim illic criminum judicia agitari ubi facinus dicatur admissum. Peregrina autem judicia præsentibus legibus coercemus.*
[2] Placed in 375.

night and day, I beseech the Lord in your behalf, that I may have boldness in the day of our Lord Jesus Christ through your salvation, and that when your work is tried by the just judgment of God you may shine forth in the brightness of the saints. At the same time the difficulties of the day cause me deep anxiety, for all Churches have been tossed to and fro, and all souls are being sifted. Some have even opened their mouths without any reserve against their fellow servants. Lies are boldly uttered, and the truth has been hidden. The accused are being condemned without a trial, and the accusers are believed without evidence. I had heard that many letters are being carried about against myself, stinging, gibbeting, and attacking me for matters about which I have my defence ready for the tribunal of truth ; and I had intended to keep silence, as indeed I have done ; for now for three years I have been bearing the blows of calumny and the whips of accusation, content to think that I have the Lord, Who knows all secrets, as witness of its falsehood. But I see now that many men have taken my silence as a corroboration of these slanders, and have formed the idea that my silence was due, not to my longsuffering, but to my inability to open my lips in opposition to the truth. For these reasons I have attempted to write to you, beseeching your love in Christ not to accept these partial calumnies as true, because, as it is written, the law judges no man unless it have first heard and known his actions.[1]

2. Nevertheless before a fair judge the facts themselves are a sufficient demonstration of the truth. Wherefore, even if I be silent, you can look at events. The very men who are now indicting me for heterodoxy have been seen openly numbered with the heretical faction. The very accusers who condemn me for other men's writings, are plainly contravening their own confessions, given to me by them in writing. Look at the conduct of the exhibitors of this audacity. It is their invariable custom to go over to the party in power, to trample on their weaker friends, and to court the strong. The writers of those famous letters against Eudoxius and all his faction, the senders of them to all the brotherhood, the protesters that they shun their communion as fatal to souls, and would not accept the votes given for their deposition, because they were given by heretics, as they persuaded me then, — these very men, completely forgetful of all this, have joined

their faction.[1] No room for denial is left them. They laid their mind bare when they embraced private communion with them at Ancyra, when they had not yet been publicly received by them. Ask them, then, if Basilides, who gave communion to Ecdicius, is now orthodox, why when returning from Dardania, did they overthrow his altars in the territory of Gangra, and set up their own tables?[2] Why have they comparatively recently[3] attacked the churches of Amasea and Zela and appointed presbyters and deacons there themselves? If they communicate with them as orthodox, why do they attack them as heretical? If they hold them to be heretical. how is it that they do not shun communion with them? Is it not, my honourable brethren, plain even to the intelligence of a child, that it is always with a view to some personal advantage that they endeavour to calumniate or to give support? So they have stood off from me, not because I did not write in reply (which is alleged to be the main ground of offence), nor because I did not receive the chorepiscopi whom they assert they sent. Those who are trumping up the tale will render an account to the Lord. One man, Eustathius,[4] was sent and gave a letter to the court of the vicar, and spent three days in the city. When he was on the point of going home, it is said that he came to my house late in the evening, when I was asleep. On hearing that I was asleep, he went away ; he did not come near me on the next day, and after thus going through the mere form of discharging his duty to me, departed. This is the charge under which I am guilty. This is the sin against which these longsuffering people have neglected to weigh the previous service wherein I served them in love. For this error they have made their wrath against me so severe that they have caused me to be denounced in all the Churches throughout the world — at least, that is, wherever they could.

---

[1] The events referred to happened ten years before the date assigned for this letter, when the Semi-Arians summoned Eudoxius to Lampsacus, and sentenced him to deprivation in his absence. (Soc. H.E. iv. 2-4; Soz. H.E. vi. 7.) On the refusal of Valens to ratify the deposition and ultimate banishment of the Anti-Eudoxians, Eustathius went to Rome to seek communion with Liberius, subscribed the Nicene Confession, and received commendatory letters from Liberius to the Easterns. Soc. H.E. iv. 12. Eudoxius died in 370.

[2] On the action of Eustathius on this occasion, cf. Letter ccli. Basilides is described as a Paphlagonian. On Ecdicius, intruded by Demosthenes into the see of Parnassus, cf. Letter ccxxxvii.

[3] So the Ben. ed. for μέγοι νῦν, with the idea that the action of Eustathius in currying favour with the Catholics of Amasea and Zela by opposing the Arian bishops occupying those sees, must have taken place before he had quite broken with Basil. Tillemont (ix. 236) takes νῦν to mean 375. Amasea and Zela (in Migne erroneously Zeli. On the name, see Ramsay's Hist. Geog. Asia M. 260) are both on the Iris.

[4] A chorepiscopus; not of course to be confounded with Eustathius of Sebaste.

---

[1] cf. John vii. 51.

3. But of course this is not the real cause of our separation. It was when they found that they would recommend themselves to Euzoius [1] if they were alienated from me, that they devised these pretences. The object was to find some ground of recommendation with the authorities for their attack upon me. Now they are beginning to run down even the Nicene Creed, and nickname me *Homoousiast*, because in that creed the Only begotten Son is said to be *homoousios* with God the Father. Not that one essence is divided into two kindred parts; God forbid! This was not the meaning of that holy and God-beloved synod; their meaning was that what the Father is in essence, such is the Son. And thus they themselves have explained it to us, in the phrase *Light of Light*. Now it is the Nicene Creed, brought by themselves from the west, which they presented to the Synod at Tyana, by which they were received.[2] But they have an ingenious theory as to changes of this kind; they use the words of the creed as physicians use a remedy for the particular moment, and substitute now one and now another to suit particular diseases. The unsoundness of such a sophism it is rather for you to consider than for me to prove. For "the Lord will give you understanding"[3] to know what is the right doctrine, and what the crooked and perverse. If indeed we are to subscribe one creed to-day and another to-morrow, and shift with the seasons, then is the declaration false of him who said, "One Lord, one faith, one baptism."[4] But if it is true, then " Let no man deceive you with [these] vain words." They falsely accuse me of introducing novelties about the Holy Spirit. Ask what the novelty is. I confess what I have received, that the Paraclete is ranked with Father and Son, and not numbered with created beings. We have made profession of our faith in Father, Son, and Holy Ghost, and we are baptized in the name of Father, Son, and Holy Ghost. Wherefore we never separate the Spirit from conjunction [5] with the Father and the Son. For our mind, enlightened by the Spirit, looks at the Son, and in Him, as in an image, beholds the Father. And I do not invent names of myself, but call the Holy Ghost Paraclete; nor do I consent to destroy His due glory. These are truly my doctrines. If any one wishes to accuse me for them, let him accuse me; let my persecutor persecute me. Let him who believes in the slanders against me be ready for the judgment. " The Lord is at hand." " I am careful for nothing." [1]

4. If any one in Syria is writing, this is nothing to me. For it is said " By thy words thou shalt be justified, and by thy words thou shalt be condemned." [2] Let my own words judge me. Let no one condemn me for other men's errors, nor adduce letters written twenty years ago in proof that I would allow communion to the writers of such things. Before these things were written, and before any suspicion of this kind had been stirred against them, I did write as layman to layman. I wrote nothing about the faith in any way like that which they are now carrying about to calumniate me. I sent nothing but a mere greeting to return a friendly communication, for I shun and anathematize as impious alike all who are affected with the unsoundness of Sabellius, and all who maintain the opinions of Arius. If any one says that Father, Son, and Holy Ghost are the same, and supposes one thing under several names, and one hypostasis described by three persons, I rank such an one as belonging to the faction of the Jews.[3] Similarly, if any one says that the Son is in essence unlike the Father, or degrades the Holy Ghost into a creature, I anathematize him, and say that he is coming near to the heathen error. But it is impossible for the mouths of my accusers to be restrained by my letter; rather is it likely that they are being irritated at my defence, and are getting up new and more violent attacks against me. But it is not difficult for your ears to be guarded. Wherefore, as far as in you lies, do as I bid you. Keep your heart clear and unprejudiced by their calumnies; and insist on my rendering an account to meet the charges laid against me. If you find that truth is on my side do not yield to lies; if on the other hand you feel that I am feeble in defending myself, then believe my accusers as being worthy of credit. They pass sleepless nights to do me mischief. I do not ask this of you. They are taking to a commercial career, and turning their slanders against me into a means of profit. I implore you on the other hand to stop at home, and to lead a decorous life, quietly doing Christ's work.[4] I advise you to avoid communication with them, for it always tends to the perversion of their hearers. I say this that you may keep your affection for me uncontaminated, may preserve the faith of the Fathers in its integrity, and may appear approved before the Lord as friends of the truth.

---

1 *cf.* note on p. 265.
2 *i.e.* after their return from Rome, and another Synod in Sicily, in 367.
3 2 Tim. ii. 7.   4 Eph. iv. 5.
5 συνάφεια. *cf.* note on p. 16.

1 Phil. iv. 5 and 6.   3 *cf. Letter* ccx. p. 249.
2 Matt. xii. 37.   4 *cf.* 1 Thess. iv. 11.

LETTER CCXXVII.[1]

Consolatory, to the clergy of Colonia.[2]

WHAT is so goodly and honourable before God and men as perfect love, which, as we are told by the wise teacher, is the fulfilling of the law?[3] I therefore approve of your warm affection for your bishop, for, as to an affectionate son the loss of a good father is unendurable, so Christ's Church cannot bear the departure of a pastor and teacher. Thus, in your exceeding affection for your bishop, you are giving proof of a good and noble disposition. But this your good will towards your spiritual father is to be approved so long as it is shewn in reason and moderation; once let it begin to overstep this line, and it is no longer deserving of the same commendation. In the case of your very God-beloved brother, our fellow-minister Euphronius, good government has been shewn by those to whom has been committed the administration of the Church; they have acted as the occasion compelled them, to the gain alike of the Church to which he has been removed and of yourselves from whom he has been taken. Do not look at this as merely of man's ordaining, nor as having been originated by the calculations of men who regard earthly things. Believe that those to whom the anxious care of the Churches belongs have acted, as they have, with the aid of the Holy Spirit; impress this inception of the proceedings on your hearts and do your best to perfect it. Accept quietly and thankfully what has happened, with the conviction that all, who refuse to accept what is ordered in God's Churches by the Churches, are resisting the ordinance of God.[4] Do not enter into a dispute with your Mother Church at Nicopolis. Do not exasperate yourselves against those who have taken the anxious responsibility of your souls. In the firm establishment of things at Nicopolis your part in them may also be preserved; but if some disturbance affects them, though you have protectors beyond number, with the head the heart will be destroyed. It is like men who live on the riverside; when they see some one far up the stream making a strong dam against the current, they know that, in stopping the inrush of the current, he is providing for their safety. Just so those who have now undertaken the weight of the care of the Churches, by protecting the rest, are

providing for your own security. You will be sheltered from every storm, while others have to bear the brunt of the attack. But you ought also to consider this; he has not cast you off; he has taken others into his charge. I am not so invidious as to compel the man, who is able to give a share of his good gifts to others, also to confine his favour to you, and to limit it to your own city. A man who puts a fence round a spring, and spoils the outpour of the waters, is not free from the disease of envy, and it is just the same with him who tries to prevent the further flow of abundant teaching. Let him have some care for Nicopolis too, and let your interests be added to his anxieties there. He has received an addition of labour, but there is no diminution in his diligence on your behalf. I am really distressed at one thing that you have said, which seems to me quite extravagant, namely, that if you cannot obtain your object, you will betake yourselves to the tribunals, and put the matter into the hands of men, the great object of whose prayers is the overthrow of the Churches. Take heed lest men, carried away by unwise passions, persuade you, to your hurt, to put in any plea before the courts, and so some catastrophe may ensue, and the weight of the result fall upon the heads of those who have occasioned it. Take my advice. It is offered you in a fatherly spirit. Consent to the arrangement with the very God-beloved bishops, which has been made in accordance with God's will. Wait for my arrival. When I am with you, with God's help, I will give you in person all the exhortations which it has been impossible for me to express in my letter, and will do my utmost to give you all possible consolation, not by word but in deed.

LETTER CCXXVIII.[1]

To the magistrates of Colonia.

I HAVE received your lordships' letter, and offered thanks to God most holy, that you, occupied as you are with affairs of state, should not put those of the Church in the second place. I am grateful to think that every one of you has shewn anxiety as though he were acting in his own private interest, nay, in defence of his own life, and that you have written to me in your distress at the removal of your very God-beloved bishop Euphronius. Nicopolis has not really stolen him from you; were she pleading her cause before

---

[1] Placed in 375.
[2] *i.e.* in Armenia. *cf. Letter* cxcv. p. 234. The removal of Euphronius to Nicopolis was occasioned by the death of Theodotus and the consecration of Fronto by the Eustathians, to whom the orthodox Colonians would not submit.
[3] Rom. xiii. 10.   [4] *cf.* Rom. xiii. 2.

[1] Of the same date as the preceding.

a judge she might say that she was recovering what is her own. If honourably treated she will tell you, as becomes an affectionate mother, that she will share with you the Father who will give a portion of his grace to each of you: he will not suffer the one to be in any way harmed by the invasion of their adversaries, and at the same time will not deprive you, the other, of the care to which you have been accustomed. Bethink you then of the emergency of the time; apply your best intelligence to understand how good government necessitates a certain course of action; and then pardon the bishops who have adopted this course for the establishment of the Churches of our Lord Jesus Christ. Suggest to yourselves what is becoming you. Your own intelligence needs no instruction. You know how to adopt the counsels of those who love you. It is only natural that you should be unaware of many of the questions that are being agitated, because of your being situated far away in Armenia; but we who are in the midst of affairs and have our ears dinned every day on all sides with news of Churches that are being overthrown, are in deep anxiety lest the common enemy, in envy at the protracted peace of our life, should be able to sow his tares in your ground too, and Armenia, as well as other places, be given over to our adversaries to devour. For the present be still, as not refusing to allow your neighbours to share with you the use of a goodly vessel. Ere long, if the Lord allow me to come to you, you shall, if it seem necessary to you, receive yet greater consolation for what has come to pass.

LETTER CCXXIX.[1]

To the clergy of Nicopolis.

1. I AM sure that a work done by one or two pious men is not done without the coöperation of the Holy Spirit. For when nothing merely human is put before us, when holy men are moved to action with no thought of their own personal gratification, and with the sole object of pleasing God, it is plain that it is the Lord Who is directing their hearts. When spiritually-minded men take the lead in counsel, and the Lord's people follow them with consentient hearts, there can be no doubt that their decisions are arrived at with the participation of our Lord Jesus Christ, Who poured out His blood for the Churches' sake. You are therefore right in supposing that our very God-beloved brother

and fellow minister Pœmenius,[1] who arrived among you at an opportune moment, and discovered this means of consoling you, has been divinely moved. I not only praise his discovery of the right course to take; I much admire the firmness with which, without allowing any delay to intervene, so as to slacken the energy of the petitioners, or to give the opposite party an opportunity of taking precautions, and to set in motion the counterplots of secret foes, he at once crowned his happy course with a successful conclusion. The Lord of His especial grace keep him and his, so that the Church, as becomes her, may remain in a succession in no way degenerate, and not give place to the evil one, who now, if ever, is vexed at the firm establishment of the Churches.

2. I have also written at length to exhort our brethren at Colonia. You, moreover, are bound rather to put up with their frame of mind than to increase their irritation, as though you despised them for their insignificance, or provoked them to a quarrel by your contempt. It is only natural for disputants to act without due counsel, and to manage their own affairs ill with the object of vexing their opponents. And no one is so small as not to be now able to give an occasion, to those who want an occasion, for great troubles. I do not speak at random. I speak from my own experience of my own troubles. From these may God keep you in answer to your prayers. Pray also for me, that I may have a successful journey, and, on my arrival, may share your joy in your present pastor, and with you may find consolation at the departure of our common father.[2]

LETTER CCXXX.[3]

To the magistrates of Nicopolis.

THE government of the Churches is carried on by those to whom the chief offices in them have been entrusted, but their hands are strengthened by the laity. The measures which lay with the God-beloved bishops have been taken. The rest concerns you, if you deign to accord a hearty reception to the bishop who has been given you, and to make a vigorous resistance to attacks from outside. For nothing is so likely to cause discouragement to all, whether rulers or the rest who envy your peaceful position, as agreement in affection to the appointed bishop, and firmness in maintaining your ground. They are

---

[1] On Pœmenius, bishop of Satala in Armenia, cf. p. 185.
[2] i.e. Theodotus. cf. Letter cxxi. and cxxx. pp. 193 and 198.
[3] Of the same date as the preceding.

likely to despair of every evil attempt, if they see that their counsels are accepted neither by clergy nor by laity. Bring it about then that your own sentiments as to the right[1] may be shared by all the city, and so speak to the citizens, and to all the inhabitants of the district, in confirmation of their good sentiments, that the genuineness of your love to God may be everywhere known. I trust that it may be permitted me one day to visit and inspect a Church which is the nursing mother of true religion, honoured by me as a metropolis of orthodoxy, because it has from of old been under the government of men right honourable and the elect of God, who have held fast to " the faithful word as we have been taught."[2] You have approved him who has just been appointed as worthy of these predecessors, and I have agreed. May you be preserved by God's grace. May He scatter the evil counsels of your enemies, and fix in your souls strength and constancy to preserve what has been rightly determined on.

LETTER CCXXXI.[3]

To Amphilochius, bishop of Iconium.

I FIND few opportunities of writing to your reverence, and this causes me no little trouble. It is just the same as if, when it was in my power to see you and enjoy your society very often, I did so but seldom. But it is impossible for me to write to you because so few travel hence to you, otherwise there is no reason why my letter should not be a kind of journal of my life, to tell you, my dear friend, everything that happens to me day by day. It is a comfort to me to tell you my affairs, and I know that you care for nothing more than for what concerns me. Now, however, Elpidius[4] is going home to his own master, to refute the calumnies falsely got up against him by certain enemies, and he has asked me for a letter. I therefore salute your reverence by him and commend to you a man who deserves your protection, at once for the sake of justice and for my own sake. Although I could say nothing else in his favour, yet, because he has made it of very great importance to be the bearer of my letter, reckon him among our friends, and remember me and pray for the Church.

You must know that my very God-beloved brother is in exile, for he could not endure the annoyance caused him by shameless per-

sons.[1] Doara[2] is in a state of agitation, for the fat sea monster[3] is throwing everything into confusion. My enemies, as I am informed by those who know, are plotting against me at court. But hitherto the hand of the Lord has been over me. Only pray that I be not abandoned in the end. My brother is taking things quietly. Doara has received the old muleteer.[4] She can do no more. The Lord will scatter the counsels of my enemies. The one cure for all my troubles present and to come is to set eyes on you. If you possibly can, while I am still alive, do come to see me. The book on the Spirit has been written by me, and is finished, as you know. My brethren here have prevented me from sending it to you written on paper, and have told me that they had your excellency's orders to engross it on parchment.[5] Not, then, to appear to do anything against your injunctions, I have delayed now, but I will send it a little later, if only I find any suitable person to convey it. May you be granted to me and to God's Church by the kindness of the Holy One, in all health and happiness, and praying for me to the Lord.

LETTER CCXXXII.[6]

To Amphilochius, bishop of Iconium.

EVERY day that brings me a letter from you is a feast day, the very greatest of feast days. And when symbols of the feast are brought, what can I call it but a feast of feasts, as the old law used to speak of Sabbath of Sabbaths? I thank the Lord that you are quite well, and that you have celebrated the commemoration of the œconomy of salvation[7] in a Church at peace. I have been disturbed by some troubles; and have not been without distress from the fact of my God-beloved brother being in exile. Pray for him that God may one day grant him to see his Church healed from the wounds of

---

[1] τοῦ καλοῦ, or "the good man:" i.e. Euphronius.
[2] Tit. i. 9. cf. 1 Tim. i. 15; 1 Tim. iii. 1; 2 Tim. ii. 11; and Tit. iii. 8.   [3] Placed in 375.
[4] It is doubtful whether this Elpidius is to be identified with any other of the same name mentioned in the letters.

[1] On the withdrawal of Gregory of Nyssa, cf. note, p. 267.
[2] Doara was one of the bishoprics in Cappadocia Secunda under Tyana; now Hadji Bektash. Ramsay, Hist. Geog. Asia Minor, p. 287.
[3] i.e. Demosthenes. Such language may seem inconsistent with the tone of Letter ccxxv., but that, it will be remembered, was an official and formal document, while the present letter is addressed to an intimate friend.
[4] Possibly another hit at Demosthenes. The name might be thought to fit Anthimus, but with him Basil had made peace. cf. Letter ccx.
[5] ἐν σωματίῳ, i.e. in a volume, not on leaves of papyrus, but in book form, as e.g. the Cod. Alexandrinus in the B.M.
[6] Placed in 376. Maran, Vit. Bas. xxxv., thinks that this letter is to be placed either in the last days of 375, if the Nativity was celebrated on December 25, or in the beginning of 376, if it followed after the Epiphany. The Oriental usage, up to the end of the fourth century, was to celebrate the Nativity and Baptism on January 6. St. Chrysostom, in the homily on the birthday of our Saviour, delivered c. 386, speaks of the separation of the celebration of the Nativity from that of the Epiphany as comparatively recent. cf. D.C.A., 1, pp. 361, 617.   [7] i.e. the incarnation. cf. pp. 7 and 12, n.

heretical bites. Do come to see me while I am yet upon this earth. Act in accordance with your own wishes and with my most earnest prayers. I may be allowed to be astonished at the meaning of your blessings, inasmuch as you have mysteriously wished me a vigorous old age. By your lamps [1] you rouse me to nightly toil; and by your sweet meats you seem to pledge yourself securely that all my body is in good case. But there is no munching for me at my time of life, for my teeth have long ago been worn away by time and bad health. As to what you have asked me there are some replies in the document I send you, written to the best of my ability, and as opportunity has allowed.

LETTER CCXXXIII.

To Amphilochius, in reply to certain questions.

1. I KNOW that I have myself heard of this, and I am aware of the constitution of mankind. What shall I say? The mind is a wonderful thing, and therein we possess that which is after the image of the Creator. And the operation of the mind is wonderful; in that, in its perpetual motion, it frequently forms imaginations about things non-existent as though they were existent, and is frequently carried straight to the truth. But there are in it two faculties; in accordance with the view of us who believe in God, the one evil, that of the dæmons which draws us on to their own apostasy; and the divine and the good, which brings us to the likeness of God. When, therefore, the mind remains alone and unaided, it contemplates small things, commensurate with itself. When it yields to those who deceive it, it nullifies its proper judgment, and is concerned with monstrous fancies. Then it considers wood to be no longer wood, but a god; then it looks on gold no longer as money, but as an object of worship.[3] If on the other hand it assents to its diviner part, and accepts the boons of the Spirit. then, so far as its nature admits, it becomes perceptive of the divine. There are, as it were, three conditions of life, and three operations of the mind. Our ways may be wicked, and the movements of our mind wicked; such as adulteries, thefts,

idolatries, slanders, strife, passion, sedition, vain-glory, and all that the apostle Paul enumerates among the works of the flesh.[1] Or the soul's operation is, as it were, in a mean, and has nothing about it either damnable or laudable, as the perception of such mechanical crafts as we commonly speak of as indifferent, and, of their own character, inclining neither towards virtue nor towards vice. For what vice is there in the craft of the helmsman or the physician? Neither are these operations in themselves virtues, but they incline in one direction or the other in accordance with the will of those who use them. But the mind which is impregnated with the Godhead of the Spirit is at once capable of viewing great objects; it beholds the divine beauty, though only so far as grace imparts and its nature receives.

2. Let them dismiss, therefore, these questions of dialectics and examine the truth, not with mischievous exactness but with reverence. The judgment of our mind is given us for the understanding of the truth. Now our God is the very truth.[2] So the primary function of our mind is to know one God, but to know Him so far as the infinitely great can be known by the very small. When our eyes are first brought to the perception of visible objects, all visible objects are not at once brought into sight. The hemisphere of heaven is not beheld with one glance, but we are surrounded by a certain appearance, though in reality many things, not to say all things, in it are unperceived; — the nature of the stars, their greatness, their distances, their movements, their conjunctions, their intervals, their other conditions, the actual essence of the firmament, the distance of depth from the concave circumference to the convex surface. Nevertheless, no one would allege the heaven to be invisible because of what is unknown; it would be said to be visible on account of our limited perception of it. It is just the same in the case of God. If the mind has been injured by devils it will be guilty of idolatry, or will be perverted to some other form of impiety. But if it has yielded to the aid of the Spirit, it will have understanding of the truth, and will know God. But it will know Him, as the Apostle says, in part; and in the life to come more perfectly. For "when that which is perfect is come, then that which is in part shall be done away." [3] The judgment of the mind is, therefore, good and given us for a good end—the perception of God; but it operates only so far as it can.

[1] The reading of the Ben. ed. is λαμπηνῶν The only meaning of λαμπήνη in Class. Greek is a kind of *covered carriage*, and the cognate adj. λαμπηνικος is used for the *covered* waggons of Numb. vii. 3 in the LXX. But the context necessitates some such meaning as *lamp* or candle. Ducange *s.v.* quotes John de Janua "*Lampenæ sunt stellæ fulgentes.*" *cf.* Italian *Lampana, i.e.* lamp.
[2] Placed in 376.
[3] St. Basil's words may point either at the worshippers of a golden image in a shrine in the ordinary sense, or at the state of things where, as A. H. Clough has it, "no golden images may be worshipped except the currency."

[1] *cf.* Gal. v. 19, 20, 21.   [3] 1 Cor. xiii. 10.
[2] ἡ αὐτοαλήθεια.

LETTER CCXXXIV.[1]

To the same, in answer to another question.

Do you worship what you know or what you do not know? If I answer, I worship what I know, they immediately reply, What is the essence of the object of worship? Then, if I confess that I am ignorant of the essence, they turn on me again and say, So you worship you know not what. I answer that the word *to know* has many meanings. We say that we know the greatness of God, His power, His wisdom, His goodness, His providence over us, and the justness of His judgment; but not His very essence. The question is, therefore, only put for the sake of dispute. For he who denies that he knows the essence does not confess himself to be ignorant of God, because our idea of God is gathered from all the attributes which I have enumerated. But God, he says, is simple, and whatever attribute of Him you have reckoned as knowable is of His essence. But the absurdities involved in this sophism are innumerable. When all these high attributes have been enumerated, are they all names of one essence? And is there the same mutual force in His awfulness and His loving-kindness, His justice and His creative power, His providence and His foreknowledge, and His bestowal of rewards and punishments, His majesty and His providence? In mentioning any one of these do we declare His essence? If they say, yes, let them not ask if we know the essence of God, but let them enquire of us whether we know God to be awful, or just, or merciful. These we confess that we know. If they say that essence is something distinct, let them not put us in the wrong on the score of simplicity. For they confess themselves that there is a distinction between the essence and each one of the attributes enumerated. The operations are various, and the essence simple, but we say that we know our God from His operations, but do not undertake to approach near to His essence. His operations come down to us, but His essence remains beyond our reach.

2. But, it is replied, if you are ignorant of the essence, you are ignorant of Himself. Retort, If you say that you know His essence, you are ignorant of Himself. A man who has been bitten by a mad dog, and sees a dog in a dish, does not really see any more than is seen by people in good health; he is to be pitied because he thinks he sees what he does not see. Do not then

admire him for his announcement, but pity him for his insanity. Recognise that the voice is the voice of mockers, when they say, if you are ignorant of the essence of God, you worship what you do not know. I do know that He exists; what His essence is, I look at as beyond intelligence. How then am I saved? Through faith. It is faith sufficient to know that God exists, without knowing what He is; and "He is a rewarder of them that seek Him."[1] So knowledge of the divine essence involves perception of His incomprehensibility, and the object of our worship is not that of which we comprehend the essence, but of which we comprehend that the essence exists.

3. And the following counter question may also be put to them. "No man hath seen God at any time, the Only-begotten which is in the bosom of the Father he hath declared him."[2] What of the Father did the Only-begotten Son declare? His essence or His power? If His power, we know so much as He declared to us. If His essence, tell me where He said that His essence was the being unbegotten?[3] When did Abraham worship? Was it not when he believed? And when did he believe? Was it not when he was called? Where in this place is there any testimony in Scripture to Abraham's comprehending? When did the disciples worship Him? Was it not when they saw creation subject to Him? It was from the obedience of sea and winds to Him that they recognised His Godhead. Therefore the knowledge came from the operations, and the worship from the knowledge. "Believest thou that I am able to do this?" "I believe, Lord;"[4] and he worshipped Him. So worship follows faith, and faith is confirmed by power. But if you say that the believer also knows, he knows from what he believes; and *vice versa* he believes from what he knows. We know God from His power. We, therefore, believe in Him who is known, and we worship Him who is believed in.

LETTER CCXXXV.[5]

To the same, in answer to another question.

1. WHICH is first in order, knowledge or faith? I reply that generally, in the case of disciples, faith precedes knowledge. But, in our teaching, if any one asserts knowledge to come before faith, I make no objec-

[1] Heb. xi. 6.
[2] John i. 18.
[3] ἀγεννησία. *cf.* Prolegomena on the Books against Eunomius, and p. 39 n.
[4] *cf.* Matt. ix. 28.   [5] Placed in 376.

tion; understanding knowledge so far as is within the bounds of human comprehension. In our lessons we must first believe that the letter *a* is said to us; then we learn the characters and their pronunciation, and last of all we get the distinct idea of the force of the letter. But in our belief about God, first comes the idea that God is. This we gather from His works. For, as we perceive His wisdom, His goodness, and all His invisible things from the creation of the world,[1] so we know Him. So, too, we accept Him as our Lord. For since God is the Creator of the whole world, and we are a part of the world, God is our Creator. This knowledge is followed by faith, and this faith by worship.

2. But the word knowledge has many meanings, and so those who make sport of simpler minds, and like to make themselves remarkable by astounding statements (just like jugglers who get the balls out of sight before men's very eyes), hastily included everything in their general enquiry. Knowledge, I say, has a very wide application, and knowledge may be got of what a thing is, by number, by bulk, by force, by its mode of existence, by the period of its generation, by its essence. When then our opponents include the whole in their question, if they catch us in the confession that we know, they straightway demand from us knowledge of the essence; if, on the contrary, they see us cautious as to making any assertion on the subject, they affix on us the stigma of impiety. I, however, confess that I know what is knowable of God, and that I know what it is which is beyond my comprehension.[2] So if you ask me if I know what sand is, and I reply that I do, you will obviously be slandering me, if you straightway ask me the number of the sand; inasmuch as your first enquiry bore only on the form of sand, while your second unfair objection bore upon its number. The quibble is just as though any one were to say, Do you know Timothy? Oh, if you know Timothy you know his nature. Since you have acknowledged that you know Timothy, give me an account of Timothy's nature. Yes; but I at the same time both know and do not know Timothy, though not in the same way and in the same degree. It is not that I do not know in the same way in which I do know; but I know in one way and am ignorant in one way. I know him according to his form and other properties; but I am ignorant

of his essence. Indeed, in this way too, I both know, and am ignorant of, myself. I know indeed who I am, but, so far as I am ignorant of my essence I do not know myself.

3. Let them tell me in what sense Paul says, "Now we know in part";[1] do we know His essence in part, as knowing parts of His essence? No. This is absurd; for God is without parts. But do we know the whole essence? How then "When that which is perfect is come, then that which is in part shall be done away."[2] Why are idolaters found fault with? Is it not because they knew God and did not honour Him as God? Why are the "foolish Galatians"[3] reproached by Paul in the words, "After that ye have known God, or rather are known of God, how turn ye again to the weak and beggarly elements?"[4] How was God known in Jewry? Was it because in Jewry it was known what His essence is? "The ox," it is said, "knoweth his owner."[5] According to your argument the ox knows his lord's essence. "And the ass his master's crib."[6] So the ass knows the essence of the crib, but "Israel doth not know me." So, according to you, Israel is found fault with for not knowing what the essence of God is. "Pour out thy wrath upon the heathen that have not known thee,"[7] that is, who have not comprehended thy essence. But, I repeat, knowledge is manifold — it involves perception of our Creator, recognition of His wonderful works, observance of His commandments and intimate communion with Him. All this they thrust on one side and force knowledge into one single meaning, the contemplation of God's essence. Thou shalt put them, it is said, before the testimony and I shall be known of thee thence.[8] Is the term, "I shall be known of thee," instead of, "I will reveal my essence"? "The Lord knoweth them that are his."[9] Does He know the essence of them that are His, but is ignorant of the essence of those who disobey Him? "Adam knew his wife."[10] Did he know her essence? It is said of Rebekah "She was a virgin, neither had any man known her,"[11] and "How shall this be seeing I know not a man?"[12] Did no man know Rebekah's essence? Does Mary mean "I do not know the essence of any man"? Is it not the custom of Scripture to use the word "know" of nuptial embraces? The statement that God shall be

---

[1] cf. Rom. i. 20.
[2] A various reading gives the sense "but do not know what is beyond my comprehension."

[1] 1 Cor. xiii. 9.
[2] 1 Cor. xiii. 10.
[3] Gal. iii. 1.
[4] Gal. iv. 9.
[5] Is. i. 3.
[6] Is. i. 3.
[7] Ps. lxxix. 6.
[8] Referred by the Ben. Ed. to Ex. xxv. 21 and 22. The first clause is apparently introduced from Ex. xvi. 34.
[9] 2 Tim. ii. 19.
[10] Gen. iv. 1.
[11] Gen. xxiv. 16.
[12] Luke i. 34.

known from the mercy seat means that He will be known to His worshippers. And the Lord knoweth them that are His, means that on account of their good works He receives them into intimate communion with Him.

LETTER CCXXXVI.[1]

To the same Amphilochius.

1. ENQUIRY has already frequently been made concerning the saying of the gospels as to our Lord Jesus Christ's ignorance of the day and of the hour of the end;[2] an objection constantly put forward by the Anomœans to the destruction of the glory of the Only-Begotten, in order to show Him to be unlike in essence and subordinate in dignity; inasmuch as, if He know not all things, He cannot possess the same nature nor be regarded as of one likeness with Him, who by His own prescience and faculty of forecasting the future has knowledge coextensive with the universe. This question has now been proposed to me by your intelligence as a new one. I can give in reply the answer which I heard from our fathers when I was a boy, and which on account of my love for what is good, I have received without question. I do not expect that it can undo the shamelessness of them that fight against Christ, for where is the reasoning strong enough to stand their attack? It may, however, suffice to convince all that love the Lord, and in whom the previous assurance supplied them by faith is stronger than any demonstration of reason.

Now "no man" seems to be a general expression, so that not even one person is excepted by it, but this is not its use in Scripture, as I have observed in the passage "there is none good but one, that is, God."[3] For even in this passage the Son does not so speak to the exclusion of Himself from the good nature. But, since the Father is the first good, we believe the words "no man" to have been uttered with the understood addition of "first."[4] So with the passage "No man knoweth the Son but the Father;"[5] even here there is no charge of ignorance against the Spirit, but only a testimony that knowledge of His own nature naturally belongs to the Father first. Thus also we understand

"No man knoweth,"[1] to refer to the Father the first knowledge of things, both present and to be, and generally to exhibit to men the first cause. Otherwise how can this passage fall in with the rest of the evidence of Scripture, or agree with the common notions of us who believe that the Only-Begotten is the image of the invisible God, and image not of the bodily figure, but of the very Godhead and of the mighty qualities attributed to the essence of God, image of power, image of wisdom, as Christ is called "the power of God and the wisdom of God"?[2] Now of wisdom knowledge is plainly a part; and if in any part He falls short, He is not an image of the whole; and how can we understand the Father not to have shewn that day and that hour — the smallest portion of the ages — to Him through Whom He made the ages? How can the Creator of the universe fall short of the knowledge of the smallest portion of the things created by Him? How can He who says, when the end is near, that such and such signs shall appear in heaven and in earth, be ignorant of the end itself? When He says, "The end is not yet."[3] He makes a definite statement, as though with knowledge and not in doubt. Then further, it is plain to the fair enquirer that our Lord says many things to men, in the character of man; as for instance, "give me to drink"[4] is a saying of our Lord, expressive of His bodily necessity; and yet the asker was not soulless flesh, but Godhead using flesh endued with soul.[5] So in the present instance no one will be carried beyond the bounds of the interpretation of true religion, who understands the ignorance of him who had received all things according to the œconomy,[6] and was advancing with God and man in favour and wisdom.[7]

2. It would be worthy of your diligence to set the phrases of the Gospel side by side, and compare together those of Matthew and those of Mark, for these two alone are found in concurrence in this passage. The wording of Matthew is "of that day and hour knoweth no man, no, not the angels of heaven, but my Father only."[8] That of Mark runs, "But of that day and that hour knoweth no man, no, not the angels which are in heaven, neither the Son, but the

---

[1] This letter is also dated in 376, and treats of further subjects not immediately raised by the *De Spiritu Sancto*: How Christ can be said to be ignorant of the day and the hour; Of the prediction of Jeremiah concerning Jeconiah; Of an objection of the Encratites; Of fate; Of emerging in baptism; Of the accentuation of the word φάγος; Of essence and hypostasis; Of the ordaining of things neutral and indifferent.
[2] Mark xiii. 32.
[3] Mark x. 18. *i.e.* in *Adv. Eunom.* iv. *vide* Proleg.
[4] The manuscripts at this point are corrupt and divergent.
[5] Matt. xi. 27.

[1] Matt. xxiv. 36.   [3] Matt. xxiv. 6.
[2] 1 Cor. i. 24.   [4] John iv. 7.
[5] *cf. Ep.* cclxi. 2. The reference is to the system of Apollinarius, which denied to the Son a ψυχὴ λογική or reasonable soul.
[6] οἰκονομικῶς, *i.e.* according to the œconomy of the incarnation. *cf.* note on p. 7.   [7] *cf.* Luke ii. 52.
[8] Matt. xxiv. 36. R.V. in this passage inserts "Neither the Son," on the authority of ℵ, *B.D.* Plainly St. Basil knew no such difference of reading. On the general view taken by the Fathers on the self-limitation of the Saviour, *cf.* C. Gore's *Bampton Lectures* (vi. p. 163, and notes 48 and 49, p. 267).

Father." [1] What is noticeable in these passages is this; that Matthew says nothing about the ignorance of the Son, and seems to agree with Mark as to sense in saying " but my Father only." Now I understand the word " only " to have been used in contradistinction to the angels, but that the Son is not included with His own servants in ignorance.

He could not say what is false Who said, " All things that the Father hath are Mine," [2] but one of the things which the Father hath is knowledge of that day and of that hour. In the passage in Matthew, then, the Lord made no mention of His own Person, as a matter beyond controversy, and said that the angels knew not and that His Father alone knew, tacitly asserting the knowledge of His Father to be His own knowledge too, because of what He had said elsewhere, " as the Father knoweth me even so know I the Father," [3] and if the Father has complete knowledge of the Son, nothing excepted, so that He knows all knowledge to dwell in Him, He will clearly be known as fully by the Son with all His inherent wisdom and all His knowledge of things to come. This modification, I think, may be given to the. words of Matthew, " but my Father only." Now as to the words of Mark, who appears distinctly to exclude the Son from the knowledge, my opinion is this. No man knoweth, neither the angels of God ; nor yet the Son would have known unless the Father had known : that is, the cause of the Son's knowing comes from the Father. To a fair hearer there is no violence in this interpretation, because the word " only " is not added as it is in Matthew. Mark's sense, then, is as follows : of that day and of that hour knoweth no man, nor the angels of God ; but even the Son would not have known if the Father had not known, for the knowledge naturally His was given by the Father. This is very decorous and becoming the divine nature to say of the Son, because He has, His knowledge and His being, beheld in all the wisdom and glory which become His Godhead, from Him with Whom He is consubstantial.

3. As to Jeconias, whom the prophet Jeremiah declares in these words to have been rejected from the land of Judah, ''Jeconias was dishonoured like a vessel for which there is no more use ; and because he was cast out he and his seed ; and none shall rise from his seed sitting upon the throne of David and ruling in Judah," [4] the matter

is plain and clear. On the destruction of Jerusalem by Nebuchadnezzar, the kingdom had been destroyed, and there was no longer an hereditary succession of reigns as before. Nevertheless, at that time, the deposed descendants of David were living in captivity. On the return of Salathiel and Zerubbabel the supreme government rested to a greater degree with the people, and the sovereignty was afterwards transferred to the priesthood, on account of the intermingling of the priestly and royal tribes ; whence the Lord, in things pertaining, to God, is both King and High Priest. Moreover, the royal tribe did not fail until the coming of the Christ ; nevertheless, the seed of Jeconias sat no longer upon the throne of David. Plainly it is the royal dignity which is described by the term " throne." You remember the history, how all Judæa, Idumæa, Moab, both the neighbouring regions of Syria and the further countries up to Mesopotamia, and the country on the other side as far as the river of Egypt, were all tributary to David. If then none of his descendants appeared with a sovereignty so wide, how is not the word of the prophet true that no one of the seed of Jeconias should any longer sit upon the throne of David, for none of his descendants appears to have attained this dignity. Nevertheless, the tribe of Judah did not fail, until He for whom it was destined came. But even He did not sit upon the material throne. The kingdom of Judæa was transferred to Herod, the son of Antipater the Ascalonite, and his sons who divided Judæa into four principalities, when Pilate was Procurator and Tiberius was Master of the Roman Empire. It is the indestructible kingdom which he calls the throne of David on which the Lord sat. He is the expectation of the Gentiles [1] and not of the smallest division of the world, for it is written, " In that day there shall be a root of Jesse which shall stand for an ensign of the people ; to it shall the Gentiles seek." [2] " I have called thee . . . for a covenant of the people for a light of the Gentiles " ; [3] and thus then God remained a priest, although He did not receive the sceptre of Judah, and King of all the earth ; so the blessing of Jacob was fulfilled, and in Him [4] " shall all the nations of the earth be blessed," and all the nations shall call the Christ blessed.

4. And as to the tremendous question put by the facetious Encratites, why we do

---

[1] Mark xiii. 32.
[2] John xvi. 15.
[3] John x. 15.
[4] Jer. xxii. 28-30, LXX.

[1] Gen. xlix. 10.
[2] Is. xi. 10. The LXX. is καὶ ὁ ἀνιστάμενος ἄρχειν ἐθνῶν.
[3] Is. xlii. 6, and 2 Kings vii. 13.   [4] Gen. xxii. 18.

not eat everything? Let this answer be given, that we turn with disgust from our excrements. As far as dignity goes, to us flesh is grass; but as to distinction between what is and what is not serviceable, just as in vegetables, we separate the unwholesome from the wholesome, so in flesh we distinguish between that which is good and that which is bad for food. Hemlock is a vegetable, just as vulture's flesh is flesh; yet no one in his senses would eat henbane nor dog's flesh unless he were in very great straits. If he did, however, he would not sin.

5. Next as to those who maintain that human affairs are governed by fate, do not ask information from me, but stab them with their own shafts of rhetoric. The question is too long for my present infirmity. With regard to emerging in baptism — I do not know how it came into your mind to ask such a question, if indeed you understood immersion to fulfil the figure of the three days. It is impossible for any one to be immersed three times, without emerging three times.

We write the word φάγος paroxytone.[1]

6. The distinction between οὐσία and ὑπόστασις is the same as that between the general and the particular; as, for instance, between the animal and the particular man. Wherefore, in the case of the Godhead, we confess one essence or substance so as not to give a variant definition of existence, but we confess a particular hypostasis, in order that our conception of Father, Son and Holy Spirit may be without confusion and clear.[2] If we have no distinct perception of the separate characteristics, namely, fatherhood, sonship, and sanctification, but form our conception of God from the general idea of existence, we cannot possibly give a sound account of our faith. We must, therefore, confess the faith by adding the particular to the common. The Godhead is common; the fatherhood particular. We must therefore combine the two and say, " I believe in God the Father." The like course must be pursued in the confession of the Son; we must combine the particular with the common and say " I believe in God the Son," so in the case of the Holy Ghost we must make our utterance conform to the appellation and say " in God [3] the Holy Ghost." Hence it results

that there is a satisfactory preservation of the unity by the confession of the one Godhead, while in the distinction of the individual properties regarded in each there is the confession of the peculiar properties of the Persons. On the other hand those who identify essence or substance and hypostasis are compelled to confess only three Persons,[1] and, in their hesitation to speak of three hypostases, are convicted of failure to avoid the error of Sabellius, for even Sabellius himself, who in many places confuses the conception, yet, by asserting that the same hypostasis changed its form [2] to meet the needs of the moment, does endeavour to distinguish persons.

7. Lastly as to your enquiry in what manner things neutral and indifferent are ordained for us, whether by some chance working by its own accord, or by the righteous providence of God, my answer is this: Health and sickness, riches and poverty, credit and discredit, inasmuch as they do not render their possessors good, are not in the category of things naturally good, but, in so far as in any way they make life's current flow more easily, in each case the former is to be preferred to its contrary, and has a certain kind of value. To some men these things are given by God for stewardship's sake,[3] as for instance to Abraham, to Job and such like. To inferior characters they are a challenge to improvement. For the man who persists in unrighteousness, after so goodly a token of love from God, subjects himself to condemnation without defence. The good man, however,

---

of MSS. is noted and *Ep.* cxli, both written before he was bishop. *cf.* Proleg. Gregory of Nazianzus, *Or.* xliii., explains the rationale of St. Basil's use of the word " God," of the Holy Ghost; alike in his public and private teaching he never shrank from using it, whenever he could with impunity, and his opinions were perfectly well known, but he sought to avoid the sentence of exile at the hands of the Arians by its unnecessary obtrusion. He never uses it in his homily *De Fide*, and the whole treatise *De Spiritu Sancto*, while it exhaustively vindicates the doctrine, ingeniously steers clear of the phrase.

[1] πρόσωπα.

[2] The Ben. Edd. note " *Existimat Combefisius verbum* μετασχηματίζεσθαι *sic reddendum esse, in varias formas mutari. Sed id non dicebat Sabellius. Hoc tantum dicebat, ut legimus in Epist.* ccxiv. Unum quidem hypostasi Deum esse, sed sub diversis personis a Scripturare praesentari. According to Dante the minds of the heresiarchs were to Scripture as bad mirrors, reflecting distorted images; and, in this sense, μετασχηματίζειν might be applied rather to them.

" *Si fe Sabellio ed Arrio e quegli stolti,*
Che furon come spade alle scritture,
In render torti li diritti volti."
Par. xiii. 123 (see Cary's note).

[3] ἐξ οἰκονομίας. In *Ep.* xxxi. Basil begins a letter to Eusebius of Samosata: " The dearth has not yet left us, we are therefore compelled still to remain in the town, either for stewardship's sake or for sympathy with the afflicted." Here the Benedictines' note is *Saepe apud Basilium* οἰκονουία *dicitur id quod pauperibus distribuitur. Vituperat in Comment. in Isa.* praesules *qui male partam pecuniam accipiunt vel ad suos usus,* ἡ ἐπὶ λόγῳ τῆς τῶν πτωχευόντων ἐν τῇ Ἐκκλησίᾳ οἰκονουίας, *vel per causam distribuendi pauperibus Ecclesiae. In Epistola* 92 *Orientales inter mala Ecclesiae illud etiam deplorant quod ambitiosi praesules* οἰκονου ας πτωχων, *pecunias pauperibus destinatas in suos usus convertant.*

---

[1] Amphilochius's doubt may have arisen from the fact that φαγός, the Doric form of φηγός, the esculent oak of Homer, is oxytone.

[2] " ἀσύγχυτος," *unconfounded,* or *without confusion,* is the title of *Dialogue II.* of Theodoret. *cf.* p. 195 n.

[3] The Benedictine note is *Videtur in Harlaeano codice scriptum prima manu* εἰς τὸν θεόν Their reading is εἰς τὸ θεῖον πνεῦμα τὸ ἅγιον. *cf. Ep.* viii., § 2, where no variation

neither turns his heart to wealth when he has it, nor seeks after it if he has it not. He treats what is given him as given him not for his selfish enjoyment, but for wise administration. No one in his senses runs after the trouble of distributing other people's property, unless he is trying to get the praise of the world, which admires and envies anybody in authority.

Good men take sickness as athletes take their contest, waiting for the crowns that are to reward their endurance. To ascribe the dispensation of these things to any one else is as inconsistent with true religion as it is with common sense.

LETTER CCXXXVII.[1]

To Eusebius, bishop of Samosata.

1. I BOTH wrote to your reverence by the vicar of Thrace, and sent other letters by one of the officers of the treasury of Philippopolis, who was starting from our country into Thrace, and begged him to take them on his departure. But the vicar never received my letter, for while I was visiting my diocese,[2] he came into town in the evening and started early in the morning, so that the church officers did not know of his coming, and the letter remained at my house. The treasurer, too, on account of some unexpected and urgent business, set out without seeing me or taking my letters. No one else could be found; so I remained, sorry at not being able to write to you and at not receiving any letter from your reverence. Yet I was wishful, were it possible, to tell you all that happens to me day by day. So many astonishing things happen as to need a daily narrative, and you may be sure that I would have written one, unless my mind had been diverted from its purpose by the pressure of events.

2. The first and greatest of my troubles was the visit of the Vicar. As to whether he is a man really heretically minded I do not know; for I think that he is quite unversed in doctrine, and has not the slightest interest or experience in such things, for I see him day and night busy, both in body and soul, in other things. But he is certainly a friend of heretics; and he is not more friendly to them than he is ill-disposed to me. He has summoned a synod of wicked men in midwinter in Galatia.[3] He has deposed Hypsinus and set up Ecdicius in his place.[4]

He has ordered the removal of my brother on the accusation of one man, and that one quite insignificant. Then, after being occupied for some little time about the army, he came to us again breathing rage and slaughter,[1] and, in one sentence, delivered all the Church of Cæsarea to the Senate. He settled for several days at Sebaste, separating friends from foes,[2] calling those in communion with me senators, and condemning them to the public service, while he advanced the adherents of Eustathius. He has ordered a second synod of bishops of Galatia and Pontus to be assembled at Nyssa.[3] They have submitted, have met, and have sent to the Churches a man of whose character I do not like to speak; but your reverence can well understand what sort of a man he must be who would put himself at the disposal of such counsels of men.[4] Now, while I am thus writing, the same gang have hurried to Sebaste to unite with Eustathius, and, with him, to upset the Church of Nicopolis. For the blessed Theodotus has fallen asleep. Hitherto the Nicopolitans have bravely and stoutly resisted the vicar's first assault; for he tried to persuade them to receive Eustathius, and to accept their bishop on his appointment. But, on seeing them unwilling to yield, he is now trying, by yet more violent action, to effect the establishment of the bishop whom it has been attempted to give them.[5] There is, moreover, said to be some rumoured expectation of a synod, by which means they mean to summon me to receive them into communion, or to be friendly with them. Such is the position of the Churches. As to my own health, I think it better to say nothing. I cannot bear not to tell the truth, and by telling the truth I shall only grieve you.

LETTER CCXXXVIII.[6]

To the presbyters of Nicopolis.[7]

I HAVE received your letter, my reverend brethren, but it told me nothing that I did not already know. for the whole country round about was already full of the report

1 Placed in 376.   3 i.e. at Ancyra.
2 παροικία. cf. p. 163, n.
4 i.e. at Parnassus. Parnassus is placed by Ramsay at a ford a few miles higher up the Halys than Tchikin Aghyl. (Hist. Geog. of Asia Minor, p. 255.)

1 cf. Acts ix. 1.
2 φυλοκρινῶν. The word occurs also in the De Sp. S. § 74, and in Letter cciv. § 2. Another reading in this place is φιλοκρινῶν, "picking out his friends."
3 Mansi iii. 502. The fruitlessness of Ancyra necessitated a second. On Gregory's deposition and banishment, see Greg. Nyss., De Vit Macr. ii. 192, and Ep. xviii. and xxii. Also Greg. Naz., Ep. cxlii.
4 Tillemont supposes this to refer to some one sent on a visitation to the Churches. The Ben. note prefers to apply it to the unknown intruder into the see of Nyssa, of whom Basil speaks with yet greater contempt in Letter ccxxxix.
5 i.e. Fronto. 6 Placed in 376.
7 On the appointment of Fronto to succeed Theodotus.

announcing the disgrace of that one among you who has fallen, and through lust of vain glory has brought on himself very shameful dishonour, and has through his self-love lost the rewards promised to faith. Nay, through the just hatred of them that fear the Lord, he misses even that contemptible little glory for lust of which he has been sold to impiety. By the character he has now shown he has very plainly proved, concerning all his life, that he has never at any time lived in hope of the promises laid up for us by the Lord, but, in all his transactions of human affairs, has used words of faith and mockery of piety, all to deceive every one whom he met. But how are you injured? Are you any worse off for this than you were before? One of your number has fallen away, and if one or two others have gone with him, they are to be pitied for their fall, but, by God's grace, your body is whole. The useless part has gone, and what is left has not suffered mutilation. You are haply distressed that you are driven without the walls, but you shall dwell under the protection of the God of Heaven,[1] and the angel who watches over the Church has gone out with you. So they lie down in empty places day by day, bringing upon themselves heavy judgment through the dispersion of the people. And, if in all this there is sorrow to be borne, I trust in the Lord that it will not be without its use to you. Therefore, the more have been your trials, look for a more perfect reward from your just Judge. Do not take your present troubles ill. Do not lose hope. Yet a little while and your Helper will come to you and will not tarry.[2]

LETTER CCXXXIX.[3]

To Eusebius, bishop of Samosata.

1. The Lord has granted me the privilege of now saluting your holiness by our beloved and very reverend brother, the presbyter Antiochus, of exhorting you to pray for me as you are wont, and offering in our communication by letter some consolation for our long separation. And, when you pray, I ask you to beg from the Lord this as the first and greatest boon, that I may be delivered from vile and wicked men, who have gained such power over the people that now I seem to see, indeed, a repetition of the events of the taking of Jerusalem.[4] For the weaker grow the Churches the more does men's lust for power increase. And now

the very title of bishop has been conferred on wretched slaves, for no servant of God would choose to come forward in opposition to claim the see; — no one but miserable fellows like the emissaries of Anysius the creature of Euippius, and of Ecdicius of Parnassus: whoever has appointed him[1] has sent into the Churches a poor means of aiding his own entry into the life to come.

They have expelled my brother from Nyssa, and into his place have introduced hardly a man — a mere scamp[2] worth only an obol or two, but, so far as regards the ruin of the faith, a match for those who have put him where he is.

At the town of Doara they have brought shame upon the poor name of bishop, and have sent there a wretch, an orphans' domestic, a runaway from his own masters, to flatter a godless woman, who formerly used George as she liked, and now has got this fellow to succeed him.

And who could properly lament the occurrences at Nicopolis? That unhappy Fronto did, indeed, for a while pretend to be on the side of the truth, but now he has shamefully betrayed both the faith and himself, and for the price of his betrayal has got a name of disgrace. He imagines that he has obtained from these men the rank of bishop; in reality he has become, by God's grace, the abomination of all Armenia. But there is nothing that they will not dare; nothing wherein they are at a loss for worthy accomplices. But the rest of the news of Syria my brother knows better, and can tell you better, than I.

2. The news of the West you know already, on the recital of brother Dorotheus. What sort of letters are to be given him on his departure? Perhaps he will travel with the excellent Sanctissimus, who is full of enthusiasm, journeying through the East, and collecting letters and signatures from all the men of mark.[3] What ought to be written by them, or how I can come to an agreement with those who are writing, I do not know. If you hear of any one soon travelling my way, be so good as to let me know. I am moved to say, as Diomede said,

" Would God, Atrides, thy request were yet to undertake;
. . . he's proud enough."[4]

Really lofty souls, when they are courted,

---

[1] Ps. xci. 1, LXX.   [2] Hab. ii. 3.   [3] Placed in 376.
[4] Ἰουδαϊκῆς ἁλώσεως, which the Ben. note is no doubt right in referring to the events of 70.

[1] The sudden change from the vaguer plural marks the strong contempt of the writer for the individual pointed at.
[2] The paronomasia in ἄνδρα and ἀνδράποδον is untranslatable.
[3] Sanctissimus, the envoy of Damasus, seems to have paid two visits to the East. For letters of introduction given him by Basil, see *Letters* cxx., ccxxi., ccxxv., ccliv., cxxxii., and ccliii.   [4] Homer, *Il.* ix. 694-5 (Chapman).

get haughtier than ever. If the Lord be propitious to us, what other thing do we need? If the anger of the Lord lasts on, what help can come to us from the frown of the West? Men who do not know the truth, and do not wish to learn it, but are prejudiced by false suspicions, are doing now as they did in the case of Marcellus,[1] when they quarrelled with men who told them the truth, and by their own action strengthened the cause of heresy. Apart from the common document, I should like to have written to their Coryphæus — nothing, indeed, about ecclesiastical affairs, except gently to suggest that they know nothing of what is going on here, and will not accept the only means whereby they might learn it. I would say, generally, that they ought not to press hard on men who are crushed by trials. They must not take dignity for pride. Sin only avails to produce enmity against God.

LETTER CCXL.[2]

To the Presbyters of Nicopolis.

1. You have done quite right in sending me a letter, and in sending it by the hands of one who, even if you had not written, would have been perfectly competent to give me considerable comfort in all my anxieties, and an authentic report as to the position of affairs. Many vague rumours were continually reaching me, and therefore I was desirous of getting information on many points from some one able to give it through accurate knowledge. Touching all these I have received a satisfactory and intelligent narrative from our well-beloved and honourable brother Theodosius the presbyter. I now write to your reverences the advice which I give myself, for in many respects our positions are identical; and that not only at the present moment, but in times gone by too, as many instances may prove. Of some of these we possess records in writing; others we have received through unwritten recollection from persons acquainted with the facts. We know how, for the sake of the name of the Lord, trials have beset alike individuals and cities that have put their trust in Him. Nevertheless, one and all have passed away, and the distress caused by the days of darkness has not been everlasting. For just as when hail-storm and flood, and all natural calamities, at once injure and destroy things that have no strength, while they are only themselves affected by falling on the

strong, so the terrible trials set in action against the Church have been proved feebler than the firm foundation of our faith in Christ. The hail-storm has passed away; the torrent has rushed over its bed; clear sky has taken the place of the former, and the latter has left the course without water and dry, over which it travelled, and has disappeared in the deep. So, too, in a little while the storm, now bursting upon us, will cease to be. But this will be on the condition of our being willing not to look to the present, but to gaze in hope at the future somewhat further off.

2. Is the trial heavy, my brethren? Let us endure the toil. No one who shuns the blows and the dust of battle wins a crown. Are those mockeries of the devil, and the enemies sent to attack us, insignificant? They are troublesome because they are his ministers, but contemptible because God has in them combined wickedness with weakness. Let us beware of being condemned for crying out too loud over a little pain. Only one thing is worth anguish, the loss of one's own self, when for the sake of the credit of the moment, if one can really call making a public disgrace of one's self credit, one has deprived one's self of the everlasting reward of the just. You are children of confessors; you are children of martyrs; you have resisted sin unto blood.[1] Use, each one of you, the examples of those near and dear to you to make you brave for true religion's sake. No one of us has been torn by lashes;[2] no one of us has suffered confiscation of his house; we have not been driven into exile; we have not suffered imprisonment. What great suffering have we undergone, unless peradventure it is grievous that we have suffered nothing, and have not been reckoned worthy of the sufferings of Christ?[3] But if you are grieved because one whom I need not name occupies the house of prayer, and you worship the Lord of heaven and earth in the open air, remember that the eleven disciples were shut up in the upper chamber, when they that had crucified the Lord were worshipping in the Jews' far-famed temple. Peradventure, Judas, who preferred death by hanging to life in disgrace, proved himself a better man than those who now meet universal condemnation without a blush.

3. Only do not be deceived by their lies

---

[1] cf. Letter lxix. p. 165.   [2] Placed in 376.

[1] cf. Heb. xii. 4.
[2] κατεξάνθη. cf. the use of καταξαίνω (=card or comb) in the Letter of the Smyrneans on the Martyrdom of Polycarp, § 2, "They were so torn by lashes that the mechanism of their flesh was visible, even as far as the veins and arteries." cf. note, p. 2, on the difference between the persecution of the Catholics by Valens and that of the earlier Christians by earlier emperors, though exile and confiscation were suffered in Basil's time.
[3] cf. Acts v. 41.

when they claim to be of the right faith. They are not Christians, but traffickers in Christ,[1] always preferring their profit in this life to living in accordance with the truth. When they thought that they should get this empty dignity, they joined the enemies of Christ: now that they have seen the indignation of the people, they are once more for pretending orthodoxy. I do not recognise as bishop—I would not count among Christ's clergy[2]—a man who has been promoted to a chief post by polluted hands, to the destruction of the faith. This is my decision. If you have any part with me, you will doubtless think as I do. If you take counsel on your own responsibility, every man is master of his own mind, and I am innocent of this blood.[3] I have written thus, not because I distrust you, but that by declaring my own mind I may strengthen some men's hesitation, and prevent any one from being prematurely received into communion, or after receiving the laying on of hands of our enemies, when peace is made, later on, trying to force me to enroll them in the ranks of the sacred ministry. Through you I salute the clergy of the city and diocese, and all the laity who fear the Lord.

LETTER CCXLI.[4]

To Eusebius, bishop of Samosata.

It is not to increase your distress that I am so lavish of painful topics in my letters to your excellency. My object is to get some comfort for myself in the lamentations which are a kind of natural means of dispersing deep-seated pain whenever they are produced, and further to rouse you, my great-hearted friend, to more earnest prayer on behalf of the Churches. We know that Moses prayed continually for the people; yet, when his battle with Amalek had begun, he did not let down his hands from morning to evening, and the uplifting of the hands of the saint only ended with the end of the fight.

LETTER CCXLII.[5]

To the Westerns.[6]

1. THE Holy God has promised a happy issue out of all their infirmities to those that trust in Him. We, therefore, though we have been cut off in a mid-ocean of troubles, though we are tossed by the great waves raised up against us by the spirits of wickedness, nevertheless hold out in Christ Who strengthens us. We have not slackened the strength of our zeal for the Churches, nor, as though despairing of our salvation, while the billows in the tempest rise above our heads, do we look to be destroyed. On the contrary, we are still holding out with all possible earnestness, remembering how even he who was swallowed by the sea monster, because he did not despair of his life, but cried to the Lord, was saved. Thus too we, though we have reached the last pitch of peril, do not give up our hope in God. On every side we see His succour round about us. For these reasons now we turn our eyes to you, right honourable brethren. In many an hour of our affliction we have expected that you would be at our side; and disappointed in that hope we have said to ourselves, "I looked for some to take pity and there was none; and for comforters but I found none."[1] Our sufferings are such as to have reached the confines of the empire; and since, when one member suffers,[2] all the members suffer, it is doubtless right that your pity should be shown to us who have been so long in trouble. For that sympathy, which we have hoped you of your charity feel for us, is caused less by nearness of place than by union of spirit.

2. How comes it to pass then that we have received nothing of what is due to us by the law of love; no letter of consolation, no visit from brethren? This is now the thirteenth year since the war of heresy began against us.[3] In this the Churches have suffered more tribulations than all those which are on record since Christ's gospel was first preached.[4] I am unwilling to de-

---

[1] χριστέμποροι. cf. the use of the cognate subst. χριστεμ ποσία in the letter of Alexander of Alexandria in Theodoret, *Ecc. Hist.* i. 3. χριστέμπορος occurs in the *Didache*, § 12, and in the *Pseud. Ig.*, e.g., *ad Mag.* ix.
[2] ἱερεῦσι. cf. note in *Letter* liv. p. 157.
[3] cf. Matt. iv. 24. [4] Placed in 376. [5] Placed in 376.
[6] This and the following letter refer to the earlier of two missions of Dorotheus to the West. In the latter he carried *Letter* cclxiii. The earlier was successful at least to the extent of winning sympathy. Maran (*Vit. Bas. cap.* xxxv.)

places it not earlier than the Easter of 376, and objects to the earlier date assigned by Tillemont.
[1] Ps. lxix. 20. [2] 1 Cor. xii. 26.
[3] Valens began the thirteenth year of his reign in the March of 376, and this fact is one of Maran's reasons for placing this letter where he does. Tillemont reckons the thirteen years from 361 to 374, but Maran points out that if the Easterns had wanted to include the persecution of Constantius they might have gone farther back, while even then the lull under Julian would have broken the continuity of the attack. *Vit. Bas.* xxxv. cf. note on p. 48.
[4] A rhetorical expression not to be taken literally. Some of the enormities committed under Valens, *e.g.* the alleged massacre of the Orthodox delegates off Bithynia in 370 (Soz. vi. 14, Theod. iv. 21), would stand out even when matched with the cruelties perpetrated under Nero and Diocletian, if the evidence for them were satisfactory. cf. Milman, *Hist. Christ.* iii. 45. The main difference between the earlier persecutions, conventionally reckoned as ten, and the persecution of the Catholics by Valens, seems to be this, that while the former were a putting in force of the law against a *religio non licita*, the latter was but the occasional result of the personal spite and partizanship of the imperial heretic and his courtiers. Valens would feel bitterly towards a Catholic who thwarted him. Basil could under Diocletian hardly have died in his bed as archbishop of Cæsarea.

scribe these one by one, lest the feebleness of my narrative should make the evidence of the calamities less convincing. It is moreover the less necessary for me to tell you of them, because you have long known what has happened from the reports which will have reached you. The sum and substance of our troubles is this: the people have left the houses of prayer and are holding congregations in the wildernesses. It is a sad sight. Women, boys, old men, and those who are in other ways infirm, remain in the open air, in heavy rain, in the snow, the gales and the frost of winter as well as in summer under the blazing heat of the sun. All this they are suffering because they refuse to have anything to do with the wicked leaven of Arius.

3. How could mere words give you any clear idea of all this without your being stirred to sympathy by personal experience and the evidence of eyewitnesses? We implore you, therefore, to stretch out a helping hand to those that have already been stricken to the ground, and to send messengers to remind us of the prizes in store for the reward of all who patiently suffer for Christ. A voice that we are used to is naturally less able to comfort us than one which sounds from afar, and that one coming from men who over all the world are known by God's grace to be among the noblest; for common report everywhere represents you as having remained steadfast, without suffering a wound in your faith, and as having kept the deposit of the apostles inviolate. This is not our case. There are among us some who, through lust of glory and that puffing up which is especially wont to destroy the souls of Christian men, have audaciously uttered certain novelties of expression with the result that the Churches have become like cracked pots and pans and have let in the inrush of heretical impurity. But do you, whom we love and long for, be to us as surgeons for the wounded, as trainers for the whole, healing the limb that is diseased, and anointing the limb that is sound for the service of the true religion.

LETTER CCXLIII.[1]

To the bishops of Italy and Gaul concerning the condition and confusion of the Churches.

1. To his brethren truly God-beloved and very dear, and fellow ministers of like mind, the bishops of Gaul and Italy, Basil,

bishop of Cæsarea in Cappadocia. Our Lord Jesus Christ, Who has deigned to style the universal Church of God His body, and has made us individually members one of another, has moreover granted to all of us to live in intimate association with one another, as befits the agreement of the members. Wherefore, although we dwell far away from one another, yet, as regards our close conjunction, we are very near. Since, then, the head cannot say to the feet, I have no need of you,[1] you will not, I am sure, endure to reject us; you will, on the contrary, sympathize with us in the troubles to which, for our sins, we have been given over, in proportion as we rejoice together with you in your glorying in the peace which the Lord has bestowed on you. Ere now we have also at another time invoked your charity to send us succour and sympathy; but our punishment was not full, and you were not suffered to rise up to succour us. One chief object of our desire is that through you the state of confusion in which we are situated should be made known to the emperor of your part of the world.[2] If this is difficult, we beseech you to send envoys to visit and comfort us in our affliction, that you may have the evidence of eyewitnesses of those sufferings of the East which cannot be told by word of mouth, because language is inadequate to give a clear report of our condition.

2. Persecution has come upon us, right honourable brethren, and persecution in the severest form. Shepherds are persecuted that their flocks may be scattered. And the worst of all is that those who are being treated ill cannot accept their sufferings in proof of their testimony, nor can the people reverence the athletes as in the army of martyrs, because the name of Christians is applied to the persecutors. The one charge which is now sure to secure severe punishment is the careful keeping of the traditions of the Fathers. For this the pious are exiled from their homes, and are sent away to dwell in distant regions. No reverence is shown by the judges of iniquity to the hoary head, to practical piety, to the life lived from boyhood to old age according to the Gospel. No malefactor is doomed without proof, but bishops have been convicted on calumny alone, and are consigned to penalties on charges wholly unsupported by evidence. Some have not even known who has accused them, nor been brought

---

[1] 1 Cor. xii. 21.
[2] *i.e.* Gratian, who succeeded Valentinian I. in 375.

before any tribunal, nor even been falsely accused at all. They have been apprehended with violence late at night, have been exiled to distant places, and, through the hardships of these remote wastes, have been given over to death.[1] The rest is notorious, though I make no mention of it; — the flight of priests; the flight of deacons; the foraying of all the clergy. Either the image must be worshipped, or we are delivered to the wicked flame of whips.[2] The laity groan; tears are falling without ceasing in public and in private; all are mutually lamenting their woes. No one's heart is so hard as to lose a father, and bear the bereavement meekly. There is a sound of them that mourn in the city — a sound in the fields, in the roads, in the deserts. But one voice is heard from all that utter sad and piteous words. Joy and spiritual gladness are taken away. Our feasts are turned into mourning.[3] Our houses of prayer are shut. The altars of the spiritual service are lying idle. Christians no longer assemble together; teachers no longer preside. The doctrines of salvation are no longer taught. We have no more solemn assemblies, no more evening hymns, no more of that blessed joy of souls which arises in the souls of all that believe in the Lord at communions, and the imparting of spiritual boons.[4] We may well say, "Neither is there at this time prince, or prophet, or reader, or offering, or incense, or place to sacrifice before thee, and to find mercy."[5]

3. We are writing to those who know these things, for there is not a region of the world which is ignorant of our calamities. Do not suppose that we are using these words as though to give information, or to recall ourselves to your recollection. We know that you could no more forget us than a mother forget the sons of her womb.[6] But all who are crushed by any weight of agony find some natural alleviation for their pain in uttering groans of distress, and it is for this that we are doing as we do. We get rid of the load of our grief in telling you of our manifold misfortunes, and in expressing the hope that you may haply be the more moved to pray for us, and may prevail on the Lord to be re-

conciled to us. And if these afflictions had been confined to ourselves, we might even have determined to keep silence, and to rejoice in our sufferings for Christ's sake, since "the sufferings of this present time are not worthy to be compared with the glory which shall be revealed in us."[1] But at the present time we are alarmed, lest the mischief growing day by day, like a flame spreading through some burning wood, when it has consumed what is close at hand, may catch distant objects too. The plague of heresy is spreading, and there is ground of apprehension lest, when it has devoured our Churches, it may afterwards creep on even so far as to the sound portion of your district.[2] Peradventure it is because with us iniquity has abounded that we have been first delivered to be devoured by the cruel teeth of the enemies of God. But the gospel of the kingdom began in our regions, and then went forth over all the world. So, peradventure — and this is most probable — the common enemy of our souls, is striving to bring it about that the seeds of apostasy, originating in the same quarter, should be distributed throughout the world. For the darkness of impiety plots to come upon the very hearts whereon the "light of the knowledge" of Christ has shone.[3]

4. Reckon then, as true disciples of the Lord, that our sufferings are yours. We are not being attacked for the sake of riches. or glory, or any temporal advantages. We stand in the arena to fight for our common heritage, for the treasure of the sound faith, derived from our Fathers. Grieve with us, all ye who love the brethren, at the shutting of the mouths of our men of true religion, and at the opening of the bold and blasphemous lips of all that utter unrighteousness against God.[4] The pillars and foundation of the truth are scattered abroad. We, whose insignificance has allowed of our being overlooked, are deprived of our right of free speech. Do ye enter into the struggle, for the people's sake. Do not think only of your being yourselves moored in a safe haven, where the grace of God gives you shelter from the tempest of the winds of wickedness. Reach out a helping hand to the Churches that are being buffeted by the storm, lest, if they be abandoned, they suffer complete shipwreck of the faith. Lament for us, in that the Only-begotten is being blasphemed, and there is none to offer contradiction. The Holy Ghost is being set at

---

[1] For the midnight banishment, cf. the story of the expulsion of Eusebius from Samosata in Theod. iv. 13. Of death following on exile Basil did not live to see the most signal instance — that of Chrysostom in 407.
[2] cf. Dan. iii. 10. The whips seem as rhetorical as the image and the flame. [3] Amos viii. 10.
[4] ἐπὶ ταῖς σύναξεσι καὶ τῇ κοινωνίᾳ τῶν πνευματικῶν χαρισμάτων.
[5] Song of the Three Children, 14. [6] Is. xlix. 15.

[1] Rom. viii. 18.
[2] παροικία. The word seems here to have a wider sense even than that of "diocese."
[3] cf. 2 Cor. iv. 6. [4] cf. Ps. lxxiii. 8, LXX.

nought and he who is able to confute the error has been sent into exile. Polytheism has prevailed. Our opponents own a great God and a small God. "Son" is no longer a name of nature, but is looked upon as a title of some kind of honour. The Holy Ghost is regarded not as complemental of the Holy Trinity, nor as participating in the divine and blessed Nature, but as in some sort one of the number of created beings, and attached to Father and Son, at mere hap-hazard and as occasion may require. " Oh that my head were waters, and mine eyes a fountain of tears,"[1] and I will weep many days for the people who are being driven to destruction by these vile doctrines. The ears of the simple are being led astray, and have now got used to heretical impiety. The nurslings of the Church are being brought up in the doctrines of iniquity. What are they to do? Our opponents have the command of baptisms; they speed the dying on their way;[2] they visit the sick; they console the sorrowful; they aid the distressed; they give succour of various kinds; they communicate the mysteries. All these things, as long as the performance of them is in their hands, are so many ties to bind the people to their views. The result will be that in a little time, even if some liberty be conceded to us, there is small hope that they who have been long under the influence of error will be recalled to recognition of the truth.

5. Under these circumstances it would have been well for many of us to have travelled to your reverences, and to have individually reported each his own position. You may now take as a proof of the sore straits in which we are placed the fact that we are not even free to travel abroad. For if any one leaves his Church, even for a very brief space, he will leave his people at the mercy of those who are plotting their ruin. By God's mercy instead of many we have sent one, our very reverend and beloved brother the presbyter Dorotheus. He is fully able to supply by his personal report whatever has been omitted in our letter, for he has carefully followed all that has occurred, and is jealous of the right faith. Receive him in

peace, and speedily send him back to us, bringing us good news of your readiness to succour the brotherhood.

LETTER CCXLIV.[1]

To Patrophilus, bishop of Ægæ.[2]

1. I HAVE read, and read with pleasure, the letter which you have sent by Strategius the presbyter. How should I not so read it, written as it is by a wise man, and dictated by a heart which has learned to observe the universal love taught by the commandment of the Lord? Possibly I am not unaware of the reasons which have hitherto kept you silent. You have been, as it were, amazed and astounded, at the idea of the change in the notorious Basil. Why, ever since he was a boy he did such and such service to such an one; at such and such times he did such and such things; he waged war against foes innumerable for the sake of his allegiance to one man; now he has become a totally different character; he has exchanged love for war; he is all that you have written; so you naturally shew considerable astonishment at the very unexpected turn of affairs. And if you have found some fault, I do not take it ill. I am not so beyond correction as to be amazed at the affectionate rebukes of my brothers. Indeed so far was I from being vexed at your letter that it really almost made me laugh to think that when there were, as I thought, so many strong causes already existing to cement our friendship, you should have expressed such very great astonishment at the trifles which have been reported to you. So truly have you suffered the fate of all those who omit to enquire into the nature of circumstances, and give heed to the men who are being discussed; of all who do not examine into the truth, but judge by the distinction of persons, in forgetfulness of the exhortation " Ye shall not respect persons in judgment."[3]

2. Nevertheless, since God in judgment of man does not accept persons, I will not refuse to make known to you the defence which I have prepared for the great tribunal. On my side, from the beginning, there has been no cause of quarrel, either small or great; but men who hate me, for what reason is best known to themselves (I must not say a word about them), incessantly ca-

---

[1] Jer. ix. 1.
[2] I suggest this rendering of προπομπαὶ τῶν ἐξοδευόντων with hesitation, and feel no certainty about the passage except that the Ben. tr., " deductiones proficiscentium," and its defence in the Ben. note, is questionable. The escort of a bishop on a journey is quite on a different plane from the ministrations which Basil has in mind. προπομπαὶ is used by Chrysostom of funerals. and Combefis explains " excedentium deductæ funebres, deducta funera ; " but the association of ideas seems to necessitate some reference to the effect of vicious teaching on the living. There may be an indirect allusion to the effect on the friends at a funeral, but to take ἐξοδευόντων to mean " the dying " seems the simplest. ἐξοδευθείς is used of Sisera in Judges v. 27, LXX. cf. p. 180 n., where perhaps this rendering might be substituted, and Canon Bright on Canon xiii of Nicæa.

[1] Placed in 376.
[2] " Aigaiai is the more correct form." Ramsay, Hist. Geog. A.M. 116. In the gulf of Issus, now Ayas. St. Julianus, son of a senator of Anazarbus, is said to have suffered there. (Basil, Menol. and, possibly, Chrysost., Hom. in Jul. Mart.)
[3] Deut. i. 17.

lumniated me. I cleared myself again and again of slanders. There seemed no end to the matter, and no good came of my continual defence, because I was far away, and the authors of the false statements, being on the spot, were able by their calumnies against me to wound a susceptible heart, and one which has never learnt to keep one ear open for the absent. When the Nicopolitans, as you yourself are partly aware, were asking for some proof of faith, I determined to have recourse to the written document.[1] I thought that I should fulfil two objects at once; I expected both to persuade the Nicopolitans not to think ill of the man,[2] and to shut the mouths of my calumniators, because agreement in faith would exclude slander on both sides. Indeed the creed had been drawn up, and it was brought from me, and signed. After it had been signed, a place was appointed for a second meeting, and another date fixed, so that my brethren in the diocese might come together and be united with one another, and our communion for the future be genuine and sincere. I, for my part, arrived at the appointed time, and, of the brethren who act with me, some were on the spot, and others were hurrying thither, all joyous and eager as though on the high road to peace.[3] Couriers and a letter from myself announced my arrival; for the spot appointed for the reception of those who were assembling was mine. But nobody appeared on the other side; no one came in advance; no one to announce the approach of the expected bishops. So those who had been sent by me returned with the report of the deep dejection and the complaints of those who were assembled, as though a new creed had been promulgated by me. They were moreover said to be for deciding, that they certainly would not suffer their bishop to go over to me. Then came a messenger bringing me a letter hastily drawn up, and containing no mention of the points originally agreed on. My brother Theophilus,[4] a man worthy of all respect and honour at my hands, sent one of his adherents, and made certain announcements, which he thought it not improper for him to utter, nor unbecoming in me to hear. He did not condescend to write, not so much because he was afraid of being convicted on written evidence, as because he was anxious not to be compelled to address me as bishop. Assuredly his language was violent, and came from a heart vehemently agitated. Under these circum-

stances I departed abashed and depressed, not knowing what to answer to my questioners. Then, without any long interval of time, there was the journey into Cilicia,[1] the return thence, and forthwith a letter repudiating communion with me.[2]

3. The cause of the rupture was the allegation that I wrote to Apollinarius and was in communion with the presbyter Diodorus. I never regarded Apollinarius as an enemy, and for some reasons I even respect him. But I never so far united myself to him as to take upon me the charges against him; indeed I have myself some accusations to bring against him after reading some of his books. I do not know that I ever asked him for a book on the Holy Spirit, or received it on his sending. I am told that he has become a most copious writer, but I have read very few of his works.[3] I have not even time to investigate such matters. Indeed I shrink from admitting any of the more recent works, for my health does not even allow of my reading the inspired Scriptures with diligence and as I ought. What, then, is it to me, if some one has written something displeasing to somebody else? Yet if one man is to render an account on behalf of another, let him who accuses me for Apollinarius' sake defend himself to me for the sake of Arius his own master and of Aetius his own disciple. I never learnt anything from, nor taught anything to this man whose guilt is laid at my door. Diodorus, as a nursling of the blessed Silvanus, I did receive from the beginning: I love him now and respect him on account of his grace of speech, whereby many who meet him are made the better men.[4]

4. At this letter I was affected in such a manner as might be expected, and astounded at so sudden and pleasant a change. I felt quite unable to reply. My heart could hardly beat; my tongue failed me, and my hand grew numb. I felt like a poor creature (for the truth shall be told; yet it is pardonable); I all but fell into a state of misanthropy; I looked on every one with suspicion and thought that there was no charity to be found

---

[1] *i.e.* the formula proposed to Eustathius by Basil, and signed in 373 by him with Fronto, Severus, and others, and appearing as *Letter* cxxv.
[2] *i.e.* Eustathius.
[3] *cf. Letter* cxxx.
[4] Theophilus of Castabala.

[1] *cf. Letter* cxxx. The journey of Eustathius to Cilicia was the occasion of his presenting an Arian creed to a certain Gelasius.
[2] *cf. Letter* ccxxvi. The letter of repudiation was conveyed by Eustathius the chorepiscopus.
[3] Fragments of Apollinarius are extant in the works of Theodoret and Gregory of Nyssa, and in Mai's *Script. Vet. Nov. col.* vii., and *Spicil. Rom.* x. 2. *cf.* Thomasius, *Christ. Dogm.* 451. *cf. Ep* cclxiii. p. 302.
[4] Diodorus, now presbyter of Antioch, did not become bishop of Tarsus till about the time of Basil's death. On his services to the Church at Antioch, *cf.* Theod., *H.E.* ii. 19. and Soc., *H.E.* vi. 8. The controversy as to his alleged Nestorianism belongs to a later date. On the relations between Diodorus and Apollinarius, *cf.* Dorner, *Christ.* i. pp. 976 and 1022.

in mankind. Charity seemed a mere specious word, serving as a kind of decoration to those who use it, while no such sentiment was really to be found in the heart of man. Could it really be that one who seemed to have disciplined himself from boyhood to old age, could be so easily brutalized on such grounds, without a thought for me, without any idea that his experience of bygone years ought to have more weight than this wretched slander? Could he really, like an unbroken colt as yet untaught to carry his rider properly, on some petty suspicion rear and unseat his rider and fling to the ground what was once his pride? If so, what must be thought of the rest with whom I had no such strong ties of friendship, and who had given no such proofs of a well trained life? All this I turned over in my soul and continually revolved in my heart, or, shall I rather say my heart was turned over by these things fighting and pricking me at the recollection of them? I wrote no answer; not that I kept silence from contempt; do not think it of me my brother, for I am not defending myself to men but I speak before God in Christ. I kept silence from utter inability to say a word commensurate with my grief.

5. While I was in this position another letter came to me, addressed to a certain Dazizas, but in reality written to all the world. This is obvious from its very rapid distribution, for in a few days it was delivered all over Pontus, and was travelling about Galatia; indeed it is said that the carriers of this good news traversed Bithynia, and reached the Hellespont itself. What was written against me to Dazizas[1] you are very well aware, for they do not reckon you as so far beyond the bounds of their friendship as to have left you alone undistinguished by this honour. However, if the letter has not reached you, I will send it to you. In it you will find me charged with craft and treachery, with corruption of Churches and with ruin of souls. The charge which they think the truest of all is, that I made that exposition of the faith for secret and dishonest reasons, not to do service to the Nicopolitans, but with the design of disingenuously extracting a confession from them. Of all this the Lord is Judge. What clear evidence can there be of the thoughts of the heart? One thing I do wonder at in them, that after signing the document presented by me, they show so much disagreement, that they confuse truth and falsehood to satisfy those who are accusing them, quite forgetful that their

written confession of the Nicene Creed is preserved at Rome, and that they with their own hand delivered to the council at Tyana the document brought from Rome which is in my hands, and contains the same creed. They forgot their own address, when they came forward and bewailed the deceit by which they had been tricked into giving their adhesion to the document drawn up by the faction of Eudoxius,[1] and so bethought them of the defence for that error, that they should go to Rome[2] and there accept the creed of the Fathers, that so they might make amends, for the mischief they had done the Church by their agreement in evil, by their introduction of something better. Now the very men who undertook long journeys for the faith's sake, and made all these fine speeches, are reviling me for walking craftily, and for playing the plotter under the cloke of love. It is plain from the Letter, now being carried about, that they have condemned the faith of Nicæa. They saw Cyzicus, and came home with another creed.[3]

6. But why say anything of mere verbal inconsistency? The practical proofs of their change of position afforded by their conduct are far stronger. They refused to yield to the sentence of fifty bishops passed against them.[4] They declined to resign the government of their Churches although the number of bishops assenting to the decree for their deposition was so many, on the alleged ground that they were not partakers of the Holy Ghost, and were not governing their Churches by the grace of God, but had clutched their dignity by the aid of human power, and through lust of vain glory. Now they are for receiving the men consecrated by these same persons as bishops. I should like you to ask them in my stead, (although they despise all mankind, as bereft of eyes, ears, and common sense), to perceive the inconsistency of their conduct, what sentiments they do really entertain in their own hearts. How can there be two bishops, one deposed by Euippius,[5] and the other consecrated by him? Both are the actions of the same man. Had he not been endowed with the grace bestowed upon Jeremiah to pull down and build again, to root out and to plant,[6] he certainly would not have rooted the one out and planted the other. Grant him the one and you must grant him the other. Their

---

[1] In *Letter* cxxxi. the name appears as Dazinas, or Dexinas. In this place the MSS. agree in the form Dazizas.

[1] ? The Creed of Ariminum.
[2] Eustathius, Silvanus, and Theophilus went to Rome after the Lampsacene Council of 365.
[3] The Synod of Tyana had been ready to recognise the Eustathians as Catholics in 374. The Semi-Arian Council of Cyzicus was held in 375 or 376 (Mansi iii. 469).
[4] *i.e.* at Constantinople in 360.
[5] *cf. Letter* ccxxviii.
[6] *cf.* Jer. i. 10.

one object, as it seems, is everywhere to look to their own advantage, and to regard every one who acts in accordance with their own wishes as a friend, while they treat any one who opposes them as an enemy, and spare no calumny to run him down.[1]

7. What measures are they now taking against the Church? For the shiftiness of their originators, shocking; for the apathy of all who are affected by them, pitiable. By a respectable commission the children and grandchildren of Euippius have been summoned from distant regions to Sebasteia, and to them the people have been entrusted.[2] They have taken possession of the altar. They have been made the leaven of that Church. I am persecuted by them as a Homoousiast. Eustathius, who brought the Homoousion in the script from Rome to Tyana, although he was not able to get admitted into their much to be coveted communion, either because they feared, or respected the authority of, the large number of persons who had agreed in condemning him, is now in intimate alliance with them. I only hope that I may never have time enough on my hands to tell of all their doings — who were gathered together, how each one had been ordained, and from what kind of earlier life each arrived at his present dignity. I have been taught to pray " that my mouth may not utter the works of the men." [3] If you enquire you will learn these things for yourself, and, if they are hidden from you, they will not assuredly continue hidden from the judges.

8. I will not, however, omit to tell you, my dear friend, in what a state I have been. Last year I suffered from a very violent fever, and came near to the gates of death. When, by God's mercy, I was restored, I was distressed at coming back to life, as I bethought me of all the troubles before me. I considered with myself for what reason, hidden in the depths of the wisdom of God, yet further days of life in the flesh had been allowed me. But when I heard of these matters I concluded that the Lord wished me to see the Churches at rest after the storm which they had previously suffered from the

alienation of the men in whom, on account of their fictitious gravity of character, every confidence had been placed. Or peradventure the Lord designed to invigorate my soul, and to render it more vigilant for the future, to the end that, instead of giving heed to men, it might be made perfect through those precepts of the Gospel which do not share in the changes and chances of human seasons and circumstances, but abide for ever the same, as they were uttered by the blessed lips that cannot lie.[1]

9. Men are like clouds, shifting hither and thither in the sky with the change of the winds.[2] And of all men who have ever come within my experience these of whom I am speaking are the most unstable. As to the other business of life, those who have lived with them may give evidence; but as to what is within my own knowledge, their inconsistency as regards the faith, I do not know that I have ever myself observed it or heard from any one else, of anything like it. Originally they were followers of Arius; then they went over to Hermogenes, who was diametrically opposed to the errors of Arius, as is evinced by the Creed originally recited by him at Nicæa.[3] Hermogenes, fell asleep, and then they went over to Eusebius, the coryphæus, as we know on personal evidence, of the Arian ring. Leaving this, for whatever reasons, they came home again, and once more concealed their Arian sentiments. After reaching the episcopate, to pass by what occurred in the interval, how many creeds did they put forth? One at Ancyra;[4] another at Seleucia;[5] another at Constantinople,[6] the famous one; another at Lampsacus,[7] then that of Nike in Thrace;[8] and now again the creed of Cyzicus.[9] Of this last I know nothing, except that I am told that they have suppressed the homoousion, and are supporting the *like in essence*, while they subscribe with Eunomius the blas-

---

[1] Contrast the famous appeal of Antigone in Soph., *Ant.* 454 to the eternal principles of right and wrong; οὐ γάρ τι νῦν γε καχθὲς, ἀλλ' ἀεί ποτε ζῆ ταῦτα κοὐδεὶς οἶδεν ἐξ ὅτου 'φάνη. The Christian saint can make the more personal reference to the ἀψευδὲς στόμα.　　　[2] *cf.* Jude 12.

[3] *cf. Letter* lxxxi. p. 172. Hermogenes was bishop of Cæsarea, in which see he preceded Dianius. He acted as secretary at Nicæa, when yet a deacon. " The actual creed was written out and read, perhaps in consideration of Hosius' ignorance of Greek, by Hermogenes." (Stanley, *Eastern Church*, p. 140, ed. 1862.)

[4] In 358, when the ὁμοιούσιον was accepted.

[5] In 359, when the Semiarians supported the Antiochene Dedication Creed of 341.

[6] In 360, when the Acacians triumphed, and Eustathius with other Semiarians was deposed. The Creed of Ariminum, as revised at Nike, was accepted.

[7] In 364, when the Creeds of Ariminum and Constantinople were condemned by the Semiarians, and the Dedication Creed was reaffirmed.

[8] The Creed of Nike in Thrace was the Creed of Ariminum revised, and it seems out of order to mention it after Lampsacus.

[9] In 375 or 6. This is the formula referred to in *Letter* cclvi. 4, as the latest. On the variety of Creeds, *cf.* p. 48, n.

---

[1] The Ben. note on this passage suggests that the reference to Jeremiah is an argument supposed to be put forward by Eustathius, and immediately answered by Basil, but there seems no necessity for this. Basil says nothing for or against the powers of the bishops who condemned Eustathius; he only points out the inconsistency of Eustathius in accepting their powers to ordain when it suited his purpose, while he refused to admit their authority to depose. It is enough for Basil's argument that Eustathius treated him as having authority. On Basil's own views as to the validity of heretical ordination, *cf.* Canon i., *Letter* clxxxviii.

[2] *i.e.* bishops and presbyters whose spiritual descent is to be traced to Euippius, *viz.*: Eustathius and his clergy. Over what see Euippius presided is unknown.

[3] Ps. xvii. 3 and 4, LXX.

phemies against the Holy Spirit. Although all of the creeds which I have enumerated may not be opposed to one another, yet they alike exhibit the inconsistency of the men's minds, from their never standing by the same words. I have said nothing as to countless other points, but this that I do say is true. Now that they have gone over to you, I beg you to write back by the same man, I mean our fellow presbyter Strategius, whether you have remained in the same mind towards me, or whether you have been alienated in consequence of your meeting them. For it was not likely that they would be silent, nor that you yourself, after writing to me as you have, would not use free speaking to them too. If you remain in communion with me, it is well ; it is what I would most earnestly pray for. If they have drawn you over to them, it is sad. How should separation from such a brother not be sad? If in nothing else, at least in bearing losses like this, we have been considerably tried at their hands.

LETTER CCXLV.[1]

To Theophilus the Bishop.[2]

It is some time since I received your letter, but I waited to be able to reply by some fit person ; that so the bearer of my answer might supply whatever might be wanting in it. Now there has arrived our much beloved and very reverend brother Strategius, and I have judged it well to make use of his services, both as knowing my mind and able to convey[3] news of me with due propriety and reverence. Know, therefore, my beloved and honoured friend, that I highly value my affection for you, and am not conscious, so far as the disposition of my heart goes, of having at any time failed in it, although I have had many serious causes of reasonable complaint. But I have decided to weigh the good against the bad, as in a balance, and to add my own mind where the better inclines. Now changes have been made by those who should least of all have allowed anything of the kind. Pardon me, therefore, for I have not changed my mind, if I have shifted my side, or rather I should say, I shall still be on the same side, but there are others who are continually changing it, and are now openly deserting to the foe. You yourself know what a value I put on their communion, so long as

they were of the sound party. If now I refuse to follow these, and shun all who think with them, I ought fairly to be forgiven. I put truth and my own salvation before everything.

LETTER CCXLVI.[1]

To the Nicopolitans.

I am filled with distress at seeing evil on the high road to success, while you, my reverend friends, are faint and failing under continuous calamity. But when again I bethink me of the mighty hand of God, and reflect that He knows how to raise up them that are broken down, to love the just, to crush the proud and to put down the mighty from their seats, then again my heart grows lighter by hope, and I know that through your prayers the calm that the Lord will show us will come soon. Only grow not weary in prayer, but in the present emergency strive to give to all a plain example by deed of whatever you teach by word.

LETTER CCXLVII.[2]

To the Nicopolitans.

When I had read the letter of your holinesses, how did I not groan and lament that I had heard of these further troubles, of blows and insults inflicted on yourselves, of destruction of homes, devastation of the city, ruin of your whole country, persecution of the Church, banishment of priests, invasion of wolves, and scattering of flocks. But I have looked to the Lord in heaven, and have ceased to groan and weep, because I am perfectly well assured, as I hope you know too, that help will speedily come and that you will not be for ever forsaken. What we have suffered, we have suffered for our sins. But our loving Lord will show us His own aid for the sake of His love and pity for the Churches. Nevertheless, I have not omitted to beseech men in authority in person. I have written to those at court, who love us, that the wrath of our ravening enemy may be stayed. I think, moreover, that from many quarters condemnation may fall upon his head, unless indeed these troublous times' allow our public men no leisure for these matters.[3]

---

[1] Placed in 376.
[2] i.e. of Castabala, who had accompanied Eustathius to Rome, and was closely associated with him. cf. p. 198.
[3] διακομίσαι. Two MSS. have διακονῆσαι.

[1] Placed in 376.   [2] Placed in 376.
[3] It is rare to find in Basil's letters even so slight an allusion as this to the general affairs of the empire. At or about the date of this letter the Goths, hitherto kept in subjection by the legions of Valens, were being driven south by the Huns and becoming a danger to the empire. Amm. Marc. xxxi. 4. *Turbido instantium studio, orbis Romani pernicies ducebatur.*

LETTER CCXLVIII.[1]

To Amphilochius, bishop of Iconium.

So far as my own wishes are concerned I am grieved at living at such a distance from your reverence. But, as regards the peace of your own life, I thank the Lord Who has kept you out of this conflagration which has specially ravaged my diocese. For the just Judge has sent me, in accordance with my works, a messenger of Satan,[2] who is buffeting me [3] severely enough, and is vigorously defending the heresy. Indeed to such a pitch has he carried the war against us, that he does not shrink even from shedding the blood of those who trust in God. You cannot fail to have heard that a man of the name of Asclepius,[4] because he would not consent to communion with Doeg,[5] has died under the blows inflicted on him by them, or rather, by their blows has been translated into life. You may suppose that the rest of their doings are of a piece with this; the persecutions of presbyters and teachers, and all that might be expected to be done by men abusing the imperial authority at their own caprice. But, in answer to your prayers, the Lord will give us release from these things, and patience to bear the weight of our trials worthily of our hope in Him. Pray write frequently to me of all that concerns yourself. If you find any one who can be trusted to carry you the book that I have finished, be so kind as to send for it, that so, when I have been cheered by your approval, I may send it on to others also. By the grace of the Holy One may you be granted to me and to the Church of the Lord in good health, rejoicing in the Lord, and praying for me.

LETTER CCXLIX.[6]

Without address. Commendatory.

I CONGRATULATE this my brother, in being delivered from our troubles here and in approaching your reverence. In choosing a good life with them that fear the Lord he has chosen a good provision for the life to come. I commend him to your excellency and by him I beseech you to pray for my wretched life, to the end that I may be delivered from these trials and begin to serve the Lord according to the Gospel.

---

[1] Placed in 376. [2] cf. 2 Cor. xii. 7.
[3] The word κατακονδυλίζω here used (it occurs in Æschines) is a synonym, slightly strengthened, for the κολαφίζω of St. Paul. St. Basil seems plainly to have the passage quoted in his mind.
[4] I have failed to find further mention of this Asclepius. An Asclepius of Cologne is commemorated on June 30.
[5] cf. 1 Sam. xxi. 18. [6] Placed in 376.

LETTER CCL.[1]

To Patrophilus, bishop of Ægæ.

THERE has been some delay in my receiving your answer to my former letter; but it has reached me through the well-beloved Strategius, and I have given thanks to the Lord for your continuance in your love to me. What you have now been kind enough to write on the same subject proves your good intentions, for you think as you ought, and you counsel me to my gain. But I see that my words will be extending too far, if I am to reply to everything written to me by your excellency. I therefore say no more than this, that, if the blessing of peace goes no further than the mere name of peace, it is ridiculous to go on picking out here one and there another, and allow them alone a share in the boon, while others beyond number are excluded from it. But if agreement with mischievous men, under the appearance of peace, really does the harm an enemy might do to all who consent to it, then only consider who those men are who have been admitted to their companionship, who have conceived an unrighteous hatred against me; who but men of the faction not in communion with me. There is no need now for me to mention them by name. They have been invited by them to Sebasteia; they have assumed the charge of the Church; they have performed service at the altar; they have given of their own bread to all the people, being proclaimed bishops by the clergy there, and escorted through all the district as saints and in communion. If one must adopt the faction of these men, it is absurd to begin at the extremities, and not rather to hold intercourse with those that are their heads.[2] If then we are to count heretic and shun no one at all, why, tell me, do you separate yourself from the communion of certain persons? But if any are to be shunned, let me be told by these people who are so logically consistent in everything, to what party those belong whom they have invited over from Galatia to join them? If such things seem grievous to you, charge the separation on those who are responsible for it. If you judge them to be of no importance, forgive me for declining to be of the leaven of the teachers of wrong doctrine.[3] Wherefore, if you will, have no more to do with those specious arguments, but with all

---

[1] Placed in 376.
[2] i.e. with Euzoius, Eudoxius, and the more pronounced Arians.
[3] τῶν ἑτεροδιδασκαλούντων. cf. 1 Tim. i. 3. The Ben. note compares Greg., Orat. xii. 203.

openness confute them that do not walk aright in the truth of the Gospel.

LETTER CCLI.[1]

To the people of Evæsæ.[2]

1. My occupations are very numerous, and my mind is full of many anxious cares, but I have never forgotten you, my dear friends, ever praying my God for your constancy in the faith, wherein ye stand and have your boasting in the hope of the glory of God. Truly nowadays it is hard to find, and extraordinary to see, a Church pure, unharmed by the troubles of the times, and preserving the apostolic doctrine in all its integrity and completeness. Such is your Church shewn at this present time by Him who in every generation makes manifest them that are worthy of His calling. May the Lord grant to you the blessings of Jerusalem which is above, in return for your flinging back at the heads of the liars their slanders against me, and your refusal to allow them entry into your hearts. I know, and am persuaded in the Lord, that "your reward is great in heaven,"[3] even on account of this very conduct. For you have wisely concluded among yourselves, as indeed is the truth, that the men who are "rewarding me evil for good, and hatred for my love,"[4] are accusing me now for the very same points which they are found to have themselves confessed and subscribed.

2. Their presenting you with their own signatures for an accusation against me is not the only contradiction into which they have fallen. They were unanimously deposed by the bishops assembled at Constantinople.[5] They refused to accept this deposition and appealed to a synod of impious men,[6] refusing to admit the episcopacy of their judges, in order not to accept the sentence passed upon them.

The reason alleged for their non-recognition was their being leaders of wicked heresy. All this[7] happened nearly seventeen years ago. The principal men of those who deposed them were Eudoxius, Euippius, George,[8] Acacius, and others unknown to you.[9]

The present tyrants of the churches are their successors, some ordained to fill their places, and others actually promoted by them.

3. Now let those who charge me with unsound doctrine tell me in what way the men whose deposition they refused to accept were heretical. Let them tell me in what way those promoted by them, and holding the same views as their fathers, are orthodox. If Euippius was orthodox, how can Eustathius, whom he deposed, be other than a layman? If Euippius was a heretic, how can any one ordained by him be in communion with Eustathius now? But all this conduct, this trying to accuse men and set them up again, is child's play, got up against the Churches of God, for their own gain.

When Eustathius was travelling through Paphlagonia, he overthrew the altars[1] of Basilides of Paphlagonia,[2] and used to perform divine service on his own tables.[3] Now he is begging Basilides to be admitted to communion. He refused to communicate with our reverend brother Elpidius, because of his alliance with the Amasenes;[4] and now he comes as a suppliant to the Amasenes, petitioning for alliance with them. Even ye yourselves know how shocking were his public utterances against Euippius: now he glorifies the holders of Euippius's opinions for their orthodoxy, if only they will co-operate in promoting his restitution. And I am all the while being calumniated, not because I am doing any wrong, but because they have imagined that they will thus be recommended to the party at Antioch. The character of those whom they sent for last year from Galatia, as being likely by their means to recover the free exercise of their episcopal powers, is only too well known to all who have lived even for a short time with them. I pray that the Lord may never allow me leisure to recount all their proceedings. I will only say that they have passed through the whole country, with the honour and attendance of bishops, escorted by their most honourable body-guard and sympathizers; and have made a grand entry into the city, and held an assembly with all authority. The people have been given over to them. The altar has been given over to them. How they went to Nicopolis, and could do nothing there of all that they had promised, and how they came, and what appearance they presented on their return, is known to those who were on the spot. They are obviously taking every single step for their own

---

[1] Placed in 376.
[2] Euassai. Possibly Ptolemy's Σεΐουα. Ramsay, *Hist. Geog.* A.M. 304. Now Yogounés, *i.e.* Ἅγιος Ἰωάννης.
[3] Matt. v. 12.   [4] Ps. cix. 5.
[5] *i.e.* in January 360. Soc. ii. 41-43; Soz. iv. 24.
[6] The Synod of Lampsacus in 365 is probably referred to, but Socrates (v. 14) mentions several synods of the Homoiousians.   [7] *i.e.* the deposition.
[8] Of uncertain see.   [9] A MS. variety is "to me."

[1] θυσιαστήρια.
[2] *i.e.* Basilides, bishop of Gangra. *cf. Letter* ccxxvi. p. 268.
[3] τραπεζῶν.
[4] *i.e.* the Arian bishop of Amasia, who was intruded into the place of Eulalius. On the state of the Amasene church at his time, *cf.* Soz. vii. 2.

gain and profit. If they say that they have
repented, let them shew their repentance in
writing; let them anathematize the Creed
of Constantinople; let them separate from
the heretics; and let them no longer trick
the simple-minded. So much for them and
theirs.

4. I, however, brethren beloved, small
and insignificant as I am, but remaining ever
by God's grace the same, have never changed
with the changes of the world. My creed
has not varied at Seleucia, at Constantinople,
at Zela,[1] at Lampsacus, and at Rome. My
present creed is not different from the former;
it has remained ever one and the same. As
we received from the Lord, so are we baptized; as we are baptized, so we make profession of our faith; as we make profession
of our faith, so do we offer our doxology,
not separating the Holy Ghost from Father
and Son, nor preferring Him in honour to
the Father, or asserting Him to be prior to
the Son, as blasphemers' tongues invent.[2]
Who could be so rash as to reject the Lord's
commandment, and boldly devise an order of
his own for the Names? But I do not call
the Spirit, Who is ranked with Father and
Son, a creature. I do not dare to call slavish
that which is royal.[3] And I beseech you to
remember the threat uttered by the Lord in
the words, "All manner of sin and blasphemy shall be forgiven unto men; but the
blasphemy against the Holy Ghost shall not
be forgiven unto men, neither in this world,
neither in the world to come."[4] Keep yourselves from dangerous teaching against the
Spirit. "Stand fast in the faith."[5] Look
over all the world, and see how small the
part is which is unsound. All the rest of
the Church which has received the Gospel,
from one end of the world to the other,
abides in this sound and unperverted doctrine. From their communion I pray that I
may never fall, and I pray that I may have
part and lot with you in the righteous day of
our Lord Jesus Christ, when He shall come
to give to every one according to his conduct.

LETTER CCLII.[6]

To the bishops of the Pontic Diocese.[7]

The honours of martyrs ought to be very
eagerly coveted by all who rest their hopes on

the Lord, and more especially by you who seek
after virtue. By your disposition towards
the great and good among your fellow servants you are shewing your affection to our
common Lord. Moreover, a special reason
for this is to be found in the tie, as it were,
of blood, which binds the life of exact discipline to those who have been made perfect
through endurance. Since then Eupsychius
and Damas and their company are most illustrious among martyrs, and their memory
is yearly kept in our city and all the neighbourhood, the Church, calling on you by my
voice, reminds you to keep up your ancient
custom of paying a visit. A great and good
work lies before you among the people, who
desire to be edified by you, and are anxious
for the reward dependent on the honour paid
to the martyrs. Receive, therefore, my supplications, and consent of your kindness to
give at the cost of small trouble to yourselves
a great boon to me.[1]

LETTER CCLIII.[2]

To the presbyters of Antioch.[3]

The anxious care which you have for
the Churches of God will to some extent be
assuaged by our very dear and very reverend brother Sanctissimus the presbyter,
when he has told you of the love and kindness felt for us by all the West. But, on the
other hand, it will be roused afresh and
made yet keener, when he has told you in
person what zeal is demanded by the present position of affairs. All other authorities
have told us, as it were, by halves, the
minds of men in the West, and the condition of things there. He is very competent
to understand men's minds, and to make
exact enquiry into the condition of affairs,
and he will tell you everything and will
guide your good will through the whole
business. You have matter before you

primate of a group of provincial churches, as it had been used
by Ibas, bishop of Edessa, at his trial in 448; alluding to the
'Eastern Council' which had resisted the council of Ephesus,
and condemned Cyril, he said, 'I followed my exarch,' meaning John of Antioch (Mansi vii. 237; compare Evagrius iv. 11,
using 'patriarchs' and 'exarchs' synonymously). Reference
is here made not to all such prelates, but to the bishops of
Ephesus, Cæsarea in Cappadocia, and Heraclea, if, as
seems possible, the see of Heraclea still nominally retained its
old relation to the bishop of Thrace." Bright, Canons of
the First Four Gen. Councils, pp. 156, 157.
The Pontic diocese was one of Constantine's thirteen civil
divisions.
[1] cf. p. 184, n. cf. Proleg. Eupsychius, a noble bridegroom
of Cæsarea, was martyred under Julian for his share in the
demolition of the temple of Fortune. Soz. v. 11. cf. Greg.
Naz., Ep. ad Bas. lviii. September 7 was the day of the feast
at Cæsarea. [2] Placed in 376.
[3] This and the three following letters are complimentary
and consolatory epistles conveyed by Sanctissimus on his
return to Rome. It does not appear quite certain whether they
are to be referred to the period of his return from his second
journey to the East in 376, or that of his earlier return in 374.
cf. Letters cxx. and ccxxi.

---

[1] cf. Letter ccxxvi. p. 268.
[2] cf. De Sp. S. chap. xii. p. 18.
[3] cf. Ps. li. 12, LXX.
[4] Matt. xii. 31, 32.
[5] 1 Cor. xvi. 13.
[6] Placed in 376.
[7] In the title the word διοίκησις is used in its oldest ecclesiastical sense of a patriarchal jurisdiction commensurate with
the civil diocese, which contained several provinces. cf. the
IXth Canon of Chalcedon, which gives an appeal from the
metropolitan, the head of the province, to the exarch of
the "diocese." "The title exarch is here applied to the

appropriate to the excellent will which you have always shewn in your anxiety on behalf of the Churches of God.

LETTER CCLIV.[1]

To Pelagius,[2] bishop of the Syrian Laodicea.

MAY the Lord grant me once again in person to behold your true piety and to supply in actual intercourse all that is wanting in my letter. I am behindhand in beginning to write and must needs make many excuses. But we have with us the well beloved and reverend brother Sanctissimus, the presbyter. He will tell you everything, both our news and the news of the West. You will be cheered by what you hear; but when he tells you of the troubles in which we are involved he will perhaps add some distress and anxiety to that which already besets your kindly soul. Yet it is not to no purpose that affliction should be felt by you, able as you are to move the Lord. Your anxiety will turn to our gain, and I know that we shall receive succour from God as long as we have the aid of your prayers. Pray, too, with me for release from my anxieties, and ask for some increase in my bodily strength; then the Lord will prosper me on my way to the fulfilment of my desires and to a sight of your excellency.

LETTER CCLV.[3]

To Vitus, bishop of Charræ.[4]

WOULD that it were possible for me to write to your reverence every day! For ever since I have had experience of your affection I have had great desire to converse with you, or, if this be impossible, at least to communicate with you by letter, that I may tell you my own news and learn in what state you are. Yet we have not what we wish but what the Lord gives, and this we ought to receive with gratitude. I have therefore thanked the holy God for giving me an opportunity for writing to your reverence on the arrival of our very well beloved and reverend brother Sanctissimus, the presbyter. He has had considerable trouble in accomplishing his journey, and will tell you with accuracy all that he has learnt in the West. For all these things we ought to thank the Lord and to beseech Him to give us too the same peace and that we may freely receive one another. Receive all the brethren in Christ in my name.

LETTER CCLVI.[1]

To the very well beloved and reverend brethren the presbyters Acacius, Aetius, Paulus, and Silvanus; the deacons Silvinus and Lucius, and the rest of the brethren the monks, Basil, the bishop.[2]

NEWS has reached me of the severe persecution carried on against you, and how directly after Easter the men who fast for strife and debate[3] attacked your homes, and gave your labours to the flames, preparing for you indeed a house in the heavens, not made with hands,[4] but for themselves laying up in store the fire which they had used to your hurt. I no sooner heard of this than I groaned over what had happened; pitying not you, my brethren, (God forbid!) but the men who are so sunk in wickedness as to carry their evil deeds to such an extent. I expected you all to hurry at once to the refuge prepared for you in my humble self; and I hoped that the Lord would give me refreshment in the midst of my continual troubles in embracing you, and in receiving on this inactive body of mine the noble sweat which you are dropping for the truth's sake, and so having some share in the prizes laid up for you by the Judge of truth. But this did not enter into your minds, and you did not even expect any relief at my hands. I was therefore at least anxious to find frequent opportunities of writing to you, to the end that like those who cheer on combatants in the arena, I might myself by letter give you some encouragement in your good fight. For two reasons, however, I have not found this easy. In the first place, I did not know where you were residing. And, secondly, but few of our people travel in your direction. Now the Lord has brought us the very well beloved and reverend brother Sanctissimus, the presbyter. By him I am able to salute you, and I beseech you to pray for me, rejoicing and exulting that your reward is great in heaven,[5] and that you have freedom with the Lord to cease not day and night calling on Him to put an end to this storm of the Churches;

[1] Placed in 376.
[2] *cf. Letter* xcii. p. 177. On Pelagius bishop of the Syrian Laodicea, see Theod., *H.E.* iv. 13, and v. S. Philostorg., *H.E.* v. 1. Sozomen, *H.E.* vi. 12, and vii. 9.
[3] Placed in 376.
[4] *cf. Letter* xcii. p. 177. Vitus of Charræ (Haran) was bishop of Constantinople in 381. (Labbe, ii. 955.) *cf.* Sozomen, *H.E.* vi. 33.

[1] Placed in 376.
[2] Maran (*Vit. Bas.* xxxvi. 5) remarks that the Acacius heading this list is probably the Acacius who in 375 had invited Basil in the name of the Church of Berœa, and was afterwards famous alike for his episcopate at Berœa and his hostility to St. Chrysostom. *cf. Letter* ccxx. p. 260.
[3] Is. lviii. 4.   [4] 2 Cor. v. 1.   [5] Matt. v. 12.

to grant the shepherds to their flocks, and
that the Church may return to her proper
dignity. I am persuaded that if a voice be
found to move our good God, He will not
make His mercy afar off, but will now
" with the temptation make a way to escape,
that ye may be able to bear it." [1] Salute all
the brethren in Christ in my name.

LETTER CCLVII.[2]

To the monks harassed by the Arians.

1. I HAVE thought it only right to announce to you by letter how I said to myself, when I heard of the trials brought upon
you by the enemies of God, that in a time
reckoned a time of peace you have won
for yourselves the blessings promised to all
who suffer persecution for the sake of the
name of Christ. In my judgment the war
that is waged against us by our fellow country-
men is the hardest to bear, because against
open and declared enemies it is easy to defend ourselves, while we are necessarily at
the mercy of those who are associated with
us, and are thus exposed to continual
danger. This has been your case. Our
fathers were persecuted, but by idolaters ;
their substance was plundered, their houses
were overthrown, they themselves were
driven into exile, by our open enemies,
for Christ's name's sake. The persecutors,
who have lately appeared, hate us no less
than they, but, to the deceiving of many,
they put forward the name of Christ, that
the persecuted may be robbed of all comfort
from its confession, because the majority of
simpler folk, while admitting that we are
being wronged, are unwilling to reckon our
death for the truth's sake to be martyrdom.
I am therefore persuaded that the reward in
store for you from the righteous Judge is
yet greater than that bestowed on those
former martyrs. They indeed both had the
public praise of men, and received the reward of God ; to you, though your good
deeds are not less, no honours are given by
the people. It is only fair that the requital
in store for you in the world to come should
be far greater.

2. I exhort you, therefore, not to faint
in your afflictions, but to be revived by
God's love, and to add daily to your zeal.
knowing that in you ought to be preserved
that remnant of true religion which the
Lord will find when He cometh on the
earth. Even if bishops are driven from

their Churches, be not dismayed. If traitors
have arisen from among the very clergy[1]
themselves, let not this undermine your
confidence in God. We are saved not by
names, but by mind and purpose, and genuine
love toward our Creator. Bethink you how
in the attack against our Lord, high priests
and scribes and elders devised the plot,
and how few of the people were found
really receiving the word. Remember that
it is not the multitude who are being saved,
but the elect of God. Be not then affrighted
at the great multitude of the people who are
carried hither and thither by winds like the
waters of the sea. If but one be saved, like
Lot at Sodom, he ought to abide in right
judgment, keeping his hope in Christ unshaken, for the Lord will not forsake His
holy ones. Salute all the brethren in Christ
from me. Pray earnestly for my miserable
soul.

LETTER CCLVIII.[2]

To Epiphanius the bishop.[3]

1. IT has long been expected that, in accordance with the prediction of our Lord,
because of iniquity abounding, the love of the
majority would wax cold.[4] Now experience
has confirmed this expectation. But though
this condition of things has already obtained
among us here, it seems to be contradicted
by the letter brought from your holiness.
For verily it is no mere ordinary proof of
love, first that you should remember an unworthy and insignificant person like myself;
and secondly, that you should send to visit
me brethren who are fit and proper ministers
of a correspondence of peace. For now,
when every man is viewing every one else with
suspicion, no spectacle is rarer than that
which you are presenting. Nowhere is pity
to be seen ; nowhere sympathy ; nowhere
a brotherly tear for a brother in distress.
Not persecutions for the truth's sake, not
Churches with all their people in tears ;
not this great tale of troubles closing round
us, are enough to stir us to anxiety for the
welfare of one another. We jump on them
that are fallen ; we scratch and tear at
wounded places ; we who are supposed to
agree with one another launch the curses that
are uttered by the heretics ; men who are in
agreement on the most important matters are

---

[1] Maran conjectures an allusion to Fronto.
[2] Placed in 377.
[3] The learned and saintly bishop of Salamis in Cyprus.
About this time he published his great work against heresy,
the Πανάριον, and also travelled to Antioch to reconcile the
Apollinarian Vitalis to Paulinus. On the failure of his efforts,
and the complicated state of parties at Antioch at this time,
cf. Epiphan., lxxvii. 20-23; Jerome. *Epp.* 57, 58. and Soz., *H.E.*
vi. 25.   [4] cf. Matt. xxiv. 12.

---

[1] 1 Cor. x. 13.   [2] Placed in 376.

wholly severed from one another on some one single point. How, then, can I do otherwise than admire him who in such circumstances shews that his love to his neighbour is pure and guileless, and, though separated from me by so great a distance of sea and land, gives my soul all the care he can?

2. I have been specially struck with admiration at your having been distressed even by the dispute of the monks on the Mount of Olives, and at your expressing a wish that some means might be found of reconciling them to one another. I have further been glad to hear that you have not been unaware of the unfortunate steps, taken by certain persons, which have caused disturbance among the brethren, and that you have keenly interested yourself even in these matters. But I have deemed it hardly worthy of your wisdom that you should entrust the rectification of matters of such importance to me: for I am not guided by the grace of God, because of my living in sin; I have no power of eloquence, because I have cheerfully withdrawn from vain studies; and I am not yet sufficiently versed in the doctrines of the truth. I have therefore already written to my beloved brethren at the Mount of Olives, our own Palladius,[1] and Innocent the Italian, in answer to their letters to me, that it is impossible for me to make even the slightest addition to the Nicene Creed, except the ascription of Glory to the Holy Ghost, because our Fathers treated this point cursorily, no question having at that time arisen concerning the Spirit. As to the additions it is proposed to make to that Creed, concerning the incarnation of our Lord, I have neither tested nor accepted them, as being beyond my comprehension.[2] I know well that, if once we begin to interfere with the simplicity of the Creed, we shall embark on interminable discussion, contradiction ever leading us on and on, and shall but disturb the souls of simpler folk by the introduction of new phrases.[3]

3. As to the Church at Antioch (I mean that which is in agreement in the same doctrine), may the Lord grant that one day we may see it united. It is in peril of being specially open to the attacks of the enemy.

who is angry with it because there the name of Christian first obtained.[1] There heresy is divided against orthodoxy, and orthodoxy is divided against herself.[2] My position, however, is this. The right reverend bishop Meletius was the first to speak boldly for the truth, and fought that good fight in the days of Constantine. Therefore my Church has felt strong affection towards him, for the sake of that brave and firm stand, and has held communion with him. I, therefore, by God's grace, have held him to be in communion up to this time; and, if God will, I shall continue to do so. Moreover the very blessed Pope Athanasius came from Alexandria, and was most anxious that communion should be established between Meletius and himself; but by the malice of counsellors their conjunction was put off to another season. Would that this had not been so! I have never accepted communion with any one of those who have since been introduced into the see, not because I count them unworthy, but because I see no ground for the condemnation of Meletius. Nevertheless I have heard many things about the brethren, without giving heed to them, because the accused were not brought face to face with their accusers, according to that which is written, "Doth our law judge any man, before it hear him, and know what he doeth?"[3] I cannot therefore at present write to them, right honourable brother, and I ought not to be forced to do so. It will be becoming to your peaceful disposition not to cause union in one direction and disunion in another, but to restore the severed member to the original union. First, then, pray; next, to the utmost of your ability, exhort, that ambition may be driven from their hearts, and that reconciliation may be effected between them both to restore strength to the Church, and to destroy the rage of our foes. It has given great comfort to my soul that, in addition to your other right and accurate statements in theology, you should acknowledge the necessity of stating that the hypostases are three. Let the brethren at Antioch be instructed by you after this manner. Indeed I am confident that they have been so instructed; for I am sure you would never have accepted communion with them unless you had carefully made sure of this point in them.

4. The Magusæans,[4] as you were good

---

[1] This Palladius may possibly be identified with the Palladius of Cæsarea of Athanasius, *Ep. ad Pall.* Migne, *Pat.* xxvi. 1167, and in the Ath. of this series, p. 580.

[2] The Ben. note remarks "*Cum nonnulli formulæ Nicenæ aliquid de Incarnatione adderent ad comprimendos Apollinaristas, id Basilius nec examinaverat,*" etc. I rather understand the present προσυφαίνομενα to refer to the proposals of Innocent to Palladius.

[3] Yet Basil will admit an addition which he holds warranted, in the case of the glorification of the Spirit, and would doubtless have acquiesced in the necessity of the additions finally victorious in 451.

[1] *cf.* note on Theodoret in this series, p. 320.

[2] In 377 Meletius was in exile, and Paulinus the bishop of the "old Catholics," or Eustathians (Soc., *H.E.* iv. 2, v. 5), opposing Vitalius, who was consecrated to the episcopate by Apollinaris. On the confusion resulting from these three nominally orthodox claimants, *vide* Jerome's *Letter* xvi. in this series, p. 20. [3] John vii. 51.

[4] From Magusa in Arabia, *cf.* Plin., *Nat. Hist.* vi. 32.

enough to point out to me in your other letter, are here in considerable numbers, scattered all over the country, settlers having long ago been introduced into these parts from Babylon. Their manners are peculiar, as they do not mix with other men. It is quite impossible to converse with them, inasmuch as they have been made the prey of the devil to do his will. They have no books; no instructors in doctrine. They are brought up in senseless institutions, piety being handed down from father to son. In addition to the characteristics which are open to general observation, they object to the slaying of animals as defilement, and they cause the animals they want for their own use to be slaughtered by other people. They are wild after illicit marriages; they consider fire divine, and so on.[1] No one hitherto has told me any fables about the descent of the Magi from Abraham: they name a certain Zarnuas as the founder of their race. I have nothing more to write to your excellency about them.

LETTER CCLIX.[2]

To the monks Palladius and Innocent.

From your affection for me you ought to be able to conjecture my affection for you. I have always desired to be a herald of peace, and, when I fail in my object, I am grieved. How could it be otherwise? I cannot feel angry with any one for this reason, because I know that the blessing of peace has long ago been withdrawn from us. If the responsibility for division lies with others, may the Lord grant that those who cause dissension may cease to do so. I cannot even ask that your visits to me may be frequent. You have therefore no reason to excuse yourselves on this score. I am well aware that men who have embraced the life of labour, and always provide with their own hands the necessities of life, cannot be long away from home; but, wherever you are, remember me, and pray for me that no cause of disturbance may dwell in my heart, and that I may be at peace with myself and with God.

LETTER CCLX.[3]

To Optimus the bishop.[4]

1. Under any circumstances I should have gladly seen the good lads, on account of both a steadiness of character beyond

their years, and their near relationship to your excellency, which might have led me to expect something remarkable in them. And, when I saw them approaching me with your letter, my affection towards them was doubled. But now that I have read the letter, now that I have seen all the anxious care for the Church that there is in it, and the evidence it affords of your zeal in reading the divine Scriptures, I thank the Lord. And I invoke blessings on those who brought me such a letter, and, even before them, on the writer himself.

2. You have asked for a solution of that famous passage which is everywhere interpreted in different senses, "Whosoever slayeth Cain will exact vengeance for seven sins."[1] Your question shews that you have yourself carefully observed the charge of Paul to Timothy,[2] for you are obviously attentive to your reading. You have moreover roused me, old man that I am, dull alike from age and bodily infirmity, and from the many afflictions which have been stirred up round about me and have weighed down my life. Fervent in spirit as you are yourself, you are rousing me, now benumbed like a beast in his den, to some little wakefulness and vital energy. The passage in question may be interpreted simply and may also receive an elaborate explanation. The simpler, and one that may occur to any one off hand, is this: that Cain ought to suffer sevenfold punishment for his sins.

For it is not the part of a righteous judge to define requital on the principle of like for like, but the originator of evil must pay his debt with addition, if he is to be made better by punishment and render other men wiser by his example. Therefore, since it is ordained that Cain pay the penalty of his sin sevenfold, he who kills him, it is said, will discharge the sentence pronounced against him by the divine judgment. This is the sense that suggests itself to us on our first reading the passage.

3. But readers, gifted with greater curiosity, are naturally inclined to probe into the question further. How, they ask, can justice be satisfied seven times? And what are the vengeances? Are they for seven sins committed? Or is the sin committed once, and are there seven punishments for the one sin? Scripture continually assigns *seven* as the number of the remission of sins. "How often," it is asked, "shall my brother sin against me and I forgive him?" (It is Peter who is speaking to the Lord.) "Till

1 With the statements of Basil may be compared those of Bardesanes in Eusebius, *Præp. Evan.* vi. 275, and of Epiphanius in his *Exp. Cathol. Fid.*
2 Placed in 377.   3 Placed in 377.
4 Bishop of Antioch in Pisidia. Soc. vii. 36; Theod. v. 8.

1 Gen. iv. 15, LXX.   2 cf. 1 Tim. iv. 13.

seven times?" Then comes the Lord's answer, "I say not unto thee, until seven times, but, until seventy times seven."[1] Our Lord did not vary the number, but multiplied the seven, and so fixed the limit of the forgiveness. After seven years the Hebrew used to be freed from slavery.[2] Seven weeks of years used in old times to make the famous jubilee,[3] in which the land rested, debts were remitted, slaves were set free, and, as it were, a new life began over again, the old life from age to age being in a sense completed at the number seven. These things are types of this present life, which revolves in seven days and passes by, wherein punishments of slighter sins are inflicted, according to the loving care of our good Lord, to save us from being delivered to punishment in the age that has no end. The expression *seven times* is therefore introduced because of its connexion with this present world, for men who love this world ought specially to be punished in the things for the sake of which they have chosen to live wicked lives. If you understand the *vengeances* to be for the sins committed by Cain, you will find those sins to be seven. Or if you understand them to mean the sentence passed on him by the Judge, you will not go far wrong. To take the crimes of Cain: the first sin is *envy* at the preference of Abel; the second is *guile*, whereby he said to his brother, "Let us go into the field: "[4] the third is *murder*, a further wickedness: the fourth, *fratricide*, a still greater iniquity: the fifth that he committed the *first murder*, and set a bad example to mankind: the sixth *wrong*, in that he grieved his parents: the seventh, his *lie* to God; for when he was asked, "Where is Abel thy brother?" he replied, "I know not."[5] Seven sins were therefore avenged in the destruction of Cain. For when the Lord said, "Cursed is the earth which has opened to receive the blood of thy brother," and "groaning and trembling shall there be on the earth," Cain said, "If thou castest me out to-day from the earth, then from thy face shall I be hid, and groaning and trembling shall I lie upon the earth, and every one that findeth me shall slay me." It is in answer to this that the Lord says, "Whosoever slayeth Cain will discharge seven vengeances."[6] Cain supposed that he would be an easy prey to every one, because of there being no safety for him in the earth (for the earth was cursed for his sake), and of his being deprived of the succour of God,

Who was angry with him for the murder, and so of there being no help for him either from earth or from heaven. Therefore he said, "It shall come to pass that every one that findeth me shall slay me." Scripture proves his error in the words, "Not so;" *i.e.* thou shall not be slain. For to men suffering punishment, death is a gain, because it brings relief from their pain. But thy life shall be prolonged, that thy punishment may be made commensurate with thy sins. Since then the word ἐκδικούμενον may be understood in two senses; both the sin for which vengeance was taken, and the manner of the punishment, let us now examine whether the criminal suffered a sevenfold torment.

4. The seven sins of Cain have been enumerated in what has been already said. Now I ask if the punishments inflicted on him were seven, and I state as follows. The Lord enquired 'Where is Abel thy brother?' not because he wished for information, but in order to give Cain an opportunity for repentance, as is proved by the words themselves, for on his denial the Lord immediately convicts him saying, "The voice of thy brother's blood crieth unto me." So the enquiry, "Where is Abel thy brother?" was not made with a view to God's information, but to give Cain an opportunity of perceiving his sin. But for God's having visited him he might have pleaded that he was left alone and had had no opportunity given him for repentance. Now the physician appeared that the patient might flee to him for help. Cain, however, not only fails to hide his sore, but makes another one in adding the lie to the murder. "I know not. Am I my brother's keeper?" Now from this point begin to reckon the punishments. "Cursed is the ground for thy sake," one punishment. "Thou shalt till the ground." This is the second punishment. Some secret necessity was imposed upon him forcing him to the tillage of the earth, so that it should never be permitted him to take rest when he might wish, but ever to suffer pain with the earth, his enemy, which, by polluting it with his brother's blood, he had made accursed. "Thou shalt till the ground." Terrible punishment, to live with those that hate one, to have for a companion an enemy, an implacable foe. "Thou shalt till the earth," that is, Thou shalt toil at the labours of the field, never resting, never released from thy work, day or night, bound down by secret necessity which is harder than any savage master, and continually urged on to labour. "And it shall not yield unto thee her

---

[1] Matt. xviii. 21, 22.   [4] Gen. iv. 8.
[2] Deut. v. 12.   [5] Gen. iv. 9.
[3] Lev. xxv. 10.   [6] Gen. iv. 11, 12, 14, 15, LXX.

strength." Although the ceaseless toil had some fruit, the labour itself were no little torture to one forced never to relax it. But the toil is ceaseless, and the labours at the earth are fruitless (for "she did not yield her strength") and this fruitlessness of labour is the third punishment. "Groaning and trembling shalt thou be on the earth." Here two more are added to the three; continual groaning, and tremblings of the body, the limbs being deprived of the steadiness that comes of strength. Cain had made a bad use of the strength of his body, and so its vigour was destroyed, and it tottered and shook, and it was hard for him to lift meat and drink to his mouth, for after his impious conduct, his wicked hand was no longer allowed to minister to his body's needs. Another punishment is that which Cain disclosed when he said, "*Thou hast driven me out from the face of the earth, and from thy face shall I be hid.*" What is the meaning of this driving out from the face of the earth? It means deprivation of the benefits which are derived from the earth. He was not transferred to another place, but he was made a stranger to all the good things of earth. "*And from thy face shall I be hid.*" The heaviest punishment for men of good heart is alienation from God. "*And it shall come to pass that every one that findeth me shall slay me.*" He infers this from what has gone before. If I am cast out of the earth, and hidden from thy face, it remains for me to be slain of every one. What says the Lord? *Not so.* But he put a mark upon him. This is the seventh punishment, that the punishment should not be hid, but that by a plain sign proclamation should be made to all, that this is the first doer of unholy deeds. To all who reason rightly the heaviest of punishments is shame. We have learned this also in the case of the judgments, when "some" shall rise "to everlasting life, and some to shame and everlasting contempt."[1]

5. Your next question is of a kindred character, concerning the words of Lamech to his wives; "*I have slain a man to my wounding, and a young man to my hurt: if Cain shall be avenged sevenfold, truly Lamech seventy and sevenfold.*"[2] Some suppose that Cain was slain by Lamech, and that he survived to this generation that he might suffer a longer punishment. But this is not the case. Lamech evidently committed two murders, from what he says himself, "I have slain a man and a young man," the man to his wounding, and the

young man to his hurt. There is a difference between wounding and hurt.[1] And there is a difference between a man and a young man. "If Cain shall be avenged sevenfold, truly Lamech seventy and sevenfold." It is right that I should undergo four hundred and ninety punishments, if God's judgment on Cain was just, that his punishments should be seven. Cain had not learned to murder from another, and had never seen a murderer undergoing punishment. But I, who had before my eyes Cain groaning and trembling, and the mightiness of the wrath of God, was not made wiser by the example before me. Wherefore I deserve to suffer four hundred and ninety punishments. There are, however, some who have gone so far as the following explanation, which does not jar with the doctrine of the Church; from Cain to the flood, they say, seven generations passed by, and the punishment was brought on the whole earth, because sin was everywhere spread abroad. But the sin of Lamech requires for its cure not a Flood, but Him Who Himself takes away the sin of the world.[2] Count the generations from Adam to the coming of Christ, and you will find, according to the genealogy of Luke, that the Lord was born in the seventy-seventh.

Thus I have investigated this point to the best of my ability, though I have passed by matters therein that might be investigated, for fear of prolonging my observations beyond the limits of my letter. But for your intelligence little seeds are enough. "Give instruction," it is said, "to a wise man, and he will be yet wiser."[3] "If a skilful man hear a wise word he will commend it, and add unto it."[4]

6. About the words of Simeon to Mary, there is no obscurity or variety of interpretation. "And Simeon blessed them, and said unto Mary His mother, Behold, this Child is set for the fall and rising again of many in Israel; and for a sign which shall be spoken against; (yea, a sword shall pierce through thine own soul also,) that the thoughts of many hearts may be revealed."[5] Here I am astonished that, after passing by the previous words as requiring no explanation, you should enquire about the expression, "Yea, a sword shall pierce through thy own soul also." To me the question, how the same child can be for the fall and rising again, and what is the sign that shall be spoken against, does not seem less perplexing than the question how a sword shall pierce through Mary's heart.

---

[1] Dan. xii. 2.   [2] Gen. iv. 23, 24.

[1] LXX. μώλωψ, *i.e.* weal.   [3] Prov. ix. 9.   [5] Luke ii. 34, 35.
[2] John i. 29.   [4] Ecclus. xx. 18.

7. My view is, that the Lord is for falling and rising again, not because some fall and others rise again, but because in us the worst falls and the better is set up. The advent[1] of the Lord is destructive of our bodily affections and it rouses the proper qualities of the soul. As when Paul says, "When I am weak, then I am strong,"[2] the same man is weak and is strong, but he is weak in the flesh and strong in the spirit. Thus the Lord does not give to some occasions of falling and to others occasions of rising. Those who fall, fall from the station in which they once were, but it is plain that the faithless man never stands, but is always dragged along the ground with the serpent whom he follows. He has then nowhere to fall from, because he has already been cast down by his unbelief. Wherefore the first boon is, that he who stands in his sin should fall and die, and then should live in righteousness and rise, both of which graces our faith in Christ confers on us. Let the worse fall that the better may have opportunity to rise. If fornication fall not, chastity does not rise. Unless our unreason be crushed our reason will not come to perfection. In this sense he is for the fall and rising again of many.

8. *For a sign that shall be spoken against.* By a sign, we properly, understand in Scripture a cross. Moses, it is said, set the serpent "upon a pole."[3] That is upon a cross. Or else a sign[4] is indicative of something strange and obscure seen by the simple but understood by the intelligent. There is no cessation of controversy about the Incarnation of the Lord; some asserting that he assumed a body, and others that his sojourn was bodiless; some that he had a passible body, and others that he fulfilled the bodily œconomy by a kind of appearance. Some say that His body was earthly, some that it was heavenly; some that He pre-existed before the ages; some that He took His beginning from Mary. It is on this account that He is a sign that shall be spoken against.

9. By a sword is meant the word which tries and judges our thoughts, which pierces even to the dividing asunder of soul and spirit and of the joints and marrow, and is a discerner of our thoughts.[5] Now every soul in the hour of the Passion was subjected, as it were, to a kind of searching. According to the word of the Lord it is said, "All ye shall be offended because of me."[6] Simeon therefore prophesies about Mary herself, that

when standing by the cross, and beholding what is being done, and hearing the voices, after the witness of Gabriel, after her secret knowledge of the divine conception, after the great exhibition of miracles, she shall feel about her soul a mighty tempest.[1] The Lord was bound to taste of death for every man — to become a propitiation for the world and to justify all men by His own blood. Even thou thyself, who hast been taught from on high the things concerning the Lord, shalt be reached by some doubt. This is the sword. "That the thoughts of many hearts may be revealed." He indicates that after the offence at the Cross of Christ a certain swift healing shall come from the Lord to the disciples and to Mary herself, confirming their heart in faith in Him. In the same way we saw Peter, after he had been offended, holding more firmly to his faith in Christ. What was human in him was proved unsound, that the power of the Lord might be shewn.

LETTER CCLXI.[2]

To the Sozopolitans.[3]

I HAVE received the letter which you, right honourable brethren, have sent me concerning the circumstances in which you are placed. I thank the Lord that you have let me share in the anxiety you feel as to your attention to things needful and deserving of serious heed. But I was distressed to hear that over and above the disturbance brought on the Churches by the Arians, and the confusion caused by them in the definition of the faith, there has appeared among you yet another innovation, throwing the brotherhood into great dejection, because, as you have informed me, certain persons are uttering, in the hearing of the faithful, novel and unfamiliar doctrines which they allege to be deduced from the teaching of Scripture. You write that there are men among you who are trying to destroy the saving incarnation[4] of our Lord Jesus Christ, and,

[1] The Ben. note strongly objects to this slur upon the constancy of the faith of the Blessed Virgin, and is sure that St. Basil's error will not be thus corrected without his own concurrence. It supposes this interpretation of the passage in question to be derived from Origen, *Hom.* xxvii. *In Lucam*, and refers to a list of commentators who have followed him in Petavius, *De Incar.* xiv. 1.

[2] This letter is placed in 377. Fessler styles it "*celeberrima.*" The Benedictine heading is "*Cum scripsissent Basilio Sozopolitani nonnullos carnem cœlestem Christo affingere et affectus humanos in ipsam divinitatem conferre; breviter hunc errorem refellit; ac demonstrat nihil nobis prodesse passiones Christi si non eandem ac nos carnem habuit. Quod spectat ad affectus humanos, probat naturales a Christo assumptos fuisse, vitiosos vero nequaquam.*"

[3] Sozopolis, or Suzupolis, in Pisidia (*cf.* Evagrius, *Hist. Ecc.* iii. 33), has been supposed to be the ancient name of Souzon, S. of Aglasoun, where ruins still exist. On its connexion with Apollonia. *cf. Hist. Geog. A.M.* p. 400. [4] οἰκονομίαν.

---

[1] ἐπιδάνεια. [3] Num. xxi. 8. [5] *cf.* Heb. iv. 12.
[2] 2 Cor. xii. 10. [4] σήμειον, LXX. [6] Matt. xxvi. 3.

so far as they can, are overthrowing the grace of the great mystery unrevealed from everlasting, but manifested in His own times, when the Lord, when He had gone through [1] all things pertaining to the cure of the human race, bestowed on all of us the boon of His own sojourn among us. For He helped His own creation, first through the patriarchs, whose lives were set forth as examples and rules to all willing to follow the footsteps of the saints, and with zeal like theirs to reach the perfection of good works. Next for succour He gave the Law, ordaining it by angels in the hand of Moses; [2] then the prophets, foretelling the salvation to come; judges, kings, and righteous men, doing great works, with a mighty [3] hand. After all these in the last days He was Himself manifested in the flesh, " made of a woman, made under the law, to redeem them that were under the law, that we might receive the adoption of sons." [4]

2. If, then, the sojourn of the Lord in flesh has never taken place, the Redeemer [5] paid not the fine to death on our behalf, nor through Himself destroyed death's reign. For if what was reigned over by death was not that which was assumed by the Lord, death would not have ceased working his own ends, nor would the sufferings of the God-bearing flesh have been made our gain; He would not have killed sin in the flesh; we who had died in Adam should not have been made alive in Christ; the fallen to pieces would not have been framed again; the shattered would not have been set up again; that which by the serpent's trick had been estranged from God would never have been made once more His own. All these boons are undone by those that assert that it was with a heavenly body that the Lord came among us. And if the God-bearing flesh was not ordained to be assumed of the lump of Adam, what need was there of the Holy Virgin? But who has the hardihood now once again to renew by the help of sophistical arguments and, of course, by scriptural evidence, that old dogma [6] of Valentinus, now long ago silenced? For this impious doctrine of the seeming [7] is no

novelty. It was started long ago by the feeble-minded Valentinus, who, after tearing off a few of the Apostle's statements, constructed for himself this impious fabrication, asserting that the Lord assumed the " form of a servant," [1] and not the servant himself, and that He was made in the " likeness," but that actual manhood was not assumed by Him. Similar sentiments are expressed by these men who can only be pitied for bringing new troubles upon you. [2]

3. As to the statement that human feelings are transmitted to the actual Godhead, it is one made by men who preserve no order in their thoughts, and are ignorant that there is a distinction between the feelings of flesh, of flesh endowed with soul, and of soul using a body. [3] It is the property of flesh to undergo division, diminution, dissolution; of flesh endowed with soul to feel weariness, pain, hunger, thirst, and to be overcome by sleep; of soul using body to feel grief, heaviness, anxiety, and such like. Of these some are natural and necessary to every living creature; others come of evil will, and are superinduced because of life's lacking proper discipline and training for virtue. Hence it is evident that our Lord assumed the natural affections to establish His real incarnation, and not by way of semblance of incarnation, and that all the affections derived from evil that besmirch the purity of our life, He rejected as unworthy of His unsullied Godhead. It is on this account that He is said to have been " made in the likeness of flesh of sin;" [4] not, as these men hold, in likeness of flesh, but of flesh of sin. It follows that He took our flesh with its natural affections, but " did no sin." [5] Just as the death which is in the flesh, transmitted to us through Adam, was swallowed up by the Godhead, so was the sin taken away by the righteousness which is in Christ Jesus, [6] so that in the resurrection we receive back the flesh neither liable to death nor subject to sin.

These, brethren, are the mysteries of the

---

1 Here the Ben. Ed. call attention to the fact that St. Basil may by this word indicate the appearance of the Son to the patriarchs before the Birth from the Virgin, and compares a similar statement in his Book *Cont. Eunom.* II.. as well as the words of Clemens Alex. in the work *Quis Dives Salvandus*, n. 8, in which the Son is described as ἀπὸ γενέσεως μέχρι τοῦ σημείου τὴν ἀνθρωπότητα διατρέχων. 2 *cf.* Gal. iii. 19.
3 κραταιᾷ with the ed. Par. seems to make better sense than κρυφαίᾳ, which has better authority. 4 Gal. iv. 4, 5.
5 Λυτρωτής. *cf.* Acts vii. 35, where R.V. gives redeemer as a marginal rendering. Λυτρωτής = payer of the λύτρον, which is the means of release (λύω). The word is used of Moses in the Acts in a looser sense than here of the Saviour.
6 On the use of " dogma" for heretical opinion, *cf. De Sp. S.* note on § 66. 7 δόκησις.

1 Phil. ii. 7.
2 On the Docetism of Valentinus *vide* Dr. Salmon in *D.C. Biog.* i. 869. " According to V. (Irenæus i. 7) our Lord's nature was fourfold: (1) He had a ψυχή or animal soul; (2) He had a πνεῦμα or spiritual principle derived from Achamoth; (3) He had a body, but not a material body, but a heavenly one. . . . (4) The pre-existent Saviour descended on Him in the form of a dove at His Baptism. When our Lord was brought before Pilate, this Saviour as being incapable of suffering withdrew His power;" (*cf.* the *Gospel of Peter*, "The Lord cried, saying, ' My Power, my Power, Thou hast left me.' ") " and the spiritual part which was also impassible was likewise dismissed; the animal soul and the wonderfully contrived body alone remaining to suffer, and to exhibit on the cross on earth a representation of what had previously taken place on the heavenly Stauros. It thus appears that Valentinus was only partially docetic." But *cf.* Iren. v. 1, 2, and iii. 22.
3 *cf. De Sp. S.* § 12. p. 7. 5 1 Pet. ii. 22.
4 Rom. viii. 3, R.V. marg. 6 *cf.* Rom. v. 12 *ad fin.*

Church; these are the traditions of the Fathers. Every man who fears the Lord, and is awaiting God's judgment, I charge not to be carried away by various doctrines. If any one teaches a different doctrine, and refuses to accede to the sound words of the faith, rejecting the oracles of the Spirit, and making his own teaching of more authority than the lessons of the Gospels, of such an one beware. May the Lord grant that one day we may meet, so that all that my argument has let slip I may supply when we stand face to face! I have written little when there was much to say, for I did not like to go beyond my letter's bounds. At the same time I do not doubt that to all that fear the Lord a brief reminder is enough.

LETTER CCLXII.[1]

To the Monk Urbicius.[2]

1. You have done well to write to me. You have shewn how great is the fruit of charity. Continue so to do. Do not think that, when you write to me, you need offer excuses. I recognise my own position, and I know that by nature every man is of equal honour with all the rest. Whatever excellence there is in me is not of family, nor of superfluous wealth, nor of physical condition; it comes only of superiority in the fear of God. What, then, hinders you from fearing the Lord yet more, and so, in this respect, being greater than I am? Write often to me, and acquaint me with the condition of the brotherhood with you. Tell me what members of the Church in your parts are sound, that I may know to whom I ought to write, and in whom I may confide. I am told that there are some who are endeavouring to deprave the right doctrine of the Lord's incarnation by perverse opinions, and I therefore call upon them through you to hold off from those unreasonable views, which some are reported to me to hold. I mean that God Himself was turned into flesh; that He did not assume, through the Holy Mary, the nature[3] of Adam, but, in His own proper Godhead, was changed into a material nature.[4]

2. This absurd position can be easily confuted. The blasphemy is its own conviction, and I therefore think that, for one who fears the Lord, the mere reminder is enough. If He was turned, then He was changed. But far be it from me to say or think such a thing, when God has declared,

"I am the Lord, I change not."[1] Moreover, how could the benefit of the incarnation be conveyed to us, unless our body, joined to the Godhead, was made superior to the dominion of death? If He was changed, He no longer constituted a proper body, such as subsisted after the combination with it of the divine body.[2] But how, if all the nature of the Only-begotten was changed, could the incomprehensible Godhead be circumscribed within the limit of the mass of a little body? I am sure that no one who is in his senses, and has the fear of God, is suffering from this unsoundness. But the report has reached me that some of your company are afflicted with this mental infirmity, and I have therefore thought it necessary, not to send you a mere formal greeting, but to include in my letter something which may even build up the souls of them that fear the Lord. I therefore urge that these errors receive ecclesiastical correction, and that you abstain from communion with the heretics. I know that we are deprived of our liberty in Christ by indifference on these points.

LETTER CCLXIII.[3]

To the Westerns.

1. May the Lord God, in Whom we have put our trust, give to each of you grace sufficient to enable you to realize your hope, in proportion to the joy wherewith you have filled my heart, both by the letter which you have sent me by the hands of the well-beloved fellow-presbyters, and by the sympathy which you have felt for me in my distress, like men who have put on bowels of mercy,[4] as you have been described to me by the presbyters afore-mentioned. Although my wounds remain the same, nevertheless it does bring alleviation to me that I should have leeches at hand, able, should they find an opportunity, to apply rapid remedies to my hurts. Wherefore in return I salute you by our beloved friends, and exhort you, if the Lord puts it into your power to come to me, not to hesitate to visit me. For part of the greatest commandment is the visitation of the sick. But if the good God and wise

---

[1] Mal. iii. 6.
[2] The sentence in all the MSS. (except the *Codex Coislin.* II., which has ὁ τραπείς) begins οὐ τραπείς. The Ben. Ed. propose simply to substitute εἰ for οὐ, and render " *Si enim conversus est, proprium constituit corpus, quod videlicet densata in ipsa deitate, substitit.*" I have endeavoured to force a possible meaning on the Greek as it stands, though παχυνθείσης more naturally refers to the unorthodox *change* than to the orthodox *conjunction.* The original is οὐ γὰρ τραπεὶς οἰκεῖον ὑπεστήσατο σῶμα, ὅπερ, παχυνθείσης αὐτῷ τῆς θείκῆς φύσεως, ὑπέστη.
[3] Placed in 377. [4] Col. iii. 12.

---

[1] Placed in 377.
[2] cf. *Letters* cxxiii. and ccclxvi.
[3] φύραμα.
[4] φύσις.

Dispenser of our lives reserves this boon for another season, at all events write to me whatever it is proper for you to write for the consolation of the oppressed and the lifting up of those that are crushed down. Already the Church has suffered many severe blows, and great has been my affliction at them. Nowhere is there expectation of succour, unless the Lord sends us a remedy by you who are his true servants.

2. The bold and shameless heresy of the Arians, after being publicly cut off from the body of the Church, still abides in its own error, and does not do us much harm because its impiety is notorious to all. Nevertheless, men clad in sheep's clothing, and presenting a mild and amiable appearance, but within unsparingly ravaging Christ's flocks, find it easy to do hurt to the simpler ones, because they came out from us. It is these who are grievous and hard to guard against. It is these that we implore your diligence to denounce publicly to all the Churches of the East; to the end that they may either turn to the right way and join with us in genuine alliance, or, if they abide in their perversity, may keep their mischief to themselves alone, and be unable to communicate their own plague to their neighbours by unguarded communion. I am constrained to mention them by name, in order that you may yourselves recognise those who are stirring up disturbance here, and may make them known to our Churches. My own words are suspected by most men, as though I had an ill will towards them on account of some private quarrel. You, however, have all the more credit with the people, in proportion to the distance that separates your home from theirs, besides the fact that you are gifted with God's grace to help those who are distressed. If more of you concur in uttering the same opinions, it is clear that the number of those who have expressed them will make it impossible to oppose their acceptance.

3. One of those who have caused me great sorrow is Eustathius of Sebasteia in Lesser Armenia; formerly a disciple of Arius, and a follower of him at the time when he flourished in Alexandria, and concocted his infamous blasphemies against the Only-begotten, he was numbered among his most faithful disciples. On his return to his own country he submitted a confession of the sound faith to Hermogenes, the very blessed Bishop of Cæsarea, who was on the point of condemning him for false doctrine. Under these circumstances he was ordained by Hermogenes, and, on the death of that

bishop, hastened to Eusebius of Constantinople, who himself yielded to none in the energy of his support of the impious doctrine of Arius. From Constantinople he was expelled for some reason or another, returned to his own country and a second time made his defence, attempting to conceal his impious sentiments and cloking them under a certain verbal orthodoxy. He no sooner obtained the rank of bishop than he straightway appeared writing an anathema on the Homoousion in the Arians' synod at Ancyra.[1] From thence he went to Seleucia and took part in the notorious measures of his fellow heretics. At Constantinople he assented a second time to the propositions of the heretics. On being ejected from his episcopate, on the ground of his former deposition at Melitine,[2] he hit upon a journey to you as a means of restitution for himself. What propositions were made to him by the blessed bishop Liberius, and to what he agreed, I am ignorant. I only know that he brought a letter restoring him, which he shewed to the synod at Tyana, and was restored to his see. He is now defaming the very creed for which he was received; he is consorting with those who are anathematizing the Homoousion, and is prime leader of the heresy of the pneumatomachi. As it is from the west that he derives his power to injure the Churches, and uses the authority given him by you to the overthrow of the many, it is necessary that his correction should come from the same quarter, and that a letter be sent to the Churches stating on what terms he was received, and in what manner he has changed his conduct and nullifies the favour given him by the Fathers at that time.

4. Next comes Apollinarius, who is no less a cause of sorrow to the Churches. With his facility of writing, and a tongue ready to argue on any subject, he has filled the world with his works, in disregard of the advice of him who said, "Beware of making many books."[3] In their multitude there are certainly many errors. How is it possible to avoid sin in a multitude of words?[4] And the theological works of Apollinarius are founded on Scriptural proof, but are based on a human origin. He has written about the resurrection, from a mythical, or rather Jewish, point of view; urging that we shall return again to the worship of the Law, be circumcised, keep the Sabbath, abstain from meats, offer sacrifices to God,

---

[1] In 358, when the homoiousion was accepted, and twelve anathemas formulated against all who rejected it.
[2] Before 359. Mansi iii. 201.   [4] cf. Prov. x. 19.
[3] Ecc. xii. 12, LXX. cf. Ep. ccxliv. p. 286.

worship in the Temple at Jerusalem, and be altogether turned from Christians into Jews. What could be more ridiculous? Or, rather, what could be more contrary to the doctrines of the Gospel? Then, further, he has made such confusion among the brethren about the incarnation, that few of his readers preserve the old mark of true religion; but the more part, in their eagerness for novelty, have been diverted into investigations and quarrelsome discussions of his unprofitable treatises.

5. As to whether there is anything objectionable about the conversation of Paulinus, you can say yourselves. What distresses me is that he should shew an inclination for the doctrine of Marcellus, and unreservedly admit his followers to communion. You know, most honourable brethren, that the reversal of all our hope is involved in the doctrine of Marcellus, for it does not confess the Son in His proper hypostasis, but represents Him as having been sent forth, and as having again returned to Him from Whom He came; neither does it admit that the Paraclete has His own subsistence. It follows that no one could be wrong in declaring this heresy to be all at variance with Christianity, and in styling it a corrupt Judaism. Of these things I implore you to take due heed. This will be the case if you will consent to write to all the Churches of the East that those who have perverted these doctrines are in communion with you, if they amend; but that if they contentiously determine to abide by their innovations, you are separated from them. I am myself well aware, that it had been fitting for me to treat of these matters, sitting in synod with you in common deliberation. But this the time does not allow. Delay is dangerous, for the mischief they have caused has taken root. I have therefore been constrained to dispatch these brethren, that you may learn from them all that has been omitted in my letter, and that they may rouse you to afford the succour which we pray for to the Churches of the East.

LETTER CCLXIV.[1]

To Barses, bishop of Edessa, in exile.[2]

To Barses the bishop, truly God-beloved and worthy of all reverence and honour, Basil sends greeting in the Lord. As my

dear brother Domninus[1] is setting out to you, I gladly seize the opportunity of writing, and I greet you by him, praying the holy God that we may be so long preserved in this life as to be permitted to see you, and to enjoy the good gifts which you possess. Only pray, I beseech you, that the Lord may not deliver us for aye to the enemies of the Cross of Christ, but that He will keep His Churches, until the time of, that peace which the just Judge Himself knows when He will bestow. For He will bestow it. He will not always abandon us. As He limited seventy years[2] for the period of captivity for the Israelites in punishment for their sins, so peradventure the Mighty One, after giving us up for some appointed time, will recall us once again, and will restore us to the peace of the beginning — unless indeed the apostasy is now nigh at hand, and the events that have lately happened are the beginnings of the approach of Antichrist. If this be so, pray that the good Lord will either take away our afflictions, or preserve us through our afflictions unvanquished. Through you I greet all those who have been thought worthy to be associated with you. All who are with me salute your reverence. May you, by the grace of the Holy One, be preserved to the Church of God in good health, trusting in the Lord, and praying for me.

LETTER CCLXV.[3]

To Eulogius, Alexander, and Harpocration, bishops of Egypt, in exile.

1. In all things we find that the providence exercised by our good God over His Churches is mighty, and that thus the very things which seem to be gloomy, and do not turn out as we should like, are ordained for the advantage of most, in the hidden wisdom of God, and in the unsearchable judgments of His righteousness. Now the Lord has removed you from the regions of Egypt, and has brought you and established you in the midst of Palestine, after the manner of Israel of old, whom He carried away by captivity into the land of the Assyrians, and there extinguished idolatry through the sojourn of His saints. Now too we find the same thing, when we observe that the Lord is making known your struggle for the sake of true religion, opening to you through your exile the arena of your blessed contests, and

[1] Placed in 377.
[2] See Soz., *H.E.* vi. 34, who says that Barses, with Eulogius, was not consecrated to any definite see. *cf.* also Theodoret, *H.E.* iv. 16, where it is stated that his bed was preserved at Aradus.

[1] Domninus was a not uncommon name, and there are several mentioned about the same time, *e.g.* Nilus, *Epp.* iii. 43 and 144. [2] Jer. xxv. 12. [3] Placed in 377.

to all who see before them your noble constancy, giving the boon of your good example to lead them to salvation. By God's grace, I have heard of the correctness of your faith, and of your zeal for the brethren, and that it is in no careless or perfunctory spirit that you provide what is profitable and necessary for salvation, and that you support all that conduces to the edification of the Churches. I have therefore thought it right that I should be brought into communion with your goodness, and be united to your reverences by letter. For these reasons I have sent my very dear brother the deacon Elpidius, who not only conveys my letter, but is moreover fully qualified to announce to you whatever may have been omitted in my letter.

2. I have been specially moved to desire union with you by the report of the zeal of your reverences in the cause of orthodoxy. The constancy of your hearts has been stirred neither by multiplicity of books nor by variety of ingenious arguments. You have, on the contrary, recognised those who endeavoured to introduce innovations in opposition to the apostolic doctrines, and you have refused to keep silence concerning the mischief which they are causing. I have in truth found great distress among all who cleave to the peace of the Lord at the divers innovations of Apollinarius of Laodicea. He has all the more distressed me from the fact that he seemed at the beginning on our side. A sufferer can in a certain sense endure what comes to him from an open enemy, even though it be exceedingly painful, as it is written, "For it was not an enemy that reproached me; then I could have borne it."[1] But it is intolerable, and beyond the power of comfort, to be wronged by a close and sympathetic friend. Now that very man whom I have expected to have at my right hand in defence of the truth, I have found in many ways hindering those who are being saved, by seducing their minds and drawing them away from direct doctrine. What rash and hasty deed has he not done? What ill considered and dangerous argument has he not risked? Is not all the Church divided against herself, specially since the day when men have been sent by him to the Churches governed by orthodox bishops, to rend them asunder and to set up some peculiar and illegal service? Is not ridicule brought upon the great mystery of true religion when bishops go about without people and clergy, having nothing but

the mere name and title, and effecting nothing for the advancement of the Gospel of peace and salvation? Are not his discourses about God full of impious doctrines, the old impiety of the insane Sabellius being now renewed by him in his writings? For if the works which are current among the Sebastenes are not the forgery of foes, and are really his composition, he has reached a height of impiety which cannot be surpassed, in saying that Father, Son, and Spirit are the same, and other dark pieces of irreverence which I have declined even to hear, praying that I may have nothing to do with those who have uttered them. Does he not confuse the doctrine of the incarnation? Has not the œconomy of salvation been made doubtful to the many on account of his dark and cloudy speculations about it? To collect them all, and refute them, requires long time and much discussion. But where have the promises of the Gospel been blunted and destroyed as by his figments? So meanly and poorly has he dared to explain the blessed hope laid up for all who live according to the Gospel of Christ, as to reduce it to mere old wives' fables and doctrines of Jews. He proclaims the renewal of the Temple, the observance of the worship of the Law, a typical high priest over again after the real High Priest, and a sacrifice for sins after the Lamb of God Who taketh away the sin of the world.[1] He preaches partial baptisms after the one baptism, and the ashes of a heifer sprinkling the Church which, through its faith in Christ, has not spot or wrinkle, or any such thing;[2] cleansing of leprosy after the painless state of the resurrection; an offering of jealousy[3] when they neither marry nor are given in marriage; shew-bread after the Bread from heaven; burning lamps after the true Light. In a word, if the law of the Commandments has been done away with by dogmas, it is plain that under these circumstances the dogmas of Christ will be nullified by the injunctions of the law.[4] At these things shame and disgrace have covered my face,[5] and heavy grief hath filled my heart. Wherefore, I beseech you, as skilful physicians, and instructed how to discipline antagonists with gentleness, to try and bring him back to the right order of the Church, and to persuade him to despise the wordiness of his own works; for he has proved the truth of the proverb " in the multitude of words there wanteth not sin."[6] Put boldly before

---

1 John i. 29.   2 Eph. v. 27.   3 cf. Num. v. 15.
4 This passage shews in what sense St. Basil understands δόγματα in Eph. ii. 15, and Col. ii. 14.   cf. note on p. 41.
5 cf. Ps. lxiv. 7.   6 Prov. x. 19.

him the doctrines of orthodoxy, in order that his amendment may be published abroad, and his repentance made known to his brethren.

3. It is also desirable that I should remind your reverence about the followers of Marcellus, in order that you may decide nothing in their case rashly or inconsiderately. On account· of his impious doctrines he has gone out from the Church.[1] It is therefore necessary that his followers should only be received into communion on condition that they anathematize that heresy, in order that those who are united to me through you may be accepted by all the brethren. And now most men are moved to no small grief on hearing that you have both received them and admitted them to ecclesiastical communion on their coming to your excellency. Nevertheless you ought to have known that by God's grace you do not stand alone in the East, but have many in communion with you, who vindicate the orthodoxy of the Fathers, and who put forth the pious doctrine of the Faith at Nicæa. The Westerns also all agree with you and with me, whose exposition of the Faith I have received and keep with me, assenting to their sound doctrine. You ought, then, to have satisfied all who are in agreement with you, that the action which is being taken may be ratified by the general consent, and that peace may not be broken by the acceptance of some while others are kept apart. Thus you ought to have at the same time seriously and gently taken counsel about matters which are of importance to all the Churches throughout the world. Praise is not due to him who hastily determines any point, but rather to him who

rules every detail firmly and unalterably, so that when his judgment is enquired into, even at a later time, it may be the more esteemed. This is the man who is acceptable both to God and man as one who guides his words with discretion.[1] Thus I have addressed your reverence in such terms as are possible in a letter. May the Lord grant that one day we may meet, that so, after arranging everything together with you for the government of the Churches, I may with you receive the reward prepared by the righteous Judge for faithful and wise stewards. In the mean time be so good as to let me know with what intention you have received the followers of Marcellus, knowing this, that even if you secure everything, so far as you yourselves are concerned, you ought not to deal with a matter of such importance on your own sole responsibility. It is further necessary that the Westerns, and those who are in communion with them in the East, should concur in the restoration of these men.

LETTER CCLXVI.[2]

To Petrus, bishop of Alexandria.[3]

1. YOU have very properly rebuked me, and in a manner becoming a spiritual brother who has been taught genuine love by the Lord, because I am not giving you exact and detailed information of all that is going on here, for it is both your part to be interested in what concerns me, and mine to tell you all that concerns myself. But I must tell you, right honourable and well-beloved brother, that our continuous afflictions, and this mighty agitation which is now shaking the Churches, result in my taking all that is happening as a matter of course. Just as in smithies where men whose ears are deafened get accustomed to the sound, so by the frequency of the strange tidings that reach me I have now grown accustomed to be undisturbed and undismayed at extraordinary events. So the policy which has been for a long time pursued by the Arians to the detriment of the Church, although their achievements have been many and great and noised abroad through all the world, has nevertheless been endurable to me, because of their being the work of open foes and enemies of the word of truth. It is when these men do something unusual that I am astonished, not when they attempt something great and audacious against

---

[1] Here the Ben. note is *Mirum id videtur ac prima specie vix credibile, Marcellum ob impios errores ex ecclesia exiisse. Nam S. Athanasius suspectum illum quidem, sed tamen purgatum habuit, teste Epiphanio, Hæres.* lxxii. p. 837. *Hinc illius discipuli communicatorias beatissimi papæ Athanasii litteras ostenderunt confessoribus Ægyptiis, ibid.* p. 843. *Testatur idem Epiphanius varia esse Catholicorum de Marcello judicia, aliis eum accusantibus, aliis defendentibus,* p. 834. *Paulinus ejus discipulos sine discrimine recipiebat, ut in superiore epistola vidimus. Ipse Basilius in epist.* 69 *queritur quod eum Ecclesia Romana in communionem ab initio suscepisset. Quomodo ergo exiise dicitur ex Ecclesia qui tot habuit communicatores? Sed tamen S. Basilii testimonium cum sua sponte magni est momenti (non enim ut in dijudicandis Marcelli scriptis, ita in ejusmodi facto proclive fuit errare), tum etiam hoc argumento confirmatur quod Athanasius extremis vitæ suæ annis Marcellum a communione sua removerit. Neque enim, si semper cum eo communicasset Athanasius, opus habuissent illius discipuli confessione fidei ad impetrandam confessorum Ægyptiorum communionem: nec Petrus Athanasii successor canones violatos, concessa illis communione, quereretur, ut videmus in epistola sequenti, si Ægyptum inter ac Marcellum ejusque clerum et plebem non fuisset rupta communio. Videtur ergo Marcellus sub finem vitæ aliquid peccasse, quod Athanasium ab ejus communione discedere cogeret : et cum jamdudum a tota fere oriente damnatus esset, amissa Athanasii communione, quæ unicum fere illius refugium erat, desertus ab omnibus videri debuit, nec ei nova ignominia notato prodesse poterat concessa olim a Romana Ecclesia communio.*

[1] Ps. cxii. 5.
[2] Placed in 377.
[3] *cf. Letter* cxxxiii. p. 200.

true religion. But I am grieved and troubled at what is being done by men who feel and think with me. Yet their doings are so frequent and so constantly reported to me, that even they do not appear surprising. So it comes about that I was not agitated at the recent disorderly proceedings, partly because I knew perfectly well that common report would carry them to you without my help, and partly because I preferred to wait for somebody else to give you disagreeable news. And yet, further, I did not think it reasonable that I should show indignation at such proceedings, as though I were annoyed at suffering a slight. To the actual agents in the matter I have written in becoming terms, exhorting them, because of the dissension arising among some of the brethren there, not to fall away from charity, but to wait for the matter to be set right by those who have authority to remedy disorders in due ecclesiastical form. That you should have so acted, stirred by honourable and becoming motives, calls for my commendation, and moves my gratitude to the Lord that there remains preserved in you a relic of the ancient discipline, and that the Church has not lost her own might in my persecution. The canons have not suffered persecution as well as I. Though importuned again by the Galatians, I was never able to give them an answer, because I waited for your decision. Now, if the Lord so will, and they will consent to listen to me, I hope that I shall be able to bring the people to the Church. It cannot then be cast in my teeth that I have gone over to the Marcellians, and they on the contrary will become limbs of the body of the Church of Christ. Thus the disgrace caused by heresy will be made to disappear by the method I adopt, and I shall escape the opprobrium of having gone over to them.

2. I have also been grieved by our brother Dorotheus, because, as he has himself written, he has not gently and mildly reported everything to your excellency. I set this down to the difficulty of the times. I seem to be deprived by my sins of all success in my undertakings, if indeed the best of my brethren are proved ill-disposed and incompetent, by their failure to perform their duties in accordance with my wishes. On his return Dorotheus reported to me the conversation which he had had with your excellency in the presence of the very venerable bishop Damasus, and he caused me distress by saying that our God-beloved brethren and fellow-ministers, Meletius and

Eusebius, had been reckoned among the Ariomaniacs.[1] If their orthodoxy were established by nothing else, the attacks made upon them by the Arians are, to the minds of all right thinking people, no small proof of their rectitude. Even your participation with them in sufferings endured for Christ's sake ought to unite your reverence to them in love. Be assured of this, right honourable sir, that there is no word of orthodoxy which has not been proclaimed by these men with all boldness. God is my witness. I have heard them myself. I should not certainly have now admitted them to communion, if I had caught them tripping in the faith. But, if it seem good to you, let us leave the past alone. Let us make a peaceful start for the future. For we have need one of another in the fellowship of the members, and specially now, when the Churches of the East are looking to us, and will take your agreement as a pledge of strength and consolation. If, on the other hand, they perceive that you are in a state of mutual suspicion, they will drop their hands, and slacken in their resistance to the enemies of the faith.[2]

LETTER CCLXVII.[3]

To Barses, bishop of Edessa, in exile.

For the sake of the affection which I entertain for you, I long to be with you, to embrace you, my dear friend, in person, and to glorify the Lord Who is magnified in you, and has made your honourable old age renowned among all them that fear Him throughout the world. But severe sickness afflicts me, and to a greater degree than I can express in words, I am weighed down by the care of the Churches. I am not my own master, to go whither I will, and to visit whom I will. Therefore I am trying to satisfy the longing I have for the good gifts in you by writing to you, and I beseech your reverence to pray for me and for the Church, that the Lord may grant to me to pass the remaining days or hours of my sojourn here without offence. May He permit me to see the peace of His Churches. Of your fellow-ministers and fellow-athletes may I hear all that I pray for, and of yourself that you are granted such a lot as the people under

---

[1] The Ben. note points out that the accusation against Eusebius (of Samosata) and Meletius was monstrous, and remarks on the delicacy with which Basil approaches it, without directly charging Petrus, from whom it must have come, with the slander involved.

[2] One MS. contains a note to the effect that this letter was never sent. Maran (*Vit. Bas.* xxxvii.) thinks the internal evidence is in favour of its having been delivered.

[3] Placed in 377, or in the beginning of 378.

you seek for by day and by night from the Lord of righteousness. I have not written often, not even so often as I ought, but I have written to your reverence. Possibly the brethren to whom I committed my greetings were not able to preserve them. But now that I have found some of my brethren travelling to your excellency, I have readily entrusted my letter to them, and I have sent some messages which I beg you to receive from my humility without disdain, and to bless me after the manner of the patriarch Isaac.[1] I have been much occupied, and have had my mind drowned in a multiplicity of cares. So it may well be that I have omitted something which I ought to have said. If so, do not reckon it against me; and do not be grieved. Act in all things up to your own high character, that I, like every one else, may enjoy the fruit of your virtue. May you be granted to me and to the Church, in good health, rejoicing in the Lord, praying for me.

LETTER CCLXVIII.[2]

To Eusebius, in exile.

EVEN in our time the Lord has taught us, by protecting with His great and powerful hand the life of your holiness, that He does not abandon His holy ones. I reckon your case to be almost like that of the saint remaining unhurt in the belly of the monster of the deep, or that of the men who feared the Lord, living unscathed in the fierce fire. For though the war is round about you on every side, He, as I hear, has kept you unharmed. May the mighty God keep you, if I live longer, to fulfil my earnest prayer that I may see you! If not for me, may He keep you for the rest, who wait for your return as they might for their own salvation. I am persuaded that the Lord in His loving-kindness will give heed to the tears of the Churches, and to the sighs which all are heaving over you, and will preserve you in life until He grant the prayer of all who night and day are praying to Him. Of all the measures taken against you, up to the arrival of our beloved brother Libanius the deacon,[3] I have been sufficiently informed by him while on his way. I am anxious to learn what happened afterwards. I hear that in the meanwhile still greater troubles have occurred where you are; about all this, sooner if possible, but, if not, at least by our

reverend brother Paul the presbyter, on his return, may I learn, as I pray that I may, that your life is preserved safe and sound. But on account of the report that all the roads are infested with thieves and deserters,[1] I have been afraid to entrust anything to the brother's keeping, for fear of causing his death. If the Lord grant a little quiet, (as I am told of the coming of the army), I will try to send you one of my own men, to visit you, to bring me back news of everything about you.

LETTER CCLXIX.[2]

To the wife of Arinthæus, the General. Consolatory.

1. IT had been only proper, and due to your affection, that I should have been on the spot, and have taken part in the present occurrences. Thus I might have at once assuaged my own sorrow, and given some consolation to your excellency. But my body will no longer endure long journeys, and so I am driven to approach you by letter, that I seem not to count what has happened as altogether of no interest to me. Who has not mourned for that man? Who is so stony of heart as not to have shed a warm tear over him? I especially have been filled with mourning at the thought of all the marks of respect which I have received from him, and of the general protection which he has extended to the Churches of God. Nevertheless, I have bethought me that he was human, and had done the work he had to do in this life, and now in the appointed time has been taken back again by God Who ordains our lots. All this, I beseech you, in your wisdom, to take to heart, and to meet the event with meekness, and, so far as is possible, to endure your loss with moderation. Time may be able to soothe your heart, and allow the approach of reason. At the same time your great love for your husband, and your goodness to all, lead me to fear that, from the very simplicity of your character, the wound of your grief may pierce you deeply, and that you may give yourself up entirely to your feelings. The teaching of Scripture is always useful, and specially at times like this. Remember, then, the sentence passed by our Creator. By it all we who are dust shall return to dust.[3] No one is so great as to be superior to dissolution.

2. Your admirable husband was a good and great man, and his bodily strength

---

[1] Gen. xxvii. 27.   [2] Placed in 378.
[3] To be distinguished from Libanius the bishop, p. 177, and Libanius the professor, mentioned later.

[1] Δησερόρων, or Δεσερτόρων, the accepted reading, is a curious Latinism for the Greek αὐτόμολοι. Eusebius was in exile in Thrace, and there now the Goths were closing round Valens.
[2] Placed in 378.   [3] Gen. iii. 19.

rivalled the virtues of his soul. He was unsurpassed, I must own, in both respects. But he was human, and he is dead; like Adam, like Abel, like Noah, like Abraham, like Moses, or any one else of like nature that you can name. Let us not then complain because he has been taken from us. Let us rather thank Him, who joined us to him, that we dwelt with him from the beginning. To lose a husband is a lot which you share with other women; but to have been united to such a husband is a boast which I do not think any other woman can make. In truth our Creator fashioned that man for us as a model of what human nature ought to be. All eyes were attracted towards him, and every tongue told of his deeds. Painters and sculptors fell short of his excellence, and historians, when they tell the story of his achievements in war, seem to fall into the region of the mythical and the incredible. Thus it has come about that most men have not even been able to give credit to the report conveying the sad tidings, or to accept the truth of the news that Arinthæus is dead. Nevertheless Arinthæus has suffered what will happen to heaven and to sun and to earth. He has died a bright death; not bowed down by old age; without losing one whit of his honour; great in this life; great in the life to come; deprived of nothing of his present splendour in view of the glory hoped for, because he washed away all the stain of his soul, in the very moment of his departure hence, in the laver of regeneration. That you should have arranged and joined in this rite is cause of supreme consolation. Turn now your thoughts from the present to the future, that you may be worthy through good works to obtain a place of rest like his. Spare an aged mother; spare a tender daughter, to whom you are now the sole comfort. Be an example of fortitude to other women, and so regulate your grief that you may neither eject it from your heart, nor be overwhelmed by your distress. Ever keep your eyes fixed on the great reward of patience, promised, as the requital of the deeds of this life, by our Lord Jesus Christ.[1]

LETTER CCLXX.[2]

Without Address. Concerning Raptus.[3]

I AM distressed to find that you are by no means indignant at the sins forbidden, and

that you seem incapable of understanding, how this *raptus*, which has been committed, is an act of unlawfulness and tyranny against society and human nature, and an outrage on free men. I am sure that if you had all been of one mind in this matter, there would have been nothing to prevent this bad custom from being long ago driven out of your country. Do thou at the present time shew the zeal of a Christian man, and be moved as the wrong deserves. Wherever you find the girl, insist on taking her away, and restore her to her parents, shut out the man from the prayers, and make him excommunicate. His accomplices, according to the canon[1] which I have already put forth, cut off, with all their household, from the prayers. The village which received the girl after the abduction, and kept her, or even fought against her restitution, shut out with all its inhabitants from the prayers; to the end that all may know that we regard the ravisher as a common foe, like a snake or any other wild beast, and so hunt him out, and help those whom he has wronged.

LETTER CCLXXI.[2]

To Eusebius,[3] *my comrade, to recommend Cyriacus the presbyter.*

AT once and in haste, after your departure, I came to the town. Why need I tell a man not needing to be told, because he knows by experience, how distressed I was not to find you? How delightful it would have been to me to see once more the excellent Eusebius, to embrace him, to travel once again in memory to our young days, and to be reminded of old times when for both of us there was one home, one hearth, the same schoolmaster, the same leisure, the same work, the same treats, the same hardships, and everything shared in common! What do you think I would not have given to recall all this by actually meeting you, to rid me of the heavy weight of my old age, and to seem to be turned from an old man into a lad again? But I have lost this pleasure. At least of the privilege of meeting your excellency in correspondence,

---

[1] cf. Ep. clxxix and Theod., *H. E.* iv. 30.
[2] Placed after 374.
[3] On this subject see before *Letters* cxcix. and ccxvii. pp. 238 and 256. See Preb. Meyrick in *D.C.A.* ii. 1102: "It means not exactly the same as our word ravishment, but the violent

removal of a woman to a place where her actions are no longer free, for the sake of inducing her or compelling her to marry. . . . By some *raptus* is distinguished into the two classes of *raptus seductionis* and *raptus violentiæ.*" cf. Cod. Theod. ix. *tit.* xxiv. *legg.* 1, 2, and *Cod. Justin.* ix.–xiii. *leg.* 1 Corp. *Juris.* ii. 832.
[1] κήρυγμα. The Ben. note is no doubt right in understanding the word not to refer to any decree on this particular case, but to Basil's general rule in Canon xxx. *cf.* p. 239. On the use of κήουγμα by Basil, see note on p. 41.
[2] Placed at the end of Basil's life.
[3] Apparently a schoolfellow of Basil, not to be identified with any of the others of the name.

and of consoling myself by the best means at my disposal, I am not deprived. I am so fortunate as to meet the very reverend presbyter Cyriacus. I am ashamed to recommend him to you, and to make him, through me, your own, lest I seem to be performing a superfluous task in offering to you what you already possess and value as your own. But it is my duty to witness to the truth, and to give the best boons I have to those who are spiritually united to me. I think that the man's blamelessness in his sacred position is well known to you; but I confirm it, for I do not know that any charge is brought against him by those who do not fear the Lord and are laying their hands upon all. Even if they had done anything of the kind, the man would not have been unworthy, for the enemies of the Lord rather vindicate the orders of those whom they attack than deprive them of any of the grace given them by the Spirit. However, as I said, nothing has even been thought of against the man. Be so good then as to look upon him as a blameless presbyter, in union with me, and worthy of all reverence. Thus will you benefit yourself and gratify me.

LETTER CCLXXII.[1]

To Sophronius the magister officiorum.[2]

1. It has been reported to me by Actiacus the deacon, that certain men have moved you to anger against me, by falsely stating me to· be ill-disposed towards your excellency. I cannot be astonished at a man in your position being followed by certain sycophants. High position seems to be in some way naturally attended by miserable hangers-on of this kind. Destitute as they are of any good quality of their own whereby they may be known, they endeavour to recommend themselves by means of other people's ills. Peradventure, just as mildew is a blight which grows in corn, so flattery stealing upon friendship is a blight of friendship. So, as I said, I am by no means astonished that these men should buzz about your bright and distinguished hearth, as drones do about the· hives. But what has moved my wonderment, and has seemed altogether astounding, is that a man like yourself, specially distinguished by the seriousness of your character, should have been induced to give both your ears to these people and to accept their calumny against

me. From my youth up to this my old age I have felt affection for many men, but I am not aware that I have ever felt greater affection for any one than for your excellency. Even had not my reason induced me to regard a man of such a character, our intimacy from boyhood would have sufficed to attach me to your soul. You know yourself how much custom has to do with friendship. Pardon my deficiency, if I can show nothing worthy of this preference. You will not ask some deed from me in proof of my good will; you will be satisfied with a temper of mind which assuredly prays for you that you may have all that is best. May your fortunes never fall so low, as that you should need the aid of any one so insignificant as myself!

2. How then was I likely to say anything against you, or to take any action in the matter of Memnonius? These points were reported to me by the deacon. How could I put the wealth of Hymetius before the friendship of one so prodigal of his substance as you are? There is no truth in any of these things. I have neither said nor done anything against you. Possibly some ground may have been given for some of the lies that are being told, by my remarking to some of those who are causing disturbance, "If the man has determined to accomplish what he has in mind, then, whether you make disturbance or not, what he means to be done will certainly be done. You will speak, or hold your tongues; it will make no difference. If he changes his mind, beware how you defame my friend's honourable name. Do not, under the pretence of zeal in your patron's cause, attempt to make some personal profit out of your attempts to threaten and alarm." As to that person's making his will, I have never said one word, great or small, directly or indirectly, about the matter.

3. You must not refuse to believe what I say, unless you regard me as quite a desperate character, who thinks nothing of the great sin of lying. Put away all suspicion of me in relation to the business, and for the future reckon my affection for you as beyond the reach of all calumny. Imitate Alexander, who received a letter, saying that his physician was plotting his death, at the very moment when he was just about to drink his medicine, and was so far from believing the slanderer that he at one and the same time read the letter and drank the draught.[1] I refuse to admit that I am in any

[1] Written in the last years of Basil's life.
[2] cf. p. 134, n.

[1] Plut., Alex.

way inferior to the men who have been famous for their friendship, for I have never been detected in any breach of mine; and, besides this, I have received from my God the commandment of love, and owe you love not only as part of mankind in general, but because I recognise you individually as a benefactor both of my country and of myself.

LETTER CCLXXIII.[1]

Without address. Concerning Hera.

I AM sure that your excellency loves me well enough to regard all that concerns me as concerning you. Therefore I commend to your great kindness and high consideration my very reverend brother Hera, whom I do not merely call brother by any conventional phrase, but because of his boundless affection. I beseech you to regard him as though he were nearly connected with yourself, and, so far as you can, to give him your protection in the matters in which he requires your generous and thoughtful aid. I shall then have this one more kindness to reckon in addition to the many which I have already received at your hands.

LETTER CCLXXIV.[2]

To Himerius, the master.

THAT my friendship and affection for the very reverend brother Hera began when I was quite a boy, and has, by God's grace, continued up to my old age, no one knows better than yourself. For the Lord granted me the affection of your excellency at about the same time that He allowed me to become acquainted with Hera. He now needs your patronage, and I therefore beseech and supplicate you to do a favour for the sake of our old affection, and to heed the necessity under which we now lie. I beg you to make his cause your own, that he may need no other protection, but may return to me, successful in all that he is praying for. Then to the many kindnesses which I have received at your hands I shall be able to add yet this one more. I could not claim any favour more important to myself, or one more nearly touching my own interests.

LETTER CCLXXV.[3]

Without address. Concerning Hera.

YOU have anticipated my entreaties in

your affection for my very reverend brother Hera, and you have been better to him than I could have prayed for you to be in the abundant honour which you have shewn him, and the protection which you have extended to him on every occasion. But I cannot allow his affairs to go unnoticed by a word, and I must beseech your excellency that for my sake you will add something to the interest you have shewn in him, and will send him back to his own country victorious over the revilings of his enemies. Now many are trying to insult the peacefulness of his life, and he is not beyond the reach of envy's shafts. Against his foes we shall find one sure means of safety, if you will consent to extend your protection over him.

LETTER CCLXXVI.[1]

To the great Harmatius.

THE common law of human nature makes elders fathers to youngsters, and the special peculiar law of us Christians puts us old men in the place of parents to the younger. Do not, then, think that I am impertinent or shew myself indefensibly meddlesome, if I plead with you on behalf of your son. In other respects I think it only right that you should exact obedience from him; for, so far as his body is concerned, he is subject to you, both by the law of nature, and by the civil law under which we live. His soul, however, is derived from a diviner source, and may properly be held to be subject to another authority. The debts which it owes to God have a higher claim than any others. Since, then, he has preferred the God of us Christians, the true God, to your many gods which are worshipped by the help of material symbols, be not angry with him. Rather admire his noble firmness of soul, in sacrificing the fear and respect due to his father to close conjunction with God, through true knowledge and a life of virtue. Nature herself will move you, as well as your invariable gentleness and kindliness of disposition, not to allow yourself to feel angry with him even to a small extent. And I am sure that you will not set my mediation at naught, —or rather, I should say, the mediation of your townsmen of which I am the exponent. They all love you so well, and pray so earnestly for all blessings for you, that they suppose that in you they have welcomed a Christian too. So overjoyed have they been at the report which has suddenly reached the town.

[1] Written in the last years of Basil's life.
[2] Of the same time as the preceding.
[3] Placed at the same time as the preceding.
[1] Placed in the last years of Basil's life.

LETTER CCLXXVII.[1]

To the learned Maximus.

THE excellent Theotecnus has given me an account of your highness, whereby he has inspired me with a longing for your acquaintance, so clearly do his words delineate the character of your mind. He has enkindled in me so ardent an affection for you, that were it not that I am weighed down with age, that I am the victim of a congenital ailment, that I am bound hand and foot by the numberless cares of the Church, nothing would have hindered my coming to you. For indeed it is no small gain that a member of a great house, a man of illustrious lineage, in adopting the life of the gospel, should bridle the propensities of youth by reflection, and subject to reason the affections of the flesh; should display a humility consistent with his Christian profession, bethinking himself, as is his duty, whence he is come and whither he is going. For it is this consideration of our nature that reduces the swelling of the mind, and banishes all boastfulness and arrogance. In a word it renders one a disciple of our Lord, Who said, " Learn of me, for I am meek and lowly in heart."[2] And in truth, very dear son, the only thing that deserves our exertions and praises is our everlasting welfare; and this is the honour that comes from God.

Human affairs are fainter than a shadow; more deceitful than a dream. Youth fades more quickly than the flowers of spring; our beauty wastes with age or sickness. Riches are uncertain; glory is fickle. The pursuit of arts and sciences is bounded by the present life; the charm of eloquence, which all covet, reaches but the ear: whereas the practice of virtue is a precious possession for its owner, a delightful spectacle for all who witness it. Make this your study; so will you be worthy of the good things promised by the Lord.

But a recital of the means whereby to make the acquisition, and secure the enjoyment of these blessings, lies beyond the intention of this present letter. Thus much however, after what I heard from my brother Theotecnus, it occurred to me to write to you. I pray that he may always speak the truth, especially in his accounts of you; that the Lord may be the more glorified in you, abounding as you do in the most precious fruits of piety, although derived from a foreign root.

---

[1] Placed at the end of Basil's life.
[2] Matt. xi. 29.

LETTER CCLXXVIII.[1]

To Valerianus.

I DESIRED, when in Orphanene,[2] to see your excellency; I had also hoped that while you were living at Corsagæna, there would have been nothing to hinder your coming to me at a synod which I had expected to hold at Attagæna; since, however, I failed to hold it, my desire was to see you in the hill-country; for here again Evesus,[3] being in that neighbourhood, held out hopes of our meeting. But since I have been disappointed on both occasions, I determined to write and beg that you would deign to visit me; for I think it is but right and proper that the young man should come to the old. Furthermore, at our meeting, I would make you a tender of my advice, touching your negotiations with certain at Cæsarea: a right conclusion of the matter calls for my intervention. If agreeable then, do not be backward in coming to me.

LETTER CCLXXIX.[4]

To Modestus the Prefect.

ALTHOUGH so numerous are my letters, conveyed to your excellency by as many bearers, yet, having regard to the especial honour you have shewn me, I cannot think that their large number causes you any annoyance.

I do not hesitate therefore to entrust to this brother the accompanying letter: I know that he will meet with all that he wishes, and that you will count me but as a benefactor in furnishing occasion for the gratification of your kind inclinations. He craves your advocacy. His cause he will explain in person, if you but deign to regard him with a favourable eye, and embolden him to speak freely in the presence of so august an authority. Accept my assurance that any kindness shewn to him, I shall regard as personal to myself. His special reason for leaving Tyana and coming to me was the high value he attached to the presentation of a letter written by myself in support of his application. That he may not be disappointed of his hope; that I may continue in the enjoyment of your consideration; that your interest in all that is good may, in this present matter, find scope for its full exercise — are the

---

[1] Placed in the episcopate.
[2] A district in Armenia Minor. Ramsay, *Hist. Geog. A.M.* 314.
[3] *cf. Ep.* ccli. p. 291. Euassai or Evesus is about fifty miles north of Cæsarea.
[4] Placed in the episcopate.

grounds on which I crave a gracious reception for him, and a place amongst those nearest to you.

LETTER CCLXXX.[1]

To Modestus the Prefect.

I FEEL my boldness in pressing my suit by letter upon a man in your position; still the honour that you have paid me in the past has banished all my scruples. Accordingly I write with confidence.

My plea is for a relative of mine, a man worthy of respect for his integrity. He is the bearer of this letter, and he stands to me in the place of a son. Your favour is all that he requires for the fulfilment of his wishes. Deign therefore to receive, at the hands of the aforesaid bearer, my letter in furtherance of his plea. I pray you to give him an opportunity of explaining his affairs at an interview with those in a position to help him. So by your direction shall he quickly obtain his desires; while I shall have occasion for boasting that by God's favour I have found a champion who regards the entreaties of my friends as personal claims to his protection.

LETTER CCLXXXI.[2]

To Modestus the Prefect.

I AM mindful of the great honour I received in the encouragement you gave me, along with others, to address your excellency. I avail myself of the privilege and the enjoyment of your gracious favour.

I congratulate myself upon having such a correspondent, as also upon the opportunity afforded your excellency of conferring an honour on me by your reply.

I claim your clemency on behalf of Helladius my special friend. I pray that he may be relieved from the anxieties of Tax-assessor, and so be enabled to work in the interests of our country.

You have already so far given a gracious consent, that I now repeat my request, and pray you to send instructions to the governor of the Province, that Helladius may be released from this infliction.

LETTER CCLXXXII.[3]

To a bishop.

You blame me for not inviting you; and, when invited, you do not attend. That your former excuse was an empty one is clear from your conduct on the second occasion. For had you been invited before, in all probability you would never have come.

Act not again unadvisedly, but obey this present invitation; since you know that its repetition strengthens an indictment, and that a second lends credibility to a previous accusation.

I exhort you always to bear with me; or even if you cannot, at any rate it is your duty not to neglect the Martyrs, to join in whose commemoration you are invited. Render therefore your service to us both; or if you will not consent to this, at any rate to the more worthy.

LETTER CCLXXXIII.[1]

To a widow.

I HOPE to find a suitable day for the conference, after those which I intend to fix for the hill-country. I see no opportunity for our meeting (unless the Lord so order it beyond my expectation), other than at a public conference.

You may imagine my position from your own experience. If in the care of a single household you are beset with such a crowd of anxieties, how many distractions, think you, each day brings to me?

Your dream, I think, reveals more perfectly the necessity of making provision for spiritual contemplation, and cultivating that mental vision by which God is wont to be seen. Enjoying as you do the consolation of the Holy Scriptures, you stand in need neither of my assistance nor of that of anybody else to help you to comprehend your duty. You have the all-sufficient counsel and guidance of the Holy Spirit to lead you to what is right.

LETTER CCLXXXIV.[2]

To the assessor in the case of monks.

CONCERNING the monks, your excellency has, I believe, already rules in force, so that I need ask for no special favour on their behalf.

It is enough that they share with others the enjoyment of your general beneficence; still I feel it incumbent upon me too to interest myself in their case. I therefore submit it to your more perfect judgment,

---

1 Placed in the episcopate.　3 Placed in the episcopate.
2 Placed in the episcopate.

1 Placed in the episcopate.　2 Placed in the episcopate.

that men who have long since taken leave of this life, who have mortified their own bodies, so that they have neither money to spend nor bodily service to render in the interests of the common weal, should be exempted from taxation. For if their lives are consistent with their profession, they possess neither money nor bodies; for the former is spent in communicating to the needy; while their bodies are worn away in prayer and fasting.

Men living such lives you will, I know, regard with special reverence; nay you will wish to secure their intervention, since by their life in the Gospel they are able to prevail with God.

LETTER CCLXXXV.[1]

Without Address.

THE bearer of this letter is one on whom rests the care of our Church and the management of its property — our beloved son.

Deign to grant him freedom of speech on those points that are referred to your holiness, and attention to the expression of his own views; so shall our Church at length recover herself, and henceforth be released from this many-headed Hydra.

Our property is our poverty; so much so that we are ever in search of one to relieve us of it; for the expenses of the Church property amount to more than any profit that she derives from it.

LETTER CCLXXXVI.[2]

To the Commentariensis.[3]

WHEREAS certain vagabonds have been arrested in the church for stealing, in defiance of God's commandment, some poor men's clothing, of little value otherwise, yet such as they had rather have on than off their backs; and whereas you consider that in virtue of your office you yourself should have the custody of the offenders : — I hereby declare, that I would have you know that for offences committed in the church it is our business to mete out punishment, and that the intervention of the civil authorities is in these cases superfluous. Wherefore, the stolen property, as set forth in the document in your possession and in the transcript made in the presence of eye-

witnesses, I enjoin you to retain, reserving part for future claims, and distributing the rest among the present applicants.

As for the offenders, — that they be corrected in the discipline and admonition of the Lord. By this means I hope to work their successive reformations. For where the stripes of human tribunals have failed, I have often known the fearful judgments of God to be effectual. If it is, however, your wish to refer this matter also to the count, such is my confidence in his justice and uprightness that I leave you to follow your own counsels.

LETTER CCLXXXVII.[1]

Without address.

IT is difficult to deal with this man. I scarcely know how to treat so shifty, and, to judge from the evidence, so desperate a character. When summoned before the court, he fails to appear; and if he does attend, he is gifted with such volubility of words and oaths, that I think myself well off to be quickly rid of him. I have often known him twist round his accusations upon his accusers. In a word, there is no creature living upon earth so subtile and versatile in villainy. A slight acquaintance with him suffices to prove this. Why then do you appeal to me? Why not at once bring yourselves to submit to his ill-treatment, as to a visitation of God's anger?

At the same time you must not be contaminated by contact with wickedness.

I enjoin therefore that he and all his household be forbidden the services of the Church, and all other communion with her ministers. Being thus made an example of, he may haply be brought to a sense of his enormities.

LETTER CCLXXXVIII.

Without address. Excommunicatory.

WHEN public punishment fails to bring a man to his senses, or exclusion from the prayers of the Church to drive him to repentance, it only remains to treat him in accordance with our Lord's directions — as it is written, " If thy brother shall trespass against thee, . . . tell him his fault between thee and him; . . . if he will not hear thee, take with thee another;" " and if he shall" then " neglect to hear, tell it unto

---

1 Placed in the episcopate.
2 Placed in the episcopate.
3 A registrar of prisons, or prison superintendent. *Cod.*
Just. ix. 4. 4. *Dis.* xlviii. 20. 6.

1 Placed in the episcopate.
2 Placed in the episcopate.

the Church ; but if he neglect to hear even the Church, let him be unto thee henceforth as an heathen man, and as a publican." [1] Now all this we have done in the case of this fellow. First, he was accused of his fault ; then he was convicted in the presence of one or two witnesses ; thirdly, in the presence of the Church. Thus we have made our solemn protest, and he has not listened to it. Henceforth let him be excommunicated.

Further, let proclamation be made throughout the district, that he be excluded from participation in any of the ordinary relations of life ; so that by our withholding ourselves from all intercourse with him he may become altogether food for the devil.[2]

LETTER CCLXXXIX.[3]

Without address. Concerning an afflicted woman.

I CONSIDER it an equal mistake, to let the guilty go unpunished, and to exceed the proper limits of punishment. I accordingly passed upon this man the sentence I considered it incumbent on me to pass — excommunication from the Church. The sufferer I exhorted not to avenge herself; but to leave to God the redressing of her wrongs. Thus if my admonitions had possessed any weight, I should then have been obeyed, for the language I employed was far more likely to ensure credit, than any letter to enforce compliance.

So, even after listening to her statements that contained matter sufficiently grave, I still held my peace ; and even now I am not sure that it becomes me to treat again of this same question.

For, she says, I have foregone husband, children, all the enjoyments of life, for the attainment of this single object, the favour of God, and good repute amongst men. Yet one day the offender, an adept from boyhood in corrupting families, with the impudence habitual to him, forced an entrance into my house; and thus within the bare limits of an interview an acquaintanceship was formed. It was only owing to my ignorance of the man, and to that timidity which comes from inexperience, that I hesitated openly to turn him out of doors. Yet to such a pitch of impiety and insolence did he come, that he filled the whole city with slanders, and publicly inveighed against me by affixing to the church doors libellous placards.

For this conduct, it is true, he incurred the displeasure of the law ; but, nevertheless, he returned to his slanderous attacks on me. Once more the market-place was filled with his abuse, as well as the gymnasia, theatres, and houses whose congeniality of habits gained him an admittance. Nor did his very extravagance lead men to recognise those virtues wherein I was conspicuous, so universally had I been represented as being of an incontinent disposition. In these calumnies, she goes on to say, some find a delight — such is the pleasure men naturally feel in the disparagement of others ; some profess to be pained, but shew no sympathy ; others believe the truth of these slanders ; others again, having regard to the persistency of his oaths, are undecided. But sympathy I have none. And now indeed I begin to realise my loneliness, and bewail myself. I have no brother, friend, relation, no servant, bond or free, in a word, no one whatever to share my grief. And yet, I think, I am more than any one else an object of pity, in a city where the haters of wickedness are so few. They bandy violence ; but violence, though they fail to see it, moves in a circle, and in time will overtake each one of them.

In such and still more appealing terms she told her tale, with countless tears, and so departed. Nor did she altogether acquit me of blame ; thinking that, when I ought to sympathise with her like a father, I am indifferent to her troubles, and regard the sufferings of others too philosophically.

For it is not, she urged, the loss of money that you bid me disregard ; nor the endurance of bodily sufferings ; but a damaged reputation, an injury involving loss upon the Church at large.

This is her appeal ; and now I pray you, most excellent sir, consider what answer you would have me make her. The decision I have come to in my own mind is, not to surrender offenders to the magistrates ; yet not to rescue those already in their custody, since it has long ago been declared by the Apostle, that the magistrates should be a terror to them in their evildoings ; for, it is said, " he beareth not the sword in vain." [1] To surrender him, then, is contrary to my humanity ; while to release him would be an encouragement to his violence.

Perhaps, however, you will defer taking action until my arrival. I will then shew you that I can effect nothing from there being none to obey me.

[1] Matt. xviii. 15-17.　　[3] Placed in the episcopate.
[2] Contrast 1 Tim. i. 20.

[1] Rom. xiii. 4.

LETTER CCXC.[1]

To Nectarius.

MAY many blessings rest on those who encourage your excellency in maintaining a constant correspondence with me! And regard not such a wish as conventional merely, but as expressing my sincere conviction of the value of your utterances. Whom could I honour above Nectarius — known to me from his earliest days as a child of fairest promise, who now through the exercise of every virtue has reached a position of the highest eminence? — So much so, that of all my friends the dearest is the bearer of your letter.

Touching the election of those set over districts,[2] God forbid that I should do anything for the gratification of man, through listening to importunities or yielding to fear. In that case I should be not a steward, but a huckster, bartering the gift of God for the favour of man. But seeing that votes are given but by mortals, who can only bear such testimony as they do from outward appearances, while the choice of fit persons is committed in all humility to Him Who knows the secrets of the heart, haply it is best for everybody, when he has tendered the evidence of his vote, to abstain from all heat and contention, as though some self-interest were involved in the testimony, and to pray to God that what is advantageous may not remain unknown. Thus the result is no longer attributable to man, but a cause for thankfulness to God. For these things, if they be of man, cannot be said to be; but are pretence only, altogether void of reality.

Consider also, that when a man strives with might and main to gain his end, there is no small danger of his drawing even sinners to his side; and there is much sinfulness, such is the weakness of man's nature, even where we should least expect it.

Again, in private consultation we often offer our friends good advice, and, though we do not find them taking it, yet we are not angry. Where then it is not man that counsels, but God that determines, shall we feel indignation at not being preferred before the determination of God?

And if these things were given to man by man, what need were there for us to ask them of ourselves? Were it not better for each to take them from himself? But if they are the gift of God, we ought to pray and not to grieve. And in our prayer we should not seek our own will, but leave it to God who disposes for the best.

Now may the holy God keep from your home all taste of sorrow; and grant to you and to your family a life exempt from harm and sickness.

LETTER CCXCI.[1]

To Timotheus the Chorepiscopus.[2]

THE due limits of a letter, and that mode of addressing you, render it inconvenient for me to write all I think; at the same time to pass over my thoughts in silence, while my heart is burning with righteous indignation against you, is well-nigh impossible. I will adopt the midway course: I will write some things; others I will omit. For I wish to chide you, if so I may, in terms both frank and friendly.

Yes! that Timotheus whom I have known from boyhood, so intent upon an upright and ascetic life, as even to be accused of excess therein, now forsakes the enquiry after those means whereby we may be united to God; now makes it his first thought what some one else may think of him, and lives a life of dependence upon the opinions of others; is mainly anxious how to serve his friends, without incurring the ridicule of enemies; and fears disgrace with the world as a great misfortune. Does he not know, that while he is occupied with these trifles he is unconsciously neglecting his highest interests? For, that we cannot be engaged with both at once — the things of this world and of Heaven — the holy Scriptures are full of teaching for us. Nay, Nature herself is full of such instances. In the exercise of the mental faculty, to think two thoughts at the same time is quite impossible. In the perceptions of our senses, to admit two sounds falling upon our ears at the same moment, and to distinguish them, although we are provided with two open passages, is impossible. Our eyes, again, unless they are both fixed upon the object of our vision, are unable to perform their action accurately.

Thus much for Nature; but to recite to you the evidence of the Scriptures were as

[1] Placed in the episcopate.
[2] On the word συμμορίας the Ben. note is: "*Hac voce non designatur tota diocesis, sed certos quidam pagorum numerus chorepiscopo commissus, ut patet ex epist.* cxlii.," *q.v.,* "*erat autem chorepiscoporum sedes insigni alicui affixa pago, cui alii pagi attribuebantur. Unde Basilius in epist.* clxxxviii. § 10. *Auctor est Amphilochio ut agrum Mestiæ subjectum Vasodis subjiciat.*"

[1] Placed in the episcopate. [2] *cf.* note on p. 156.

ridiculous as, so runs the proverb, ' to carry owls to Athens.'[1]   Why then combine things incompatible — the tumults of civil life and the practice of religion?

Withdraw from clamour; be no more the cause or object of annoyance; let us keep ourselves to ourselves. We long since proposed religion as our aim; let us make the attainment of it our practice, and shew those who have the wish to insult us that it does not lie with them to annoy us at their will. But this will only be when we have clearly shewn them that we afford no handle for abuse.

For the present enough of this! Would that some day we might meet and more perfectly consider those things that be for our souls' welfare; so may we not be too much occupied with thoughts of vanity, since death must one day overtake us.

I was greatly pleased with the gifts you kindly sent me. They were most welcome on their own account; the thought of who it was that sent them made them many times more welcome. The gifts from Pontus, the tablets and medicines, kindly accept when I send them. At present they are not by me.

N.B. The letters numbered CCXCII.–CCCLXVI. are included by the Ben. Ed. in a "Classis Tertia," having no note of time. Some are doubtful, and some plainly spurious. Of these I include such as seem most important.

LETTER CCXCII.

To Palladius.

THE one-half of my desire has God fulfilled in the interview He granted me with our fair sister, your wife. The other half He is able to accomplish; and so with the sight of your excellency I shall render my full thanks to God.

And I am the more desirous of seeing you, now that I hear you have been adorned with that great ornament, the clothing of immortality, which clokes our mortality, and puts out of sight the death of the flesh; by virtue of which the corruptible is swallowed up in incorruption.

Thus God of His goodness has now alienated you from sin, united you to Himself, has opened the doors of Heaven, and pointed out the paths that lead to heavenly bliss. I entreat you therefore by that wisdom wherein

you excel all other men, that you receive the divine favour circumspectly, proving a faithful guardian of this treasure, as the repository of this royal gift, keeping watch over it with all carefulness. Preserve this seal of righteousness unsullied, that so you may stand before God, shining in the brightness of the Saints. Let no spot or wrinkle defile the pure robe of immortality; but keep holiness in all your members, as having put on Christ. " For," it is said, " as many of you as have been baptized into Christ, have put on Christ."[1] Wherefore let all your members be holy as becomes their investment in a raiment of holiness and light.

LETTER CCXCIII.

To Julianus.

How fare you this long while? Have you altogether recovered the use of your hand? And how do other things prosper? According to your wishes and my prayers? In accordance with your purposes?

Where men are readily disposed to change, it is only natural that their lives are not well ordered: but where their minds are fixed, steadfast and unalterable, it follows that their lives should be conformable to their purposes.

True, it is not in the helmsman's power to make a calm when he wishes; but with us, it is quite easy to render our lives tranquil by stilling the storms of passion that surge within, by rising superior to those that assail us from without. The upright man is touched by neither loss, nor sickness, nor the other ills of life; for he walks in heart with God, keeps his gaze fixed upon the future, and easily and lightly weathers the storms that rise from earth.

Be not troubled with the cares of earth. Such men are like fat birds, in vain endowed with flight, that creep like beasts upon the ground. But you — for I have witnessed you in difficulties — are like swimmers racing out at sea.

A single claw reveals the whole lion: so from a slight acquaintance I think I know you fully. And I count it a great thing, that you set some store by me, that I am not absent from your thoughts, but constantly in your recollection.

Now writing is a proof of recollection; and the oftener you write, the better pleased I am.

---

[1] γλαῦκ' Ἀθήναζε. Arist., *Av.* 301.

[1] Gal. iii. 27.

LETTER CCXCIV.

To Festus and Magnus.

It is doubtless a father's duty to make provision for his children; a husbandman's to tend his plants and crops; a teacher's to bestow care upon his pupils, especially when innate goodness shews signs of promise for them.

The husbandman finds toil a pleasure when he sees the ears ripen or the plants increase; the teacher is gladdened at his pupils' growth in knowledge, the father at his son's in stature. But greater is the care I feel for you; higher the hopes I entertain; in proportion as piety is more excellent than all the arts, than all the animals and fruits together.

And piety I planted in your heart while still pure and tender, and I matured it in the hopes of seeing it reach maturity and bearing fruits in due season. My prayers meanwhile were furthered by your love of learning. And you know well that you have my good wishes, and that God's favour rests upon your endeavours; for when rightly directed, called or uncalled, God is at hand to further them.

Now every man that loves God is prone to teaching; nay, where there is the power to teach things profitable, their eagerness is well nigh uncontrollable; but first their hearers' minds must be cleared of all resistance.

Not that separation in the body is a hindrance to instruction. The Creator, in the fulness of His love and wisdom, did not confine our minds within our bodies, nor the power of speaking to our tongues. Ability to profit derives some advantage even from lapse of time; thus we are able to transmit instruction, not only to those who are dwelling far away, but even to those who are hereafter to be born. And experience proves my words: those who lived many years before teach posterity by instruction preserved in their writings; and we, though so far separated in the body, are always near in thought, and converse together with ease.

Instruction is bounded neither by sea nor land, if only we have a care for our souls' profit.

LETTER CCXCV.

To monks.

I do not think that I need further commend you to God's grace, after the words that I addressed to you in person. I then bade you adopt the life in common, after the manner of living of the Apostles. This you accepted as wholesome instruction, and gave God thanks for it.

Thus your conduct was due, not so much to the words I spoke, as to my instructions to put them into practice, conducive at once to your advantage who accepted, to my comfort who gave you the advice, and to the glory and praise of Christ, by Whose name we are called.

For this reason I have sent to you our well-beloved brother, that he may learn of your zeal, may quicken your sloth, may report to me of opposition. For great is my desire to see you all united in one body, and to hear that you are not content to live a life without witness; but have undertaken to be both watchful of each other's diligence, and witnesses of each other's success.

Thus will each of you receive a reward in full, not only on his own behalf, but also for his brother's progress. And, as is fitting, you will be a source of mutual profit, both by your words and deeds, as a result of constant intercourse and exhortation.

But above all I exhort you to be mindful of the faith of the Fathers, and not to be shaken by those who in your retirement would try to wrest you from it. For you know that unless illumined by faith in God, strictness of life availeth nothing; nor will a right confession of faith, if void of good works, be able to present you before the Lord.

Faith and works must be joined: so shall the man of God be perfect, and his life not halt through any imperfection.

For the faith which saves us, as saith the Apostle, is that which worketh by love.

LETTER CCXCVI.

To a widow.

[A short letter in which Basil excuses himself for making use of the widow's mules.]

LETTER CCXCVII.

To a widow.

[A short letter of introduction.]

LETTER CCXCVIII.

Without address.

[A short letter of commendation.]

LETTER CCXCIX.

To a Censitor.[1]

I was aware, before you told me, that you do not like your employment in public affairs. It is an old saying that those who are anxious to lead a pious life do not throw themselves with pleasure into office. The case of magistrates seems to me like that of physicians. They see awful sights; they meet with bad smells; they get trouble for themselves out of other people's calamities. This is at least the case with those who are real magistrates. All men who are engaged in business, look also to make a profit, and are excited about this kind of glory, count it the greatest possible advantage to acquire some power and influence by which they may be able to benefit their friends, punish their enemies, and get what they want for themselves. You are not a man of this kind. How should you be? You have voluntarily withdrawn from even high office in the State. You might have ruled the city like one single house, but you have preferred a life free from care and anxiety. You have placed a higher value on having no troubles yourself and not troubling other people, than other people do on making themselves disagreeable. But it has seemed good to the Lord that the district of Ibora[2] should not be under the power of hucksters, nor be turned into a mere slave market. It is His will that every individual in it should be enrolled, as is right. Do you therefore accept this responsibility? It is vexatious, I know, but it is one which may bring you the approbation of God. Neither fawn upon the great and powerful, nor despise the poor and needy. Show to all under your rule an impartiality of mind, balanced more exactly than any scales. Thus in the sight of those who have entrusted you with these responsibilities your zeal for justice will be made evident, and they will view you with exceptional admiration. And even though you go unnoticed by them, you will not be unnoticed by our God. The prizes which He has put before us for good works are great.

LETTER CCC.

Without address.

[A consolatory letter to a father.]

LETTER CCCI.

To Maximus.

[Consolatory on the death of his wife.]

LETTER CCCII.

To the wife of Briso.

[Consolatory on the death of her husband. These three consolatory letters present no features different from those contained in previous letters of a similar character.]

LETTER CCCIII.

To the Comes Privatarum.

You have, I think, been led to impose a contribution of mares[1] on these people by false information on the part of the inhabitants. What is going on is quite unfair. It cannot but be displeasing to your excellency, and is distressing to me on account of my intimate connexion with the victims of the wrong. I have therefore lost no time in begging your lordship not to allow these promoters of iniquity to succeed in their malevolence.

LETTER CCCIV.

To Aburgius.

[A few unimportant words of introduction.]

LETTER CCCV.

Without address.

[An unimportant letter of recommendation.]

LETTER CCCVI.

To the Governor of Sebasteia.[2]

I am aware that your excellency is favourably receiving my letters, and I understand why. You love all that is good; you are

1 φοράδων τέλεσμα. " *Recte Scultetum castigat Combefisius quod* raptim vectigal *reddiderit. At idem immerito putat ob equarum possessionem tributum aliquod ejusmodi hominibus impositum fuisse. Perspicuum est equas ipsas iis, quibus patrocinatur Basilius, imperatas fuisse, idque in multæ magis quam in tributi loco; si quidem eos comes rei privatæ falsis criminationibus deceptus damnaverat. Sic etiam Greg. Naz., Ep.* clxxxiv. *Nemesium flectere conatur qui Valentiniano equarum multam ob aliquod delictum inflexerat. Nec mirum est in Cappadocia, quæ optimos equos alebat, ejusmodi multas impossitas fuisse.*" Ben. note.
2 Ἡγεμόνι Σεβαστείας. The Ben. Ed. think that here and in *Letter* lxiii. ἡγεμών means not governor but Head of the Senate. *cf. Cod. Theod.* xii., i. 127, 171, 189. So in *Letter* lxxxvi. The "*præpositus pagorum*" is styled ἡγεμών.

ready in doing kindnesses. So whenever I give you the opportunity of shewing your magnanimity, you are eager for my letters, because you know that they furnish an occasion for good deeds. Now, once more, behold an occasion for your shewing all the signs of rectitude, and at the same time for the public exhibition of your virtues! Certain persons have come from Alexandria for the discharge of a necessary duty which is due from all men to the dead. They ask your excellency to give orders that it may be permitted them to have conveyed away, under official sanction, the corpse of a relative who departed this life at Sebasteia, while the troops were quartered there. They further beg that, as far as possible, aid may be given them for travelling at the public expense, so that, of your bounty, they may find some help and solace in their long journey. The tidings of this will travel as far as to great Alexandria, and will convey thither the report of your excellency's astonishing kindness. This you well understand without my mentioning it. I shall add gratitude for this one more favour to that which I feel for all which you have done me.

LETTER CCCVII.

Without address.

[A request to mediate between two litigants.]

LETTER CCCVIII.

Without address.

[Commendatory, with the mention of a place called Capralis.]

LETTER CCCIX.

Without address.

[Commendatory on behalf of a man reduced from wealth to poverty, with three children, and anxious about his rating.]

LETTER CCCX.

Without address.

[Commendatory on behalf of some kinsfolk, and of the people of Ariarathia, a place in the Sargaransene, about 60 m. E. of Cæsarea.[1]]

LETTER CCCXI.

[Commendatory: short and of no importance.]

LETTER CCCXII.

[Commendatory: short and unimportant.]

LETTER CCCXIII.

[Commendatory of the interests of Sulpicius.]

LETTER CCCXIV.

Without address.

[Commendatory.]

LETTER CCCXV.

Without address.

[Commendatory of a widow.]

LETTERS CCCXVI., CCCXVII., CCCXVIII., CCCXIX.

Without address.

[Commendatory; short.]

LETTER CCCXX.

Without address.

[A salutation.]

LETTER CCCXXI.

To Thecla.

[Included among the Letters of Gregory of Nazianzus, who is assumed by the Ben. Ed. to be indubitably the writer.[1]]

LETTER CCCXXII.

Without address.

[Asking a friend to come with his wife and spend Easter with him.]

LETTER CCCXXIII.

To Philagrius Arcenus.

LETTER CCCXXIV.

To Pasinicus, the Physician.

LETTER CCCXXV.

To Magninianus.

LETTER CCCXXVI.

Without address.

[Monitory.]

[1] Ramsay, *Hist. Geog. A.M.* p. 55.

[1] *Vide* Greg. Naz., *Ep.* lvii.

LETTER CCCXXVII.

Without address.

[Hortatory.]

LETTER CCCXXVIII.

To Hyperectius.

[On Basil's health.]

LETTER CCCXXIX.

To Phalirius.

[With thanks for a present of fish.]

LETTERS CCCXXX., CCCXXXI., CCCXXXII., CCCXXXIII.

[All short and without address. Letters from CCCXXIII. to CCCXXXIII. have no importance.]

LETTER CCCXXXIV.

To a writer.

Write straight, and make the lines straight. Do not let your hand go too high or too low. Avoid forcing the pen to travel slantwise, like Æsop's crab. Advance straight on, as if following the line of the carpenter's rule, which always preserves exactitude and prevents any irregularity. The oblique is ungraceful. It is the straight which pleases the eye, and does not allow the reader's eyes to go nodding up and down like a swing-beam. This has been my fate in reading your writing. As the lines lie ladderwise, I was obliged, when I had to go from one to another, to mount up to the end of the last: then, when no connexion was to be found, I had to go back, and seek for the right order again, retreating and following the furrow,[1] like Theseus in the story following Ariadne's thread.[2] Write straight, and do not confuse our mind by your slanting and irregular writing.

LETTER CCCXXXV.

Basil to Libanius.[3]

I am really ashamed of sending you the Cappadocians one by one. I should prefer to induce all our youths to devote themselves to letters and learning, and to avail themselves of your instruction in their training. But it is impracticable to get hold of them all at once, while they choose what suits themselves. I therefore send you those who from time to time are won over; and this I do with the assurance that I am conferring on them a boon as great as that which is given by those who bring thirsty men to the fountain. The lad, whom I am now sending, will be highly valued for his own sake when he has been in your society. He is already well known on account of his father, who has won a name among us both for rectitude of life and for authority in our community. He is, moreover, a close friend of my own. To requite him for his friendship to me, I am conferring on his son the benefit of an introduction to you — a boon well worthy of being earnestly prayed for by all who are competent to judge of a man's high character.

LETTER CCCXXXVI.

Libanius to Basilius.

1. After some little time a young Cappadocian has reached me. One gain to me is that he is a Cappadocian. But this Cappadocian is one of the first rank. This is another gain. Further, he brings me a letter from the admirable Basil. This is the greatest gain of all. You think that I have forgotten you. I had great respect for you in your youth. I saw you vying with old men in self-restraint, and this in a city teeming with pleasures. I saw you already in possession of considerable learning. Then you thought that you ought also to see Athens, and you persuaded Celsus to accompany you. Happy Celsus, to be dear to you! Then you returned, and lived at home, and I said to myself, What, I wonder, is Basil about now? To what occupation has he betaken himself? Is he following the ancient orators, and practising in the courts? Or is he turning the sons of fortunate fathers into orators? Then there came

---

[1] Of the use of this word to indicate the lines in MSS., *cf.* Aristoph., *Thesm.* 782, and Anth., *Pal.* vi. 82.

[2] *i.e.* in the Labyrinth of Crete.

Ope virginea, nullis iterata priorum,
Janua difficilis filo est inventa relecto.
                                Ov., *Metam.* viii. 172.

[3] "Basilii et Libanii epistolæ mutuæ, quas magni facit Tillemontius, probatque ut genuinas, maxime dubiæ videntur Garnier, in *Vit. Bas. cap.* 39, p. 172, seqq., is tamen illas spartim edidit. . . . Schroeckh Garn. dubitationi de omnium illarum epist. mutuarum νοθείᾳ quædam opponit." Fabricius. Harles., *Tom.* ix.

Maran (*Vit. Bas.* xxxix. 2) thinks that the Libanian correspondence, assuming it to be genuine, is to be assigned partly to the period of the retreat, partly to that of the presbyterate, while two only, the one a complaint on the part of Libanius that bishops are avaricious, and Basil's retort, may perhaps have been written during the episcopate. He would see no reason for rejecting them on the ground merely of the unlikelihood of Basil's corresponding with a heathen philosopher, but he is of opinion that the style of most of them is unworthy both of the sophist and of the archbishop. Yet there seems no reason why they should have been invented. It is intelligible enough that they should have been preserved, considering the reputation of the writers; but they suggest no motive for forgery. The life of Libanius extended from 314 to nearly the end of the fourth century. J. R. Mozley, in *D.C.B.* (iv. 712) refers to G. R. Siever (*Das Leben des Libanius*, Berlin, 1868) as the fullest biographer.

those who reported to me that you were adopting a course of life better than any of these, and were, rather, bethinking you how you might win the friendship of God than heaps of gold, I blessed both you and the Cappadocians; you, for making this your aim; them, for being able to point to so noble a fellow-countryman.

2. I am aware that the Firmus, whom you mention, has continually won everywhere; [1] hence his great power as a speaker. But with all the eulogies that have been bestowed on him, I am not aware that he has ever received such praise as I have heard of in your letter. For what a credit it is to him, that it should be you who declare that his reputation is inferior to none!

Apparently, you have despatched this young man to me before seeing Firminus; had you done so, your letters would not have failed to mention him. What is Firminus now doing or intending to do? Is he still anxious to be married? Or is all that over now? Are the claims of the senate heavy on him? Is he obliged to stay where he is? Is there any hope of his taking to study again? Let him send me an answer, and I trust it may be satisfactory. If it be a distressing one, at least it will relieve him from seeing me at his door. And if Firminus had been now at Athens, what would your senators have done? Would they have sent the Salaminia [2] after him? You see that it is only by your fellow-countrymen that I am wronged. Yet I shall never cease to love and praise the Cappadocians. I should like them to be better disposed to me, but, if they continue to act as they do, I shall bear it. Firminus was four months with me, and was not a day idle. You will know how much he has acquired, and perhaps will not complain. As to his being able to come here again, what ally can I call in? If your senators are right-minded, as men of education ought to be, they will honour me in the second case, since they grieved me in the first.

LETTER CCCXXXVII.

Basil to Libanius.

Lo and behold, yet another Cappadocian has come to you; a son of my own! For my present position makes all men my sons.

On this ground he may be regarded as a brother of the former one, and worthy of the same attention alike from me his father, and from you his instructor — if really it is possible for these young men, who come from me, to obtain any further favours. I do not mean that it is not possible for your excellency to give anything more to your old comrades, but because your services are so lavishly bestowed upon all. It will be sufficient for the lad before he gets experience if he be numbered among those who are intimately known to you. I trust you may send him back to me worthy of my prayers and of your great reputation in learning and eloquence. He is accompanied by a young man of his own age, and of like zeal for instruction; a youth of good family, and closely associated with myself. I am sure he will be in every way as well treated, though his means are smaller than is the case with the rest.

LETTER CCCXXXVIII.

Libanius to Basil.

I KNOW you will often write, "Here is another Cappadocian for you!" I expect that you will send me many. I am sure that you are everywhere putting pressure on both fathers and sons by all your complimentary expressions about me. But it would not be kind on my part not to mention what happened about your good letter. There were sitting with me not a few of our people of distinction, and among them the very excellent Alypius, Hierocles' cousin. The messengers gave in the letter. I read it right through without a word; then with a smile, and evidently gratified, I exclaimed, "I am vanquished!" "How? When? Where?" they asked. "How is it that you are not distressed at being vanquished?" "I am beaten," I replied, "in beautiful letter writing. Basil has won. But I love him; and so I am delighted." On hearing this, they all wanted to hear of the victory from the letter itself. It was read by Alypius, while all listened. It was voted that what I had said was quite true. Then the reader went out, with the letter still in his hand, to shew it, I suppose, to others. I had some difficulty in getting it back. Go on writing others like it; go on winning. This is for me to win. You are quite right in thinking that my services are not measured by money. Enough for him who has nothing to give, that he is as wishful to receive. If I perceive any one who is poor to be a lover of learning, he takes precedence of the rich. True, I

---

[1] πανταχοῦ διετέλεσε κοατῶν. "*Ubique constantem perdurasse.*" Ben. Ed. "*Ubique firma memoria fuerit.*" Combefis Firmus may possibly be the father of the young student.

[2] The allusion is to the "Salaminia," one of the two sacred or state vessels of the Athenian government. The "Paralus" and the "Salaminia" were both Triremes, the latter being called also "Delia" and "Theoris," because it was used to convey the Θεωροὶ to Delos. State criminals were conveyed by them.

never found such instructors; but nothing shall stand in the way of my being, at least in that respect, an improvement on mine. Let no one, then, hesitate to come hither because he is poor, if only he possesses the one qualification of knowing how to work.

LETTER CCCXXXIX.

Basil to Libanius.

WHAT could not a sophist say? And such a sophist! One whose peculiar art is, whenever he likes, to make great things small, and to give greatness to small things! This is what you have shewn in my case. That dirty little letter of mine, as, perhaps, you who live in all luxury of eloquence would call it, a letter in no way more tolerable than the one you hold in your hands now, you have so extolled as, forsooth, to be beaten by it, and to be yielding me the prize for composition! You are acting much as fathers do, when they join in their boys' games, and let the little fellows be proud of the victories which they have let them win, without any loss to themselves, and with much gain to the children's emulation. Really and truly the delight your speech must have given, when you were joking about me, must have been indescribable! It is as though some Polydamas[1] or Milo[2] were to decline the pancratium or a wrestling bout with me![3] After carefully examining, I have found no sign of weakness. So those who look for exaggeration are the more astonished at your being able to descend in sport to my level, than if you had led the barbarian in full sail over Athos.[4] I, however, my dear sir, am now spending my time with Moses and Elias, and saints like them, who tell me their stories in a barbarous tongue,[5] and I utter what I learnt from them, true, indeed, in sense, though rude in phrase, as what I am writing testifies. If ever I learned anything from you, I have forgotten it in the course of time. But do you continue to write to me, and so suggest other topics for correspondence. Your letter will exhibit you, and will not convict me. I have

[1] A famous athlete of Scotussa. Paus. vi. 5.
[2] The athlete of Crotona, who was crowned again and again at the Pythian and Olympian games.
[3] ὁ θλίβειν καὶ κατέχειν δυνάμενος, παλαιστικός· ὁ δὲ ῶσαι τῇ πληγῇ, πυστικός· ὁ δὲ ἀμφοτέροις τούτοις, παγκρατιαστικός. Arist., *Rhet.* i. v. 14.
[4] The story that Xerxes had made a canal through the isthmus of Athos is supposed to be an instance of gross exaggeration. cf. Juv. x. 174: "*Creditur olim Velificatus Athos et quidquid Græcia mendax Audet in historia,*" and Claudian iii. 336: "*Remige Medo solicitatus Athos.*" But traces of the canal are said to be still visible.
[5] This might lead to the idea that Basil knew some Hebrew, but the close of the sentence indicates that he means the Greek of the LXX., in which he always quotes Scripture.

already introduced to you the son of Anysius, as a son of my own. If he is my son, he is the child of his father, poor, and a poor man's son. What I am saying is well known to one who is wise as well as a sophist.[1]

LETTER CCCXL.

Libanius to Basil.

HAD you been for a long time considering how best you could reply to my letter about yours, you could not in my judgment have acquitted yourself better than by writing as you have written now. You call me a sophist, and you allege that it is a sophist's business to make small things great and great things small. And you maintain that the object of my letter was to prove yours a good one, when it was not a good one, and that it was no better than the one which you have sent last, and, in a word that you have no power of expression, the books which you have now in hand producing no such effect, and the eloquence which you once possessed having all disappeared. Now, in the endeavour to prove this, you have made this epistle too, which you are reviling, so admirable, that my visitors could not refrain from leaping with admiration as it was being read. I was astonished that after your trying to run down the former one by this, by saying that the former one was like it, you have really complimented the former by it. To carry out your object, you ought to have made this one worse, that you might slander the former. But it is not like you, I think, to do despite to the truth. It would have been done despite to, if you had purposely written badly, and not put out the powers you have. It would be characteristic of you not to find fault with what is worthy of praise, lest in your attempt to make great things insignificant, your proceedings reduce you to the rank of the sophists. Keep to the books which you say are inferior in style, though better in sense. No one hinders you. But of the principles which are ever mine, and once were yours, the roots both remain and will remain, as long as you exist. Though you water them ever so little, no length of time will ever completely destroy them.

LETTER CCCXLI.

Libanius to Basil.

YOU have not yet ceased to be offended with me, and so I tremble as I write. If you

[1] σοφῷ τε καὶ σοφιστῇ.

have cared, why, my dear sir, do you not write? If you are still offended, a thing alien from any reasonable soul and from your own, why, while you are preaching to others, that they must not keep their anger till sundown,[1] have you kept yours during many suns? Peradventure you have meant to punish me by depriving me of the sound of your sweet voice? Nay; excellent sir, be gentle, and let me enjoy your golden tongue.

LETTER CCCXLII.

Basil to Libanius.

ALL who are attached to the rose, as might be expected in the case of lovers of the beautiful, are not displeased even at the thorns from out of which the flower blows. I have even heard it said about roses by some one, perhaps in jest, or, it may be, even in earnest, that nature has furnished the bloom with those delicate thorns, like stings of love to lovers, to excite those who pluck them to intenser longing by these ingeniously adapted pricks.[2] But what do I mean by this introduction of the rose into my letter? You do not need telling, when you remember your own letter. It had indeed the bloom of the rose, and, by its fair speech, opened out all spring to me; but it was bethorned with certain fault findings and charges against me. But even the thorn of your words is delightful to me, for it enkindles in me a greater longing for your friendship.

LETTER CCCXLIII.

Libanius to Basil.

IF these are the words of an untrained tongue, what would you be if you would polish them? On your lips live fountains of words better than the flowing of springs. I, on the contrary, if I am not daily watered, am silent.

LETTER CCCXLIV.

Basil to Libanius.

I AM dissuaded from writing often to you, learned as you are, by my timidity and my ignorance. But your persistent silence is different. What excuse can be offered for it? If any one takes into account that you are slow to write to me, living as you do in the midst of letters, he will condemn you for forgetfulness of me. He who is ready at speaking is not unprepared to write. And if a man so endowed is silent, it is plain that he acts either from forgetfulness or from contempt. I will, however, requite your silence with a greeting. Farewell, most honoured sir. Write if you like. If you prefer it, do not write.

LETTER CCCXLV.

Libanius to Basil.

IT is, I think, more needful for me to defend myself for not having begun to write to you long ago, than to offer any excuse for beginning now. I am that same man who always used to run up whenever you put in an appearance, and who listened with the greatest delight to the stream of your eloquence; rejoicing to hear you; with difficulty tearing myself away; saying to my friends, This man is thus far superior to the daughters of Achelous, in that, like them, he soothes, but he does not hurt as they do. Truly it is no great thing not to hurt; but this man's songs are a positive gain to the hearer. That I should be in this state of mind, should think that I am regarded with affection, and should seem able to speak, and yet should not venture to write, is the mark of a man guilty of extreme idleness, and, at the same time, inflicting punishment on himself. For it is clear that you will requite my poor little letter with a fine large one, and will take care not to wrong me again. At this word, I fancy, many will cry out, and will crowd round with the shout, What! has Basil done any wrong — even a small wrong? Then so have Œacus, and Minos, and his brother.[1] In other points I admit that you have won. Who ever saw you that does not envy you? But in one thing you have sinned against me; and, if I remind you of it, induce those who are indignant thereat not to make a public outcry. No one has ever come to you and asked a favour which it was easy to give, and gone away unsuccessful. But I am one of those who have craved a boon without receiving it. What then did I ask? Often when I was with you in camp, I was desirous of entering, with the aid of your wisdom, into the depth of Homer's frenzy. If the whole is impossible, I said, do you bring me to a portion of what I

---

[1] *cf.* Eph. iv. 27, and the passage quoted by Alford from Plut., *De Am. Frat.* 488 B., to the effect that the Pythagoreans, whenever anger had caused unkindly words, shook hands before sundown, and were reconciled.

[2] MS. vary between ἐνπλήκτοις, ἐνπλέκτοις, ἀπλήκτοις, ἀπράκτοις.

[1] Rhadamanthus and Minos were both said to be sons of Zeus and Europa. *cf.* Verg., *Æn.* vi. 566 and Pind., *Ol.* ii. 75.

want. I was anxious for a part, wherein, when things have gone ill with the Greeks, Agamemnon courts with gifts the man whom he has insulted. When I so spoke, you laughed, because you could not deny that you could if you liked, but were unwilling to give. Do I really seem to be wronged to you and to your friends, who were indignant at my saying that you were doing a wrong?

LETTER CCCXLVI.

Libanius to Basil.

You yourself will judge whether I have added anything in the way of learning to the young men whom you have sent. I hope that this addition, however little it be, will get the credit of being great, for the sake of your friendship towards me. But inasmuch as you give less praise to learning than to temperance and to a refusal to abandon our souls to dishonourable pleasures, they have devoted their main attention to this, and have lived, as indeed they ought, with due recollection of the friend who sent them hither.

So welcome what is your own, and give praise to men who by their mode of life have done credit both to you and to me. But to ask you to be serviceable to them is like asking a father to be serviceable to his children.

LETTER CCCXLVII.

Libanius to Basil.

Every bishop is a thing out of which it is very hard to get anything.[1] The further you have advanced beyond other people in learning, the more you make me afraid that you will refuse what I ask. I want some rafters.[2] Any other sophist would have called them stakes, or poles, not because he wanted stakes or poles, but rather for shewing off his wordlets than out of any real need. If you do not supply them, I shall have to winter in the open air.

LETTER CCCXLVIII.

Basil to Libanius.

If γριπίζειν is the same thing as to gain, and this is the meaning of the phrase which your sophistic ingenuity has got from the depths of Plato, consider, my dear sir,

who is the more hard to be got from, I who am thus impaled[1] by your epistolary skill, or the tribe of Sophists, whose craft is to make money out of their words. What bishop ever imposed tribute by his words? What bishop ever made his disciples pay taxes? It is you who make your words marketable, as confectioners make honey-cakes. See how you have made the old man leap and bound! However, to you who make such a fuss about your declamations, I have ordered as many rafters to be supplied as there were fighters at Thermopylæ,[2] all of goodly length, and, as Homer has it, "long-shadowing,"[3] which the sacred Alphæus has promised to restore.[4]

LETTER CCCXLIX.

Libanius to Basil.

Will you not give over, Basil, packing this sacred haunt of the Muses with Cappadocians, and these redolent of the frost[5] and snow and all Cappadocia's good things? They have almost made me a Cappadocian too, always chanting their "I salute you." But I must endure, since it is Basil who commands. Know, however, that I am making a careful study of the manners and customs of the country, and that I mean to metamorphose the men into the nobility and the harmony of my Calliope, that they may seem to you to be turned from pigeons into doves.

LETTER CCCL.

Basil to Libanius.

Your annoyance is over. Let this be the beginning of my letter. Go on mocking and abusing me and mine, whether laughing or in earnest. Why say anything about frost[5] or snow, when you might be luxuriating in mockery? For my part, Libanius, that I may rouse you to a hearty laugh, I have written my letter enveloped in a snow-white veil. When you take the letter in your hand, you will feel how cold it is, and how it symbolizes the condition of the sender — kept at home and not able to put his head out of doors. For my house is a grave till spring comes and brings us back from death to life, and once more gives to us, as to plants, the boon of existence.

---

[1] With a play on χάραξ, the word used for stakes.
[2] i.e. three hundred.
[3] Hom. iii. 346.
[4] *Non illepide auctor epistolæ fluvium obstringit restituendi promisso, ut gratuito a se dari ostendat.*" Ben. note.
[5] γριπή, an unknown word. Perhaps akin to κρίοτη. cf. Ducange s.v.

---

[1] πρᾶγμα δυσγρίπιστον. γριπίζω = I catch fish, from γρῖφος, a creel. [2] στρωτήρ.

LETTER CCCLI.

Basil to Libanius.

MANY, who have come to me from where you are, have admired your oratorical power. They were remarking that there has been a very brilliant specimen of this, and a very great contest, as they alleged, with the result that all crowded together, and no one appeared in the whole city but Libanius alone in the lists, and everybody, young and old, listening. For no one was willing to be absent — not a man of rank — not a distinguished soldier — not an artisan. Even women hurried to be present at the struggle. And what was it? What was the speech which brought together this vast assembly? I have been told that it contained a description of a man of peevish temper. Pray lose no time in sending me this much admired speech, in order that I too may join in praising your eloquence. If I am a praiser of Libanius without his works, what am I likely to become after receiving the grounds on which to praise him?

LETTER CCCLII.

Libanius to Basil.

BEHOLD! I have sent you my speech, all streaming with sweat as I am! How should I be otherwise, when sending my speech to one who by his skill in oratory is able to shew that the wisdom of Plato and the ability of Demosthenes were belauded in vain? I feel like a gnat compared with an elephant. How I shiver and shake, as I reckon up the day when you will inspect my performance! I am almost out of my wits!

LETTER CCCLIII.

Basil to Libanius.

I HAVE read your speech, and have immensely admired it. O muses; O learning; O Athens; what do you not give to those who love you! What fruits do not they gather who spend even a short time with you! Oh for your copiously flowing fountain! What men all who drink of it are shewn to be! I seemed to see the man himself in your speech, in the company of his chattering little woman. A living story has been written on the ground by Libanius, who alone has bestowed the gift of life upon his words.

LETTER CCCLIV.

Libanius to Basil.

Now I recognise men's description of me! Basil has praised me, and I am hailed victor over all! Now that I have received your vote, I am entitled to walk with the proud gait of a man who haughtily looks down on all the world. You have composed an oration against drunkenness. I should like to read it. But I am unwilling to try to say anything clever. When I have seen your speech it will teach me the art of expressing myself.

LETTER CCCLV.

Libanius to Basil.

ARE you living at Athens, Basil? Have you forgotten yourself? The sons of the Cæsareans could not endure to hear these things. My tongue was not accustomed to them. Just as though I were treading some dangerous ground, and were struck at the novelty of the sounds, it said to me its father, "My father, you never taught this! This man is Homer, or Plato, or Aristotle, or Susarion. He knows everything." So far my tongue. I only wish, Basil, that you could praise me in the same manner!

LETTER CCCLVI.

Basil to Libanius.

I AM delighted at receiving what you write, but when you ask me to reply, I am in a difficulty. What could I say in answer to so Attic a tongue, except that I confess, and confess with joy, that I am a pupil of fishermen?

LETTER CCCLVII.

Libanius to Basil.

WHAT has made Basil object to the letter, the proof of philosophy? I have learned to make fun from you, but nevertheless your fun is venerable and, so to say, hoary with age. But, by our very friendship, by our common pastimes, do away, I charge you, with the distress caused by your letter . . . in nothing differing.[1]

LETTER CCCLVIII.

Libanius to Basil.

OH, for the old days in which we were all in all to one another! Now we are sadly

---

[1] Incomplete in original.

separated! Ye have one another. I have
no one like you to replace you. I hear that
Alcimus in his old age is venturing on a
young man's exploits, and is hurrying to
Rome, after imposing on you the labour of
remaining with the lads. You, who are
always so kind, will not take this ill. You
were not even angry with me for having to
write first.

LETTER CCCLIX.

Basil to Libanius.

You, who have included all the art of the
ancients in your own mind, are so silent,
that you do not even let me get any gain in a
letter. I, if the art of Dædalus had only
been safe, would have made me Icarus'
wings and come to you. But wax cannot
be entrusted to the sun, and so, instead of
Icarus' wings, I send you words to prove my
affection. It is the nature of words to indicate the love of the heart. So far, words.[1]
You do with them what you will, and, possessing all the power you do, are silent. But
pray transfer to me the fountains of words
that spring from your mouth.

LETTER CCCLX.[2]

*Of the Holy Trinity, the Incarnation, the
invocation of Saints, and their Images.*

According to the blameless faith of the
Christians which we have obtained from God,
I confess and agree that I believe in one
God the Father Almighty; God the Father,
God the Son, God the Holy Ghost; I adore and
worship one God, the Three.[3] I confess to
the œconomy of the Son in the flesh,[4] and
that the holy Mary, who gave birth to Him
according to the flesh, was Mother of God.[5]
I acknowledge also the holy apostles, prophets, and martyrs; and I invoke them to
supplication to God, that through them, that
is, through their mediation. the merciful
God may be propitious to me, and that a
ransom may be made and given me for my
sins. Wherefore also I honour and kiss the

features of their images, inasmuch as they
have been handed down from the holy
apostles, and are not forbidden, but are in
all our churches.

Letters CCCLXI. and CCCLXIII., to
Apollinarius, and Letters CCCLXII. and
CCCLXIV., from Apollinarius to Basil, are
condemned as indubitably spurious, not
only on internal evidence, but also on the
ground of Basil's asseveration that he had
never written but once to Apollinarius, and
that "as layman to layman."[1] Letter
CCCLXV., "to the great emperor Theodosius," on an inundation in Cappadocia, is
also condemned by the Ben. Ed. as spurious,
and contains nothing of ecclesiastical or
theological interest. Tillemont however
(vol. v., p. 739) thought its style not unworthy
of a young man a rhetorician, and conjectures the Theodosius to whom it is addressed to be not the great emperor, but
some magistrate of Cappadocia.

LETTER CCCLXVI.[2]

*Basil to Urbicius the monk, concerning
continency.*

You do well in making exact definitions
for us, so that we may recognise not only
continency, but its fruit. Now its fruit is
the companionship of God. For not to be
corrupted, is to have part with God; just as
to be corrupted is the companionship of the
world. Continency is denial of the body,
and confession to God. It withdraws from
anything mortal, like a body which has the
Spirit of God. It is without rivalry and
envy, and causes us to be united to God.
He who loves a body envies another. He
who has not admitted the disease of corruption into his heart, is for the future strong
enough to endure any labour, and though he
have died in the body, he lives in incorruption. Verily, if I rightly apprehend the
matter, God seems to me to be continency,
because He desires nothing, but has all
things in Himself. He reaches after nothing,
nor has any sense in eyes or ears; wanting

---

[1] Corrupt in original.
[2] This letter is almost undoubtedly spurious, but it has a certain interest, from the fact of its having been quoted at the so-called 7th Council (2d of Nicæa) in 787. Maran (*Vit. Bas.* xxxix.) is of opinion that it is proved by internal evidence to be the work of some Greek writer at the time of the Icono-clastic controversy. The vocabulary and style are unlike that of Basil.
[3] Neuter *sc.* πρόσωπα, not ὑποστάσεις, as we should expect in Basil.
[4] ἔνσαρκον οἰκονουίαν an expression I do not recall in Basil's genuine writings.
[5] Θεοτόκον. the watchword of the Nestorian controversy, which was after Basil's time.

[1] *Ep.* ccxxiv. § 2.
[2] Introduced by the Ben. with the following preface: "*En magni Basilii epistolam, ex prisco codice* lxi, *f.* 324, *a me exscriptam, quæ olim clarissimis quoque viris Marcianæ bibliothecæ descriptoribus Zannetto atque Morellio inedita visa est; atque utrum sit alicubi postremis his annis edita, mihi non constat, sed certe in plenissima Garnerii editione desid-eratur. Ea scribitur ad Urbicum monachum, ad quem aliæ duæ Basilii epistolæ exstant, nempe* 123 *and* 262, *in Garneriana editione. Argumentum titulusque est De Continentia, neque vero scriptum hoc Basilianum diutius ego celandum arbitror præsertim quia Suidas ac Photius nihil præstantius aut epistolari charactere accommodatius Basilii epistolis esse judicarunt. Mai, biblioth. nov. patr.* iii. 450.*

nothing, He is in all respects complete and full. Concupiscence is a disease of the soul; but continency is its health. And continency must not be regarded only in one species, as, for instance, in matters of sensual love. It must be regarded in everything which the soul lusts after in an evil manner, not being content with what is needful for it. Envy is caused for the sake of gold, and innumerable wrongs for the sake of other lusts. Not to be drunken is continency. Not to overeat one's self is continency. To subdue the body is continency, and to keep evil thoughts in subjection, whenever the soul is disturbed by any fancy false and bad, and the heart is distracted by vain cares. Continency makes men free, being at once a medicine and a power, for it does not teach temperance; it gives it. Continency is a grace of God. Jesus seemed to be continency, when He was made light to land and sea; for He was carried neither by earth nor ocean, and just as He walked on the sea, so He did not weigh down the earth. For if death comes of corruption, and not dying comes of not having corruption, then Jesus wrought not mortality but divinity.[1] He ate and drank in a peculiar manner, without rendering his food.[1] So mighty a power in Him was continency, that His food was not corrupted in Him, since He had no corruption. If only there be a little continency in us, we are higher than all. We have been told that angels were ejected from heaven because of concupiscence and became incontinent. They were vanquished; they did not come down. What could that plague have effected there, if an eye such as I am thinking of had been there? Wherefore I said, If we have a little patience, and do not love the world, but the life above, we shall be found there where we direct our mind. For it is the mind, apparently, which is the eye that seeth unseen things. For we say "the mind sees;" "the mind hears." I have written at length, though it may seem little to you. But there is meaning in all that I have said, and, when you have read it, you will see it.

---

[1] θεότητα οὐ θνητότητα.

[1] The Ben. note is: "*Hac super re reverentissime theologiceque scribit Athanasius Corinthi episcopus in fragmento quod nos edidimus AA.* class l. x. p. 499–500, *quod incipit:* Ζητοῦμεν, εἰ ἡ πλήρωσις τῶν βρωμάτων ἐπὶ Χριστοῦ ἐκέκτητο καὶ κένωσιν. *Erat enim hæc quoque una ex objectionibus hæreticorum. Definit autem, corpus Christi hac in re fuisse cæteris superius, sicuti etiam in insolita nativitate. Utitur quoque Athanasius exemplo trinitatis illius apud Abrahamum convivantis, neque tamen naturali necessitati obtemperantis; quod item de Christo post resurrectionem edente intelligendum dicit.*

INDEXES.

ST. BASIL.

INDEX TO TEXTS.

LETTERS OF ST. BASIL.

INDEX.

ACCORDING TO THE PLACE THEY OCCUPY IN THIS VOLUME.

LETTERS OF ST. BASIL.

INDEX OF THE PERSONS WHOSE CORRESPONDENCE WITH ST. BASIL IS PRESERVED.

[THE NUMBER OF THE LETTER IS IN ROMAN NUMERALS.]

Abramius, bp. of Batnæ, to, cxxxii. 199.

Aburgius, to, xxxiii. 135: lxxv. 170: cxlvii. 206: cxcvi. 234: clxxviii. 221: ccciv. 318.

Acacius, Aetius, Paulus, and Silvanus, to the very well beloved and reverend brethren the presbyters: the deacons Silvinus and Lucius, and the rest of the brethren the monks, Basil, the bishop, cclvi. 293.

Accountant, to the prefect's, cxli. 205.

Accountant, to another, cxliii. 205.

Aetius, presbyter (Acacius, etc.), to, cclvi. 293.

Alexander, Eulogius, Harpocration, bishops of Egypt, in exile, to, cclxv. 303.

Alexandrians, to the, cxxxix. 303.

Ambrose, bp. of Milan, to, cxcvii. 234.

Amphilochius, bishop of Iconium, to, clxi. 214: clxxvi. 220: cxc. 232: cxci. 233: cc. 240: cci. ccii. 24: ccxviii. 259: ccxxxi. ccxxxii. 272: ccxxxiii. 273: ccxxxiv. ccxxxv. 274: ccxxxvi. 276: ccxlviii. 290.

Amphilochius, concerning the canons, to (*Canonica prima*) clxxxviii. 223: (*canonica secunda*) cxcix. 236: (*canonica tertia*) ccxvii. 255.

Amphilochius, in the name of Heraclidas, to, cl. 207.

Ancyra, to the Church of, consolatory, xxix. 133.

Andronicus, a general, to, cxii. 188.

Antioch, to the Church of Antioch, cxl. 203.

Antioch, to the presbyters, celiii. 292.

Antiochus, to, cxlvi. 206: clvii. clviii. 211: clxviii. 217.

Antipater, the governor, clxxxvi. 223.

Antipater, on his assuming the governorship of Cappadocia, cxxxvii. 201.

Antipater to Basil, clxxxvii. 223.

Arcadius, the bishop, to, xlix. 153.

Arcadius, imperial treasurer, xv. 125.

Arinthæus, to, clxxix. 221.

Arinthæus, the general, to the wife of, consolatory, cclxix. 307.

Ascetics under him (Basil), to the, ccxxvi. 267.

Ascholius, bishop of Thessalonica, to, cliv. 209: clxiv. 215.

Assessor in the case of monks, to the, cclxxxiv. 312.

Atarbius, to, lxv. 162: cxxvi. 196.

Athanasius, bishop of Alexandria, to, lxi. 161: lxvi. 163: lxviii. 164: lxix. 165.

Athanasius, bp. of Ancyra, to, xxv. 130.

Athanasius, father of Athanasius, bishop of Ancyra, to, xxiv. 130.

Barses, bishop of Edessa, in exile, to, cclxiv. 303.

Beræans, to the, ccx. 260: ccxxi. 261.

Bishop, to a, cclxxxii. 312.

Bosporius, to bishop, li. 154.

Briso, to the wife of, cccii. 318.

Cæsaræans, to the, viii. 115.

Cæsaria, to the patrician, concerning communion, xciii. 179.

Cæsarius, brother of Gregory, to, xxvi. 131.

Callisthenes, to, lxxiii. 168.

Candidianus, to, iii. 112.

Canonica prima, clxxxviii. 223: *secunda,* cxcix. 236: *tertia,* ccxvii. 255.

Canonicæ, to the, lii. 155.

Censitor, to a, ccxcix. 318.

Chalcis, to the people of, ccxxii. 261.

Chilo, his disciple, to, xlii. 143.

Chorepiscopi, to the, liii. 156: liv. 157.

Colonia, consolatory, to the clergy of, ccxxvii. 270.

Colonia, to the magistrates of, ccxxviii. 270.

Comes Privatarum, to the ccciii. 318.

Commentariensis, to the, cclxxxvi. 313.

Consolatory, ci. 184.

Cyriacus, at Tarsus, to, cxiv. 190.

Demosthenes, as from the synod of bishops, to, ccxxv. 267.

Diodorus, the presbyter of Antioch, to, cxxxv. 200: clx. 212.

Dorotheus to the presbyter, ccxv. 254.

Elias, governor of the province, to, xciv. 179.

Elpidius the bishop, to, ccv. 245: ccvi. 246.

Epiphanius the bishop, to, cclviii. 294.

Eulancius, to, ccviii. 248.

Eulogius, Alexander, and Harpocration, bishops of Egypt, in exile, to, cclxv. 303.

Eunomius the heretic, against, xvi. 125.

Eupaterius and his daughter, to, clix. 212.

Euphronius, bishop of Colonia Armeniæ, to, cxcv. 234.

Eusebius, bishop of Samosata, to, xxvii. 131: xxx. xxxi. 134: xxxiv. 135: xlvii. 152: xlviii. 153: xcv. 180: xcviii. 182: c. 184: cxxvii. cxxviii. 196: cxxxvi. 201: cxxxviii. 202: cxli. 204: cxlv. 205: clxii. 215: clxvi. clxvii. 217: cxcviii. 235: ccxxxvii. 279: ccxxxix. 280: ccxli. 282: cclxviii. 307.

Eusebius, my comrade, to recommend Cyriacus the presbyter, to, cclxxi. 308.

Eustathius, bishop of Himmeria, to, clxxxiv. 222.

Eustathius of Sebasteia, against, ccxxiii. 262.

Eustathius, bishop of Sebastia, to, lxxix. 171: cxix. 192.

Eustathius, the philosopher, to, i. 109.

Eustathius, the physician, to, clxxxix. 228: cli. 209.

Evæsæ, to the people of, ccli. 291.

Evagrius, to the presbyter, clvi. 210.

Faith (a transcript of the) as dictated by Saint Basil, and subscribed by Eustathius, bishop of Sebasteia, cxxv. 194.

Festus and Magnus, to, ccxciv. 317.

Firminius, to, cxvi. 191.

Gaul, to the bishops of Italy and, concerning the condition and confusion of the churches, ccxliii. 283.

Gauls, to the Italians and, xcii. 177.

Genethlius, to the presbyter, ccxxiv. 265.

Governor, to the, lxxxvi. 174.

Gregory, to, ii. 110: clxix. 217; clxxi. 218.

Gregory, to his brother, concerning the difference between οὐσια and ὑπόστασις, xxxviii. 137.

(338)

INDEX OF AUTHORS QUOTED.

ST. BASIL.

INDEX OF SUBJECTS.

Cæsarea at the deposition of Elias the governor, 181.
its relation to the early life of Basil, xiv. xv. xx. xxi.
identification of its site, xxi.
its position as a city, xxiv. n.
suffered from the Carnival indulgences, lxii. n.
Cæsarius, letter to, 131.
his life, 131 n.
his executory caused Gregory Naz. much trouble, 135.
Cain, a question upon his punishment, 296–8.
Calendar, the Julian, and its adjustments, 87 n.
the Greek, 87.
Callisthenes, friend of Basil, 167, 168.
letter to, 168.
had been set upon by slaves, 168.
Calypso's island, 124.
Camel, a type of revenge, 95.
Canaan, why made a servant, 32.
Canal through Egypt, 73.
difference of level imagined as an obstacle, 73.
the Suez, 73 n.
Candidianus, governor of Cappadocia letter to, 112.
friend of Basil and Gregory, 112 n.
praised for his open courts, 265 n.
Canonicæ, 155 n., 219 n.
distinguished from nuns and deaconesses, 219 n.
questions as to marriage, 155 n.
calumnies regarding, 155.
letter to, 155, cf. 219.
Cappadocia, its division opposed by Basil, 168, 169, 170, 182.
abounded with altars and martyr memorials, 241 n.
persecutions in, xxiii. 261, 261 n.
oppressed by Basil, xxiii.
divided by Valens, xxiii. xxv.
why it remained so orthodox, xxix. n.
Cappadocians, character of the, 153, 153 n.
several sent by Basil to Libanius. 320 sq.
"the three Cappadocians," xiv.
Captivity, ransoming from, 166.
Carthusian silence, 128 n.
Caspian sea, 74.
Catacombs, rearranged by Pope Damasus, xxxii. n.
Cataphrygian, 223 n.
Catechumen, one for baptism blessed, 42.
his name registered, 17.
the renunciation and professions of faith, 17 n.

Cathari, followers of Novatian, 223, 223 n.
their baptism, 223.
were schismatics, 224.
Catholics, persecuted by Arians, 152 n.
Cattle, prone by nature, 102, 104.
their digestive organs, 104.
Caucasus, Mount, 68.
Causality, 56 n., 92 n.
Cause, four kinds of, 4 n.
six given by Basil, 4 n.
the Supreme, 5, 56, 68.
voluntary in God, 56, 59, 60.
Celebration of Eucharist at home forbidden, 236 n.
Celts, 69.
Censitor, letter to, 318.
as assessor of taxes, his work unpleasant, 173 n., 318.
Censure, gentleness in, 111.
Cetaceans, produced from the water, 90, 91.
Chalcis, letter to the people of, 261.
Chaldæan star-reading, 84, 85, 93.
Chamanene, 175.
Chance did not create the world, 55, 92 n.
χαρακτήρ, 14 n.
Chariot with three riders, 233.
Charity, administration of, 208.
Chastity, how honoured, 257 n.
χειρόγραφον, 17 n.
χειροτονητή, ἐχειροτονήθη, 231 n.
Children, on what condition admitted into monasteries, lii. liv.
Chilo, disciple of Basil, letter to, 143.
Chinese silk, 100.
Choaspes, 68.
Chorepiscopus, 130, 156 n., 157, 205, 210, 268, 315.
his duties under the bishop, xxi. 157.
his district, 315 n.
if accused of simony, 156, 157.
had charge of the hospital, xxi.
Chosroes, bishop, signed the letter to the West, 177.
Chremetes, 69.
Chrism, only if blessed, 42.
Christ, names and terms applied to Him, 11, 12.
His incarnation for us, 12, 21.
His glory in redemption, 11.
as the Word, 24.
His body real and not as a spirit, 7.
bore witness to purity of life, 34, 122.
His body in the unity of the Spirit, 38.
to be glorified with the saints, 41.
to be our judge, 10.
if neither honoured nor feared, 48.
held by Arians as only a titular deity, 49.
His Eternal Generation, 13.
His incarnation true and perfect, 10, 21, 104 n.

Christ, purpose of His incarnation, 21, 104 n.
the image of God, 15.
His pattern life for man's perfection, 21, 104 n.
perfect as our pattern, 21.
His relation to birth sin, 104 n.
His œconomy, 117.
is God, 117, 138.
interpretation of his words, 122 n.
He made all things, 138.
Saviour, with the sinner to return, 147, 152.
the pattern of duty, xxxix. 241.
His self-limitation, 276 n.
His Not-knowing discussed, xxxviii. 276, 277.
our Redeemer, 300.
His prayer in the Agony, xxxix.
His brethren, xli. n.
Himself the Vine, xxxix.
χριστέμποροι, 282 n.
Christians, made such in baptism, 18.
some apostatise, 17, 294.
proper Christian behaviour, 127 sq., 284, 290, 294.
unworthy, have no good from the name, 239.
made on the pattern of Christ, 241, 294.
some only traffickers in Christ, 282.
all require fortitude in their calamities, lxii.
Christmas and Epiphany, xxiv. n., 272 n.
χριστοφόνοι, 16 n.
Chrysippus of Tarsus, 54.
Chrysostom, his death in exile, 284 n.
Church, one body in Christ, 39, 189, 211, 241, 242, 245, 283.
preserves the tradition of teaching, 40 sq., 132.
like a battle field, 48, 290.
like a battle at sea in a tempest, 48, 242, 282.
as pictured in Basil's experience, 48, 49, 50, 178, 216, 294.
an object of beauty, 75, 216.
her public worship, 75.
falling into a worse condition, 163, 178, 189, 190, 268, 280.
her unity most desirable, 189, 190, 211, 241, 242, 245.
persecuted in Egypt, 203, 303 sq.
its picture in peace, 216.
as Catholic, 224, 245, 283.
in schism, 223, 224.
funds and treasures of, 267.
only one communion in, 245, 283.
in persecution, 268, 280, 281 sq., 290, 294.
her mutual sympathy, 282, 283.
her assemblies deserted through persecution, 284, 290, 294.